M000006887

101 Classic Cookbooks

501 CLASSIC RECIPES

COOK

101 Classic Cookbooks

501 CLASSIC RECIPES

THE FALES LIBRARY, NEW YORK UNIVERSITY

Marvin J. Taylor and Clark Wolf, Editors

Text by Marvin J. Taylor

RIZZOLI
NEW YORK
New York · Paris · London · Milan

First published in the United States of America
in 2012
by Rizzoli International Publications, Inc.
300 Park Avenue South
New York, NY 10010
www.rizzoliusa.com

The publisher has made its best efforts at contacting all rightsholders for the use of their material in this work. Please contact the publisher at the address above for any omissions, which will be corrected at the next opportunity.

2012 2013 2014 2015 / 10 9 8 7 6 5 4 3 2 1

Distributed in the U.S. trade by Random House, New York

Printed in China

ISBN: 978-0-8478-3793-9

Library of Congress Control Number: 2012940384

ADVISORY COMMITTEE

CONTENTS

501 CLASSIC RECIPES 305

COOKBOOKS AND FOOD STUDIES CANONS

Within my academic lifetime, the use of food as a means to examine critical questions about the causes and consequences of production and consumption has grown dramatically. Indeed, the growth of scholarly interest in food has been so rapid and extensive that the various approaches to such questions—historical, cultural, behavioral, biological, and socioeconomic—are now often grouped under the rubric *food studies*. As such, food studies can be considered to constitute a new movement, not only as an academic discipline but also as a means to change society.

Food studies has deep roots in foodways and other aspects of the humanities and social sciences. Nevertheless, it was only in 1996 that this collective term began to describe a legitimate field of academic study. That year, my department at New York University (NYU) recruited Amy Bentley as its first food studies professor and admitted its first undergraduate, master's, and doctoral students to food studies programs accredited by New York State.

How we were able to create programs under this title was a matter of fortuitous circumstances and a certain amount of preparation. The department, then known as Nutrition, Food, and Hotel Management, already offered courses in food and nutrition. The administrative transfer of its hotel programs to another school at NYU created a vacuum that new food programs could fill. A few years earlier, Julia Child had inspired development of the gastronomy master's program at Boston University. We thought we could something similar at NYU, but more academically focused. Because "studies" would be consistent with existing programs in such fields as Africana, cinema, French, gender, and liberal studies, we were certain that the title "food studies" would work better.

From the start, we considered food studies to encompass foodways, gastronomy, and culinary history, as well as discipline-based approaches to investigating critical social questions about food production or consumption. Today NYU food studies students can focus their research along the entire spectrum, from food culture to food systems.

Also from the start, this broad definition of food studies immediately raised questions about its scope, methods, and content. To deal with such questions, our department's advisory committee suggested that we identify a food studies "canon"—a set of books that every food scholar should be expected to read, understand, and use. In our innocence of the minefields of such a suggestion, we embarked on the project. For some months, we sent out questionnaires, collected suggestions, and struggled with the responses. At the end of this process, beyond Sidney Mintz's *Sweetness and Power*, we could not agree on which books—or whose—should be in or out, and we abandoned the idea.

Subsequently, food studies has expanded into the academy in the United States and elsewhere. I visited the former program at the University of Adelaide and the one still going strong at the University of Gastronomy in Italy. In addition to NYU's food studies programs and the gastronomy program at Boston University, new programs, some formal and some relatively informal, have emerged at the New School in New York (general studies) and at Indiana University (anthropology). Others are under development in Minnesota, the University of California at Davis, and elsewhere. Dillard University in New Orleans has appointed food scholar Jessica Harris to the Ray Charles Chair at the new Institute for the Study of Culinary Cultures. Although I don't have data, I have plenty of anecdotal evidence that it is much easier for doctoral students in humanities and social sciences to develop food dissertation projects now than it was in 1996 when we started all this at NYU.

Even so, something was missing. Many academic libraries did not collect primary texts about food other than those published by academic presses or the occasional title by journalists like Michael Pollan. Bibliographies of books about food were scarce. One notable exception was William Cagle's 1999 catalogue of the thousand or so rare international books on food and drink in the Gernon collection, housed at Indiana University's Lilly Library. We needed a collection of books to support graduate and doctoral level research at NYU. In seeking ways to support that research in our emergent food studies programs, we had another lucky break. The Fales Library and Special Collections section of the NYU Libraries chose food studies as a new focus. Since 2003 the Fales has acquired more than 55,000 books about food and cooking and more than 7,000 pamphlets, and is actively engaged in collecting restaurant menus, food brochures, personal papers, oral histories, and other such documents. The Fales Library now has the largest collection of food studies materials held by any library in the United States and has become a center for food research.

Today we have a better sense of the canon of books that make up the core knowledge that every food studies scholar should know. But we had not tackled the same question for cookbooks. So many are published, more each year than any other type of book. Yet food history is inscribed in cookbooks. Recipes are gateways to understanding how people ate and thought about foodways in the past. *101 Classic Cookbooks* brings together some of the most important cookbooks that shaped American eating in the past century. The selection advisory committee includes the top food writers, historians, journalists, academics, and chefs working in food studies today. They have done the seemingly impossible: They have suggested a canon of some of the most influential cookbooks that explain who we are, why we eat what we do, and why we should advocate for the best possible foods and diets for everyone.

—Marion Nestle

PREFACE

It's hard to imagine a time when food studies was not an academic discipline or program, much less a national obsession. But it was less than twenty years ago that I had the extreme pleasure of helping Dr. Marion Nestle "food up" the nutrition program (as she said) at New York University. We gathered smart, articulate, and thoughtful folks, and took their advice. The result was a bachelor's, master's, and doctoral juggernaut that has helped further educate some truly talented people.

One thing that eluded us was a required or even preferred reading list. Fearful of proscribing or deciding (or acknowledging) a canon, even the department's academics played refusenik. This treasury is certainly not that list. It would need to include some revealing memoirs and some frightening exposés, not to mention anything by Wendell Berry. Rather, it is a selection from the collection. It's a sort of "greatest hits" from an extraordinary cache that has been built into the largest collection of its kind in the United States. It's a tasty sampling from the cookery side of things that has turned into an amusing, delicious, and sometimes surprising cookbook all on its own.

We accomplished this book in somewhat the same way as the department got "fooded up." We invited some brilliant, accomplished, and broadly acknowledged leaders (movers and shakers) to aid us in building the list. These folks are our colleagues and friends, and a sort of extended informal faculty of the Critical Topics in Food Series I have enjoyed hosting at the library since the collection was launched. It's a "Really Good Friends of the Fales Library and Special Collections at the NYU Libraries" list.

Anyone who works in the broad and complex field of food knows that one mind cannot carry all of the necessary information, prioritized for usefulness and applicability, nor can it keep all of it in its cultural context. Food is, after all, the largest industry in the world and, as much as some would like to minimize something so enjoyable, the most important thing in the world—without food we would all cease to exist. Certainly, in the restaurant industry, there's little time for the deepest sort of research. It is a business that requires a tight set of evolving skills and a broad but constant view of the competition. That's why it's so important to have a "go-to" list of the people in your life who know the most about bread, or beef, or pastry, or veggies. Even a generalist needs to have specialties. Some are a phone call or e-mail away. Many of these precious resources live in the books kept closest to the stove.

Starting from my own shelves, Tosca Giamatti, a graduate of the NYU food studies master's program and then my assistant, helped cull the core, which turned out to be fifty or so nearly obvious choices that I've seen or put onto the shelves of chefs and shopkeepers all across the country over the last thirty years. We made sure we had all of the top volumes Marvin Taylor has at home and cooks from personally, then Tosca helped me go through every single title nominated by the International Association of Culinary Professionals and the James Beard Foundation Awards. This brought the total number of books to about ninety. We then sent the list to the Advisory Committee members, who had a chance to add, vote, veto, comment, and cajole. The result was more than 200 choices (all of which are listed at the back of this book). Our rule was simple: to be included on the big list, a book had to be recommended from at least two sources and confirmed by Marvin Taylor and me. Then we rated the books by how our committee had responded, how well a decade or topic was covered, how the overall list reflected the range and depth of the collection as a whole, and, let's face it, how the graphic presentation would enhance a treasury published by Rizzoli, legendary for stylish and beautiful, as well as rich and timeless, books.

Then the fun began. Once the final list emerged, Marvin set about performing his curatorial magic, writing entries for every volume. We discussed and assigned an engaging and in some cases historically significant collection of essays. Each is from a unique voice with an incomparable vantage point. Close in and close up, they are stories of mentors and partners, special interests and special friends, all from acclaimed writers, editors, historians, and cooks.

Then came what seemed like yet another impossible task. Who would dare to select and collate star recipes from each of these legendary books? For this, too, we turned to an education well built. With the hard work of Janet Lo and Waverley Aufmuth—both recent master's graduates of the food studies program—we pulled the most often mentioned, touted, repeated, praised, and reproduced recipes from every one of the books. This was no Google search and click. Yes, much of it was done on the computer, but it still took a lot of crisscross referencing and research to discover the value and reliability of sources. Oh, and they went to the library.

In the end, we gathered and organized the recipes into a recipe table of contents in a way that reflects how many of us in the industries of food think about dishes and how they're considered, prepared, and presented, on menus, in kitchens, and at the table. It's not completely traditional (which itself is traditional now), but it sure is fun to peruse. Our hope is that this will become one of everyone's reference guides and family cookbooks. We hope for a spot on the chef's desk and the professor's syllabus.

Most people don't realize the strong connection between what are sometimes called cookery books and the life of a professional chef. We're in an era in which we want home-style foods when eating in restaurants and professional ingredients, equipment, and quality at home. The interchange and conversation have never been greater. So it's therefore even more fascinating to see this list start with Fannie Merritt Farmer and end with Thomas Keller. But I'm quick to add that this list is from that last century that we've all heard so much about. The deluge of cooking and food books from this most recent decade or so—many from well-known restaurant chefs—will need to settle some before we can even begin to sift through it. That's an adventure and a collection yet to come.

—Clark Wolf

INTRODUCTION

Onions sautéed in butter. That's my first food memory. I was four years old and my grandmother, in whose house I grew up, was in a wheelchair by that point, so I helped her in the kitchen. Because she couldn't stand, I took the onions to her at the table, where she pared them. I put a chair up to the sink and another up to the stove in order to reach their tops. I washed the potatoes and delivered them to her too. Then I took the heavy soup pot from the lower cabinet, lit the fire, and set it on the stove. I added the butter and, once it had melted, the onions. Then the potatoes and whatever else she told me to add. Every time I put onions into butter, the smell returns me to my grandmother's kitchen and that pot of soup. I was hooked. And I've been cooking ever since.

I was blessed as a child because I had two grandmothers who were both great cooks. My maternal grandmother, Verda Hampton, of the onion soup fame, was a solid English/German–style cook as her Quaker upbringing made her. Her father, my great-grandfather Ulysses Miller, was a farmer and ran the general store in the small Indiana town where I grew up. Fresh vegetables and local meats were all we knew. My paternal grandmother, Hattie Taylor, was a Southern cook from Virginia; her fried chicken was outstanding, mostly, I believe, because the chickens were dressed just before they were fried. She and my grandfather, William, were also farmers. Some of my favorite memories of early childhood are from the farm. The two- or three-acre kitchen garden that provided vegetables for the family and for sale. The apple and peach trees behind the farmhouse that sat up on a small knoll surrounded by maple trees. The Concord grape arbor, whose grapes made perfect jelly. The hen house where I was sent to collect the eggs, moving the hens off their roosts with an upward twitch of the back of my hand while they rustled and complained. Then, into the basket draped on my other arm went the still-warm egg. To this day when I cut up a chicken I think fondly—and mischievously—of the Rhode Island red rooster who chased me from the chicken coop all the way to the backdoor, pecking at my back and legs for having invaded his domain.

Grandma Hampton had literary aspirations. She wrote short articles for women's magazines, read copiously, and entertained her lady friends. Books were everywhere in our home, and she taught me to read before I entered kindergarten. It was inevitable that I would fall in love with books, and with cookbooks in particular. Grandma had several volumes of handwritten family recipes in splattered notebooks that showed their use. I still have them, along with an 1842 Quaker Bible my grandmother gave to me.

Fast-forward to college, where I fell in with a group of friends who all liked to cook. We joked about teaching a course, C101: Introduction to Culture and Cuisine, thinking such a thing would never happen. Such was the status of food in academia in the early 1980s. For my part, I went into rare books librarianship and had the good fortune to work at the Lilly Library at Indiana University. While I was there, William Cagle, the director, successfully courted Mr. and Mrs. John Talbot Gernon for their outstanding collection of historical cookbooks. Bill was a great gourmet and oenophile, as well as a visionary collector of rare materials. I learned a great deal from observing the kinds of collections he acquired for the Lilly and even more from how he ignored the criticisms people launched at him for his decisions. Few people in the mid-1980s thought a food collection was really important for a major rare book library.

That has all changed, happily. In 2003 Marion Nestle came to see me at the Fales Library, New York University's primary rare book and manuscript collection in the arts and humanities, because she had heard of a major collection of cookbooks that was for sale. Marion's vision for the academic study of food had led her in the mid-1990s to create the first undergraduate, master's, and doctoral programs in food studies in what is now the Department of Nutrition, Food Studies, and Public Health at NYU. It was as though my college fantasy had come true! Here, standing in my office, was someone who not only realized the centrality of food to our everyday lives, but who also had created a whole field to study it. As was still typical at the time, the libraries were hesitant to build cookbook collections. Many librarians still thought of these books as sources for recipes that belonged under the purview of public libraries. Cookbooks are, of course—in addition to providing recipes—one of the most important places to go to see how a culture thinks about its food. Race, gender, ethnicity, religion, sexuality, age, and a host of other topics inform cookbooks, if you know how to look for the signs. Marion wanted to know if I might be interested in building a collection to support food studies. "Yes!" I said.

The Fales Library and Special Collections at NYU began as the personal collection of DeCoursey Fales, who was a banker and a lawyer in New York City. As an undergraduate at Harvard University in 1908, Fales took a course on the development of the novel from the scholar Bliss Perry. Perry was the first person to teach fiction in an American university. The novel was considered popular entertainment and not suitable for serious study. If you studied literature, you studied the classics, meaning Greek and Roman texts, and possibly Chaucer and Shakespeare. Fales became fascinated with the novel and began collecting first editions of the authors he read in Bliss Perry's class: Dickens, Trollope, and Scott for the British novel and Paulding, Irving, and Cooper for the American. To teach the British novel was thought of as crazy at the time; to teach the American novel was simply insane. But Fales continued to collect, using a methodology he developed from Perry. Fales was interested in literary circles and in what people actually read. This was a time before the literary canon of fiction had been established. Between 1908 and 1956, Fales amassed some 50,000 volumes in his private library. He offered the collection to Harvard, but the library turned it down, for the prejudice against fiction was still strong in the 1950s. Fales's grandfather had moved part of the family from Boston to New York in 1849, where they lived just off Washington Square. With the encouragement of his son Timothy and his friend Gordon Ray, a well-known book collector and faculty member at NYU, Fales offered the collection to the university, and we accepted. Today the collection comprises some 250,000 volumes, 12,000 linear feet of archives, and 70,000 media elements.

DeCoursey Fales's faith in his collection of fiction has been a source of inspiration for me as director. Over the years, his collection has come to be seen as one of the most important in the country. The novel is not only an entertainment; it is a way of understanding what people were thinking in a given period. Novelists can help us understand what it was like to be in London in the 1830s or India in 1900. They can also teach us about style, fashion, and popular expressions. In fact, Fales's willingness to build large collections of cultural materials led me to create the Downtown New York collection, which documents the New York City art scene from the 1970s through the 1990s. It also provided me the perfect model for collecting food materials. Certainly we weren't going to reject the possibility of building a major collection for food studies.

So Marion and I went to visit Cecily Brownstone, who was for thirty-nine years the Associated Press syndicated food columnist, as well as a close friend of James Beard. Cecily was bedridden at the time, but we did get to meet and speak with her. She was a small woman with a sharp mind and quick wit. Over her career she amassed more than seven thousand cookbooks and five thousand pamphlets, which she used as her personal research library about food. Her four-story townhouse on Jane Street in Greenwich Village was stuffed with the materials. We walked into a collection that had been carefully curated for more than sixty years. I knew instantly that this would be the foundation for a major food studies collection. We found a donor who was able to help us, and NYU purchased the collection in toto. The funds helped to take care of Cecily for the remaining years of her life.

We were strategic about how we were going to build the food studies collection. Historically, such collections—the few that existed—were built on one of two models: Some, like the wonderful collection at Harvard's Schlesinger Library, began as repositories for women's history; others, like the Texas Women's University collection, began as home economics libraries. At Fales we needed a different approach. Our New York City location inspired us to look at food in a more comprehensive way, taking into account restaurants, ethnic foods, chefs, farmers' markets, women's organizations, professional chefs, and so forth. The book collections needed to be as comprehensive as possible to support wide-ranging research by students and faculty, while our archival holdings could focus on the New York City area and the city's role in changing Americans' thinking about food in the post–World War II era. With the help of food consultant Clark Wolf and Marion Nestle, we launched the Critical Topics in Food Series, which presents at least three panels on current topics in food each year. These events regularly attract 150 people interested in food history, politics, and trends. They also attract cookbook collectors.

Today the food studies collection at the Fales Library stands at more than 55,000 printed items, 7,000 pamphlets, and 642 linear feet of archival materials. New Yorkers were hoarding cookbooks in amazing personal collections that they made accessible to students and scholars because there was no major repository in the city for food research.

Dalia Carmel Goldstein is a perfect example. Since about 1960, Dalia has amassed a collection of more than 11,000 books, which she has already donated to Fales. Her collection perfectly dovetails with Cecily Brownstone's, filling in later titles and showing Dalia's love of international cuisines, especially Middle Eastern and Mediterranean foods. The *Ladies' Home Journal* decided it no longer needed its cookbook collection, and donated one of the most important magazine food collections to Fales. The James Beard Foundation, which had maintained a library for food scholars in a small space at its offices, realized that Fales was becoming a major center for food in New York, so it donated its collection. Rozanne Gold generously made a donation that allowed us to purchase the library of *Gourmet* magazine just days before Condé Nast was slated to throw it out. Andrew F. Smith's outstanding collection of eighteenth- and nineteenth-century American cookery is now also a part of the collection, filling in our historical holdings. Les Dames d'Escoffier of New York, the first organization for women in the food industry, has not only donated its papers, but has also created a fund in honor of Carol Brock, its founder, to acquire major titles for the library. The largest collection, however, came from George and Jenifer Lang, the impresarios behind New York's famous Café des Artistes. George began collecting books about food as a young man, building an astonishing collection of more than 22,000 European and American volumes, which he and Jenifer donated to the library. There are many, many other donors who have helped us along the way, enabling us to quickly build the largest collection of food materials in the country.

And these materials are used heavily. Students, faculty, food writers, biographers, playwrights, and many others make appointments to visit Fales every day. Some of my favorite topics that people have researched include: the first appearance of ice cream in Japan; death row inmates' requests for their last meal; the meaning of table settings in Jane Austen's novels; kosher Ethiopian cooking; food and citizenship during World War II; early, Americanized ethnic cookbooks; food and identity in the Middle East; food and memory in the Jewish community; television cooks and their influence on cookbooks. Food research is no longer just the province of food studies students and faculty. We regularly see patrons from history, English, anthropology, performance studies, gender studies, Jewish studies, Asian Pacific American studies, and a variety of other disciplines using the collection. Of course, all of this reflects the larger cultural interest in all aspects of food that has developed over the past thirty years.

Which brings me to the list of the 101 great cookbooks included in this book. When I began writing the entries for the books, I purposefully had no agenda or outline other than the chronological arrangement of the titles. Yet a narrative did emerge, one that sheds light on our current interest in healthy, sustainable, organic foods.

The narrative begins with Fannie Farmer, the maven of domestic science, whose foods were meant to be not only nutritious but also tasty. To our palate today, it seems implausible that Farmer's bland menus were meant to be tasty, but that was her agenda. In her own way, Farmer was a food activist. She was trying to improve the lives of women and the food they served. This theme recurs throughout the list in the titles Marion Nestle mentions in her essay, and even in the early hippie cookbooks. There is a sense that food is not only for enjoyment, but it also should be nutritious. Seemingly at odds with this is the tradition of the gourmet as someone who wants only the very best and is extremely fussy. Here I'm thinking of the tradition of Louis De Gouy, Dione Lucas, Crosby Gaige, Earle MacAusland, and Victor Hirtzler, for instance, who all look to France as having the only truly worthwhile cuisine.

At the same time, Americans like Sheila Hibben, James Beard, Clementine Paddleford, and Cecily Brownstone were arguing for the importance of American cookery, showing how it, too, was sophisticated. They were more like gourmands, who want to taste everything that is good rather than judge what is traditionally thought of as the best.

Julia Child demystified haute cuisine to a large extent with *Mastering the Art of French Cooking*, in 1961. She opened the way for Americans to begin preparing traditional French foods at home. Suddenly, as though the floodgates had opened, other authors created serious cookbooks that investigated other cuisines. The 1970s exploded with Italian, Indian, Chinese, Mexican, Szechwan, Japanese, Jewish, and other ethnic cookbooks.

At the same time, the hippie-inspired vegetarian and eco-friendly activist cookbooks raised our awareness of the need for humanely and organically produced foods. Alice Waters led the way at her flagship restaurant, Chez Panisse, where only local, sustainable produce and meats were served. In time, other chefs rallied to her battle cry and the new California cuisine and food activism spread across the country.

The 1980s represented the heyday of the new ingredients. Arugula appeared at Dean & DeLuca in 1977. Elizabeth Schneider's *Uncommon Fruits & Vegetables* appeared in 1986. We all began to enjoy new Asian flavors like wasabi and lemongrass. Our palate was expanding to include what were once called "exotic" cuisines. As we are wont to do, we picked and chose from these, pushing the American palate further and further. In the 1980s and 1990s regional cuisines from Italy, Mexico, India, and Southeast Asia appeared on our tables. Craig Claiborne had foreseen this development in 1960 in his monumental *New York Times Cook Book*, but Mark Bittman would present them in a contemporary way to a whole new audience with his *How to Cook Everything*, which Jonathan Gold has called the "dude's *Joy of Cooking*."

Importantly, beginning in the 1980s, men began to cook for leisure. No longer was the kitchen solely gendered feminine. With men came stainless steel and industrial-size appliances, but also a new kind of manly man, who saw food as another area to conquer. My father never lifted a skillet in his life. I was always suspect because I liked to. Today it's a badge of honor to have a son who wants to be a chef.

As the century ended, American food was on top of the world. Thomas Keller opened the French Laundry in a small town, Yountville, California, and served a witty, postmodern riff on American foods using only the best ingredients, many of them from local farmers, if not from the extensive gardens at the restaurant, and French culinary technique. Keller won three stars from Michelin for the French Laundry. He went on to open Per Se in New York, again winning three stars—the only chef in America to do so.

From Fannie Farmer to Thomas Keller, we forged a new cuisine. We preserved the best of American foods, applied French culinary techniques, returned to the best, organic, local produce and meats, and borrowed new ingredients and new techniques from all the world's food. A new American palate was born. These books will show you how it happened.

—Marvin J. Taylor
Director, Fales Library and Special Collections

101 CLASSIC AMERICAN COOKBOOKS OF THE TWENTIETH CENTURY

1 Fannie Merritt Farmer, *The Boston Cooking-School Cook Book*, 1896.
2 Ella Kellogg. *Every-day Dishes and Every-day Work*, 1897.
3 Hugo Ziemann and Mrs. F. L. Gilette. *The White House Cook Book*, 1900.
4 The Times-Picayune. *The Original Picayune Creole Cook Book*, 1901.
5 Mrs. Simon Kander and Others. *"The Settlement" Cook Book*, 1901.
6 Sarah Tyson Rorer. *Mrs. Rorer's New Cook Book*, 1902.
7 Isabel Gordon Curtis. *Good Housekeeping Everyday Cook Book*, 1903.
8 Rufus Estes. *Good Things to Eat, as Suggested by Rufus*, 1911.
9 Ida Cogswell Bailey Allen. *Mrs. Allen's Cook Book*, 1917.
10 Lulu Hunt Peters. *Diet and Health with Key to the Calories*, 1918.
11 Victor Hirtzler. *The Hotel St. Francis Cook Book*, 1919.
12 Mrs. S. R. Dull. *Southern Cooking*, 1928.
13 Harry Craddock. *The Savoy Cocktail Book*, 1930.
14 Irma Rombauer. *The Joy of Cooking*, 1931.
15 Sheila Hibben. *The National Cookbook*, 1932.
16 Mme. Bégué. *Mme. Bégué's Recipes of Old New Orleans Creole Cookery*, 1937.
17 Cora, Rose, and Robert Brown. *The South American Cook Book*, 1939.
18 Crosby Gaige. *New York World's Fair Cook Book*, 1939.
19 Junior League of Augusta. *Old and New Recipes from the South*, 1940.
20 James Beard. *Cook It Outdoors*, 1941.
21 Genevieve Callahan. *The California Cook Book for Indoor and Outdoor Eating*, 1946.
22 Louis Pullig de Gouy. *The Gold Cook Book*, 1947.
23 Dione Lucas. *The Cordon Bleu Cook Book*, 1947.
24 James Beard. *The Fireside Cook Book*, 1949.
25 Junior League of Charleston. *Charleston Receipts*, 1950.
26 Betty Crocker. *Betty Crocker's Picture Cook Book*, 1950.
27 Earle R. MacAusland. *The Gourmet Cookbook*, 1950.
28 Jan Mitchell. *Lüchow's German Cookbook*, 1952.
29 Helen Evans Brown. *Helen Brown's West Coast Cook Book*, 1952.
30 Alice B. Toklas. *The Alice B. Toklas Cook Book*, 1954.
31 M.F.K. Fisher. *The Art of Eating*, 1954.
32 Carol Truax. *Ladies' Home Journal Cookbook*, 1960.
33 Clementine Paddleford. *How America Eats*, 1960.
34 Craig Claiborne. *The New York Times Cook Book*, 1961.
35 Julia Child, Louisette Bertholle, and Simone Beck. *Mastering the Art of French Cooking, Volumes I and II*, 1961–1970.
36 Paula Peck. *The Art of Fine Baking*, 1961.
37 Elizabeth David. *French Provincial Cooking*, 1962.
38 Roy Andries de Groot. *Feasts for All Seasons*, 1966.
39 Marian Burros. *The Elegant But Easy Cookbook*, 1967.
40 Edward Espe Brown. *The Tassajara Bread Book*, 1970.

41 Alicia Bay Laurel. *Living on the Earth*, 1971.
42 George Lang. *The Cuisine of Hungary*, 1971.
43 Frances Moore Lappé. *Diet for a Small Planet*, 1971.
44 Time-Life Books. *Foods of the World*, 1968–1970.
45 Anna Thomas. *The Vegetarian Epicure*, 1972.
46 Claudia Roden. *A Book of Middle Eastern Food*, 1972.
47 James Beard. *American Cookery*, 1972.
48 Cecily Brownstone. *The Associated Press Cookbook*, 1972.
49 Julia Child. *From Julia Child's Kitchen*, 1972.
50 Craig Claiborne and Virginia Lee. *The Chinese Cookbook*, 1972.
51 Diana Kennedy. *The Cuisines of Mexico*, 1972.
52 Bernard Clayton, Jr. *The Complete Book of Breads*, 1973.
53 Marcella Hazan. *The Classic Italian Cook Book*, 1973.
54 Paula Wolfert. *Couscous and Other Good Food from Morocco*, 1973.
55 Madhur Jaffrey. *An Invitation to Indian Cooking*, 1973.
56 Maida Heatter. *Maida Heatter's Book of Great Desserts*, 1974.
57 Robert A. Delfs. *The Good Food of Szechwan*, 1974.
58 Richard Olney. *Simple French Food*, 1974.
59 Jeanne Lesem. *The Pleasures of Preserving and Pickling*, 1975.
60 Laurel Robertson, Carol Flinders, and Bronwen Godfrey. *Laurel's Kitchen*, 1976.
61 Edna Lewis. *The Taste of Country Cooking*, 1976.
62 Jacques Pépin. *La Technique*, 1976.
63 Mollie Katzen. *The Moosewood Cookbook*, 1977.
64 Giuliano Bugialli. *The Fine Art of Italian Cooking*, 1977.
65 Mimi Sheraton. *From My Mother's Kitchen*, 1979.
66 Shizuo Tsuji. *Japanese Cooking*, 1980.
67 Abby Mandel. *Abby Mandel's Cuisinart Classroom*, 1980.
68 Jennifer Brennan. *The Original Thai Cookbook*, 1981.
69 Penelope Casas. *The Foods and Wines of Spain*, 1982.
70 Julee Rosso and Sheila Lukins. *The Silver Palate Cookbook*, 1982.
71 Barbara Tropp. *The Modern Art of Chinese Cooking*, 1982.
72 Lee Bailey. *Lee Bailey's Country Weekends*, 1983.
73 Viana La Place and Evan Kleiman. *Cucina Fresca*, 1983.
74 Bert Greene. *Greene on Greens*, 1984.
75 Paul Prudhomme. *Chef Paul Prudhomme's Louisiana Kitchen*, 1984.
76 Carol Field. *The Italian Baker*, 1985.
77 Julie Sahni. *Classic Indian Vegetarian and Grain Cooking*, 1985.
78 Elizabeth Schneider. *Uncommon Fruits & Vegetables*, 1986.
79 Marion Cunningham. *The Breakfast Book*, 1987.
80 Barbara Kafka. *Microwave Gourmet*, 1987.
81 Deborah Madison. *The Greens Cook Book*, 1987.
82 Martha Stewart. *Weddings*, 1987.
83 Colman Andrews. *Catalan Cuisine*, 1988.
84 Rose Levy Beranbaum. *The Cake Bible*, 1988.
85 Patricia Wells. *Bistro Cooking*, 1989.
86 Bruce Cost. *Bruce Cost's Asian Ingredients*, 1989.
87 Bruce Aidells. *Hot Links and Country Flavors*, 1990.
88 Lidia Bastianich. *La Cucina di Lidia*, 1990.
89 Alice Medrich. *Cocolat*, 1990.
90 Felipe Rojas-Lombardi. *The Art of South American Cooking*, 1991.
91 Lynne Rossetto Kasper. *The Splendid Table*, 1992.
92 Emeril Lagasse. *Emeril's New New Orleans Cooking*, 1993.
93 William Woys Weaver. *Pennsylvania Dutch Country Cooking*, 1993.
94 Joan Nathan. *Jewish Cooking in America*, 1994.
95 Richard Sax. *Classic Home Desserts*, 1994.
96 Cara de Silva, ed. *In Memory's Kitchen*, 1996.
97 Alice Waters. *Chez Panisse Vegetables*, 1996.
98 Rick Bayless. *Rick Bayless's Mexican Kitchen*, 1996.
99 Jeffrey Alford and Naomi Duguid. *Seductions of Rice*, 1998.
100 Mark Bittman. *How to Cook Everything*, 1998.
101 Thomas Keller. *The French Laundry Cookbook*, 1999.

101 Classic Cookbooks

FANNIE MERRITT FARMER

The Boston Cooking-School Cook Book, 1896

Fannie Merritt Farmer probably never thought of herself as a feminist or as an activist, but she was both. Farmer was part of the domestic science movement in late-nineteenth-century America, a movement that sought to elevate the work of women in the home by the application of scientific principles that were transforming nearly every aspect of American life. Efficiency, cleanliness, thrift, and economy were all words that circulated through the magazines and books published by women of the movement.

Farmer began teaching cooking as a way to help educate young girls who could then find positions as cooks in the kitchens of the upper-middle and upper classes. She also planned menus based on the latest theories about healthy foods. Unlike some of her more strident peers, Farmer believed that the foods should be not only nutritious but also tasty, and that they should be elegantly presented at the table. She was known for her monochromatic dinners where everything would be pink or white, for instance. She is also noted for the creation of "perfection salad," which had fruits and other foods encased in gellatine—the precursor of the 1950s Jell-O salad.

Farmer's *Boston Cooking-School Cook Book* was the textbook for her school and became one of the first compendiums of American cooking. It has gone through many different editions, including a complete reworking by Marion Cunningham during the 1970s.

NOTABLE RECIPES: Angel Cake (page 609) • **Baked Cod with Oyster Stuffing** (page 478) • **Boston Baked Beans** (page 428) • **Boston Brown Bread** (page 568) • Brownies • Chocolate Cake • Corned Beef Hash • **Custard Pie** (page 606) • **Fried Corn Meal Mush/Fried Hominy** (page 428) • **Mint Julep** (page 312) • **Peanut Butter Cookies** (page 632) • **Snow Pudding** (page 649) • Tipsy Pudding

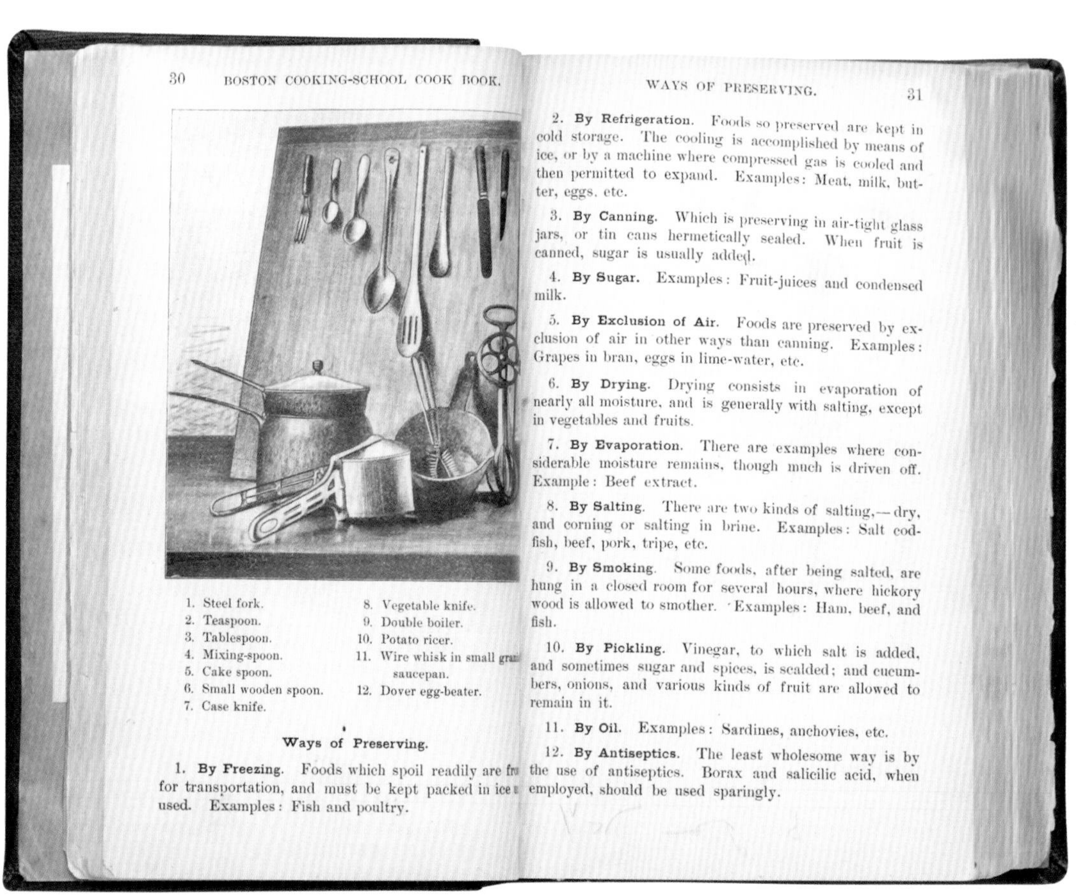

30 BOSTON COOKING-SCHOOL COOK BOOK.

1. Steel fork.
2. Teaspoon.
3. Tablespoon.
4. Mixing-spoon.
5. Cake spoon.
6. Small wooden spoon.
7. Case knife.
8. Vegetable knife.
9. Double boiler.
10. Potato ricer.
11. Wire whisk in small gra[...] saucepan.
12. Dover egg-beater.

Ways of Preserving.

1. **By Freezing.** Foods which spoil readily are fr[...] for transportation, and must be kept packed in ice [...] used. Examples: Fish and poultry.

WAYS OF PRESERVING. 31

2. **By Refrigeration.** Foods so preserved are kept in cold storage. The cooling is accomplished by means of ice, or by a machine where compressed gas is cooled and then permitted to expand. Examples: Meat, milk, butter, eggs, etc.

3. **By Canning.** Which is preserving in air-tight glass jars, or tin cans hermetically sealed. When fruit is canned, sugar is usually added.

4. **By Sugar.** Examples: Fruit-juices and condensed milk.

5. **By Exclusion of Air.** Foods are preserved by exclusion of air in other ways than canning. Examples: Grapes in bran, eggs in lime-water, etc.

6. **By Drying.** Drying consists in evaporation of nearly all moisture, and is generally with salting, except in vegetables and fruits.

7. **By Evaporation.** There are examples where considerable moisture remains, though much is driven off. Example: Beef extract.

8. **By Salting.** There are two kinds of salting,—dry, and corning or salting in brine. Examples: Salt codfish, beef, pork, tripe, etc.

9. **By Smoking.** Some foods, after being salted, are hung in a closed room for several hours, where hickory wood is allowed to smother. Examples: Ham, beef, and fish.

10. **By Pickling.** Vinegar, to which salt is added, and sometimes sugar and spices, is scalded; and cucumbers, onions, and various kinds of fruit are allowed to remain in it.

11. **By Oil.** Examples: Sardines, anchovies, etc.

12. **By Antiseptics.** The least wholesome way is by the use of antiseptics. Borax and salicilic acid, when employed, should be used sparingly.

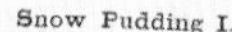

Snow Pudding I.

¼ box gelatine or
1¼ tablespoons granulated gelatine.
¼ cup cold water.
1 cup boiling water.
1 cup sugar.
¼ cup lemon juice.
Whites 3 eggs.

Soak gelatine in cold water, dissolve in boiling water, add sugar and lemon juice, strain, and set aside in cool place; occasionally stir mixture, and when quite thick, beat with wire spoon or whisk until frothy; add whites of eggs beaten stiff, and continue beating until stiff enough to hold its shape. Mould, or pile by spoonfuls on glass dish; serve cold with Boiled Custard. A very attractive dish may be prepared by coloring half the mixture with fruit red.

Amber Pudding.

Make as Snow Pudding I., using cider instead of boiling water, and one-fourth cup boiling water to dissolve gelatine, omitting lemon juice.

Snow Pudding II.

Beat whites of four eggs until stiff, add one-half tablespoon granulated gelatine dissolved in three tablespoons boiling water, beat until thoroughly mixed, add one-fourth cup powdered sugar, and flavor with one-half teaspoon lemon extract. Pile lightly on dish, serve with Boiled Custard.

Pudding à la Macédoine.

Make fruit or wine jelly mixture. Place a mould in pan of ice water, pour in mixture one-half inch deep; when firm, decorate with slices of banana from which radiate thin strips of figs (seed side down), cover fruit, adding mixture by spoonfuls lest the fruit be disarranged. When firm, add more fruit and mixture; repeat until all is used, each time allowing mixture to stiffen before fruit

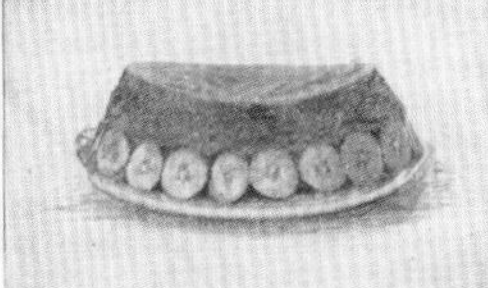

Pudding à la Macédoine.

is added. In preparing this dish various fruits may be used: oranges, bananas, dates, figs, and English walnuts. Serve with Cream Sauce I.

Fruit Chartreuse.

Make fruit or wine jelly mixture. Place a mould in pan of ice water, pour in mixture one-half inch deep; when firm, decorate with candied cherries and angelica; add by spoonfuls more mixture to cover fruit; when this is firm, place a smaller mould in the centre on jelly, and fill with ice water. Pour gradually remaining jelly mixture between moulds; when firm, invert to empty smaller mould of ice water; then pour in some tepid water; let stand a few seconds, when small mould may easily be removed. Fill space thus made with fresh sweetened fruit, using shredded pineapple, sliced bananas, and strawberries.

Spanish Cream.

¼ box gelatine or
1¼ tablespoons granulated gelatine.
3 cups milk.
Whites 3 eggs.
Yolks 3 eggs.
½ cup sugar (scant).
¼ teaspoon salt.
1 teaspoon vanilla or
3 tablespoons wine.

Scald milk with gelatine, add sugar, pour slowly on yolks of eggs slightly beaten. Return to double boiler

CHAPTER XXXIX.

SUITABLE COMBINATIONS FOR SERVING.

BREAKFAST MENUS.

Oranges.
Oatmeal with Sugar and Cream.
Broiled Ham. Creamed Potatoes. Pop-overs or Fadges.
Coffee.

Quaker Rolled Oats with Baked Apples, Sugar and Cream.
Creamed Fish. Baked Potatoes. Golden Corn Cake.
Coffee.

Bananas.
Toasted Wheat with Sugar and Cream.
Scrambled Eggs. Sautéd Potatoes. Graham Gems.
Griddle Cakes.
Coffee.

Grape Fruit.
Wheatlet with Sugar and Cream.
Beefsteak. Lyonnaise Potatoes. Twin Mountain Muffins.
Coffee.

Sliced Oranges.
Wheat Germ with Sugar and Cream.
Warmed over Lamb. French Fried Potatoes. Raised Biscuits.
Buckwheat Cakes with Maple Syrup.
Coffee.

Strawberries.
Hominy with Sugar and Cream.
Bacon and Fried Eggs. Baked Potatoes. Rye Muffins.
Coffee.

Raspberries.
Shredded Wheat Biscuit.
Dried Smoked Beef in Cream. Hashed Brown Potatoes.
Baking-Powder Biscuit.
Coffee.

Watermelon.
Wheat Germ with Sugar and Cream.
Broiled Halibut. Potato Cakes. Sliced Cucumbers.
Quaker Biscuit.
Coffee.

Canteloupe.
Pettijohns with Sugar and Cream.
Fecils with Tomato Sauce. Potato Balls. Rice Muffins.
Coffee.

Peaches.
Farinose with Sugar and Cream.
Omelette. Potatoes à la Maître d' Hôtel. Berry Muffins.
Coffee.

Blackberries.
H-O with Sugar and Cream. Dropped Eggs on Toast.
Waffles with Maple Syrup.
Coffee.

Pears.
Wheatena with Sugar and Cream.
Corned Beef Hash. Milk Toast.
Coffee.

33

LAURA SHAPIRO *on* FANNIE FARMER *and* MARION CUNNINGHAM

Fannie Merritt Farmer, a genteel Bostonian proud of her association with the nation's most high-minded city, would have been startled to glance down from that great kitchen in the sky sixty-five years after her death and see that her name and legacy had been entrusted to a pony-tailed Californian with fond memories of a wartime job in a gas station. But Marion Cunningham, who revised Farmer's classic book in the 1970s, turned out to be the best possible choice to retrofit the 1896 culinary bible. Today The Fannie Farmer Cookbook *runs perfectly in a modern home, while its comforting aura of tradition and reliability is unchanged.*

One reason Farmer and Cunningham were able to collaborate so successfully, despite being separated by more than half a century, was a shared sense of mission: Both these food lovers put teaching at the heart of their work. Farmer (1857–1915) had contracted polio as a teenager and couldn't finish high school, much less go on to college, as she had hoped. Few respectable careers were open to a young woman with a limp who lacked a high school diploma, but graduates of the Boston Cooking-School were finding employment in the new and dignified career of cooking teacher. Farmer enrolled, and did so well that she was invited to become assistant principal of the school as soon as she graduated. In 1893 she became principal, and the immense popularity of her public lecture-demonstrations, as well as her skills in classroom teaching, quickly made her a local legend. Three years later she published The Boston Cooking-School Cook Book, *which would come to be known simply as* The Fannie Farmer Cookbook. *Unabashedly a teaching text, it covered every kitchen procedure, from blacking the stove and making whole-wheat bread to molding a crème de menthe ice and decorating it with spun sugar, all in a tone of calm, plainspoken authority. It was the first comprehensive American cookbook to become an enduring best-seller and an influential reference work for generations of home cooks.*

Cunningham, born in 1922, was also handicapped as a young woman, but in her case she was crippled by phobias, which kept her close to home for years. She did marry and raise a family, however, and during those years she became an accomplished cook and baker, eventually offering lessons in her own kitchen. Finally, at age forty-five, shaking with fear, she managed to get on a plane and fly to Oregon to take a cooking class with James Beard. The trip opened up a new world. She went back a year later for another class, and in time became Beard's assistant, traveling and teaching with him. Like Beard, she appreciated the lasting value of uncomplicated recipes based on excellent ingredients, and she shared with her mentor a deep affection for the tastes and traditions of American cooking. Meanwhile, The Fannie Farmer Cookbook, *once a symbol of those very traditions, had lost both substance and character after numerous revisions at various hands, and Judith Jones, the cookbook editor at Knopf, was looking for the right person to overhaul it. To the surprise of most culinary insiders, Beard suggested the little-known Cunningham: A perfect match was made.*

Compatible though they were, Farmer and Cunningham also represented different moments in the history of American attitudes toward the kitchen. Farmer, from her stance in the late nineteenth century, looked toward a bright technological future. She had become a professional just as science was emerging as a popular template for every realm of life, including food and domesticity, and the new sensibility suited her. She was a trained expert, not an instinctive one, with a brisk, businesslike mind. As far as she was concerned, clear instructions based on the principles of nutrition and food chemistry could turn anyone into a fine, up-to-date cook. Rather than relying on such time-honored but impressionistic terms as "butter the size of an egg" or "a heaping spoonful," for instance, she insisted that her pupils and readers use standardized measuring cups and spoons—a revolution that became a definitive feature of American cooking and earned her the title "the mother of level measurements." At the same time she openly enjoyed food, to an extent that was unusual in the community of science-minded cooks, and often said that home cooks should delight their families as well as nourish them. Her public lectures, as well as her nonpedagogical food writing, were notable for an array of salads and desserts bedecked as if they were fashionable hats. The practical and the frivolous, the rational and the startling—it was an unwieldy combination, but Farmer led the way toward making it a hallmark of culinary Americana.

Cunningham, by contrast, was painfully aware of how much American cookery had lost under the reign of speed and efficiency, and she took much of her culinary inspiration from the past. By the time she began revising The Fannie Farmer Cookbook, the food industry had been hard at work for decades trying to persuade homemakers that they had neither the time nor the skill to prepare meals from scratch. Although home cooking never disappeared, it was plainly struggling, and the prospect of preparing a full meal from fresh ingredients seemed to intimidate more people every year. Cunningham wanted to restore ordinary good cooking to its once-honorable place in everyday life. Her goal was to open the kitchen door and keep it open; she didn't want anyone, ever, to back away nervously from the notion of filling a cookie jar with homemade cookies. Her revision emphasized genuine simplicity: The recipes were concise but easy to follow, and she jettisoned the pointless shortcuts that had been hardening like cement over successive editions of the book. Much of the food remained comfortably old-fashioned, but the roasts and fricassees, white sauce and gingerbread, were joined by tacos, spaghetti carbonara, and hundreds more dishes representing contemporary American tastes. Most of all, the book reflected Cunningham herself—confident, unpretentious, and thoroughly hospitable. In her hands, the best in American cooking found its way back home.

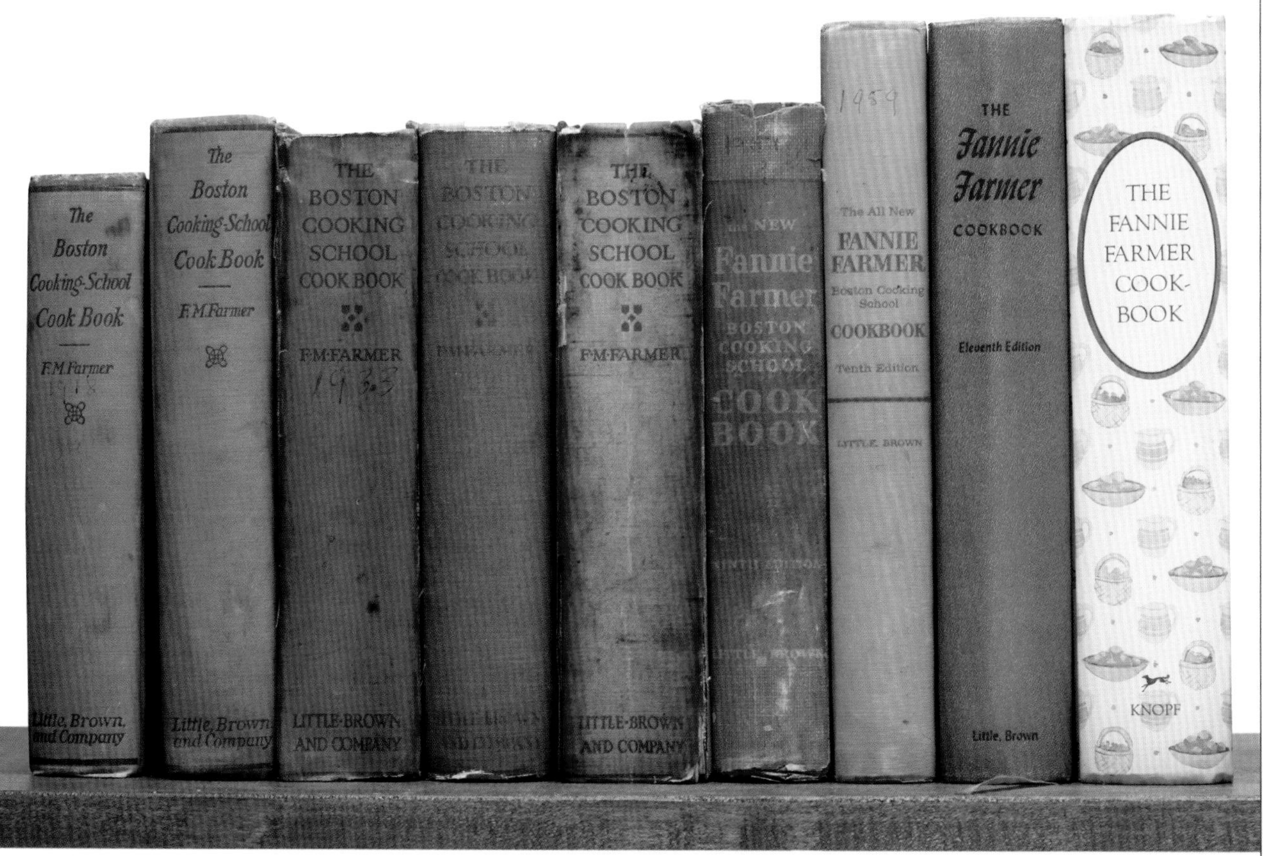

ELLA KELLOGG

Every-day Dishes and Every-day Work, 1897

Ella Eaton Kellogg was born in Alfred, New York, where she attended Alfred University, receiving both an undergraduate and a master's degree by 1885. She and her sister made a summer trip to Battle Creek, Michigan, in 1876, during which her sister contracted typhoid fever and was taken to Battle Creek Sanitarium, a reform medical institution established by Seventh-day Adventists. At the sanitarium she met Dr. John Harvey Kellogg, who invited her to enroll as a charter member of his new School of Hygiene. She agreed, and began work with the sanitarium. On February 22, 1879, she married Kellogg, and the two became partners in their own health, diet, and medical reform institute.

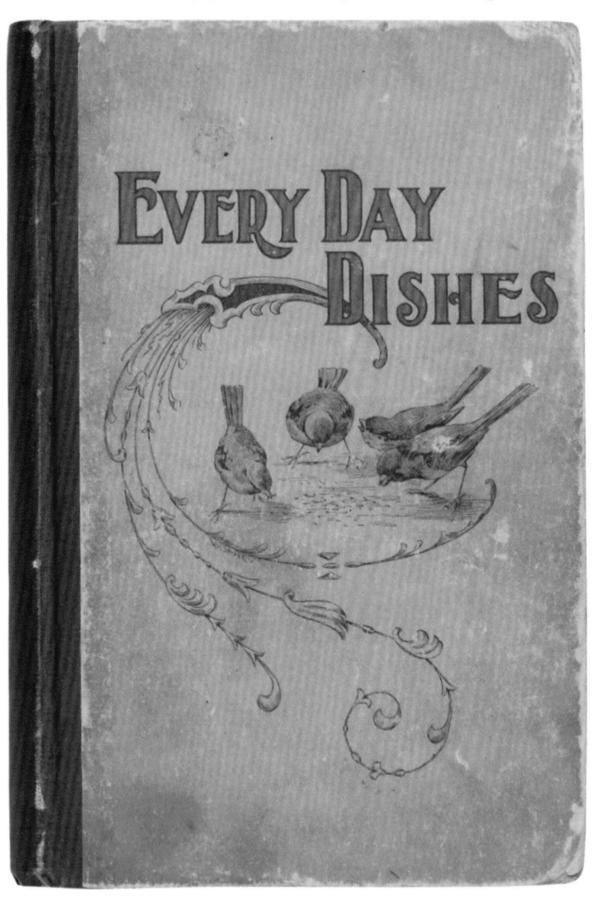

Dr. Kellogg was encouraged by Adventist leaders Ellen and James White to pursue professional training to legitimize the group's ideas on health and natural remedies. He published two books on dietary reform in 1874, including one that promoted vegetarianism. Kellogg's dietary suggestions limited many of the tastiest foods in the name of health. His patients found the diet inedible. Ella Kellogg attempted to create more appetizing menus based on her husband's principles. In 1893 she published *Science in the Kitchen*, based on her "Experimental Kitchen" at the sanitarium. One product of the "Experimental Kitchen" was the establishment of a cooking school, based on other cooking schools that were cropping up across the country, including the Boston Cooking-School operated by Fannie Farmer. Kellogg's school developed into the Battle Creek Sanitarium School of Home Economics, following the trend to view housework as scientific and on par with men's labor.

Ella Kellogg wrote *Every-day Dishes and Every-day Work* to help the average housewife cook healthy meals on a daily basis. Her recipes are simple, relying on the mostly grain diet promoted by her husband. Her preface states clearly that her food was about nutrition, not taste: "The purposes of food are to promote growth, to supply force and heat, and to furnish material to repair the waste which is constantly taking place in the body." Two pages later she includes a "Table Showing the Nutritive Values of Some Common Food Substances." Interestingly, the front and back sections of the book are filled with advertisements for foodstuffs available for sale by the Battle Creek Sanitarium Health Food Company.

Ella Kellogg's work represents one of the major strains of thinking about food that shaped what Americans ate in the twentieth century.

NOTABLE RECIPES: Cerealine Flakes • Cooked Peanuts • Graham Grits • **Granola** (page 469) • **Nut Butter Sandwiches** (page 372) • **Oatmeal Mush** (page 469) • **Succotash** (page 381)

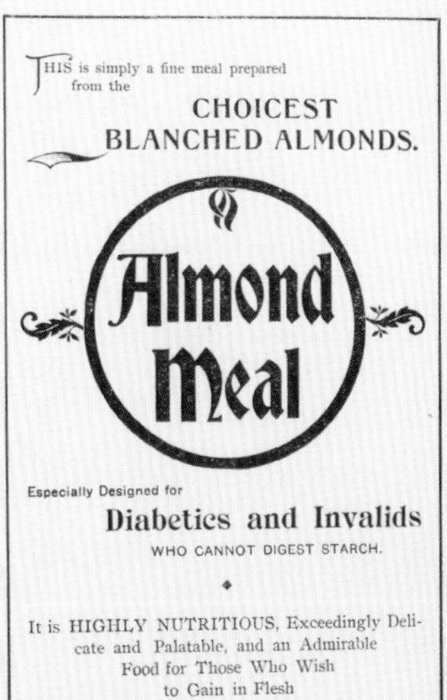

Each of these different groups of elements has a particular work to perform in the maintenance of health, so it is especially necessary that our food should contain some of each kind of elements. It is likewise essential that these elements, particularly the nitrogenous and carbonaceous, should be supplied to the system in certain definite proportions, as the body is able to appropriate only a certain amount of each. More of the carbonaceous than of the nitrogenous elements are needed. One part nitrogenous material to every eight or ten parts carbonaceous, is, according to the latest authorities, a good proportion.

Of the different nutritive elements, the nitrogenous is physiologically the most important, as these elements especially nourish the brain, nerves, muscles, and all the more highly vitalized and active tissues of the body, and also serve as a stimulus to tissue change. Hence it may be said that a food deficient in these elements is a particularly poor food. The carbonaceous elements furnish material for the production of heat and energy when used in connection with other food elements.

The mineral elements aid in furnishing the requisite building material for bones and nerves. Most food substances are deficient in one or another of the food elements, and need to be supplemented by other foods containing the deficient element in superabundance, since to employ a dietary in which any one of the nutritive elements is lacking, although in bulk it may be all the digestive organs can manage, is really starvation, and will in time occasion serious results.

It will thus be apparent that great care should be exercised in the selection and combination of food ma-

TABLE SHOWING THE NUTRITIVE VALUES OF SOME COMMON FOOD SUBSTANCES.

	FOOD SUBSTANCES.	Water.	Albuminous Elements.	Starch.	Grape Sugar.	Cane Sugar.	Free Fat.	Salts.	Cellulose.	Propor. Carbon. to Nitrogenous	Total Nutritive Value.
GRAINS.	Wheat, Poland	13.2	21.5	61.9	...	...	1.5	1.9	...	2.9	86.8
	Mich. White	12.8	11.6	71.	...	...	1.3	1.6	1.7	6.2	85.5
	Rye	8.7	11.	74.6	...	...	1.9	2.3	1.5	6.9	89.8
	Barley	14.	10.5	66.7	...	...	2.4	2.6	3.8	6.5	82.2
	Oats	12.	10.7	58.3	...	...	7.8	3.3	17.9	6.1	89.1
	Corn	13.1	10.2	68.5	...	...	4.8	1.4	1.7	7.1	84.9
	Rice	12.6	6.7	78.5	...	...	.9	.8	.5	11.8	86.9
	Macaroni	13.1	9.	76.8			.3	.8	...	8.5	86.9
FRESH FRUITS.	Apple	84.8	.4	...	7.2		...	.5	1.5	18.	13.7
	Apricot	81.2	.5	...	4.6		...	.8	5.3	9.2	13.5
	Blackberry	86.4	.5	...	4.1		...	.4	7.	8.2	6.6
	Banana	73.	1.0	...	...		.6	1.	.3	12.5	26.7
	Cherry	79.8	.7	...	10.2		...	.7	5.9	14.5	14.8
	Grape	78.2	.6	...	14.3		...	.5	3.6	23.8	18.2
	Pear	83.2	.4	...	8.2		...	.3	4.4	20.5	12.4
	Prune	81.2	.8	...	6.2		...	.7	5.4	7.7	13.4
	Plum	84.9	.4	...	3.6		...	.7	4.3	9.	10.8
	Peach	80.	.7	...	4.5		...	.7	6.1	6.4	13.9
	Raspberry	85.7	.4	...	3.9		...	.5	7.4	9.7	6.9
	Strawberry	87.6	1.1	...	6.3		.5	.8	2.3	6.1	10.1
NUTS.	Chestnut	7.3	14.6	69.	...		2.4	3.3	3.4	4.8	89.3
	Walnut	7.2	15.8	13.	...		57.4	2.	4.6	4.4	88.2
	Hazelnut	7.1	17.4	7.2	...		62.6	2.5	3.2	4.	89.7
	Sweet Almond	6.2	23.5	7.8	...		53.	3.	6.5	2.6	87.3
	Peanut	6.5	28.3	1.8	...		46.2	3.3	13.9	1.7	79.6
	Cocoanut	46.6	5.6	8.	...		35.9	1.	2.9	7.8	50.5
VEGETABLES.	Winter Cabbage	89.	4.	...	1.2		.9	1.6	1.9	3.1	18.1
	Spinach	88.5	3.5	...	.1		.6	2.	1.	1.4	10.5
	Potato	75.	2.2	...	...		.2	1.	.6	9.6	24.4
	White Turnip	92.5	1.5	...	...		.2	.7	2.1	2.1	5.4
	Beet	87.5	1.3	...	...		.1	1.1	1.	.1	11.5
	Parsnip	82.	1.2	...	...		.6	1.	8.	6.5	10.
	Sweet Potato	71.8	1.	...	...		.2	.7	1.	23.5	27.2
	Asparagus	93.7	1.8	...	.4		.3	.5	1.	1.6	5.3
	Squash	90.3	1.1	...	1.4		.1	.7	1.2	6.1	8.5
	Onion	86.	1.7	...	2.8		.1	.7	.7	6.4	13.3
	Tomato	92.4	1.6	...	2.5		.3	.6	.8	2.8	6.8
LEGUMES.	Peas, small	10.3	24.6	52.6	...	...	3.5	2.6	6.4	2.2	83.3
	Beans, field	13.5	23.	48.3	...	...	1.7	3.5	8.	2.	78.5
	French or Kidney	11.	23.7	55.6	...	...	2.2	3.7	3.8	2.4	85.2
	Lima	9.	21.9	60.6	...	...	1.6	2.9	4.	2.8	87.
	Lentils	12.3	25.9	53.	...	...	1.9	3.	3.9	2.1	83.8
						Milk Sug.					
MILK.	Cows' milk	86.	4.1	...	...	5.2	3.9	.8	...	2.2	14.
	Cream	66.	2.7	...	...	2.8	26.7	1.8	...	11.	34.
	Skimmed milk	88	4.	...	...	3.8	1.8	.8	...	1.4	10.4
	Buttermilk	88.	4.1	...	...	3.6	.7	.8	...	1.	9.2
MEATS.	Lean Beef	72.	19.3	...	...	...	3.6	5.1	...	.18	28.
	Lean Mutton	72.	18.3	...	...	...	4.9	4.8	...	.26	28.
	Veal	63.	16.5	...	...	...	15.8	4.7	...	.93	37.
	Pork	39.	9.8	...	...	...	48.9	2.3	...	4.9	61.
	Poultry	74.	21.	...	...	...	3.8	1.2	...	.18	26.
	White Fish	78.	18.1	...	...	...	2.9	1.	...	.16	22.
	Entire Egg	74.	14	...	...	...	10.5	1.5	...	.75	26.

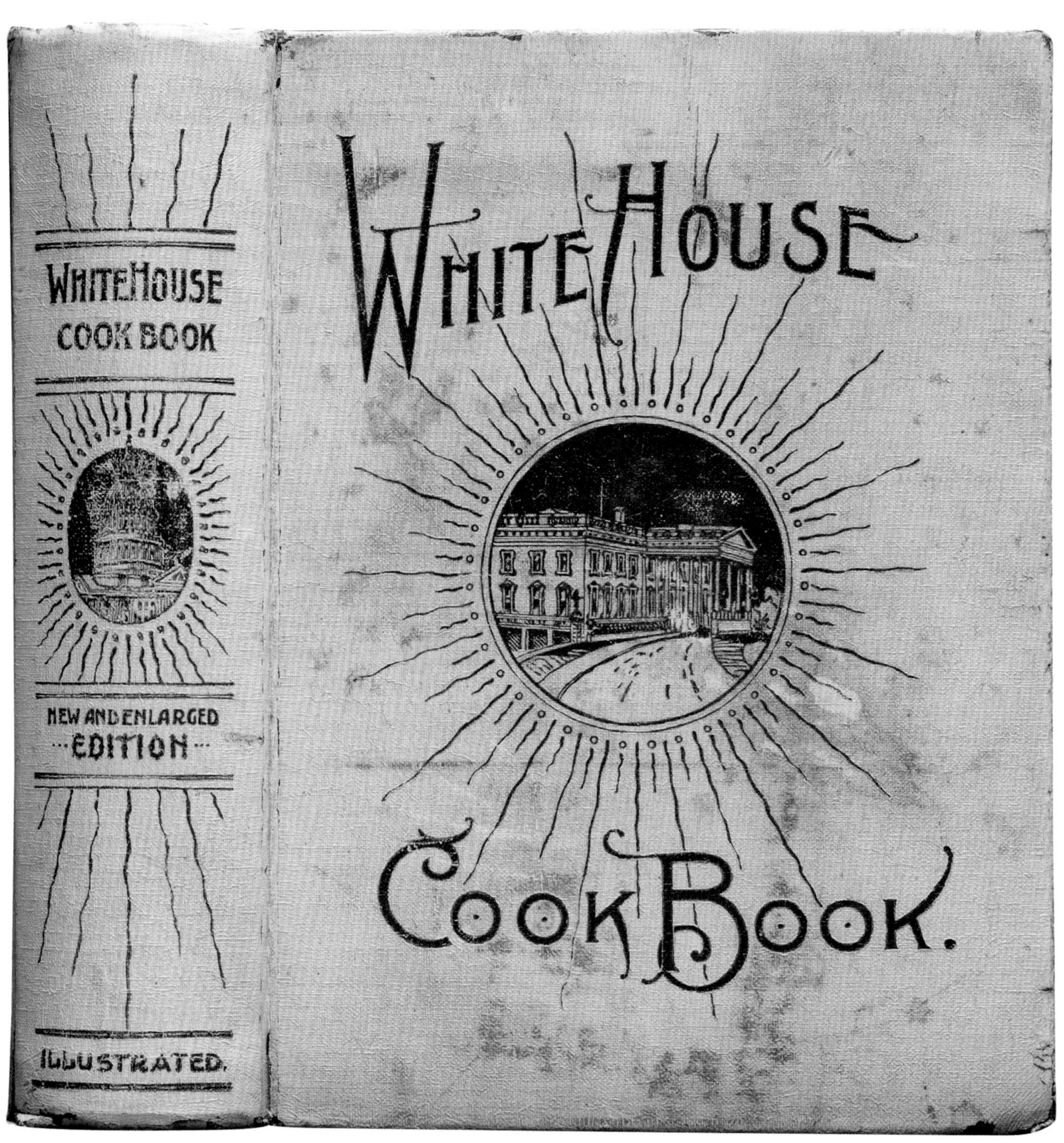

NOTABLE RECIPES: **Boston Cream Pie** (page 603) • Corn Pudding • **Dessert Puffs** (page 636) • **Election Cake** (page 612) • Lemon Raisin Pie • **Mock Turtle Soup of Calf's Head** (page 355) • **Pigeon Pie** (page 496) • **Tomato Catsup, No. 1** (page 432)

HUGO ZIEMANN AND MRS. F. L. GILETTE

The White House Cook Book

A Comprehensive Cyclopedia of Information for the Home, Containing Cooking, Toilet and Household Recipes, Menus, Dinner-giving, Table Etiquette, Care of the Sick, Health Suggestions, Facts Worth Knowing, etc, 1900

The first *White House Cook Book* was published in 1887, and it was a continually updated and published volume for more than fifty years. More than a cookbook, it is, as the title indicates, an attempt to be a cyclopedia for the home for "housekeepers of all classes," and thus it includes sections as disparate as "cooking for the sick; miscellaneous recipes for using ammonia, killing vermin, starching shirts, freshening up furs, removing stains; facts worth knowing about how to prevent mold, applying raw beef steak to easy bruises, curing hiccoughs; and points on etiquette." This last section declaims: "There is no position where the innate refinement of a person is more fully exhibited than at the table, and nowhere that those who have not been trained in table etiquette feel more keenly their deficiencies." Also covered in great detail are plans for state dinners and table settings, which were probably of little use to the average housewife but add to the general impression that the standards for American food behavior were set by the White House.

Especially interesting in this edition from 1900, which has a frontispiece portrait of Mrs. Ida Saxton McKinley, is the inclusion called "Seasonable Food," which tells what foods are in season when and how they should be incorporated into menus. Finally, the publisher's introduction stresses that the White House chef, Hugo Ziemann, has an outstanding French pedigree, having served as a caterer to Prince Napoleon and afterward as a steward at "the famous Hotel Splendide in Paris . . . the Brunswick Café in New York . . . [and] the Hotel Richelieu in Chicago." Chef Ziemann has also provided a list of "French Words in Cooking." Clearly, at the White House, French culinary traditions, if not French recipes, signified the highest form of American taste in 1900.

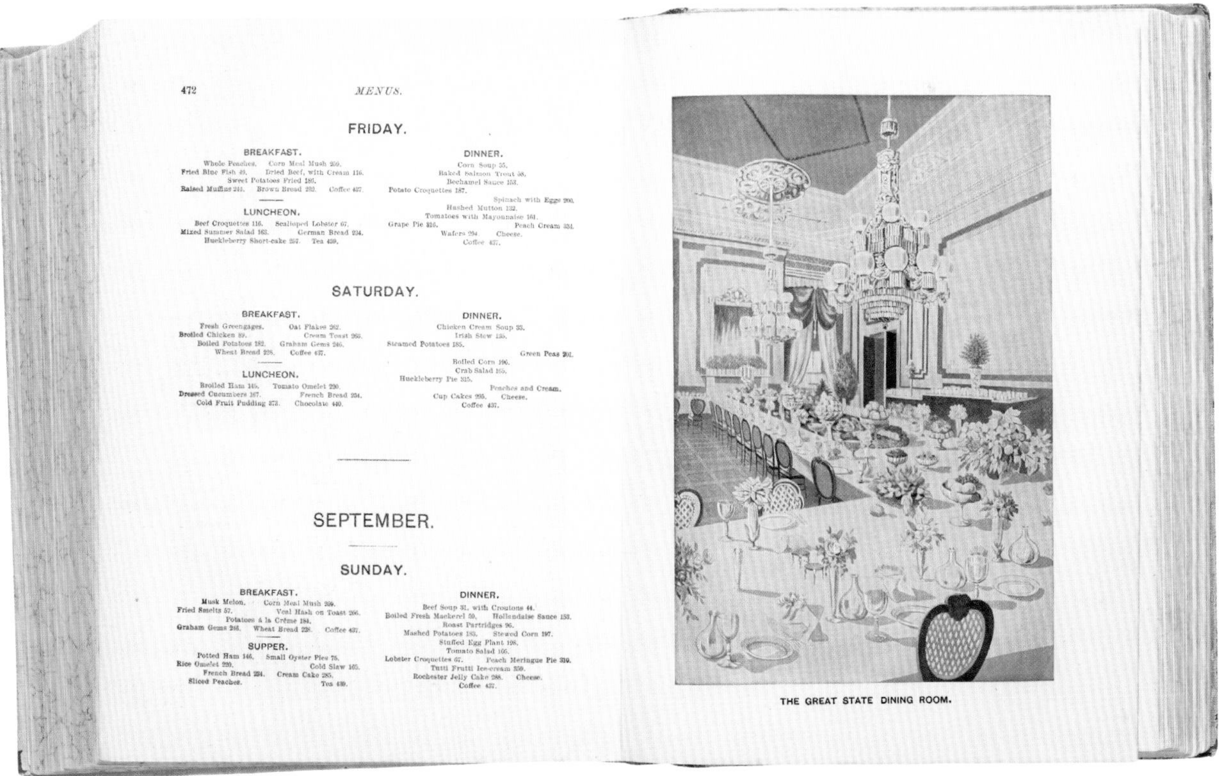

472 *MENUS.*

FRIDAY.

BREAKFAST.
Whole Peaches. Corn Meal Mush 259.
Fried Blue Fish 49. Dried Beef, with Cream 116.
Sweet Potatoes Fried 186.
Raised Muffins 244. Brown Bread 232. Coffee 437.

LUNCHEON.
Beef Croquettes 116. Scalloped Lobster 67.
Mixed Summer Salad 163. German Bread 234.
Huckleberry Short-cake 257. Tea 439.

DINNER.
Corn Soup 35.
Baked Salmon Trout 58.
Bechamel Sauce 153.
Potato Croquettes 187.
Spinach with Eggs 200.
Hashed Mutton 132.
Tomatoes with Mayonnaise 161.
Grape Pie 316. Peach Cream 334.
Wafers 294. Cheese.
Coffee 437.

SATURDAY.

BREAKFAST.
Fresh Greengages. Oat Flakes 262.
Broiled Chicken 89. Cream Toast 265.
Boiled Potatoes 182. Graham Gems 246.
Wheat Bread 228. Coffee 437.

LUNCHEON.
Broiled Ham 145. Tomato Omelet 230.
Dressed Cucumbers 167. French Bread 234.
Cold Fruit Pudding 373. Chocolate 440.

DINNER.
Chicken Cream Soup 33.
Irish Stew 135.
Steamed Potatoes 185.
Green Peas 201.
Boiled Corn 196.
Crab Salad 165.
Huckleberry Pie 315.
Peaches and Cream.
Cup Cakes 295. Cheese.
Coffee 437.

SEPTEMBER.

SUNDAY.

BREAKFAST.
Musk Melon. Corn Meal Mush 259.
Fried Smelts 57. Veal Hash on Toast 266.
Potatoes à la Crême 184.
Graham Gems 248. Wheat Bread 228. Coffee 437.

SUPPER.
Potted Ham 146. Small Oyster Pies 75.
Rice Omelet 220. Cold Slaw 165.
French Bread 234. Cream Cake 285.
Sliced Peaches. Tea 439.

DINNER.
Beef Soup 31, with Croutons 44.
Boiled Fresh Mackerel 59. Hollandaise Sauce 153.
Roast Partridges 96.
Mashed Potatoes 183. Stewed Corn 197.
Stuffed Egg Plant 198.
Tomato Salad 166.
Lobster Croquettes 67. Peach Meringue Pie 319.
Tutti Frutti Ice-cream 359.
Rochester Jelly Cake 288. Cheese.
Coffee 437.

THE GREAT STATE DINING ROOM.

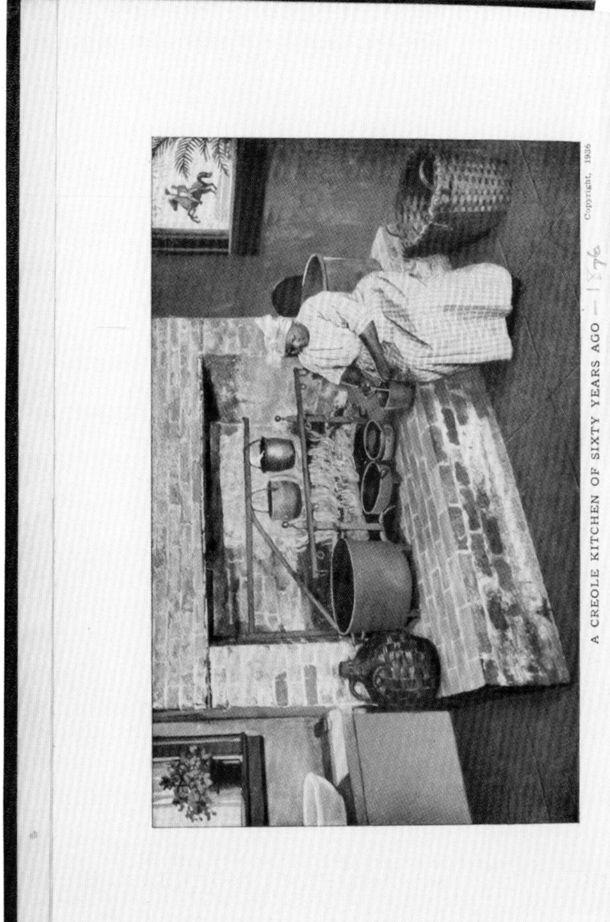

A CREOLE KITCHEN OF SIXTY YEARS AGO —
Copyright, 1936

The
Original Picayune
Creole Cook Book

NINTH EDITION

Reprinted from the Fifth Edition, Containing Recipes Using Wines and Liquors Customary Before Prohibition

To assist the good housewives of the present day and to preserve to future generations the many excellent and matchless recipes of the New Orleans cuisine by gathering up from the old Creole cooks and the old housekeepers the best of Creole cookery, with all its delightful combinations and possibilities, is the object of this book.

Price, Per Copy - $1.50

Copyright 1901, 1906, 1916, 1922, 1928, 1936 and 1938 by
THE TIMES-PICAYUNE PUBLISHING CO.
NEW ORLEANS, LA.

THE TIMES-PICAYUNE

The Original Picayune Creole Cook Book

Containing Recipes Using Wines and Liquors Customary in Early Creole Cookery, 1901

New Orleans has long been held in the imagination of Americans as the place for great food. The serendipitous historical mix of French, Spanish, African, and Caribbean food traditions brought by each successive owner of this small strip of land between the bay and the river produced Creole cooking—one of the treasures of American food.

By the end of the nineteenth century, however, the old-time Creole cooks were all passing on and there was a fear that the recipes "that your mother used, and her mother, and her grandmother, and the grandmother got it from the old-time 'Mammy,' who could work magic in that black-raftered kitchen of long ago" would disappear with them. It was not just the home cooking that was in danger but also the tradition of the great chefs of New Orleans, people like Mme. Eugene, Alex Hause, Arthur Gray, John Straner, Charles Rhodes, and, of course, Madame Bégué. The *Times-Picayune* newspaper decided to preserve these recipes and gathered more than eight hundred of them into the first edition of *The Original Picayune Creole Cook Book*, in 1901.

NOTABLE RECIPES: Beignets • **Bonbons et Sucreries** (page 634) • **Crab Gumbo** (page 378) • **Creole Coffee** (page 315) • **Okra Gumbo** (page 377) • **Oyster Loaf** (page 373) • Pain Perdu • **Peanut Pralines** (page 636) • **Red Beans and Rice** (page 380) • King's Cake

ter, two hard-boiled eggs, two cold (left-over) potatoes, a half pint of water, and salt and pepper to taste. Chop the potatoes, onions and eggs fine and put them into the stewing pan with the meat, adding by degrees the butter, salt and one-half pod of Red Pepper, without the seeds, with a little dash of Cayenne. Stew very slowly for about fifteen or twenty minutes and serve hot.

CHAPTER VII

Gombo à la Créole

Gumbo, of all other products of the New Orleans cuisine, represents a most distinctive type of the evolution of good cookery under the hands of the famous Creole cuisinieres of old New Orleans. Indeed, the word "evolution" fails to apply when speaking of Gumbo, for it is an original conception, a something sui generis in cooking, peculiar to this ancient Creole city alone, and to the manner born. With equal ability the olden Creole cooks saw the possibilities of exquisite and delicious combinations in making Gumbo, and hence we have many varieties, till the occult science of making a good "Gombo a la Creole" seems too fine an inheritance of gastronomic lore to remain forever hidden away in the cuisines of this old Southern metropolis. The following recipes, gathered with care from the best Creole housekeepers of New Orleans, have been handed down from generation to generation. They need only to be tried to prove their perfect claim to the admiration of the many distinguished visitors and epicures who have paid tribute to our Creole Gumbo.

Gombo Filé

First, it will be necessary to explain here, for the benefit of many, that "File" is a powder manufactured by the remaining tribe of Choctaw Indians in Louisiana, from the young and tender leaves of the sassafras. The Indian squaws gather the leaves and spread them out on a stone mortar to dry. When thoroughly dried, they pound them into a fine powder, pass them through a hair sieve, and then bring the File to New Orleans to sell, coming twice a week to the French Market, from the old reservation set aside for their home on Bayou Lacombe, near Mandeville, La. The Indians used sassafras leaves and the sassafras for many medicinal purposes, and still sell bunches of the dried roots in the French Market. The Creoles, quick to discover and apply, found the possibilities of the powdered sassafras, or "File," and originated the well-known dish, "Gombo File."

To make a good "Gombo File," use

1 Large Tender Chicken.
2 Large Slices or ½ Pound Lean Ham.
2 Tablespoonfuls of Butter or 1 of Shortening.
1 Bay Leaf. 3 Sprigs of Parsley.
3 Dozen Oysters.
1 Large Onion. 1 Sprig of Thyme.
2 Quarts of Oyster Water.
2 Quarts of Boiling Water.
1 Half Pod of Red Pepper Without the Seeds.
Salt and Pepper and Cayenne to Taste.

Clean and cut up the chicken as for a fricassee. Dredge with salt and black pepper, judging according to taste. Cut the ham into dice shape and chop the onion, parsley and thyme very fine. Put the shortening or butter into the soup kettle or deep stewing pot, and when hot, put in the ham and chicken. Cover closely and fry for about five or ten minutes. Then add the onion and parsley and thyme, stirring occasionally to prevent burning. When nicely browned add the boiling water and throw in the oyster stock, which has been thoroughly heated. Add the bay leaf, chopped very fine, and the pepper pod, cut in two, and set the Gumbo back to simmer for about an hour longer. When nearly ready to serve dinner, and while the Gumbo is boiling, add the fresh oys-

ters. Let the Gumbo remain on the stove for about three minutes longer, and then remove the pot from the fire. Have ready the tureen, set in a "bain-marie," or hot water bath, for once the File is added the Gumbo must never be warmed over. Take two tablespoonfuls of the File and drop gradually into the pot of boiling hot Gumbo, stirring slowly to mix thoroughly; pour into the tureen, or tureens, if there should be a second demand, and serve with boiled rice. (See recipe.) The rice, it should be remarked, must be boiled so that the grains stand quite apart, and brought to the table in a separate dish, covered. Serve about two spoonfuls of rice to one plate of Gumbo.

The above recipe is for a family of six. Increase quantities in proportion as required. Never boil the Gumbo with the rice, and never add the File while the Gumbo is on the fire, as boiling after the File is added tends to make the Gumbo stringy and unfit for use, else the File is precipitated to the bottom of the pot, which is equally to be avoided.

Where families cannot afford a fowl, a good Gumbo may be made by substituting the round of the beef for the chicken.

Turkey Gumbo

Gombo de Dinde

The Remains of a Turkey.
½ Pound of Lean Ham.
2 Tablespoons of Butter or 1 of Shortening.
1 Bay Leaf. 3 Sprigs of Parsley.
3 Dozen Oysters.
1 Large Onion. 1 Sprig of Thyme.
2 Quarts of Oyster Water.
½ Pod of Red Pepper, Without the Seeds.
Salt, Pepper and Cayenne to Taste.

Nothing is ever lost in a well-regulated Creole kitchen. When turkey is served one day, the remains or "left-over" are saved and made into that most excellent dish—a Turkey Gumbo. It is made in the same manner as Chicken Gumbo, only instead of the chicken the turkey meat, black and white, that is left over, is stripped from the bones and carcass. Chop fine and add to the hot shortening, and then put in the ham, cut fine into dice shape. Proceed exactly as in the recipe above, only after adding the boiling water, throw in the bones and carcass of the turkey. At the proper time remove the carcass and bones, add the oysters, and then remove the pot and "File" the Gumbo. Serve with boiled rice. Turkey Gumbo, when made from the remains of wild turkey, has a delicious flavor.

Squirrel or Rabbit Gumbo

Gombo d'Ecureuil ou de Lapin

These are famous Creole Gumbos. The following ingredients are used:

1 Fine Squirrel or Rabbit.
2 Slices or ½ Pound of Lean Ham.
3 Sprigs of Parsley. 1 Sprig of Thyme.
1 Bay Leaf. 1 Large Onion.
3 Dozen Oysters.
2 Quarts of Oyster Water.
½ Pod of Red Pepper, Without the Seed
A Dash of Cayenne.
Salt and Pepper to Taste.

Skin, clean and cut up the squirrel or rabbit, as for a fricassee. Dredge well with salt and black pepper. Cut the ham into dice shape, and chop the onion, parsley and thyme very fine. Put the shortening or butter into a deep stew pot and when hot, put in the squirrel or rabbit. Cover closely and fry for about eight or 10 minutes. Then proceed in exactly the same manner as for Chicken Gumbo; add the "File" at the time indicated, and serve with boiled Louisiana rice. (See recipe.)

Okra Gumbo

Gombo Févi

1 Chicken. 1 Onion.
6 Large Fresh Tomatoes.
2 Pints of Okra, or Fifty Counted.
½ Pod of Red Pepper, Without the Seeds.
2 Large Slices of Ham.
1 Bay Leaf. 1 Sprig of Thyme or Parsley.
1 Tablespoonful of Shortening or 2 Level Spoons of Butter.
Salt and Cayenne to Taste.

Clean and cut up the chicken. Cut the ham into small squares or dice and chop the onions, parsley and thyme. Skin the tomatoes, and chop fine, saving the juice. Wash and stem the okra and slice into thin layers of one-half inch each. Put the shortening or butter into the soup kettle, and when hot add the chicken and the ham. Cover closely and let it simmer for about ten minutes. Then add the chopped onions, parsley, thyme and tomatoes, stirring frequently to prevent scorching. Then add the okra, and, when well browned, add the juice of the tomatoes, which imparts a superior flavor. The okra is

2 Cloves of Garlic.
6 Green Sweet Peppers.
Cup of Consomme or Boiling Water.
Salt and Pepper to Taste.

Wash the Frog legs. Put two tablespoonfuls of butter into a saucepan and add the legs. Let this brown well, being careful not to burn. After ten minutes of very slow cooking on a good fire, take three large onions and slice them and let them brown with the frogs. Then add one-half dozen nice large fresh tomatoes, or a half can; cover and let these brown. Cook very slowly adding salt and pepper to taste, thyme, bay leaf, two cloves of garlic, all chopped very fine indeed. Let the mixture smother slowly over the fire, and, if possible, add one-half dozen green sweet peppers sliced very fine, being careful to extract all the seeds. Stir well and let it smother twenty minutes longer, stirring frequently to prevent burning. When well smothered—that is, when the Frog legs are tender, which is easily ascertained by touching with a fork—add one cup of broth, if you have it, or consomme; if not, add one cup of boiling water, and let it cook again for half an hour very slowly and well covered. Serve hot.

Broiled Frogs

Grenouilles Grillées

6 Frog Legs.
A Cup of Boiling Lemon Juice and Salt.
1 Tablespoonful of Olive Oil.
1 Tablespoonful of Black Pepper.
1 Tablespoonful of Butter.
Salt and Pepper to Taste.
Lettuce Leaves and Parsley, or Sliced Lemons and Olives to Garnish.

Clean and skin the Frogs; scald well in boiling lemon juice and salt. Dry with a clean towel. Mix thoroughly a little black pepper, salt and olive oil, or butter melted, and rub the Frogs thoroughly, rolling them over and over. Take out and put on a double wire broiler, being careful to turn frequently to prevent scorching. When done, place in a platter of delicate lettuce leaves or parsley and garnish with sliced lemons and olives.

Fried Frogs

Grenouilles Frites

6 Frog Legs.
½ Cup of Lemon Juice and a Teaspoonful of Salt.
2 Eggs. 1 Cup of Sifted Bread Crumbs
Parsley, Sliced Lemon and Radishes to Garnish.
Salt and Pepper to Taste.

Scald the Frog legs about three minutes in boiling water and add a half cup of lemon juice and salt. Take out of the water and dry with a clean towel. Season with salt and pepper and dip into a batter made of the well-beaten yolks and whites of two eggs and sifted bread crumbs. Pat the Frogs well and drop into the shortening, heated to a boiling point and fry to a golden brown. Take them from the shortening and drain well by placing on a soft brown paper, heated. Place a snow-white folded napkin in a dish, and lay the frogs upon it and garnish with fried parsley and sliced lemon, or place the frogs in a bed of fried parsley laid in the dish and garnish with decorated radishes and sliced lemons.

Stewed Frogs

Grenouilles en Fricassée

1 Dozen Frog Legs.
1 Tablespoonful of Butter.
1 Tablespoonful of Flour. 1 Cup of Water.
1 Cup of Oyster Water.
1 Sprig of Thyme. 1 Sprig of Parsley.
1 Bay Leaf. 1 Sprig of Sweet Marjoram. 10 Allspice, 1 Clove.
The Yolk of an Egg. Croutons.
2 Dozen Oysters.

Take the legs of one dozen Frogs and prepare the same as for frying. Take a tablespoonful of butter and put in a frying pan. When it begins to melt, add a tablespoonful of flour and stir constantly. When it begins to brown nicely, add one cup of water and a pint of oyster water. Throw in the Frog legs as it begins to boil, and add salt and pepper, a little Cayenne, a sprig of thyme, bay leaf and sweet marjoram, eight or ten allspice, one clove. Let it simmer about fifteen minutes and take off the fire. Have ready the yolk of a beaten egg, and add, blending well, and serve immediately with garnishes of Croutons, and fried in a little butter, with oysters laid upon them.

CHAPTER IX

Des Crustacés

Under this heading are classed the shellfish found in our Louisiana waters and those of the Mississippi Sound adjacent to New Orleans. Oysters, Shrimp, Crabs and Crawfish and the famous Green Turtle—these are the delightful varieties that are common articles of food among the people and which are to be had for the fishing.

That delicious bivalve, the Oyster, has its home among us. Everyone who has visited New Orleans in winter has noted the exceptionally palatable oysters that are sold in every restaurant and by the numerous small vendors on almost every other corner or so throughout the lower section of the city. In the cafes, the hotels, the oyster saloons, they are served in every conceivable style known to epicures and caterers. The oyster beds adjacent to New Orleans send to our markets Oysters that are highly prized for exquisite flavor and rated by epicures as unsurpassed in quality. The Mississippi Sound is stocked with oysters from one end to the other, and millions of cans are shipped yearly from Biloxi and other points to every point of the United States. Houma, La., and Morgan City, La., are important shipping points for fresh Oysters in bulk. And so with our celebrated Lake and River Shrimp.

So strict are the laws governing the use of dredges in the Mississippi Sound that a watchman accompanies each dredgeboat to see that no attempt is made to use the dredge in less than fourteen feet of water. Thus are preserved, in all their splendid flavor and almost inexhaustible supply, our far-famed oysters. While the yearly increase in consumption of this delicious bivalve has tended to alarm scientists and to raise the question as to whether the American oyster beds may not likely become depleted, modern methods of renewing the beds by planting "seed" oysters give assurance of a permanently adequate supply. The railroad facilities for handling oysters can hardly be improved, and, fresh and fine and ready to be eaten, they arrive in our markets. Oysters from the Louisiana bays and bayous are with us all summer, and New Orleans oyster lovers enjoy the succulent bivalve the year around.

New Orleans opened the eyes of the United States to the possibilities of the oyster in every variety and form of cooking. Her chefs evolved the most dainty and palatable ways of preparing them, and while raw oysters remained practically an unknown quantity in aristocratic centers in other states of the Union, the Creoles, quick to discover and apply, placed the raw oyster on their tables as one of the greatest delicacies that could be offered the most fastidious appetite.

Probably no one item of seafood lends itself so well to the ministrations of the ingenious chef as the oyster. It is prepared in a great number of ways, and in each it is a dish fit for the gods.

In the following recipes are given the most delightful manner of serving

OYSTERS

Huitres à la Créole

There has already been given, in the chapter devoted to soups, the several ways that the Creoles have of preparing oysters in this style. (See Oyster Soups.) In a general treatment of oysters, it presents, first, that famous but exceptionally palatable manner in which oysters can be eaten at all hours, day or night, without overloading the stomach or causing the least symptom of indigestion, viz:

Raw Oysters on Half Shell

Huitres en Coquilles

6 Oysters to Each Plate. Cracked Ice.

MRS. SIMON KANDER AND OTHERS

"The Settlement" Cook Book

The Way to a Man's Heart, 1901

"The Settlement" Cook Book stands along with Fannie Farmer's *The Boston Cooking-School Cook Book* as one of the most important cookbooks of the early twentieth century. Milwaukee, Wisconsin, was a mostly German immigrant city by the late 1800s. The population included a large wealthy German Jewish community of established businessmen who tended to practice American Reform Judaism. During this period, however, an influx of working-class German and Russian Jews also settled in ghetto areas of the city.

Enter Lizzie Black Kander (1858–1940), who was born into one of the wealthy German Jewish families and who felt that social work was not strictly the province of Christians. By the 1890s Kander was heavily involved in improving the lives of young immigrant Jewish women, helping to educate them and to assimilate them into American society. Kander had two obsessions: food and cleanliness. By 1895 she had built a public bathhouse for immigrant children next to the Schlitz Brewery, utilizing the excess hot water from the bottle sterilization process to provide hot baths for up to one hundred children a day. In 1901 she moved her operation to a location on North Fifth Street that became known as The Settlement. The new space was funded for the first year by a board of directors, whose members each gave thousand-dollar subscriptions. Kander knew this would not be enough to run the operation. Realizing that her most popular programs were her cooking classes, Kander proposed to do a charity cookbook, the proceeds from which would go to fund The Settlement. She approached the board with the idea to seek funding and was rejected. With assistance from her father, she privately printed the book, and it sold out in the first year. It has been reprinted ever since and has sold more than 1.5 million copies worldwide.

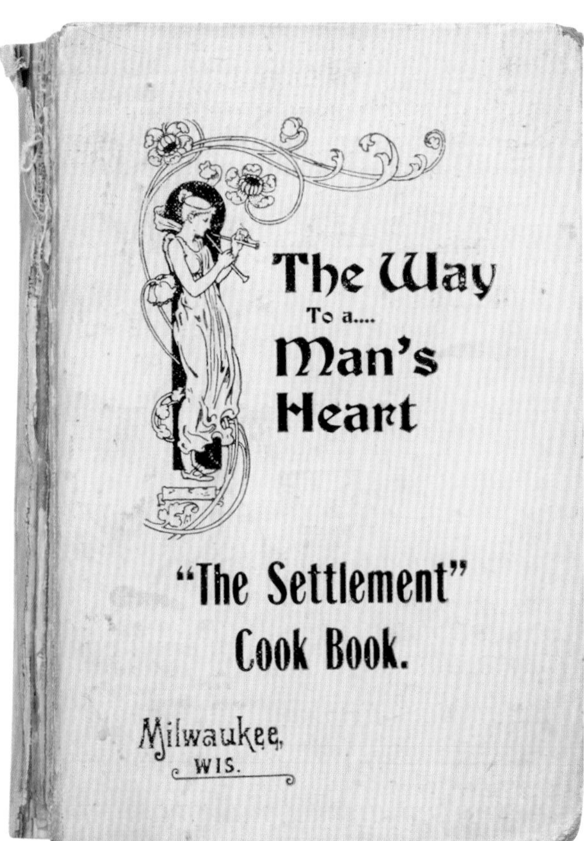

"The Settlement" Cook Book Americanized many traditional Jewish dishes, breaking with strict dietary laws; it also included recipes for shellfish, cream and meat dishes, and nonkosher cuts of meat. Largely German in inspiration, the book presented more than five hundred "heirloom recipes" collected from "some of the finest tables in Milwaukee" that were tested by Kander herself in her home kitchen. *"The Settlement" Cook Book,* more than any other, is the foundation on which twentieth-century Jewish American cooking rests.

NOTABLE RECIPES: Berliner Pfann Kuchen (Filled Doughnuts) • Casserole of Rice and Meat • **Gingerbread No. 1** (page 589) • **German Pancakes** (page 594) • **Good Kuchen Roll** (page 639) • Matzos Pancakes • Muffins • **Potato Cakes** (page 419)

For high grade instruction in

BUSINESS AND SHORTHAND

ATTEND THE

GILBERT

Commercial College

Cor. Broadway and Mason St. A. L. GILBERT, *Principal.*

ADOLPH EHRLER'S

Cafe and Confectionery,

276 Third Street. MILWAUKEE. Telephone, 1714 Main.

Specialty in Wedding and Birthday Cakes, also a great assortment in all kinds of small fancy cakes.

Milwaukee-Western Fuel Co.,

SUCCESSOR TO
B. Uhrig Fuel Co.,
The R. P. Elmore Co.,
H. M. Benjamin Coal Co.,
F. R. Buell Coal Co.,
Geo. S. Eastman.

AGENT FOR
D. L. & W. R. R. Co.'s Scranton Coal,
The W. L. Scott Co.'s Lackawanna Coal
C. C. & B.'s Pocahontas Smokeless Coal

GENERAL OFFICES:
2 TO 12 GRAND AVENUE. MILWAUKEE.

EYES EXAMINED FREE OF CHARGE.

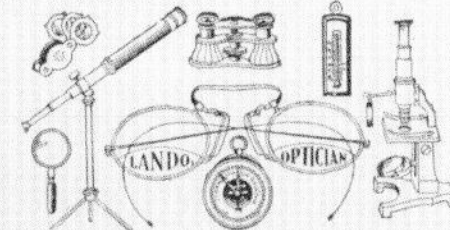

JULIUS LANDO, Optician,

419 East Water Street, Telephone, 8654 White.

Kabo Corsets

Have No Brass Eyelets.

It Would be Absurd to assert that nobody can make as good corsets as *Kabo*, but it is quite safe to say *nobody is doing so*, and further that there is no other line

So Extensive,

So well balanced,

So popular—

Proof positive that the models are always the precise things decreed by fashion. *Over one hundred* of the most alluringly dainty *straight front styles* at $1.00 to $10.00, and intermediate prices.
Write for catalog de luxe.

Kabo Corset Co.

For sale at all leading Dry Goods stores.

UP-TO-DATE CHINA WARE,
GLASSES, SILVERWARE AND
DECORATIONS.

Telephone Main 1421.

George Nedtweg,

CATERER.

448 Jefferson Street,

Milwaukee.

Special Attention Given to Weddings,
Receptions, Dinners, Suppers, Etc.
in any part of the State

Campbell Laundry Co.,

514 Grand Ave., Milwaukee.

10 "THE SETTLEMENT" COOK BOOK.

RHUBARB WATER.

Wash the rhubarb, cut in one-half inch lengths. Put into a bowl, add the peel, sugar and boiling water. Cover and set away to cool. Strain and serve cold. Pink stalks will give the water a pretty color.

GRAPE CORDIAL.

¼ cup grape juice,
1 teaspoon lemon juice,
¾ cup cold water,
Sugar to taste.

Mix sugar with strained grape juice, add lemon juice and water. A slice of orange or pineapple may also be added.

ALBUMENIZED MILK.

½ cup milk.
White of 1 egg.

Put white of egg in a tumbler, add milk, cover tightly, and shake thoroughly until well mixed.

EGG NOG.

Beat the yolk of one egg, add one tablespoon sugar, and beat until light. Add one-half cup of milk. Beat the white of the egg well and fold it in lightly. Add one-half teaspoon vanilla or a little grated nutmeg.

MANHATTAN COCKTAIL.

⅓ whiskey (Sheridan rye).
⅓ Vermuth bitters,
⅓ water.

And add a dash of angostura, apricotine and orange bitters, and a slice of lemon peel. Sweeten to taste.

WASHINGTON PUNCH FOR 12 PEOPLE.

One-half pineapple, sliced fine and sprinkle liberally with granulated sugar. Add one-half bottle Rhine or Moselle wine, and set aside for twenty-four hours to ripen; then strain and add two bottles Rhine wine, one bottle claret, and the remainder of the pineapple, sliced fine. Just before serving, add one quart champagne. Either use a large piece of ice to cool, or have the wines ice cold before mixing.

BEVERAGES. 11

EGG MILK PUNCH.

One egg, three teaspoons fine sugar, fill half full ice, one wineglass brandy, two tablespoons St. Croix rum, fill with milk, shake well and strain into large glass, grating nutmeg on top.

CHAMPAGNE PUNCH FOR 12 PEOPLE.

3 qts. champagne,
¼ pt. maraschino,
½ pt. imported brandy,
¼ lb. loaf sugar,
2 lemons, sliced fine,
2 oranges, sliced fine,

Or any fruit in season. If not sweet enough, add more sugar. Just before using, add a large piece of ice.

CLARET CUP No. 1.

3 lemons (juice),
6 tablespoons sugar,
1 sherry glass curacoa,
1 slice cucumber rind, and a bunch of fresh mint,
3 pts. claret,
1 pt. apollinaris,
1 finely sliced orange, strawberries, pineapple.

CLARET CUP No. 2.

1 pt. claret,
1 cup sugar,
1 pt. sparkling Moselle,
Juice of 1 orange,
1 slice cucumber rind,
1 pt. apollinaris.

POUSSE CAFE.

⅔ crême de café,
⅙ crême de menthe,
⅙ apricotine or vanilla.

Pour the café first and slowly add apricotine or vanilla and then the mint.

ORANGE JULEP.

Peel very thin one-half fine orange rind, put it into a glass with a little finely chopped ice, two teaspoonfuls of powdered sugar. Stir two minutes to extract the oil. Fill the glass with chopped ice, two sprigs of fresh mint, one small teaspoon of crême de menthe, four tablespoonfuls good whiskey—Sheridan rye is the best.

SARAH TYSON RORER

Mrs. Rorer's New Cook Book

A Manual of Housekeeping, 1902

Sarah Tyson Rorer was a member of the early domestic science movement, which included such figures as Fannie Farmer and Mary J. Lincoln. These enterprising, educated women saw a possibility for elevating women's work in the home by applying the rigors of science—the nineteenth century's supreme justification for just about everything—to the domestic sphere.

Rorer was born in October 1849 in Bucks County, Pennsylvania. Her father was a chemist, and her own early interest in chemistry led her to focus on food and its effects on the body. She is considered to be America's first dietician. Rorer was also a teacher of domestic science, a lecturer on food and on health, an author, and an editor. She wrote columns for the popular Philadelphia magazine *Table Talk* and served as an editor for the *Ladies' Home Journal* for fourteen years. Like many of her peers, she opened a cooking school, the Philadelphia Cooking School.

While Rorer wrote many books, pamphlets, and articles, she is best known for the book shown here. Rorer was a staunch advocate for fresh vegetables, not overcooked lest they lose much of their nutritional value. She was also a great defender of rice, because it was higher in protein than potatoes and could be digested within an hour. Laura Shapiro notes in her excellent book on the early domestic scientists, *Perfection Salad: Women and Cooking at the Turn of the Century*: "Mrs. Rorer had a special fondness for the all-white meal, which she didn't mind going to some lengths to achieve. Cream soups, cream sauces, boiled poultry, and white fish dominated her dinners, with vanilla ice cream, whipped cream, and angel cake for dessert." This dreadful concoction was not uncommon among the domestic science menus and cooking schools, where color-themed dinners were popular. While we have difficulty today imagining how we would prepare, let alone serve, these recipes, that was no problem for the domestic scientists, whose influence was pervasive in the first half of the twentieth century. The focus on nutritional values, vitamins, and additives that overshadowed taste and enjoyment of food still haunts us every time we go to the grocery store today. Sadly, for all her contributions, Rorer lost all her financial holdings during the Depression. She died destitute in 1937, having lived the last years of her life dependent on her children and former students.

NOTABLE RECIPES: Banana Pudding (page 650) • **Cream of Peanut Soup** (page 348) • **Cream of Salsify Soup** (page 347) • **Dandelion Salad, German Fashion** (page 360) • **Mushroom Catsup** (page 432) • Nut and Fruit Crackers • Nut Sausage • **Peanut Wafers** (page 633) • Stuffed Cucumbers

Breakfast Table, Last Course

MRS RORER'S NEW COOK BOOK

A MANUAL OF HOUSEKEEPING

By

SARAH TYSON RORER

Author of Mrs. Rorer's Philadelphia Cook Book, Canning and Preserving, Bread and Bread Making, and other valuable works on cookery; Principal of Philadelphia Cooking School

PHILADELPHIA
ARNOLD AND COMPANY
420 SANSOM STREET

24 MRS. RORER'S NEW COOK BOOK

NAMES OF FRUITS AND VEGETABLES IN VARIOUS LANGUAGES

ENGLISH	FRENCH	GERMAN	SPANISH
Almond	Amandier	Mandel	Almendra
Apple	Pomme	Apfel	Manzana
Apricot	Abricote	Aprikose	Albaricoque
Artichoke	Artichaut	Artischöke	Cinauco
Asparagus	Asperge	Spargel	Esparrago
Banana	Banane	Pisang	(Guineo)
Bean, Broad	Fève de Marais	Grosse Bohne, Garten Bohne	Haba
Bean, Kidney	Haricot	Türkische Bohne	Judias and Fasoles
Beet	Betterave	Rothe Rübe	Betarraga
Berberry	Épine vinette	Berberitzen	Berberis
Black Currant	Cassis and Groseille noir	Schwarze Johannisbeere	Grosella negro
Borecole	Chou vert, or Non pommé	Grüner Kohl	Col
Broccoli	Broccoli and Chou brocoli	Italienischer Kohl	Broculi
Brussels Sprouts	Chou de Bruxelles or à jets	Sprossen Kohl	
Cabbage	Chou pommé or Cabus	Kopfkohl	Berza
Cardoon	Cardon	Kardon	Cardo
Carrot	Carotte	Möhre or Gelbe Rübe	Chirivia
Cauliflower	Chou-fleur	Blumen Kohl	Berza florida
Celery	Céleri	Sellerie	Appio hortense
Cherry	Cerise	Kirsche	Cerezo
Chicory or Succory	Chicorée Sauvage	Gemeine Cichorie	Achicoria
Cress, Garden	Cresson	Gemeine Garten Kresse	Mastuerzo
Cress, Water	Cresson de Fontaine	Brunnen Kresse	Berro
Cress, Winter	Cresson de Terre	Winter Kresse	Hierba de Santa Barbbara
Cucumber	Concombre	Gurke	Pepino or Cohombro
Eggplant	Melongène Aubergine	Tollapfel and Eierpflanze	Berengena
Endive	Chicorée des Jardins, Endive	Endivie	Endivia
Fig	Figue	Feige	Higuera
Filbert	Noisette	Haselnuss	Avellano
Garlic	Ail	Knoblauch	Ajo
Gooseberry	Groseille	Stachelbeere	Uva-Crespas
Grape	Vigne	Traube and Weintrauben	Vina
Horseradish	Cranson or le Grand Raifort	Meerrettig	Rabano Picante
Kohlrabi or Turnip Cabbage	Chou-rave	Kohl Rabi	
Leek	Poireau	Gemeiner Lauch or Porro Zwiebel	Puerro
Lemon	Limon	Citrone	Limon
Lettuce	Laitue	Gartensalat and Lattich	Lechuga
Melon, Musk	Melon	Melone	Melon
Mint, Common	Menthe des Jardins	Münze	Menta
Mulberry	Mûre	Maulbeere	Moral
Mushroom	Champignon comestible	Essbare Blätter Schwämme	Seta
Mustard	Moutarde	Senf	Mostaza
Nectarine	Pêche lisse	Nectarpfirsich	Especie de Duramo
Olive	Olive	Olive	Olivo

KITCHEN CALENDAR 25

ENGLISH	FRENCH	GERMAN	SPANISH
Onion	Oignon	Zwiebel	Cebolla
Orange	Oranger	Pomeranze	Naranja
Orach	Arroche	Meldekraut	Armuelle
Parsley	Persil	Petersilie	Perejil
Parsnip	Panais	Pastinake	Chirivia and Pastinaca
Pea	Pois	Erbse	Guisante
Peach	Pêche	Pfirsiche	Alberchigo
Pear	Poire	Birne	Pera
Pepper, Red or Chile	Piment	Spanischer Pfeffer	Pimiento
Pineapple	Ananas	Ananas	Pina
Plum	Prune	Pflaume	Ciruelo
Pomegranate	Grenade	Granate	Granada
Potato	Pomme de Terre	Kartoffel	Batatas Inglezas
Pumpkin or Gourd	Courge	Kürbis	Calabaza
Quince	Coignassier	Quitte	Membrillo
Radish	Radis and Rave	Rettig and Radies	Rabano
Rape	Navette	Repskohl	Naba silvestre
Red Currant	Groseille rouge	Gemeine Johannisbeere	Grosella
Rhubarb	Rhubarbe	Rhabarber	Ruibarbo
Sage	Sauge	Salbei	Salvia
Salsify	Salsifis	Haferwurzel and Bocksbart	Barba Cabruna
Savoy	Chou de Milan or pommé fraisé	Wirsing or Herzkohl	Berza de Saboya
Sea-kale	Chou Marin and Crambé	Meerkohl	Col marina
Spinach	Épinard	Spinat	Espinaca
Strawberry	Fraise	Erdbeere	Fresa
Sweet Chestnut	Marron	Castanie	Castano
Thyme	Thym	Thimian	Tomillo
Tomato	Tomate	Liebesapfel	Tomate
Turnip	Navet	Rübe	Nabo
Walnut	Noyer	Wallnuss	Noguera
White Currant	Groseille blanche	Gemeine Johannisbeere	Grosella
Watermelon	Melon d'Eau	Wassermelone	Sandia

ISABEL GORDON CURTIS

Good Housekeeping Everyday Cook Book

A Combined Memorandum Cook Book and Scrap Book, 1903

Isabel Gordon Curtis was an associate editor at *Good Housekeeping* at the turn of the twentieth century. In her introduction to this book, which is "The Good Housekeeping Library Number One," Curtis outlines how her book "represents several new ideas in cook book writing." Its unusual narrow and tall size allows it to "lie open without taking too much room" on the table. It also includes blank pages interleaved between the recipes so readers can copy or paste in other recipes. Curtis notes: "these memorandum pages will be particularly popular with subscribers to *Good Housekeeping*, who will now be able to put into this book in proper place all their favorite recipes from *Good Housekeeping* every month."

The *Good Housekeeping Everyday Cook Book* is one of the earliest ladies' magazine cookbooks. Many of the cooking schools, such as Fannie Farmer's Boston Cooking-School, published magazines directed at the average homemaker. *Good Housekeeping* was affiliated with the New England School of Cookery, where all the recipes in this volume were tested. As with many cookbooks of this period, the recipes are narrative in style and don't list the ingredients at the beginning.

NOTABLE RECIPES: Buttermilk Biscuits (page 590) • **Cheese Straws** (page 317) • Chicken en Casserole • **A Club Sandwich** (page 372) • **Cold Slaw** (page 358) • Corn Oysters • Devil's Food Cake • **Strawberry Salad** (page 361) • **Tomatoes Stuffed** (page 412)

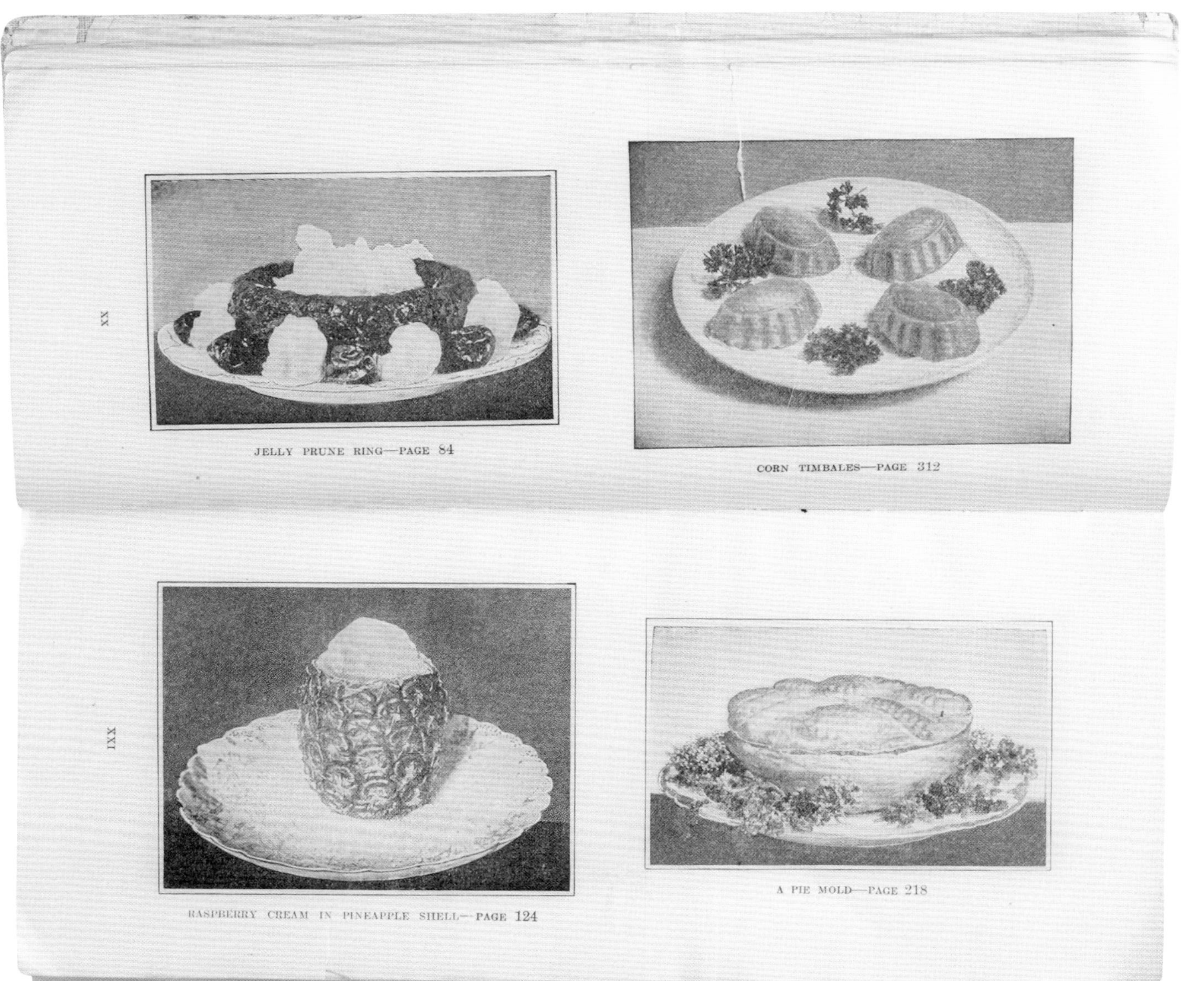

XX

JELLY PRUNE RING—PAGE 84

CORN TIMBALES—PAGE 312

XXI

RASPBERRY CREAM IN PINEAPPLE SHELL—PAGE 124

A PIE MOLD—PAGE 218

answer the purpose), then add the well-beaten yolks of the eggs, and add the flour, a little at a time, beating very thoroughly all the while, lastly add the whites of the eggs which have been beaten to a stiff froth that can be cut with a knife, or that will adhere to the vessel in which it has been beaten, being careful not to beat the cake after the whites have been added, but merely to fold in the puff. Flavor with one-fourth of a grated nutmeg, which should be put in before the whites of eggs. Bake in a very moderate oven for one hour. The only improvement that could be made on this recipe would be to use pastry flour (which was not used in mother's time). The best authorities on cake baking declare that good results cannot be obtained without the use of pastry flour.—Mrs P. L. Sherman, Chicago.

Orange Cake

Two cups of sugar, two and one-quarter cups of flour, one-half cup of water, yolks of five eggs, whites of four eggs, grated rind of one orange, one teaspoon of cream tartar, one-half teaspoon of soda. Bake in four tins.

Filling: Whites of two eggs, add pulverized sugar till stiff, the grated rind of one orange and the juice of two, to which add sufficient sugar to spread. —Mrs J. B. Hobbs, Chicago.

Extra Nice Walnut Cake

Beat to a cream one-half cup of butter and one cup of sugar. Dissolve one-half cup of cornstarch in one-half cup of milk, and add to butter and sugar, then add one cup of flour with one teaspoon of baking powder and the whites of two eggs beaten stiff. At the last add one cup of chopped walnut meats, and flavor with vanilla.

Cocoanut Loaf Cake

One cup of sugar, one-half cup of butter, three-quarters cup of milk, three

Burnt Leather Cake

Caramel part

2/3 cup sugar put on the stove and cooked until thick & dark like molasses

Cake part

1½ cup white sugar
½ " butter
3 Eggs
1 cup water
3 teaspoons of the Caramel
2 " " Vanilla
3 " " Baking powder
2½ cups Flour

Filling

1½ cup sugar 2/3 cup water
Boil until it threads
Pour over the beaten whites of 2 eggs beat until creamy
add rest of the caramel & 1 teaspoon vanilla

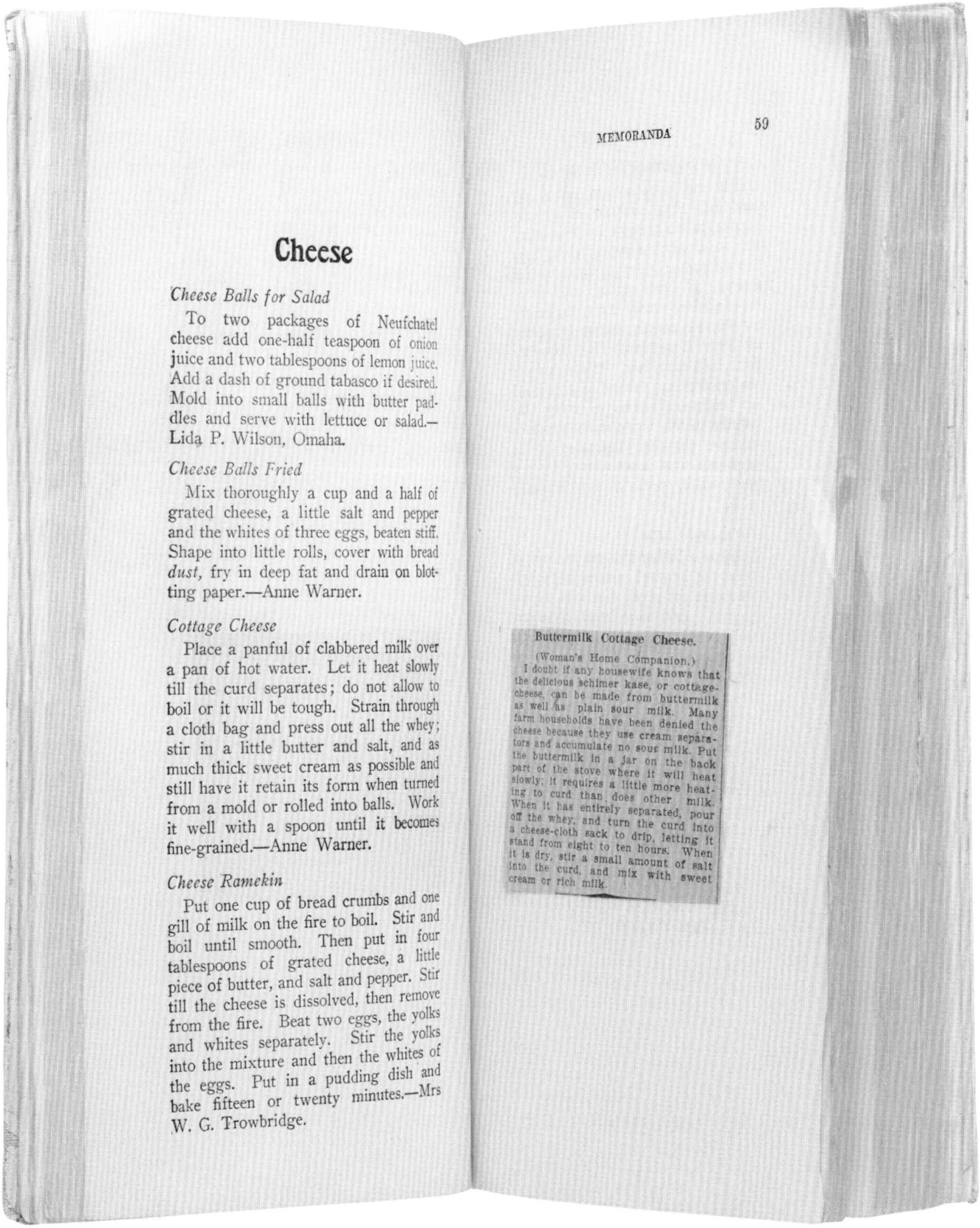

Cheese

Cheese Balls for Salad

To two packages of Neufchatel cheese add one-half teaspoon of onion juice and two tablespoons of lemon juice. Add a dash of ground tabasco if desired. Mold into small balls with butter paddles and serve with lettuce or salad.—Lida P. Wilson, Omaha.

Cheese Balls Fried

Mix thoroughly a cup and a half of grated cheese, a little salt and pepper and the whites of three eggs, beaten stiff. Shape into little rolls, cover with bread *dust,* fry in deep fat and drain on blotting paper.—Anne Warner.

Cottage Cheese

Place a panful of clabbered milk over a pan of hot water. Let it heat slowly till the curd separates; do not allow to boil or it will be tough. Strain through a cloth bag and press out all the whey; stir in a little butter and salt, and as much thick sweet cream as possible and still have it retain its form when turned from a mold or rolled into balls. Work it well with a spoon until it becomes fine-grained.—Anne Warner.

Cheese Ramekin

Put one cup of bread crumbs and one gill of milk on the fire to boil. Stir and boil until smooth. Then put in four tablespoons of grated cheese, a little piece of butter, and salt and pepper. Stir till the cheese is dissolved, then remove from the fire. Beat two eggs, the yolks and whites separately. Stir the yolks into the mixture and then the whites of the eggs. Put in a pudding dish and bake fifteen or twenty minutes.—Mrs W. G. Trowbridge.

Buttermilk Cottage Cheese.

(Woman's Home Companion.)

I doubt if any housewife knows that the delicious schimer kase, or cottage-cheese, can be made from buttermilk as well as plain sour milk. Many farm households have been denied the cheese because they use cream separators and accumulate no sour milk. Put the buttermilk in a jar on the back part of the stove where it will heat slowly; it requires a little more heating to curd than does other milk. When it has entirely separated, pour off the whey, and turn the curd into a cheese-cloth sack to drip, letting it stand from eight to ten hours. When it is dry, stir a small amount of salt into the curd, and mix with sweet cream or rich milk.

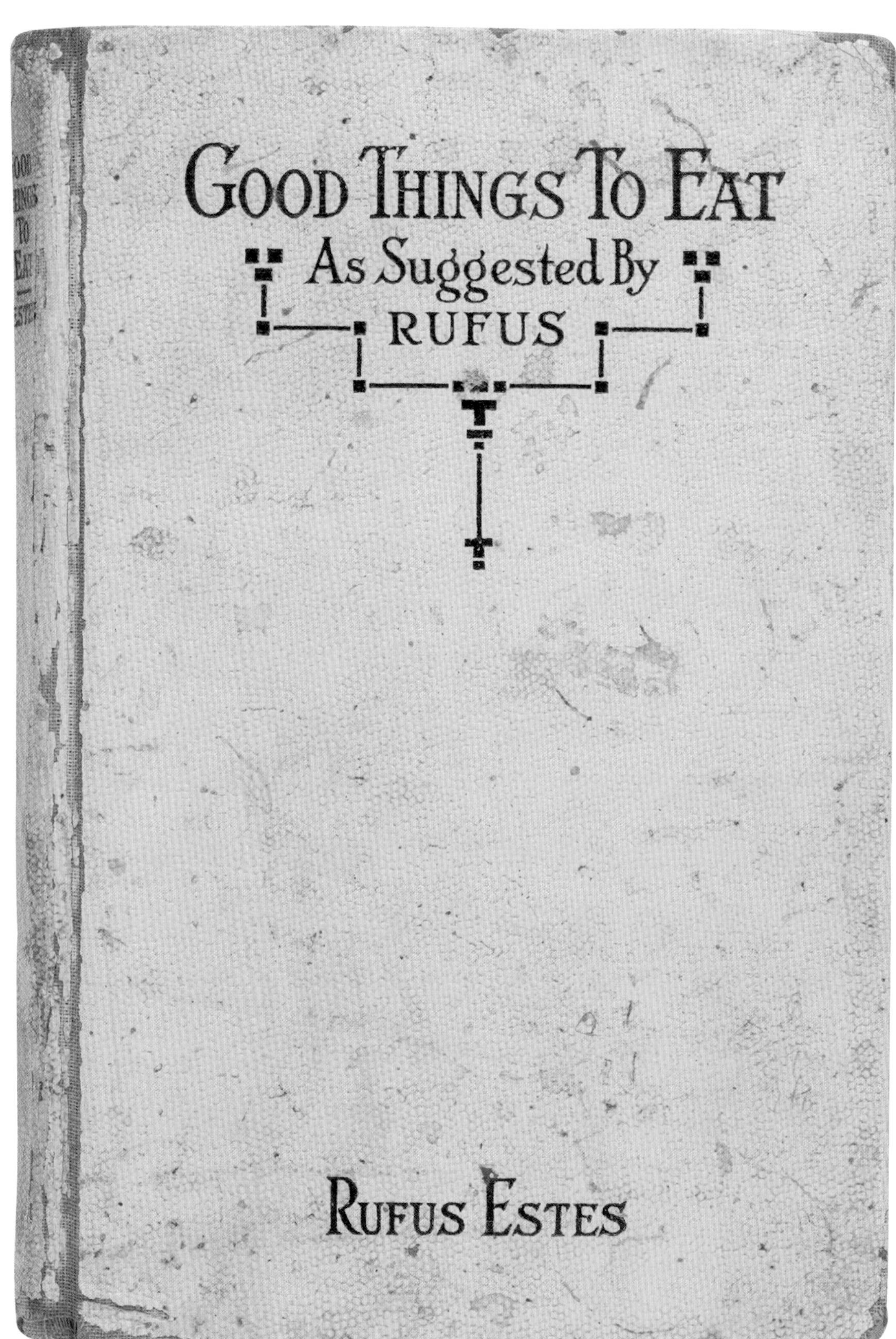
GOOD THINGS TO EAT
As Suggested By
RUFUS
RUFUS ESTES

RUFUS ESTES

Good Things to Eat, as Suggested by Rufus

A Collection of Practical Recipes for Preparing Meats, Game, Fowl, Fish, Puddings, Pastries, etc., 1911

The story of Rufus Estes is one of the most amazing of any cookbook author in American history. His life and work follow the sweep of a nation that nearly fell apart during the Civil War and then began modernizing at a dizzying rate to become one of the leading industrial powers of the world. Estes was born into slavery in Murray County, Tennessee, in 1857, as one of nine children. Two of his brothers escaped to fight for the North during the Civil War. Both were killed. His mother suffered a breakdown after their deaths. Following the Emancipation Proclamation, Rufus and his mother moved the family to Nashville to be near a grandmother. He worked a series of menial jobs, eventually finding work in a restaurant, where he began to pursue cooking seriously. He spent five years working in the restaurant before moving to Chicago.

In Chicago, Estes was hired by the Pullman Private Car Service in 1883 and spent fourteen years with the company. As a cook for the private cars that carried the country's wealthy, powerful, and elite class, he prepared food for Grover Cleveland, Benjamin Harrison, Adelina Patti, and Ignace Paderewski, among many others. Estes worked briefly in 1897 for the president of the Pittsburgh & Gould Railroad, but it went into receivership and was sold to the John W. Gates syndicate. Gates was so impressed with Estes's cooking that he kept him on as the cook for his private car. He also encouraged Estes to compile his recipes into a cookbook. In 1907 Estes was hired as chef of the executive dining room at U.S. Steel Corporation's offices in Chicago. He continued to compile his cookbook, which was privately published in 1911 under the title *Good Things to Eat*. It is also one of the rarest and scarcest of all cookbooks: Only twelve copies of the first edition are known to exist. Luckily there is a 1999 reprint that allows us to appreciate the culinary genius of this extraordinary man.

NOTABLE RECIPES: Candied Violets • **Cranberry Sherbet** (page 641) • **Maple Parfait** (page 640) • **Roasted Canvas-Back Duck** (page 492) • **Turkey Truffles** (page 496)

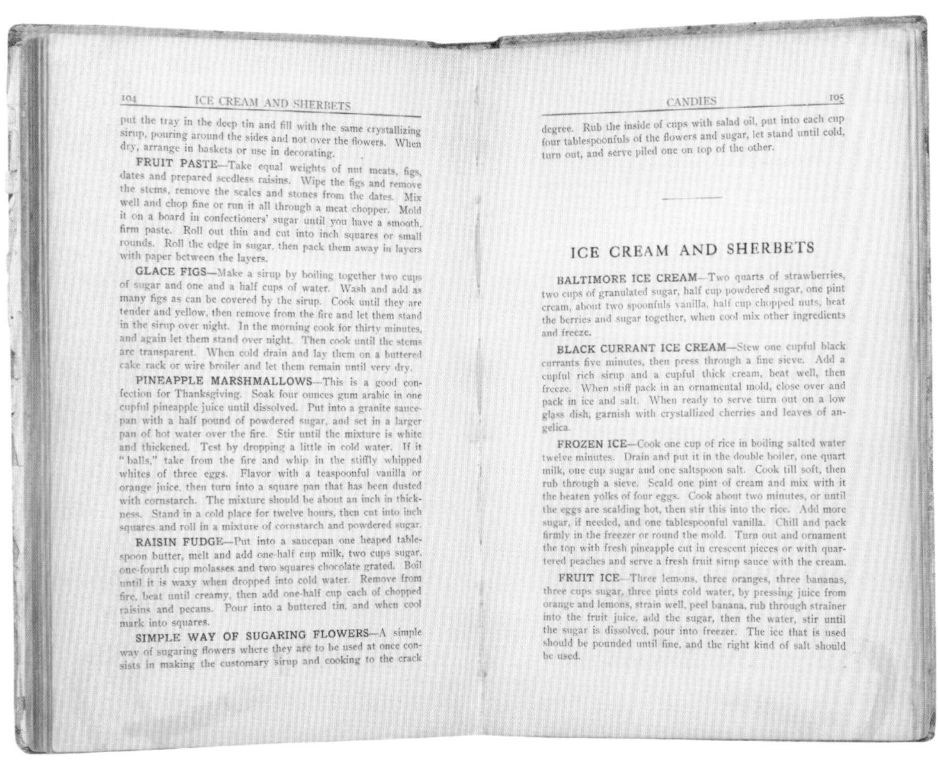

104 ICE CREAM AND SHERBETS

put the tray in the deep tin and fill with the same crystallizing sirup, pouring around the sides and not over the flowers. When dry, arrange in baskets or use in decorating.

FRUIT PASTE—Take equal weights of nut meats, figs, dates and prepared seedless raisins. Wipe the figs and remove the stems, remove the scales and stones from the dates. Mix well and chop fine or run it all through a meat chopper. Mold it on a board in confectioners' sugar until you have a smooth, firm paste. Roll out thin and cut into inch squares or small rounds. Roll the edge in sugar, then pack them away in layers with paper between the layers.

GLACE FIGS—Make a sirup by boiling together two cups of sugar and one and a half cups of water. Wash and add as many figs as can be covered by the sirup. Cook until they are tender and yellow, then remove from the fire and let them stand in the sirup over night. In the morning cook for thirty minutes, and again let them stand over night. Then cook until the stems are transparent. When cold drain and lay them on a buttered cake rack or wire broiler and let them remain until very dry.

PINEAPPLE MARSHMALLOWS—This is a good confection for Thanksgiving. Soak four ounces gum arabic in one cupful pineapple juice until dissolved. Put into a granite saucepan with a half pound of powdered sugar, and set in a larger pan of hot water over the fire. Stir until the mixture is white and thickened. Test by dropping a little in cold water. If it "balls," take from the fire and whip in the stiffly whipped whites of three eggs. Flavor with a teaspoonful vanilla or orange juice, then turn into a square pan that has been dusted with cornstarch. The mixture should be about an inch in thickness. Stand in a cold place for twelve hours, then cut into inch squares and roll in a mixture of cornstarch and powdered sugar.

RAISIN FUDGE—Put into a saucepan one heaped tablespoon butter, melt and add one-half cup milk, two cups sugar, one-fourth cup molasses and two squares chocolate grated. Boil until it is waxy when dropped into cold water. Remove from fire, beat until creamy, then add one-half cup each of chopped raisins and pecans. Pour into a buttered tin, and when cool mark into squares.

SIMPLE WAY OF SUGARING FLOWERS—A simple way of sugaring flowers where they are to be used at once consists in making the customary sirup and cooking to the crack

CANDIES 105

degree. Rub the inside of cups with salad oil, put into each cup four tablespoonfuls of the flowers and sugar, let stand until cold, turn out, and serve piled one on top of the other.

ICE CREAM AND SHERBETS

BALTIMORE ICE CREAM—Two quarts of strawberries, two cups of granulated sugar, half cup powdered sugar, one pint cream, about two spoonfuls vanilla, half cup chopped nuts, heat the berries and sugar together, when cool mix other ingredients and freeze.

BLACK CURRANT ICE CREAM—Stew one cupful black currants five minutes, then press through a fine sieve. Add a cupful rich sirup and a cupful thick cream, beat well, then freeze. When stiff pack in an ornamental mold, close over and pack in ice and salt. When ready to serve turn out on a low glass dish, garnish with crystallized cherries and leaves of angelica.

FROZEN ICE—Cook one cup of rice in boiling salted water twelve minutes. Drain and put it in the double boiler, one quart milk, one cup sugar and one saltspoon salt. Cook till soft, then rub through a sieve. Scald one pint of cream and mix with it the beaten yolks of four eggs. Cook about two minutes, or until the eggs are scalding hot, then stir this into the rice. Add more sugar, if needed, and one tablespoonful vanilla. Chill and pack firmly in the freezer or round the mold. Turn out and ornament the top with fresh pineapple cut in crescent pieces or with quartered peaches and serve a fresh fruit sirup sauce with the cream.

FRUIT ICE—Three lemons, three oranges, three bananas, three cups sugar, three pints cold water, by pressing juice from orange and lemons, strain well, peel banana, rub through strainer into the fruit juice, add the sugar, then the water, stir until the sugar is dissolved, pour into freezer. The ice that is used should be pounded until fine, and the right kind of salt should be used.

JESSICA B. HARRIS *on* RUFUS ESTES

Rufus Estes's 1911 classic cookbook, Good Things to Eat, as Suggested by Rufus, *is representative of the untold hundreds of African American cooks and chefs of the first quarter of the twentieth century. The genial face that peers out proudly from the first edition of this self-published book belies the travails of his life story. Estes's tale is harrowing, but it is not unusual. It is a story lived over and over again by African Americans in the years following the Civil War and the end of Reconstruction.*

We know little of Estes. Most of our information comes from the "Sketch of My Life" that forms one of the introductions to his book. He was born into slavery in Murray County, Tennessee, in 1857, and given the surname of his slaveholder, Estes. A youngster at the time of the Civil War, he was put to work early and by the age of five was already engaged in chores around the farm. After Emancipation, his family moved to Nashville, where he continued to display entrepreneurial skills by taking a job that consisted of bringing hot meals to laborers for a fee of twenty-five cents a month. He took this job so he could care for his mother, who was in poor health. By the age of sixteen, Estes was an accomplished worker. At this time, he entered into food service at a restaurant called Hemphill and discovered his true calling: He wanted to be a chef. Estes stayed at Hemphill for five years, learning the trade. When he was twenty-four, he relocated to Chicago. The Reconstruction had ended in the South in 1877, and the Estes family joined the northward trickle of Southerners that would soon become a tidal wave. Upon his arrival in the Windy City, Estes's culinary skills enabled him to find work in restaurants. The year was 1881—the same year Abby Fisher published What Mrs. Fisher Knows about Old Southern Cooking, *a work long thought to be the first African American cookbook.*

Two years later, like many African Americans trained in the culinary and service industries in the post–Civil War period, Estes took a position in the Pullman company, which manufactured railroad cars and had a large African American staff that served food on trains. He remained with the company until 1897, becoming one of its top chefs. Estes served many notables of the day, including two presidents (Harrison and Cleveland), the opera singer Adelina Patti, and the Princess of Spain when she visited the Chicago World's Fair. Estes continued to work on the railroads, both with Pullman and subsequently with private individuals. When he self-published his cookbook in 1911, he was the chef of the subsidiary companies of the U.S. Steel Corporation in Chicago.

While little else is known of Estes's life, the recipes he offers in Good Things to Eat, as Suggested by Rufus *speak volumes. Coupled with the advice for garnishing and service that he offers, the recipes give us a vivid picture of his talent and expertise. Estes presents them with evident "parental" pride in his introduction and reminds the reader that they're tested and true:*

> The recipes given in the following pages represent the labor of years. Their worth has been demonstrated, not experimentally, but by actual tests, day by day and month by month, under dissimilar, and, in many instances, not too favorable conditions.

Estes is meticulous in his attention to detail, and his suggestions to kitchen maids about food combining and menu pairings seem almost contemporary:

> For a roast beef dinner serve vegetable soup as the first course, with a relish of vegetables in season and horseradish or chow-chow pickle, unless you serve salad.
>
> If quail or ducks are to be served for dinner, an old Indian dish, wild rice, is very desirable.

He is also mindful of the necessary balance of a meal and enjoins them: "Do not serve dishes at the same meal that conflict. For instance, if you have sliced tomatoes, do not serve tomato soup."

Finally, in keeping with notions of hygiene that are central to all African American kitchens, he reminds them at the beginning of his advice section:

> It is always necessary to keep your kitchen in the best condition.

Very much the culinary perfectionist, Estes created recipes that display attention to detail and concern for taste. Situated midway between the culinary

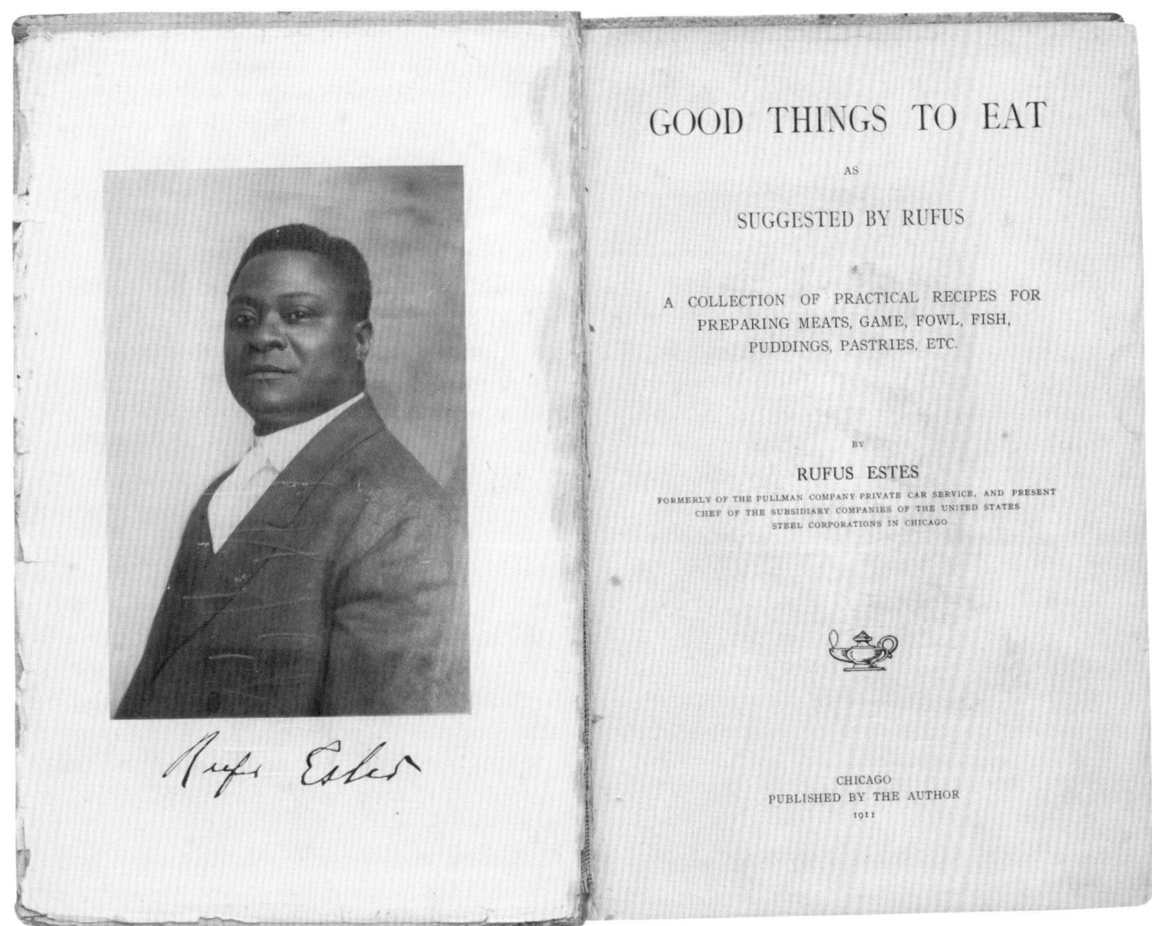

GOOD THINGS TO EAT

AS

SUGGESTED BY RUFUS

A COLLECTION OF PRACTICAL RECIPES FOR PREPARING MEATS, GAME, FOWL, FISH, PUDDINGS, PASTRIES, ETC.

BY

RUFUS ESTES

FORMERLY OF THE PULLMAN COMPANY PRIVATE CAR SERVICE, AND PRESENT CHEF OF THE SUBSIDIARY COMPANIES OF THE UNITED STATES STEEL CORPORATIONS IN CHICAGO

CHICAGO
PUBLISHED BY THE AUTHOR
1911

assumptions of the two earlier African American volumes, Abby Fisher's What Mrs. Fisher Knows about Old Southern Cooking *and Malinda Russell's* A Domestic Cook Book Containing a Careful Selection of Useful Receipts for the Kitchen *(1866), and the domestic science approach espoused by Fannie Farmer at the turn of the twentieth century, Estes's work often gives precise measurements and occasionally even offers yields for the recipes, as in his version of Chicken Gumbo, Creole Style.*

There are also recipes, such as the curious trompe l'oeil Bird's Nest Salad, that testify to the fact that Estes is situated firmly in the tradition of African Americans who earned their living by cooking for the country's elite and were bound by the aesthetic whims of their clientele:

> BIRDS NEST SALAD—Have ready as many crisp leaves of lettuce as may be required to make a dainty little nest for each person. Curl them into shape and in each one place tiny speckled eggs made by rolling cream cheese into shape, then sprinkle with fine chopped parsley. Serve with French dressing hidden under the leaves of the nest.

There are further indications of the rarefied culinary world in which Estes worked, such as an extravagant chestnut and truffle stuffing that calls for a quarter pound of truffles for every half pound of chestnuts. Estes, however, was no food snob. There are also occasional forays into more traditional African American cookery, such as his recipes for snap and beans, fried chicken, macaroni and cheese, and a wide range of fritters. International recipes such as kedgeree, beef marrow quenelles, and Italian ravioli highlight his culinary range.

In the 1920s, African American poet James Weldon Johnson sang paeans to "Black and Unknown Bards." Rufus Estes's Good Things to Eat, as Suggested by Rufus *is a culinary equivalent and a celebration of all the African American and other unknown cooks who stood facing the stoves in houses grand and humble in the twentieth century.*

IDA COGSWELL BAILEY ALLEN

Mrs. Allen's Cook Book, 1917

Ida Cogswell Bailey Allen was an early food media maven—Rachael Ray for the 1920s, if you will. Born in 1885, she was, by 1912, a columnist, food editor, and eventually, from 1928 to 1935, radio host of her own cooking program, *The National Radio Homemaker's Club*. Allen was a household name because of her more than fifty cookbooks and her writing for companies such as Pillsbury Flour, Sunshine Biscuits, and Coca-Cola, as well as her position as an editor at *Good Housekeeping* magazine. One of Allen's major interests was in making cooking "modern" and, thus, easier for the homemaker. As she notes in the introduction to her 1926 book *104 Prize Radio Recipes*:

> *There are twenty million of us—Home-Makers. That is our job. Sometimes we become so enmeshed in it that we cannot look beyond the narrow confines of our own home. Then it is that the flapper daughter—the "too modern" son—the gayety-loving husband—present real problems—we have not their viewpoint. To be a successful Home-Maker one must keep up. Any woman who has the wish can do it. Magic is not confined to myths or the Dark Ages. There is Magic today. The Magic of great manufacturers who have taken drudgery away—the Magic of gas and electricity—the Magic of books and libraries—and we have the Radio—that makes the Whole World Kin.*

Mrs. Allen reached a huge audience because of her savvy use of magazines, newspapers, printed books, and the relatively new medium of radio. Her influence on cooking of the 1920s and 1930s was immense. Her cookbooks went into second and third editions, and her publisher speculated that more than twenty million copies of her books had been printed. Allen believed so strongly in her "modern" cooking that she went so far as to say that good home cooking was an antidote to the rising divorce rate! Today her "modern" food looks like the beginning of the "box and can" cuisine we have come to distrust. To women of her time, she must have been a godsend.

NOTABLE RECIPES: Banana Fritters • Bread and Ham Timbales • Chop Suey • Coddled Apples • Consomme • **Fried Liver and Bacon / with Onions** (page 559) • Lamb Pasty • Macaroni Custard • **Old-Fashioned Chicken Pot-Pie** (page 500) • **Old-Fashioned Strawberry Shortcake** (page 589) • **Shirred Eggs** (page 461) • Shrimp Pie (with anchovies and peas) • **Waldorf Salad** (page 357)

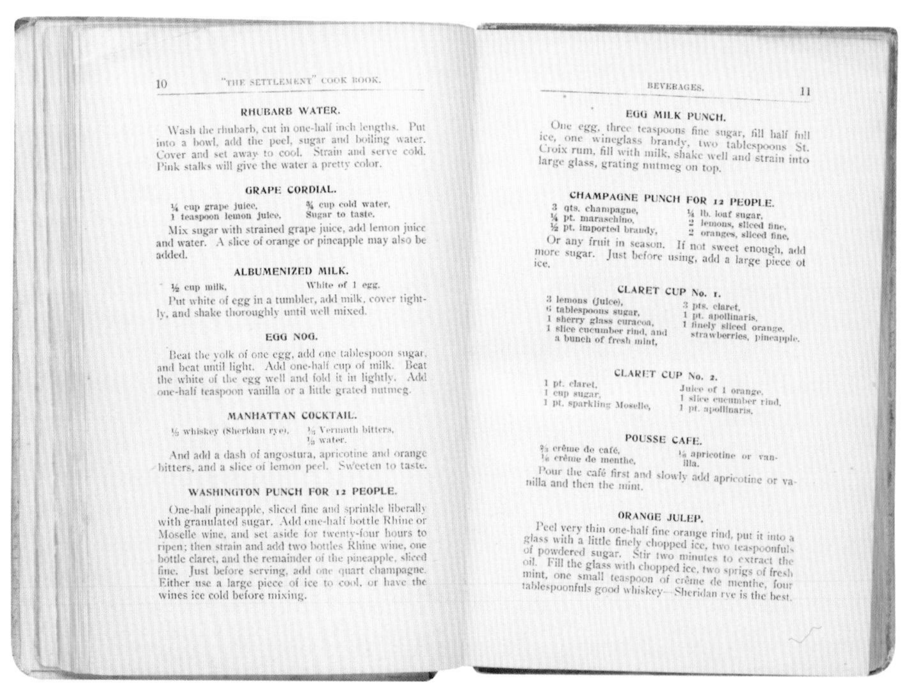

10 "THE SETTLEMENT" COOK BOOK.

RHUBARB WATER.

Wash the rhubarb, cut in one-half inch lengths. Put into a bowl, add the peel, sugar and boiling water. Cover and set away to cool. Strain and serve cold. Pink stalks will give the water a pretty color.

GRAPE CORDIAL.

¼ cup grape juice, ¾ cup cold water,
1 teaspoon lemon juice, Sugar to taste.

Mix sugar with strained grape juice, add lemon juice and water. A slice of orange or pineapple may also be added.

ALBUMENIZED MILK.

½ cup milk, White of 1 egg.

Put white of egg in a tumbler, add milk, cover tightly, and shake thoroughly until well mixed.

EGG NOG.

Beat the yolk of one egg, add one tablespoon sugar, and beat until light. Add one-half cup of milk. Beat the white of the egg well and fold it in lightly. Add one-half teaspoon vanilla or a little grated nutmeg.

MANHATTAN COCKTAIL.

⅓ whiskey (Sheridan rye), ⅓ Vermuth bitters,
⅓ water.

And add a dash of angostura, apricotine and orange bitters, and a slice of lemon peel. Sweeten to taste.

WASHINGTON PUNCH FOR 12 PEOPLE.

One-half pineapple, sliced fine and sprinkle liberally with granulated sugar. Add one-half bottle Rhine or Moselle wine, and set aside for twenty-four hours to ripen; then strain and add two bottles Rhine wine, one bottle claret, and the remainder of the pineapple, sliced fine. Just before serving, add one quart champagne. Either use a large piece of ice to cool, or have the wines ice cold before mixing.

BEVERAGES. 11

EGG MILK PUNCH.

One egg, three teaspoons fine sugar, fill half full ice, one wineglass brandy, two tablespoons St. Croix rum, fill with milk, shake well and strain into large glass, grating nutmeg on top.

CHAMPAGNE PUNCH FOR 12 PEOPLE.

3 qts. champagne, ¼ lb. loaf sugar,
¼ pt. maraschino, 2 lemons, sliced fine,
½ pt. imported brandy, 2 oranges, sliced fine,

Or any fruit in season. If not sweet enough, add more sugar. Just before using, add a large piece of ice.

CLARET CUP No. 1.

3 lemons (juice), 3 pts. claret,
6 tablespoons sugar, 1 pt. apollinaris,
1 sherry glass curacoa, 1 finely sliced orange,
1 slice cucumber rind, and a bunch of fresh mint, strawberries, pineapple.

CLARET CUP No. 2.

1 pt. claret, Juice of 1 orange,
1 cup sugar, 1 slice cucumber rind,
1 pt. sparkling Moselle, 1 pt. apollinaris.

POUSSE CAFE.

⅔ crême de café, ⅙ apricotine or vanilla.
⅙ crême de menthe,

Pour the café first and slowly add apricotine or vanilla and then the mint.

ORANGE JULEP.

Peel very thin one-half fine orange rind, put it into a glass with a little finely chopped ice, two teaspoonfuls of powdered sugar. Stir two minutes to extract the oil. Fill the glass with chopped ice, two sprigs of fresh mint, one small teaspoon of crême de menthe, four tablespoonfuls good whiskey—Sheridan rye is the best.

II

Chicken *à la* King (Chafing Dish) — Hot Toast
Salted Nuts — Olives
Waldorf Salad — Unsweetened Wafers
Pineapple Lemonade

III

Bouillon (Chafing Dish)
Creamed Halibut (Chafing Dish) with Pimentoes
Olive, Grapefruit, Celery and Endive Salad
Whipped Cream Cake — Coffee

Menus for Chafing Dish Luncheons

I

Cream of Celery Soup — Wafers
Chicken and Mushrooms (Chafing Dish) — Saratoga Chips — Rolls
Tomato, Cucumber and Lettuce Salad
Cherry and Pineapple Fruit Cup — Little Nut Cakes
Coffee

II

Grapefruit Cocktail
Oyster and Celery Bisque (Chafing Dish) — Crackers
Salted Nuts — Olives
Stuffed Egg and Pimento Salad
Graham Bread Sandwiches — Little Rolls
Little Apple Tarts — Cream Cheese Balls
Tea

III

Cream of Chicken Soup — Croutons
Spanish Omelet (Chafing Dish) — Little Rolls
Banana, Pineapple and Nut Salad — Cheese Sticks
Eclairs — Coffee

The chafing dish is usually adopted when there is no maid in attendance, and, because of this, food for the entire meal is often placed on the table at once.

The first course is in position when the guests are called to the table, the chafing dish, with ingredients, is set in place, with a pile of serving plates beside it. The salad, arranged on a platter or in a bowl, is set at the place opposite, the plates being at the left of it while the dessert (unless an ice) is served individually, and set at the right of each guest; the *hors d'œuvers* and plates of sandwiches, cake, etc., are set where it is convenient. Extra butter and a carafe or pitcher of water are also on the table, while the service for coffee, tea, or any other drink to be served

TABLE SET FOR INFORMAL CHAFING DISH SUPPER

in French dressing for thirty minutes. Then arrange the lettuce in a salad bowl, pour over the rest of the dressing and mix well with the radishes and onions. Garnish with radish roses made from the remaining radishes.

Red Cabbage and Celery Salad

- 3 cupfuls shredded red cabbage
- 1 tablespoonful chopped chives or Bermuda onion
- 2 cupfuls diced celery
- Curry or French dressing

Let the cabbage and celery crisp separately in cold, salted water. Drain thoroughly, mix and toss with the dressing, garnish with celery tips or lettuce and serve immediately.

Plain Potato Salad

- 3 cupfuls thinly sliced and diced boiled potatoes
- 2 hard-cooked eggs
- 1 onion (medium sized) grated
- 1 cupful diced celery (optional)
- $1\frac{1}{4}$ teaspoonfuls salt
- $\frac{1}{4}$ teaspoonful pepper
- 5 tablespoonfuls olive oil
- 2 tablespoonfuls vinegar
- Parsley

Chop the eggs and mix with the potato, celery, onion and seasonings. Then pour over the oil and toss it in. Add the vinegar, mix lightly and let stand to become very cold. Serve garnished with parsley.

Potato Salad (New York)

- $2\frac{1}{2}$ cupfuls small cooked potato cubes
- 1 cucumber, pared and diced, or
- 1 cupful diced celery
- 2 hard-cooked eggs
- Boiled salad dressing
- Oil and vinegar
- Lettuce
- Salt and cayenne to taste

Dress the cucumber and potato separately with oil and vinegar, using $1\frac{1}{2}$ tablespoonfuls of oil to $\frac{1}{2}$ tablespoonful of vinegar. Let stand thirty minutes. Drain them thoroughly; dust with salt and cayenne pepper, and toss together with the eggs, chopped, and salad dressing to moisten thoroughly. Arrange on lettuce and garnish as desired with olives or pimento strips, and extra dressing.

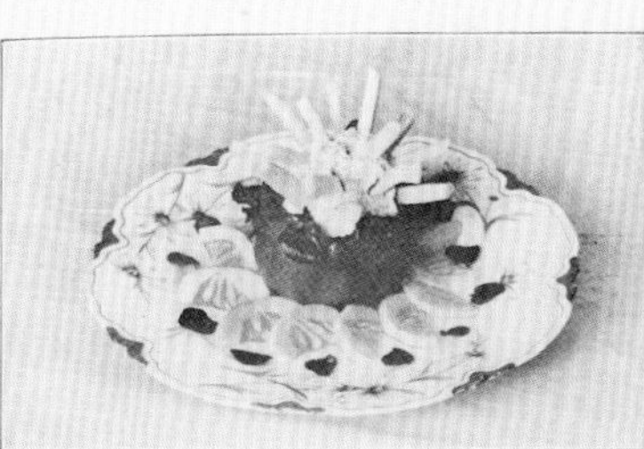

TOMATO CREAM SALAD

TOMATO AND SARDINE SALAD

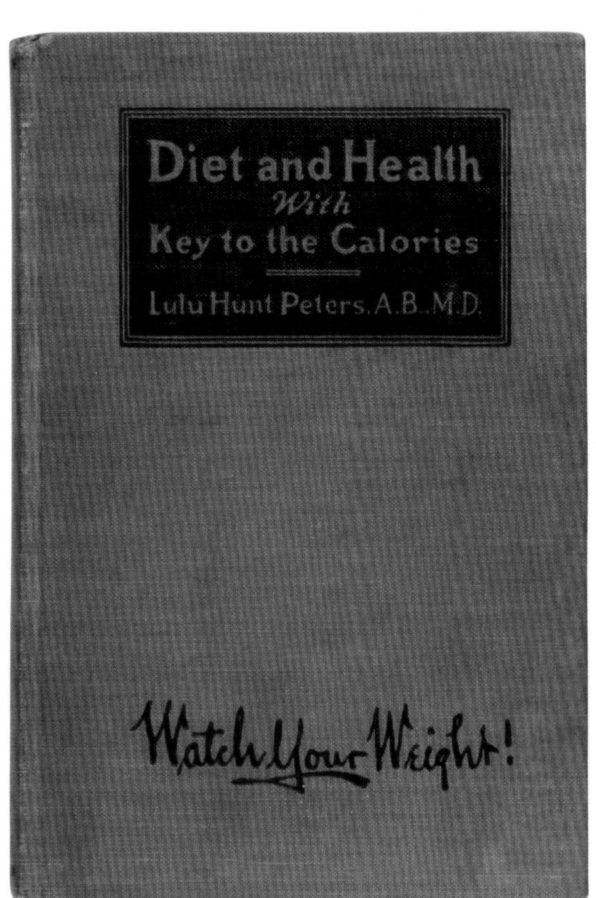

LULU HUNT PETERS

Diet and Health with Key to the Calories, 1918

Lulu Hunt Peters was a stout woman who wanted to lose weight. At one point she weighed 220 pounds, which, because she was a doctor, she knew was not good for her health—or for her looks. By thinking of food as calories, she was one of the first people to promote calorie counting as a means to structure what you eat.

She published her program in a small book called *Diet and Health with Key to the Calories* in 1918, then left the United States to help fight in Bosnia during World War I. When she returned to Los Angeles after the war, she found that her book had become a best-seller with more than 800,000 copies sold. Peters was one of the first writers to link caloric intake to obesity and to propose menus and recipes to combat excessive weight gain.

NOTABLE RECIPES: Celery, Olives, Corn Bread, Buttermilk • Creamed Dried Beef on Toast, Raw Cabbage, Skim Milk • Eggs Fried in Bacon Fat, Whole Wheat Bread, Butter, Tea • Menu of 100 Calories: Half Grapefruit or 5 Prunes with Coffee • Oysters, Beaten Egg with Cracker Crumbs Fried in Bacon Fat, Bacon, Chow Chow, Baked Apple

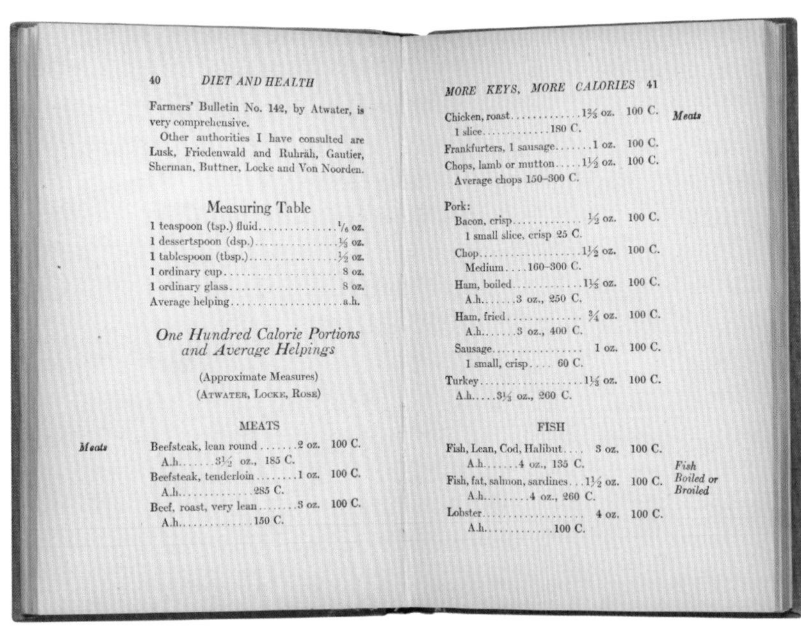
40 *DIET AND HEALTH*

Farmers' Bulletin No. 142, by Atwater, is very comprehensive.

Other authorities I have consulted are Lusk, Friedenwald and Ruhräh, Gautier, Sherman, Buttner, Locke and Von Noorden.

Measuring Table

1 teaspoon (tsp.) fluid................1/6 oz.
1 dessertspoon (dsp.)................1/3 oz.
1 tablespoon (tbsp.)................1/2 oz.
1 ordinary cup................8 oz.
1 ordinary glass................8 oz.
Average helping................a.h.

One Hundred Calorie Portions and Average Helpings

(Approximate Measures)
(Atwater, Locke, Rose)

MEATS

Meats
Beefsteak, lean round.......2 oz. 100 C.
A.h.......3½ oz., 185 C.
Beefsteak, tenderloin........1 oz. 100 C.
A.h..............285 C.
Beef, roast, very lean........3 oz. 100 C.
A.h..............150 C.

MORE KEYS, MORE CALORIES 41

Chicken, roast.............1⅔ oz. 100 C. *Meats*
1 slice............180 C.
Frankfurters, 1 sausage.......1 oz. 100 C.
Chops, lamb or mutton.....1½ oz. 100 C.
Average chops 150–300 C.

Pork:
Bacon, crisp............. ½ oz. 100 C.
1 small slice, crisp 25 C.
Chop..................1½ oz. 100 C.
Medium....160–300 C.
Ham, boiled............1⅓ oz. 100 C.
A.h.......3 oz., 250 C.
Ham, fried.............. ¾ oz. 100 C.
A.h.......3 oz., 400 C.
Sausage................. 1 oz. 100 C.
1 small, crisp.... 60 C.
Turkey..................1⅓ oz. 100 C.
A.h....3⅓ oz., 260 C.

FISH

Fish, Lean, Cod, Halibut.... 3 oz. 100 C.
A.h.......4 oz., 135 C. *Fish Boiled or Broiled*
Fish, fat, salmon, sardines...1½ oz. 100 C.
A.h.........4 oz., 260 C.
Lobster................... 4 oz. 100 C.
A.h.............100 C.

12 DIET AND HEALTH

been constrained to give you advice. You won't find it spontaneous nor from the heart, but if you follow my directions I will guarantee that you will gain; providing, of course, you have no organic trouble; and the chances are that by giving proper attention to your diet you will gain anyway, and maybe in passing lose your trouble. Who knows?

Bad Business

In war time it is a crime to hoard food, and fines and imprisonment have followed the exposé of such practices. Yet there are hundreds of thousands of individuals all over America who are hoarding food, and that one of the most precious of all foods! *They have vast amounts of this valuable commodity stored away in their own anatomy.*

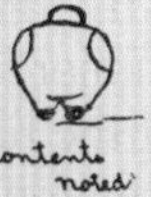

Now fat individuals have always been considered a joke, but you are a joke no longer. Instead of being looked upon with friendly tolerance and amusement, you are now viewed with distrust, suspicion, and even aversion. How dare you hoard fat when our

PRELIMINARY BOUT 13

nation needs it? You don't dare to any longer. You never wanted to be fat anyway, but you did not know how to reduce, and it is proverbial how little you eat. Why, there is Mrs. Natty B. Slymm, who is beautifully thin, and she eats twice as much as you do, and does not gain an ounce. You know positively that eating has nothing to do with it, for one time you dieted, didn't eat a thing but what the doctor ordered, besides your regular meals, and you actually gained.

You are in despair about being anything but fat, and—! how you hate it. But cheer up. I will save you; yea, even as I have saved myself and many, many others, so will I save you.

Spirituality vs. Materiality

It is not in vain that all my life I have had to fight the too, too solid. Why, I can remember when I was a child I was always being consoled by being told that I would outgrow it, and that when I matured I would have some shape. Never can I tell pathetically "when I was married I weighed only one hundred eighteen, and look at me now." No, I was a delicate slip of one hundred and sixty-five when I was taken.

A Long, Long Battle

I never will tell you how much I have weighed, I am so thoroughly ashamed of it, but my normal weight is one hundred and fifty pounds, and at one time there was seventy

72 DIET AND HEALTH

three cents to go with his two cents so that he could buy a Thrift Stamp. He is given due credit on the title page.)

Turn On Your Music

These exercises executed with vim, vigor, and vip—deep breathing between each set—will take ten to fifteen minutes. Re-read my warning.

Little Movements with Meanings All Their Own

1. Feet together, arms outstretched, palms up, describe as large a circle as possible. Fine for round shoulders and fat backs. Do slowly and stretch fifteen times. Smile.

2. Arms outstretched, swing to right and to left as far as possible at least 15 times each.

EXERCISE 73

Important! Keep Facial Expression Throughout as per Artist's Idea

3. Bend sideways, to right and left, alternately, as far as possible at least 15 times each.

4. Revolve the body upon the hips from right to left at least 10 times, and left to right the same.

5. Bend and touch the floor with your fingers, without bending your knees, at least 15 times.

MARION NESTLE *on the* EARLY NUTRITIONISTS

Cookbooks have always aimed to keep readers happy and healthy, but basing them on concepts of nutrition is a twentieth-century phenomenon. Although the origins of nutrition science can be traced to Hippocrates in ancient Greece and the work of eighteenth- and nineteenth-century chemists and physiologists, most of what is known about nutrients and their functions in the body was discovered in the last century. Scientists identified the role of calories in energy production, "micronutrients" (vitamins and minerals) in deficiency diseases, and "macronutrients" (proteins, fats, and carbohydrates) in chronic diseases. Cookbook authors quickly translated these discoveries into dietary advice and recipes.

Calorie science begins with the USDA (United States Department of Agriculture) scientist Wilbur Atwater in the 1890s. Atwater measured the number of calories provided by macronutrients in hundreds of foods, and those needed by people of different occupations. His discoveries made Atwater the most famous scientist in America.

Knowing nothing about nutrition, however, his contemporaries had strong opinions about diet and health. Horace Fletcher, the "Great Masticator," insisted that food must be chewed until it liquefied. The Seventh-day Adventist Kellogg brothers, John Harvey and W.K., ran a sanitarium in Battle Creek, Michigan, where they fed the rich and famous vegetarian diets, nut butters, and early versions of Corn Flakes, accompanied by yogurt enemas.

Nutrition science entered diet books in 1918 when a California doctor, Lulu Hunt Peters, published Diet and Health with Key to the Calories. *Her title echoed Mary Baker Eddy's Christian Science text of 1875,* Science and Health with Key to the Scriptures, *but Peters based her book firmly on Atwater. She divided the food world into 100-calorie portions and 1,200-calorie reducing diets. That the book went through seventeen editions by 1922 surprised Peters, who had gone to work with the Red Cross in Bosnia during World War I and returned to find herself famous. Her advice was sensible and recognized the need for foods containing the newly discovered but not yet named "vital elements" (micronutrients), and the book was illustrated with charming stick figures drawn by her ten-year-old nephew. Peters continued the Fletcherist tradition:* "If there is one thing more important than another, it is through mastication" *[her emphasis].*

Until the early 1900s, scientists understood that diseases such as scurvy, beriberi, and pellagra were caused by diet but did not know how. As they identified vitamins and minerals one after another, government agencies and cookbook writers enthusiastically embraced these discoveries. In 1917 the USDA issued How to Select Foods, *a pamphlet that organized the principal food sources of micronutrients in groups: fruit, vegetables, meat, dairy, cereals, and so forth. Balanced diets were to include foods from all groups.*

J. I. Rodale and other proponents of organic farming and sustainable agriculture argued that vital nutrients were destroyed by industrial farming and processing methods. White bread, they said, offered nothing but "empty calories." Clive McCay, a professor of animal nutrition at Cornell University, thought the nutritional deficiencies of white bread could be solved by adding soy flour, dry milk solids, and wheat germ to the dough. He demonstrated that laboratory rats survived splendidly when fed nothing but his bread topped with butter or margarine, and bread baked according to his formula was served to great acclaim at a state dinner in Albany in 1943.

The nutritionist Adelle Davis seized on the importance of micronutrients in her 1947 Let's Cook It Right, *a book that ruined the childhoods of many of my friends whose parents packed every meal with whole-grain bread, wheat germ, cod liver oil, brewers' yeast, blackstrap molasses, peanut flour, chopped-up green vegetables, and as much protein as possible. "Serve eggs and cheese daily," Davis insisted, but vitamins mattered most. Her* Let's Eat Right to Keep Fit *(1954) attributed allergies, poison ivy, fatigue, leg cramps, heart disease, and even polio to vitamin deficiencies.*

When Marion Becker signed on as coauthor of the 1951 edition of the Joy of Cooking, *the influence of Adelle Davis was evident, if not acknowledged. The nutrition section that begins on page 931 describes the hazards of vitamin deficiencies and the dangers of incomplete vegetable protein. Joy advised readers to reduce sweets, starchy foods, and sweetened beverages not because of their calories but because they would lead to a "deficiency of vitamin B complex."*

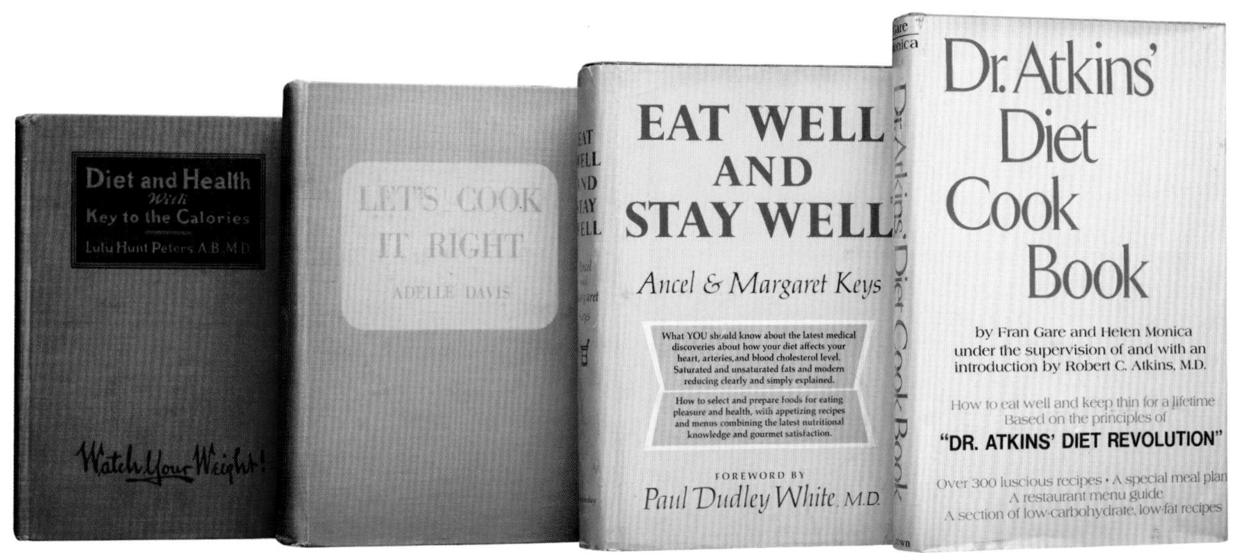

The 1962 Joy of Cooking *moved nutrition to the front of the book, still echoing Davis. It bemoaned the "devitalizing" effects of additives, chemicals, and preserving methods, and called for protein foods in every meal. It even included a recipe for McCay's Cornell Triple-Rich Flour Formula (which lasted until the 1997 edition). But precepts such as "fill your market basket so that it holds a minimum of 2 fruits and 3 vegetables daily" seem thoroughly modern even though their purpose was to stave off nutrient deficiencies. Today such advice aims to prevent obesity, heart disease, diabetes, and other chronic diseases that have become the leading health problems related to diet.*

Following World War II, cardiologists were confronted with rising rates of heart disease. Noting how little heart disease occurred in Italy, the Minnesota cardiologist Ancel Keys judged the cause of the American epidemic as eating too much meat, sugar, and processed foods. In 1959 he and his wife, Margaret, wrote Eat Well and Stay Well. *Although by no means the first cookbook aimed at preventing heart disease, this one proposed a Mediterranean approach that seems quite contemporary: Avoid obesity, saturated fats, salt, and refined sugars; eat plenty of fresh vegetables and fruit; and "be sensible about cigarettes, alcohol, excitement, business strain."*

During the 1960s and 1970s, public health authorities gradually recognized the relevance of diet to chronic diseases, and diet books flooded the marketplace. In 1967 I. M. Stillman published The Doctor's Quick Weight-Loss Diet *(high protein, low fat and carbohydrate). Robert Atkins's* Dr. Atkins' Diet Revolution *(high fat and protein, low carbohydrate) followed in 1972. Both sold in the millions.*

To make sense of conflicting popular advice, a Senate committee chaired by George McGovern issued Dietary Goals for the United States *in 1977. This report shifted the focus of dietary advice from "eat more" to prevent nutrient deficiencies to "eat less" (of foods with fat, saturated fat, salt, and sugar) to prevent chronic diseases. Jane Brody's 1981 best-seller,* Jane Brody's Nutrition Book, *promoted these principles.*

I spent two years in Washington, DC, editing the 1988 Surgeon General's Report on Nutrition and Health, *which summarized research supporting those ideas and identified eating less fat as the primary nutrition priority. Public health officials assumed that if people reduced overall fat intake, they would automatically reduce calories and saturated fat and eat more carbohydrates from whole grains. It did not occur to us that the food industry would interpret the low-fat message as a license to invent products low in fat but loaded with sugars, refined starches, and calories, thereby taking Americans into the present era of obesity.*

Today thousands of "healthy" cookbooks promote diets high or low in protein, fat, or carbohydrate (take your pick), or devoid of animal products, gluten, and anything unnatural. As the wave of the future, the best cookbooks put taste first, call for relatively unprocessed ingredients produced locally, seasonally, and sustainably, and promote age-old nutritional principles of dietary variety and balance—always in moderation, of course.

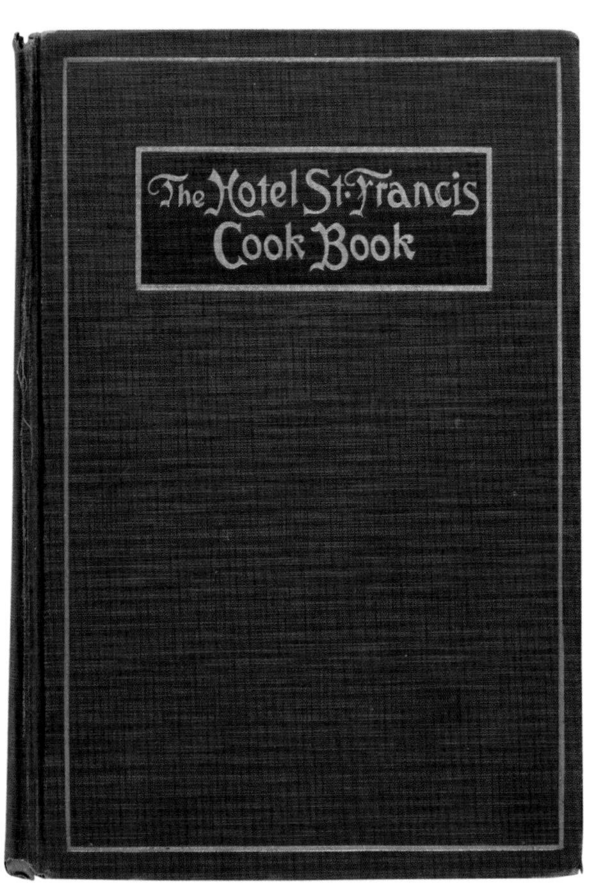

VICTOR HIRTZLER

The Hotel St. Francis Cook Book, 1919

Long before the Food Network, celebrity chefs reigned supreme in the imagination of American "foodies." Names such as "Oscar of the Waldorf" and Charles Ranhofer at Delmonico's were internationally known chefs. Perhaps no chef of the period was as flamboyant as Victor Hirtzler, who helped create the stereotype of the French chef. Hirtzler was born in Strasbourg and trained at the Grand Hotel in Paris. He served as a cook and food taster for Czar Nicholas II and a chef de cuisine for Carlos I of Portugal. He then moved to New York, working for Louis Sherry, the caterer to "The Four Hundred," New York's elite of the Belle Epoque, and at the Waldorf-Astoria Hotel. In 1904 Hirtzler was named head chef at San Francisco's new St. Francis Hotel on Union Square.

The St. Francis Hotel was a tribute to the wealth of San Francisco as a major trading port. Its grand marble beaux-arts decor was matched by the excess of Hirtzler's menus, which, he boasted, typically

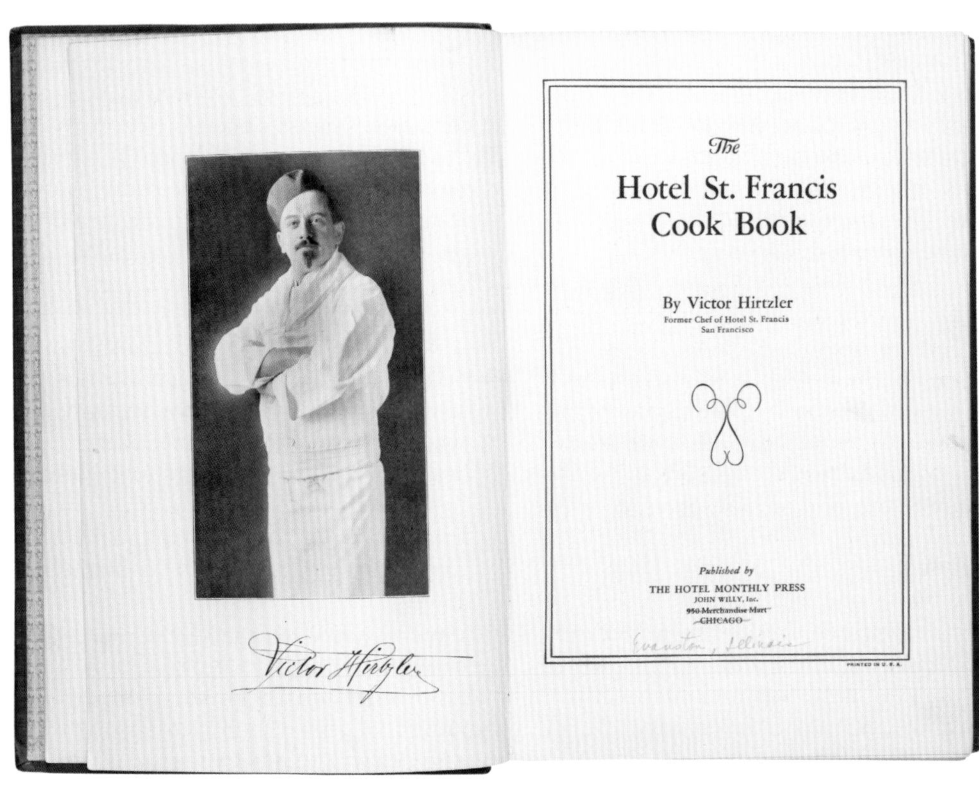
The
Hotel St. Francis
Cook Book

By Victor Hirtzler
Former Chef of Hotel St. Francis
San Francisco

Published by
THE HOTEL MONTHLY PRESS
JOHN WILLY, Inc.
~~950 Merchandise Mart~~
~~CHICAGO~~

PRINTED IN U.S.A.

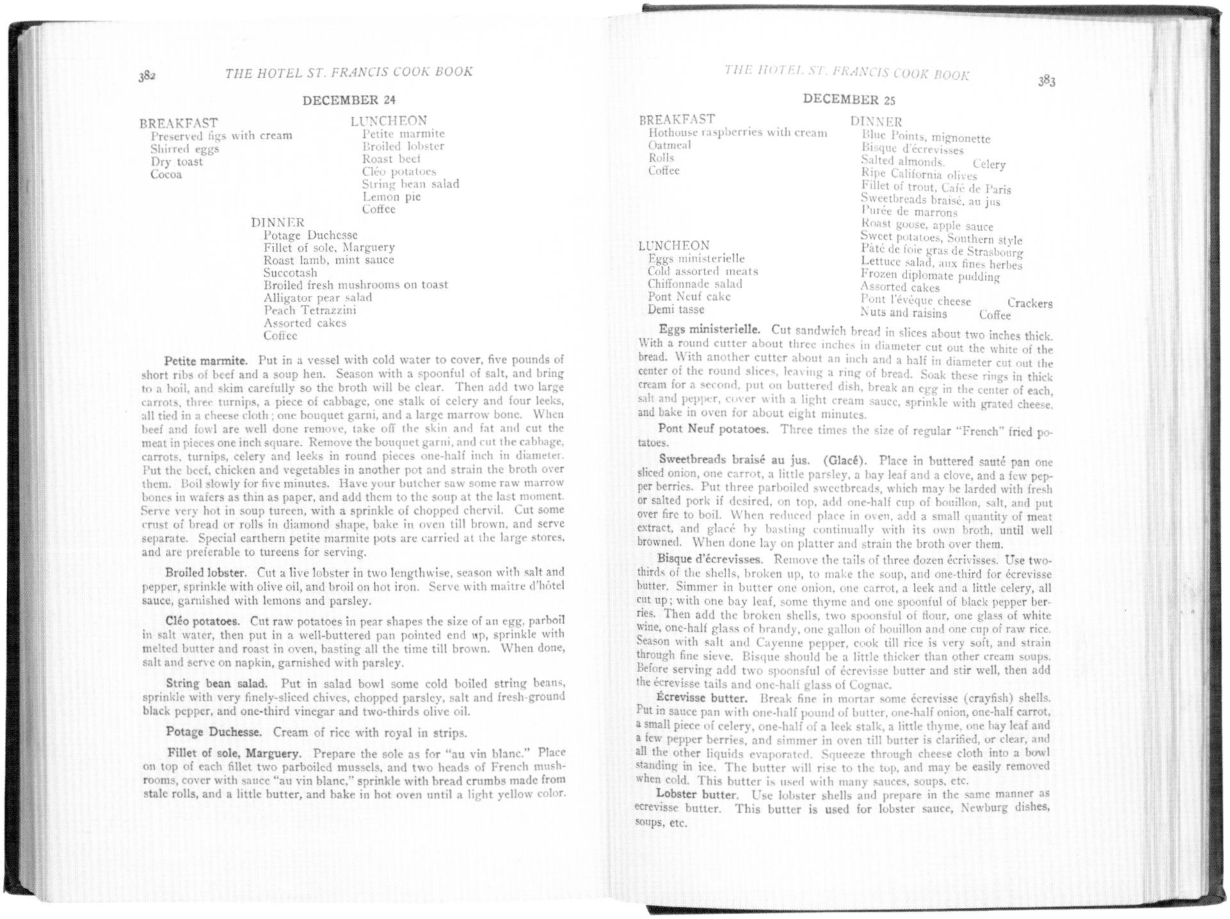

382 THE HOTEL ST. FRANCIS COOK BOOK

DECEMBER 24

BREAKFAST
Preserved figs with cream
Shirred eggs
Dry toast
Cocoa

LUNCHEON
Petite marmite
Broiled lobster
Roast beef
Cléo potatoes
String bean salad
Lemon pie
Coffee

DINNER
Potage Duchesse
Fillet of sole, Marguery
Roast lamb, mint sauce
Succotash
Broiled fresh mushrooms on toast
Alligator pear salad
Peach Tetrazzini
Assorted cakes
Coffee

Petite marmite. Put in a vessel with cold water to cover, five pounds of short ribs of beef and a soup hen. Season with a spoonful of salt, and bring to a boil, and skim carefully so the broth will be clear. Then add two large carrots, three turnips, a piece of cabbage, one stalk of celery and four leeks, all tied in a cheese cloth; one bouquet garni, and a large marrow bone. When beef and fowl are well done remove, take off the skin and fat and cut the meat in pieces one inch square. Remove the bouquet garni, and cut the cabbage, carrots, turnips, celery and leeks in round pieces one-half inch in diameter. Put the beef, chicken and vegetables in another pot and strain the broth over them. Boil slowly for five minutes. Have your butcher saw some raw marrow bones in wafers as thin as paper, and add them to the soup at the last moment. Serve very hot in soup tureen, with a sprinkle of chopped chervil. Cut some crust of bread or rolls in diamond shape, bake in oven till brown, and serve separate. Special earthern petite marmite pots are carried at the large stores, and are preferable to tureens for serving.

Broiled lobster. Cut a live lobster in two lengthwise, season with salt and pepper, sprinkle with olive oil, and broil on hot iron. Serve with maitre d'hôtel sauce, garnished with lemons and parsley.

Cléo potatoes. Cut raw potatoes in pear shapes the size of an egg, parboil in salt water, then put in a well-buttered pan pointed end up, sprinkle with melted butter and roast in oven, basting all the time till brown. When done, salt and serve on napkin, garnished with parsley.

String bean salad. Put in salad bowl some cold boiled string beans, sprinkle with very finely-sliced chives, chopped parsley, salt and fresh-ground black pepper, and one-third vinegar and two-thirds olive oil.

Potage Duchesse. Cream of rice with royal in strips.

Fillet of sole, Marguery. Prepare the sole as for "au vin blanc." Place on top of each fillet two parboiled mussels, and two heads of French mushrooms, cover with sauce "au vin blanc," sprinkle with bread crumbs made from stale rolls, and a little butter, and bake in hot oven until a light yellow color.

THE HOTEL ST. FRANCIS COOK BOOK 383

DECEMBER 25

BREAKFAST
Hothouse raspberries with cream
Oatmeal
Rolls
Coffee

LUNCHEON
Eggs ministerielle
Cold assorted meats
Chiffonnade salad
Pont Neuf cake
Demi tasse

DINNER
Blue Points, mignonette
Bisque d'écrevisses
Salted almonds. Celery
Ripe California olives
Fillet of trout, Café de Paris
Sweetbreads braisé, au jus
Purée de marrons
Roast goose, apple sauce
Sweet potatoes, Southern style
Pâté de foie gras de Strasbourg
Lettuce salad, aux fines herbes
Frozen diplomate pudding
Assorted cakes
Pont l'évêque cheese Crackers
Nuts and raisins Coffee

Eggs ministerielle. Cut sandwich bread in slices about two inches thick. With a round cutter about three inches in diameter cut out the white of the bread. With another cutter about an inch and a half in diameter cut out the center of the round slices, leaving a ring of bread. Soak these rings in thick cream for a second, put on buttered dish, break an egg in the center of each, salt and pepper, cover with a light cream sauce, sprinkle with grated cheese, and bake in oven for about eight minutes.

Pont Neuf potatoes. Three times the size of regular "French" fried potatoes.

Sweetbreads braisé au jus. (Glacé). Place in buttered sauté pan one sliced onion, one carrot, a little parsley, a bay leaf and a clove, and a few pepper berries. Put three parboiled sweetbreads, which may be larded with fresh or salted pork if desired, on top, add one-half cup of bouillon, salt, and put over fire to boil. When reduced place in oven, add a small quantity of meat extract, and glacé by basting continually with its own broth, until well browned. When done lay on platter and strain the broth over them.

Bisque d'écrevisses. Remove the tails of three dozen écrivisses. Use two-thirds of the shells, broken up, to make the soup, and one-third for écrevisse butter. Simmer in butter one onion, one carrot, a leek and a little celery, all cut up; with one bay leaf, some thyme and one spoonful of black pepper berries. Then add the broken shells, two spoonsful of flour, one glass of white wine, one-half glass of brandy, one gallon of bouillon and one cup of raw rice. Season with salt and Cayenne pepper, cook till rice is very soft, and strain through fine sieve. Bisque should be a little thicker than other cream soups. Before serving add two spoonsful of écrevisse butter and stir well, then add the écrevisse tails and one-half glass of Cognac.

Écrevisse butter. Break fine in mortar some écrevisse (crayfish) shells. Put in sauce pan with one-half pound of butter, one-half onion, one-half carrot, a small piece of celery, one-half of a leek stalk, a little thyme, one bay leaf and a few pepper berries, and simmer in oven till butter is clarified, or clear, and all the other liquids evaporated. Squeeze through cheese cloth into a bowl standing in ice. The butter will rise to the top, and may be easily removed when cold. This butter is used with many sauces, soups, etc.

Lobster butter. Use lobster shells and prepare in the same manner as ecrevisse butter. This butter is used for lobster sauce, Newburg dishes, soups, etc.

included "a choice of fourteen cheeses, twenty clam or oyster dishes, eleven soups, twenty-four relishes, seventeen kinds of fish, and fifty-eight entrées from hamburger to Bohemian ham."

The St. Francis survived the San Francisco Earthquake of 1906, and opened for breakfast that morning, serving such dishes as chilled rhubarb stew, southern hominy with cream, and eggs with black truffles in puff pastry. Later that day the hotel was severely damaged by the fires that followed the quake, but was rebuilt to its former elegance. In later years Hirtzler's menu for breakfast was represented to commemorate the disaster.

Ever the savvy publicist, Hirtzler started publishing cookbooks to promote the hotel and, of course, himself. His *L'Art Culinaire* appeared in both a popular (cheap) and a subscription (expensive, with a lengthy list of patrons) version. The title is a reference to Escoffier's masterpiece of French cooking, *Le Guide Culinaire*. Hirtzler considered himself on par and even a rival of Escoffier. *The Hotel St. Francis Cook Book* is the best known of Hirtzler's books.

NOTABLE RECIPES: Boston Baked Beans • **Celery Victor** (page 406) • **Chicken Salad, Victor** (page 369) • **Crab Meat, à la Louise** (page 367) • **Eggs Benedict** (page 464) • **Peach Melba** (page 641) • Pink Pudding Victor • **Strawberries Romanoff** (page 641) • Thousand Island Dressing • Waldorf Salad

---

Mrs. S. R. Dull

SOUTHERN COOKING

By

MRS. S. R. DULL

Former Editor of the Home Economics page in the Magazine Section of the Atlanta Journal, and Cooking School Instructor

Illustrated by

LUCINA WAKEFIELD

GROSSET & DUNLAP

Publishers NEW YORK

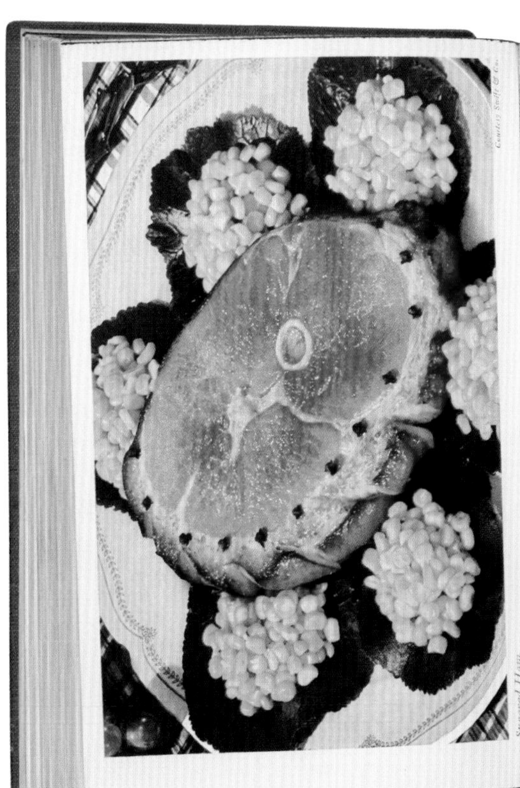

Sugared Ham

eggs, omelets, souffles and cheese dishes

MRS. S. R. DULL

Southern Cooking, 1928

Southern cooking has long been a specialty appreciated by all Americans. By the early nineteenth century, books such as *Carolina Receipts* brought the tradition of Southern food preparation to the North as a kind of delicacy. The mother of twentieth-century Southern cooking is Henrietta Stanley (Mrs. S. R.) Dull, who published, locally, a compilation of Georgia recipes under the title *Southern Cooking*.

Henrietta Celeste Stanley was born on her family's plantation near Chappells Mill in Laurens County, Georgia. As a child she watched the slaves prepare all the food for the family and became interested in making the recipes herself, later trying to re-create the tastes from memory. At age twenty-three, Henrietta married Samuel Rice Dull; ten years later he began to show signs of mental illness and Henrietta had to support him and their six children. She turned to her love of cooking and began catering small parties for local socialites. Word spread and her business grew. At the same time the Atlanta Gas Light Company asked her to demonstrate the newly invented gas stoves, which she did to help support her family. She was fond of comparing a gas range to a husband, saying, "You couldn't get the best out of either until you learn how to manage them." In 1920 she became an editor at the *Atlanta Journal*'s Sunday magazine and, for twenty-five years, wrote a weekly column called "Mrs. Dull's Cooking Lessons."

In 1941 the New York publisher Grosset & Dunlap printed an expanded and reworked edition of *Southern Cooking* containing 1,300 recipes. It sold 150,000 copies, establishing Mrs. Dull's book as the bible of Southern cuisine.

NOTABLE RECIPES: Alma's Recipe for 'Possum • **Brunswick Stew No. 1** (page 380) • Cheese Straws • Cornmeal Bread • Drop Biscuits (Beaten Biscuits) • **Fried Chicken** (page 498) • Fried Okra • **Macaroni and Cheese** (page 445) • **Mother Dull's Tea Cakes** (page 633) • **Tea** (page 316) • **Watermelon Rind Pickles** (page 438)

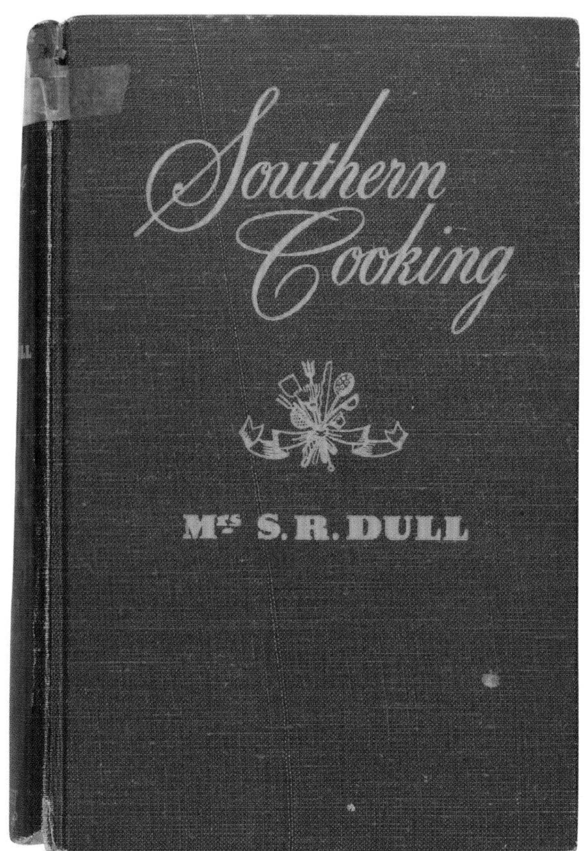

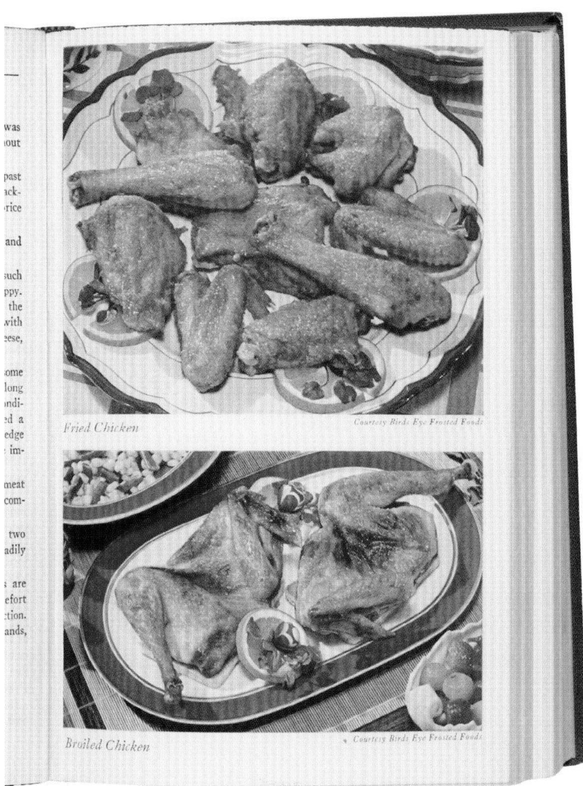

the kitchen

cocktails

salads

milk and cheese

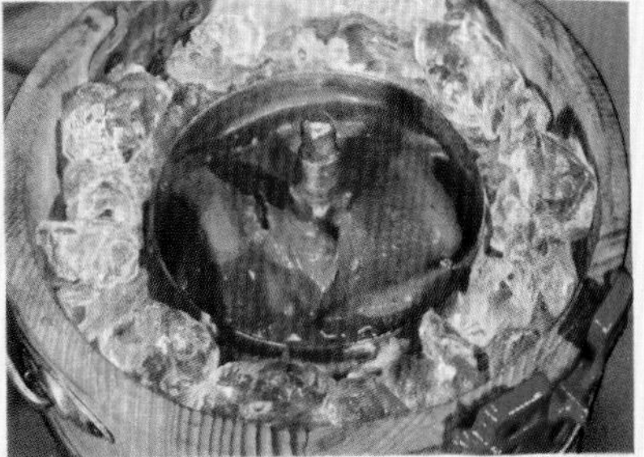

Chocolate Ice Cream — Courtesy Walter Baker's Chocolate

Chocolate Pie — Courtesy Walter Baker's Chocolate

bake thirty to forty minutes. If gas oven is used, place under blaze until slightly browned, then into oven about center, with moderate heat. Serve with vegetables.

BROWN BREADS

Annie's Reliable Brown Bread

2½ cups graham flour	½ cup of molasses
1 cup of white flour	1 cup of raisins
1 cup of buttermilk	½ teaspoon salt
½ cup sugar	1 teaspoon soda

Mix all dry ingredients together, mix liquids, combine the two. Grease one-pound baking powder cans well, fill half-full, put on tops, steam two hours, or until done.

Place cans on rack or trivet so they will be entirely surrounded by water, let water come up half-way the depth of can. Keep a constant boiling.

Steamed Bread

3½ cups cornmeal	1 teaspoon soda
1 cup flour	1 teaspoon salt
2 cups sweet milk (or water)	1 teaspoon baking powder
1 cup buttermilk	¾ cup molasses

If not thick enough, add more meal.

Steam three hours. Have water cold in steamer. Bread will rise while water heats.

Mrs. H's Brown Bread

2 cups white flour	½ cup milk
2 cups graham flour	1 cup raisins
½ cup molasses (black)	1 cup nut meats
½ cup shortening, lard or oil	½ teaspoon soda
½ cup sugar	6 teaspoons baking powder

Mix soda and baking powder into the flour, mix all dry ingredients into flour. Mix syrup and milk with melted shortening, add the two mixtures together. Mix well and fill one-pound baking powder cans half full. Steam two hours. Have water come up half way the depth of cans, which must be set on a rack while boiling. When boiled, place in oven, dry out half hour.

NUT BREADS

Nut Bread

4 cups flour	2 eggs
1 cup chopped pecan meats	2 teaspoons salt
¼ cup sugar	4 teaspoons baking powder
2 cups sweet milk (or half water)	3 tablespoons melted shortening

Mix all dry ingredients together. Beat eggs together well; add liquid

Tomato Canape

Prepare toast. Peel and cut slice of very firm tomato to fit toast.

Butter toast, place tomato, spread with mayonnaise. Cover center with grated egg yolk and border with the grated white. Drop a small portion of mayonnaise in center and stick a small stuffed olive in top.

Caviar Canape

One small jar caviar. Add lemon juice and salad oil until a smooth paste is made. Spread on slice of bread and cover top with grated hard boiled egg.

Caviar and Cream Cheese Canape

1 small jar caviar	1 package cream cheese

Mix caviar and cream cheese, whipping the mixture until light. Use for canapes.

Ham Canape

Grind cooked lean ham. Prepare toast and cover with minced ham.

Have ready a cup of whipped cream. Add to cream freshly grated horseradish to flavor highly, salt and pepper. With a forcing bag and tube make a rosette on the ham and sprinkle with more ham or paprika.

The toast must have something to hold the ham in place—soft butter or mayonnaise.

Any other tasty meat may be used in place of ham.

Artichoke Canape

Use the canned artichoke bottoms. Soak in highly seasoned French dressing about 1 hour. Rub butter soft with minced pimento until smooth.

Spread toast with butter, place choke, and decorate top with strip of pimento or rings of stuffed olives.

SANDWICHES

The sandwiches given in this book are more for afternoon teas than for feeding real hungry people.

Sandwiches should be made of bread 24 hours old and of a sandwich loaf. The sandwich loaf gives better slices, is whiter, and the grain closer than in the ordinary loaf bread.

Brown, white and rye breads are those generally used. Nut breads are easily made at home and very effectively used with a light spread—sweet or plain.

Bread should be cut in thin slices and all crust removed. The shapes are cut to suit the individual. When using cutters if they are kept damp by dipping in warm water, the slices are not ragged around the edges, and the work is more easily done.

Courtesy Swans Down Cake Flour

White Layer Cake with Orange Filling and Spongy White Icing, decorated with orange slices

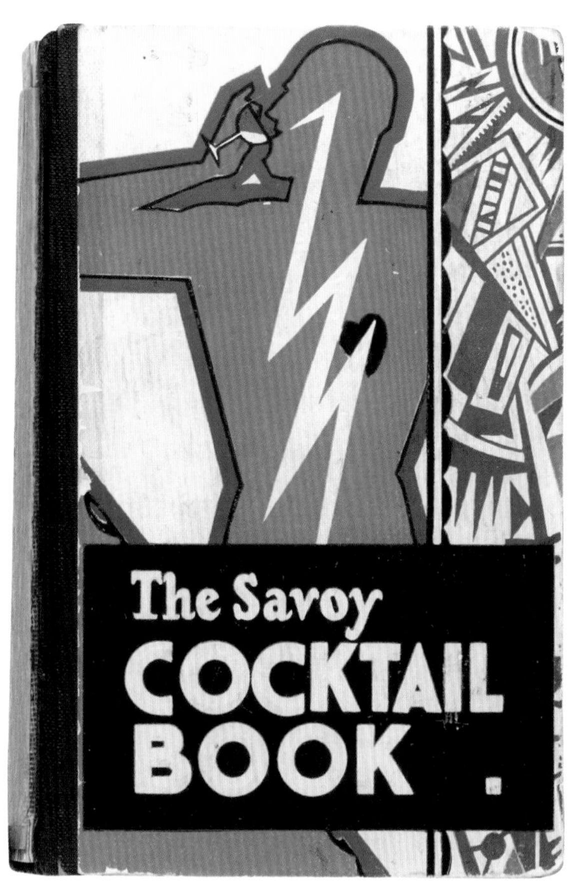

HARRY CRADDOCK

The Savoy Cocktail Book, 1930

People have been drinking mixtures of wine, spirits, and other flavors—the ingredients that make up the dictionary definition of the "cocktail"—for centuries, but the term "cocktail" is a distinctly American appellation. The first printed reference to a "cocktail" appeared in the April 28, 1803, issue of the *Farmer's Cabinet*, published in Amherst, New Hampshire. The origin of the word is obscure. Fanciful myths claim the name derives from the use of cock feathers to decorate these early potables, or from the cutting of horses' tails so they stand up, presumably like the feeling you get with your first sip of a drink; another asserts that it comes from the moniker for an appealing woman who was of low repute. Perhaps we require that an air of mystery surround the cocktail. Think of the myriad stories about who created the first margarita or the first martini.

Whatever the origin, Americans created cocktail culture in the early twentieth century and gave it to the world. Cookbooks from the mid-century are chock-a-block with recipes for hors d'oeuvres to

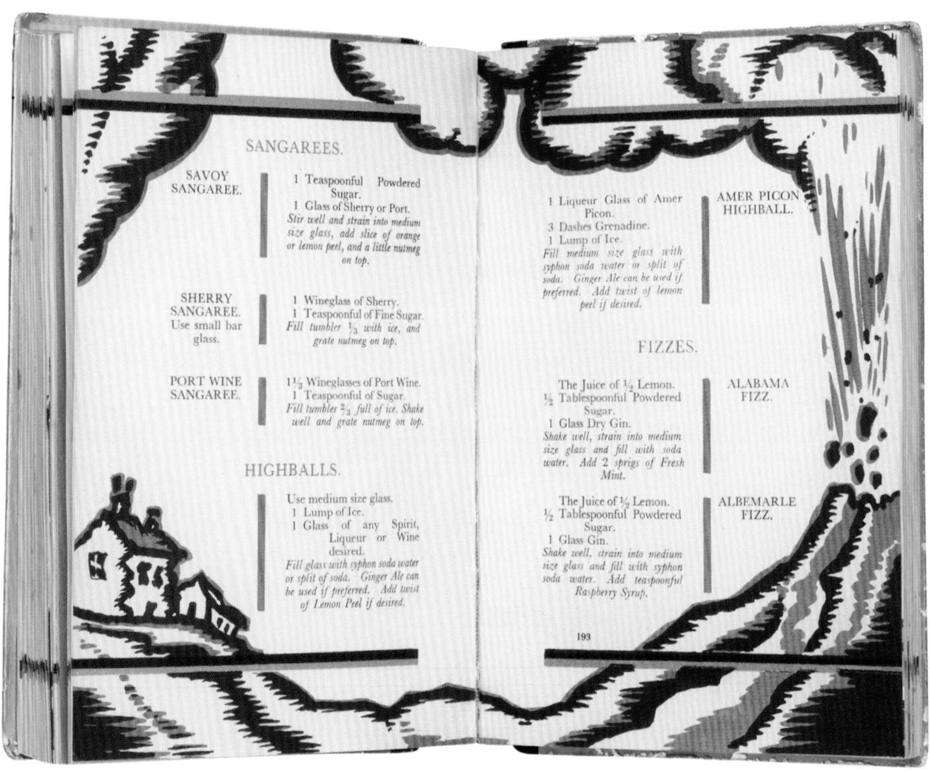

SANGAREES.

SAVOY SANGAREE.

1 Teaspoonful Powdered Sugar.
1 Glass of Sherry or Port.
Stir well and strain into medium size glass, add slice of orange or lemon peel, and a little nutmeg on top.

SHERRY SANGAREE. Use small bar glass.

1 Wineglass of Sherry.
1 Teaspoonful of Fine Sugar.
Fill tumbler ⅓ with ice, and grate nutmeg on top.

PORT WINE SANGAREE.

1⅓ Wineglasses of Port Wine.
1 Teaspoonful of Sugar.
Fill tumbler ⅔ full of ice. Shake well and grate nutmeg on top.

HIGHBALLS.

Use medium size glass.
1 Lump of Ice.
1 Glass of any Spirit, Liqueur or Wine desired.
Fill glass with syphon soda water or split of soda. Ginger Ale can be used if preferred. Add twist of Lemon Peel if desired.

AMER PICON HIGHBALL.

1 Liqueur Glass of Amer Picon.
3 Dashes Grenadine.
1 Lump of Ice.
Fill medium size glass with syphon soda water or split of soda. Ginger Ale can be used if preferred. Add twist of lemon peel if desired.

FIZZES.

ALABAMA FIZZ.

The Juice of ½ Lemon.
½ Tablespoonful Powdered Sugar.
1 Glass Dry Gin.
Shake well, strain into medium size glass and fill with soda water. Add 2 sprigs of Fresh Mint.

ALBEMARLE FIZZ.

The Juice of ½ Lemon.
½ Tablespoonful Powdered Sugar.
1 Glass Gin.
Shake well, strain into medium size glass and fill with syphon soda water. Add teaspoonful Raspberry Syrup.

193

serve with cocktails before dinner. (James Beard, a self-confessed lover of gin, wrote his first cookbook, *Hors d'Oeuvre and Canapés*, about these dainty cocktail accompaniments.)

The most important book about the cocktail is Harry Craddock's *Savoy Cocktail Book*. (This particular copy was owned by Ray Wellington, the sommelier and cocktail specialist at Windows on the World, the restaurant at the top of the former World Trade Center.) Not much is known about Craddock other than he was a New York mixologist who left for London when Prohibition was inflicted upon the American public. He became the master bartender at the famous Savoy Hotel and was renowned for his concoctions. This charmingly illustrated book was popular in its time and has become the bible of the late-century cocktail revival in the United States.

NOTABLE RECIPES: Corpse Reviver (No. 1) (page 313) • **Dry Martini Cocktail** (page 312) • **Hanky Panky Cocktail** (page 313) • **Bombay Punch** (page 313) • Queen Elizabeth Cocktail • Savoy Hotel Cocktail • **Sidecar Cocktail** (page 312) • **White Lady Cocktail** (page 313)

" If all be true that I do think,
There are five reasons why men drink,
Good wine, a friend, or being dry,
Or lest we should be by-and-by,
Or any other reason why."

Henry Aldrich (1647—1710).

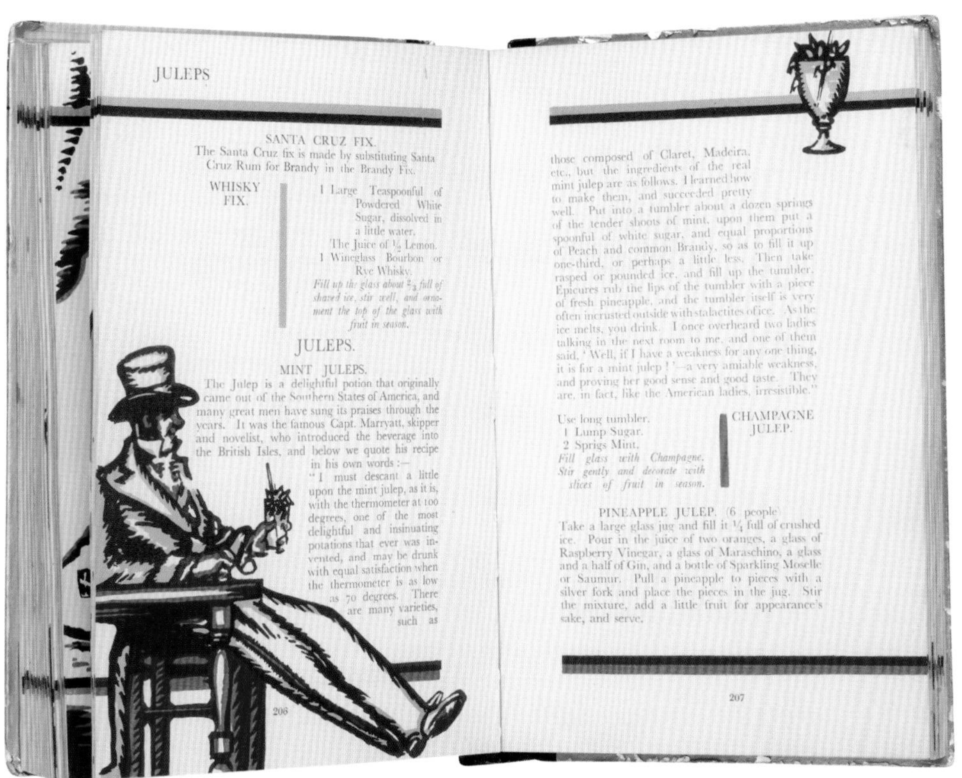

JULEPS

SANTA CRUZ FIX.

The Santa Cruz fix is made by substituting Santa Cruz Rum for Brandy in the Brandy Fix.

WHISKY FIX.

1 Large Teaspoonful of Powdered White Sugar, dissolved in a little water.
The Juice of ½ Lemon.
1 Wineglass Bourbon or Rye Whisky.
Fill up the glass about ⅔ full of shaved ice, stir well, and ornament the top of the glass with fruit in season.

JULEPS.

MINT JULEPS.

The Julep is a delightful potion that originally came out of the Southern States of America, and many great men have sung its praises through the years. It was the famous Capt. Marryatt, skipper and novelist, who introduced the beverage into the British Isles, and below we quote his recipe in his own words:—

"I must descant a little upon the mint julep, as it is, with the thermometer at 100 degrees, one of the most delightful and insinuating potations that ever was invented, and may be drunk with equal satisfaction when the thermometer is as low as 70 degrees. There are many varieties, such as

206

those composed of Claret, Madeira, etc., but the ingredients of the real mint julep are as follows. I learned how to make them, and succeeded pretty well. Put into a tumbler about a dozen springs of the tender shoots of mint, upon them put a spoonful of white sugar, and equal proportions of Peach and common Brandy, so as to fill it up one-third, or perhaps a little less. Then take rasped or pounded ice, and fill up the tumbler. Epicures rub the lips of the tumbler with a piece of fresh pineapple, and the tumbler itself is very often incrusted outside with stalactites of ice. As the ice melts, you drink. I once overheard two ladies talking in the next room to me, and one of them said, 'Well, if I have a weakness for any one thing, it is for a mint julep!'—a very amiable weakness, and proving her good sense and good taste. They are, in fact, like the American ladies, irresistible."

CHAMPAGNE JULEP.

Use long tumbler.
1 Lump Sugar.
2 Sprigs Mint.
Fill glass with Champagne. Stir gently and decorate with slices of fruit in season.

PINEAPPLE JULEP. (6 people)

Take a large glass jug and fill it ¼ full of crushed ice. Pour in the juice of two oranges, a glass of Raspberry Vinegar, a glass of Maraschino, a glass and a half of Gin, and a bottle of Sparkling Moselle or Saumur. Pull a pineapple to pieces with a silver fork and place the pieces in the jug. Stir the mixture, add a little fruit for appearance's sake, and serve.

207

The JOY of COOKING
Rombauer
the JOY OF COOKING
ROMBAUER
BECKER
BOBBS • MERRILL

joy
OF
COOKING
ROMBAUER
BECKER

JOY
OF COOKING
ROMBAUER
BECKER

WARRANTY
Satisfaction guaranteed or your money back. Try any dozen recipes in JOY OF COOKING. If for any reason you are not completely satisfied, you may return the book and get your money back.

BOBBS · MERRILL
Rombauer
and
Becker
THE
JOY
OF COOKING
The
All-Purpose
Cookbook
REVISED
ENLARGED
EDITION
DENT

IRMA ROMBAUER

The Joy of Cooking, 1931

The Joy of Cooking has been America's cooking bible since its first publication in 1931. Early editions of *Joy* amused readers because of Irma Rombauer's witty and playful texts that read almost like kitchen-table, coffee-klatch banter. Over the years, the work grew to become a compendium of all kinds of American cooking, preserving historical recipes for such things as opossum while also adding newer ethnic dishes that found a place on the average American table. This was the book received by every new bride as a wedding shower present. And for good reason, as it is one of the most reliable reference books for standard American cooking and has a place on every cookbook shelf in every American home.

NOTABLE RECIPES: Beef Wellington or Filet de Boeuf en Croute (page 548) • Butterscotch Ice Box Cookies • **Chocolate Custard Cake—Devils' Food** (page 619) • Crown Roast of Pork • **Roast Turkey** (page 496) • **Rule for Meringue** (page 603)

ANNE MENDELSON *on* IRMA ROMBAUER *and* MARION ROMBAUER BECKER

Irma Starkloff Rombauer (1877–1962), a product of Victorian-era St. Louis, had either no qualifications or every qualification for launching the twentieth century's most beloved American kitchen bible during the depths of the Great Depression. As her daughter, Marion Rombauer Becker (1903–1976), once wrote, "All through her life—and, as I have found, in mine—the most unlikely enthusiasms, the most far-fetched experiences, have, after long dormancy, suddenly burst into applicable attitudes."

The Joy of Cooking *was not born out of either joy or crack cooking skills. It started life in 1930 as Irma Rombauer's first desperate stratagem to make money in the aftermath of her husband's suicide. Dashing, impulsive, and endowed with outrageous charm, she flung herself into collecting and arranging recipes with the headlong energy that had marked her life as a mighty power in St. Louis women's club circles.*

She planned to produce and publish the book at her own expense, a tall order for a woman who had never held a job or learned to use a typewriter. (Girls in her parents' affluent St. Louis German-American set accomplished their destiny by marrying.) But the more practical Marion, who was living with her mother while teaching art at a nearby progressive school, provided crucial moral and logistical support. An earlier job as a local stringer for Women's Wear Daily *had familiarized her with layouts and typography; she also designed a dust jacket and paper cutout silhouettes to be used as chapter headings. "Mazie" (Mary) Whyte, longtime secretary to Irma's late husband, loyally typed recipes as pages in loose-leaf binders. A bridge-playing friend steered them to a family connection who owned a small printing company, and* The Joy of Cooking: A Compilation of Reliable Recipes with a Casual Culinary Chat *saw the light of day in November 1931.*

Today the selection of materials in this maiden effort looks oddly chosen, and the instruction often haphazard. But a certain advantage over the competition is clear, at least in hindsight. Irma was not reputed to be one of St. Louis's most virtuosic cooks. But from pure instinct, she imbued Joy *with something unique. It conveyed the sense of a real person—no great culinary authority, just a whimsical and interesting companion who had alighted on the subject of cooking—conversing with other real people. (About liquor-based cocktails, for instance, which generally "are made today"—Prohibition-bound 1931—"with gin and ingenuity.") Other cookbooks of the day either ignored such goals (the institutional* Boston Cooking-School Cook Book*) or ineptly counterfeited them (the gushy Ida Bailey Allen's* Modern Cook Book*).*

Chiefly by word of mouth, Irma managed to sell out her 3,000-copy run in a couple of years. By then she was primed with concrete plans for an expanded version, with a new recipe format of her own invention. Many bootless appeals to trade publishers finally paid off when the Bobbs-Merrill Company of Indianapolis and New York issued her revision in 1936. Astonishingly, she had contrived to whack the small original into a respectable kitchen manual while not only retaining but also heightening its personality-driven irreverence toward ordinary cookbook conventions. The result was an illogical amalgam of elements (Jell-O salads, anything-goes soufflés, old-fashioned German Christmas cookies, a favorite Sauerbraten recipe) somehow marshaled into a convincing whole. Writing in the first person, Rombauer's charm beamed through, and the book appealed to a huge group of readers without consciously setting out to do so.

Irma herself remained the great drawing card of the first Joy *edition to achieve nationwide bestsellerdom: a hefty retooling, published in 1943 during the bleak food-rationing days of World War II, that interwove the contents of the 1936 version with those of a short 1937 book on quickie cooking. But even as the fact of success sank in, by the war's end, it was clear that at nearly seventy she would need younger help to carry the work into another era. The collaborator she finally settled on was both the likeliest and the unlikeliest person imaginable: Marion.*

Marion, who had married her longtime fiancé John Becker and moved to Cincinnati in 1932, was Irma's opposite in aspects ranging from looks and manner (outgoing, stylishly petite, captivating mother; heavy, plain-featured, introspective, earnest daughter) to convictions about food (Irma never tried to impose any special agenda; Marion had adopted "health food" and organic gardening principles). The joint effort that they brought out in 1951 threw several new ingredients into an already miscellaneous bouillabaisse. Advice about conserving vitamins in cooking or finding out how vegetables had been grown suddenly rubbed elbows with throwaway Irmaisms such as "Here, like Charlie McCarthy, we are torn 'between vice and versa.'" Dozens of flavored gelatin and canned soup recipes had been deleted to make room for material on making your own yogurt or putting whole grains to use. Even so, Irma's voice contrived to gloss over all incongruities.

The series of strokes that Irma suffered in the late 1950s left Marion to shape Joy's future path. She chose a forbiddingly difficult one: to throw out still more old recipes, work in huge swathes of explanatory material ("Know Your Ingredients"; "About Thickeners for Sauces"), and add many cosmopolitan dishes, from carbonnade flamande to huevos rancheros, all while trying to retain something like Irma's persona.

Her complex effort appeared in 1963 after long battles with Bobbs-Merrill, which actually released a mangled version without Marion's authorization at the height of their author-publisher hostilities in 1962, while Irma lay dying. It did not sound precisely or consistently like Irma. But Marion and her husband (an important contributor to the work) had come closer to replicating the Irma spirit than anyone else could have done. In the edition of 1975, they went still further in turning the beloved work into an extraordinary reference tool—a one-of-a-kind encyclopedic resource that improbably managed to find room for family stories, puns ("What foods these morsels be!"), and many priceless Irmaisms from earlier editions.

Despite the publication of a post-Marion edition incorporating the work of several dozen contributors (1997) and another that attempted to restore some of the book's family character (2006), it seems safe to say that no future version will ever inspire the sheer affection that Joy evoked among a loyal, wildly heterogeneous public over more than half of the twentieth century.

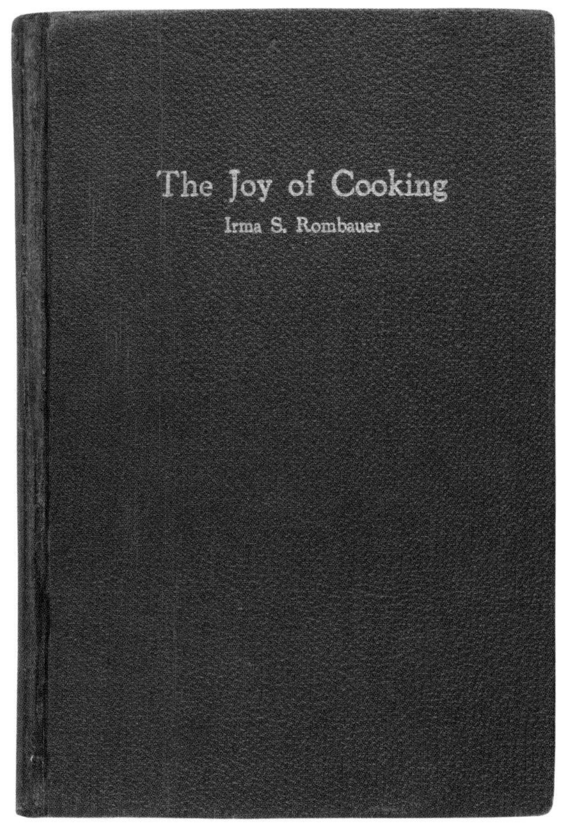

General Rules

The recipes in this book call for standard measuring cups and spoons.

The majority of these recipes will serve from four to six people.

All the measurements given are level, unless indicated otherwise.

A standard measuring cup equals ½ pint.

TABLE OF WEIGHTS AND MEASURES

1 salt spoon	= ¼ teaspoon	Butter the size of an egg	= ¼ cup
3 teaspoons	= 1 tablespoon	1 square bitter chocolate	= 1 ounce
1 rounding tablespoon	= 2 tablespoons	1 ounce chocolate	= 1/3 cup cocoa
2 tablespoons	= ⅛ cup	1 cup raisins	= 6 ounces
4 tablespoons	= ¼ cup	1 cup shelled walnuts	= ¼ pound
16 tablespoons	= 1 cup	1 cup shelled pecans	= 1/3 pound
2 gills	= 1 cup	1 cup shelled almonds	= ¼ pound
1 cup	= ½ pint	3 cups of macaroni	= 1 pound
2 cups	= 1 pint	1 cup grated cheese	= ¼ pound
2 pints	= 1 quart	1 pound green peas, hulled	= 1 cup
4 quarts	= 1 gallon	1 cup macaroni, cooked	= 2 cups
8 quarts	= 1 peck	1 cup rice, cooked	= 3 cups
4 pecks	= 1 bushel	1 cup noodles, cooked	= 1¼ cups
16 ounces	= 1 pound	1 lemon, juiced	= Approximately 3½ tablespoons
16 liquid ounces	= 1 pint (2 cups)	1 orange, juiced	= Approximately 6 tablespoons
4 cups flour	= 1 pound		
2 cups granulated sugar	= 1 pound		
2-2/3 cups powdered sugar	= 1 pound		
2-2/3 cups brown sugar	= 1 pound		
2 cups solid meat	= 1 pound		
8 egg whites	= 1 cup		
16 egg yolks	= 1 cup		
2 cups butter	= 1 pound		

The following chart is sometimes helpful:

No. 1 can contains	1½ cups	No. 2½ can contains	3½ cups
No. 2 can contains	2½ cups	No. 3 can contains	4 cups

Condensed Milk.

Substitute ½ cup condensed milk and ½ cup of water for 1 cup of fresh milk.

I

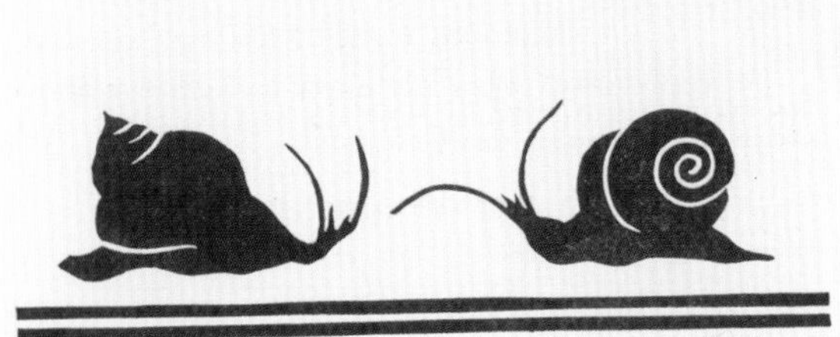

I. Cream the butter and the sugar, beat in the eggs and add the vanilla.

II. Sift the dry ingredients.

III. Add the dry ingredients, alternately with the milk, to No. I.

Serve the waffles with chocolate sauce and vanilla ice cream, or whipped cream. The ice cream may be made with condensed milk.

208

Pies

CHART FOR BAKING PIES

Double crust fruit pies; Hot oven 450° for 30 minutes. Slow oven 325° for an additional 10 minutes.

Minced Pie, or any other double crust pie with a previously cooked filling; Hot oven 450° for 30 minutes.

Open Fruit Pies; Hot oven 450° for 20 minutes.

Custard Pie, Pumpkin Pie and other open pies; Hot oven 450° for 15 minutes, Slow oven 325° for an additional 30 minutes.

Deep Fruit Pies; 450° for 30 minutes, 325° for an additional 10 minutes.

Pie shells without filling; Very hot oven 500° for 12 minutes.

Dumplings or Turnovers; 450° for 15 minutes.

Meringue; 300° for 12 minutes.

PIE CRUST

1¾ cups cake flour
1 teaspoon baking powder
½ teaspoon salt
4 tablespoons lard
2 tablespoons butter
¼ cup ice water

RULE FOR MAKING PIE CRUST

All the materials should be as cold as possible. Sift the dry ingredients and cut in the shortening with a knife, or work it with a fork until it is the size of a pea. The less it is handled, the better. Do not work it until it is fine, or the crust will not be flaky. Add the ice water very slowly, using less

209

LOGANBERRY OR RASPBERRY JUICE

Add
1 cup of sugar to
1 quart of berries and
2 tablespoons of water

Cook the berries until they are soft. Then strain the juice from them.

CANNED LOGANBERRY OR RASPBERRY JUICE

Strain the juice from canned loganberries, or raspberries.

326

Ice Creams, Ices and Frozen Desserts

Ice Creams and Ices to be Frozen in an Ice Cream Freezer

RULES FOR MAKING ICE CREAM AND ICES IN A FREEZER

Use cream that is twenty-four hours old, as it makes a finer grain than fresh cream. When it is possible to do so, dissolve the sugar in liquid over heat before adding it to the cream.

Add ¼ teaspoonful, or more, of salt to the syrup. Cool the syrup before adding it to the cream. Chill the mixture to be frozen before placing it in the ice cream container.

Fill the ice cream container only three-fourths full to allow for the expansion of the frozen cream.

Allow from three to six measures of ice to one measure of coarse (rock) salt, according to the rapidity with which you wish to freeze the cream. The larger proportion of salt will bring quicker results, but the cream is finer grained when it is frozen slowly. Pack the freezer one-third full of ice before adding any salt, then add the salt and the remaining ice and salt in alternate layers around the container until the freezer is filled.

Turn the cream slowly at first until a slight pull is felt, then turn it rapidly.

If the ice cream is to be used at once, turn it until it is very stiff. If the ice cream is to be packed, turn it only until it is the consistency of thick sauce.

327

Breakfast Table, First Course

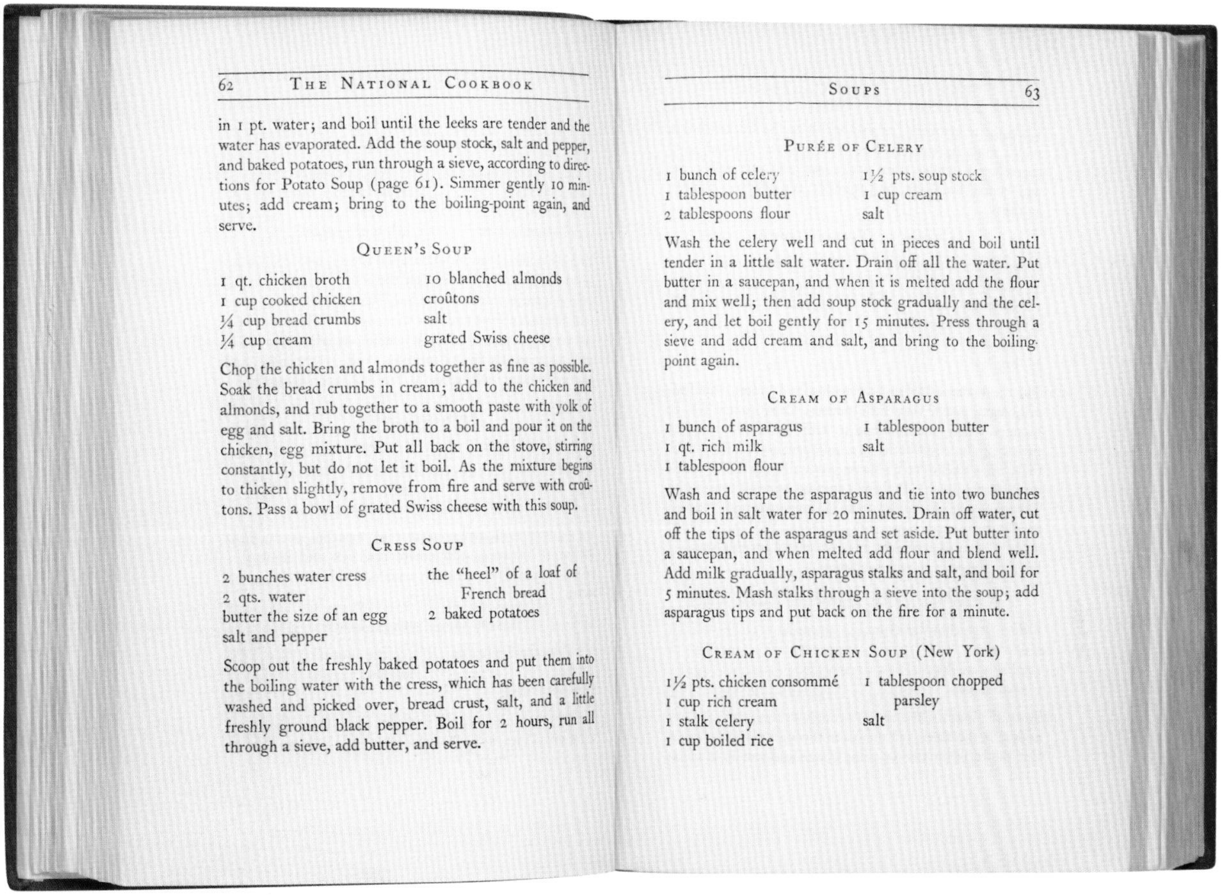

62 THE NATIONAL COOKBOOK

in 1 pt. water; and boil until the leeks are tender and the water has evaporated. Add the soup stock, salt and pepper, and baked potatoes, run through a sieve, according to directions for Potato Soup (page 61). Simmer gently 10 minutes; add cream; bring to the boiling-point again, and serve.

QUEEN'S SOUP

1 qt. chicken broth	10 blanched almonds
1 cup cooked chicken	croûtons
¼ cup bread crumbs	salt
¼ cup cream	grated Swiss cheese

Chop the chicken and almonds together as fine as possible. Soak the bread crumbs in cream; add to the chicken and almonds, and rub together to a smooth paste with yolk of egg and salt. Bring the broth to a boil and pour it on the chicken, egg mixture. Put all back on the stove, stirring constantly, but do not let it boil. As the mixture begins to thicken slightly, remove from fire and serve with croûtons. Pass a bowl of grated Swiss cheese with this soup.

CRESS SOUP

2 bunches water cress	the "heel" of a loaf of French bread
2 qts. water	
butter the size of an egg	2 baked potatoes
salt and pepper	

Scoop out the freshly baked potatoes and put them into the boiling water with the cress, which has been carefully washed and picked over, bread crust, salt, and a little freshly ground black pepper. Boil for 2 hours, run all through a sieve, add butter, and serve.

SOUPS 63

PURÉE OF CELERY

1 bunch of celery	1½ pts. soup stock
1 tablespoon butter	1 cup cream
2 tablespoons flour	salt

Wash the celery well and cut in pieces and boil until tender in a little salt water. Drain off all the water. Put butter in a saucepan, and when it is melted add the flour and mix well; then add soup stock gradually and the celery, and let boil gently for 15 minutes. Press through a sieve and add cream and salt, and bring to the boiling-point again.

CREAM OF ASPARAGUS

1 bunch of asparagus	1 tablespoon butter
1 qt. rich milk	salt
1 tablespoon flour	

Wash and scrape the asparagus and tie into two bunches and boil in salt water for 20 minutes. Drain off water, cut off the tips of the asparagus and set aside. Put butter into a saucepan, and when melted add flour and blend well. Add milk gradually, asparagus stalks and salt, and boil for 5 minutes. Mash stalks through a sieve into the soup; add asparagus tips and put back on the fire for a minute.

CREAM OF CHICKEN SOUP (New York)

1½ pts. chicken consommé	1 tablespoon chopped parsley
1 cup rich cream	
1 stalk celery	salt
1 cup boiled rice	

SHEILA HIBBEN

The National Cookbook

A Kitchen Americana, 1932

Sheila Hibben was one of the early proponents of American food during the time when cooking from just about anywhere else was considered superior to our homegrown cuisines. Like James Beard, she spoke out for the use of fresh, local ingredients. In a 1946 interview with Jane Nickerson for the *New York Times*, Hibben spoke about cooking in mid-century America: "No one can ever talk me out of my belief that real American cookery is at its best great. But the ready-mixes and the bottled sauces are standardizing what was once anything but uniform in the various sections of this country. It seems to be that one way to revive the different culinary traditions is to turn our backs on the 'quickies' and everything synthetic, and concentrate on indigenous dishes." She focused on learning to taste: "I think that the best way to learn to cook is to become perceptive about flavor. No one needs to be taste-blind. Whatever and whenever you eat, reflect—Is this good with that, or would something else be better." Her advice still stands today.

Despite being an editor at the *New Yorker*, where she created the restaurant column, and being asked by Eleanor Roosevelt to consult on menus for the White House, Hibben didn't have much of a direct effect on American food in general but was very influential on the smaller circle of food writers in the period. Beard would play that role in the following decades but on a more public stage. But Hibben was right: American cuisines were just as legitimate as French cooking.

NOTABLE RECIPES: Crab-Flake Cakes (Baltimore) (page 480) • **Jelly Pie (Arkansas)** (page 603) • **Muffin Cakes (Colorado)** (page 587) • Ole Koeks • **Rhode Island Johnny Cake** (page 592)

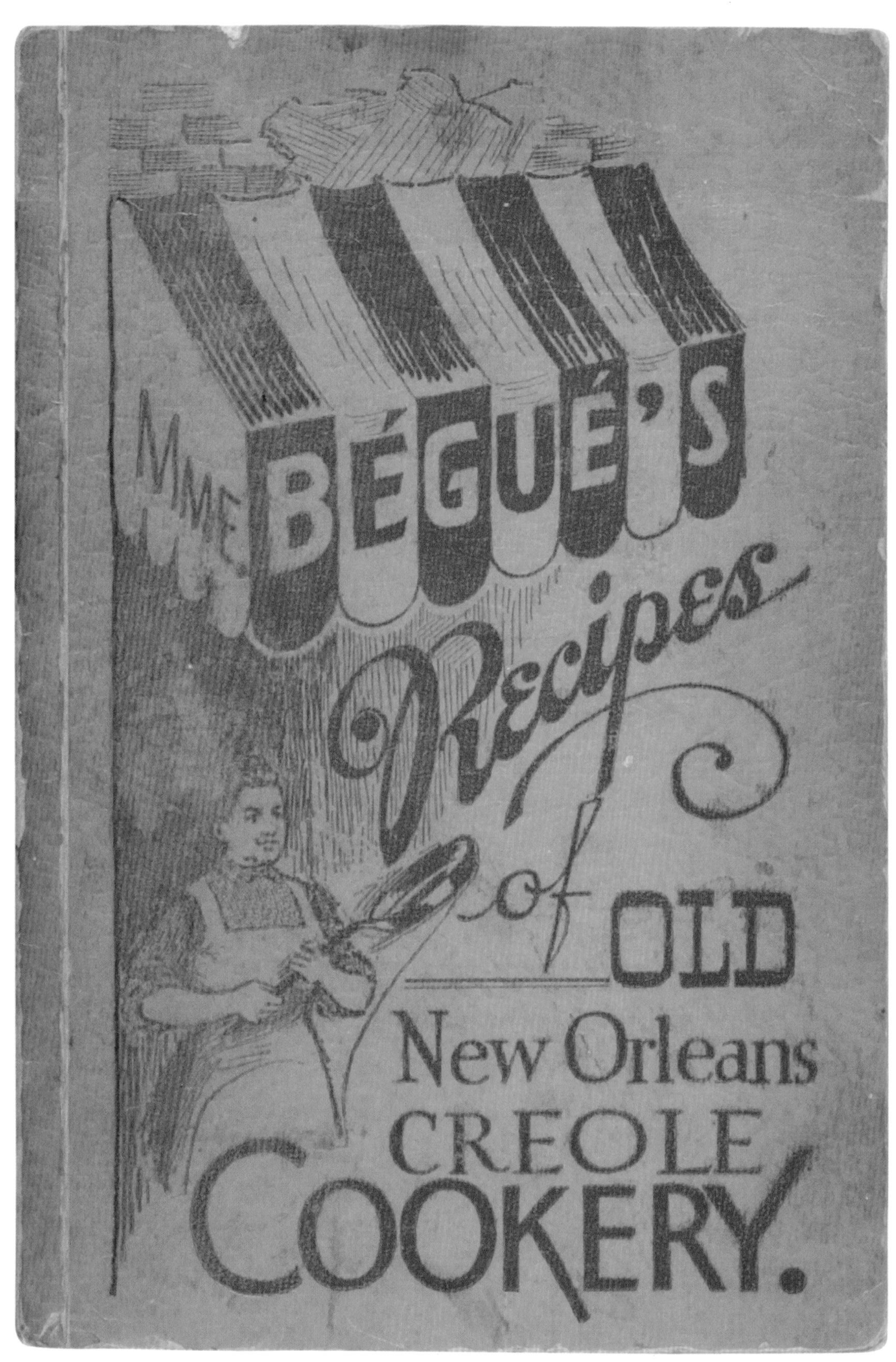
MME. BÉGUÉ'S
Recipes
of
OLD
New Orleans
CREOLE
COOKERY.

MME. BÉGUÉ

Mme. Bégué's Recipes of Old New Orleans Creole Cookery, 1937

Madame Bégué's name is synonymous with the grand tradition of "Old New Orleans" cooking. Born Elizabeth Kettering in Bavaria, the future Mme. Bégué immigrated to New Orleans, where she married a butcher named Louis Dutrey. In 1863 the couple opened a coffeehouse called Dutrey's near the markets of the French Quarter.

Following Dutrey's death, Elizabeth married another butcher, Hypolite Bégué, and changed the name of the restaurant to Mme. Bégué's. She began serving a late or "second breakfast" at 11 a.m. each day. This unusual hour was popular with both those who shopped at the markets and the butchers and other purveyors who sold products at the markets because it came at the end of shopping time. Neither just a breakfast nor really a lunch, the meals are now cited as the origin of the idea for brunch. A typical second breakfast consisted of an egg dish, including various kinds of omelets, French toast, crawfish bisque, and Creole gumbo and jambalaya, followed by coffee and brandy.

Breakfast at Mme. Bégué's was a local tradition until 1884, when the Centennial Cotton Exposition was held in New Orleans. Tourists discovered the amazing and delicious food, and the restaurant became a destination for anyone interested in New Orleans cuisine. Mme. Bégué reigned over her kitchen for forty-three years, until her death in 1906. Hypolite Bégué continued to serve the second breakfast until his death in 1917. Mme. Bégué's cookbook preserves the great recipes she prepared at the restaurant. It is like a peek back into a particularly personal, nineteenth-century New Orleans kitchen and a great chronicle of the heyday of Old New Orleans cooking.

NOTABLE RECIPES: Bisque of Crayfish (page 349) • **Jambalaya of Chicken** (page 380) • Chicken à la Créole • Creole Gumbo • **Liver à la Bégué** (page 560) • Oyster Stew • **Pain Perdu** (page 594) • **Shrimp Remoulade** (page 322) • **Turtle Soup** (page 350)

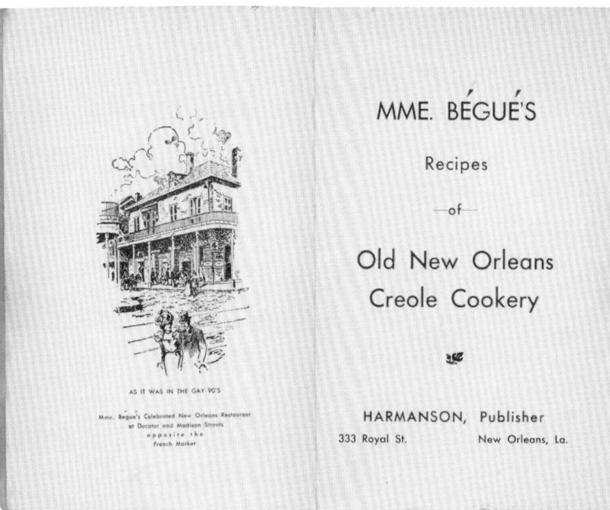

AS IT WAS IN THE GAY 90'S

Mme. Begue's Celebrated New Orleans Restaurant
at Decatur and Madison Streets
opposite the
French Market

MME. BÉGUÉ'S
Recipes
of
Old New Orleans
Creole Cookery

HARMANSON, Publisher
333 Royal St. New Orleans, La.

gué's," the place began its march to culinary fame. It was not until 1884 that Madame Bégué's breakfasts became famous outside of the French Market trade. During the Cotton Centennial Exposition in 1884, tourists doing the Vieux Carré "discovered" Madame Bégue's "second breakfasts," and gave all credit for them to Elizabeth Kettenring, the woman from Germany, for the success the place attained. In a few years the "breakfasts" attained a reputation outside of New Orleans—for visitors to the Crescent City spread her fame far and wide.

October 19, 1906, the place was closed for the first time in 31 years, for Madame Bégué had laid down her pots and her pans and had passed on to solve the silent mystery of death. However, the doors were not closed for good and all, as Hypolite Bégué carried on and, as is so frequently the case, the traditional breakfasts which had become established in the thirty-odd years Elizabeth Kettenring had presided over the kitchen. Hypolite's second wife was Françoise Lafforgue, widow of Jean Pierre Laporte, a butcher in the French Market and, as she had served an apprenticeship under the first Madame Bégué, the famed breakfasts continued.

"Bégué's," and the Bégué breakfasts remained an institution in New Orleans' colorful and tasteful history of cookery through the years until finally, on April 4, 1917, Hypolite Bégué passed on to join the first Madame Bégué in a plot in Metairie Cemetery.

In 1900, six years before her death, the recipes of the dishes that made Bégué's so famous were set to paper by Elizabeth Kettenring. In spite of her German birth she spoke French fluently, but she never became proficient in the English tongue, so when she set down in words the secrets of her cookery they were written in the language of France.

For years these prized recipes for Creole cookery have been out of print and an original copy of Madame Bégué's Cook Book has become a collector's item. The demand for Madame Begué's recipes has become insistent and it is to meet this

Twelve

demand that they have been reproduced by the present publisher.

The sturdy brick building, built in 1826 on the site of the Old French, Spanish, and United States Arsenal, still stands at the self-same corner, although the name Bégué is now missing. Today it is called "Tujagues Restaurant," and here John Castet, who worked for years for Hypolite Bégué, serves many of the dishes that made the place a dining shrine. The celebrated "breakfasts" of Madame Bégué, however, are memories of the past, they live only in the remembrance of thousands who climbed the narrow stairway to do homage to Old New Orleans' queen of the kitchen—Elizabeth Kettenring Dutrey Bégué.

For those puzzled by names in New Orleans of French flavor:
Bégué can best be pronounced "bay-gay."
Tujagues may be called "two jacks."

Thirteen

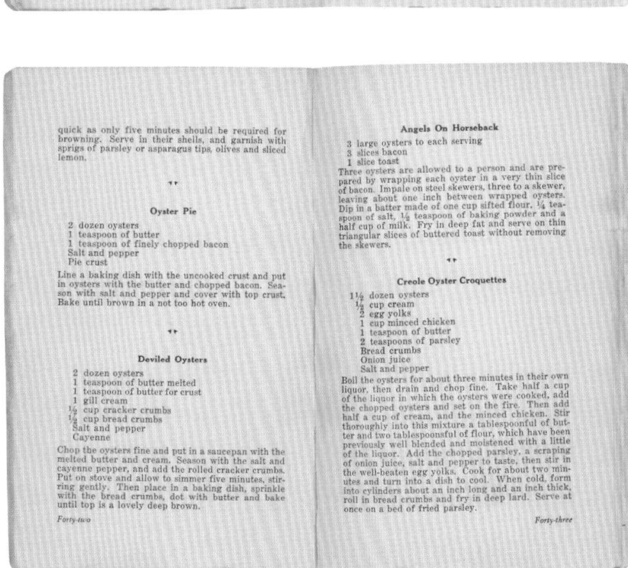

quick as only five minutes should be required for browning. Serve in their shells, and garnish with sprigs of parsley or asparagus tips, olives and sliced lemon.

Oyster Pie

2 dozen oysters
1 teaspoon of butter
1 teaspoon of finely chopped bacon
Salt and pepper
Pie crust

Line a baking dish with the uncooked crust and put in oysters with the butter and chopped bacon. Season with salt and pepper and cover with top crust. Bake until brown in a not too hot oven.

Deviled Oysters

2 dozen oysters
1 teaspoon of butter melted
1 teaspoon of butter for crust
1 gill cream
½ cup cracker crumbs
½ cup bread crumbs
Salt and pepper
Cayenne

Chop the oysters fine and put in a saucepan with the melted butter and cream. Season with the salt and cayenne pepper, and add the rolled cracker crumbs. Put on stove and allow to simmer five minutes, stirring gently. Then place in a baking dish, sprinkle with the bread crumbs, dot with butter and bake until top is a lovely deep brown.

Forty-two

Angels On Horseback

3 large oysters to each serving
3 slices bacon
1 slice toast

Three oysters are allowed to a person and are prepared by wrapping each oyster in a very thin slice of bacon. Impale on steel skewers, three to a skewer, leaving about one inch between wrapped oysters. Dip in a batter made of one cup sifted flour, ¼ teaspoon of salt, ½ teaspoon of baking powder and a half cup of milk. Fry in deep fat and serve on thin triangular slices of buttered toast without removing the skewers.

Creole Oyster Croquettes

1½ dozen oysters
½ cup cream
2 egg yolks
1 cup minced chicken
1 teaspoon of butter
2 teaspoons of parsley
Bread crumbs
Onion juice
Salt and pepper

Boil the oysters for about three minutes in their own liquor, then drain and chop fine. Take half a cup of the liquor in which the oysters were cooked, add the chopped oysters and set on the fire. Then add half a cup of cream, and the minced chicken. Stir thoroughly into this mixture a tablespoonful of butter and two tablespoonsful of flour, which have been previously well blended and moistened with a little of the liquor. Add the chopped parsley, a scraping of onion juice, salt and pepper to taste, then stir in the well-beaten egg yolks. Cook for about two minutes and turn into a dish to cool. When cold, form into cylinders about an inch long and an inch thick, roll in bread crumbs and fry in deep lard. Serve at once on a bed of fried parsley.

Forty-three

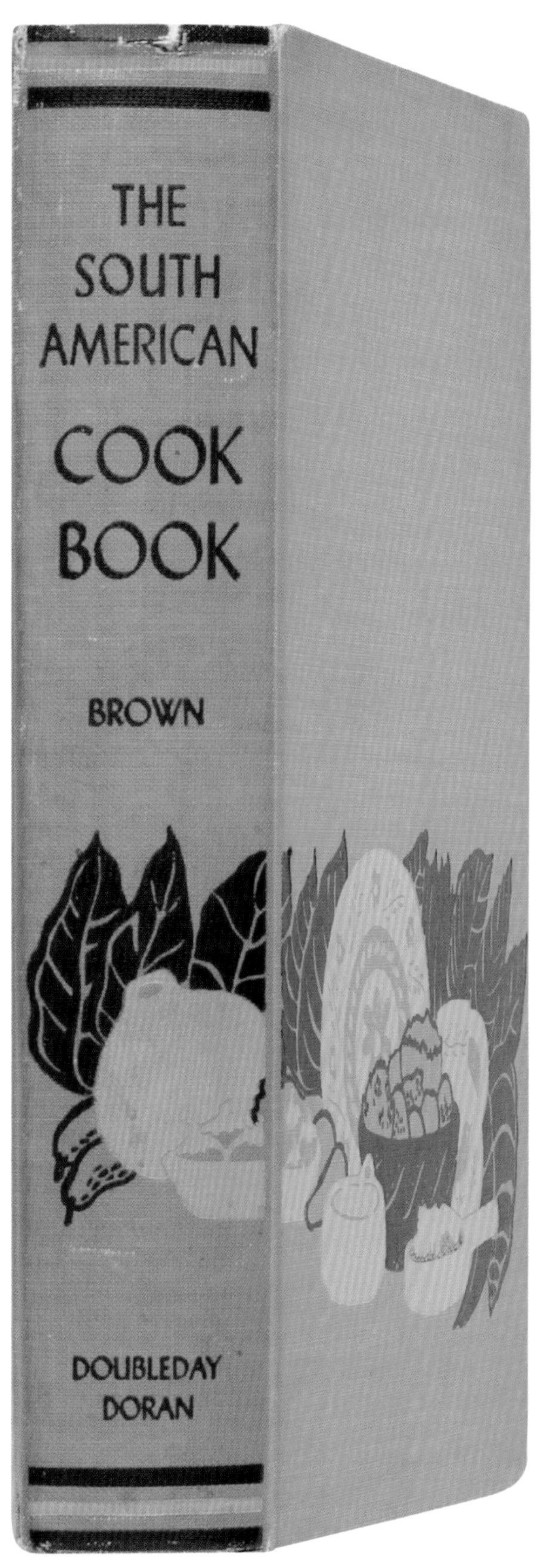

CORA, ROSE, AND ROBERT BROWN

The South American Cook Book

Including Central America, Mexico, and the West Indies, 1939

Robert Carlton Brown (1886–1959) was a writer, editor, publisher, and traveler. From 1908 to 1917, he wrote poetry and prose for numerous magazines and newspapers in New York City, publishing two pulp novels, *What Happened to Mary* (1913) and *The Remarkable Adventures of Christopher Poe* (1913), and one volume of poetry, *My Marjonary* (1916).

In the 1910s Brown was involved with a group of artists and poets in New York's Greenwich Village that included Alfred Kreymborg, Walter Arensberg, Maxwell Bodenheim, Malcolm Cowley, Man Ray, William Carlos Williams, and Marcel Duchamp. During 1918 he traveled extensively in Mexico and Central America, writing for the U.S. Committee of Public Information in Santiago de Chile. In 1919 he moved with his wife, Rose Brown, to Rio de Janeiro, where they founded *Brazilian American*, a weekly magazine that ran until 1929. With Brown's mother, Cora, the Browns also established magazines in Mexico City and London: *Mexican American* (1924–29) and *British American* (1926–29). Following the 1929 stock market crash, the Browns moved to Paris, where Robert became friends with the literary avant-garde, especially those like Gertrude Stein and Ezra Pound who were experimenting with visual poetry, something he himself liked to write.

During the 1930s Robert, Cora, and Rose wrote a series of international cookbooks based on their travels. *The South American Cook Book* remains an important introduction to the cuisines of the region, and is based on the Browns' research into the foods. Robert Brown continued to vacillate between the worlds of commerce, avant-garde poetry, and food writing for the rest of his career.

NOTABLE RECIPES: Rice with Palm Hearts (Arroz con Palmito) (page 453) • **Argentine Lamb Stew (Cazuela de Cordero)** (page 538) • **Paraguayan Eggs with Tomato Sauce (Huevos con Salsa de Tomate)** (page 465)

living in burrows along streams and sallying forth at night to browse in sugar and rice fields. It is gentle and so easily tamed that specimens kept for sale often run about underfoot in country markets. Since it is supposed to eat fish as well as green stuffs the fat under the skin and in its insides has a rank taste. When this is removed the rest of the flesh is sweet and delicious. Its preparation illustrates the patience of the Brazilian cook, for it is marinated 24 hours (See Marinating Mixture for Rabbit.), soaked in water under a dripping tap another 24 hours, parboiled, drained, dried and then soaked in the juice of the wild orange 6–8 hours, when it is at last ready for cooking. Then it is browned in fat or butter, put into boiling water with a glass of white rum, seasonings, including herbs, onion, cloves and ginger, and cooked until done. The proper accompaniment is a wilted salad of wild greens.

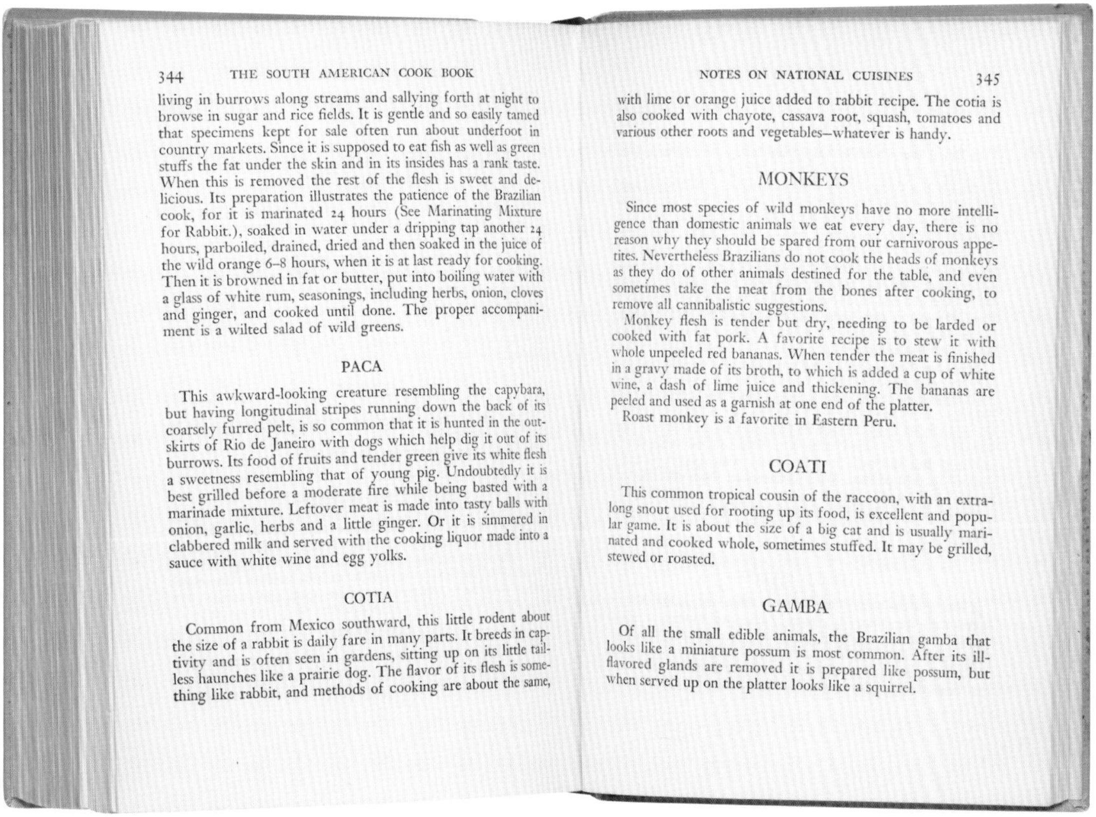

PACA

This awkward-looking creature resembling the capybara, but having longitudinal stripes running down the back of its coarsely furred pelt, is so common that it is hunted in the outskirts of Rio de Janeiro with dogs which help dig it out of its burrows. Its food of fruits and tender green give its white flesh a sweetness resembling that of young pig. Undoubtedly it is best grilled before a moderate fire while being basted with a marinade mixture. Leftover meat is made into tasty balls with onion, garlic, herbs and a little ginger. Or it is simmered in clabbered milk and served with the cooking liquor made into a sauce with white wine and egg yolks.

COTIA

Common from Mexico southward, this little rodent about the size of a rabbit is daily fare in many parts. It breeds in captivity and is often seen in gardens, sitting up on its little tail-less haunches like a prairie dog. The flavor of its flesh is something like rabbit, and methods of cooking are about the same,

with lime or orange juice added to rabbit recipe. The cotia is also cooked with chayote, cassava root, squash, tomatoes and various other roots and vegetables—whatever is handy.

MONKEYS

Since most species of wild monkeys have no more intelligence than domestic animals we eat every day, there is no reason why they should be spared from our carnivorous appetites. Nevertheless Brazilians do not cook the heads of monkeys as they do of other animals destined for the table, and even sometimes take the meat from the bones after cooking, to remove all cannibalistic suggestions.

Monkey flesh is tender but dry, needing to be larded or cooked with fat pork. A favorite recipe is to stew it with whole unpeeled red bananas. When tender the meat is finished in a gravy made of its broth, to which is added a cup of white wine, a dash of lime juice and thickening. The bananas are peeled and used as a garnish at one end of the platter.

Roast monkey is a favorite in Eastern Peru.

COATI

This common tropical cousin of the raccoon, with an extra-long snout used for rooting up its food, is excellent and popular game. It is about the size of a big cat and is usually marinated and cooked whole, sometimes stuffed. It may be grilled, stewed or roasted.

GAMBA

Of all the small edible animals, the Brazilian gamba that looks like a miniature possum is most common. After its ill-flavored glands are removed it is prepared like possum, but when served up on the platter looks like a squirrel.

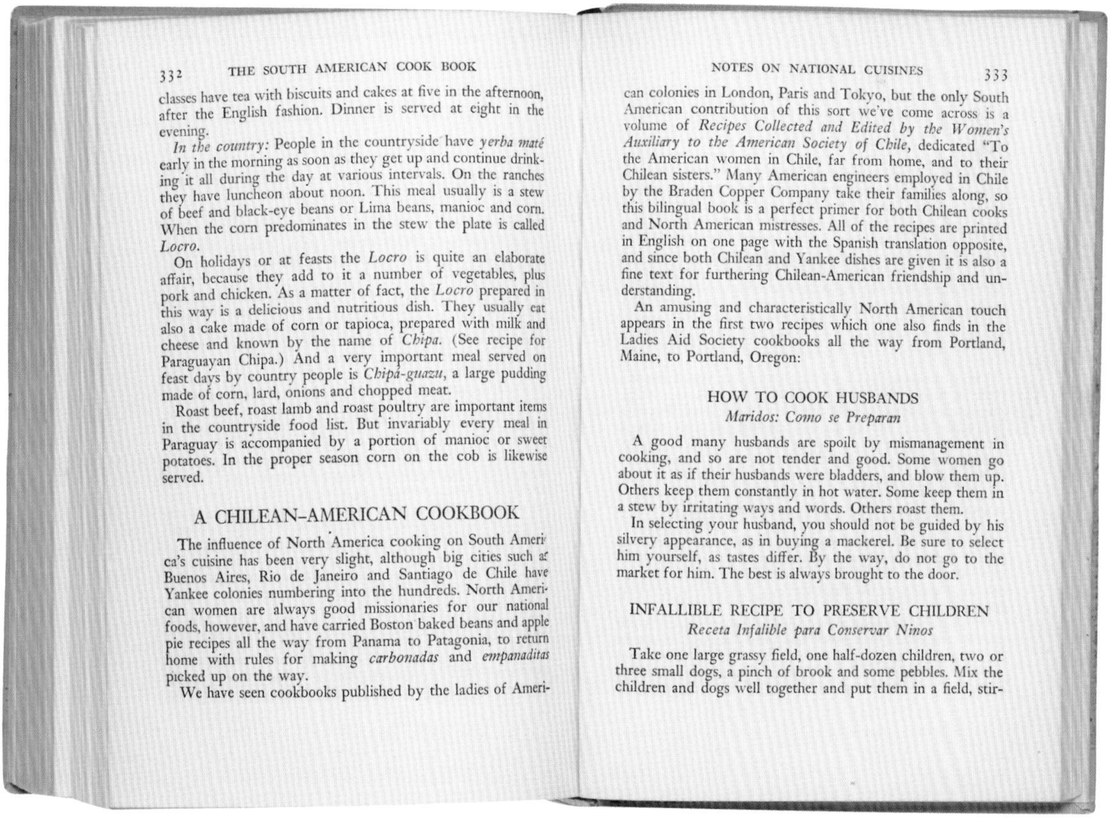

classes have tea with biscuits and cakes at five in the afternoon, after the English fashion. Dinner is served at eight in the evening.

In the country: People in the countryside have *yerba maté* early in the morning as soon as they get up and continue drinking it all during the day at various intervals. On the ranches they have luncheon about noon. This meal usually is a stew of beef and black-eye beans or Lima beans, manioc and corn. When the corn predominates in the stew the plate is called *Locro.*

On holidays or at feasts the *Locro* is quite an elaborate affair, because they add to it a number of vegetables, plus pork and chicken. As a matter of fact, the *Locro* prepared in this way is a delicious and nutritious dish. They usually eat also a cake made of corn or tapioca, prepared with milk and cheese and known by the name of *Chipa.* (See recipe for Paraguayan Chipa.) And a very important meal served on feast days by country people is *Chipa-guazu,* a large pudding made of corn, lard, onions and chopped meat.

Roast beef, roast lamb and roast poultry are important items in the countryside food list. But invariably every meal in Paraguay is accompanied by a portion of manioc or sweet potatoes. In the proper season corn on the cob is likewise served.

A CHILEAN-AMERICAN COOKBOOK

The influence of North America cooking on South America's cuisine has been very slight, although big cities such as Buenos Aires, Rio de Janeiro and Santiago de Chile have Yankee colonies numbering into the hundreds. North American women are always good missionaries for our national foods, however, and have carried Boston baked beans and apple pie recipes all the way from Panama to Patagonia, to return home with rules for making *carbonadas* and *empanaditas* picked up on the way.

We have seen cookbooks published by the ladies of Ameri-

can colonies in London, Paris and Tokyo, but the only South American contribution of this sort we've come across is a volume of *Recipes Collected and Edited by the Women's Auxiliary to the American Society of Chile,* dedicated "To the American women in Chile, far from home, and to their Chilean sisters." Many American engineers employed in Chile by the Braden Copper Company take their families along, so this bilingual book is a perfect primer for both Chilean cooks and North American mistresses. All of the recipes are printed in English on one page with the Spanish translation opposite, and since both Chilean and Yankee dishes are given it is also a fine text for furthering Chilean-American friendship and understanding.

An amusing and characteristically North American touch appears in the first two recipes which one also finds in the Ladies Aid Society cookbooks all the way from Portland, Maine, to Portland, Oregon:

HOW TO COOK HUSBANDS

Maridos: Como se Preparan

A good many husbands are spoilt by mismanagement in cooking, and so are not tender and good. Some women go about it as if their husbands were bladders, and blow them up. Others keep them constantly in hot water. Some keep them in a stew by irritating ways and words. Others roast them.

In selecting your husband, you should not be guided by his silvery appearance, as in buying a mackerel. Be sure to select him yourself, as tastes differ. By the way, do not go to the market for him. The best is always brought to the door.

INFALLIBLE RECIPE TO PRESERVE CHILDREN

Receta Infalible para Conservar Ninos

Take one large grassy field, one half-dozen children, two or three small dogs, a pinch of brook and some pebbles. Mix the children and dogs well together and put them in a field, stir-

CROSBY GAIGE

New York World's Fair Cook Book

The American Kitchen, 1939

Crosby Gaige, born Roscoe Conkling Gaige, was a theatrical producer who thought of himself as New York's greatest gourmet and oenophile. He was a member of a group of almost exclusively male epicureans who looked back to the Golden Age of New York hotel restaurants from the turn of the century and promoted anything elite and European. The New York chapter of the International Wine & Food Society had its headquarters in his offices. Gaige was born in Skunk Hollow, New York, attended Columbia University, and later worked in the offices of theatrical agent Elisabeth Marbury. He joined the producers Edgar and Arch Selwyn, producing such Broadway hits as, appropriately, *The Butter and Egg Man* (1925) and many other plays.

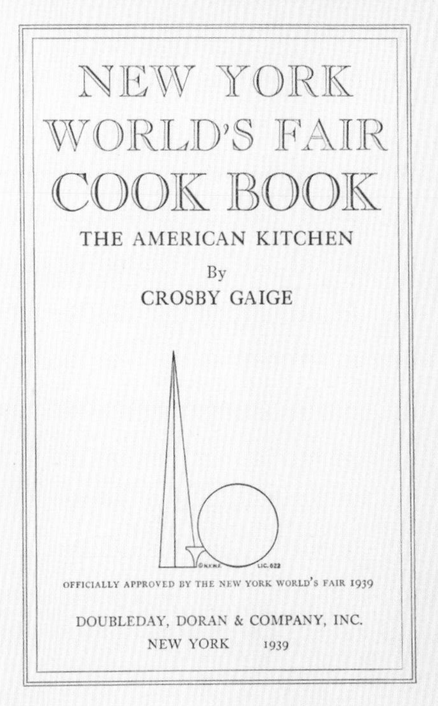
NEW YORK WORLD'S FAIR COOK BOOK

THE AMERICAN KITCHEN

By

CROSBY GAIGE

OFFICIALLY APPROVED BY THE NEW YORK WORLD'S FAIR 1939

DOUBLEDAY, DORAN & COMPANY, INC.

NEW YORK 1939

4 NEW YORK WORLD'S FAIR COOK BOOK

enough bouillon to make pliable but not wet. Stuff fish and sew up. Lay several slices of salt pork in a greased and heated baking pan. Put in the fish. Dredge with flour, salt and pepper. Lay two slices of the salt pork over the fish. Bake in moderately hot oven (300° F.), allowing fifteen minutes to each pound of fish. Baste often with drippings in pan.

Boston fish wharves are responsible for much of the halibut eaten in this country. But all New England follows this truly British recipe, and it is also a favorite in New York City.

BOILED HALIBUT WITH EGG SAUCE

2 or more pounds of fish, cut for boiling
2 tablespoons melted butter
1½ tablespoons flour
1 cup hot milk
2 hard-boiled eggs
salt, pepper

To boil, cover the prepared fish with hot broth (see Broth for Poaching Fish) and simmer very gently until the flesh begins to separate from the bones. Never boil fish hard. Allow six to ten minutes for each pound for boiling, depending on the thickness of the fish. A large fish should be cut into fillets of a size for serving, before boiling.

Make a sauce of the butter, flour and milk. When well blended add the seasonings and the eggs cut into slices. Serve very hot, poured over the fish.

Beloved of Maine and Massachusetts cooks, the shad is also a favorite of New York and New Jersey chefs. This is a Jersey dish, as given, but much like the Southern way too:

BAKED SHAD

1 large shad
2 cups bread crumbs
1 egg yolk, beaten
1 tablespoon minced onion
lemon juice
1 tablespoon melted butter
slices of fat salt pork
salt, pepper, flour

Remove the scales from the fish and clean it. Make a dressing of the bread crumbs, egg yolk, butter, onion and seasonings. Stuff and sew up the fish. As shad is inclined to be dry, cover the fish with slices of salt pork when you lay it in the greased baking pan. Dredge the fish with flour, salt and pepper. Add a cup of boiling water or bouillon to the pan. Use a moderate oven (350° F.). Baste with this every ten minutes during the baking. When the fish is tender remove it with the pork scraps and make a gravy of the sauce in the pan. Brown one or two tablespoons of flour in a pan and add gradually the liquid in the fish pan. Stir and cook until well combined.

In baking shad, allow one hour for each two and one half pounds

FROM EARLY NEW ENGLAND KITCHENS 5

of fish. Put into a hot oven (400° F. to 450° F.) at first, then reduce heat to 350° F. after the first fifteen minutes.

I like to add chopped almonds to the stuffing; or peanuts; or I add the nuts to the sauce. Also I garnish the platter with thin lemon slices sprinkled with paprika.

And the fried roe is known in every coastal state on the Eastern seaboard:

FRIED SHAD ROE

shad roe
1 teaspoon salt
1 tablespoon vinegar
2 cups water
salt, pepper
flour

Pour the water over the shad roe (more if necessary, as the water must cover the roe), then add salt and vinegar. Boil for twenty minutes. Drain, then add enough cold water to cover and let stand for five minutes. Drain again, sprinkle with salt and pepper and dip in flour, and fry in deep hot fat until a light brown.

Rhode Island, Long Island, Massachusetts and up along Maine, produce this dish, from time to time described as *Italian!* Actually is Italian in origin, but known to all fishermen wherever scallops are caught. Add garlic for pep!

BUTTERED SCALLOPS

1 or 2 cups small scallops
2 tablespoons butter
2 slices onion
minced parsley, salt, pepper
slices of toasted bread

Parboil the scallops, drain and dry well. Melt the butter in a saucepan, add the onion and cook until yellow. Remove the onion. Put in the scallops. Cover with the melted butter and let brown on all sides. Season well and serve on hot toast. Tartare sauce is an excellent sauce with these.

New Englanders will not agree, but the southern part of our Eastern shore is responsible for this particular recipe, although it has been made for so long in the North that it is claimed by New Englanders too:

DEVILED CRABS

2 cups crab meat
1 tablespoon butter
1 tablespoon flour
1 cup cream
grated onion
salt, pepper
dash of nutmeg
2 eggs, well beaten
crab shells
bread crumbs
melted butter

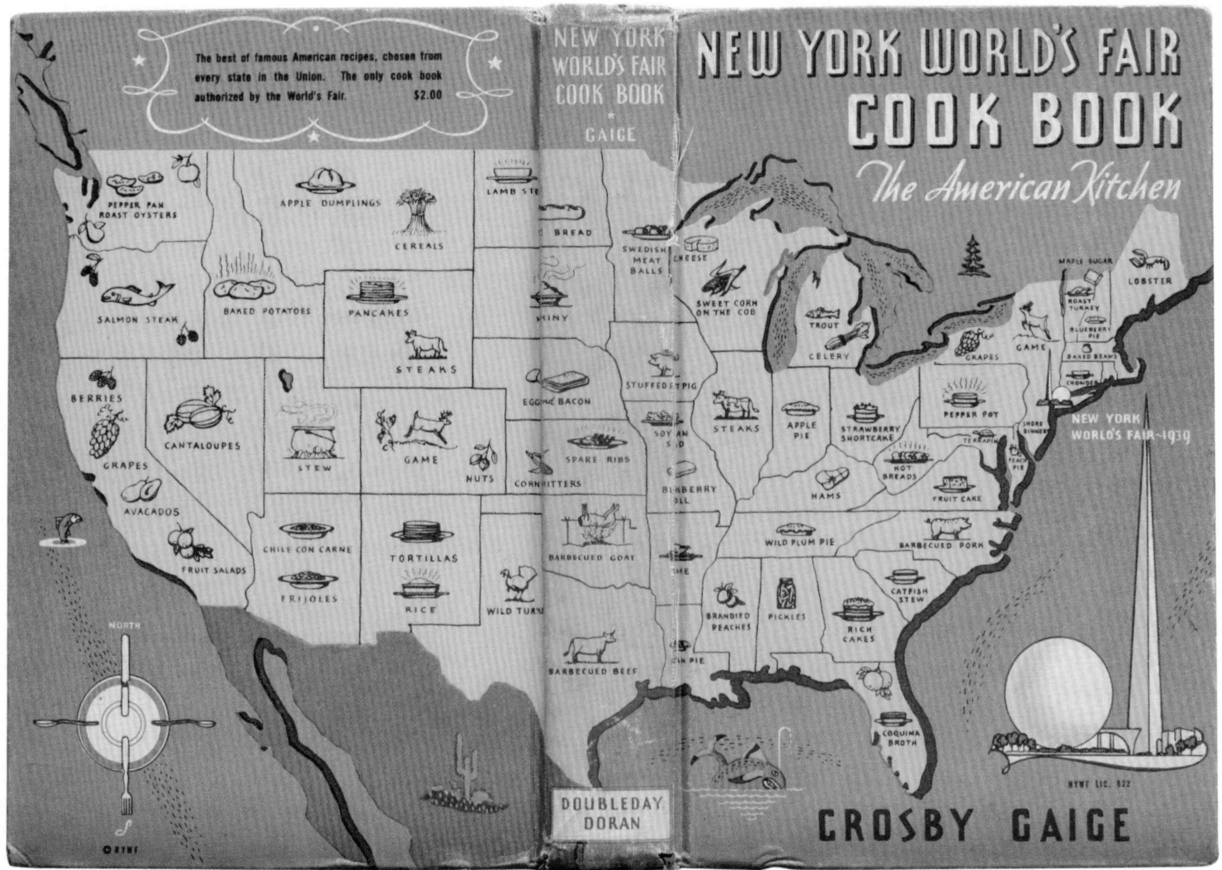

Gaige counted among his friends the famous Lucius Beebe—Luscious Lucius, as he was known—syndicated columnist for the *New York Herald Tribune* from the 1930s through 1944. Beebe's column, called "This New York," chronicled the fashionable society of New York's most famous restaurants, such as the 21 Club, the Stork Club, and the Colony. Beebe popularized the term "café society," which he used to describe his milieu. Gaige and Beebe both dined at the Restaurant Français during the 1939 World's Fair in Flushing, Queens. The restaurant was a reawakening of fine food in America following Prohibition and the Great Depression. Restaurant Français served more than 200,000 meals in its two-year run and became the foundation on which Henri Soulé would found his famous temple to haute cuisine, Le Pavillon, the grandfather of all New York French restaurants. Gaige's final book, *Dining with My Friends*, is a who's who of café society from his and Beebe's reign as arbiters of taste.

NOTABLE RECIPES: Baltimore Crab Cakes (page 480) • **Elephants' Ears** (page 636) • **Leavenworth Corn-Bread Sticks** (page 592)

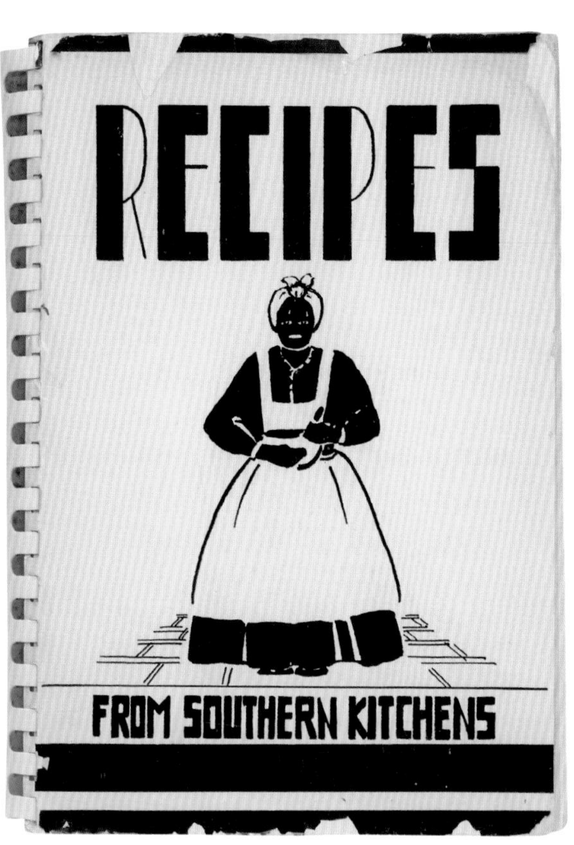

JUNIOR LEAGUE OF AUGUSTA

Old and New Recipes from the South, 1940

The first Junior League was founded in New York City in 1901 by Mary Harriman, a nineteen-year-old debutante. Harriman was aware of the need for social services such as child health, nutrition, and literacy among the immigrant population of Manhattan's Lower East Side. She convinced a group of eighty other young women to volunteer their time and support for these projects. In the following decades, groups formed in cities across the country, and eventually in Canada, Mexico, and Great Britain.

In 1940 the Junior League of Augusta compiled and published a cookbook titled *Old and New Recipes from the South* as a fundraising venture. It was the first Junior League cookbook and was very popular. Soon other chapters began to publish cookbooks, and they became a trend. Featuring recipes from community members, the cookbooks served as a way to bring the community together. They also documented the foods prepared in the average kitchen at a given time, making them invaluable for anyone studying the history of cooking in America.

NOTABLE RECIPES: Ambrosia (page 361) • Baked Country Ham • Bourbon Balls • **Deviled Eggs** (page 320) • **Eggnog** (page 314) • **Green Goddess Salad** (page 357) • **Green Tomato Pickle** (page 438) • **Ramos Gin Fizz** (page 312) • Rena's Deviled Crab • Virginia Ham

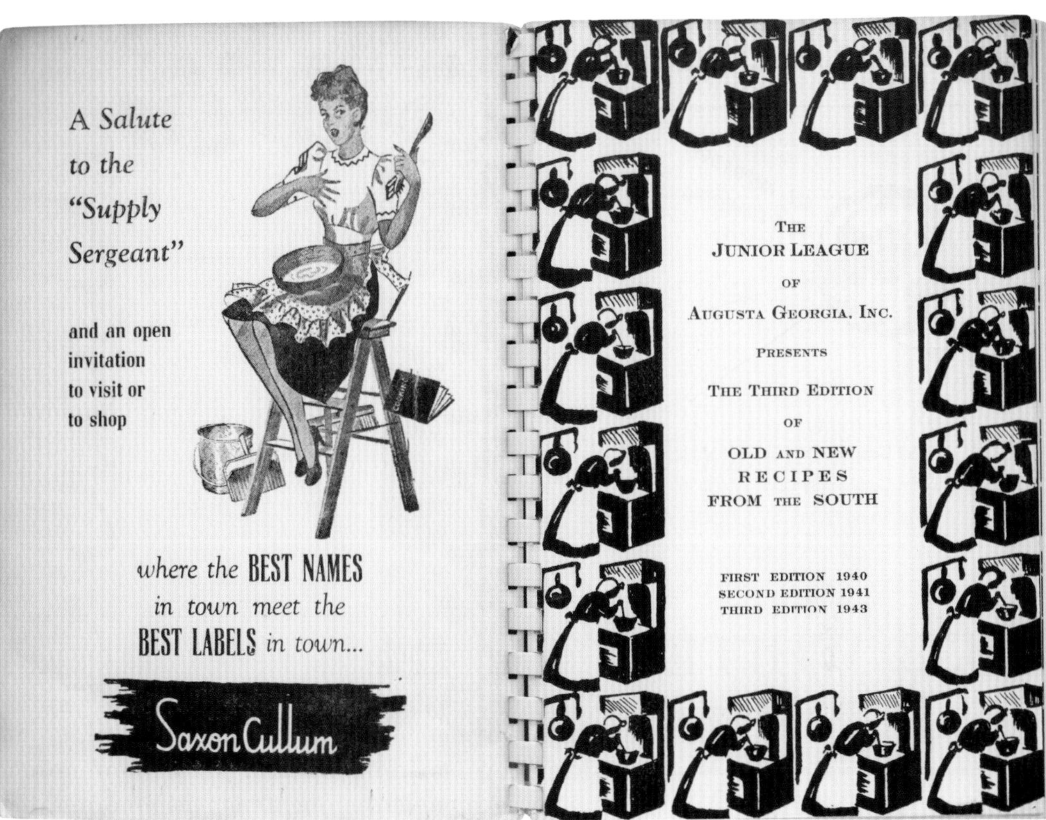

A Salute to the "Supply Sergeant"

and an open invitation to visit or to shop

where the BEST NAMES in town meet the BEST LABELS in town...

Saxon Cullum

THE
JUNIOR LEAGUE
OF
AUGUSTA GEORGIA, INC.
PRESENTS
THE THIRD EDITION
OF
OLD AND NEW
RECIPES
FROM THE SOUTH

FIRST EDITION 1940
SECOND EDITION 1941
THIRD EDITION 1943

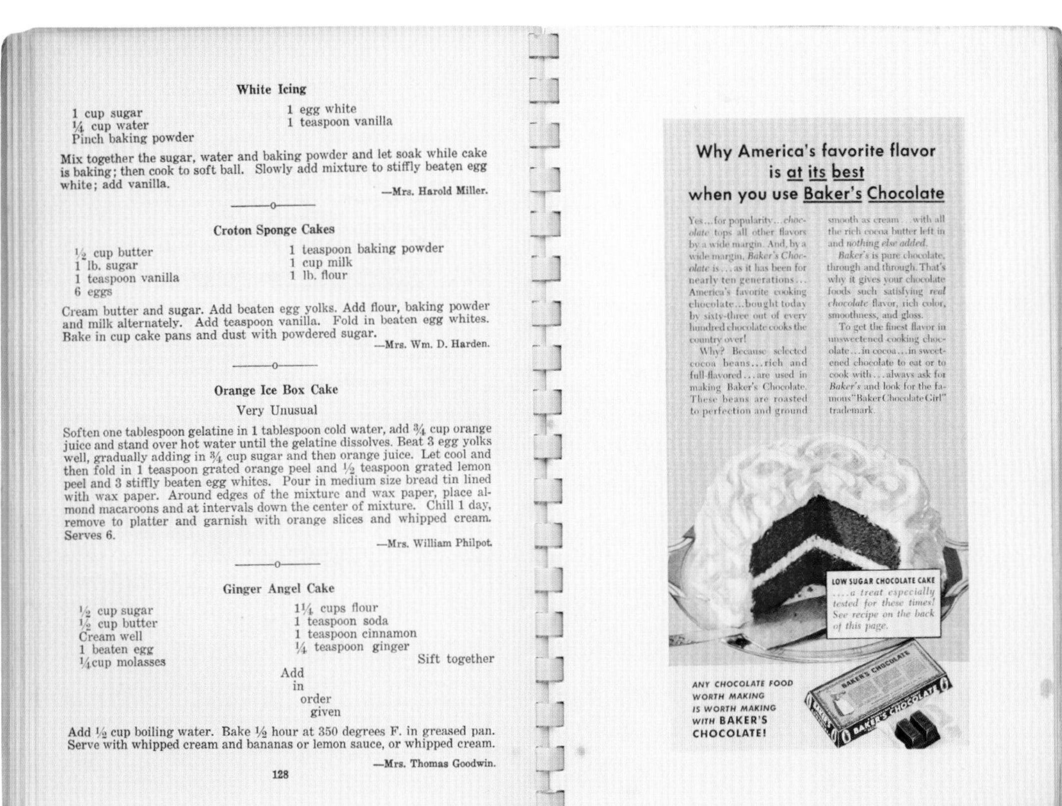

White Icing

1 cup sugar	1 egg white
¼ cup water	1 teaspoon vanilla
Pinch baking powder	

Mix together the sugar, water and baking powder and let soak while cake is baking; then cook to soft ball. Slowly add mixture to stiffly beaten egg white; add vanilla.

—Mrs. Harold Miller.

———o———

Croton Sponge Cakes

½ cup butter	1 teaspoon baking powder
1 lb. sugar	1 cup milk
1 teaspoon vanilla	1 lb. flour
6 eggs	

Cream butter and sugar. Add beaten egg yolks. Add flour, baking powder and milk alternately. Add teaspoon vanilla. Fold in beaten egg whites. Bake in cup cake pans and dust with powdered sugar.

—Mrs. Wm. D. Harden.

———o———

Orange Ice Box Cake

Very Unusual

Soften one tablespoon gelatine in 1 tablespoon cold water, add ¾ cup orange juice and stand over hot water until the gelatine dissolves. Beat 3 egg yolks well, gradually adding in ¾ cup sugar and then orange juice. Let cool and then fold in 1 teaspoon grated orange peel and ½ teaspoon grated lemon peel and 3 stiffly beaten egg whites. Pour in medium size bread tin lined with wax paper. Around edges of the mixture and wax paper, place almond macaroons and at intervals down the center of mixture. Chill 1 day, remove to platter and garnish with orange slices and whipped cream. Serves 6.

—Mrs. William Philpot.

———o———

Ginger Angel Cake

½ cup sugar	1¼ cups flour
½ cup butter	1 teaspoon soda
Cream well	1 teaspoon cinnamon
1 beaten egg	¼ teaspoon ginger
¼cup molasses	Sift together

Add in order given

Add ½ cup boiling water. Bake ½ hour at 350 degrees F. in greased pan. Serve with whipped cream and bananas or lemon sauce, or whipped cream.

—Mrs. Thomas Goodwin.

128

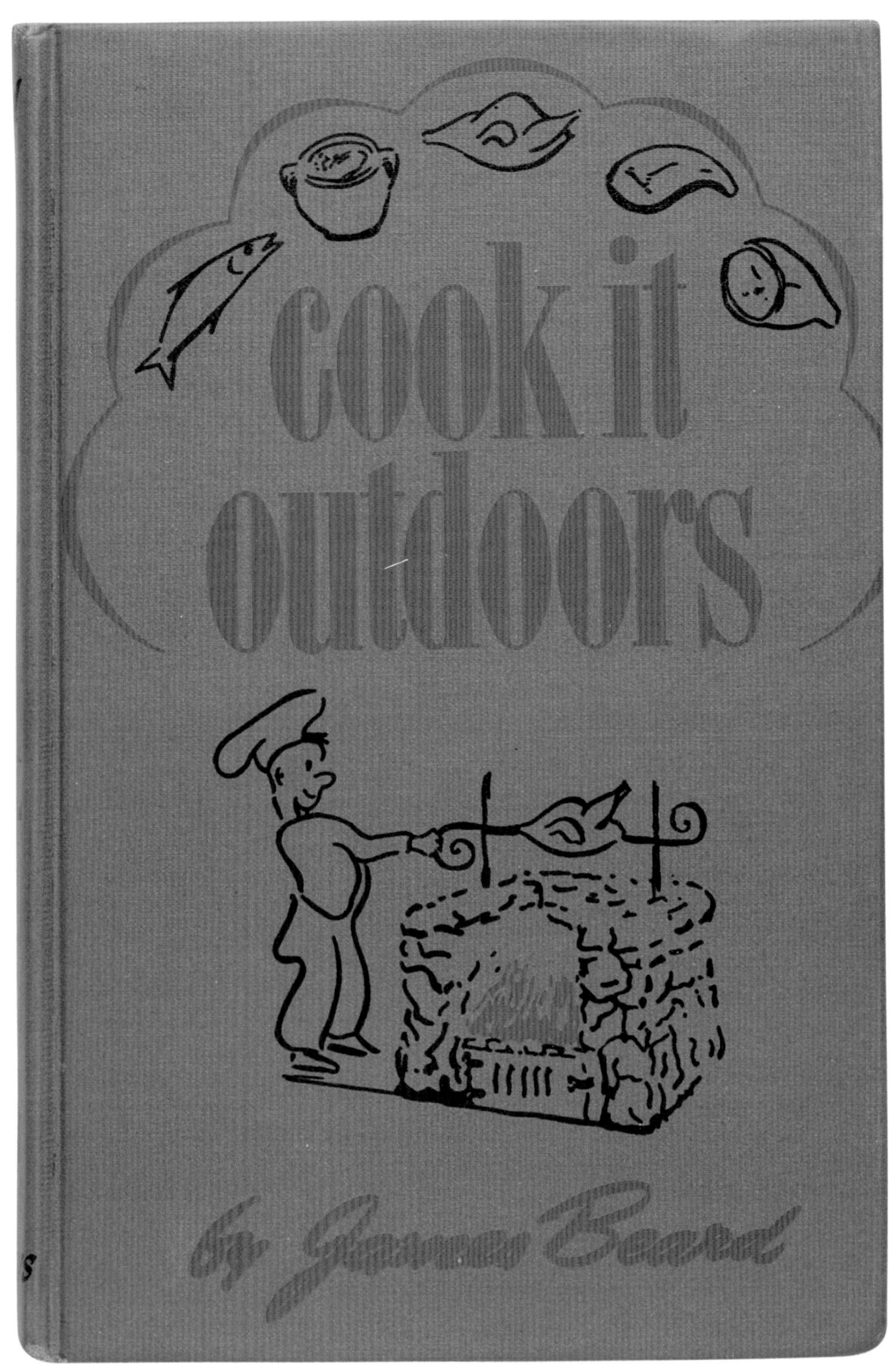
cook it
outdoors
by James Beard

JAMES BEARD

Cook It Outdoors, 1941

Cooking in America was largely considered women's work until the late twentieth century—with one major exception: grilling and barbecuing. Outdoor cooking was the man's prerogative, at least when it came to grilling meat. Wives could fuss about salads and desserts, but when it came time to overcook a side of beef and serve it piping from the grill, it was man's work.

Interestingly, James Beard's second book—his first was on hors d'oeuvre and canapés—was about grilling. Beard had grown up in the West, and his love of grilling came from his early childhood. The book begins with instructions on how to build your own stone grill, complete with diagrams and illustrations. This hands-on approach appealed to GIs returning from World War II, for thousands of these grills graced backyards across the country in the 1950s as the cult of grilling outdoors grew.

The gendered nature of grilling is fascinating, as are the gender issues surrounding Beard himself. He was a big man with a hearty appetite. He didn't give off the airs of a gourmet. He was a gourmand. He wanted to taste and try everything that was good. It didn't have to be buried in a cream sauce. It is probable that Beard was so successful and so important to American food precisely because he was a big man. The irony of it all, of course, is that he was also gay—a fact that was little known outside of the food world at the time.

NOTABLE RECIPES: Bagdad Hamburgers (page 373) • **If You Should Run Over an Old Hen** (page 395) • Goose • New England Clambake • **The Pascal Burger** (page 374) • Pickled Salmon • **Pig Hamburgers** (page 374) • Ragout of Lamb with Vegetables • **San Francisco Style** (page 373)

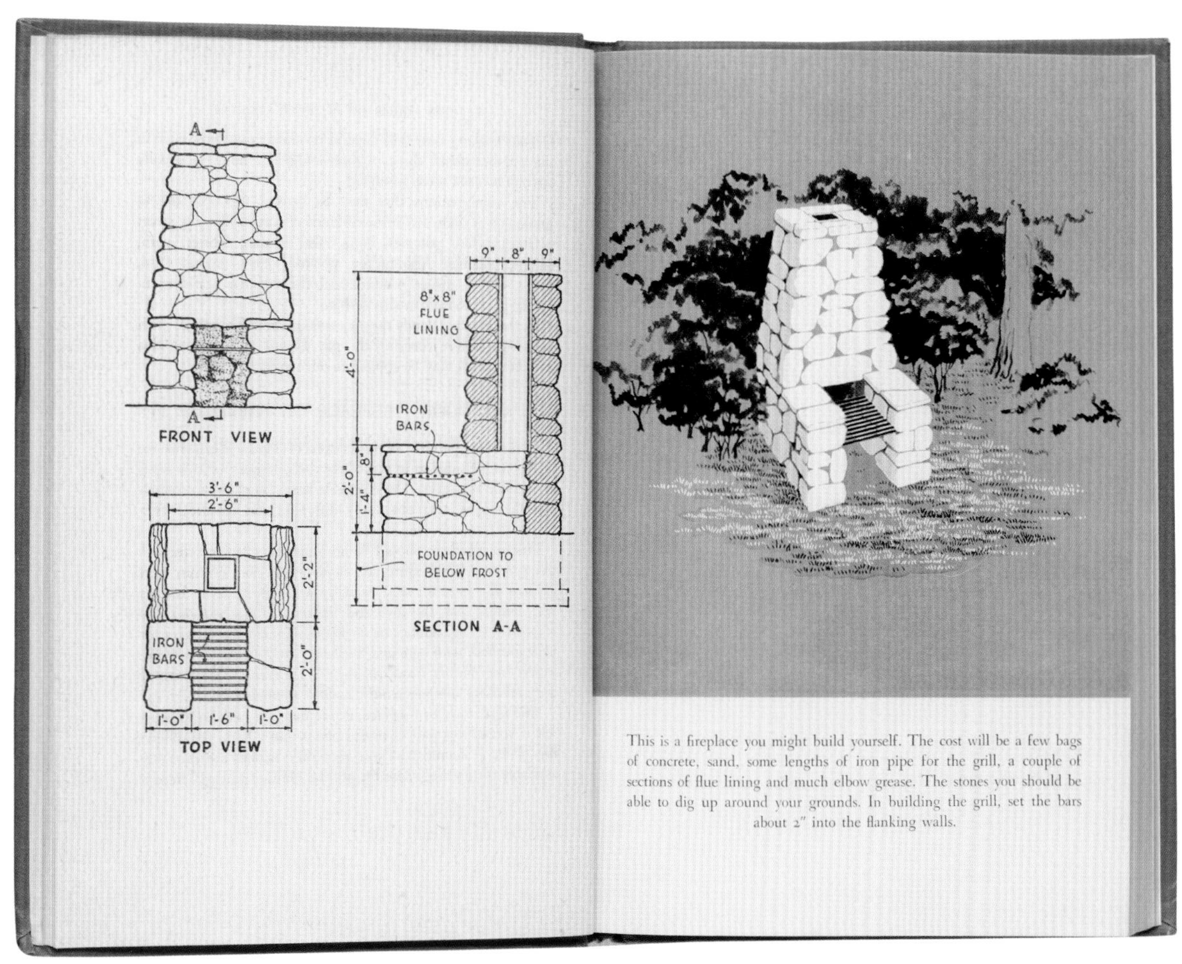
A
A
FRONT VIEW
3'-6"
2'-6"
2'-2"
2'-0"
IRON BARS
1'-0"
1'-6"
1'-0"
TOP VIEW
9"
8"
9"
8"x8" FLUE LINING
4'-0"
IRON BARS
2'-0"
8"
1'-4"
FOUNDATION TO BELOW FROST
SECTION A-A
This is a fireplace you might build yourself. The cost will be a few bags of concrete, sand, some lengths of iron pipe for the grill, a couple of sections of flue lining and much elbow grease. The stones you should be able to dig up around your grounds. In building the grill, set the bars about 2" into the flanking walls.

GENEVIEVE CALLAHAN

The California Cook Book for Indoor and Outdoor Eating,

1946

Genevieve Callahan opens *The California Cook Book* by quoting an advertisement for sports clothes: "California is more than a state—it's a way of life." This may seem an odd way to begin a cookbook, but it's telling.

The *California Cook Book* was selling a way of life that it proposes is truly Californian. But why? To answer that question we need to look at the history of *Sunset* magazine, which began in 1898 as a promotional magazine for the Southern Pacific Transportation Company as a way to counter negative impressions of California as the "Wild West." By the 1920s the magazine had accomplished its mission. Visitors flocked to the state without fear of gunfights and native insurrections. But the magazine was losing money. Lawrence W. Lane, who had been an advertising executive at *Better Homes and Gardens*, bought *Sunset* in 1929 and shifted the focus to the "Western lifestyle." In 1943 the magazine became *Sunset: The Magazine of Western Living*, reflecting the shift in thinking about California.

Among the innovations *Sunset* introduced was the ranch-style house. Enter Genevieve Callahan, who was an editor for *Sunset*. She saw that there was a new style of cooking and eating emerging, at once more casual and outdoorsy than the rest of the country, but just as interested in tasty food. Her *California Cook Book for Indoor and Outdoor Eating* reflects this new style of eating, dining, and entertaining. Interestingly, Callahan spends part of her introduction discussing why California cooking is "gourmet":

> It's an informal cook book, you will find—as informal as patio living. But for all its informality and its uninhibited, undictatorial attitude toward recipes and cookery, I think you will agree that this is a gourmet cook book in the true sense—a book for a connoisseur of good food. Every good home economist, nutritionist, and dietitian knows, food simply has to taste good, otherwise it won't be eaten.

CALIFORNIA

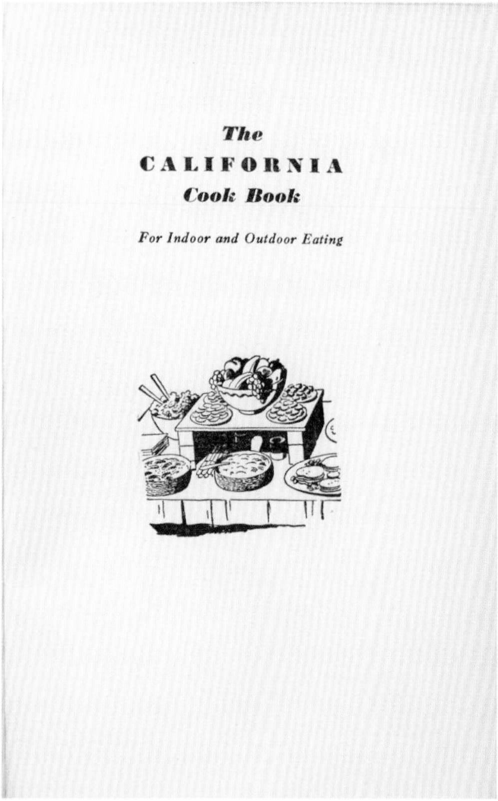

The
CALIFORNIA
Cook Book

For Indoor and Outdoor Eating

In trying to justify California cooking as a gourmet endeavor, Callahan clearly describes the most important, and conflicting, influences on American cooking in the twentieth century: home economics and nutrition versus gourmet foods and fine dining. Her distrust of "vitamin-saving" preparations and "beautiful" arrangement on the plate is a jab at the East Coast cooking schools, such as Fannie Farmer's Boston Cooking-School, and the kind of meals they proposed. Callahan would rather her California cooking be aligned with gourmet eating. Prophetically, she identifies the two strands that would come together in the return to local, farm-based foods in the 1960s and the development of California cuisine by Alice Waters and others.

NOTABLE RECIPES: Arrowhead Casserole • **Chinatown Spareribs** (page 534) • Green Goddess Dressing • Guacamole • **Mexican Chiles Rellenos** (page 407) • **Syrian Stuffed Eggplant** (page 414)

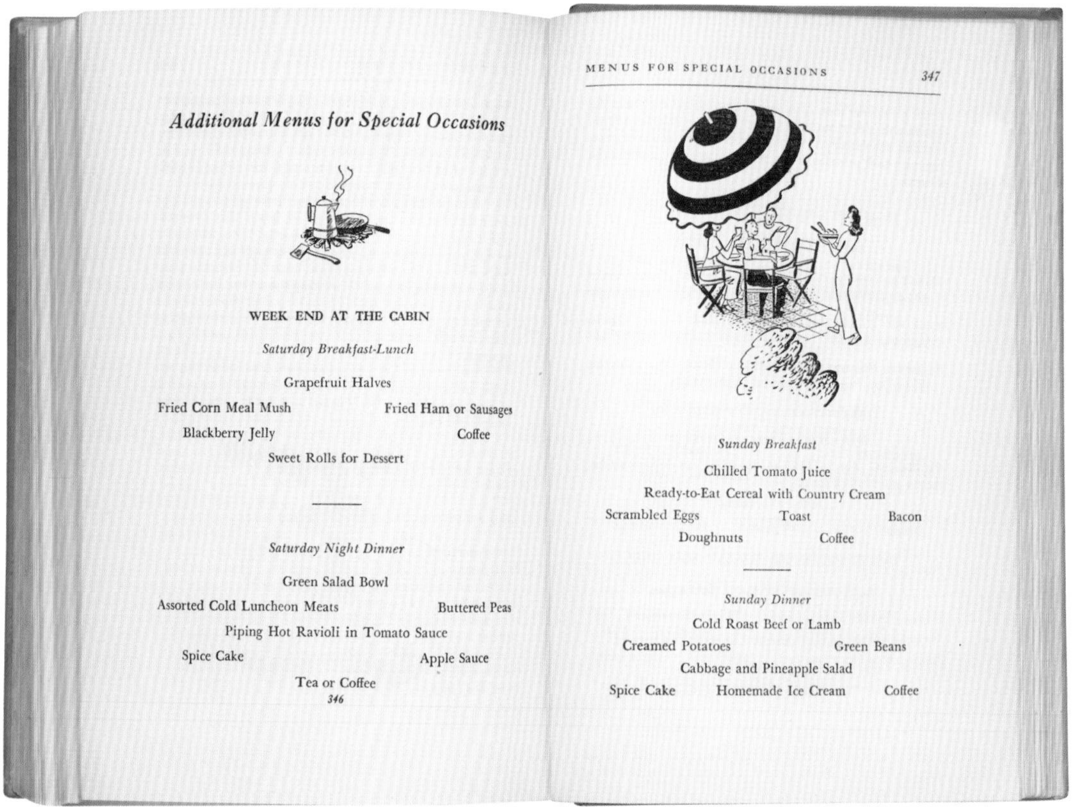

Additional Menus for Special Occasions

WEEK END AT THE CABIN

Saturday Breakfast-Lunch

Grapefruit Halves
Fried Corn Meal Mush　Fried Ham or Sausages
Blackberry Jelly　Coffee
Sweet Rolls for Dessert

Saturday Night Dinner

Green Salad Bowl
Assorted Cold Luncheon Meats　Buttered Peas
Piping Hot Ravioli in Tomato Sauce
Spice Cake　Apple Sauce
Tea or Coffee

346

MENUS FOR SPECIAL OCCASIONS　347

Sunday Breakfast

Chilled Tomato Juice
Ready-to-Eat Cereal with Country Cream
Scrambled Eggs　Toast　Bacon
Doughnuts　Coffee

Sunday Dinner

Cold Roast Beef or Lamb
Creamed Potatoes　Green Beans
Cabbage and Pineapple Salad
Spice Cake　Homemade Ice Cream　Coffee

Fry the ham, celery, green pepper, and onion in the butter until soft. Add rice and cook, stirring, 5 minutes. Add flour, blend, then stir in broth and heat. Add remaining ingredients, season to taste with salt and pepper, cover, and let simmer 40 minutes. Makes about 2 1/2 quarts, or 10 generous servings.

TRICKS WITH CANNED SOUPS

Follow directions on cans accurately. Don't add more salt without first tasting!

Make jellied consommé by leaving cans of consommé in refrigerator for several hours. Open can, pour out the jellied contents, stir lightly with a fork to break it up and make it sparkle, and serve in cups with lemon wedges. So good on a hot day.

Chapter 3

Recipes Featuring Western Fish and Sea Food

Which way is best to cook a certain variety of fish depends chiefly on whether that particular fish is fat and oily, or lean and dry. *Fat fish* are usually best broiled or baked. Salmon, mackerel, halibut, rock cod and other rock fishes; tuna, albacore, barracuda, and yellowtail; pilchard and other herrings—all these are classed as fat fish. *Lean fish* are usually best fried, or "poached" in water or other liquid and served with a sauce. Sole, flounder, and other flat fish; hake, trout and steelhead (ocean-going trout); swordfish—these are classed as lean fish. *Shellfish* of all kinds are rich in flavor, and are usually prepared in some way which does not obscure their own character, but which does stretch a small amount of sea food to make a reasonable number of servings.

The following general directions apply to fresh and quick-frozen fish, from either salt water or fresh water. Ways of pre-

Chapter 5

Indoor and Outdoor Cooking of Poultry and Wild Fowl

Chickens and turkeys are among the tremendously important products of the state of California. Drive along any road near Petaluma and you see batteries of chicken houses that turn out broilers and fryers and roasters on an endless production line. Drive through the San Joaquin or Sacramento Valley and you see vast turkey ranches that keep the market supplied not merely at holiday time, but every month in the year. Not all of these fine-feathered friends are shipped to other parts of the country—not by any means. Millions of pounds of them stay right here each year to be barbecued, roasted, fried, and made into all sorts of delicious dishes, California style.

lated sugar, 6 tablespoons top milk and 2 tablespoons light corn syrup to very soft ball stage (236° F.). Add 1 teaspoon vanilla, 1 tablespoon butter, 2 to 3 cups walnuts. Beat until creamy. Turn out and separate.

LOUIS PULLIG DE GOUY

The Gold Cook Book, 1947

Born in 1875, Louis Pullig de Gouy was one of the first chefs to bring true haute cuisine experience to the U.S. table. He began cooking as a child, working with his father, who was Squire of Cuisine to Emperor Franz Josef of Austria, and went on to become a student of the great master chef Auguste Escoffier (1846–1935). Escoffier had transformed French cooking at his various restaurants, limiting the number of courses, arranging the menu by the way courses should be eaten, restructuring the kitchen staff, and overhauling the recipes and sauces.

De Gouy brought all this knowledge—and that which he gained by working at many fine restaurants in France, Belgium, and Austria—to the United States. Here, he worked variously at the Hotel Belmont and the Waldorf-Astoria in New York City, Indian Harbor Yacht Club in Greenwich, Connecticut, and La Tour d'Argent in Chicago. His most important position was as master chef at the Waldorf-Astoria, where he worked for more than forty years.

The Gold Cook Book was de Gouy's last and most lasting contribution to American food. With more than 2,400 recipes, it was an encyclopedic summing up of his training in French cookery, simplified for the American housewife. Oscar of the Waldorf, the famous maître d'hôtel at the Waldorf-Astoria, wrote the introduction to *The Gold Cook Book*, adding celebrity to the publication. Sadly, de Gouy didn't live to see the effects of his masterpiece. He died suddenly of a heart attack the week after it was published while attending the Annual Hotel Exposition at New York's Grand Central Palace Hotel in 1947.

NOTABLE RECIPES: Almond Fritters (page 639) • **Asparagus Tip Omelet** (page 463) • Homemade Tagliatelli • Lime Ladyfingers • **Lobster Thermidor** (page 482) • **Mornay Sauce** (page 525) • **Mussels Mariniere** (page 481) • **Pecan Pie** (page 601) • **Swiss Steak** (page 542)

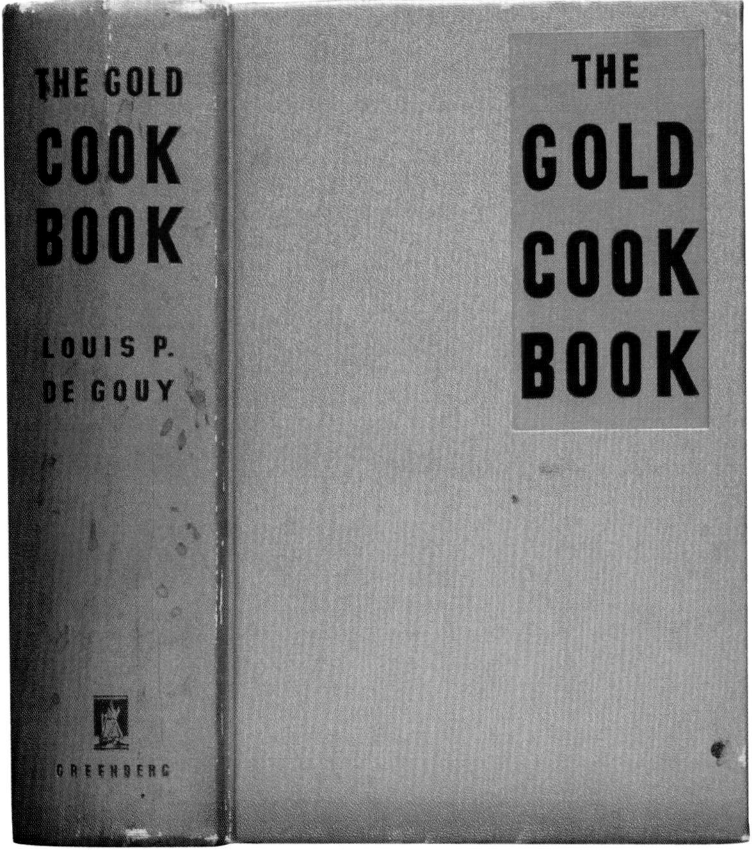

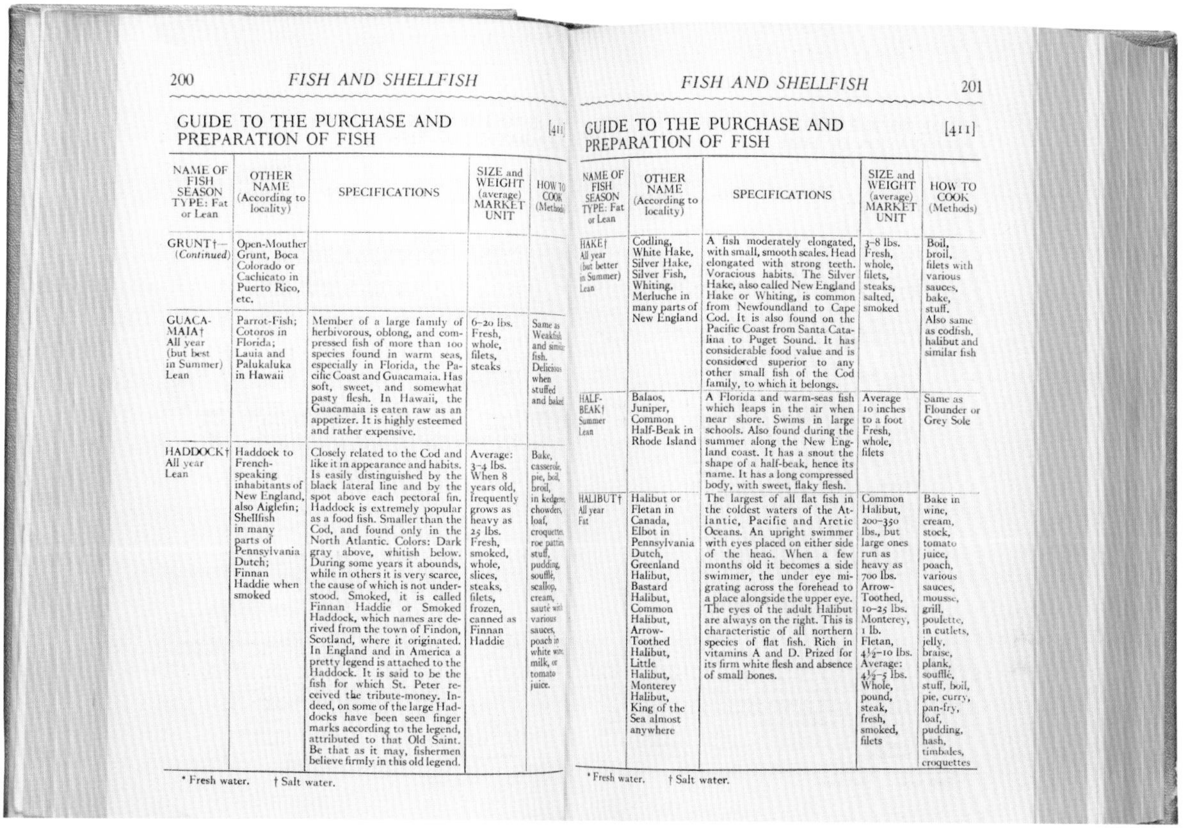

GUIDE TO THE PURCHASE AND PREPARATION OF FISH [411]

NAME OF FISH SEASON TYPE: Fat or Lean	OTHER NAME (According to locality)	SPECIFICATIONS	SIZE and WEIGHT (average) MARKET UNIT	HOW TO COOK (Methods)
GRUNT†—(*Continued*)	Open-Mouther Grunt, Boca Colorado or Cachicato in Puerto Rico, etc.			
GUACAMAIA† All year (but best in Summer) Lean	Parrot-Fish; Cotoros in Florida; Lauia and Palukaluka in Hawaii	Member of a large family of herbivorous, oblong, and compressed fish of more than 100 species found in warm seas, especially in Florida, the Pacific Coast and Guacamaia. Has soft, sweet, and somewhat pasty flesh. In Hawaii, the Guacamaia is eaten raw as an appetizer. It is highly esteemed and rather expensive.	6–20 lbs. Fresh, whole, filets, steaks	Same as Weakfish and similar fish. Delicious when stuffed and baked
HADDOCK† All year Lean	Haddock to French-speaking inhabitants of New England, also Aiglefin; Shellfish in many parts of Pennsylvania Dutch; Finnan Haddie when smoked	Closely related to the Cod and like it in appearance and habits. Is easily distinguished by the black lateral line and by the spot above each pectoral fin. Haddock is extremely popular as a food fish. Smaller than the Cod, and found only in the North Atlantic. Colors: Dark gray above, whitish below. During some years it abounds, while in others it is very scarce, the cause of which is not understood. Smoked, it is called Finnan Haddie or Smoked Haddock, which names are derived from the town of Findon, Scotland, where it originated. In England and in America a pretty legend is attached to the Haddock. It is said to be the fish for which St. Peter received the tribute-money. Indeed, on some of the large Haddocks have been seen finger marks according to the legend, attributed to that Old Saint. Be that as it may, fishermen believe firmly in this old legend.	Average: 3–4 lbs. When 8 years old, frequently grows as heavy as 25 lbs. Fresh, smoked, whole, slices, steaks, filets, frozen, canned as Finnan Haddie	Bake, casserole, pie, boil, broil, in kedgeree, chowders, loaf, croquettes, roe patties, stuff, pudding, soufflé, scallop, cream, sauté with various sauces, poach in white wine, milk, or tomato juice.

* Fresh water. † Salt water.

GUIDE TO THE PURCHASE AND PREPARATION OF FISH [411]

NAME OF FISH SEASON TYPE: Fat or Lean	OTHER NAME (According to locality)	SPECIFICATIONS	SIZE and WEIGHT (average) MARKET UNIT	HOW TO COOK (Methods)
HAKE† All year (but better in Summer) Lean	Codling, White Hake, Silver Hake, Silver Fish, Whiting, Merluche in many parts of New England	A fish moderately elongated, with small, smooth scales. Head elongated with strong teeth. Voracious habits. The Silver Hake, also called New England Hake or Whiting, is common from Newfoundland to Cape Cod. It is also found on the Pacific Coast from Santa Catalina to Puget Sound. It has considerable food value and is considered superior to any other small fish of the Cod family, to which it belongs.	3–8 lbs. Fresh, whole, filets, steaks, salted, smoked	Boil, broil, filets with various sauces, bake, stuff. Also same as codfish, halibut and similar fish
HALF-BEAK† Summer Lean	Balaos, Juniper, Common Half-Beak in Rhode Island	A Florida and warm-seas fish which leaps in the air when near shore. Swims in large schools. Also found during the summer along the New England coast. It has a snout the shape of a half-beak, hence its name. It has a long compressed body, with sweet, flaky flesh.	Average 10 inches to a foot Fresh, whole, filets	Same as Flounder or Grey Sole
HALIBUT† All year Fat	Halibut or Fletan in Canada, Elbot in Pennsylvania Dutch, Greenland Halibut, Bastard Halibut, Common Halibut, Arrow-Toothed Halibut, Little Halibut, Monterey Halibut, King of the Sea almost anywhere	The largest of all flat fish in the coldest waters of the Atlantic, Pacific and Arctic Oceans. An upright swimmer with eyes placed on either side of the head. When a few months old it becomes a side swimmer, the under eye migrating across the forehead to a place alongside the upper eye. The eyes of the adult Halibut are always on the right. This is characteristic of all northern species of flat fish. Rich in vitamins A and D. Prized for its firm white flesh and absence of small bones.	Common Halibut, 200–350 lbs., but large ones run as heavy as 700 lbs. Arrow-Toothed, 10–25 lbs. Monterey, 1 lb. Fletan, 4½–10 lbs. Average: 4½–5 lbs. Whole, pound, steak, fresh, smoked, filets	Bake in wine, cream, stock, tomato juice, poach, various sauces, mousse, grill, poulette, in cutlets, jelly, braise, plank, soufflé, stuff, boil, pie, curry, pan-fry, loaf, pudding, hash, timbales, croquettes

* Fresh water. † Salt water.

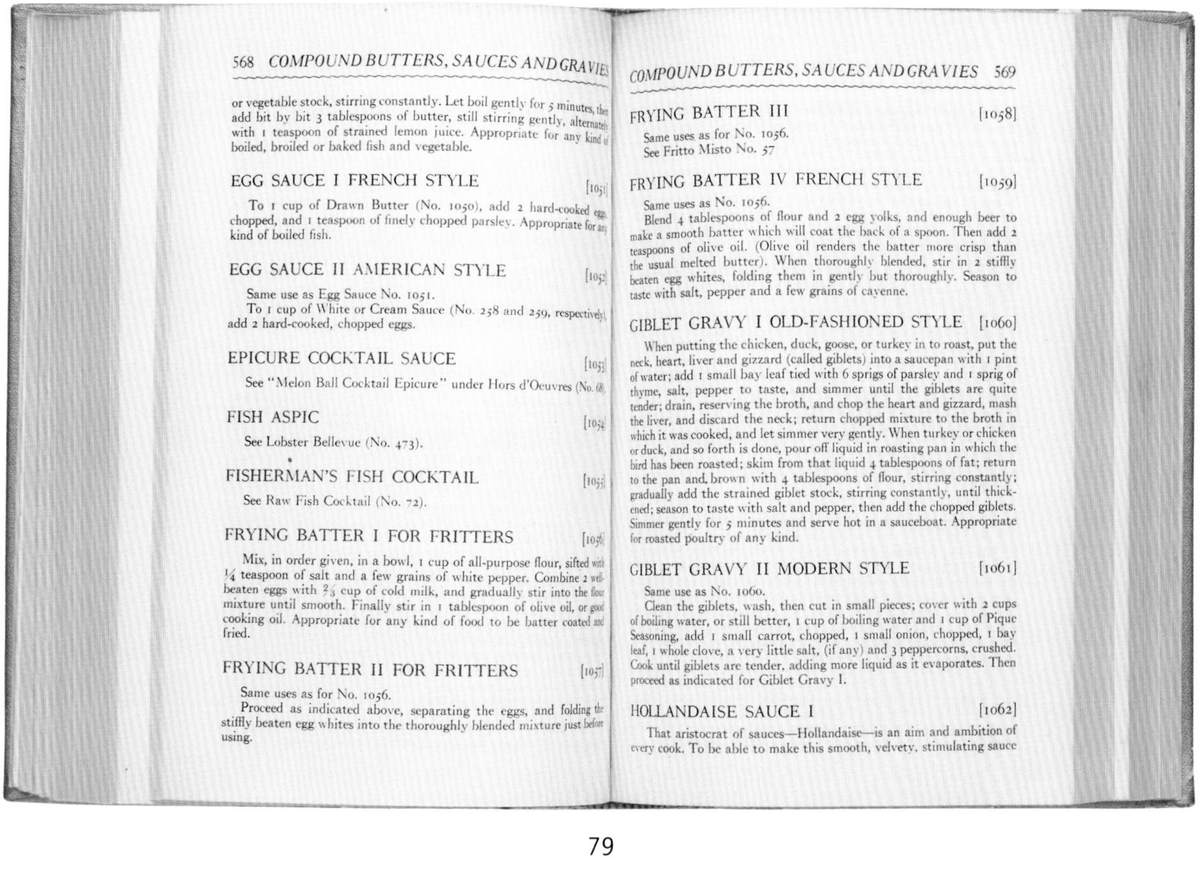

or vegetable stock, stirring constantly. Let boil gently for 5 minutes, then add bit by bit 3 tablespoons of butter, still stirring gently, alternately with 1 teaspoon of strained lemon juice. Appropriate for any kind of boiled, broiled or baked fish and vegetable.

EGG SAUCE I FRENCH STYLE [1051]

To 1 cup of Drawn Butter (No. 1050), add 2 hard-cooked eggs, chopped, and 1 teaspoon of finely chopped parsley. Appropriate for any kind of boiled fish.

EGG SAUCE II AMERICAN STYLE [1052]

Same use as Egg Sauce No. 1051.

To 1 cup of White or Cream Sauce (No. 258 and 259, respectively), add 2 hard-cooked, chopped eggs.

EPICURE COCKTAIL SAUCE [1053]

See "Melon Ball Cocktail Epicure" under Hors d'Oeuvres (No. 68).

FISH ASPIC [1054]

See Lobster Bellevue (No. 473).

FISHERMAN'S FISH COCKTAIL [1055]

See Raw Fish Cocktail (No. 72).

FRYING BATTER I FOR FRITTERS [1056]

Mix, in order given, in a bowl, 1 cup of all-purpose flour, sifted with ¼ teaspoon of salt and a few grains of white pepper. Combine 2 well-beaten eggs with ⅔ cup of cold milk, and gradually stir into the flour mixture until smooth. Finally stir in 1 tablespoon of olive oil, or good cooking oil. Appropriate for any kind of food to be batter coated and fried.

FRYING BATTER II FOR FRITTERS [1057]

Same uses as for No. 1056.

Proceed as indicated above, separating the eggs, and folding the stiffly beaten egg whites into the thoroughly blended mixture just before using.

FRYING BATTER III [1058]

Same uses as for No. 1056.

See Fritto Misto No. 57

FRYING BATTER IV FRENCH STYLE [1059]

Same uses as No. 1056.

Blend 4 tablespoons of flour and 2 egg yolks, and enough beer to make a smooth batter which will coat the back of a spoon. Then add 2 teaspoons of olive oil. (Olive oil renders the batter more crisp than the usual melted butter). When thoroughly blended, stir in 2 stiffly beaten egg whites, folding them in gently but thoroughly. Season to taste with salt, pepper and a few grains of cayenne.

GIBLET GRAVY I OLD-FASHIONED STYLE [1060]

When putting the chicken, duck, goose, or turkey in to roast, put the neck, heart, liver and gizzard (called giblets) into a saucepan with 1 pint of water; add 1 small bay leaf tied with 6 sprigs of parsley and 1 sprig of thyme, salt, pepper to taste, and simmer until the giblets are quite tender; drain, reserving the broth, and chop the heart and gizzard, mash the liver, and discard the neck; return chopped mixture to the broth in which it was cooked, and let simmer very gently. When turkey or chicken or duck, and so forth is done, pour off liquid in roasting pan in which the bird has been roasted; skim from that liquid 4 tablespoons of fat; return to the pan and brown with 4 tablespoons of flour, stirring constantly; gradually add the strained giblet stock, stirring constantly, until thickened; season to taste with salt and pepper, then add the chopped giblets. Simmer gently for 5 minutes and serve hot in a sauceboat. Appropriate for roasted poultry of any kind.

GIBLET GRAVY II MODERN STYLE [1061]

Same use as No. 1060.

Clean the giblets, wash, then cut in small pieces; cover with 2 cups of boiling water, or still better, 1 cup of boiling water and 1 cup of Pique Seasoning, add 1 small carrot, chopped, 1 small onion, chopped, 1 bay leaf, 1 whole clove, a very little salt, (if any) and 3 peppercorns, crushed. Cook until giblets are tender, adding more liquid as it evaporates. Then proceed as indicated for Giblet Gravy I.

HOLLANDAISE SAUCE I [1062]

That aristocrat of sauces—Hollandaise—is an aim and ambition of every cook. To be able to make this smooth, velvety, stimulating sauce

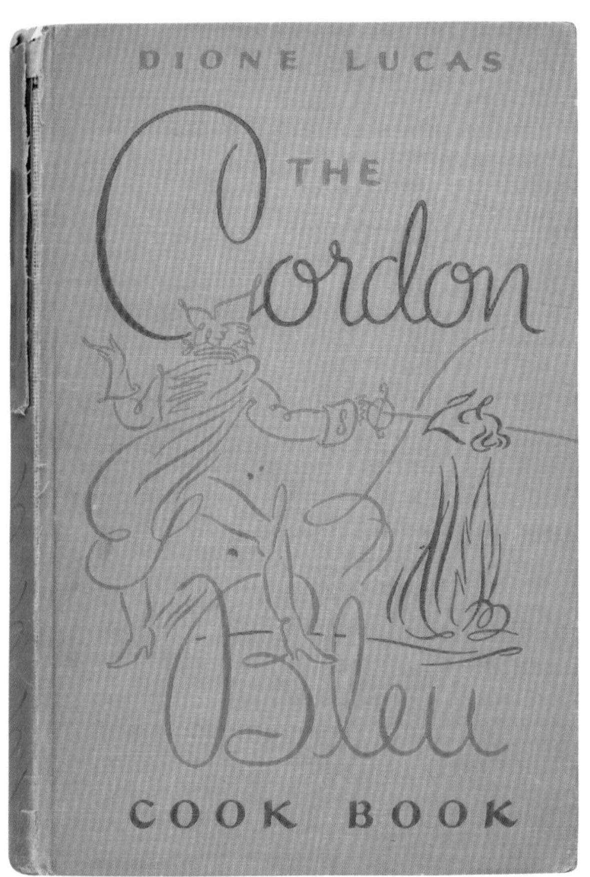

DIONE LUCAS

The Cordon Bleu Cook Book, 1947

Dione Lucas was born in London in 1909. She studied under Henri-Paul Pellaprat at the Cordon Bleu in Paris and apprenticed at Drouant Restaurant, also in Paris, before becoming the first woman to graduate from the Cordon Bleu. She returned to London during the 1930s and opened Le Petit Cordon Bleu Restaurant and Cooking School, which was authorized by the Cordon Bleu.

In 1940 she moved to New York City and, in 1942, opened the Cordon Bleu Cooking School and Restaurant in Manhattan. In 1946 Lucas became the first woman to host her own television cooking show, *To the Queen's Taste*. She was affiliated with several restaurants in Manhattan, including the Egg Basket, the Ginger Man, and the Brasserie Restaurant. In many ways, Lucas was the precursor to Julia Child in bringing French cuisine to the American public. She wrote many cookbooks, but this one, based on her training at the Cordon Bleu, is her best known.

NOTABLE RECIPES: Clam and Oyster Chowder (page 350) • **Quiches Lorraine** (page 465) • Oysters Rockefeller

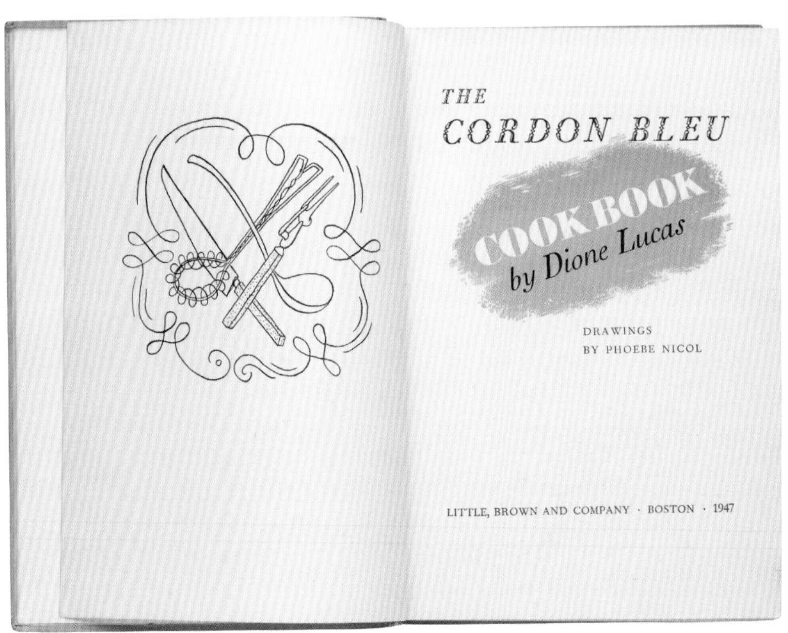

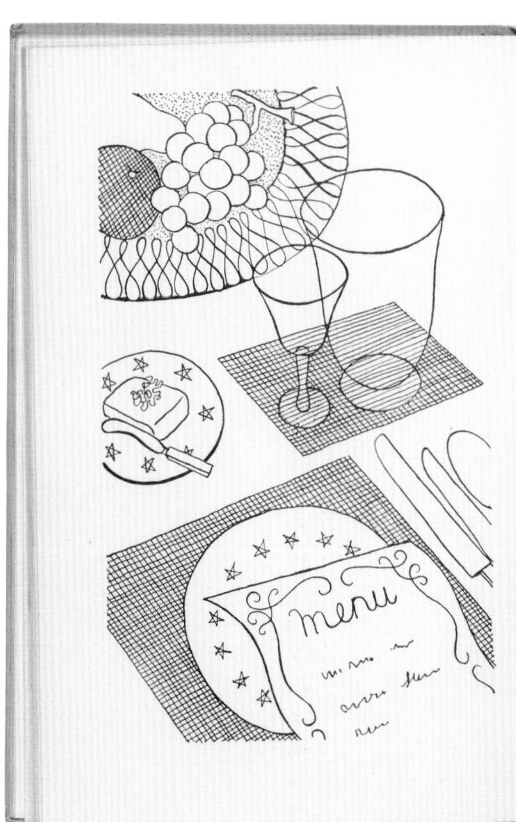

CHAPTER I

MENUS

First comes the building of your meal. It is a good idea to plan menus well ahead so that there is no last-minute rushing to the store for missing ingredients. Try to visualize your meal beforehand, for the good cook always plans with an eye to contrasting color, shape, and texture of foods. For example, the monotony of plain boiled potatoes, chicken à la king and creamed onions would detract from any appetite, no matter how keen. But garnish those potatoes with the vivid green of freshly chopped herbs, place them alongside crisp, golden corn on the cob, and serve with well-browned chicken leg from a *poulet en casserole*, and you have contrasting colors, shapes and texture, with all the makings of an attractive dinner plate.

Connoisseurs of good food recognize that the fairly formal patterns of our luncheons and dinners have evolved because they have been found most agreeable to the majority. Luncheon is a smaller meal than dinner, since it is gastronomically sound to eat lightly in the middle of the day (this does not apply to those engaged in heavy manual work, of course). So we have for luncheon menus, the cold *hors d'oeuvre* or perhaps a consommé, followed by a fairly simple main dish, a light dessert and coffee. At dinner, however, the day's work is done, there is a feeling of relaxation, and appetites are keener. So we serve for our average dinner menu a soup, hot or iced depending on the season, to whet the appetite further, a small serving of fish perhaps, followed by a substantial main dish with vegetables. The keen tang of crisp, chilled salad serves as a stimulant to the palate after the main course. *Entremets* should be light, and if occasionally a rich *gâteau* is served, small portions are the rule. We know from experience that ending the meal with a sweet food gives it greater "staying" value. The French habit of a *corbeille de fruits* is a sound custom, the natural sugars supplying the necessary sweetness.

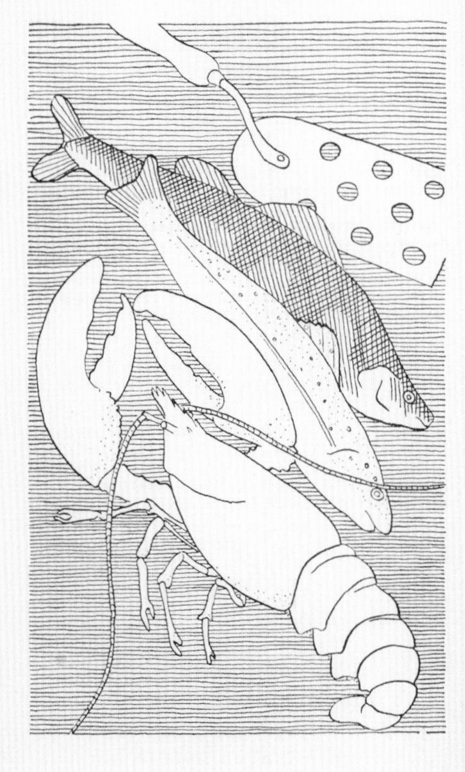

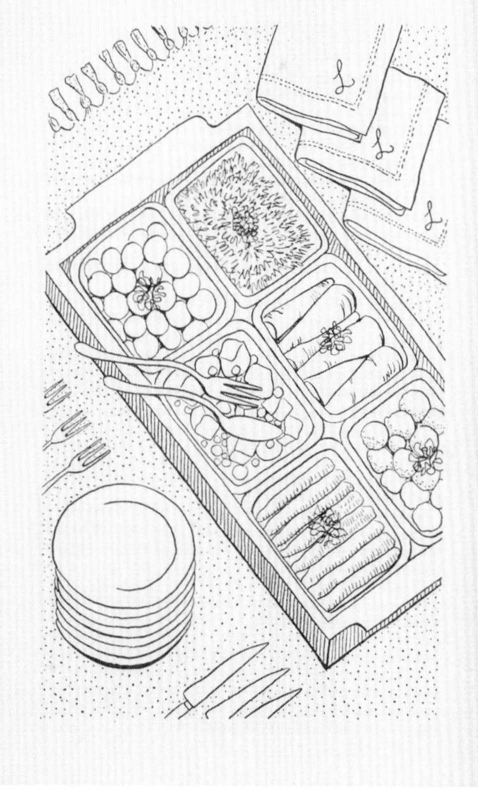

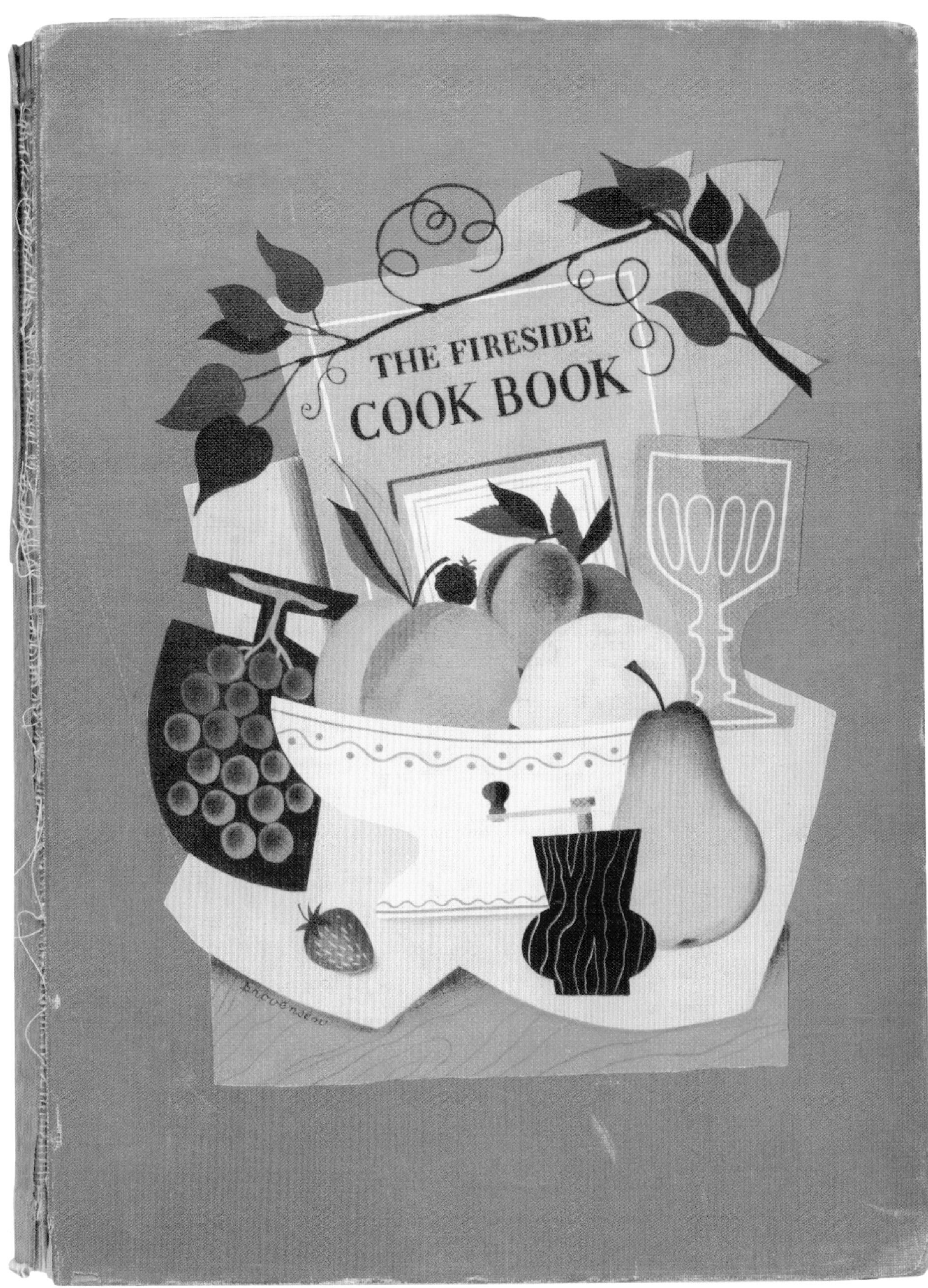
THE FIRESIDE
COOK BOOK

JAMES BEARD

The Fireside Cook Book, 1949

The Fireside Cook Book was one of James Beard's first attempts to create a cookbook for both the novice cook and the seasoned gourmand. Unlike his previous works, which focused on a single type of food, such as hors d'oeuvre or outdoor cooking, *The Fireside Cook Book* included more than 1,200 American recipes of all kinds that were easy to make and delicious. It was also Beard's first book to stake a claim for the importance of American cooking.

NOTABLE RECIPES: Calf's Liver • **Cream of Celery** (page 348) • **Cream of Corn** (page 348) • Fresh Beef Tongue • **Leftover Roast Beef** (page 543) • Meatloaf, Lamb Loaf, and Veal Loaf • **Pot Roast of Beef** (page 543) • Roasted Pork Loin • **Spareribs** (page 534) • **Tongue Rolls** (page 561)

TO GAIN WEIGHT
increase calorie intake 500 to 1000 calories per day.
½ avocado = 300 calories
1 cup strawberries = 90 calories
1 slice chocolate cake = 350 calories
1 cup fruit sundae = 800 calories
1 muffin = 125 calories
1 piece of pie = 350 calories
1 plain cookie = 75 calories
TO LOSE WEIGHT
decrease calorie intake 500 to 1000 calories per day.

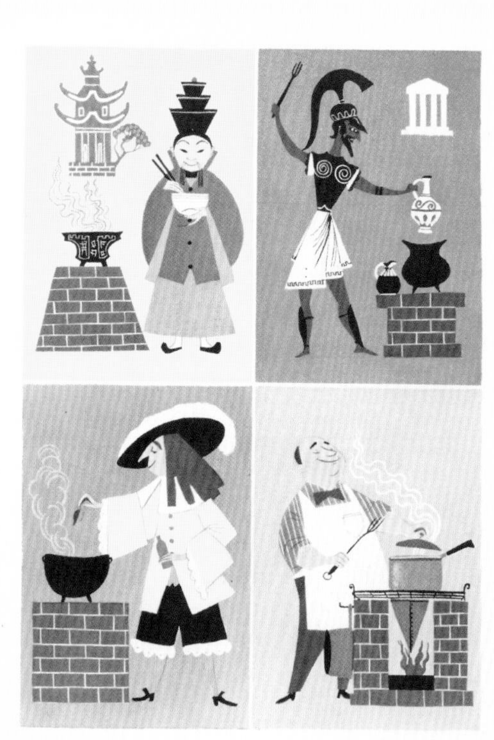

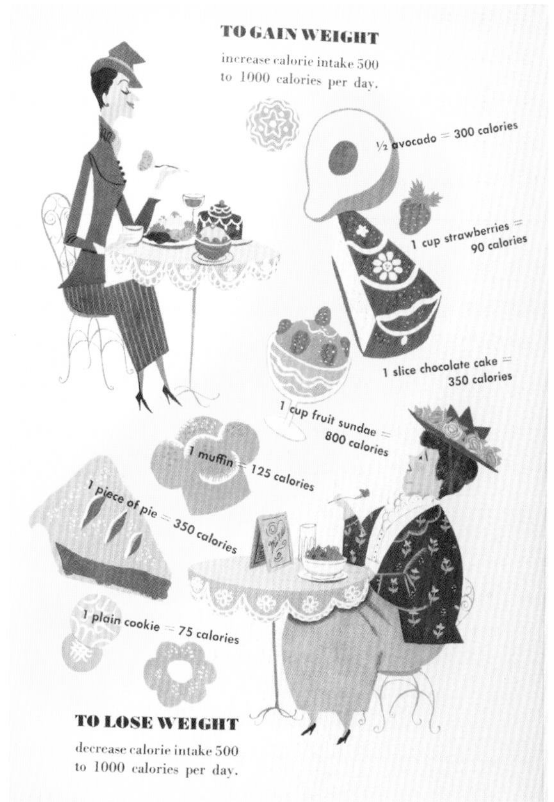

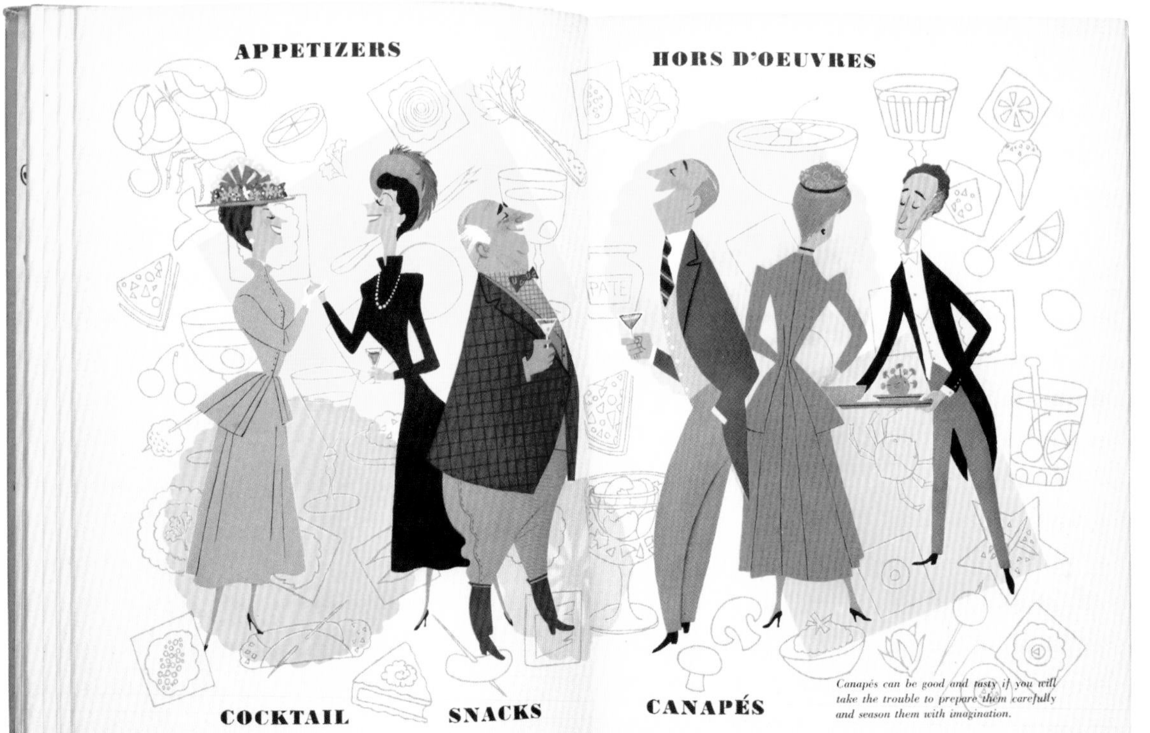

APPETIZERS
HORS D'OEUVRES
PATE
COCKTAIL
SNACKS
CANAPÉS
Canapés can be good and tasty if you will take the trouble to prepare them carefully and season them with imagination.

Boiled Eggs

(1) Place in a saucepan enough water to cover the eggs. Bring the water to a simmer, not a boil. Place the eggs in the saucepan with a spoon and allow the eggs to simmer for 3½ minutes or more depending on the degree of softness desired.

(2) Cover eggs with cold water. Place them over medium heat and allow the water to come to a full boil. Remove the eggs at once.

(3) Put the eggs in boiling water. Allow 1 minute of boiling and then remove the pan from the heat and let the eggs stand 3 minutes in the hot water.

Hard-Cooked Eggs

Allow eggs to boil, completely covered with water, for 8 to 10 minutes. Remove from heat and plunge into cold water. If you crack the shells slightly before cooling, the eggs will peel with greater ease.

Poached Eggs

A skillet or flat saucepan is the best utensil for poaching eggs, unless you have a patented poacher of one type or another. You should have water deep enough to cover the eggs. Add a little salt and a tablespoon of vinegar to the water. When it is boiling rapidly, break the eggs and drop them in carefully or slide them from a saucer and let them cook until set. Lift them out with a large perforated spoon or skimmer.

Eggs may be poached until fairly hard for use in salads or jellies or for a first course.

Eggs Benedict

For each person toast 1 English muffin split in half. Top each muffin half, which has been well buttered just at serving time, with a round slice of sautéed or boiled Virginia ham. Top the ham with poached eggs and cover with Hollandaise sauce. Sprinkle with chopped parsley and serve.

Eggs Italian

Place poached eggs on crisp buttered toast, allowing 2 eggs per person. Add Italian tomato sauce, sprinkle liberally with grated Parmesan cheese, and put under the broiler for a few minutes to brown. Serve at once.

Eggs in Nest

Boil 8 ounces of fine noodles until just tender. Drain and mix with 4 tablespoons butter, salt, and pepper to taste, and 4 truffles, finely cut. Sprinkle liberally with chopped parsley. Form into nests on serving plates or platter and add 1 poached egg to each nest. Dot with softened butter and sprinkle liberally with finely chopped truffles. *(Serves 4.)*

Eggs Mornay

Poach 2 eggs per person and place the cooked eggs in a shallow baking dish. Cover the eggs with sauce Mornay, sprinkle liberally with grated Parmesan cheese, and put under the broiler for a few minutes to brown. Serve at once.

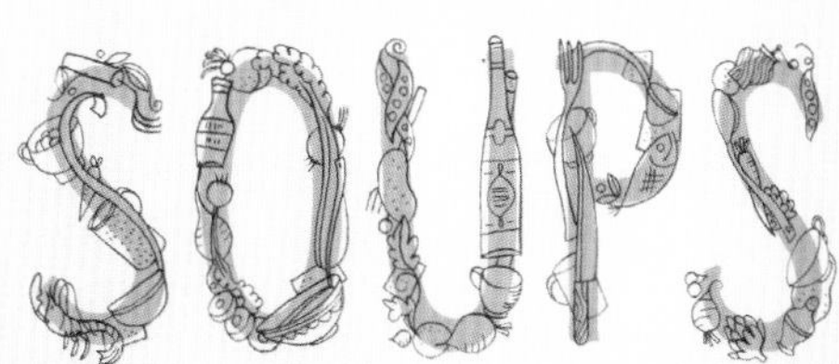

In these days of small kitchens there is seldom the space for the soup or stock pot which was a permanent fixture in the kitchens of other days. Now, too, one may purchase tins of consommé or chicken broth, or prepare a quick substitute for stock with powders or cubes. For much of the cooking where stock is required this is the ideal arrangement for most housekeepers. Dehydrated broth will also serve the purpose, and the value of the pressure cooker is ideally demonstrated when stock is required, for it cuts the time required for cooking and gives a concentrated essence which is ideal for most requirements.

Basic Beef Stock

4 pounds beef shin (including 1½ pounds marrow bone)
3 tablespoons butter or oil
3 quarts cold water
1 tablespoon salt
2 onions
2 cloves
3 or 4 carrots
Celery
Parsley
Bay leaf
2 leeks
Thyme
2 egg whites (optional)
Crushed egg shells (optional)

Shin is excellent for this, together with the marrow bone, which should be sawed into small pieces. Purchase about 2½ pounds of meat and 1½ pounds of bone.

Cut the beef into small pieces so that you will get all the good from it. Brown the meat very quickly in butter or oil and place in a deep kettle (an 8-quart one will do). Add the marrow bone and cold water. Bring this to a boil and allow it to boil briskly for 5 minutes; then skim the top of the liquid. Reduce the heat to simmering and allow the meat to cook slowly for at least 3 hours. The scum which will form should be skimmed from time to time during the cooking process. Keep the kettle covered except when you are skimming the surface.

After 1 hour of cooking, add salt (coarse salt is far more flavorful for this type of cookery). After salting the stock, add onions stuck with cloves, the carrots, a few branches of celery with their leaves, a few sprigs of parsley, a bay leaf, the leeks, and a few sprigs of thyme.

Strain the soup through cheesecloth and allow it to cool very quickly without cover. Skim off the fat from the top. Use absorbent paper to collect the small particles of fat that float on the surface after you have skimmed it.

If you wish to clarify the broth, add 2 egg whites, lightly beaten, and the crushed shells of the eggs. Allow this to come to a boil and boil briskly for 2 minutes. Strain through two thicknesses of cheesecloth.

Remove the marrow from the bones and add it to the broth, or serve it on toast with the broth.

MEAT SOUPS 39

VARIATIONS

With Cooked Bird: You may add the carcass of a cooked bird (chicken, turkey, duck, goose, or game) to the beef and proceed as above. Bones from a roast or steak may be used, or from any cooked meat except mutton or lamb scraps with a great deal of fat or corned or smoked meat.

With Vegetables (I): For a vegetable soup, proceed as above, but cut the meat in very fine dice and brown well. Make a small bag of cheesecloth for the herbs and seasonings, and add it after 1 hour's cooking. An hour before serving time, add 1 cup each of finely diced carrots, finely cut onions, sliced leeks, finely diced turnip, finely cut celery, and finely shredded snap beans. Allow to cook until vegetables are just tender.

Now remove the seasoning bag and then the marrow bones; extract the marrow and add it to the soup. Skim off the fat, but do not strain. Pour into large soup plates and add well-dried stale bread which has been warmed in the oven, or croutons if you wish. Sprinkle generously with chopped parsley.

With Vegetables (II): Prepare soup: strain, cool, and clarify as directed. Bring 1 quart of the stock to the boiling point and add ½ cup each of finely shredded carrots, finely diced onions, finely shredded snap beans, and finely cut celery. Simmer until vegetables are just tender and add ½ cup tender green peas or ½ package frozen peas which have been thawed (page 261). Taste for seasoning, add a generous quantity of chopped parsley, and serve at once.

Pressure Cooker Beef Stock

1½ pounds lean beef
3 or 4 tablespoons butter or oil
Knuckle bone
1 tablespoon salt
Bay leaf
2 or 3 small carrots
1 onion
2 cloves
Parsley
Thyme
6 cups water

Brown the lean beef (from the shank or the round) in butter or oil. This may be done in the pressure cooker. Add a knuckle bone, salt, a bay leaf, carrots, onion stuck with cloves, 1 or 2 sprigs parsley, a sprig of thyme, and the water. Cover and secure the cooker, and cook at 15 pounds for 15 to 20 minutes.

Allow to cool in the cooker before removing cover. Strain through a double cheesecloth and skim off all fat. Use as you do other stock.

JUNIOR LEAGUE OF CHARLESTON

Charleston Receipts, 1950

Junior League cookbooks serve as a barometer of what the average American prepared for supper. Like all community or congregation cookbooks, they reside somewhere between manuscripts; recipe card files; and printed, edited cookbooks. They are both fascinating and revealing in what they say about the taste of the period. As such, they are some of the best documentation of our food habits.

Because many congregational cookbooks are often ethnic cookbooks, we can chart the assimilation of immigrant groups into American culture by observing how recipes change from edition to edition. As Dalia Carmel, the noted cookbook collector who amassed a collection of thousands of these home-grown volumes, has said: "Sooner or later, there's a Jello recipe." Once a Jell-O recipe appears, the immigrant community has assimilated to the point where "American" recipes are allowed with the ethnic group's "traditional" fare. Carmel has donated more than 11,000 books to the Food Studies Collection at the Fales Library.

Edited by Mary Vereen Huguenin and Anne Montague Stoney, *Charleston Receipts* reflected a Low Country character and was first published on November 1, 1950, as a fundraising project by a committee of twenty-one sustaining members. The proceeds from sales of the book went to support the Charleston Speech and Hearing Center—the first center of its kind in South Carolina. The first edition was 350 pages long, contained 750 recipes, and cost $150 to produce. Two thousand copies were printed, and it sold out in two days. To date, an estimated 792,000 copies have been printed, and the cookbook has never gone out of print.

NOTABLE RECIPES: Benne Seed Wafers (page 633) • **Breakfast Shrimp** (page 470) • **Chicken Tetrazzini** (page 394) • Harriet Stoney Simons's Pilau • **Hopping John** (page 371) • Mrs. Harold G. Dotterer Scripture Cake • Mrs. James Hagood's Quail and Oysters • **Roast 'possum** (page 555) • **She-Crab Soup** (page 350) • **Shrimp Paste** (page 438)

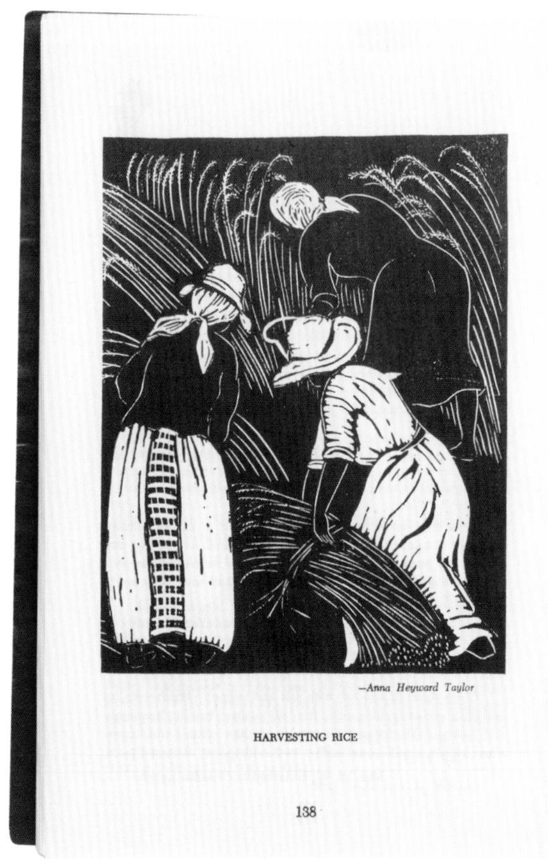

HOMINY & RICE
CHEESE & EGGS

Man, w'en 'e hongry, 'e teck sum egg or cheese an' ting an' eat till e' full. But 'ooman boun' fuh meck wuck an' trouble. 'E duh cook!

Never call it "Hominy Grits"
Or you will give Charlestonians fits!
When it comes from the mill, it's "grist";
After you cook it well, I wist,
You serve "*hominy*"! Do not skimp;
Serve butter with it and lots of shrimp.

Hominy

Hominy has long been a favorite in the Carolina Low-Country. This corn preparation, boiled with water and salt, was served in almost every household for breakfast—not as a cereal with sugar and cream, but mixed with butter and eaten with a relish such as bacon, eggs or fish cakes. It was not frequently used for dinner, but was often on the supper table, either cooked in the same manner, or, more often, in the form of fried hominy, baked hominy or "Awendaw." These concoctions were usually made from the hominy left "in the pot" after breakfast and were served for the evening meal with ham, shrimp, crab, or the like. Hominy is still used a great deal in Charleston and its vicinity, and may be prepared in any of the following ways:

139

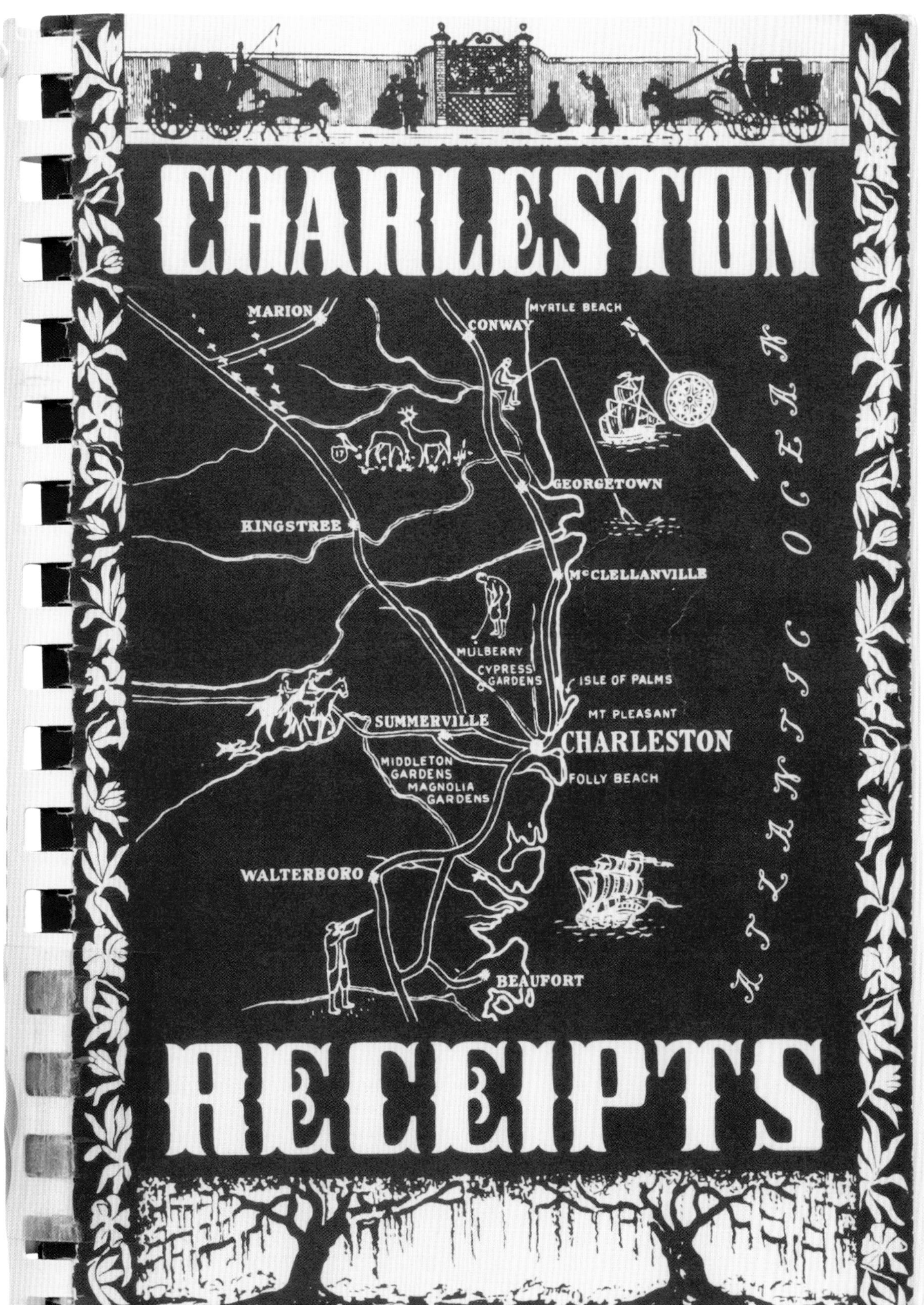
CHARLESTON
MARION
CONWAY
MYRTLE BEACH
N
ATLANTIC OCEAN
17
GEORGETOWN
KINGSTREE
McCLELLANVILLE
MULBERRY
CYPRESS GARDENS
ISLE OF PALMS
MT PLEASANT
SUMMERVILLE
CHARLESTON
MIDDLETON GARDENS
MAGNOLIA GARDENS
FOLLY BEACH
WALTERBORO
BEAUFORT
RECEIPTS

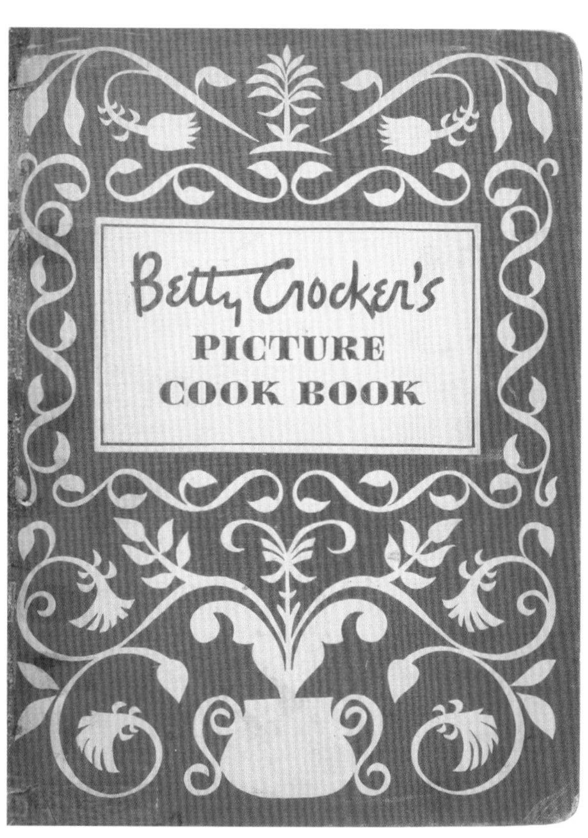

BETTY CROCKER

Betty Crocker's Picture Cook Book, 1950

It is common knowledge that Betty Crocker never existed. She was a creation of the Washburn-Crosby Company of Minneapolis in 1921, which produced flour. Beginning in the late 1910s and early 1920s, the company received thousands of letters asking questions about baking. Managers at Washburn-Crosby thought it would be better to actually sign the letters, as a personal touch, so they took the surname of William Crocker, a retired executive at the firm, and the name "Betty" because it was "warm and friendly," and—voilà—America's most beloved home cook was born. Her classic signature came from one of the secretaries at the mill and was the result of a company contest.

Betty found a voice on the radio in 1924 when she debuted in the nation's first cooking show. *The Betty Crocker School of the Air* ran for twenty-four years. When the Washburn-Crosby Company and six other major mills merged into General Mills in 1928, Betty Crocker went along with them. In 1936 an artist named Neysa McMein combined the features of several women at General Mills to create the likeness of Betty. From 1949 to 1964, Adelaide Hawley Cumming portrayed Crocker on television.

Perhaps the most important event for Betty Crocker, however, was the 1950 publication of *Betty Crocker's Picture Cook Book*. "Big Red," as it is known, was an instant success and became the essential book given to every new bride who moved to the rapidly expanding suburbs to set up her new home. The rest is history. With more than two hundred cookbooks and millions of copies sold, Betty Crocker is one of the most important women who never lived.

NOTABLE RECIPES: Apple Pie • Berries and Cream Pie • Black Devil's Food Cake • Blueberry Pie • Butter Cookies • **Chocolate Chip Cookies** (page 632) • **Maraschino Cherry Cake/Poppy Seed Cake** (page 612) • Peach Cobbler • Pie Crust Recipe • Pigs in Blanket • Snickerdoodles • Spaghetti with Meatballs • Spritz Cookies • **Sugar Jumbles** (page 632) • **Sweet Dough Yeast Breads for Delectable Rolls and Coffee Cakes** (page 564) • **Upside Down Cake** (page 616)

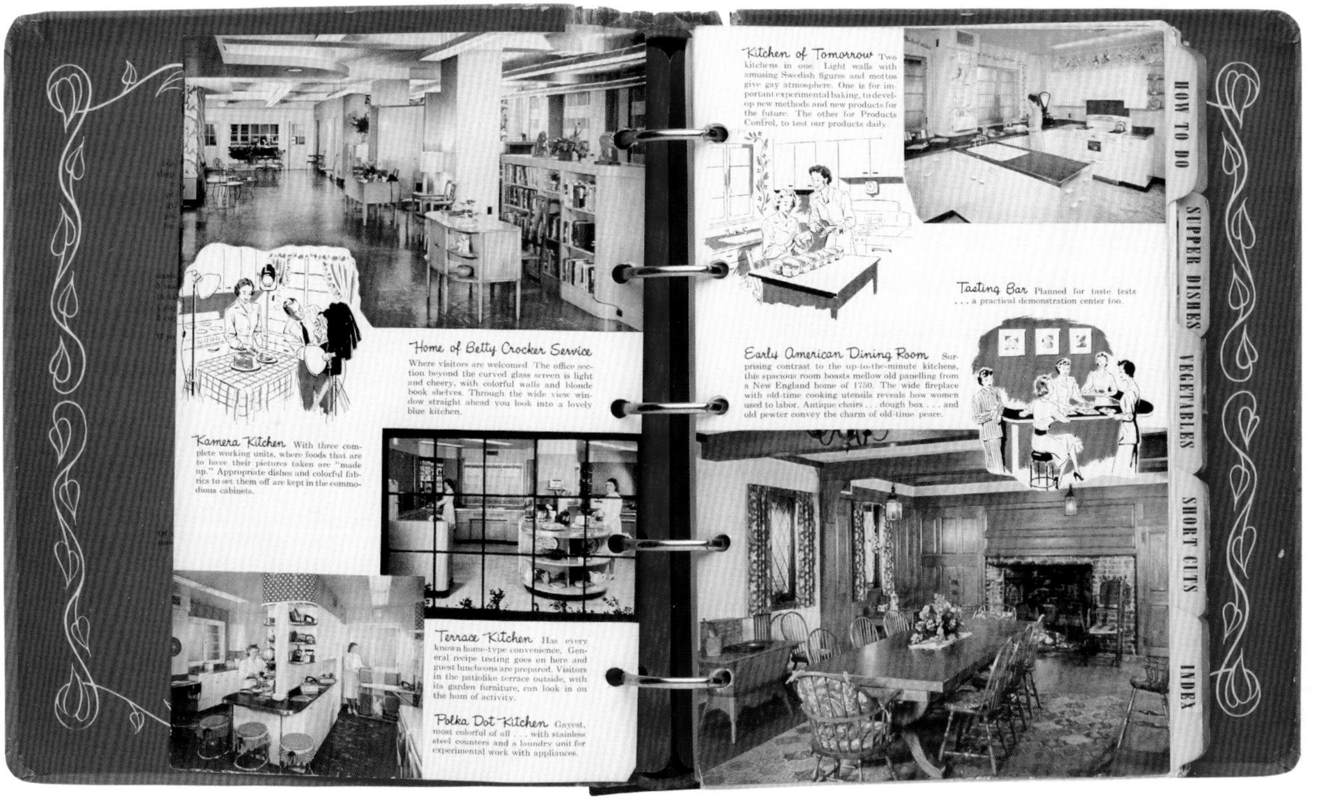

Home of Betty Crocker Service Where visitors are welcomed. The office section beyond the curved glass screen is light and cheery, with colorful walls and blonde book shelves. Through the wide view window straight ahead you look into a lovely blue kitchen.

Kamera Kitchen With three complete working units, where foods that are to have their pictures taken are "made up." Appropriate dishes and colorful fabrics to set them off are kept in the commodious cabinets.

Terrace Kitchen Has every known home-type convenience. General recipe testing goes on here and guest luncheons are prepared. Visitors in the patiolike terrace outside, with its garden furniture, can look in on the hum of activity.

Polka Dot Kitchen Gayest, most colorful of all . . . with stainless steel counters and a laundry unit for experimental work with appliances.

Kitchen of Tomorrow Two kitchens in one. Light walls with amusing Swedish figures and mottos give gay atmosphere. One is for important experimental baking, to develop new methods and new products for the future. The other for Products Control, to test our products daily.

Tasting Bar Planned for taste tests . . . a practical demonstration center too.

Early American Dining Room Surprising contrast to the up-to-the-minute kitchens, this spacious room boasts mellow old panelling from a New England home of 1750. The wide fireplace with old-time cooking utensils reveals how women used to labor. Antique chairs . . . dough box . . . and old pewter convey the charm of old-time peace.

SHORT CUTS Make every motion count.

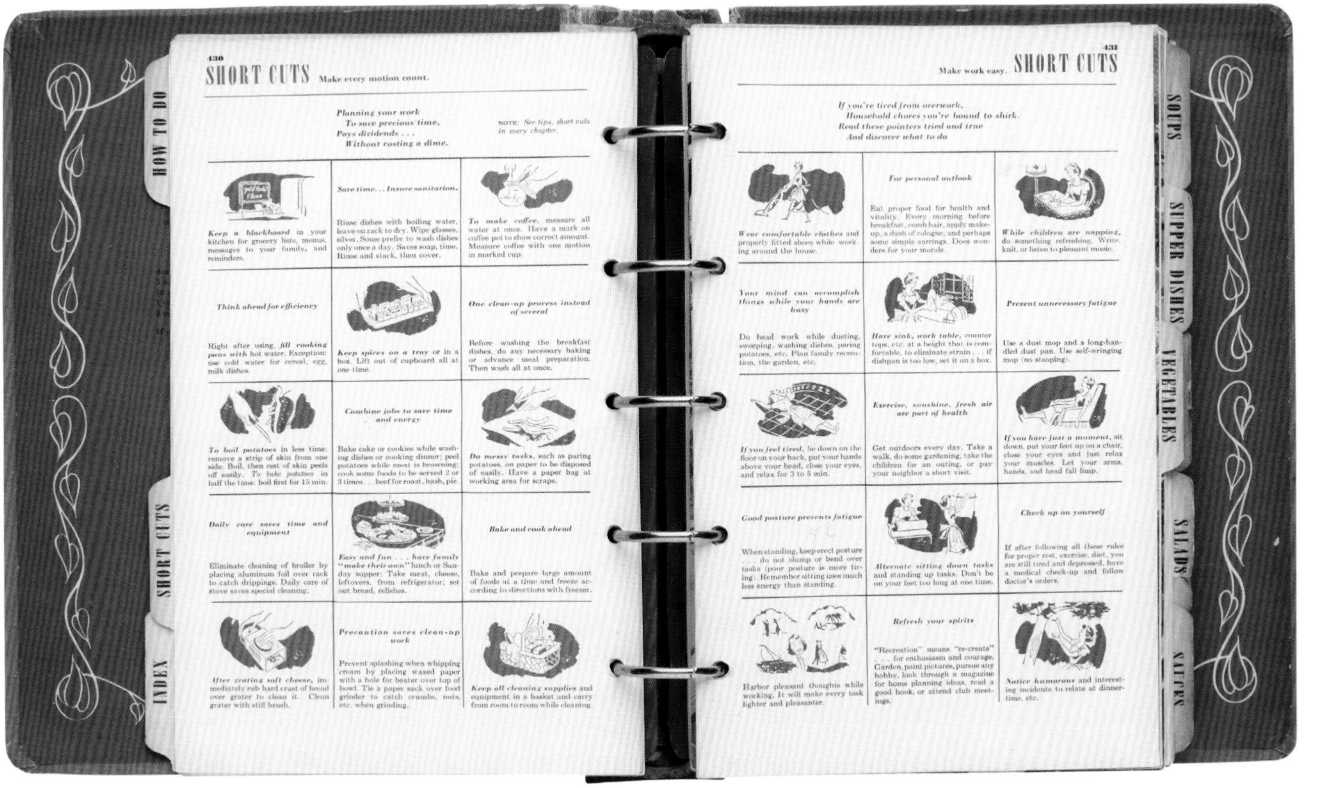

Planning your work
To save precious time,
Pays dividends . . .
Without costing a dime.

NOTE: *See tips, short cuts in every chapter.*

Keep a blackboard in your kitchen for grocery lists, menus, messages to your family, and reminders.

Save time . . . Insure sanitation. Rinse dishes with boiling water, leave on rack to dry. Wipe glasses, silver. Some prefer to wash dishes only once a day. Saves soap, time. Rinse and stack, then cover.

To make coffee, measure all water at once. Have a mark on coffee pot to show correct amount. Measure coffee with one motion in marked cup.

Think ahead for efficiency Right after using, ***fill cooking pans with*** hot water. Exception: use cold water for cereal, egg, milk dishes.

Keep spices on a tray or in a box. Lift out of cupboard all at one time.

One clean-up process instead of several Before washing the breakfast dishes, do any necessary baking or advance meal preparation. Then wash all at once.

To boil potatoes in less time: remove a strip of skin from one side. Boil, then rest of skin peels off easily. *To bake potatoes* in half the time: boil first for 15 min.

Combine jobs to save time and energy Bake cake or cookies while washing dishes or cooking dinner; peel potatoes while meat is browning; cook some foods to be served 2 or 3 times . . . beef for roast, hash, pie.

Do messy tasks, such as paring potatoes, on paper to be disposed of easily. Have a paper bag at working area for scraps.

Daily care saves time and equipment Eliminate cleaning of broiler by placing aluminum foil over rack to catch drippings. Daily care of stove saves special cleaning.

Easy and fun . . . have family "make their own" lunch or Sunday supper: Take meat, cheese, leftovers, from refrigerator; set out bread, relishes.

Bake and cook ahead Bake and prepare large amount of foods at a time and freeze according to directions with freezer.

After grating soft cheese, immediately rub hard crust of bread over grater to clean it. Clean grater with stiff brush.

Precaution saves clean-up work Prevent splashing when whipping cream by placing waxed paper with a hole for beater over top of bowl. Tie a paper sack over food grinder to catch crumbs, nuts, etc. when grinding.

Keep all cleaning supplies and equipment in a basket and carry from room to room while cleaning.

Make work easy. SHORT CUTS

If you're tired from overwork,
Household chores you're bound to shirk.
Read these pointers tried and true
And discover what to do

Wear comfortable clothes and properly fitted shoes while working around the house.

For personal outlook Eat proper food for health and vitality. Every morning before breakfast, comb hair, apply make-up, a dash of cologne, and perhaps some simple earrings. Does wonders for your morale.

While children are napping, do something refreshing. Write, knit, or listen to pleasant music.

Your mind can accomplish things while your hands are busy Do head work while dusting, sweeping, washing dishes, paring potatoes, etc. Plan family recreation, the garden, etc.

Have sink, work table, counter tops, etc. at a height that is comfortable, to eliminate strain . . . if dishpan is too low, set it on a box.

Prevent unnecessary fatigue Use a dust mop and a long-handled dust pan. Use self-wringing mop (no stooping).

If you feel tired, lie down on the floor on your back, put your hands above your head, close your eyes, and relax for 3 to 5 min.

Exercise, sunshine, fresh air are part of health Get outdoors every day. Take a walk, do some gardening, take the children for an outing, or pay your neighbor a short visit.

If you have just a moment, sit down, put your feet up on a chair, close your eyes and just relax your muscles. Let your arms, hands, and head fall limp.

Good posture prevents fatigue When standing, keep erect posture . . . do not slump or bend over tasks (poor posture is more tiring). Remember sitting uses much less energy than standing.

Alternate sitting down tasks and standing up tasks. Don't be on your feet too long at one time.

Check up on yourself If after following all these rules for proper rest, exercise, diet, you are still tired and depressed, have a medical check-up and follow doctor's orders.

Harbor pleasant thoughts while working. It will make every task lighter and pleasanter.

Refresh your spirits "Recreation" means "re-create" . . . for enthusiasm and courage. Garden, paint pictures, pursue any hobby, look through a magazine for home planning ideas, read a good book, or attend club meetings.

Notice humorous and interesting incidents to relate at dinnertime, etc.

338

MIXED GREEN SALADS For every day in the year.

HOW-TO-MAKE THE EASIEST, QUICKEST GREEN SALAD

1 For a faint whisper of garlic flavor, rub chilled bowl with garlic bud.

2 Pluck apart and break up crisp salad greens and place in bowl.

3 Add attractive sized pieces (to retain their identity) of vegetables, fruits, seafoods, etc.

4 Just before serving, add dressing . . . only enough to make leaves of greens glisten.

5 Gently toss ingredients so that every piece is coated with dressing.

6 Add juicy tomato sections at the last.

7 Serve in large bowl or in individual bowls or on individual salad plates.

339

SALADS MIXED GREEN

THERE CAN ALWAYS BE A SALAD

A glance in your refrigerator, cupboard, or garden will convince you that you always have ingredients available. Follow the general plan on opposite page, using whatever you happen to have on hand.

Commonly used with salad greens (*p. 337*) in mixed green salads, are the following:

RAW VEGETABLES: Thinly sliced radishes. Thinly sliced cucumbers. Diced celery. Tomato slices or sections. Thinly sliced carrots or thin carrot strips. Little new onions. Finely cut chives. Minced parsley. Rings of green or red pepper. Strips of pimiento. Flowerets of cauliflower. Wafer-thin slices of turnips. Shredded cabbage. Finely shredded baby beets. Shredded raw parsnips. Sliced raw mushrooms.

AMOUNTS FOR GREEN SALADS

For 6	*For 3*
1 head lettuce (or equivalent of other salad greens)	½ head
½ cucumber, thinly sliced	¼
6 radishes, thinly sliced	3
2 stalks celery, diced	1 stalk
3 ripe tomatoes, sectioned	1 (large)

COOKED VEGETABLES: Peas. Green beans. Lima beans. Beets. Asparagus tips. Artichoke hearts. Broccoli. Cauliflower flowerets. Hearts of palm.

BITS OF FRUIT: Grapefruit or orange sections. Little seedless green grapes. Tokay grapes. Melon balls or cubes (honeydew, cantaloupe, watermelon). Pomegranate seeds. Apple. Plum. Peach. Pear. Cherries. Avocado.

GARNISH: Remember that a bit of color contrast steps up appetite appeal. Add shiny black or green olives, gay radish roses, strips of red pimiento, or a sprig of dark green mint or watercress. Bits of colorful fruit such as slices of bright orange can also serve as garnish.

WESTERN WAY SALAD

A connoisseur's salad, made for our Staff by a delightful visitor, famous home economist Essie L. Elliott of California.

Place 3 qt. salad greens in large bowl. Add ⅓ cup each salad oil, grated dry cheese and crumbled blue cheese. Salt and pepper to taste. Break one raw egg over greens. Squeeze juice from 2 lemons over egg. Toss well. Dribble 2 tbsp. oil with garlic steeped in it over 1 pt. crisp croutons (bread cubes browned), and add just before serving. *Serves 8.*

CHEF'S SALAD

Julienne strips of meat with mixed greens make a hearty main dish salad. Served in many smart restaurants.

Follow recipe for Mixed Green Salad (*opposite page*) and add 1 cup match-like strips of cold baked ham and chicken or other meat (slices cut ¼" wide, 3" long). Just before serving, toss with Mayonnaise. Place ½ cup meat strips over the top. Garnish with quartered hard-cooked egg, radishes, and sliced olives or pickles.

SEAFOOD, CHEESE, OR EGGS

Any of these added to a salad of mixed greens makes of it a "meal-in-one-dish" for luncheon or supper.

Follow recipe for Mixed Green Salad (*opposite page*) and add, just before tossing together with Mayonnaise, boned seafood in large pieces (crab, lobster, shrimp, tuna, salmon, anchovy, or sardines, etc.); *or* strips of American cheese; *or* coarsely cut-up or sliced hard-cooked eggs.

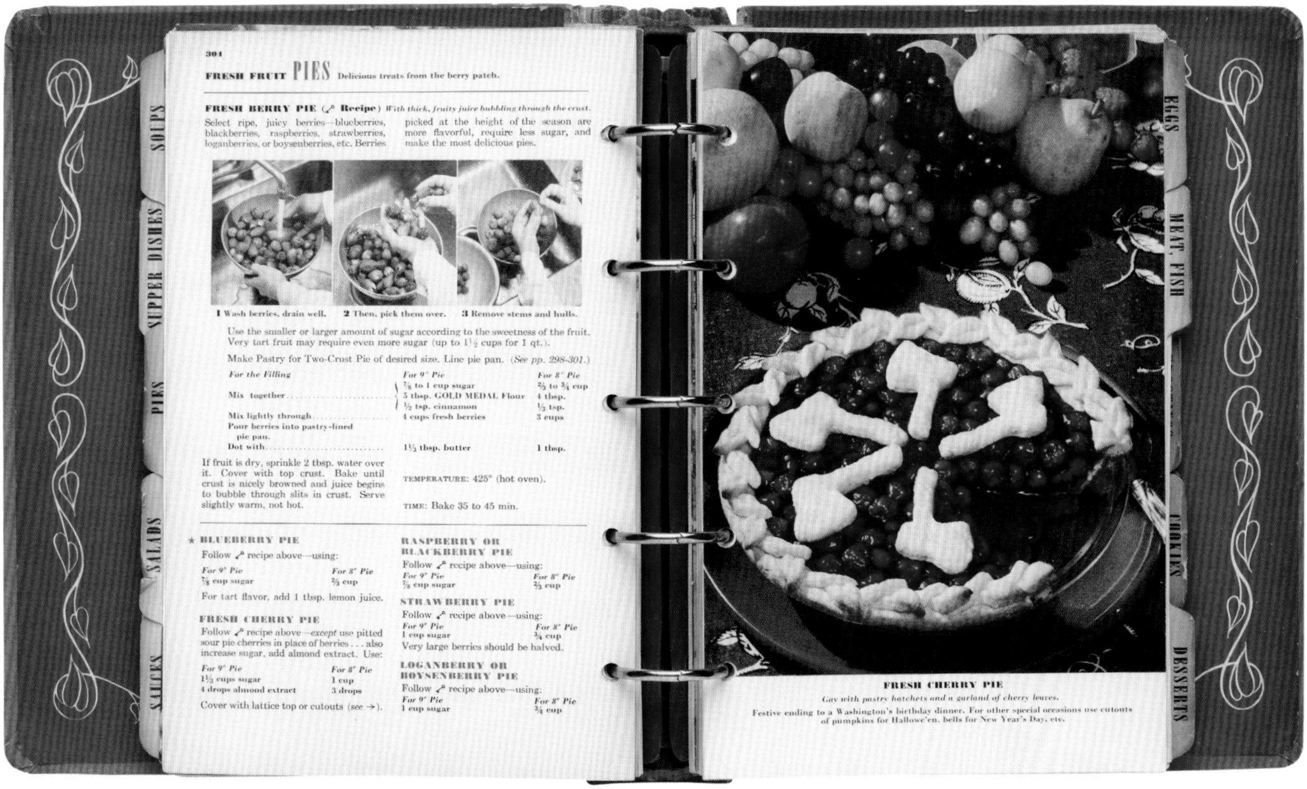

304

FRESH FRUIT PIES Delicious treats from the berry patch.

FRESH BERRY PIE (Recipe) *With thick, fruity juice bubbling through the crust.*

Select ripe, juicy berries—blueberries, blackberries, raspberries, strawberries, loganberries, or boysenberries, etc. Berries picked at the height of the season are more flavorful, require less sugar, and make the most delicious pies.

1 Wash berries, drain well. 2 Then, pick them over. 3 Remove stems and hulls.

Use the smaller or larger amount of sugar according to the sweetness of the fruit. Very tart fruit may require even more sugar (up to 1½ cups for 1 qt.).

Make Pastry for Two-Crust Pie of desired size. Line pie pan. (See pp. 298-301.)

For the Filling	*For 9" Pie*	*For 8" Pie*
Mix together	⅞ to 1 cup sugar	⅔ to ¾ cup
	5 tbsp. GOLD MEDAL Flour	4 tbsp.
	½ tsp. cinnamon	⅓ tsp.
Mix lightly through	4 cups fresh berries	3 cups
Pour berries into pastry-lined pie pan.		
Dot with	1⅓ tbsp. butter	1 tbsp.

If fruit is dry, sprinkle 2 tbsp. water over it. Cover with top crust. Bake until crust is nicely browned and juice begins to bubble through slits in crust. Serve slightly warm, not hot.

TEMPERATURE: 425° (hot oven).

TIME: Bake 35 to 45 min.

★ **BLUEBERRY PIE**

Follow recipe above—using:

For 9" Pie	*For 8" Pie*
⅞ cup sugar	⅔ cup

For tart flavor, add 1 tbsp. lemon juice.

FRESH CHERRY PIE

Follow recipe above—*except* use pitted sour pie cherries in place of berries . . . also increase sugar, add almond extract. Use:

For 9" Pie	*For 8" Pie*
1⅓ cups sugar	1 cup
4 drops almond extract	3 drops

Cover with lattice top or cutouts (see →).

RASPBERRY OR BLACKBERRY PIE

Follow recipe above—using:

For 9" Pie	*For 8" Pie*
⅞ cup sugar	⅔ cup

STRAWBERRY PIE

Follow recipe above—using:

For 9" Pie	*For 8" Pie*
1 cup sugar	¾ cup

Very large berries should be halved.

LOGANBERRY OR BOYSENBERRY PIE

Follow recipe above—using:

For 9" Pie	*For 8" Pie*
1 cup sugar	¾ cup

FRESH CHERRY PIE

Gay with pastry hatchets and a garland of cherry leaves.

Festive ending to a Washington's birthday dinner. For other special occasions use cutouts of pumpkins for Hallowe'en, bells for New Year's Day, etc.

201

Gay shapes . . . for holiday cheer. COOKIES ROLLED

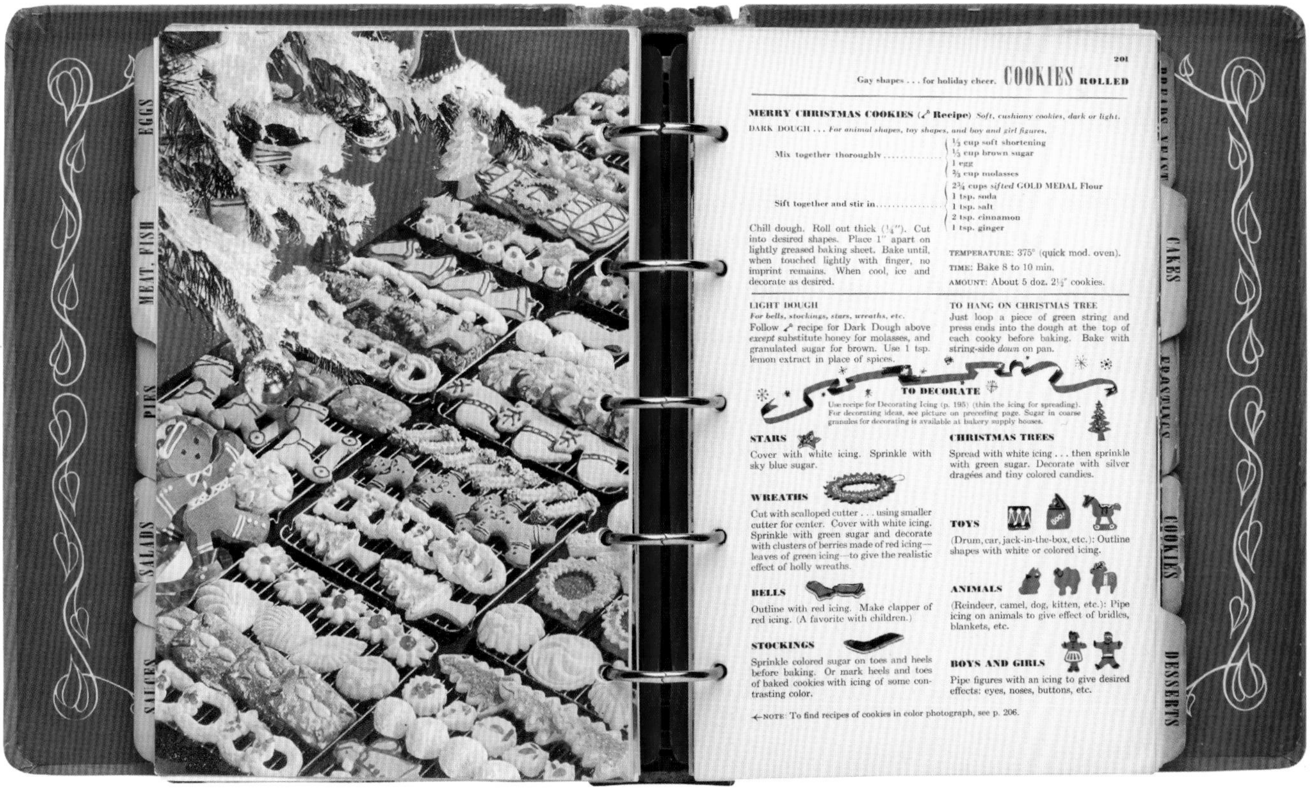

MERRY CHRISTMAS COOKIES (Recipe) *Soft, cushiony cookies, dark or light.*

DARK DOUGH . . . *For animal shapes, toy shapes, and boy and girl figures.*

Mix together thoroughly	⅓ cup soft shortening
	⅓ cup brown sugar
	1 egg
	⅔ cup molasses
Sift together and stir in	2¾ cups *sifted* GOLD MEDAL Flour
	1 tsp. soda
	1 tsp. salt
	2 tsp. cinnamon
	1 tsp. ginger

Chill dough. Roll out thick (¼"). Cut into desired shapes. Place 1" apart on lightly greased baking sheet. Bake until, when touched lightly with finger, no imprint remains. When cool, ice and decorate as desired.

TEMPERATURE: 375° (quick mod. oven).

TIME: Bake 8 to 10 min.

AMOUNT: About 5 doz. 2½" cookies.

LIGHT DOUGH

For bells, stockings, stars, wreaths, etc.

Follow recipe for Dark Dough above *except* substitute honey for molasses, and granulated sugar for brown. Use 1 tsp. lemon extract in place of spices.

TO HANG ON CHRISTMAS TREE

Just loop a piece of green string and press ends into the dough at the top of each cooky before baking. Bake with string-side *down* on pan.

TO DECORATE

Use recipe for Decorating Icing (p. 195) (thin the icing for spreading). For decorating ideas, see picture on preceding page. Sugar in coarse granules for decorating is available at bakery supply houses.

STARS

Cover with white icing. Sprinkle with sky blue sugar.

WREATHS

Cut with scalloped cutter . . . using smaller cutter for center. Cover with white icing. Sprinkle with green sugar and decorate with clusters of berries made of red icing—leaves of green icing—to give the realistic effect of holly wreaths.

BELLS

Outline with red icing. Make clapper of red icing. (A favorite with children.)

STOCKINGS

Sprinkle colored sugar on toes and heels before baking. Or mark heels and toes of baked cookies with icing of some contrasting color.

CHRISTMAS TREES

Spread with white icing . . . then sprinkle with green sugar. Decorate with silver dragées and tiny colored candies.

TOYS

(Drum, car, jack-in-the-box, etc.): Outline shapes with white or colored icing.

ANIMALS

(Reindeer, camel, dog, kitten, etc.): Pipe icing on animals to give effect of bridles, blankets, etc.

BOYS AND GIRLS

Pipe figures with an icing to give desired effects: eyes, noses, buttons, etc.

←NOTE: To find recipes of cookies in color photograph, see p. 206.

ANDREW F. SMITH *on* BETTY CROCKER *and* HER SISTERS

For the first 150 years or so of this country's history, Americans grew or raised much of their own food; what they couldn't produce themselves, they bought or bartered from farmers or general stores. Food was usually local and unbranded: Cheese was chiseled from an unlabeled wheel, beans scooped from a bin into a plain brown bag, milk ladled from a big can into a pail that the housewife had brought from home.

In the late nineteenth century this began to change, as processed and manufactured foods became more common and their producers felt the need to identify these novel comestibles and ingredients as unique. Even companies that packaged "generic" foods, such as flour or spices, saw the advantage of branding their products to distinguish them from those of lesser quality. And manufacturers of kitchen appliances and gadgets—which were being patented at a record pace—wanted to establish the superiority (and explain the proper use) of their "improved" stove, eggbeater, food chopper, or cake pan.

The newly created processed foods—breakfast cereals, baking powders, vegetable shortenings—had no generic equivalents and no precedent in the kitchen or on the table. How to convince potential consumers to buy a new product that they did not know how to prepare or serve? The food companies tried, through magazines and newspaper ads, to show the public how to make the most of their new products, but it was an expensive way to go, and there really wasn't space in a quarter- or half-page to tell the full story.

The invention of the rotary press in 1846 made high-speed, low-cost printing possible; at around the same time there were major advances in color lithography and photography. So some food companies took the route of publishing promotional literature, ranging from tiny bifold pamphlets to substantial, lengthy brochures. These "cookbooklets" introduced previously unfamiliar products and supplied recipes and serving suggestions. They also encouraged customers to demand specific brand-name products at local grocery stores rather than

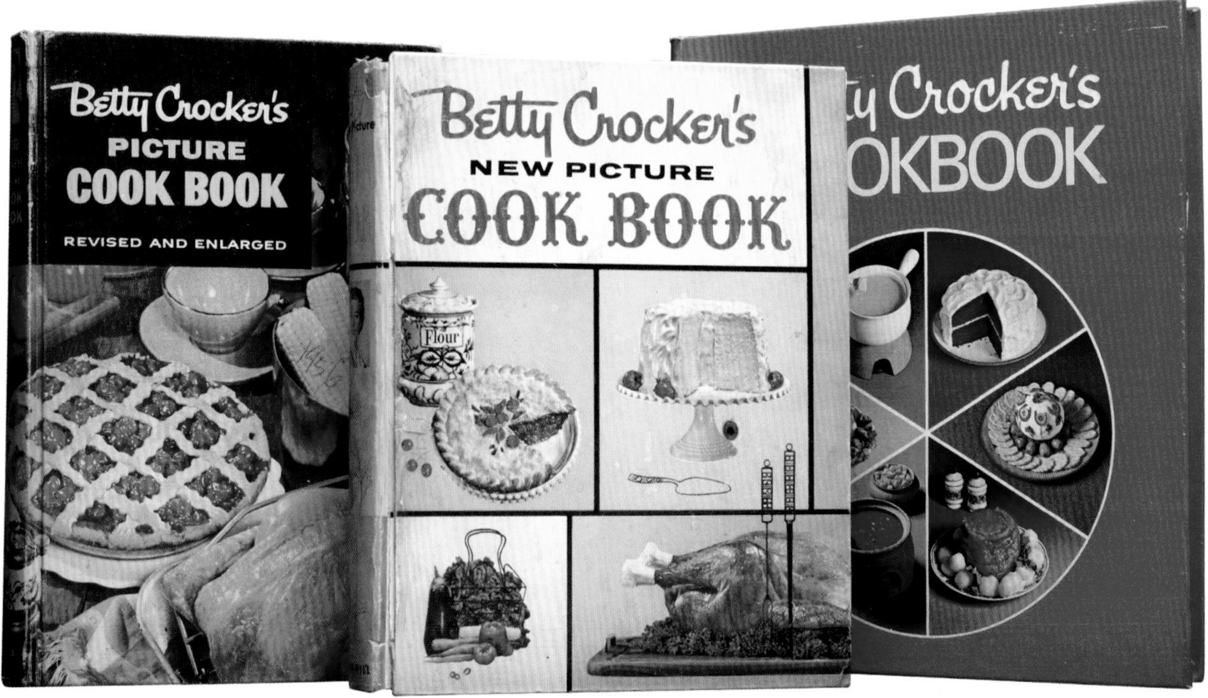

accept unbranded bulk goods, which were inevitably portrayed as inferior.

This literature was circulated in a variety of ways. Sometimes the booklet was packed with the product—tucked right into or affixed to the box or bag. Or the customer could send away for the booklet at no charge or for the price of a stamp, which allowed the manufacturer to develop a mailing list for future promotions. For kitchen equipment, an accompanying instruction booklet would include recipes that took advantage of the gadget's features.

Because cookbooklets were intended primarily as advertising, they were more attractively designed than the trade cookbooks of the day. They usually included illustrations or photographs of the product (or the full product line), pictures of prepared dishes, awards won at fairs and expositions, and sometimes a depiction of the corporate headquarters or factory, demonstrating its modernity and cleanliness. Although the earliest examples were relatively simple black-and-white affairs devoid of artwork, cookbooklets soon became more colorful, elaborate, and attractive, offering—along with recipes—anecdotes, jokes or riddles, helpful advice, and florid testimonials. The booklets introduced new color-processing techniques in illustration and photography. Full-color artwork was an irresistible eye-catcher in the early twentieth century, and food advertising in particular was designed to whet the consumer's appetite.

The reliability of the recipes was also very important: If the homemaker decided to try a new product and the dish she used it in was a failure, she would doubtless blame the product and probably never buy it again. So the recipes published in advertising booklets were well tested (and sometimes "guaranteed")—unlike those that appeared in trade cookbooks of the period.

Some of the earliest advertising cookbooklets were produced by the Shredded Wheat Company, whose product was revolutionary for its time. Provocatively titled The Vital Question, an information-packed (148 pages) yet diminutive 1905 booklet in green covers tied with a purple string featured hundreds of creative ways to serve Shredded Wheat, as well as kitchen tips, nutrition charts, menus, an essay on the product's healthful qualities, and a few brilliant lithographed plates showing some of the more colorful dishes, such as Raspberries in Biscuit Basket and Jellied Apple Sandwich.

The Genesee Pure Food Company, makers of Jell-O, showcased their product's jewel-like colors in some of the most strikingly beautiful cookbooklets ever published. Jell-O booklets have been enlivened by some of America's most beloved artists and illustrators—Rose O'Neill (creator of the Kewpie doll), Norman Rockwell, Maxfield Parrish, and, more recently, Seymour Chwast. One of the first Jell-O booklets, Desserts of the World, was published in 1909. Finely lithographed in full color with gold accents, the illustrations showed (theoretical, mostly) uses of the product in myriad cultures throughout history. Hawaii, Russia, Holland, and Middle Eastern countries are represented, and so is the Garden of Eden, where, we are told, Apple Snow Jell-O was served. On the center pages, the dainty, dreamy-eyed Jell-O Girl, reminiscent of the angels in Renaissance paintings, demonstrates how easy the product is to mix and mold.

Another company that showed great confidence in cookbooklets was Campbell's Soup. Early publications emphasized ways to combine, enhance, and garnish the soups, and showed how to incorporate them as ingredients in other dishes. The 1910 Campbell's Menu Book asserts that the success of dinner depends on the selection of the soup. This booklet offers menus "of educational value" for housewives "not conversant with the kinds of soups that may be appropriately and correctly served with certain meats." Its forty-eight pages offer thirteen menus, along with recipes developed by Cornelia C. Bedford, "an eminent authority on culinary topics." For instance, classic Campbell's Tomato Soup could be fortified or gussied up with cheese, noodles, parsley, celery, vermicelli, rice, or whipped cream. The pantry staple could also go into croquettes, jellies, and sauces for fish, hamburger, steak, and codfish balls.

The promotional cookbooklet was an effective medium for introducing unfamiliar foods to American consumers. In 1900, for example, few Americans had ever tasted canned tuna, but within a decade it had become a staple of the American diet, thanks largely to the recipe booklets published by tuna canners. Likewise, few Americans ate avocados until the 1920s, when Calavo Growers of California began to publish avocado cookbooklets. (The growers even tried to brand the fruits as "Calavos," but it didn't stick.) Although most Americans had eaten oranges—often found in the toe of a Christmas stocking—it wasn't until California and Florida citrus growers began issuing cookbooklets in the 1920s and 1930s that orange juice became a fixture on the American breakfast table.

At first, advertising messages concentrated on saving time and energy; later the focus shifted to economy and nutrition, and finally they focused on celebrities. In 1933 a new General Mills product was promoted via Betty Crocker's 101 Delicious Bisquick Creations as Made and Served by Well-Known Gracious Hostesses; Famous Chefs; Distinguished Epicures and Smart Luminaries of Movieland. *The booklet included many recipes "signed" by Hollywood movie stars. Two years later, General Mills followed up with* Let the Stars Show You How to Take a Trick a Day with Bisquick as Told to Betty Crocker. *Of course, the "as told to Betty Crocker" tag is disingenuous: Betty Crocker was a product of the fertile imagination of General Mills advertisers in 1922. The creation of a fictional character proved successful, and other companies followed suit. Betty's sisters include Ann Page and Jane Parker (A&P), Mary Blake (Carnation Evaporated Milk), and Aunt Jenny (Spry Vegetable Shortening). Betty Crocker's image—her hairstyle, makeup, and wardrobe evolving over the years—is all but gone from General Mills products and promotions, but her name lives on as one of the great successes in American commerce.*

As the twentieth century came to a close, advertising cookbooklets faded from the scene. Some companies, such as Campbell's Soup, began offering bigger, more durable hardcover cookbooks. Brand-name products were subtly integrated into editorial copy and recipes in shelter magazines. The ever-expanding mass media—radio, then television, and now the Internet—often pack more punch than the printed word. Still, in their heyday, these handsome, useful booklets had a profound influence on American cookery. Today those that have proven not so ephemeral—the folders and pamphlets that survive, tucked away in a kitchen drawer or an apron pocket—offer a fertile field for collectors of cookbooks and food-related items and for historians of American industry and foodways.

The
DEL MONTE FRUIT BOOK
Containing the FAVORITE FRUIT
RECIPES of AMERICA'S BEST
KNOWN COOKING AUTHORITIES

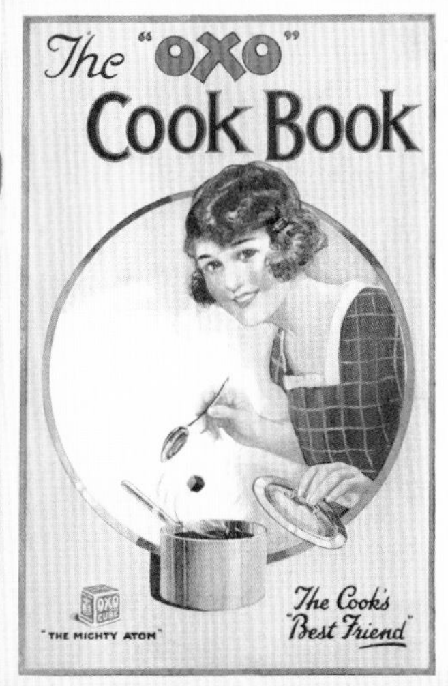
The "OXO" Cook Book
"THE MIGHTY ATOM"
The Cook's "Best Friend"

DEL MONTE
TOMATO SAUCE
RECIPES
TOMATO SAUCE
FOR COOKING USES

Around the World
with Mr. Peanut
MR. PEANUT

FROZEN
DAINTIES
PUBLISHED BY THE WHITE MOUNTAIN FREEZER CO.

JELL-O
AMERICA'S MOST FAMOUS
DESSERT

Sunkist Recipes
Oranges-Lemons

CRISP AND TASTY!
TRISCUIT
The
Shredded
Wheat
Cracker
TRISCUIT
Delicious with butter
soft cheese or marmalades

EARLE R. MACAUSLAND

The Gourmet Cookbook, 1950

Food in America changed with the first publication of *Gourmet* magazine. Hyperbolic, perhaps, but it was Earle R. MacAusland's brainchild, dreamed up in his suite at New York's Plaza Hotel, that brought the world of "good living" and good eating to a larger U.S. audience than ever before.

Prior to *Gourmet*—and, some would say, even during MacAusland's tenure as publisher—the world of the gourmet in America was mostly restricted to a small group of male Francophiles who lived in New York City, when not in Paris, and who traveled in the elite society of "The Four Hundred," New York's aristocratic class of the late nineteenth century. Such names as Crosby Gaige and Lucius Beebe come to mind when thinking about these early days.

While MacAusland was a Francophile and a part of this boys' club, his desire to create a magazine about fine eating had a democratizing effect. We can't ignore that *Gourmet* was first published in 1941, either. Following World War II, American GIs returned from Europe with a very different approach to eating. Many had been stationed in France, Italy, and the Mediterranean and came back with a palate that was no longer satisfied by the Anglo-Germanic cookery that had prevailed in America until then. They wanted garlic. Not too much, but garlic. Through its recipes, food writing, and travel coverage, *Gourmet* appealed to these men—for it remained largely a men's magazine for a long time. It helped launch the careers of such food writers as M.F.K. Fisher, Clementine Paddleford, Louis P. de Gouy, Samuel Chamberlain, and James Beard.

The magazine changed as the times changed, but it never gave up its mission of finding the best food, no matter where or how humble the origin. Condé Nast purchased *Gourmet* in 1983 and published it until 2009, when this beloved, venerable guide to all that is good in food was closed. NYU acquired the *Gourmet* office library through a generous gift from Rozanne Gold, literally a day before it was headed to the Dumpster. The books are now part of the Food Studies Collection in the Fales Library.

The Gourmet Cookbook is a compilation of recipes from the first ten years of the magazine's history. In his jovial introduction, MacAusland reminds us

that the famous French gourmand Brillat-Savarin weathered the French Revolution in America, as if to give a foundation for good cooking on American soil. He then notes that there are three kinds of gourmets: "good cooks who refuse to compromise with quality; good cooks who constantly improvise or improve, create or adapt, a recipe; cooks who are artists in still life." He offers up the best of *Gourmet*'s early recipes with a generous caveat: "No recipe is so sacred that it cannot be adjusted to individual taste or contemporary exigency." In other words, American gourmets have a calling not to reduce every food experience to rules and codifications, but to go forth, experiment, and create a gourmet style that is founded in tradition, but that is also distinctly American.

NOTABLE RECIPES: Black Bean Soup Creole • Brandy Black Bottom Chiffon Pie • **Caneton à l'Orange** (page 492) • **Chicken Cacciatore** (page 505) • Chicken Tetrazzini • Chocolate Bavarian Cream • **Crêpes Suzette** (page 596) • **Jellied Egg Salad Gourmet** (page 466) • **Lobster Newberg** (page 483) • **Petits Pots de Crème à la Vanille** (page 644) • **Soupe à l'Oignon au Fromage** (page 341)

CRAYFISH IN THE BUSH
(Page 252)

SEA FOOD SALAD
(Page 161)

BOUILLABAISSE MARSEILLAISE
(Page 283)

SALMON IN ASPIC NORWEGIAN
(Page 272)

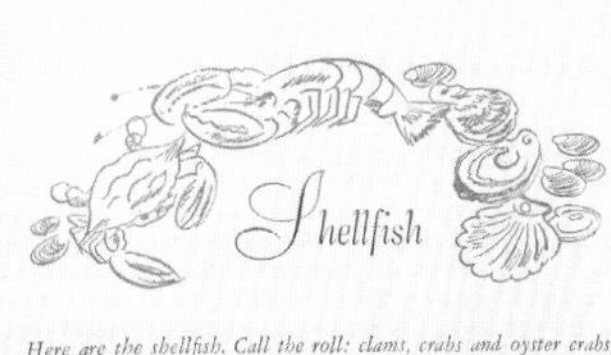

Shellfish

Here are the shellfish. Call the roll: clams, crabs and oyster crabs, crayfish, lobster, mussels, oysters, scallops, shrimp. All are present in many versions, some simple, some complex, all eminently delicious. Present also are the odd fellows, the aquatic turtle and terrapin, the amphibious frog, the succulent snail.

Court-Bouillon for Shellfish

MELT 2 tablespoons butter in a saucepan and in it cook 1 large onion, 1 large carrot, and 3 stalks celery, all finely chopped, until the vegetables are browned. Add 2 quarts water, 1 bay leaf tied with 2 sprigs of parsley, 6 peppercorns, and 2 cloves. Acidulate with 2 tablespoons white wine vinegar and bring to a boil. Cover the pan tightly and simmer the *court-bouillon* for 30 minutes or longer. Strain and cool before using.

Steamed Clams

WASH and scrub as many clams in the shell as are required. Put them in a large kettle with 1/4 cup water, cover, and steam until the shells open. Serve the clams with individual dishes of melted butter. Strain the broth through several thicknesses of cheesecloth, season to taste, and serve in a bouillon cup to accompany the clams.

Clams Casino

OPEN 3 dozen cherrystone clams. Loosen the clams and in the bottom of each shell place a nugget of anchovy butter, made by creaming 3 tablespoons butter with 1/2 teaspoon anchovy paste. Place the clams over the anchovy butter and set the shells firmly on a layer of rock salt in a shallow baking pan. Top each clam with a pinch each of finely chopped green pepper and canned pimiento. Cover with a piece of raw bacon the size of the clam. Broil 3 inches

247

JAN MITCHELL

Lüchow's German Cookbook,

1952

German food has long played a major role in American cooking. In the nineteenth century the largest restaurants were German beer halls that served as many as four thousand people at a time. Americans drank copious amounts of beer, produced in the German style. Think: Pabst, Budweiser, Schlitz, Miller. New York, Chicago, Milwaukee, Cincinnati, and many other cities had large German populations with German-language newspapers and publishers. Pennsylvania Dutch cooking, long a favorite among American eaters, celebrated its German roots. This all changed with World War I. Fear of Germans (including Poles, Swedes, and others with "German" accents) rose to horrific heights after the United States entered into the war, in 1917. Many Germans changed their names, anglicizing them. Streets in Chicago, New Orleans, and elsewhere were retitled to remove their German names. Hamburgers were called "liberty sandwiches" and dachshunds, always a popular American pooch, became "liberty pups." Anti-German sentiment reached its apex in the April 4, 1918, lynching of Robert Prager, a German immigrant who worked in the coal mines in Collinsville, Illinois. Suddenly German food was verboten. It passed out of the eating habits of many Americans, never to return.

In New York City, however, there was one legendary establishment that reintroduced the delicacies of German cuisine to Americans following World War II—Lüchow's. August Lüchow emigrated from Hanover, Germany, arriving in New York in 1879. In 1882 he opened a massive restaurant and beer hall at 110–112 Fourteenth Street in the heart of what was then New York's theater district. Lüchow's stood out for its elegance in Gay Nineties New York, attracting many stars and important socialites. It weathered both world wars, and found a new clientele after World War II. As the 1950s and 1960s wore on, the German population of New York fled to the suburbs. Lüchow's closed in 1982 after one hundred years in business.

NOTABLE RECIPES: Barley Soup with Giblets (page 353) • **Breaded Veal Cutlet** (page 552) • **Cold Sauerbraten à la Mode in Aspic** (page 545) • **Goulash Spätzle** (page 451) • **Hot Potato Salad with Bacon** (page 367) • **Pork and Veal Sausage** (page 556)

WILLIAM GRIMES *on* LÜCHOW'S

It's easy to forget that New York was once a profoundly German city. In the middle of the nineteenth century, political unrest and instability drove thousands of Germans to seek a better life in the United States. Manhattan was home to 200,000 Germans by 1860, a number that doubled by 1880, when only Vienna and Berlin had larger German-speaking populations.

Until World War I, German culture and the cuisine of Germany and the Austro-Hungarian empire enjoyed enormous prestige in New York. German poets, philosophers, singers, musicians, conductors, and scientists enjoyed celebrity status. German taverns, beer halls, delicatessens, and restaurants, most of them concentrated in the streets along lower Second Avenue and the Bowery, known as Kleindeutschland, drew crowds of appreciative diners. Any list of the city's top restaurants included establishments like Janssen's Hofbrau, Pabst's Grand Circle, Little Hungary, Fleischmann's Vienna Model Bakery, and, towering over the culinary landscape, Lüchow's, the inspiration for Lüchow's German Cookbook, *published in 1952.*

By the 1950s, of course, Lüchow's was already an elder statesman among restaurants. It had begun in the nineteenth century as a humble tavern on Fourteenth Street, operated by the Baron von Mehlbach, and it sat in prime cultural territory. Fourteenth Street was the heart of Manhattan's musical life, with the Academy of Music and Steinway Hall attracting a constant flow of the world's leading singers, virtuosos, composers, and conductors.

In 1879 Mehlbach made a fateful hiring decision when he took on a waiter from Hanover named August Lüchow. Within three years, backed by a loan from William Steinway, the piano magnate, Lüchow bought out his boss and embarked on a twenty-year expansion that would transform the modest tavern into a sprawling temple of German cuisine, its warren of dining rooms including the Hunt Room, with twenty-one stuffed stag heads on the walls, and the Nibelungen Room, decorated with murals from Wagner's Ring Cycle. A small orchestra organized by the composer Victor Herbert played light classics. Around the turn of the century, with renovations complete, Lüchow's entered its glory years. "For a musician not to be seen at Lüchow's argued that he was unknown in the social world of tone," the eminent critic James Hunecker wrote.

The menu was surprisingly varied. Lüchow's German Cookbook *deliberately emphasized the Germanness of the restaurant, highlighting dishes like medallion of goose liver à la Lüchow. These were indeed the heart and soul of the restaurant, but like most large-scale establishments of the era, Lüchow's aimed to please just about everyone. Diners could order oysters in multiple varieties, boiled New England dinner, baked blue fish à l'Italienne, braised oxtail bourgeoise, or croustade of sweetbreads with truffles.*

Obviously, there were diners who treated Lüchow's as a fancy continental restaurant. But the avid patrons, and there were many, went straight to the purely German offerings: roast suckling pig with sauerkraut, sauerbraten and potatoes, quail smothered in weinkraut, Tyrolean ragout, beef brisket with horseradish sauce, and, at the bargain end of the menu, pig's knuckle with sauerkraut and potatoes.

The liquid accompaniment was beer. August Lüchow made one of his most profitable decisions when he secured the American rights to sell Würzburger, one of Germany's finest brands, and Pilsner from Bohemia. The beer flowed in torrents, and so did the profits. The Würzburger connection even inspired a popular song in 1902, "Down Where the Würzburger Flows," which became a kind of anthem for the restaurant. "Take me down, down, down where the Wurzburger flows, flows, flows," the rousing chorus began. "It goes down, down, down but nobody knows where it goes."

The good times came to a halt with the outbreak of World War I, and when American doughboys began sailing for France in 1917 anything remotely German quickly lost its appeal. In 1915 in a panicked communiqué to the press, Lüchow and his fellow restaurateur August Janssen reassured diners that no one, despite press reports, had cheered the sinking of the Lusitania *at either of their restaurants. Two years later, Lüchow removed the umlaut in response to anti-German sentiment. Unfortunately, the name now looked Chinese to many diners, who gave the waiters fits when they sat down and ordered chow mein and fried rice.*

Prohibition dealt a severe blow to the restaurant's fortunes. In 1923 August Lüchow died.

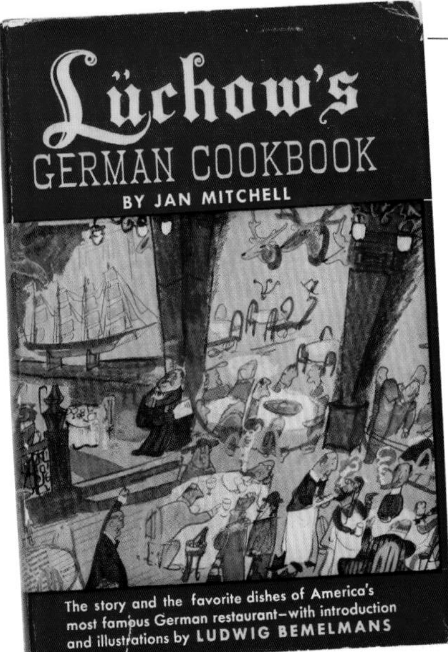

By this time, Kleindeutschland was but a distant memory. Germans prospered and dispersed, their streets occupied by new immigrants from Eastern Europe. The city's musical life moved uptown, away from Fourteenth Street. And a new German area coalesced uptown, along Eighty-Sixth Street, in a neighborhood known as Yorkville. The pastry shops and restaurants that ran up and down the street struck a decidedly more populist tone than majestic Lüchow's. The cuisine was strictly sausages, sauerkraut, and beer, served to the exuberant accompaniment of oompah music. Lüchow's, adrift but physically imposing, sailed on, a shadow of its former self, its labyrinthine halls haunted by Wagnernian spirits and the now fading strains of "Down Where the Würzburger Flows."

Determined to arrest the decline, a plucky restaurant owner named Jan Mitchell entered the picture in 1950. He was a somewhat inscrutable figure. Born in Latvia, he liked to imply that he had grown up on vast baronial estates owned by his family in Sweden and Finland, and had studied law at the University of Stockholm. It is hard not to suspect some myth-making here. In 1939 he arrived in New York and found a series of jobs waiting tables at the city's best hotels before buying the Olmsted Restaurant in Washington in 1942, with $25,000 in borrowed money.

But he nourished an infatuation with Lüchow's, where he had dined during his earliest days in New York, and, after protracted and strenuous negotiations with the founder's heirs, he bought the restaurant, pledging to remain faithful to its German roots.

And so he was. In truth, Mitchell was attempting the most difficult task in the restaurant business: restoring the reputation of a faded legend. But he was passionate, energetic, and determined, and, against the odds, he really did conceive a second act for Lüchow's, this time as a gaudy flagship of Wagnerian kitsch.

1.

APPETIZERS

Old hands who have been eating at Lüchow's for more years than they can readily remember have developed a capacity which does not shrink at the generosity of the restaurant's appetizers. The uninitiated, however, thinking to nibble at a modest beginning to a hearty meal are likely to find themselves overwhelmed by a small mountain of herring salad, a substantial plate of head cheese covered with a special vinaigrette sauce, or some other dish which dampens their enthusiasm for whatever follows. Be warned, then. Unless you are a trencherman of proved capacity, deal humbly with the appetizers.

What is true of the appetizers is true also of the entire menu. Mr. Seute's philosophy is that old customers should have the best and new ones the same, consequently everyone gets the ample portions which have filled and satisfied Lüchow's patrons for seventy years.

It takes twenty-eight cooks, masters from Austria and South Germany, some of them in Lüchow service for thirty-five years, to produce the Lüchow cuisine. None of these cooks would dream of modifying or changing the traditional European recipes which are as much a part of the restaurant as Mr. Seute himself.

German cuisine and culture no longer played the role they once did in the city's life. Nothing was going to change that. But Mitchell did his utmost to bring excitement back to the old restaurant. He reinstated the popular weekly events, like the venison festival, the bock beer festival, and the May wine festival. Diners sitting down for the venison festival were issued feathered Tyrolean caps. He brought back old menu favorites like roast goose and pig's knuckles schlemmerschnitte.

Shrewdly, Mitchell put the umlaut back over the u. And he signaled the restaurant's comeback with a cookbook dedicated to its most venerable German dishes. Illustrated by Ludwig Bemelmans, the cookbook celebrated German cooking without apology.

Somehow, Manhattan-style clam chowder found its way into the book, but by and large Mitchell wanted Lüchow's German Cookbook to live up to its name. It gladdens the heart to see recipes for liver biscuits, Berlin-style eel soup, boiled carp with horseradish sauce, Wiener backhändl, Hamburg-style goose in wine aspic, boiled beef Hanover style, hasenpfeffer, and one of the great set-piece dishes, beef roulade August Lüchow.

With pizzazz and marketing flair, Mitchell kept the great Lüchow's afloat for another twenty years, before selling it in 1971 to a restaurant corporation that seemed to have no idea what to do with the place. It limped along, increasingly anachronistic on a street entering into steep decline, until the early 1980s, when a midtown branch replaced it. The new venture failed, and the abandoned Lüchow's, denied landmark status, became a den for squatters. In 1994 a fire gutted the building. The site is now occupied by one of New York University's student residences.

In New York, restaurants come and go. Very quickly. But in a more deliberate, less fickle age, when customers pledged their loyalty decade after decade, restaurants like Lüchow's could remain a commanding presence seemingly forever. They added continuity and the pleasure of old memories to the city's dining culture. Lüchow's added something else, a Teutonic flavor that once reminded New Yorkers that their city, once upon a time, had roots that extended to the land of Grimm, Heine, Schopenhauer, and Brahms.

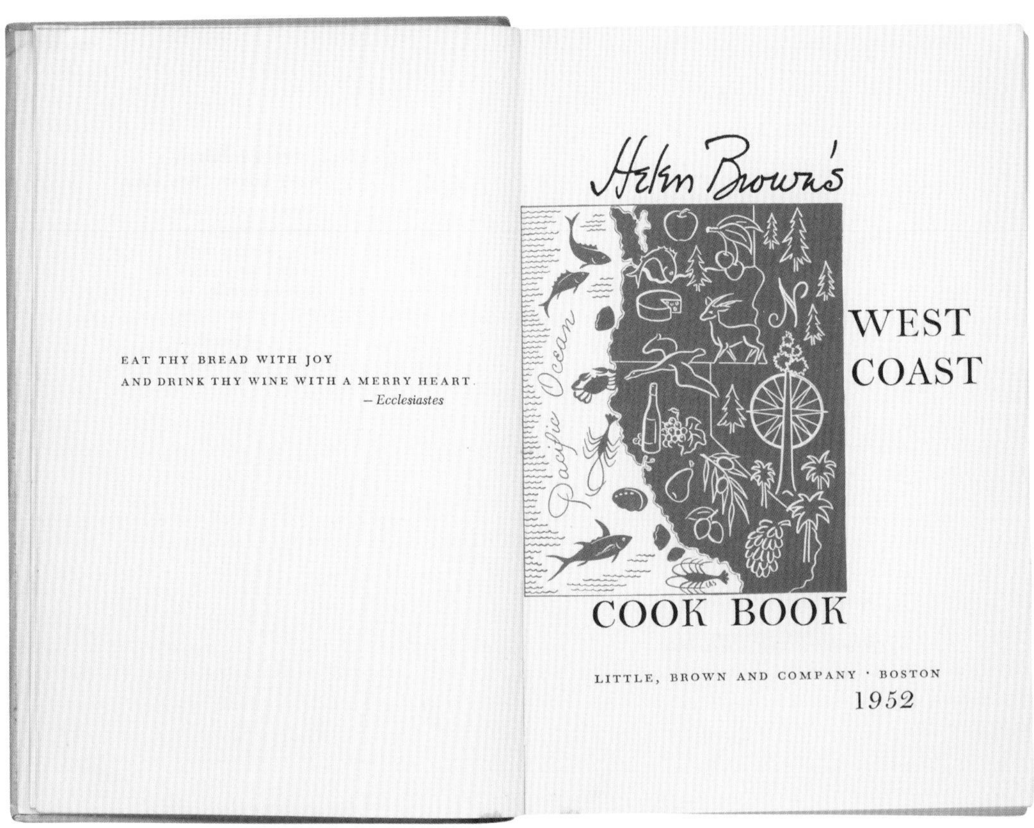

EAT THY BREAD WITH JOY
AND DRINK THY WINE WITH A MERRY HEART.
– Ecclesiastes
Helen Brown's
WEST
COAST
COOK BOOK
Pacific Ocean
LITTLE, BROWN AND COMPANY · BOSTON
1952

HELEN EVANS BROWN

Helen Brown's West Coast Cook Book, 1952

Helen Evans Brown, a close confidant of James Beard, became known in food circles during the 1930s for the parties and dinners she threw at her Pasadena home. Her husband, who was a rare book dealer, served as her secretary, typist, and librarian, helping her build a very large and important collection of books on food. Brown wrote for *Sunset* magazine and had an abiding love of the foods from the Pacific coast, with their mix of Chinese, Mexican, and other cuisines. She also appreciated the wonderful produce of California and seafood of the Pacific Northwest. She set about collecting and documenting these distinctly American cuisines.

Her book stands alongside *The Joy of Cooking* and James Beard's later tome *American Cooking* as one of the monuments to a thoroughly American style of food. So important was Brown on the West Coast that the New York food mafia referred to her simply as "the West Coast food establishment." Alfred A. Knopf reprinted this landmark book in 1991, introducing it to a new generation of American cooks.

NOTABLE RECIPES: A California Pioneer Apple Pie (page 597) • **Figs and Bacon** (page 412) • **Fried Cream** (page 643) • **Guacamole** (page 320) • Lumber Camp Doughnuts • **Monte Cristo and Monte Carlo Sandwiches** (page 373) • **Sourdough Biscuits** (page 591)

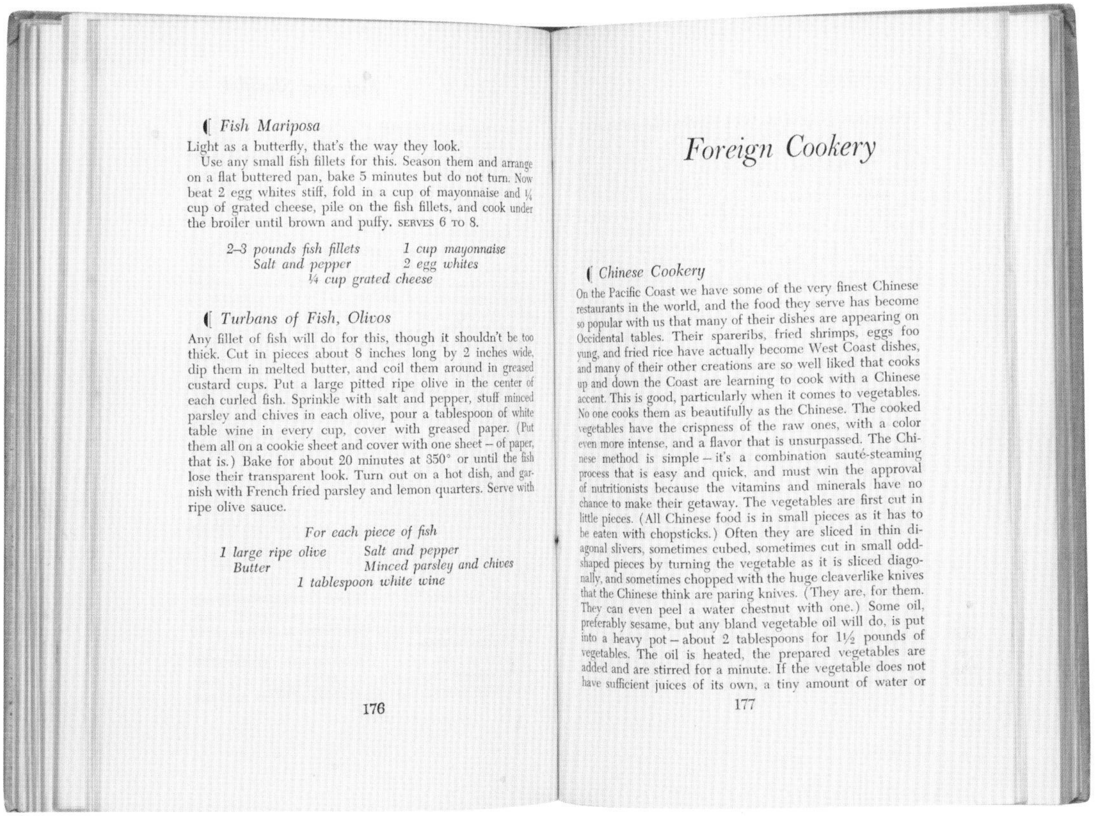

Fish Mariposa

Light as a butterfly, that's the way they look.

Use any small fish fillets for this. Season them and arrange on a flat buttered pan, bake 5 minutes but do not turn. Now beat 2 egg whites stiff, fold in a cup of mayonnaise and ¼ cup of grated cheese, pile on the fish fillets, and cook under the broiler until brown and puffy. SERVES 6 TO 8.

2–3 pounds fish fillets	*1 cup mayonnaise*
Salt and pepper	*2 egg whites*

¼ cup grated cheese

Turbans of Fish, Olivos

Any fillet of fish will do for this, though it shouldn't be too thick. Cut in pieces about 8 inches long by 2 inches wide, dip them in melted butter, and coil them around in greased custard cups. Put a large pitted ripe olive in the center of each curled fish. Sprinkle with salt and pepper, stuff minced parsley and chives in each olive, pour a tablespoon of white table wine in every cup, cover with greased paper. (Put them all on a cookie sheet and cover with one sheet – of paper, that is.) Bake for about 20 minutes at 350° or until the fish lose their transparent look. Turn out on a hot dish, and garnish with French fried parsley and lemon quarters. Serve with ripe olive sauce.

For each piece of fish

1 large ripe olive	*Salt and pepper*
Butter	*Minced parsley and chives*

1 tablespoon white wine

176

Foreign Cookery

Chinese Cookery

On the Pacific Coast we have some of the very finest Chinese restaurants in the world, and the food they serve has become so popular with us that many of their dishes are appearing on Occidental tables. Their spareribs, fried shrimps, eggs foo yung, and fried rice have actually become West Coast dishes, and many of their other creations are so well liked that cooks up and down the Coast are learning to cook with a Chinese accent. This is good, particularly when it comes to vegetables. No one cooks them as beautifully as the Chinese. The cooked vegetables have the crispness of the raw ones, with a color even more intense, and a flavor that is unsurpassed. The Chinese method is simple – it's a combination sauté-steaming process that is easy and quick, and must win the approval of nutritionists because the vitamins and minerals have no chance to make their getaway. The vegetables are first cut in little pieces. (All Chinese food is in small pieces as it has to be eaten with chopsticks.) Often they are sliced in thin diagonal slivers, sometimes cubed, sometimes cut in small odd-shaped pieces by turning the vegetable as it is sliced diagonally, and sometimes chopped with the huge cleaverlike knives that the Chinese think are paring knives. (They are, for them. They can even peel a water chestnut with one.) Some oil, preferably sesame, but any bland vegetable oil will do, is put into a heavy pot – about 2 tablespoons for 1½ pounds of vegetables. The oil is heated, the prepared vegetables are added and are stirred for a minute. If the vegetable does not have sufficient juices of its own, a tiny amount of water or

177

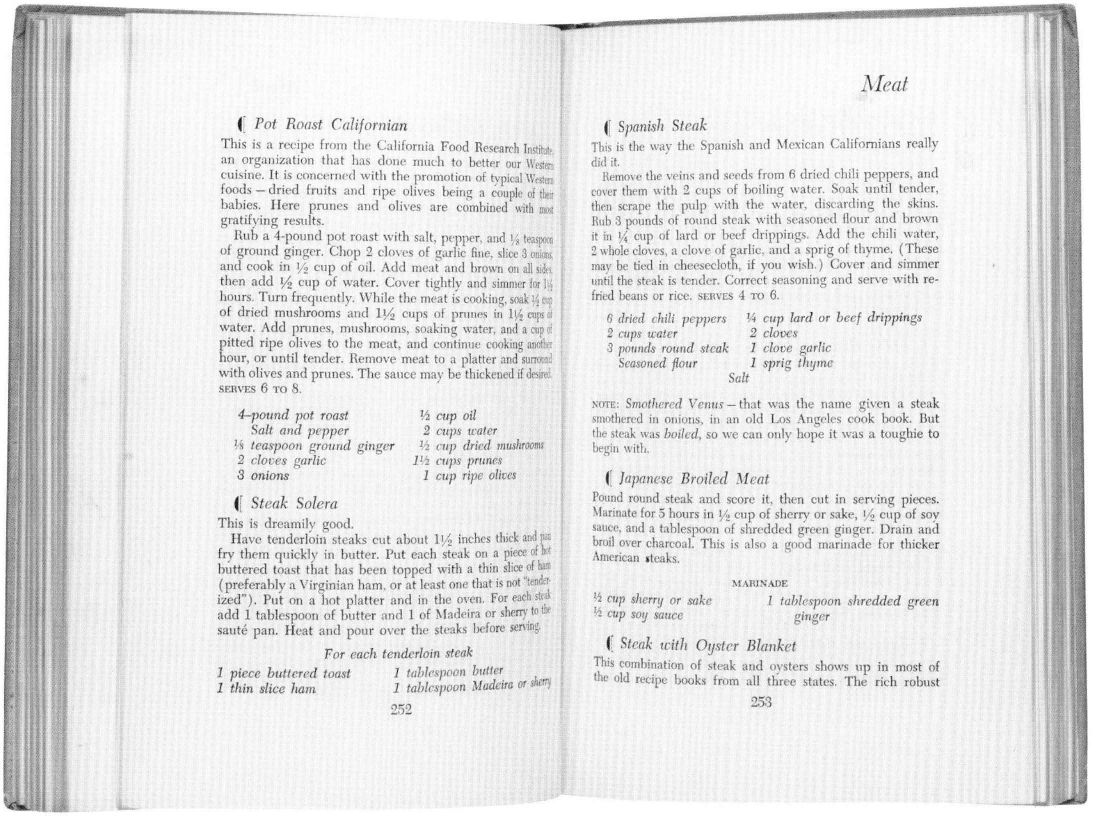

Pot Roast Californian

This is a recipe from the California Food Research Institute, an organization that has done much to better our Western cuisine. It is concerned with the promotion of typical Western foods – dried fruits and ripe olives being a couple of their babies. Here prunes and olives are combined with most gratifying results.

Rub a 4-pound pot roast with salt, pepper, and ⅛ teaspoon of ground ginger. Chop 2 cloves of garlic fine, slice 3 onions, and cook in ½ cup of oil. Add meat and brown on all sides, then add ½ cup of water. Cover tightly and simmer for 1½ hours. Turn frequently. While the meat is cooking, soak ½ cup of dried mushrooms and 1½ cups of prunes in 1½ cups of water. Add prunes, mushrooms, soaking water, and a cup of pitted ripe olives to the meat, and continue cooking another hour, or until tender. Remove meat to a platter and surround with olives and prunes. The sauce may be thickened if desired. SERVES 6 TO 8.

4-pound pot roast	*½ cup oil*
Salt and pepper	*2 cups water*
⅛ teaspoon ground ginger	*½ cup dried mushrooms*
2 cloves garlic	*1½ cups prunes*
3 onions	*1 cup ripe olives*

Steak Solera

This is dreamily good.

Have tenderloin steaks cut about 1½ inches thick and pan fry them quickly in butter. Put each steak on a piece of hot buttered toast that has been topped with a thin slice of ham (preferably a Virginian ham, or at least one that is not "tenderized"). Put on a hot platter and in the oven. For each steak add 1 tablespoon of butter and 1 of Madeira or sherry to the sauté pan. Heat and pour over the steaks before serving.

For each tenderloin steak

1 piece buttered toast	*1 tablespoon butter*
1 thin slice ham	*1 tablespoon Madeira or sherry*

252

Meat

Spanish Steak

This is the way the Spanish and Mexican Californians really did it.

Remove the veins and seeds from 6 dried chili peppers, and cover them with 2 cups of boiling water. Soak until tender, then scrape the pulp with the water, discarding the skins. Rub 3 pounds of round steak with seasoned flour and brown it in ¼ cup of lard or beef drippings. Add the chili water, 2 whole cloves, a clove of garlic, and a sprig of thyme. (These may be tied in cheesecloth, if you wish.) Cover and simmer until the steak is tender. Correct seasoning and serve with refried beans or rice. SERVES 4 TO 6.

6 dried chili peppers	*¼ cup lard or beef drippings*
2 cups water	*2 cloves*
3 pounds round steak	*1 clove garlic*
Seasoned flour	*1 sprig thyme*

Salt

NOTE: *Smothered Venus* – that was the name given a steak smothered in onions, in an old Los Angeles cook book. But the steak was *boiled*, so we can only hope it was a toughie to begin with.

Japanese Broiled Meat

Pound round steak and score it, then cut in serving pieces. Marinate for 5 hours in ½ cup of sherry or sake, ½ cup of soy sauce, and a tablespoon of shredded green ginger. Drain and broil over charcoal. This is also a good marinade for thicker American steaks.

MARINADE

½ cup sherry or sake	*1 tablespoon shredded green ginger*
½ cup soy sauce	

Steak with Oyster Blanket

This combination of steak and oysters shows up in most of the old recipe books from all three states. The rich robust

253

ALICE B. TOKLAS

The Alice B. Toklas Cook Book, 1954

Gertrude Stein and Alice B. Toklas were probably the most important couple of the modernist period. They met in 1907, on Toklas's first day in Paris. In 1910 Toklas moved in with Stein and her brother—and partner in collecting contemporary art—Leo. Stein and Toklas's home at 27 Rue de Fleurus became the major gathering place for the modernist avant-garde in Paris from about 1915 to 1945. Hemingway, Picasso, Braque, Gris, Apollinaire, Sherwood Anderson, Thornton Wilder, and a host of other artists and writers came for dinner or to the salons at the Stein/Toklas home.

When Stein died in 1946 of stomach cancer, Toklas was crushed. But in her own, strong-willed way, she continued to support Gertrude's friends and to find a new life for herself. Around 1950 she wrote to Sam Steward, the novelist and tattoo artist who had forged a close bond with both Stein and Toklas, encouraging him to keep writing at a time when he was not feeling sanguine about his literary efforts—something Gertrude had always encouraged him to do. Toklas, too, had taken her own advice and was working on a cookbook/memoir. Her dinners were famous among the expatriates in Paris, for she was an excellent French cook. (Stein recounts the dinners and the salons in her book *The Autobiography of Alice B. Toklas*.)

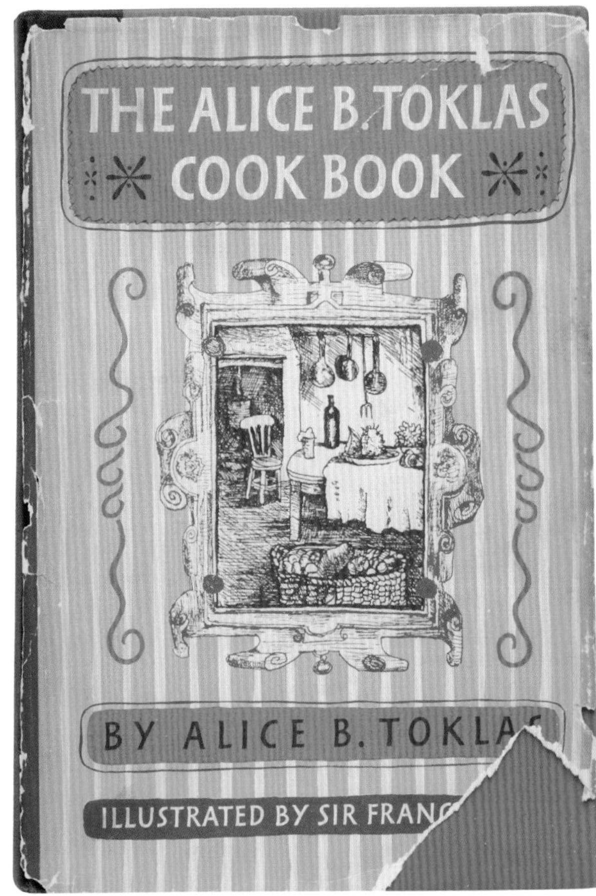

Toklas's cookbook, which included her recipes as well as those of her friends, was an instant underground success. Each later generation of intellectuals who fantasize about the bohemian culture of modernist Paris discover Toklas's book for themselves. (Of course, it is known for the infamous "hash brownie" recipe, which wasn't by Toklas, in fact, but by the artist Brion Gysin. It appeared in the first edition, published in England, and Toklas was furious. It was removed from the first American edition.) Toklas's wonderful cookbook is a testament to the central role food played in her and Stein's relationship and in the creation of the modern avant-garde.

NOTABLE RECIPES: Cock in Wine • **Gazpacho of Malaga** (page 335) • **Gigot de la Clinique** (page 539) • **Green Peas à la Goodwife** (page 404) • **Haschich Fudge** (page 645) • Hearts of Artichokes à la Isman Bavaldy • **Oeufs Francis Picabia** (page 467)• **Scheherezade's Melon** (page 641) • Sole de la Maison

brussels sprouts and cauliflower. There were potatoes, to be sure, and apple sauce, which was considered a vegetable.

At Cernay we were helped in our distribution by little *Abbé* Hick, who had returned after the Armistice to find his church bombed, and the presbytery with the exception of one room in ruins. He asked us however to lunch with him the next time we were distributing in his neighbourhood. He met us at the door of his room and said, Welcome, come into the salon and warm yourselves. Excuse me while I go into the bedroom and wash my hands. He went to the far end of the room past a set dining-room table. Presently he returned and said, Now we will go into the dining-room and have lunch. All this without the least suspicion of the ludicrous. A refugee had cooked the simple but succulent lunch. The *abbé's* mother had sent him some good white wine from Riquewehr where she lived.

On Sundays we frequently lunched with the hospitable Mulhouseens who were gradually returning to the lives they had led before the war. Everything was in the French manner, with great elegance and luxury. They had really kept the manner of living of pre-1870. They had refused everything German. It was the memory of the way our French friends in San Francisco had lived come to life again.

At Monsieur B.'s there was for dessert, to my delight, a

TARTE CHAMBORD

Beat until foamy and thick with a rotary beater 1 cup and 1 tablespoon sugar and 8 eggs, gently stir in 2 cups and 3 tablespoons thrice-sifted flour. Add 1 cup and 1 tablespoon melted unsalted butter. Bake in a deep buttered and floured cake pan in 350° preheated oven for 30 minutes. Take from oven, let stand for 10 minutes, take out of pan, place on grill. When cold, cut horizontally four times, making five layers.

CREAM FOR CAKE

Turn with a wooden spoon in an enamelled saucepan the yolks of 10 eggs and very slowly add 1 ½ cups icing sugar. Turn until thick and pale yellow. Put over lowest flame with 4 tablespoons butter for 2 minutes and as soon as butter is melted, stirring constantly, remove from flame and when the mixture is cold add drop by drop 3 tablespoons cold

hot with chopped parsley and fine chopped spring onion sprinkled on them.

And this way:

STRING BEANS BROWNED IN THE OVEN

Boil in salted water uncovered 4 cups string beans. Do not overcook, but when tender remove from heat and drain thoroughly. Butter a fireproof earthenware dish. Sprinkle generously with grated Swiss cheese. Mix 1 ½ cups *Béchamel* sauce with 2 yolks of eggs. Pour ¼ cup of this on the cheese in the earthenware dish, then the string beans and on them the rest of the sauce. Sprinkle ⅓ cup grated Swiss cheese on the string beans, dot with 3 tablespoons melted butter and put in preheated 450° oven for 15 minutes.

These are very nice ways to cook string beans but they interfere with the poor vegetable's leading a life of its own. As for the cooking of lettuces, with or without sauce, the easiest way to accept this is to consider lettuce as two vegetables, raw lettuce and cooked lettuce. To me cooking lettuces is the sacrifice of the innocents. If cooked they must be, this way is always received with appreciation:

LETTUCE IN RIBBONS WITH CREAM

For 4 cups shredded lettuce put 4 tablespoons butter in a saucepan over medium flame, put the shredded lettuce in the butter and turn with a wooden spoon until all the lettuce is covered with butter. Reduce the heat to low, add ¼ teaspoon salt. Cover and simmer until all the moisture in the lettuce has been absorbed. Add 1 ½ cups thick cream sauce and 1 teaspoon onion juice. Stir well together. Place on a serving dish in a mound, and surround by large triangular *croûtons*.

BRAISED LETTUCE WITH ITALIAN SAUCE

Wash and dry 4 large lettuces having removed the green outer leaves. Put into 4 tablespoons butter melted in a saucepan. Stir, reduce

TRAC
DUCLAIR
CREAM

La France
ROUEN
PARIS
MONTEREAU
ANGERS
BILLIGNAN
LES BAUX
PERPIGNAN

M.F.K. FISHER

The Art of Eating, 1954

"It seems to me that our three basic needs, for food, and security and love, are so mixed and mingled and entwined that we cannot straightly think of one without the others, so it happens that when I write of hunger, I am really writing about love and the hunger for it, and warmth and the love of it and the hunger for it."

So writes M.F.K. Fisher (1908–1992) in her 1943 book *The Gastronomical Me*. This Stein-like passage gives a glimpse into the writing style of "America's greatest writer," as W. H. Auden called her. It is commonplace to say that Fisher's career suffered because she chose to write about the pleasures of the table. Literary critics, mostly men, rejected her because of her subject matter. Just as damning, however, were the women critics who tried to say that Fisher used food as merely metaphors for larger, more important issues. Clearly, Fisher herself saw food as a perfectly acceptable topic for serious writing—a stance that seems traditionally to elude many of her critics.

Fisher first developed her love for food while she and her first husband, Alfred Fisher, spent time in Dijon during the 1930s. Alfred had a teaching appointment at the University of Dijon, and Mary Frances (née Kennedy) Fisher threw herself into cooking and writing about food. Her first published work was a combination cookbook/story book, *Serve It Forth* (1937). She went on to write fifteen books of essays and reminiscences and to do a superb English translation of Brillat-Savarin's *Physiology of Taste*, one of the most important books on food and eating.

The Art of Eating marked the high point of her early career, bringing together all her previous books about food and her times in France during the 1930s and 1940s. Included in this volume is her famous essay "How to Cook a Wolf," which she wrote during World War II when rationing and food shortages made preparing foods difficult for many Americans. Fisher spent the last years of her life on a farm in California. When she died on June 22, 1992, Ruth Reichl wrote in the *Los Angeles Times Book Review*: "Her genius has been her absolute insistence that life's small moments are the important ones."

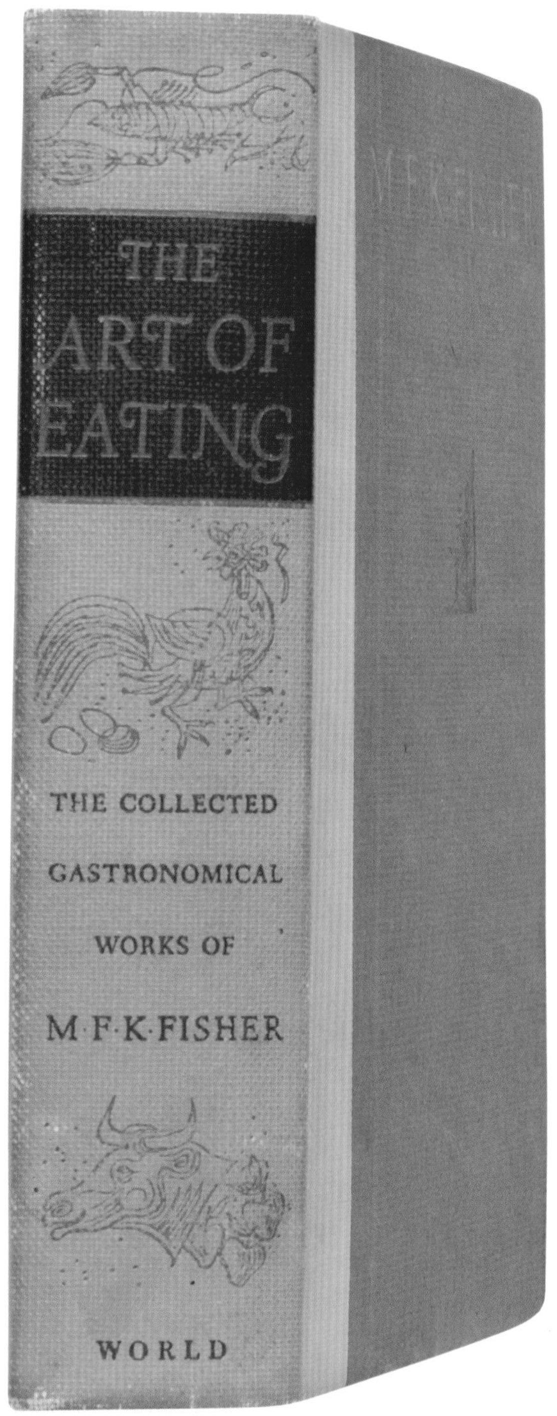

NOTABLE RECIPES: Cold Buttermilk Soup (page 334) • Eggs in Hell • Milk Toast • **Petit Pois à la Française** (page 404) • Raspberries Romanoff • **Sausage Pie** (page 497) • Scrambled Eggs • **Tomato Soup Cake** (page 614) • Warmed Orange on a Radiator

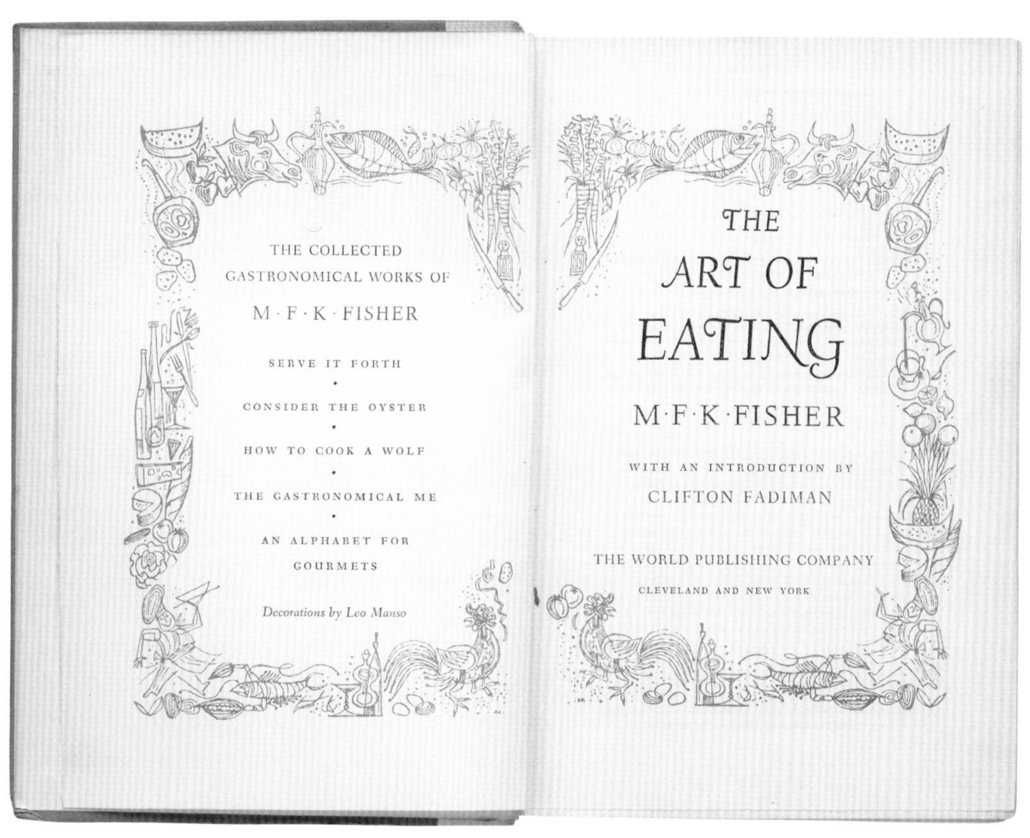

THE COLLECTED
GASTRONOMICAL WORKS OF
M·F·K·FISHER

SERVE IT FORTH
•
CONSIDER THE OYSTER
•
HOW TO COOK A WOLF
•
THE GASTRONOMICAL ME
•
AN ALPHABET FOR
GOURMETS

Decorations by Leo Manso

THE
ART OF
EATING

M·F·K·FISHER

WITH AN INTRODUCTION BY
CLIFTON FADIMAN

THE WORLD PUBLISHING COMPANY
CLEVELAND AND NEW YORK

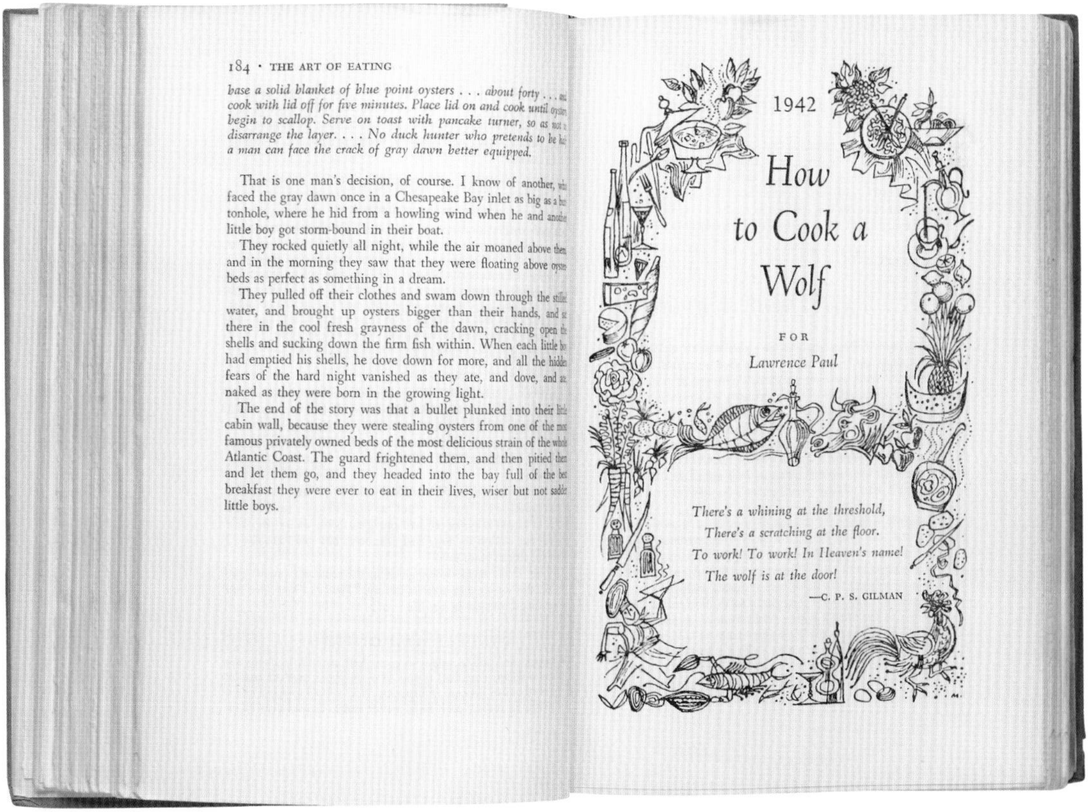

184 · THE ART OF EATING

base a solid blanket of blue point oysters . . . about forty . . . and cook with lid off for five minutes. Place lid on and cook until oysters begin to scallop. Serve on toast with pancake turner, so as not to disarrange the layer. . . . No duck hunter who pretends to be [illegible] a man can face the crack of gray dawn better equipped.

That is one man's decision, of course. I know of another, who faced the gray dawn once in a Chesapeake Bay inlet as big as a buttonhole, where he hid from a howling wind when he and another little boy got storm-bound in their boat.

They rocked quietly all night, while the air moaned above them, and in the morning they saw that they were floating above oyster beds as perfect as something in a dream.

They pulled off their clothes and swam down through the stiller water, and brought up oysters bigger than their hands, and sat there in the cool fresh grayness of the dawn, cracking open the shells and sucking down the firm fish within. When each little boy had emptied his shells, he dove down for more, and all the hidden fears of the hard night vanished as they ate, and dove, and as naked as they were born in the growing light.

The end of the story was that a bullet plunked into their little cabin wall, because they were stealing oysters from one of the most famous privately owned beds of the most delicious strain of the whole Atlantic Coast. The guard frightened them, and then pitied them and let them go, and they headed into the bay full of the best breakfast they were ever to eat in their lives, wiser but not sadder little boys.

1942

How to Cook a Wolf

FOR

Lawrence Paul

There's a whining at the threshold,
There's a scratching at the floor.
To work! To work! In Heaven's name!
The wolf is at the door!

—C. P. S. GILMAN

CAROL TRUAX

Ladies' Home Journal Cookbook, 1960

During the late nineteenth century, America was littered with magazines of all types, appealing to the rising numbers of literate, middle-class readers. One of the most important targets for publishers was the average housewife. Sensing this eager market, Cyrus H. K. Curtis, one of the major magazine publishers, and his wife, Louisa Knapp Curtis, began to publish a one-page supplement to the magazine *Tribune and Farmer*, which they called *Women at Home*, in 1883. Mrs. Curtis wrote the content for the early issues. Within a year, the supplement became its own magazine under the titles *Ladies' Home Journal* and *Practical Housekeeper.*

Within ten years, the magazine became the best of its kind, with a circulation of more than one million copies. While *Ladies' Home Journal* had competitors, such as *Better Homes and Gardens*, *Family Circle*, *Good Housekeeping*, *McCall's*, *Redbook*, and *Woman's Day*, the *Journal* enjoyed the strongest reputation for writing about food. In fact, Sarah Tyson Rorer, the famous cooking school maven, was the first food editor at the *Journal,* from 1897 to 1911. In time, most of the magazines published cookbooks and series about food. The *Ladies' Home Journal Cook Book* stands out as the best of the women's magazine–based books.

NOTABLE RECIPES: Apricot Nut Bread (page 570) • **Artichoke Hearts in Lemon Butter** (page 404) • **Bran Muffins** (page 587) • Blueberry Oat Bran Muffins • **Burnt-Sugar Cake** (page 631) • **Cream Puffs** (page 640) • Molasses Custard • Rum Butterscotch Sauce

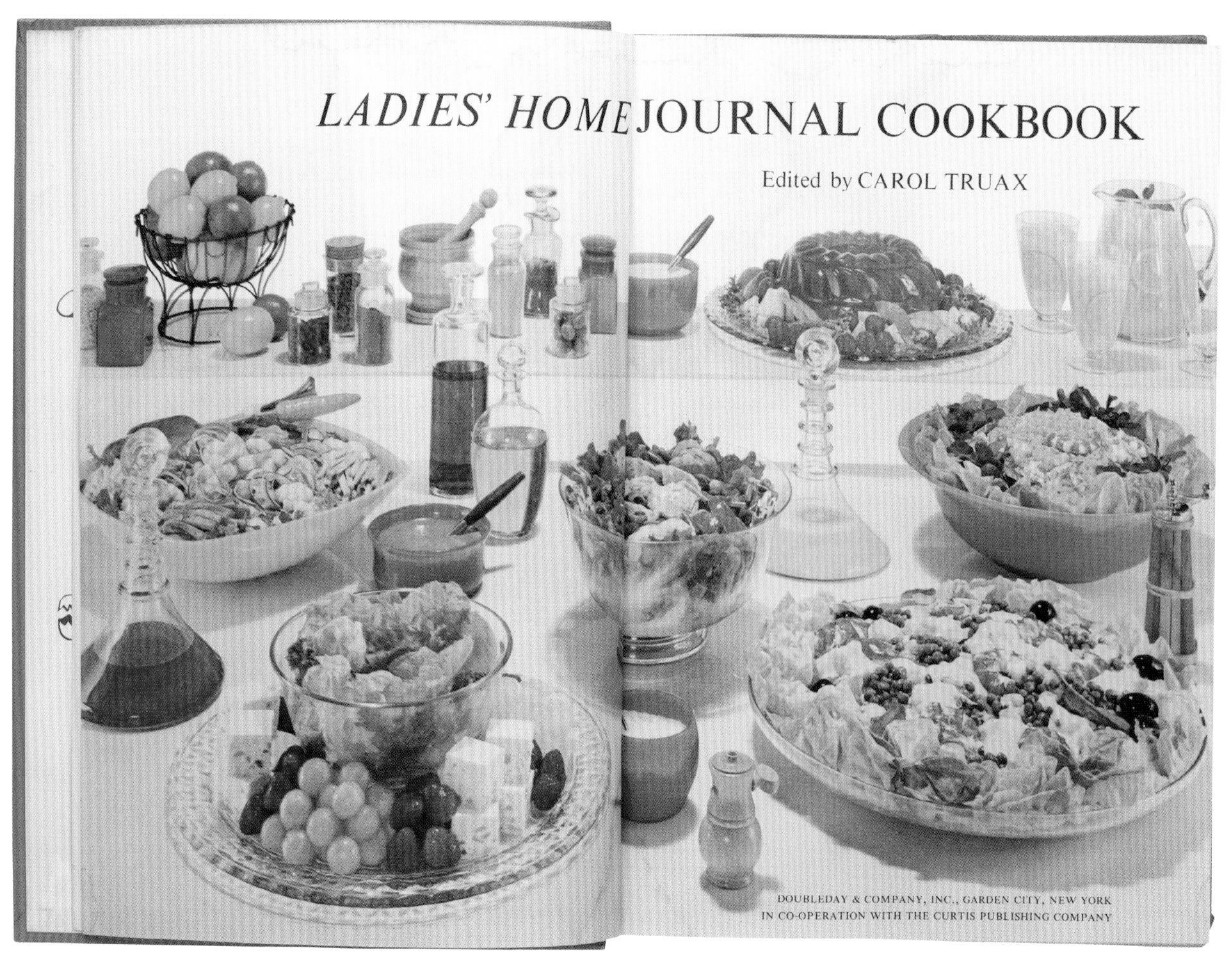

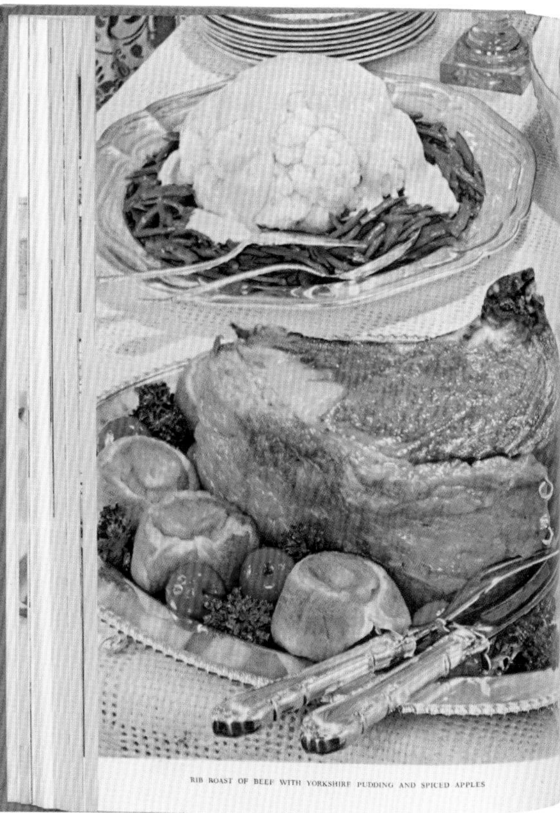

RIB ROAST OF BEEF WITH YORKSHIRE PUDDING AND SPICED APPLES

BITOCHKI

1 pound ground beef
Stale bread
1 teaspoon salt
Dash pepper
2 tablespoons chopped onion
2 tablespoons sour cream
1 egg
Fine dry bread crumbs
Shortening

Sauce

1 tablespoon butter
½ cup water
1 cup sour cream or 1 (10½ oz.) can cream of mushroom soup
½ cup milk

Cut the crusts off the bread and break into pieces. You will need 2 cups. Soak the bread in water and squeeze almost dry. Mix the beef and bread and add salt, pepper, onion, sour cream and an egg if you wish. Blend well. Make little balls and roll in bread crumbs. Sauté in hot shortening, and as they are ready, remove to another pan. *Sauce.* Add the butter and water to the drippings. Bring to a boil. Add the sour cream or mushroom soup and milk. Don't let the sour cream boil. Blend thoroughly and pour over meat and let it stand. The flavor improves with standing. Warm gently to serve. Good with noodles, elbow macaroni or rice. Four servings.

BROILED BEEF LOAF

1½ pounds ground beef
2 teaspoons salt
¼ teaspoon pepper
⅛ pound sliced Cheddar cheese
2 tablespoons chopped scallion
2 tablespoons catchup
¼ teaspoon orégano
5 slices bacon

Season the beef with 1½ teaspoons salt and ⅛ teaspoon pepper. Divide the hamburger into 2 portions. Flatten each out on waxed paper, shaping into 2 rectangular pieces about ½ inch thick. Lay the sliced Cheddar cheese on one of the portions. Sprinkle with the scallion, catchup and orégano. Season lightly with salt and pepper. Turn the other piece of hamburger over onto the seasoned layer. Press edges of beef together. Lift onto the broiler pan with 2 wide spatulas. Broil about 5 minutes on each side. Lay bacon slices on top of beef after turning. Bacon will crisp in that time. Four to six servings.

FRANKFURTERS WITH TOMATOES

6 frankfurters sliced ½ inch thick
4 onions sliced thin
2 green peppers diced fine
1 tablespoon salad oil
2 (1 lb. 4 oz.) cans tomatoes
1 (6 oz.) can tomato paste
4 potatoes diced
1 teaspoon salt
1 teaspoon orégano
½ teaspoon monosodium glutamate
Dash pepper

Sauté the onions and green peppers in the salad oil in a large skillet. When the onions are golden, add the tomatoes and tomato paste. Put in the potatoes and season with salt, orégano, monosodium glutamate and pepper. Cover and simmer gently for 15 minutes; then add the sliced frankfurters. Simmer 15 minutes more. Season to taste. Six servings.

FRANKFURTERS WITH BAKED BEANS

6 frankfurters
1 medium onion minced fine
3 tablespoons butter
2 (1 lb.) cans baked beans
3 tablespoons molasses
Juice ½ lemon
½ teaspoon dry mustard
¼ teaspoon nutmeg
Pinch baking soda
½ lemon cut into thin slices

Sauté the onion in 2 tablespoons butter until tender but not brown. In a shallow round or rectangular casserole (about 10 inches in diameter and 2 inches deep) combine the beans, molasses, lemon juice, sautéed onion, mustard, nutmeg and baking soda. Score the frankfurters on one side crisscross fashion. Arrange on top of the beans with the lemon slices. Bake in moderately hot oven, 375°, for an hour, brushing the franks from time to time with a little melted butter. Four servings.

COOKTIP

Ground round steak, chuck or flank are all satisfactory for hamburgers. The flavor varies as does the price. Buy it lean. If selecting packaged beef, be sure it has a good fresh color.

HAM BAKED WITH MAPLE SIRUP

1 (12–14 lb.) ready-to-eat ham
Cloves
1½ cups maple sirup
½ cup cider
Candied cherries (optional)

Trim off most of the skin, leaving skin on the shank end. Score the fat in a crisscross pattern and stud with cloves. Brush the ham with maple sirup. Put it in a large open roasting pan and bake in moderately slow oven, 325°, allowing 20 minutes per pound. Pour around the ham a mixture of 1 cup maple sirup and the cider. Baste every 10 minutes with this mixture. When the ham is baked, decorate it with the cherries if you wish. Twelve servings.

BAKED HAM APRICOTS PIQUANTE

1 ready-to-eat ham
1 (1 lb. 13 oz.) can whole apricots
1½ cups light brown sugar
Cloves
Candied cherries cut in halves (optional)

Trim the rind and a little fat off the ham. Score the top and stud with cloves and, if you wish, decorate with cherries. Cook the apricot sirup, brown sugar and ¼ cup ham fat to a thin sirup to use for basting the ham. Place ham in a roasting pan in a moderate oven, 350°, for about an hour, basting frequently with apricot sirup to glaze and brown the ham. If you wish, apricots can be glazed with brown sugar and butter and served with the ham. Twelve servings.

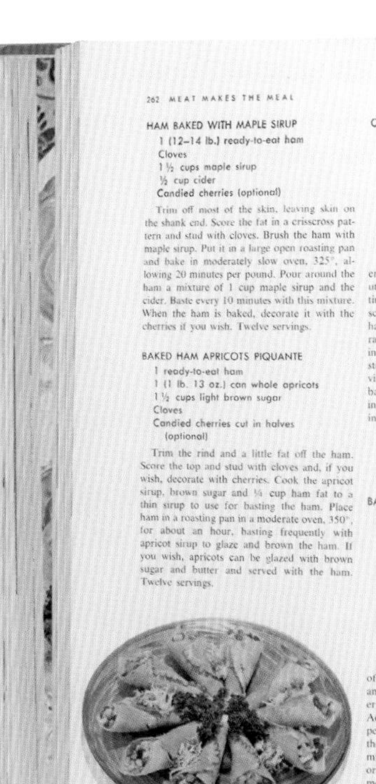

CUMBERLAND BAKED HAM

Shank half ready-to-eat ham (6–8 pounds)
Cloves
½ cup raisins
½ cup water

Sauce

1 (12 oz.) jar currant jelly
¼ cup vinegar
1 tablespoon prepared mustard

Place ham in a roasting pan in a moderately slow oven, 325°, and bake 14 minutes per pound. Toward the end of baking time, remove ham from oven, take off rind, score fat and stud it with whole cloves. Put the ham in a shallow baking pan. Simmer the raisins in water until plump and arrange them in the scored slits of fat. Push them in so they stick. *Sauce.* Beat together the currant jelly, vinegar and mustard. Use half the sauce to baste the ham during the last half hour of baking, raising temperature to 350°. Serve remaining sauce with the ham. Ten servings.

"Go little book, and wish to all
Flowers in the garden, meat in the hall."
ROBERT LOUIS STEVENSON, *Underwoods*

BAKED HAM WITH CURRANT GLAZE

1 ham
⅓ cup prepared mustard
½ cup water
½ cup sugar
1 (12 oz.) glass currant jelly
½ cup sirup drained from pickled crab apples, peaches or pears
Blanched almonds
Cloves
Strips of angelica or tinted citron (optional)

Cook ham according to directions for type of ham you buy. After the ham has been skinned and scored, prepare the glaze by mixing together the mustard, water, sugar and currant jelly. Add the sirup from the crab apples, peaches or pears. Heat together until well blended. Baste the ham frequently with the glaze for about 25 minutes in a moderately slow oven, 325°. Decorate the ham, if you wish, with blanched almond halves, using the cloves to form the center part of blossoms. In alternate squares use the strips of angelica or citron, if you like. Glaze again and bake another 15 minutes. Twelve to fifteen servings.

Clementine
Paddleford
HOW
AMERICA
EATS

CLEMENTINE PADDLEFORD

How America Eats, 1960

By all accounts, Clementine Paddleford was a force of nature. Born in Stockdale, Kansas, in 1898, Paddleford showed an early interest in food and writing. She graduated from Kansas State Agricultural College in 1921 with a degree in industrial journalism. From there she moved to New York City and enrolled in the Columbia University School of Journalism while taking night classes at New York University. Paddleford worked as a journalist for the *New York Sun* and the *New York Telegram*, and from 1936 to 1966 she was food editor for the *New York Herald-Tribune*. During her time at the *Herald-Tribune*, she published well-researched articles about American regional cooking, of which she became a major proponent.

In 1949 Paddleford wrote: "We all have hometown appetites. Every other person is a bundle of longing for the simplicities of good taste once enjoyed on the farm or in the hometown they left behind." And she set about to find these good, local dishes in her Piper Cub airplane that she flew across the country, sometimes covering 50,000 miles a year. Paddleford had an expansive sense of American food, not unlike her peer James Beard. In her columns, she also wrote about the wonderful ethnic foods of New York City, bringing such things as pizza, which she notes is pronounced "peet-za," to her readers.

How America Eats is Paddleford's major book, and offers a great overview of American cooking. Unfortunately, it was published in late 1960. Craig Claiborne's *New York Times Cookbook* and Julia Child's *Mastering the Art of French Cooking* both appeared in 1961, overshadowing *How America Eats*. She is remembered today as one of the early pioneers in good eating in the United States, along with James Beard, Cecily Brownstone, and other New Yorkers of the 1950s and 1960s.

NOTABLE RECIPES: Aunt Sabella's Black Chocolate Cake (page 619) • **Boston Marlborough Pie** (page 604) • Butterhorn Rolls • Chicken Hash on Flannel Cakes • Citrus Spareribs • **Ellin North's Plum Pudding** (page 650) • Fruited Baked Ham • Haman Taschen • **Iowa Ice Cream** (page 651)

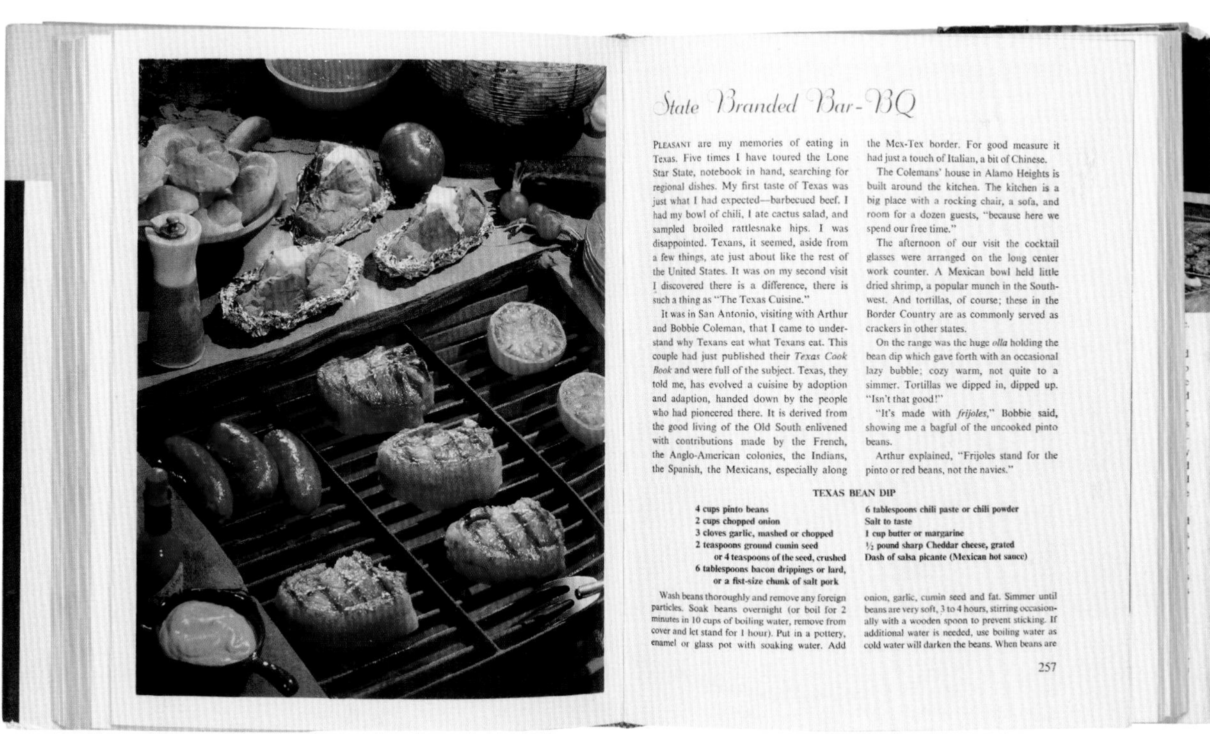

State Branded Bar-BQ

PLEASANT are my memories of eating in Texas. Five times I have toured the Lone Star State, notebook in hand, searching for regional dishes. My first taste of Texas was just what I had expected—barbecued beef. I had my bowl of chili, I ate cactus salad, and sampled broiled rattlesnake hips. I was disappointed. Texans, it seemed, aside from a few things, ate just about like the rest of the United States. It was on my second visit I discovered there is a difference, there is such a thing as "The Texas Cuisine."

It was in San Antonio, visiting with Arthur and Bobbie Coleman, that I came to understand why Texans eat what Texans eat. This couple had just published their *Texas Cook Book* and were full of the subject. Texas, they told me, has evolved a cuisine by adoption and adaption, handed down by the people who had pioneered there. It is derived from the good living of the Old South enlivened with contributions made by the French, the Anglo-American colonies, the Indians, the Spanish, the Mexicans, especially along the Mex-Tex border. For good measure it had just a touch of Italian, a bit of Chinese.

The Colemans' house in Alamo Heights is built around the kitchen. The kitchen is a big place with a rocking chair, a sofa, and room for a dozen guests, "because here we spend our free time."

The afternoon of our visit the cocktail glasses were arranged on the long center work counter. A Mexican bowl held little dried shrimp, a popular munch in the Southwest. And tortillas, of course; these in the Border Country are as commonly served as crackers in other states.

On the range was the huge *olla* holding the bean dip which gave forth with an occasional lazy bubble; cozy warm, not quite to a simmer. Tortillas we dipped in, dipped up. "Isn't that good!"

"It's made with *frijoles*," Bobbie said, showing me a bagful of the uncooked pinto beans.

Arthur explained, "Frijoles stand for the pinto or red beans, not the navies."

TEXAS BEAN DIP

4 cups pinto beans
2 cups chopped onion
3 cloves garlic, mashed or chopped
2 teaspoons ground cumin seed or 4 teaspoons of the seed, crushed
6 tablespoons bacon drippings or lard, or a fist-size chunk of salt pork
6 tablespoons chili paste or chili powder
Salt to taste
1 cup butter or margarine
½ pound sharp Cheddar cheese, grated
Dash of salsa picante (Mexican hot sauce)

Wash beans thoroughly and remove any foreign particles. Soak beans overnight (or boil for 2 minutes in 10 cups of boiling water, remove from cover and let stand for 1 hour). Put in a pottery, enamel or glass pot with soaking water. Add onion, garlic, cumin seed and fat. Simmer until beans are very soft, 3 to 4 hours, stirring occasionally with a wooden spoon to prevent sticking. If additional water is needed, use boiling water as cold water will darken the beans. When beans are

257

CRAIG CLAIBORNE

The New York Times Cook Book, 1961

In the pantheon of American food experts, Craig Claiborne is one of the gods. Claiborne was born in a small Mississippi town and grew up eating the legendary cuisine of the South. During his service in the Navy in World War II, Claiborne experienced the wonders of French food. After serving in the Korean War, he attended the École Hôtelière in Lausanne, Switzerland, to seriously study cooking.

After settling in New York, he began working for *Gourmet* magazine as a contributor. By 1957 he had accepted the position as editor of the food page for the *New York Times*. He was the first man to hold such a position—the food page had usually been thought of as a women's section. Under Claiborne's guidance the *New York Times* food section became the most important arbiter of food trends, restaurants to try, and chefs to follow. Claiborne's rise as a tastemaker was due not just to his culinary expertise but also to his ability to network in New York society. It was a heady time for food writers in America. James Beard was promoting American cookery. Julia Child was about to publish *Mastering the Art of French Cooking*. Restaurant Associates, under the leadership of Joe Baum, was transforming New Yorkers' notions of what a restaurant could be.

What Claiborne understood was that American food traditions, especially those in New York City, were heavily inflected by ethnic cooking. While Paris had better French restaurants, New York had Italian, Chinese, Japanese, German, Russian, and a host of others that all blended into the American palate. He applied rigorous standards in all his reviews and sought out the best, most interesting, and tastiest restaurants for his reviews. While he wrote more than twenty cookbooks, it is his *New York Times Cook Book* that everyone remembers and refers to. Coauthored with chef Pierre Franey, *The New York Times Cook Book* is a paean to the diversity of New York cooking. A single page contains recipes for braised pork and sauerkraut, porc au rosmarin, and Vietnamese grilled pork patties with lettuce leaves.

NOTABLE RECIPES: Arroz con Pollo • **Basic Tomato Sauce** (page 526) • **Beef Stroganoff** (page 547) • Coconut Cream Pie • **Chicken à la Kiev** (page 509) • **Chili con Carne** (page 393) • **Flank Steak with Herb Stuffing** (page 542) • **Herbed Pork Chops** (page 530) • **Key West Port Chops** (page 530) • Lemon Meringue Pie • **Pork Chops with Basil** (page 530) • **Pork Chops with Paprika** (page 530)

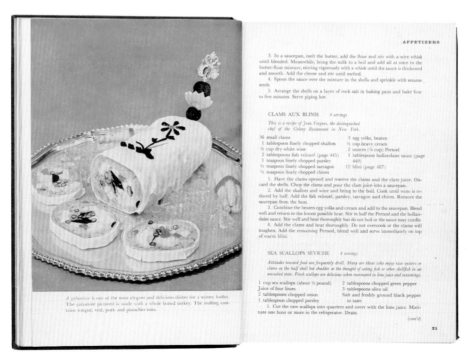

A galantine is one of the most elegant and delicious dishes for a winter buffet. The galantine pictured is made with a whole boned turkey. The stuffing contains tongue, veal, pork and pistachio nuts.

APPETIZERS

3. In a saucepan, melt the butter, add the flour and stir with a wire whisk until blended. Meanwhile, bring the milk to a boil and add all at once to the butter-flour mixture, stirring vigorously with a whisk until the sauce is thickened and smooth. Add the cheese and stir until melted.

4. Spoon the sauce over the mixture in the shells and sprinkle with sesame seeds.

5. Arrange the shells on a layer of rock salt in baking pans and bake four to five minutes. Serve piping hot.

CLAMS AUX BLINIS *4 servings*

This is a recipe of Jean Vergnes, the distinguished chef of the Colony Restaurant in New York.

36 small clams
1 tablespoon finely chopped shallots
½ cup dry white wine
2 tablespoons fish velouté (page 445)
1 teaspoon finely chopped parsley
½ teaspoon finely chopped tarragon
½ teaspoon finely chopped chives
3 egg yolks, beaten
½ cup heavy cream
2 ounces (¼ cup) Pernod
1 tablespoon hollandaise sauce (page 449)
12 blini (page 487)

1. Have the clams opened and reserve the clams and the clam juice. Discard the shells. Chop the clams and pour the clam juice into a saucepan.

2. Add the shallots and wine and bring to the boil. Cook until wine is reduced by half. Add the fish velouté, parsley, tarragon and chives. Remove the saucepan from the heat.

3. Combine the beaten egg yolks and cream and add to the saucepan. Blend well and return to the lowest possible heat. Stir in half the Pernod and the hollandaise sauce. Stir well and heat thoroughly but do not boil or the sauce may curdle.

4. Add the clams and heat thoroughly. Do not overcook or the clams will toughen. Add the remaining Pernod, blend well and serve immediately on top of warm blini.

SEA SCALLOPS SEVICHE *4 servings*

Attitudes toward food are frequently droll. Many are those who enjoy raw oysters or clams on the half shell but shudder at the thought of eating fish or other shellfish in an uncooked state. Fresh scallops are delicious when marinated in lime juice and seasonings.

1 cup sea scallops (about ½ pound)
Juice of four limes
2 tablespoons chopped onion
1 tablespoon chopped parsley
2 tablespoons chopped green pepper
3 tablespoons olive oil
Salt and freshly ground black pepper to taste

1. Cut the raw scallops into quarters and cover with the lime juice. Marinate one hour or more in the refrigerator. Drain.

(cont'd)

21

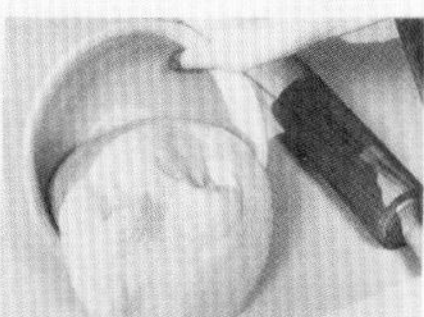

1. To make a tasty spiral loaf of bread the dough is allowed to rise. It is punched down and turned out on a smooth surface.

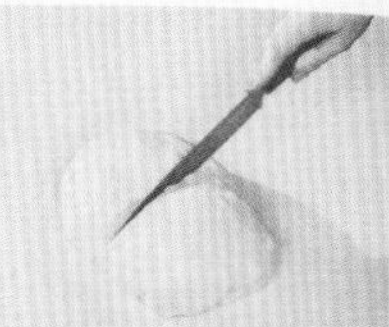

2. The dough is allowed to rest ten minutes. It is then cut in half with a knife. Each half is shaped into a ball.

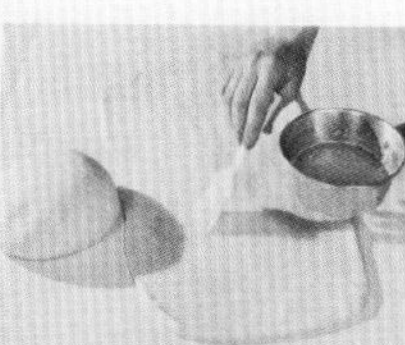

3. Each ball of dough is rolled into a rectangle about one-quarter inch thick. It is then brushed with lightly beaten egg.

4. A selected filling such as chopped parsley and scallions is spread over the dough to about one inch from the edges.

5. The dough is rolled somewhat tightly in a jelly-roll fashion. It is placed in greased pans, with sealed edges underneath.

6. After the loaves are left to rise about fifty to sixty minutes, they are baked one hour until brown in a 400° oven.

The American spice shelf has undergone a minor revolution in two decades. Whole spices and ground spices, many of them little known until recent years, are now in common use. Seen here are a green salad with mixed herbs, tomato soup with basil.

1. *To make cream puffs or éclairs,* flour is added all at once to boiling water and butter. Mixture is stirred rapidly until paste ball forms.

2. Eggs are added one at a time. Mixture is beaten well after each addition until the paste is waxy, firm, and exceptionally smooth.

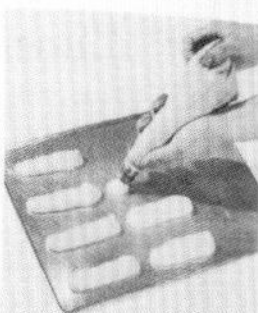

3. To make éclairs, the paste is forced out of a pastry tube onto a baking sheet. To make cream puffs it is dropped from a spoon.

4. Cream puffs or éclairs are baked in a hot oven. When they are done, no bubbles of fat remain on surface; sides feel rigid.

5. Many fillings complement cream puff shells. Here shells are filled with smooth pastry cream, then frosted and chilled.

Cream puffs (on compote) and éclairs filled with pastry cream.

and bake until no bubbles of fat remain on the surface and the sides of the puffs feel rigid, about thirty minutes longer. Cool. Cut a cap off each puff and fill with pastry cream (see below). Replace the cap.

VARIATIONS:

Eclairs: Using a spoon or large round pastry tube, shape the cream puff mixture on a baking sheet into finger lengths. Bake, cool and slit each puff at the side. Fill with pastry cream (see below) and frost with melted chocolate or any chocolate icing.

Beignets Soufflés: Flavor cream puff mixture with one-quarter teaspoon orange extract or one tablespoon rum and drop by tablespoons into deep hot fat (370° F.). Fry until brown on all sides. Serve hot, sprinkled with confectioners' sugar.

PASTRY CREAM: *About 3 cups*

⅓ cup sugar
3½ tablespoons cornstarch or
6 tablespoons flour
6 lightly beaten egg yolks
2 cups milk
1 teaspoon vanilla extract

1. Mix sugar, cornstarch and egg yolks in a saucepan. Scald the milk and pour it gradually over the egg yolk mixture, stirring rapidly with a wire whisk.

2. Cook over low heat or in the top of a double boiler, stirring rapidly with the whisk, until the mixture is thickened and smooth. Do not allow the pastry cream to boil. Cool and stir in the vanilla.

DANISH PASTRY *About 24 pastries*

4¾ cups sifted all-purpose flour, approximately
1½ cups butter
1½ packages dry yeast
1¼ cups lukewarm milk
¼ cup sugar
1 egg, beaten

1. Measure one-third cup flour onto a board or into a bowl. Add the butter and chop the flour and butter together with a pastry blender or two knives. Roll the mixture between two sheets of waxed paper into a twelve-by-six-inch rectangle. Chill.

2. Sprinkle the yeast on the warm milk and let stand until softened and the mixture has cooled. Add the sugar and egg. Add the remaining flour gradually and mix with a wooden spoon until a soft dough is formed. Turn the dough onto a floured surface and knead until smooth.

3. Roll the dough on a generously floured board into a fourteen-inch square. Place the butter-flour mixture on one half of the dough and fold the other half of the dough over it. Press around the edges to seal.

4. Pat the dough with a rolling pin and then roll it out into a paper-thin sheet. Fold the sheet of dough into thirds. Repeat the patting, rolling and folding process three times. If the butter mixture softens and begins to ooze out upon rolling, chill the dough before continuing.

(cont'd)

FLORENCE FABRICANT *on* CRAIG CLAIBORNE

There is no Craig Claiborne foundation raising money for culinary scholarships. His home, with its lavish kitchen, never became foodie theater and was not donated to the Smithsonian.

And his legacy is not a high-profile, fundraising machine sponsored by Champagne houses and cookware companies, or a series of delectable public television segments spanning decades. Instead, it exists mainly in more than twenty books, and especially in the memories of those, the keepers of the flame, who loved him, depended on him, and sought his journalistic blessing. But today's generation of the food crazed who stand on line for cupcakes at flea markets do not revere him.

Nonetheless, Craig Claiborne, a quirky, sometimes flamboyant, often cranky character who wrote for the New York Times *from 1957 to 1986 and was notable for creating restaurant criticism as it is still practiced in objective dining circles, did as much, if not more, than his peers to encourage Americans to explore new cuisines, recognize rising chefs and restaurants, try new recipes, and be unafraid of cooking.*

It was Claiborne's pen—or typewriter—that first put Paul Prudhomme, Zarela Martinez, Michael Tong, Maida Heatter, André Soltner, Sirio Maccioni, Alain Chapel, Paul Bocuse, Roger Fessaguet, and Joseph Baum on the culinary map. And he did not ignore little places either, including Bo Bo in Chinatown, which received three stars.

He was also available for his readers. Once, in East Hampton, where he had a vacation house with a listed phone number, a desperate cook, attempting one of Claiborne's recipes for his guests, called him because the sauce did not seem to be doing what it should. "What kind of heat do you have it on?" Claiborne asked. "Kind of a simmer," replied the cook. "Well, boil the bejesus out of it!" came roaring through the phone. Claiborne did not mince words.

Craig Claiborne was born in Sunflower, Mississippi, in 1920, and had a troubled childhood. He discovered the allure of the kitchen at his mother's boardinghouse in nearby Indianola, but it would take decades for him to build this interest into a career. He studied journalism at the University of Missouri, joined the Navy in World War II, and then held jobs in public relations, which allowed him to sample fine food on an expense account. Then, not knowing what to do, in 1949 he moved to France, where he described the food, even the modest fare he could afford, as "heavenly."

He went back into the service during the Korean War and after his discharge took the step that would change his life more than any omelet or glass of wine in a Paris café. He enrolled in the École Hôtelière de la Société Suisse in Lausanne, Switzerland, and after graduation returned to New York. His first job in food was as a receptionist at Gourmet. *Eventually he became an editor. In 1957 he moved to the* New York Times, *where the executive editor and fellow Southerner Turner Catledge hired him as food editor, the very job that Claiborne had dreamed of years before.*

He wrote features, recipe stories, and restaurant reviews. A few years after he started at the Times, *he asked the editors for permission to use the* Times *logo on a cookbook,* The New York Times Cook Book. *They said yes without giving it too much thought, but eventually came to resent the money that Claiborne, not the* Times, *was making on the book. It led the* Times *to go into the book publishing business.*

Claiborne changed restaurant reviewing. Without him, Gael Greene would not have needed to bother with hats, Ruth Reichl with wigs, and just about every other reviewer with phony names. When Claiborne started, reviewers' photos were not restaurant kitchen pinups, and he went about his job mostly under the radar. But his standards were high.

He visited restaurants anonymously, making reservations in assumed names, accepting no favors and paying for his meals. The zero-to-four-star rating system that he established still holds sway. Not just the food but the ambiance and the quality of the service were subjected to his scrutiny, and not once, but on at least two visits. But there was much less foodie frenzy in those days. He finally got around to reviewing Lutèce a few months after it opened, giving it one star (it eventually would earn the top rating of four).

It was while he was interviewing Henri Soulé, the chef and proprietor of Le Pavillon, which Claiborne considered to be the best restaurant in New York at the time, that he met a thirty-eight-year-old French chef, Pierre Franey. Soon Franey, who quit Le Pavillon and went to work for the Howard Johnson chain, became a dining companion. That association turned into a professional relationship. Franey joined the Times and worked with Claiborne for decades, helping to develop the recipes that would appear, under their joint byline, in the Sunday Times Magazine.

Since Franey also had a home in East Hampton, the two would get together for working sessions, Franey at the professional stove, manning the copper sauté pans and calling out the ingredients and steps, as Claiborne sat at the typewriter nearby and took it all down. Some of these sessions evolved into contretemps, like the time that the French chef Alain Chapel came to visit and prepare calves' ears. They had four heads to work with, and when they were done, they threw them into Gardiners Bay. When they washed up on the beach weeks later, the police were called in and it took days to discover exactly who was responsible, with all sorts of mysterious speculation in the press.

It was with Franey that Claiborne enjoyed his famous $4,000 dinner in Paris in 1975—a princely sum for dinner for two even at today's dollar. It was a $300 prize that Claiborne had bought in an auction for Channel 13, donated by American Express for a dinner anywhere in the world. The front-page report of the dinner had mail pouring into the Times office.

Claiborne eventually sold that fairly modest house and built a 5,000-square-foot home elsewhere in East Hampton. It was there, in the summer of 1982, that chefs from around the country came, set up cooking stations in the driveway, and served food to guests for a party to celebrate the publication of Claiborne's controversial autobiography, A Feast Made for Laughter.

The management at the Times did not find the book easy to swallow, what with Claiborne's frank discussion of his homosexuality. His relationship with the Times soured after that. Around that time he and Franey also had a falling-out. A few years later he retired with, as he put it, "not so much as a gold watch."

But in 1990, for his seventieth birthday, Alain Ducasse, one of the French chefs that Claiborne wrote about glowingly, threw a magnificent three-day party in Monte Carlo and on the Riviera, which included a sumptuous lunch at a Rothschild estate and a formal dinner in the Hôtel de Paris. It was a memorable, well-deserved celebration of a lifetime of devotion to food, and, at the end of the day, great honesty.

He died in 2000, just short of his eightieth birthday. Now that would have been some party!

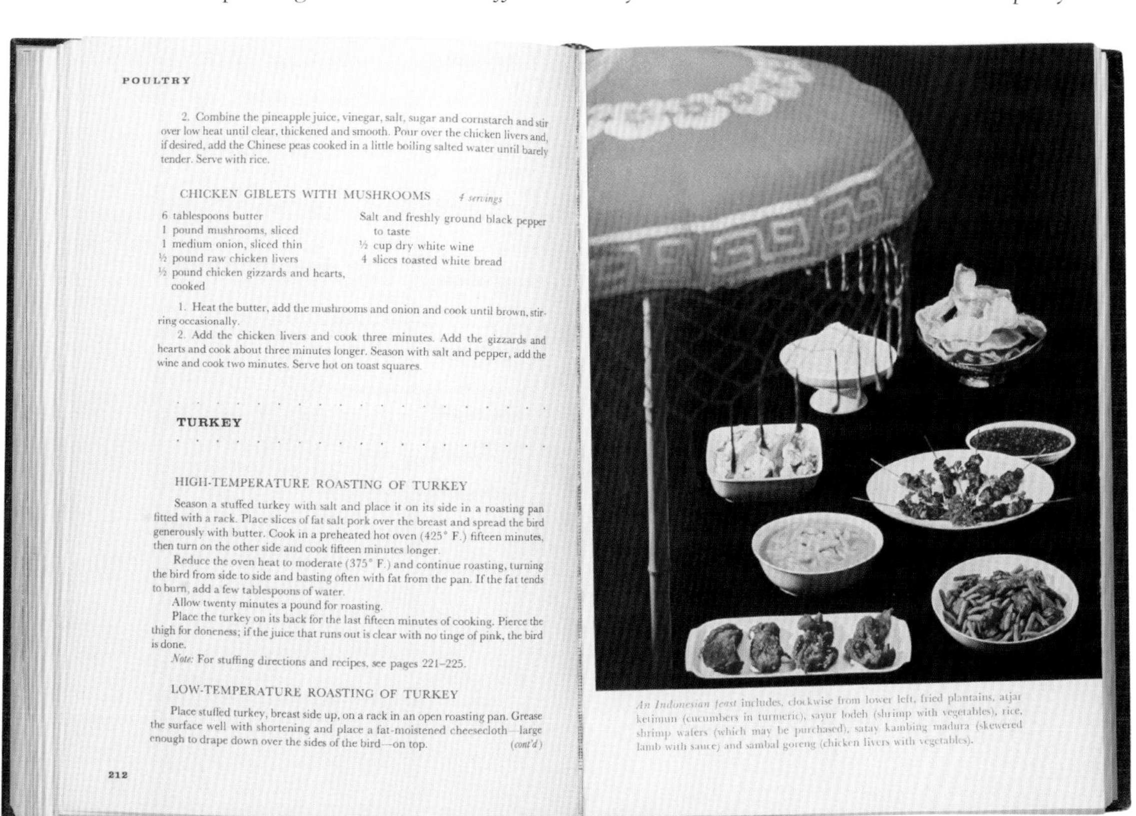

POULTRY

2. Combine the pineapple juice, vinegar, salt, sugar and cornstarch and stir over low heat until clear, thickened and smooth. Pour over the chicken livers and, if desired, add the Chinese peas cooked in a little boiling salted water until barely tender. Serve with rice.

CHICKEN GIBLETS WITH MUSHROOMS *4 servings*

6 tablespoons butter
1 pound mushrooms, sliced
1 medium onion, sliced thin
½ pound raw chicken livers
½ pound chicken gizzards and hearts, cooked
Salt and freshly ground black pepper to taste
½ cup dry white wine
4 slices toasted white bread

1. Heat the butter, add the mushrooms and onion and cook until brown, stirring occasionally.

2. Add the chicken livers and cook three minutes. Add the gizzards and hearts and cook about three minutes longer. Season with salt and pepper, add the wine and cook two minutes. Serve hot on toast squares.

TURKEY

HIGH-TEMPERATURE ROASTING OF TURKEY

Season a stuffed turkey with salt and place it on its side in a roasting pan fitted with a rack. Place slices of fat salt pork over the breast and spread the bird generously with butter. Cook in a preheated hot oven (425° F.) fifteen minutes, then turn on the other side and cook fifteen minutes longer.

Reduce the oven heat to moderate (375° F.) and continue roasting, turning the bird from side to side and basting often with fat from the pan. If the fat tends to burn, add a few tablespoons of water.

Allow twenty minutes a pound for roasting.

Place the turkey on its back for the last fifteen minutes of cooking. Pierce the thigh for doneness; if the juice that runs out is clear with no tinge of pink, the bird is done.

Note: For stuffing directions and recipes, see pages 221–225.

LOW-TEMPERATURE ROASTING OF TURKEY

Place stuffed turkey, breast side up, on a rack in an open roasting pan. Grease the surface well with shortening and place a fat-moistened cheesecloth—large enough to drape down over the sides of the bird—on top. *(cont'd)*

212

An Indonesian feast includes, clockwise from lower left, fried plantains, atjar ketimun (cucumbers in turmeric), sayur lodeh (shrimp with vegetables), rice, shrimp wafers (which may be purchased), satay kambing madura (skewered lamb with sauce) and sambal goreng (chicken livers with vegetables).

Julia and Jacques Cooking at Home
JULIA CHILD and JACQUES PEPIN
KNOPF
JULIA CHILD
THE WAY TO COOK
KNOPF
IN JULIA'S KITCHEN WITH MASTER CHEFS
BY JULIA CHILD
Knopf
FROM JULIA CHILD'S KITCHEN
by Julia Child
KNOPF
MASTERING THE ART OF French Cooking
BECK BERTHOLLE CHILD
Alfred · A · Knopf
MASTERING THE ART OF French Cooking
* *
JULIA CHILD AND SIMONE BECK
Alfred · A · Knopf

JULIA CHILD, LOUISETTE BERTHOLLE, AND SIMONE BECK

Mastering the Art of French Cooking,

Volumes I and II, 1961–1970

Mastering the Art of French Cooking is unquestionably the most important American cookbook of the twentieth century. In the first printings, the authors' names appeared in alphabetical order, but soon Julia Child's name moved to the top, once she gained notoriety. This is as it should be since Child conceived of the book and wrote most of it. She wanted to demystify French cooking for the average American cook. Her unpretentious but detailed explanations of French culinary techniques and her careful adaptations of ingredients, measurements, and cooking temperatures ensured that anyone could make an outstanding boeuf bourguignon or tarte tatin in their home kitchen. French food was no longer available only in the bastions of haute cuisine, such as Henri Soulé's Le Pavillon restaurant. For a whole generation of American cooks, the stranglehold English and German cooking had over the palate finally was broken.

Child's book opened the door for other writers to create "ethnic" cookbooks based on either their native cuisine or a cuisine about which they had extensive knowledge. Child gave the average cook an attitude toward food that shaped the way America ate for the rest of the century.

NOTABLE RECIPES: Boeuf Bourguignon (page 400) • **Cassoulet** (page 397) • **Soufflé au Fromage** (page 387) • **Goose** (page 492) • **La Tarte des Demoiselles Tatin** (page 596) • **Omelettes** (page 461)

JUDITH JONES *on* JULIA CHILD

Julia Child used to say to me: "Judith, you and I were born at the right time."

It's true. America was fertile ground for the food revolution that took root after World War II. The GIs had come home from Europe and from the Far East, where they had experienced new exciting flavors, and once their taste buds were awakened they wanted more. Now anyone could save their pennies and take an economy flight to Paris, where real French food could be had in inexpensive bistros—and they wanted to duplicate those dishes at home. Jackie Kennedy had a French chef in the White House and elegant state dinners made the news. America was ready to shake off its puritanical attitude toward food and embrace the sensuous pleasures of good cooking.

But while it is lucky to be born at the right time, you have to act upon your convictions and seize the moment. And that is what Julia did instinctively. After her own epiphany over that famous sole meunière that she tasted en route to Paris for the first time, she felt driven not only to learn the secrets of French cooking so that she could become a better cook, she also wanted to awaken her fellow Americans to the mastery of this art. She was the perfect person to take on this crusade. She had never learned to cook at her mother's knee and now, at over thirty, she found herself living in Paris with a husband who loved good food. In other words, she was one of us, wanting to cook but finding herself alone in the kitchen without the tools and the knowledge to achieve that soigné finish that was the key to French cooking.

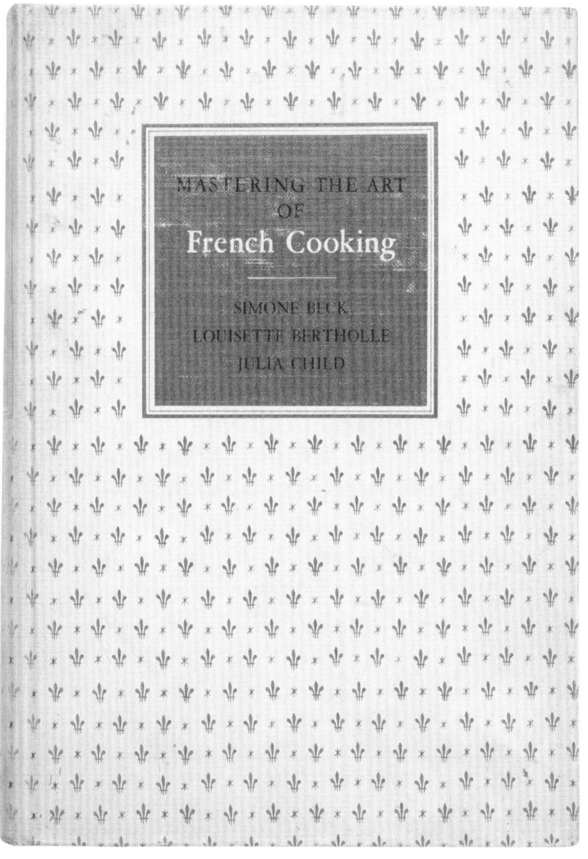

So she enlisted in the famous Cordon Bleu, where she was the only female student, along with several GIs. Then she teamed up with two French women who were doing a book for an American publisher on French cooking. Right away she realized that just producing a collection of good recipes would not suffice. The more she got into the task, the more she realized that she had to explain classic techniques, ingredients, timing, and equipment. The book had to be a basic teaching book in order for it to work for Americans. It was a daunting task, but she was not willing to compromise, even when the publisher who had backed them bowed out, telling Mrs. Child that no American woman wanted to know that much about French cooking.

Well, I did. I longed for just such a book, and by one of those lucky coincidences this huge tome landed on my desk at Knopf, where I was a young editor working mostly on translations of French writers that Blanche Knopf had acquired. But word had gotten out that I liked to cook, so I was asked to take a look at this submission from Avis DeVoto, our literary scout in Cambridge. Like Julia, I had spent several years in Paris and had fallen in love with food and the French way of life. When I returned to the States with my husband, who shared my passion for la cuisine, we were distressed at the wasteland we found in the supermarkets. Where were the plump garlic cloves, shallots, mushrooms, good cheeses, fresh herbs and parsley, all so essential to French cooking? We couldn't even get a crusty baguette in New York City to mop up our plates. Moreover, the few books we could find on French cooking offered little guidance on technique.

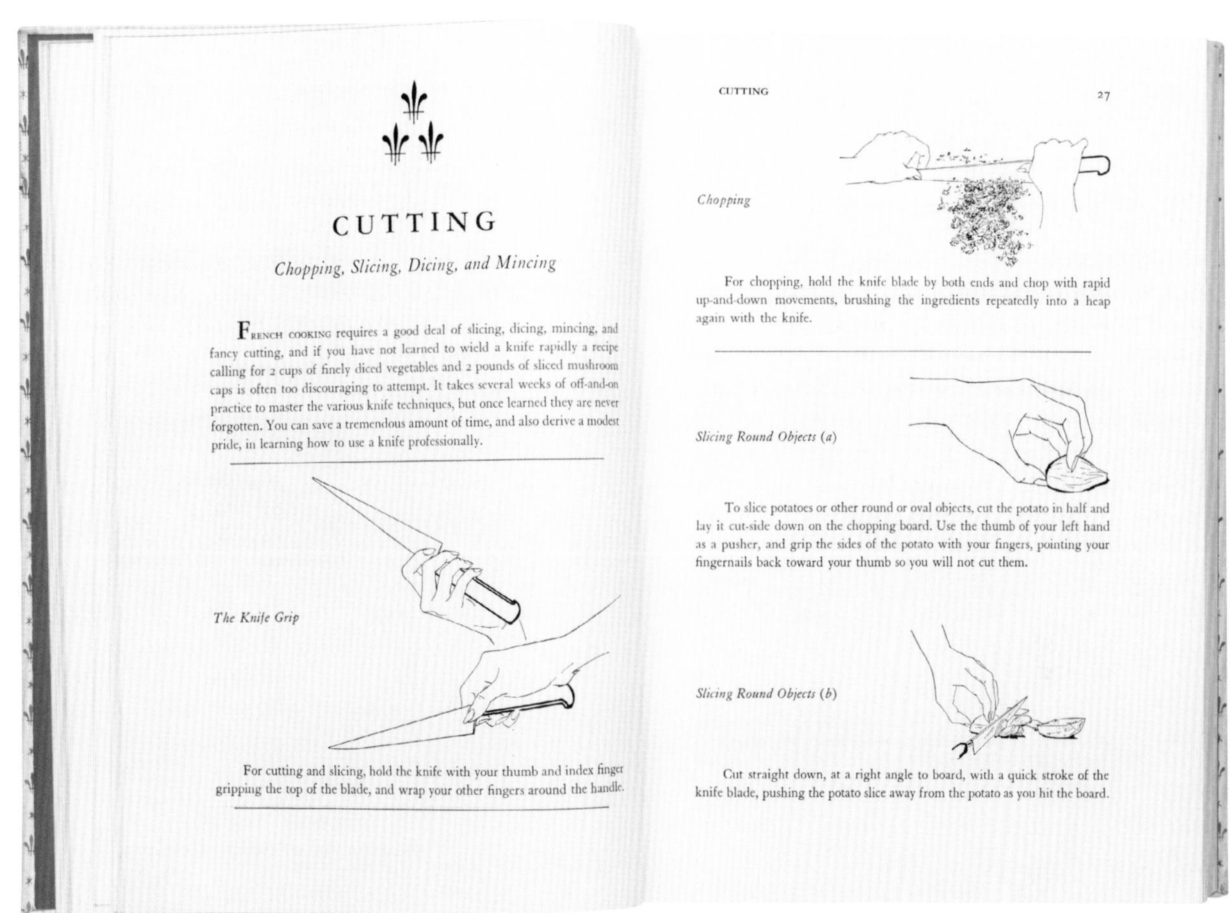

CUTTING

Chopping, Slicing, Dicing, and Mincing

French cooking requires a good deal of slicing, dicing, mincing, and fancy cutting, and if you have not learned to wield a knife rapidly a recipe calling for 2 cups of finely diced vegetables and 2 pounds of sliced mushroom caps is often too discouraging to attempt. It takes several weeks of off-and-on practice to master the various knife techniques, but once learned they are never forgotten. You can save a tremendous amount of time, and also derive a modest pride, in learning how to use a knife professionally.

The Knife Grip

For cutting and slicing, hold the knife with your thumb and index finger gripping the top of the blade, and wrap your other fingers around the handle.

CUTTING 27

Chopping

For chopping, hold the knife blade by both ends and chop with rapid up-and-down movements, brushing the ingredients repeatedly into a heap again with the knife.

Slicing Round Objects (a)

To slice potatoes or other round or oval objects, cut the potato in half and lay it cut-side down on the chopping board. Use the thumb of your left hand as a pusher, and grip the sides of the potato with your fingers, pointing your fingernails back toward your thumb so you will not cut them.

Slicing Round Objects (b)

Cut straight down, at a right angle to board, with a quick stroke of the knife blade, pushing the potato slice away from the potato as you hit the board.

So I was enthralled as I read this revolutionary manuscript and took home sample pages to put some of the recipes to the test. The winey boeuf bourguignon I made first was as delicious as any we had eaten in Paris. Why? Because for the first time I understood what I was doing. I learned what cuts of meat were best to use, how to blanch bacon, extract its fat, and make lardons, how to dry the beef and brown it a little at a time, not crowding the pan, the importance of glazing the vegetables separately and using a decent wine. And so on.

I was fully convinced that if I felt this enthusiastic, there must be others out there like me, and that we had to publish the book. Fortunately Knopf was a small family business and Alfred was a food and wine connoisseur—who never set foot in the kitchen, of course. But I sensed he would be intrigued and, being a very junior editor, I enlisted the support of veteran editor Angus Cameron, who got his start at Bobbs-Merrill, where he had helped market The Joy of Cooking *so successfully. One of our ploys was to convince the Knopfs that this was such a great teaching book that it could make the recipes in other cookbooks work, all of which had inadequate directions (including those that we had published). It worked, and Alfred agreed to give "Mrs. Jones" a chance.*

The rest is history. In the fall of 1961 we published what we called Mastering the Art of French Cooking. *(Alfred didn't like the title and said to me that if a book with such a title sold, he would eat his hat.) But Craig Claiborne, the much-esteemed food editor of the* New York Times, *declared it a classic, and the book took off. We even went back to print before Christmas. And that was well before Julia went on Public Television and seduced us with the sensuous pleasure she got out of massaging a chicken breast and flipping an omelet.*

PREPARING AN ARTICHOKE

No one is quite sure who first discovered that this relative of the thistle family is edible, but it certainly dates back to ancient times. We know it was cultivated by Greeks in Sicily and that it is native to the Mediterranean and other parts of southern Europe. Preparing one for cooking is not hard, but until you have seen it done, it can seem impossible. Several cookbooks illustrate how to remove the thorns and the heart or "choke," which is inedible in larger artichokes. Here are some of the most instructive illustrations.

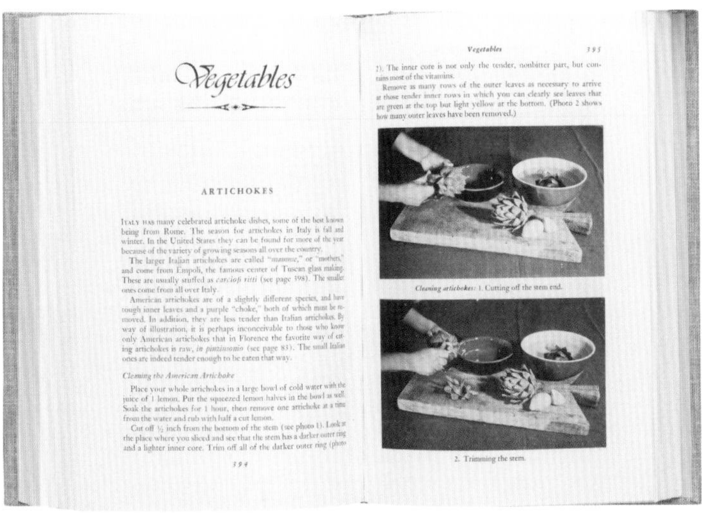

Vegetables

ARTICHOKES

ITALY HAS many celebrated artichoke dishes, some of the best known being from Rome. The season for artichokes in Italy is fall and winter. In the United States they can be found for more of the year because of the variety of growing seasons all over the country.

The larger Italian artichokes are called "*mamme*," or "mothers," and come from Empoli, the famous center of Tuscan glass making. These are usually stuffed as *carciofi ritti* (see page 398). The smaller ones come from all over Italy.

American artichokes are of a slightly different species, and have tough inner leaves and a purple "choke," both of which must be removed. In addition, they are less tender than Italian artichokes. By way of illustration, it is perhaps inconceivable to those who know only American artichokes that in Florence the favorite way of eating artichokes is raw, *in pinzimonio* (see page 83). The small Italian ones are indeed tender enough to be eaten that way.

Cleaning the American Artichoke

Place your whole artichokes in a large bowl of cold water with the juice of 1 lemon. Put the squeezed lemon halves in the bowl as well. Soak the artichokes for 1 hour, then remove one artichoke at a time from the water and rub with half a cut lemon.

Cut off ½ inch from the bottom of the stem (see photo 1). Look at the place where you sliced and see that the stem has a darker outer ring and a lighter inner core. Trim off all of the darker outer ring (photo

394

Vegetables 395

2). The inner core is not only the tender, nonbitter part, but contains most of the vitamins.

Remove as many rows of the outer leaves as necessary to arrive at those tender inner rows in which you can clearly see leaves that are green at the top but light yellow at the bottom. (Photo 2 shows how many outer leaves have been removed.)

Cleaning artichokes: 1. Cutting off the stem end.

2. Trimming the stem.

ARTICHOKE BOTTOMS

Then, holding artichoke bottom up, bend a lower leaf back on itself until it snaps; peel it off toward base leaving meat at bottom of leaf attached to bottom of artichoke.

Proceed all around until you have gone beyond the curve where leaves fold inward over top of artichoke bottom; cut off remaining cone of leaves just above this curve, as illustrated.

Rub cuts with lemon to prevent discoloration, and trim all bits of green off bottom to expose whitish tender flesh, frequently rubbing with lemon as you do so.

Drop prepared bottom into bowl of acidulated water, and continue with the other artichokes. The chokes will be removed after cooking.

Cooking. Gradually beat 1 cup of cold water into the flour and bring to the boil; pour in 3 cups more water and simmer a moment, stirring, to be sure liquid is smooth and lump free. Add the lemon juice and salt, the prepared artichoke bottoms, and a little more water if they are not completely covered with liquid. Simmer 30 to 40 minutes, until artichokes are tender when pierced with a knife. Let cool in liquid, and refrigerate until needed. They will keep perfectly for 2 or 3 days in their cooking liquid.

Just before using, wash under cold water, and scoop out choke with a teaspoon; trim off any tough leaf ends. Reheat as indicated in your recipe.

Fonds d'artichauts farcis, béarnaise

ARTICHOKE BOTTOMS STUFFED WITH MUSHROOMS AND POACHED EGGS, TOPPED WITH BÉARNAISE SAUCE

All parts of this dish may be cooked in advance, then reheated and assembled at the last minute. This was the first course for our televised sit-down dinner party, followed by a roast tenderloin of beef with fresh vegetables, and a pretty dessert, a pear and meringue fantasy. The artichoke combination is equally good as the main course for a smart luncheon and you could, of course, omit the poached eggs in either case, though their soft yolks blending with sauce, mushrooms, and artichokes are a luscious experience. Serve a chilled dry white wine here, one with some body, like a Pouilly Fumé, Pouilly Fuissé, or Chablis—again, there are some who declare wine goes with neither eggs nor artichokes and again I say to you, serve such old harpies plain water and there will be more wine for your glass.

For 8 people

The mushroom duxelles filling

½ lb. fresh mushrooms, washed and finely minced (2 cups)
3 Tb butter in a no-stick medium-sized frying pan
2 Tb minced shallots or scallions
Salt and pepper
¼ tsp dried tarragon
2 Tb flour
¼ cup dry Port wine
½ cup heavy cream

For the sauce béarnaise, about 1 cup

A small saucepan containing ¼ cup each excellent wine vinegar and dry white Vermouth

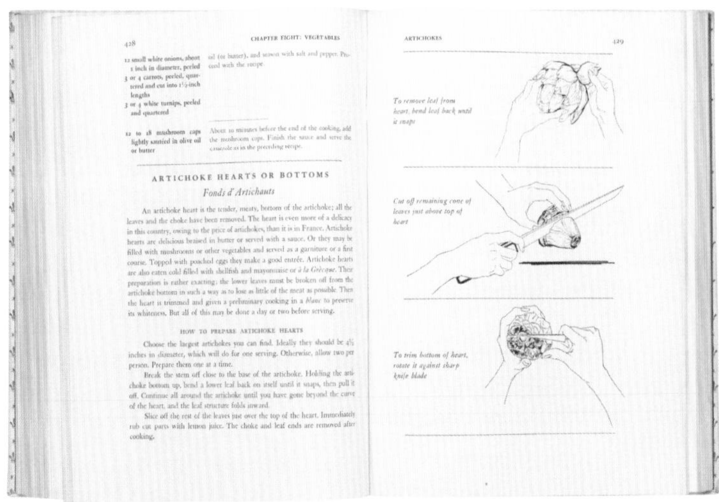

428 CHAPTER EIGHT: VEGETABLES

12 small white onions, about 1 inch in diameter, peeled
3 or 4 carrots, peeled, quartered and cut into 1½-inch lengths
3 or 4 white turnips, peeled and quartered

oil (or butter), and season with salt and pepper. Proceed with the recipe.

12 to 18 mushroom caps lightly sautéed in olive oil or butter

About 10 minutes before the end of the cooking, add the mushroom caps. Finish the sauce and serve the casserole as in the preceding recipe.

ARTICHOKE HEARTS OR BOTTOMS

Fonds d'Artichauts

An artichoke heart is the tender, meaty, bottom of the artichoke; all the leaves and the choke have been removed. The heart is even more of a delicacy in this country, owing to the price of artichokes, than it is in France. Artichoke hearts are delicious braised in butter or served with a sauce. Or they may be filled with mushrooms or other vegetables and served as a garniture or a first course. Topped with poached eggs they make a good entrée. Artichoke hearts are also eaten cold filled with shellfish and mayonnaise or *à la Grècque*. Their preparation is rather exacting; the lower leaves must be broken off from the artichoke bottom in such a way as to lose as little of the meat as possible. Then the heart is trimmed and given a preliminary cooking in a *blanc* to preserve its whiteness. But all of this may be done a day or two before serving.

HOW TO PREPARE ARTICHOKE HEARTS

Choose the largest artichokes you can find. Ideally they should be 4½ inches in diameter, which will do for one serving. Otherwise, allow two per person. Prepare them one at a time.

Break the stem off close to the base of the artichoke. Holding the artichoke bottom up, bend a lower leaf back on itself until it snaps, then pull it off. Continue all around the artichoke until you have gone beyond the curve of the heart, and the leaf structure folds inward.

Slice off the rest of the leaves just over the top of the heart. Immediately rub cut parts with lemon juice. The choke and leaf ends are removed after cooking.

ARTICHOKES 429

To remove leaf from heart, bend leaf back until it snaps

Cut off remaining cone of leaves just above top of heart

To trim bottom of heart, rotate it against sharp knife blade

FROM TOP:

Giuliano Bugialli
The Fine Art of Italian Cooking

Julia Child
From Julia Child's Kitchen

Julia Child, Louisette Bertholle, and Simone Beck
Mastering the Art of French Cooking

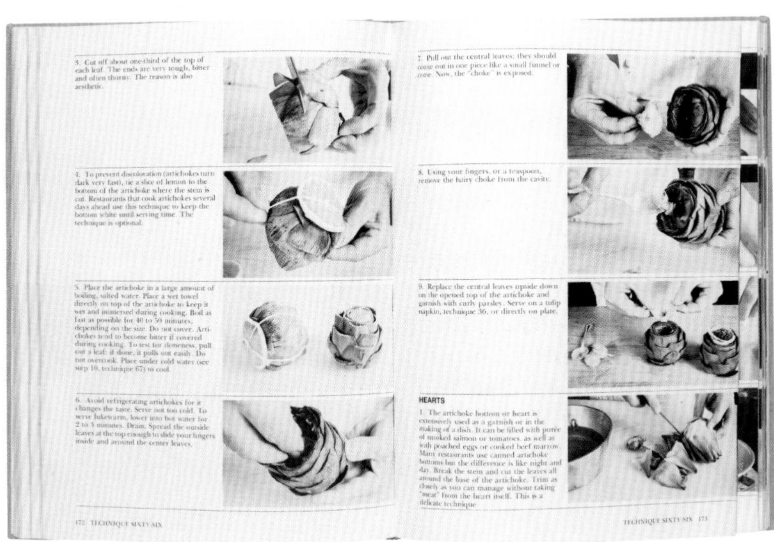

3. Cut off about one-third of the top of each leaf. The ends are very tough, bitter and often thorny. The reason is also aesthetic.

4. To prevent discoloration (artichokes turn dark very fast), tie a slice of lemon to the bottom of the artichoke where the stem is cut. Restaurants that cook artichokes several days ahead use this technique to keep the bottom white until serving time. The technique is optional.

5. Place the artichoke in a large amount of boiling, salted water. Place a wet towel directly on top of the artichoke to keep it wet and immersed during cooking. Boil as fast as possible for 40 to 50 minutes, depending on the size. Do not cover. Artichokes tend to become bitter if covered during cooking. To test for doneness, pull out a leaf: if done, it pulls out easily. Do not overcook. Place under cold water (see step 10, technique 67) to cool.

6. Avoid refrigerating artichokes for it changes the taste. Serve not too cold. To serve lukewarm, lower into hot water for 2 to 3 minutes. Drain. Spread the outside leaves at the top enough to slide your fingers inside and around the center leaves.

7. Pull out the central leaves; they should come out in one piece like a small funnel or cone. Now, the "choke" is exposed.

8. Using your fingers, or a teaspoon, remove the hairy choke from the cavity.

9. Replace the central leaves upside down on the opened top of the artichoke and garnish with curly parsley. Serve on a tulip napkin, technique 36, or directly on plate.

HEARTS

1. The artichoke bottom or heart is extensively used as a garnish or in the making of a dish. It can be filled with purée of smoked salmon or tomatoes, as well as with poached eggs or cooked beef marrow. Many restaurants use canned artichoke bottoms but the difference is like night and day. Break the stem and cut the leaves all around the base of the artichoke. Trim as closely as you can manage without taking "meat" from the heart itself. This is a delicate technique

172 TECHNIQUE SIXTY-SIX

TECHNIQUE SIXTY-SIX 173

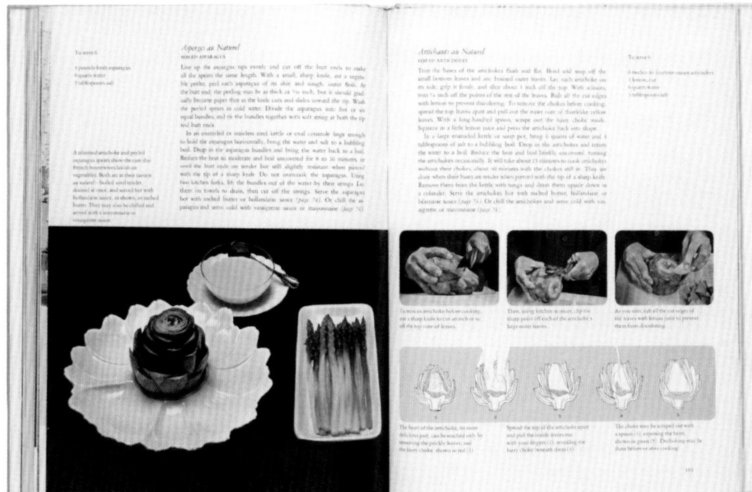

Asperges au Naturel

Artichauts au Naturel

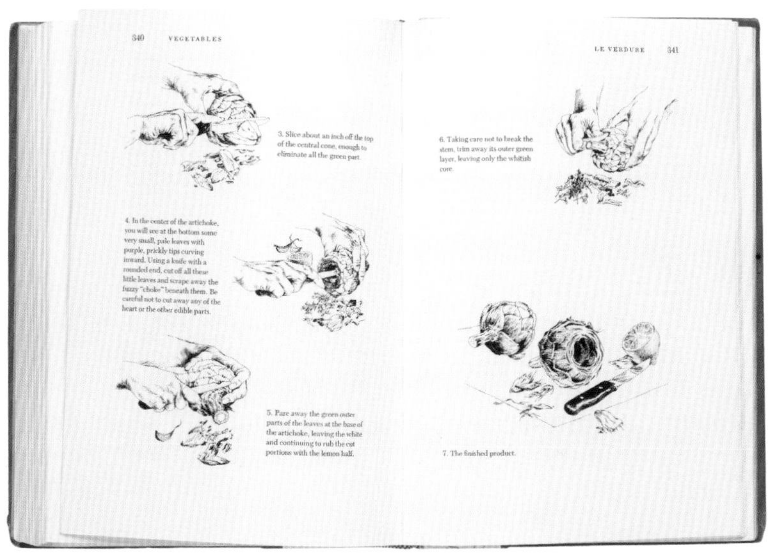

340 VEGETABLES

3. Slice about an inch off the top of the central cone, enough to eliminate all the green part.

4. In the center of the artichoke, you will see at the bottom some very small, pale leaves with purple, prickly tips curving inward. Using a knife with a rounded end, cut off all these little leaves and scrape away the fuzzy "choke" beneath them. Be careful not to cut away any of the heart or the other edible parts.

5. Pare away the green outer parts of the leaves at the base of the artichoke, leaving the white and continuing to rub the cut portions with the lemon half.

LE VERDURE 341

6. Taking care not to break the stem, trim away its outer green layer, leaving only the whitish core.

7. The finished product.

FROM TOP:

Jacques Pépin
La Technique

Time-Life Foods of the World Series
Cooking of Provincial France

Marcella Hazan
The Classic Italian Cook Book

THE ART
OF
FINE BAKING

BY PAULA PECK

ILLUSTRATIONS BY GRAMBS MILLER

PAULA PECK

The Art of Fine Baking, 1961

Paula Peck was on her way to becoming a food-world star, but her career was cut short by illness and she died in 1972, at only forty-five years old. James Beard realized Peck's amazing talent for baking and encouraged her, as he did so many people, to follow her bliss, which in Peck's case was the world of eggs, flour, and yeast. The result was *The Art of Fine Baking*, about which Beard said in his introduction to the book: "This book is as complete a treatise on the art of baking as you will find in the English language." And so it is. Writing in a clear, concise, no-nonsense style, Peck makes even the most difficult baking recipes seem easy and within grasp of the home cook. Her illustrations help demystify some of the most complicated techniques. Though it's now fifty years old, *The Art of Fine Baking* still deserves a place on the bookshelf of any serious baker.

NOTABLE RECIPES: Apricot Cream Filling • Chocolate Brownies • Chocolate Truffles • **Croissants** (page 588) • **Gênoise** (page 621) • **Linzer Torte** (page 601) • **Swiss Meringue** (page 650)

ELIZABETH DAVID

French Provincial Cooking, 1962

The most important writers who influenced American food in the twentieth century include one Briton, Elizabeth David. David's heavily researched and impeccably written books on Mediterranean food changed not only how the English eat but also how Americans eat.

Born Elizabeth Gwynne, in 1913, into a very wealthy English family, David was a bit of a rebel from the start. Showing some talent as a teenager, she was sent by her mother to painting classes at the Sorbonne. Following graduation, she decided to take to the stage but realized quickly it was not for her. While in the Oxford Repertory Company in 1933, she met Charles Gibson-Cowan, who was nine years older than she and flouted convention as much as she did. The two began an affair, despite his being married. In 1938 they bought a boat and sailed off, planning to go to Greece. They traveled throughout France, spending time in Marseille. In Antibes David became close friends with Norman Douglas, the writer and aesthete. Her appreciation of cooking, already strong while in England, blossomed in the Mediterranean. From Douglas she learned never to accept anything but the very best of foods. David and Gibson-Cowan made it to Greece, only to be captured by the Nazis as possible spies. After their release, they went to Egypt, where they had an amicable split. David met Lieutenant-Colonel Tony David in Cairo and accepted his proposal of marriage.

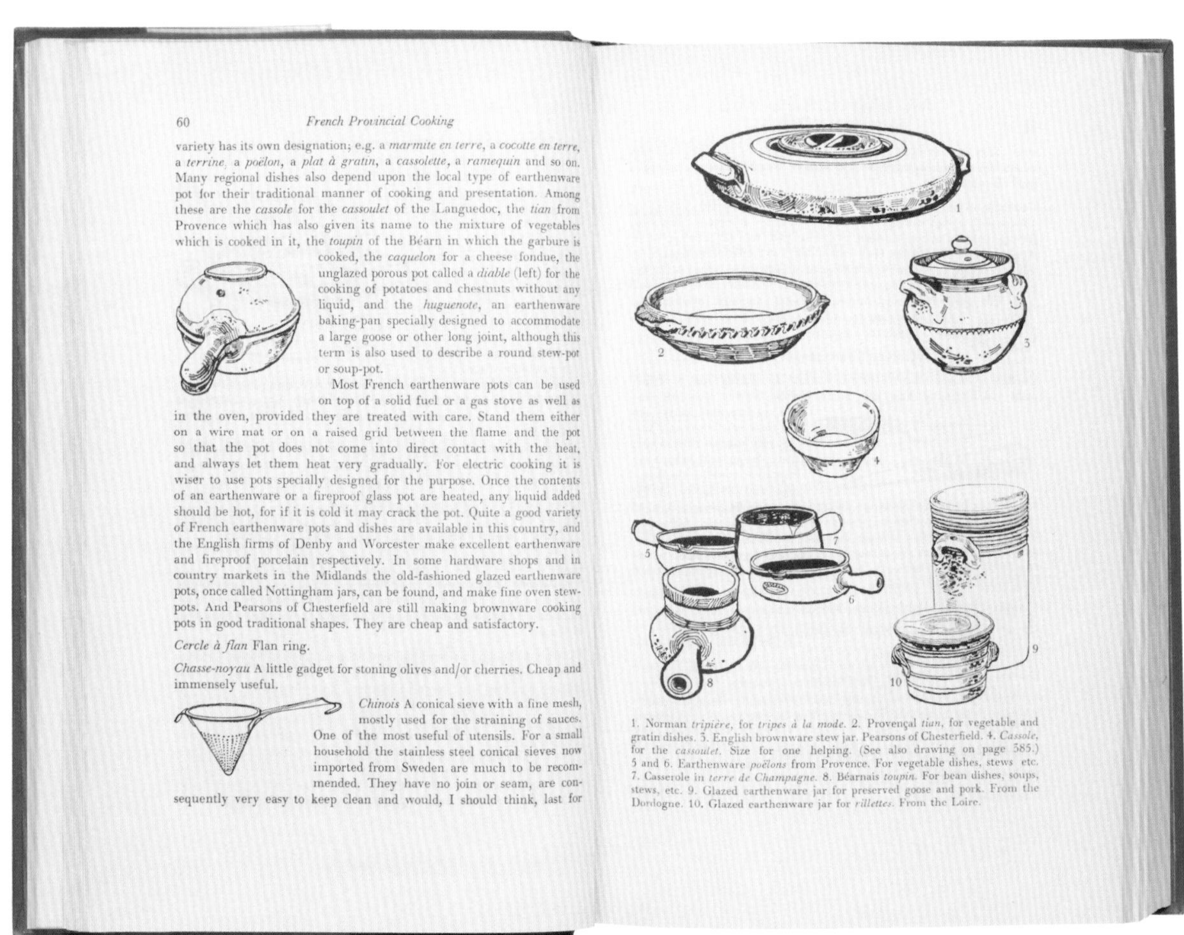

60 *French Provincial Cooking*

variety has its own designation; e.g. a *marmite en terre*, a *cocotte en terre*, a *terrine*, a *poëlon*, a *plat à gratin*, a *cassolette*, a *ramequin* and so on. Many regional dishes also depend upon the local type of earthenware pot for their traditional manner of cooking and presentation. Among these are the *cassole* for the *cassoulet* of the Languedoc, the *tian* from Provence which has also given its name to the mixture of vegetables which is cooked in it, the *toupin* of the Béarn in which the garbure is cooked, the *caquelon* for a cheese fondue, the unglazed porous pot called a *diable* (left) for the cooking of potatoes and chestnuts without any liquid, and the *huguenote*, an earthenware baking-pan specially designed to accommodate a large goose or other long joint, although this term is also used to describe a round stew-pot or soup-pot.

Most French earthenware pots can be used on top of a solid fuel or a gas stove as well as in the oven, provided they are treated with care. Stand them either on a wire mat or on a raised grid between the flame and the pot so that the pot does not come into direct contact with the heat, and always let them heat very gradually. For electric cooking it is wiser to use pots specially designed for the purpose. Once the contents of an earthenware or a fireproof glass pot are heated, any liquid added should be hot, for if it is cold it may crack the pot. Quite a good variety of French earthenware pots and dishes are available in this country, and the English firms of Denby and Worcester make excellent earthenware and fireproof porcelain respectively. In some hardware shops and in country markets in the Midlands the old-fashioned glazed earthenware pots, once called Nottingham jars, can be found, and make fine oven stew-pots. And Pearsons of Chesterfield are still making brownware cooking pots in good traditional shapes. They are cheap and satisfactory.

Cercle à flan Flan ring.

Chasse-noyau A little gadget for stoning olives and/or cherries. Cheap and immensely useful.

Chinois A conical sieve with a fine mesh, mostly used for the straining of sauces. One of the most useful of utensils. For a small household the stainless steel conical sieves now imported from Sweden are much to be recommended. They have no join or seam, are consequently very easy to keep clean and would, I should think, last for

1. Norman *tripière*, for *tripes à la mode*. 2. Provençal *tian*, for vegetable and gratin dishes. 3. English brownware stew jar. Pearsons of Chesterfield. 4. *Cassole*, for the *cassoulet*. Size for one helping. (See also drawing on page 585.) 5 and 6. Earthenware *poëlons* from Provence. For vegetable dishes, stews etc. 7. Casserole in *terre de Champagne*. 8. Béarnais *toupin*. For bean dishes, soups, stews, etc. 9. Glazed earthenware jar for preserved goose and pork. From the Dordogne. 10. Glazed earthenware jar for *rillettes*. From the Loire.

Finally, after some time in India, David returned to England in 1947 to find the state of food and eating a disaster. The war had destroyed the English food traditions, in which she'd had little interest anyway. David found her calling. She would introduce to the English table the cuisines of the Mediterranean that she knew and loved so well.

Her first book, titled *A Book of Mediterranean Food*, was a success, and she began work on her second, *French Country Cooking*. The publication in 1962 of *French Provincial Cooking* took America by storm. David's writing became known to all those seriously interested in food in the United States. Near the end of her life, David began visiting San Francisco, which she found to be as close to the markets of Italy and France as she had ever seen. She had long been a proponent of seasonal eating, that is, eating only what is in season when it is in season, and the bounteous produce of California was like a dream come true. Alice Waters has often cited the importance of David's writing on her own career and on the founding of Chez Panisse. Finally, David found a man preparing meals in an alley in San Francisco and loved his food. She told others about it and his business boomed. He moved into the adjacent restaurant space, which became San Francisco's beloved Zuni Café, now run and owned by celebrated chef Judy Rogers and a stopping-off point for knowledgeable food lovers from all over the world.

NOTABLE RECIPES: Cassoulet de Toulouse • Chocolate Cake • **La Bouillabaisse** (page 351) • **Poulet à l'Estragon** (page 504) • Quiche Lorraine • **Tarte à l'Oignon, or Zewelwaï** (page 416) • **Terrine de Campagne** (page 560)

Les Œufs, et les Hors-d'œuvre Chauds

Eggs, cheese dishes and hot hors-d'œuvre

'THEY reckon 685 ways of dressing eggs in the French kitchen; we hope our half-dozen recipes give sufficient variety for the English kitchen.' Doctor William Kitchiner, who wrote these words in *The Cook's Oracle*, round about 1821, therewith betrays himself as a pretty smug fellow.

For the life of me I cannot see why, if our neighbours 21 miles across the Channel have 685 ways of cooking eggs, we should have to make do with six. Six recipes would no more than cover the basic ways of cooking eggs common to all countries, but Dr. Kitchiner was certainly right in so far as it is important to understand these methods thoroughly before embarking on the 679 remaining variations.

'Have ready twelve freshly poached eggs,' says the cookery book, and with a shudder you turn over the page, knowing that, allowing for

180

Eggs, Cheese Dishes and Hot Hors-d'œuvre 181

disasters, those twelve eggs will probably turn into twenty and that your kitchen will be a charnel house of eggshells and a shambles of running egg yolks. Or 'shell eight *œufs mollets*,' they say, 'lay each in a puff pastry case and mask with an hollandaise sauce. Pour a cordon of melted meat glaze round each egg and brown with a salamander.' And one begins to agree with old Dr. Kitchiner. For elaborate dishes of this sort are not really to be recommended for household cookery. Leave them to the restaurant kitchens where there is a *chef-pâtissier* to prepare the pastry cases, a larder cook to provide the meat glaze, a sauce cook ready with the hollandaise, and half a dozen kitchen boys to clear away, to say nothing of the waiters ready to rush it from the kitchen to the tables.

There are still plenty of lovely egg dishes of a much simpler kind to be made at home; with constant practice and given the time, it is perfectly possible to poach a few eggs successfully; an omelette is very easily made, in spite of all the talk about light hands and heavy frying pans; and once you know the trick, the shelling of *œufs mollets* is quite easy, provided you have a steady hand.

I shall try to explain these things, and others connected with the successful manipulation of eggs, for they are well worth the practice needed and the time and money you must spend. From unsuccessful attempts there is much to be learnt, so one must count an occasional wasted egg or failed soufflé as profit rather than loss. Egg dishes have a kind of elegance, a freshness, an allure, which sets them quite apart from any other kind of food, so that it becomes a great pleasure to be able to cook them properly and to serve them in just the right condition.

Eggs in their own right, as well as all those allied dishes such as the onion tarts of Alsace, the cream and bacon *quiches* of Lorraine and all the various cheese and egg, potato and cream, and hot pastry confections of the different provinces of France which come under the heading of hot hors-d'œuvre make the best possible dishes to serve as a first course at luncheon on the occasions when something hot is required. But it cannot be claimed that these are particularly *light* dishes. Eggs, and especially eggs with cheese or cream, are very filling. So if you are starting with a soufflé, or an onion tart, or a *pipérade*, it is best to make the second course something not too rich, and certainly not one requiring an egg or cream sauce.

ŒUFS À LA COQUE

BOILED EGGS

Although eggs are cooked in such a variety of exquisite ways by French cooks, the ordinary boiled egg is not their strong point. One would be

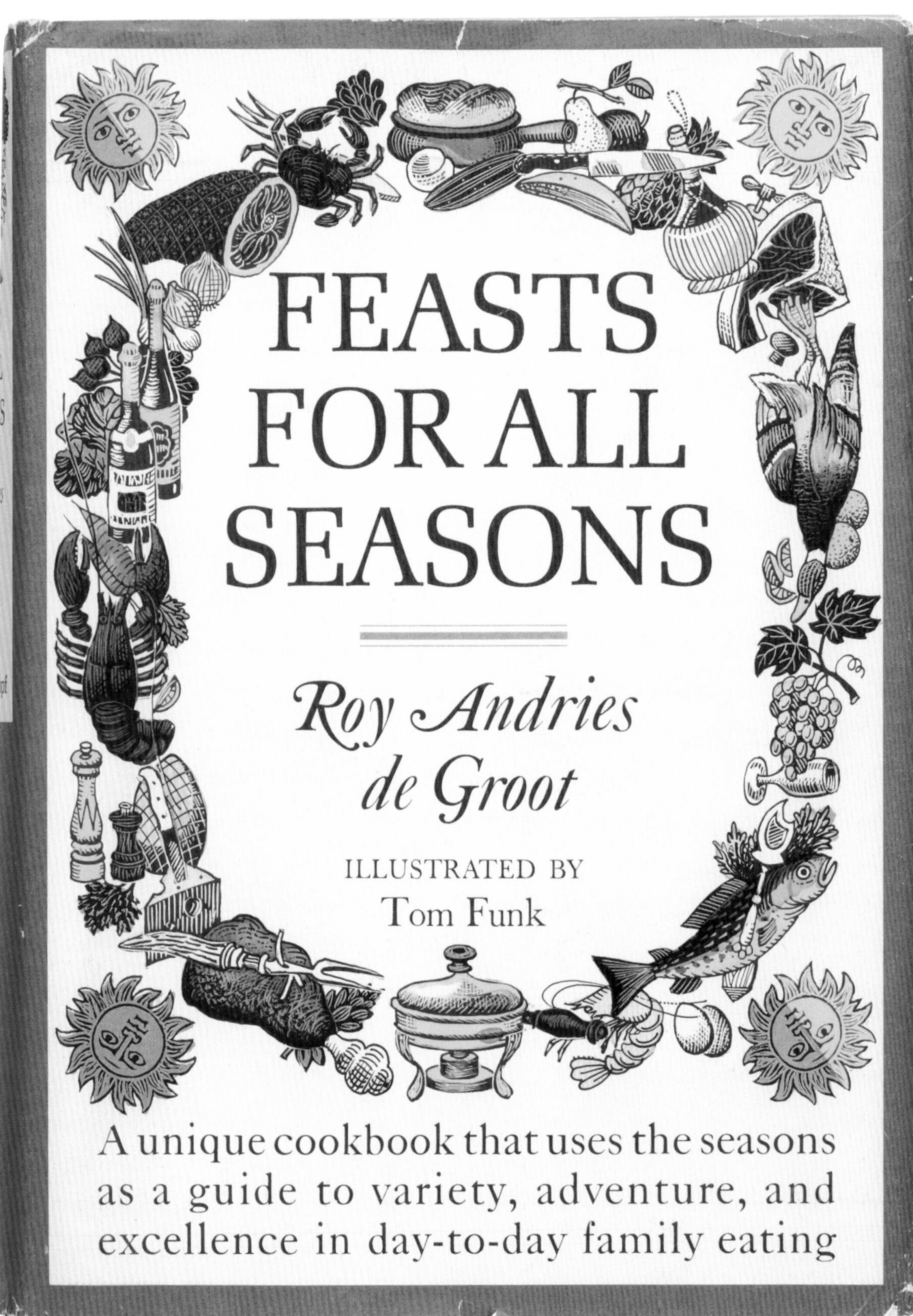
FEASTS
FOR ALL
SEASONS
Roy Andries
de Groot
ILLUSTRATED BY
Tom Funk
A unique cookbook that uses the seasons
as a guide to variety, adventure, and
excellence in day-to-day family eating

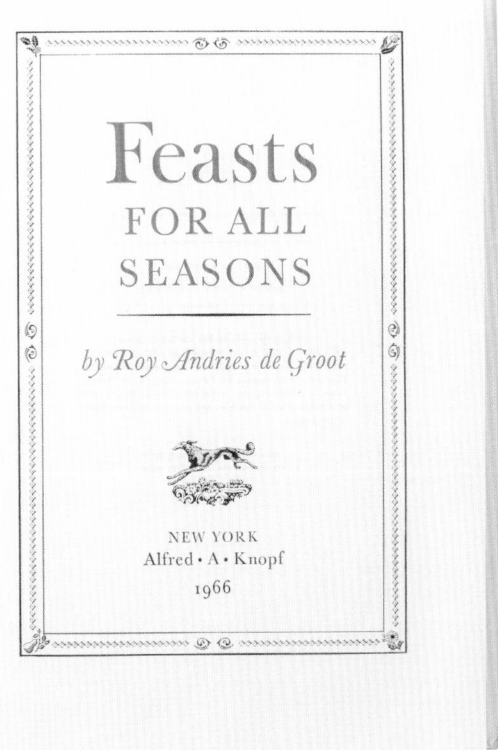

Feasts
FOR ALL
SEASONS

by Roy Andries de Groot

NEW YORK
Alfred · A · Knopf
1966

ROY ANDRIES DE GROOT

Feasts for All Seasons, 1966

Roy Andries de Groot's *Feasts for All Seasons* is one of the early cookbooks organized around seasonal eating. It's not that this was really a new conceit. Many European cuisines, which rely on absolutely fresh produce, say, are by their very nature seasonal. This was true historically of American cooking, too. With the advent of boxed, canned, and frozen foods and the invention of refrigerated train cars and trucks, however, habits changed. Inferior produce, meat, fruit, and other edibles were available year-round.

De Groot, in his imperious way, wrote *Feasts for All Seasons* to challenge the use of these lesser products. Audaciously, he begins the book with cooking for winter, notoriously difficult for Northeasterners, whose growing season is so short. It's the longest and most inventive section of the book.

De Groot was a bit of an eccentric. Born in London in 1910, he was part Dutch by birth, went through the English school system, and attended Oxford University. After graduation he worked for the BBC as a writer, producer, and announcer. In 1940 he suffered eye damage during the Blitz and began to go blind. At this point he decided to turn his attention to food and wine, two of his great passions, and remade himself as a culinary expert with an elegant writing style. Although he held the title of Baron de Groot, he stopped using it after he became a U.S. citizen in 1945. In addition to *Feasts for All Seasons*, De Groot wrote several other books, including *Revolutionizing French Cooking* and *The Wines of California, the Pacific Northwest and New York.*

NOTABLE RECIPES: Chicken Paprikas • Clafoutis • **Cseresznyeleves—Cold Cherry Soup** (page 334) • **Fruit and Chestnut Stuffing** (page 425) • **Lemon-Cream Spaghetti with Fish Stuffing** (page 394) • Sicilian Onions in Marsala

The Elegant But Easy Cookbook

By Marian Fox Burros and Lois Levine

Revised and greatly expanded, a new version of the best-selling cookbook "*Elegant But Easy, A Cookbook for Hostesses.*"

MARIAN BURROS

The Elegant But Easy Cookbook, 1967

Long before Mark Bittman became "the minimalist," Mari an Burros was promoting simple, quick meals that had big flavor. After completing her undergraduate degree in English at Wellesley College, Burros became a cooking instructor, but her real love was writing about food. Her cookbooks include *The Elegant But Easy Cookbook* (MacMillan, 1967), *Freeze with Ease* (MacMillan, 1967), *Come for Cocktails, Stay for Supper* (MacMillan, 1970), *The Summertime Cookbook* (MacMillan, 1972), *Pure & Simple* (William Morrow, 1978), *Keep It Simple* (William Morrow, 1981), *You've Got It Made* (William Morrow, 1984), *The Best of De Gustibus* (Simon & Schuster, 1988), and *20-Minute Menus* (Simon & Schuster, 1989). She wrote for the *Washington Post*, the *Washington Daily News*, and the *Washington Star*, among many other newspapers.

In 1981 she became a reporter for the *New York Times*, and in 1983 was named the *Times*'s food columnist. In some ways, Burros's cookbooks are the antidote to Julia Child's recipes in *Mastering the Art of French Cooking*. Burros understood that not everyone who loves good food has the time to make stock or to braise a pork shoulder for three hours. Women's and men's lives had changed by the late 1960s. Perhaps over the weekend the committed home cook could undertake one of Child's elaborate dishes to serve guests for a Saturday evening supper, but on the average weeknight, twenty minutes of preparation was about what you had to fix a meal. *Elegant But Easy* delivered a group of recipes and a way of thinking about food that reflected the realities of a new lifestyle. And the recipes are as valid today as they were in 1967.

NOTABLE RECIPES: Chafing-Dish Meatballs (page 329) • **Chicken Florentine** (page 499) • **Fruit Torte** (page 599) • Grand Marnier Soufflé • Lasagna • **Sherley's Parmesan Puffs** (page 318)

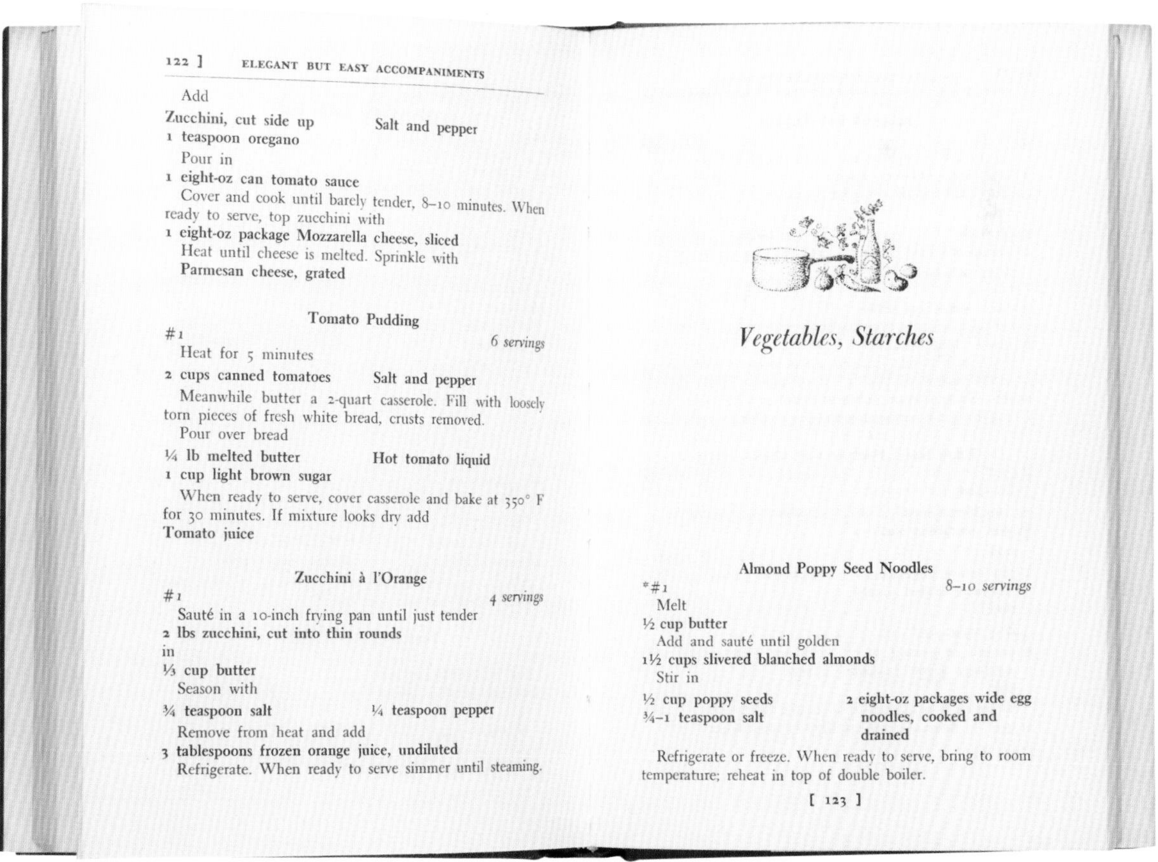

122] ELEGANT BUT EASY ACCOMPANIMENTS

Add

Zucchini, cut side up **Salt and pepper**
1 teaspoon oregano

Pour in

1 eight-oz can tomato sauce

Cover and cook until barely tender, 8–10 minutes. When ready to serve, top zucchini with

1 eight-oz package Mozzarella cheese, sliced

Heat until cheese is melted. Sprinkle with

Parmesan cheese, grated

Tomato Pudding

#1 *6 servings*

Heat for 5 minutes

2 cups canned tomatoes **Salt and pepper**

Meanwhile butter a 2-quart casserole. Fill with loosely torn pieces of fresh white bread, crusts removed.

Pour over bread

¼ lb melted butter **Hot tomato liquid**
1 cup light brown sugar

When ready to serve, cover casserole and bake at 350° F for 30 minutes. If mixture looks dry add

Tomato juice

Zucchini à l'Orange

#1 *4 servings*

Sauté in a 10-inch frying pan until just tender

2 lbs zucchini, cut into thin rounds

in

⅓ cup butter

Season with

¾ teaspoon salt **¼ teaspoon pepper**

Remove from heat and add

3 tablespoons frozen orange juice, undiluted

Refrigerate. When ready to serve simmer until steaming.

Vegetables, Starches

Almond Poppy Seed Noodles

*#1 *8–10 servings*

Melt

½ cup butter

Add and sauté until golden

1½ cups slivered blanched almonds

Stir in

½ cup poppy seeds **2 eight-oz packages wide egg noodles, cooked and drained**
¾–1 teaspoon salt

Refrigerate or freeze. When ready to serve, bring to room temperature; reheat in top of double boiler.

[123]

EDWARD ESPE BROWN

The Tassajara Bread Book, 1970

Whatever your feelings about the hippie movement of the 1960s, one thing is certain: The movement's emphasis on food, on a return to nature, and on activism created the American food revolution today. There would be no organic, return-to-the-farm, locavore, foodie identity to inhabit without the hippie counterculture.

Baking bread, for example, became a moral statement. No longer was it acceptable to eat over-processed Wonder Bread. The alternative: Bake your own bread—preferably with lots of whole, nutritious grains. Unfortunately, these loaves often had the consistency of a brick. *The Tassajara Bread Book* changed all that. Edward Espe Brown was a student at a Zen retreat named Tassajara in Monterey, California, in the late 1960s, where he asked the cooks to teach him how to bake. He became a master baker and published *The Tassajara Bread Book* in 1970 in an edition of 3,000 copies. The book was an immediate success because it taught a generation of willing, radically minded bakers how to create good bread that supported their moral convictions. *The Tassajara Bread Book has* sold more than 750,000 copies since it was first published. Brown went on to publish other cookbooks and to open the famous vegetarian restaurant Greens, with Deborah Madison. His mix of good food with good ethics still stands as a model today.

NOTABLE RECIPES: Banana Sandwich Bread • Corn Sesame Breakfast Cake • **Flakey Biscuits** (page 590) • Honey Bars • **Mustard Gingerbread** (page 589) • **Tassajara Yeasted Bread** (page 569)

folding until oil and salt are incorporated (Figures 8, 9, 10).

Sprinkle DRY INGREDIENTS on surface of dough about a cup at a time. Fold wet mixture from sides of bowl on top of dry ingredients. Turn the bowl ¼ turn between folds (Figures 8, 9, 10). When dry ingredients are moistened by the dough, add some more dry ingredients (Figures 11 and 12). Continue folding. After adding 6–8 cups of wheat flour, the dough will become very thick and heavy, but don't be intimidated. Continue folding in flour until dough comes away from (does not stick to) sides and bottom of bowl, sitting up in bowl in a big lump (Figure 12). The dough is ready for kneading when it can be turned out of bowl in pretty much of a piece, except for a few remaining scraps (Figure 13). Take time to scrape bowl carefully, and lay scrapings on top of dough on floured board. It is not necessary to wash the bread bowl at this point, simply oil it lightly.

(B) KNEADING THE DOUGH

The kneading surface, board or table should be at a height on which your hands rest comfortably when you are standing straight (mid-thigh). Keep the surface floured sufficiently to prevent the dough from sticking during kneading. The purpose of kneading is to get the dough well-mixed, of a smooth, even texture, and to further develop the elasticity of the dough.

Beginning with a lump of dough not entirely of a piece, somewhat ragged and limply-lying, commence kneading. Flour your hands.

26

14

15

16

27

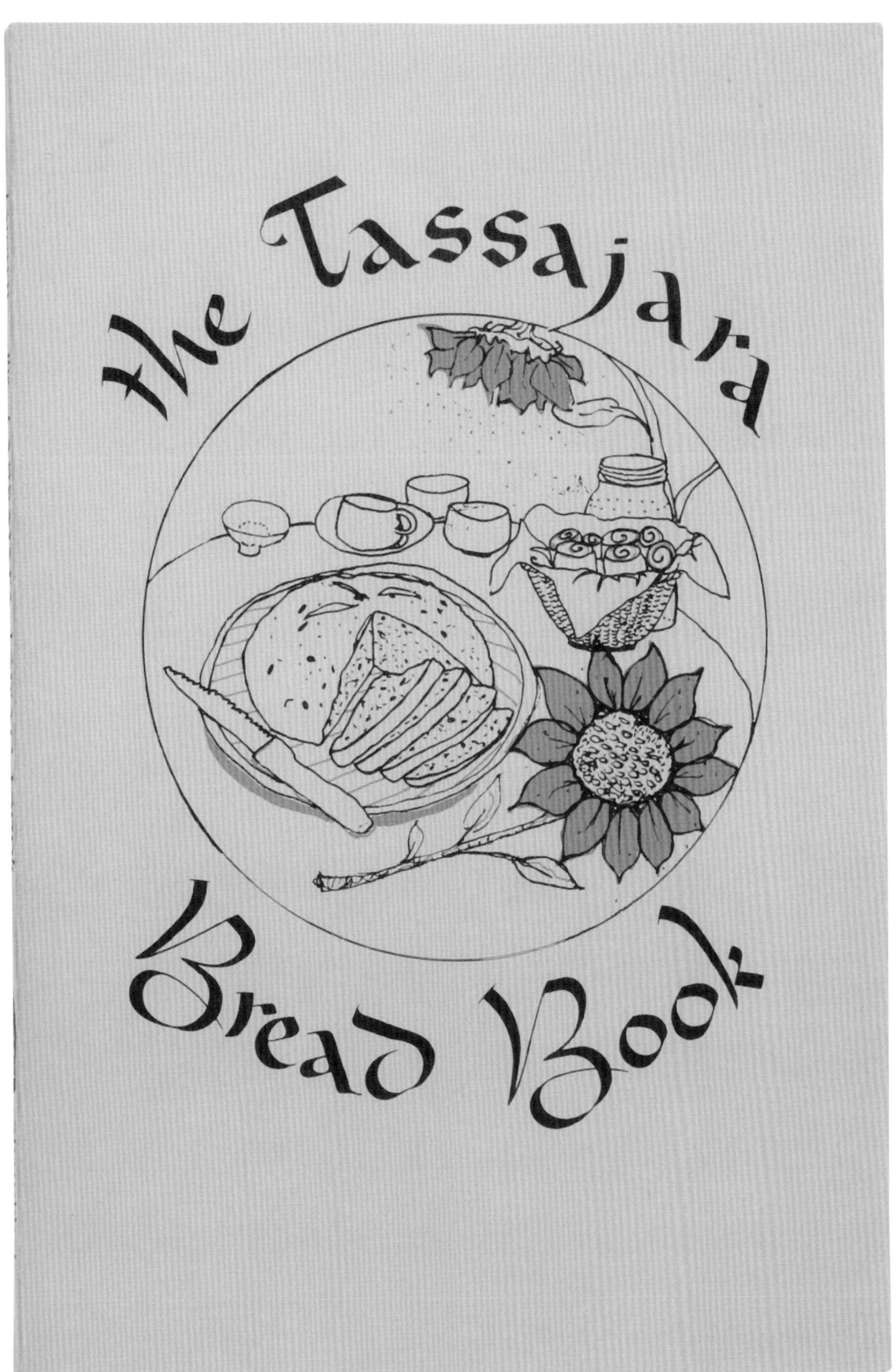
The Tassajara
Bread Book

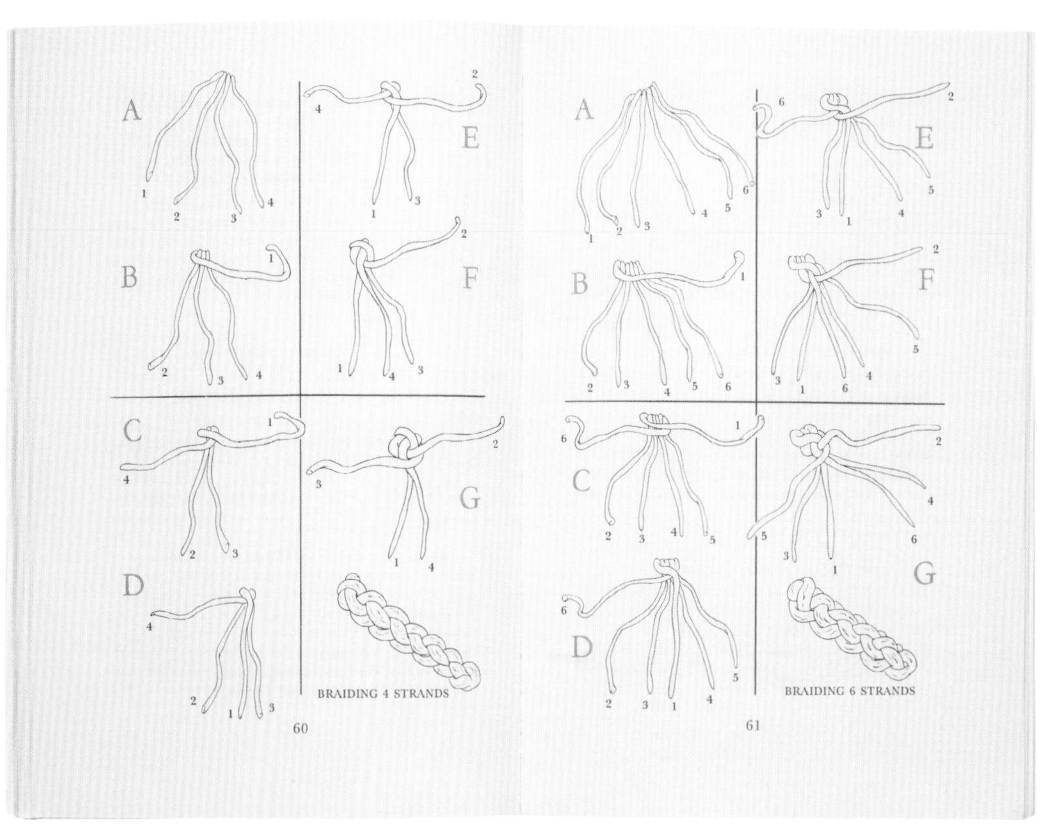

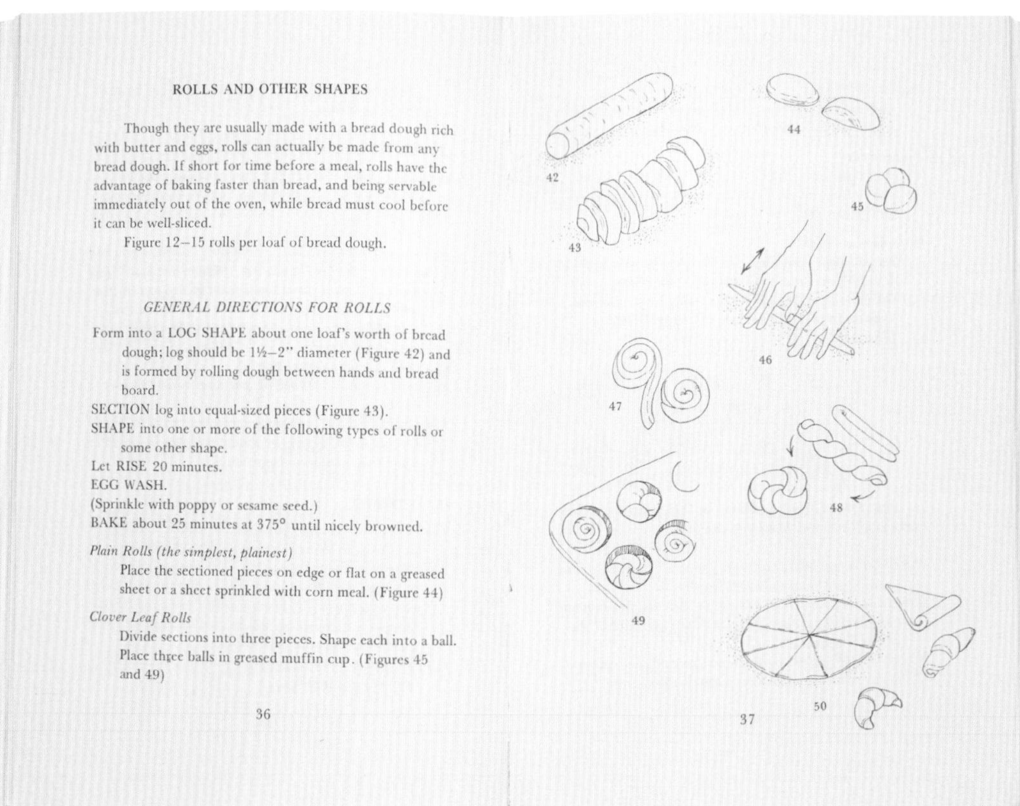

ROLLS AND OTHER SHAPES

Though they are usually made with a bread dough rich with butter and eggs, rolls can actually be made from any bread dough. If short for time before a meal, rolls have the advantage of baking faster than bread, and being servable immediately out of the oven, while bread must cool before it can be well-sliced.

Figure 12–15 rolls per loaf of bread dough.

GENERAL DIRECTIONS FOR ROLLS

Form into a LOG SHAPE about one loaf's worth of bread dough; log should be 1½–2" diameter (Figure 42) and is formed by rolling dough between hands and bread board.
SECTION log into equal-sized pieces (Figure 43).
SHAPE into one or more of the following types of rolls or some other shape.
Let RISE 20 minutes.
EGG WASH.
(Sprinkle with poppy or sesame seed.)
BAKE about 25 minutes at 375° until nicely browned.

Plain Rolls (the simplest, plainest)
Place the sectioned pieces on edge or flat on a greased sheet or a sheet sprinkled with corn meal. (Figure 44)

Clover Leaf Rolls
Divide sections into three pieces. Shape each into a ball. Place three balls in greased muffin cup. (Figures 45 and 49)

36

37

ALICIA BAY LAUREL

Living on the Earth

Celebrations, Storm Warnings, Formulas, Recipes, Rumors, Country Dances Harvested by Alicia Bay Laurel, 1971

In 1969 Alicia Bay Laurel wrote, designed, and illustrated *Living on the Earth*, the first hippie cookbook. It is now a legendary guide to sustainable living. In the spring of 1971 *Living on the Earth* was the first paperback book included on the *New York Times* best-seller list. Its calligraphic style, reproducing Laurel's handwriting, launched a trend for other homespun and, occasionally, psychedelic designs.

NOTABLE RECIPES: Dandelion Wine (page 313) • **How to Smoke Fish** (page 472) • Plum Pudding • Sourdough Starter/Bread • **Sunflower Milk** (page 317) • **Yogurt** (page 433)

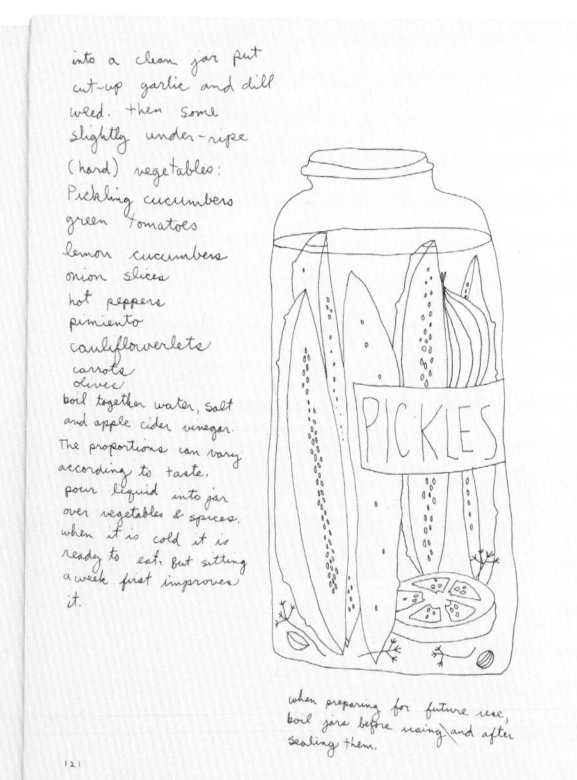

into a clean jar put cut-up garlic and dill weed. then some slightly under-ripe (hard) vegetables:
Pickling cucumbers
green tomatoes
lemon cucumbers
onion slices
hot peppers
pimiento
cauliflowerlets
carrots
olives
boil together water, salt and apple cider vinegar. The proportions can vary according to taste. pour liquid into jar over vegetables & spices. when it is cold it is ready to eat, but sitting a week first improves it.

when preparing for future use, boil jars before using and after sealing them.

121

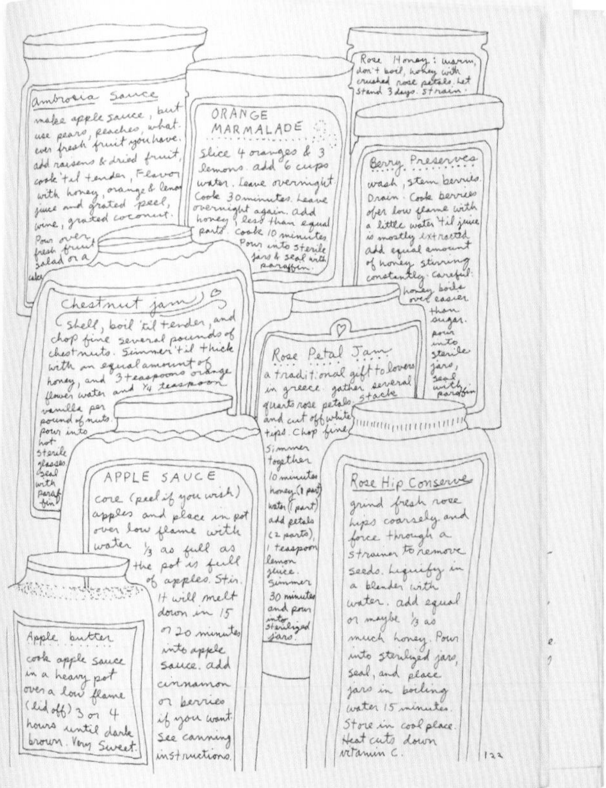

Ambrosia Sauce
make apple sauce, but use pears, peaches, whatever fresh fruit you have. add raisens & dried fruit, cook 'til tender, Flavor with honey, orange & lemon juice and grated peel, wine, grated coconut. Pour over fresh fruit salad or a cake

ORANGE MARMALADE
Slice 4 oranges & 3 lemons. add 6 cups water. Leave overnight. Cook 30 minutes. Leave overnight again. add honey, less than equal parts. Cook 10 minutes. Pour into sterile jars & seal with paraffin.

Rose Honey: warm, don't boil, honey with crushed rose petals. Let stand 3 days. Strain.

Berry Preserves
wash, stem berries. Drain. Cook berries over low flame with a little water 'til juice is mostly extracted. add equal amount of honey, stirring constantly. careful: honey boils over easier than sugar. pour into sterile jars, seal with paraffin

Chestnut jam
Shell, boil 'til tender, and chop fine several pounds of chestnuts. Simmer 'til thick with an equal amount of honey, and 3 teaspoons orange flower water and 1/4 teaspoon vanilla per pound of nuts. pour into hot sterile glasses. seal with paraffin

Rose Petal Jam
a traditional gift to lovers in greece. gather several quarts rose petals, stack and cut off white tips. Chop fine. Simmer together 10 minutes honey (1 part) water (1 part) add petals (2 parts), 1 teaspoon lemon juice. Simmer 30 minutes and pour into sterilized jars.

APPLE SAUCE
core (peel if you wish) apples and place in pot over low flame with water 1/3 as full as the pot is full of apples. Stir. It will melt down in 15 or 20 minutes into apple sauce. add cinnamon or berries if you want. See canning instructions.

Apple butter
cook apple sauce in a heavy pot over a low flame (lid off) 3 or 4 hours until dark brown. Very Sweet.

Rose Hip Conserve
grind fresh rose hips coarsely and force through a strainer to remove seeds. Liquify in a blender with water. add equal or maybe 1/3 as much honey. Pour into sterilized jars, seal, and place jars in boiling water 15 minutes. Store in cool place. Heat cuts down vitamin C.

122

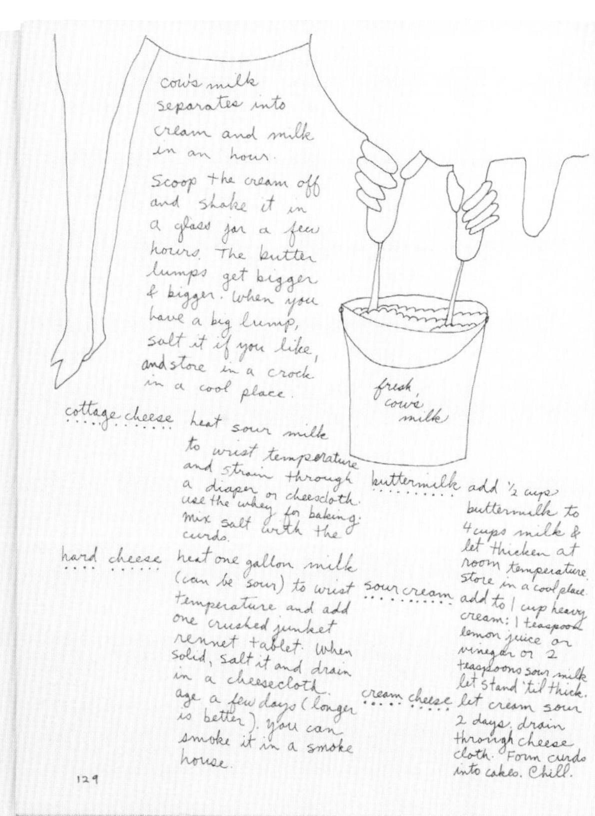

cow's milk separates into cream and milk in an hour.

Scoop the cream off and shake it in a glass jar a few hours. The butter lumps get bigger & bigger. When you have a big lump, salt it if you like, and store in a crock in a cool place.

cottage cheese — heat sour milk to wrist temperature and strain through a diaper or cheesecloth. use the whey for baking. mix salt with the curds.

buttermilk — add ½ cups buttermilk to 4 cups milk & let thicken at room temperature. store in a cool place.

hard cheese — heat one gallon milk (can be sour) to wrist temperature and add one crushed junket rennet tablet. When solid, salt it and drain in a cheesecloth. age a few days (longer is better). You can smoke it in a smoke house.

sour cream — add to 1 cup heavy cream: 1 teaspoon lemon juice or vinegar or 2 teaspoons sour milk. let stand 'til thick.

cream cheese — let cream sour 2 days, drain through cheese cloth. Form curds into cakes. Chill.

129

heat milk to wrist temperature (don't boil) and stir in one tablespoon yogurt per pint of milk. Pour into small glass jars. Leave them in the sun all day if it is warm and sunny. Or leave in a warm place (near stove). Or if it's sunny, but not warm, leave jars in a black box in the sun all day. Or put yogurt in a thermos bottle. Instant milk can also be used - or even evaporated milk - restored to normal consistency.

Store in a cool place after it reaches desired tanginess. Yogurt culture distroys toxic bacteria in the colon.

130

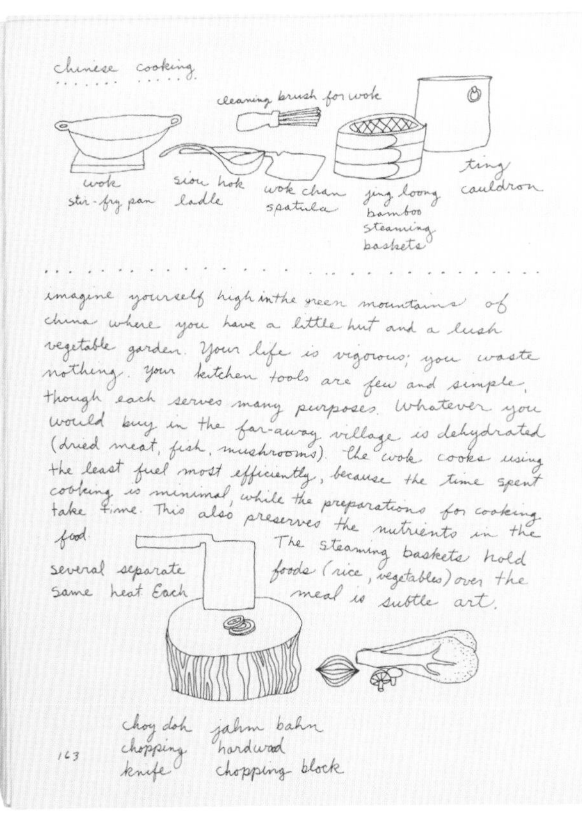

chinese cooking

imagine yourself high in the green mountains of china where you have a little hut and a lush vegetable garden. Your life is vigorous; you waste nothing. Your kitchen tools are few and simple, though each serves many purposes. Whatever you would buy in the far-away village is dehydrated (dried meat, fish, mushrooms). the wok cooks using the least fuel most efficiently, because the time spent cooking is minimal, while the preparations for cooking take time. This also preserves the nutrients in the food. The steaming baskets hold several separate foods (rice, vegetables) over the same heat. Each meal is subtle art.

163

felafel are the arabic taco. pita is a flat yeast bread - hollow in the middle. In it you put deep-fried balls of garbanzo bean purée, over that a salad of tomato, onion and cucumber or else eggplant cooked according to the recipe in this book, and over that a sauce of garbanzo purée and garlic.

an israeli-arabic recipe...

felafel:

combine the following and roll into balls one inch in diameter:

4 cups puréed cooked garbanzo beans
1 teaspoon salt
½ teaspoon white pepper
one mashed pickled red pepper
½ teaspoon basil & thyme & marjoram - mixed
½ cup fine crumbs
4 eggs
4 tablespoons tahini (ground sesame)

Roll balls in one cup dry crumbs and deep fry.

pita

dissolve one teaspoon yeast in ½ cup warm water with one teaspoon sugar. When foamy add a beaten egg, and 2 cups flour sifted with a pinch of salt, and 3 tablespoons oil and ½ cup warm water. Cover and let rise 'til it doubles. Form 12 flat cakes and place on a greased & floured pan. let rise until double again, pat them flat, brush with oil and bake 20 minutes at 375° until light brown and puffy.

Nahit Sauce

mix together:

one cup garbanzo purée
½ cup cooking liquid from beans
4 tablespoons tahini
¼ teaspoon raw garlic juice.

164

New Years' Day Family Meals Served at the Table of Count Sztaniszlo Thurzo

In the Town of Galgoc, January 1, 1603

Luncheon

1. Beef Meat with Horseradish
2. Capon with Honeyed Noodles
3. Soup with Sausage and Bread
4. Pike in Salt
5. Beaver Tail in Fruit Broth
6. Walnut Stuffed Indian Chicken (1)
7. Salmon cooked with Gooseberries
8. Calf's Lung with Pure Black Pepper
9. Lamb with Lemon
10. Peppered Duck with Girl's Sprouts (2)
11. Calf with Bacon
12. Sourkraut with Flourmeat
13. Roast Duck
14. Little Birds of Pork Tenderloin
15. Roast Grouse
16. Pate
17. Stuffed Wafers (3)
18. Tiny Pastries

Dinner

1. Duck with Roux
2. Chopped Capon
3. Peppered Tuna
4. Vinegared and Herbed Sheep's Meat
5. Eels Cooked with Cabbage
6. Veal with Saffron
7. Pike with Chicken Broth but Honest
8. Capon with Sour Cream
9. Fillet of Beef
10. Turnip with Meat
11. Breaded Fish Fried in Butter
12. Rice Gruel with Brains
13. Pork Tenderloin
14. Steak with Priest' Salad
15. Doughnut Fried in Butter
16. Stuffed Wafers (3)
17. Plum Torte
18. Rabbit in Black Juice

New Year's Day family meals. Calligraphy by the author.

GEORGE LANG

The Cuisine of Hungary, 1971

At age nineteen, in June 1944, George Lang was forced to leave his Hungarian home and enter a labor camp. His parents died in Auschwitz, but Lang managed to escape to New York, where he began his career in American food as a dishwasher. Lang brought three cherished books along with him: *The Selected Writings of Epictetus, Morning Serenade* by Arpad Toth, and *Ethics* by Epicurus. Almost as soon as he entered the food world in New York, Lang became known for organizing large, sold-out banquets. By 1956, just twelve years after he was sent to the Hungarian labor camp, the Waldorf-Astoria appointed Lang chef and assistant banquet manager. In 1960 Joe Baum's famed Restaurant Associates hired Lang to help open two new avant-garde restaurants, including the Tower Suite in the Time-Life Building. A few years later, Lang found himself director of the Four Seasons, soon to become one of the most distinguished restaurants in New York. In 1971 he resigned from his position with Restaurant Associates and started one of the first-ever fine dining consulting businesses. Lang would go on to own a trademark restaurant of New York City, Café des Artistes, and later purchase, renovate, and open the historic Gundel in Budapest in 1992.

The Cuisine of Hungary introduced Americans to the rich heritage of Hungarian cooking. Lang never lost his great love of books about food. He, along with his wife and business partner, Jenifer Lang, amassed a collection of more than 22,000 volumes, which they donated to the Fales Library in 2010.

NOTABLE RECIPES: Ilona Torte (page 625) • **Inces' Stuffed Cabbage** (page 420) • **Layered Cabbage Basic Recipe, or Kolosvàri Layered Cabbage** (page 384) • Marosszeki Heranytokany • **Lecsó** (page 418) • **Paprika Chicken** (page 510) • Túrós Pogácsa (Biscuits with Cottage Cheese) • Veal Paprikas • **Veal Pörkölt** (page 554)

FRANCES MOORE LAPPÉ

Diet for a Small Planet, 1971

The most revolutionary cookbook of the American twentieth century wasn't intended to be a cookbook, though it has recipes in it; it was a political manifesto about global hunger and the wastefulness of American beef production.

In 1971 Frances Lappé, a graduate student at the University of California, Berkeley, saw that part of the problem of world hunger was the distribution of foods. Americans in particular wasted natural resources and land to sate their love of beef. Cattle ranching is very expensive and requires huge amounts of land to produce a small portion of protein. Lappé famously noted that "spinach . . . can produce up to 26 times more protein per acre than can beef." Her message was seen as a call to vegetarianism by many, but it was, in actuality, much more. In the spirit of the time, Lappé tied the issue of global hunger to the personal acts of individuals. If you were eating industrially produced beef, you were a part of the problem. She helped make eating a political statement: "It's very liberating to realize that you can choose good food, that you don't have to be led around by advertising."

Lappé's book was an instant success and has sold more than three million copies. At first glance, her manifesto seems like a rejection of fine dining and the gourmet tradition in the United States. In fact, many of her recipes, like those of other "hippie" cookbooks, aren't very appealing to the average American. (It would take time for the wondrous vegetarian dishes of the world to entice Americans away from their high-protein diet.) But that's almost beside the point. Without Lappé's work, and those of others like her who combined activism with food, we would not be as focused on, for example, organic farming, locavorism, grass-fed beef, heirloom pork, cage-free hens, and our contemporary conscience about what we eat. Dan Imhoff's work to change the Farm Bill, the single greatest deterrent to healthy eating in the United States, wouldn't have such a large following.

Lappé suggested how politics prevents us from eating well, and Marion Nestle proved exactly how that happens in *Food Politics*. Michael Pollan followed in Lappé's footsteps when he published *The Omnivore's Dilemma*, showing a new generation the ethical and health implications of industrial meat production. In short, we would not think and act about food the way we do today without this slim paperback.

NOTABLE RECIPES: Egg and Potato Bake • Hearty Vegetable Soup • Leafy Chinese Tofu • Lentils Monastery Style • **Roman Rice and Beans** (page 382) • **Tabouli** (page 365) • **Turkish Barley-Buttermilk Soup** (page 344)

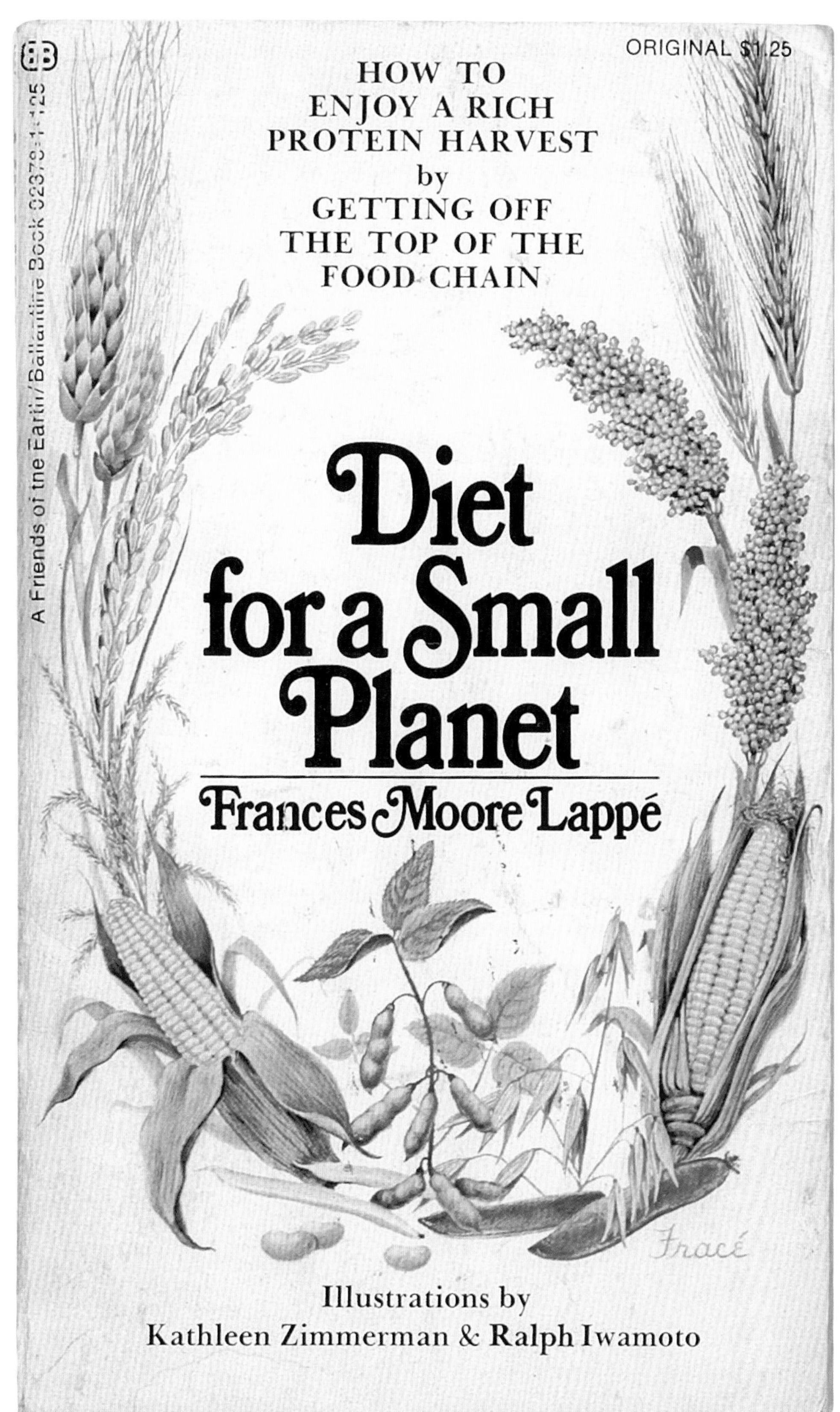
A Friends of the Earth/Ballantine Book 02378-1-125
ORIGINAL $1.25
HOW TO
ENJOY A RICH
PROTEIN HARVEST
by
GETTING OFF
THE TOP OF THE
FOOD CHAIN
Diet
for a Small
Planet
Frances Moore Lappé
Illustrations by
Kathleen Zimmerman & Ralph Iwamoto

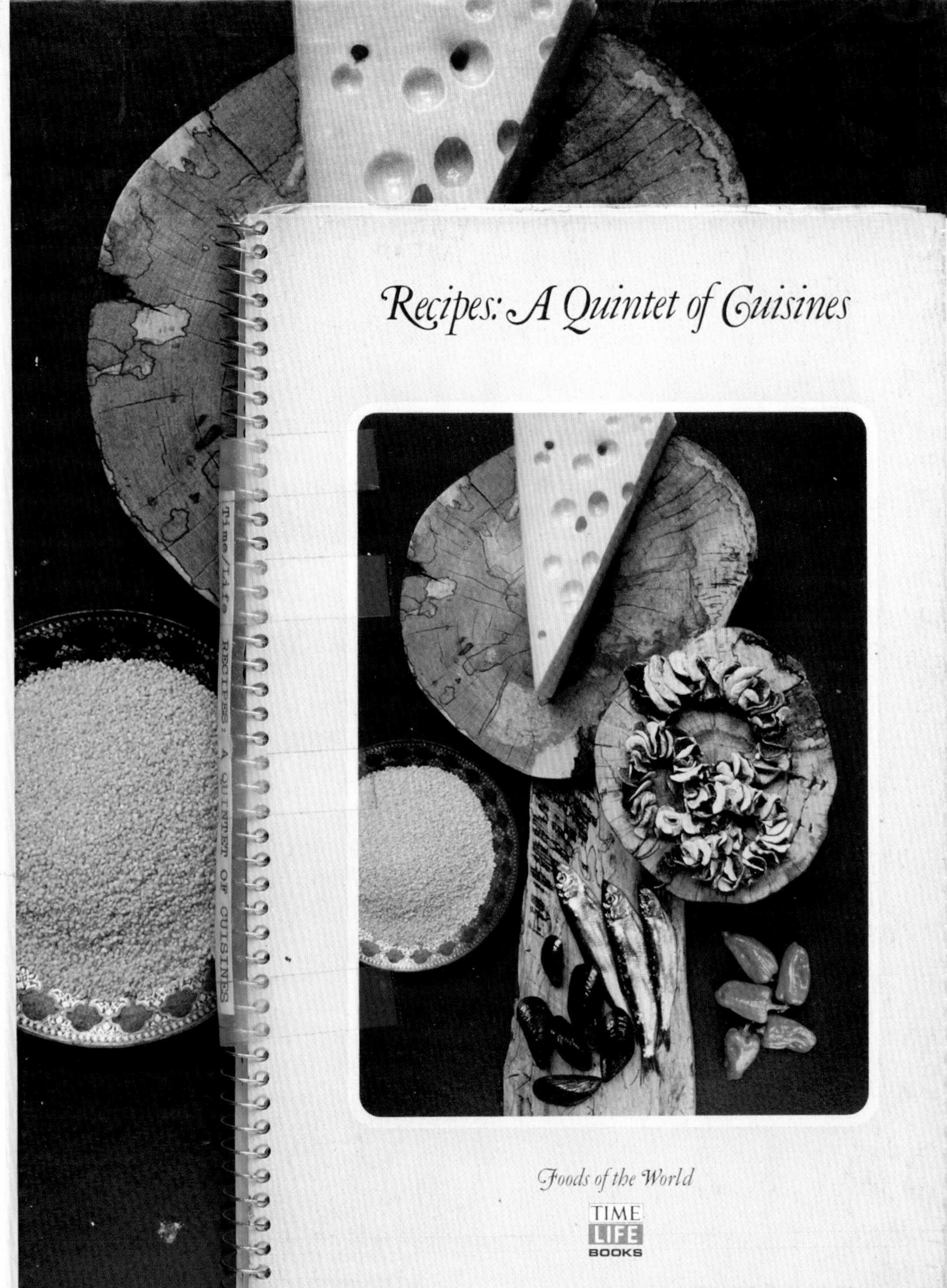
A Quintet of Cuisines by Michael and Frances Field
Recipes: A Quintet of Cuisines
Foods of the World
TIME
LIFE
BOOKS
Time/Life RECIPES: A QUINTET OF CUISINES

TIME-LIFE BOOKS

Foods of the World

27 Volumes, 1968–1970

Many American food writers of the 1940s, '50s, and '60s were obsessed with what constitutes American food. People like Sheila Hibben, Clementine Paddleford, and James Beard all wrote cookbooks that showed the breadth and depth of American cooking. It's not as if no international cookbooks were published during this time, but they were the exception.

In 1961 Julia Child's *Mastering the Art of French Cooking* taught American cooks that French food could be made at home and was no longer solely the province of chefs and haute cuisine restaurants. With the cultural revolution of the late 1960s and '70s, which questioned so many of our traditions, the American palate opened up and began to explore world foods. Perhaps no single publication expresses this so well as the Time-Life Foods of the World Series, consisting of twenty-seven volumes, edited by the outstanding author and food maven Richard Olney. For many Americans, these cookbooks were the first chance they had to hear about food from Africa, India, or Japan. This was also a time when Americans liked to purchase things by installment. Time-Life had several similar series on topics such as Ancient Civilizations, World War II, and the Emergence of Man. If you subscribed, you received a volume every month. In the case of Foods of the World, you received not only a large-format hardbound book, profusely illustrated and with text about the food of a particular region, but also a smaller, spiral-bound book of recipes. Following is a list of the complete set.

Bailey, Adrian. *Cooking of the British Isles.* 1969.
Brown, Dale. *American Cooking.* 1968.
Brown, Dale. *American Cooking: The Northwest.* 1970.
Brown, Dale. *Cooking of Scandinavia.* 1968.
Claiborne, Craig. *Classic French Cooking.* 1970.
Feibleman, Peter S. American *Cooking: Creole and Acadian.* 1971.
Feibleman, Peter S. *Cooking of Spain and Portugal.* 1969.
Field, Michael. *Quintet of Cuisines.* 1970.
Fisher, M.F.K. *Cooking of Provincial France.* 1968.
Hahn, Emily. *Cooking of China.* 1973.
Hazelton, Nika Standen. *Cooking of Germany.* 1968.
Leonard, Jonathan Norton. *American Cooking: The Great West.* 1971.
Leonard, Jonathan Norton. *American Cooking: New England.* 1970.
Leonard, Jonathan Norton. *Latin American Cooking.* 1968.
Nickles, Harry G. *Middle Eastern Cooking.* 1969.
Papashvily, Helen Waite. *Russian Cooking.* 1969.
Rau, Santha Rama. *Cooking of India.* 1969.
Root, Waverley. *Cooking of Italy.* 1968.
Shenton, James Patrick. *American Cooking: The Melting Pot.* 1971.
Steinberg, Rafael. *Cooking of Japan.* 1969.
Steinberg, Rafael. *Pacific and Southeast Asian Cooking.* 1970.
Van der Post, Laurens. *African Cooking.* 1970.
Walter, Eugene. *American Cooking: Southern Style.* 1971.
Waugh, Alec. *Wines and Spirits.* 1968.
Wechsberg, Joseph. *Cooking of Vienna's Empire.* 1968.
Wilson, José. *American Cooking: The Eastern Heartland.* 1971.
Wolfe, Linda. *Cooking of the Caribbean Islands.* 1970.

NOTABLE RECIPES: Endive Stuffed with Chicken in Mornay Sauce Wrapped in Ham Gratineed (Quintet of Cuisines) • **Irish Soda Bread** (Cooking of the British Isles) (page 570) • **Kulebiaka** (Russian Cooking) (page 477) • Lacey Potato Cakes (Cooking of Scandinavia) • **Pizza** (Cooking of Italy) (page 571) • **Potage Crème d'Asperges** (Cooking of Provincial France) (page 347) • Potato Roesti (Quintet of Cuisines) • **Prune and Apricot Pie** (American Cooking) (page 598) • **Rårakor med Gråslök** (Russian Cooking) (page 417) • **Potato Roesti** (Quintet of Cuisines) (page 419) • **Sachertorte** (Cooking of Vienna's Empire) (page 622) • **Swedish Meatballs** (Cooking of Scandinavia) (page 545)

A Smörgåsbord Sampler

Step-by-Step to the Best in Danish Pastry

The four baked pastries and the cake shown in the making on these pages are all confected from the Danish pastry dough whose preparation is presented on the preceding page. Each pastry recipe calls for a quarter of the dough. The cake recipe alone calls for one half of it. (The dough is most easily handled in quarter parts.) A floured pastry board or a muslin or canvas pastry cloth are the best working surfaces. The cloth is helpful, as several of the pictures show, in rolling up the dough or in flipping one side over the other because it can be lifted and used to ease the dough along. But on the floured board the flat surface of a narrow spatula will prove just as useful in making the dough behave. Because of the chilling and rechilling, making the basic dough takes time and is exacting, but not difficult. The results are worth the time and effort; these are the finest Danish pastries to be found outside Denmark itself.

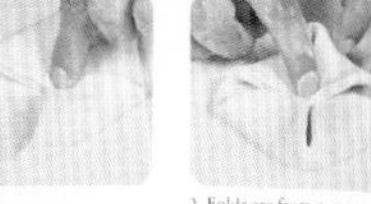

ENVELOPES
1 Cut rolled-out dough into 4-inch squares and fold.

2 Folds are from corners to the middle, where gentle finger pressure seals them.

3 Fill the center of each folded square with a tablespoon of pastry cream.

4 Add a dab of red currant jelly and bake to produce the delicacy at right.

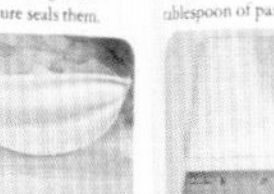
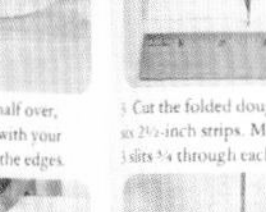

COCKS COMBS
1 Cover one half of a sheet of dough with frangipane.

2 Fold the other half over, seal edges closed with your fingers, then trim the edges.

3 Cut the folded dough into six 2½-inch strips. Make 3 slits ¾ through each strip.

4 Bend strips slightly. The baked pastry *(right)* has been sprinkled with sugar.

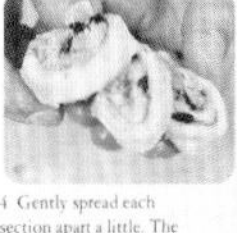

SNAILS
1 Cover filling with wax paper and roll into dough.

2 Use pastry cloth to help roll dough up into a long, fat cigar shape.

3 Make 2 half cuts and then a full cut ½ inch apart along the roll's length.

4 Gently spread each section apart a little. The baked pastry is at right.

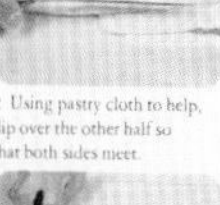

APRICOT SLIPS
1 Cover one half of a sheet of dough with apricot preserve.

2 Using pastry cloth to help, flip over the other half so that both sides meet.

3 Cut into 2-by-5-inch strips and make a 3-inch slit lengthwise in each strip.

4 Tuck one end of each strip under, and pull up and out through its slit.

5 Gently press the slip down with your hands, slightly flattening it.

6 Brush with egg white and sprinkle with sugar; then bake the pastry *(right)*.

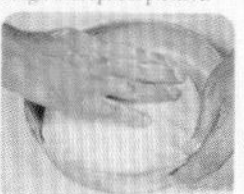
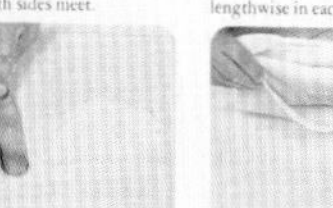
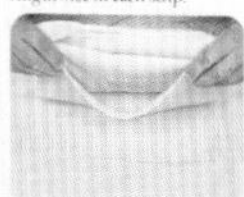
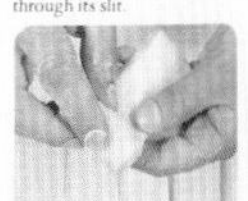
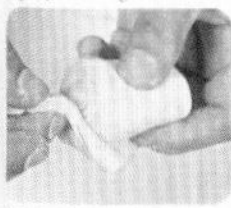

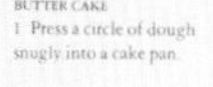

BUTTER CAKE
1 Press a circle of dough snugly into a cake pan.

2 Spread a butter-sugar mixture over half a 14-by-14-inch sheet of dough.

3 Now fold unspread half of dough over spread half; seal edges with your fingers.

4 After cutting the folded dough into 2-inch strips, roll up each strip.

5 Take a flap of dough at one end of each roll, tuck under, and press gently to secure.

6 Set rolls on the dough in the pan, bake, and spread butter cake with icing *(right)*.

Chef Persson grows so fond of the geese he feeds that he stays away for the three days in the fall when they are killed.

Geese and Eels Cooked at an Ancient Village Inn

Like most other countries, Sweden can be divided into gastronomic regions. Easily the most lavishly endowed of these is the southern province of Skåne. At the Skanör Gästgifvaregården, a tavern in the ancient fishing village of Skanör, all the best of this area's splendid cookery may be tasted—like roast goose stuffed with apples and prunes. Here are found, regularly, 15 different kinds of herring dishes, and in the chill days of autumn the chef *(right)* prepares eel in one of the several variations he offers. But because eel is a rich food the inn offers a traditional remedy against indigestion—aquavit in which a branch of wormwood *(opposite)* has been steeped. The bitter herb, in combination with the alcohol, is said to help "cut" the fatty food and rouse the appetite.

Chef Börje Lennart Persson samples his chervil-flavored eel soup. *Opposite:* smoked eels, with shears for clipping off a piece of any desired length; eel baked in a copper pan; and—behind the frosted glasses ready for the aquavit—eel soup and eel baked on straw.

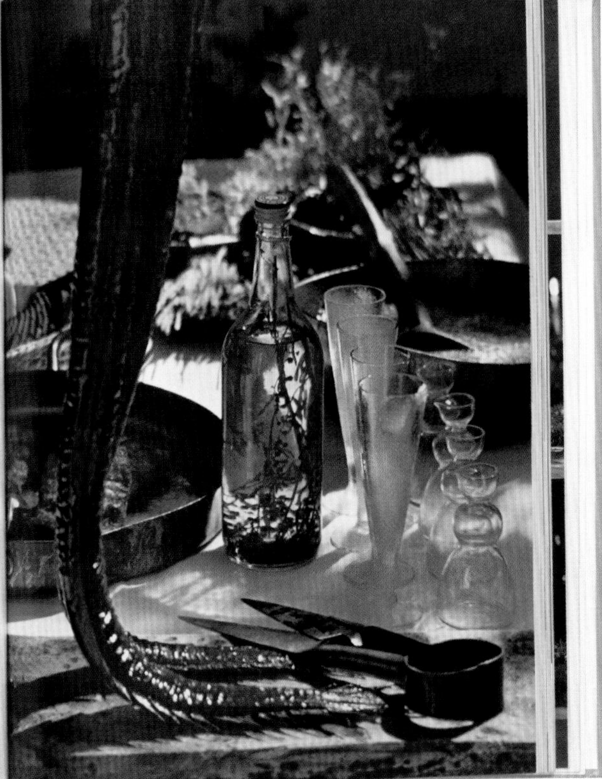

THE PERFECT OMELET

A perfect omelet is one of the great delights of French cooking. Light and tender, tasting of fresh eggs and rich butter, few things evoke the cafés and bars of Paris so completely. Making one requires some skill—and a lot of experience. Cookbooks often show the French technique for flipping the omelet.

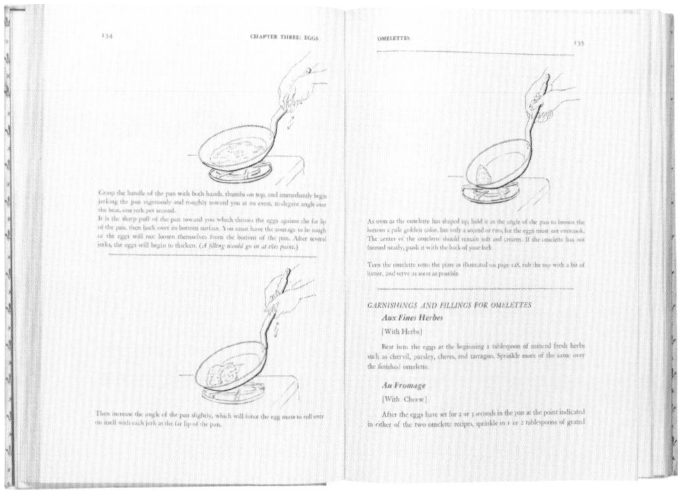

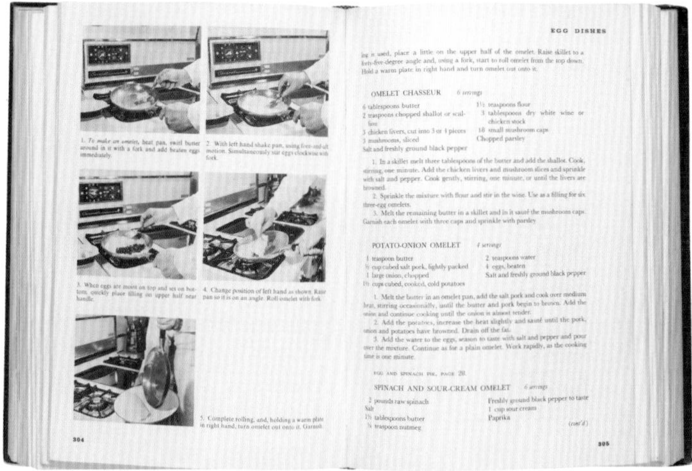

FROM TOP:

Julia Child, Louisette Bertholle, and Simone Beck
Mastering the Art of French Cooking

Craig Claiborne
The New York Times Cook Book

Time-Life Foods of the World Series
Cooking of Provincial France

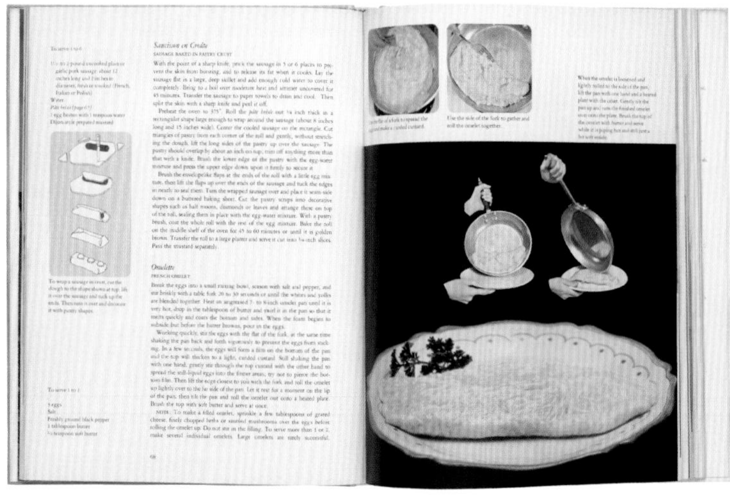

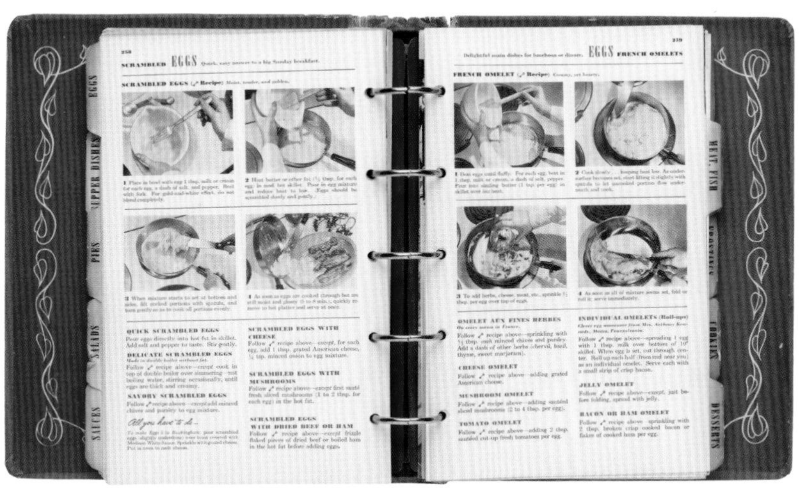

plate when cooked. Be sure to use the highest possible heat, be careful not to overbeat the eggs and do not use too much butter, or the omelet will be wrinkled. The whole operation should not take you more than 1 minute.

PLAIN OMELET

1. Using a fork, beat 3 whole eggs with salt and freshly ground pepper until well mixed. Add 1 tablespoon water (optional) to lighten the omelet. Place 1 tablespoon sweet butter in the pan on high heat. When the foaming has subsided, and the butter has a nice hazelnut color, pour in the eggs. They should sizzle. Let the eggs coagulate for about 6 to 8 seconds.

2. With the flat side of a fork in one hand, stir the eggs in a circular motion. Simultaneously, with the other hand, shake the pan back and forth in a continuous movement so that the eggs coagulate uniformly. Lift up the pan slightly while the eggs are cooking so that the "scrambled" eggs end up piled up toward the front of the pan. If the pan is kept flat, and the whole surface is covered with a uniform layer of eggs, then the omelet will roll like a jelly roll or a carpet, and it will not be moist inside.

3. Fold the lower "lips" back onto the omelet, shaping it in a nice half-moon shape as you go along.

98 TECHNIQUE FORTY-SIX

4. Run your fork along the side of the pan under the front of the omelet.

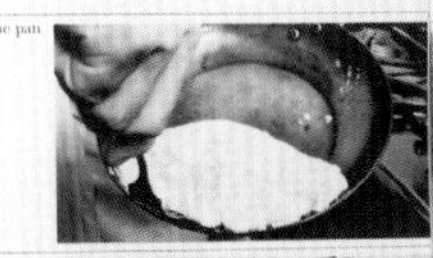

5. Tap the handle of the pan to encourage the omelet to lift up in the front

6. and, using the fork, fold the upper lip onto the center, taking care to see that it comes to a point at each end.

7. At this time, the omelet can be stuffed. Arrange the solid pieces, whether you use chicken livers, creamed chicken, spinach or whatever, in a line along the center of the omelet.

TECHNIQUE FORTY-SIX 99

FROM TOP:

Betty Crocker
Betty Crocker's Picture Cook Book

Jacques Pépin
La Technique

Julia Child
From Julia Child's Kitchen

OMELETTES 100

However, if you do succumb, be sure the measurements are as stated above; if it is of plain aluminum, the interior should be highly polished, and you should use this type of pan only for omelettes. The French heavy-gauge iron pan should also be reserved only for omelettes: before using it, heat to warm, scrub thoroughly with scouring powder and steel wool, and dry it; heat again until it is warm to your hand, rub with olive oil, let sit overnight, heat again, rub with salt, wipe clean, and the pan is ready to use. With both plain aluminum and iron pans, never scour after use; simply wipe clean with an oiled paper towel—if it is necessary to wash them, however, do so in warm water only, then heat, dry, and rub with oil.

L'omelette nature

PLAIN FRENCH OMELETTE

The best omelettes are single servings made from 2 or 3 eggs, since tenderness depends on the speed with which you make them. You will find the scrambled omelette-making technique (shaking the pan in one hand and stirring the eggs with the back of a fork in the other hand) both in Volume I of *Mastering* and in *The French Chef Cookbook*. The following no-hands technique forces the omelette to form itself by the manner in which you toss and shake the omelette pan. The whole process takes but a few seconds.

For each omelette

2 eggs (or 3 eggs, but start first with 2 "large" eggs until you are expert)
Salt and pepper
Optional: 1 Tb water
2 Tb butter

Equipment: A beating bowl and a table fork; a nonsticking frying pan 7 to 7½ inches bottom diameter; a warm dinner plate beside you.

Break the eggs into the bowl, add a pinch of salt and pepper, the optional water (to make a more perfect blending) and beat vigorously about 30 strokes of the fork to mix yolks and whites. Set the omelette pan over highest heat, add 1½ tablespoons of the butter; tilt pan in all

101

directions to film bottom and sides. When melted, the butter will foam; when foam begins to subside and butter is on the point of browning, pour in the beaten eggs. They should sizzle as they hit the pan, indicating pan is hot enough.

Wait 4 or 5 seconds for a film of coagulated egg to form in the bottom of the pan.

Grasp pan by its handle and swish it about right and left to distribute the eggs for several seconds.

Then jerk pan roughly toward you several times, throwing egg mass against far edge of pan, and forcing it to roll over upon itself; continue the movement, lifting handle slightly up as you do so.

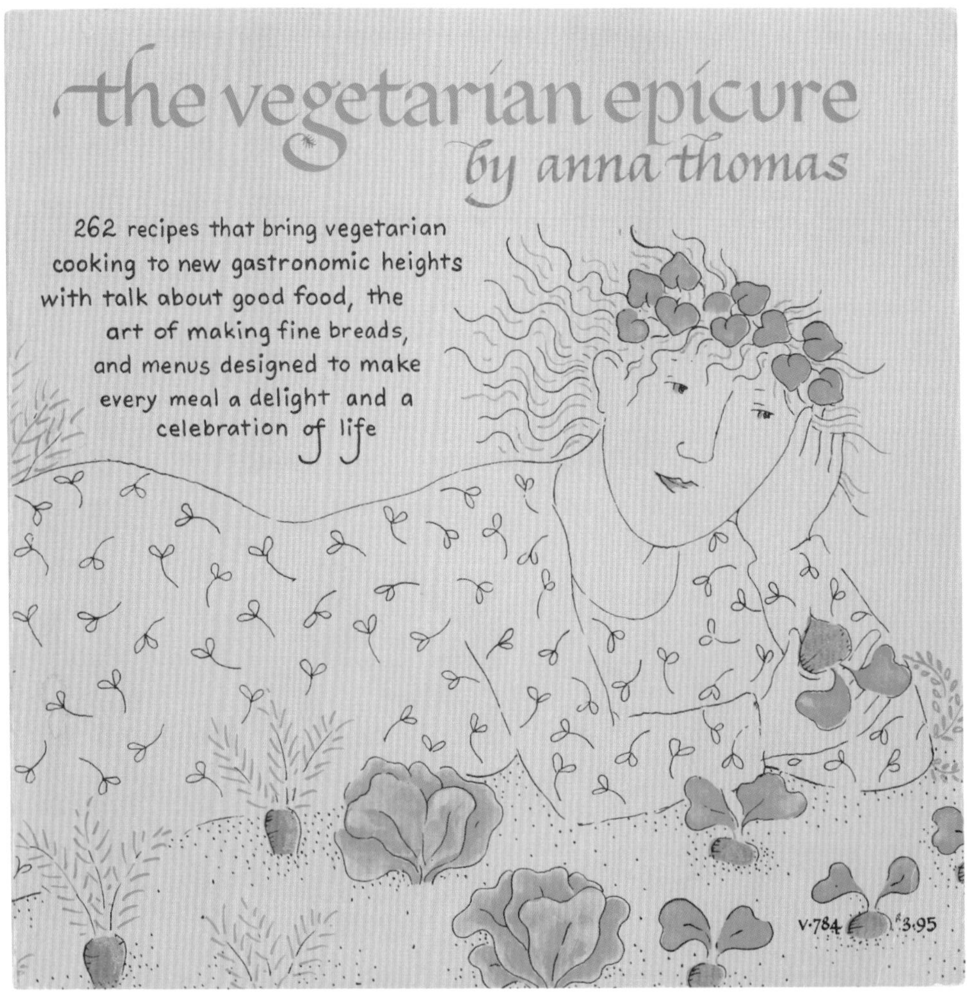

the vegetarian epicure
by anna thomas
262 recipes that bring vegetarian cooking to new gastronomic heights with talk about good food, the art of making fine breads, and menus designed to make every meal a delight and a celebration of life
V-784 $3.95

124 vegetables

beets in citrus sauce

1½ to 2 lb. very young beets
1¼ cups liquid from beets
1 lemon
1 Tbs. orange peel, freshly grated
2½ Tbs. sugar
½ tsp. salt
½ tsp. ground cloves
2 Tbs. frozen orange juice concentrate
1½ Tbs. cornstarch
1 Tbs. butter

Cook the beets whole until just tender. Drain, reserving liquid, peel and slice thin. (Or slice equivalent amount of canned beets.) Pour liquid from the beets (either from the can or the cooking water) into a pot, add the grated peel and the juice of 1 lemon, the grated orange peel, sugar, salt, cloves, and frozen orange juice concentrate. Dissolve the cornstarch in just enough water to make a smooth paste and add that also. Beat the mixture lightly with a whisk and cook until it becomes clear.

Add the sliced beets and the butter, heat it through, correct the seasoning, and serve very hot. Serves 6 to 8.

artichokes vinaigrette

To cook artichokes:

Wash them and remove the tough outer leaves; trim off the stem and the pointy tops of the remaining outer leaves. Put them into a large kettle of vigorously boiling salted water, to which you have added a little olive oil and a little lemon juice. Cover and let cook for about 40 minutes, or until a leaf will slip out easily. When they are tender, take them out and turn them upside-down to drain. They may be served hot or cold, and a sauce should be passed in a bowl for dipping. I recommend vinaigrette, or lemon butter with some fresh herbs.

To eat the artichoke, pull off one leaf at a time, dip it in the sauce, and eat the tender, meaty part of the vegetable at the base of the leaf. When leaves are gone, scrape off the fuzz (choke), and eat the heart.

(See also Creamed Artichoke Soup—page 70.)

vegetables 125

greek stewed artichokes

6 to 8 tiny artichokes or 4 large ones
2 lemons
¼ cup olive oil
1 onion, finely chopped
4 large carrots
12 to 16 tiny whole onions
4 large potatoes
1 tsp. flour
1 bunch fresh dill, chopped, or 1 Tbs. dried dill
salt and fresh-ground black pepper

Trim the artichokes, cutting off the stem, the tough outer leaves, and the tops of the other leaves. Scrub them, rub them with lemon, and put them into well-salted water to keep them from turning black.

Put the olive oil in a very large, fireproof casserole or skillet and sauté the chopped onion in it while you prepare the other vegetables. Scrape the carrots and cut them into 1-inch pieces. Peel the whole small onions. Peel the potatoes and cut them into about 6 pieces each.

Add all the vegetables except the artichokes to the hot oil and turn them over and over for a few minutes until the potatoes begin to turn golden. Add the flour and dill and stir very well.

Take the skillet off the heat and arrange the artichokes in it, fitting the onions and pieces of carrot and potato around them. Squeeze in the juice of 1 lemon, add some salt and pepper, and add enough hot water to just cover the vegetables. Put on a tight-fitting lid, and bake at 375 degrees for 50 minutes to 1½ hours, depending on the size of the artichokes. The water should be simmering gently.

Serve very hot. The liquid becomes a delicious sauce, just a bit thickened by the potatoes.

This recipe makes 4 to 6 servings.

ANNA THOMAS

The Vegetarian Epicure, 1972

While still in college, Anna Thomas wrote *The Vegetarian Epicure*, which brought vegetarian cooking into the gourmet world. The *Los Angeles Times* considers it "the bible of vegetarians in the 1970s." *The Vegetarian Epicure* has sold more than one million copies and remains in print. It features more than 262 recipes, including chestnut soufflé, Russian vegetable pie, ratatouille, German apple pancake, pasta e fagioli, zabaglione, and Linzertorte. Thomas went on to write *The Vegetarian Epicure, Book Two* (1978), *The New Vegetarian Epicure* (1996), and *Love Soup* (2009), which won a James Beard Award in 2010.

NOTABLE RECIPES: Baked Macaroni and Cheese • Corn and Cheddar Cheese Chowder • Cottage Cheese Pancakes • Creamed Artichoke Soup • Eggplant Parmigiana • **Lasagne** (page 395) • **Pea Soup with Butter Dumplings** (page 343) • **Spanakopita** (page 318) • **Russian Vegetable Pie** (page 424)

pasta 231

"Every individual who is not perfectly imbecile and void of understanding, is an epicure in his way; the epicures in boiling potatoes are innumerable." Dr. Kitchener, quoted in *The Greedy Book*.

The epicures in preparing pasta are just as plentiful, and it is worth a little effort to join their ranks. This country is blessed with a large Italian population. It is well represented in restaurants, but most Italians, understanding the delicate nature of the art, wisely partake of their pasta at home. Follow their example. Remember how wonderful is the privacy of home, even when shared with friends, for such a voluptuous activity as the eating of pasta.

Pasta is quite manageable if you only recognize the few nonnegotiable demands it makes. If you start with the best materials you can anticipate the best results—again, look to the Italians. Good pasta can be obtained from the bins of an Italian grocery, and there is probably one near you if you only look around. Otherwise, good pasta can be magically created from the simplest ingredients in your own kitchen. (It is not found in supermarkets where visually convincing imitations nestle against envelopes of vile "sauce" mixes.) Having secured your pasta, get some ripe Italian plum tomatoes, fresh if you are lucky, or else in cans. Herbs from your herb garden are preferred, but dried ones—well cared for—are fine. Virgin, pure olive oil is worth the extra pennies it costs, and should be purchased at the same Italian grocery where your favorite pasta waits in the barrel. Finally, the cheeses must be chosen. Pregrated cheese is an insult to pasta and to cheese. The Italian grocer will slice off a wedge of pungent Romano or Parmesan for you, which you can take home whole or have grated there. Delicatessen Mozzarella is reliable, but Ricotta should be purchased really fresh, sliced from a block rather than prepackaged.

When you have procured the finest ingredients, handle them respectfully. The sauces take some time to prepare. You have heard that spaghetti sauce must be simmered very slowly for hours to blend and marry the flavors. That is quite true—with a notable

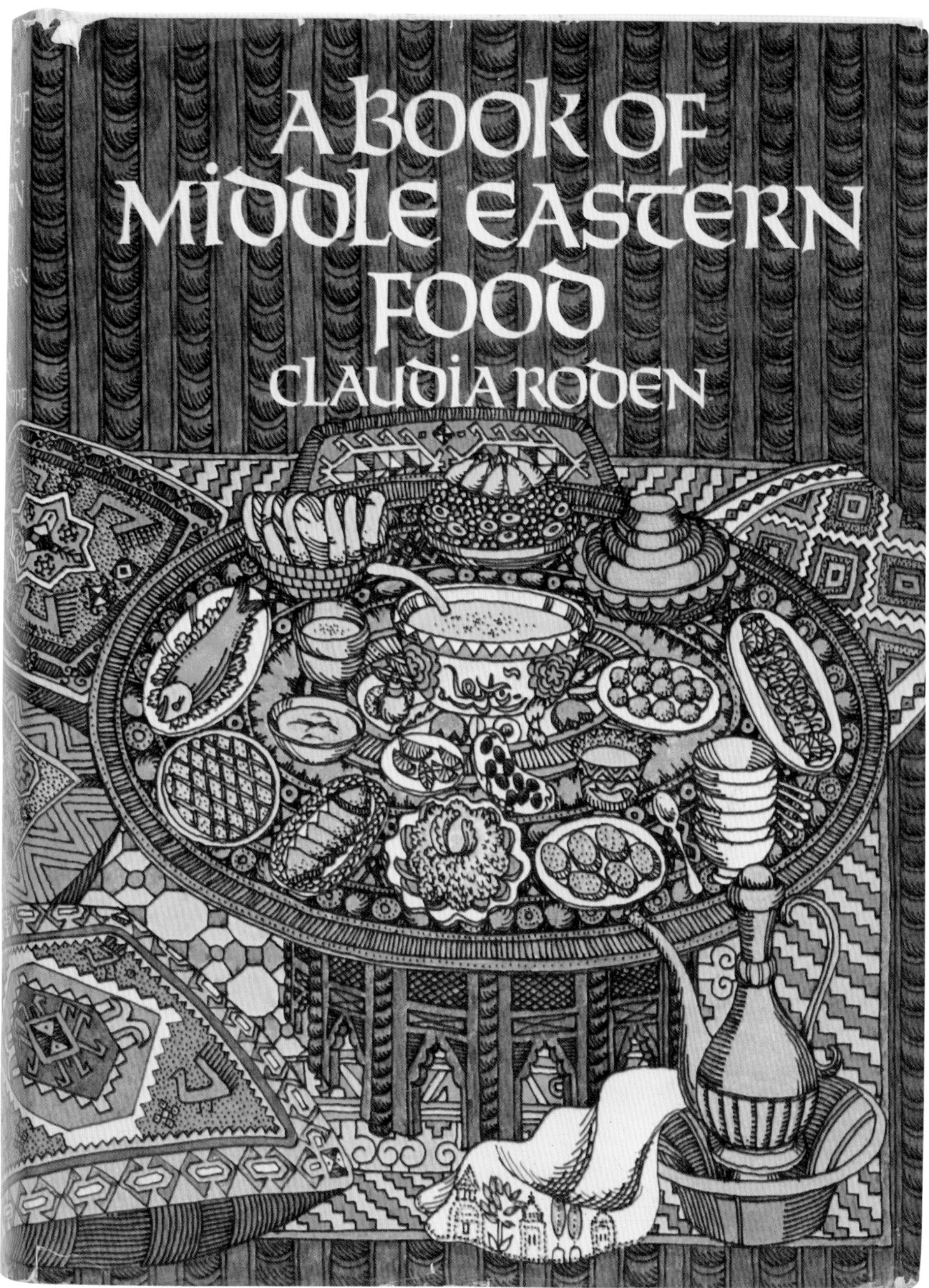
A BOOK OF
MIDDLE EASTERN
FOOD
CLAUDIA RODEN

CLAUDIA RODEN

A Book of Middle Eastern Food, 1972

Claudia Roden's *A Book of Middle Eastern Food* was an instant classic. Published originally in England by Penguin Books in 1968, the first edition is quite rare. The book went through several editions in the first five years, including the first American edition, published by Alfred A. Knopf in 1972.

Roden was born in Egypt, but immigrated to England, where she found herself among a large number of Middle Eastern immigrants. She longed for the food of her childhood and began to study the history of Egyptian cooking. She quickly realized, however, that dishes she thought were solely Egyptian were, in fact, of Turkish, Lebanese, or Syrian origin. She decided to think about the Middle East, with all of its diversity, as sharing certain kinds of food traditions and to research these foodways. The outcome was *A Book of Middle Eastern Food*, presenting recipes for more than five hundred dishes.

NOTABLE RECIPES: Ataïf (Atayef) (Arab Pancakes) • **Beid bi Lamoun (Avgolemono Sauce)** (page 337) • **Imam Bayildi** (page 415) • **Megadarra** (page 430) • Orange and Almond Cake • **Sephardic Cakes** (page 617) • Tagine of Chicken with Preserved Lemons • Torshi Left (Pickled Turnips)

Beid Masluq / Hard-boiled Eggs with Cumin

Prepare hard-boiled eggs in the usual way, packing several tightly in a pan to prevent them from moving about too much and cracking. Peel them. Cut in half and sprinkle with salt and ground cumin; or serve whole, accompanied by a small bowl of salt mixed with about twice as much cumin, to dip the eggs in. Serve as an appetizer.

In Morocco, vendors sell these eggs in the streets, sprinkled with the same seasoning.

Baid Mutajjan / Fried Hard-boiled Eggs

A medieval recipe from al-Baghdadi advises hard-boiling the eggs, then peeling them, frying them in oil, and sprinkling them with, or dipping them in, a mixture of dried ground coriander (1 teaspoon), cinnamon (½ teaspoon), cumin (1 teaspoon), and salt to taste. This type of egg is still sold in the streets in Egypt and Morocco today, and many families prepare these eggs (without the strong seasoning) as a garnish for meat and potato dishes.

Beid Hamine / Hamine Eggs

Great favorites of ancient origin.

Put the eggs and skins from several onions in a very large saucepan. Fill the pan with water, cover, and simmer very gently over the lowest heat possible for at least 6 hours, even overnight. A layer of oil poured over the surface is a good way of preventing the water from evaporating too quickly. This lengthy cooking produces deliciously creamy eggs. The whites acquire a soft beige color from the onion skins, and the yolks are very creamy and pale yellow. The flavor is delicate and excitingly different from eggs cooked in any other way.

Some people add ground coffee to the water, to obtain a slightly darker color.

My mother sometimes uses a pressure cooker to prepare *hamine* eggs in a hurry. In this case, it is advisable to hard-boil the eggs first, and then cook them under pressure with the onion skins. They will

136 | EGG DISHES

BEID | 137

JAMES BEARD

American Cookery, 1972

American Cookery is James Beard's masterwork. It comprises all aspects of American cooking and contains the summation of his knowledge about our cuisine. The recipes are the best for any given dish. No one so completely explains the preparation of a country ham, one of Beard's favorite dishes and one of our national food treasures, as Beard does here. From several days of soaking, to boiling, baking, and serving the ham with homemade biscuits, Beard never misses a step. *American Cookery* became an instant classic. It remains so and should be on every bookshelf.

NOTABLE RECIPES: Baked Ham (page 536) • Baked Stuffed Artichokes • **Baking Powder Biscuits** (page 590) • Cherry Pie • Cream Biscuits • Favorite Hamburgers • **Fresh Fruit Pie (Two-Crust)** (page 599) • **Oyster Stew** (page 376) • Peach Pie • **Pound Cake** (page 607) • **Scotch Eggs** (page 467) • Stir-fried String Beans

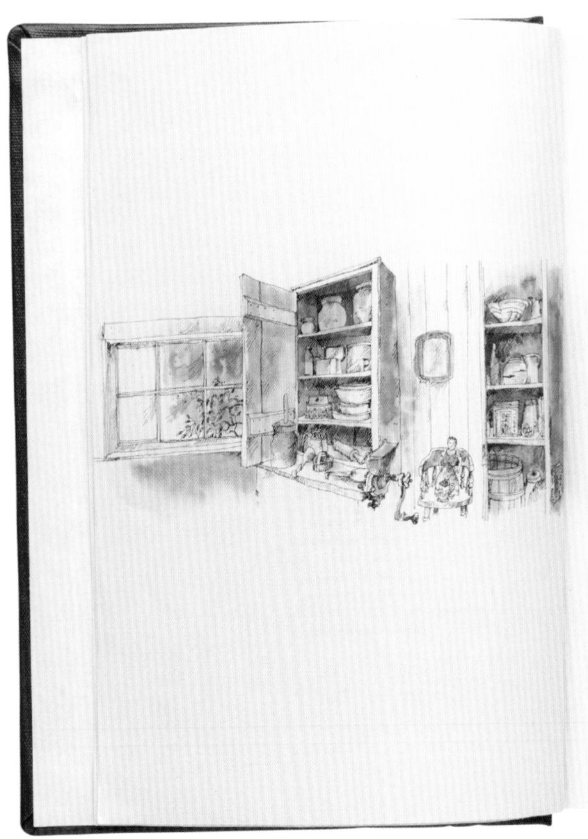

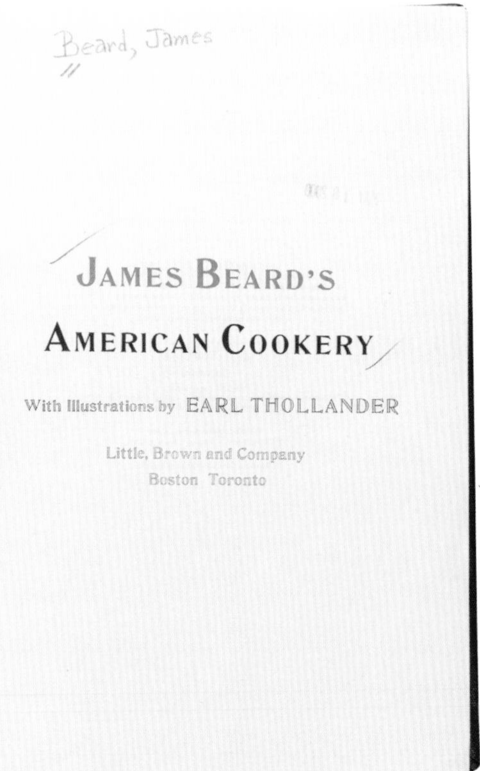

Roast Beef

Beef was largely spit-roasted in this country until the early nineteenth century when the reflector oven was introduced. This was a small metal piece, rounded in shape, which could be set before the coals of a fireplace. The roast, salted and peppered, was placed upon a trivet or muffin rings, with a dripping pan underneath, filled with boiling water. It was then positioned between the reflector and the coals. The roast thus had both direct and reflected heat. It roasted rather quickly in this fashion, for Mrs. Crowen gives directions for roasting 15 minutes per pound. The secret of its success was frequent basting with the drippings. When the meat was half done, it was often pushed nearer the coals, the thickest part foremost. The pan was kept replenished with boiling water, so that at least a pint of dripping would remain at the end of the roasting period. Fifteen minutes before the roast was done, its fatty covering was dredged with flour. This in turn was basted with drippings to make a crusty finish. The roast was then removed to a hot platter and covered while the drippings were mixed with a bit of flour and strained into a small sauceboat. Mrs. Crowen adds that the correct accompaniments were plain boiled or mashed potatoes, boiled spinach, beets or dressed celery, mashed turnips or squash. Pickles or horseradish were also allowed.

In the eighteenth and nineteenth centuries it was necessary to baste a good deal when roasting a major cut of beef, largely because the heat of most wood or coal fires was so uneven and beef was not as well marbled with fat as it is today. It was not unusual to find a recipe that called for a cup of boiling water to be thrown over the roast, after which it was to be basted copiously with the water and pan juices. Nowadays this procedure is unnecessary.

By the mid-nineteenth century ovens were becoming more common, but they were primarily used for baking. When they were put into use for meat, the results were called "baked meats." Mrs. Crowen states that with proper handling a good piece of meat could be baked in a stove oven so nearly to resemble a roast as to be mistaken for it! Here, too, the meat was placed on a trivet or muffin rings to bake. There was little means for controlling heat, but cooks were warned that if the oven became too hot, the oven door should be opened to cool it a bit.

In both the 1886 and 1902 editions of her book, Mrs. Rorer of Philadelphia still refers to the "tin kitchen," which was a more modern form of the reflector oven. It had more space and a deeper well for the dripping pan. Also it is interesting to note that Mrs. Rorer suggests maintaining a temperature of 300 degrees for beef after searing it. And for baking in the oven, this same culinary genius suggests 400 degrees to start and 240 degrees after the meat is well browned. This was quite advanced thinking for her day, and unfortunately most cooks went on testing the oven with the hand, and thus roasting was largely a hit or miss affair. Even Miss Farmer, up to the 1914 edition of her book, had no thoughts on meat temperature at all and simply recommended an hour and five minutes for a 5-pound roast and one hour and thirty minutes for a 10-pound roast in a hot oven. Only since the development of good ranges and accurate oven thermometers has the subject of meat temperatures become essential.

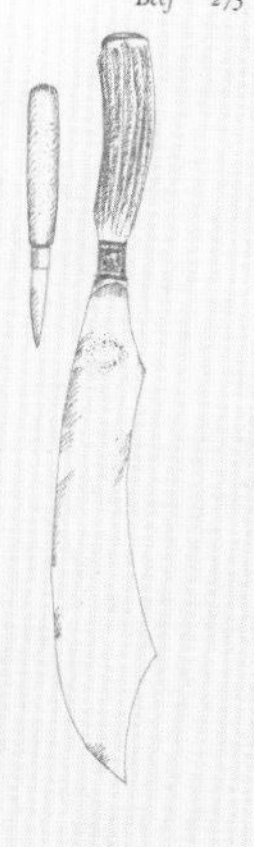

Today there are four or five favorite attacks on the roasting of beef. Each is successful in its way, and it remains for the cook to compare results.

To buy beef for roasting

Look for cherry red, well-trimmed beef with good marbling in it and with creamy fat. It should be U.S. *Choice* or *Prime*. If you have a butcher who indulges you, order your roast well ahead and ask him to hang it a little longer than is customary nowadays.

Estimate ¾ to 1 pound of meat per person, especially if there is much bone. Have no fear of leftover roast. To many palates it is even better cold than hot and can be used in a variety of ways.

Boned roasts. It is still common practice for the French and Italians to bone out roasts, and bard and tie them. The idea went with them to the New World, and thus in earlier days butcher shops offered boned and barded rump roasts or boned and rolled ribs of beef. Rolled roasts are less common today (although at this writing I have a piece of contre-filet, thinly barded and beautifully tied, roasting in the oven), except in food shops and delicatessens where beef is machine-sliced. If you are serving a large roast, it is always handsomer to see it carved from the bones, and the bones themselves can be saved for delectable leftovers, deviled beef bones.

Prime (Standing) Rib Roast

The first three ribs are considered the best, although in my opinion a larger roast is preferable — the first five ribs, well trimmed, so that carving will be easy. This means a "7-inch cut," with the

Puddings, Ice Creams, and Dessert Sauces

We have been one of the most dessert-minded of all countries except England. "What shall we have for dessert?" has been the cry of hostesses and family heads for generations, and the sweet tooth has been entertained in sundry ways. Shortage of the more refined ingredients led to experimentation with rougher meals and sweeteners — corn, whole meal, maple syrup, and molasses — and resulted in puddings and other sweets that still linger in our repertoire. Indian pudding, blueberry buckle, flummery, and steamed puddings are some of these holdovers, as well as custards and creams of various types. Perhaps the most extreme refinement of all appeared in the early part of this century when gelatine desserts became popular. "Dainty desserts for dainty people" became the catch phrase of one of the major manufacturers of gelatine. Certain rather doubtful inventions issued forth from kitchens during this period. Some of these gelatine concoctions have stayed with us on our daily round of menus, and others have become, shall we say, museum pieces.

Even with the surge of dieters in this country, when it comes to sweets the weakness of will shown by most people is striking, to say the least. The way of the transgressor is straight through the pastry tray.

Apple Brown Betty

3 cups coarse breadcrumbs
½ cup butter
3 large apples
1¼ cups sugar
½ teaspoon cinnamon
½ teaspoon nutmeg

Apple Brown Betty has many different guises. I don't think any two of the old recipes are alike. They all have unusual bits of personality attached to them. This one I like very much.

Toast the breadcrumbs. Cut the butter into small pieces. Peel and core the apples and cut them into thin slices. Combine the sugar and spices. Divide the crumbs into three parts, the butter into four, the apples into two, and the combined sugar and spices into three. Butter a 2-quart baking dish and arrange in it layers of, in order: 1 part each of crumbs, butter, apples, spices, butter, crumbs, butter, apples, spices, crumbs, butter, and spices. Bake 30 minutes at 375 degrees, or until the apples are tender and the crumb topping is well browned. Serve hot with heavy cream.

Apple Charlotte

12 tart apples
Sugar
¼ teaspoon vanilla
Thin slices of white bread
Melted butter

Wash the apples, cut them into quarters, and remove the cores but not the peel. Cook the apples in a little boiling water in a saucepan over moderate heat until they are soft. Drain them and force them through a sieve. Discard the residue. Measure the purée and combine it in the saucepan with an equal amount of sugar and the vanilla. Reduce the purée over moderate heat until it is very thick. Trim off the bread crusts, dip the slices in melted butter, and brown them on both sides in a skillet. Cut enough of the browned slices into triangles to fit tightly over the bottom of a 1½-quart mold, and set them in place. Cut enough additional slices into strips 2 inches wide to cover the sides completely and fit them around, overlapping them slightly. Fill the mold with the prepared purée and cover the top with more of the browned bread. Place the mold in a pan of hot water in a 350-degree oven and bake the charlotte 30 minutes, or until the bread lining is firm enough to support the filling. Unmold the charlotte and serve it, warm or cooled, with whipped cream or hard sauce.

Apple Dumplings

2 cups sifted flour
1 teaspoon salt
⅔ cup shortening
5 to 6 tablespoons ice water
6 small baking apples
⅓ cup sugar
½ cup butter
Nutmeg
1½ cups firmly packed brown sugar

Prepare pastry with the flour, salt, shortening, and as much of the ice water as may be needed (page 634). Roll the pastry ¼ inch thick and cut it into 6 squares, each large enough to enclose one of the baking apples. Peel and core the apples and fill the cavities with the sugar and butter combined. The cavities should be thoroughly filled. Use more butter and sugar if necessary. Sprinkle the fillings each with nutmeg. Enclose each apple in a square of the prepared pastry by molding the pastry around it. Chill the apples 30 minutes. Preheat the oven to 425 degrees. In a saucepan combine the brown sugar, water, and additional butter, and cook them at a gentle boil 5 minutes. Brush the pastry-enclosed apples each with

MITCHELL DAVIS *on* JAMES BEARD

"America's first foodie." That's how we describe James Beard to the growing legions of young food enthusiasts who may have heard his name but who don't really know the man or what he stood for. Of course, the term "foodie" wouldn't be coined by journalist Paul Levy until 1984, the year before Jim died, and long before clusters of culinarians would congregate at farmers' markets and food festivals, from Brooklyn to San Francisco's Mission and everywhere in between. But the truth is, whether you are enjoying a fine, regional American meal in Louisville or a cookout in Charleston, American foodies everywhere owe a debt to James Beard.

Beard was born in Portland, Oregon, in 1903, and his early food impressions—shaped by his mother, Mary Elizabeth, a gifted cook who ran a boarding house, and her Chinese chef, Let, as well as by his West Coast environs—would never recede from his memory. The sweet flavor of huckleberries and the delicate flesh of sand dabs were part of his dining DNA, where they fused with classical Cantonese cooking and fine French food to form the foundation of his palate.

When Beard arrived in New York in the 1930s, it was to act and sing, not to cook. But like many stage lovers before and since, he ended up in the food service industry, opening a small catering company that specialized in hors d'oeuvre for cocktail parties on Manhattan's Upper East Side in 1939. (Accepting author and gourmet Alexandre Dumas's admonition, he never pluralized that word with an "s.")

By 1940 Beard had written his first book, appropriately titled Hors d'Oeuvre and Canapés, *which immediately evidenced his definitive, tell-it-like-it-is approach to cooking, eating, and entertaining. "The hors d'oeuvre is a rite rather than a course and its duty is to enchant the eye, please the palate, and excite the flow of the gastric juices . . . so that the meal to follow will seem doubly tempting and flavorful," was how he began. And it was a telling taste of the kitchen wisdom to come.*

It didn't take long for Cook It Outdoors *(M. Barrows and Company, 1941) to appear on bookstore shelves. Groundbreaking in that, as the book jacket announced, it was "a man's book written by a man," this handsome guide to grilling was filled with oversized photographs and tips to master "the subtle nuances of tricky flavoring." Between dozens of recipes for different hamburgers appeared some marital advice, as well. "Let the husband control the fire, and the wife the kitchen," said Beard, a confirmed bachelor (as some high-profile gay men were called in those days).*

In 1949 Simon & Schuster published The Fireside Cookbook, *a charming, general how-to book for beginner and expert alike that reflected Beard's personality and his American culinary leanings. "America has the opportunity, as well as the resources, to create for herself a truly national cuisine that will incorporate all that is best in the traditions of the many people who have crossed the seas to form our new, still young nation," wrote the future "dean of American cookery." Beard's biographer and friend Evan Jones called it "the most lavishly produced American cookbook to date, due in large part to the whimsical illustrations by Alice and Martin Provensen, which appeared throughout the book, from endpaper to endpaper, and that even found their way onto wallpaper.*

Beard wrote more than two dozen books—an exact number is difficult to pinpoint because of multiple printings and repackaging—most of which are still in print today. Their topics range the entire gourmet gamut from game cookery to economical entertaining, from bread to pasta to fish.

Although Beard inspired several generations of chefs, he was not really a chef himself. He had a photographic food memory, an encyclopedic and ever-expanding knowledge, and a perfect-pitch palate, which, coupled with his generosity and larger-than-life size and demeanor, made him an icon of American cuisine. It was the New York Times *that in 1957 deemed him the "dean of American cookery." But it was with the publication in 1972 of his nine-hundred-page chef d'oeuvre,* American Cookery, *that he really embraced his role as America's first foodie.*

American Cookery *was a massive project with more than 1,500 recipes from around the country, from Beard's memory and from his kitchen. As he described it, "This is not a book of regional cookery, it is not a collection of family recipes, it is not primarily a critique of American cuisine. It is simply a record of good eating in this country with some of its lore." Reviewing it for the* Times, *Nika Hazelton praised the book and Beard himself: "The value of the year, and as good for us as it will be for our* children. The author, who has done more than anybody else to popularize good food in America, puts a lifetime of experience into the page."

Beard was first in many other ways too. He was one of the first regular columnists hired by Gourmet magazine when it debuted in 1942. He was the first to cook on television, a medium that was barely a year old when he had guest spots on Radio City Matinee in April 1946, and the first to have his own show dedicated to food, I Love to Eat, which debuted later that same year.

Beard may have laid the groundwork for what would have evolved into the sophisticated, regional American cuisine we are fortunate to enjoy today, but he was a lifelong lover of France. An unforgettable Rolleiflex photograph of him picnicking in the French countryside with Alice B. Toklas and some friends shows him in all his awkwardness and glee. He is five times Toklas's size, and seems uncomfortable to be sitting on the ground. But in the company of famous people and close friends, eating outdoors, which he loved to do, and no doubt enjoying simple French charcuterie, cheese, bread, and wine, nothing could be wrong in Jim's world.

Of course, life is not as tidy as a photograph or a book, and like everyone's, Beard's life was punctuated with many travails. A lifelong freelancer—he was ahead of the curve in that regard, as well—Beard was always worried about when and from where his next paycheck would come. He was gay long before the concept of gay marriage would ever enter anyone's mind, let alone be considered an acceptable lifestyle, and his love life seems perhaps the least satisfying part of his otherwise well-sated life. Though adept at good living, Beard lived hard, and his consumption patterns took their toll, landing him periodically in the hospital with various ailments, including gout, which might have been avoided.

If anything, Beard's legacy was to engender both appreciation and pride in the produce and skill of the American culinary scene. He called it "an American attitude toward food," which is something he embodied with his generosity, his energy, and his endlessly enjoyable quotations. A perennial lover of oysters, Jim issued forth many pearls:

> "I believe that if ever I had to practice cannibalism, I might manage if there were enough tarragon around."
>
> "Two of my best friends are a stripper and a zester."
>
> "Good bread is the most fundamentally satisfying of all foods; and good bread with fresh butter, the greatest of feasts."
>
> "The only thing that will make a soufflé fall is if it knows you're afraid of it."
>
> "Be simple. Be honest. Don't overcook and don't undercook, but it's better to undercook than overcook."

Simple, honest, and perfectly cooked food was James Beard's favorite. As Julia Child said often, "In the beginning, there was James Beard." And we are ever grateful he helped lay the foundation for the great American cuisine we relish today.

Cecily
Brownstone's
ASSOCIATED PRESS
COOK
BOOK
This book is based on the Cecily Brownstone food columns that have appeared
in Associated Press member newspapers throughout the United States.

CECILY BROWNSTONE
The Associated Press Cookbook, 1972

Cecily Brownstone served as the Associated Press syndicated food writer for thirty-nine years. Upon her retirement, *New York Times* food editor Jane Nickerson wrote: "Of syndicated food writers, she's been the most widely read." Nickerson added that Brownstone's recipes were always "unusual, appetizing, and accurate down to the last one-eighth of a teaspoon of salt."

Brownstone was born in Plum Coulee, Manitoba, Canada, in 1909. After attending the University of Manitoba, she made her way to New York City and into the food world. Brownstone was a close friend and confidant of James Beard; the *Joy of Cooking* authors, Irma Rombauer and Marion Rombauer Becker; and other noted cookbook and food writers. She and Beard telephoned each other almost daily, at 8 a.m. Brownstone's personal papers include ninety-three letters and postcards from Irma Rombauer and about forty-five from Marion Becker.

Brownstone's books include inscribed copies of almost every edition of *The Joy of Cooking*, sent to her first by Irma Rombauer and later by Marion Becker. During her career, Brownstone amassed a private library of more than six thousand volumes, which she used to develop the recipes she published each week for the Associated Press. A meticulous critic of recipes—the marks in many of her books demonstrate her attention to detail—she carefully tested all those she published. The recipes in this book work reliably. The Fales Library acquired Brownstone's books as the cornerstone of the food studies collection at New York University.

NOTABLE RECIPES: Country Captain (page 500) • **Jennie's Rice Torta** (page 382) • **Strawberry Deep Dish Pie** (page 598)

Carrot Soufflé

138

Carrot Soufflé

½ pound carrots (5 medium)
3 tablespoons butter
2 tablespoons minced onion
3 tablespoons flour
½ teaspoon salt
⅛ teaspoon pepper
¼ teaspoon nutmeg
1 cup milk
3 eggs, separated

With a vegetable brush, wash and scrub carrots; do not peel. Cut off a small slice from each top and cut carrots into 1½-inch pieces. Cook carrots, covered, in boiling salted water until very tender—about 20 minutes. Drain. Strain through a food mill. There should be ¾ cup strained carrot.

In a saucepan, melt butter. Add onion and cook gently until wilted but not browned. Stir in flour, salt, pepper and nutmeg. Remove from heat; gradually stir in milk, keeping smooth. Return to moderately low heat and cook, stirring constantly, until thickened. Stir in carrots. Set aside until cool to the touch.

Beat egg yolks until thick and lemon color. With a clean beater, beat egg whites until they hold straight stiff peaks when beater is slowly withdrawn. Stir beaten yolks into cooled carrot mixture. Fold in beaten whites. Turn into an ungreased 1-quart baking dish. Bake in a preheated 350-degree oven until golden-brown and mixture in center does not shake—35 to 40 minutes.

Makes 4 to 6 servings.

Cauliflower with Coral Sauce

Delicate flavor and bright color distinguish a sauce.

1 medium-size cauliflower
1 cup boiling water
1 teaspoon salt
1 jar (4 ounces) pimientos, drained
2 tablespoons each butter and flour
1 cup milk

Separate cauliflower into small flowerets; wash in cold water. In a medium saucepan boil the cauliflower, covered, with the boiling water and ½ teaspoon of the salt just until tender-crisp—about 8 minutes. Drain and keep warm.

In an electric blender, blend together the pimientos and milk until combined.

In a 1-quart saucepan over low heat melt the butter; stir in the flour, then the pimiento mixture; cook and stir constantly until thickened and bubbly; stir in the remaining ½ teaspoon salt. Pour sauce over cauliflower so that some of the white flowerets show.

Makes 6 servings.

139

Strawberry Rhubarb Pie

278

Strawberry Deep Dish Pie

1¼ cups sugar
⅓ cup cornstarch
¼ teaspoon salt
4 pints fresh strawberries, halved
2 tablespoons butter, melted
1⅓ cups flour, stir before measuring
½ teaspoon salt
½ cup solid all-vegetable shortening
2 tablespoons butter
3 tablespoons water
½ egg white, beaten slightly
1 teaspoon sugar

In a large bowl stir together 1¼ cups sugar, cornstarch and salt. Add strawberries and melted butter; mix well; let stand while you prepare pastry.

In a medium sized bowl stir together the flour and salt. Cut in shortening until the size of small peas; cut in butter until the size of large peas. Sprinkle with water, toss with a fork and press into a square. On a lightly floured surface roll out pastry to a 10-inch square. Cut 10 1-inch strips with pastry wheel.

Turn strawberry mixture into a 9-inch square (2 quart) oven-glass baking dish. Weave pastry strips over strawberries to form lattice top. Brush with egg white; sprinkle with 1 teaspoon sugar. Bake in a preheated 425-degree oven 30 minutes or until crust is golden brown. Serve warm in bowls with vanilla ice cream.

Makes 8 servings.

Note: Toward the end of the baking time, if the strawberry juice bubbles up and looks as if it's going to run over, place a piece of foil on a lower rack under the baking dish to collect the syrup and save you oven washing.

Strawberry Rhubarb Pie

Don't expect a firmer-than-firm filling for this pie, even if you allow it to stand until cold before cutting and serving—as we suggest. The filling may be a little runny. But who cares? Old-fashioned eaters, who knew a good fresh fruit pie when they tasted one, believed this runniness made the pie delectable.

Pastry
2 cups granulated sugar
1 cup unsifted flour
1 quart strawberries, hulled
2 cups pink or red rhubarb, cut crosswise into ½-inch pieces
2 tablespoons lemon juice
2 tablespoons butter, soft
2 tablespoons light brown sugar
¼ teaspoon cinnamon

Roll out pastry to make a shell with a high fluted edge to fit a 10-inch oven-glass pie plate; refrigerate.

In a mixing bowl, thoroughly stir together the granulated sugar and ½ cup of the flour; add strawberries and rhubarb and toss together; let stand at room temperature for 30 minutes.

Meanwhile blend the butter, brown sugar and cinnamon; work in the remaining ½ cup flour to make a crumbly mixture.

Turn the strawberry and rhubarb mixture into the pastry-lined pie plate. Sprinkle the fruit with the lemon juice, then with the crumbly flour mixture.

Bake in a preheated 425-degree oven for 1 hour. Place pie on wire rack; allow to stand at room temperature until cold so filling can "set."

Note: We baked this pie on the middle rack of our range for 40 minutes; then we covered the top of the pie with foil and finished the baking on the rack just below the middle rack for the last 20 minutes. This method produced a well browned crust.

279

JULIA CHILD

From Julia Child's Kitchen, 1972

During the production of the color television version of her show *The French Chef*, Julia Child collected notes, recipes, and other musings about the foods she prepared. *From Julia Child's Kitchen* is a compendium of those notes, illustrated with photographs by her husband, Paul Child. It was Child's favorite among her many cookbooks. On one program Child prepared coq au vin and chicken fricassee together, revisiting the recipes from *Mastering the Art of French Cooking*. Child shows that the two recipes are basically the same: a chicken (or all of the same parts) braised in wine with herbs: one in red wine, one in white. One with bacon, thyme, and tomato. One with tarragon finished with lemon. It is a classic example of how Child demystified French cooking for American audiences. The coq au vin recipe, in particular, became wildly popular.

NOTABLE RECIPES: Coq au vin/Chicken fricassée (page 501) • **L'omelette Nature** (page 462) • **Mrs. Child's Famous Sticky Fruitcake** (page 585) • **Salade Niçoise** (page 368) • Sauce Hollandaise • Soubise • **Vichyssoise** (page 346)

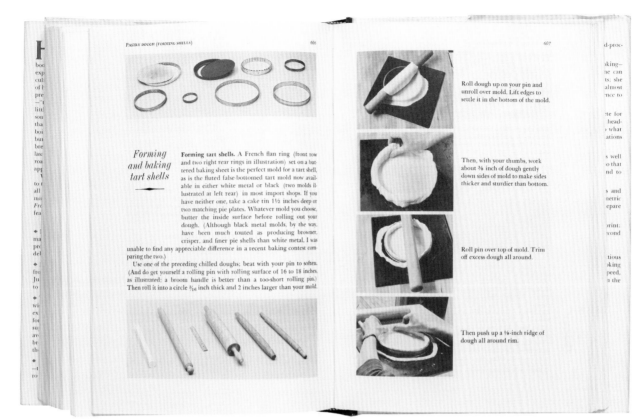

Forming and baking tart shells

Forming tart shells. A French flan ring (front row and two right rear rings in illustration) set on a buttered baking sheet is the perfect mold for a tart shell, as is the fluted false-bottomed tart mold now available in either white metal or black (two molds illustrated at left rear) in most import shops. If you have neither one, take a cake tin 1½ inches deep or two matching pie plates. Whatever mold you choose, butter the inside surface before rolling out your dough. (Although black metal molds, by the way, have been much touted as producing browner, crisper, and finer pie shells than white metal, I was unable to find any appreciable difference in a recent baking contest comparing the two.)

Use one of the preceding chilled doughs; beat with your pin to soften. (And do get yourself a rolling pin with rolling surface of 16 to 18 inches, as illustrated; a broom handle is better than a too-short rolling pin.) Then roll it into a circle 3/16 inch thick and 2 inches larger than your mold.

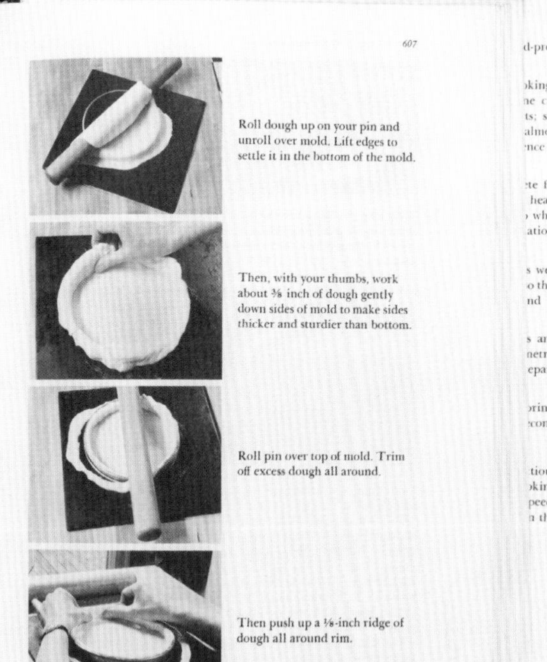

Roll dough up on your pin and unroll over mold. Lift edges to settle it in the bottom of the mold.

Then, with your thumbs, work about 3/8 inch of dough gently down sides of mold to make sides thicker and sturdier than bottom.

Roll pin over top of mold. Trim off excess dough all around.

Then push up a 1/8-inch ridge of dough all around rim.

occasionally, just to check on it. Rabbit should take 1 to 1½ hours of simmering, depending on its youth and tenderness; it is done when a sharp fork pierces the flesh easily, but do not let it overcook or flesh will fall from bone.

Finishing the dish. When rabbit is tender, carefully skim all accumulated fat off surface of sauce–remove meat to a side dish, if necessary. You should have almost 2 cups of sauce just thick enough to coat the rabbit lightly. If too thick, thin out with a little chicken stock. If too thin, remove from heat, and make a *beurre manié* (1 tablespoon of flour worked into a smooth paste with 1 tablespoon of butter); blend it into the sauce, and bring to the simmer, basting rabbit with sauce until it thickens–a minute or two. Very carefully correct seasoning, adding salt and pepper as you see fit. To serve, arrange rabbit on a platter and spread over it the lemon slices from the simmering, or rearrange attractively in a cooking dish. Decorate, if you wish, with sprigs of parsley or watercress.

☼ May be cooked a day or two in advance; when cold, cover and refrigerate. To serve, reheat slowly basting with sauce, then cover and keep at the barest simmer 5 minutes or so. You may have to thin out the sauce with a little bouillon; retaste for seasoning.

Chicken breasts

We are all so used to buying chicken breasts it's hard to remember what a luxury they used to be when Great-grandmother, and even Grandmother, had to buy the whole bird just to get those two tender morsels. Boned breasts are so fast to cook they are a boon when you are pressed for time, and if your market doesn't package them boned, you'll find them quick to do yourself. Boned breasts are called *suprêmes*–the supreme delicacy the chicken has to offer (unless, of course, you are a dark-meat-only type).

TO BONE A CHICKEN BREAST

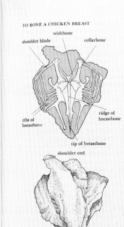

When you buy chicken breasts you may find them whole, as illustrated, or split in half the length of the breastbone. Once in a while the wings will be on, and sometimes the breastbone will have been snapped out, leaving just the cartilage at the tip. The whole breast pictured here is the easiest to bone because you can see what you are doing. However, in whatever form you have bought them, boning is a simple matter following the general procedures outlined: remember the cardinal rule of cutting and scraping against the bones wherever you find them, and you will make out, ending up with the boned breast and its two flaps of meat, shown in the final drawing of this series.

WINGS. If the wings have been left on, locate the ball joint attaching wing to shoulder by wiggling the wing back and forth and feeling for the joint with your finger; cut through the joint from the shoulder side, and you will detach the wing from the breast.

SKIN. Rip the skin off the meat, grasping it in a towel to get a firm hold.

WISHBONE. Locate the wishbone buried in the flesh, feeling it with your finger. Cut flesh from around each fork, cut through attachments at end of each fork, then around top of wishbone, and twist it out. (If you have a half breast, don't bother.)

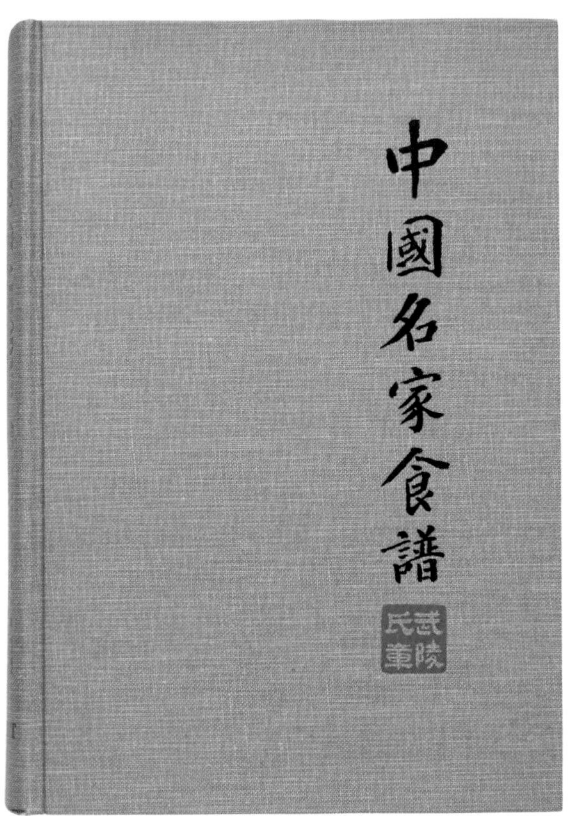

CRAIG CLAIBORNE AND VIRGINIA LEE

The Chinese Cookbook, 1972

Americans have had a love of Chinese food for at least the last 150 years. Some of the earliest Chinese restaurants were in San Francisco and New York, whose "Chinatowns" were culinary destinations not just for gourmands, but also for the public at large. Surprisingly, there are a number of Chinese cookbooks from early in the twentieth century, but most of them catered to American tastes.

The first serious book about foods from all over China is *The Chinese Cookbook*. Craig Claiborne, the noted food writer for the *New York Times*, first experienced Chinese food as a child when his family took him to a Chinese restaurant. So began a love affair with the tastes and smells of this amazing set of cuisines. Like many Americans, however, Claiborne was at first intimidated to "cook Chinese" because his training was in French cooking and the methods were so completely different. So he decided simply not to "cook Chinese." But when he met Virginia Lee, everything changed. Lee was an expert Chinese chef and had an amazing talent for teaching how to prepare traditional Chinese foods. As Claiborne did so many times on so many projects, he encouraged Lee to work on a cookbook about her food. In this instance, he coauthored *The Chinese Cookbook*, though he said he was more like a midwife to the project. The outcome was the most comprehensive and clear introduction to Chinese food to date.

NOTABLE RECIPES: Abalone with Oyster Sauce • The Best Fried Rice • **Cantonese Roast Pork** (page 531) • **Cold Noodles with Spicy Sauce** (page 451) • **Hot and Sour Soup** (page 340) • **Kung Pao Chicken** (page 511) • **Shrimp Toast with Sesame Seed Topping** (page 317) • Stir Fry Crabmeat • **Sweet and Sour Pork** (page 533)

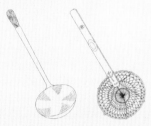

12 *The Chinese Cookbook*

Many Chinese dishes require that an ingredient be scooped out of the fat and drained at some point during the cooking. There are special sieves designed for this purpose, and one of the best is a heavy round metal sieve with fairly large holes and a handle. This can be placed over a large bowl to catch the drippings when food such as shrimp or chicken is scooped into the sieve. However, any large Western-style sieve, or even a colander, can be adapted for the purpose.

Chinese Cooking: Equipment, Methods, and Tips 13

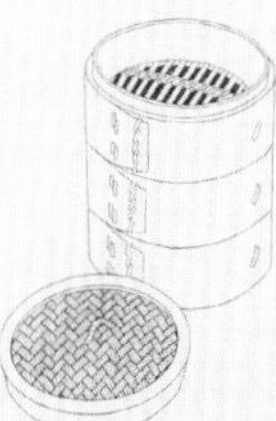

Steaming plays a large and important role in Chinese cooking, and bamboo steamers are ideal. These steamers, which come in many sizes, have no base and are made to be set onto a wok containing boiling water. They are convenient in that they come in layers, so that several dishes can be steamed at once. They are attractive enough that steamed dumplings, for instance, can be served directly out of their steaming vessel.

Western-style steamers can, of course, be substituted, and if you have none at all you can improvise by setting the dish to be steamed onto a bowl or some other kind of pedestal in a pot of boiling water. The pot should have a cover to keep the steam in, and enough room should be left around the dish so that the steam circulates freely.

Where rice is concerned, we offer the traditional recipe for rice in this book. On the other hand, we would like to add that there are some very good electric rice cookers on the market, most, if not all, made in the Orient and all of them designed to turn out quite acceptable rice for the Chinese table. They are simplicity itself to operate, and once the rice and water are added to the cooker it can be forgotten. They are wholly automatic, and cooking time is about 20 minutes.

HOW TO CUT COOKED POULTRY FOR SERVING, CHINESE STYLE:

1. Cut off the head, if any, and reserve or discard. Cut off the neck and reserve.
2. Cut off the wings close to the body and reserve.
3. Lay the fowl on its back, breast side up, and cut it in two down the center of the breast. A rubber mallet to pound the cleaver through the bone, and a pair of kitchen shears, are helpful.

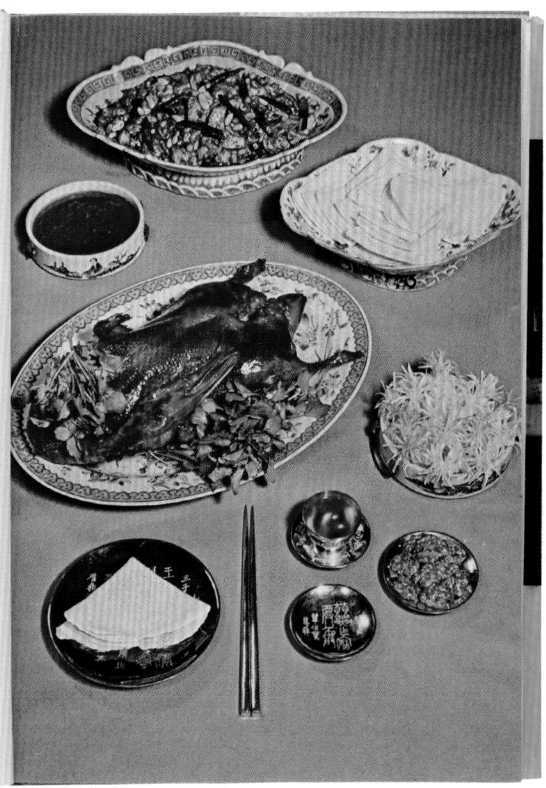

DIANA KENNEDY

The Cuisines of Mexico, 1972

Diana Kennedy became an expert on Mexican cooking almost by accident. Born in England, she met Paul Kennedy, a Latin American news correspondent for the *New York Times*, in Haiti during a trip there. The two fell in love, married, and Diana followed her husband to his new appointment in Mexico City. The Kennedy home became an international center for American and Latin American journalists, writers, and others passing through Mexico.

Craig Claiborne, who was the *New York Times* food editor in this period, was a frequent visitor. A lover of Mexican food from his childhood—when he would buy tamales from a street cart, despite worries about what kind of meat was in them—Claiborne encouraged Diana Kennedy to pursue her near-maniacal love of Mexican food and its history. When Paul died in 1967, Diana turned her attention to the study of Mexican food. By 1969 she had moved to New York City and was teaching Mexican cooking classes out of her apartment on Sunday afternoons. With Claiborne's encouragement, she turned her research into the most authoritative guide to Mexican cuisines published up to that time, *The Cuisines of Mexico*. The book remains one of the most comprehensive studies of these amazing traditions.

NOTABLE RECIPES: Flan a la Antigua (page 644) • Mexican Rice • **Mole Poblano de Guajolote** (page 391) • Pato en Mole Verde de Pepita • **Pozole de Jalisco** (page 352) • **Salsa de Jitomate Cocida** (page 527) • **Sopa de Lima** (page 354)

Diana Kennedy

The Cuisines of Mexico

Foreword by Craig Claiborne

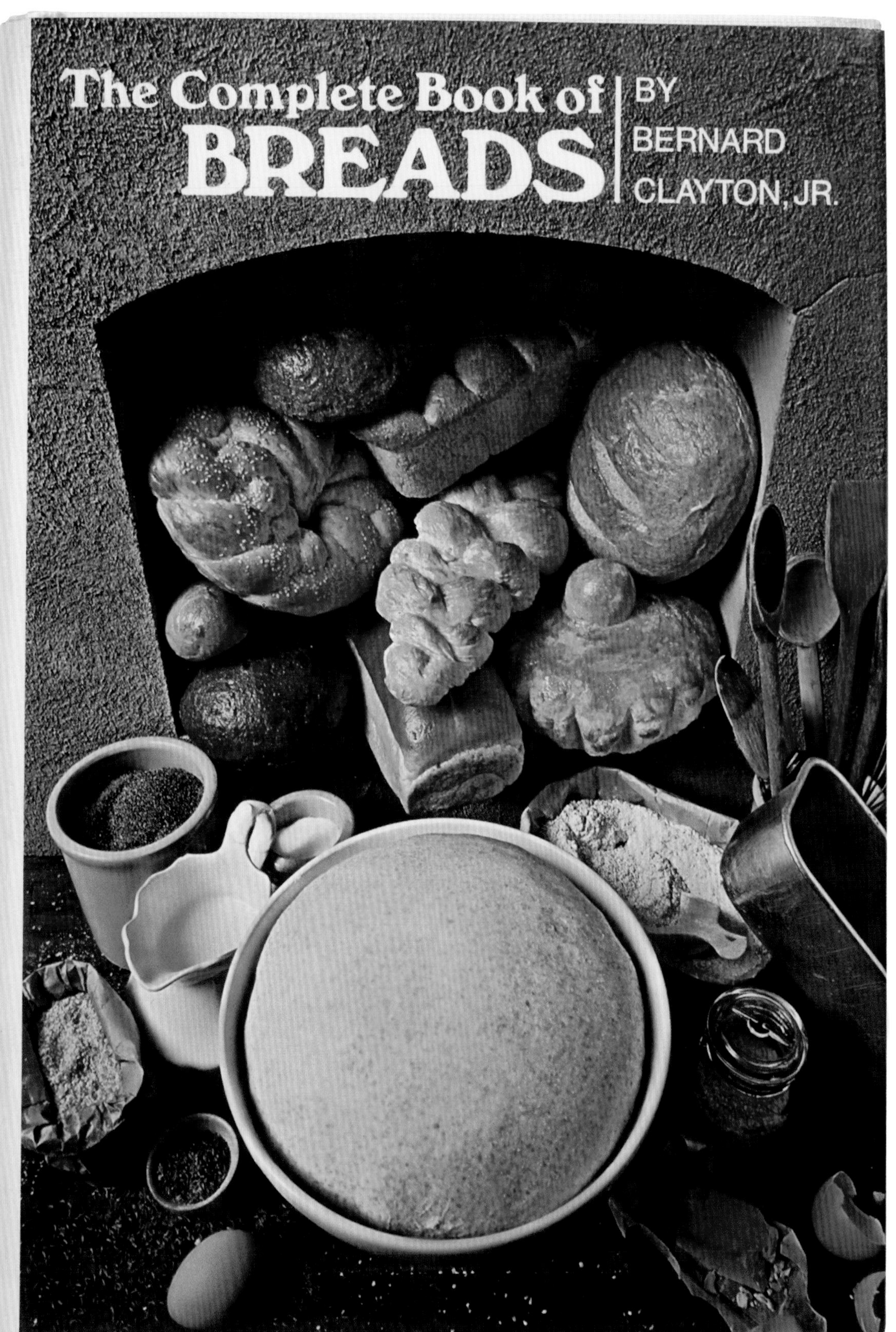
The Complete Book of
BREADS
BY
BERNARD
CLAYTON, JR.

BERNARD CLAYTON, JR.

The Complete Book of Breads, 1973

We all have an image of a Frenchman on his bicycle with a baguette lovingly tucked into a basket, heading home for lunch. Bernard Clayton, Jr., could have been a model for such a photograph. Clayton was an avid cyclist and went on a bike tour of Europe in 1965 with his wife. At that time, he was a successful journalist and had no aspirations to become a master baker. His cycling trip through France changed everything. Clayton became obsessed with the outstanding breads he found at every stop and began trying to replicate them when he returned stateside. Over the next ten years, Clayton traveled around the world seeking out the secrets to good baking.

His obsession turned into a second career when he brought out *The Complete Book of Breads* in 1973. The volume quickly became a best-seller and a twin to James Beard's *Beard on Bread*. Clayton's next project, *The Breads of France*, published in 1978, involved a seven-thousand-mile research trip that produced a comprehensive guide to the various French bread styles. Craig Claiborne, the *New York Times* food critic, likened Clayton's knowledge of baking to Marcella Hazan's knowledge of Italian food and Diana Kennedy's knowledge of Mexican food. While perhaps a bit dated now, Clayton's book stands as one of the monuments of home bread baking.

NOTABLE RECIPES: Challah (page 576) • Dilly Casserole Bread • **Dresden Christmas Fruit Bread** (page 584) • Grandma's Oatmeal Bread • Honey-Lemon Whole Wheat • **Old Milwaukee Rye Bread** (page 568) • Pane Italiano • Panettone • Pepper Cheese Loaf • **Sprouted Wheat Bread** (page 566) • White Breads • White Bread with Chocolate

28 THE COMPLETE BOOK OF BREADS

Thermometer

Until you are familiar with every nook and cranny of the oven, use either a columnar or dial-type thermometer to gauge the uniformity of the heat. You may find the oven thermometer does not always agree with a good thermometer like a Taylor, so adjust the heat accordingly. And, move the loaves once or twice during the baking period to expose them to the various heats in the oven.

Bread Knife

A fine loaf of bread deserves to be sliced with a razor-sharp knife. Invest in a good one; there is none better than a 14-inch knife with a serrated blade made by a Swiss firm and sold in the U.S. by R. H. Forschner Co. It is the Victorinox #460-9 and sells for about $5. Reserve it for bread *only* and it will stay sharp for several years.

Toaster

Home-baked breads adapt more easily to the old-fashioned toaster, with sides that fold out to accommodate a variety of slice sizes and textures, than to the more modern ones. While you must watch the toast in the old model, it does a custom job that an automatic machine cannot equal. I use a Canadian toaster manufactured by the Toastess Corporation, Model 202.

Standard Weights and Measures

Herbman
Strasbourg, 1529

Make certain all measurements are level.

Dash	= 8 drops
1 tablespoon	= 3 teaspoons
4 tablespoons	= ¼ cup
5⅓ tablespoons	= ⅓ cup
8 tablespoons	= ½ cup
16 tablespoons	= 1 cup (dry)
1 fluid ounce	= 2 tablespoons
1 cup (liquid)	= ½ pint
2 cups (16 ounces)	= 1 pint
2 pints (4 cups)	= 1 quart
4 quarts	= 1 gallon
8 quarts	= 1 peck (dry)
4 pecks	= 1 bushel
16 ounces (dry measure)	= 1 pound

U.S.	EUROPEAN
1 teaspoon	= 1 coffee spoon
1 tablespoon	= 1 soup spoon
2 tablespoons	= 1 English tablespoon
2 teaspoons	= 1 English teaspoon
20 fluid ounces	= 1 English pint
10 ounces (dry measure)	= 1 English cup

29

MARCELLA HAZAN

The Classic Italian Cook Book

The Art of Italian Cooking, 1973

If you have only one Italian cookbook, it should be Marcella Hazan's *Essentials of Classic Italian Cooking.* While Americans have been enjoying the richness of Italy's food traditions since the eighteenth century, by the early twentieth century Italian food had come to be thought of as secondary, garlicky, ethnic, and "red sauce," or, even worse, frozen pizza or pasta from a can. That all changed with the publication of *The Classic Italian Cook Book.* Hazan carefully, clearly, and lovingly shares the simplicity of preparations, the focus on fresh ingredients, and the complexity of taste that is the essence of food from all the regions of Italy. Make your own pasta? Why not! It's easy and the result is transformative. Try the recipe for arrosto di maiale al latte if you want to taste one of the most delicious of all pork roasts.

She went on to write *More Classic Italian Cooking* (1978), *Marcella's Italian Kitchen* (1986), and *Essentials of Classic Italian Cooking* (1992), which is a compilation of the other volumes, often referred to as "the green Marcella." If you really love Italian food, you'll want all of Hazan's books on your shelf.

NOTABLE RECIPES: Arrosto di maiale al latte (page 535) • Baby Lamb Chops Fried in Parmesan Cheese • **Blender Pesto** (page 432) • Chicken al diavolo • **Coniglio in padella** (page 555) • Fried Artichoke Wedges • Home-Made Egg Pasta • **Ossobucco alla milanese** (page 550) • **Ragù** (page 527) • **Scaloppine di vittelo al marsala** (page 549) • **Vitello tonnato** (page 552) • **Zuppa di scarole e riso** (page 342)

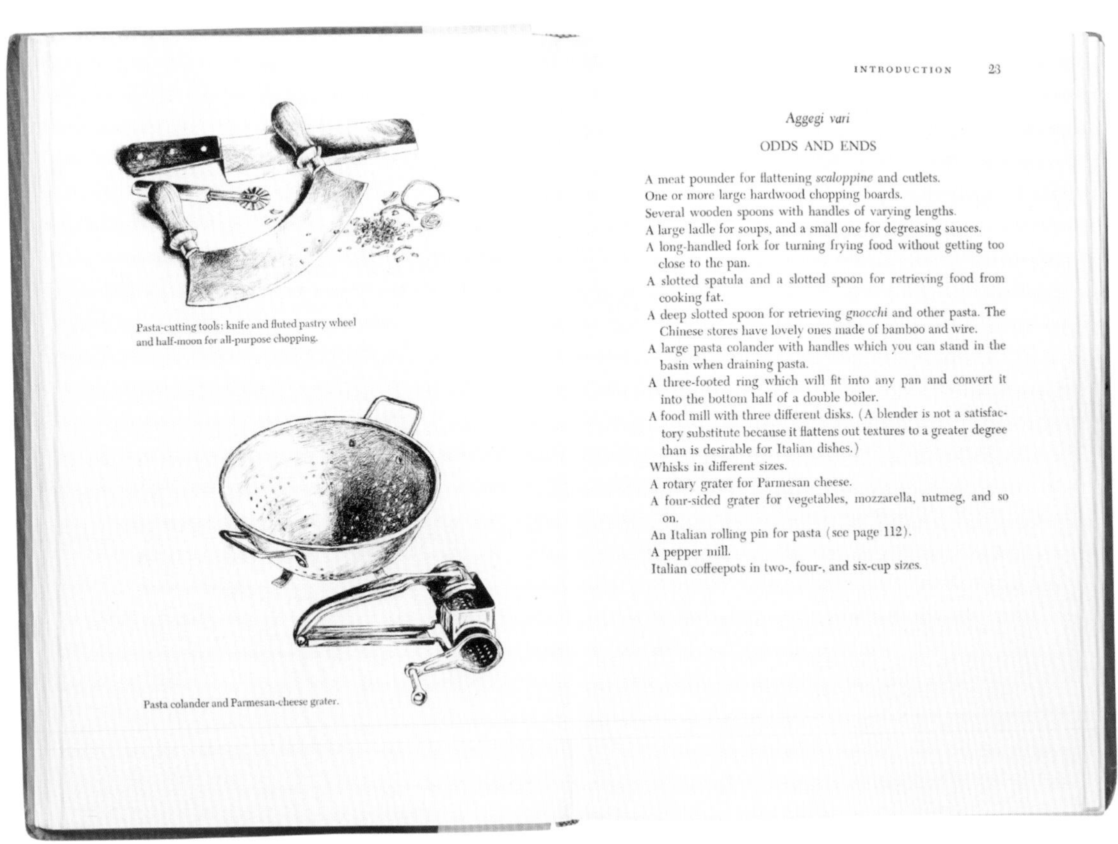

Pasta-cutting tools: knife and fluted pastry wheel and half-moon for all-purpose chopping.

Pasta colander and Parmesan-cheese grater.

INTRODUCTION 23

Aggegi vari

ODDS AND ENDS

A meat pounder for flattening *scaloppine* and cutlets.
One or more large hardwood chopping boards.
Several wooden spoons with handles of varying lengths.
A large ladle for soups, and a small one for degreasing sauces.
A long-handled fork for turning frying food without getting too close to the pan.
A slotted spatula and a slotted spoon for retrieving food from cooking fat.
A deep slotted spoon for retrieving *gnocchi* and other pasta. The Chinese stores have lovely ones made of bamboo and wire.
A large pasta colander with handles which you can stand in the basin when draining pasta.
A three-footed ring which will fit into any pan and convert it into the bottom half of a double boiler.
A food mill with three different disks. (A blender is not a satisfactory substitute because it flattens out textures to a greater degree than is desirable for Italian dishes.)
Whisks in different sizes.
A rotary grater for Parmesan cheese.
A four-sided grater for vegetables, mozzarella, nutmeg, and so on.
An Italian rolling pin for pasta (see page 112).
A pepper mill.
Italian coffeepots in two-, four-, and six-cup sizes.

2. While the *cappelletti* are cooking, choose an enameled cast-iron or other flameproof cook-and-serve pan that will later accommodate all the *cappelletti* without stacking them too high. Put in half the cream and all the butter and simmer over moderate heat for less than a minute, until the cream and butter have thickened. Turn off the heat.

3. Fresh *cappelletti* are done within 5 minutes after the water returns to a boil, while dry *cappelletti* may take 15 to 20 minutes. When done—they should be firm, but cooked throughout—transfer them with a large slotted spoon or colander to the pan containing the cream and butter and turn the heat on to low. Turn the *cappelletti* to coat them all with the cream and butter sauce. Add the rest of the cream and all the grated cheese, and continue turning the *cappelletti* until they are evenly coated and all the cream has thickened. Serve immediately from the same pan, with a bowl of additional grated cheese on the side.

MENU SUGGESTIONS

See the ones for Fettuccine Tossed in Cream and Butter (page 131).

TORTELLINI

Some people prefer the rounder, more compact shape of *tortellini*. If you would like to make *tortellini alla panna* or *tortellini in brodo*, follow every direction in the above recipes except for cutting the pasta. Instead of cutting the pasta into squares, cut it into 2-inch disks, using juice glass, cookie cutter, or any circular instrument with that diameter. The disks are stuffed, folded, wrapped, and sealed exactly as the squares are.

Tortellini begin as circles. When stuffed and folded over, the edges do not come exactly together.

Bend around the finger and press one corner over the other.

5. These shrimps require brisk, rapid cooking. Wait until the broiler has been on for 15 minutes. Cook the shrimps no more than 3 minutes on one side and 2 minutes on the other, and even less if the shrimps are very small. Each side is done as soon as a crisp, golden crust forms.

6. Serve piping hot, on the skewers, with lemon wedges on the side.

MENU SUGGESTIONS

Very tiny shrimps broiled in this manner are a frequent part of Italian "shore dinners," served together with a mixture of broiled and fried fish. American shrimps are frequently sufficiently large to suffice as a course of their own. The dish can be preceded by a Risotto with Clams (page 192), Clam Soup (page 53), Mussel Soup (page 56), or Trenette with Potatoes and Pesto (page 142). Generally no vegetable is served with it, but the Sautéed Mushrooms with Garlic and Parsley (page 379) can be a very agreeable accompaniment. Follow the shrimp with Mixed Salad (page 408).

Calamari
SQUID

It is odd how New Englanders, who consume clams by the ton, dread the thought of eating another excellent mollusk, the squid. Actually, the flesh of the squid, when properly cooked, is far more delicate and tender than most clams. It is no accident that fish-loving countries from Italy to Japan regard the squid and its numerous relatives as one of the sea's most delectable offerings. If you are open minded about experimenting with food, you will be well rewarded by the taste of squid.

The squid most commonly available here corresponds to the large Italian squid, *Calamari* and *calamaroni*. Its sac, exclusive of tentacles, measures from 3½ inches to 6 or 7 inches in length. It is available either fresh or frozen, and both are good. In Italy, freshly caught large squid is kept in the refrigerator one or two days before cooking, to relax its rigid flesh. In this country it is probably already that old before it reaches the market. Use squid only when it is a pure, milky white in color. The tastiest, sweetest squid, whether fresh or frozen, comes to the markets in early spring.

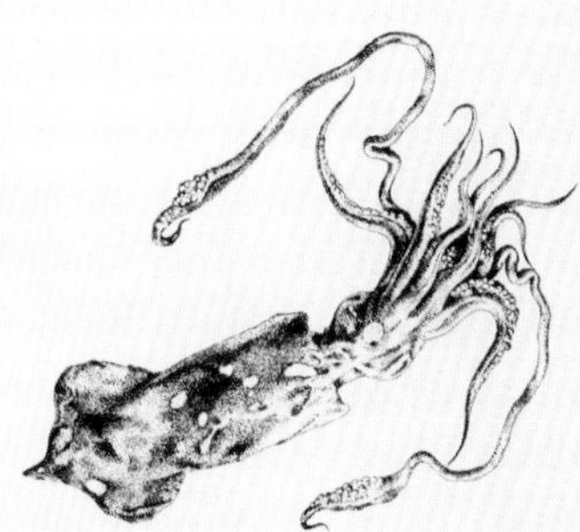

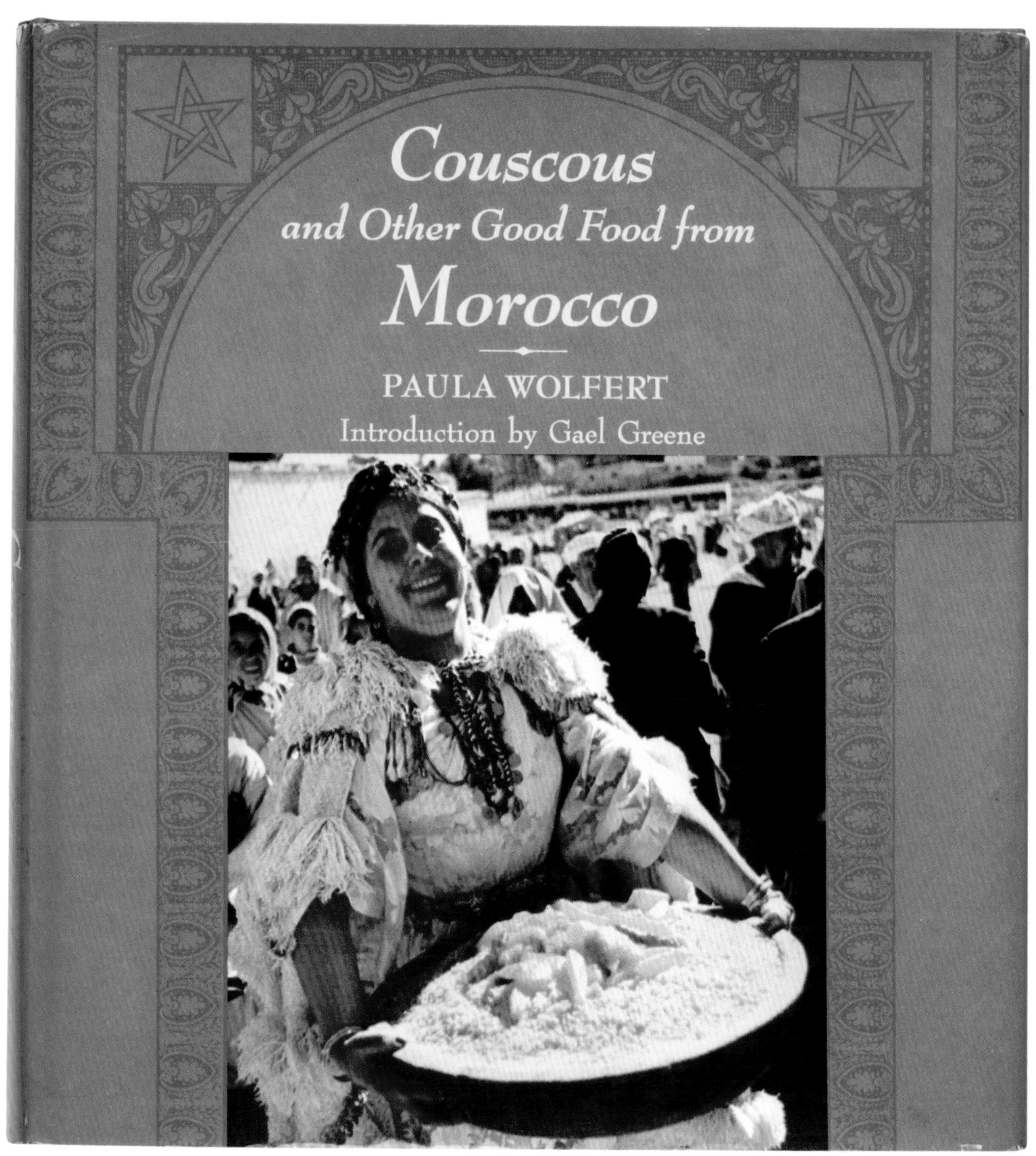
Couscous
and Other Good Food from
Morocco
PAULA WOLFERT
Introduction by Gael Greene

PAULA WOLFERT

Couscous and Other Good Food from Morocco, 1973

Nearly all of Paula Wolfert's cookbooks are classics, but none is more important than her first, *Couscous and Other Good Food from Morocco*. One of the reasons her books are so well received is her meticulous research. Her books have a scholarly quality—almost an ethnographic feel—about the regional foods she writes about. While some critics have accused her of elitism and being an "absolutist," she's said, "If it calls for mace, I'm not going to use nutmeg."

Wolfert's credentials for Moroccan food are hard to argue with. After leaving Columbia University to marry Michael Wolfert, a Harvard graduate, she enrolled in cooking classes taught by the famous Dione Lucas, the first woman to receive a degree from the Cordon Bleu in Paris. From Lucas she got a solid foundation in French cooking techniques. In a stroke of luck, Michael Wolfert was transferred to Morocco for work and the couple moved to North Africa, where they lived for three years. Paula became fascinated with the flavors of Moroccan food. She began collecting recipes that eventually became *Couscous and Other Good Food from Morocco*.

The timing was perfect. Americans were more adventurous than they had ever been about international foods. International groceries were making it easier to find "exotic" ingredients. Wolfert's book opened the way for preserved lemons, couscous, and, later, duck confit, as well as all manner of animal fat, to enter into the American palate with her books *The Cooking of the Eastern Mediterranean* and *The Cooking of Southwest France*.

NOTABLE RECIPES: Bisteeya (page 514) • Chicken Tagine with Prunes and Almonds • **Four Different Ways to Make Chicken with Lemon and Olives** (page 506) • Couscous with Seven Vegetables in the Fez Manner • Eggplant Salad • Harira (Lentil) Soup • **Lamb Tagine with Artichokes, Lemon, and Olives** (page 539) • Moroccan Bread • **Orange Salads** (page 362) • **Preserved Lemons** (page 434) • The Snake

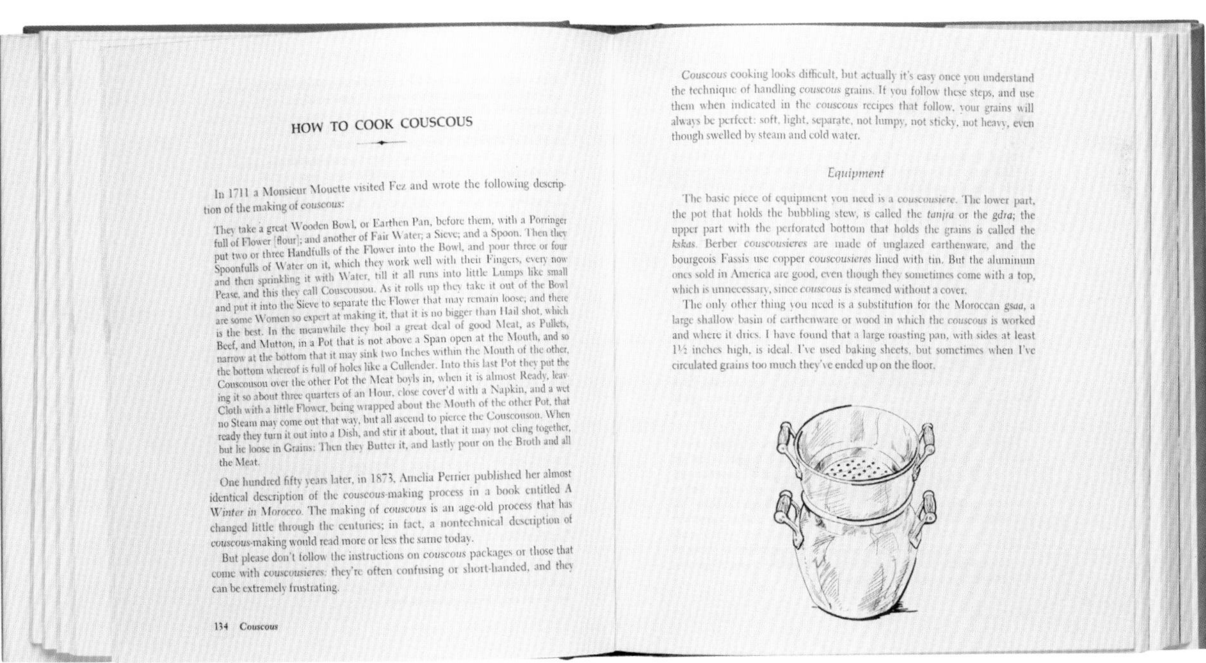

HOW TO COOK COUSCOUS

In 1711 a Monsieur Mouette visited Fez and wrote the following description of the making of *couscous*:

> They take a great Wooden Bowl, or Earthen Pan, before them, with a Porringer full of Flower [flour]; and another of Fair Water; a Sieve; and a Spoon. Then they put two or three Handfulls of the Flower into the Bowl, and pour three or four Spoonfulls of Water on it, which they work well with their Fingers, every now and then sprinkling it with Water, till it all runs into little Lumps like small Pease, and this they call Couscousou. As it rolls up they take it out of the Bowl and put it into the Sieve to separate the Flower that may remain loose; and there are some Women so expert at making it, that it is no bigger than Hail shot, which is the best. In the meanwhile they boil a great deal of good Meat, as Pullets, Beef, and Mutton, in a Pot that is not above a Span open at the Mouth, and so narrow at the bottom that it may sink two Inches within the Mouth of the other, the bottom whereof is full of holes like a Cullender. Into this last Pot they put the Couscousou over the other Pot the Meat boyls in, when it is almost Ready, leaving it so about three quarters of an Hour, close cover'd with a Napkin, and a wet Cloth with a little Flower, being wrapped about the Mouth of the other Pot, that no Steam may come out that way, but all ascend to pierce the Couscousou. When ready they turn it out into a Dish, and stir it about, that it may not cling together, but lie loose in Grains: Then they Butter it, and lastly pour on the Broth and all the Meat.

One hundred fifty years later, in 1873, Amelia Perrier published her almost identical description of the *couscous*-making process in a book entitled *A Winter in Morocco*. The making of *couscous* is an age-old process that has changed little through the centuries; in fact, a nontechnical description of *couscous*-making would read more or less the same today.

But please don't follow the instructions on *couscous* packages or those that come with *couscousieres*: they're often confusing or short-handed, and they can be extremely frustrating.

134 *Couscous*

Couscous cooking looks difficult, but actually it's easy once you understand the technique of handling *couscous* grains. If you follow these steps, and use them when indicated in the *couscous* recipes that follow, your grains will always be perfect: soft, light, separate, not lumpy, not sticky, not heavy, even though swelled by steam and cold water.

Equipment

The basic piece of equipment you need is a *couscousiere*. The lower part, the pot that holds the bubbling stew, is called the *tanjra* or the *gdra*; the upper part with the perforated bottom that holds the grains is called the *kskas*. Berber *couscousieres* are made of unglazed earthenware, and the bourgeois Fassis use copper *couscousieres* lined with tin. But the aluminum ones sold in America are good, even though they sometimes come with a top, which is unnecessary, since *couscous* is steamed without a cover.

The only other thing you need is a substitution for the Moroccan *gsaa*, a large shallow basin of earthenware or wood in which the *couscous* is worked and where it dries. I have found that a large roasting pan, with sides at least 1½ inches high, is ideal. I've used baking sheets, but sometimes when I've circulated grains too much they've ended up on the floor.

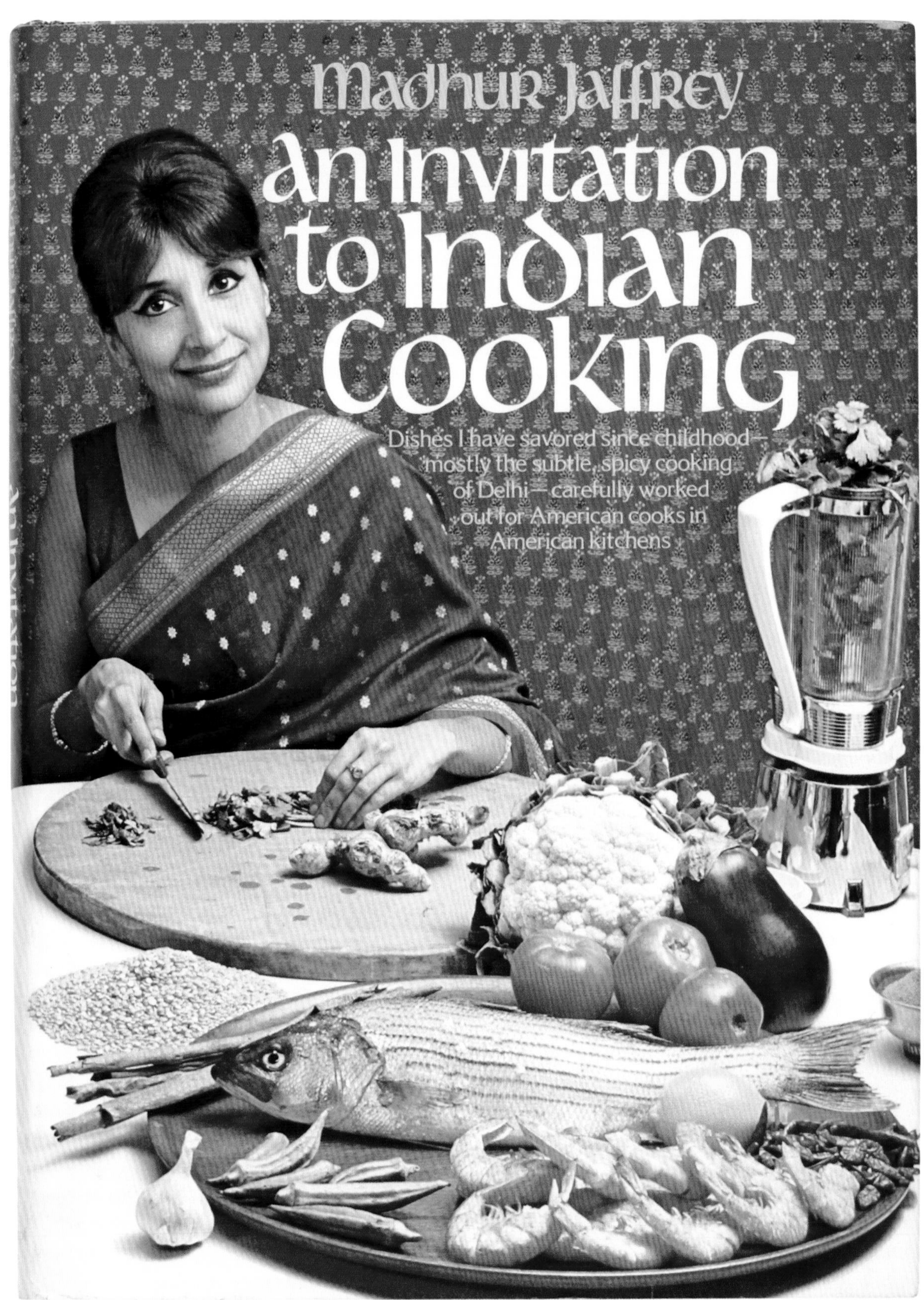
Madhur Jaffrey
An Invitation to Indian Cooking
Dishes I have savored since childhood—mostly the subtle, spicy cooking of Delhi—carefully worked out for American cooks in American kitchens

MADHUR JAFFREY

An Invitation to Indian Cooking, 1973

Madhur Jaffrey gave us all a great gift with this book. When it was first published, Craig Claiborne of the *New York Times* described it as "one of the finest, most lucid and comprehensive books on Indian cooking ever published." Jaffrey has done more than any other person to make the complex and rich traditions of Indian cooking accessible to the American palate.

Jaffrey was an unlikely spokesperson for food. As a child she didn't learn to cook (but was always fascinated by the kitchen). Jaffrey was born Madhur Bahadur in Delhi and attended the University of Delhi. She went to London to study at the Royal Academy of Dramatic Art, from which she graduated with honors. During her time there she missed the food she grew up with and so learned to cook, receiving recipes in letters from her mother.

Jaffrey's first career was as an actress. She starred in many films made by Ismail Merchant and James Ivory, such as *Shakespeare Wallah* (1965), *The Guru* (1969), *Autobiography of a Princess* (1976), and *Heat and Dust* (1983). After her performance in *Shakespeare Wallah*, she became known as the "actress who could cook." She created a show for the BBC about Indian cooking, which was very popular, and she did the same for U.S. television. Following an article about her in the *New York Times*, she received an offer from Alfred A. Knopf publishers to do a book about Indian food for the American market. Jaffrey did for Indian cooking what Julia Child did for French cooking. This book is one of the essential cookbooks and should be on every shelf.

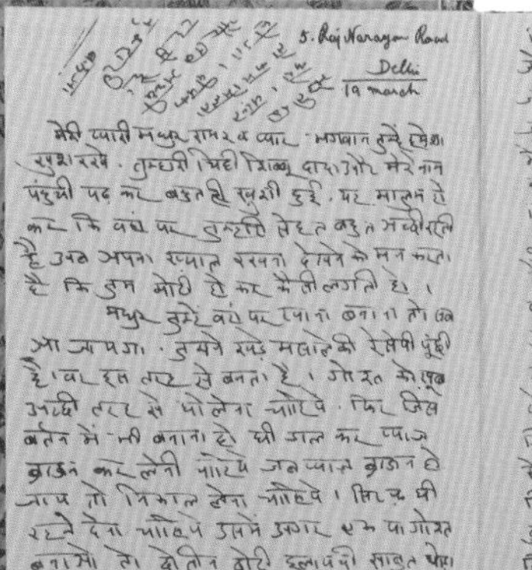

5, Raj Narayan Road
Delhi
19 march

NOTABLE RECIPES: Butterflied Leg of Lamb • **Cucumber Raita** (page 434) • Lamb Chops with Whole Spices and Yogurt • Lamb Korma with Almonds, Pecans, and Sour Cream • **Naan** (page 572) • Sweet Rice • **Stuffed Whole Okra** (page 412) • **Tandoori Chicken** (page 516) • Tomato Tamarind Chutney • **Whole-Wheat Samosas** (page 319)

MAIDA HEATTER

Maida Heatter's Book of Great Desserts, 1974

For anyone who loves to bake and to eat desserts, *Maida Heatter's Book of Great Desserts* is a sacred text. You don't have to be a pastry chef to make Heatter's recipes work with magical results.

Heatter didn't set out to have a career in food—far from it. While she always liked to cook, and credits her mother as her teacher, Heatter attended the Pratt Institute in New York to become a fashion illustrator. Following graduation, she got a job at the *New York Herald Tribune* as an illustrator for the Retail-Merchandising Services. In the late 1940s she moved to Miami Beach, where she met and married Ralph Daniels. She won his heart with a brownie she had in her purse—something she often carried with her wherever she went. To make money, Heatter had spent many years designing and making jewelry. When her father moved in after her mother's death in the early 1960s, Heatter needed something else to do. She had an idea to open a restaurant with her husband, though neither of them knew anything about the restaurant business. Nevertheless, they opened a small restaurant that got big press in 1968 when the Republican Party held its presidential convention in Miami. As a joke, Heatter and her husband decided to put elephant on the menu during the convention. While no one ordered any of the meat (which came from a few cans) the stunt caught the attention of the press, including Craig Claiborne, who visited the restaurant to cover the story for the *New York Times*. Claiborne was immediately struck by Heatter's outstanding desserts. She showed him her recipes and he convinced her to write a cookbook. (Again and again throughout his career, Claiborne encouraged very talented cooks to share their recipes. Many of the books they produced became best-sellers. Claiborne clearly had a sense of who the most important and capable home cooks were and how they could influence American food.) And so, Maida Heatter's practical wisdom about baking desserts and her carefully crafted recipes became mainstays of American baking. Everyone who loves desserts should own this book.

NOTABLE RECIPES: Brownies • Chocolate Cupcakes • **Chocolate Mousse Heatter** (page 646) • Hot Fudge Sauce • **Queen Mother's Cake** (page 620) • **Raspberry-Strawberry Bavarian** (page 640) • **Texas Fruitcake** (page 586) • **Walnut Fudge Pie à la Mode with Hot Fudge Sauce** (page 606)

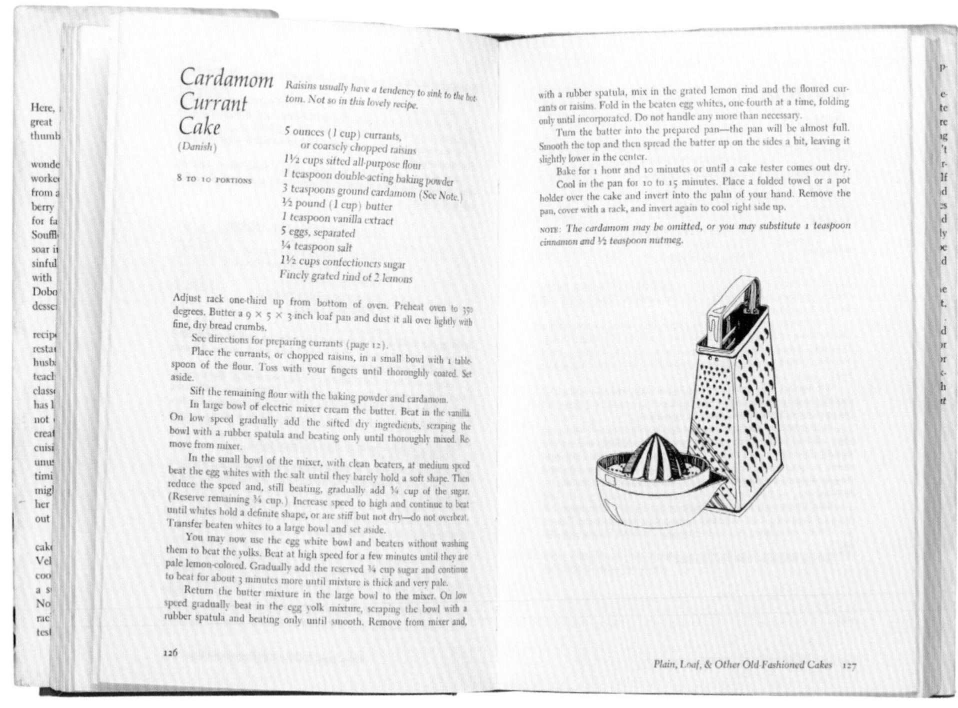

Cardamom Currant Cake
(*Danish*)

8 TO 10 PORTIONS

Raisins usually have a tendency to sink to the bottom. Not so in this lovely recipe.

5 ounces (1 cup) currants, or coarsely chopped raisins
1½ cups sifted all-purpose flour
1 teaspoon double-acting baking powder
3 teaspoons ground cardamom (See Note.)
½ pound (1 cup) butter
1 teaspoon vanilla extract
5 eggs, separated
¼ teaspoon salt
1½ cups confectioners sugar
Finely grated rind of 2 lemons

Adjust rack one-third up from bottom of oven. Preheat oven to 350 degrees. Butter a 9 × 5 × 3-inch loaf pan and dust it all over lightly with fine, dry bread crumbs.

See directions for preparing currants (page 12).

Place the currants, or chopped raisins, in a small bowl with 1 tablespoon of the flour. Toss with your fingers until thoroughly coated. Set aside.

Sift the remaining flour with the baking powder and cardamom.

In large bowl of electric mixer cream the butter. Beat in the vanilla. On low speed gradually add the sifted dry ingredients, scraping the bowl with a rubber spatula and beating only until thoroughly mixed. Remove from mixer.

In the small bowl of the mixer, with clean beaters, at medium speed beat the egg whites with the salt until they barely hold a soft shape. Then reduce the speed and, still beating, gradually add ¾ cup of the sugar. (Reserve remaining ¾ cup.) Increase speed to high and continue to beat until whites hold a definite shape, or are stiff but not dry—do not overbeat. Transfer beaten whites to a large bowl and set aside.

You may now use the egg white bowl and beaters without washing them to beat the yolks. Beat at high speed for a few minutes until they are pale lemon-colored. Gradually add the reserved ¾ cup sugar and continue to beat for about 3 minutes more until mixture is thick and very pale.

Return the butter mixture in the large bowl to the mixer. On low speed gradually beat in the egg yolk mixture, scraping the bowl with a rubber spatula and beating only until smooth. Remove from mixer and,

126

with a rubber spatula, mix in the grated lemon rind and the floured currants or raisins. Fold in the beaten egg whites, one-fourth at a time, folding only until incorporated. Do not handle any more than necessary.

Turn the batter into the prepared pan—the pan will be almost full. Smooth the top and then spread the batter up on the sides a bit, leaving it slightly lower in the center.

Bake for 1 hour and 10 minutes or until a cake tester comes out dry.

Cool in the pan for 10 to 15 minutes. Place a folded towel or a pot holder over the cake and invert into the palm of your hand. Remove the pan, cover with a rack, and invert again to cool right side up.

NOTE: *The cardamom may be omitted, or you may substitute 1 teaspoon cinnamon and ½ teaspoon nutmeg.*

Plain, Loaf, & Other Old-Fashioned Cakes 127

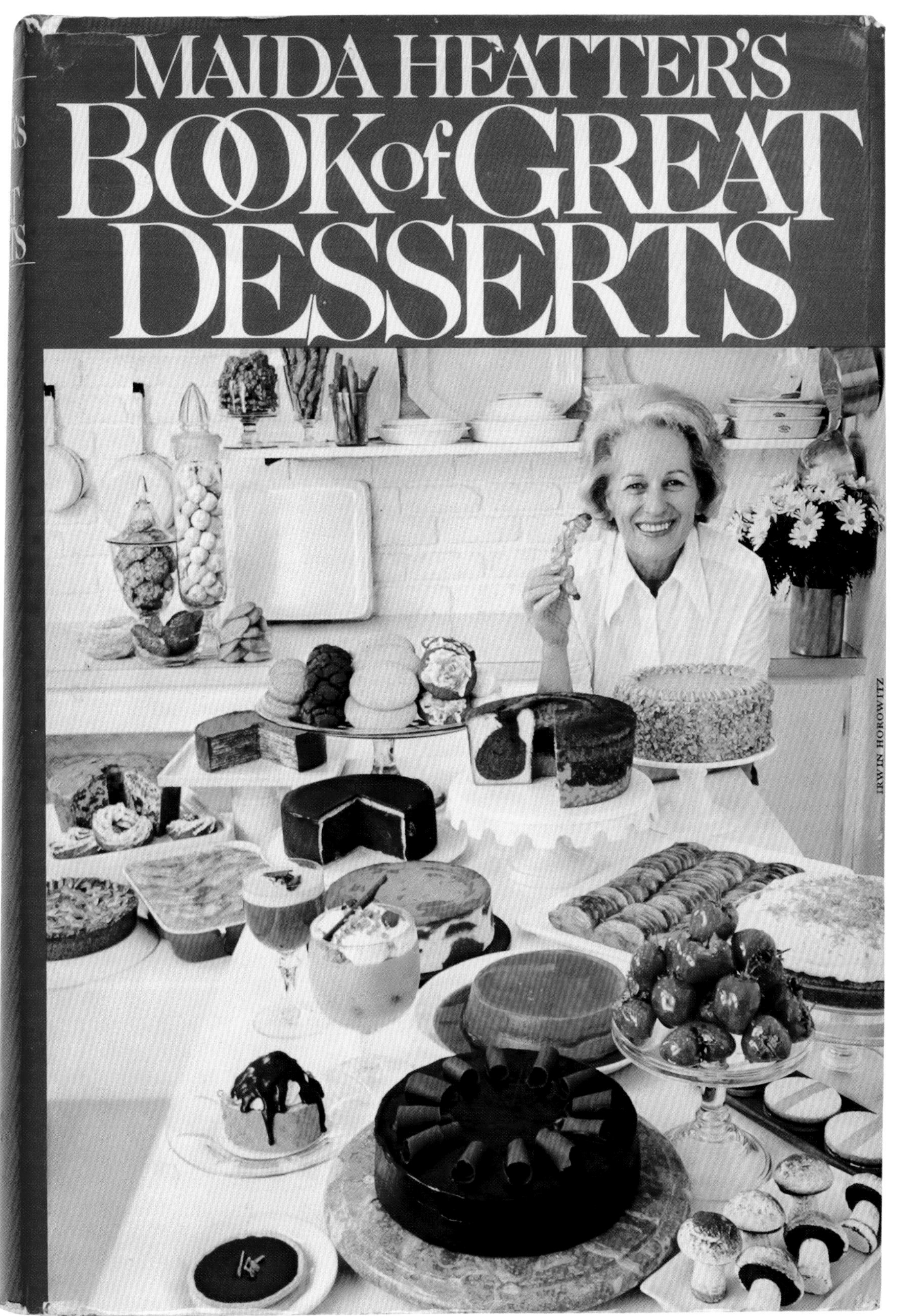
MAIDA HEATTER'S
BOOK of GREAT
DESSERTS
IRWIN HOROWITZ

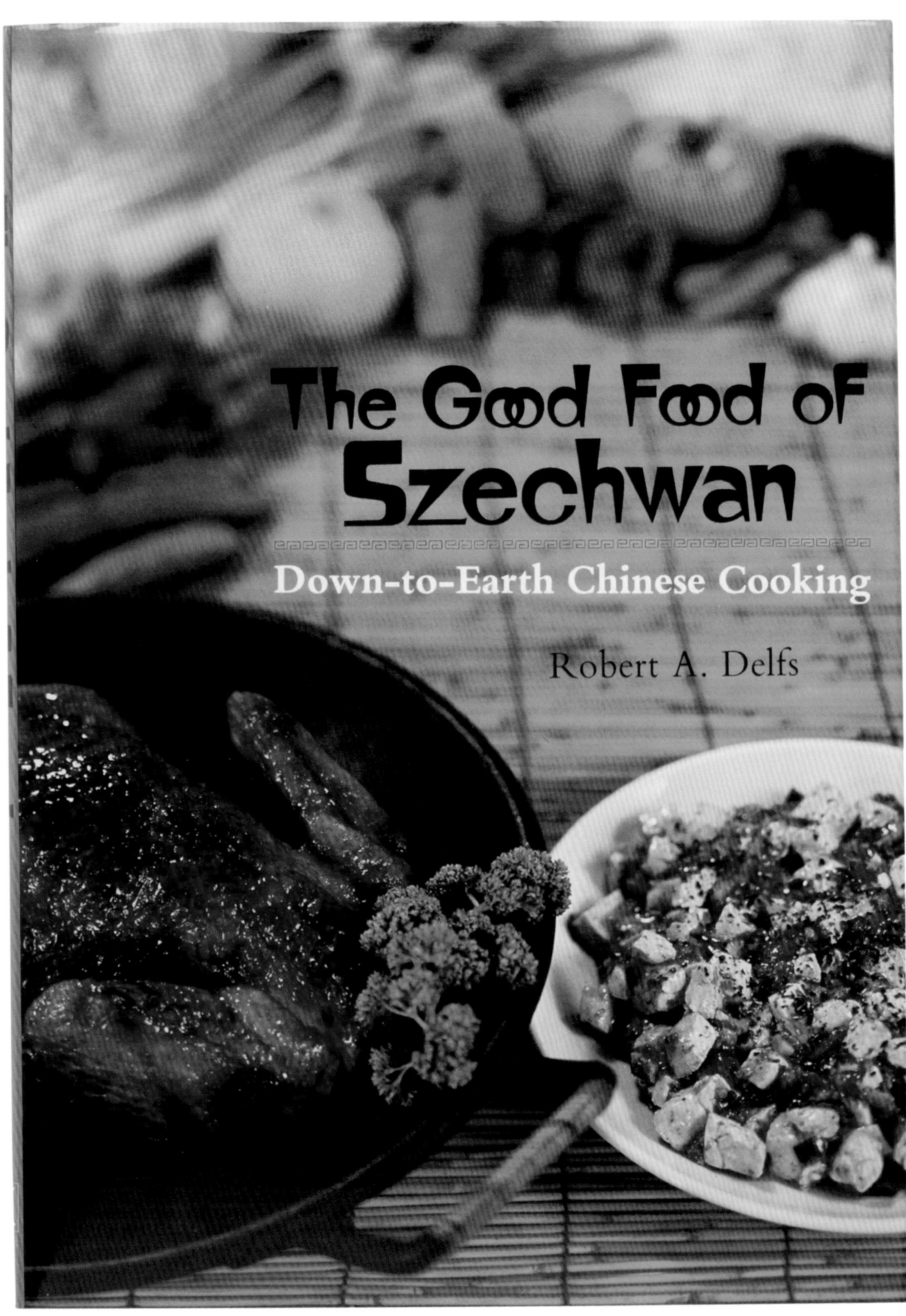
The Good Food of
Szechwan
Down-to-Earth Chinese Cooking
Robert A. Delfs

ROBERT A. DELFS

The Good Food of Szechwan

Down-to-Earth Chinese Cooking, 1974

Americans have always loved Chinese food—well, actually Chinese American food, for many dishes were altered by Chinese immigrants based on availability of ingredients. And, famously, some dishes are completely American fabrications of Chinese-style food: think chop suey. Until the 1970s, most Chinese American food was Cantonese, reflecting the fact that historically many Chinese immigrants came from this southeastern part of China. In the seventies, however, food from the western provinces of Szechwan and Hunan began to appear—and Americans were smitten. These dishes have a distinct flavor from the use of Szechwan peppercorns, fermented bean paste, sesame oil, and other ingredients. Overnight we became obsessed with Szechwan cooking. One of the best books about this cuisine is *The Good Food of Szechwan* by Robert A. Delfs. Delfs was a student at Princeton University who spent two years in Taiwan. While there, he fell in love with Szechwan cooking and began to translate traditional recipes into English. He finally produced this book, which has detailed descriptions of ingredients, cooking techniques, food traditions, and easy-to-follow recipes for the major Szechwan dishes. It remains one of the best introductions to Szechwan cooking for the home cook.

NOTABLE RECIPES: Chicken with Charred Red Peppers and Cashews (page 512) • Cold Chicken with Sesame and Sechuan Pepper • **Dry-Fried Beef with Carrots and Celery** (page 546)• **Dry-Fried String Beans** (page 406) • Eggplant with Yu Xiang Sauce • Hot and Sour Zucchini • Ma Po Tofu • Twice Cooked Pork

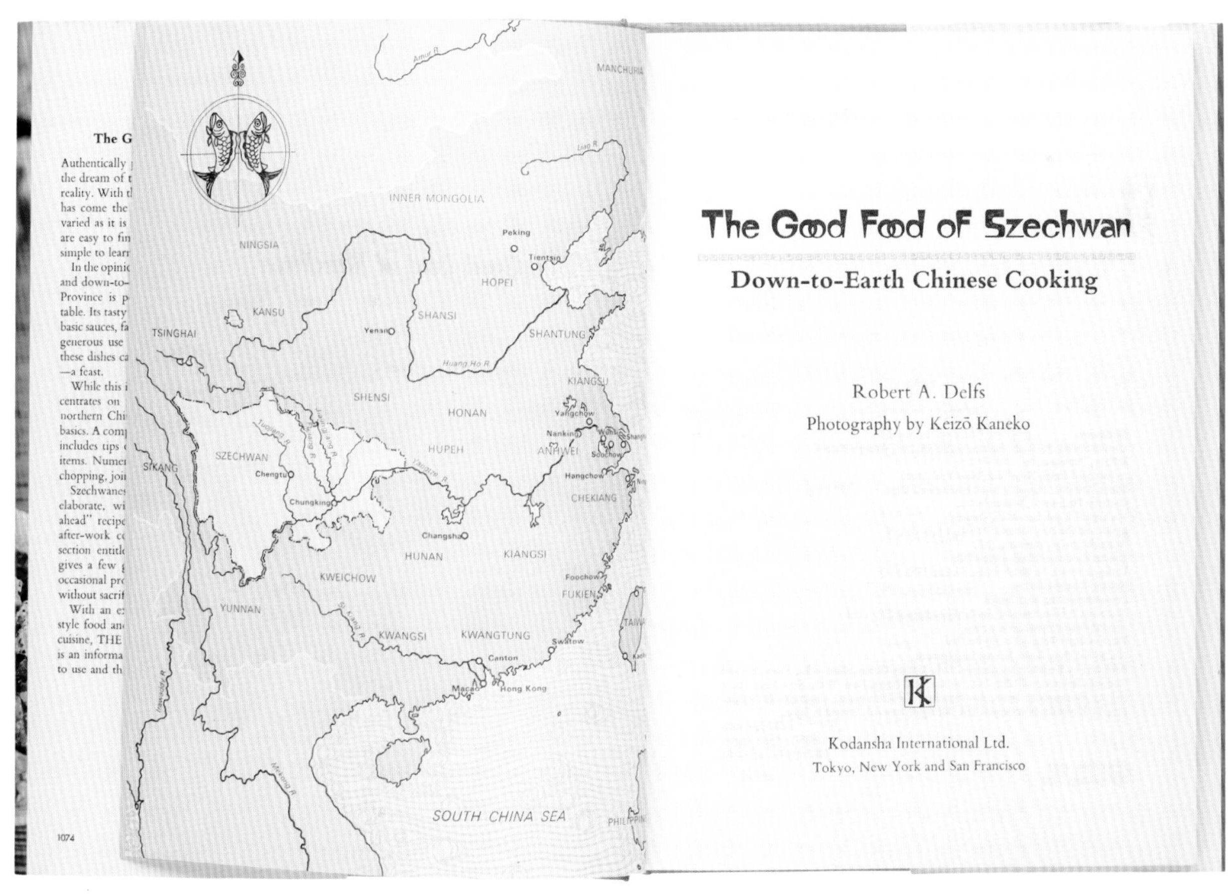

—the ring-stand just moves the *wok* further away from an already inadequate heat source. Keep the ring, however, for use in camping as you cook over a fire or coals with no grill.

Cleaning: Treat the *wok* as you would a good French omelette pan. Do not use detergents. Cylindrical *wok*-cleaners made from bamboo slivers bound at one end are available at Chinese grocery stores. They are preferable to nylon scouring pads because they can be used while the *wok* is still hot. Avoid using metal scouring pads. To clean, just run water into the *wok* and with the *wok*-cleaner or nylon pad loosen any food or grease adhering to the sides. Rinse, then replace on the fire and wipe out excess water with a rag if you are going to use *wok* immediately for preparing another dish. Heat for a few seconds to evaporate any remaining moisture before adding oil. Clean and wipe before storing.

Residual oil absorbed into the charred black layer which develops on the inside of the *wok* is what keeps food from sticking and the *wok* from rusting. If the *wok* does rust or if food does stick, scour the rust or foreign matter away, then wipe with a little oil and heat briefly. To season a new *wok*, scour thoroughly then heat ½ cup oil or so over low heat for about ½ hour, tilting the *wok* occasionally. Wipe and store.

SPATULA/LADLE: Cooks in Chinese restaurants use a ladle to stir food. They keep oil, soy sauce, salt and various ingredients in pots in front of them and the ladle functions both as a stirrer and as a measuring and transferring device. At home, a shovel-shaped, wooden-handled utensil may work better. A wooden spatula or flat-bottomed spoon is excellent, because it is less likely to scratch the charred surface of the *wok*.

WIRE SPOON: The Chinese kind is made of twisted wire in various sizes from about 6-inches in diameter (the bowl of the spoon) and up. It is impossible to clean thoroughly, but it doesn't matter because the hot oil kill the "bad guys." A slotted spoon is a satisfactory substitute but is less efficient. An 8-inch wire scoop is a good thing for deep frying and it doubles for retrieving French fries too.

RICE COOKER: Optional equipment. Automatic and makes perfect rice every time. It does not take up a burner and it is easy to clean. You can leave the extra rice in it and reheat it with a little water the next day. Also doubles as a steamer and can be used for reheating things you don't want to fry.

OIL DRAINER: Optional. A colander will double, but if the holes are small, it is hard to clean.

The Chinese drainer is usually iron, shaped like a small, shallow *wok* with numerous holes about ½-inch apart. It should be placed over a medium-sized saucepan or a coffee can somewhere within easy reach of the stove. When you stir-fry vegetables, superior results can be obtained by using an excess of oil, thus making it possible to cook the vegetables very quickly. This is especially important if you are using an American stove—the inadequate heating power makes it advisable to use more oil because the introduction of the food tends to cool the oil faster than the flame can reheat it. After a few moments, the entire contents of the *wok* can be dumped into the oil drainer. This is much easier and faster than picking the food out with chopsticks or a wire spoon. Afterwards, the cooled oil that has collected in the bottom of the saucepan through the drainer can be reused. (For directions on how to reclaim oil, see page 30.)

CHINESE CLEAVER, or *Dao*: Absolutely essential. If you try to do all the chopping with a kitchen knife, it will take so long you'll never want to cook Chinese food again.

Buy a fairly heavy cleaver, wooden-handled if possible—one with a thick blade of carbon steel, not stainless. Stainless steel blades are almost impossible to sharpen once they lose their edge. The best size is one with about a 10-inch blade and about 4-inches high. Cleavers come in three weights: "big" (*da*, 大), "medium" (*chong*, 中) and "small" (*shao*, 小). The medium weight, or *chong*, is best for most purposes, but the big, or heavyweight, cleaver is good for cutting through light bones.

Buy a whetstone and use it occasionally. If you don't have one, try to find a curb made of fine concrete and use that. Hold the blade with both hands at about a 20-degree angle over the whetstone and with a circular motion sharpen the entire length of blade on both sides. Between sharpenings, the edge of the cleaver can be restored by running the blade across the chopping board at about a 45-degree angle, like a strap, using considerable force.

COOKING CHOPSTICKS: Nice looking when they get old and used. Sometimes convenient, but unnecessary.

CHOPPING BLOCK: Chinese cooks use a 6-inch thick round cut from a hardwood tree trunk. While these can be purchased at some Oriental provisions stores, any good cutting board will do. The surface should be wide enough to hold some volume of chopped ingredients, and it should be thick and heavy enough not to skate across the table while using the cleaver.

chopstick, which moves in a pincerlike motion against the lower chopstick, rests between the tips of your forefinger and middle finger. Follow these directions or devise your own method of handling chopsticks.

As to the best beverage to drink with a Szechwan-style meal, I'm convinced that nothing is better than beer and I invariably serve or order beer with a Szechwanese meal. Tea, in my opinion, is something to drink before or after a meal, not with it—but that is a matter of taste. If you want to serve wine, I would suggest a dry red, powerful enough to stand up to the garlic and peppers—which is asking a lot of any wine. Chinese wines from the People's Republic of China and from Taiwan are now becoming more and more available in the United States, though few Americans are truly fond of them. If you do serve Chinese wine or Japanese saké, warm it first by placing it in a heat-proof container or decanter and lowering it into a simmering hot-water bath. If you place the entire commercial bottle in the hot-water bath, crack open the top first. The stronger Chinese beverages such as *mao-tai* and *gao-liang* (color: page 40) are not really wines at all—some varieties of *gao-liang* are as powerful as 180 proof. Most of these beverages should be heated as directed above. Serve in tiny wine cups and treat with respect.

1. Fresh bamboo shoot
2. and 5. Hot bean sauce
3. Sesame paste
4. Sesame oil
6. Chinese cabbage
7. Green onions
8. Winter melon
9. Dried mushrooms
10. Eggplants
11. Canned bamboo shoot
12. Green peppers
13. Transparent vermicelli
14. Fresh ginger
15. Fresh garlic cloves
16. Snow peas
17. Fresh mushrooms
18. Canned water chestnuts
19. Dried red peppers
20. Cashews
21. Fresh noodles
22. *Dou-fu*, or bean curd
23. Sweet bean sauce
24. Szechwan vegetable
25. Star anise
26. Dried orange peel
27. Fermented black beans
28. Wood ear
29. Dried shrimps
30. Szechwan pepper
31. Straw mushrooms
32. Dried scallops

Clockwise: Steamed Bread (p. 106), Dry-fried Beef with Carrots and Celery (p. 61), Crispy-skin Chicken (p. 52), Braised Eel with Bamboo Shoot (p. 84), Hot and Sour Soup (p. 104)

34

35

Jiang-bao Qing-xie
蟹爆青蟹
FRESH CRAB WITH PEKING SAUCE

- ½–¾ lb. fresh hard-shell crab, or crab legs
- 2 tsps. finely chopped fresh ginger
- 1 tsp. finely chopped green onion
- 1 Tbsp. sweet bean sauce mixed with 1 Tbsp. water
- ½ cup fish or chicken stock
- 2 tsps. rice wine or dry sherry
- 1 tsp. salt
- ½ tsp. sugar
- 2 tsps. soy sauce
- 2 tsps. cornstarch mixed with 2 tsps. water
- ½–1 cup oil

TO PREPARE: 1. If desired, parboil the crab in boiling water for a minute or so before dismembering it. Crack open the shell of the crab, clean and remove the entrails. Wash thoroughly in cold water. Detach the claws and legs. Discard the lower part of the legs and crack the shells of the claws and legs but do not remove the meat. Using a cleaver, cut the body of the crab in half from front to back. Then cut each half into several pieces. Do not remove the meat from the shell.
2. Chop the green onion and ginger finely. Mix the sweet bean sauce with the water. Mix the cornstarch with the water. Have the other ingredients on hand.

TO COOK: 1. Heat ½ to 1 cup cooking oil in a *wok* or large frying pan over a medium-high flame. Add the crab pieces and deep fry, stirring, for 15–20 seconds. Remove and drain.
2. Leave only 4–6 Tbsps. of the cooking oil in the *wok*. (For instructions in how to reclaim cooking oil, See page 30.) Heat the oil over a medium flame, then add the green onion and ginger. Stir-fry briefly, then return the deep-fried crab to the *wok*. Stir-fry for a few moments.
3. Add the stock, wine and salt. Stir well for a few seconds, then pull the crab pieces up from the center of the *wok* onto the sides. Add sweet bean sauce-water, sugar and soy sauce to the liquid in the bottom of the *wok*. Stir well, then let the pieces of crab return to the bottom of the *wok*. Stir.
4. Give the cornstarch and water mixture a stir and then add this to the contents of the *wok*. Stir over heat until the sauce thickens and adheres to the crab pieces. Remove to a serving dish and serve hot.

90

VEGETABLES AND DOU-FU

This section has been intentionally limited to dishes which are reasonably well known or require special techniques. Since many of the so-called meat dishes contain vegetables, this category is further restricted to those dishes which principally, if not exclusively, consist of vegetables. Obviously, any fresh vegetable may be stir-fried in a bit of cooking oil and served as a course at a Chinese meal. The following section includes simple recipes of this type, for example Quick-fried Fresh Spinach and Fried Celery.

Dou-fu, or bean curd, is a high-protein food made from soy beans and is very commonly seen as a main dish on Chinese tables. A good meat substitute, *dou-fu* is sold in soft cakes or blocks at Chinese grocery stores and sometimes at health food stores.

Chao Jie-cai
炒芹菜
FRIED CELERY

This is an example of how to cook firm green vegetables. You can apply this basic procedure to fresh asparagus, snow peas (in this case omit the green onion and Szechwan pepper), Swiss chard, green beans, and so on. If you like, add a few drops of sesame oil for flavoring just before serving.

- 1 lb. celery
- 5–8 Szechwan peppercorns
- 2 Tbsps. finely chopped green onion
- SEASONINGS
  - 2 tsps. rice wine or dry sherry
  - 1–2 Tbsps. soy sauce
  - 1 tsp. sugar
  - ½–1 tsp. salt
- 4–6 Tbsps. oil

TO PREPARE: 1. Wash and clean the celery. Remove the base and cut off the leafy top. If desired, remove the strings. Cut the celery into ¾-inch lengths. Chop the green onion finely.
2. Mix the SEASONINGS in a cup or small bowl.

TO COOK: 1. Heat 4–6 Tbsps. cooking oil in a *wok* or large frying pan until very hot. Add the Szechwan peppercorns and fry for 15–20 seconds. Remove and discard the peppercorns, using a spoon, fine wire mesh or spatula. If you decide to leave the peppercorns in the dish, be careful not to eat them—they are for flavoring the cooking oil only.
2. Add the green onion and stir-fry briefly. Add the celery pieces and stir-fry for up to 1 minute. Add the SEASONINGS. Stir-fry briefly, remove to a serving dish and serve hot.

91

SIMPLE FRENCH FOOD

RICHARD OLNEY

Author of The French Menu Cookbook

Foreword by James Beard

RICHARD OLNEY

Simple French Food, 1974

Jonathan Gold has said that "there's more wisdom in a paragraph by Richard Olney than in whole books by other writers about food." And Gold is not alone. Nearly every reviewer praised Olney's outstanding knowledge of true French food and his great skill as a writer when *Simple French Food* first appeared. Critics still rave about this book, especially about how it explains the essence of French cooking and relies on true French proportions to achieve the perfect taste and texture required for each dish. Only one book comes close to matching Olney's masterpiece—Elizabeth David's *French Provincial Cooking*.

NOTABLE RECIPES: Garlic Chicken (page 503) • Eggs in Aspic with Sorrel Mousse • Fennel Marinated Roast Pork • Fresh Fig and Mint Salad • **Hot Onion Omelet with Vinegar** (page 464) • Potato and Leek Soup • **Rabbit Sausages** (page 556) • Sautéed Chicken with Fennel • **Scrambled Eggs** (page 460) • **Shanks with Garlic** (page 537) • Sorrel Tart • Vegetable Soup with Pistou

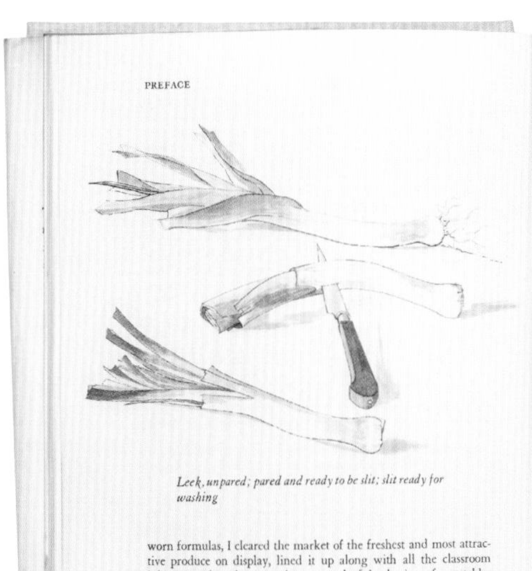

PREFACE

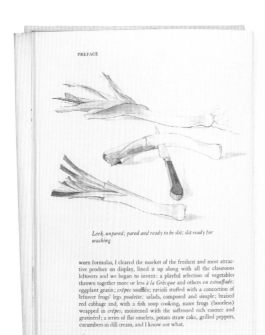

Leek, unpared; pared and ready to be slit; slit ready for washing

worn formulas, I cleared the market of the freshest and most attractive produce on display, lined it up along with all the classroom leftovers and we began to invent: a playful selection of vegetables thrown together more or less *à la Grècque* and others *en estouffade;* eggplant gratin; *crêpes* soufflés; ravioli stuffed with a concoction of leftover frogs' legs *poulette;* salads, composed and simple; braised red cabbage and, with a fish soup cooking, more frogs (boneless) wrapped in *crêpes,* moistened with the saffroned rich essence and gratinéed; a series of flat omelets, potato straw cake, grilled peppers, cucumbers in dill cream, and I know not what.

18

PREFACE

Another day we were faced with leftover braised lamb shoulder and a quantity of generously truffled fresh egg noodles. After taking an inventory of the larder, several pounds of zucchini, a quart of heavy cream, and a block of Parmesan were retained. A heavy round copper utensil some 6 inches high and 2½ feet in diameter was unearthed and in it were thoroughly mixed the noodles (already freely buttered), the slivered meat and its juices, the zucchini, first coarsely grated, salted, squeezed, and tossed in butter, a healthy amount of freshly ground pepper, a memory of nutmeg, the whole smoothed down, smeared thick with cream, and thickly dusted with Parmesan. An hour later the vast expanse of golden crispness was glorious to behold. The zucchini juliènne, imitating the form of the noodles, was meltingly different in texture and its delicate flavor fused happily, holding its own with the penetrating heady truffle, providing a unique taste experience that is stamped the more clearly in my memory thanks to the class's enthusiasm.

HERBS

For my part, the classroom has been instructive in many ways. One forgets so easily and I had long since come to think of herbs as an unquestioned presence in the kitchen. I discovered that, for the students, the summer course was a revelation in "herb cookery." The "recommended improvements" forms filled out at the end of the course nearly all suggested a series of herb lectures, and many of my students returned home to plant herb gardens.

Interesting books on herbs are not lacking, although a number of them are better informed in the ways of religious rites, witchcraft, and medicine than in those of the kitchen. For practical purposes, Tom Stobart's *The International Wine and Food Society's Guide to Herbs, Spices and Flavorings* (London: David and Charles; 1970) seems particularly good. *Of Herbs and Spices,* by Colin Clair (London: Abelard-Schuman; 1961) I have enjoyed for its historical and anecdotal content and another, *Les Soleils de la Cuisine* by Robert

19

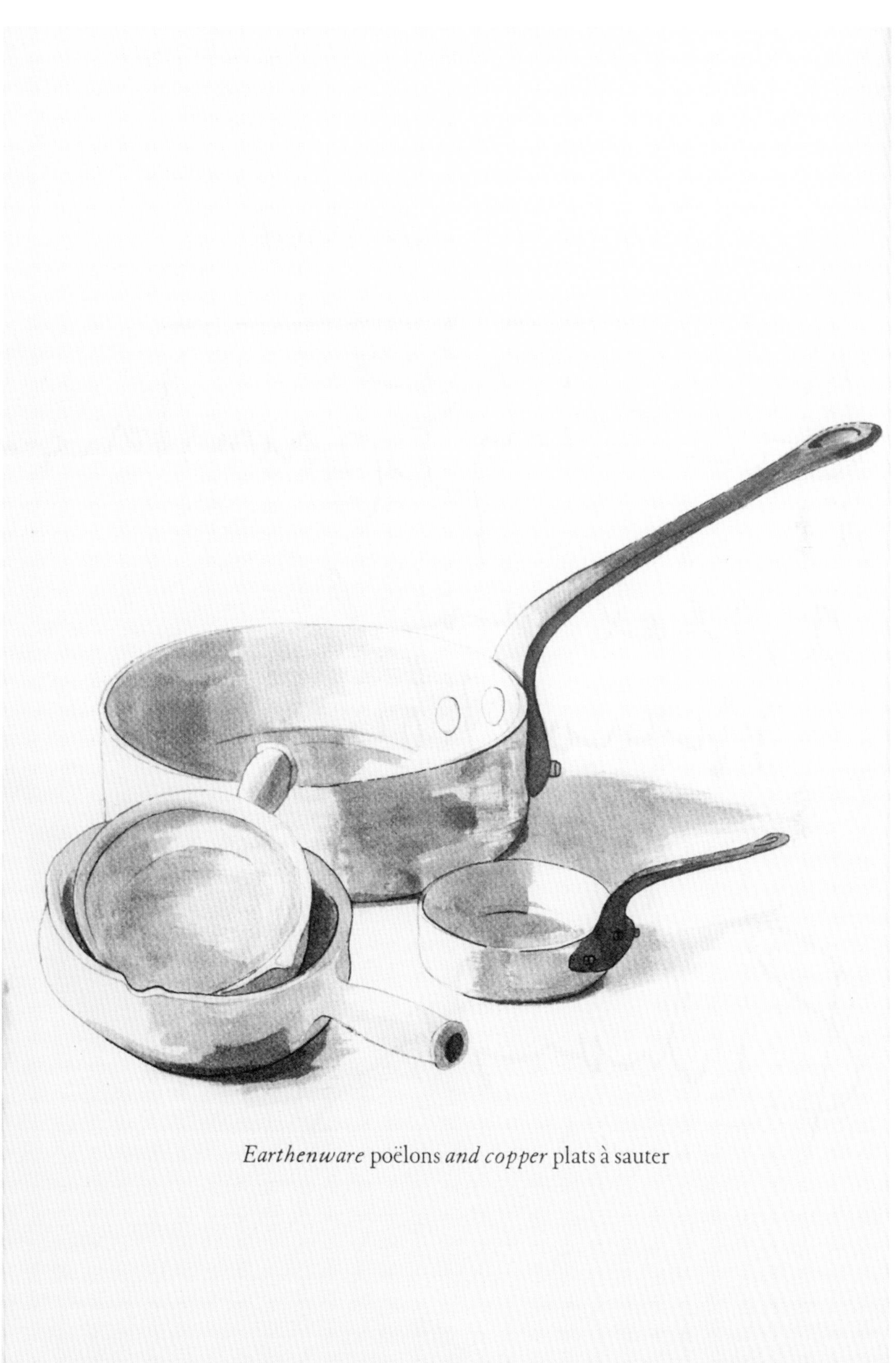

Earthenware poëlons *and copper* plats à sauter

ALICE WATERS *on* RICHARD OLNEY

Almost thirty years ago, when I was becoming a restaurantrice, one of my partners gave me a copy of Richard Olney's first book, The French Menu Cookbook. *We had recently dared to open a restaurant with a simple format: At Chez Panisse we offered our guests no choice, serving instead one meal only, at a fixed price, composed of four or five courses, using only the best ingredients we could find. The menu changed daily, following the seasons and the market; our culinary inspiration was the regional cooking of France. We were amateurs and wildly inexperienced, but we were impassioned by food and wine.*

Reading The French Menu Cookbook *was like receiving unexpected validation. With intense conviction, it articulated precisely what we were struggling to demonstrate: that "one can only eat marvelously by respecting the seasons," that menus must be composed "in terms of what may be called 'gastronomic aesthetic,'" and that "good and honest cooking and good and honest French cooking are the same thing." The gastronomic aesthetic revealed throughout the book was exuberant, sensual, and, at the same time, deeply knowledgeable and rigorously uncompromising. We immediately began cooking recipes from the book, but it yielded more than additions to our repertoire: It reminded us that we had much to learn, and it gave us courage by confirming our implausibly high standards.*

Naturally, I wanted to meet the author, and a few years later, when Simple French Food *was published and Richard traveled to San Francisco to promote his new book, I managed to invite him to Chez Panisse and arranged a surprise reunion with his old friend Kenneth Anger, whom he had not seen for twenty years. This endeared me to Richard and helped get me invited the following summer to his Provençal* mas, *hidden away in the rocky hillside above Toulon.*

Richard Olney is known primarily as a writer of cookbooks. However, he has also written indispensible books about wine, and, what is more, he is a painter, a mentor, a guide, and a gardener. In a word, he is an artist, and one whose artistry is evident in everything he has created, from his wine cellar, hewn with his own hands from rock and stocked with irresistible vintages, to his elegant prose, with its occasional Gallic turns of phrase. His artistry as a host is unforgettable.

My first visit to Solliès-Toucas began in that state of extreme self-consciousness and absorbent, heightened awareness that sometimes accompanies a first visit to the house of someone who is very important to you. I remember every detail: the climb up the steep hill to his little house set amid terraces of ancient olive trees; the clicking of the cicadas, the rustle of the leaves in the wind, the aroma of the wild herbs all around us, mixed with the smell of Richard's Gauloise.

Richard received us wearing nothing but an open shirt, his skimpy bathing suit, a kitchen towel at his waist, and a pair of worn espadrilles. He invited us into his house, which consists basically of one room in which he works, eats, and entertains when weather prohibits dining on his idyllic terrace. I can close my eyes and see the boulders with which Richard and his brothers had built the fireplace at the head of the house, the copper pots hanging above, the marble mortars on the mantelpiece, the column by the table papered with wine labels, the lovely platters and tureens displayed on hard-to-reach shelves, the windows out to the garden where the table under the grape arbor had been laid with beautiful linens. He served us a spectacular salad, full of Provençal greens that were new to me—rocket, anise, hyssop—with perfectly tender green beans and bright nasturtium flowers tossed in, and dressed with vinegar he makes himself from the ends of bottles of great wine. (That salad was a revelation, and inspired countless salades composées *in the years to come.) My first visit ended, many hours later, in the same way all my subsequent visits have ended: in a kind of ecstatic paralysis brought on by extraordinary food, astonishing wines, and dancing until dawn to seventy-eights of Edith Piaf and* bal musette *music.*

In conversation, Richard can be blunt in his judgments—and he's always right. In print, on the other hand, although he is still always right, his judgments are expressed with discretion and finesse. He has never pursued celebrity; he has neither the patience nor the appetite for it. He has lived to please himself, and in so doing, he has created an irreplaceable body of work. His generosity to like-minded gastronomes is legendary. Through Richard I have made the acquaintance of some of the soulful and spirited people in his circle, including the remarkable Peyraud family of the Domaine Tempier at Bandol,

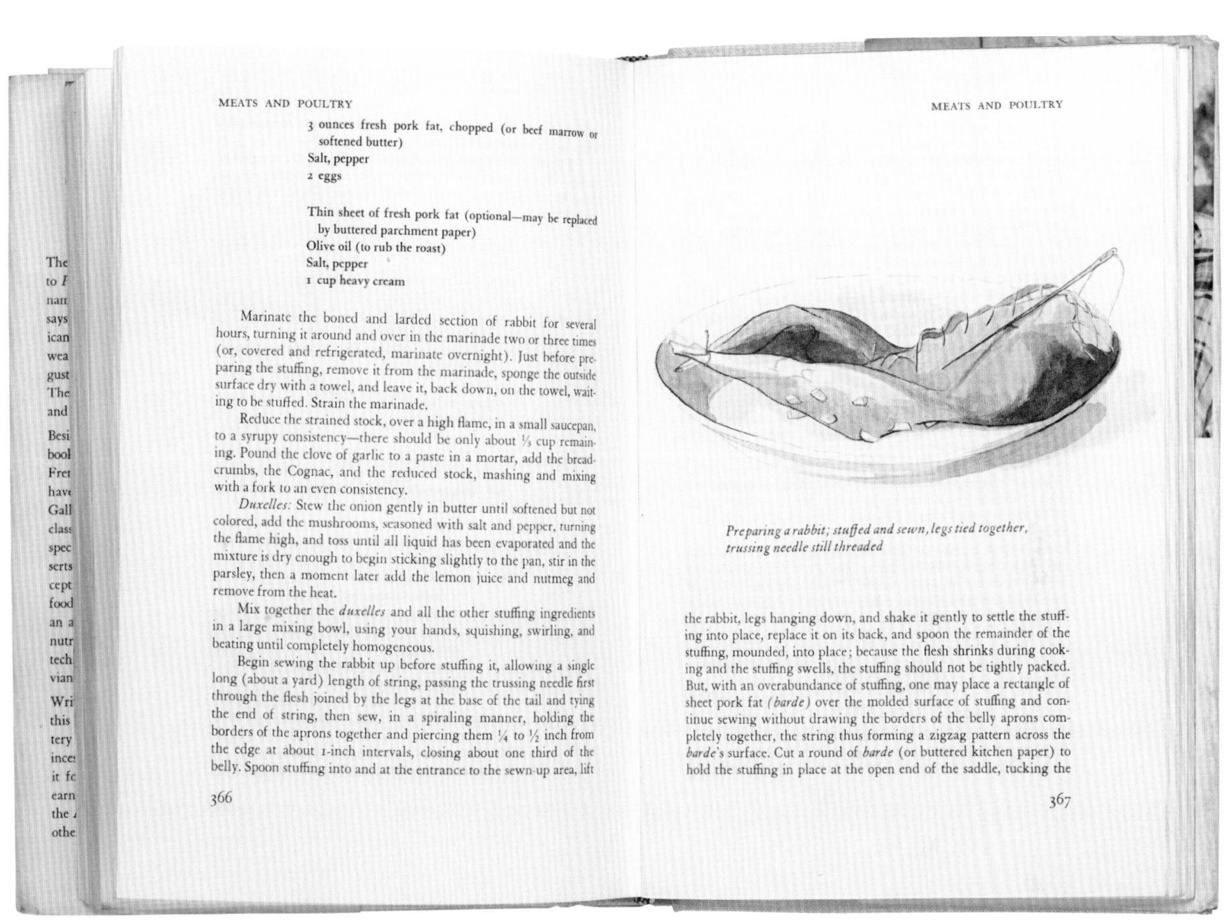

MEATS AND POULTRY

3 ounces fresh pork fat, chopped (or beef marrow or softened butter)
Salt, pepper
2 eggs

Thin sheet of fresh pork fat (optional—may be replaced by buttered parchment paper)
Olive oil (to rub the roast)
Salt, pepper
1 cup heavy cream

Marinate the boned and larded section of rabbit for several hours, turning it around and over in the marinade two or three times (or, covered and refrigerated, marinate overnight). Just before preparing the stuffing, remove it from the marinade, sponge the outside surface dry with a towel, and leave it, back down, on the towel, waiting to be stuffed. Strain the marinade.

Reduce the strained stock, over a high flame, in a small saucepan, to a syrupy consistency—there should be only about ⅓ cup remaining. Pound the clove of garlic to a paste in a mortar, add the breadcrumbs, the Cognac, and the reduced stock, mashing and mixing with a fork to an even consistency.

Duxelles: Stew the onion gently in butter until softened but not colored, add the mushrooms, seasoned with salt and pepper, turning the flame high, and toss until all liquid has been evaporated and the mixture is dry enough to begin sticking slightly to the pan, stir in the parsley, then a moment later add the lemon juice and nutmeg and remove from the heat.

Mix together the *duxelles* and all the other stuffing ingredients in a large mixing bowl, using your hands, squishing, swirling, and beating until completely homogeneous.

Begin sewing the rabbit up before stuffing it, allowing a single long (about a yard) length of string, passing the trussing needle first through the flesh joined by the legs at the base of the tail and tying the end of string, then sew, in a spiraling manner, holding the borders of the aprons together and piercing them ¼ to ½ inch from the edge at about 1-inch intervals, closing about one third of the belly. Spoon stuffing into and at the entrance to the sewn-up area, lift

366

MEATS AND POULTRY

Preparing a rabbit; stuffed and sewn, legs tied together, trussing needle still threaded

the rabbit, legs hanging down, and shake it gently to settle the stuffing into place, replace it on its back, and spoon the remainder of the stuffing, mounded, into place; because the flesh shrinks during cooking and the stuffing swells, the stuffing should not be tightly packed. But, with an overabundance of stuffing, one may place a rectangle of sheet pork fat *(barde)* over the molded surface of stuffing and continue sewing without drawing the borders of the belly aprons completely together, the string thus forming a zigzag pattern across the *barde*'s surface. Cut a round of *barde* (or buttered kitchen paper) to hold the stuffing in place at the open end of the saddle, tucking the

367

who have become my surrogate family in France. Twenty-five years ago, scarcely anyone in America knew what an Hermitage or a Bandol or a Côte-Rôtie was, but, because he took an interest in the education of my friend Kermit Lynch, an audacious young wine importer, and introduced him to many of France's most steadfastly traditional winemakers, today there is a thriving market in this country for their wines. During the same quarter century, the demand for fresh, local produce that has led to the rebirth of farmers' markets has surely been stimulated by Richard's fervor for the seasonal and the authentic.

My proudest moment as a seasoned restauratrice took place one afternoon at Chez Panisse some years ago, when Richard rose to speak to a group of French winemakers he was accompanying on a tour of California wineries. We had just cleared away the remnants of the last course of a special lunch over which we had taken great pains. Richard's appreciation of the wines, as always, was eloquent and succinct, but when he spoke of the food, he praised Chez Panisse with particular warmth. Readers will have some sense of what it must be like to receive a tribute from someone whose discrimination is so artful and whose enthusiasms are so passionate; and, above all, they will learn something of what it means to lead a life so honest, so pure in taste, and so fine in judgment.

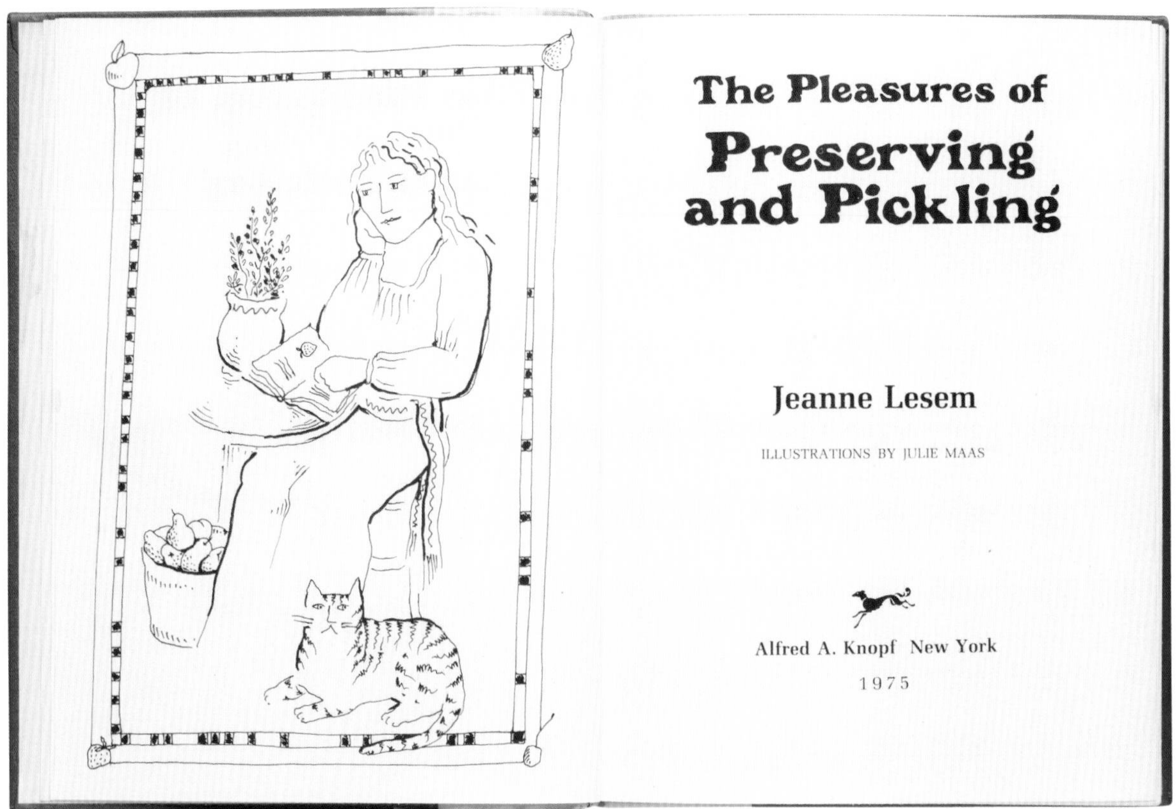

JEANNE LESEM

The Pleasures of Preserving and Pickling, 1975

Canned and preserved foods have been staples in American farmhouses since the nineteenth century. The bountiful harvests of beans, corn, tomatoes, cucumbers, onions, strawberries, blueberries, quinces—you name it, we'll can it—were lovingly cleaned, cooked, put into sterilized glass jars, and boiled again in water baths during the hottest days of August and September each year. The benefit was a quince pie in January. Cherry pies for Thanksgiving. Strawberry jams for breakfast on Christmas morning.

Many authors have written books about "puttin' up," as canning is called in the South, but Jeanne Lesem made it a lifelong study. Her library contained six shelves of books on food preservation. Her own books on the topic are the best researched and usable for the home canner who is no longer putting up forty quarts of beans a day but wants to make six pints of strawberry and rhubarb jam to give to friends. Jeanne Lesem's extensive library of books on food is part of the Food Studies Collection at the Fales Library.

NOTABLE RECIPES: Bermuda Marmalade, Amber Marmalade • Carrot Marmalade • Citrus Marmalades (Pink Grapefruit, Orange) • Cornichons • Honeyed Marmalade • **Mustard Pickles** (page 439) • **Mystery Marmalade** (page 437) • Rose Geranium Jelly • Peppery Pear Relish • **Spiced Cherries** (page 435)

tials; the second, of optional articles that can make your work faster and/or easier.

ESSENTIAL

Sterilizer (an 8-quart Dutch oven with tight-fitting cover is adequate)
Saucepans

Mixing bowls
A large slotted metal spoon
A large metal spoon with solid bowl
Eyedropper
Wooden spoons reserved only for preserving or pickling (those you use for general cooking sometimes retain odors and flavors)
Jar lifter or tongs (see source list, page 201)
Colander or large, fine-meshed strainer
Graduated measuring spoons, preferably a 6-unit set that includes measures for 1/8 teaspoon and 1/2 tablespoon
Graduated measuring cups
Food grinder, manual or electric
Heatproof glass measuring cups, preferably a 1-cup and a 1-quart size
Chopping board
Small, sharp, stainless steel paring knife
Stainless steel kitchen knife with 6- or 7-inch blade for chopping
Carving knife with serrated blade
Swivel-blade vegetable peeler
Reamer or electric juicer
Food mill or electric blender

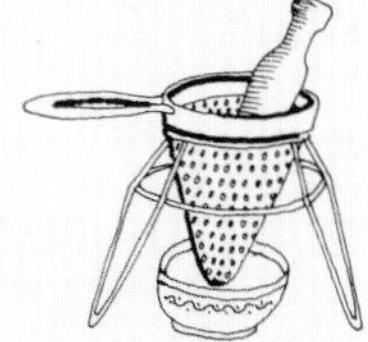

Jelly bag or clean cheesecloth
Jar funnel
Grater with assorted size holes
Jars, glasses, paraffin, and labels
Scales—kitchen, diet, postal or bathroom (listed in order of preference)

Country Chutney

This relish is based on a prize-winning English recipe of more than a generation ago. It is less sweet than traditional chutneys; most of its sweetness comes not from sugar, but from apples, dates, and parsnips. I generally use Winesap apples but any well-flavored, crisp eating apple will do.

- 1 1/4 pounds parsnips
- 1 pound (3 medium) apples, peeled, cored, and sliced
- 1/2 pound (2 medium) onions, peeled and chopped (about 1 cup)
- 1/2 pound (2 medium) ripe tomatoes, peeled and finely chopped (about 1 cup)
- 1/2 teaspoon dried cracked ginger or 1 piece (1-inch) dried whole ginger
- 1 teaspoon mustard seed
- 2 1/4 cups cider vinegar
- 1 cup, packed, dark brown sugar
- 1 cup (4 ounces) lightly packed, dried currants
- 1/2 cup (4 ounces) packed, finely cut pitted dates
- 1/4 cup (about 2 ounces) packed, finely diced crystallized ginger
- 1 teaspoon table salt
- 1 large pinch cayenne

Cook the unpeeled parsnips 30 to 40 minutes in boiling water, to cover, in a saucepan or skillet wide enough to permit them to lie flat. They should be soft enough to mash. When the parsnips can be pierced easily with a fork, drain and cover with cold water until cool enough to handle. Peel and mash.

Simmer the apple slices with 1/2 cup water in a covered 1 1/2-quart saucepan 12 to 15 minutes, or until soft enough to mash. Do not drain.

Place the mashed parsnips and apples in a wide 4-quart saucepan. Add onions and tomatoes; tie ginger and mustard seed loosely in a double thickness of dampened cheesecloth or place in a metal tea ball and add to the pan, along with vinegar. Bring to boil over medium heat and simmer slowly 1 hour, stirring occasionally.

Add remaining ingredients and simmer 1 hour more, or until thick. Stir occasionally to prevent sticking. The chutney will darken considerably.

Remove from heat and spoon at once into hot, sterilized half-pint or pint jars and seal. Store at least 1 month before opening. Makes about 7 cups.

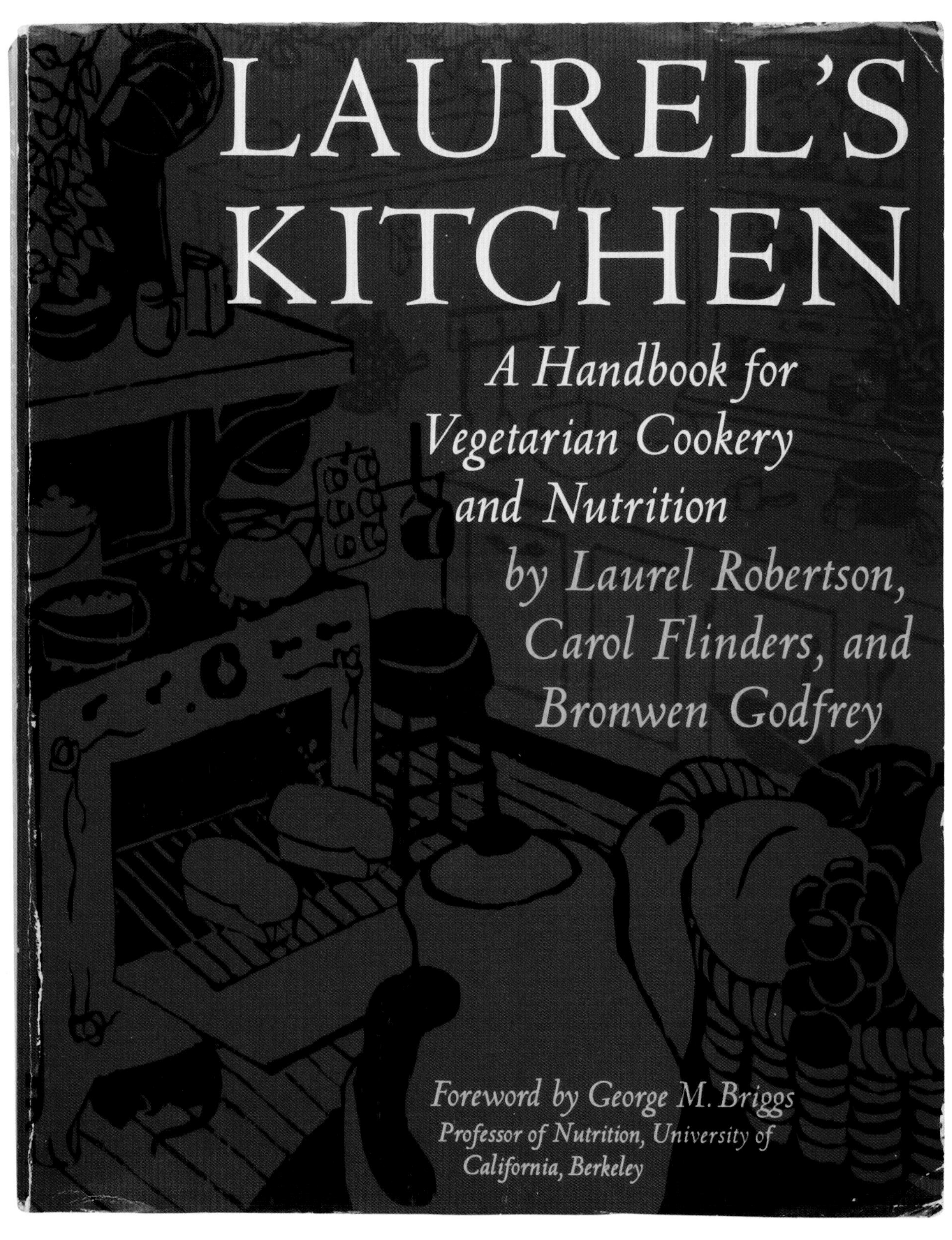
LAUREL'S
KITCHEN
A Handbook for
Vegetarian Cookery
and Nutrition
by Laurel Robertson,
Carol Flinders, and
Bronwen Godfrey
Foreword by George M. Briggs
Professor of Nutrition, University of
California, Berkeley

Dinner

If breakfast is the most important meal to the body, dinner may be to the spirit: not the food so much as the simple, precious fact of coming together with those you love. The world we live in now is so rushed and hectic that by the end of a day, people very often find themselves feeling depleted, confused, and fragmented. This is the time of day when the warmth and conviviality of a family meal can make all the difference in the world.

Be fierce as a mother lion to protect the sanctity of this hour. Fight football coaches, drama teachers, and scout leaders if you must, but keep the dinner hour intact. Actually, the most insidious opposition may well come from right within the home. By absorbing our attention so that we don't really see or hear one another, by filling our minds with the most ignoble trivia, and by giving our daily life a backdrop of continual violence, television exerts a ceaseless, disintegrating influence upon individual consciousness and family unity.

Strong language, and startling, maybe, in the middle of a cookbook. But people's lives are all of a piece—good health involves much more than B vitamins. Put your television set on dry ice for a month, by whatever ruse will work. Withdrawal symptoms are inevitable, and people will be at a loss for a while. Make a conscious effort, though, to foster activities that develop your minds and hands and draw you closer to one another. See whether at the end of the month you wouldn't like to pack the nuisance off for good.

Dinner should be a leisurely affair—slow, gracious, and calm. There are sound physiological reasons for eating slowly. One is obvious: eating in haste interferes with thorough digestion and assimilation of food. The other is more subtle, and of special interest to those of us who have to watch our weight. Many nutritionists believe that our appetite mechanism is regulated by the level of glucose in our bloodstream. As we eat a meal, the blood sugar level rises slowly, and when we've eaten what our body needs, the signal goes to the brain to stop

144 DINNER

eating. If we eat very rapidly, we may outstrip the mechanism and overeat before the body can give a warning.

Tired nerves need time to relax, and laughter helps, so encourage family members to cull little stories from their day to share with one another. There's definitely an art to this, so don't be disappointed if the conversation falters a little at first. It seems so obvious, yet we have to remind ourselves continually how important it is to give our full attention to one another. The full, healthy development of children depends on their parents' capacity and willingness to do this. An eight-year-old's anecdote may be pretty roundabout, but an attentive listener, asking the right questions, will gradually make a fluent conversationalist out of him or her.

If the deeper purpose of the evening meal is to draw a family together, it stands to reason that they will want to eat the same food. However well-intentioned the effort might be, when we cater too solicitously to individual likes and dislikes we end up emphasizing the differences between family members at just the moment when we want to bring out their fellow feeling. We realize that this is not a popular line of reasoning. The restaurant business is bigger than ever now, and as if ordering from a restaurant menu didn't give full enough scope to personal preferences, we now have international restaurants in every town, where Junior can have a pizza while his mother eats crepes. A small thing, perhaps, but eating the same food is a quiet but effective force for family unity.

DINNER 145

LAUREL ROBERTSON, CAROL FLINDERS, AND BRONWEN GODFREY

Laurel's Kitchen

A Handbook for Vegetarian Cookery and Nutrition, 1976

The history of American vegetarianism is much longer and more complex than many people suspect, for there are many nineteenth-century texts that advocate an all-vegetable diet for ethical and/or nutritional reasons. Contrary to popular opinion, not all vegetarians historically were influenced by Eastern philosophical and religious thought, either. The trendiness of vegetarians during the last quarter of the twentieth century is partially a response to the horrors of industrial meat production, but also the result of a more and more sophisticated understanding of how to eat good, delicious, nutritional vegetarian diets.

Laurel's Kitchen was one of the earliest and most popular introductions to good vegetarian cooking. It is more than just a cookbook, however. Its impact on American food is summed up best by scholar Megan Elias, who said, "*Laurel's Kitchen* was as much a lifestyle guide as it was a cookbook." Laurel Robertson and her coauthors were pioneers in understanding how food gets from farm to table and in criticizing that process. They also helped create our current desire to eat sustainable, healthy, and ethically sound foods.

NOTABLE RECIPES: Carrot Fruitcake • **Cauliflower Eggplant Curry** (page 415) • **Chinese Vegetables and Tofu** (page 410) • **Falafel** (page 427) • **Greek Lentil Soup** (page 344) • Green Bean Stroganoff • Many-a-Bean Stew • Oatmeal Pancakes • Potato Cheese Soup • **Tennessee Corn Pone** (page 593) • **Tomato Ginger Sauce** (page 527) • Winter Squash Soup

Artichokes

Artichokes are California's own. The highway south from Berkeley to Big Sur takes you through Castroville, with its funky banner telling you that you've finally made it to the Artichoke Capital of the World. Well might they brag—they're on to a good thing.

It can take anywhere from a half hour to an hour to steam artichokes, depending on size and age. For a gourmet touch, slip a few drops of olive oil down into the leaves and hide a few slivers of garlic clove here and there before cooking. If you have a few minutes, trim the thorns with a sharp knife: the artichoke is much prettier without them, though of course they soften quite adequately with cooking. Serve artichokes hot or cold.

People seem to have rather strong opinions about how best to enjoy artichokes. Some like to have mayonnaise to dip the leaves in; others prefer drawn butter. Still others insist you miss the real joys of artichokes if you drench them in fat. In any case, don't forget to provide a bowl for the gnawed-up byproducts—though it's fascinating to see how differently people cope with them if you don't.

Asparagus

Asparagus ranks right alongside the hyacinth as a sure, spriggy herald of spring. Its season is so brief we never have time to tire of its delicate appeal.

Break the stalks off just above the white part, at the place where they choose to snap. If they're too long to lie across your steamer basket, stand them upright in a coffee pot, with just ½ inch of water in the bottom. Steam for no more than

20 minutes, if that. They should still be bright green, and flexible but not limp. Serve with Lemon Butter, or just lemon, or sprinkle lightly with Parmesan cheese. If you'd like the piquancy of hollandaise sauce without all its calories, try our Buttermilk Sauce or Sunshine Sauce.

For ASPARAGUS CHINOISE, slice asparagus diagonally into 2-inch lengths and sauté in a little oil; add sliced water chestnuts at the very last minute, and a few drops of soy sauce.

Give a new twist to Ratatouille (p. 216) by stirring in a cup of asparagus pieces for the last 10 minutes of cooking time—and before the season is past, make Asparagus Soup at least once.

Slivered and toasted almonds are an especially tasty garnish for cooked asparagus spears. They've found their way into the following recipe, too, in small but effective measure.

Asparagus Patties

1 pound asparagus
2 or 3 green onions, chopped
2 tablespoons oil
2 tablespoons chopped parsley or coriander leaves
1 teaspoon basil
¼ cup toasted almond meal
½ cup bread crumbs
½ teaspoon salt
¼ cup cooked bulgur wheat or rice
2 eggs, separated

Slice asparagus lengthwise and cut small. Steam just until tender.

Sauté onions in oil until soft. Add parsley; stir to wilt.

Combine almond meal, bread crumbs, salt, and cooked grain. Stir in beaten egg yolks. Add the steamed asparagus, making sure it has cooled somewhat so that it doesn't cook the eggs. Stir in the onions and herbs. Beat egg whites until stiff and fold into asparagus mixture.

Heat a lightly greased Teflon skillet or well-seasoned iron one. Drop batter by spoonfuls and spread to form patties. Brown on each side over medium heat.

Makes about 8 patties.

ZUCCHINI PATTIES

Substitute 2 cups coarsely grated zucchini for asparagus, and sunflower seed meal for almond meal. Increase bread crumbs to 1 cup.

Spanakopita

2 or 3 bunches spinach
3 cups low-fat cottage cheese
3 eggs
1 teaspoon salt

2½ cups whole wheat flour
¼ cup oil
2 teaspoons salt
1 cup warm water
½ cup melted margarine or Better-Butter

Over the years, our friend Sultana's pita has gradually outstripped all contenders for the title of Most Requested Dish. There is a knack to making it, we admit, but it's a knack you'll be glad to have developed. You will need a pizza pan and a 4-foot piece of ¾- or 1-inch doweling to roll out the dough. If you have neither a pita pan nor a pizza pan, don't be daunted. Use pie plates or tins, and since you'll be working on a smaller scale, a rolling pin will do. One recipe will make two 9- or 10-inch "pies."

Wash and dry the spinach and chop it fine. Sprinkle with salt and squeeze or wring to wilt it. Add the cottage cheese and eggs. Mix very well and set aside.

Sift the flour and save the bran for tomorrow morning's porridge. Mix flour, salt, oil, and water, and knead briefly until you have a soft dough.

Divide dough into two balls, one larger than the other. Pat the larger ball flat and roll it into an 8-inch circle, using a rolling pin. Now, beginning with the edge closest to you, roll the dough over the dowel as shown. Use the sifted flour only as needed to keep dough from sticking.

Start with your hands in the center and move them forward and backward, working outward, towards the ends of the dowel. When your hands reach the edge of the dough, unroll it gently so that it is flat again. Turn the crust (larger now, but lopsided) a ⅛ turn, and repeat this rolling operation until the dough is very round, paper-thin, even, and 3 inches bigger all around than your pan. The tricky part is to do all this without making holes in the dough.

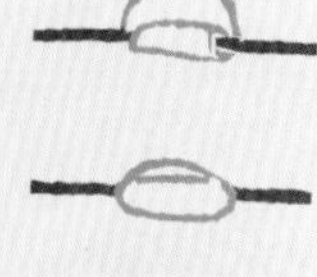

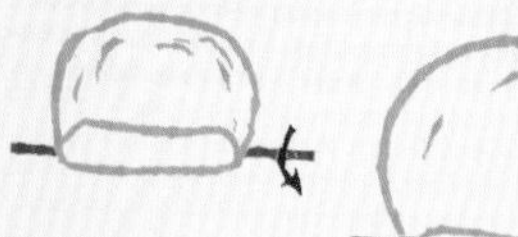

Grease a pizza pan. Preheat oven to 400°.

Place the dowel with the dough wrapped around it on one edge of the pan, and unroll the dough over the pan. Gently fold the excess edge of the crust in, towards the center, so that it won't break while you're preparing the second crust.

Now roll the smaller ball similarly, until it is slightly smaller than the other. Set it aside carefully.

Unfold the edges of the dough in the pan and spread with a tablespoonful or two of the melted margarine. Put in the filling and drizzle again with a little margarine. Place the second piece of dough over the top, leaving it loose with plenty of wrinkles. Pour half the remaining margarine over the edges and fold the under-crust edge around the upper-crust edge as shown.

Drizzle the last of the margarine over the top, particularly around the edges. Be sure to poke holes all over the top crust with a fork or a sharp paring knife.

Bake the pita on the bottom rack of the oven for 45 minutes, until just brown. Cover it with a towel and let it stand for 10 minutes before serving. Cut in wedges.

Serves 6 to 8.

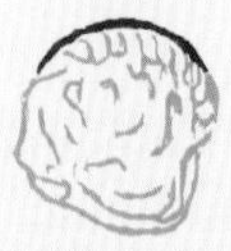

CHARD PITA

6 green onions, chopped
3 tablespoons melted margarine
4 quarts chopped chard leaves
3 cups low-fat cottage cheese
3 eggs
1 teaspoon salt
pinch pepper
3 tablespoons grated Parmesan or other sharp cheese

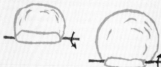

We're very fond of chard, which grows abundantly in our gardens. With a few changes, the spanakopita recipe adapts very nicely. The crust is the same; here is the filling.

Sauté green onions in a large pan until soft. Add the chopped chard and cook until wilted. Drain off the liquid (save it for soup). Combine all ingredients and mix well. Prepare crust and then fill and bake just as you would spanakopita.

Four Food Groups for a Meatless Diet: A Daily Guide

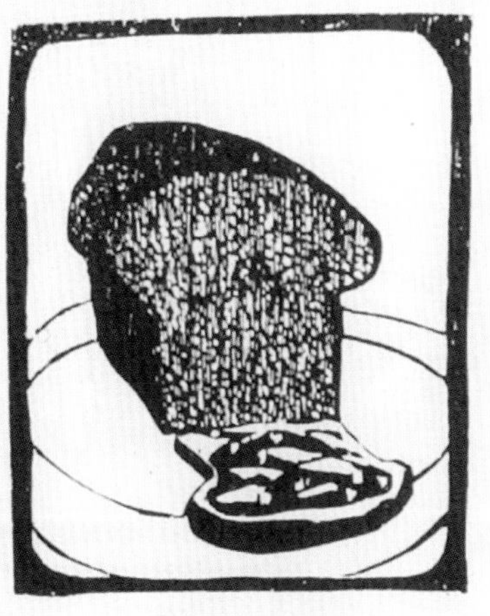

Grains, Legumes, Nuts, & Seeds

Six servings or more. Include several slices of yeast-raised, whole-grain bread, a serving of beans, and a few nuts or seeds.

Vegetables

Three servings or more. Include one or more servings of dark leafy greens, like romaine, spinach, or chard.

Fruit

One to four pieces. Include a raw source of vitamin C, like citrus fruits, strawberries, or cantaloupe.

Milk & Eggs

Two or more glasses of fresh milk for adults, three or more for children. (Children under nine use smaller glasses.) Other dairy products or an egg may be used to meet part of the milk requirement. Eggs are optional—up to four per week.

The Taste of Country Cooking

She evokes the tantalizing aromas of a farm kitchen. She brings back the fresh, natural tastes of the wonderful cooking she was raised on in Virginia. She shares old family recipes in menus that make the most of each season's bounty...

★ By Edna Lewis ★

EDNA LEWIS

The Taste of Country Cooking, 1976

Edna Lewis was born in Orange County, Virginia, in 1916, the daughter of emancipated slaves. After her father's death, she moved to Washington, D.C., and, eventually to New York City, where she first worked as a seamstress. In 1949, a friend of hers, Johnny Nicholson, an antiques dealer by trade, decided to open a restaurant called Café Nicholson on the east side of Manhattan. Lewis became the cook. Before long the restaurant attracted such café society figures as Marlon Brando, Richard Avedon, Gore Vidal, Marlene Dietrich, Gloria Vanderbilt, and Tennessee Williams. Café Nicholson was an important breakthrough on the American dining scene. Nicholson had a flair for interior design and let it shine in the restaurant, which is often cited as the first completely designed American restaurant. Lewis worked with Nicholson until the late 1950s before moving on. Her luscious renditions of Southern cooking captivated the imagination of the foodies of the day. *The Edna Lewis Cookbook*, based on the dishes of the restaurant, appeared in 1972. Then, Judith Jones, who had edited Julia Child's *Mastering the Art of French Cooking*, convinced Lewis to write a cookbook focused on her memories of growing up in Virginia. *The Taste of Country Cooking* came out in 1976. Lewis's name became synonymous with the very best of Southern cooking. Her legacy is carried on today by the world-famous chef Scott Peacock.

NOTABLE RECIPES: Blueberry Cake with Blueberry Sauce (page 618) • **Caramel Layer Cake** (page 611) • Chicken with Dumplings • **Coconut Layer Cake** (page 610) • **Ham Biscuits** (page 591) • **Oven Brisket or Rolled Chuck** (page 544) • **Parker House Rolls** (page 564) • Pork-Flavored Green Beans • Purple Plum Tart • **Spoon Bread** (page 593) • Sweet Potato Casserole • Sweet Potato Pie • Summer Vegetable Soup • Watermelon Rind Pickles • **Wilted Lettuce with Hot Vinegar Dressing** (page 361)

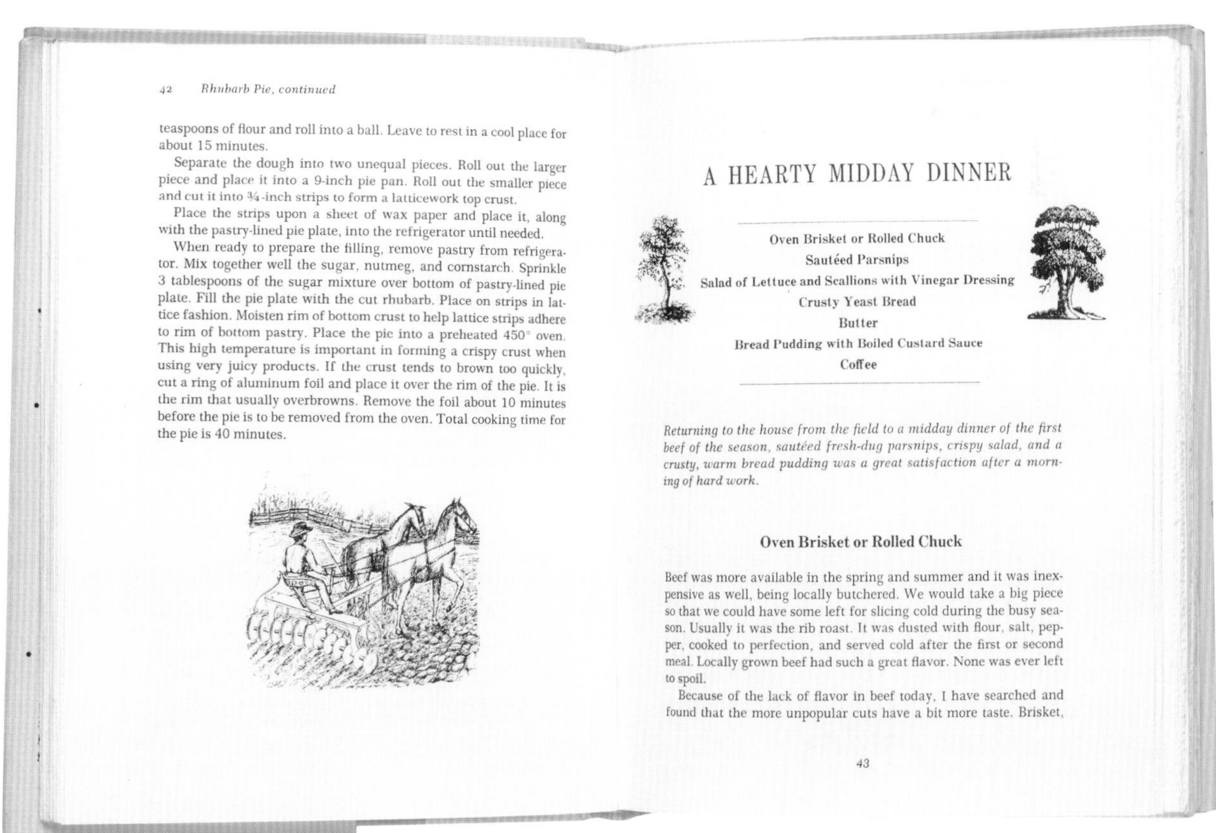

42 *Rhubarb Pie, continued*

teaspoons of flour and roll into a ball. Leave to rest in a cool place for about 15 minutes.

Separate the dough into two unequal pieces. Roll out the larger piece and place it into a 9-inch pie pan. Roll out the smaller piece and cut it into ¾-inch strips to form a latticework top crust.

Place the strips upon a sheet of wax paper and place it, along with the pastry-lined pie plate, into the refrigerator until needed.

When ready to prepare the filling, remove pastry from refrigerator. Mix together well the sugar, nutmeg, and cornstarch. Sprinkle 3 tablespoons of the sugar mixture over bottom of pastry-lined pie plate. Fill the pie plate with the cut rhubarb. Place on strips in lattice fashion. Moisten rim of bottom crust to help lattice strips adhere to rim of bottom pastry. Place the pie into a preheated 450° oven. This high temperature is important in forming a crispy crust when using very juicy products. If the crust tends to brown too quickly, cut a ring of aluminum foil and place it over the rim of the pie. It is the rim that usually overbrowns. Remove the foil about 10 minutes before the pie is to be removed from the oven. Total cooking time for the pie is 40 minutes.

A HEARTY MIDDAY DINNER

Oven Brisket or Rolled Chuck
Sautéed Parsnips
Salad of Lettuce and Scallions with Vinegar Dressing
Crusty Yeast Bread
Butter
Bread Pudding with Boiled Custard Sauce
Coffee

Returning to the house from the field to a midday dinner of the first beef of the season, sautéed fresh-dug parsnips, crispy salad, and a crusty, warm bread pudding was a great satisfaction after a morning of hard work.

Oven Brisket or Rolled Chuck

Beef was more available in the spring and summer and it was inexpensive as well, being locally butchered. We would take a big piece so that we could have some left for slicing cold during the busy season. Usually it was the rib roast. It was dusted with flour, salt, pepper, cooked to perfection, and served cold after the first or second meal. Locally grown beef had such a great flavor. None was ever left to spoil.

Because of the lack of flavor in beef today, I have searched and found that the more unpopular cuts have a bit more taste. Brisket,

43

SCOTT PEACOCK *on* EDNA LEWIS

The Taste of Country Cooking *was first released in 1976. Among serious gastronomes, it was a revelation. It was unlike any Southern cookbook that had been published prior. Indeed, it was unlike any other cookbook. Period. James Beard proclaimed it "a delicately drawn picture of an interesting period when American cooking was a series of family events." M.F.K. Fisher went further: "It is in the best sense American, with an innate dignity, and freedom from prejudice and hatred, and it is reassuring to be told again that although we may have lost some of all this simplicity, it still exists here . . . and may be attainable again."*

In the nearly forty years since, Edna Lewis's story continues to resonate in food circles everywhere. She was the Virginia-born granddaughter of freed slaves who, in the 1940s, rose to fame as the chef and partner of Café Nicholson on Manhattan's Upper East Side. The restaurant quickly became a favorite haunt of the café society of the day. Eleanor Roosevelt, Salvador Dalí, Lillian Hellman, and Marlon Brando swooned over her roast chicken and chocolate soufflé that New York food writer Clementine Paddleford described as "light as a dandelion seed in a high wind." William Faulkner once flattered her by asking her if she had studied cooking in Paris.

In the late 1960s Miss Lewis slipped on an icy New York sidewalk and broke her leg badly. To combat boredom in the hospital, she began writing down recipes. Later, with the help of a former student, Evangeline Peterson, she turned them into a cookbook. With recipes ranging from cold poached lobster to chicken Kiev, The Edna Lewis Cookbook *was heavy on classic European technique, but revealed little of the author's rich personal history and voice.*

As that book was going to print, Miss Lewis was introduced to Judith Jones, the longtime editor of Julia Child and novelist John Updike, among many other luminaries. As the two became acquainted, Miss Lewis's poignant childhood recollections of rural life in Virginia began to unfold. Jones was enthralled by her vivid accounts of bygone annual events unknown to much of the rest of the world, like wheat-threshing, ice-cutting, and Emancipation Day. She had a poetic way of distilling the daily rituals and the rhythm of the seasons onto a plate, making even hog-butchering sound beautiful. For several years, Miss Lewis, who was then working as a teaching assistant in the African Hall of the Museum of Natural History, would meet with Jones in her Manhattan office to talk through these memories, and then go home and write them down long-hand on yellow legal pads. These recipes and recollections would become The Taste of Country Cooking.

At the time of its release, I was in junior high school and had never heard of Edna Lewis. In Hartford, the small town in southeast Alabama where I grew up, I ate a traditional Southern diet, while aspiring to cook like Julia Child did on television. By the time cooking became a career for me, my eyes were set on Italy, France, and the American food revolution Alice Waters was leading in California. Though I enjoyed the food prepared by my mother and grandmothers, I took it for granted and saw nothing special about it at all. My overriding notion of Southern food at the time was of overcooked, often canned, vegetables slathered in bacon grease, deep-fried everything, and overly sweet tea and desserts.

In 1988, while working as chef at the Georgia Governor's Mansion in Atlanta, I read about a Southern food festival in which Edna Lewis would be participating. Some time earlier, I had seen an article about her in a cooking magazine, and purchased her most recent cookbook, In Pursuit of Flavor. *Drawn to both her striking appearance and her refined and sophisticated recipes in that volume—inspired as much by the greenmarkets of New York as her Southern childhood—I was riveted by the idea of meeting her. I finagled an invite to a fancy cocktail party where she was being honored. Standing in the center of the courtyard garden, wearing one of her trademark African-print dresses, she appeared regal and ten feet tall.*

Upon introduction, Miss Lewis asked me where I had gone to cooking school. Embarrassed, I confessed to her I'd never been. At that she lit up, and said, "Oh good! Let's go have a drink." As we ate fried soft-shell crawfish and sipped mint juleps, she asked me about where I was from, and the foods I was raised on. I told her that I had cut okra, shelled field peas, and watched my mother and grandmothers bake elaborate layer cakes in rural Alabama.

She spoke intensely about the importance of food organically grown from open-pollinated seed, and how her brother, a farmer in Virginia, had told her that corn grown today yields three times as much as it did when they were children. "But he also told me that he noticed the cows eat twice as much of it, because they're not satisfied," she said. This was something I had never heard anyone speak about before.

The following year, Miss Lewis returned to Atlanta to cook again, and this time I was asked to assist her in the kitchen. I was practically jumping up and down with excitement. For three days we scoured farmers' markets for the ripest blackberries, rhubarb, and peaches we could find, and baked them into dozens of extraordinarily fine lattice-topped cobblers and pies.

Though taken with Miss Lewis as a person and a cook, I remained perplexed by her fierce devotion to Southern food and cooking, primarily because I still had a very narrow vision of what that meant. That same weekend, I was given a copy of The Taste of Country Cooking, *which would expand my view and challenge my understanding of Southern food. Leafing through its pages, I noticed that, alongside recipes familiar to me, like fried chicken and pound cake, there were other exotic-sounding dishes I had never heard of: blanc mange, sugared black raspberries, wild purslane and watercress cooked in pork stock, beef à la mode. It occurred to me that, before I met Miss Lewis, I didn't have a firm grasp that Virginia—or anything north of Tennessee, for that matter—was considered part of the South.*

Several months later, I visited Miss Lewis for the first time in New York, where she was then chef at the historic Brooklyn restaurant Gage and Tollner. Over coffee one afternoon, I told Miss Lewis I had been reading about how Italian food was so revered because of the short distance it travels from field to table. I said that it reminded me of my childhood, and the large vegetable garden my father grew in the field behind our house. Corn was eaten the day it was picked, or not at all. Our family's standards for okra were so particular, my sister and I were sent into the field with pen knives to cut pods both early in the morning and again at dusk.

Throughout our visit, Miss Lewis was relentless in extolling the virtues of Southern food. But I still didn't get it. Then, the morning of my departure, a revelation came to me: What if Southern cooking was approached using the same principles of immediacy and integrity that Alice Waters was practicing at Chez Panisse—and that Edna Lewis and my very own ancestors had been implementing their whole lives? Suddenly I was a convert.

Back home, I started to look seriously to my own roots for inspiration. I began perusing old cookbooks and plantation journals, and talking with my parents and older members of my community about the dishes and food traditions of their youth. Over time, I began to see the lovingly rolled pie crusts, greaseless fried chicken, tiny lady peas, peach pickles, and fifteen-layer chocolate cakes of my childhood in a different light.

This, I believe, is exactly what Miss Lewis sought to accomplish in writing The Taste of Country Cooking: *to inspire all of us to value our own place in the world, wherever that might be.*

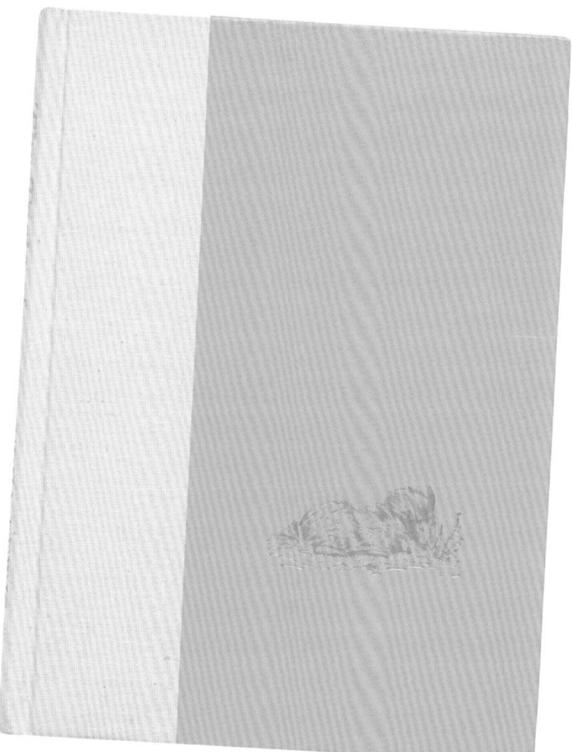

AN EARLY SUMMER BREAKFAST

Ham in Heavy Cream Sauce
Covered Fried Eggs
Pan-Fried Sweet Potatoes
Biscuits
Butter
Green Tomato Preserves
Coffee

Ham in Heavy Cream Sauce

Ham in heavy cream sauce was the most delicious combination one could ever hope to taste in leftovers. After carving away all the nice slices, the base of the ham was left with a lot of rough pieces. These were cut into 1-inch sizes and put into a saucepan containing heavy cream. The cream, which was skimmed from a crock of milk two days old, was much heavier than what we know as heavy cream, which is separated by a machine at the time of milking. The ham and cream mixture was then set on the back of the stove to heat without even reaching a simmer. When ready, the sauce would be thick and flavored by the pieces of ham—no other flavor added. It was served with hot biscuits or, if one liked, spooned over an open-faced biscuit. If you are having a Virginia ham you can still use the broken pieces, but not the bottom of the ham because that is usually dry and stringy. I don't think any other type of ham is any good. They just don't have the same flavor.

1 cup cut-up ham
2 cups heavy cream

Serves 4 to 5

Heat the cream to a scald, add the ham pieces, mix lightly, and set the saucepan on a low burner. The ham and cream mixture will more or less dry out in about ½ hour. Remove from the burner and serve piping hot.

Covered Fried Eggs

Covered fried eggs were developed by women who loved the outdoors and were anxious to get into the field or flower garden. When the meat was about ready in the oven and the coffee and the bread were all ready, a big skillet was set on the hot section of the stove—that is, over the fire box. Some fat from cooking bacon was added and when the pan began to smoke, a dozen eggs were broken one by one and carefully slipped in. A cover was placed on top. When the rest of the food was served up, the eggs were ready, beautiful, and looked as if they had been poached. They were placed upon a platter and decorated with delicious crisp bacon, or placed surrounding the ham.

Unlike other seasons of the year, the coming of fall was looked upon with mixed feelings. When the leaves began to fall, all the visitors were gone, and the whistle from the train passing through Orange gave a long, lonesome, shrill sound as it rolled through without stopping to let off any passengers.

But our spirits always lifted when my father would announce at the breakfast table on a Sunday morning in late September that he was bringing the stock home that day from the community pasture where they had grazed lazily all summer. As soon as my father and my older brother came in sight of the house we would rush out to greet them, admiring how much the calves had grown and how fat and sleek all of the animals were. After patting and stroking them, they were herded into their winter lots and left to get used to being back home.

Our thoughts turned to the opening of school in mid-October and to the harvesting of vegetable root crops, like sweet potatoes, peanuts, the cutting of field corn. After school started, we would rush home, change our clothes, and help gather in the potatoes and do other daily chores.

Once the corn was all cut and stacked in shocks, a group of high-school students who loved my mother would come on the first moonlit night and help us with the corn shucking. They thought it great fun, boys and girls with their favorite friends. After the shucking they would return to the house and be given a festive meal that my mother had had in preparation all afternoon: one of fried chicken, baked ham, roasted, newly dug sweet potatoes, baked tomatoes, green beans, cake, and apple pie—the apple pie being the favorite. The young people ate heartily and left late, thanking my mother and promising to come back the next fall. The next morning the corn field was dotted over with mounds of yellow corn, ready to be picked up and hauled to the corn crib.

Before we fully realized it, we were deep into fall and the other activities related to it, such as Race Day, hunting season, and rehearsing for the Annual Community Concert of Winter.

BREAKFAST BEFORE LEAVING FOR RACE DAY

Sour-Milk Griddle Cakes with Warm Blueberry Sauce and Maple Syrup
Sausage Patties
Biscuits
Pear Preserves
Damson Plum Preserves
Coffee

194 PREPARATIONS FOR CHRISTMAS

Mincemeat

We always made our mincemeat three or four weeks before Christmas and stored it in a big stone crock. It would keep a year or more —but it was always eaten up during the winter.

Makes about 8 cups

½ pound bottom round of beef
2 ounces suet (from veal kidney is best)
2 ounces currants
1 ounce seedless raisins
1 ounce seeded raisins
1 ounce candied lemon peel
1 ounce candied orange peel
1 cup finely chopped tart apples
3½ ounces soft brown sugar
½ teaspoon each cinnamon, allspice, cloves, ginger
½ nutmeg, grated
½ teaspoon salt
½ cup each Madeira, rum, and brandy

1 ½-gallon stone crock, or bowl or glass jars of approximately same quantity

Place the beef in a saucepan of boiling water just enough to cover. Simmer the meat 1 hour until tender, remove from burner, and leave to become really cold. Then chop fine and put through a meat grinder. Remove skin from suet and chop by hand until it becomes almost as smooth as lard. In a large mixing bowl mix the fruits well with a clean wooden spoon. Sprinkle over the brown sugar and spices, salt, and suet. Continue to stir. Pour together the rum, Madeira, and brandy. Add chopped beef to fruit mixture, sprinkle over the rum mixture, and stir well. Spoon the mixture into the clean 5-gallon stone jar or smaller glass jars. Tie over with a heavy, clean cloth. Store in a cold, dry place for 3 to 4 weeks.

Winter

240 *Lemon Meringue Pie, continued*

tinue to bake until the crust is lightly browned. Remove from the oven and set upon a wire rack to cool. When the crust is cold, fill it with the lemon filling.

FILLING
1 cup sugar
¼ teaspoon salt
¼ cup hot water
½ cup lemon juice, strained through a fine strainer
1 tablespoon butter
5 egg yolks, beaten

Put the sugar, salt, water, and lemon juice into a 2-quart, non-aluminum saucepan, and set over a medium burner, stirring until the sugar is completely dissolved. Then add the butter. Have the beaten yolks in a bowl. Pour some of the hot mixture into the yolks, stirring the yolks as you pour to prevent curdling. Then pour the yolk mixture back into the saucepan. Return the pan to the stove and cook carefully, stirring continuously until the contents become transparent and definitely coat the spoon. Set the filling out to cool.

MERINGUE TOPPING
2 egg whites
3 tablespoons sugar
1 teaspoon vanilla

Put the egg whites on a platter and beat them with a wire whisk or a fork. Beat until foamy. Add sugar and continue to beat until whites hold in stiff peaks. Add the vanilla and spoon the meringue onto the filling. Spread it in the desired design and set into a preheated 325° oven. Bake until lightly browned, about 15 minutes.

A WINTER DINNER

Beef à la Mode
Salad of Wild Watercress with Vinegar and Oil
Crusty Bread
Butter
Deep-Dish Apple Pie with Nutmeg Sauce
Coffee

In early winter we would get a quarter of beef in the hide and hang it, using pieces of it during the coldest months. Beef à la mode was a special-occasion dish served hot with lots of sauce, our own canned green beans, and a dessert of deep-dish apple pie with nutmeg.

241

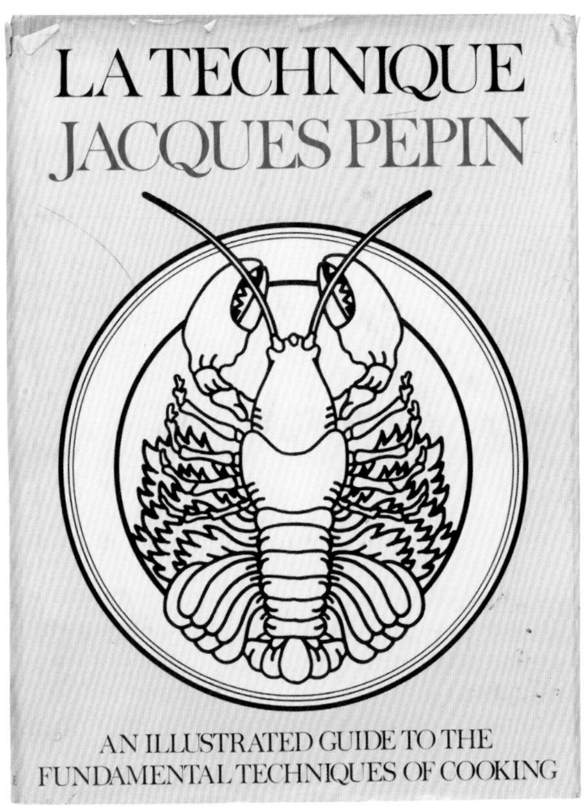

JACQUES PEPIN
La Technique, 1976

As strange as it sounds, chefs are the new rock stars. With a "bam!" this and a "bam!" that, you can practically hear the bass line and the wailing sax picking up the beat. With all this clatter, it's important to remember that there are still some chefs who still want to show you how to cook. Jacques Pépin is one of those.

Pépin came from a cooking family. His parents owned a restaurant in Bourg-en-Bresse, his hometown, near Lyon, France. At age thirteen he began an apprenticeship at the Grand Hôtel d'Europe, also in Bourg-en-Bresse. From there he worked in Paris under Lucien Diat at the Plaza Athénée. In 1959 Pépin came to the United States to work at the famed Le Pavillon restaurant in New York and as a consultant for the Howard Johnson Company. During this time he returned to complete his education and attended Columbia University. He received a master's degree in eighteenth-century French literature in 1972.

As all chefs know, there are two distinct elements of French cooking that have influenced food worldwide. First, French cuisine is based on a simple but radical idea: Remove the meat from the bone, prepare each separately, and bring them together at the end and serve. The bones are used to make stock, a basic ingredient in all French sauces. The second element is *la technique*, which includes knife skills, making stock, baking, carving—everything that you do in the process of cooking. Jacques Pépin's *La Technique* illustrates all of the major French culinary techniques with photographs and descriptions of the work. For those who don't prepare a rabbit every day, for instance, this is the ultimate "go-to" book. It's both a textbook and a reference book for cooking. In fact, it is still used to teach French technique. Pépin realized that his book would translate very well into a television series, and in 1997 PBS produced *The Complete Pépin*, a very popular series about how to cook. Pépin went on to do several other series for PBS, including the 1999 *Julia and Jacques Cooking at Home*, with the grande dame of American cooking, Julia Child.

NOTABLE RECIPES: Crepes Suzettes • **Gravlax à la Française** (page 472) • **Oeufs à la Neige** (page 651) • **Pâté à Brioche** (page 573) • Plain Omelette • **Saumon Poché en Gelée** (page 476) • **Sole Meunière** (page 475)

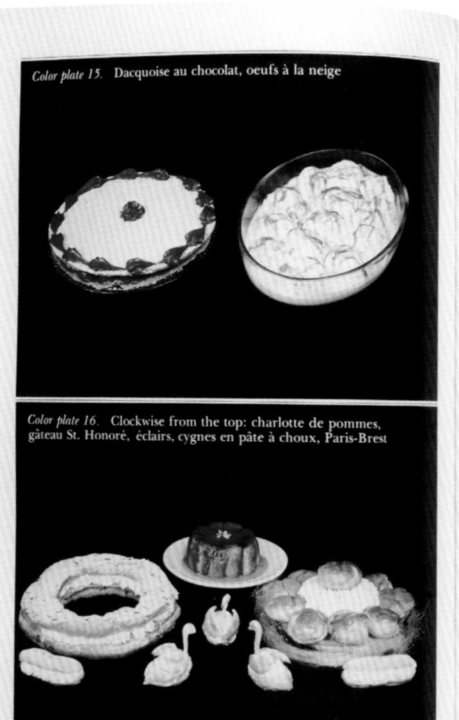

Color plate 15. Dacquoise au chocolat, oeufs à la neige

Color plate 16. Clockwise from the top: charlotte de pommes, gâteau St. Honoré, éclairs, cygnes en pâte à choux, Paris-Brest

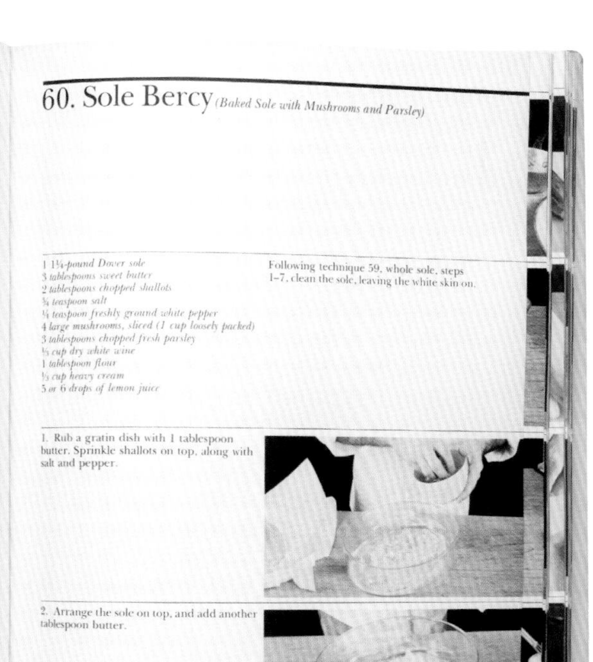

60. Sole Bercy *(Baked Sole with Mushrooms and Parsley)*

1 1¼-pound Dover sole
3 tablespoons sweet butter
2 tablespoons chopped shallots
¾ teaspoon salt
¼ teaspoon freshly ground white pepper
4 large mushrooms, sliced (1 cup loosely packed)
3 tablespoons chopped fresh parsley
⅓ cup dry white wine
1 tablespoon flour
⅓ cup heavy cream
5 or 6 drops of lemon juice

Following technique 59, whole sole, steps 1–7, clean the sole, leaving the white skin on.

1. Rub a gratin dish with 1 tablespoon butter. Sprinkle shallots on top, along with salt and pepper.

2. Arrange the sole on top, and add another tablespoon butter.

3. Fold the mixture into the *crème pâtissière*, technique 125.

127. Oeufs à la Neige *(Floating Islands)*

1. To make tender floating islands, the egg whites should be poached in water that doesn't exceed a temperature of 170 degrees. Beat 6 egg whites with a dash of salt in the electric mixer or by hand. When the egg whites are firm, add ¾ cup sugar and continue beating for 30 seconds. Stop the beating and fold in another ¼ cup sugar (see technique 128, step 1).

2. Using an ice-cream scoop, dish the whites out. Round the top of the scoop with your finger to get an "egg" as round as possible.

3. Drop the eggs into the hot (170 degrees) water.

4. Poach for 1½ to 2 minutes on one side, then turn the eggs on the other side.

5. Poach for another 1½ to 2 minutes; then lift the eggs onto a paper-lined tray.

6. Prepare a *crème anglaise*, technique 124, let it cool and place in the bottom of an oval or round dish. Arrange the cold eggs on top of the cream.

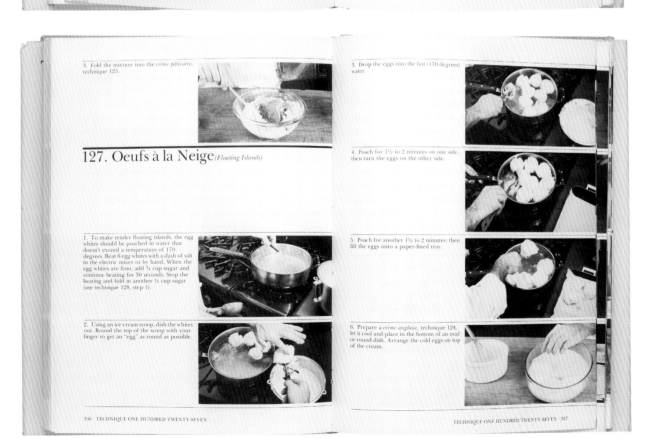

CARVING A CHICKEN

Few foods are as satisfying and as lovely to serve as a perfect roast chicken. Prepared correctly, the bird is a delight of tender, juicy meat encased in crispy, flavorful skin that emits an aroma of herbs, butter, and heaven. Traditionally the bird was carved at the table following its presentation. Cookbook authors love to illustrate how to carve the bird, assuring that this ancient and honorable skill is passed down to subsequent generations. Of course, most chicken recipes call for chicken parts. There are many different national styles for cutting up a chicken; most vary on how to carve the back. The illustrations here show how to cut a chicken in the French style. The major benefit of buying whole chickens and cutting them yourself is that you can retain the neck, back, wing tips, and other parts for making homemade chicken stock.

FROM TOP:

James Beard
American Cookery

Giuliano Bugialli
The Fine Art of Italian Cooking

Julia Child
From Julia Child's Kitchen

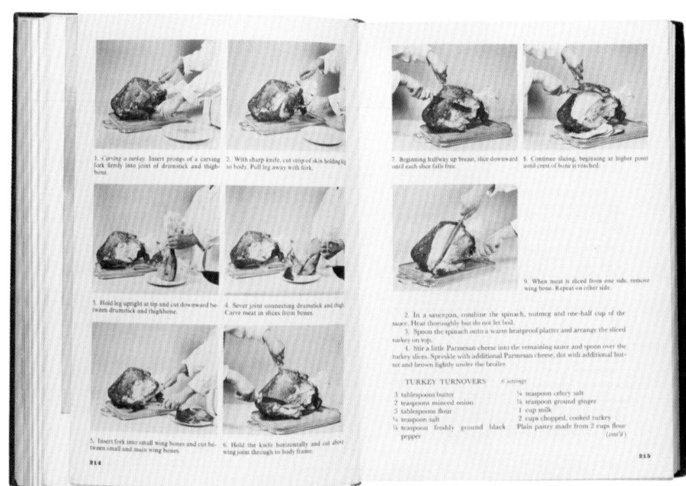
1. *Carving a turkey.* Insert prongs of a carving fork firmly into joint of drumstick and thighbone.

2. With sharp knife, cut strip of skin holding leg to body. Pull leg away with fork.

3. Hold leg upright at tip and cut downward between drumstick and thighbone.

4. Sever joint connecting drumstick and thigh. Carve meat in slices from bones.

5. Insert fork into small wing bones and cut between small and main wing bones.

6. Hold the knife horizontally and cut above wing joint through to body frame.

214

7. Beginning halfway up breast, slice downward until each slice falls free.

8. Continue slicing, beginning at higher point until crest of bone is reached.

9. When meat is sliced from one side, remove wing bone. Repeat on other side.

2. In a saucepan, combine the spinach, nutmeg and one-half cup of the sauce. Heat thoroughly but do not let boil.

3. Spoon the spinach onto a warm heatproof platter and arrange the sliced turkey on top.

4. Stir a little Parmesan cheese into the remaining sauce and spoon over the turkey slices. Sprinkle with additional Parmesan cheese, dot with additional butter and brown lightly under the broiler.

TURKEY TURNOVERS *6 servings*

3 tablespoons butter
2 teaspoons minced onion
3 tablespoons flour
¼ teaspoon salt
⅛ teaspoon freshly ground black pepper
¼ teaspoon celery salt
⅛ teaspoon ground ginger
1 cup milk
2 cups chopped, cooked turkey
Plain pastry made from 2 cups flour
(cont'd)

215

Pollo disossato ripieno: 1. Cutting the tendon at the end of the leg.

2. Freeing the leg bone on the inside.

3. Pushing the thigh bone from one end and pulling from the other.

310

4. Scraping the meat from the rib cage.

5. Removing the carcass.

6. Cutting off the two outer sections of the wing.

311

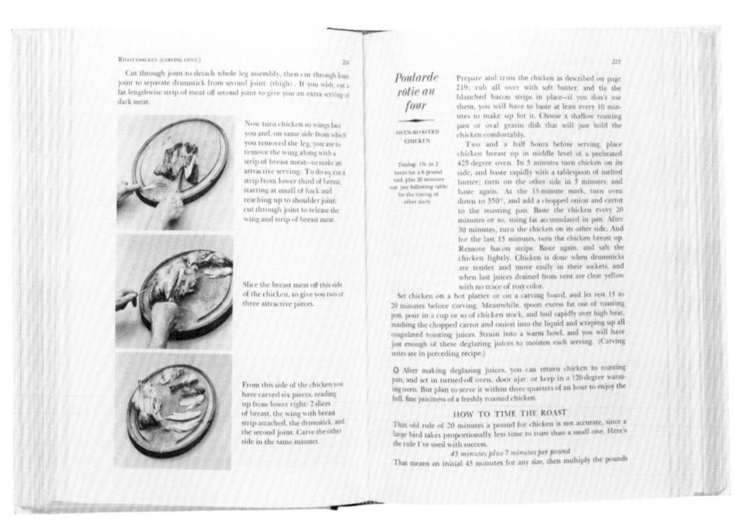
ROAST CHICKEN (CARVING CONT.) 224

Cut through joint to detach whole leg assembly, then cut through knee joint to separate drumstick from second joint (thigh). If you wish, cut a fat lengthwise strip of meat off second joint to give you an extra serving of dark meat.

Now turn chicken so wings face you and, on same side from which you removed the leg, you are to remove the wing along with a strip of breast meat—to make an attractive serving: To do so, cut a strip from lower third of breast, starting at small of back and reaching up to shoulder joint; cut through joint to release the wing and strip of breast meat.

Slice the breast meat off this side of the chicken, to give you two or three attractive pieces.

From this side of the chicken you have carved six pieces, reading up from lower right: 2 slices of breast, the wing with breast strip attached, the drumstick, and the second joint. Carve the other side in the same manner.

225

Poularde rôtie au four

OVEN-ROASTED CHICKEN

Timing: 1¾ to 2 hours for a 6-pound bird, plus 20 minutes rest (see following table for the timing of other sizes)

Prepare and truss the chicken as described on page 219; rub all over with soft butter, and tie the blanched bacon strips in place—if you don't use them, you will have to baste at least every 10 minutes to make up for it. Choose a shallow roasting pan or oval gratin dish that will just hold the chicken comfortably.

Two and a half hours before serving, place chicken breast up in middle level of a preheated 425-degree oven. In 5 minutes turn chicken on its side, and baste rapidly with a tablespoon of melted butter; turn on the other side in 5 minutes, and baste again. At the 15-minute mark, turn oven down to 350°, and add a chopped onion and carrot to the roasting pan. Baste the chicken every 20 minutes or so, using fat accumulated in pan. After 30 minutes, turn the chicken on its other side. And for the last 15 minutes, turn the chicken breast up. Remove bacon strips. Baste again, and salt the chicken lightly. Chicken is done when drumsticks are tender and move easily in their sockets, and when last juices drained from vent are clear yellow with no trace of rosy color.

Set chicken on a hot platter or on a carving board, and let rest 15 to 20 minutes before carving. Meanwhile, spoon excess fat out of roasting pan, pour in a cup or so of chicken stock, and boil rapidly over high heat, mashing the chopped carrot and onion into the liquid and scraping up all coagulated roasting juices. Strain into a warm bowl, and you will have just enough of these deglazing juices to moisten each serving. (Carving notes are in preceding recipe.)

✿ After making deglazing juices, you can return chicken to roasting pan, and set in turned-off oven, door ajar; or keep in a 120-degree warming oven. But plan to serve it within three quarters of an hour to enjoy the full, fine juiciness of a freshly roasted chicken.

HOW TO TIME THE ROAST

That old rule of 20 minutes a pound for chicken is not accurate, since a large bird takes proportionally less time to roast than a small one. Here's the rule I've used with success.

45 minutes plus 7 minutes per pound

That means an initial 45 minutes for any size, then multiply the pounds

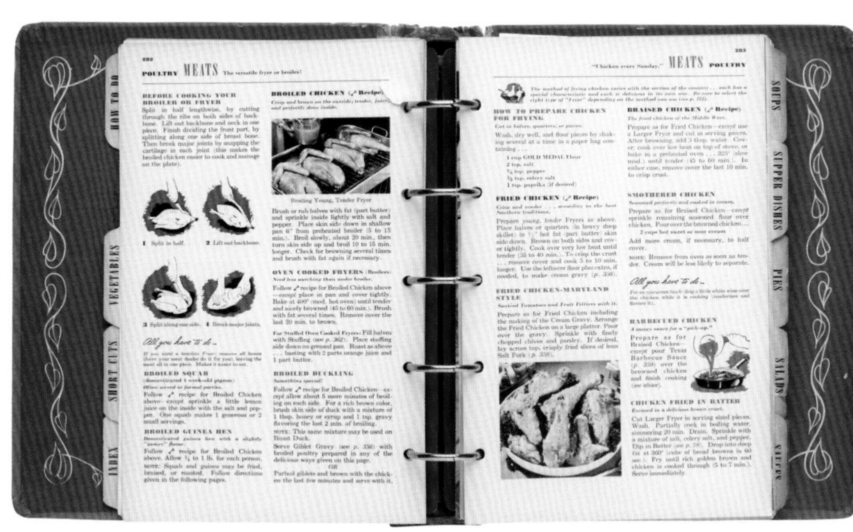

FROM TOP:

Betty Crocker
Betty Crocker's Picture Cook Book

Mark Bittman
How to Cook Everything

Jacques Pépin
La Technique

MOOSEWOOD COOKBOOK
By Mollie Katzen

MOLLIE KATZEN
The Moosewood Cookbook, 1977

Moosewood, Inc., is a business collective born out of the heady days of late-1960s student radicalism. The collective's restaurant was one of the first to promote what has been called "healthful natural foods cuisine" and to focus on fresh produce, whole grains, beans, soy, and other natural foods. Noting that "vegetarianism as a life-style choice was a strong influence on the development of the restaurant's repertoire," members of the collective sought out interesting recipes from around the world to produce a corpus of meals that helped a generation turn to meatless diets. The collective has published eleven books in total, but it was the original *Moosewood Cookbook* that many people purchased and that radically changed the way Americans think about vegetarian foods.

NOTABLE RECIPES: Gado-Gado (page 365) • **Gypsy Soup** (page 384) • Hungarian Mushroom Soup • Hummus • **Minestrone** (page 343) • Ratatouille • Refritos/Refried Beans • Spinach-Ricotta Pie • Tabouli • **Vegetarian Chili** (page 381)

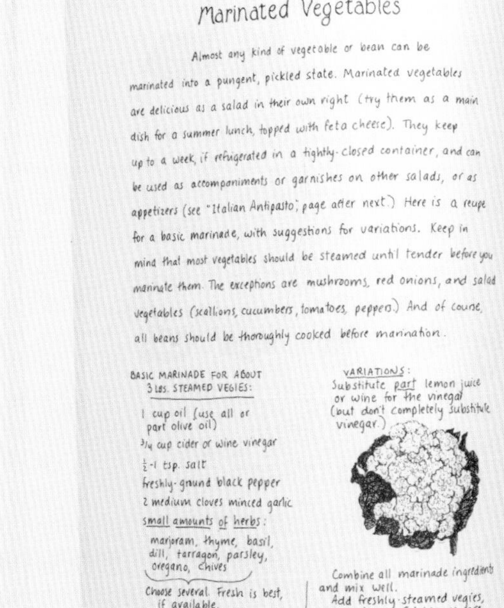

Marinated Vegetables

Almost any kind of vegetable or bean can be marinated into a pungent, pickled state. Marinated vegetables are delicious as a salad in their own right (try them as a main dish for a summer lunch, topped with feta cheese). They keep up to a week, if refrigerated in a tightly-closed container, and can be used as accompaniments or garnishes on other salads, or as appetizers (see "Italian Antipasto," page after next.) Here is a recipe for a basic marinade, with suggestions for variations. Keep in mind that most vegetables should be steamed until tender before you marinate them. The exceptions are mushrooms, red onions, and salad vegetables (scallions, cucumbers, tomatoes, peppers.) And of course, all beans should be thoroughly cooked before marination.

BASIC MARINADE FOR ABOUT 3 LBS. STEAMED VEGIES:

1 cup oil (use all or part olive oil)
3/4 cup cider or wine vinegar
½-1 tsp. salt
freshly-ground black pepper
2 medium cloves minced garlic
small amounts of herbs:
marjoram, thyme, basil, dill, tarragon, parsley, oregano, chives
Choose several. Fresh is best, if available.

VARIATIONS:
Substitute part lemon juice or wine for the vinegar (but don't completely substitute vinegar.)

Combine all marinade ingredients and mix well.
Add freshly-steamed vegies, cooked beans (chickpeas are best) and raw salad stuff in amounts desired.

58

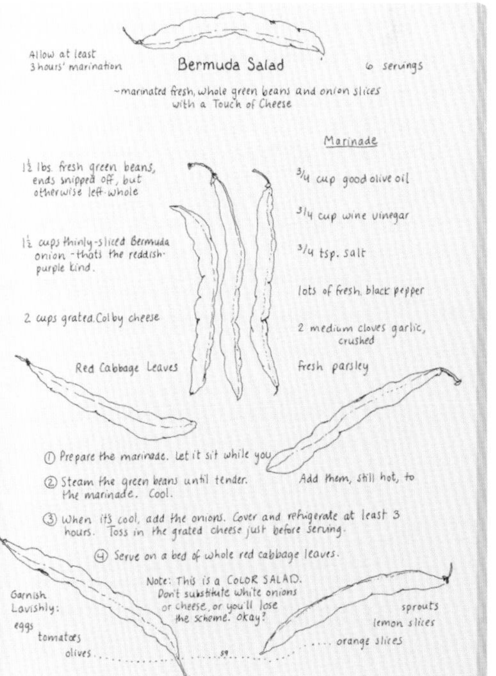

Allow at least 3 hours' marination

Bermuda Salad

6 servings

~marinated fresh, whole green beans and onion slices with a Touch of Cheese

1½ lbs. fresh green beans, ends snipped off, but otherwise left whole
1½ cups thinly-sliced Bermuda onion - that's the reddish-purple kind.
2 cups grated Colby cheese
Red Cabbage Leaves

Marinade
3/4 cup good olive oil
3/4 cup wine vinegar
3/4 tsp. salt
lots of fresh black pepper
2 medium cloves garlic, crushed
fresh parsley

① Prepare the marinade. Let it sit while you
② Steam the green beans until tender. Add them, still hot, to the marinade. Cool.
③ When it's cool, add the onions. Cover and refrigerate at least 3 hours. Toss in the grated cheese just before serving.
④ Serve on a bed of whole red cabbage leaves.

Note: This is a COLOR SALAD. Don't substitute white onions or cheese, or you'll lose the scheme. okay?

Garnish Lavishly:
eggs
tomatoes
olives
sprouts
lemon slices
orange slices

59

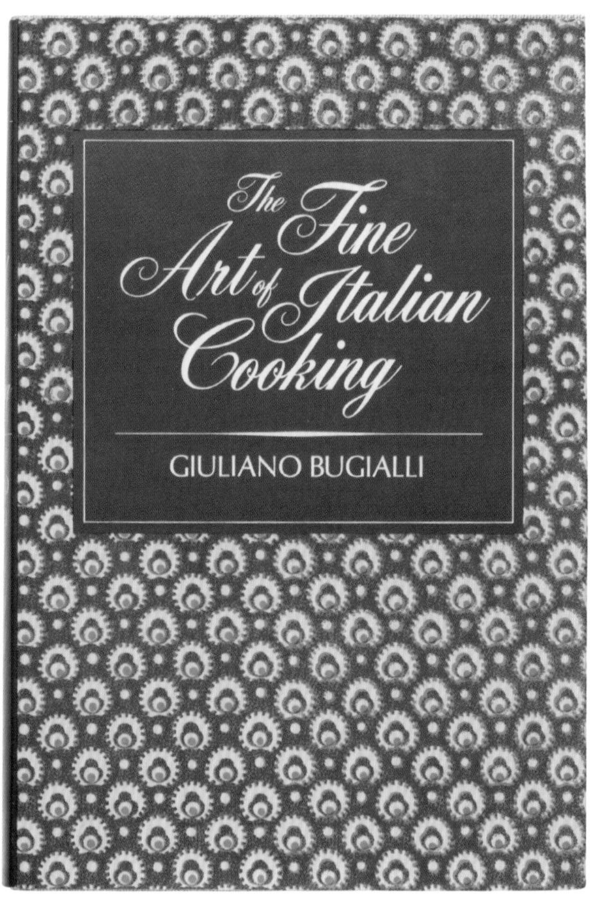

NOTABLE RECIPES: Balsamella (page 525) • Duck Lasagna • **Fresh Pasta** (page 442) • Lasagna al Forno • **Pollo in Porchetta** (page 517) • Scallopine ai Capperi • **Spaghetti alla Carbonara** (page 444) • **Spaghetti alla Fiaccheraia** (page 443) • Tagliatelle alla Panna (Cream Sauce/Alfredo)

GIULIANO BUGIALLI

The Fine Art of Italian Cooking, 1977

It is a commonplace that many Americans think Italian food is pizza or spaghetti with red sauce and meatballs. And for a good reason; if made well, these are treasured Italian-American specialties. Beginning in the 1970s, however, and exploding in the 1980s, was the realization that there are many, many food traditions in Italy that vary widely from region to region. Italian-American food tends to be influenced by cooking from the south and from Sicily, the homelands of many Italian-American immigrants. Guiliano Bugialli is one of the important Italian cooks who came to the United States preaching the gospel of Tuscan cooking.

Bugialli grew up outside of Florence, where his father had a large winery. Following studies in literature and languages, Bugialli found his true calling making and promoting Italian food, founding a cooking school in Florence in 1972 aimed at an international audience. When his first book, *The Fine Art of Italian Cooking*, was published in 1977, it was a major success. Suddenly there was a rage for anything Italian. New ingredients, such as arugula, began appearing in high-end groceries, such as New York's Dean & DeLuca. Extra virgin olive oils with a distinct bite to their finish appeared on tables. Italian breads were coveted by the growing group of gourmets who were increasingly dissatisfied with French cooking and saw something both healthier and more "honest," in the sense of more aligned with home cooking, in the unpretentious foods of Italy. Italian food effectively ceased to be ethnic and became gourmet. Bugialli helped make this change happen. And we're all better for it. On the other hand, the rise of interest in Italian food came at the cost of interest in the Italian-American food traditions, which were a different cuisine specific to the United States. Sadly, many of the traditional Italian-American cooks are dying, and with them goes this truly American food.

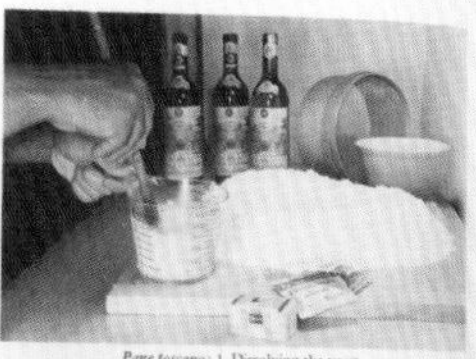

Pane toscano: 1. Dissolving the yeast.

2. The sponge doubled in size.

With a wooden spoon, carefully mix together all the ingredients in the well, then add the remaining water and start mixing with your hands, absorbing the flour from the inside rim of the well little by little (see photo 3).

Keep mixing until all but 4 or 5 tablespoons of the flour are incorporated (about 15 minutes), then knead the dough with the palms of your hands, in a folding motion, until it is homogenous and smooth (about 20 minutes), incorporating the remaining flour, if necessary, to keep the dough from being sticky (see photo 4).

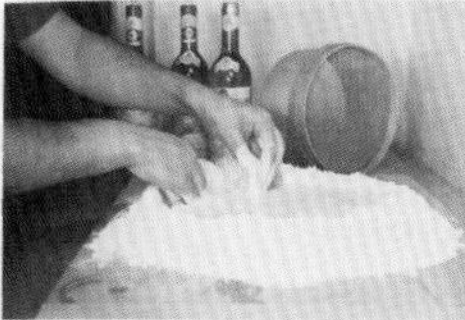

3. Combining the flour and sponge.

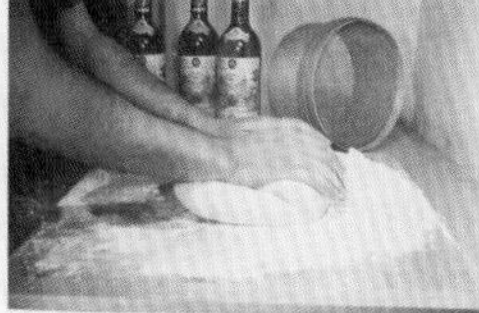

4. Kneading the dough.

PHOTO BY STUDIO BENCINI, FLORENCE

A SUGGESTED DINNER

WINE
Chianti Classico Castell'in Villa

Risotto con funghi (see page 215)
Fritto misto alla fiorentina (see below)
Insalata verde (see page 387)
Pesche al vino (see page 496)

Fritto Misto alla Fiorentina
(Mixed Fry, Florentine Style)

The fried-dish counterpart to the *bollito misto* is called *fritto misto*. It is again a holdover from the days when the boiled course and the fried course were the *primi e secondi*.

The most usual mixture, if only two dishes are included, is that of fried calf's brain (see page 277) and fried artichokes (see page 398), a combination that appears on most restaurant menus as *fritto alla fiorentina*. However, the *misto* can be a more elaborate combination. For a really grand *misto*, you may include, for meats, fried chicken (see page 275), croquettes (see page 278), and the brains, for vegetables, zucchini (see page 426), zucchini flowers (see page 425), cauliflower (see page 410), potatoes, or any combination thereof.

To serve *fritto misto*, divide the serving dish into as many wedges (like slices of a pie) as there are different dishes. Separate each wedge from the next by a row of lemon wedges. As much as possible, alternate wedges of meats with those of vegetables.

A SUGGESTED DINNER

WINE
Chianti Classico Montagliari

Tortelli alla menta (see page 168)
Braciole fritte (see below)
Fiori di zucca fritti (see page 425)
or *Insalata mista* (see page 387)
Schiacciata unta di Berlingaccio (see page 472)

Braciole Fritte
(Deep-Fried Veal or Beef Cutlets) (SERVES 4)

This dish is the Florentine counterpart of *cotolette alla milanese*. Cookbooks from the turn of the century mention that a *milanese* has a bone when it is cut from the loin, and is boneless when it is cut from the upper leg. (These are called respectively *costola* and *noce*.) At that time the *milanese* was cooked in enough butter so that it was really deep-fried. Nowadays, most *milanese* are made with the bone and use less butter, so they are almost sautéed rather than deep-fried.

This recipe is for a dish that the Florentines sometimes call a *milanese*, but I believe that, though they were once the same, both it and the *milanese* have changed in the past century. I call it *braciola* because it is made from meat, either veal or young beef, without the bone, pounded thin and tender with the *batticarne* (meat pounder). In Milan the dish is often swimming in butter; some recommend that the butter in which it has been cooked be poured over the dish when served. This obviously would not appeal to the Florentines with their horror of fat and heaviness. So, in Florence, the deep frying of the old days remains, but done with the lighter *olio di semi*. The butter flavor is replaced by lemon juice and a little salt, which are added when the dish is served. It is also the practice there to marinate the meat in the beaten egg, rather than just dipping it.

PHOTO BY STUDIO BENCINI, FLORENCE

in the well along with the other ingredients. Follow the remaining directions exactly, but allow the pasta to dry for 15 or 16 minutes instead of 10.

Green pasta may be used for *tagliatelle* and *taglierini*. To cut pasta into those shapes, see pages 138–139.

To cut green pasta for lasagne or cannelloni, see *cannelloni con carne* (page 178).

Green pasta and red pasta: spinach for green, beets for red.

Pasta Rossa
(Red Pasta) (SERVES 3)

1 medium-sized red beet
3½ cups all-purpose flour, preferably unbleached
2 "extra-large" eggs
2 teaspoons olive or other vegetable oil
Pinch of salt

Discard the stem of the beet and wash the beet very well.

Place a saucepan containing a large quantity of cold salted water on the heat. When the water has reached the boiling point, add the beet and cook for 1 to 1½ hours, until soft. Peel off the beet's outer layer under cold running water, then chop the beet extremely fine. Measure 1 heaping tablespoon of finely chopped beet. (If there is a little left over, discard it.)

At this point, using the remaining ingredients, follow the directions on pages 133–138, noting that this recipe uses 1¾ cups of flour to each egg instead of 1 cup. Place the chopped beet in the well along with the other ingredients. Follow the remaining directions exactly, but allow the pasta to dry for 15 to 16 minutes instead of 10.

Red pasta may be used for *taglierini*, *tagliatelle*, or even cannelloni. To cut pasta into these shapes, see pages 138–139 and 178.

Taglierini al Pomodoro Fresco
(Taglierini with Fresh Tomato Sauce) (SERVES 4)

The thinly cut, delicate *taglierini* go best with the lightest sauce, one made from ripe, fresh tomatoes, cooked very lightly and then adorned only with fresh basil leaves to bring out the quality of the tomatoes.

With good imported Italian canned plum tomatoes, and basil preserved in salt, a very creditable version can also be made in the winter. The fresh *taglierini* need be cooked for only 15 seconds. Green *tagliolini* (see page 143) are also used to good advantage in this dish.

For the pasta

2 cups all-purpose flour, preferably unbleached
2 "extra-large" eggs
2 teaspoons olive or other vegetable oil
Pinch of salt

Sugo di pomodoro fresco (see page 69)
Coarse salt
4 tablespoons (½ stick) butter or ¼ cup olive oil
¼ cup freshly grated Parmigiano cheese
Freshly ground black pepper
3 or 4 leaves fresh basil (see note below)

Make the *taglierini*, using the quantities listed above, according to directions on pages 133–138. To cut into *taglierini*, see page 138. Let the *taglierini* stand on a pasta board, covered with a cotton dishtowel, until needed.

PHOTO BY STUDIO BENCINI, FLORENCE

MIMI SHERATON

From My Mother's Kitchen

Recipes and Reminiscences, 1979

Mimi Sheraton has had a lot to say about American food over the years, and she's said it with confidence and brass. Though she grew up in a house where food was very important, Sheraton went New York University to study business, majoring in marketing and minoring in journalism. She got a job writing advertising copy about home furnishings at an ad agency, eventually leaving it to write for *Good Housekeeping*. She then studied interior design at the New School of Interior Design, became a certified professional decorator, and finally ended up as home furnishings editor for *Seventeen* magazine. At *Seventeen* she traveled often, searching out new furniture, silver, and tableware. On the side, she did her own food research, going to restaurants and markets, photographing and tasting world foods, and bringing home cookbooks and utensils for her own kitchen. Soon she began testing recipes in the kitchen at *Good Housekeeping* (another Hearst-owned magazine) and was named food editor. Even though her next job was as managing editor of *House Beautiful*'s supplements division, she continued to write about food.

Finally her desire to write about food won out: She spent twenty years as a freelance food writer, traveling the world and writing. Sheraton studied cooking at the Cordon Bleu in Paris, and she has taken classes in Copenhagen, Beirut, Phnom Penh, and Istanbul. She was the food critic for the *New York Times* from 1975 to 1983. Sheraton is the author of many cookbooks, including *The German Cookbook*, *The Whole World Loves Chicken Soup*, *From My Mother's Kitchen*, and an autobiography, *Eating My Words*.

NOTABLE RECIPES: Aunt Estelle's Date and Nut Bread • **Black Radish and Onion Salad** (page 363) • **Cheese Blintzes** (page 326) • Chicken Soup • Chopped Chicken Livers • **Cold Beet Borscht** (page 334) • **Eggplant Caviar, Two Ways** (page 416) • Gefilte Fish • Kosher Garlic Dill Pickles • May's Sour Cream Coffee Cake • Poppy Seed Coffee Cake • Potato Cakes • Soft Passover Almond Macaroons

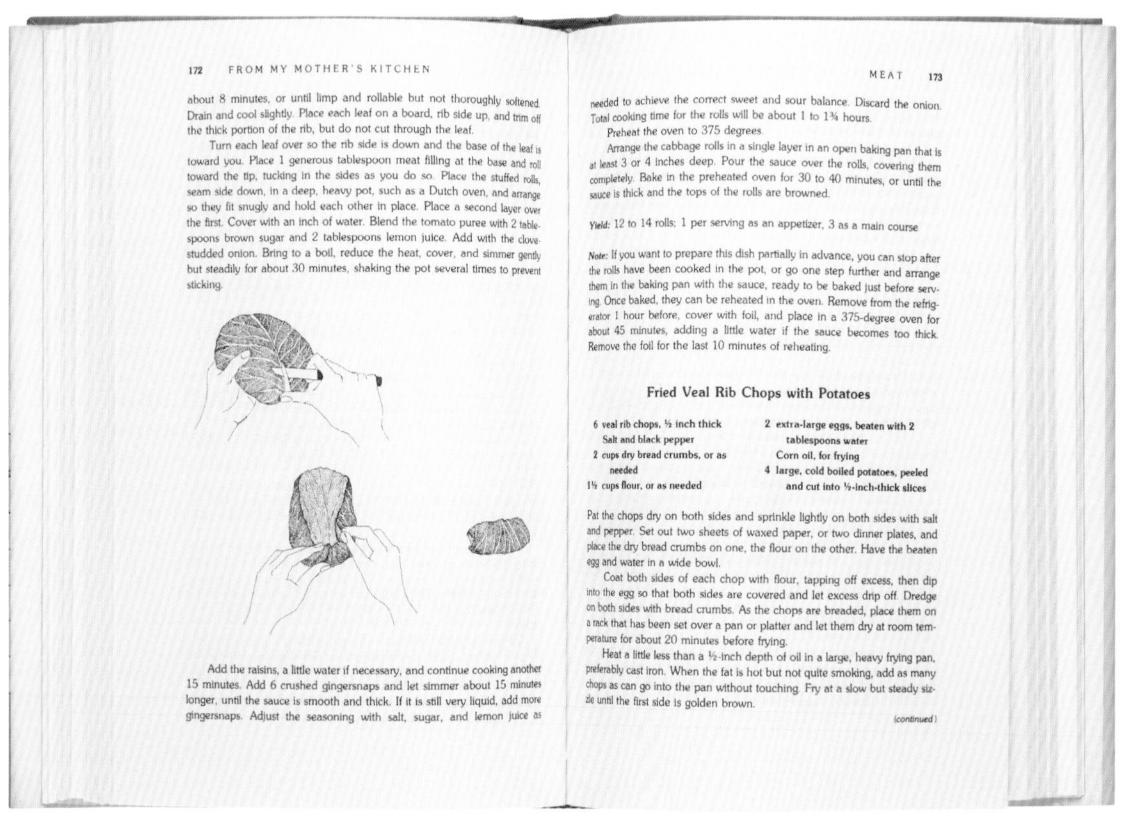

172 FROM MY MOTHER'S KITCHEN

about 8 minutes, or until limp and rollable but not thoroughly softened. Drain and cool slightly. Place each leaf on a board, rib side up, and trim off the thick portion of the rib, but do not cut through the leaf.

Turn each leaf over so the rib side is down and the base of the leaf is toward you. Place 1 generous tablespoon meat filling at the base and roll toward the tip, tucking in the sides as you do so. Place the stuffed rolls, seam side down, in a deep, heavy pot, such as a Dutch oven, and arrange so they fit snugly and hold each other in place. Place a second layer over the first. Cover with an inch of water. Blend the tomato puree with 2 tablespoons brown sugar and 2 tablespoons lemon juice. Add with the clove-studded onion. Bring to a boil, reduce the heat, cover, and simmer gently but steadily for about 30 minutes, shaking the pot several times to prevent sticking.

Add the raisins, a little water if necessary, and continue cooking another 15 minutes. Add 6 crushed gingersnaps and let simmer about 15 minutes longer, until the sauce is smooth and thick. If it is still very liquid, add more gingersnaps. Adjust the seasoning with salt, sugar, and lemon juice as

MEAT 173

needed to achieve the correct sweet and sour balance. Discard the onion. Total cooking time for the rolls will be about 1 to 1¾ hours.

Preheat the oven to 375 degrees.

Arrange the cabbage rolls in a single layer in an open baking pan that is at least 3 or 4 inches deep. Pour the sauce over the rolls, covering them completely. Bake in the preheated oven for 30 to 40 minutes, or until the sauce is thick and the tops of the rolls are browned.

Yield: 12 to 14 rolls; 1 per serving as an appetizer, 3 as a main course

Note: If you want to prepare this dish partially in advance, you can stop after the rolls have been cooked in the pot, or go one step further and arrange them in the baking pan with the sauce, ready to be baked just before serving. Once baked, they can be reheated in the oven. Remove from the refrigerator 1 hour before, cover with foil, and place in a 375-degree oven for about 45 minutes, adding a little water if the sauce becomes too thick. Remove the foil for the last 10 minutes of reheating.

Fried Veal Rib Chops with Potatoes

6 veal rib chops, ½ inch thick
Salt and black pepper
2 cups dry bread crumbs, or as needed
1½ cups flour, or as needed
2 extra-large eggs, beaten with 2 tablespoons water
Corn oil, for frying
4 large, cold boiled potatoes, peeled and cut into ½-inch-thick slices

Pat the chops dry on both sides and sprinkle lightly on both sides with salt and pepper. Set out two sheets of waxed paper, or two dinner plates, and place the dry bread crumbs on one, the flour on the other. Have the beaten egg and water in a wide bowl.

Coat both sides of each chop with flour, tapping off excess, then dip into the egg so that both sides are covered and let excess drip off. Dredge on both sides with bread crumbs. As the chops are breaded, place them on a rack that has been set over a pan or platter and let them dry at room temperature for about 20 minutes before frying.

Heat a little less than a ½-inch depth of oil in a large, heavy frying pan, preferably cast iron. When the fat is hot but not quite smoking, add as many chops as can go into the pan without touching. Fry at a slow but steady sizzle until the first side is golden brown.

(continued)

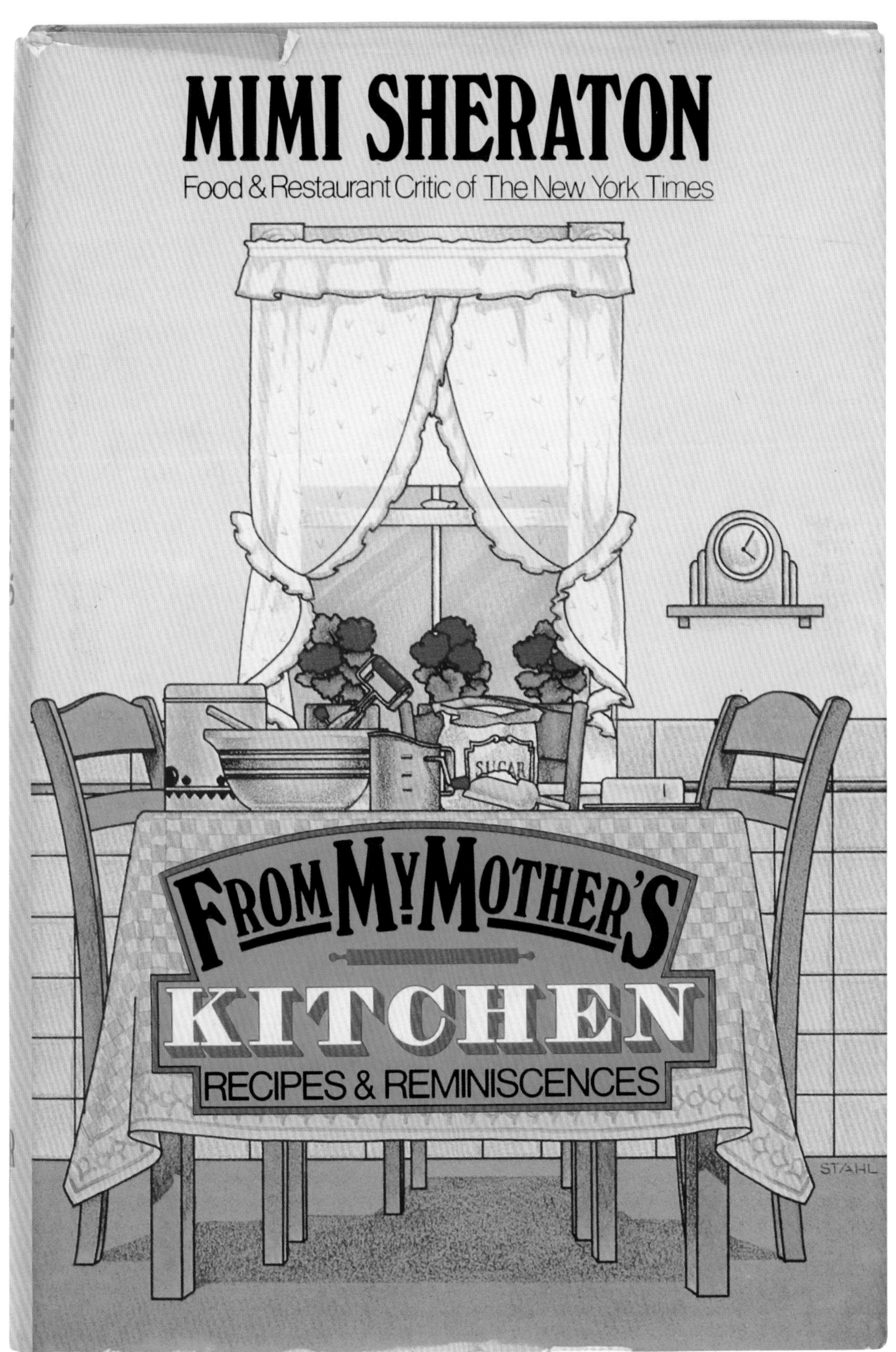
MIMI SHERATON
Food & Restaurant Critic of The New York Times
SUGAR
FROM MY MOTHER'S
KITCHEN
RECIPES & REMINISCENCES
STAHL

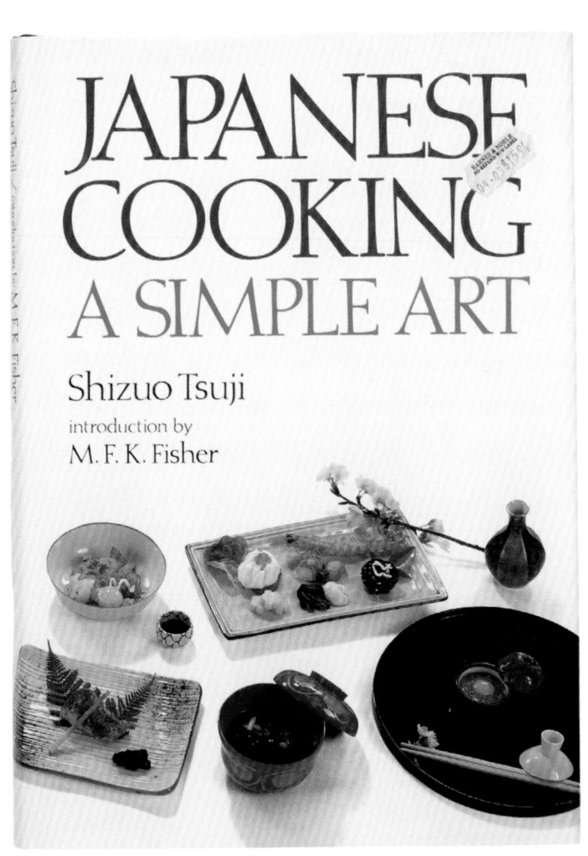

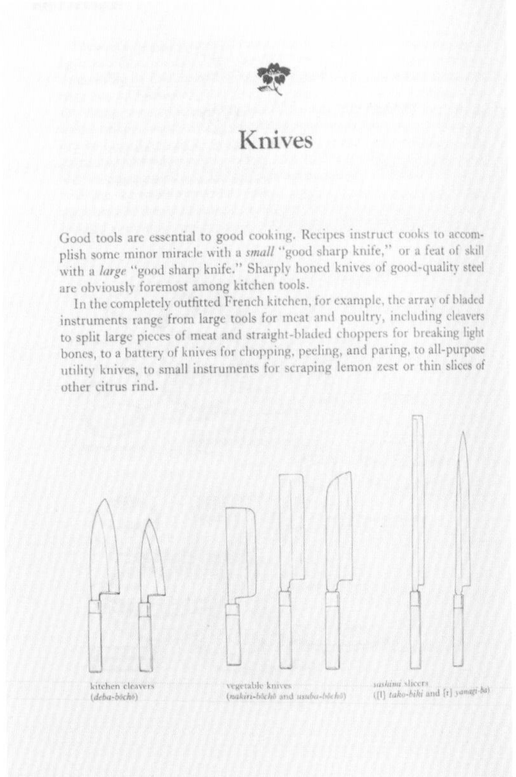

Knives

Good tools are essential to good cooking. Recipes instruct cooks to accomplish some minor miracle with a *small* "good sharp knife," or a feat of skill with a *large* "good sharp knife." Sharply honed knives of good-quality steel are obviously foremost among kitchen tools.

In the completely outfitted French kitchen, for example, the array of bladed instruments range from large tools for meat and poultry, including cleavers to split large pieces of meat and straight-bladed choppers for breaking light bones, to a battery of knives for chopping, peeling, and paring, to all-purpose utility knives, to small instruments for scraping lemon zest or thin slices of other citrus rind.

SHIZUO TSUJI

Japanese Cooking

A Simple Art, 1980

It is hard today to imagine a world without a sushi bar on every other corner, for Americans have completely embraced Japanese cuisine, and sushi in particular, as essential to the American palate. One book is largely responsible for this change: *Japanese Cooking*. Tsuji's text showed the food world that sushi was not just an ethnic Japanese form of cooking, but as sophisticated as haute cuisine. M.F.K. Fisher wrote the introduction to the first edition. Ruth Reichl, in her foreword to the anniversary edition, wrote:

> This is much more than a cookbook. It is a philosophical treatise about the simple art of Japanese cooking. Appreciate the lessons of this book, and you will understand that while *sushi* and *sashimi* were becoming part of American culture, we were absorbing much larger lessons from the Japanese. We were learning to think about food in an entirely new way.

Perhaps Reichl's statement best sums up what happened in American food in the last quarter of the twentieth century. As editor of *Gourmet* magazine, Reichl helped lead the way.

NOTABLE RECIPES: Basic Stock (page 520) • **Grilled Mushrooms with Ponzu Sauce** (page 413) • **Homemade Japanese Noodles** (page 452) • **Miso Soup** (page 340) • **Ponzu Sauce** (page 522) • **Savory Cup Custard** (page 468) • Steamed Salmon • **Steak Teriyaki** (page 547) • Sushi Rice • Vinegared Octopus

Fish

Plate 2

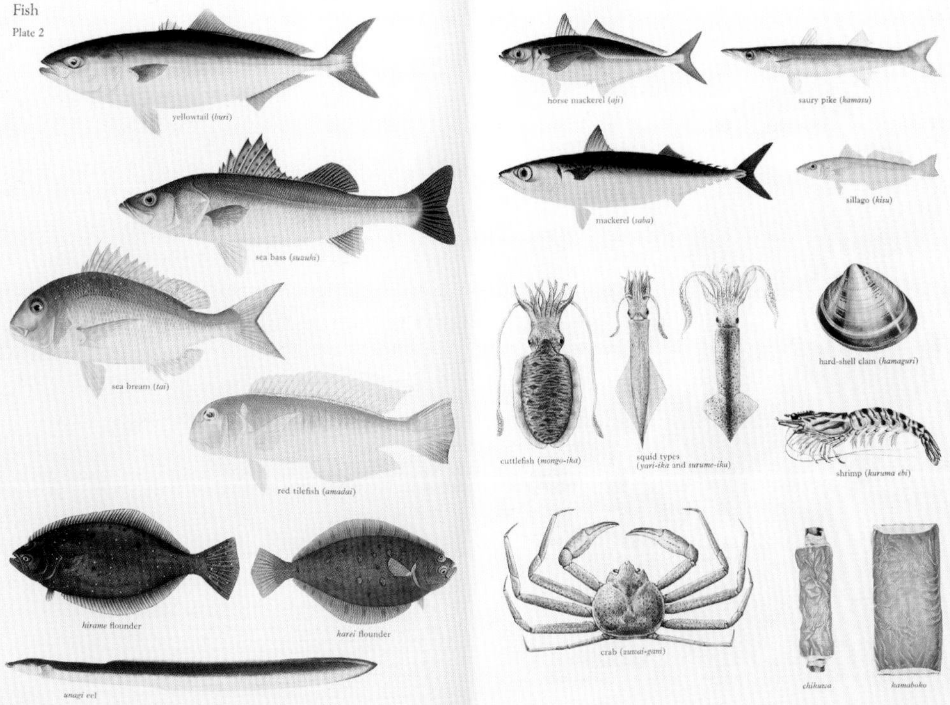

yellowtail (*buri*)

sea bass (*suzuki*)

sea bream (*tai*)

red tilefish (*amadai*)

hirame flounder

karei flounder

unagi eel

horse mackerel (*aji*)

saury pike (*kamasu*)

mackerel (*saba*)

sillago (*kisu*)

cuttlefish (*mongo-ika*)

squid types
(*yari-ika* and *surume-ika*)

hard-shell clam (*hamaguri*)

shrimp (*kuruma ebi*)

crab (*zuwai-gani*)

chikuwa

kamaboko

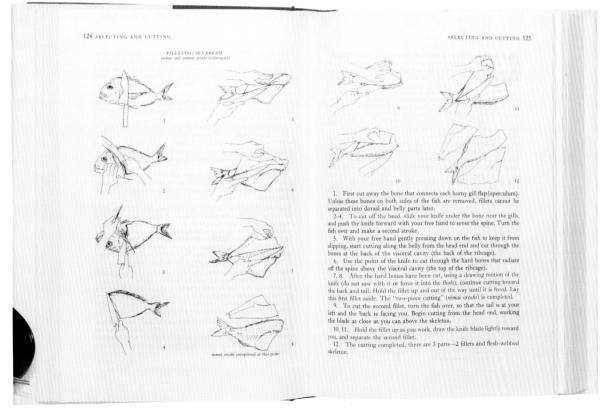

FILLETING SEA BREAM
(*nimai* and *sanmai oroshi* techniques)

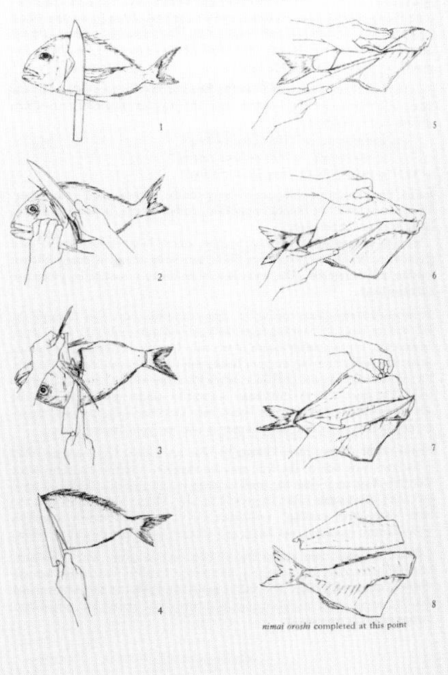

1 2 3 4 5 6 7 8

nimai oroshi completed at this point

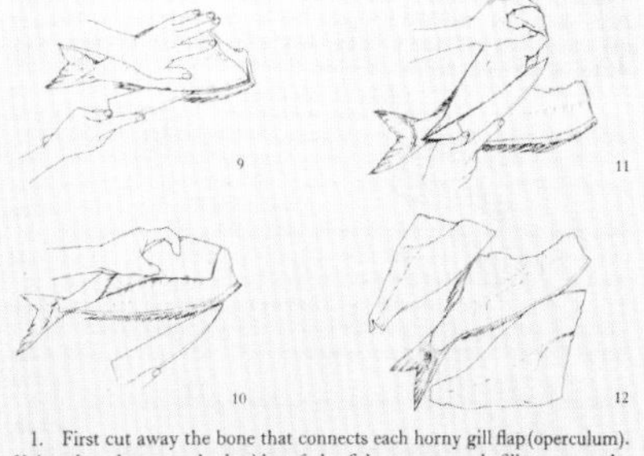

9 10 11 12

1. First cut away the bone that connects each horny gill flap (operculum). Unless these bones on both sides of the fish are removed, fillets cannot be separated into dorsal and belly parts later.

2–4. To cut off the head, slide your knife under the bone near the gills, and push the knife forward with your free hand to sever the spine. Turn the fish over and make a second stroke.

5. With your free hand gently pressing down on the fish to keep it from slipping, start cutting along the belly from the head end and cut through the bones at the back of the visceral cavity (the back of the ribcage).

6. Use the point of the knife to cut through the hard bones that radiate off the spine above the visceral cavity (the top of the ribcage).

7, 8. After the hard bones have been cut, using a drawing motion of the knife (do not saw with it or force it into the flesh), continue cutting toward the back and tail. Hold the fillet up and out of the way until it is freed. Lay this first fillet aside. The "two-piece cutting" (*nimai oroshi*) is completed.

9. To cut the second fillet, turn the fish over, so that the tail is at your left and the back is facing you. Begin cutting from the head end, working the blade as close as you can above the skeleton.

10, 11. Hold the fillet up as you work, draw the knife blade lightly toward you, and separate the second fillet.

12. The cutting completed, there are 3 parts—2 fillets and flesh-webbed skeleton.

Winter

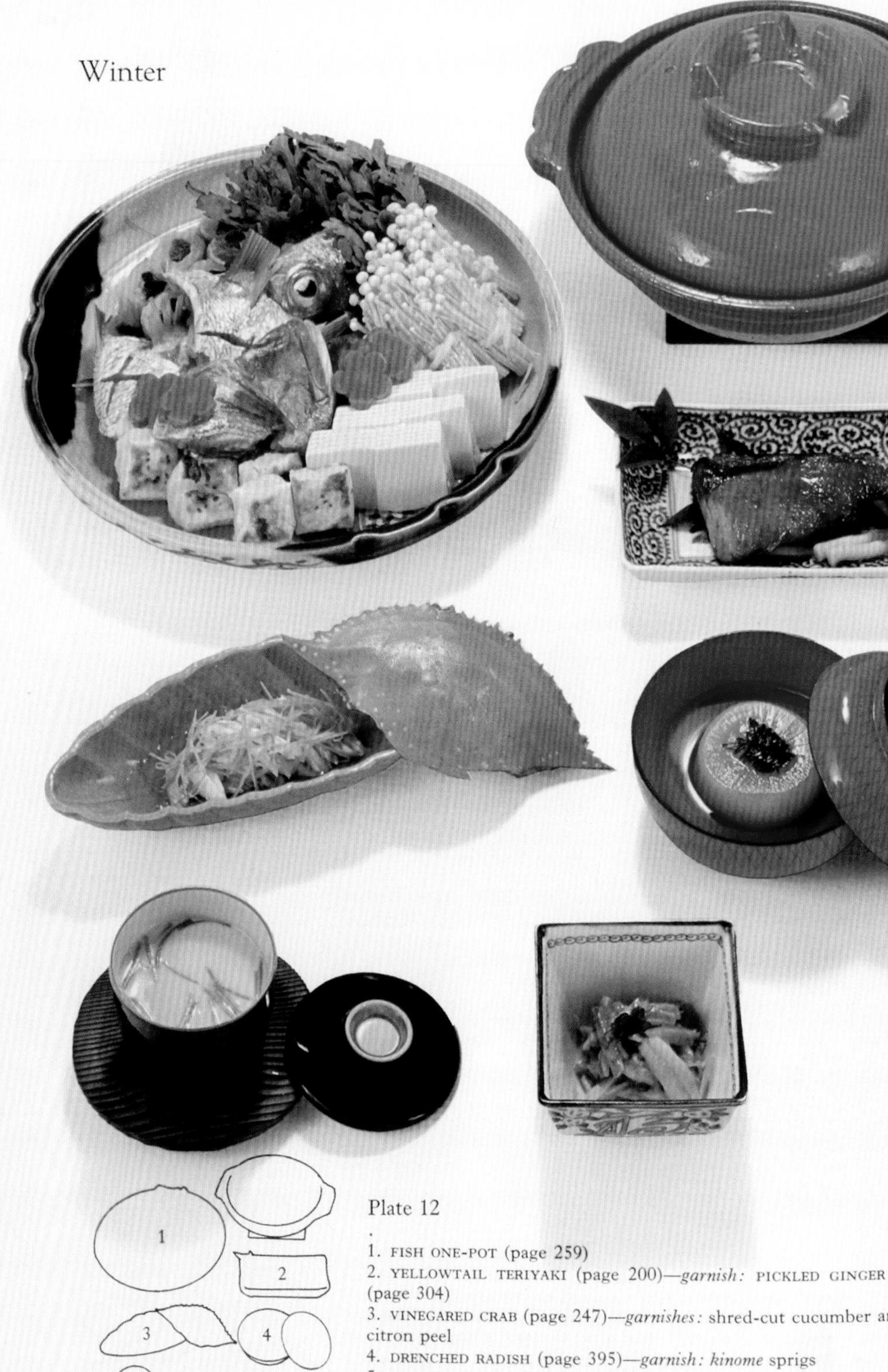

Plate 12

1. FISH ONE-POT (page 259)
2. YELLOWTAIL TERIYAKI (page 200)—*garnish:* PICKLED GINGER SH
(page 304)
3. VINEGARED CRAB (page 247)—*garnishes:* shred-cut cucumber and
citron peel
4. DRENCHED RADISH (page 395)—*garnish: kinome* sprigs
5. SAVORY CUP CUSTARD (page 214)
6. SHELLFISH WITH MISO DRESSING (page 252)—*garnish: benitade*

Fish

Plate 13

1. SAKÉ-SIMMERED FLOUNDER (page 224)—*garnish: kinome* sprigs
2. FLOUNDER TREASURE SHIPS (page 405)—*garnishes:* small green peppers; noodle "whisk"; lemon wedge; *dip:* salt
3. SEA BREAM STEAMED WITH BUCKWHEAT NOODLES (page 375)—*garnishes:* chopped green onion; *wasabi* horseradish; shreds of toasted *nori* seaweed
4. SEA BREAM SASHIMI (page 164)—*garnishes:* RED MAPLE RADISH (page 170); chopped green onion
5. GRILLED RED TILEFISH "WAKASA" (page 363)—*garnishes:* lemon wedge; pickled ginger shoot
6. YELLOWTAIL LEMON SASHIMI (page 352)—*garnishes: shiso* buds; *bōfu*; carrot curl; *wasabi* horseradish; *dip:* Tosa soy sauce

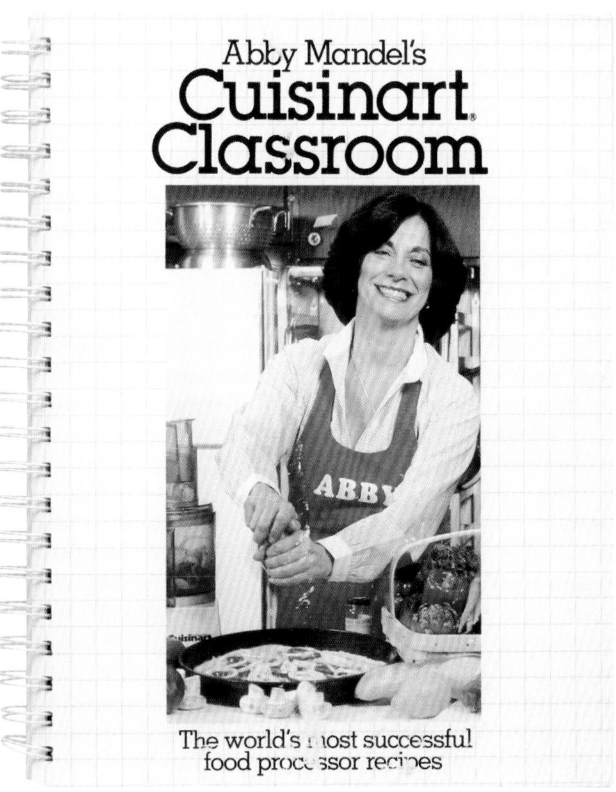

ABBY MANDEL

Abby Mandel's Cuisinart Classroom

The World's Most Successful Food Processor Recipes, 1980

Abby Mandel was fond of quoting from Ecclesiastes: "A man hath no better thing under the sun than to eat, drink and be merry." And she spent her life helping make this proverb a reality for the average home cook.

Most people know her from *Abby Mandel's Cuisinart Classroom,* because this book taught us how to make the best use of the newfangled Cuisinart food processors we bought in the late 1970s and early 1980s.

In the early 1970s, Carl Sontheimer, a retired physicist, had a brilliant idea. He had seen the large-scale food processors used in mass food production that chopped, sliced, and diced foods. These machines could do in seconds what would take sous-chefs hours of manual labor. Sontheimer, who was a hobby cook, thought: Why not make a home version of the food processor? So he set about creating the Cuisinart. The early machines, which were very expensive, became the signature gadget for anyone with gourmet pretentions. Julia Child, James Beard, and Craig Claiborne all weighed in on how efficient and useful the new machine was. But it was Abby Mandel, with *Cuisinart Classroom* and the demonstrations she gave across the country, who actually taught people how to get the most out of the machine.

Cooking was not Mandel's first profession. She received a bachelor's degree in sociology and a master's in social work. In the early 1970s she met Julia Child and decided to switch careers and pursue her love of cooking. Mandel enrolled in La Varenne cooking school in Paris and trained in a variety of restaurants in France, Switzerland, and Belgium. She found, however, that haute cuisine was not where her heart lay. She was more interested in the home cook who wanted to make delicious, elegant food with good, fresh ingredients. To that end, she wrote for a host of newspapers and magazines, including the *Chicago Tribune* and *Bon Appétit,* sharing her love of simple food. During the 1980s Mandel became very active in the farmers' market and sustainable agriculture movement. She was the driving force behind Chicago's Green City Market, including creating a foundation to help sustain the market year-round.

NOTABLE RECIPES: Banana Bread (page 571) • **Béarnaise Sauce** (page 526) • **Eleven-Layer Salad** (page 364) • Glazed Chocolate Torte • Mushroom, Green Pepper, and Pepperoni Pizza/Pizza Dough • Pie Crust • **Ratatouille** (page 396)

JENNIFER BRENNAN

The Original Thai Cookbook,

1981

Americans have had a longstanding love of Asian foods, but from the 1970s on, Indian, Thai, Vietnamese, Malaysian, Cambodian, and other Southeast Asian restaurants began to appear in American cities and to displace Chinese food. We can't seem to get enough of the aroma of lemongrass, the heat of chiles, or the tang of fish sauce. Certainly, immigration of Southeast Asians to the United States is responsible for part of the interest in these foods, but perhaps the Vietnam War taught a generation of men and women just how amazing these cuisines are, as World War II had done for their parents with French and Italian food. Whatever the cause, we crave sticky rice, satay, summer rolls, peanut sauce. Thai cooking in particular has become a mainstay of the American diet. In our health-conscious, weight-conscious world of the late twentieth century, Thai food offered a lighter, brighter option for tasting Asian flavors than the often deep-fried Chinese cooking. Jennifer Brennan's *Original Thai Cookbook* is one of the early publications about this tantalizing cuisine that made the dishes accessible to home cooks.

NOTABLE RECIPES: Beef Balls in Peanut Sauce (page 546) • Chicken and Coconut Milk Soup • Chicken Lemongrass Soup • Combination Thai Fried Rice • Fried Broccoli with Shrimp/Pak Pad Gup Gung • **Green Chicken Curry** (page 510) • Green Curry Paste • **Hot and Sour Shrimp Soup** (page 339) • Red Curry Paste • Thai Beef Salad • Satay • Tom Yom Gong Soup

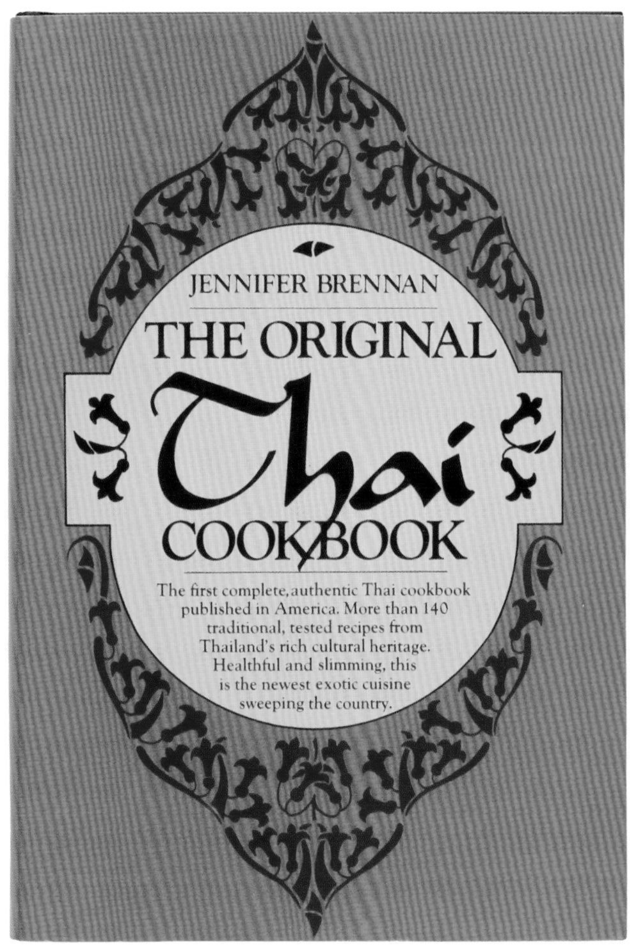

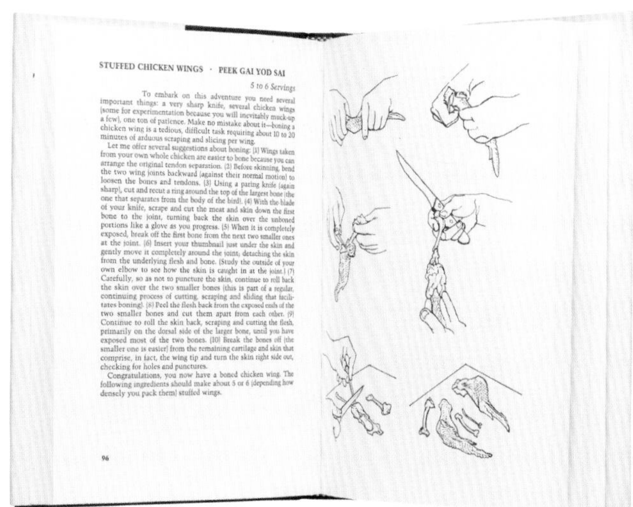

STUFFED CHICKEN WINGS · PEEK GAI YOD SAI

5 to 6 Servings

To embark on this adventure you need several important things: a very sharp knife, several chicken wings (some for experimentation because you will inevitably muck-up a few), one ton of patience. Make no mistake about it—boning a chicken wing is a tedious, difficult task requiring about 10 to 20 minutes of arduous scraping and slicing per wing.

Let me offer several suggestions about boning: (1) Wings taken from your own whole chicken are easier to bone because you can arrange the original tendon separation. (2) Before skinning, bend the two wing joints backward (against their normal motion) to loosen the bones and tendons. (3) Using a paring knife (again sharp), cut and recut a ring around the top of the largest bone (the one that separates from the body of the bird). (4) With the blade of your knife, scrape and cut the meat and skin down the first bone to the joint, turning back the skin over the unboned portions like a glove as you progress. (5) When it is completely exposed, break off the first bone from the next two smaller ones at the joint. (6) Insert your thumbnail just under the skin and gently move it completely around the joint, detaching the skin from the underlying flesh and bone. (Study the outside of your own elbow to see how the skin is caught in at the joint.) (7) Carefully, so as not to puncture the skin, continue to roll back the skin over the two smaller bones (this is part of a regular, continuing process of cutting, scraping and sliding that facilitates boning). (8) Peel the flesh back from the exposed ends of the two smaller bones and cut them apart from each other. (9) Continue to roll the skin back, scraping and cutting the flesh, primarily on the dorsal side of the larger bone, until you have exposed most of the two bones. (10) Break the bones off (the smaller one is easier) from the remaining cartilage and skin that comprise, in fact, the wing tip and turn the skin right side out, checking for holes and punctures.

Congratulations, you now have a boned chicken wing. The following ingredients should make about 5 or 6 (depending how densely you pack them) stuffed wings.

96

PENELOPE CASAS

The Foods and Wines of Spain, 1982

Americans did not warm to Spanish cuisines as readily as they did to French, Chinese, and Italian cuisines. When asked why, Penelope Casas, who has been promoting Spanish foods since the 1970s, said: "People hear 'Spanish' and they think 'Mexican.' And while Mexican food is delicious, it has nothing in common with Spanish food, which uses almost no corn and much more delicate seasoning." She predicted that the 1992 Olympic Games, which were held in Barcelona, and the celebrations of the five-hundredth anniversary of Columbus's "discovery" of the New World would change all that. And to a certain extent, it did. Manchego cheese, Serrano ham, and Spanish olive oils hit the American markets and are sought out by foodies everywhere.

Casas learned about Spanish food because she married a Spanish doctor and moved to Spain. She notes that her editor at Knopf, Judith Jones, "thinks [being married to someone from another food tradition] is the perfect role for writing about a cuisine. You get to know the food from the inside, through the people who grew up with it. But because you're American, you know how to present it to American readers." She also points out the Moorish influences in Spanish cooking, such as the use of saffron, cinnamon, and cumin, which hark back to the centuries when Spain was occupied by Arabs.

Casas's book was the first major American text about true Spanish food. And it was prescient, for now Americans not only love Spanish foods and cooking, but they also look to Spain for new techniques.

NOTABLE RECIPES: Arroz a Banda • **Arroz con Pollo** (page 457) • Catalan-Style Salad • **Chorizo** (page 558) • **Gambas al Ajillo "Rincon de España"** (page 490) • Gazpacho • **Empanadillas de Carne** (page 327) • Paella a la Valenciana • Pollo en Pepitoria • **Sangria** (page 313) • **Tortilla Española** (page 466) • Veal Extremena

THE LAY OF THE LAND

The word terroir usually refers to the specific qualities of the land where wines are produced. The term has come to mean any specific area that imparts a distinctive quality to foods grown or raised there. There is no question that the integrity of most food traditions relies on the land where the ingredients are grown. Cookbooks often reproduce maps of the geographic regions where their foods are from, reminding us of the important connection between what we eat and where it is grown.

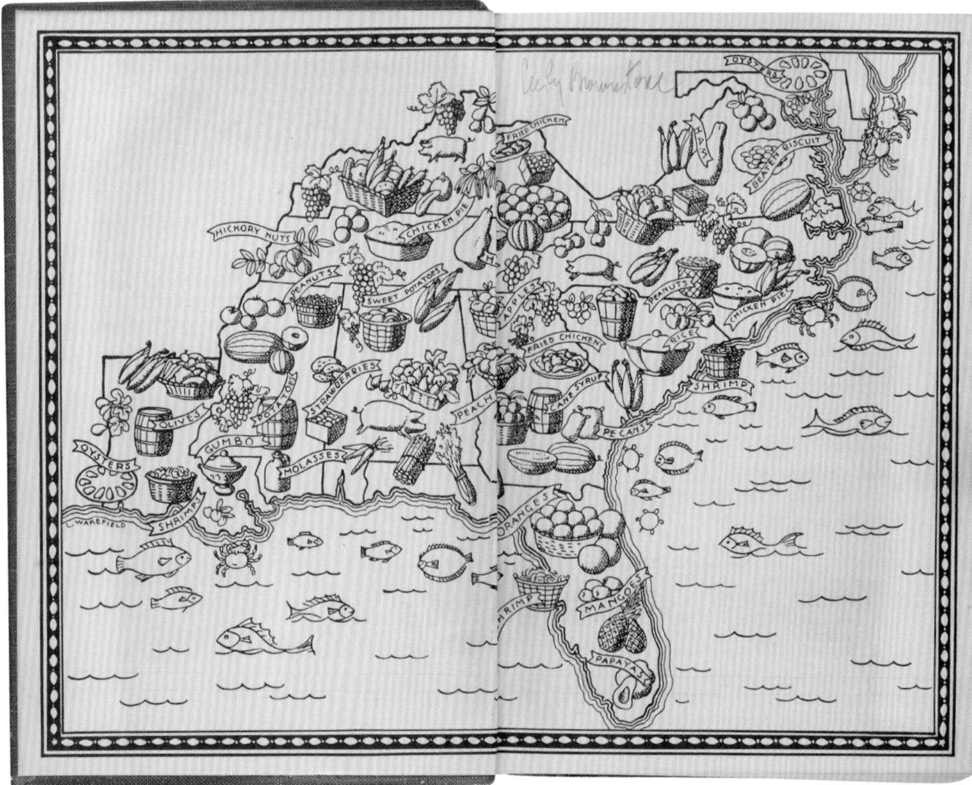

THIS PAGE, FROM TOP:

Penelope Casas, *The Foods and Wines of Spain*

Mrs. S.R. Dull, *Southern Cooking*

OPPOSITE PAGE, FROM TOP:

Lynne Rossetto Kasper, *The Splendid Table*

George Lang, *The Cuisine of Hungary*

EMILIAROMAGNA
PIACENZA
PARMA
REGGIO
MODENA
BOLOGNA
FERRARA
RAVENNA
FORLI
RIMINI
Scale
30 miles
48 kilometers

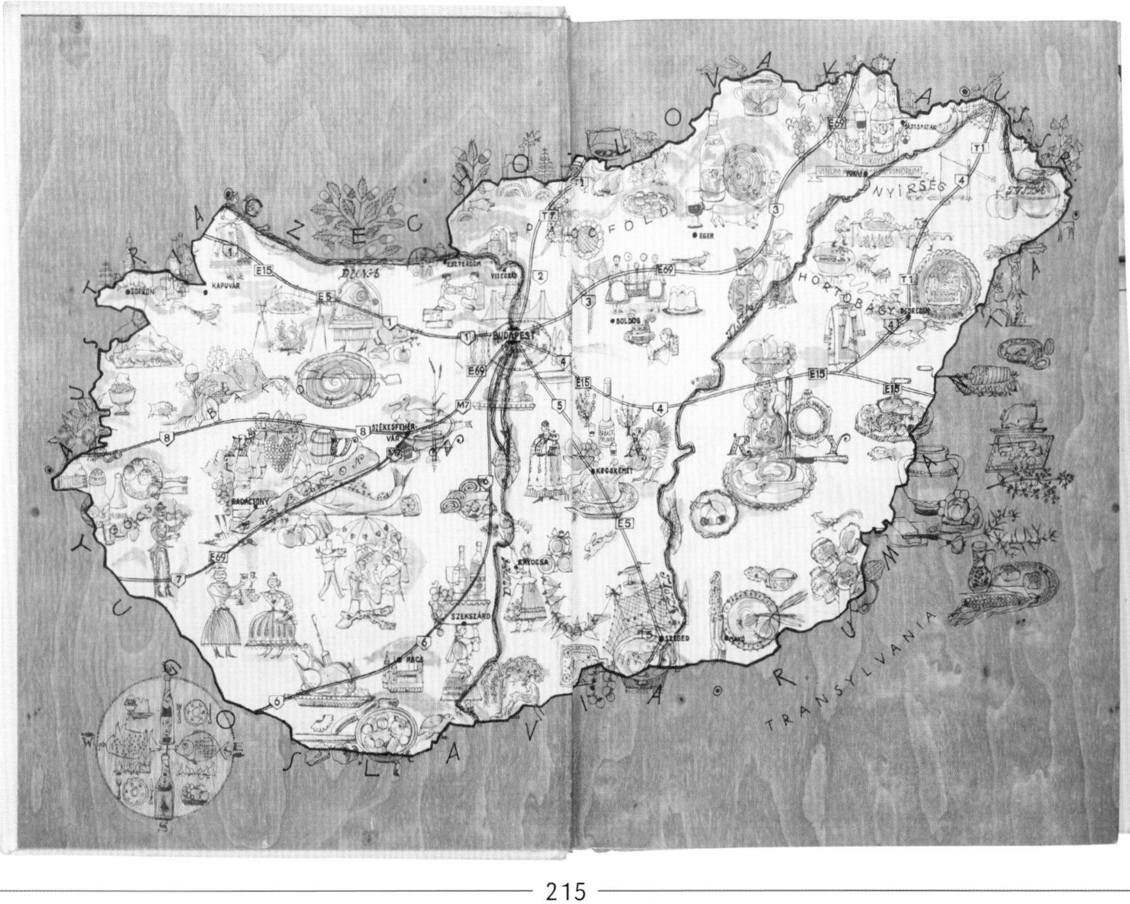

BUDAPEST
EGER
SZEGED
SOPRON
KAPUVÁR
ESZTERGOM
VISEGRÁD
SZÉKESFEHÉRVÁR
BADACSONY
KECSKEMÉT
KALOCSA
SZEKSZÁRD
NYÍRSÉG
HORTOBÁGY
TRANSYLVANIA
E15
E5
E69
M7

THE
SILVER PALATE
C·O·O·K·B·O·O·K

Delicious recipes, menus, tips, lore from Manhattan's celebrated gourmet food shop.

JULEE ROSSO & SHEILA LUKINS
WITH MICHAEL McLAUGHLIN

JULEE ROSSO AND SHEILA LUKINS

The Silver Palate Cookbook, 1982

"Ah, the eighties" Jonathan Gold said about *The Silver Palate Cookbook*. Nothing captures the new spirit of cooking that took America by storm in the 1980s like *The Silver Palate*. By the mid-1970s, Sheila Lukins, who graduated from New York University in 1970 and studied at the Cordon Bleu, was a divorced mother of two, making a living as the owner of the Other Woman Catering Company, which she ran out of her apartment in the famous Dakota apartment building on the Upper West Side of Manhattan.

Julee Rosso, who was Lukins's business partner, said of the seventies, "Back then, New York bachelors would throw dinner parties, but all they really wanted to do was pick out the wine." Lukins began cooking menus that expanded the palates of her clients, including dishes such as curried soups and Greek and Moroccan main courses. Lukins and Rosso realized there was a new group of educated, working women who didn't have time to cook, but who were still interested in good, tasty food. So they decided to open a store that would appeal to this new class of New York professionals. They initially planned to call it Seaboard Deluxe, which is coffee-shop slang for an order to go, but food writer Florence Fabricant suggested they call it the Silver Palate. The store was an instant hit, spawning a line of food products under the same name, and its boldly flavored dishes sparked cooking as a hobby.

Suddenly an interest in preparing gourmet foods at home expanded beyond the relatively small coterie of food insiders who huddled together in Greenwich Village near the Florence Meat Market—Balducci's, Ottomanelli's, Faicco's, Murray's Cheese Shop, and the wonderful grocers of Little Italy and Chinatown, not to mention Di Palo's, the famous cheese shop on Mulberry and Grand. In the relative food wasteland of the Upper West Side, at Seventy-third and Columbus Avenue, to be exact, the Silver Palate was an oasis of taste for the food adventurer.

In 1982 Workman published *The Silver Palate Cookbook*, and suddenly across the country everyone was serving one of the signature dishes, Chicken Marbella, with its prunes and capers. Lukins went on to write several other cookbooks, but it was *The Silver Palate*—translated into many languages and selling more than two and a half million copies—that defined a turning point in American food and cooking. Sheila Lukins passed away at the young age of sixty-six in 2009. Her family generously donated her books, including copies of all the editions and translations of *The Silver Palate Cookbook*, to the Fales Library.

NOTABLE RECIPES: Chicken Marbella (page 501) • Chili for a Crowd • **Curried Butternut Squash Soup** (page 348) • Decadent Chocolate Cake • **Pasta Puttanesca** (page 444) • Roast Lamb with Peppercorn Crust • **Salmon Mousse** (page 322) • Six Onion Soup • **Tarragon Chicken Salad** (page 369) • Tomato, Montrachet and Basil Salad

GOUGERE

Gougère, the splendid hot cheese pastry from the Burgundy region of France, makes a spectacularly easy cocktail snack. Of course it is delicious with a glass of red wine, but we also love to serve it with the best vintage Port we can muster. Traditionally it is baked into a large, wreathlike ring, but it is easier to handle at cocktail time if formed into tiny individual puffs.

1 cup milk
8 tablespoons (1 stick) sweet butter
1 teaspoon salt
1 cup sifted unbleached, all-purpose flour
5 eggs
1½ cups grated imported Parmesan cheese (or half Parmesan, half Gruyère), plus an additional ½ cup grated Parmesan to top puffs (optional)

1. Combine milk, butter and salt in a small saucepan and bring to a boil. Remove pan from heat and add the flour all at once. Whisk vigorously for a few moments, then return the pan to medium heat and cook, stirring constantly, until the batter has thickened and is pulling away from the sides and bottom of the pan—5 minutes or less.
2. Again remove pan from the heat and stir in 4 eggs, one at a time, making certain the first egg is completely incorporated before adding the second. Then stir in the cheese or cheeses.
3. Preheat oven to 375°F. Lightly butter a baking sheet.
4. Drop the batter by tablespoons onto baking sheet, spacing the puffs at least 1 inch apart.
5. Beat remaining egg in a small bowl. Brush the tops of the puffs with the beaten egg, and sprinkle with additional Parmesan if you use it.
6. Set baking sheet on the center rack of the oven, reduce heat to 350°F., and bake for 15 to 20 minutes, or until *gougères* are puffed and well browned. Serve immediately.

About 20 puffs

COCKTAIL PUFFS

Any number of soft, savory mixtures can be used to fill a tiny cocktail puff. For the puffs, use Pâte à Choux (see page 335). Elsewhere in this book you will find recipes for Tapenade, Pâté Maison, Taramosalata, Salmon Mousse and Peasant Caviar. We have tried them all in puffs at one time or another with great success.

STUFFED GRAPE LEAVES

50 medium-size preserved grape leaves (1 or 2 jars)
1 pound very lean lamb, ground
16 ounces canned Italian plum tomatoes, crushed
1 cup raw long-grain rice
1 cup best-quality olive oil
2 bunches of scallions (green onions), chopped
3 cups loosely packed fresh mint leaves, chopped
juice of 2 lemons

1. Drain the grape leaves, separate them and rinse them under running water, being careful not to tear them. Reserve.
2. Combine lamb, crushed tomatoes and their liquid, rice, olive oil, scallions and mint.
3. Lay a grape leaf, vein side up, stem toward you, on your work surface. Place 1 tablespoon of filling at the base of the leaf and roll up, tucking in excess leaf at the sides to make a tiny bundle. Repeat with remaining filling and leaves, packing each bundle seam side down into a small kettle.
4. Squeeze lemon juice over the leaf bundles, and add water nearly to cover. Weight with 1 or 2 small plates or saucers. Cover, bring to a boil, reduce heat, and simmer for 1 hour, or until rice in stuffing is completely cooked.
5. Serve hot, or cool and refrigerate the leaves in their cooking liquid. Offer plain yogurt seasoned to taste with lemon juice and coarse salt as a dip or sauce.

Approximately 50 grape leaves

STUFFED MUSHROOMS

Easterners like them whiter than white, while Westerners prefer them a bit beige, but in any case the widely cultivated American button mushroom must always be at its freshest for the cocktail hour. It is terrific raw, marinated or cooked. When stuffed, it becomes a perfect finger food. It is quiet, attractive and completely self-contained.

SAUSAGE-STUFFED MUSHROOMS

2 Italian sweet sausages, about ⅓ pound
¼ teaspoon fennel seeds
pinch of red pepper flakes (optional)
¼ cup finely minced yellow onion
1 garlic clove, peeled and minced
olive oil, as necessary
¼ cup chopped parsley
¼ cup chopped black olives, preferably imported
⅓ cup thick Béchamel Sauce (see page 341)
salt and freshly ground black pepper, to taste
12 large white mushrooms
imported Parmesan cheese to taste

1. Remove sausage meat from casings and crumble into a small skillet. Sauté gently, stirring often, until meat is thoroughly done. Season with fennel and, if desired, red pepper flakes. With a slotted spoon, remove sausage to a bowl, leaving the rendered fat in the skillet.
2. Sauté onion and garlic in the rendered fat, adding a little olive oil if necessary, until tender and golden, about 25 minutes. Stir in chopped parsley and add to reserved sausage meat.
3. Stir olives and béchamel into the sausage mixture; combine thoroughly. Taste the mixture, and season with salt and pepper if necessary.
4. Pull the stems off the mushrooms and save for another use. Wipe mushroom caps with a damp cloth and season lightly with salt and pepper.
5. Fill each cap generously with the stuffing. Arrange caps in a lightly oiled baking dish. Sprinkle the tops of the stuffing with Parmesan cheese to taste.
6. Bake at 450°F. for about 15 minutes, or until bubbling and well browned. Let settle for 5 minutes before serving.

3 or 4 portions

AN AIOLI PLATTER

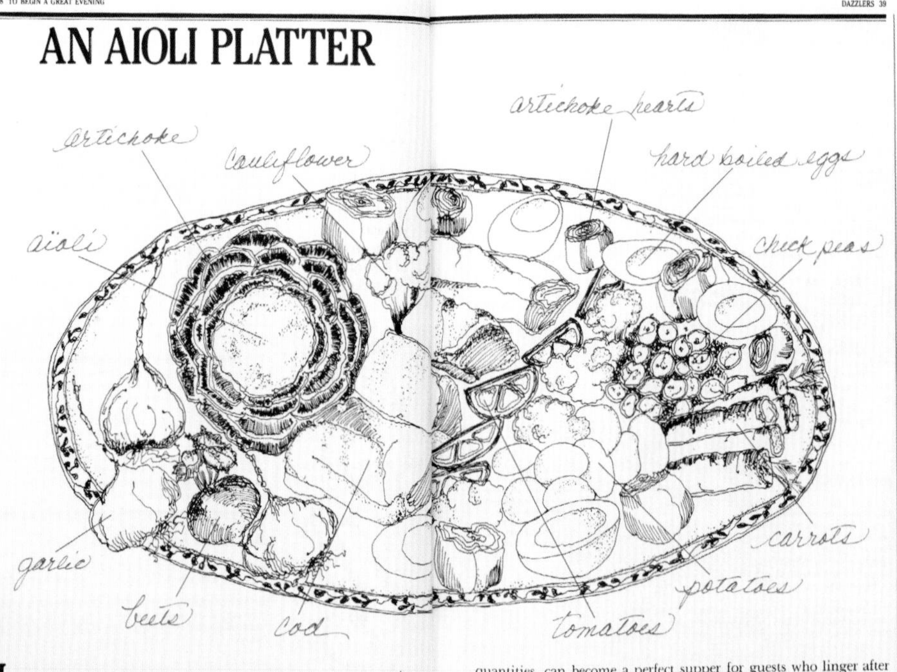

In Provence, feast days are often celebrated by a lusty community meal in which poached fish, cooked vegetables and a garlicky Aïoli sauce are the main components. This same feast, arranged in smaller quantities, can become a perfect supper for guests who linger after drinks. The colors are intense, the flavors powerful. Aïoli brings Provence to your buffet. (Recipe follows.)

CHICKEN MARBELLA

This was the first main-course dish to be offered at The Silver Palate, and the distinctive colors and flavors of the prunes, olives and capers have kept it a favorite for years. It's good hot or at room temperature. When prepared with small drumsticks and wings, it makes a delicious hors d'oeuvre.

The overnight marination is essential to the moistness of the finished product: the chicken keeps and even improves over several days of refrigeration; it travels well and makes excellent picnic fare.

Since Chicken Marbella is such a spectacular party dish, we give quantities to serve 10 to 12, but the recipe can successfully be divided to make a smaller amount if you wish.

4 chickens, 2½ pounds each, quartered
1 head of garlic, peeled and finely puréed
¼ cup dried oregano
coarse salt and freshly ground black pepper to taste
½ cup red wine vinegar
½ cup olive oil
1 cup pitted prunes
½ cup pitted Spanish green olives
½ cup capers with a bit of juice
6 bay leaves
1 cup brown sugar
1 cup white wine
¼ cup Italian parsley or fresh coriander (cilantro), finely chopped

1. In a large bowl combine chicken quarters, garlic, oregano, pepper and coarse salt to taste, vinegar, olive oil, prunes, olives, capers and juice, and bay leaves. Cover and let marinate, refrigerated, overnight.
2. Preheat oven to 350°F.
3. Arrange chicken in a single layer in one or two large, shallow baking pans and spoon marinade over it evenly. Sprinkle chicken pieces with brown sugar and pour white wine around them.
4. Bake for 50 minutes to 1 hour, basting frequently with pan juices. Chicken is done when thigh pieces, pricked with a fork at their thickest, yield clear yellow (rather than pink) juice.
5. With a slotted spoon transfer chicken, prunes, olives and capers to a serving platter. Moisten with a few spoonfuls of pan juices and sprinkle generously with parsley or cilantro. Pass remaining pan juices in a sauceboat.
6. To serve Chicken Marbella cold, cool to room temperature in cooking juices before transferring to a serving platter. If chicken has been covered and refrigerated, allow it to return to room temperature before serving. Spoon some of the reserved juice over chicken.

16 pieces, 10 or more portions

THE CHICKEN CHART

BROILERS:
1 to 2½ pounds; young chickens with little fat.

BROILERS/FRYERS:
2½ to 3½ pounds. Butchers use these terms interchangeably. If you prepare them well, these chickens may be cooked either way. Look for yellow fat and plump breasts.

ROASTERS/PULLETS:
3½ to 6½ pounds; good for roasting, baking, barbecuing and quick cooking. Bred for tenderness and very meaty.

HENS AND FOWL:
Up to 8 pounds; best for stock or chicken salad. They require longer and slower cooking but are by far the most flavorful.

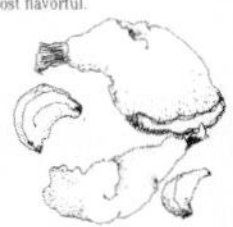

COUNTRY WEEKEND LUNCH

Cheese Straws
Crudités and assorted dips

Chicken Marbella
Semolina Bread
Boucheron cheese

Lime Mousse
Chocolate Chip Cookies

✣ FROM THE SILVER PALATE NOTEBOOK

Successful flavoring depends on many things. To appreciate this fully you must experiment. Try some lemon in the rice. Grate an orange on the broccoli. Next time combine meat with fresh fruit. You may feel the need to experiment with small batches at first; as your confidence and your palate develop, you will learn to create boldly, trusting in the results. You will be a cook.

RASPBERRY CHICKEN

Boneless chicken breasts are quick and economical to serve but often dull to eat. In this recipe, ready in minutes, raspberry vinegar lends a bit of welcome tartness, mellowed by chicken stock and heavy cream. A handful of fresh raspberries, poached briefly in the sauce just before serving, adds an elegant note. Wild rice and a simply sautéed green vegetable would be good accompaniments.

2 whole boneless, skinless chicken breasts, about 2 pounds
2 tablespoons sweet butter
¼ cup finely chopped yellow onion
*4 tablespoons raspberry vinegar**
¼ cup Chicken Stock (see page 342), or canned chicken broth
¼ cup heavy cream, or Crème Fraîche (see page 339)
1 tablespoon canned crushed tomatoes
16 fresh raspberries (optional)

1. Cut each chicken breast into halves along the breastbone line. Remove the filet mignon, the finger-size muscle on the back of each half, and reserve for another use. Flatten each breast half or *suprême* by pressing it gently with the palm of your hand.
2. Melt the butter in a large skillet. Raise the heat, add the *suprêmes*, and cook for about 3 minutes per side, or until they are lightly colored. Remove from the skillet and reserve.
3. Add the onion to the fat in the pan and cook, covered, over low heat until tender, about 15 minutes.
4. Add the vinegar, raise the heat and cook, uncovered, stirring occasionally, until vinegar is reduced to a syrupy spoonful. Whisk in the chicken stock, heavy cream or *crème fraîche*, and crushed tomatoes and simmer for 1 minute.
5. Return *suprêmes* to the skillet and simmer them gently in the sauce, basting often, until they are just done and the sauce has been reduced and thickened slightly, about 5 minutes; do not overcook.
6. Remove *suprêmes* with a slotted spoon and arrange on a heated serving platter. Add the raspberries to the sauce in the skillet and cook over low heat for 1 minute. Do not stir the berries with a spoon, merely swirl them in the sauce by shaking the skillet.
7. Pour sauce over *suprêmes* and serve immediately.

2 to 4 portions

*Available in specialty food stores. The intensity of vinegars varies from brand to brand. Be prepared to adjust this quantity to suit your own taste.

SALADS ON THE GREEN

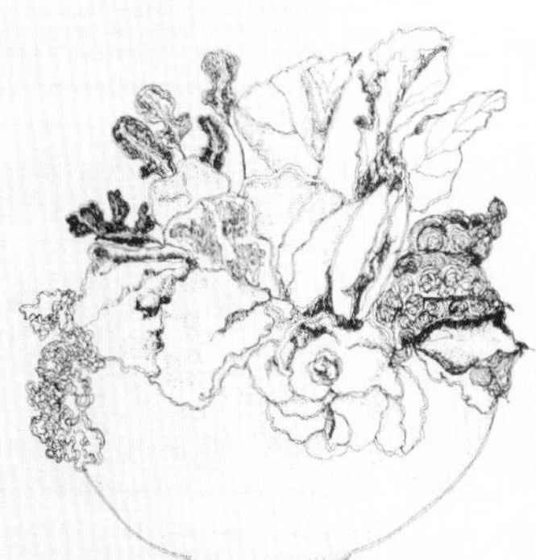

The salads that come after the main course are most often green salads, and while they are called the relief of the dinner, they should by no means be boring.

Need we say that iceberg lettuce from the salad bar, laden with this garnish and that, is not our idea of a "tossed green salad"? It should instead consist of everything cool, green and crisp, gently tossed at the last moment with a superb vinaigrette.

Be adventurous but wise in combining the glorious greens available to you from market and garden. Use a judiciously light dressing, made by hand from fresh, good-quality ingredients. Always serve salads as soon as they are tossed.

Treated thus with imagination and respect, the simple green salad can become one of the glories of your table. Our favorite green combinations and dressings follow.

A GREEN SAMPLER

Salad greens vary dramatically in taste, texture and color. When combined with other summer foods and endless vinaigrettes they can match every mood and occasion.

Be certain to rinse the greens carefully and dry them thoroughly. Keep them crisp in the refrigerator, wrapped in a towel, or stored in a covered bowl until serving time.

ARUGULA: Intense in color and pungent in flavor, it is an ideal companion to softer and sweeter leaves and wonderful on its own. Toss with a strong vinaigrette and sprinkle with sieved, hard-cooked egg.

BELGIAN ENDIVE: Crisp and opalescent, it is so special it makes a great first course combined with thinly sliced prosciutto and red wine basil vinaigrette.

BIBB LETTUCE: Delectably small, tight leaves with a crunchy sweetness. Bibb leaves are best on their own with a light vinaigrette.

BOSTON LETTUCE: Pale green, loosely packed and tender, this fragile green has a pleasing hearty flavor.

CHICORY: Tart and crunchy, it combines well with other vegetables for a salad or entree course.

CRESS ALBISEOIS: The most delicate of cresses, it deserves a delicate vinaigrette. Watch for it in the market.

DANDELION GREENS: Wild or cultivated, they have a refreshing tart taste alone or in a combination with other greens. Be certain they're young and fresh.

ESCAROLE: Yellow-white leaves with a pleasantly tart flavor that can take stronger dressings than other leaves.

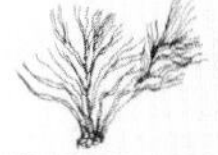

FENNEL GREENS: Snip the feathery tips of anise-flavored fennel into mixed green salads as a seasoning.

FIELD LETTUCE or LAMB'S TONGUE (MACHE): A lovely fall and winter green that comes in small bunches. Combine with other greens.

ICEBERG LETTUCE: As a last resort, we think.

LEAF LETTUCE: Curly, green- or red-tipped, the tasty, tender leaves of the various leaf lettuces are rather soft in texture. Especially delicious when young.

NASTURTIUM LEAVES: Use sparingly with milder greens. They give a surprising peppery flavor.

PURSLANE: Vinegary flavor, crisp texture that complements milder greens.

RADICCHIO: A ruby-red miniature leaf with a slightly bitter flavor. This mixes color and flavor with other greens and can stand a hearty vinaigrette.

RED LEAF LETTUCE: Purple-red, it is a soft crinkly lettuce that is good to eat as well as

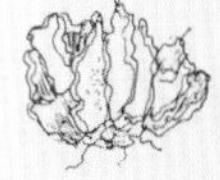

aesthetically pleasing. Use it combined with other sturdier greens.

ROMAINE: Firm tight leaves with a robust nutty flavor. This green can be dressed with a strong vinaigrette.

SORREL: The taste of lemons and light vinegar. This bright green leaf is tart, and should be mixed sparingly with milder leaves.

SPINACH: Dense, small, rounded leaves, and the crinkliest. Don't limit its complements to bacon bits and hard-cooked eggs; its flavor blends well in many combinations.

WATERCRESS: Dark green and spicy with cloverlike leaves, it is becoming a staple. Alone or mixed with others, cress has a beautiful color and is a good taste balancer.

We have some very favorite green salad combinations. Tossed with complementary vinaigrettes (see Index for recipes), the possibilities are endless.

Allow ⅓ to ½ cup of vinaigrette for every 6 servings. The dressing should gently coat the greens, not smother them.

- ♥ Watercress, Belgian endive cut into julienne, and walnut halves. Serve with Walnut Oil Vinaigrette.
- ♥ Fresh dark green arugula and delicate Bibb lettuce leaves. Serve with Garlic Dressing.

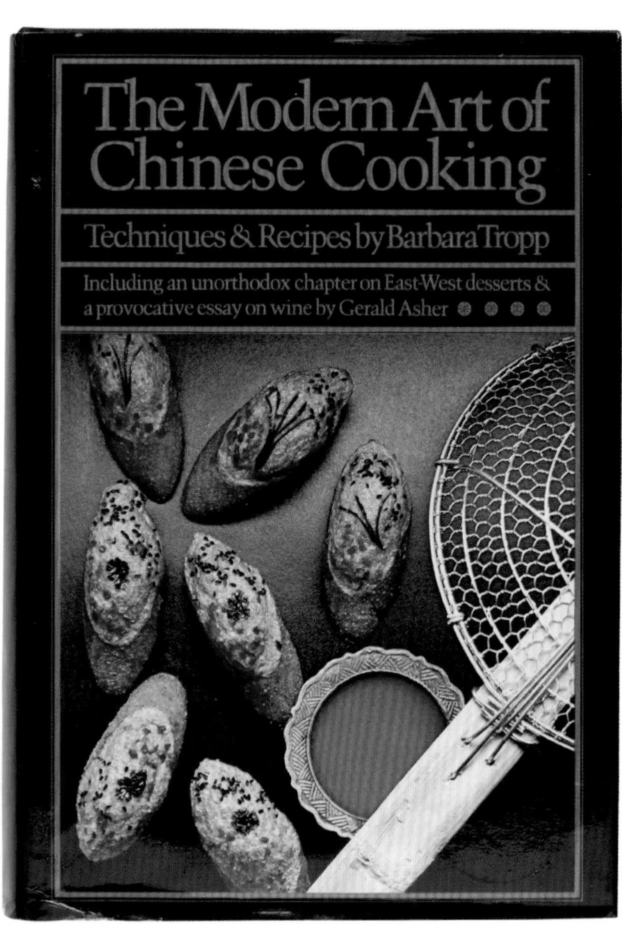

BARBARA TROPP

The Modern Art of Chinese Cooking, 1982

Barbara Tropp became fascinated with Chinese culture when she took an art history course in high school. Her adolescent interest led her to study Chinese in college and to pursue a PhD in Chinese at Princeton University. During her doctoral studies, she spent two years in Taiwan, staying with families who turned out to be obsessed with Chinese cuisine. She found her calling.

Returning to the United States, she dropped out of the doctoral program and moved to San Francisco, with its large Chinese American community and excellent Asian markets. The writer in her won out, and she soon had a book contract to write *The Modern Art of Chinese Cooking*. James Beard described the book as "a unique achievement. Her intelligent and thorough explanations are detailed and truly great. The choice of recipes is exciting. This is a magnum opus for any cooking addict." Tropp was meticulous in her attention to detail, reflecting her life as a scholar.

Her book is one of the great explanations of Chinese cuisine, and it helped her become one of the leading English-speaking experts on Chinese food. Tropp went on to open China Moon Café, a California-Chinese fusion restaurant, in San Francisco, which attracted Julia Child, who became a friend. Tropp nurtured a number of cooks who would go on to become leading chefs. Sadly, she died of ovarian cancer in 2001 at the age of fifty-three.

NOTABLE RECIPES: **Bong-Bong Chicken** (page 513) • **Dry-Fried Szechuan String Beans** (page 408) • Everyday Chinese Rice • **Hunan Pork Dumplings with Hot Sauce** (page 330) • **Mendocino Lemon Tart** (page 601) • Pan-Fried Scallion Breads • Sesame Noodles with Spicy Peanut Sauce • Smoked Chicken • Spicy Szechuan Peanut Sauce • **Strange Flavor Eggplant** (page 323)

A variation on this theme, involving the modest purchase of a flat, metal, and circular *perforated Chinese steaming tray,* is to put the metal tray on top of the stockpot, and then pile the steamer tiers on top of the tray. The tray makes a stable base for the steamer, especially useful when the diameter of the stockpot is exactly that or just a bit larger than the diameter of the steamer.

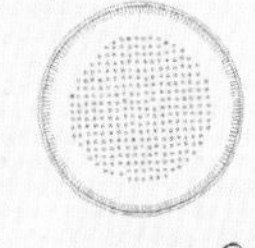
a flat, metal Chinese perforated steaming tray (top view)

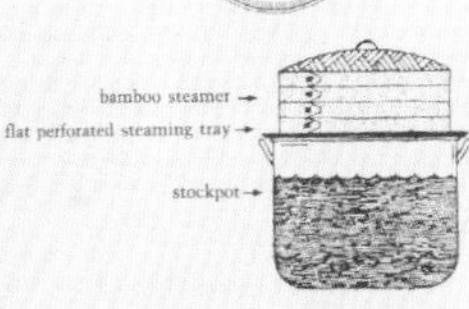

There is yet another way of using a bamboo steamer, and that is to perch it atop a *metal* steamer. This, in fact, is what I do most often in my own kitchen, where I have both sorts of steamers and frequently juggle them in combination. Sometimes, I simply borrow the metal pot as the base for the bamboo steamer when the one matches the other and there are no handles in the way. At other times, I put the bamboo tier on top of one or two of the metal tiers. This is useful either when a protruding handle gets in the way of the bamboo tier balancing directly atop the pot, or when I need a full array of steaming racks, some for steaming small items, and others for steaming larger items in a deeper space. Steamers are to the kitchen what modular book shelves are to the study, a flexible way to rearrange space imaginatively to suit your needs.

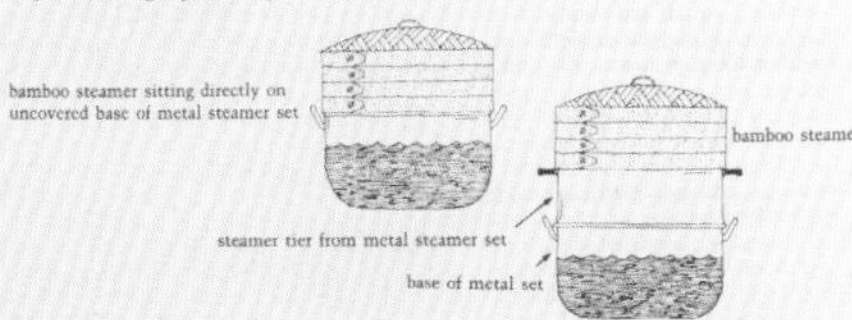

Now to the question of *improvising a steamer.* You don't have or you don't want to purchase a metal steamer set or a bamboo steamer. You want to tackle some of these recipes *right now,* so what do you do? There are several possibilities, all more or less workable, many using things snatched from one's usual cache of kitchen objects.

Most primitive and capable of being erected over a campstove is the partnership of *one large pot and several tin cans,* the cans emptied of contents and with both ends cut away. The pot must be wide enough to hold whatever you are steaming with room to spare, and the cans must be tall enough to hoist the dish you are steaming at least ¾ inch above the water. The two typical combinations are a stockpot outfitted with tall cans, or a roasting pan outfitted with short cans, the choice depending upon the size of the thing to be steamed. For instance, a plump chicken requiring an hour of steaming would do best in a stockpot with an ample amount of water beneath it, while a long fish that will steam to doneness in minutes can better recline in a roaster and requires only a shallow bit of water. Being a bad one for balance, I prefer 3 cans to the usual recommended 2, or the conscription of one large can on the order of the sort which holds vegetable shortening. With this system, you need to put the cans in the pot and hold them in place with a dish *prior* to adding boiling water to the pot, or else they will be washed askew by the bubbling of the water.

stockpot–tin can steamer

roasting pan–tin can steamer

Owing to this, I encourage the consideration of one of two helpful items, cheaply bought in a Chinese hardware store or in many Oriental markets, and bound to ease the life of any steam-it-yourselfer. Both provide a single, stable steaming base for an improvised steamer, with no need to worry about float-away cans.

The first, designed expressly for this purpose, is a *long-legged steaming trivet,* a simple rack or arrangement of metal bars permanently attached to 4 tall legs. Designed to be put into a wok, it may also be used in a stockpot (preferably, in my thinking, for the reasons stated above). Be sure it is sturdily made! My first resembled a squashed grasshopper when it collapsed on its maiden voyage under the weight of a plump duck. The longer the legs and broader the platform, the better, as you can thus fill the steamer with more water and balance the dish you are steaming more securely on top.

Soy-Dipped Red Radish Fans
涼拌紅蘿蔔

This is the Chinese version of our radish "roses," a delicate fan of crisp radish that unfolds in a zestily flavored sauce rather than in ice water. Beautiful looking and delicious, they are excellent as an edible garnish, a wine-chaser hors d'oeuvre, or a crunchy, colorful addition to any meal. ◆ The best radishes are those sold with their green, leafy tops intact. Choose them fat, firm, and unblemished, and store in a misted plastic bag until ready to use. ◆ Radish fans are best made 8–24 hours in advance, though if you're in a hurry you may use light brown sugar to season them instead of white. That quickens the marinating process somehow, though the radishes then become quite strong the next day.

TECHNIQUE NOTES:
For a fast, foolproof method of cutting fans, put a pair of wooden chopsticks flat on a cutting surface, then place a radish between the thinner (round) ends. (Most Chinese chopsticks have one round and one square end, emblematic, some say, of heaven and earth.) Pinch the thick ends of the chopsticks together, as illustrated, so the radish is held in the V-shaped wedge. Put your hand on top, simultaneously anchoring the chopsticks and grasping the radish, then cut the radish as directed. The chopsticks will prevent the knife from slicing through the fans—an altogether neat trick.

For "salting" a vegetable with salt and sugar, see TECHNIQUE NOTES, page 117.

Serves 2–3 as a nice munch, 4–6 as a smaller nibble.

INGREDIENTS:

1 dozen large, pretty red radishes

Salting ingredients:
½ teaspoon coarse kosher salt
½ teaspoon sugar

Seasonings:
2 teaspoons thin (regular) soy sauce
3–4 teaspoons brown or white sugar, to taste
¼ teaspoon Chinese or Japanese sesame oil
⅛–¼ teaspoon hot chili oil

Slicing and salting the radishes:
Trim the root and stem ends of each radish neatly, so that any green is cut away and the two ends are stark white. (If the radishes aren't perfectly fresh and hard, plump them for several hours or overnight in the refrigerator in a bowl of cold water.)

To cut the radishes into fans, hold the radish clamped between a pair of chopsticks as described above in TECHNIQUE NOTES. With a sharp, thin-bladed knife make a series of cuts $\frac{1}{16}$ inch apart across the width of the radish, cutting down to the chop-

sticks, until the top is cut like a fan. (If your fingers get in the way when you near the end, turn the radish around and complete the cuts.)

Toss the radishes in a glass or stainless bowl with the salt and sugar, then put aside for 45 minutes at room temperature, tossing occasionally.

Seasoning the fans:
Whisk the seasonings until blended and slightly thick, tasting for desired sweetness. Put aside to develop for 10 minutes.

Drain the radishes, then squeeze several at a time between your palms to extract excess liquid. Press; do not wring. Put the radishes in a clean dry bowl, then scrape the seasonings on top and toss well to mix. For best flavor, marinate 5–6 hours at room temperature or overnight in the refrigerator, to give the seasonings time to penetrate and enlarge. Toss occasionally while marinating, or place the radishes fan side down in the liquid for even absorption.

Serve chilled. Press gently with your fingers to spread the fans, and present them on a plate or in a bowl of contrasting color, with a bit of the sauce drizzled on top.

The radishes keep 2–3 days, sealed and refrigerated, and grow a bit stronger if you store them in the sauce.

MENU SUGGESTIONS:
The crunch and color of the radish fans make them a perfect garnish for dishes like *Orchid's Tangy Cool Noodles* (page 356), *Master Sauce Chicken* (page 153), *Tea and Spice Smoked Chicken* (page 158), and *Tea and Spice Smoked Fish* (page 256), or any of the mildly spiced cold noodle dishes. For picnics, they are ideal tote-alongs with *Marbelized Tea Eggs* (page 325) or *Master Sauce Eggs* (page 327). As openers for a meal, I like the radishes with a chilled, dry white wine, either alone or in tandem with *Fire-Dried Walnuts or Pecans* (page 105). Try them also with vodka or gin-based drinks—a good Martini or an ice-cold glass of vodka.

Sweet and Crunchy Red Bell Pepper Cubes
糖醋紅椒

This is a simple, crunchy "pickle" of bell pepper cubes marinated in a light dressing of soy sauce, sugar, and rice vinegar. Its bright color and clean, fresh taste would make it a welcome addition to a barbecue, a simple dinner, or a Chinese feast starring a constellation of "Little Dishes." I much prefer red to green bell pepper, but you may do this dish with either, or even mix the two, if you wish. ◆ This dish is a good discovery if you like or need to cook ahead. The peppers require 2 full days to reach their flavor peak, so you can stash them in the refrigerator and forget about them until it's time to eat.

TECHNIQUE NOTES:
When shopping for bell peppers, look for ones with vivid color, unbroken skin, and a uniform firmness. When cutting them, take care to remove any fleshy white ribs with a sharp paring knife. If the peppers are firm and the ribs are carefully removed, you are assured of a crunchy pickle.

For the use of coarse kosher salt to transform vegetables to a special crispness, see TECHNIQUE NOTES, page 110.

Yields 2 cups pepper cubes, enough to serve 4–8 as a cold dish, 10–15 as a cold nibble with a host of other dishes.

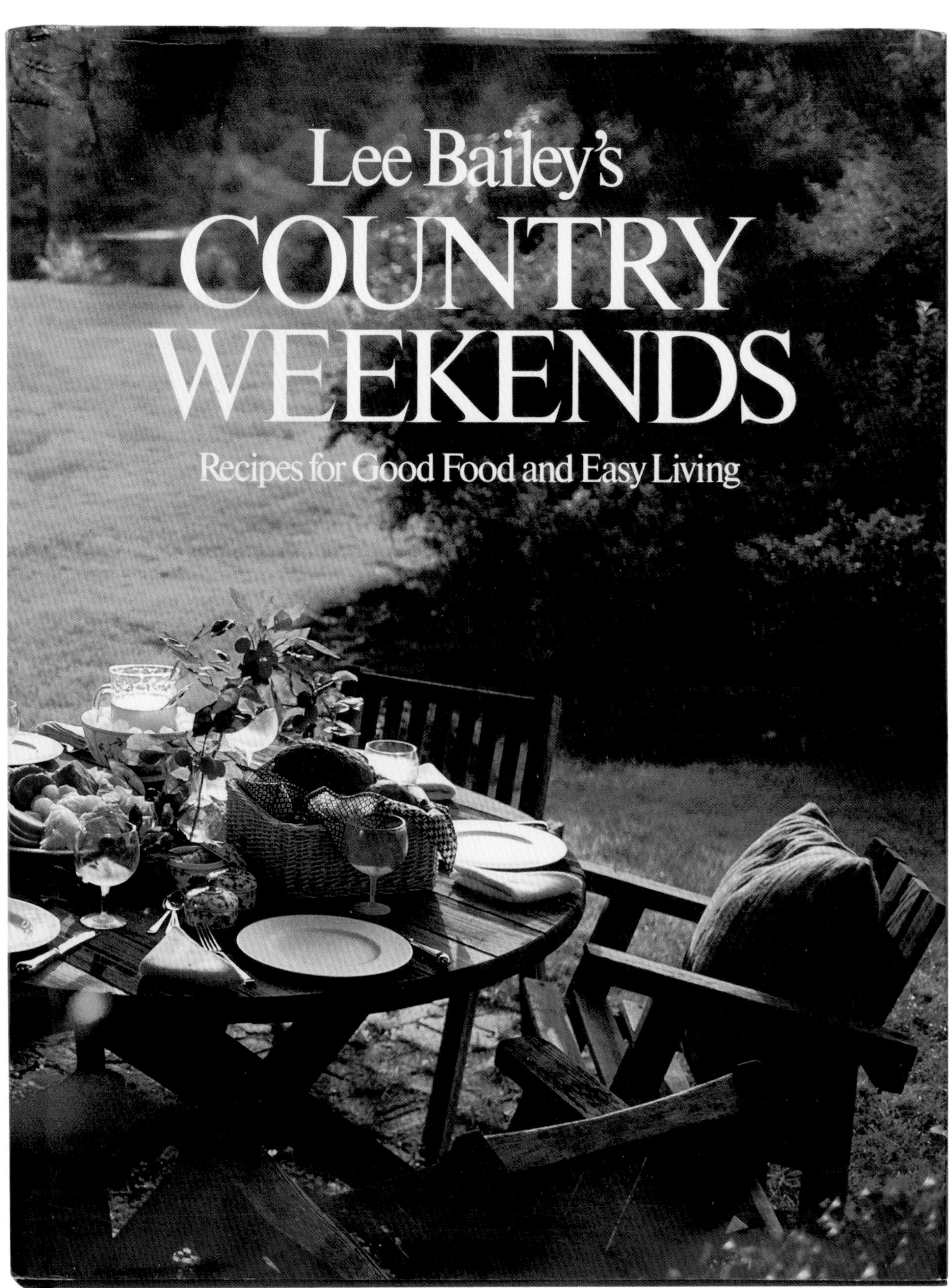
Lee Bailey's
COUNTRY
WEEKENDS
Recipes for Good Food and Easy Living

LEE BAILEY

Lee Bailey's Country Weekends,

Recipes for Good Food and Easy Living, 1983

Long before Martha Stewart became the maven of entertaining, Lee Bailey had made a career out of stylish living. Born in Bunkie, Louisiana, in 1926, Bailey served in the Army from 1945 to 1946, then attended the Parsons School of Design, graduating in 1950. He taught at Tulane University and later at Parsons. From 1974 to 1987 he owned and operated the Lee Bailey Shop in New York City, and for some years he also had a design business in Manhattan and a boutique in Southampton, New York. Bailey also worked as a columnist for such publications as *House and Garden*, the *Los Angeles Times*, the *New York Times*, and *Australian Vogue*, and as a contributing editor for *Food and Wine*.

He published eighteen books in all, but the most important was *Lee Bailey's Country Weekends*, which provided not only recipes for foods to serve for weekend guests but also photographs and ideas for making everything about the weekend a special event, including ideas for places to dine, tableware, linens, and floral arrangements. The book is lavishly illustrated with exquisite photographs of lunches by the oceanside under gay colored umbrellas and dinners on the deck overlooking the countryside.

The *New York Times* summed up Bailey's style by writing that his *Country Weekends* "included practical and easily reproduced touches like using bunches of field flowers casually stuck in a pitcher to garnish the table." Lee Bailey helped us all realize that you can't just "boil it, butter it, and dish it out." That's just food. A beautiful setting, nice table arrangements, well-composed menus, and a planned—but not taxing—schedule make for a perfect meal and a perfect weekend.

NOTABLE RECIPES: Chopped Beet, Endive, and Red Onion Salad (page 363) • Double Crust Chicken and Dumpling Pie • Green Bean and Potato Purée • **Lord Baltimore Cake** (page 630) • **Peppered Peaches** (page 412) • Sour Cream Corn Bread with Onions and Cheddar Cheese • **Turnip Custard** (page 423) • **Veal-Stuffed Sweet Red Peppers** (page 553)

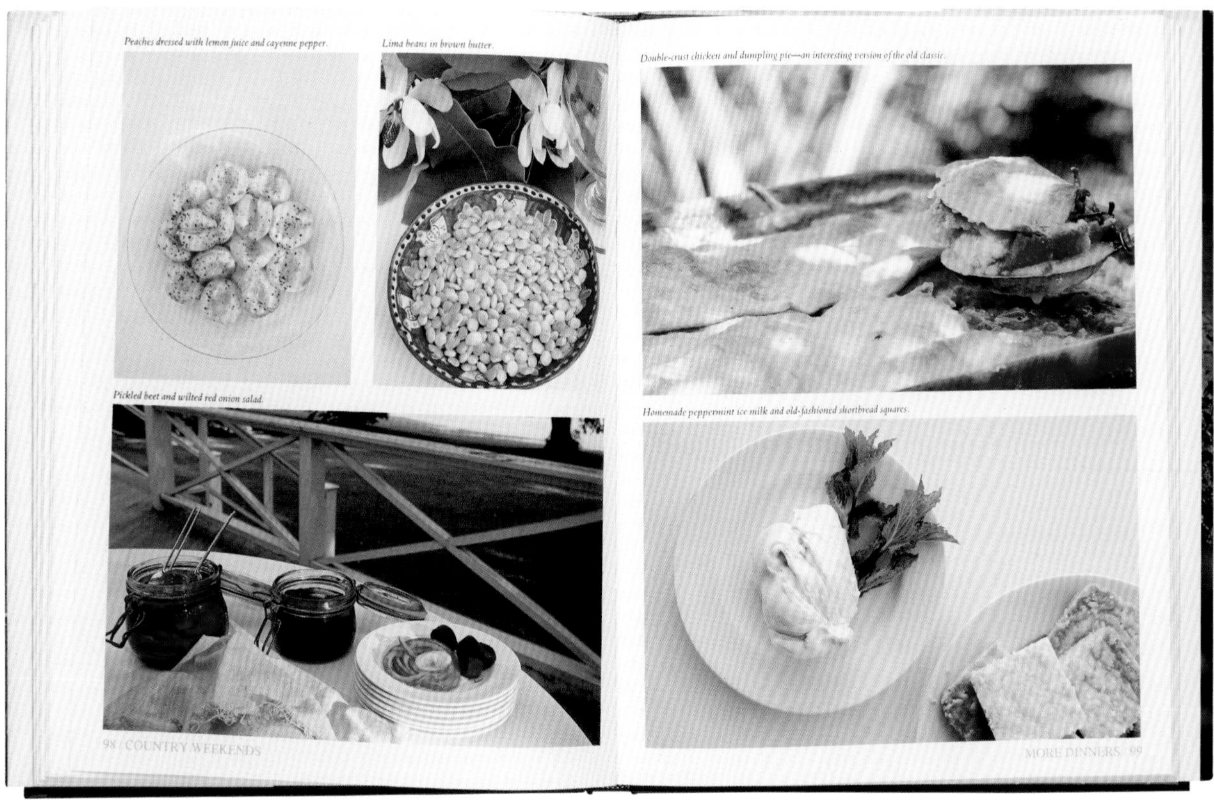

Peaches dressed with lemon juice and cayenne pepper.
Lima beans in brown butter.
Double-crust chicken and dumpling pie—an interesting version of the old classic.
Pickled beet and wilted red onion salad.
Homemade peppermint ice milk and old-fashioned shortbread squares.
98 COUNTRY WEEKENDS
MORE DINNERS 99

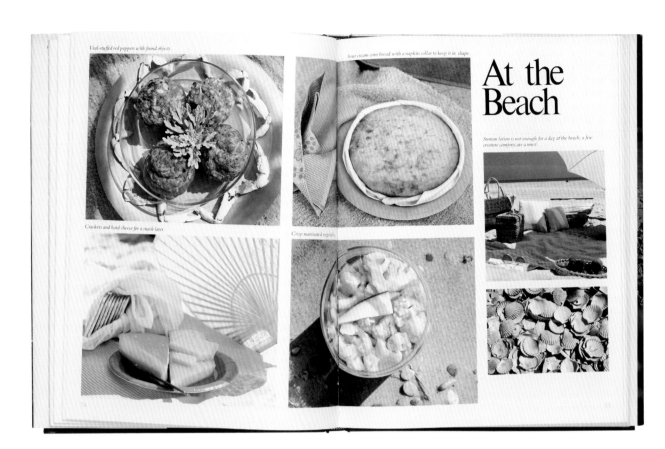

Veal-stuffed red peppers with found objects.

Sour cream corn bread with a napkin collar to keep it in shape.

At the Beach

Suntan lotion is not enough for a day at the beach; a few creature comforts are a must.

Crackers and hard cheese for a snack later.

Crisp marinated vegeta

In the Meadow

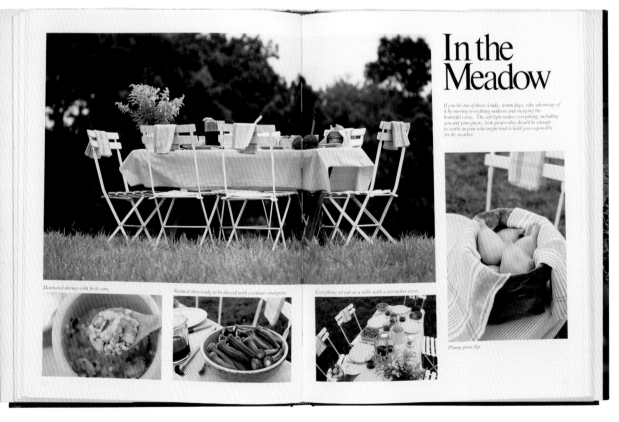

If you hit one of those cloudy, warm days, take advantage of it by moving everything outdoors and enjoying the beautiful vistas. The soft light makes everything, including you and your guests, look great—this should be enough to soothe anyone who might tend to hold you responsible for the weather.

Marinated shrimp with fresh corn.

Steamed okra ready to be dressed with a tomato vinaigrette.

Everything set out on a table with a seersucker cover.

Plump green figs.

In the Yard

Dining in the backyard can be great fun if the spirit is right. Hang the radio in the trees, and if you don't have exactly the right kind of outdoor furniture for the occasion, don't worry. Move the dining room table and chairs outside and pretend it is a Swedish movie.

MENU
(for 6 to 8)

Barbecued Veal
Warm String Bean and New Potato Salad
Okra-Corn Fritters
Brandy Custard with Fresh Berries
Wine
Coffee

Start this dinner right after lunch and then you can forget about it. Since the veal must marinate for 4 or 5 hours, longer if you like, just be sure you allow enough time. The bean and potato salad is served warm or at room temperature, and since the meat can rest for about 30 minutes after it cooks, you have plenty of leeway. The fritters must be done last so they will be hot. Dessert is finished and put aside in the afternoon.

Brandy custard topped with a generous grind of nutmeg.

Crispy okra and corn fritters.

Barbecued veal with string beans and new potatoes.

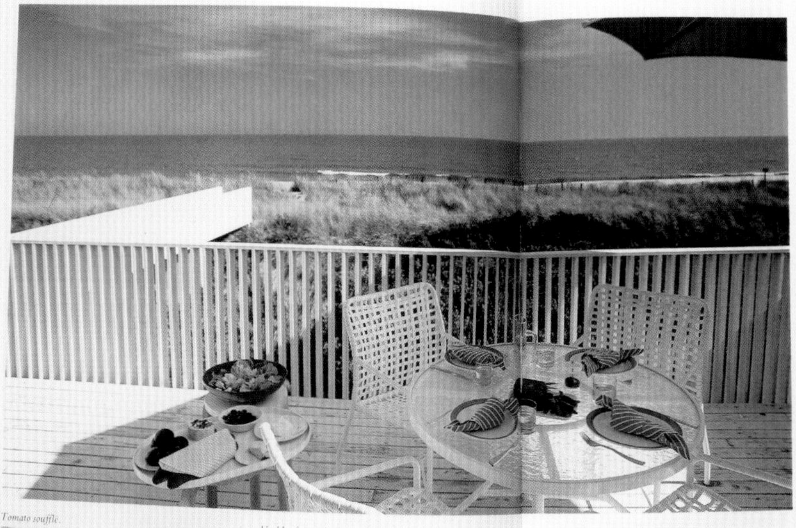

Saturday Lunch

If you are fortunate enough to have a deck facing the ocean, it makes the perfect place to entertain intimate or large groups of guests. During the day, always shade the dining table; nobody really likes to sit in the hot summer sun to eat.

Tomato soufflé.

Veal loaf garnished with sage.

Left: *green salad, black olives, cheeses, crisp French bread and sweet butter, and big purple plums.*

cucina fresca

Italian food, simply prepared and served cold or at room temperature

VIANA LA PLACE & EVAN KLEIMAN

VIANA LA PLACE AND EVAN KLEIMAN

Cucina Fresca, 1983

In a May 3, 1990, article titled "Rustic Italian: Fresh produce. Grilled meat. Seasonal ingredients," the *Los Angeles Times* explained how the American palate began to shift from the influence of French cuisine to Italian:

> Something happened in the middle of the food revolution: our tastes changed. Simplicity became the hallmark of California cooking. We began to crave fresh clear flavors, to favor grilling over slow-cooking, to replace the richness of butter with the strength of olive oil. Sauces started to disappear; pasta became paramount. We wanted food that fit into the lives we were leading and that didn't have a lot to do with France. Suddenly French food seemed too rich, too fussy, too contrived. For the first time Americans trusted their own taste; we began to look for the sort of food that we really wanted to eat. All at once we were looking across France and straight into Italy.

One of the first books to lead the way was Viana La Place and Evan Kleiman's *Cucina Fresca*. Both women had a distrust of "gourmetness," as Kleiman called it. They preferred the simple food of the Italian trattoria, with the focus on perfect vegetables, outstanding grilled meats, and sprightly flavored herbs. This book opened a new set of possibilities for the American palate, introducing true Italian food. It's no surprise that the best restaurants in nearly every American city are now serving Italian-inspired cuisine.

NOTABLE RECIPES: Artichokes Roman-Style (page 405) • Chilled Poached Veal With Tuna Sauce • **Homemade Ricotta** (page 433) • **Panzanella** (page 366) • Rosemary Chicken • Tomato, Avocado and Red Onion Salad • **Torta Rustica** (page 577) • **White Beans with Sage** (page 429)

salads

Radicchio, Mâche, and Arugola

Radicchio is an extraordinarily dramatic head lettuce. The first time we saw the amazing vegetable was in an open-air market in Northern Italy. An Italian friend laughed when we asked why the sellers had taken all the stems off the "gorgeous red flowers." He explained that the "flowers" were heads of winter lettuce. Cultivated in Treviso and Verona, Italy, where it is a traditional Christmas dish, radicchio is now available as an import nearly year round.

Characterized by a full rounded head, radicchio is the size of Bibb lettuce, with compact, curled leaves. The color ranges from a dark magenta to light pink, and often the leaves are boldly streaked with white or mottled with small white speckles. Radicchio has a

FRITTATA WITH FOUR FLAVORS

A light dish with the sweet presence of herbs.

6–8 eggs
¼ cup grated Parmesan cheese
Coarse salt and freshly ground pepper to taste
2 teaspoons chopped fresh tarragon leaves, or ½ teaspoon dried tarragon leaves, crumbled
1 tablespoon each chopped fresh mint leaves, fresh flat-leaf parsley, and fresh marjoram leaves, or 1 teaspoon each dried mint leaves, basil leaves, and marjoram leaves, crumbled
2 tablespoons olive oil

Lightly beat the eggs in a bowl with the Parmesan, salt and pepper, and herbs. Heat the olive oil in a small, nonstick, ovenproof skillet. Swirl the oil in the pan to coat all sides. Add the egg mixture. Lower the heat.

TO COOK ALL FRITTATAS:
Cook slowly, stirring frequently, until the eggs have formed small curds and the frittata is firm except for the top. To cook the top, place the pan under a hot broiler or into a preheated 400° oven until the frittata browns lightly. Remove the pan from the broiler or oven. Let cool in the pan 1 or 2 minutes. Place a plate over the top of pan and invert the frittata onto it. Serve the frittata at room temperature, cut into wedges. *Serves 4.*

RICOTTA FRITTATA

Lightly beating the ricotta into the egg mixture helps the frittata puff and stay puffed. The cheese will form lovely white streaks throughout the eggs.

6–8 eggs
½ cup ricotta
¼ cup grated Parmesan cheese
2 tablespoons finely chopped fresh parsley
2 teaspoons chopped fresh thyme leaves, or ¾ teaspoon dried whole thyme leaves, crumbled
Coarse salt and freshly ground pepper to taste
2 tablespoons olive oil

Lightly beat the eggs in a bowl with the ricotta, Parmesan, parsley, thyme, salt, and pepper. Heat the oil in a small, nonstick, ovenproof skillet. Swirl the oil in the pan to coat all sides. Add the egg mixture. Lower the heat. Cook and unmold according to the general frittata recipe (see page 104). Serve at room temperature, cut into wedges. *Serves 4.*

ZUCCHINI AND BASIL FRITTATA

The basil adds a light, sweet taste to this frittata. Shredding, salting, and squeezing the zucchini dry allows a very brief cooking time, thus reducing the amount of oil the zucchini absorbs.

TO COOK ALL ASPARAGUS:
Using kitchen twine, tie the asparagus into a bundle, one tie just below the tips and another 2 inches from the bottom. Blanch the bundled asparagus in an abundant amount of boiling water in a large pot for 5 to 7 minutes or until the spears are tender yet firm to the bite. Plunge them immediately into a large bowl filled with ice and water and untie. When the asparagus feel cool to the touch, remove from the water and drain. The asparagus may be cooked the day before serving. Refrigerate covered with a damp (*not wet*) cloth. *Serves 6 to 8.*

ASPARAGUS WITH TOMATOES AND PINE NUTS

The bright ribbon of tomatoes makes a pretty presentation.

2 pounds thin asparagus
2 tomatoes, peeled, seeded, and diced fine
1 shallot, peeled and minced fine
2 tablespoons pine nuts
Simple Virgin Dressing made with 2 tablespoons roughly chopped basil (see page 263)

Cook the asparagus according to the directions above. Combine the tomatoes, shallot, and pine nuts in a small bowl and moisten with a bit of the Simple Virgin Dressing. Arrange the asparagus on a serving platter. Spoon the tomato mixture across the center of the asparagus in a stripe. Just before serving, drench the asparagus with

the Simple Virgin Dressing. Vinegar discolors asparagus, so wait until the last minute to dress them. *Serves 6 to 8 as a first course.*

WHITE BEANS WITH SAGE

This dish is served at the most elegant Florentine restaurants. Americans tend to scorn the bean, considering it a lowly budget-stretcher. That it is economical cannot be denied, but served as a side dish with a tablespoon of fine extra-virgin olive oil, White Beans with Sage often outclasses the accompanying entrée. The elegance of the dish, however, rests in its whole-bean presentation. Overcooked, or cooked too rapidly, the beans can split and become mushy and unappealing. They should be cooked slowly over very low heat so that they do not move with the movement of the water. Cooked this way just until tender, each bean remains separate and whole.

1 pound dry small white, or Great Northern beans
2½ quarts water
1 large garlic clove, peeled
1 handful fresh sage leaves, or 1 teaspoon dried sage leaves, crumbled
Coarse salt and freshly ground pepper to taste
Fruity olive oil

Place the beans, water, garlic, sage, and salt in a heavy cooking pot, preferably earthenware. Cover and place on heat so low that it will take almost an hour for the water to boil. Once the liquid comes to a boil, regulate the heat so that the liquid barely simmers. The

BERT GREENE

Greene on Greens, 1984

Bert Greene called this book "a love letter to the 30 or so vegetables, green and otherwise, that I prize most in all the world." It was his love for fresh, local vegetables, usually plucked from his own garden in Amagansett, Long Island, that distinguished Greene's well-written cookbooks.

In 1966 Greene and Denis Vaughan opened a high-end takeout store called The Store in Amagansett, which catered to the Hamptons set—New Yorkers who had summer or weekend homes in the scenic east end of Long Island. This was one of the first stores of its kind in the United States. Greene sought out recipes from around the world that would titillate the taste buds of adventurous New York eaters.

His first cookbook, with Denis Vaughan, *The Store Cookbook*, was based on the first seven years of work at The Store. He went on to write *Bert Greene's Kitchen Bouquets* (1979), *Honest American Fare* (1984), *Greene on Greens* (1984), and the posthumously published *The Grains Cookbook* (1989).

In 1980 Greene and his longtime companion, Phillip Schulz, collaborated on a syndicated column about food that appeared in the New York *Daily News*, as well as many other papers. Barbara Haber, the visionary curator of the culinary collections at the Schlesinger Library at Radcliffe, notes that Greene was an excellent writer who wrote about food with "feeling, wit, style, and grace." Greene himself remarked: "Cooking fame does not last forever. With luck, recipes do!"

NOTABLE RECIPES: Bashed Neeps (page 422) • Brazilian Avocado Cream • **Broccoli Frittata, Parma Style** (page 465) • **Drunken Leeks in Red Wine** (page 406) • **Farm-Style Braised Kale** (page 409) • French Fried Asparagus • **Frittera** (page 417) • Tomato Devil's Food Cake with Tomato Buttercream Frosting • Turkish Squash Cakes (Gozleme) • **Winter Squash Crème Brûlée** (page 422)

126

CORN

The Sooner It's Cooked the Better It Tastes

Gastronomes have different notions of paradise than do mortal men, it seems. The grandest treat for a deep-dyed epicure, I have been reasonably assured, is dining *al fresco* on a freshly dug truffle in Perigord or slurping malossol caviar from a just-caught sterlet along the Volga. My own likes are a darn sight more pedestrian, although the same optimum state of freshness certainly applies. Greene's dream meal? Half a dozen ears of sweet summer corn (preferably picked before sundown) from a cornfield in Iowa. If the geography seems a tad imprecise, I will confess that I have only minimal first-hand knowledge of the Great Plains. I simply chose that territory because it is obviously the "in place" to sample lots and lots of corn—something I have done before, albeit not in Iowa—and therein lies a tale, of course.

I left home to be completely on my own when I was twenty-two. Many things conspired to arrange my independence. The war ended; my father died unexpectedly; and after a cursory period of mourning, my mother remarried. "For security reasons only," she announced, to ward off any infelicitous hint of romance that might be construed by this rash action. Though she was still exceedingly attractive at forty-eight, my parent seemed openly offended at any sexual implication inherent in her second union. That my stepfather (and her choice for matrimony) turned out to be wildly eccentric seemed beside the point in her view. He was a former suitor who had not only pined after her for thirty years but also managed to accrue some solid assets with which to press his suit.

CORN 127

When my mother announced her plans to marry, I moved. Actually I had been paying rent on an apartment for some time, but put off taking occupancy when my father became ill. No conventional studio, my first home was once the ballroom of a grand mansion off upper Fifth Avenue. From a carved stone balustrade I could even see a stretch of Central Park. Aside from that, and its vast size, this apartment had very few virtues. There was no kitchen or closet, and the bathroom was a mahogany cave equipped with turn-of-the-century fixtures. However, I was young and adventurous, the rent was reasonable, and the building had a private elevator. True, it accommodated only two persons at a time, but it certainly added a touch of class to my bachelor existence.

When I settled into my first apartment I had no furniture whatsoever. In time I acquired a large bed and a bookcase. I had planned to add more household goods before I entertained but natural gregariousness and a new girlfriend, Norma, changed my plans. Norma had recently arrived in New York as well (from a small town in New England), and she lived in a hotel for women where males were forbidden above the lobby floor. Of necessity much of our courtship took place in my quarters.

Norma did not cook. I did, of course, but had nowhere to do it. In the end we spent most of our time like picnickers, roasting our dinner over a log fire in one of the most opulent marble fireplaces ever carved.

Our romance had one other setback. Norma was a vegetarian. We grilled an awful lot of corn (and potatoes) between kisses and I will never forget the flavor of a single singed kernel, though in time my tastebuds rebelled at the diet and I also gained twenty pounds. I enrolled Norma in the best cooking school I knew at the time: Dione Lucas Cordon Bleu, where she shortly gave up her vegetarian principles, and me too, for she married a more aggressive fellow that she met in class. All of which sounds *corny* but is absolutely true!

Norma never heard of it, but there is a tart New England adage that puts down the cooking instructions for corn very concisely. "You may stroll to the garden to cut the corn but you had darn well better run back to the kitchen to cook it!"

That is no exaggeration. As soon as a corn's cob is cut, natural sugar in the kernel's fiber starts to convert to starch. Consequently, the longer the cut corn sits, the mealier each bite will be!

Vegetable Roots

Corn—on the cob and off—antedated Columbus's discovery of America by three thousand years at least—some hint even longer. The first Indian corn, maize *(Zea mays)*, was the chief staple of the Mayan, Aztec, and Incan diets. Corn's origin is traced so far back in Indian history, in fact, that it may date from the very first appearance of man in the western world—when he ate grass seeds to survive.

Food sleuths assert that these precious food seeds, planted along the way of his migration to warmer climes, crossbred; and the result was early corn. Other historians cast a cold eye on that theory, however, insisting that maize, rather than being a wild hybrid, was developed through centuries of cultivation—plus nature's unerring sense of selectivity, of course. Whatever its

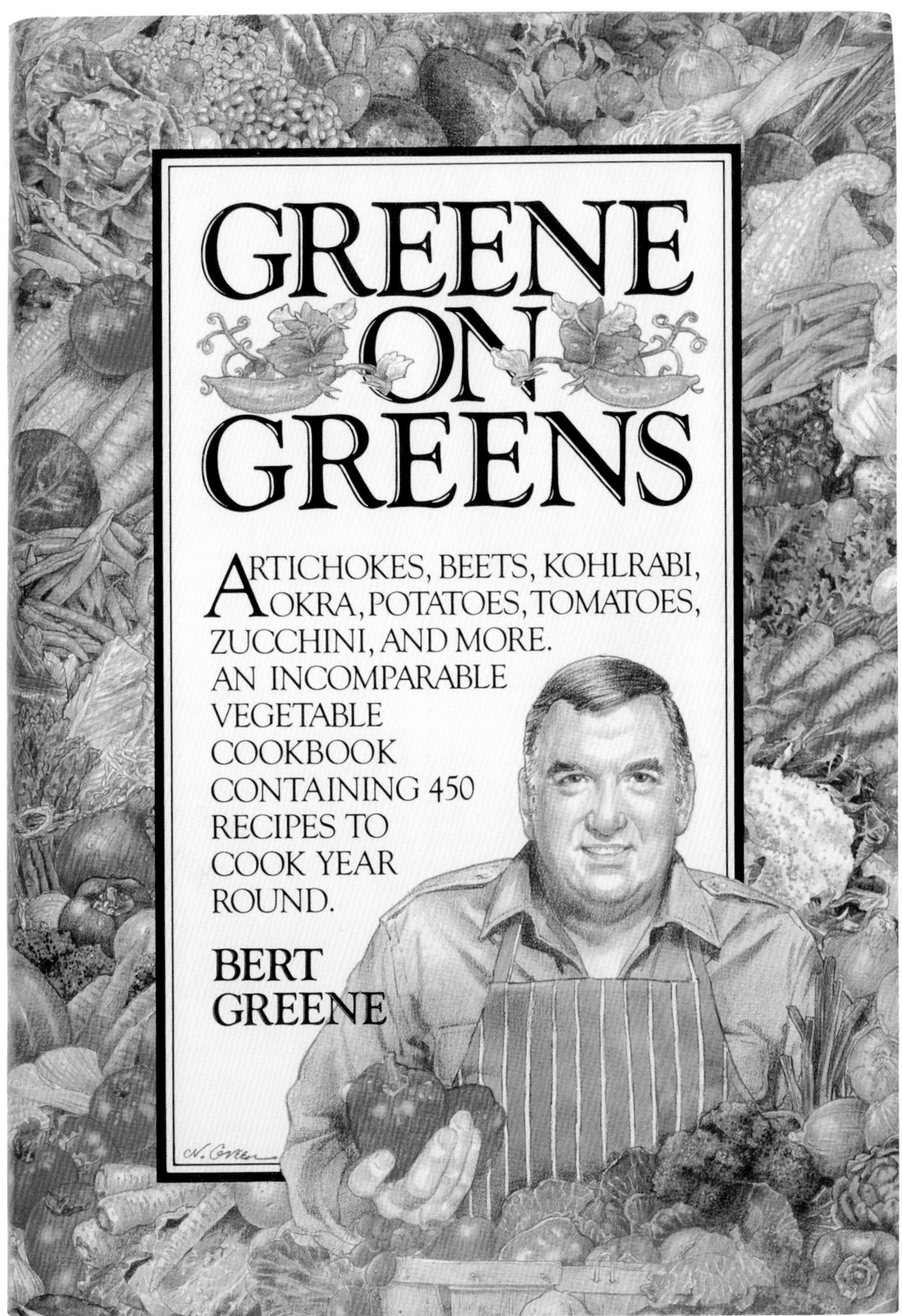
GREENE ON GREENS
ARTICHOKES, BEETS, KOHLRABI, OKRA, POTATOES, TOMATOES, ZUCCHINI, AND MORE. AN INCOMPARABLE VEGETABLE COOKBOOK CONTAINING 450 RECIPES TO COOK YEAR ROUND.
BERT GREENE

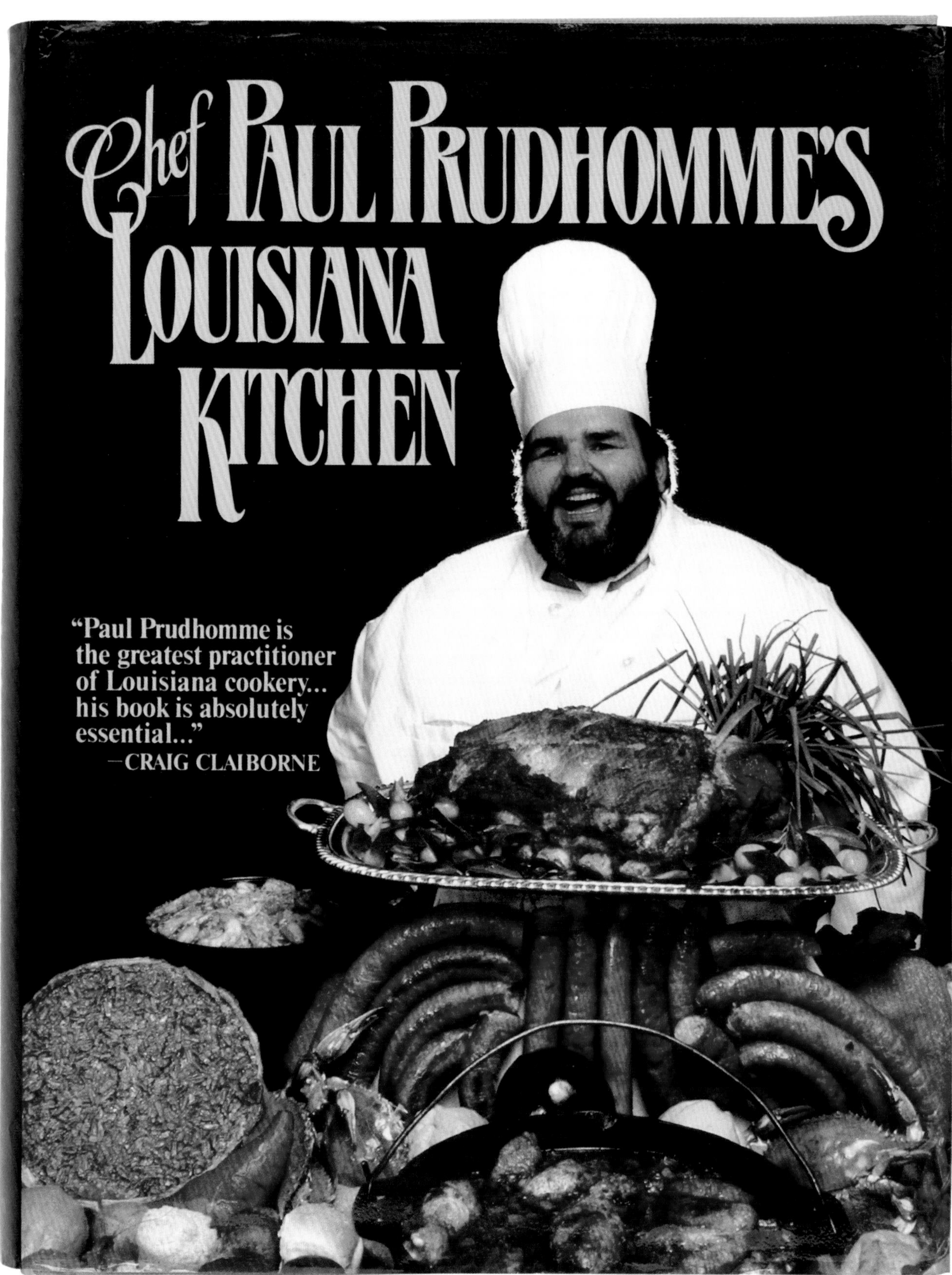
Chef Paul Prudhomme's
Louisiana
Kitchen
"Paul Prudhomme is
the greatest practitioner
of Louisiana cookery...
his book is absolutely
essential..."
—CRAIG CLAIBORNE

PAUL PRUDHOMME

Chef Paul Prudhomme's Louisiana Kitchen, 1984

The craze for Cajun cooking took over in the 1980s thanks to Paul Prudhomme, the corpulent conjurer of his native Louisiana cuisine.

Prudhomme was discovered by Craig Claiborne, who loved the chef's use of perfectly fresh ingredients, loving attention to preparation, and sheer force of taste that this country-style cooking provided. Suddenly the country was ablaze with Cajun cooking. Blackened redfish was so popular we nearly depleted the redfish stock. Americans' taste buds tingled to the timbres of red, black, and white pepper, each hitting a different spot on the tongue. Behind it all was the master chef at K-Paul's Louisiana Kitchen in New Orleans. The smell of blackened fish and steak, okra, and gumbo filé hung in the street outside the restaurant. In his loving tribute to Cajun food, Prudhomme demystified such dishes as red, brown, and black roux, rabbit etouffée, and chicken and andouille smoked sausage gumbo—sometimes known as "barnyard" gumbo because it has no shellfish. If you want the best cornbread dressing ever, you need look no further than page 227 of this book. It's a meal of its own. Prudhomme's book meticulously re-creates those Cajun flavors in their pure taste.

NOTABLE RECIPES: Barbecued Shrimp • **Cajun Meat Loaf** (page 544) • Cajun Sheppard's Pie • **Chicken and Seafood Jambalaya** (page 379) • **Chicken and Andouille Smoked Sausage Gumbo** (page 378) • **Crawfish (or Shrimp) Étouffée** (page 489) • Potato Salad with Green Onion Dressing • Seafood Dirty Rice • **Shrimp Diane** (page 487) • Sweet Potato Pecan Pie

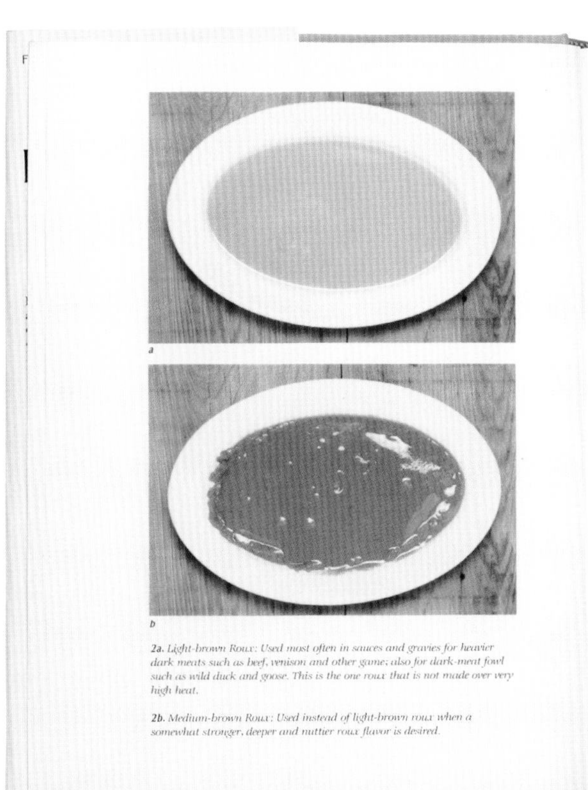

a
b
2a. Light-brown Roux: Used most often in sauces and gravies for heavier dark meats such as beef, venison and other game; also for dark-meat fowl such as wild duck and goose. This is the one roux that is not made over very high heat.
2b. Medium-brown Roux: Used instead of light-brown roux when a somewhat stronger, deeper and nuttier roux flavor is desired.

c
d
2c. Dark Red-brown Roux: Used for light, sweet meats such as domesticated fowl and rabbit, pork, veal and seafoods. You may also use it for gumbos.
2d. Black Roux: Used when you want a stronger flavor than dark red-brown roux gives. It takes practice to make a black roux without burning it, but it's really the right color roux for a gumbo.

CAROL FIELD

The Italian Baker, 1985

"Do you know the land where the lemon trees bloom?" So wrote Wolfgang von Goethe, invoking his transformative trip to Italy (1786–88). Like Winckelmann and so many others before him, Goethe went to Italy to seek out the ancient world. What he found was a culture of such depth that it startled even his overwhelming intellect. Every thinking person who goes to Italy has such an epiphany.

Carol Field's came in 1972, when she accompanied her husband, who was helping shoot a film for PBS. Smog from the factories in Northern Italy delayed the production, forcing the crew to return the following year. Realizing that they had no translator, Field decided to learn Italian, and her love affair with Italy began. Then there was the food. Field never learned to cook at home, but as a young wife taught herself the basics by working through such cookbooks as Julia Child's *Mastering the Art of French Cooking*. In the process, she realized she loved to cook.

Having studied English at Wellesley College, Field was a good writer. She decided to turn her love of Italy into a book, *The Hill Towns of Italy*, a historical description of the Tuscan and Umbrian fortified towns, many of which were Etruscan and, thus, predated the Roman period. Increasingly, Field began to understand the role food plays in the life of Italians and how it is so completely different for Americans. For Italians, food is their history, their culture, their family. She wanted to write about this experience and to bring it to the attention of Americans.

Her books, including *The Italian Baker, Italy in Small Bites, Focaccia*, and *In Nonna's Kitchen*, are some of the finest explanations of Italian food and culture ever written. Field appreciates the traditional Italian foods and recipes, which were always based on seasonal, organic fruits and vegetables, locally produced meats, and the freshest ingredients. There is a simple reason why this was the case with Italian foods: Refrigeration came to most parts of Italy only after the economic upswing following

World War II. Sadly, with greater prosperity, Italy began to lose some of its important traditional foodways. It comes as no surprise that the Slow Food movement, with its turn back to traditional cooking, organic produce, and ethically prepared meats, began in Italy.

Field seems to have divined the Slow Food movement. In her book about *nonnas* (Italian grandmothers), she quotes an old woman who says, "Si stava meglio quando si stave peggio" or "We were better off when we were worse off"—a perfect example of what the Italians call the *saggezza di contadini*, the wisdom of the farmers. Field helped to preserve many of these traditional Italian recipes and to bring the Italian love of food to the American table.

NOTABLE RECIPES: Ciabatta (page 574) • Chocolate Bread • **Grissini Torinesi** (page 578) • Pane al'Olio • **Panettone** (page 581) • Pane Pugliese • **Panforte** (page 583) • **Panmarino** (page 575) • Pappa al Pomodoro

Pane Siciliano (continued)

Shaping and Second Rise. Punch the dough down, knead it briefly, and let it rest for 5 minutes. Flatten it with your forearm into a square. Roll it into a long, fairly narrow rope, about 20 to 22 inches long. The dough should be so elastic that it could almost be swung and stretched like a jump rope. Cut the dough in half and shape each half into a loaf, choosing from the following shapes:

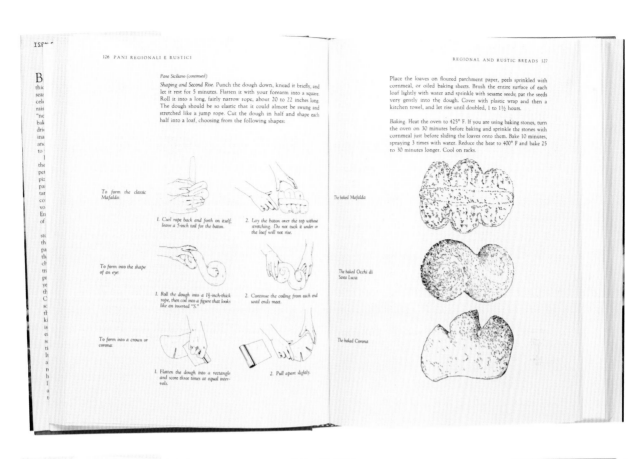

To form the classic Mafalda:

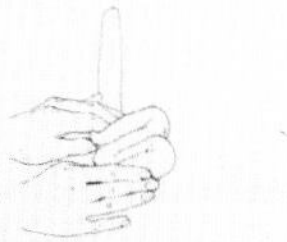

1. Curl rope back and forth on itself; leave a 5-inch tail for the baton.

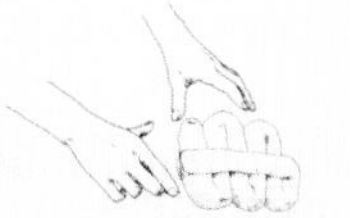

2. Lay the baton over the top without stretching. Do not tuck it under or the loaf will not rise.

To form into the shape of an eye:

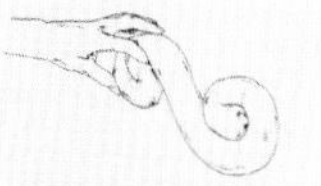

1. Roll the dough into a 1½-inch-thick rope, then coil into a figure that looks like an inverted "S."

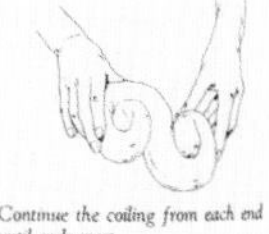

2. Continue the coiling from each end until ends meet.

To form into a crown or corona:

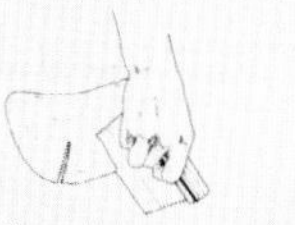

1. Flatten the dough into a rectangle and score three times at equal intervals.

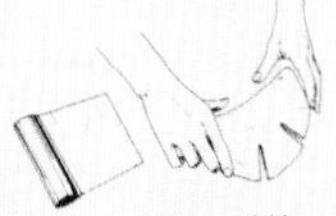

2. Pull apart slightly.

Place the loaves on floured parchment paper, peels sprinkled with cornmeal, or oiled baking sheets. Brush the entire surface of each loaf lightly with water and sprinkle with sesame seeds; pat the seeds very gently into the dough. Cover with plastic wrap and then a kitchen towel, and let rise until doubled, 1 to 1½ hours.

Baking. Heat the oven to 425° F. If you are using baking stones, turn the oven on 30 minutes before baking and sprinkle the stones with cornmeal just before sliding the loaves onto them. Bake 10 minutes, spraying 3 times with water. Reduce the heat to 400° F and bake 25 to 30 minutes longer. Cool on racks.

The baked Mafalda

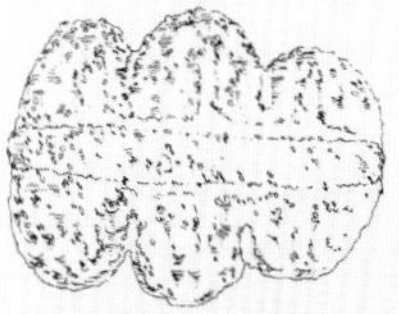

The baked Occhi di Santa Lucia

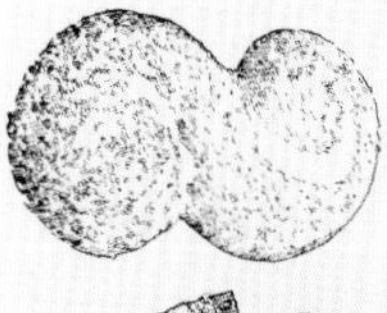

The baked Corona

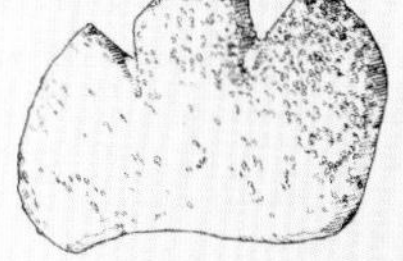

Pani Festivi
Celebration Breads

Fruit and nut breads are among the oldest country loaves, invented by poor Italians who used raw and dried fruits and nuts to give sweetness to their doughs in the days when there was no such thing as sugar. I like the thought of medieval peasants, whose lives were difficult at best, adding a bit of sweetness to their days with special breads bursting with fat raisins or figs or studded with walnuts. It was common in those times and much later as well to make regular doughs during the week and then enrich them on Sunday with a splash of milk, an egg or two, and a few handfuls of candied fruit and nuts. Of course, such exotic ingredients as chocolate did not make an appearance until the seventeenth century.

Many of these rich, eggy doughs are very similar. The *colomba* has more butter and is sprinkled with almonds, the *civitavecchia* is flavored with port and anise, and the panettone is studded with raisins, citron, and candied orange peel, but all are essentially variations on a theme of flour, eggs, butter, and yeast. In Italy every bakery has bottles of powerful essences labelled *aroma di panettone, aroma di colomba, aroma di limone,* and *aroma di arancia dolce,* which give the breads their memorable tastes, but some of the finest bakers I met prefer using freshly grated lemon and orange zests or a splash of vanilla extract for flavoring, which is the approach I have used to replicate the mysterious essence of these Italian holiday breads.

The doughs are delicate and complex, and almost all need fairly long rises to create the high, airy loaves. But that does not mean that they cannot be made in a day. I like to start baking right after breakfast and work out a schedule for the first and second rises that fits into the rest of my day. The dough can go in the refrigerator if you have other things to do; the action of the yeast will be slowed down, but the dough will develop more flavor.

Actually, it isn't putting the ingredients together that is time-consuming, but rather the time required for the yeast to do its magical work, which is true for all breads but especially for these loaves which are heavy with eggs and butter as well as fruits and

nuts. I have found several ways to encourage the process, however. Covering the bowl tightly with plastic wrap for the dough's first rise traps the heat given off as the yeast begins to work. I never place the dough directly over the pilot of my gas stove, but it can certainly be set near the source of heat. I also have taken note of the warm, moist proofers in bakeries and approximated the method by turning the oven on at 150° F for three minutes and then immediately placing the shaped loaves in the oven along with a pan of steaming water. The warm moisture is a wonderful incentive for the expansion of the dough.

The holiday bread doughs (pages 220-245) must be made by hand or by mixer, for the food processor simply will not create the right airy texture. Don't be daunted by their seeming complexity. After you've tried one recipe, you'll find that the process is not as complicated as it reads. And, when you take a bite of the finished bread, close your eyes and you'll find you're tasting the true flavor of Italy.

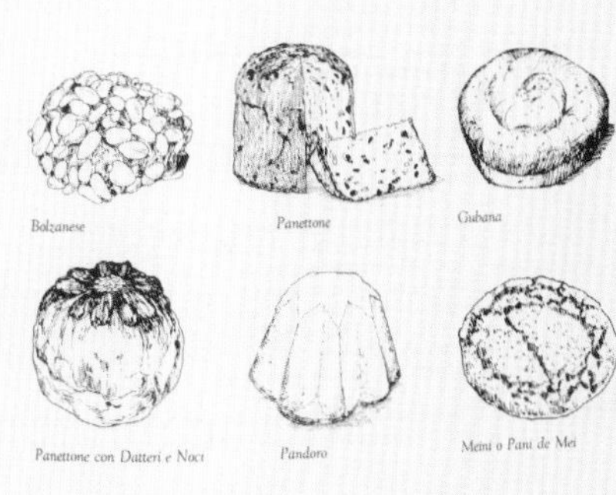

Bolzanese — *Panettone* — *Gubana*

Panettone con Datteri e Noci — *Pandoro* — *Meini o Pani de Mei*

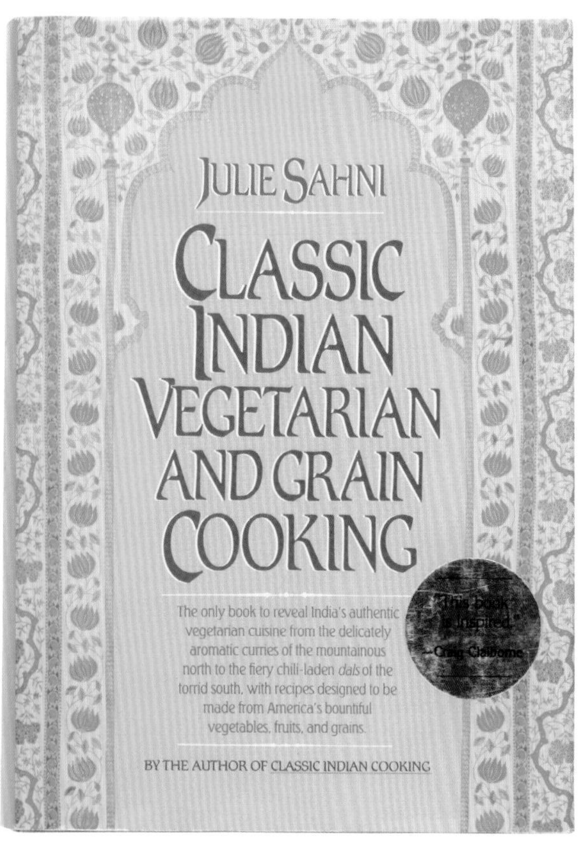

VEGETABLE-LEGUME-DAIRY-GRAIN COMBINATIONS

FRAGRANT RICE AND MUNG BEAN PORRIDGE WITH POTATOES AND SWEET PEPPERS

(Khichdee)

Khichdee is a creamy porridge of rice and yellow mung beans laced with turmeric and cumin butter. It is the first solid food given to an infant in India because it is mild flavored and easy to digest. It is also the basic diet of a person at home with a cold or the flu. I love the creamy consistency and subtle flavor of this dish. If I have it at lunch, I like to add a little sautéed sweet peppers and potatoes to make it more interesting.

273

JULIE SAHNI

Classic Indian Vegetarian and Grain Cooking, 1985

Nineteen seventy-three was an auspicious year for Indian food in America. Madhur Jaffrey published her seminal book, *An Invitation to Indian Cooking*, and Julie Sahni opened her Indian Cooking School in New York City. The time had come for Americans to taste the "exotic" flavors of curries, chutneys, dosas, and vindaloos. Through her cooking school and her cookbooks, Sahni established herself as an expert on Indian foods and cooking during the 1970s and 1980s.

From the 1970s onward, Americans began expanding their palates to include foods from around the world in their authentic, non-Americanized versions. At the same time, a subset of Americans turned to vegetarianism for social and ethical reasons. Sahni's *Classic Indian Cooking*, published in 1980, provided a step-by-step guide for all those interested in Indian cooking. Her 1985 book, *Classic Indian Vegetarian and Grain Cooking*, opened up the possibilities for delicious, traditional Indian vegetarian eating that became popular not only among vegetarians, but also among the food cognoscenti. Sahni has gone on to become a media spokesperson for Indian food of all kinds. Since 1987, she has been leading annual cultural and gastronomic tours of India.

NOTABLE RECIPES: Bengal Red Lentils with Spices (page 429) • **Bengali Green Beans and Potatoes Smothered in Mustard Oil** (page 411) • Coconut Relish with Tomatoes • **Cucumber and Peanut Salad, Maharashtrian-Style** (page 362) • **Eggplant and Potatoes Laced with Fenugreek** (page 420) • Idlee Sambaar (Steamed Rice and Bean Dumplings in Spicy Lentil and Radish Sauce) • Indian Cheese and Red Peppers in Fragrant Spinach Sauce • Sabzi Dhan Shak (Parsi Vegetable and Lentil Stew) • **Sweet and Spicy Tamarind Chutney** (page 437)

Bitter Melon ***(Karela)***

The bitter melon with its green, very coarsely wrinkled rind, like the skin of a crocodile, has been growing in India since ancient times. There are two distinct varieties of bitter melon plants, *Momordica charantia* and *Momordica balsamina*. The former yields cucumberlike fruits, while the latter, ovoid-shaped fruits with narrow pointed ends.

Only the cucumber-shaped bitter melon is available in the United States in Indian and Oriental grocery stores. Make sure you buy small young ones because they are more flavorful. Also take care to select firm melons that are not spongy to the touch. The color of the skin should be as dark green as you can find. Bitter melon, as the name suggests, has a characteristic bitterness that is an acquired taste. Much of its bitterness is removed by soaking or boiling the vegetable in a salt-turmeric mixture before cooking.

Bitter melon contains many medicinal properties. It is believed to be anti-diabetic and cardiotonic. It is also rich in iron and vitamins.

In Indian cooking bitter melon is usually cooked dry and stuffed with spices and seasonings or with other vegetables. This method enhances its flavor. Bitter melon is the principal vegetable in the classic Bengali vegetarian dish *Shokhto* (p. 296). My personal favorite is Bitter Melon with Spicy Onion Stuffing (p. 297).

Green Black-eyed Peas ***(Hara Lobbia)***

The young, tender seeds of the pod of *Vigna unguiculata* (the black-eyed pea plant) are regarded as a delicacy by the vegetarians in the western and southwestern regions of India. Indians handle this vegetable much the same way as green peas; they serve them in green salads, pilafs, braised dishes with spices, as well as in desserts.

Green or fresh black-eyed peas are commonly available at greengroceries that sell Latin American and West Indian products. They are also available frozen or in one-pound plastic bags in some supermarket chains. Select crisp-looking peas that have no brown spots and, most important of all, that exude a fresh pinelike fragrance.

Green Chick-peas ***(Phalian)***

Green chick-peas are the young tender pods (containing seeds) of the plant *Cicer arietinum*, which, when mature and dry, are what we know as chick-peas (*channa*). In the province of Uttar Pradesh, where most of the chick-peas in India are grown, these green delicacies are particularly prized. The seeds from the pods are munched raw, served in a spicy salad by themselves, or cooked with herbs and seasonings like any lentil preparation. Green chick-peas have a wonderful earthy scent and a delightful crunch. They do not have the heavy, mealy quality of dried chick-peas. Green chick-peas are not commercially available in this country, although you may find them in some farms in the Midwest. Young, uncooked fava beans and tiny lima beans (lightly steamed) make fine substitutes.

Drumstick ***(Sehjana ki Phali)***

Sehjana ki Phali is called drumstick not because of its similarity to a turkey leg but because the pods, the edible part of this plant *Moringa oleifara*, are shaped, when dried, like the sticks used to beat a drum. The green pods, ¼ inch thick and 12 inches to 18 inches long, have thick, rubbery skins and fleshy pulp and seeds. The flavor is often compared with asparagus and drumstick is considered a delicacy in Gujarat, Bengal, and southern India. A native of India, the drumstick plant grows wild in southern California and Florida, often as a decorative ornamental tree. Fresh drumsticks are sometimes found in Indian grocery stores in the summer months. Canned drumsticks imported from India are almost always available. They are acceptable, since for most vegetarian dishes in this book, drumsticks are parboiled before being added to a dish at the end of cooking.

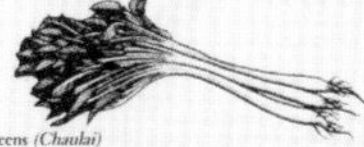

Amaranth Greens ***(Chaulai)***

Amaranth, also known as Indian summer spinach, is commonly referred to in India as *chaulai*. It looks and tastes very much like Indian spinach except for its

SILKY RICE AND BEAN BATTER CREPES WITH SPICY POTATO FILLING

(Masala Dosai)

◆

This is a slightly more substantial version of *dosai*, in which the crepes are filled with a spicy stuffing of potatoes laced with fresh ginger, chilies, turmeric, and other herbs. They are great for lunch or a light supper. *Masala dosai* is a very popular item on the menus of tiffin houses, known as Madras coffee houses, that are all over India. These restaurants feature several other classic southern India delicacies on their menus.

FOR 8 PERSONS

Spicy Potato Filling:

- 2 pounds potatoes (about 8, medium-size), boiled, peeled, and cubed
- ⅔ cup cooked chopped carrots
- ⅔ cup cooked green peas (fresh or frozen)
- 4 tablespoons light sesame oil or light vegetable oil
- 1½ teaspoons black mustard seeds
- 1 teaspoon yellow split peas (*channa dal*, optional)
- 1½ teaspoons white split gram beans (*urad dal*, optional)
- 4–6 hot green chilies, chopped
- 4 medium-size onions, peeled and chopped
- 1 tablespoon chopped fresh ginger
- ¼ teaspoon turmeric or curry powder
- 8 curry (*kari*) leaves, fresh or dry (optional)
- 2 teaspoons coarse salt, or to taste
- Juice of 1 small lemon, or to taste
- 2 tablespoons chopped fresh coriander (optional)

Dosai Batter:

All ingredients for Silky Rice and Bean Batter Crepes, p. 154

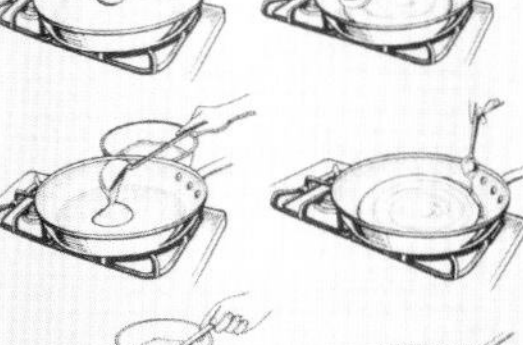

MAKES 1 PINT

- 1 pound fresh mango ginger (or use ½ pound fresh tender ginger and 1 medium-size unripe, tart mango)
- 1 tablespoon coarse salt
- 4 tablespoons light sesame oil
- 12 dry red chili pods, broken into large pieces
- 1 teaspoon ground asafetida
- ½ teaspoon turmeric

1. Peel the mango ginger and either dice into ½-inch pieces or cut into ⅛-inch-thick slices. If you are using a plain ginger and unripe mango combination, prepare the ginger the same way. Peel and pit the mango. Cut the pulp in the same manner as the ginger. Put ginger (and mango) in a nonmetallic bowl, sprinkle on the salt, and toss well.
2. Heat the oil in a small frying pan over high heat. When it is hot, add the chili pieces, asafetida, and turmeric, and immediately pour the entire contents of the pan over the prepared vegetables.

Mix well and let rest for a half-hour before serving.

THE STAPLES: BREADS AND RICE

◇

रोटी और चावल

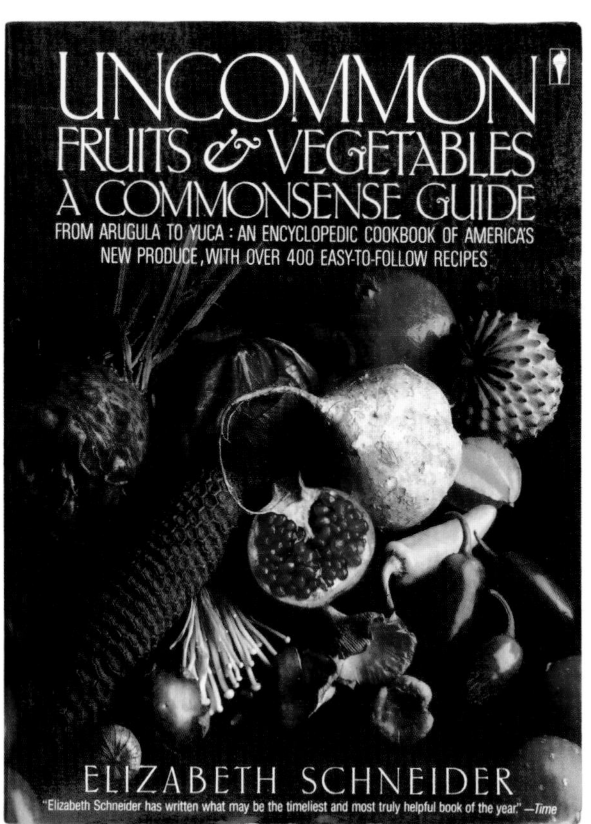

ELIZABETH SCHNEIDER

Uncommon Fruits & Vegetables, 1986

Yuppies (young urban professionals) of the 1980s were interested in anything new, and were willing to pay for it. Perhaps nowhere was this as evident as in their interest in restaurants, cooking, cookware, and unusual new cuisines and ingredients. The modern "foodie" was born, expanding beyond anyone's wildest dreams the audience for food, which had once been the province of a small number of gourmets. The American palate was going well beyond the "world cuisines" of the 1970s.

Elizabeth Schneider clearly understood that a sea change was happening in American taste. Her book *Uncommon Fruits and Vegetables* is an encyclopedia of world ingredients, many of which were unheard of to most people when the book came out in 1986. Today many of these delicacies, such as kiwis, tomatillos, star fruit, and jicama, are common in our homes. Schneider was a champion of the exotic, and her detailed descriptions and useful recipes opened up a new world of taste to us. Can you imagine a world without lemongrass?

NOTABLE RECIPES: **Basic Fiddlehead Ferns** (page 359) • Cape Scallops with Cape Gooseberries • **Felipe Rojas-Lombardi's Dandelions with Penn Dutch Dressing** (page 360) • Lemon Grass Seasoning Paste • **Plantain Baked in Its Skin** (page 424) • **Richards' Mashed Celeriac and Potatoes** (page 423) • **Sorrel Cream Sauce for Vegetables** (page 526) • **Sour Cherry Ratafia** (page 314) • **Spaghetti with Radicchio, Anchovies, and Garlic** (page 448)

PHYSALIS

See Cape Gooseberry

PLANTAIN

(Musa X paradisiaca)

also Plátano, Plátano Macho, Cooking Banana

In much of the southern hemisphere a good part of dinner is made up of cooking banana, not in a pudding or cake, but as a staple starch or main dish—whether crisply fried, baked tender, formed into spicy fritters or dumpling-like balls (kofta in India, fufu in Cuba), or simmered with a garlicky coconut-chili sauce. Northerners, just lately

introduced to some of the members of the Musa family (which has been on earth longer than mere mortals), have begun to discover the banana's diversity, thanks to the Latin American, Caribbean, and Asian restaurants that have sprung up throughout the country. It is the cooking banana that is most popular in the tropics, the hard green or black fruit that is often passed over by many in North American markets, who believe it to be too green, too bruised, too large, or too black. Elsewhere the situation is reversed: it is the sweet dessert banana that we know so well that is eaten in moderation.

Dubbed *plantain* in North America, this vegetable-banana (called *banane-légume* in the French West Indies—where one type of banana is called a fig!) can be eaten, and tastes different, at every stage of development. The interior color of the fruit will remain creamy, yellowish, or lightly pink. When the plantain's peel is green to yellow, the flavor of the flesh is bland and its texture simply starchy, the uses similar to those for a potato. As the peel changes from yellow-brown through black, plantain

plays the role of both fruit and vegetable, having a sweetness and banana aroma, but keeping a firm shape when cooked. Only experience can teach you which stages suit your taste, and consequently how you wish to incorporate the plantain in your meals.

Multiple personalities come naturally to the banana or plantain, which is, surprisingly, classified as a large berry. This botanical berry that certainly resembles no other hangs from an enormous herb, or so it is called. What appears to be a tree trunk is actually the sheathed bases of spirally arranged broad leaves, which form at ground level. The trunk-like tube of overlapping sheaths supports the mass of upper leaves and drooping clusters of fruit. The real stem is a large underground rhizome, a bulblike growth that extends massive roots from its underside. When the fruit is picked, the plant is cut down. It then develops suckers that become new "trunks," then flowers, then fruits—for up to fifty years in some areas.

SELECTION AND STORAGE: As far as I can tell, unless a plantain is dry-hard, squishy, moldy, or cracked, it's good for eating. Do not be put off by any amount of browning or blackening; that's the way plantains look. What state of ripeness you choose depends upon how you plan to cook the fruit. Kept at room temperature, it will slowly ripen through every phase and store for a considerable time, as well. (Occasionally plantains do not ripen properly, but harden instead; fully ripe black plantains should give like firm bananas. If they are hard, throw them out.) It pays to buy an oversupply if you don't regularly find plantains in your market.

Do not refrigerate plantains unless they are at the stage you wish to use them, or they will stop ripening. Even when ripe, they'll hold for a bit; so unless you have a mass of fruit and a heat wave, there's no reason to fill up the refrigerator with them.

Like bananas, plantains freeze well. When sufficiently ripe, peel, wrap each tightly in plastic, then freeze.

USE: Green or greenish plantains, which are very hard and starchy, have little banana flavor and no sweetness. They are generally cooked in the same ways as potatoes and require comparable cooking time. They are best when thin-fried as chips, made into tostones (see recipe), or boiled in chunks to be added to salty, spicy soups or stews.

Yellow-ripe plantains can be used in these same ways, and will have a lovely creamy texture and light banana scent, once cooked. They are more tender than green plantains, but nowhere near as soft as bananas. You can rinse them, cut in fairly wide crosswise sections, and boil; then peel and serve as a side dish. Add them to soups, stews, and vegetable mixtures—peeling before or after cooking, as you prefer (they hold their shape better with peel). Mash the cooked, peeled plantain, mixing with squash or apple or sweet potato. Make irresistible *tostones* (see recipe) and fritters. Sauté or deep-fry plantain slices—diagonals, rounds, or full lengths—to accompany roasts, stews, or broiled meat. Or rinse the plantain, trim the ends, and slit it lengthwise; bake about 45 minutes in a moderate oven and serve as you would a sweet potato.

An unusual and useful way to cook half-ripe plantains is to grill them. Cuban cook Maricel Presilla cooks the peeled and diagonally halved fruit over a low fire, basting

SQUASH AND SQUASH FLOWER PUDDING

This adaptation of a traditional Niçois specialty includes yellow summer squash, squash blossoms, and a thickening of rice, eggs, and cheese. The saffron-golden dish is sunny, casual, straightforward—ideal for a rustic buffet. The soft bites of squash flower hidden in the rather firm, moist pudding lend a sweet, fresh flavor.

6 servings

2 pounds small yellow summer squash, scrubbed
⅓ cup white rice
2 tablespoons olive oil
1 large onion, coarsely chopped
1 large garlic clove, minced
3 eggs
3 ounces Parmesan cheese, grated (¾ cup)
¾ teaspoon salt
White pepper
8 large basil leaves, slivered (about 2 tablespoons), plus sprigs for garnish
15 large or 20 medium squash flowers (5–6 ounces), cleaned (see Preparation)
Optional: A few small squash flowers for garnish

1. Drop squash into boiling salted water; continue boiling until just tender, about 4–5 minutes. Lift out with tongs; drop in cold water. Add rice to boiling water and cook until tender, about 10 minutes. Drain rice and trim squash.

2. Heat oil in skillet over moderate heat and sauté onions until softened, about 5 minutes. Add garlic and stir for a minute. Transfer to processor.

3. Blend eggs in a mixing bowl. Add rice, cheese, salt, and pepper; blend well. Roughly purée onion mixture. Add basil and squash, chunked; roughly purée, in batches, keeping some texture. Add to egg mixture.

4. Slice blossoms across into ½-inch slices (you should have about 2 cups). Add to bowl and blend well.

5. Scrape into oiled shallow 8-cup baking-serving dish. Set in middle of preheated 350-degree oven. Bake 45 minutes, until set in center and very lightly browned. Cool to lukewarm or room temperature; garnish with small basil leaves. Garnish with pretty, fresh squash flowers—or if they are less than perfect, fry them.

STAR FRUIT

See Carambola

SUGAR PEA (both SUGAR SNAP PEA and SNOW PEA)

(*Pisum sativum* variety *macrocarpon*)

also Edible-Podded Pea; Snow Pea is also called Mangetout, Chinese Snow Pea, and Chinese Pea

Snow peas and sugar snap peas (although *Sugar Snap*, properly speaking, only applies to one cultivar, the term is now used to mean any pea of this type) are both edible-podded (or sugar) peas. They differ from shelling peas in that the pods do not develop a tough, supportive lining (an alternative French name for the group is *pois sans parchemin*, or peas without parchment). As a result, the entire vegetable is

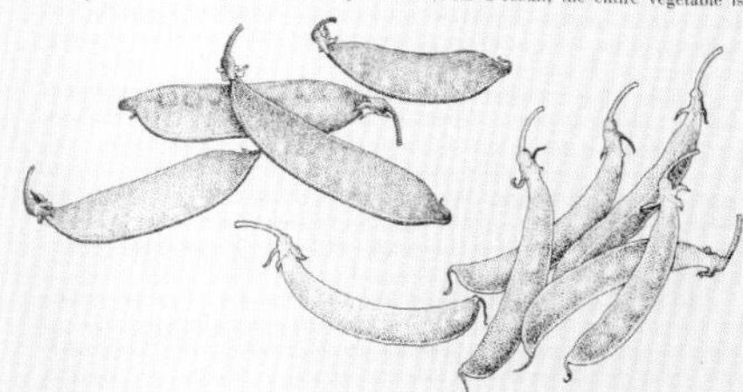

tender-edible. Ribbon-flat snow peas must be harvested when the immature peas are the size of peppercorns and the translucent straight-sided pods show only a suggestion of bumps within, or the whole will be fibrous and starchy. Sugar snap peas develop fat peas that tightly fill the curved, thick-walled pods, but both remain sweet and tender when mature.

Although relatively new in the American marketplace, edible-podded peas are no upstarts, having been fashionable in Europe as early as the sixteenth century (shelling peas have been around since ancient times).

Snow peas, generally assumed to be Chinese in origin, were most likely first cultivated in Europe, according to many sources. I have read that the Cantonese name for the vegetable, *ho laan* (as in Holland), is a likely clue to the source of the variety first planted. In support of this theory is the fact that French horticul-

THE BREAKFAST BOOK

An invitation to breakfast—with 288 recipes, from the best-ever sticky buns to scones, coddled eggs, pancakes, and new delights like Bridge Creek Heavenly Hots and Fresh Ginger Muffins

MARION CUNNINGHAM

MARION CUNNINGHAM

The Breakfast Book, 1987

Marion Cunningham is best known for her revision of *The Fannie Farmer Cook Book*, which she undertook at the suggestion of James Beard. Cunningham took cooking courses with Beard and eventually worked with him, helping him teach.

Cunningham has a no-nonsense approach to cooking good food that is simple but delicious. She brought this sensibility to her updated version of *Fannie Farmer*, and she brings it to *The Breakfast Book*. By the 1980s, cooking breakfast and having the family sit down together in the morning was quickly becoming a thing of the past. With both parents working and children going off to different schools, soccer, ballet, rugby, or tennis, no one had time to sit down together for a meal, let alone breakfast. Cunningham found this preposterous. She knew that there are many breakfast foods that can be made ahead, such as oatmeal, muffins, and pies. Eggs take very little time to prepare. Breakfast is really just about planning and thinking that it's important to eat something nutritious and tasty in the morning—and that it's important to sit down as a family first thing in the day. Here are recipes that signify home and comfort. Even if you can only make a big breakfast on Sunday or when friends are over, it's well worth having these scrumptious recipes at hand.

NOTABLE RECIPES: Bridge Creek Ginger Muffins • **Bridge Creek Heavenly Hots** (page 594) • **Buttermilk Pancakes** (page 594) • **The Coach House Bread and Butter Pudding** (page 469) • **Dried Fruit Cream Scones** (page 592) • **Great Coffee Cake** (page 612) • **Oatmeal Bran Breakfast Cookies** (page 632) • **Rhubarb Ginger Jam** (page 438) • Shirred Lemon Eggs

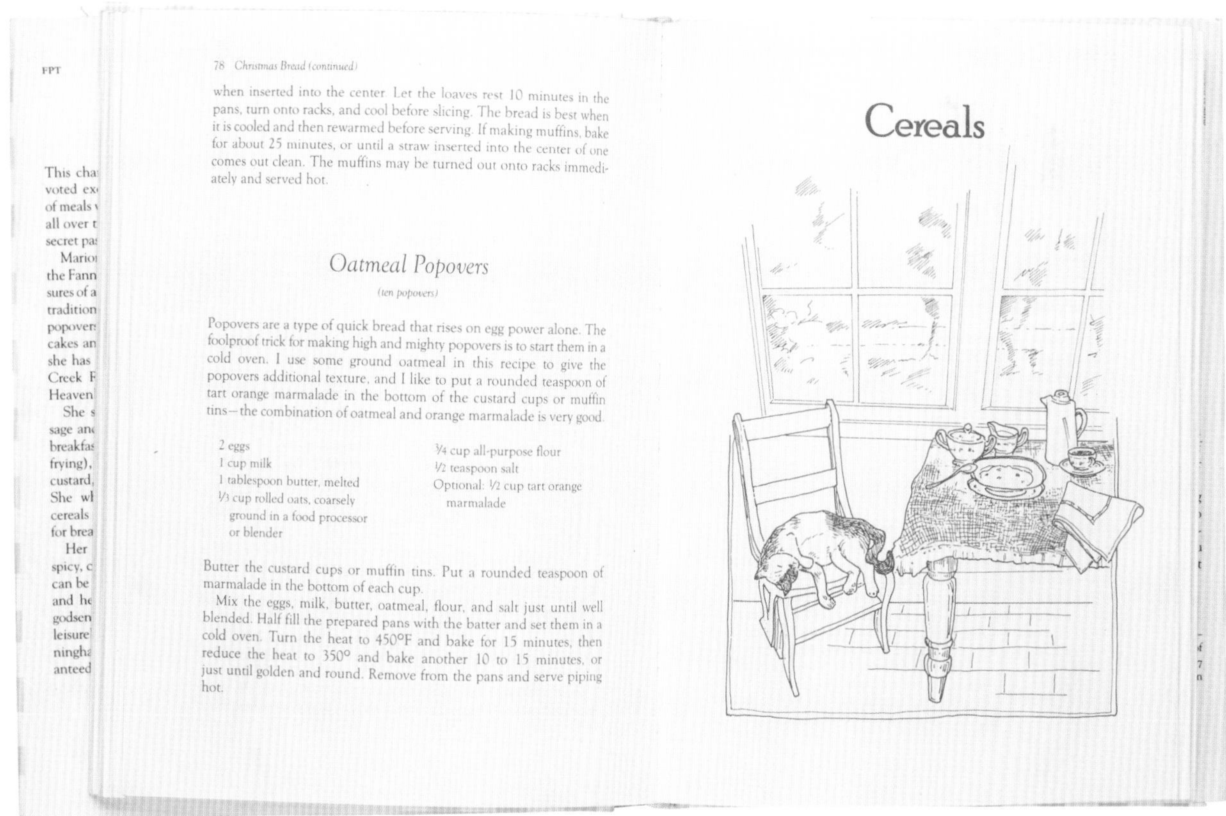

78 *Christmas Bread (continued)*

when inserted into the center. Let the loaves rest 10 minutes in the pans, turn onto racks, and cool before slicing. The bread is best when it is cooled and then rewarmed before serving. If making muffins, bake for about 25 minutes, or until a straw inserted into the center of one comes out clean. The muffins may be turned out onto racks immediately and served hot.

Oatmeal Popovers

(ten popovers)

Popovers are a type of quick bread that rises on egg power alone. The foolproof trick for making high and mighty popovers is to start them in a cold oven. I use some ground oatmeal in this recipe to give the popovers additional texture, and I like to put a rounded teaspoon of tart orange marmalade in the bottom of the custard cups or muffin tins—the combination of oatmeal and orange marmalade is very good.

2 eggs
1 cup milk
1 tablespoon butter, melted
1/3 cup rolled oats, coarsely ground in a food processor or blender
3/4 cup all-purpose flour
1/2 teaspoon salt
Optional: 1/2 cup tart orange marmalade

Butter the custard cups or muffin tins. Put a rounded teaspoon of marmalade in the bottom of each cup.

Mix the eggs, milk, butter, oatmeal, flour, and salt just until well blended. Half fill the prepared pans with the batter and set them in a cold oven. Turn the heat to 450°F and bake for 15 minutes, then reduce the heat to 350° and bake another 10 to 15 minutes, or just until golden and round. Remove from the pans and serve piping hot.

Cereals

BARBARA KAFKA

Microwave Gourmet, 1987

Whatever one thinks about the culinary uses (or abuses) of the microwave oven, there can be no doubt that it changed how Americans eat. Microwave ovens operate on a principle of dielectric heating; that is, they use microwave radiation to heat polarized molecules in food. This causes a more even heating in most foods than any other type of cooking. While the technology dates from 1934, its use in cooking is much more recent.

The first attempt to create a home microwave oven was made by Tappan in 1955. With a price tag of more than $1,200, it didn't sell. The Amana Corporation brought out the first successful home microwave oven in 1967—the Amana "Radar Range." Today estimates show that nearly 90 percent of U.S. homes have a microwave oven. What happened? Enter Barbara Kafka, an internationally known food writer and teacher who taught for many years with James Beard. Among her many successful cookbooks are *Microwave Gourmet* and *Microwave Gourmet Healthstyle Cookbook*, both of which were *New York Times* best-sellers and Book-of-the-Month Club selections, selling out in mass paperback editions in the United States and England. Her book *Roasting: A Simple Art* won a Julia Child Cookbook Award. Kafka continues to write for the *New York Times, Family Circle*, and *Vogue*, among many other publications.

NOTABLE RECIPES: Basic Risotto • Light Poached Pears • Maple Syrup Baked Apples • **Shrimp and Spring Vegetable Risotto** (page 456) • **Soft Polenta** (page 427) • **Steamed Chocolate Pudding** (page 648) • Traditional Hot Borscht

POACHED CHICKEN BREASTS

With this simple recipe, you can create an endless series of dinners by adding different sauces or vegetables. This is also the way to cook breast meat for chicken salads or to substitute in Turkey à la King (page 216).

Poached chicken breasts are very good and elegant with Braised Lettuce (page 273) and Sauce Suprême (page 351). Plain rice and Velouté (page 350) work well. Think about snipping some fresh herbs into the sauce. Allow ¼ cup sauce for each half breast and 1 teaspoon minced herbs for each ¼ cup sauce. If you are putting tarragon on the chicken, add tarragon to the sauce. The lavish can top each half breast with thin slices of black truffle and add some chopped truffle to the sauce. Another possibility is to stir ½ teaspoon tomato paste or 1 teaspoon Chunky Tomato Sauce (page 356) into each ¼ cup of Velouté for a gently pink dish that can be sharpened with a few drops of fresh lemon juice and hot red-pepper sauce. Parsley Sauce (page 352) and Watercress Sauce (page 352) provide nice color contrasts.

How many half breasts to prepare depends on individual appetites and what else you are serving. If there is going to be a first course, count on 1½ half breasts per person, 2 half breasts per person if there is no first course. *Serves 4 to 8*

4 whole chicken breasts, skinned, split and boned
½ cup Chicken Broth (page 314) or canned chicken broth
3 sprigs fresh tarragon (optional)
Sauce Suprême (page 351), for serving

1 Arrange chicken petal-fashion in a 12″ × 1½″ round dish, with thin ends toward the center. Pour broth over chicken and scatter tarragon on top.

2 Cover tightly with microwave plastic wrap. Cook at 100% for 8 minutes.

3 Remove from oven. Uncover and serve with sauce; you may stir a tablespoon or two of the cooking liquid into the sauce, if you like.

To make 1 half breast. Place breast on a small plate with ¼ cup broth and a sprig of tarragon, if desired. Cover and cook at 100% for 3 minutes.

To make 2 half breasts. Place half breasts, thin edges toward each other, on a dinner plate with ¼ cup broth and a sprig of tarragon, if desired. Cover and cook at 100% for 4 minutes.

To make 4 half breasts. Arrange half breasts spoke-fashion in a 9-inch quiche dish with the thick ends toward the outside of the dish. Add ¼ cup broth and 2 sprigs of tarragon, if desired. Cover and cook at 100% for 6 minutes.

To make 6 half breasts. Arrange half breasts spoke-fashion in a large round serving dish about 3 inches deep, with the thick ends toward the outside of the dish. Add ¼ cup broth and 3 sprigs of tarragon, if desired. Cover and cook at 100% for 7 minutes.

A whole, skinned, boneless chicken breast, cut in half, thick sides facing

Split chicken breast cooked with the thick sides toward the edge of dish

used in the production of liquor. It is a nice change from rice and potatoes both as a side dish (see Creamy Barley) and as a soup ingredient (see Mushroom Barley Soup).

In cooking, we generally use pearl barley, which is husked, cooks rapidly and has a pleasant texture. If you have had the barley on the shelf for along time, it is liable to be very hard and dry. Add 5 minutes to the cooking times below and add more liquid if needed.

COOKING TIMES FOR MEDIUM PEARL BARLEY

Risotto technique Uncovered.

¼ c. barley with 1 c. broth (8″ × 6″ flat oval dish) — *16 min.*
1 c. barley with 3 c. broth (12″ × 9″ × 2″ flat oval dish) — *27 min.*
1 c. barley as above — *43 min. (small oven)*

Boiled Cook in a 2½-qt. soufflé; cover tightly with 2 sheets microwave plastic wrap; omit resting time.

1 c. barley with 4 c. water — *30 min.*
2 c. barley with 6 c. water — *30 min.*

BASIL I use this loveliest of herbs frequently, and I am delighted that it is now available fresh, year-round, in many supermarkets. There are two basic varieties, the large-leaf French basil and the smaller-leaf bush basil, which is generally used to make pesto in the Genoan style. Bush basil is more peppery and aromatic. Look for crisp leaves without any black spots. Wash thoroughly and, if cutting, cut across the veins in the leaves. Often, basil leaves are nicest when used whole. They make a wonderful addition to salads. See DRYING, herbs.

BASS OR STRIPED BASS One of the world's best eating fish, with flesh that is white and firm without being chewy. Unfortunately, this means that it is often expensive. Rockfish from the West Coast and red snapper can be substituted; this is important to know since recently bass supplies have often been restricted due to overfishing and pollution. I look forward to the day when aquaculturists figure out that they can farm bass. See FISH for cooking times. See also SEA BASS.

BATTER Batter-based breads, cakes and pancakes are almost useless in microwave cooking; batters to coat food for frying are useful. See Tempura and FRYING.

BAY LEAF Even more than with the other dried herbs, be careful with this one or you will get a bitter flavor. If in doubt, use less. Most recipes call for too much bay leaf in any case. Consider adding it only for the last 4 to 5 minutes of the cooking time. Remember to remove any leaves before serving or reheating a dish; people can choke on them.

BEAN CURD See SOY.

BEANS When I first started using the microwave oven, I was so infatuated with its speed that I dismissed any usage that wasn't super-quick. After I calmed down a little, I realized that the reduced time involved in soaking dried beans and cooking them the microwave way was the difference between almost never cooking them from scratch and feeling free to use them as an ingredient.

Some legumes cook as beans do. See LEGUMES or specific kind of legume.

Canned beans are obviously no problem; you are just reheating.

FRESH BEANS

GREEN, WAX, HARICOT VERT, YARD-LONG BEANS and other fresh pole and bush beans are quick, not watery, and retain their color in the microwave oven. Top, tail and string as necessary. If the beans are very large, or if the recipe calls for it, cut either into lengths or halve (French) lengthwise. Cooking times are by weight, tight wrapped in microwave plastic wrap or microwave-safe plastic bags.

BROAD BEANS

Dried BROAD, FAVA and LIMA BEANS do not cook to best advantage in the microwave oven. You blanch them to make shelling easier. Cook them on top of the stove.

DRIED BEANS

Dried-bean cooking times are determined by the size of the beans. It seems odd, but smaller beans take slightly longer to cook because there are more of them to the pound. The cooking times for these beans follow.

Never salt the beans before cooking, as it toughens the skin. All dried beans must be soaked before cooking.

Large dried beans: black beans, black-eyed peas, cannellini, kidney beans, red beans, pink beans, pinto beans.

Small dried beans: flageolets, navy beans, white beans.

Legumes: broad (fava) beans, chick-peas, lentils, lima beans, split peas.

SOAKING DRIED BEANS AND LEGUMES

To soak 1 or 2 cups dried beans of any size or legumes, place in a 2-quart soufflé dish with 2 cups water. Cover tightly with microwave plastic wrap. Cook at 100% for 15 minutes. Remove from oven and let stand, covered, for 5 minutes. Uncover and add 2 cups very hot water. Re-cover and let stand for 1 hour. Drain.

COOKING TIMES FOR LARGE DRIED BEANS

Put *presoaked* beans in 2-qt. soufflé; cover tightly with 2 sheets microwave plastic wrap.

1 c. beans with 4 c. warm water — *35 min. (rest 20 min.)*
2 c. beans with 6 c. warm water — *45 min. (rest 20 min.)*

Yields

6¼ oz., dried — *1 c., dried*
1 c., dried — *2½ c., cooked*
2½ c., cooked — *2½ c. purée*

COOKING TIMES FOR SMALL DRIED BEANS

Put *presoaked* beans in a 2-qt. soufflé; cover tightly with 2 sheets microwave plastic wrap.

1 or 2 c. beans with 4 c. warm water — *40 min. (rest 30 min.)*

Yields

1 c., dried — *3 c., cooked*
3 c., cooked — *3 c. purée*

COOKING TIMES FOR FRESH BEANS

Whole green and wax beans, trimmed Wrap tightly in ¼-lb. amounts sprinkled with water.

¼ lb. beans — *3 min. 30 sec. to 4 min.*
¼ lb. beans — *5 min. (small oven)*
½ lb. beans — *4 min. to 4 min. 30 sec.*
½ lb. beans — *6 min. (small oven)*
1 lb. — *6 to 8 min.*

Yields

1 lb. — *5 c., raw*
5 c., raw — *4 c., cooked*

Whole haricots verts and yard-long beans, trimmed Arrange in a single layer; cover tightly.

¼ lb. beans with 1 c. water (4-c. measure) — *6 min.*
1 lb. beans with 3 c. water (14″ × 11″ × 2″ dish) — *15 min.*

BEEF This may still be America's favorite food, no matter what we have learned about limiting its ingestion for our health's sake. When it comes to cooking those most favorite cuts of all, the steaks and roasts, the microwave oven is of no earthly use at all; no amount of browning mixture or glaze will conceal the fact that these cuts would have cooked better in a conventional oven, on a grill, in a sauté

DEBORAH MADISON

The Greens Cook Book,

Extraordinary Vegetarian Cuisine from the Celebrated Restaurant, 1987

In her introduction to *The Greens Cook Book*, Marion Cunningham confesses she was skeptical about eating at yet another vegetarian restaurant when she first went to Greens. Too often these bastions of progressive thinking won on ethical grounds but served "rather dismal, lackluster meals." Cunningham was surprised when "the food turned out to be better than I could have possibly imagined."

Deborah Madison and Edward Espe Brown wrote *The Greens Cook Book* to share not just the recipes from Greens but also their belief in using local produce and cooking seasonally, while demonstrating that there was a whole range of delicious vegetarian dishes from around the world that could satisfy the American desire for a meat-centered meal. As Jonathan Gold has said, this book was "a shot across the bow of American cooking." Greens could not have existed without the San Francisco Zen Center, which provided assistance in founding the restaurant, not to mention a steady clientele. Importantly, the Zen Center's Tassajara Bread Bakery, already famous for its high-quality baked goods, supplied breads and desserts to Greens.

Reading this book you get a sense of community, of people who love the food they prepare, and of sharing the joy of cooking and eating. Madison's and Brown's voice rings with a kind of poetry: "Anyone who knows the fragrance of tomatoes ripening in the sun, the sweetness of berries so ripe they practically fall into the hand, or the flavor of asparagus and corn when picked right away knows food at its pleasurable best." After reading that, who can resist the sprightly, dazzling recipes Madison and Brown share with us? Try the black bean chili. It's Madison's favorite. Most copies of the book fall open to it. It's used that often.

NOTABLE RECIPES: Black Bean Chili • **Black Bean Enchiladas** (page 388) • Chili Butter • Chinese Noodle Salad with Roasted Eggplant • **Hummous** (page 320) • New Potatoes and Garlic Baked in Parchment • Phyllo Pastry with Goat Cheese and Spinach • **Semolina Pudding with Blood Orange Syrup** (page 649) • **Summer Vegetable Stock** (page 520) • White Bread and Fresh Tomato Soup with Parsley Sauce • **Wilted Spinach Salad** (page 360) • **Winter Vegetable Stew** (page 383)

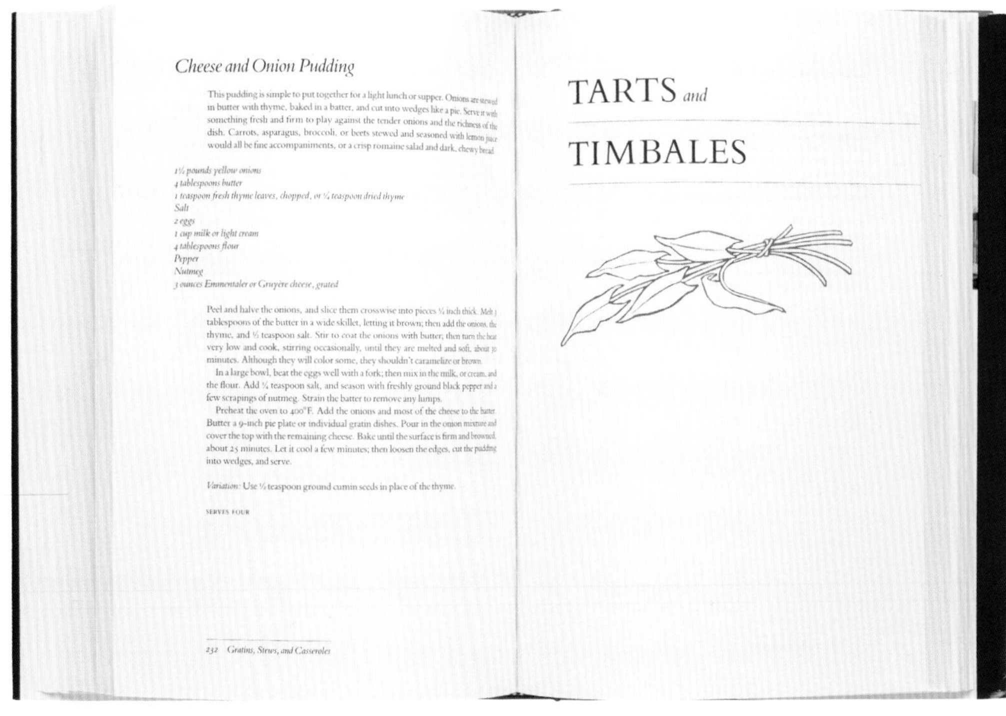

Cheese and Onion Pudding

This pudding is simple to put together for a light lunch or supper. Onions are stewed in butter with thyme, baked in a batter, and cut into wedges like a pie. Serve it with something fresh and firm to play against the tender onions and the richness of the dish. Carrots, asparagus, broccoli, or beets stewed and seasoned with lemon juice would all be fine accompaniments, or a crisp romaine salad and dark, chewy bread.

1½ pounds yellow onions
4 tablespoons butter
1 teaspoon fresh thyme leaves, chopped, or ½ teaspoon dried thyme
Salt
2 eggs
1 cup milk or light cream
4 tablespoons flour
Pepper
Nutmeg
3 ounces Emmentaler or Gruyère cheese, grated

Peel and halve the onions, and slice them crosswise into pieces ¼ inch thick. Melt 3 tablespoons of the butter in a wide skillet, letting it brown; then add the onions, the thyme, and ½ teaspoon salt. Stir to coat the onions with butter; then turn the heat very low and cook, stirring occasionally, until they are melted and soft, about 30 minutes. Although they will color some, they shouldn't caramelize or brown.

In a large bowl, beat the eggs well with a fork; then mix in the milk, or cream, and the flour. Add ¼ teaspoon salt, and season with freshly ground black pepper and a few scrapings of nutmeg. Strain the batter to remove any lumps.

Preheat the oven to 400°F. Add the onions and most of the cheese to the batter. Butter a 9-inch pie plate or individual gratin dishes. Pour in the onion mixture and cover the top with the remaining cheese. Bake until the surface is firm and browned, about 25 minutes. Let it cool a few minutes; then loosen the edges, cut the pudding into wedges, and serve.

Variation: Use ½ teaspoon ground cumin seeds in place of the thyme.

SERVES FOUR

232 *Gratins, Stews, and Casseroles*

TARTS *and*

TIMBALES

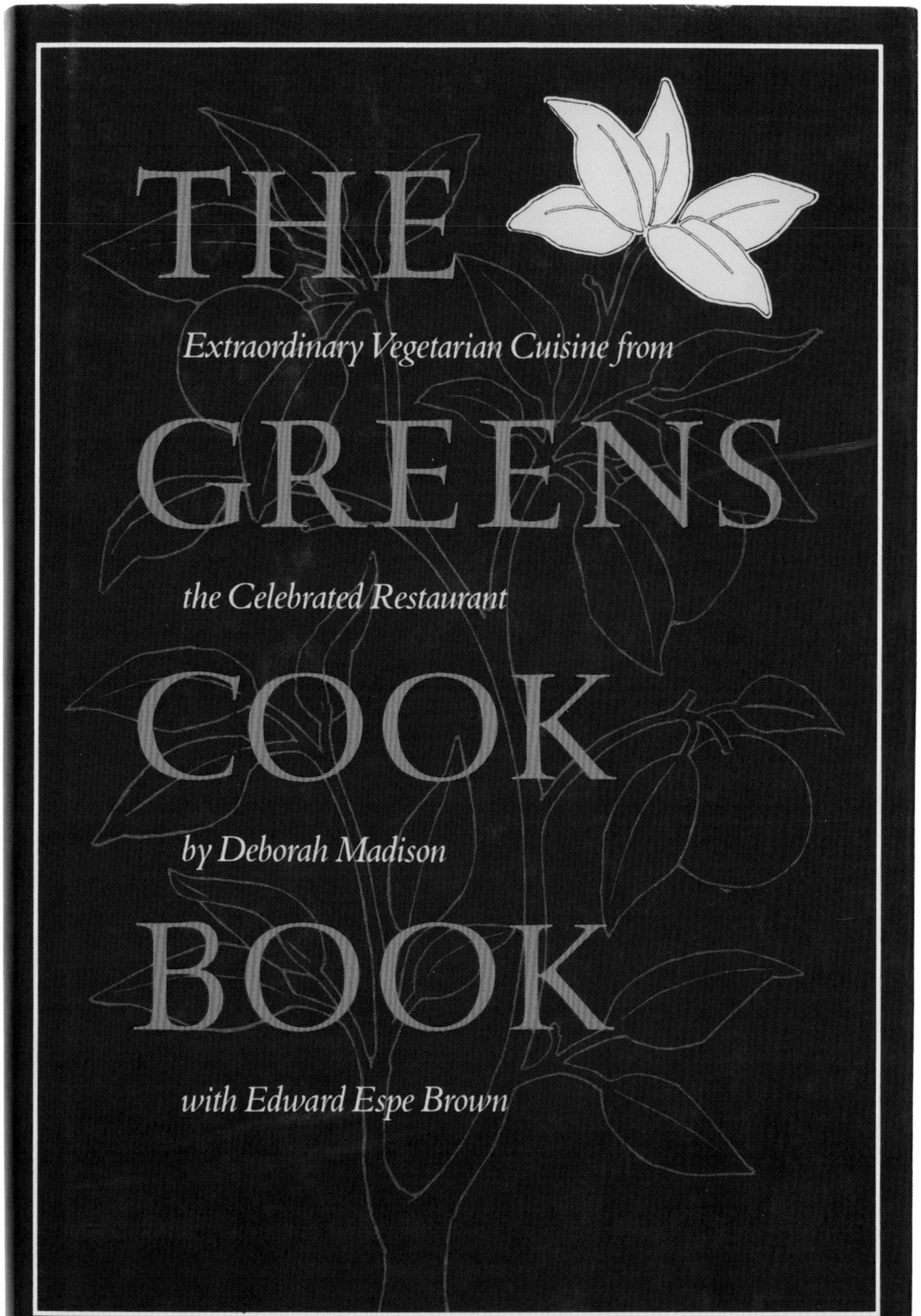

THE

Extraordinary Vegetarian Cuisine from

GREENS

the Celebrated Restaurant

COOK

by Deborah Madison

BOOK

with Edward Espe Brown

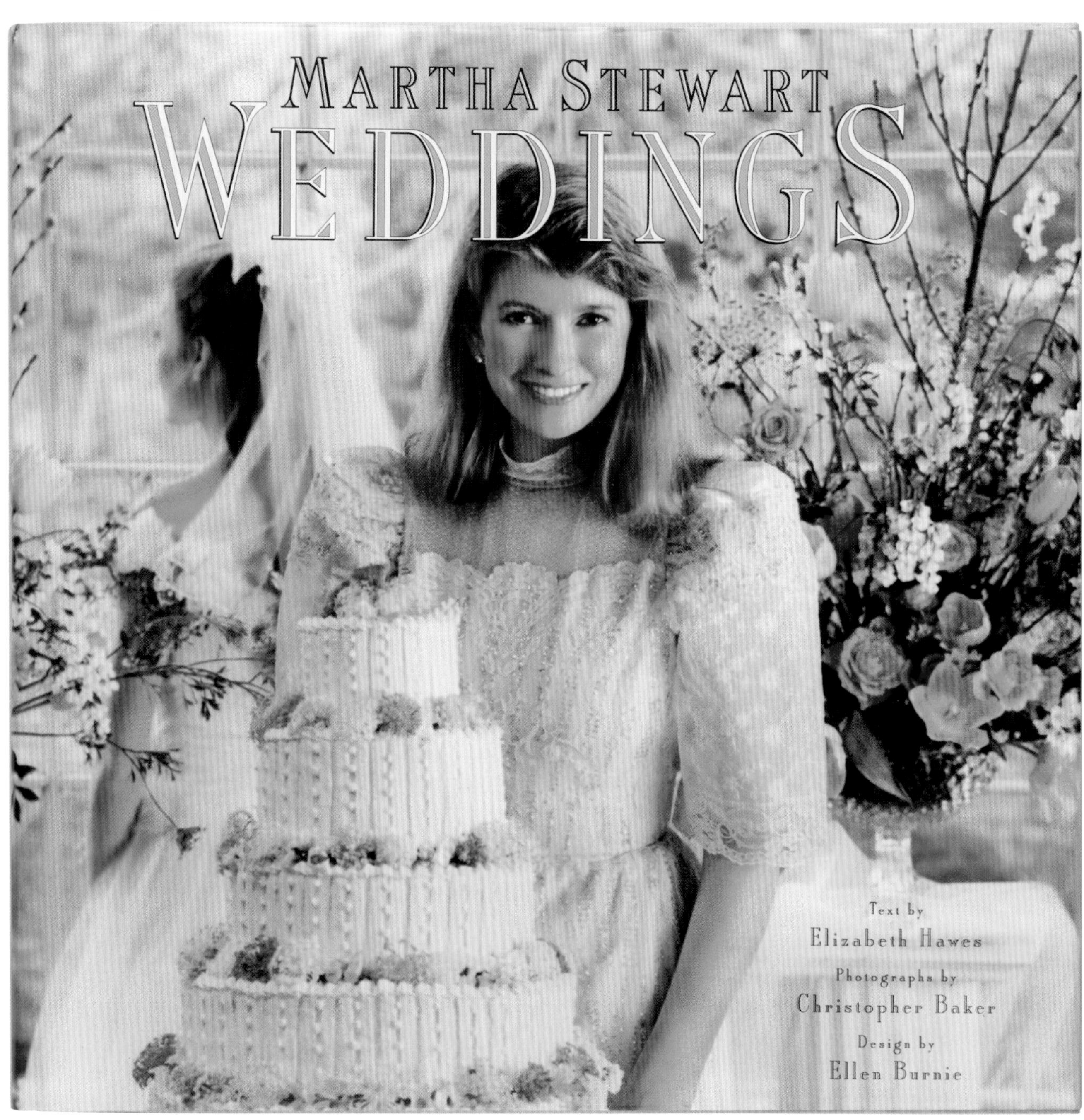
MARTHA STEWART
WEDDINGS
Text by
Elizabeth Hawes
Photographs by
Christopher Baker
Design by
Ellen Burnie

MARTHA STEWART

Weddings, 1987

Martha Stewart is a media phenomenon. Born in Jersey City, New Jersey, as Martha Kostyra, Stewart was one of six children; they grew up in the working-class town of Nutley, New Jersey. As a teen she worked as a model for television and print advertising. An excellent student, she earned a degree from Barnard College in Manhattan. During college she met Andy Stewart, who was pursuing a law degree from Yale, and the two married. Stewart spent the late 1960s working as a stockbroker for the Wall Street firm Monness, Williams, and Sidel.

She left Wall Street in 1972 when she moved to Westport, Connecticut, where she and Andy began to restore a nineteenth-century farmhouse. Stewart turned her attention to cooking, teaching herself recipes from *Mastering the Art of French Cooking* by Julia Child, and opened a catering business, which was a major success and quickly became the main focus of her life.

She began publishing cookbooks; the first one, *Entertaining*, was a best-seller. With *Weddings*, Stewart found her voice. In 1991 Stewart created Martha Stewart Living Omnimedia, Inc., and started the magazine *Martha Stewart Living*, which offered helpful hints about homemaking and lifestyle. It, too, was a major success. Soon Stewart had a television show, a syndicated news column, a radio show, and a Web presence. Her business brought in more than $763 million per year in sales. Stewart's media empire has been valued at an estimated $1.2 billion.

NOTABLE RECIPES: Chocolate Ganache Groom's Cake (page 631) • **Croquembouche** (page 629) • Hazelnut Genoise • **Orange Almond Cake** (page 628) • **Whipped Cream Cake** (page 609)

Garden Party in Pink

Caroline Damerell and Carmine Santandrea travel a great deal in Europe and the United States, and eat varied, sophisticated foods. They wanted their wedding menu to reflect their fondness for fresh, colorful regional foods and eclectic ethnic cuisines.

Because they live in Connecticut and sail every weekend, they asked for clams and lobsters. Because it was summer, they asked for lots of fresh vegetables. And because Caroline loves pink, all the desserts were some shade of her favorite color. Even the wine was pink! The chocolate petits fours were for Carmine.

The hors d'oeuvres were all very pretty and delicate, from the raw littleneck clams with a shallot-flavored cocktail sauce to the carefully sliced anise-flavored salmon gravlax, to the heart-shaped toasts with herbed cheese topping. The hors d'oeuvres were served simply, garnished with sprigs of herbs.

MENU

HORS D'OEUVRES

Raw Clam Bar with Shallot-Flavored Cocktail Sauce

Gravlax on Black Bread with Mustard-Fennel Sauce

Heart Toasts with Herb Cheese

Smoked Salmon Mousse on Cucumber Hearts

BUFFET

Poached Lobster Halves with Red Pepper Sauce

Peasant Salad · Filet of Beef Salad

Sesame Noodles with Tree-Ear Mushrooms and Cucumbers

Endive, Beet, and Orange Salad

Homemade French Bread with Pink Strawberry Butter

DESSERT

Fraises des Bois Sorbet · Long-Stemmed Strawberries

Chocolate Petit Fours · Wedding Cake

The buffet was displayed on a sixteen-foot-long table. (This table was later used as the dessert buffet, and a new pale pink cloth was placed over the original white buffet cloth.) Silver trays and baskets were used as the serving dishes. Salads were mounded on the silver trays and garnished with greenery—curly kale, radicchio, watercress, ferns, and tansy. More branches of herbs and fronds of ferns were used to decorate the table itself. The platters of lobster halves were garnished with whole, plump pink pears that had been poached in red wine. The red pepper sauce was gently pink, and the strawberry butter was pink as well.

The finale of the meal was the Rose Cake, a lemon pound cake interior with an Italian meringue exterior, lavishly swathed in old roses. A silver-footed compote was filled to brimming with more roses. Caroline gasped with pleasure at the sight of so many of her favorite flowers.

240

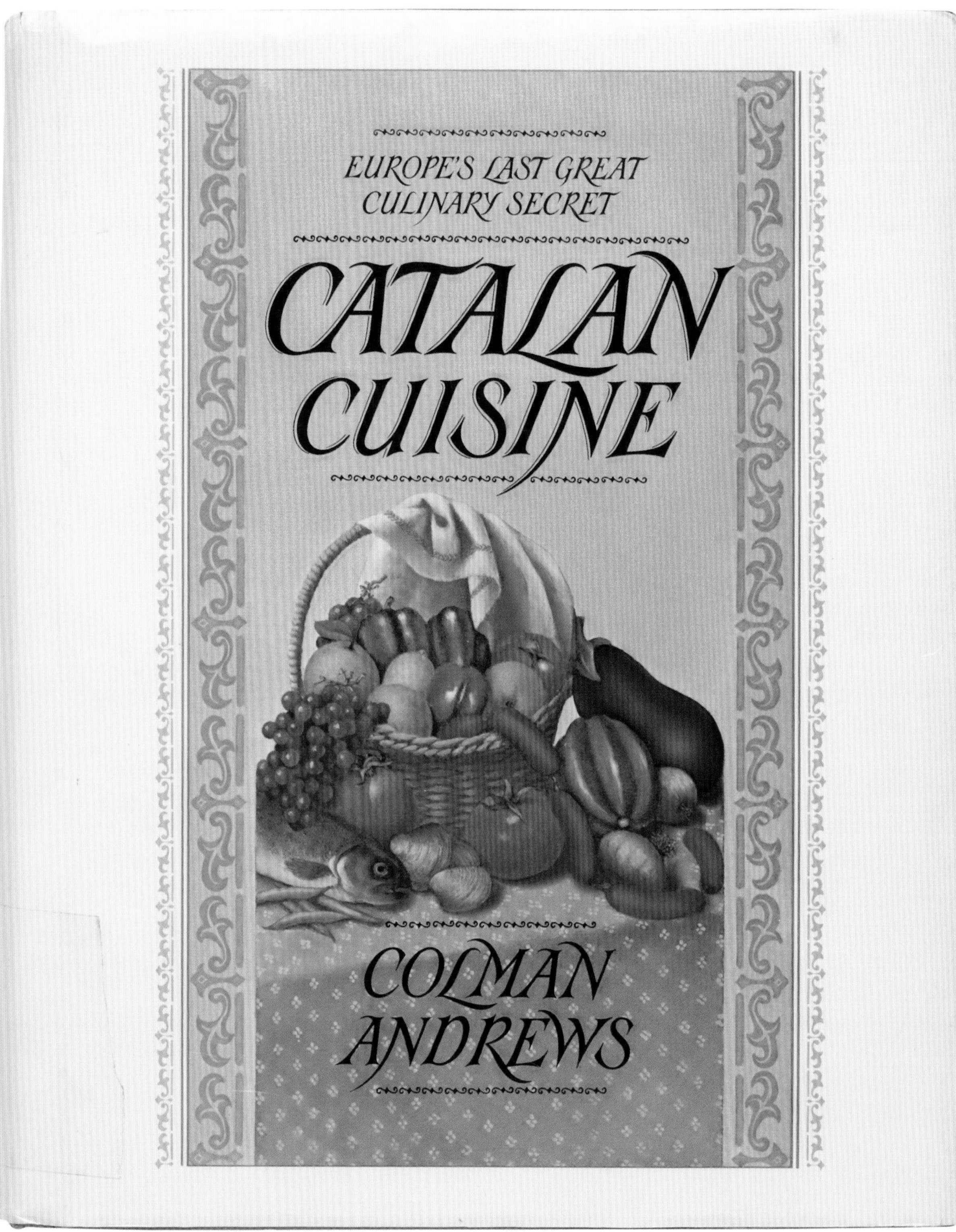
EUROPE'S LAST GREAT
CULINARY SECRET
CATALAN
CUISINE
COLMAN
ANDREWS

COLMAN ANDREWS

Catalan Cuisine, 1988

Americans have been enjoying the rich food traditions of the Iberian peninsula for a very long time, especially those that entered American food through Creole cooking in the South and, at least in some East Coast cities, the restaurants of Spaniards who immigrated to the United States when Francisco Franco came to power in their homeland. Of course, not unlike Italy or France, Spain's food traditions are not easily definable. Rather, they share the same regional distinctions as their other Latinate sister countries. Colman Andrews became obsessed with what he called "Europe's last great undiscovered cuisine."

The definition of Catalonia is itself much contested, but it generally refers to the cooking of northeastern Spain and any region where Catalans ruled and took their food traditions. Catalan cuisine dates back to the fourteenth century, but it bears a strong resemblance to Roman food—more so than any other European food tradition—for the Romans brought olives and grapes to the region and the food remains close to its origins. One thing that distinguishes Catalan food is a surprising mixing of ingredients. Nuts are pulverized to thicken sauces. Chocolate and cinnamon appear in savory dishes. Poultry is cooked with fruit. Pork sausage is served with lemon and sugar as a dessert. Andrews's book opened up these new flavor sensations for Americans in a clear, approachable style. This is a book for anyone who loves complex flavors, hearty meals, and pork—for the pig features heavily in Catalan cooking.

NOTABLE RECIPES: **Allioli** (page 522) • **Bacallà amb Mel (Salt Cod with Honey)** (page 479) • Bunyols de Bacalla (Salt Cod Fritters) • Catalan Tomato Bread • **Civet de Llogosta (Spiny Lobster Stew)** (page 484) • **Escudella i Carn d'Olla (Catalan Soup with Boiled Meats and Vegetables)** (page 355) • Espinas d'Anxoves Fregides (Deep Fried Anchovy Spines) • **Paella Valenciana amb Mariscos** (page 456) • **Stuffed Squid with Chocolate Sauce** (page 481)

WHERE, WHO, AND WHAT

sandy coves to flat vineyard and orchard land to pine-covered hills and real mountains 5,000 feet or so above sea level. The capital, Palma de Mallorca, is a handsome, cosmopolitan city, facing a wide bay and watched over by a magnificent buttressed cathedral (partially restored by Gaudí) on a hill above the port. Majorca was an important wine-producing center in the eighteenth and early nineteenth centuries, and there are limited efforts now to revive the industry. Majorcan almonds are famous, as are the island's figs and tomatoes. Majorcan gastronomy, which has a long and fascinating history and boasts many extraordinary dishes, is, alas, today, as a Majorcan winemaker of my acquaintance puts it, "mostly a family matter."

The last little bit of *els països catalans* is the city of Alghero (l'Alguer in Catalan) on the Italian island of Sardinia—sometimes called Sardinia's "little Barcelona." Alghero was first occupied by Catalan-Aragonese forces in the mid-fourteenth century, and remained part of the Catalan-speaking empire for nearly 400 years. As a result, the city is full of Catalan-style houses, religious edifices, and fortifications, and some Catalan street names—Carrer del Forn, Plaça del Portal, etc.—are still used. The local citizenry even continued to speak Catalan (albeit in an archaic and somewhat Italian-flavored form) until recent years—though it is seldom heard on the streets today. Catalan culinary influence was strong throughout Sardinia, to the point that one expert on the island's customs has written that "Sardinian gastronomy in general is specifically Catalan." Recipes for several Algherese Catalan dishes appear in the pages that follow.

II. THE CATALANS AND THEIR LANGUAGE

If food is of and from a place, it is even more so of and from—and by—a people. And it is axiomatic, I think, that the more complex and colorful a people's history—and the more other races it has come into contact with—the richer and more varied its cuisine will be. (The English, a cynic might point out, are something of an anomaly in this regard.) And the history of the Catalans, needless to say, is nothing if not complex and colorful.

Not much is known about the Iberian tribes that originally inhabited the region, but it *is* known that there were Phocaean Greek settlements on the Catalan coast as early as the sixth century B.C., and that Carthaginians followed in the late fourth or early third century B.C. The first full-scale foreign occupation of the area began in 218 B.C., when Roman armies landed on the Catalan coast at the start of the bloody Second Punic War—whence, in time, they conquered the entire Iberian Peninsula, remaining in power there until A.D. 476.

In a sense, Rome made Catalonia; it *certainly* helped make Catalan gastronomy. Romans introduced the first large-scale plantings of olive trees and grapevines to the region, for instance, as well as techniques for the production of oil and wine—subsequently so important to the local table. They also brought leavened bread to Catalonia for the first time, as well as favas, chick-peas, lentils, and other

17

Stir in the ham and chicken, mix well, sauté on low heat for about 5 minutes, then remove pan from heat, and set aside to cool.

Stir the butter and egg yolk into the mashed potatoes, and salt and pepper to taste, then place in the refrigerator for 20–30 minutes or until moldable.

Shape the potato mixture into 12–16 balls about 1½–2 inches in diameter, then form each into a small flat patty between your hands. Place 1 teaspoon of the chicken mixture in the center of each patty, then close the potatoes around it, cupping each croquette in the palm of your hand and forming it into a bell or cone shape.

Gently flatten the bottom of each croquette, dip them in beaten egg, roll in breadcrumbs, then fry in at least 1 inch of oil heated to 375° in a cassola or deep pan (or use deep fryer), turning them to brown on all sides.

Drain on paper towels as cooked, then sprinkle with parsley. Squeeze a few drops of fresh lemon juice over each croquette if desired.

Pintada a la Catalana

(GUINEA HEN IN LEMON AND GARLIC SAUCE)

Ely Buxeda is a French Catalan entertainer, who once toured Europe with his crooning vocals and syrupy saxophone but who now confines his performances to an occasional turn at the pleasant restaurant he runs in the seaside wine town of Banyuls, a few miles north of the Spanish border. I have a certain affection for his establishment—which is called Le Sardinal, "The Sardine Net"—because it was the first Catalan restaurant I ever visited, a good three years before I first set foot in Spanish Catalonia.

I must admit that I don't remember what I ate my first time at Le Sardinal, other than some rich Collioure anchovies—but when I went back, five years later, in the company of one of the directors of the Templers union of Banyuls wine cooperatives, I tasted this guinea hen dish and immediately begged for the recipe. Le Sardinal's chef, Jean-Marie Patrouix, who isn't Catalan but who knows how to cook as if he were (which I mean as a compliment), promptly scribbled it out for me.

TO SERVE 4 (AS MAIN COURSE)

One 3–4-pound guinea hen or chicken
Olive oil
1 onion, chopped
2–3 heads garlic, separated into cloves and peeled
¼ pound European-style ham (prosciutto or Black Forest type), cut into julienne strips about 2 inches long
1 lemon rind, grated
Juice of 1 lemon
2½ cups rich chicken or veal stock
Orange extract
1 cup dry white wine
Salt and pepper
8–12 rounds (3 inches in diameter) French or Italian bread, lightly toasted and allowed to dry to crispness
4 paper-thin slices lemon (optional)

Cut the guinea hen or chicken into 8 serving pieces.

Sauté the pieces in olive oil in a cassola or large skillet until golden-brown, then remove, and set aside.

In the same oil, make a *sofregit* (see page 38) of the onion, whole garlic cloves, and ham.

Return the guinea hen or chicken to the cassola and add the lemon rind, lemon juice, stock, a few drops of orange extract, the wine, and salt and pepper to taste.

Simmer partially covered until the chicken is very tender and the liquid is reduced by half (about 1½–2 hours).

Garnish with the dried bread and, if you wish, with lemon slices.

Gall Dindi Farcit Nadelenc

(STUFFED CHRISTMAS TURKEY)

As noted earlier, turkey is associated with Christmas in Catalonia as much as it is in the United States. The context in which it is traditionally presented on that holiday (or that holiday's eve) is, however, somewhat different from the American version. An old-fashioned Catalan Christmas banquet would invariably begin with *Escudella i Carn d'Olla* (see page 231), the Ur-Catalan specialty of assorted meats and vegetables cooked in stock and then served in two courses—broth first, meats later.

CATALONIA

Alella: Marqués de Alella (w).
Empordà-Costa Brava: Cavas del Ampurdán Blanc Pescador (w); Gran Recosind (r); Oliveda Garnatxa de la Bota del Racó (d); Corinosa Garnatxa de l'Empordà Reserva (d).
Penedès (*cava* or *méthode champenoise* sparkling wine): Codorníu Blanc de Blanc, Brut Noir, Gran Codorníu, and Brut Classico; Raïmat Brut Grapa; Freixenet Cordon Negro, Brut Nature, and Brut Barocco; Segura Viudas Reserva Heredad; Castellblanch Brut Zero and Gran Cremant; Cavas Hill Brut de Brut; Juvé y Camps Reserva de la Familia; Mont-Marçal Brut Tradición and Brut Gran Reserva; Marqués de Monistrol Brut Nature; Lembey Brut; Nadal Brut; Gramona Celler Batlle; Torello Brut and Brut Nature; Llopart Reserva; Mascaró Brut.
Penedès (table wines): Masia Bach Viña Extrísima Reserva (r) and Extrísimo Gran Reserva (d); Parnàs Xaloc Blanc (w); Torres Viña Sol (w), Gran Viña Sol Reserva Etiqueta Verde (w), De Casta (r), Sangre de Toro (r), Gran Sangre de Toro (r), Gran Coronas (r), and Gran Coronas Etiqueta Negra (r); Jean Leon Chardonnay (w) and Cabernet (r); Cavas Hill Gran Toc (r) and Castell de Foc (ro); Juvé y Camps Ermita d'Espiells (w); Mont-Marçal Cabernet Sauvignon (r); Quinter & Ventosa Montgros (w); Josep Ferrer Mateu Viña Laranda "Bodegas del Foix" (r); Freixedas & Pomés Tinto 5° Año (r); Valldosera Blanc Argent (w); Josep Maris Torres i Blanco Mas Rabassa (w).
Tarragona: De Muller Garnacha Solera 1926 (d), Priorato Dulce Extra Rancio Solera 1918 (d), and Dom Juan Fort Extra Rancio Solera 1865 (a/d).
Priorat: Cartoixa Scala Dei Reserva (r).
Sitges: Bodegas Robert Moscatel (d), Malvasía (d), and Malvasía Reserva (d).

VALENCIA

Valencia: C. Augusto Eglí Alto Turia (w).
Alicante: Salvador Poveda Fondillon (d).

BALEARIC ISLANDS

Majorca: Jaime Mesquida Cabernet Sauvignon (r), Vinya Esther Rosat (ro), and Xenoy Generoso Dulce (d); Jose L. Ferrer Binisalem Auténtico Tinto (r); Viños Oliver Mont Ferrutx (r).
Ibiza: Can del Mulo Alghibiza (w), Tinto del Mulo (r), and Pep Daifa (*cava*).

ROUSSILLON

(Most producers make wines from several appellations.) Château de Jau Côtes-du-Roussillon (r), Muscat de Rivesaltes (d), and Banyuls (d); Templers Banyuls Perlé (a), Cuvée Amiral François Vilarem Banyuls (d), Ancestral Banyuls (d), Mas de la Serra "Demi-Sec" Banyuls (d), Cuvée Viviane le Roy "Dry" Banyuls (a), Castell des Templers Grand Vin des Hospices de Banyuls (d), and Aphrodis Muscat de Rivesaltes (d); Cazes Frères Côtes-du-Roussillon (r), Muscat de Rivesaltes (d), and Rivesaltes Tres Vieux "Cuvée Aîme Cazes" (d); Domaine de Mas Blanc (Dr. Parcé) Cuvée Les Piloumes Collioure (r), Cosprons Levant Collioure (r), Mas Blanc "Dry" Banyuls (a), and Banyuls Rimage (a/d); Vignerons Catalans Taïchat Côtes-du-Roussillon Blanc (w), Côtes-du-Roussillon Rosé (ro), Côtes-du-Roussillon Rouge Guittard-Rodor (r), and Côtes-du-Roussillon Caramany "Cuvée Caveau de Presbytère" (r); Mas Chichet Cuvée Spéciale Cabernet.

BRANDY, ETC.

Among the good alcohols distilled in the *països catalans* are these: an *estomacal* or *digèstif* called Bonet, from the Costa Brava town of Sant Feliu de Guixols; a whole line of excellent liqueurs and Alsatian-style *eaux-de-vie* made by Joaquim Vich under the Gerunda label in Girona; *marc* or grape-pomace brandy in the style of France's *marc de champagne* made by Segura Viudas and several other *cava* producers in the Penedès; a line of dry, sophisticated brandies from Torres, also in the Penedès; three brandies from the Penedès *cava* producer Mascaró—the cheapest of which, Marivaux, is particularly good; Suau brandy from Pont d'Inca, Majorca; and the old-fashioned French *apéritif* called Byrrh (pronounced "beer"), from the town of Thuir, southwest of Perpignan, in the Roussillon.

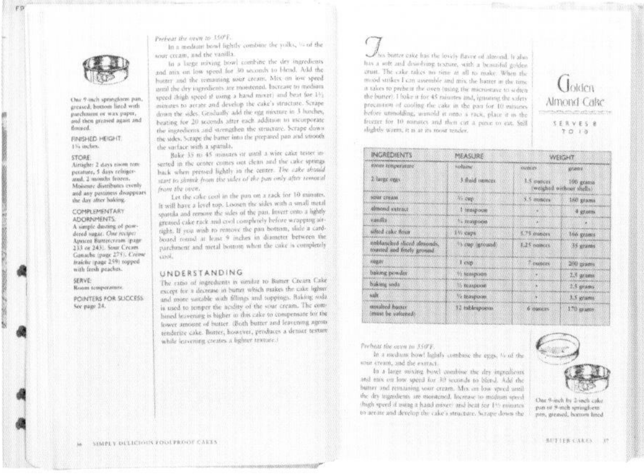

ROSE LEVY BERANBAUM

The Cake Bible, 1988

Rose Levy Beranbaum is the "Diva of Desserts." *The Cake Bible*, her aptly named first book, appeared in 1988 and changed the way a generation made cakes. Beranbaum wanted to make cakes that had the same texture as those from manufacturers, but that had truly delicious flavors. After years of experimenting, she decided to abandon all common wisdom about how to mix a cake. Rather than creaming the butter and sugar, then adding the flour and liquid, Beranbaum began to blend all the dry ingredients with the butter and a small amount of liquid, then beat in the rest of the liquid. Her technique prevents overbeating, which is a danger when the flour is added, and creates a lighter, higher cake. The result is a perfect texture and a buttery flavor that sets her cakes apart. She adds one caveat: "If you don't soften the butter you've had it."

The Cake Bible won the International Association of Culinary Professionals Book of the Year award. It was printed in an original edition of 100,000 copies and is now in its forty-seventh printing. The James Beard Foundation named it among the top thirteen baking books on its "Essential Book List." Beranbaum's description of why she is a great baker pretty much sums up the essential baking personality: "Baking captured all the things I'm interested in and was good at. It requires a certain kind of exacting personality, people who like to follow rules. It suited me perfectly. And you can do so many things with so few ingredients. A cake is something that's created, transformed from ingredients. No matter what you do to it, a lamb chop is always a lamb chop."

NOTABLE RECIPES: All-Occasion Downy Yellow Butter Cake (page 608) • **Blueberry Swan Lake Cake** (page 627) • **Cordon Rose Chocolate Christmas Log** (page 628) • Chocolate Oblivion Truffle Torte • Cordon Rose Banana Cake • Cordon Rose Cream Cheesecake • Golden Almond Cake • **Lemon Poppy Seed Pound Cake** (page 614) • Neoclassic Buttercream • **Orange-Glow Chiffon Cake** (page 616) • Pineapple Upside-Down Cake • **Swiss Black Forest Cake** (page 626)

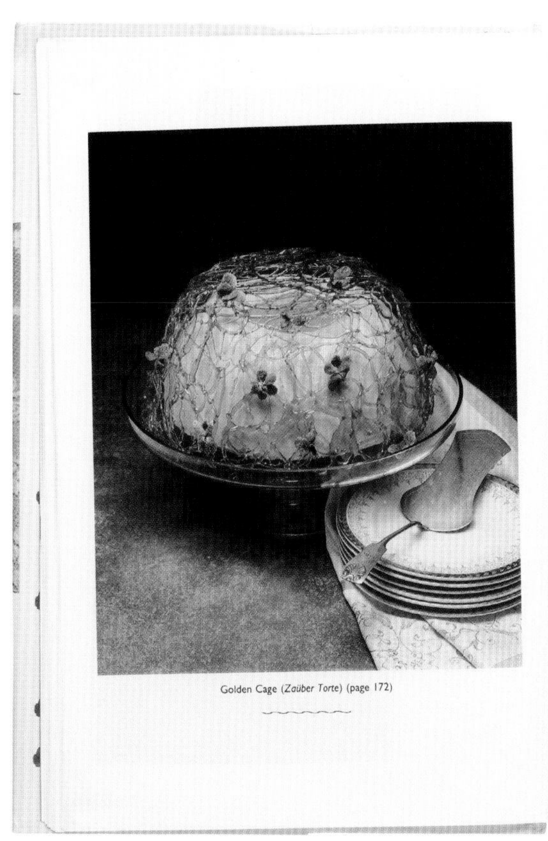

Golden Cage (*Zaüber Torte*) (page 172)

Scarlet Empress (page 177)

Chocolate Chip Charlotte (page 179)

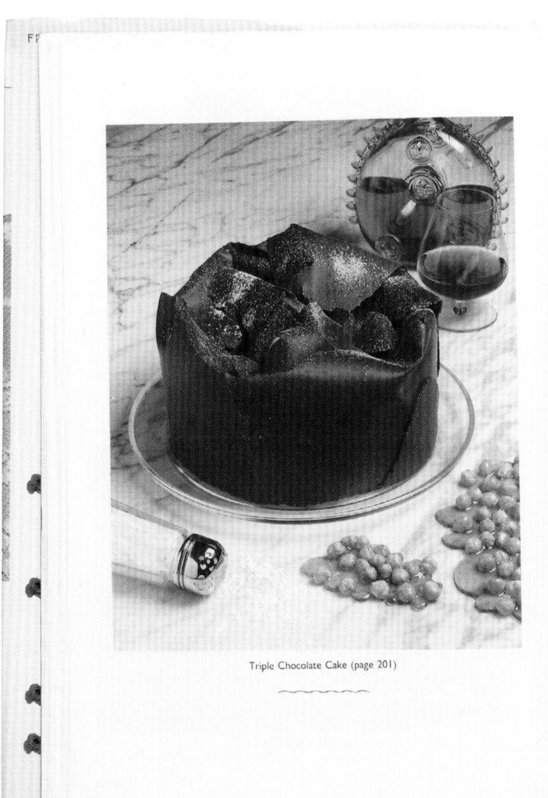

Triple Chocolate Cake (page 201)

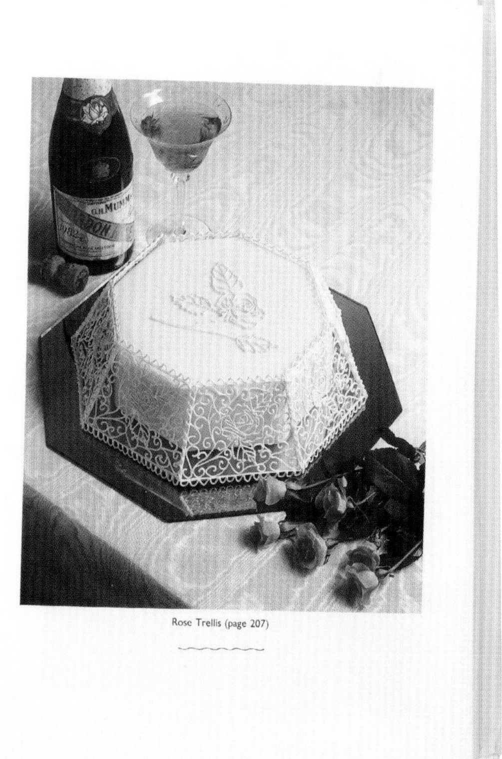

Rose Trellis (page 207)

Checkerboard Fantasy Cake (page 52)

Golden Grand Marnier Cake (page 44)

Chocolate Lover's Angel Food Cake (page 160)

Lemon Poppy Seed Pound Cake (page 27)

PATRICIA WELLS

Bistro Cooking, 1989

Patricia Wells is perhaps best known for her book *The Food Lover's Guide to Paris*, which "cracked the code" of Parisian restaurants, allowing the average American foodie to gain access to this closed world of French gourmands.

Wells was living in Paris at the height of the nouvelle cuisine craze in the late 1970s to early 1980s and reviewed it from her position as restaurant critic for the *International Herald Tribune*. (She is also the only woman and only foreigner to serve as a restaurant critic for a major French publication, the news weekly *L'Express*.) Wells found herself frequenting the mom-and-pop restaurants in Paris when she wasn't dining out for her columns. The simple fare, lovingly prepared, could have come from someone's kitchen. It was a like a blast of spring air in the arid world of nouvelle cuisine and fine dining. Bistro dining seemed egalitarian compared to the remnants of haute cuisine that informed the nouvelle, for it was the average Frenchman who frequented these noisy, familiar, neighborhood joints. It was a prescription for success in the United States. Patric Kuh, in his articulate and fascinating book *The Last Days of Haute Cuisine*, notes that Americans had always riled just a bit at the exclusiveness of haute cuisine restaurants. Access to these places was carefully guarded by the likes of Henri Soulé, the chef and host of New York's famous Le Pavillon, who was notorious for pandering to his upper-class denizens while sneering at anyone who might merely be interested in food. There was something downright un-American about Soulé and, by extension, haute cuisine. Kuh thinks this is one of the reasons that the old haute cuisine restaurants have nearly all vanished from the United States. In their place came the more democratic restaurants, like those Joe Baum created with Restaurant Associates.

By the 1980s the foodie community was expanding rapidly. People still wanted to eat wonderful French food, but not at the stuffy, class-conscious restaurants. The bistro provided the perfect setting for Americans to eat French cooking. And they appeared on nearly every street corner—90 percent of them not really serving anything like bistro food. Wells's book provides recipes that are the real thing. A salad of frisée, bacon, and vinegar, followed by steak frites, and chocolate mousse for dessert was wonderful to eat in the limelight of a bistro or in the comfort of your own dining room. Finally, French food Americans could appreciate without feeling *prétentieux*.

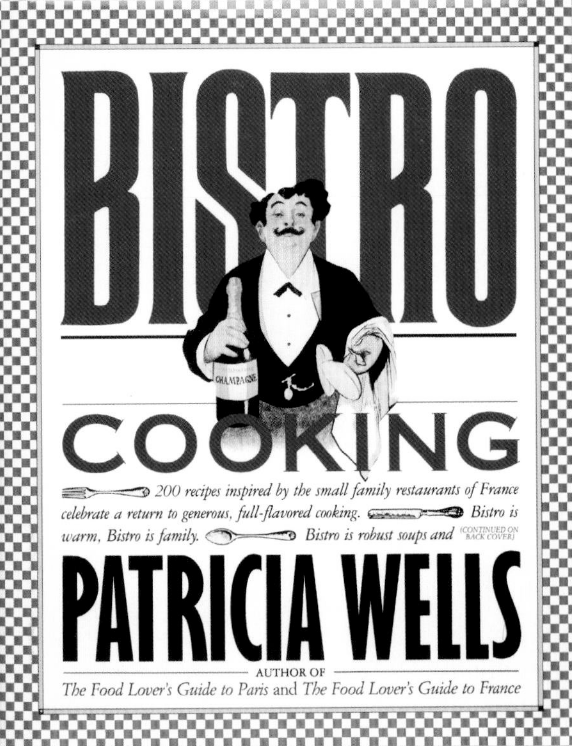

NOTABLE RECIPES: Choux Rouges Braises • **Daube de Boeuf Auberge de la Madone aux Cèpes et à l'Orange** (page 401) • **Gigot Rôti au Gratin de Monsieur Henry** (page 549) • **Gratin Dauphinois Madame Cartet** (page 386) • **Gratin Dauphinois Madame Laracine** (page 387) • Moules à la Provençale • **Poulet au Vinaigre Le Petit Truc** (page 503) • Potage aux Lentilles avec Saucisses de Porc • Roasted Tomatoes Provençales • Tarte au Citron

10
Les Hors d'Oeuvres, Pour Vous Mettre en Appétit

served with warm, sliced potatoes tossed with vinaigrette and parsley.

At home, herring marinated in oil serves as a great luncheon dish, or as a first course for a more elaborate meal. The oil reacts in a lovely way with the sweet, smoked herring, serving to soften and enrich it, while also softening and tenderizing the onions. We've found that the best brand of herring to use in the United States is King Oscar canned smoked herring or fresh-cured unsmoked matjes herring from a delicatessen. For this dish, you'll need about four 3½-ounce cans. Don't worry if the herring tends to fall apart as you take it out of the can. It's inevitable, but won't alter the flavors of this marvelous dish!

16 small herring fillets (about 12 ounces; 360 g)
2 onions, sliced into thin rounds
2 carrots, peeled and sliced into thin rounds
2 lemons, sliced into thin rounds
2 bay leaves
1 teaspoon dried thyme
12 whole black peppercorns
2 to 3 cups (50 to 75 cl) peanut oil

1. In a 1-quart (1 l) oval or rectangular terrine, layer half of each of the ingredients in this order: herring, onions, carrots, lemon, bay leaf, thyme, and peppercorns. Add a second layer, in the same order. Pour on enough peanut oil to thoroughly cover all of the ingredients; cover securely and refrigerate. Marinate for 2 to 4 days before serving. (You might want to sample it after 2 days, to see how the flavors are developing.) As long as the container is carefully sealed, the herring will stay fresh and delicious up to 2 weeks.

2. Remove from the refrigerator about 1 hour before serving.

Yield: 8 servings

11
Appetizers, First Courses, and Palate Teasers

TABOULÉ PROVENÇAL

Seasoned Couscous Salad

The French seem to have adopted couscous as their own, as nations tend to do with all foods that they love. Couscous, the fine semolina grain that is part of all good North African and Middle Eastern cooking, appears in many forms in modern French bistro cooking. One of the most popular dishes—found in charcuteries, supermarkets, on café menus—is *salade de couscous*, or *taboulé*. While most of us are more familiar with the version made with bulgur—coarse, cracked whole wheat—the French version is generally made with the slightly more refined couscous, or semolina. This French version, seen often in Provence, also generally includes tomatoes. It's a refreshing summer salad that can be served as is, or as an accompaniment to a platter of raw vegetables or crudités, such as red bell peppers, strips of fresh fennel, carrots, cucumbers, and scallions.

1 cup (about 160 g) medium-grain precooked couscous (or use bulgur)
1 cup (25 cl) flat-leaf parsley leaves
1 cup (25 cl) fresh mint leaves (or substitute ¼ cup dried crushed mint leaves)
4 medium tomatoes, peeled, cored, seeded, and chopped
10 thin scallions, white bulb cut into thin rounds
¼ cup (6 cl) freshly squeezed lemon juice
¼ cup (6 cl) extra-virgin olive oil
Salt

1. Combine the couscous with 2 cups (50 cl) cold water. Let stand at room temperature until all of the liquid has been absorbed, about 30 minutes. If any liquid remains after 30 minutes, place the couscous in a cheesecloth-lined sieve and drain off any excess.

2. In a food processor, chop the parsley and mint. Transfer to a small bowl. Add the remaining dressing ingredients, except the salt, to the bowl and stir to blend. Season with salt to taste and set aside.

3. Place the couscous in a medium-size bowl; fluff with a fork to separate the grains. Stir in the dressing; taste for seasoning. Cover and refrigerate for at least 1 hour, but not more than 4 hours. Adjust the seasoning before serving, adding additional lemon juice or salt to taste.

Yield: 4 to 6 servings

140
Les Poissons et les Fruits de Mer

1. Several hours before you plan to serve the haddock, soak the haddock: Place the fillets in a very shallow skillet, and cover with about 2 cups (50 cl) of water and 2 cups (50 cl) of the milk. Soak for about 1 hour.

2. Prepare the cabbage: Bring a large pot of salted water to a boil. Trim the cabbage, quarter it, and remove the thick center rib. Cut each quarter in half. After the water returns to a boil, cook the cabbage for 10 minutes.

3. Meanwhile, bring a second pot of salted water to a boil. Drain the cabbage and boil again for 10 minutes more. Drain well. Set aside and keep warm.

4. Meanwhile, prepare the haddock: Drain the haddock, discarding the soaking liquid. Return the fish to the skillet and cover with the remaining 2 cups (50 cl) milk. If necessary, add enough water to cover. Bring just to a simmer over medium heat. Simmer gently for 10 minutes; do not allow the liquid to boil.

5. Melt 6 tablespoons (3 ounces; 90 g) of the butter in a large, shallow saucepan over medium heat. Add the cabbage and cook gently, stirring just to coat with the butter. Remove to a warmed platter.

6. Carefully drain the haddock fillets; remove the skin. Place the fish on top of the cabbage. Keep warm.

7. In a small saucepan, melt the remaining 6 tablespoons (3 ounces; 90 g) butter over medium heat. Cook the butter just until pale brown. Remove from the heat, stir in the lemon juice, and season with salt and pepper to taste. Spoon the sauce over the haddock, sprinkle on the parsley, and serve immediately.

Yield: 6 servings

THON GRILLÉ SAUCE VIERGE

Grilled Tuna with Herbed Tomato, Garlic, Oil, and Lemon Sauce

Throughout France, the fish markets are filled with giant fresh red tuna, or *thon rouge*, which is wonderful for slicing into thick steaks and grilling or broiling rare. This sauce—known as *sauce vierge*—is a marvelous accompaniment, one that sings with the flavors and aromas of the south. This is a variation of the deliciously fresh grilled tuna I was first served at the waterside fisherman's bistro Arrantzaleak in the fishing

141
Fish and Shellfish

port of Saint-Jean-de-Luz, in the Pays Basque. Serve this dish with a good red Côtes-du-Rhone, such as Château de Fonsalette.

Sauce:
3 tomatoes, peeled, cored, seeded, and chopped
½ cup (12.5 cl) extra-virgin olive oil
3 tablespoons freshly squeezed lemon juice
3 garlic cloves, minced
Salt
Large handful of fresh herbs, preferably a blend of chervil, chives, tarragon, and parsley

Tuna:
1 pound (500 g) fresh tuna steak, sliced 3 inches (7.5 cm) thick
1 tablespoon extra-virgin olive oil

1. Prepare the sauce: Combine the tomatoes, olive oil, lemon juice, and garlic in a bowl; stir to blend. Season with salt to taste; set aside for 1 to 2 hours to allow the flavors to blend. Just before cooking the tuna, add the herbs and stir to blend.

2. Preheat the broiler, prepare a grill for grilling, or heat a dry cast-iron skillet over high heat.

3. Brush the tuna with the olive oil. Cook the tuna for just 1 minute on each side; the tuna will be very rosy and rare on the inside and charred on the outside.

4. Remove the tuna to a large preheated platter and top with half of the sauce. Then, cut the tuna into thick strips and serve with additional sauce. This is delicious cold the next day, served as is, or mixed with warm pasta.

Yield: 4 servings

"Aïoli concentrates all the warmth, the strength, the sun-loving gaiety of Provence in its essence, but it also has a particular virtue: It keeps flies away. Those who don't like it, those whose stomachs rise at the thought of our oil and garlic, won't come buzzing around us, wasting our time. There will only be family."

—FRÉDÉRIC MISTRAL

146
Les Poissons et les Fruits de Mer

without turning, until the skin is brown and crusty and the salmon has just begun to turn color, about 6 minutes. The salmon will be quite rare. (For salmon that is cooked through, put a lid on the skillet and cook for 2 to 3 minutes more.) Sprinkle with the salt. Serve immediately.

Yield: 4 servings

SMOKED POTATOES

Chef José Lampreia of Paris's Maison Blanche suggests baking potatoes—washed but not peeled—in a covered casserole with a thick slice of smoked country bacon. Cook for an hour, at about 400°F (205°C). Finely chop the bacon and serve with the potatoes to accompany grilled or roasted salmon.

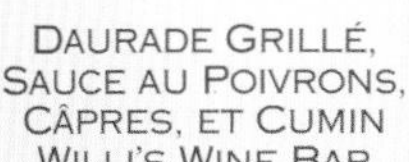

DAURADE GRILLÉ, SAUCE AU POIVRONS, CÂPRES, ET CUMIN WILLI'S WINE BAR

Willi's Wine Bar's Grilled Porgy with Red Peppers, Capers, and Cumin

One wintry Saturday morning my husband and I set off for B.H.V., the gigantic Parisian department store that specializes in hardware and things for the home. Of course Saturday is the worst day to go, for that's when every Parisian, handy or not, decides he needs a nail, a lightbulb, a ladder, or an electric extension cord. I hate going there: The crowds are suffocating and the clerks nasty.

I didn't want the day to be a total waste, so I suggested we stop at Willi's Wine Bar for a late lunch. That day, I sampled this wonderful grilled porgy: It was so fresh it tasted as though it had jumped from the

147
Fish and Shellfish

water only moments earlier, and it was so perfectly cooked—light and flavorful as could be. I loved the sauce, a pretty and lively, fragrant blend of cubed red peppers, faintly salty capers, and a touch of toasted cumin. The sauce, of course, could be served with any small fish, which I actually pan-fry rather than grill. Good substitutes include sea bream or rainbow trout. With this, sample a nice sturdy white, such as a Châteauneuf-du-Pape from Beaucastel.

5 to 6 tablespoons extra-virgin olive oil
2 large red bell peppers, cored, seeded, and diced
2 tablespoons drained capers
2 teaspoons cumin seeds
4 whole porgy, each weighing about 10 ounces (300 g), cleaned, with heads on (or substitute sea bream, or rainbow trout)
Salt and freshly ground black pepper

1. In a medium-size nonstick skillet, heat 1 tablespoon of the oil over medium heat. When the oil is hot but not smoking, add the peppers and sauté until cooked through, 4 to 5 minutes. Off the heat, stir in the capers and cumin. The sauce can be prepared ahead and reheated at serving time.

2. Rinse the fish and pat dry. Generously season the cavity of each porgy with salt and pepper. Generously brush the fish with oil.

3. In a large nonstick skillet heat 2 tablespoons of oil over medium-high heat. When hot but not smoking, add 2 of the fish and cook until opaque through but not firm or dry, 4 to 5 minutes per side. Keep the fish warm while you cook the other 2 fish, adding more oil as needed.

4. Meanwhile, reheat the sauce. Also, heat 4 dinner plates until very hot and brush the hot plates with olive oil.

5. When the fish are cooked, season with salt and pepper and place them on the hot oiled dinner plates. Spoon the warmed sauce alongside and serve immediately.

Yield: 4 servings

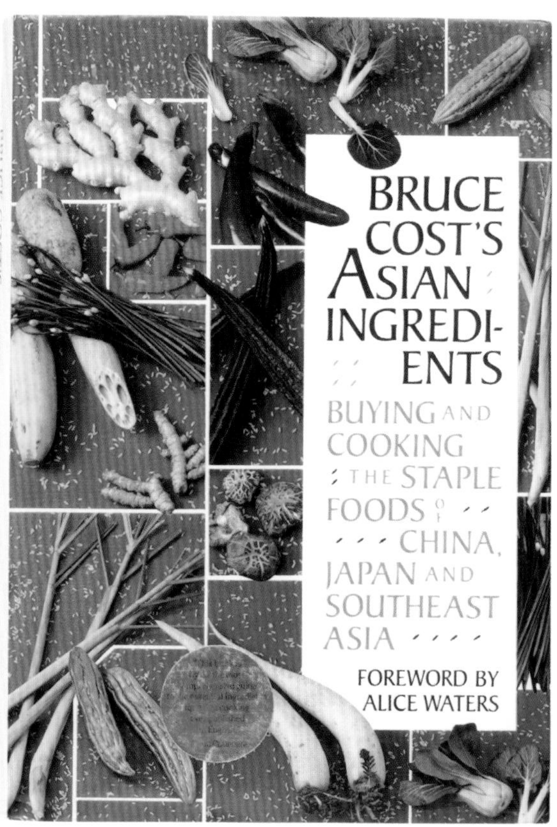

THE GINGER FAMILY

GINGER

(Zingiber officinale)

OTHER NAMES: Gingerroot, Shōga (Japanese), King or khing (Thai), Geung (Cantonese)

REGION OF USE: China, Japan, Korea, Southeast Asia

It's not an exaggeration to say you can't cook Asian food without ginger. It has extraordinary culinary value. Its clean spiciness makes the freshest seafood taste fresher; it suppresses any hint of rankness in meat; it cuts the richness of fatty dishes; and it works in wonderful harmony with garlic. All Asian countries use ginger, which can't be said of any other seasoning except salt.

Mistakenly called a root, ginger is a tropical rhizome (underground stem) that is thought to be native to Southeast Asia, although it has been cultivated for so long, no one can say for sure where it originated. For millennia it has been valued as a medicinal in every Asian culture. It is thought to aid digestion, alleviate nausea, combat colds, and stimulate the appetite for both food and sex.

In China, which perhaps has more varied uses for ginger than any other culture, the texture of the fresh rhizome counts. It's cut into fine matchsticks, chopped finely, or used in slices that are smashed. In Japan, ginger has its own tool, called an *oroshigane*, on which it's grated, and slices of pink pickled ginger, *gari*, are a familiar accompaniment to sushi. In Southeast Asia, ginger is smashed into a paste with other seasonings at the start of a dish, or it's used cut up as in Chinese cooking.

Fresh ginger is rapidly being adopted by American cooks, and it can be found in most supermarkets. In fact it's now an American product: Some of

HERBS AND SEASONINGS 27

BRUCE COST

Bruce Cost's Asian Ingredients

Buying and Cooking the Staple Foods of China, Japan, and Southeast Asia, 1989

It is hard to overestimate the influence that Chinese and other Asian cuisines, especially Thai and Japanese, have had on the American palate since the 1970s.

Bruce Cost was a student of Virginia Lee, the master chef of Chinese cooking who cowrote *The Chinese Cookbook* with Craig Claiborne in 1972. After spending seven years working with Lee, Cost set out on his own to teach and promote the understanding of Asian foods. In *Bruce Cost's Asian Ingredients*, he brought together his extensive knowledge of Asian cooking and explained the new ingredients that were beginning to flood the American grocery market. Cost had planned for the book to be half its length, but while he was writing it, the influx of Vietnamese, Thais, and Cambodians to the United States expanded the range of new ingredients significantly, and he added them to the manuscript. This guide is essential for anyone interested in cooking Asian foods.

NOTABLE RECIPES: **Asian "Pesto"** (page 433) • Coconut Egg Jam with Sticky Rice • Honeyed Pecans with Sesame Seeds • Lemon and Black Beans • **Sautéed Eggplant with Black Vinegar** (page 414) • Simple Roast Chicken with Sichuan Pepper • **Soft-Shell Crabs with Ginger, Lemon, and Black Beans** (page 480) • **Tea-Smoked Squabs** (page 496) • **Yow Choy with Black Vinegar** (page 407)

CHINESE MUSTARD CABBAGE OR GAI CHOY

(Brassica juncea)

OTHER NAMES: Chinese mustard greens, Leaf mustard, Indian mustard

REGION OF USE: China, Southeast Asia

Because of their antiquity, mustards hold a special place in Chinese (and Indian) culinary history. Among the earliest cultivated greens, they were first raised, it is thought, for the oil in their seeds. Because the leafy plants themselves are exceptionally nutritious, their cultivation has been continually refined over the centuries. Most of these mustard cabbages—and this makes them unique among leafy vegetables—are, like olives, raised to be preserved.

Among the innumerable varieties, each seems to have its own specialty. Some are raised just to make particular kinds of pickles, such as Sichuan Province's famous Preserved Vegetable (see page 178) or the chopped and salted leaves known as Red-in-Snow (see page 180). The stems of some mustards are delicious when pickled in vinegar and sugar.

Of the mustards eaten fresh, a large, bulky plant known as Swatow mustard is grown for its heart, which is expensive. With some mustards, the fresh stems are prized for banquet-style vegetable dishes—they are usually parboiled first in water to which a little bicarbonate of soda is added to turn them a brilliant green; yet the leaves of the same plant may be considered useful only in a mundane soup.

It should be noted that most mustard green leaves, cut into strips and deep-fried briefly until they're translucent and crisp, make an excellent bed for fried seafood as they look like seaweed.

The fresh mustards available on produce stands here are as follows:

BROAD-LEAF MUSTARD CABBAGE (DAI GAI CHOY)—Curved stem or semi-closed head variety. Often just the bottoms of these are sold, cut off where the leaves

start, since the stems are valued for salting and drying. That's why they're often a little more ragged looking than other produce. Sometimes the stems are cooked fresh. If the whole large plant is sold, it all may be salted and dried, or the leaves can be shredded and tossed in a soup.

BROAD-LEAF MUSTARD CABBAGE (DAI GAI CHOY)—Straight stem. After the leaves are carefully cut away, the inch-wide stems of this mustard are delicious parboiled in water with a little baking soda, then stir-fried and served in a light sauce; or they make one of the world's great sweet pickles. The leaves are best shredded for soups or for salting.

GAI CHOY SUM—This skinny-stemmed mustard looks like yow choy. However, its leaves are slightly serrated, its stems have subtle ridges characteristic of mustard, and its flowers are not readily apparent. This mustard can be stir-fried, leaves and all.

A specialty of Tung Fong, a small jewel of a *dim sum* parlor in San Francisco, these pickles are sweet with a mustardy bite—addictive is the word.

PICKLED MUSTARD GREEN STEMS

Yield: 1 quart

- 3 *bunches mustard greens, preferably with long, straight stems*
- 1⅓ *tablespoons salt*
- 2 *cups mild white rice vinegar*
- 1½ *cups sugar*
- 6 *dried red chili peppers*

Carefully trim the leaves from the stems (save the leaves for Salted Mustard Green Leaves, page 66, or another recipe). Cut the stems into 3-inch lengths and sprinkle with 1 tablespoon of the salt. Let stand for 1 hour.

Transfer the stems to a clean quart jar, leaving behind any accumulated liquid. Bring the vinegar, sugar, chilis, and remaining 1 teaspoon salt to a boil, and pour over the stems. Allow to cool, cover the jar, and refrigerate. They'll be delicious after a day or two.

GROUND FISH SAUCE

OTHER NAMES: Anchovy cream, Ground preserved fish, Mâ'm Nêm Xay or Mâ'm Nêm

REGION OF USE: Southeast Asia, principally Vietnam, Thailand, and Kampuchea

This sauce, expensive relative to fish sauce, is a suspension of ground anchovies in liquid fish sauce. "Creamed anchovies" is an apt description. The flavor and smell of this sauce is less the briny cheesiness of fish sauce and more like a fine anchovy paste we might use in Italian cooking. If you favor this sort of sauce, you should find it luxuriantly rich and delicious. It can be substituted for fish sauce, particularly in Southeast Asian curried dishes or other stewlike dishes made with coconut cream. In fact it seems ripe for experimentation in Western cooking.

RECOMMENDED: Viêt-Mỹ Corporation "Mâ'm Nêm Xay 'Phú-Quô'c,'" available in 10-ounce bottles; "Mâ'm Nêm Viet-Nam," available in 7-ounce bottles.

WHOLE FISH SAUCE

OTHER NAMES: Mâ'm nêm, Whole preserved fish

REGION OF USE: Southeast Asia, principally Vietnam, Thailand, and Kampuchea

Just as whole beans were to be found in the first soybean sauce, whole fish or fish pieces fermented in brine were undoubtedly the first fish sauces. As with liquid fish sauce, anchovies are the fish of choice—except away from the sea, in Laos for example, where freshwater fish are preserved this way. The result,

called *padek*, is used in cooking by removing the fish and pounding it with other seasonings as a base for a stew; or the liquid alone may be used like fish sauce.

RECOMMENDED: Viêt-Mỹ Corporation "Mâ'm Nêm 'Phú Quô'c,'" available in 8-ounce jars.

NOTE: Various Southeast Asian fishes—such as gourami and mudfish—are sold "pickled" in jars in Southeast Asian markets. These condiments may be used to flavor sauces and stews.

OYSTER SAUCE

OTHER NAMES: Oyster flavored sauce

REGION OF USE: Southern China

A Cantonese staple made of oysters, water, salt, and, these days, cornstarch and caramel coloring, it was the flavor of this sauce that lent an exotic touch to the first Chinese-American food such as chow mein and chop suey. Depending on its quality, it can be an excellent all-purpose seasoning for noodle, meat, seafood, and vegetable dishes.

Originally the sauce was just oysters, water, and salt, and as such was a kind of gray suspension in liquid. It was extremely flavorful but it was none too appetizing looking, which explains the caramel and cornstarch. The cornstarch homogenizes the sauce, and in the case of cheaper sauces, fewer oysters can then be used.

The quality and corresponding price for a 14-ounce bottle of oyster sauce —the standard size for home use—varies widely, and you get what you pay for in terms of rich oyster flavor. The Hop Sing Lung Oyster Sauce Company

BRUCE AIDELLS

Hot Links and Country Flavors, 1990

Hogs can be, and are, raised in nearly every climate in the world. They are one of the most adaptable of all domesticated animals. Consequently, nearly every cuisine has a tradition of making sausage. Of course, not all sausages are made with pork, but the majority include the meat of this most delicious porcine creature.

Bruce Aidells is a man who knows sausages. His line of sausage products has changed the way many Americans think about their links. It's not just Jimmy Dean for breakfast. There's a whole world of different flavors and traditions of sausage making in the United States alone. Aidells's *Hot Links and Country Flavors* is a survey of American sausage-making from the Northeast's Italian, Portuguese, and Jewish traditions to the Midwest's brats and Chicago's Polish links to the prized bulk Kentucky and Tennessee sausages that are perfect for making biscuits and gravy. Aidells shows convincingly that America is a land of sausage, and a happy thing it is, too.

NOTABLE RECIPES: Cajun-Style Andouille Sausage • Sheboygan Brats • Smoked Bratwurst • Smoked Kielbasa • **Smoked Country Sausage** (page 556) • Texas Smoky Link • **Wild Rice and Pecan Salad with Grilled Venison Sausage** (page 372) • **Venison Sausage** (page 558)

· cold beer, hot brats ·

It's a muggy Wisconsin night in late summer somewhere outside Sheboygan. A red neon sign looms through the darkness, "Cold Beer Hot Brats." We're on our way to the Sheboygan Bratwurst Festival, and our '55 Buick Roadmaster (affectionately termed The Wurstmobile) lurches off the highway into yet another parking lot. We pile into the tavern for a taste test of Sheboygan brats and the inevitable accompaniment, foaming steins of cold Wisconsin lager.

A long, dimly lit bar stretches back into the darkness. Men in shirtsleeves nurse tall seidels of pale golden beer, beads of moisture clinging to the sides of the glasses. Nobody's saying much, staring into the mirrors flanked by naked nymphs and angels, watching the neon beer signs revolve, waiting for a cool breeze off the river.

We pick a spot at the bar and wave the bartender over. "Beer and brats," we say. "Doubles all around, with the works." He nods, smiling.

The beer arrives first, pale and clean, with the bitter tang of hops in the nose, the rich sweetness of malt across the palate. As we sip our beers, we all find ourselves staring into the ornate mirrors, dreaming of bratwurst, of ancient festivals, the works.

A flurry of activity erupts in the quiet bar. Heads turn, suddenly smiling, as the bartender's wife (mother, girlfriend, sister) sweeps up behind us, balancing plates on her plump and lovely arms; blonde hair piled up around her face, red cheeks, pale blue eyes, cheerful and bold and beautiful, saying, "You the boys ordered brats, doubles, works all around?"

She lays the plates down along the bar. Two grilled brats bulge between halves of the hard roll; a slice of pale white onion sticks out underneath; hot brown mustard, coarse-ground with horseradish, opens up the sinuses; long thin slices of sour dill pickles crisscross the brats. This is the best of Sheboygan's wursts: a double brat with the works!

The first question, as with any good sausage sandwich, is the mode of attack. That is to say, how to get all these gustatory wonders into your mouth with a minimum of hassle and a modicum of dignity. At the first bite, however, all hopes of decorum and clean shirts fade. You just open your mouth as wide as you can, and bite down.

And suddenly it all becomes clear. Why everyone seems so peaceful here, so happy. As the spiced juicy meat mingles with the sweet onions, hot mustard, and sour pickles you experience a kind of heavenly harmony, a clear perception of rightness, of how things should be. "This might just be the ultimate sausage sandwich," I say, sipping my beer pensively. "It can't get any better than this."

· The Midwest ·

·152· HOT LINKS & COUNTRY FLAVORS ·153·

time, grind and season all the mixtures, refrigerate, and then stuff them into the casings all at once. When making sausage, the temperature of the meat should not get above 50° F for any extended period of time.

· sanitation ·

1. After washing the grinder and stuffer with hot water, cool them in the refrigerator or freezer before use. Have all your cutting boards, tables, equipment, and knives scrupulously clean. Sterilize wooden cutting boards with bleach and water periodically and rinse with clean water. Wash hands frequently with plenty of soap and hot water during sausage making.

2. When making several varieties of sausage, preweigh the meats and fat, and store them in labeled bowls in the refrigerator until you are ready to grind them. Work on only one batch at a time, and keep the other batches refrigerated. After the meat has been ground and the spices mixed in, store it in the refrigerator until ready to stuff into the casings.

3. Make your sausages during the cooler times of the day, morning or evening. If possible, the room temperature should not be above 70° F.

4. Have all the ingredients ready to go, spice mix made in advance.

5. Don't let the grinder or stuffer sit with meat in it. If you are going to take a break or move on to something else, take the grinder apart, and remove and discard any residual meat or fat. Wash and dry the grinder and reassemble it when you are ready to use it again. Meat should not sit in a grinder or stuffer for more than 15–20 minutes at 70° F room temperature, less time if the room is hotter.

6. When smoking or drying sausage, do not dry them in too warm a place. Always hang sausage on clean sticks.

· step-by-step method for making sausage at home ·

· using a meat grinder ·

1. If you have a meat grinder, hand operated or electric, attach the size plate (with holes of ⅛ inch, ¼ inch, or ⅜ inch) that the recipe calls for. Cut the meat and fat into ¾ x ¾-inch-wide strips (no larger than the mouth of the grinder), 1 to 6 inches long. While cutting up the meat, take care to remove any gristle and connective tissue. The mixture should come off the grinder plate in "worms." If the meat looks mushy, it means the grinder knife is not making good contact with the plate or the knife is dull. Remove the plate and knife, clean away any gristle, and reassemble, making sure the plate is reasonably tight against the knife. If you continue to have this problem, you might have to buy a new knife.

2. Grind the meat and the fat together into a large bowl. Add salt and spices, and mix in any liquid and optional curing salts. Knead the sausage meat with your hands, squeezing and turning the mixture. Do not overmix, as this could cause the fat to melt and might give the sausage a white, fatty appearance.

3. Make a small patty of the sausage meat and fry it. Taste and adjust the salt or other seasonings. Cover and refrigerate the meat mixture until you are ready to stuff it into the casings or use in a recipe. You should try to stuff the sausage meat into the casings on the same day it was ground, since it gets quite stiff and difficult to handle if refrigerated too long.

using a food processor ·

1. Cut the meat and fat into ¾-inch cubes to get reasonably consistent chopping. Process in very small batches of 1 pound or less by using the pulse switch or turning on and off until the desired consistency is reached. Do not overprocess the meat. For 3–4 pounds of sausage you will probably need to process 3 or 4 batches, depending on the size of your food processor. Mini food processors or blenders should not be used to make sausage.

2. In a large bowl, mix the meat and fat together with the salt, spices, any liquid, and optional curing salts. Knead by hand as described above until well blended. Refrigerate until ready to use.

·332· HOT LINKS & COUNTRY FLAVORS ·333·

LIDIA BASTIANICH

La Cucina di Lidia

Distinctive Regional Cuisine from the North of Italy, 1990

For Lidia Matticchio Bastianich, food is family. Anyone who has watched her television programs has seen her mother, son, grandchildren, and other family members all working in the kitchen. In one brilliant episode, two of her grandsons help roll out and shape gnocchi. What better way to demystify one of Italy's most delicate creations! And if Bastianich's grandchildren can make them, so can we. Bastianich's focus on family and food derives from her amazing life.

She was born in Pula, Istria, a small town that is now a part of Croatia. When Lidia was nine years old, her father sent the family to Trieste, Italy, but he had to stay behind because Marshall Tito's communist government required that one family member be kept as a hostage. He managed to escape, and the family lived in the former World War II Nazi concentration camp of Risiera di San Sabba. While Lidia's mother found work as a cook for a wealthy Trieste family, the Matticchios lived in the camp with other refugees until they were allowed to immigrate to the United States in 1958. They settled in North Bergen, New Jersey, later moving to Astoria, Queens. Lidia, now a teenager, began working in Italian restaurants and shortly thereafter married Felice Bastianich, a fellow Istrian immigrant. The Bastianich family opened their first restaurant, Buonavia, in 1971, serving the best of Italian-American cuisine. Lidia added traditional Istrian dishes to the menu, and Buonavia was a success. They then opened a second restaurant, Villa Secondo. Lidia gained recognition from food critics and, at this time, also began to give cooking classes. Following her father's death, in 1981, the family sold the two restaurants in Queens and opened Felidia, the restaurant that would make Lidia famous in the food world. The *New York Times* awarded Felidia a prestigious three stars upon its opening.

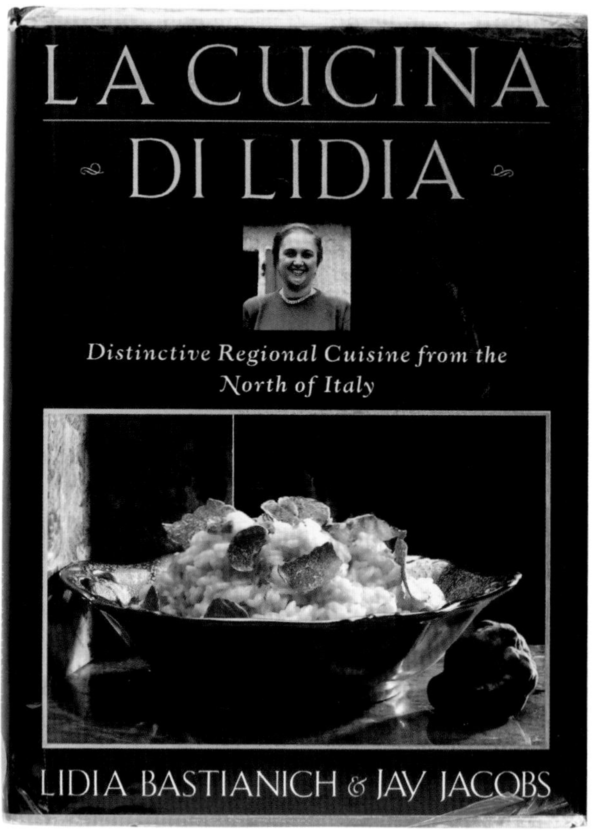

When asked about the importance of family food traditions, Lidia has said: "Food for me was a connecting link to my grandmother, to my childhood, to my past. And what I found out is that for everybody, food is a connector to their roots, to their past in different ways. It gives you security; it gives you a profile of who you are, where you come from." And we're all glad she's shared her family with ours. "Tutti a tavolo a mangiare!"

NOTABLE RECIPES: Duck Roasted with Sauerkraut • **Espresso Mousse** (page 648) • **Plum Gnocchi** (page 448) • **Polenta with Fontina and Porcini Mushrooms** (page 428) • **Roast Baby Lamb** (page 538) • Shrimp and Mixed Bean Salad • **Ricotta Cheesecake** (page 606) • Trieste Style Sauerkraut and Bean Soup • **Wild Mushroom Soup** (page 344)

LA CUCINA DI
LIDIA

Distinctive Regional Cuisine
from the North of Italy

Lidia Bastianich
and Jay Jacobs

Photography by
John Dominis

DOUBLEDAY
New York London Toronto Sydney Auckland

5

Le Carni

Meats

Minestra di Verdure Miste con Finocchio

Vegetable Soup with Fennel

SERVES 12–16

At home in Istria, this fragrant soup is eaten in the spring and early summer, when the fennel shoots are still young and tender. During my childhood, wild fennel, which I haven't seen in this country, was used, and the soup often was served as a meal in itself, sometimes with sausage added. (Sausage and fennel have a natural affinity.) Because its preparation takes some time and its character develops after a night or two in the refrigerator, when it is *riposada*, or rested, I always make this soup in big batches to be enjoyed over two or three days.

2 cups Great Northern white beans
2 fresh pork hocks (see Note)
2 large Idaho potatoes, peeled
2 large carrots
5 fresh bay leaves
4 cloves garlic, chopped fine
4 tablespoons olive oil
1 cup chopped peeled tomatoes
1 pound spinach, shredded
1 pound Swiss chard, shredded
10 ounces corn kernels, frozen if need be (see Note)
10 ounces fresh peas, or frozen (see Note)
1 pound fennel, diced fine
Salt and freshly ground pepper to taste

Pick over and rinse the beans, and soak them overnight in plenty of water.

In a large pot, bring 5 quarts water to a boil. Add the drained beans, pork hocks, potatoes, carrots, and bay leaves.

In a skillet, lightly sauté the garlic in the olive oil until golden, add the tomatoes and sauté 10 minutes longer. Add the contents of the pan to the boiling pot, lower the heat, and simmer gently, covered, 1 hour.

Meanwhile, in a large saucepan, bring 3 quarts water to a boil. Add the spinach, Swiss chard, corn, peas, and fennel, and parboil 10 minutes. Drain, and set aside.

At the end of the first hour, remove the carrots and potatoes from the pot, mash them together with a fork, and return them to the soup. Add the reserved vegetables, season to taste, and simmer another 30 minutes, uncovered, skimming and stirring occasionally. Remove the pork hocks (which may be eaten separately) and the bay leaves. Adjust the seasoning and serve with crusty Italian bread or focaccia (recipe page 229).

Note: One fresh and one smoked pork hock may be used to invest the soup with a somewhat more intriguing flavor. If frozen corn kernels and peas are used, they should not be parboiled and their final cooking time should be halved.

Minestra di Funghi Selvatici

Wild Mushroom Soup

SERVES 6

Every cook in our part of Istria had her own version of wild mushroom soup. This one was devised by my Great Aunt Santola, a widow, who cooked the soup for the whole courtyard at Busoler. She would come home and pick over the mushrooms she had gathered, separating those to be sautéed from those earmarked for other uses. Mostly trimmings and stems were reserved for her soup. When I was old enough to begin gathering my own mushrooms, I was allowed to pick only the unmistakably safe varieties, like champignons and porcini, and forbidden to eat any before my aunt approved them. The traditional belief was that the poisonous mushrooms could be detected by cooking them in water with a piece of brass; if the brass turned green, the mushrooms were unsafe. As a further precaution, the oldest woman in a household had the dubious honor of tasting the mushrooms before they were served to other members of the family.

Note: The soup is best when made with several varieties of fresh wild mushrooms (porcini, shiitake, chanterelle, hen-of-the-woods, etc.), but even a single variety will produce an excellent soup. Other types of dried mushrooms may be substituted for the dried porcini specified, but porcini are preferable.

Mountain forager weighing mushrooms, Udine.

coli, zucchini, or any other combination of ingredients can be added to cooked polenta.

Polenta almost never is eaten straight out of the pot, but is allowed to rest for a few minutes. Traditionally, it's poured onto a wooden board *(tagliere)* and cut with a taut string when it has begun to set, but while the interior is still warm. Polenta also can be served with a spoon dipped in water, or it can be chilled overnight, then sliced and grilled or fried and served as a main course garnish or accompaniment, a base for various toppings and sauces, or a breakfast food to be dipped in milk. It will keep for three days, covered, in the refrigerator, and is even eaten as dessert in Istria, with a sprinkling of sugar and cinnamon.

As a general rule, the proportion of grain to water is one to two, allowing for absorption and evaporation of the water. A successful batch of polenta requires about forty minutes of close attention, which may account for its scarcity on Italian menus in the United States. The cooking time can be reduced appreciably by using "instant" (partially precooked) polenta, which yields an acceptable result but lacks the roughness and resistant texture I prefer. When you shop for the makings of polenta, I'd recommend a medium- or coarse-grind meal, but a trip to an ethnic grocery for coarser unlabeled meal is worth the time it takes. Polenta, incidentally, can be made from white or yellow meal. Istrians prefer yellow, which makes a more attractive presentation on the plate.

Although more flavorful than pasta or rice, polenta is neutral enough to serve as a vehicle for a wide variety of sauced foods.

Cozze in Salsa Verde

Mussels in Parsley Vinaigrette

51

Capriolo in Sguazet

Venison *in Sguazet*

SERVES 4

As with most *sguazet* preparations, this venison treatment normally would be reserved for the tougher, more flavorful cuts, whereas the legs, fillets, chops, and the like would be roasted, grilled, or sautéed. At our restaurant, however, our customers expect choice cuts and are served accordingly. This is one of Felice's favorite dishes and a popular seller at Felidia. See "About Sguazet," page 210.

2 pounds venison leg or shoulder
½ cup dried porcini mushrooms
1 medium onion, minced
¼ cup minced pancetta or bacon
¼ cup olive oil
Salt and freshly ground pepper to taste
2 bay leaves
1 sprig fresh rosemary, or 1 teaspoon dried
2 whole cloves
½ cup dry red wine (preferably Barolo)
2 tablespoons tomato paste
3½ cups chicken stock (recipe page 69)

Cut the venison into 1" cubes.

Soak the porcini in 2 cups of hot water about 20 minutes. While the porcini are soaking, in a large casserole, over moderately high heat, sauté the onion and pancetta or bacon in the olive oil until golden, about 8 minutes. Season lightly with salt and pepper, add the venison, and cook until all the meat liquids have evaporated, about 15 minutes.

Pick out the porcini and chop them coarsely, reserving the liquid (except for the last 2 tablespoons of gritty sediment).

Add the porcini to the casserole, along with the bay leaves, rosemary, cloves, and wine, and cook, stirring, 5 minutes, until the wine is nearly evaporated.

Stir in the tomato paste and season lightly with salt and pepper. Add the chicken stock and reserved mushroom liquid, bring to a boil, reduce the heat to moderately low, and simmer, partially covered, until the meat is tender and the sauce is thickened, about 1½ hours.

Remove the bay leaves and rosemary, adjust the seasoning, and serve with gnocchi (recipe page 117) or polenta (recipe page 129).

Gamberoni alla Griglia
Broiled Shrimp
148

Crema di Caffè

Espresso Mousse

SERVES 8

Italians in general are passionate about coffee in almost any form and make particularly good use of it in all sorts of desserts. I wish I could remember where I picked up this recipe, but I can't. I think you'll like the flavor of the dish as much as I do.

1 tablespoon unflavored gelatin
½ cup cold water
1 cup sugar
3 drops fresh lemon juice
1 cup milk
1¾ cups heavy cream
3 eggs, separated
½ cup strong espresso coffee (see Note)
¼ teaspoon vanilla extract
Coffee beans or shaved chocolate for garnish

Sprinkle the gelatin over ¼ cup of the cold water and allow it to soften.

In a medium-size heavy saucepan, combine the sugar with ¼ cup of water and the lemon juice. Bring to a boil and cook until the sugar caramelizes to a rich dark brown, about 7 minutes. (Do not stir as it cooks.)

Meanwhile, in a second pan, scald the milk. When the caramel is ready, remove it from the heat and immediately add ¾ cup of the heavy cream. (Stand back because it may splatter.) Whisk the cream and caramel together, blending thoroughly, then whisk in the scalded milk.

In a bowl, beat the egg yolks. Add some of the caramel mixture and whisk well, then pour the contents of the bowl into the saucepan and whisk to blend. Return to moderately low heat and cook, stirring with a wooden spoon, until the custard coats the back of a spoon, about 9 minutes.

Off the heat, blend in the softened gelatin and stir well until thoroughly dissolved. Add the coffee and vanilla extract and combine well. Transfer the mixture to a bowl and refrigerate 30 minutes, stirring occasionally, until it begins to thicken.

Meanwhile, whip the remaining 1 cup heavy cream until stiff and keep chilled. When the mousse mixture has thickened, beat the egg whites until stiff. Fold them into the espresso custard, then fold in the whipped cream, lightly but thoroughly.

Pour into individual serving dishes or a large serving bowl and chill 3–4 hours. To serve, allow the mousse to rest about 10 minutes at room temperature to develop flavor, and decorate with coffee beans or shaved chocolate.

Note: 2 tablespoons instant espresso dissolved in ½ cup water can be substituted.

Fagiano Arrosto
Roast Pheasant
214

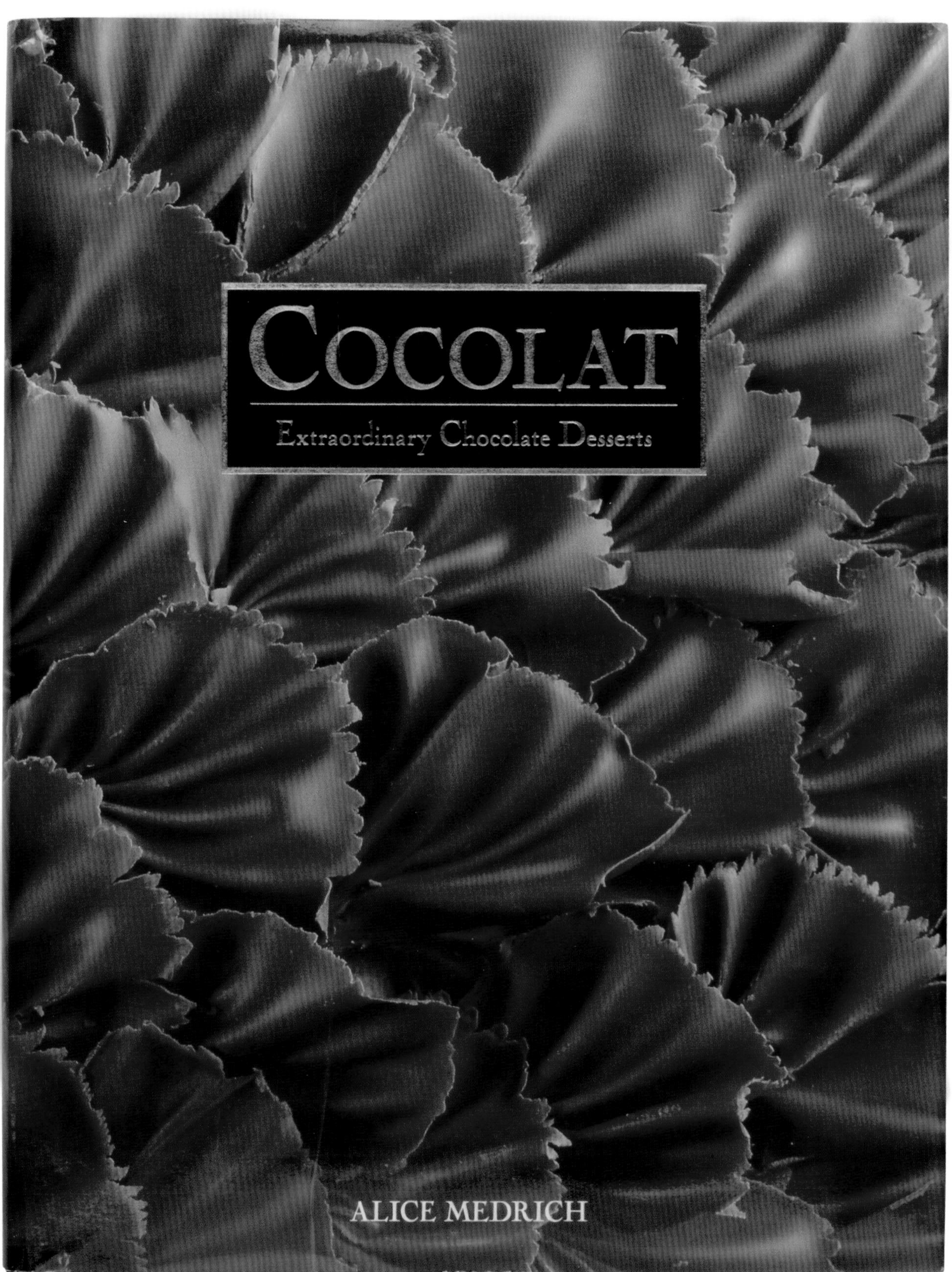
COCOLAT
Extraordinary Chocolate Desserts
ALICE MEDRICH

ALICE MEDRICH

Cocolat

Extraordinary Chocolate Desserts, 1990

Alice Medrich, sometimes referred to as "the First Lady of Chocolate," introduced chocolate truffles to Americans in 1973, when she started making and selling them in Berkeley, California. She first tasted a truffle in Paris in 1972, when her landlady served her the smaller, French-style treats: dark chocolate, eggs, and sweet butter, delicately combined and rolled in cocoa powder. Medrich was astonished at the flavor and sense of luxury the truffles effused. Upon her return to the States, she realized others might enjoy these tasty morsels. It was also at a time when people were beginning to delight in high-end desserts, a trend that would only increase during the 1980s. From her original cottage industry, Medrich built a chain of eleven stores called Cocolat in the San Francisco Bay area and also sold her confections at Zabar's in Manhattan, through Macy's stores, and at Jacquisine in Los Angeles. She is credited with creating the "California truffle," which is larger than the French variety and has a hard chocolate covering. She added a selection of liqueurs, nuts, and other delicacies to the filling, further removing them from the French tradition. Americans were crazy for her truffles.

The *New York Times Magazine* reported that Americans ate nine pounds of chocolate per capita in 1976. By 1983, ten years after Medrich opened her first store, per capita consumption was up to 11.2 pounds of chocolate per year. The average cost of that chocolate increased twofold over the same period. Chocolate was big business.

In 1990 Medrich authored *Cocolat*, which describes how to make some of the truffles that made her famous. Medrich had already made a change in Americans' eating habits; high-end chocolate desserts were here to stay.

NOTABLE RECIPES: Black and White Cheesecake • **Chocolate Banana Charlotte** (page 618) • **Chocolate Hazelnut Torte** (page 622) • **Chocolate Velvet Mousse** (page 647) • **Classic Chocolate Truffles** (page 646) • Mocha Pecan Torte • **Queen of Sheba** (page 626)

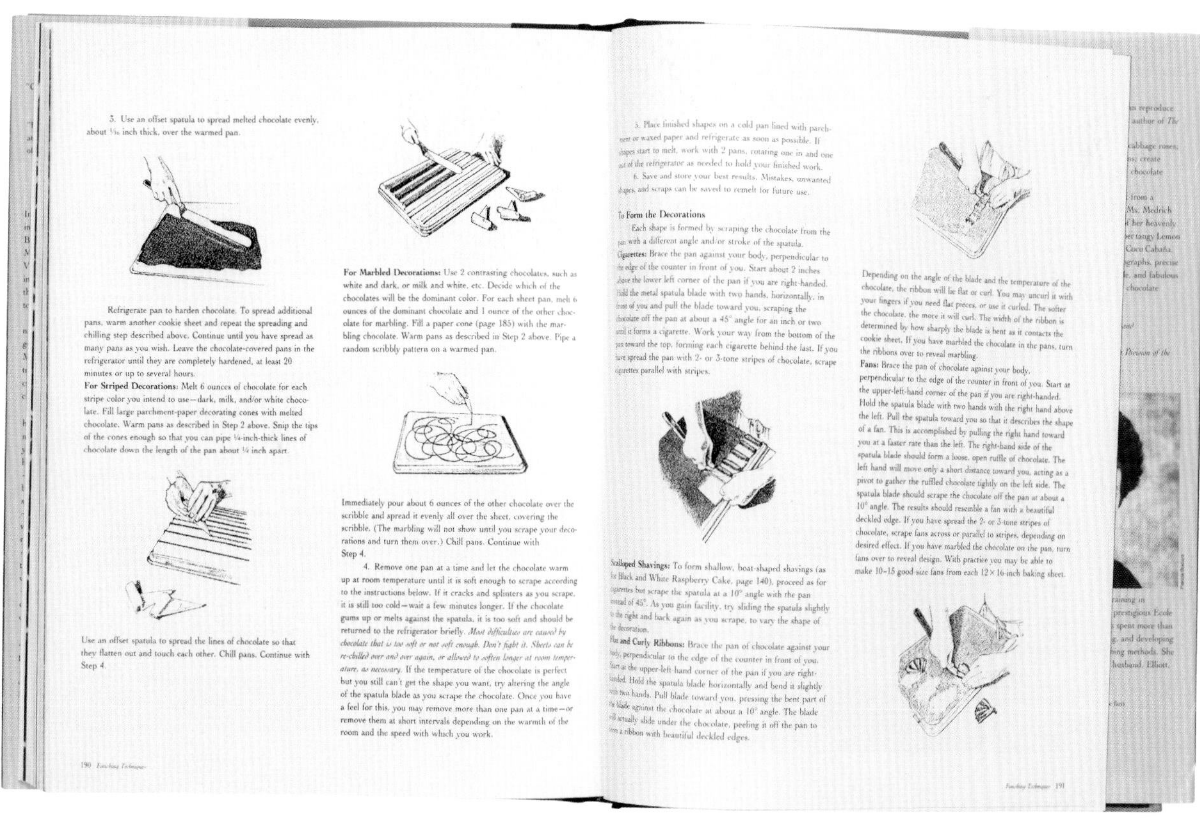

3. Use an offset spatula to spread melted chocolate evenly, about 1/16 inch thick, over the warmed pan.

Refrigerate pan to harden chocolate. To spread additional pans, warm another cookie sheet and repeat the spreading and chilling step described above. Continue until you have spread as many pans as you wish. Leave the chocolate-covered pans in the refrigerator until they are completely hardened, at least 20 minutes or up to several hours.

For Striped Decorations: Melt 6 ounces of chocolate for each stripe color you intend to use—dark, milk, and/or white chocolate. Fill large parchment-paper decorating cones with melted chocolate. Warm pans as described in Step 2 above. Snip the tips of the cones enough so that you can pipe 1/4-inch-thick lines of chocolate down the length of the pan about 1/4 inch apart.

Use an offset spatula to spread the lines of chocolate so that they flatten out and touch each other. Chill pans. Continue with Step 4.

For Marbled Decorations: Use 2 contrasting chocolates, such as white and dark, or milk and white, etc. Decide which of the chocolates will be the dominant color. For each sheet pan, melt 6 ounces of the dominant chocolate and 1 ounce of the other chocolate for marbling. Fill a paper cone (page 185) with the marbling chocolate. Warm pans as described in Step 2 above. Pipe a random scribbly pattern on a warmed pan.

Immediately pour about 6 ounces of the other chocolate over the scribble and spread it evenly all over the sheet, covering the scribble. (The marbling will not show until you scrape your decorations and turn them over.) Chill pans. Continue with Step 4.

4. Remove one pan at a time and let the chocolate warm up at room temperature until it is soft enough to scrape according to the instructions below. If it cracks and splinters as you scrape, it is still too cold—wait a few minutes longer. If the chocolate gums up or melts against the spatula, it is too soft and should be returned to the refrigerator briefly. *Most difficulties are caused by chocolate that is too soft or not soft enough. Don't fight it. Sheets can be re-chilled over and over again, or allowed to soften longer at room temperature, as necessary.* If the temperature of the chocolate is perfect but you still can't get the shape you want, try altering the angle of the spatula blade as you scrape the chocolate. Once you have a feel for this, you may remove more than one pan at a time—or remove them at short intervals depending on the warmth of the room and the speed with which you work.

190 *Finishing Techniques*

5. Place finished shapes on a cold pan lined with parchment or waxed paper and refrigerate as soon as possible. If shapes start to melt, work with 2 pans, rotating one in and one out of the refrigerator as needed to hold your finished work.

6. Save and store your best results. Mistakes, unwanted shapes, and scraps can be saved to remelt for future use.

To Form the Decorations

Each shape is formed by scraping the chocolate from the pan with a different angle and/or stroke of the spatula.

Cigarettes: Brace the pan against your body, perpendicular to the edge of the counter in front of you. Start about 2 inches above the lower left corner of the pan if you are right-handed. Hold the metal spatula blade with two hands, horizontally, in front of you and pull the blade toward you, scraping the chocolate off the pan at about a 45° angle for an inch or two until it forms a cigarette. Work your way from the bottom of the pan toward the top, forming each cigarette behind the last. If you have spread the pan with 2- or 3-tone stripes of chocolate, scrape cigarettes parallel with stripes.

Scalloped Shavings: To form shallow, boat-shaped shavings (as for Black and White Raspberry Cake, page 140), proceed as for cigarettes but scrape the spatula at a 10° angle with the pan instead of 45°. As you gain facility, try sliding the spatula slightly to the right and back again as you scrape, to vary the shape of the decoration.

Flat and Curly Ribbons: Brace the pan of chocolate against your body, perpendicular to the edge of the counter in front of you. Start at the upper-left-hand corner of the pan if you are right-handed. Hold the spatula blade horizontally and bend it slightly with two hands. Pull blade toward you, pressing the bent part of the blade against the chocolate at about a 10° angle. The blade will actually slide under the chocolate, peeling it off the pan to form a ribbon with beautiful deckled edges.

Depending on the angle of the blade and the temperature of the chocolate, the ribbon will lie flat or curl. You may uncurl it with your fingers if you need flat pieces, or use it curled. The softer the chocolate, the more it will curl. The width of the ribbon is determined by how sharply the blade is bent as it contacts the cookie sheet. If you have marbled the chocolate in the pans, turn the ribbons over to reveal marbling.

Fans: Brace the pan of chocolate against your body, perpendicular to the edge of the counter in front of you. Start at the upper-left-hand corner of the pan if you are right-handed. Hold the spatula blade with two hands with the right hand above the left. Pull the spatula toward you so that it describes the shape of a fan. This is accomplished by pulling the right hand toward you at a faster rate than the left. The right-hand side of the spatula blade should form a loose, open ruffle of chocolate. The left hand will move only a short distance toward you, acting as a pivot to gather the ruffled chocolate tightly on the left side. The spatula blade should scrape the chocolate off the pan at about a 10° angle. The results should resemble a fan with a beautiful deckled edge. If you have spread the 2- or 3-tone stripes of chocolate, scrape fans across or parallel to stripes, depending on desired effect. If you have marbled the chocolate on the pan, turn fans over to reveal design. With practice you may be able to make 10–15 good-size fans from each 12 × 16-inch baking sheet.

Finishing Techniques 191

Chocolate Hazelnut Torte

Serves 10–12

Torte tastes best if baked at least one day ahead.

Ingredients:
6 ounces semisweet or bittersweet chocolate, cut into small pieces
6 ounces sweet butter, cut into pieces
4 large eggs, separated
¾ cup sugar
½ cup (2 ounces) ground toasted hazelnuts
¼ cup (1 ounce) flour
⅛ teaspoon cream of tartar
Bittersweet Chocolate Glaze (page 174) or Chocolate Honey Glaze (page 174)
12 plain or caramelized hazelnuts (page 172; optional), for decoration, or
1 ounce each, milk and white chocolate, for piped decoration (page 185; optional)

Special Equipment:
8-inch corrugated cake circle
Parchment paper cone(s) for piping decoration (optional)

1. Preheat oven to 375°. Line bottom of an 8 × 3-inch round cake pan or springform pan with a circle of parchment or waxed paper.

2. Melt chocolate and butter in a small bowl placed in a barely simmering water bath over low heat, stirring occasionally until completely melted. Remove from heat. Or, microwave on MEDIUM (50%) for about 2 minutes. Stir until smooth and completely melted.

3. Beat egg yolks with ½ cup of sugar until pale and thick. Stir in warm chocolate mixture, nuts, and flour. Set aside.

4. Beat the egg whites and cream of tartar at medium speed until soft peaks form. Gradually sprinkle in remaining ¼ cup sugar, beating at high speed until stiff but not dry. Fold one-fourth of whites into chocolate batter to lighten it. Quickly fold in remaining whites. Turn mixture into prepared pan and smooth top if necessary. Bake for 40–45 minutes, or until a toothpick or wooden skewer plunged into center of torte shows moist crumbs.

5. Cool torte completely in pan on a rack. It will have risen and then fallen in the center, leaving a higher rim of cake around sides and possibly some cracking. Level and unmold torte onto an 8-inch corrugated cake circle according to instructions, page 175. Torte may be completed to this point, wrapped and kept at room temperature up to 3 days in advance. Or freeze for up to 3 months. Let come to room temperature before glazing.

6. Glaze with Bittersweet Chocolate or Chocolate Honey Glaze. To decorate place plain or caramelized hazelnuts around the top edge of the cake or pipe overlapping zigzags of melted white and milk chocolate (see photograph). Do not refrigerate.

34 Chocolate Tortes

The rich flavor of toasted hazelnuts (filberts) bowled me over for the first time in a creamy gelato ice cream cone just yards from the Leaning Tower of Pisa! In this torte that memory mingles with my favorite—bittersweet chocolate.

Chocolate Tortes 35

Chocolate almond meringue cookies seem to merge with a light, buttery, chocolate mousse so it's hard to know where one starts and the other leaves off. But who cares?

102 Petite Rewards

Autumn Leaves

1. **To Make the Chocolate Almond Meringues:** Preheat oven to 200°. Stir together ¼ cup sugar with the almonds, cocoa, and cornstarch. Set aside.

2. Combine ½ cup egg whites, cream of tartar, and vanilla in a clean, dry mixing bowl. Beat at medium speed until soft peaks form. Gradually sprinkle in remaining ½ cup sugar, beating on high speed until stiff but not dry.

3. Fold dry ingredients into the stiff meringue. Scrape mixture into the pastry bag. Pipe about 24 disks, each 2½ inches in diameter and about ⅜ inch thick, spacing them ½ inch apart on the parchment-lined cookie sheet.

4. Bake for 30 minutes. Turn oven off, but leave meringues in still-warm oven until completely dry and crisp, about 30 minutes more. Let cool completely. Store airtight, at room temperature, until needed. Meringues may be completed 3–4 weeks in advance.

5. **To Make the Mousse:** Melt chocolate gently in a clean, dry container set in a barely simmering water bath or microwave on MEDIUM (50%) for about 3 minutes. Keep chocolate warm until needed.

6. Meanwhile, cream butter in the bowl of an electric mixer. Beat in eggs yolks and continue to cream until very soft and fluffy. Set aside.

7. Combine the 3 egg whites plus the additional ½ cup egg whites and the cream of tartar in a clean, dry mixing bowl. Beat at medium speed until soft peaks form. Gradually sprinkle in sugar, beating at high speed until stiff but not dry.

8. Stir the warm melted chocolate into the soft egg yolk and butter mixture with a rubber spatula. Fold one-fourth of the egg whites into chocolate mixture to lighten it. Fold in remaining whites.

9. **To Assemble and Finish the Pastries:** Scoop or pipe a mound of mousse (about 3 tablespoons) on top of 12 of the meringues. (If mousse is very soft, refrigerate meringues for 10–15 minutes to firm up the mounds of mousse and the bowl of mousse, as well.) Embed a second meringue, upside down, into the mousse on the first meringue to make a tall "sandwich" cookie about 1½ inches high. Gently pick up each sandwich with thumb and forefinger. Use a small spatula to fill in and smooth sides with more mousse, forming a cylinder. Smooth mousse on the tops as well. (If at any time the pastries are too soft or difficult to work with, refrigerate or freeze them for a few minutes to stiffen them.) You will have small cylindrical pastries, about 1½ inches tall, covered in chocolate mousse. Leftover mousse may be divvied up and spread on

Makes 12 individual pastries

For best flavor and texture, assemble pastries at least one day ahead.

Ingredients:
For Chocolate-Almond Meringues:
¾ cup sugar
¾ cup (3 ounces) ground blanched almonds
2 tablespoons plus 2 teaspoons unsweetened cocoa powder
1 tablespoon plus 1 teaspoon cornstarch
½ cup (3–4) egg whites, at room temperature
¼ teaspoon cream of tartar
1 teaspoon vanilla extract
For Mousse:
9 ounces semisweet or bittersweet chocolate, cut into bits
4 ounces sweet butter (1 stick), slightly softened
3 large eggs, separated
½ cup (3–4) additional egg whites, at room temperature
½ teaspoon cream of tartar
¼ cup sugar
Chocolate shavings made by scraping a chunk or block of chocolate (page 188)

Special Equipment:
Heavy-duty baking sheet, lined with parchment paper
Pastry bag fitted with Ateco #9 plain round tip (⅜-inch opening)

Petite Rewards 103

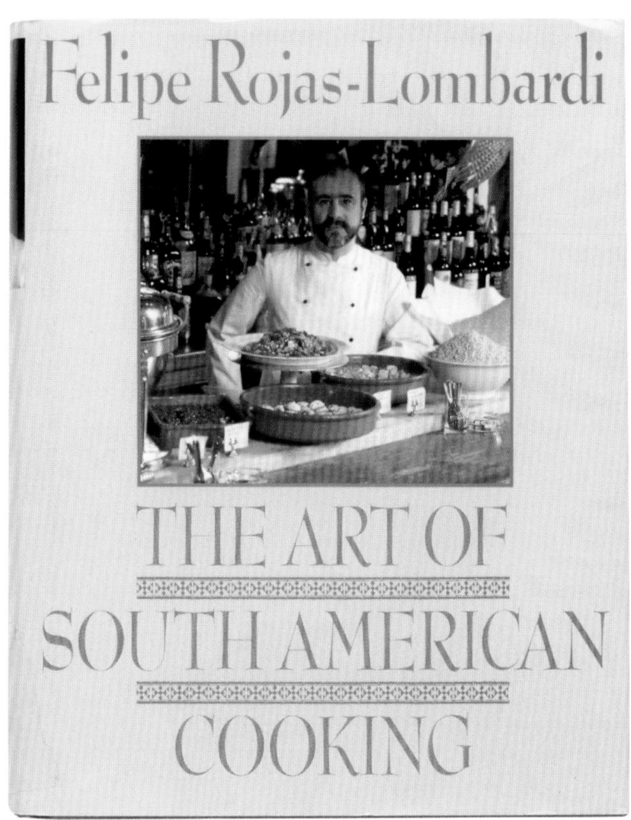

FELIPE ROJAS-LOMBARDI

The Art of South American Cooking, 1991

It's hard to believe that there was a time when there were no tapas bars, but it is true. Thankfully, Felipe Rojas-Lombardi came to New York City from Lima, Peru, in 1967 to work with James Beard at Beard's cooking school. Beard was very interested in world cuisines and encouraged many young chefs and cooks to write about these cuisines.

When Dean & DeLuca opened in 1977, Rojas-Lombardi became the store's founding chef. The following year he became a consultant for the famous restaurant and cabaret the Ballroom, located at 253 West Twenty-eighth Street in New York, which featured such legendary entertainers as Blossom Dearie. In 1982 he became executive chef and owner of the Ballroom, which the *New York Times*'s restaurant critic Bryan Miller described as exuding a "generous spirit and buoyant dining style." The Ballroom became known for its tapas, and Rojas-Lombardi is credited with introducing these small plates with powerful flavors to the American palate. Sadly, Rojas-Lombardi didn't live to see his most influential book, *The Art of South American Cooking*, published. He died 1991, at age forty-six, a few months before it appeared in print.

NOTABLE RECIPES: Caldo Verde • **Caldudas** (page 328) • **Cebiche de Atun** (page 474) • **Cebiche de Calamares** (page 487) • Chicken Escabeche • **Chupe de Quinua** (page 349) • **Ensalada de Papas** (page 367) • Lomo Horneado Con Camote y Cebollas • **Manjar Blanco** (page 644) • Mayonesa de Leche • Quinoa en Salpicon • Rabbit in Chocolate Sauce • **Sopa de Tomatitos Verdes** (page 335)

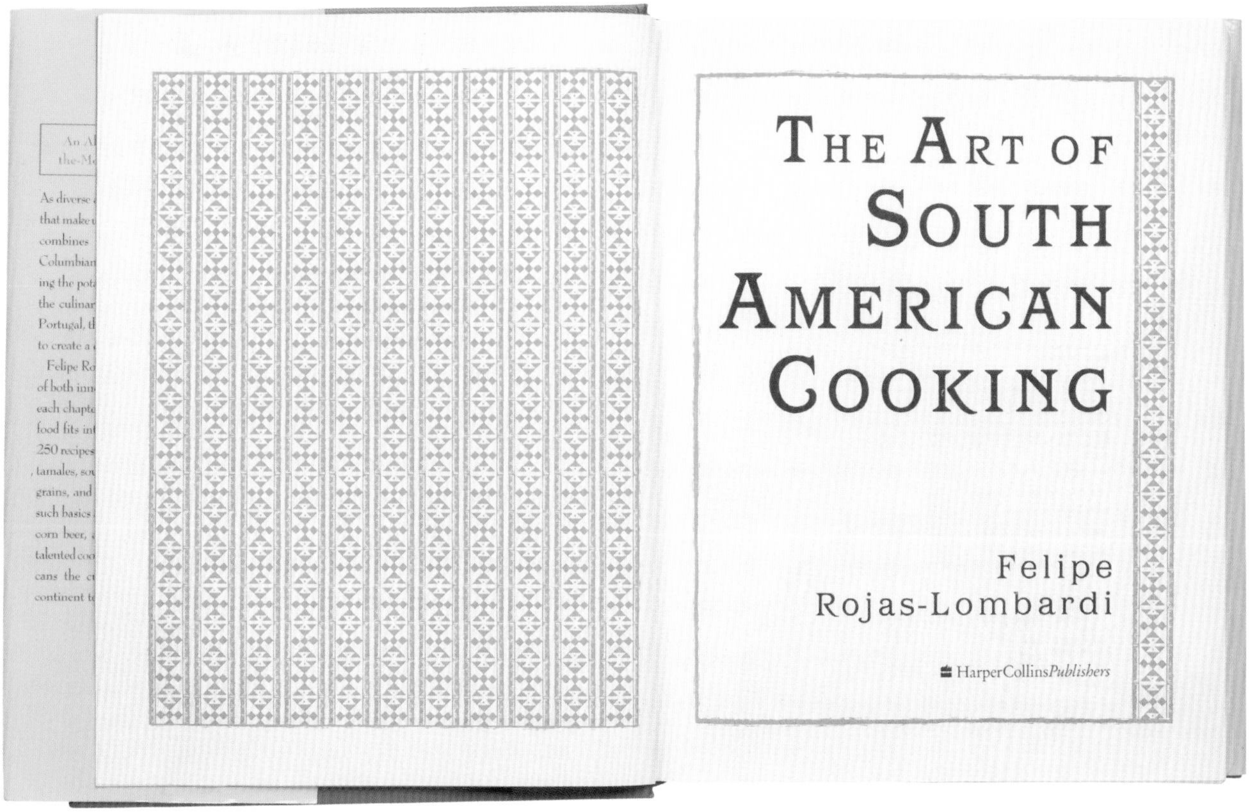
THE ART OF
SOUTH
AMERICAN
COOKING
Felipe
Rojas-Lombardi
HarperCollinsPublishers

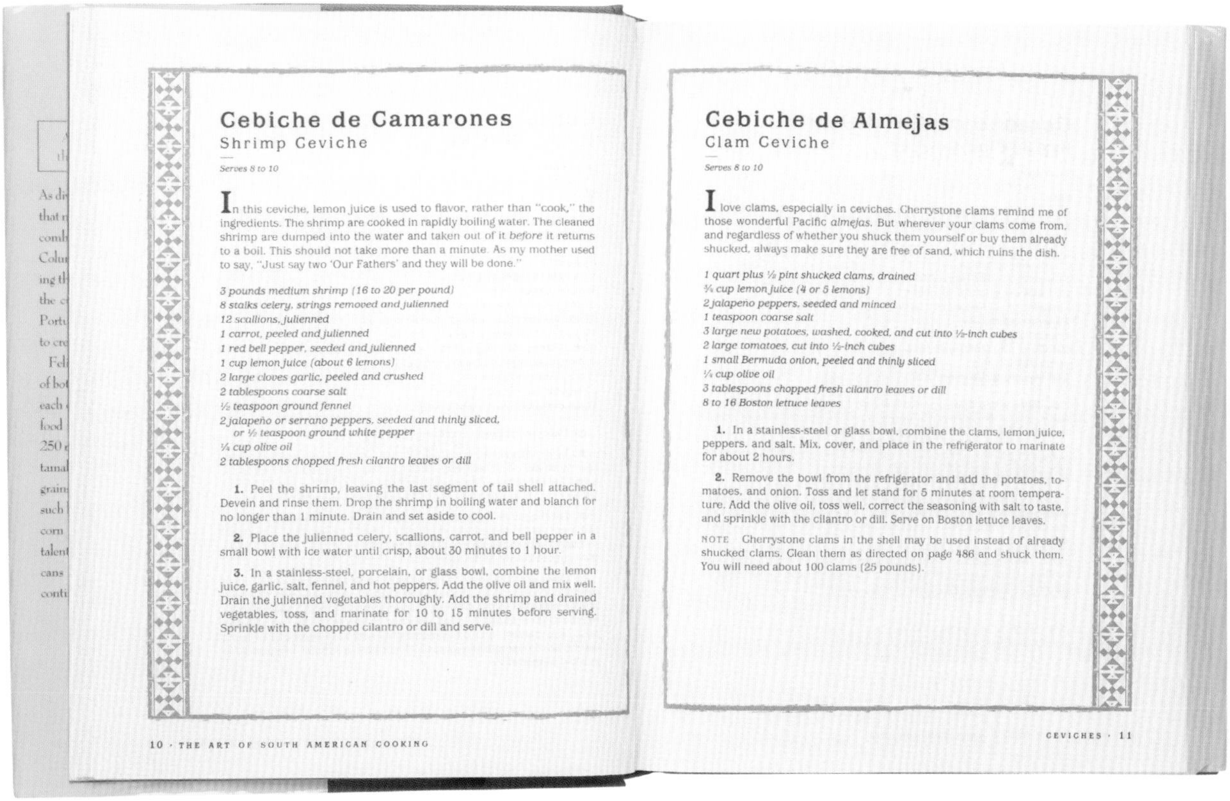

Cebiche de Camarones
Shrimp Ceviche

Serves 8 to 10

In this ceviche, lemon juice is used to flavor, rather than "cook," the ingredients. The shrimp are cooked in rapidly boiling water. The cleaned shrimp are dumped into the water and taken out of it *before* it returns to a boil. This should not take more than a minute. As my mother used to say, "Just say two 'Our Fathers' and they will be done."

3 pounds medium shrimp (16 to 20 per pound)
8 stalks celery, strings removed and julienned
12 scallions, julienned
1 carrot, peeled and julienned
1 red bell pepper, seeded and julienned
1 cup lemon juice (about 6 lemons)
2 large cloves garlic, peeled and crushed
2 tablespoons coarse salt
½ teaspoon ground fennel
2 jalapeño or serrano peppers, seeded and thinly sliced, or ½ teaspoon ground white pepper
¼ cup olive oil
2 tablespoons chopped fresh cilantro leaves or dill

1. Peel the shrimp, leaving the last segment of tail shell attached. Devein and rinse them. Drop the shrimp in boiling water and blanch for no longer than 1 minute. Drain and set aside to cool.

2. Place the julienned celery, scallions, carrot, and bell pepper in a small bowl with ice water until crisp, about 30 minutes to 1 hour.

3. In a stainless-steel, porcelain, or glass bowl, combine the lemon juice, garlic, salt, fennel, and hot peppers. Add the olive oil and mix well. Drain the julienned vegetables thoroughly. Add the shrimp and drained vegetables, toss, and marinate for 10 to 15 minutes before serving. Sprinkle with the chopped cilantro or dill and serve.

10 · THE ART OF SOUTH AMERICAN COOKING

Cebiche de Almejas
Clam Ceviche

Serves 8 to 10

I love clams, especially in ceviches. Cherrystone clams remind me of those wonderful Pacific *almejas*. But wherever your clams come from, and regardless of whether you shuck them yourself or buy them already shucked, always make sure they are free of sand, which ruins the dish.

1 quart plus ½ pint shucked clams, drained
¾ cup lemon juice (4 or 5 lemons)
2 jalapeño peppers, seeded and minced
1 teaspoon coarse salt
3 large new potatoes, washed, cooked, and cut into ½-inch cubes
2 large tomatoes, cut into ½-inch cubes
1 small Bermuda onion, peeled and thinly sliced
¼ cup olive oil
3 tablespoons chopped fresh cilantro leaves or dill
8 to 16 Boston lettuce leaves

1. In a stainless-steel or glass bowl, combine the clams, lemon juice, peppers, and salt. Mix, cover, and place in the refrigerator to marinate for about 2 hours.

2. Remove the bowl from the refrigerator and add the potatoes, tomatoes, and onion. Toss and let stand for 5 minutes at room temperature. Add the olive oil, toss well, correct the seasoning with salt to taste, and sprinkle with the cilantro or dill. Serve on Boston lettuce leaves.

NOTE Cherrystone clams in the shell may be used instead of already shucked clams. Clean them as directed on page 486 and shuck them. You will need about 100 clams (25 pounds).

CEVICHES · 11

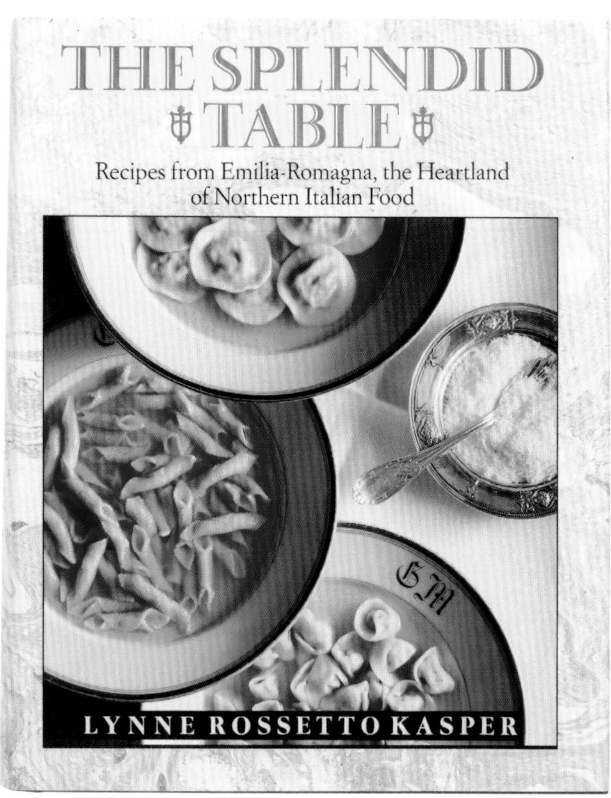

NOTABLE RECIPES: Balsamic Roast Chicken (page 505) • Cappellacci with Sweet Squash • Chestnut Ricotta Cheesecake • **Lasagne of Emilia-Romagna** (page 449) • **Linguine with Braised Garlic and Balsamic Vinegar** (page 449) • Maccheroni with Baked Grilled Vegetables • Pasta Verde (Spinach Egg Pasta) • Ragu alla Contadina (Country-Style Ragu) • Ragu Bolognese • **Salad of Tart Greens with Prosciutto and Warm Balsamic Dressing** (page 370) • **Torta Barozzi** (page 623) • **An Unusual Tortellini Pie** (page 445)

LYNNE ROSSETTO KASPER

The Splendid Table

Recipes from Emilia-Romagna, the Heartland of Northern Italian Food, 1992

No cookbook has won as many awards as Lynne Rossetto Kasper's *Splendid Table.* When published in 1992 it won the James Beard Foundation's Cookbook of the Year; the International Association of Culinary Professionals Best Cookbook of the Year; the Julia Child Award for the best first cookbook; and the Maria Luigia, Duchessa di Parma International Award. And for good reason.

Kasper spent ten years researching the history of the foods of Emilia-Romagna, the region of northern Italy that lies between Tuscany and the Alps. This region, considered by Italians to be the very best for food, gives us prosciutto di Parma, Parmigiano Reggiano, and balsamic vinegar—some of the greatest food treasures the world knows. Her focus was on food traditions and small, local producers long before our current obsession with everything local.

Americans interested in food knew virtually nothing about Emilia-Romagna until Kasper's book appeared. Suddenly a whole new array of amazing flavors burst onto the American palate. More than a quarter of the book is dedicated to pasta, which the region is known for, including Renaissance dishes for sweet pastas, something completely forgotten in American cooking. Kasper credits Marcella Hazan for opening up Northern Italian foods to a larger audience in Hazan's *Classic Italian Cook Book*; in fact, Kasper went to Bologna in 1977 to study with Hazan. One of the most important things about *The Splendid Table* is how Kasper took Hazan's project further and captures the importance of history, culture, and tradition that is the essence of Italian food.

Balsamic Vegetables

Verdure sott'Aceto

Every year when vegetables are harvested in the Modena area families put up jars of marinated peppers, cauliflower, and onions. Traditionally served as a first course with bread fritters, these can also be an unusual condiment with ham, roast pork, or any cured meat. Mix them into salads for a great boost in flavor. They are a refreshing alternative to the jarred versions sold in Italian grocery stores.

[Makes 2 quarts]

- 1 quart white wine vinegar
- 2⅔ cups water
- ½ cup extra-virgin olive oil
- 1 tablespoon coarse salt
- ¼ cup sugar
- ½ teaspoon freshly ground black pepper
- 1½ teaspoons chopped fresh basil, or ½ teaspoon dried basil
- 3 medium red bell peppers, cut into ½-inch-wide strips
- 3 medium yellow bell peppers, cut into ½-inch-wide strips
- ½ medium-size cauliflower, cut into bite-size flowerettes
- 8 to 10 pearl onions, peeled
- ⅓ cup commercial balsamic vinegar

Method

Working Ahead: *Make this at least 3 days before you intend to serve it. Cooked vegetables will keep, covered, in the refrigerator up to 3 weeks; make sure they are covered with their cooking liquid.*

Making the Marinade: In a 4-quart heavy nonaluminum saucepan, combine the white wine vinegar, water, olive oil, salt, sugar, pepper, and basil. Bring to a boil and simmer 2 to 3 minutes.

Cooking the Vegetables: Drop the peppers and cauliflower into the marinade, and bring back to a boil. Cook, uncovered, 2 to 3 minutes. Remove with a slotted spoon, leaving the marinade in the saucepan. Put the vegetables into two 1-quart glass jars. Add the onions to the hot marinade and cook 5 minutes, or until barely tender. Remove with a slotted spoon and add to the vegetables. Now boil the marinade, uncovered, 5 minutes. Remove from the heat, add the balsamic vinegar, and pour the marinade over the vegetables, making sure it completely covers all the pieces, adding a little more white wine vinegar, if necessary. Cool, cover tightly, and refrigerate.

Suggestions

Wine: The vinegar in this recipe overwhelms most wines.

Menu: Serve the vegetables as part of an antipasto, accompanying a Platter of Cured Meats (page 14) and Crispy Fritters (page 373) or with Garlic Crostini with Pancetta (page 28). They are excellent on a buffet table with roasted turkey or game.

Although created less than a decade ago, this antipasto called Salad of Tart Greens with Prosciutto and Warm Balsamic Dressing *(page 26)* plays on ancient themes.

A Classic Ragù Bolognese

Ragù Bolognese

Bologna's ragù is the most famous in Italy. According to the Bologna chapter of Italy's gastronomic society, L'Accademia Italiana della Cucina, this is the most typical and authentic-tasting rendition of the city's famed sauce. Cara De Silva, dear friend and authority on ethnic foods, researched and developed this recipe from the Academy's Bolognese original.

For our modern tastes this ragù is reserved for times of special indulgence because of its generous amounts of fat. Although a fine lower-fat version follows, I urge you to sample this recipe, if only in very small portions to experience what home cooking was like a hundred years ago in northern Italy's countryside.

[Makes enough sauce for 1½ recipes fresh pasta (pages 80 to 82) or 1½ pounds dried pasta]

- ½ cup heavy cream
- 10 ounces fresh unsalted fatback or lean salt pork, cut into small dice
- About 1 quart water
- 1 cup diced carrot (⅛- to ¼-inch dice)
- ⅔ cup diced celery (same dimensions)
- ½ cup diced onion (same dimensions)
- 1¼ pounds beef skirt steak or boneless chuck blade roast, coarsely ground
- ½ cup dry Italian white wine, preferably Trebbiano or Albana
- 2 tablespoons double or triple-concentrated imported Italian tomato paste, diluted in 10 tablespoons Poultry/Meat Stock (page 66) or Quick Stock (page 68)
- 1 cup whole milk
- Salt and freshly ground black pepper to taste

Method

Working Ahead: *The ragù is best kept warm and eaten within about 30 minutes after it has finished cooking.*

Cooking the Cream: Simmer the cream in a tiny saucepan until reduced by one-third. There should be about 6 tablespoons. Set aside.

Blanching the Salt Pork: Fresh fatback needs no blanching. If you are using salt pork, bring the water to boiling, add the salt pork, and cook for 3 minutes. Drain and pat dry.

Browning the Ragù Base: Sauté the salt pork or fatback in a 3- to 4-quart heavy saucepan over medium-low heat. Sauté 8 minutes, or until almost all its fat is rendered. Stir in the chopped vegetables. Sauté for 3 minutes over medium-low heat, or until the onion is translucent. Raise the heat to medium and stir in the beef. Brown 5 minutes, or until the meat is medium brown in color and almost, but not quite, crisp. Take care not to let the meat become overly brown or hard.

Simmering and Serving: Stir in the wine and diluted tomato paste, and reduce the heat to very low. It is critical that the mixture reduce as slowly as possible. Cook, partially covered, 2 hours. From time to time stir in a tablespoon or so of the milk. By the end of 2 hours, all the milk should be used up and the ragù should be only slightly liquid. Stir in the reduced cream. Toss the hot ragù with freshly cooked tagliatelle and serve.

Suggestions

Wine: A young red Sangue di Giuda from Lombardy's Oltrepo Pavese area, the Piedmont's "La Monella" from Braida di Giacomo Bologna, a light-bodied Merlot from the Veneto, or a young Valpolicella Classico.

Menu: Serve ragù and pasta as a main dish after a light antipasto of wedges of fresh fennel for dipping into tiny bowls of balsamic vinegar, or small portions of Spring Salad with Hazelnuts (page 21). For dessert, arrange apples, pears, and grapes on a platter, along with handfuls of unshelled nuts. Tucking clusters of glossy lemon leaves, fresh bay laurel, or evergreens around the fruit and nuts makes an appealing presentation.

BOLOGNA

Old engraving of Bologna

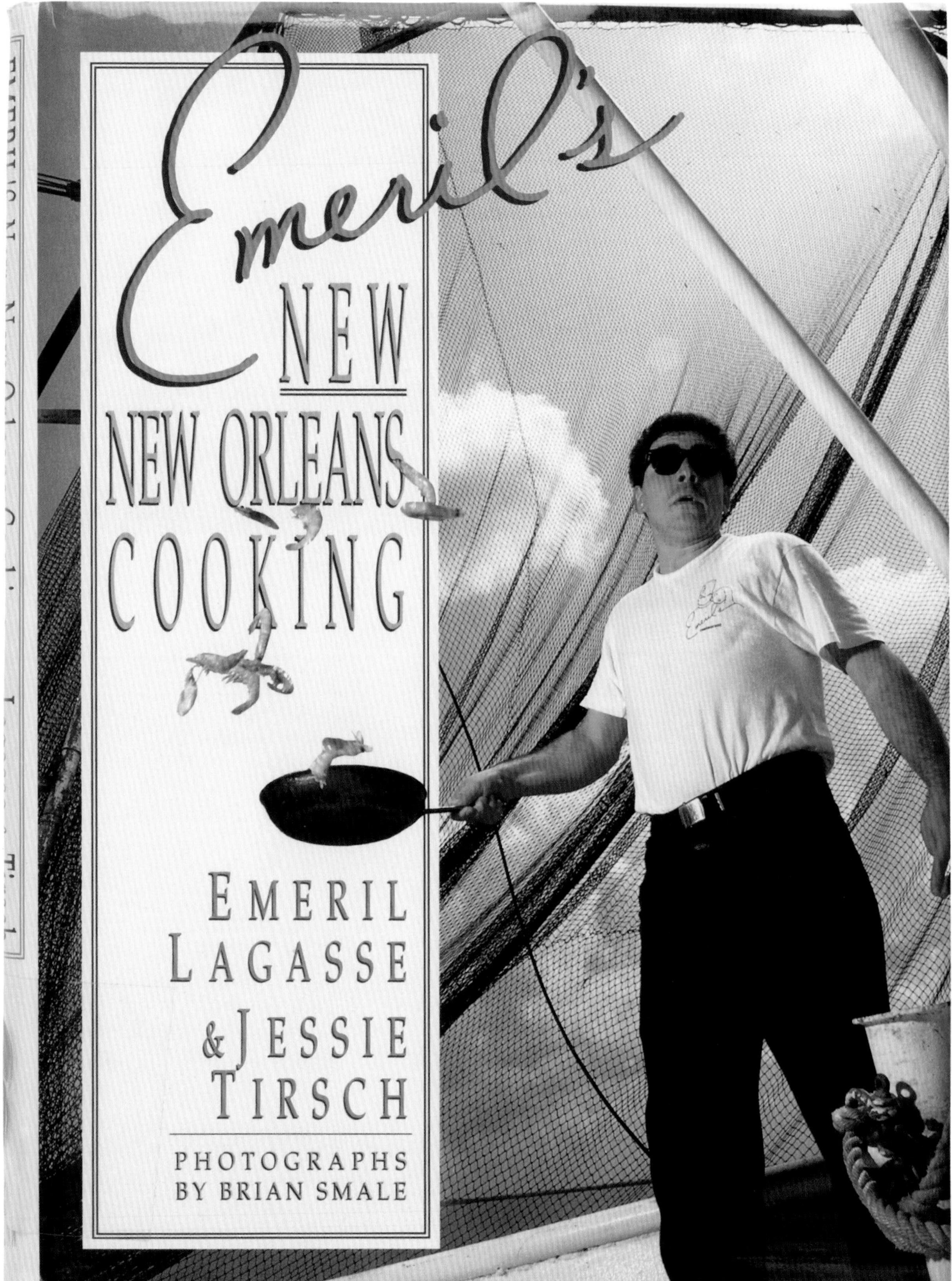
Emeril's
NEW
NEW ORLEANS
COOKING
EMERIL
LAGASSE
&JESSIE
TIRSCH
PHOTOGRAPHS
BY BRIAN SMALE

EMERIL LAGASSE

Emeril's New New Orleans Cooking, 1993

Emeril Lagasse epitomizes the contemporary star chef. He has done more than just about any other to popularize cooking through contemporary media, especially his cooking shows and his signature exclamation, "BAM!!!"

Lagasse first learned to cook from his mother, Hilda, in Fall River, Massachusetts. As a teen, he worked in a Portuguese bakery and learned the art of making breads and pastries. He attended the culinary program at Johnson & Wales University, and then worked in Paris and Lyon, learning the French culinary tradition. Dick and Ella Brennan lured Lagasse to New Orleans as the executive chef at their world-famous restaurant Commander's Palace.

In 1990 Lagasse opened Emeril's Restaurant, striking out on his own. He followed it two years later with NOLA, located in the French Quarter. He now operates thirteen restaurants nationwide. Lagasse has had a huge effect on food television, hosting more than two thousand shows for the Food Network alone. His wildly engaging *Emeril Live*, on the Cooking Channel, has captured the new audience of men who cook as a hobby and who find his jocular, jaunty, I'm-just-a-guy-who-cooks style appealing. His *New New Orleans Cooking* is full of fresh, inventive takes on Cajun and Creole cuisine.

NOTABLE RECIPES: André's Barbecued Shrimp and Homemade Biscuits (page 486) • Artichoke Seafood Salad • Banana Cream Pie with Caramel Drizzles and Chocolate Sauce • **Big Easy Seafood Okra Gumbo** (page 376) • Crawfish Egg Rolls with Sesame Drizzle • **Dr. E's Get-Well Chicken Vegetable Soup** (page 336) • **Goat Cheese Quesadilla with Guacamole and Pico di Gallo** (page 329) • **Southwest Cheese Pie with Pico di Gallo** (page 389)

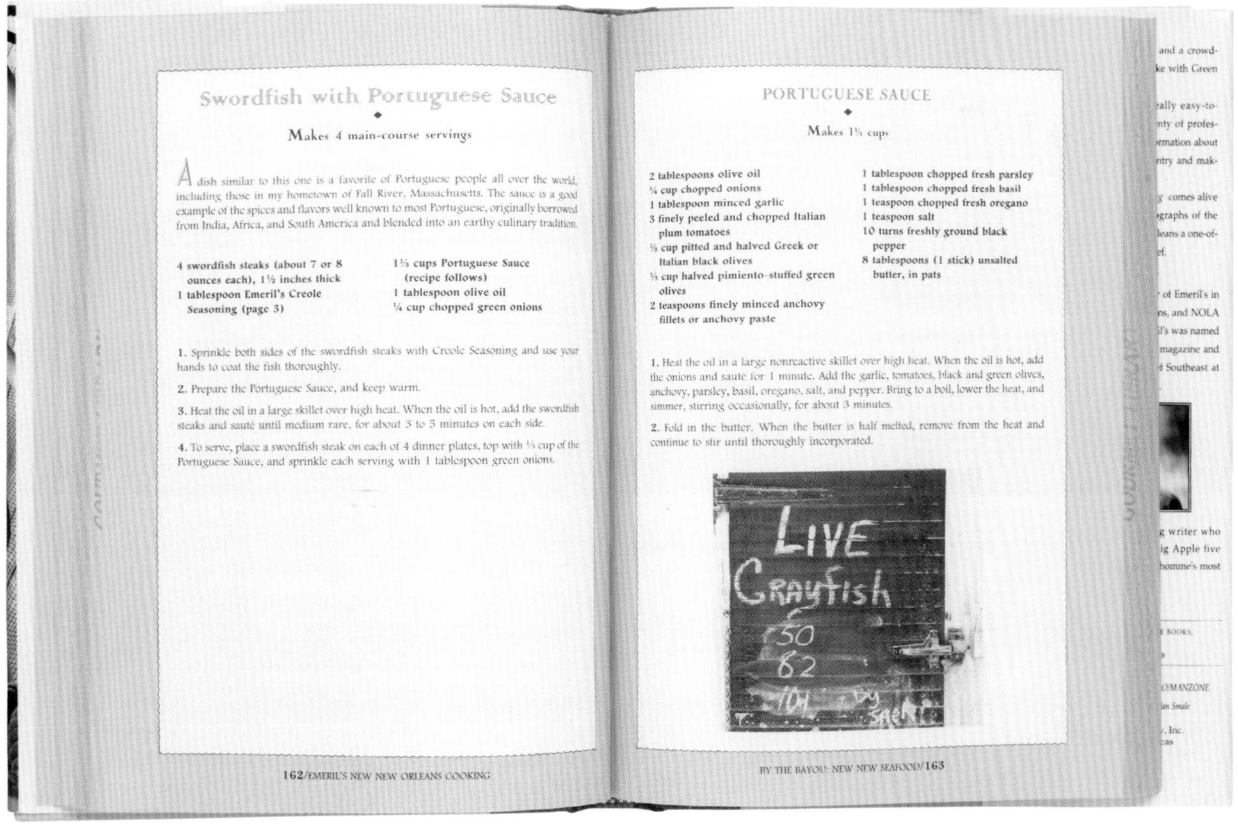

Swordfish with Portuguese Sauce

Makes 4 main-course servings

A dish similar to this one is a favorite of Portuguese people all over the world, including those in my hometown of Fall River, Massachusetts. The sauce is a good example of the spices and flavors well known to most Portuguese, originally borrowed from India, Africa, and South America and blended into an earthy culinary tradition.

4 swordfish steaks (about 7 or 8 ounces each), 1½ inches thick
1 tablespoon Emeril's Creole Seasoning (page 3)
1⅓ cups Portuguese Sauce (recipe follows)
1 tablespoon olive oil
¼ cup chopped green onions

1. Sprinkle both sides of the swordfish steaks with Creole Seasoning and use your hands to coat the fish thoroughly.
2. Prepare the Portuguese Sauce, and keep warm.
3. Heat the oil in a large skillet over high heat. When the oil is hot, add the swordfish steaks and sauté until medium rare, for about 3 to 5 minutes on each side.
4. To serve, place a swordfish steak on each of 4 dinner plates, top with ⅓ cup of the Portuguese Sauce, and sprinkle each serving with 1 tablespoon green onions.

162/EMERIL'S NEW NEW ORLEANS COOKING

PORTUGUESE SAUCE

Makes 1⅓ cups

2 tablespoons olive oil
¼ cup chopped onions
1 tablespoon minced garlic
3 finely peeled and chopped Italian plum tomatoes
⅓ cup pitted and halved Greek or Italian black olives
⅓ cup halved pimiento-stuffed green olives
2 teaspoons finely minced anchovy fillets or anchovy paste
1 tablespoon chopped fresh parsley
1 tablespoon chopped fresh basil
1 teaspoon chopped fresh oregano
1 teaspoon salt
10 turns freshly ground black pepper
8 tablespoons (1 stick) unsalted butter, in pats

1. Heat the oil in a large nonreactive skillet over high heat. When the oil is hot, add the onions and sauté for 1 minute. Add the garlic, tomatoes, black and green olives, anchovy, parsley, basil, oregano, salt, and pepper. Bring to a boil, lower the heat, and simmer, stirring occasionally, for about 3 minutes.
2. Fold in the butter. When the butter is half melted, remove from the heat and continue to stir until thoroughly incorporated.

BY THE BAYOU: NEW NEW SEAFOOD/163

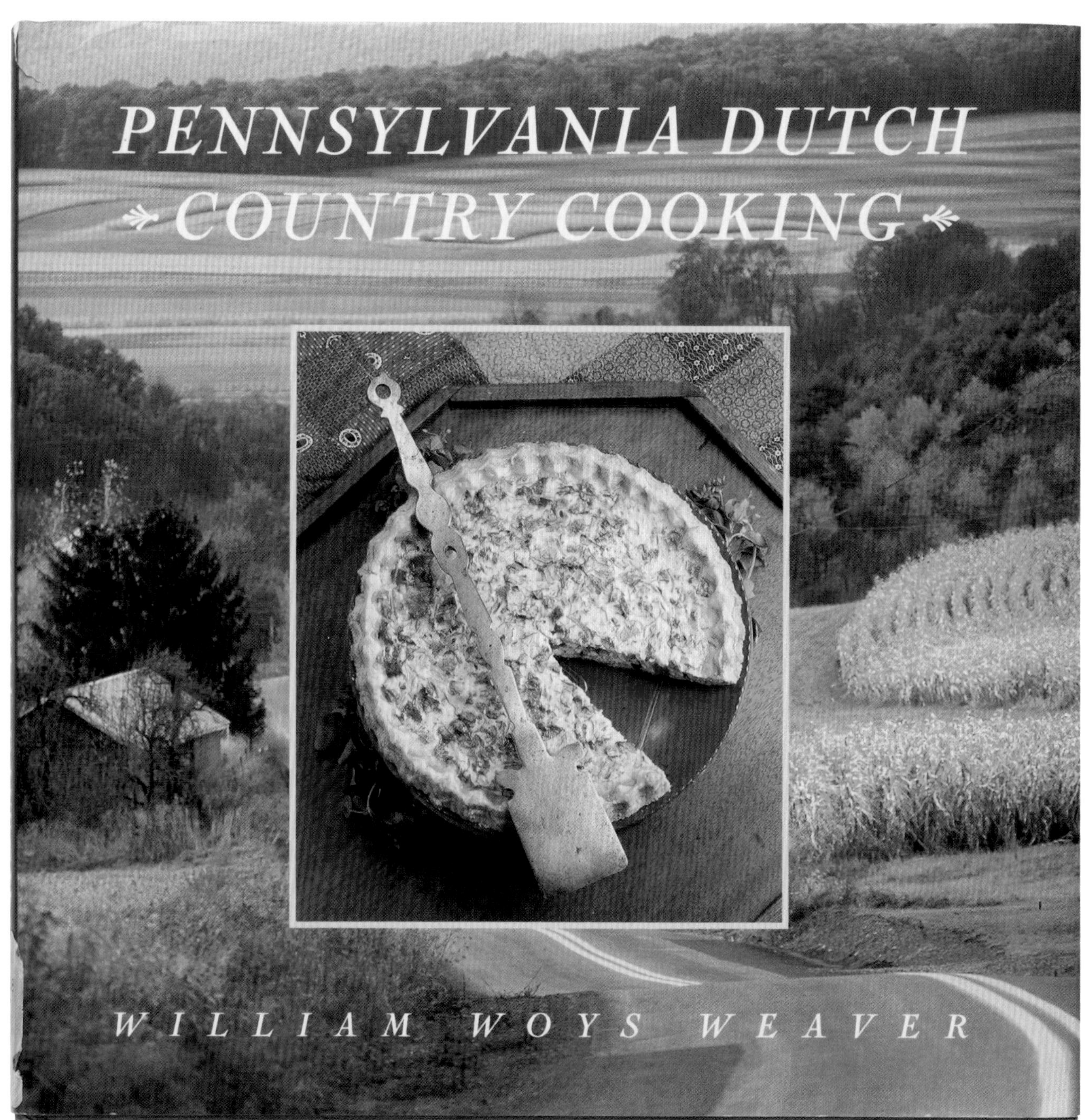
PENNSYLVANIA DUTCH
COUNTRY COOKING
WILLIAM WOYS WEAVER

WILLIAM WOYS WEAVER

Pennsylvania Dutch Country Cooking, 1993

William Woys Weaver is passionate about Pennsylvania Dutch cooking because it is his culinary heritage. As a boy, Weaver was fascinated with his grandfather's vegetable gardens, where he helped cultivate the plants. After college, Weaver began to plant a vegetable garden, which he tended on weekends in Pennsylvania, and brought the produce back to New York, where he was working as an editor. In time, Weaver left New York to follow his passion for Pennsylvania plants and food. He became a master gardener and an expert on heirloom plants. For Weaver, the beginnings of all food are in the garden.

With his penchant for historical research, Weaver turned his attention to Pennsylvania Dutch cooking, which has been recognized as an important American regional cuisine since the mid-nineteenth century. In its truest form, this kind of cooking flourishes in southeastern Pennsylvania, but it is practiced throughout the Mid-Atlantic and Midwestern states, from Virginia to Pennsylvania to Wisconsin to Iowa. Pennsylvania Dutch cooking is a conglomerate of various kinds of German cooking brought to the United States by waves of immigrants from both northern and southern Germany, with a mixture of Swiss influences, too. The use of "Dutch" in this context does not mean someone from Holland; rather, it is a broader term for those who live along the Rhine River valley. In actuality, Pennsylvania Dutch cooking is its own cuisine, created in the United States from these various sources. It's important to remember that it is not German-American cuisine. It's also important to remember that it's not Amish cooking, either.

In *Pennsylvania Dutch Country Cooking*, Weaver brings together his vast knowledge of Pennsylvania foodstuffs with historical recipes to give us a comprehensive understanding of this treasured American cuisine.

NOTABLE RECIPES: Chickweed Pie (Hinkeldarrem-kuche) (page 426) • **Gingerbread Men or "Mummeli"** (page 634) • **Green Apple Pap** (page 435) • **Hickory Nut Dumplings (Hickerniss-Gnepp)** (page 426) • Honey Jumbles • Pretzel Soup with Peanut Roux • **Scrapple** (page 534) • **Stuffed Pig's Stomach, or "Dutch Goose" (Seimawe genannt "Deitscher Gans")** (page 559)

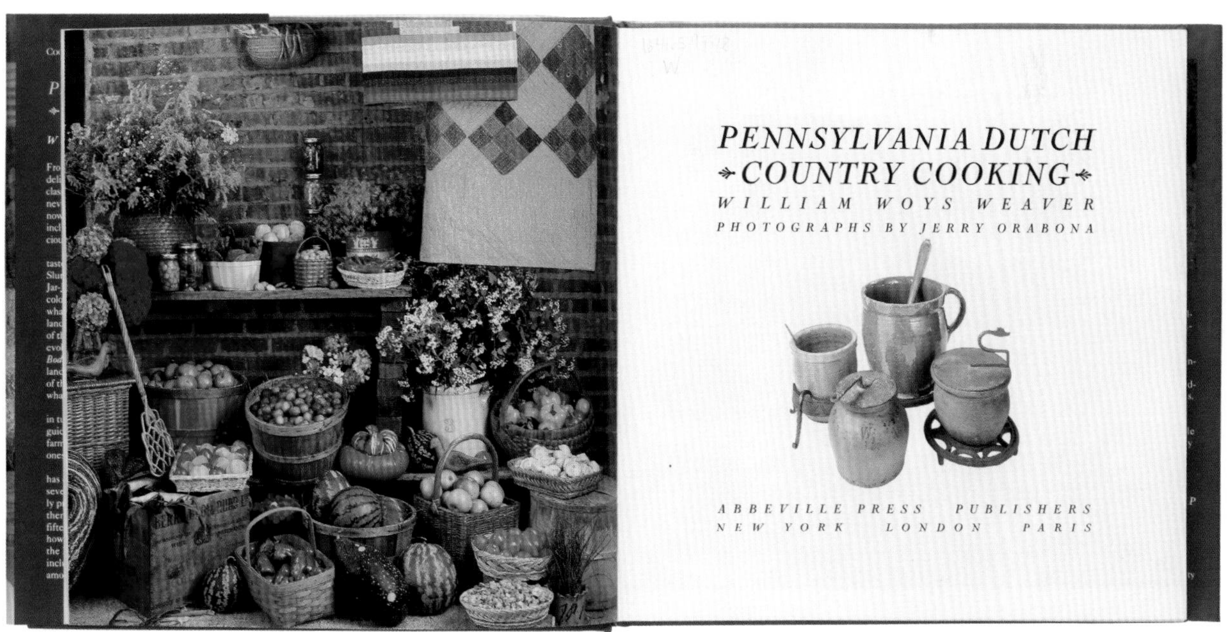

Baked Shad with Cabbage and Tomatoes

(G'backener Moifisch mit Graut un Tomatts)

This delightful shad dish comes from Dauphin County. The recipe belonged to Mrs. Carl Adam, who lived in Harrisburg at the turn of this century. Since Mrs. Adam's recipe makes quite a fulsome dinner, this may be treated as a one-pot meal.

Yield: 4 to 6 servings

3 tablespoons (45 g) unsalted butter
1 cup (100 g) plain breadcrumbs
1½ tablespoons minced fresh parsley
2 tablespoons (5 g) minced fresh chives
1 teaspoon minced fresh winter savory or ½ teaspoon dried savory
1 3- to 4-pound (1.5- to 2-kg) buck shad, gutted and cleaned but with head and tail left on
6 cups (550 g) finely shredded cabbage, resembling angel hair noodles
1 cup (65 g) shredded sorrel
1 cup (250 g) chopped onion
1 cup (150 g) peeled, seeded, and chopped fresh tomatoes
⅔ cup (160 ml) dry white wine
4 slices country smoked slab bacon

Preheat the oven to 350°F (175°C). Melt the butter in a skillet and fry the breadcrumbs until straw colored, stirring constantly to prevent scorching (3 to 4 minutes). Add the parsley, chives, and savory, and remove from the heat.

Open the shad and cut the cavity from the head toward the tail with a sharp knife so that the fish opens out flat when lying on its back. To accomplish this, press down with the point of the knife under the neck and follow the backbone so that all the "rib" bones are cut at their bases. Fill the cavity with the browned breadcrumb mixture, then sew it up with trussing thread.

Poach the cabbage in salted water for 3 to 4 minutes to tenderize it, then drain and combine with the sorrel, onion, and tomatoes. Cover the bottom of a shallow roasting pan with the cabbage mixture, then lay the stuffed shad on top of it. Pour the wine on top, then drape the bacon slices diagonally at even intervals over the fish. Bake for approximately 40 minutes, depending on the size of the fish. Baste from time to time with liquid from the pan. When the fish tests done, serve immediately.

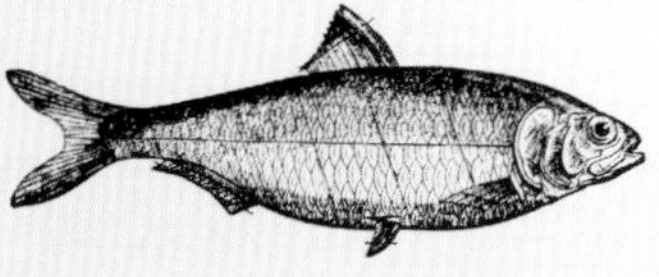

Opposite: Ball cheese filled with dry curds (foreground); pot cheese in earthenware cups; Amish farmer's cheese, a domestic version of Gruyère; and sapsago, a green cone-shaped grating cheese flavored with melilot.

SOUP AND NOODLE COOKERY

Enter the impish *Bucklich Mennli*, "Little Humped-Back Man," the eternal bane of the Pennsylvania Dutch kitchen, the designing elf who inhabits each and every Pennsylvania Dutch household. He is responsible for such mishaps as scorched toast, overturned wastepaper baskets, dumplings that fall apart, dripping faucets, chipped canning jars, and a host of other irritations, including his favorite: throwing ashes into soup.

The precautions that the Pennsylvania Dutch housewife undertook in order to create a perfect soup cannot be underestimated. Soup cookery was the centerpiece of her art, just as a hearth at worktable height was the centerpiece of the old Pennsylvania Dutch kitchen. In fact, the history of our soup cookery and the raised hearth go hand in hand.

Cumberland Valley Clafty Pudding
(Schnitzglaafdi)

As far as I can determine, this recipe first appeared in print in 1881 in The Cumberland Valley Cook and General Recipe Book *as part of the cultural revival among the Dutch then taking place.*" *Our* Glaaldi *and the French clafoutis probably share a common origin, although the Pennsylfaanisch word does not derive from French but from the past participle of* laufe, "*to run or pour.*" *A true* Glaaldi *is a batter pudding that comes out of the oven looking like a cake.*

YIELD: 6 TO 8 SERVINGS

2 cups (130 g) dried apple slices (*Schnitz*)
2 cups (500 ml) boiling water
cracker crumbs
1 cup (125 g) all-purpose flour
1 teaspoon baking powder
1 teaspoon ground cinnamon
1 teaspoon ground clove
4 large eggs
1 cup (250 g) vanilla sugar (see note)
1 cup (250 ml) unsulfured molasses
confectioners' sugar

Put the apple slices in a small heatproof bowl and cover with the boiling water. Infuse 1 hour or until the apples are soft. Drain and reserve the liquid and the fruit separately.

Preheat the oven to 375°F (190°C). Grease a 10½-inch (27 cm) porcelain baking dish and dust it with cracker crumbs. Sift together the flour, baking powder, cinnamon, and cloves. Combine the eggs and vanilla sugar in the bowl of an electric mixer and beat until frothy. Gradually beat in the molasses, reserved liquid from the infused apples, and the flour mixture.

Spread the apples evenly over the bottom of the baking dish and pour the batter on top. Bake for 30 to 35 minutes or until the top is golden and the center is set. Cool on a rack, then dust the top with confectioners' sugar. Serve warm or at room temperature.

Note: To make vanilla sugar, store 3 vanilla beans in a quart (liter) jar of granulated sugar for at least 1 month. Otherwise, mix 1 tablespoon (15 ml) of vanilla flavoring with 1 cup (250 g) granulated sugar and use as directed above.

Hickory Nut Corn Cake
(Hickerniss-Welschkannkuche)

YIELD: 10 TO 15 SERVINGS

3 cups (375 g) stone-ground organic white cornmeal
1½ cups (185 g) all-purpose flour
1½ tablespoons baking powder
1½ teaspoons sea salt
¾ cup (185 g) sugar
3 large eggs
2 cups (500 ml) whole milk
¼ cup (60 ml) unsalted butter, melted
1½ tablespoons (22 ml) vanilla extract
1 cup (125 g) finely chopped hickory nuts
½ cup (50 g) whole or partly broken hickory nuts
2 tablespoons (30 g) granulated sugar

Preheat the oven to 400°F (205°C). Sift together the cornmeal, flour, baking powder, salt, and sugar 3 times. Beat the eggs until lemon colored and combine with the milk, melted butter, and vanilla. Gently sift the cornmeal mixture, a little at a time, into the liquid ingredients to form a batter and then fold in the chopped nuts. Pour the batter into a greased baking pan measuring approximately 9 by 12 inches (23 by 30 cm). Scatter the whole or partly broken nuts over the batter and, with the back of a spoon, gently press them into it. Bake for 35 minutes or until set in the center. As soon as the cake comes from the oven, scatter the sugar over the top and cool on a rack. Serve at room temperature.

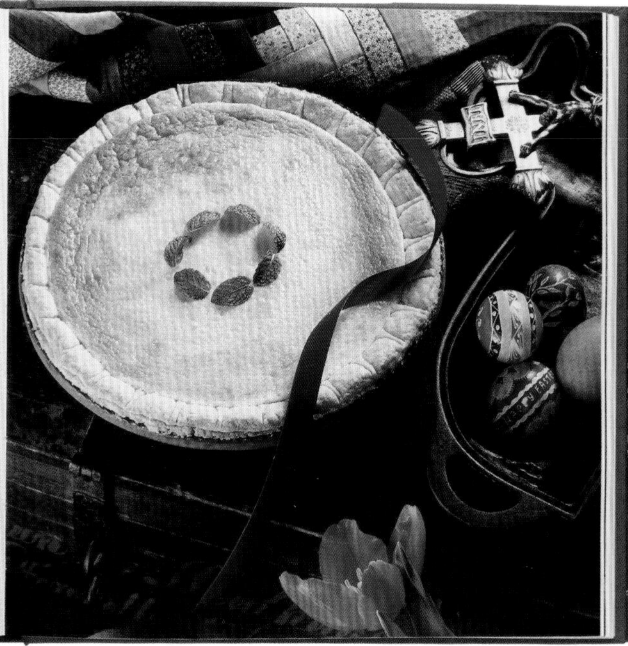

York County Peppermint Pie, an Easter favorite.

Above: Grischdaagsmoije *hanging from the ceiling of the master bedroom. Right: Switches for bad children were left under the Christmas tree.*

Foremost among these is the idea of erecting some type of tree decorated with foods and ornaments. This custom is associated with the fact that December 24 was observed as Adam and Eve Day, which focused on the Tree of Life. Most European historians of Christmas recognize this custom as a Christian reshaping of pre-Christian midwinter observances that brought greenery into the house.

The oldest forms of the Pennsylvania Dutch Christmas "tree" were not actually trees but branches. The *Grischdaagszweeg* or *Zuckerbaum* was usually a large branch of wild cherry brought into the house on St. Barbara's Day (December 4) so that it would bloom by Christmas. It was hung with cookies and candies, the main gifts children received. A variant of the *Grischdaagszweeg* was the *Grischdaagsmoije*, an evergreen bush, usually mountain laurel or juniper, set up on a table or hung from the ceiling. On page 150, I have recreated a *Grischdaagsmoije* of mountain laurel based on a woodcut printed in Philadelphia in 1845. This was the most common type of Pennsylvania Dutch Christmas tree before the Civil War.

On Christmas Eve it was customary in some households to leave empty plates on a table near the tree, one for each child in the family, so that they could be filled with cookies and candies by the *Grischtkindel* (Christ Child) during the wee hours of darkness. Bad children were left switches like the ones pictured on page 152.

Aside from the *Grischtkindel*, the other major gift bringer was the *Belschnickel*, the Pennsylvania Dutch counterpart to Santa Claus. An adult member of the family would don furs and a frightening mask, and on Christmas Eve, when all the children were assembled, this fierce-looking creature would burst into the house ringing bells, snapping whips, and tossing nuts and candy at the shrieking mob. Being spooked by the *Belschnickel* is one of the great childhood games the Pennsylvania Dutch reminisce about most when the subject of old Christmas customs comes up. The *Belschnickel* still appears now and then but has been replaced for the most part by the benign and portly Santa Claus.

An extension of the *Belschnickel* tradition was the custom of belschnickling, which took place on Second Christmas (December 26), in former times a great market day throughout the Dutch Country. The belschnicklers were usually teenagers dressed in costumes who "mummed" from house

Left: A Christmas Metzelsupp *based on the 1871 woodcut shown above.*

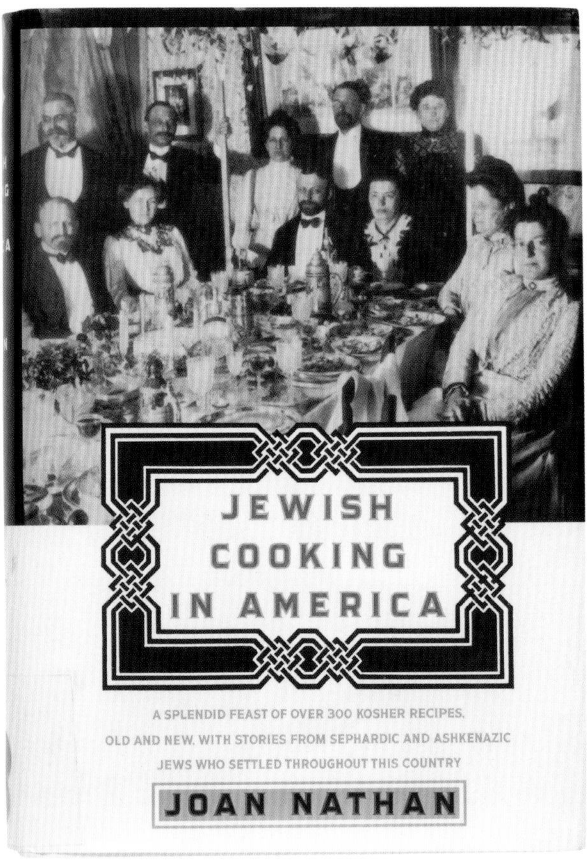

NOTABLE RECIPES: Aunt Babette's Berches (Challah) • Chocolate-filled Rugelach • Cholent (Beef and Barley Stew) • **Classic Gefilte Fish** (page 473) • **Crispy Traditional Potato Pancakes** (page 419) • **Eggplant and Green Pepper Kugel (Casserole)** (page 451) • **Fluffy Matzah Balls** (page 337) • **Mama Batalin's Potato Knishes** (page 325)• Moche's Felafel • My Favorite Brisket • Spinach and Cheese Kugel

JOAN NATHAN

Jewish Cooking in America,

1994

We are what we eat. A cliché, it's true, but it is true. No group of people understands this as well as the world's Jewish population. Their food traditions are guided by Biblical dietary laws known as *kashrut*, which determine what foods are allowed and how they must be prepared in order to be safe to eat. Jewish food traditions, thus, are directly tied to their religious beliefs and their sense of belonging, of community, and of identity.

In 1654 twenty-three Sephardic Jews arrived in New Amsterdam, bringing their cooking traditions with them and founding American Jewish cooking. Subsequent waves of Jewish immigrants would flock to American shores from all over Europe, bringing Polish, Italian, German, Syrian, Turkish, Moroccan, and other Jewish foods with them. In major centers, such as Cincinnati, Milwaukee, and New York City, Jewish delis, bakeries, and butchers tended to their own communities, but their delicious and carefully made products soon found their way into gentile American kitchens. Consider the bagel. Once found only in Jewish neighborhoods, it's now as common in American homes as white bread.

Joan Nathan traced the rich heritage of American Jewish cooking in this meticulously researched book, showing convincingly how Jewish cooking has entered into American cooking in general. Where would we be without pastrami on rye? Cheesecake? Bagels and lox? Oy! In fact, to most Americans, the word *kosher* signifies excellence, even if they have no idea that kosher just means that the food has been prepared according to the *kashrut*.

JEWISH COOKING IN AMERICA 150

Barney Greengrass's Lox, Eggs, and Onions

As a child, when I visited my grandparents in New York City, my grandmother made lox wings, onions, and hard-boiled eggs for breakfast. Lox wings, which are not as fatty as belly lox and more difficult to remove from the fish, are noticeably cheaper.

I know of no better place to eat lox, onions, and scrambled eggs than Barney Greengrass on the Upper West Side, a New York institution for over sixty years. When I visited the tiny dairy restaurant on a quiet Tuesday morning, two Baltimore ladies were sitting at a Formica table beneath the wallpaper, faded and stained with onion. They had hiked up from their downtown hotel for the Nova Scotia lox heads and wings, broiled with Spanish onions and eggs. Moe Greengrass, son of the founder, was seated at the counter across from the turn-of-the-century ice box. In the old days you could see through the mirror door cakes of ice, which would drip down and cool the butter, cheese, and eggs inside.

Mr. Greengrass took me into the back room to the black Vulcan stove. There in a huge skillet Spanish onions were cooking ever so slowly. You could just smell the sweetness leaching out of the onions. "It's a good thing you didn't come here on a Sunday," he said. "I don't know why people do it, but they wait for hours on line outside with their *New York Times*. They talk and become friends." Later they eat his lox, onions, and eggs.

Fish—From Gefilte to Grouper 151

3 Spanish onions, sliced in rounds
3 tablespoons vegetable oil
8 large eggs
*½ cup diced lox wings and heads**

*You can buy these ends at any good deli or kosher supermarket for a fraction of the price of sliced salmon. When you purchase a presliced salmon, the end and the wings are usually not sliced. Save that part for this dish.

1. Sauté the onions slowly in the oil in a frying pan with a cover. When the onions start to soften, cover, reduce the heat to low, and cook about a half hour, until the onions are very soft. Remove the cover and continue cooking until golden. This way you do not need lots of oil.
2. Beat the eggs well in a bowl. Pour over the onions. Cook slowly, stirring well. Cover for about 10 minutes. Just before the eggs have set, add the lox, and cook until just set.

Yield: 4 to 6 servings (P)

Maine Mock Lobster Salad

If you really want this to taste like a mock Maine lobster salad, serve it in a toasted hot-dog roll.

2½ pounds of a white fish like haddock or monkfish
1 16-ounce can stewed tomatoes, broken up
2 stalks celery
Salt and freshly ground pepper to taste
¼ cup mayonnaise or to taste
Paprika

1. Place the fish and tomatoes with their juice in a saucepan and simmer for 10 minutes, covered, or until done. Drain in a colander and cool.
2. Dice the celery. Break the fish into bite-size pieces and mix with the celery, salt, pepper, and mayonnaise. Sprinkle with the paprika.
3. Serve on a lettuce leaf garnished with fresh cut-up tomatoes or in the Down East fashion in a toasted hot-dog roll with mayonnaise.

Yield: 4 to 6 servings (P)

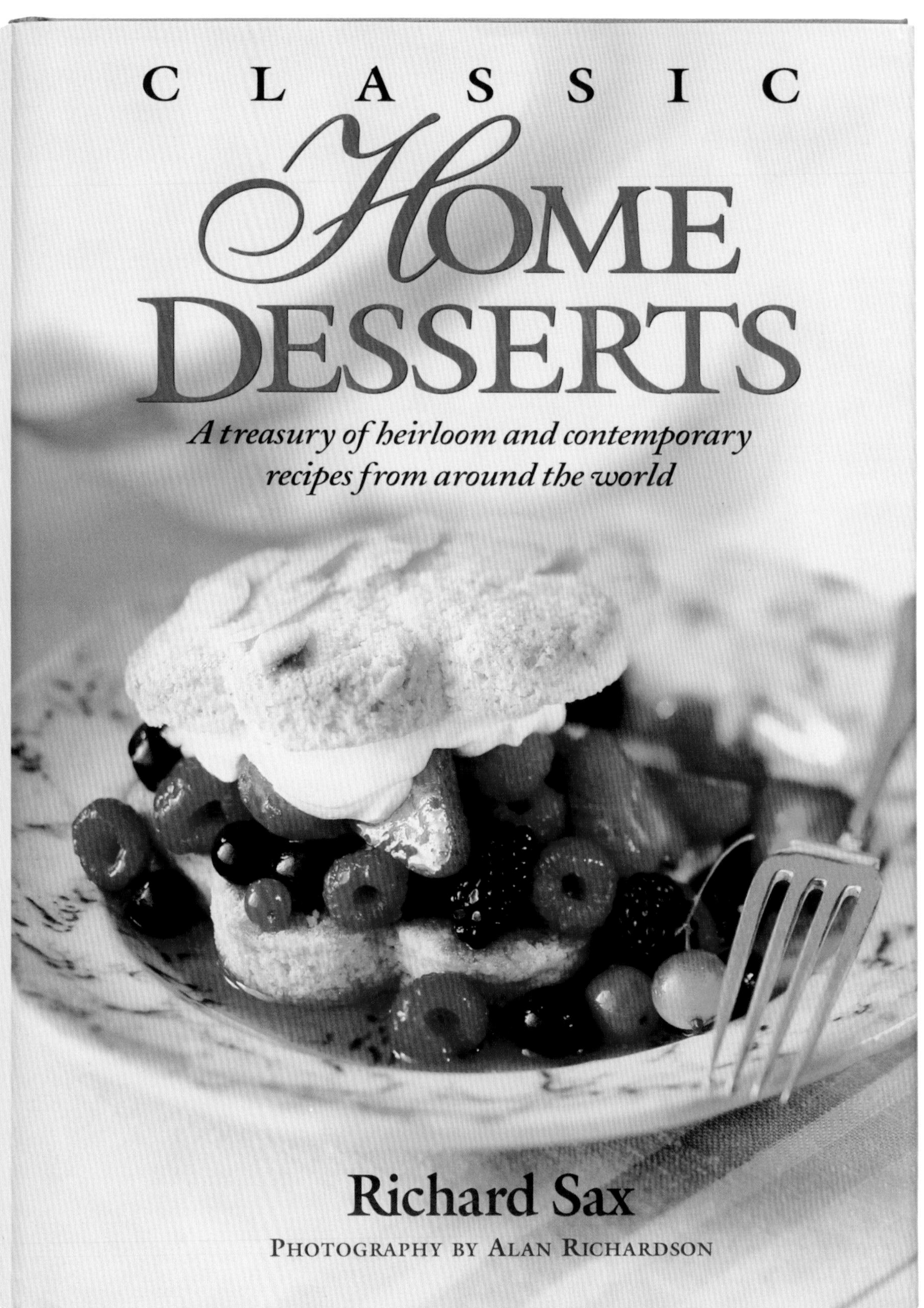
CLASSIC
HOME
DESSERTS
A treasury of heirloom and contemporary recipes from around the world
Richard Sax
PHOTOGRAPHY BY ALAN RICHARDSON

RICHARD SAX

Classic Home Desserts, 1994

Richard Sax was known for his "unadorned frankness," a term he used to describe the style of writing in old American and English recipes. Though trained as a chef both in New York and at the Cordon Bleu in Paris, Sax always thought about the home cook. In his writing for such magazines as *Bon Appétit*, *Gourmet*, *Harper's Bazaar*, *Out*, *Family Circle*, *Yankee*, and *Food and Wine*, where he was the founding director of the test kitchen, and in his cooking classes, Sax freely shared techniques and other tips on cooking that are usually kept secret by chefs. His down-to-earth approach to cooking included a focus on tasting the food as you cook and developing your own style instead of slavish adherence to recipes.

While he wrote eight cookbooks, it is *Classic Home Desserts: A Treasury of Heirloom and Contemporary Recipes from Around the World* that made him beloved to many home cooks. The recipes are straightforward in presentation, simple to follow, and produce lovely, delicious desserts fit for any table.

NOTABLE RECIPES: 1-2-3-4 Cake • All Time Best Summer Fruit Torte • **Applesauce-Carrot Cake with Lemon Cream Cheese Frosting** (page 615) • **Best-Ever Pumpkin Pie** (page 604) • Boston Cream Pie • **Buttermilk Silk Pie** (page 605) • The Chocolate Cloud Cake • **Mixed Fruit Cobbler** (page 600) • **Panna Cotta and Poached Pears in Merlot Syrup** (page 645) • **Reuben's Legendary Apple Pancake** (page 595) • **Sour Cherry Clafouti** (page 643) • White Chocolate Banana Cream Pie • **The World's Best Lemon Tart** (page 597)

To Make Jelly

Take out the great Bones of four Calves Feet, and put the Feet into a Pot with ten Quarts of Water, three Ounces of Hartshorn, three Ounces of Isinglass, a Nutmeg quarter'd, four Blades of Mace; then boil this till it comes to two Quarts, and strain it through a Flannel-Bag, let it stand twenty-four Hours, then scrape off all the Fat from the Top very clean, then slice it, and put to it the Whites of six Eggs beaten to Froth, boil it a little, and strain it again through a Flannel-Bag, then run the Jelly into little high Glasses . . . You must colour Red with Cochineal, Green with Spinage, Yellow with Saffron, Blue with Syrup of Violets, White with thick Cream, and sometimes the Jelly by itself. You may add Orange-flower Water, or Wine and Sugar, and Lemon if you please, but this is all Fancy.

HANNAH GLASSE
THE ART OF COOKERY, MADE PLAIN AND EASY
LONDON, 1747

104

CLASSIC HOME DESSERTS

ABOUT MOLDED JELLIES

Too many over-gelatinized desserts ("It's alive!!") and artificially flavored packaged versions have given gelatin-set desserts a bad name. But as long as today's easy-to-use gelatin is used with discretion, these desserts can be delicate and tasty. Just a little too much, though, can turn a limpid, quivering jelly or softly set cream to rubber.

In the days before you could sprinkle granulated gelatin from an envelope (which became available only around the turn of this century), gelatin had to be rendered at home, a culinary process possibly unmatched for sheer labor intensity. First, the home cook had to extract the gelatin from calves' feet or other natural sources, a process that required many hours of slow simmering. (Gelatin was also rendered from another natural source, hartshorn, or shavings from the horns of stag red deer.) The resulting viscous liquid was then clarified with egg whites and strained through muslin. To make a dessert jelly, the gelatin was then combined with wine, sugar, lemon and orange juice and spices.

Medieval jellies, like puddings, might contain both meat and fruit flavors in the same dish. Jellies didn't split into separate sweet (often layered in variegated colors) and savory (generally meat) versions until the days of Tudor or Stuart banquets in the 16th century. At this time, dessert jellies emerged as the third and final course of a formal dinner, served along with fruit tarts, marmalades and preserved fruits and marchpane (marzipan).

Over the years, desserts have been stabilized with other naturally jelling substances. One was isinglass, the pure gelatin extracted from the bladders of fish, especially sturgeon. Others, many of them still used today, include agar-agar, Irish moss, Iceland moss and *kanten*, Japanese seaweed. American cookbook author-teacher Mrs. Sarah Tyson Rorer, writing in 1917, advised that agar-agar "has a decided advantage over animal gelatin in the fact that it congeals quickly without ice and is less liable to contamination." While agar-agar has the benefit of being free of meat products (welcome to vegetarians and those who keep kosher, who cannot use animal-derived gelatin), it has never caught on for

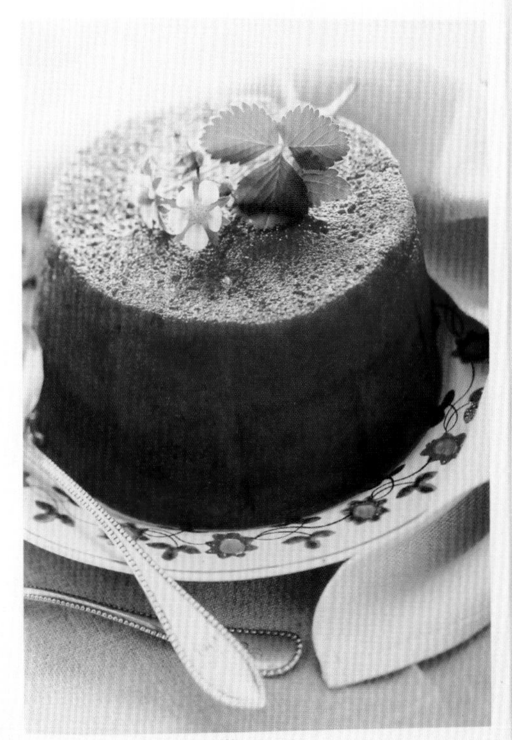

Summer Pudding of Four Red Fruits (page 230)

105

Tapioca

Wash the tapioca well, and let it steep for five or six hours, changing the water three times. Simmer it in the last water till quite clear, then season it with sugar and wine, or lemon juice.

ELIZA LESLIE
DIRECTIONS FOR COOKERY
PHILADELPHIA
1848; 1837

About Tapioca

Why don't we see tapioca more often? Clearly, all of its "fish-eye," "frog-eye" and "freshman's tears" nicknames don't help improve tapioca's reputation. But despite generations of derision, tapioca is as comforting as a pudding can be, the equal of rice pudding in innate appeal and even gentler on the palate.

Tapioca is ground from the root of the starchy cassava plant, which is also called manioc and sometimes "tapioca plant." Native to Africa, where cassava is a staple starch, the plant grows in several tropical regions.

There are two types of tapioca available:

Whole (or Pearl) Tapioca—This form of tapioca requires soaking in cold liquid until it softens, often overnight, before cooking.

Quick-Cooking Tapioca—Ground into smaller pellets than whole tapioca, the best-known is Minute brand; it needs no presoaking and literally cooks in minutes. (Note that this is not "instant" tapioca, which is available in presweetened and flavored mixes.) Quick-cooking tapioca is used for puddings and as a thickener for fruit pie fillings, where it is less starchy than cornstarch or flour. Its slightly nubbly texture, however, works best with berry pies, such as blackberry or blueberry, or with other fruits whose texture is more compatible with tapioca's grain.

The process of running whole tapioca through a commercial-size coffee grinder to make it less lumpy when cooked was developed in the mid 1890s. It was first sold as "Tapioca Superlative" and later as "Minute Tapioca." The company that produced it took on the name Minute Tapioca Company in 1908, which became part of General Foods that same year.

We shouldn't let tapioca get lost; it makes one of the best of the simple puddings.

The World's Best Lemon Tart (page 578)

That Old-Fashioned Flavor

Ilene Fields Stein says, "This recipe is from my mother, Rosetta Sikov Fields; she and my father live in Fairmont, West Virginia. My mother told me, 'It may be my recipe originally, but you are the one who got it noticed.'

"After the children grew up and my parents were the only ones at home, making blintzes became something of a chore for my mother. She came up with a way to get the old-fashioned flavor with one-tenth the effort by mixing everything together and baking it.

"The original blintz soufflé had no sugar, cinnamon or jam. It had salt and pepper and sour cream and was served with more sour cream on the side. It was the premier dish for family and company brunches. But gradually, she started to make a sweet version.

"When we visit Mom now, she's always eager to serve her 'soufflé.' We all think it tastes every bit as good as the wonderful blintzes of our childhood."

Blintz "Soufflé"

Blintzes are the Jewish pancakes that are rolled and folded around a sweetened cheese filling, then browned in butter. They're served for breakfast or for a dairy (nonmeat) supper. Russian *blinchiki* are close cousins.

This innovative spin on tradition takes the same flavors and ingredients and transforms them into a creamy "soufflé"—capturing all the buttery flavor of traditional blintzes, but without the hassle of rolling and frying, or even of beating egg whites. This luscious dessert is from Ilene Fields Stein of Rock Springs, Wyoming.

Serves 6 to 8

- 1 pound cottage cheese (Ilene uses creamed; I use low-fat)
- 3 ounces (¼ cup plus 2 tablespoons) cream cheese
- ¼ cup (½ stick) unsalted butter, melted
- ¼ cup plus 2 tablespoons sugar
- ½ cup all-purpose flour
- 3 large eggs
- ½ teaspoon fresh lemon juice
- ½ teaspoon baking powder
- ½ teaspoon ground cinnamon
- Sour cream, for serving
- Strawberry, raspberry or black currant jam, for serving

1. Preheat the oven to 350 degrees F, with a rack in the center. Butter an 8-to-9-inch baking dish; set aside.

2. In a bowl, stir together the cottage cheese, cream cheese, butter and sugar until blended. Gently stir in the flour, eggs, lemon juice and baking powder. Spoon the batter into the prepared pan; sprinkle with the cinnamon.

3. Bake until the soufflé is set and the edges are just beginning to turn light gold, 40 to 45 minutes. Cool briefly on a wire rack.

4. Serve warm, spooning the soufflé from the dish (or cut it into squares or wedges), and passing the sour cream and jam at the table.

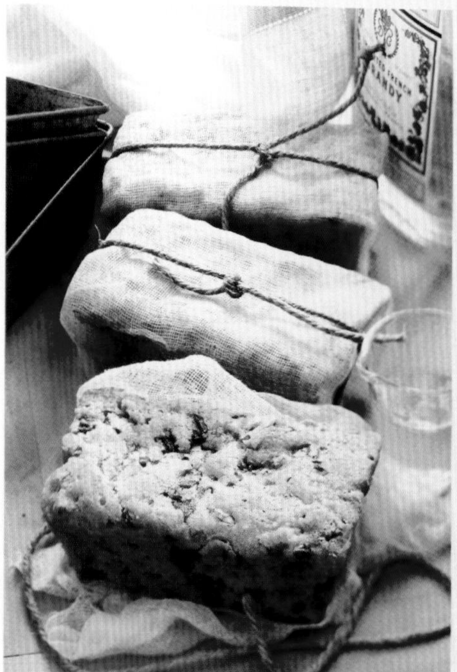

Mother Church's Spirited Dark Fruitcake (page 468)

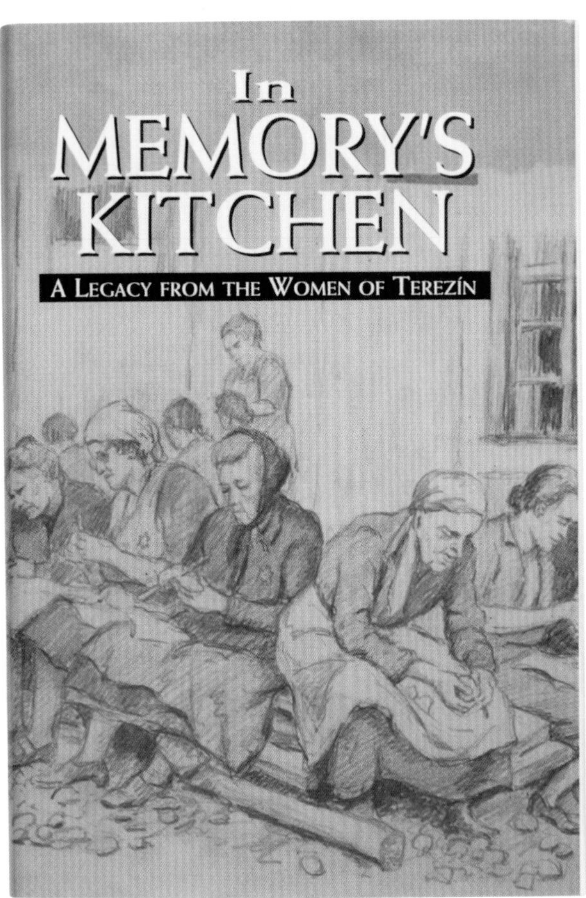

CARA DE SILVA, ED.

In Memory's Kitchen

A Legacy from the Women of Terezín, 1996

The story of the Theresienstadt cookbook is the most heart-rending tale of any cookbook. Imprisoned by the Nazis, some Jewish women in the camp compiled their favorite recipes from memory and wrote them down. Theresienstadt, located near Prague, was among the least inhumane of concentration camps. Prisoners were allowed to play music, perform theater, and engage in other artistic endeavors because the camp was used for propaganda to show reporters how well the inmates were being treated. This fact explains how Mina Pachter, one of the women who compiled the recipes, was able to have paper and pen. Though they were starving to death—Pachter died of starvation at Theresienstadt—she and the other women had hope that the volume might find its way out of the camp and to Pachter's daughter, Anny Stern, who had escaped imprisonment. It is nearly inconceivable that these starving women had the fortitude to write down recipes. We can only hope that it provided a salve to their suffering and a reminder of the better days of their youth with families and friends around a table. Dalia Carmel Goldstein, an astonishing collector of cookbooks who has donated more than 11,000 to the collection at the Fales Library, tells firsthand the account of how the cookbook was discovered. It is now at the Holocaust Museum in Washington, D.C.

NOTABLE RECIPES: Breast of Goose, Pommern Style • Chicken Galantine • **Cold Stuffed Eggs Pächter** (page 467) • **Goose Neck Stuffed with Farina** (page 495) • Health Cake • Linzer Torte • **Liver Dumplings** (page 560) • Plum Strudel • **Rich Chocolate Cake** (page 625) • War Dessert

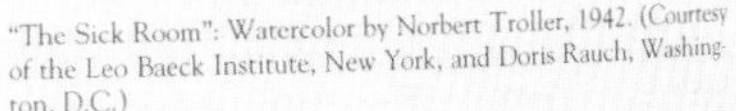

"The Sick Room": Watercolor by Norbert Troller, 1942. (Courtesy of the Leo Baeck Institute, New York, and Doris Rauch, Washington, D.C.)

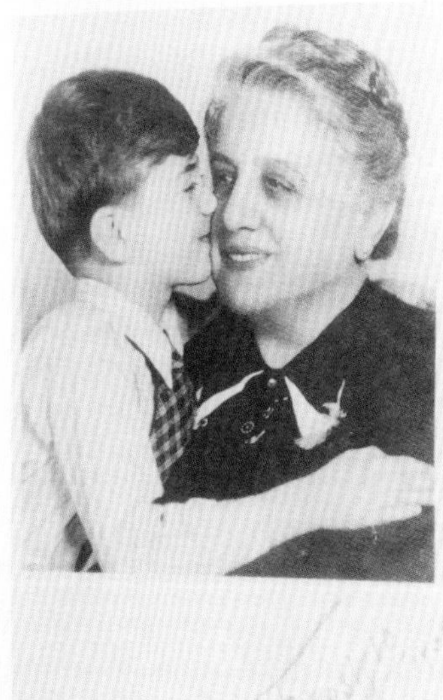

"Mina Pächter in 1939 with her grandson, David Peter Stern": Pächter died in Terezín on Yom Kippur 1944. (Courtesy of David Peter Stern.)

Ausgiebige Schokolade Torte

10 dkg Butter, 10 dkg Zucker, 4 Dotter, 14 dkg erweichte Schokol. abtreiben; 4 Schnee, 3 dkg Mehl. Eine dünne Platte in einer Tortenform backen, den Rest am Blech und zerbröseln. In der Form immer eine Lage Creme, 1 Lage Brösel obenauf Glasur, oder Sahne. Creme: 14 dkg Schok. m. 5 dkg Zucker, 2 Löffel Wasser am Feuer verrühren, ½ l Schlagsahne hinein.

Rich Chocolate Cake

Beat 10 decagrams butter, 10 decagrams sugar, 4 egg yolks, 14 decagrams softened chocolate. Fold in 4 [egg whites stiffly beaten to] snow, 3 decagrams flour. Bake a thin layer in a cake pan. [Pour] the rest [of the batter] on a baking sheet, [bake] and make crumbs [from it]. In cake pan always put a layer [of] cream, a layer [of] crumbs. Top with glaze or cream. Cream: 14 decagrams choc. with 5 decagrams sugar, 2 spoons water. Mix over fire. Fold in ½ liter whipped heavy cream.

DALIA CARMEL GOLDSTEIN *on the* WOMEN *of* TEREZIN

In the fall of 1990 my husband, Herb, and I were out running errands, and I purchased some dried fruit for my friend Anny Stern. Anny lived in our neighborhood in Manhattan, in a building that had height problems: The city agreed that the builder could keep all the unauthorized floors, provided that he rent a goodly number of them to low-income tenants. A lottery was held and Anny and her husband, George, won one of the apartments. Anny was originally from Prague. She came to New York via Israel, following her son who had been tapped by NASA to work for them. Anny was extremely hospitable, a wonderful cook and baker. She exuded warmth and love of life. Realizing that we had arrived on the night of their Bridge game, Herb and I would have delivered the fruit and departed, but Anny would not hear of it. It was not in her upbringing to let people drop in and then leave. She left the game and came to the living room to entertain us. All of a sudden she said to me, "You collect recipes—don't you?" to which I replied that I do not collect recipes, but cookbooks. Anny retorted, "It's one and the same." Then she added, "I want to show you something interesting." She rummaged in the back of a row of books in her library and fished out a school notebook wrapped in brown paper. She said that this notebook had traveled some twenty-five years before reaching her in New York.

The notebook was a collection of recipes written in the Theresienstadt concentration camp, with some poems and writings in German and Czech added on loose sheets. Anny's mother, Mrs. Mina Pachter, had been one of the writers and the owner of the notebook. Mrs. Pachter had unfortunately perished of starvation in Terezín. She had asked a fellow inmate, Mr. Buxbaum, to keep the notebook and, if he survived, to take it to her daughter in Palestine. Mr. Buxbaum was unable to honor his promise and the package sat in his New York apartment for sixteen years. He gave it to a cousin who was going to Israel to track Anny down and deliver the package. She could not find Anny, however, because Anny had immigrated to the United States. The package returned to the U.S. Eventually Mr. Buxbaum's cousin came to New York and managed to locate Anny through a B'nai B'rith New York chapter meeting. The notebook was finally delivered to Anny by a total stranger. "After all those years," said Anny, "it was like my mother's hand was reaching out to me from long ago."

The moment I opened the fragile notebook I couldn't believe my eyes. Although I could not quite read it—some of it was in German and some in Czech—I was able to read the headings of the recipes. I was struck by the foods included therein, all so typical of the Czech kitchen. It shocked my senses to think of how hungry women could think and write of their flavorful, strongly aromatic dishes. Once the shock faded, however, I understood—this was their way of facing their present lives, of holding on to the hope of a return to the riches of the past.

I said to Anny, "You cannot keep this notebook in the back of your library—the world has to see this. I don't know how or when—but it should see the light of day." To this, Herb said, "Dalia—no one will be interested in this, just don't get involved." Nevertheless, I asked Anny to borrow the notebook for twenty-four hours so I could photocopy it and run with it—where to, I had no idea.

When I got home I called Professor Barbara Kirshenblatt-Gimblett and told her that she must see this find. She joined me the next day for the photocopying adventure and promised to see what could be done with it. We made two copies of the manuscript. One thing was clear—the notebook had to be translated into English so that it could be shown to agents and publishers. A few weeks later, at an event of the Wine and Food Association, I spotted a member I hadn't been introduced to, but who I knew was Czech and was working for a recipe test kitchen in New York. Her name was Bianca Brown.

At intermission I ventured to meet her at the coffee urn and, after all necessary introductions, asked her whether she would be willing to translate the notebook into English. She responded, meekly, that she would be willing to try. Though she had no experience with translations, she was fluent in Czech, German, and recipes and most probably could take on the translation effort.

Meanwhile, I was trying to interest someone in publishing the manuscript.

Alas, whoever I approached among cookbook editors cringed at the idea. It was too ghoulish; there would be no market for such a book, they said, echoing my husband's opinion. I refused to accept his or their discouraging comments. The notebook was calling from the graves to be seen by the world at large. A few months later, while attending a meeting of the New York Culinary Historians, I made friends with Cara de Silva, a food writer for New York Newsday. I told her about the notebook, suggesting that she could write a story about it in the paper, in hopes of attracting the interest of some publisher.

Cara also cringed at the idea, but she asked her food editor, Irene Sax, whether she would be interested in such a story. Irene suggested submitting it to Part Two of the paper, rather than the food section. Cara agreed to write the story. She met with Bianca and, lo and behold, discovered that Bianca herself was a survivor of Theresienstadt. I was stunned—when I suggested the translation to her she'd given not a squeak of her own history or her familiarity with food talk among the inmates. What a coincidence!

Meanwhile, I took a trip to Israel and visited Yad Vashem to see whether such recipe collections had survived from other camps. The archivist found three such collections to show me in various languages. She could not be sure that there weren't any more, as the computer system for their holdings did not have assigned codes for recipes, food, or hunger. In order to find any such collection one had to go through the materials manually. One of the collections I saw was from Mauthausen, written on the reverse side of Hitler's propaganda leaflets.

With this information at hand I approached my dear friend and ex-neighbor Sabina Margulies, who had survived Auschwitz, and asked whether even in the death camp they'd talked about food and recipes. Amazingly, her response was affirmative. They had spent time talking and bragging about recipes, debating as to which type was really the best. All this information was given to Cara de Silva to write the story that ultimately gave birth to the book In Memory's Kitchen, published in 1996 by Jason Aronson, Inc. Unfortunately, Anny did not survive to see the book published. She was so eager for it to see the light of day, but she passed on a short time before the book came out. The book aroused a lot of interest in the United States and was covered by most newspapers and many magazines. Many TV interviews aired, featuring the editor and the translator of the book, and a movie was made about the story by Anne Georget for French TV under the title of Les carnets de Mina.

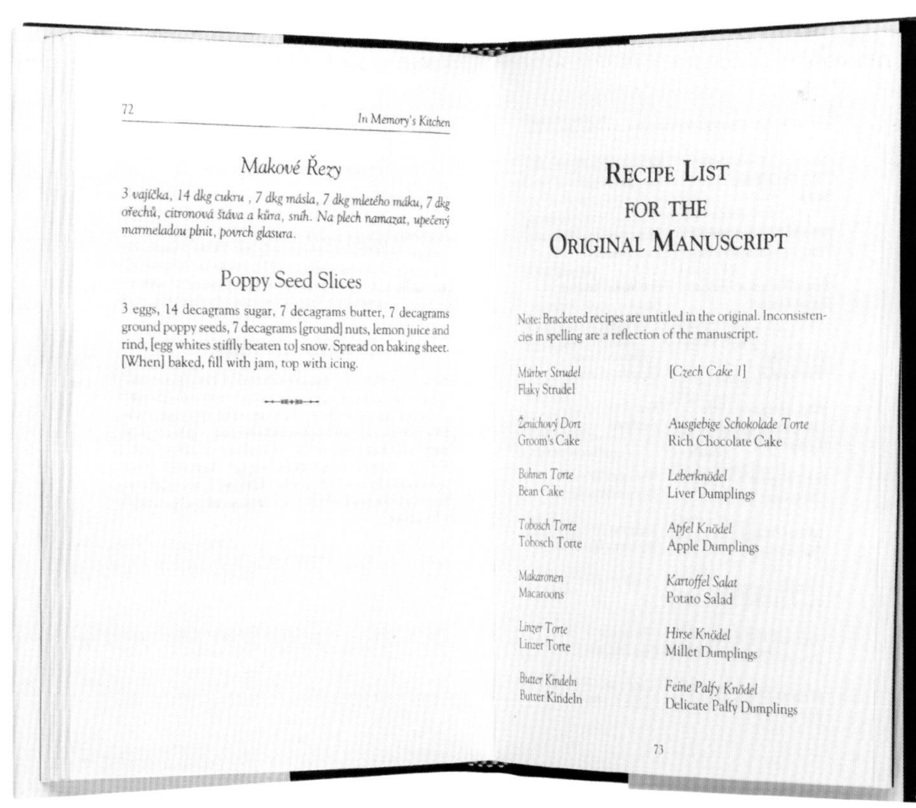

72 In Memory's Kitchen

Makové Řezy

3 vajíčka, 14 dkg cukru , 7 dkg másla, 7 dkg mletého máku, 7 dkg ořechů, citronová šťáva a kůra, sníh. Na plech namazat, upečený marmeladou plnit, povrch glasura.

Poppy Seed Slices

3 eggs, 14 decagrams sugar, 7 decagrams butter, 7 decagrams ground poppy seeds, 7 decagrams [ground] nuts, lemon juice and rind, [egg whites stiffly beaten to] snow. Spread on baking sheet. [When] baked, fill with jam, top with icing.

RECIPE LIST
FOR THE
ORIGINAL MANUSCRIPT

Note: Bracketed recipes are untitled in the original. Inconsistencies in spelling are a reflection of the manuscript.

Mürber Strudel
Flaky Strudel

Ženichový Dort
Groom's Cake

Bohnen Torte
Bean Cake

Tobosch Torte
Tobosch Torte

Makaronen
Macaroons

Linzer Torte
Linzer Torte

Butter Kindeln
Butter Kindeln

[Czech Cake 1]

Ausgiebige Schokolade Torte
Rich Chocolate Cake

Leberknödel
Liver Dumplings

Apfel Knödel
Apple Dumplings

Kartoffel Salat
Potato Salad

Hirse Knödel
Millet Dumplings

Feine Palfy Knödel
Delicate Palfy Dumplings

73

ALICE WATERS

Chez Panisse Vegetables, 1996

Chez Panisse is not just a restaurant; it is an ideology and a philosophy about food, health, joy, and ethical living. Even as industrial agriculture was producing more processed, canned, and boxed foodstuffs, there was a backlash against these products. None other than James Beard decried their use and called for a return to local, seasonal produce. But it was Alice Waters who changed the way Americans think about "local, organic, seasonal produce," the mantra of any important restaurateur, chef, or enlightened home cook today.

At Chez Panisse, which opened in Berkeley, California, in 1971, Waters pulled together two important strands of twentieth-century American cooking: the gourmet desire for exquisite ingredients and European food traditions and the California hippie/radical return-to-the-earth youth movement. The so-called American food revolution grew out of the Free Speech Movement that began at the University of California, Berkeley, in 1964. The movement was a response to the university's decision to ban all political organizations from soliciting on campus because they were inciting students to rebel. This was a time when civil rights, antinuclear, and anti-Vietnam sentiments were on the rise. Waters was directly involved in the movement, and her political activism carried over into her thoughts about food. Chez Panisse became the expression of how to prepare delicious meals with local ingredients. She championed local farmers and farmers' markets, as well as local, often little-known, ingredients. Her approach took the food world by storm. While critics noted that most of what Waters promoted was simply common practice in France and Italy, that was not the point. In the United States, this was a revolutionary idea that fit perfectly with the raised consciousness of a generation.

Chez Panisse Vegetables is Waters's personal favorite cookbook to come out of the restaurant. It is filled with tried-and-true recipes for preparing some of the best vegetable dishes imaginable.

NOTABLE RECIPES: Artichokes with Baked Anchovy Stuffing • **French Cream of Cauliflower Soup** (page 342) • **Grilled Asparagus with Blood Oranges** (page 405) • **Kale and Potato Soup** (page 341) • **Red and Golden Beets with Blood Orange, Endive, and Walnuts** (page 363) • Sautéed Kale with Garlic and Vinegar • Shaved Fennel, Artichoke, and Parmesan Salad • **Spring Onion Sandwiches** (page 372) • Oven-braised Leeks with Cream • Oven Roasted Carrots and Turnips • **Parsley Salad** (page 358) • Sage and Butternut Squash Risotto • Whole Wheat Pasta with Cauliflower, Walnuts, and Ricotta Salata • Wilted Mustard Greens and Prosciutto

ALICE WATERS

CHEZ PANISSE
VEGETABLES

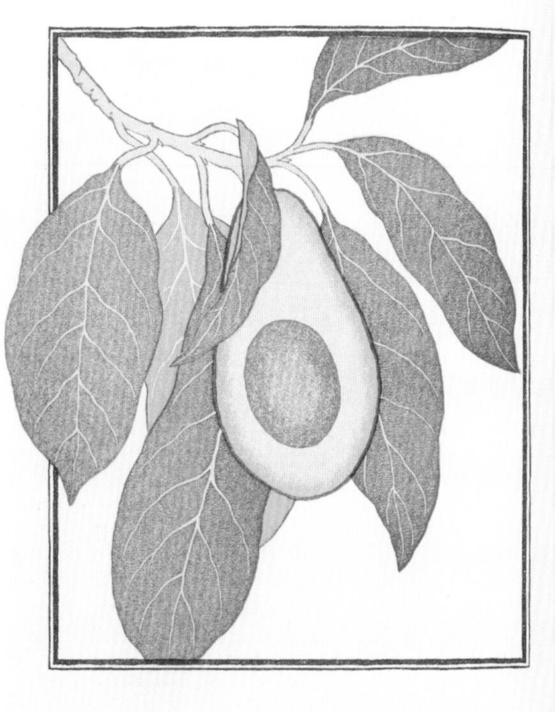
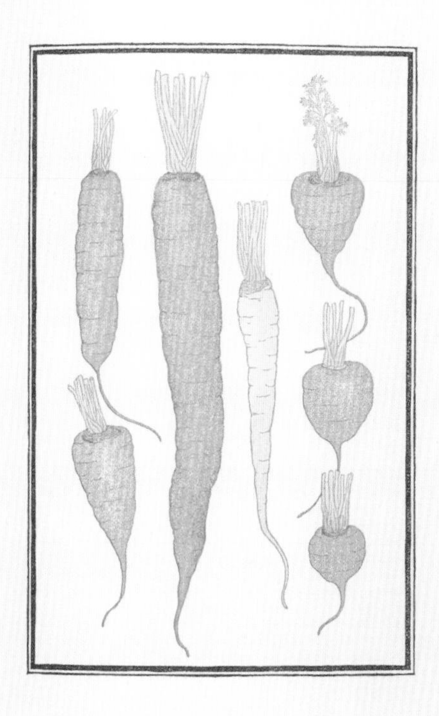

CHARD

Season: Late spring through winter

Chard is appreciated in various parts of Europe, but for some reason it is often called Swiss chard here in the United States, where it is not as well known as it deserves to be. Both its dark green leaves and their wide, thick ribs can be eaten, each cooked in different ways. The leaves can be steamed, parboiled, or sautéed, and added to soup, stuffed with meat or vegetable fillings, or used to line a pâté mold. The crisp-textured stems are delicious steamed, stewed, or gratinéed.

Most varieties of chard have medium to very dark green leaves growing from their broad white stems (or ribs). The leaves may be more or less ruffled and are rarely perfectly flat. Rhubarb chard, however, has ribs that are a brilliant red, and strongly resembles beet greens. Not surprisingly, both chard and garden beets derive from the same species, *Beta vulgaris*. France and Italy are the countries of origin for some of the choicest chard varieties, such as Paros, with curly leaves resembling those of savoy cabbage, and Argentata, which sports very dark green leaves surrounding silvery white stems.

In the colder parts of the United States, the season for chard starts in late spring and continues until late fall. In many parts of the South, and in California, chard is grown and harvested throughout the winter as well. But the chard planted in late spring seems to produce the largest and most tender leaves.

In the market, the best and most flavorful chard will have fresh, crisp, and intensely green leaves. The ribs should be stiff and free of any brown spotting. Avoid bunches that have been bundled too tightly: the leaves will be bruised. In the case of chard, baby leaves are not a guarantee of quality. In fact, the largest leaves will often be the most tender.

Unless the chard is very small and immature, it is best to separate its leaves from their ribs before cooking. This is easily accomplished by loosely folding the leaf in half along the stem, grasping the folded leaf with one hand, and pulling the rib away with the other hand. This will go very quickly once you get the hang of it. Once stripped off, the leaves are ready to be washed, drained, and used as the recipe directs. Some fastidious cooks like to peel the ribs, pulling away the strings as if from celery stalks, but this is rarely necessary. (The ribs should be washed and drained before proceeding, of course.) The ribs will look neater if their edges are trimmed a little. Chard that has been prepared for cooking can be covered or wrapped in plastic and kept refrigerated for several hours until needed.

Few vegetables look more handsome growing in a kitchen garden than chard. Both green and red varieties add terrific color and texture. A couple of plants will not take up much room, and by harvesting only the outer leaves from the plants as they mature, you can ensure a steady supply throughout the entire season from a single planting.

Sautéed Chard with Lemon and Hot Pepper

Stem the chard, wash and drain the leaves, and cut them into a rough chiffonade. Sauté in olive oil, covered, for 5 minutes or so, until the leaves are wilted and tender. Remove the cover and cook away the excess moisture. Season at the last minute with a pinch of red pepper flakes according to taste, and with salt and pepper, and squeeze lemon juice over just before serving.

Chard Stem Gratin

Chard stems are delicious. Remove their strings, if necessary, then parboil until tender, drain, and arrange in a gratin dish with bits of fried pancetta, some chopped garlic, chopped flat-leaf parsley, and a seeded, coarsely chopped tomato. Cover with a bit of béchamel sauce or cream and gratinée in a preheated 450°F. oven or under the broiler until golden.

Braised Chard

Separate the leaves and ribs of a large very fresh bunch of red or green chard. Wash, drain, and cut the leaves into a rough chiffonade. Slice a large sweet onion and start it stewing in some olive oil in a pot large enough to hold all the chard leaves. After the onion softens, add the chard leaves, season with salt and pepper, cover, and stew for 20 to 30 minutes, stirring every so often. Although additions such as garlic, pancetta, or lemon can be made, the chief virtues of chard cooked this way are its own sweet flavor and a meltingly tender texture.

Chard Gratin

2 pounds young red or green chard
1 clove garlic
3 tablespoons unsalted butter
2 cups milk
2 tablespoons flour
Whole nutmeg
Salt and pepper
¾ cup Toasted Bread Crumbs (*page 319*)

Preheat the oven to 375°F.

Wash the chard and cut off the thick ends of the stems. Parboil the chard for 1½ minutes in lightly salted boiling water. Drain, squeeze out the water from the leaves, and chop them into ¾-inch pieces. Peel the garlic and chop it very fine.

Melt the butter over medium heat in a large, nonreactive skillet and add the chard. Turn the chard in the butter as it begins to wilt, add the garlic, and continue cooking slowly, uncovered, for 7 or 8 minutes, until the leaves have begun to soften. Warm the milk in a small saucepan.

Sprinkle the flour over the chard and stir to distribute the flour evenly. Cook for 1 minute more and then begin to slowly add the milk, about ¼ cup at a time. Continue adding the milk in small amounts as it is absorbed by the chard until the milk is completely incorporated.

Season with a light grating of nutmeg, salt, and pepper; transfer to a buttered gratin dish. The layer of chard should be about 1 inch thick. Cover evenly with the bread crumbs and bake for 35 minutes, until the crumbs have browned nicely.

Serves 4.

RICK BAYLESS

Rick Bayless's Mexican Kitchen

Capturing the Vibrant Flavors of a World-Class Cuisine, 1996

Mexican food is one of the treasures of American cooking. It's not only a major influence on West Coast cooking, but those on the East Coast travel far and wide to find perfect tamales or delicate fish tacos. Rick Bayless made us rethink everything we knew about Mexican cooking with the publication of *Authentic Mexican* in 1987, but it was *Rick Bayless's Mexican Kitchen* that won the International Association of Culinary Professionals National Julia Child Cookbook of the Year Award. The *New York Times* praised him as a writer who makes "true Mexican food user-friendly for Americans," and *Time* magazine hailed him as a "cookbook superstar." For his thoughtful demystification of Mexican food, he was hailed as having done for Mexican food what Child had done in the 1960s for French food.

Bayless became fascinated with Mexican food while pursuing an undergraduate degree in Spanish and Latin American Studies and doctoral work in anthropological linguistics at the University of Michigan. From 1980 to 1986, Bayless and his wife lived in Mexico, where he wrote *Authentic Mexican*, which Craig Claiborne hailed as the "greatest contribution to the Mexican table imaginable." In 1987 Bayless opened the Frontera Grill in Chicago, which specializes in contemporary regional Mexican cooking, and in 1989 he opened the upscale Topolobampo, at the time one of America's only fine-dining Mexican restaurants.

One of the things that makes *Rick Bayless's Mexican Kitchen* so important is how he approaches the basics of Mexican cooking. He gives us the essential ingredients and techniques that are the foundation for Mexican food: dark, rich tomato sauces; tangy tomatillo salsas; deep chile pastes; and handmade tortillas. His contribution to our love of Mexican food is perfectly matched to the expanded American palate.

NOTABLE RECIPES: Achiote-Roasted Pork Tacos • Braised Turkey in Teloloapan Red Mole • **Chilied Tortilla Soup with Shredded Chard** (page 338) • **Chipotle Shrimp** (page 488) • Hearty Seven Seas Soup • **Oaxacan Black Mole with Braised Chicken** (page 389) • **Top-of-the-Line Margarita/Topolo Margarita** (page 312) • **Topolo "Caesar" Salad** (page 358) • **Very, Very Good Chili** (page 381)

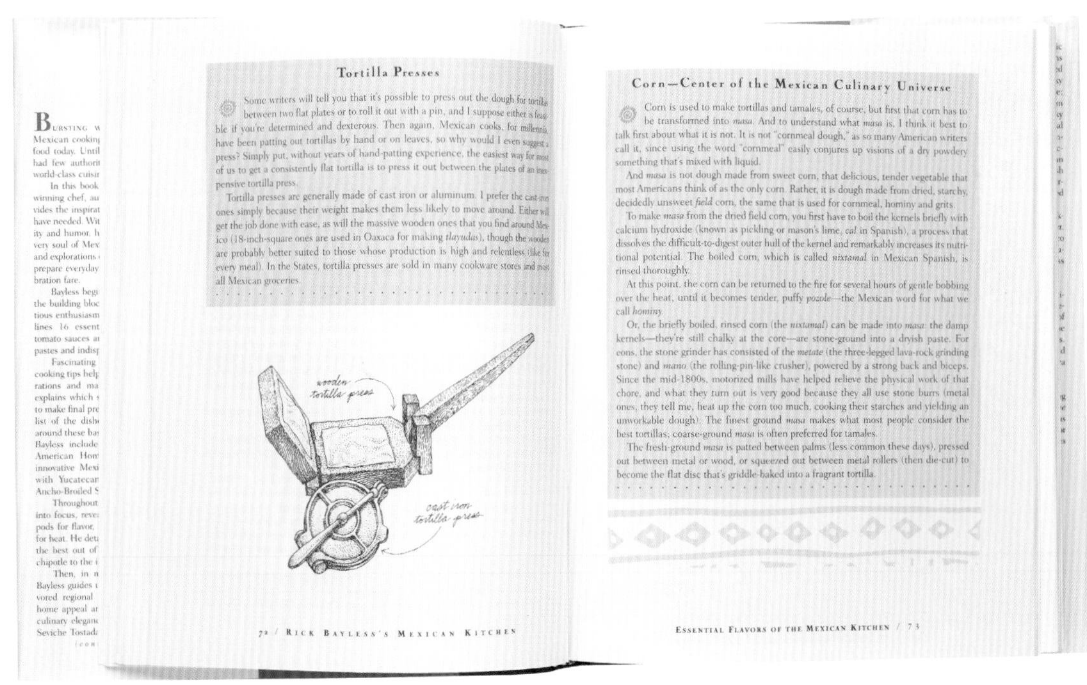

Tortilla Presses

Some writers will tell you that it's possible to press out the dough for tortillas between two flat plates or to roll it out with a pin, and I suppose either is feasible if you're determined and dexterous. Then again, Mexican cooks, for millennia, have been patting out tortillas by hand or on leaves, so why would I even suggest a press? Simply put, without years of hand-patting experience, the easiest way for most of us to get a consistently flat tortilla is to press it out between the plates of an inexpensive tortilla press.

Tortilla presses are generally made of cast iron or aluminum. I prefer the cast-iron ones simply because their weight makes them less likely to move around. Either will get the job done with ease, as will the massive wooden ones that you find around Mexico (18-inch-square ones are used in Oaxaca for making *tlayudas*), though the wooden are probably better suited to those whose production is high and relentless (like for every meal). In the States, tortilla presses are sold in many cookware stores and most all Mexican groceries.

Corn—Center of the Mexican Culinary Universe

Corn is used to make tortillas and tamales, of course, but first that corn has to be transformed into *masa*. And to understand what *masa* is, I think it best to talk first about what it is not. It is not "cornmeal dough," as so many American writers call it, since using the word "cornmeal" easily conjures up visions of a dry powdery something that's mixed with liquid.

And *masa* is not dough made from sweet corn, that delicious, tender vegetable that most Americans think of as the only corn. Rather, it is dough made from dried, starchy, decidedly unsweet *field* corn, the same that is used for cornmeal, hominy and grits.

To make *masa* from the dried field corn, you first have to boil the kernels briefly with calcium hydroxide (known as pickling or mason's lime, *cal* in Spanish), a process that dissolves the difficult-to-digest outer hull of the kernel and remarkably increases its nutritional potential. The boiled corn, which is called *nixtamal* in Mexican Spanish, is rinsed thoroughly.

At this point, the corn can be returned to the fire for several hours of gentle bobbing over the heat, until it becomes tender, puffy *pozole*—the Mexican word for what we call *hominy*.

Or, the briefly boiled, rinsed corn (the *nixtamal*) can be made into *masa*: the damp kernels—they're still chalky at the core—are stone-ground into a dryish paste. For eons, the stone grinder has consisted of the *metate* (the three-legged lava-rock grinding stone) and *mano* (the rolling-pin-like crusher), powered by a strong back and biceps. Since the mid-1800s, motorized mills have helped relieve the physical work of that chore, and what they turn out is very good because they all use stone burrs (metal ones, they tell me, heat up the corn too much, cooking their starches and yielding an unworkable dough). The finest ground *masa* makes what most people consider the best tortillas; coarse-ground *masa* is often preferred for tamales.

The fresh-ground *masa* is patted between palms (less common these days), pressed out between metal or wood, or squeezed out between metal rollers (then die-cut) to become the flat disc that's griddle-baked into a fragrant tortilla.

72 / Rick Bayless's Mexican Kitchen

Essential Flavors of the Mexican Kitchen / 73

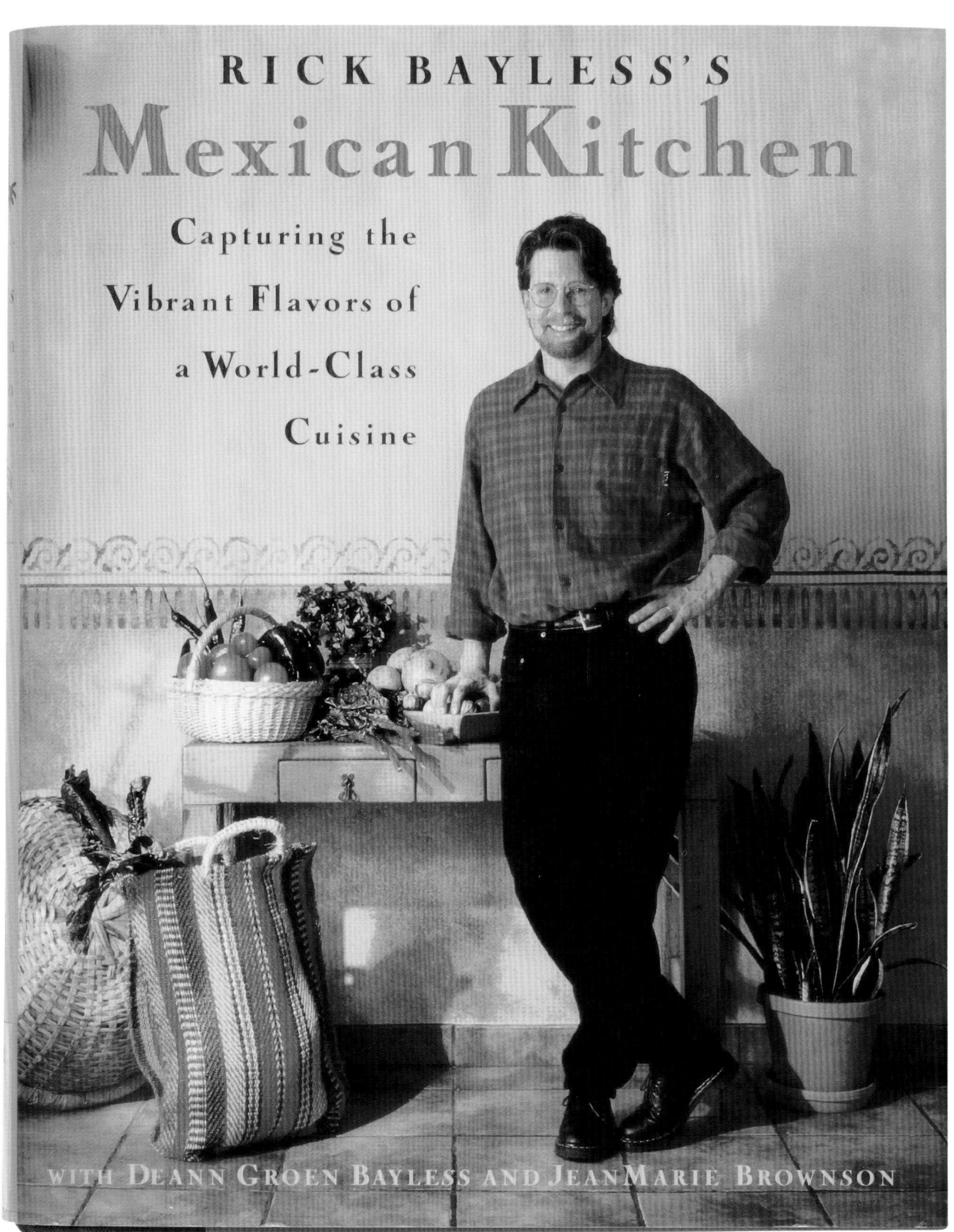
RICK BAYLESS'S
Mexican Kitchen
Capturing the
Vibrant Flavors of
a World-Class
Cuisine
WITH DEANN GROEN BAYLESS AND JEANMARIE BROWNSON

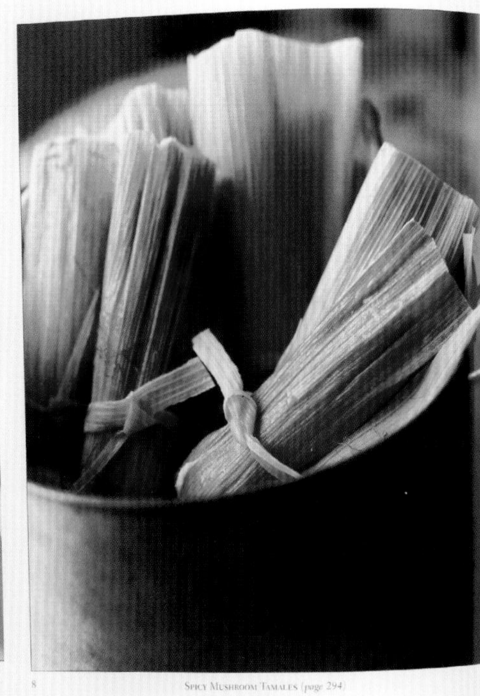

Spicy Mushroom Tamales (page 294)

TACOS OF GARLICKY MEXICAN GREENS WITH SEARED ONION AND FRESH CHEESE

Tacos de Quelites

Ever since I first ate *quelites* tacos at a market stall in Toluca, they've been high on my list. I know a taco of Mexican greens sounds trendy or made-up, so I encourage you to go to Toluca on a Friday morning (market day) and taste handmade, just-baked blue-corn tortillas wrapped around emerald-green *quelites* (lamb's quarters) dashed with red chile salsa. There they think of this rustic earthy taco as old-fashioned (poor people's) food. I think of it as some of the best food on the face of the earth.

Chard makes a nice substitute for lamb's quarters, though it doesn't have as much body or richness and won't hold the green color as well. Don't use these greens only as a taco filling; they make a wonderful accompaniment to *moles* and such.

Be sure to have all your ingredients ready before you warm the tortillas; the cooking of the filling goes very quickly.

Makes a generous 2 cups of filling, enough for 8 to 10 soft tacos

8 to 10 corn tortillas (plus a few extra, in case some break)

9 cups (about 1 pound) loosely packed, stemmed lamb's quarters (quelites)

or *6 cups loosely packed, sliced green or red chard leaves (slice them 1/2 inch thick; you'll need a 12-ounce bunch)*

1 tablespoon olive or vegetable oil

1 medium white onion, sliced 1/4 inch thick

3 garlic cloves, peeled and finely chopped

Salt, about 1/2 teaspoon

1/4 cup finely crumbled Mexican queso fresco, queso añejo, *dry feta, pressed, salted farmer's cheese or Parmesan*

About 3/4 cup salsa (I love the Essential Roasted Tomatillo-Chipotle Salsa, page 45, with these greens), for serving

1. *Warming the tortillas.* Set up a steamer (a vegetable steamer in a large saucepan filled with 1/2 inch of water works well); heat to a boil. Wrap the tortillas in a heavy kitchen towel, lay in the steamer and cover with a tight lid. Boil 1 minute, turn off the heat and let stand without opening the steamer for about 15 minutes.

2. *The greens-and-onion filling.* While the tortillas are steaming, prepare the filling. Bring 3 quarts of salted water to a boil in a large pot. Add the greens and cook until barely tender,

Yucatecan Grilled Fish Tacos (page 153)

Street-Style Red Chile Enchiladas with Zucchini, Aged Cheese and Crunchy Garnishes (page 182)

4 Tangy Seared Fish Fillets with woodland mushrooms and pickled jalapeños (page 144)

Lamb *Barbacoa* from the Backyard Grill (page 176) 5

8 Slow-Simmered Fava Bean Soup with mint and pasilla chile (page 132)

TOPOLO "CAESAR" SALAD

Ensalada Estilo Topolobampo

Though we're sure this was invented in Mexico (by Italian immigrant Caesar Cardini), I'd never call it traditionally Mexican. In Puebla or Chilpancingo or Oaxaca, its existence is still hearsay. I've included it because I love the Mexicanized version I came up with for our restaurant, Topolobampo—green chile and lime, not lemon, in the dressing, cilantro with the greens and *queso añejo* or Vella's dry Jack cheese (see Sources, page 425), not Parmesan, over everything.

It seems there are numerous "original" versions of Caesar salad around, though for me truth always lies with Julia. How can you doubt the one who taught you to master hollandaise and puff pastry? *From Julia Child's Kitchen* details a very good original formula that was my starting point here. I've chosen to add a raw egg to the dressing, but to keep it from becoming too thick and mayonnaisy, I whisk in half the oil by hand. If using raw eggs bothers you, make a spicy vinaigrette without the egg for a very good, but different, salad.

Serves 4 to 6; about 1 1/2 cups dressing

For the dressing (this is the minimum quantity manageable, though it makes enough for 4 rounds of this salad)

1 cup fruity olive oil

1 1/2 tablespoons vinegar, preferably sherry vinegar

4 teaspoons Worcestershire sauce

1 fresh serrano chile, stemmed and halved

The zest (colored part only) of 1 1/2 limes

1 egg

Salt, about 1/2 teaspoon

For the croutons

1/4 cup olive oil

4 garlic cloves, peeled and roughly chopped

2 cups firm bread (preferably sourdough) crusts removed, cut into 1/2-inch cubes

For finishing the salad

2 medium-small heads romaine lettuce, tough outer leaves removed, inner leaves rinsed and dried

or *8 ounces (about 8 cups moderately packed) mixed young greens, rinsed and dried*

3/4 cup finely crumbled Mexican queso añejo, *dry Jack or Parmesan cheese*

1/2 cup roughly chopped cilantro

1. *The dressing.* Combine *1/2 cup* of the olive oil plus all other dressing ingredients in a food processor or blender and process one full minute. Scrape into a small bowl and slowly whisk in the remaining *1/2 cup* olive oil. Taste and add more salt if you think necessary.

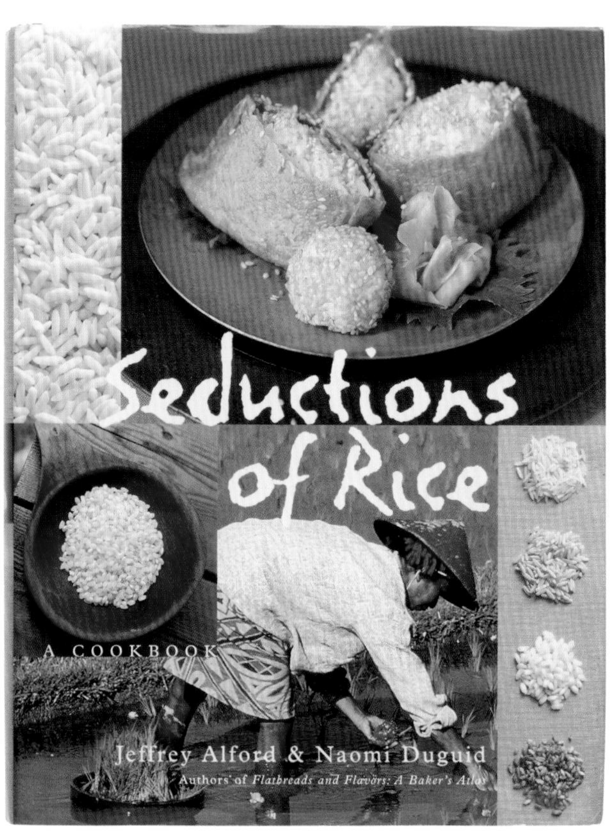

JEFFREY ALFORD AND NAOMI DUGUID

Seductions of Rice, 1998

The story of authors Naomi Duguid and Jeffrey Alford is marked with serendipitous discoveries. The couple first met on a rooftop while treking through the mountains of Tibet in 1985. They quickly realized that they shared a love of travel, photography, and Asian culture. Within a year they were married and back on the road again together. Duguid and Alford decided to document their journeys and food excursions with images and recipes. The result is a series of beautiful, informative, and enticing books about foods, mostly of Asia.

Their first cookbook, *Flatbreads and Flavors*, won the James Beard Cookbook of the Year and also the Julia Child First Book Award. Their second book, *Seductions of Rice*, took this elemental ingredient as a jumping-off point to explore different ethnic traditions around the world. The opening sections describe the various kinds of rice, how they are graded, and how they taste. The book follows the couple's journeys through China, Thailand, Japan, India, central Asia, Persia, the Mediterranean, Senegal, and finally to North America. It opened up a whole new way of thinking about this versatile grain, expanding our repertoire to basmati, jasmine, arborio, and other great varieties of rice once considered exotic. But it is also important because Alford and Duguid created a new template for the cookbook as travelogue and anthropological survey. Using photographs to document not just the dishes but the people who make the food and their time-honed techniques, the authors convey their culinary wanderlust to the home cook. It is a type of cookbook all their own—one that stresses the cultural context of food.

NOTABLE RECIPES: Baked Persian Rice with Chicken (page 457) • Central Asian Rice and Bean Stew • **Classic Thai Fried Rice** (page 455) • **Grilled Beef Salad** (page 370) • Grilled Eggplant Salad • Grilled Pork Satay • Hot and Sweet Dipping Sauce • Red Curry Sauce • Senegalese Lemon Chicken • Special Everyday Persian Rice (Chelo) • **Spring Pilaf with Fresh Greens** (page 366) • Thai Grilled Chicken (Gai Yang) • **Thai Sticky Rice** (page 454) • Thai Style Sprouted Rice and Herb Salad

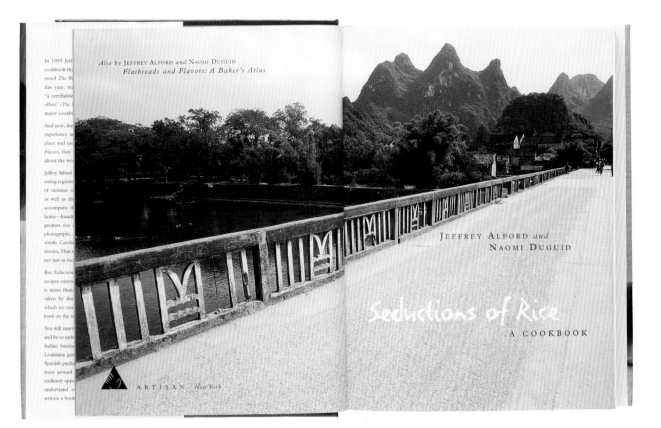

Also by Jeffrey Alford *and* Naomi Duguid
Flatbreads and Flavors: A Baker's Atlas

Jeffrey Alford *and*
Naomi Duguid

Seductions of Rice
A Cookbook

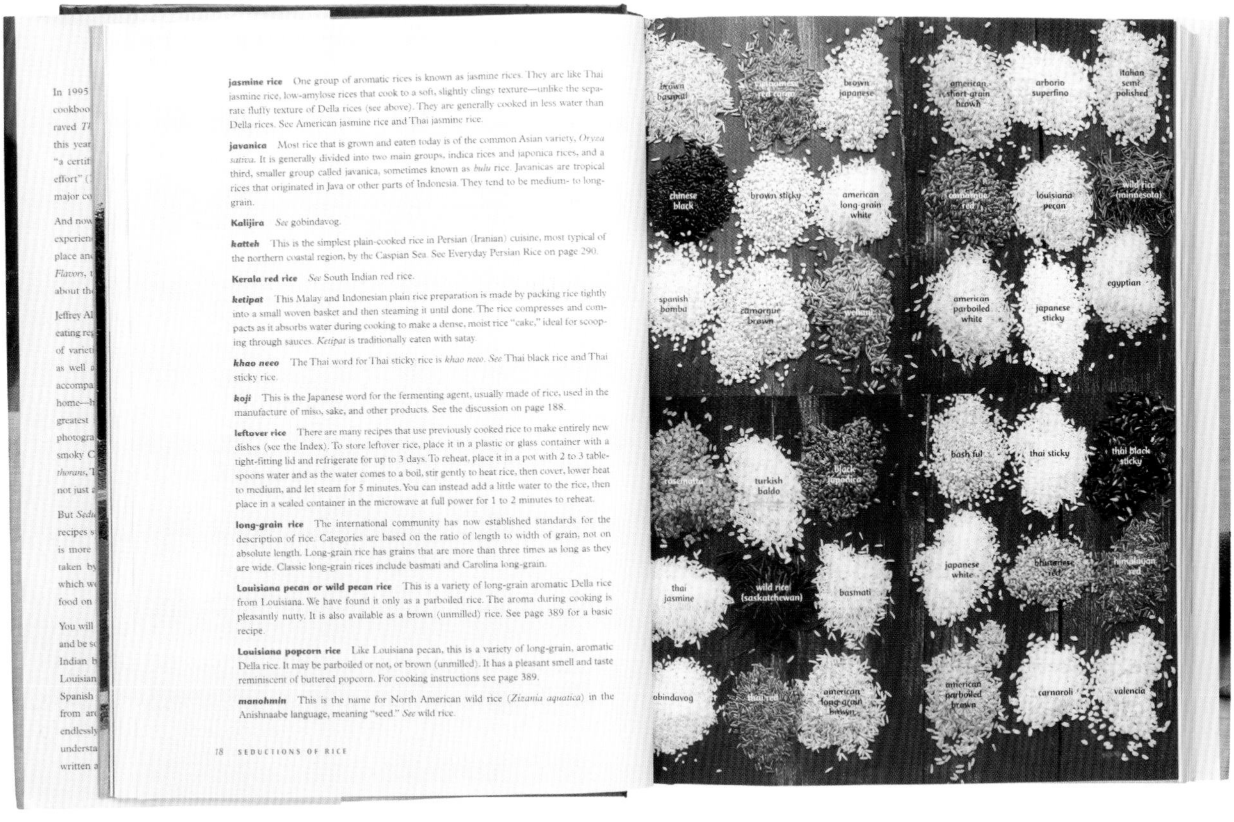

Artisan *New York*

jasmine rice One group of aromatic rices is known as jasmine rices. They are like Thai jasmine rice, low-amylose rices that cook to a soft, slightly clingy texture—unlike the separate fluffy texture of Della rices (see above). They are generally cooked in less water than Della rices. See American jasmine rice and Thai jasmine rice.

javanica Most rice that is grown and eaten today is of the common Asian variety, *Oryza sativa*. It is generally divided into two main groups, indica rices and japonica rices, and a third, smaller group called javanica, sometimes known as *bulu* rice. Javanicas are tropical rices that originated in Java or other parts of Indonesia. They tend to be medium- to long-grain.

Kalijira *See* gobindavog.

katteh This is the simplest plain-cooked rice in Persian (Iranian) cuisine, most typical of the northern coastal region, by the Caspian Sea. See Everyday Persian Rice on page 290.

Kerala red rice *See* South Indian red rice.

ketipat This Malay and Indonesian plain rice preparation is made by packing rice tightly into a small woven basket and then steaming it until done. The rice compresses and compacts as it absorbs water during cooking to make a dense, moist rice "cake," ideal for scooping through sauces. *Ketipat* is traditionally eaten with satay.

khao neeo The Thai word for Thai sticky rice is *khao neeo*. *See* Thai black rice and Thai sticky rice.

koji This is the Japanese word for the fermenting agent, usually made of rice, used in the manufacture of miso, sake, and other products. See the discussion on page 188.

leftover rice There are many recipes that use previously cooked rice to make entirely new dishes (see the Index). To store leftover rice, place it in a plastic or glass container with a tight-fitting lid and refrigerate for up to 3 days. To reheat, place it in a pot with 2 to 3 tablespoons water and as the water comes to a boil, stir gently to heat rice, then cover, lower heat to medium, and let steam for 5 minutes. You can instead add a little water to the rice, then place in a sealed container in the microwave at full power for 1 to 2 minutes to reheat.

long-grain rice The international community has now established standards for the description of rice. Categories are based on the ratio of length to width of grain, not on absolute length. Long-grain rice has grains that are more than three times as long as they are wide. Classic long-grain rices include basmati and Carolina long-grain.

Louisiana pecan or wild pecan rice This is a variety of long-grain aromatic Della rice from Louisiana. We have found it only as a parboiled rice. The aroma during cooking is pleasantly nutty. It is also available as a brown (unmilled) rice. See page 389 for a basic recipe.

Louisiana popcorn rice Like Louisiana pecan, this is a variety of long-grain, aromatic Della rice. It may be parboiled or not, or brown (unmilled). It has a pleasant smell and taste reminiscent of buttered popcorn. For cooking instructions see page 389.

manohmin This is the name for North American wild rice (*Zizania aquatica*) in the Anishnaabe language, meaning "seed." *See* wild rice.

18 SEDUCTIONS OF RICE

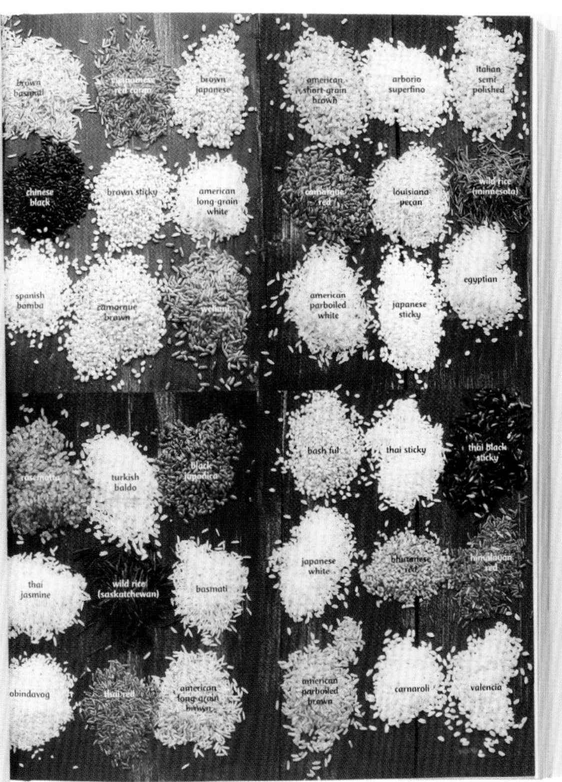

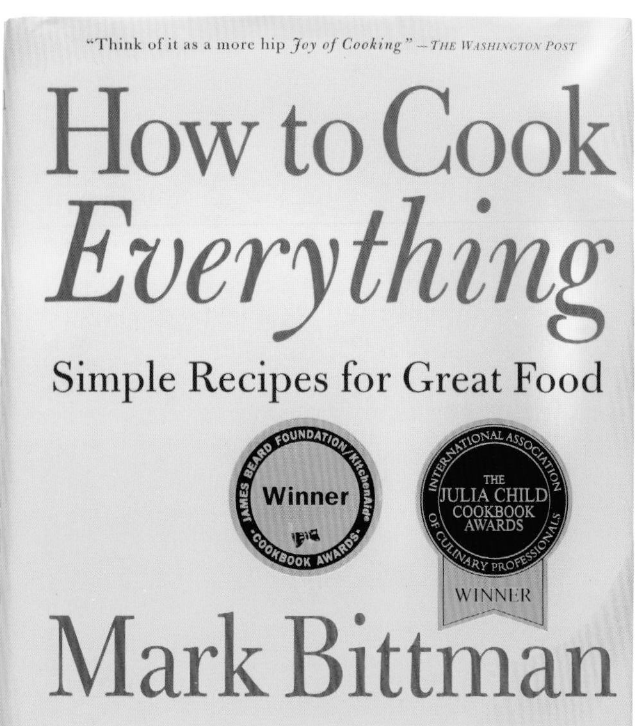

"Think of it as a more hip Joy of Cooking" —The Washington Post
How to Cook
Everything
Simple Recipes for Great Food
James Beard Foundation/KitchenAid Cookbook Awards
Winner
International Association of Culinary Professionals
The Julia Child Cookbook Awards
Winner
Mark Bittman

MARK BITTMAN

How to Cook Everything

Simple Recipes for Great Food, 1998

"The dude's *Joy of Cooking*" is how Jonathan Gold describes Mark Bittman's *How to Cook Everything*, which, when published in 1998, quickly became the new standard encyclopedic cookbook for contemporary American home cooks. *How to Cook Everything* has sold millions of copies and was revised in 2008 by Bittman to include even more dishes that were once considered "ethnic" but that now make up the American palate.

Bittman has always made a point of saying that he is not a chef. He has no formal training in the French culinary tradition and a bit of disdain for haute cuisine, which he refers to as "fancy food," and believes is best left for enjoying in restaurants. Instead, he is a home cook who is proud to make simple but delicious meals. Bittman's masculine, I'm-just-a-guy-in-the-kitchen tone appeals to a generation of men who no longer associate cooking with "women's work" and have found it to be an exciting hobby. Over the years, he's honed this narrative well, first as an editor at *Cook's Magazine* (the precursor to *Cook's Illustrated*) and then in his weekly Minimalist column for the *New York Times*. His appeal to men who cook is only a part of the success of *How to Cook Everything*. You can be assured the recipes work. They're not fussy or complicated. They're delicious.

Not unlike *Mastering the Art of French Cooking*, he gives you a recipe, then follows it with simple variations that make the dish different in taste. It's like Julia Child explaining how to make *potage parmentier*, then cutting the vegetables more evenly for *potage bonne femme*, or pureeing them for *vichyssoise*. *How to Cook Everything* should be on the top shelf of every serious cook's book collection. Bittman's first book, *Fish: The Complete Guide to Buying and Cooking*, is in its eighth printing, and for good reason. It, too, is a classic.

NOTABLE RECIPES: Banana Bread (page 570) • Basic Pancakes • **Classic Beef Stew** (page 399) • Fruit and Nut or Vegetable and Nut Bread (Cranberry Nut Bread) • **Grilled Steak, American-Style** (page 541) • **Simple Roast Chicken** (page 498) • **Skate with Brown Butter** (page 475) • **Yorkshire Pudding** (page 588)

The Basics of Baking Dishes and Roasting Pans
The Basics of Pastry Pans
The Basics of Bowls
The Basics of Cutting Boards
The Basics of Spoons, Spatulas, and More
The Basics of Measuring Devices
The Basics of Straining Devices
The Basics of Miscellaneous Tools
4 HOW TO COOK EVERYTHING
EQUIPMENT 5

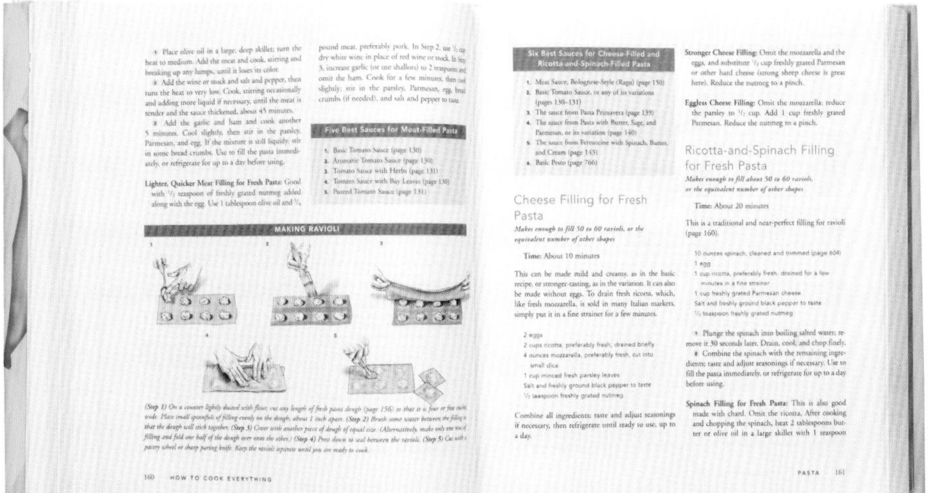
Five Best Sauces for Meat-Filled Pasta
MAKING RAVIOLI
Six Best Sauces for Cheese-Filled and Ricotta-and-Spinach-Filled Pasta
Cheese Filling for Fresh Pasta
Ricotta-and-Spinach Filling for Fresh Pasta
160 HOW TO COOK EVERYTHING
PASTA 161

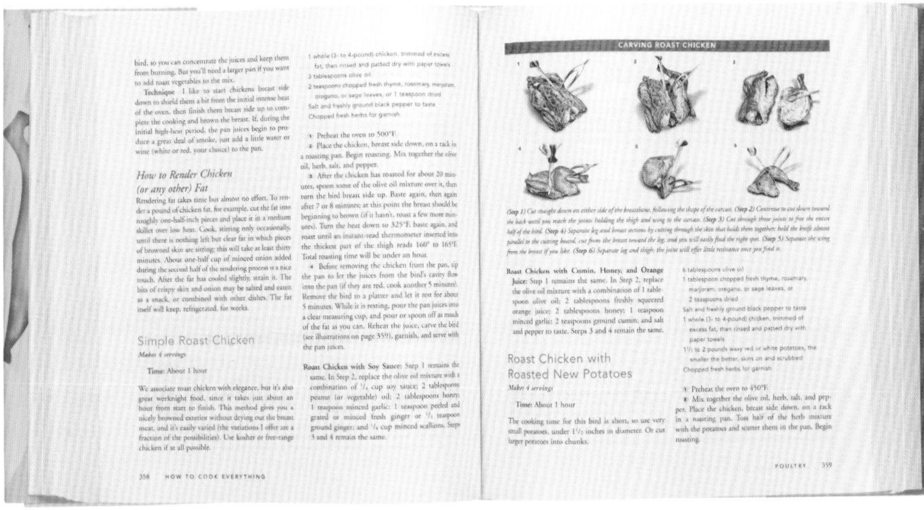
How to Render Chicken (or any other) Fat
Simple Roast Chicken
CARVING ROAST CHICKEN
Roast Chicken with Roasted New Potatoes
358 HOW TO COOK EVERYTHING
POULTRY 359

THOMAS KELLER

The French Laundry Cookbook, 1999

It's no mistake that the final great cookbook of the twentieth century is Thomas Keller's *French Laundry Cookbook*. Many would say that Keller is responsible for ushering in a new era in restaurant cuisine in the 1990s. The French Laundry restaurant, which the *New York Times* described as the most exciting place to eat in America, introduced a revolutionary dining experience—one based on a series of small courses that strive to delight all the senses in a playful way, demonstrate a rigorous attention to detail, and rely on meticulously sourced ingredients. Keller codified his style of cuisine and set a standard of excellence to which many other chefs would aspire. The book's broad popularity also signified a shift: home cooks now were ready to embrace a master chef's unadulterated recipes in all their complexity. *The French Laundry Cookbook* epitomizes just how far the nation's palate had evolved. At the beginning of the century we had Fanny Farmer's perfection salad. Now we had Keller's iconic "Cornets"—canapés that reference ice cream cones. American food finally found its own identity.

Keller started out cooking as a young man in his mother's restaurant. Then he took summer jobs at the Dunes Club in Rhode Island under the tutelage of the French master chef Roland Henin. It was here that he realized his true calling was in the kitchen. Henin recognized Keller's talent and encouraged him to pursue cooking. Keller went on to apprentice in France, perfecting his technique. Returning to the States, he opened a restaurant in New York called Rakel, which became famous and launched his career. With the stock market crash in the late 1980s, Rakel closed and Keller returned to his native California. He made a name for himself as an inventive and perfectionist chef while working at a restaurant in Checkers, a Los Angeles hotel.

In 1992 he took over a restaurant, which had been a former laundry, in Yountville, California, an hour north of San Francisco in the Napa Valley. After major renovations, the French Laundry reopened in 1994 and sent shock waves through the food world. The restaurant would win nearly every award and accolade in the business, including three Michelin stars. Keller produced *The French Laundry Cookbook* in 1999 as the summation of his philosophy of food and the experience of eating.

Keller expanded with the creation of Bouchon, then ad hoc, both in Yountville, as well as Per Se in New York City. Per Se received three Michelin stars, making Keller the only American chef ever to win that honor for two restaurants. Keller returned to simpler foods at Bouchon and ad hoc, echoing the turn that eating took in this century toward more professional foods prepared at home and more rustic foods served at restaurants. Nevertheless, the French Laundry, with its status as a world-class restaurant, remains a symbol of a new wave in thinking about food. No longer are American chefs beholden to the image of French cuisine. We may use their cooking techniques, but we have created a distinct kind of food, sense of taste, and way of eating. Even the French had to acknowledge it.

NOTABLE RECIPES: Cornets (Salmon Tartare with Sweet Red Onion Crème Fraîche) (page 321) • Cream of Walnut Soup • Heirloom Tomato Tart • **"Macaroni & Cheese" (Butter-Poached Maine Lobster with Creamy Lobster Broth and Mascarpone-Enriched Orzo)** (page 483) • **"Oysters and Pearls" (Sabayon of Pearl Tapioca with Malpeque Oysters and Osetra Caviar)** (page 324) • **"Peas and Carrots" (Maine Lobster Pancakes with Pea Shoot Salad and Ginger-Carrot Emulsion)** (page 484) • Truffle Oil Egg Custard

By then, 1967, Yountville's glamorous outlaw days had disintegrated into nothing more than a row of bars serving the veterans, trailers and ramshackle homes, and rooming houses. "It was a cesspool," said Don, who would become its mayor, orchestrate its regeneration, and, with Sally, open the French Laundry in 1978.

The late 1960s was an exciting time in the region, then a rugged territory of undeveloped farmland and abandoned prune and walnut orchards. Yountville sat like a quiet Mason-Dixon line between St. Helena lifting its eyebrows from the north at the townies of Napa in the south. And then a new wave of young winemakers arrived and tapped the power of The Grape. The grape to Napa is like the microchip to Silicon Valley, like oil to Texas. It would within thirty years transform the United States' wine business into a world-famous industry and turn the valley itself into the most sophisticated agricultural community on earth.

I gave the French Laundry a new life and it gave me a new life. I don't see us as being separate entities. Whatever the value of my skills, my knowledge, my sensibilities, they never would have come together in this book had it not been for the French Laundry.

A SAD HAPPY STORY

Autumn 1990 was a sad time in my life. I was going to be leaving New York after ten years. I would be starting life over in Los Angeles, and my new employer there wanted me to prepare a dish for a food and wine benefit there that would really wow people.

Shortly before I moved, some friends took me to our favorite restaurant in Chinatown, and, as always, we went to Baskin-Robbins for ice cream afterward. I'd been nervous about this food and wine event; I guess it had been in the back of my mind for a while. I ordered an ice-cream cone. The guy put it in a little holder—you take it from a holder—and said, "Here's your cone."

The moment he said it, I thought "There it is! We're going to take our standard tuiles, we're going to make cones with them, and we're going to fill them with tuna tartare."

And that's what we did. Now I use salmon, but you can really use anything. Eggplant caviar and roasted red peppers or tomato confit make a wonderful vegetarian version. You can do it with meat—julienne of prosciutto with some melon. The cone is just a vehicle.

Because it was a canapé that people really began to associate us with, I decided that everyone who eats at the restaurant should begin the meal with this cornet. People always smile when they get it. It makes them happy. But I wouldn't have come up with it if I hadn't been sad. I had been handed an ice-cream cone a hundred times before and it had never resulted in the cornet. I had to be sad to see it.

C A N A P É S

"CORNETS"

Salmon Tartare with Sweet Red Onion Crème Fraîche

CORNETS

1/4 cup plus 3 tablespoons all-purpose flour
1 tablespoon plus 1 teaspoon sugar
1 teaspoon kosher salt
8 tablespoons (4 ounces) unsalted butter, softened but still cool to the touch
2 large egg whites, cold
2 tablespoons black sesame seeds

SALMON TARTARE

4 ounces salmon fillet (belly preferred), skin and any pin bones removed and very finely minced
1/2 teaspoon extra virgin olive oil
1/2 teaspoon lemon oil (see Sources, page 315)
1 1/2 teaspoons finely minced chives
1 1/2 teaspoons finely minced shallots
1/4 teaspoon kosher salt, or to taste
Small pinch of freshly ground white pepper, or to taste

SWEET RED ONION CRÈME FRAÎCHE

1 tablespoon finely minced red onions
1/2 cup crème fraîche
1/4 teaspoon kosher salt, or to taste
Freshly ground white pepper to taste

24 chive tips (about 1 inch long)

This is one of my favorite dishes to serve to large groups of people—it's fun to look at, it's distinctive, delicious, and doesn't require a plate or silverware. You can eat it standing up, with a glass of Champagne or wine in one hand. At the French Laundry, I use a specially made Lucite holder to serve these cones, but you might fill a bowl with rock salt, say, or peppercorns, and stand the cones up in this to serve them.

FOR THE CORNETS: In a medium bowl, mix together the flour, sugar, and salt. In a separate bowl, whisk the softened butter until it is completely smooth and mayonnaise-like in texture. Using a stiff spatula or spoon, beat the egg whites into the dry ingredients until completely incorporated and smooth. Whisk in the softened butter by thirds, scraping the sides of the bowl as necessary and whisking until the batter is creamy and without any lumps. Transfer the batter to a smaller container, as it will be easier to work with.

Preheat the oven to 400°F.

Make a 4-inch hollow circular stencil. Place a Silpat (see Sources, page 315) on the counter (it is easier to work on the Silpat before it is put on the sheet pan). Place the stencil in one corner of the sheet and, holding the stencil flat against the Silpat, scoop some of the batter onto the back of an offset spatula and spread it in an even layer over the stencil. Then run the spatula over the entire stencil to remove any excess batter. After baking the first batch of cornets, you will be able to judge the correct thickness; you may need a little more or less batter to adjust the thickness of the cornets. There should not be any holes in the batter. Lift the stencil and repeat the process to make as many rounds as you have molds or to fill the Silpat, leaving about 1 1/2 inches between the cornets. Sprinkle each cornet with a pinch of black sesame seeds.

Place the Silpat on a heavy baking sheet and bake for 4 to 6 minutes, or until the batter is set and you see it rippling from the heat. The cornets may have browned in some areas, but they will not be evenly browned at this point.

Open the oven door and place the baking sheet on the door. This will help keep the cornets warm as you roll them and prevent them from becoming too stiff to roll. Flip a cornet over on the sheet pan, sesame seed side down, and place a 4 1/2-inch cornet mold (size #35, see Sources, page 315) at the bottom of the round. If you are right-handed, you will want the pointed end on your left and the open end on your right. The tip of the mold should touch the lower left edge (at about 7 o'clock on a clock face) of the cornet. Fold the bottom of the cornet up and around the mold and carefully roll upward and toward the left to wrap the cornet tightly around the mold; it should remain on the sheet pan as you roll. Leave the cornet wrapped around the mold and continue to roll the cornets around molds; as you proceed, arrange the rolled cornets, seam side down, on the sheet pan so they lean against each other, to prevent them from rolling.

When all the cornets are rolled, return them to the oven shelf, close the door, and bake for an additional 3 to 4 minutes to set the seams and color the cornets a golden brown. If the color is uneven, stand the cornets on end for a minute or so more, until the color is even. Remove the cornets from the oven and allow to cool just slightly, 30 seconds or so.

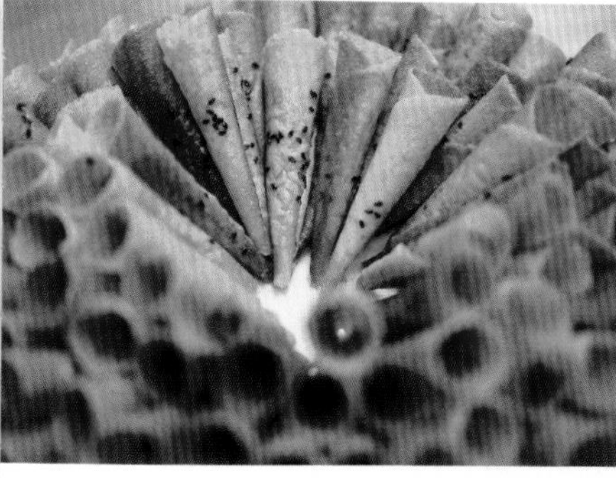

To make the stencil: Cut the rim from the top of a plastic container. Trace two concentric circles on the lid, the inner 4 inches in diameter, the outer about 4 1/2 inches. Sketch a thumb tab that will make it easy to lift the stencil off the silicon-coated Silpat. Trim around the tab and outer circle. Remove the inner circle so that you have a hollow ring. The batter gets spread to the stencil's edges, then it's lifted off, leaving perfectly shaped rounds.

Gently remove the cornets from the molds and cool for several minutes on paper towels. Remove the Silpat from the baking sheet, wipe the excess butter from it, and allow it to cool down before spreading the next batch. Store the cornets for up to 2 days (for maximum flavor) in an airtight container.

FOR THE SALMON TARTARE: With a sharp knife, finely mince the salmon fillet (do not use a food processor, as it would damage the texture of the fish) and place it in a small bowl. Stir in the remaining ingredients and taste for seasoning. Cover the bowl and refrigerate the tartare for at least 30 minutes, or up to 12 hours.

FOR THE SWEET RED ONION CRÈME FRAÎCHE: Place the red onions in a small strainer and rinse them under cold water for several seconds. Dry them on paper towels. In a small metal bowl, whisk the crème fraîche for about 30 seconds to 1 minute, or until it holds soft peaks when you lift the whisk. Fold in the chopped onions and season to taste with the salt and white pepper. Transfer the onion cream to a container, cover, and refrigerate until ready to serve or for up to 6 hours.

TO COMPLETE: Fill just the top 1/2 inch of each cornet with onion cream, leaving the bottom of the cone empty. (This is easily done using a pastry bag fitted with a 1/4-inch plain tip or with the tip of a small knife.) Spoon about 1 1/2 teaspoons of the tartare over the onion cream and mold it into a dome resembling a scoop of ice cream. Lay a chive tip against one side of the tartare to garnish.

PICTURED ON PAGE 5 MAKES 24 CORNETS

You go out to an Italian restaurant, you order something like linguine with clam sauce, and think "Why don't I do this, reduce that, do this?" And you come up with a fun new dish—"linguine" with clam sauce served in the clam shells. People can relate to the concept and flavors because they already know how it will taste.

D E S S E R T
Mache
252 The French Laundry Cookbook

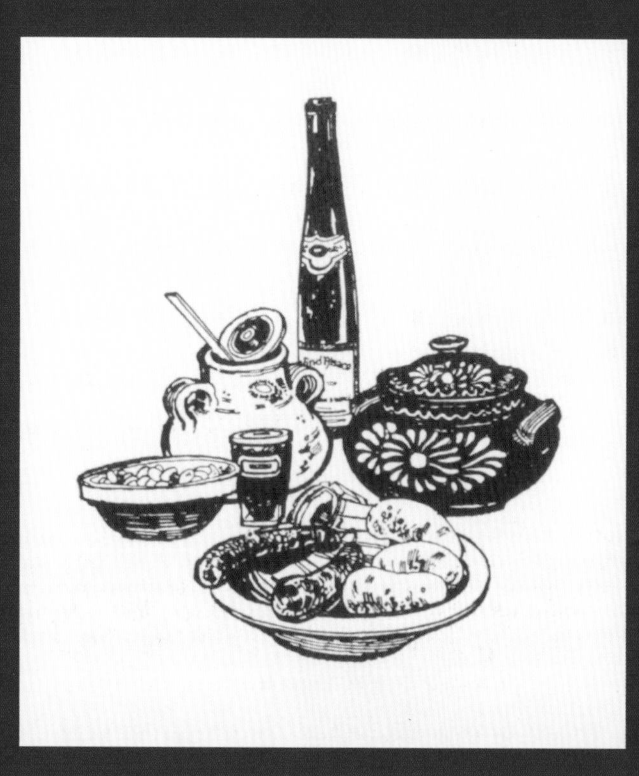

501 Classic Recipes

A RECIPE ROUNDTABLE

What makes for a good recipe?

Total clarity. Then a little bit of personal detail—where does it come from? What does it mean to the author? It should be translated not just from your own view but from that of another culture.

—**Madhur Jaffrey**

For me I need to know the history. It needs to represent a culture . . . it needs to have the wisdom of age. —**Lidia Bastianich**

It should be consistent and concise. The recipe is not creative writing: If you find a way to say something that works—cook the pasta until it's tender but not mushy (not everyone knows what al dente means), for example, it makes sense to say it that way every time. —**Mark Bittman**

An ingredient or technique that makes it stand out—fennel in the potato salad, preserved lemon with a pasta—but still makes culinary sense. No smoked vanilla beans in the lamb ragout.

—**Michael Bauer**

It depends on who the audience is. Working at *Gourmet*, I was interested to see the change over the years. In the early days it was just shorthand: "Steam a duck, and make the sauce." By the year 2000 it was two pages of how to buy a duck, two on how to steam it, and so on. If you're writing for beginners, you need to hold their hands, give them time and visual cues—how big the pot should be, for example. For an experienced audience just the ingredients and a couple of suggestions will do.

—**Ruth Reichl**

Who have you relied on in cookbooks?

James Beard and Jacques Pépin. When I read James Beard's *Theory and Practice of Good Cooking*, I remember thinking, Wow! This is everything. He explained not only how to cook things, but why things happen; there is so much there. And Jaques Pépin's two photo books, *La Technique* and *La Methode*—those images were so powerful and smart.

—**Mark Bittman**

I still go back to Madeleine Kamman's books. She's brilliant and her techniques are flawless. For searing salmon, press down and the moisture reabsorbs as it steams—something that isn't obvious that you can employ at home. —**Michael Bauer**

I got a lot of my sense of writing a recipe from the *Joy of Cooking*. —**Marian Burros**

For me it's about context. Seminal books for me were the Julia Child books, as she let you create your own context and made a sensual translation of the recipes. For example, she made yeast bread dough every morning so that those smells would be in her nose when she cooked during the day. I go back to old Elizabeth David books—I think they're hilarious because it can be difficult to figure out exactly what is being made—it's more about the sensual experience. When I was a kid I got a book called *Recipes from Around the World*, a hand-written cookbook with hand-drawn illustrations, all written with total context. I would cook whole meals, dreaming of being in those places.

—**Rick Bayless**

The first book I bought was Julia Child's *Mastering the Art of French Cooking*, simply the answer to every question. I own only five cookbooks: Julia Child, Marcella Hazan, Irene Kuo, Noriyuki Sugie, and Richard Olney's *The Good Cook* series.

—**Madhur Jaffrey**

I came to the United States as a young Italian girl. I didn't want to lose my identity, so I stuck to many of the classic Italian cookbooks, such as *Il cucchiaio d'argento* by Editoriale Domus, *Il grande libro della cucina italiana* by Alessandro Molinari Pradelli, and *L'arte di mangiar bene* by Pellegrino Artusi. In America my big influence was Julia Child—not so much the way she wrote the recipes but how she connected with people. There's also Harold McGee's *On Food and Cooking: The Science and Lore of the Kitchen*—learning the science behind what happens in a pan really helped. Why do some traditions resurface? Sometimes there's a simple scientific reason we do it over and over.

—**Lidia Bastianich**

Who should novice cooks look to?

Start with the best-known books that really work—the *Joy of Cooking, The Fannie Farmer Cookbook*—and then at a certain point you won't need them anymore, but you will be absolutely glad they were there. —**Marian Burros**

Marion Cunningham. I still check her book for a ham, a glaze . . . anything American and basic, it's just going to be good. —**Madhur Jaffrey**

Certainly not the Internet, because there's no consistency, no checks and balances. Follow a person! Someone like Jacques Pépin, a chef with a point of view you can trust, whom you can look to for advice. *Better Homes and Gardens, Joy of Cooking, The Fannie Farmer Cookbook*—a single book so you have a benchmark. —**Michael Bauer**

From Julia Child's Kitchen—I still refer back to it. Another good place to start is *The Best Recipe* from *Cook's Illustrated* magazine. —**Rick Bayless**

Which of your recipes are you most proud of?

The ones that have been easiest to follow. I learned how to write recipes so that anyone with minimal skills, who could boil water, use a knife, measure, knew what "beat until firm but not stiff" meant could make them successfully, and I haven't had many complaints over the years. **—Marian Burros**

What's the best way to present Indian dishes to Americans?

As authentically as possible—it's a vast country and there are so many regions, religions, traditions, groups, places that people don't know about. Indian has never been a hot cuisine here, though maybe soon. For me I look for the best approach to making standard dishes and new uses for unusual dishes and ingredients. **—Madhur Jaffrey**

Do you ever use cookbooks to dig into the foods of other cultures?

Well, for years that's all I did. And I still do some; but the fact is that once you learn the basic seasonings and patterns of a cuisine, you kind of have it nailed. That doesn't mean you're an expert, and it doesn't mean you can create every dish. But I'm not that interested in duplicating every traditional dish of every cuisine; I'm interested in finding ways to show people how to make a few simple Thai dishes, for example, or Mexican ones, and usually that just means understanding the basic flavors of those cuisines. **—Mark Bittman**

Is there a recipe that stands out as a building block for you?

Alice B. Toklas's Eggs Picabia. She cooks them very slowly, maybe in a double boiler. For me as an eight- or nine-year-old kid, I remember thinking, "Oh my god, it's not just scrambled eggs." I remember that as an incredible revelation. **—Ruth Reichl**

How do you feel about drawings with recipes?

Anything—anything—that makes a recipe easier to follow is fine with me. But having said that, most recipes don't need drawings or photos, though I know people like them. A recipe is a set of instructions. You don't need a drawing to show sautéing a piece of meat or boiling a vegetable, after all. **—Mark Bittman**

Were there any memorably hateful recipes you had to edit?

Yes, one of my own! At the *Los Angeles Times* every food editor had to come up with new turkey recipes every year. So one year we made fifty. The problem with turkey is when the stuffing inside is done the meat is overcooked, and if the stuffing is cooked outside the turkey it's just not as good. So we came up with a brilliant idea: Put the stuffing under the skin. Surprise: It works! But . . . you end up with very little stuffing to eat, so the recipe was really ridiculous! **—Ruth Reichl**

Do you refer back to recipes in your work?

Sometimes. If there's something I'd never get right myself, I look at other people's recipes. But almost every sort of "normal" daily recipe, I just do it, because it's better for me to create something out of my head than to try to do something someone else has written down. **—Mark Bittman**

Are there recipe writers who always knock it out of the park for you?

Marcella Hazan has been very important for me. Her recipes really work. And Marion Cunningham's *Breakfast Book* is one of the great cookbooks.

—Ruth Reichl

How do you feel about chefs' recipes for the general population?

I would think, "A chef! Chefs really know how to cook!" But when they say a handful they think everyone knows what that means. Their recipes often require being a natural cook—and most people just aren't. —**Marian Burros**

Judy Rodgers's *Zuni Café Cookbook* is very good. But most chefs don't do home cooking. More recently, Thomas Keller's *Ad Hoc at Home* is useful for home cooks even if it's a little more complicated than most people go for. It really is encouraging in many ways. —**Ruth Reichl**

You've become known for deconstructing and diagraming recipes. What gave you the idea to do that?

I like the idea of presenting recipes in nontraditional ways. To me the most important thing about teaching cooking is to show how simple it is, and how each recipe can spawn another. A goal of anyone who writes recipes or teaches cooking has to be to show that there are only a few recipes—everything grows out of everything else.

—**Mark Bittman**

What books can we find on your bookshelves?

I have forty or fifty books in my kitchen that are mostly foods I like to eat! Lot's of Thai, Japanese, Indian. —**Rick Bayless**

I have a big reference library. My collection of books is like a valued friend, a confidante I can ask advice from. *Food and Culture, Larousse Gastronomique*, Mark Bittman's books, *The Oxford Companion to Food, The Silver Spoon*, and then a whole selection on nutrition (after all, I'm feeding people!). I just love books. I think I assimilate just by sitting surrounded by books!

—**Lidia Bastianich**

Compiled by Clark Wolf

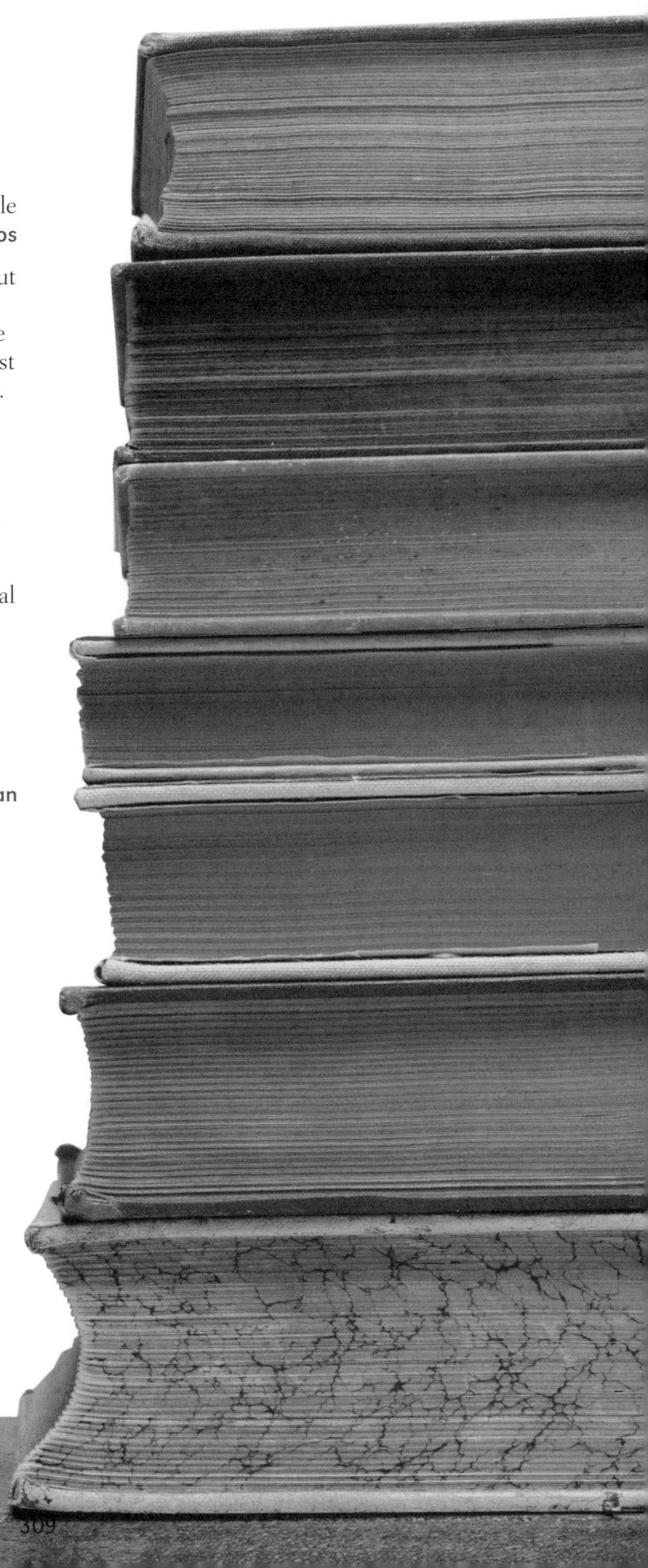

EDITOR'S NOTE

The recipes selected from each book represent those that were most often printed in reviews or that most typify the kind of food that makes that book special. We have reproduced the recipes verbatim as they appear in the original editions with a few key exceptions: If a recipe refers to another recipe or an illustration that we are not reproducing here, then we have removed the cross-reference phrase. Where we encountered an obvious typographical error, we corrected it. Lastly, some slight alterations in the typographical style of the original books were necessary in order to conform to the typography of the book in hand.

The recipes reproduced here are from a wide variety of sources and represent the wildly varying styles of recipe writing over more than one hundred years. Some of them are of purely antiquarian interest. Remember that thermometers and consistent temperatures were not very reliable until gas stoves became standard in kitchens, and that happened surprisingly late in some parts of the country. Others recipes are tried and true. Still others show the excellence of great chefs with vast kitchens and an army of sous chefs. Anyone wishing to re-create some of the older recipes will need to translate certain elements into modern terms. Not many of us regularly dress our own chickens—let alone squirrels—these days, but our grandparents or great-grandparents probably did. We hope the variety of these recipes gives insight into the diverse narratives and histories of American cooking.

Drinks, Hors d'Oeuvre, and Nibbles

COCKTAILS

CRADDOCK
The Savoy Cocktail Book

Dry Martini Cocktail

½ French Vermouth
½ Gin
1 Dash Orange Bitters

Shake well and strain into cocktail glass.

CRADDOCK
The Savoy Cocktail Book

Sidecar Cocktail

¼ Lemon Juice
¼ Cointreau
½ Brandy

Shake well and strain into cocktail glass.

JUNIOR LEAGUE OF AUGUSTA
Old and New Recipes from the South

Ramos Gin Fizz

Ramos was a famous bartender in Old New Orleans. His Ramos Gin Fizz was a closely guarded secret; even now, the receipts that are given for the fizz are not known to be exactly like the Ramos. However, those who have had the old Ramos Gin Fizz say that this one is the most nearly like the original.

1 egg white
½ teaspoon vanilla
1 teaspoon orange flower water
2 teaspoons powdered sugar
1 jigger good gin
Juice of 4 lemons
Cracked ice
2 tablespoons cream

Shake the above vigorously with the cracked ice until the mixture is foamy and cold. Strain and serve in an eight-ounce glass. Fill up with seltzer water.

—Mrs. Benjamin R. Ellis

FARMER
The Boston Cooking-School Cook Book

Mint Julep

1 quart water
2 cups sugar
1 pint claret wine
1 cup strawberry juice
1 cup orange juice
Juice 8 lemons
1½ cups boiling water
12 sprigs fresh mint

Make syrup by boiling quart of water and sugar twenty minutes. Separate mint in pieces, add to the boiling water, cover, and let stand in warm place five minutes, strain, and add to syrup; add fruit juices, and cool. Pour into punch-bowl, add claret, and chill with a large piece of ice; dilute with water. Garnish with fresh mint leaves and whole strawberries.

BAYLESS
Rick Bayless's Mexican Kitchen

Top-of-the-Line Margarita

SERVES 2 GENEROUSLY

Lime wedges
Coarse salt
¼ cup fresh lime juice, about 1 large lime
¼ cup Tesoro silver or other silver 100 percent agave tequila
¼ cup Cointreau orange liqueur
½ cup coarsely cracked ice cubes

Rub the rims of 2 martini glasses with a lime wedge, then dip the rims in a dish of coarse salt. Refrigerate the glasses if desired.

In a shaker, combine the lime juice, tequila and orange liqueur. Add ice and shake 10 to 15 seconds, then strain into the prepared glasses.

CRADDOCK
The Savoy Cocktail Book

Corpse Reviver (No. 1.)

¼ Italian Vermouth
¼ Apple Brandy or Calvados
½ Brandy

Shake well and strain into cocktail glass.

To be taken before 11 a.m., or whenever steam and energy are needed.

CRADDOCK
The Savoy Cocktail Book

Punch

"This ancient Silver bowl of mine, it tells of good old times,
Of joyous days, and jolly nights, and merry Christmas Chimes,
They were a free and jovial race, but honest, brave and true,
That dipped their ladle in the punch when this old bowl was new."

Thus runs the old drinking song by Oliver Wendell Holmes, a song among many that have lauded the old time jollity of Ye Punch Bowl.

The proper preparation of Punch requires considerable care, but there is one grand secret in its concoction that must be mastered with patience and care. It is just this, that the various subtle ingredients be thoroughly mixed in such a way, that neither the bitter, the sweet, the spirit, nor any liquor be perceptible the one over the other. This accomplishment depends not so much upon the precise proportions of the various elements, as upon the order of their addition, and the manner of mixing.

BOMBAY PUNCH

1 Qt. Brandy
1 Qt. Sherry
¼ Pt. Maraschino
¼ Pt. Orange Curaçao
4 Qts. Champagne
2 Qts. Carbonated Water

Stir gently. Surround the Punch Bowl with cracked ice and decorate with fruits in season.

CRADDOCK
The Savoy Cocktail Book

White Lady Cocktail

¼ Lemon Juice
¼ Cointreau
½ Dry Gin

Shake well and strain into cocktail glass.

CRADDOCK
The Savoy Cocktail Book

Hanky Panky Cocktail

2 Dashes Fernet Branca
½ Italian Vermouth
½ Dry Gin

Shake well and strain into cocktail glass. Squeeze orange peel on top.

LAUREL
Living on the Earth

Dandelion Wine

Combine and let stand in a covered crock 9 days: 4 quarts water and 4 quarts dandelion blossoms. Strain (squeeze) flowers. To water extract add 3 pounds honey, 3 sliced lemons, one cake yeast. Let stand in crock 9 days. Then strain it into a jug. Leave it, cork off, until it stops working, then cork it up.

CASAS
The Foods and Wines of Spain

Sangria

START PREPARATION SEVERAL HOURS IN ADVANCE.

Nothing is more satisfying in summer than an icy cold sangria. *When I think of Spain, some of my most pleasant thoughts are of beach-side restaurants, where one goes in bathing suit straight from a dip in the Mediterranean to eat paella and sip* sangria.

Sangria *slides down easily, so prepare plenty, increasing this recipe by any amount desired.*

MAKES ABOUT 4 CUPS

- 1 bottle (24 ounces) dry, full-bodied red wine, preferably of Spanish import from Valencia or Valdepeñas
- 2 tablespoons orange juice
- 2 tablespoons orange liqueur (optional), such as Gran Torres or Grand Marnier
- 1 tablespoon sugar
- Orange and lemon slices
- Apple and/or peach wedges
- 1 cup club soda or sparkling water

Mix together in a large pitcher all ingredients except the club soda. Cover and refrigerate several hours or overnight. Add the club soda and ice cubes. Serve very cold in balloon-shaped wineglasses or in Spanish earthenware mugs (without handles).

SCHNEIDER

Uncommon Fruits & Vegetables

Sour Cherry Ratafia

Cherries flavor many of the most aromatically appealing liqueurs and eaux-de-vie made—ratafia, marasquin, and kirsch. For home-made cordials, the fruit works remarkably well, thanks to the intense almondy kernel flavor, which is quickly imparted without complicated techniques or machinery.

The somewhat old-fashioned term ratafia *is used to describe liqueurs or cordials made by steeping or infusing, particularly stone fruits. The drink has been around since the Renaissance, when it was served upon the ratification of treaties and pacts—or so say the majority of authorities on spirits. The Oxford English Dictionary calls this conjecture; but it remains a most appealing derivation. Although the word is still used today in France, England, and some older American cookbooks, the meaning has expanded to include biscuits, puddings, creams, cakes, and cookies that taste of ground almonds or apricot pits or other kernel flavors.*

Serve this cherry-bright liqueur over ice, or combined with white wine or sparkling water for an aperitif; or offer it well chilled, in small glasses for dessert.

MAKES ABOUT 1 QUART

- 1 pound sour cherries, *plus ½ pound a week or two later*
- 2 cups white rum
- 1–2-inch piece vanilla bean
- 12 peppercorns
- ½ cup water
- ½ cup sugar

1. Stone 1 pound cherries, reserving pits. Enclose these in a bag, wrap in a towel, then crack with meat pounder or hammer.

2. Rinse a quart canning jar with boiling water. In it combine pits, pitted cherries, rum, vanilla, and peppercorns. Cover with baking parchment, cap tightly, and shake. Let stand in a dark place for a week or two, shaking occasionally.

3. Pour liqueur through a cheesecloth-lined sieve, then squash cherries in cheesecloth to extract most juice. Discard pulp; save vanilla and return it to the jar.

4. Prick the fresh ½ pound cherries with a clean needle. Combine in jar with liqueur. Cover as before. Leave another week or so, shaking now and then.

5. Combine water and sugar and boil for a minute; cool. Repeat squeezing and straining of ratafia as in step 3, but finish up by straining the cordial through several layers of fine cheesecloth.

6. Pour liqueur through a coffee filter in small batches, removing the filter occasionally to rinse off solids. (This is a slow job, but necessary.)

7. Gradually add cooled sugar syrup to taste. Decant into a bottle to just fit. Once you have used a good portion, transfer the cordial to a smaller bottle to prevent discoloration and loss of flavor.

JUNIOR LEAGUE OF AUGUSTA

Old and New Recipes from the South

Eggnog

(MRS. FRANK E. BEANE JR.)

12 egg whites, beaten very stiff
Add: 12 level tablespoons sugar
1 pt. of cream, whipped very stiff
12 yolks, beaten until they are light yellow
12 tablespoons brandy or whiskey, beating it in slowly. Pour into whites.

—MISS MARY ALICE BERCKMANS

DRINKS

THE TIMES-PICAYUNE

The Original Picayune Creole Cook Book

Creole Coffee

Café à la Créole

Travelers the world over unite in praise of Creole Coffee, or "Café à la Créole," as they are fond of putting it. The Creole cuisinieres succeeded far beyond even the famous chefs of France in discovering the secret of good coffee-making, and they have never yielded the palm of victory. There is no place in the world in which the use of coffee is more general than in the old Creole city of New Orleans, where, from the famous French Market, with its world-renowned coffee stands, to the old-time homes on the Bayou St. John, from Lake Pontchartrain to the verge of Southport, the cup of "Café Noir," or "Café au Lait," at morning, at noon and at night, has become a necessary and delightful part of the life of the people, and the wonder and the joy of visitors.

The morning cup of Cafe Noir is an integral part of the life of a Creole household. The Creoles hold as a physiological fact that this custom contributes to longevity, and point, day after day, to examples of old men and women of fourscore, and over, who attest to the powerful aid they have received through life from a good, fragrant cup of coffee in the early morning. The ancient residents hold, too, that, after a hearty meal, a cup of Cafe Noir, or black coffee, will relieve the sense of oppression so apt to be experienced, and enables the stomach to perform its functions with greater facility. Cafe Noir is known, too, as one of the best preventives of infectious diseases, and the ancient Creole physicians never used any other deodorizer than passing a chafing dish with burning grains of coffee through the room. As an antidote for poison the uses of coffee are too well known to be dilated upon.

Coffee is also the greatest brain food and stimulant known. Men of science, poets and scholars and journalists have testified to its beneficial effects. Coffee supported the old age of Voltaire, and enabled Fontenelle to reach his one hundredth birthday. Charles Gayarre, the illustrious Louisiana historian, at the advanced age of 80, paid tribute to the Creole cup of Cafe Noir.

How important, then, is the art of making good coffee, entering, as it does, so largely into the daily life of the American people. There is no reason why the secret should be confined to any section or city; but, with a little care and attention, every household in the land may enjoy its morning or after-dinner cup of coffee with as much real pleasure as the Creoles of New Orleans, and the thousands of visitors who yearly migrate to this old Franco-Spanish city.

THE BEST INGREDIENTS AND THE PROPER MAKING

The best ingredients are those delightful coffees grown on well-watered mountain slopes, such as the famous Java and Mocha coffees. It must be of the best quality, for Mocha and Java mixed produce a concoction of a most delightful aroma and stimulating effect. One of the first essentials is to "Parch the Coffee Grains Just Before Making the Coffee," because coffee that has been long parched and left standing loses its flavor and strength. The coffee grains should "Be Roasted to a Rich Brown," and never allowed to scorch or burn, otherwise the flavor of the coffee is at once affected or destroyed. Bear this in mind, that the GOOD CREOLE COOK NEVER BOILS COFFEE, but insists on dripping it, in a covered strainer, slowly—DRIP, DRIP, DRIP—till all the flavor is extracted.

To reach this desired end, immediately after the coffee has been roasted and allowed to cool in a covered dish, so that none of the flavor will escape, the coffee is ground—neither too fine, for that will make the coffee dreggy; nor too coarse, for that prevents the escape of the full strength of the coffee juice—but a careful medium proportion which will not allow the hot water pouring to run rapidly through, but which will admit of the water percolating slowly through the grounds, extracting every bit of the strength and aroma, and falling speedily with a "drip! drip!" into the coffee pot.

To make good coffee, the water must be "freshly boiled," and must never be poured upon the grounds until it has reached the boiling point otherwise the flavor is destroyed and subsequent pourings of boiling water can never quite succeed in extracting the superb strength and aroma.

It is of the greatest importance that "The Coffee Pot Be Kept Perfectly Clean," and the good cook will bear in mind that absolute cleanliness is as necessary for the "interior" of the coffee pot as for the shining "exterior." This fact is one too commonly overlooked, and yet the coffee pot requires more than ordinary care, for the reason that the chemical action of the coffee upon the tin or agate tends to create a substance which collects and clings to every crevice and seam, and, naturally, in the course of time, will affect the flavor of the coffee most peculiarly and unpleasantly. Very often the fact that the coffee tastes bitter or muddy arises from this fact. The "inside" of the coffee pot should, therefore, be washed as carefully "every day" as the outside.

Having observed these conditions, proceed to make the coffee according to the following unfailing

CREOLE RULE

Have the water heated to a good boil. Set the coffee pot in front of the stove, never on top, as the coffee will boil, and then the taste is destroyed.

Allow one cup, or the ordinary mill, of coffee to make four good cups of the liquid, ground and put in the strainer, being careful to keep both the strainer and the spout of the coffee pot covered to prevent the flavor from escaping. Pour, first, about two tablespoonfuls of the boiling water on the coffee grounds, or, according to the quantity of coffee used, just sufficient to settle the grounds. Wait about five minutes; then pour a little more water, and allow it to drip slowly through, but never pour water the second time until the grounds have ceased to puff or bubble, as this is an indication that the grounds have settled. Keep pouring slowly, at intervals, a little boiling water at a time, until the delightful aroma of the coffee begins to escape from the closed spout of the coffee pot. If the coffee dyes the cup it is a little too strong, but do not go far beyond this, or the coffee will be too weak. When you have produced a rich, fragrant concoction, whose delightful aroma, filling the room, is a constant, tempting invitation to taste it, serve in fine china cups, using in preference loaf sugar for sweetening. You have then a real cup of the famous Creole Cafe Noir, so extensively used at morning dawn, at breakfast, and as the "after-dinner cup."

If the coffee appears muddy, or not clear, some of the old Creoles drop a piece of charcoal an inch thick into the water, which settles it and at once makes it clear. Demonstrations prove that strength remains in the coffee grounds. A matter of economy in making coffee is to save the grounds from the meal or day before and boil these in a half gallon of water. Settle the grounds by dropping two or three drops of cold water in, and pour the water over the fresh grounds. This is a suggestion that rich and poor might heed with profit.

DULL
Southern Cooking

Tea

Most of the tea sold contains several kinds of grades blended to produce the most pleasing results.

The tea leaf contains caffeine, oil and tannin.

The average tea, if rightly made, is not harmful. Of course, too much of anything can be taken, and tea may be made harmful by drinking too much strong tea or that which is poorly made by allowing the water to stand on the leaves, or boiled.

Freshly brewed tea, after three to five minutes' infusion, is essential if a good quality is desired. The water, as for coffee, should be freshly boiled and poured over the tea for this short time. The tea in the individual bag or container is decidedly the nicest and most satisfactory way for making a cup of hot tea.

The tea leaves may be removed when the desired strength is obtained. Any bag or ball should be agitated several times to be sure the leaves are throwing off the strength and to avoid any waste which might be left in the leaf, if not thoroughly wet. Tea leaves when left in the pot or cup too long bring out the caffeine and tannin, which makes this beverage harmful.

Tea, when it is to be iced, should be made much stronger, to allow for the ice used in chilling. A medium strength tea is usually liked. A good blend and grade of black tea is most popular for iced tea, while green and black are both used for hot. The variety used depends on the individual.

The only recipe for making tea is, use a good grade of tea, freshly boiled water, to make the tea quickly, and never leave it standing on the leaves.

It is poor economy to buy cheap tea as it requires more leaves for a cup, and the flavor is not so good. Good tea may be spoiled in the making. It is not necessary to buy expensive blends put up in fancy containers, just be sure to get a reliable brand and then make it right.

Some water makes poor tea, because of the minerals it contains.

Earthenware or glass is best for brewing tea.

Teapots, like those for coffee, should never have any greasy cloth used about them.

To sweeten tea for an iced drink—less sugar is required if put in while tea is hot, but often too much is made and sweetened, so in the end there is more often a waste than saving.

A slice of lemon, cream or full milk may be used in hot tea, according to the individual taste. Iced tea is served with or without lemon, with a sprig of mint, a strawberry, a cherry, a slice of orange, or pineapple. This may be fresh or canned fruit. Milk is not used in iced tea.

LAUREL

Living on the Earth

Sunflower Milk

Commercial baby foods are not good for baby. They contain ingredients to please the mother; salt, corn syrup, white sugar, none of these benefit any human body as a steady diet.

Make your own baby food from organically grown fruits and vegetables. Just prepare them so they are soft enough to force through a sieve; use little water so that the vitamin content is not totally destroyed. Fill sterilized (boiled) baby food jars (thrift stores sell empty jars very cheap) or even large canning jars, and process them.

Make baby cereal from roasted whole grains ground fine in a grinder. Prepare as you would oatmeal. An ideal first food is mashed fresh bananas. It cures infantile diarrhea. So do strained carrots, strained cottage cheese, and rice cream.

Cow's milk is not a good food for human babies. After baby weans himself, give him soy milk or nut or seed milks. (Grind nuts or sesame or sunflower seeds and add a little water.) Orange juice is too acid a beverage for his new teeth. A better form of vitamin C is rose hips conserve. Enrich baby's food with soy powder, brewer's yeast, wheat germ oil, lecithin, wheat germ, ground alfalfa sprouts, or molasses. Sweeten only with honey.

HORS D'OEUVRE AND NIBBLES

CURTIS

Good Housekeeping Everyday Cook Book

Cheese Straws

Roll piecrust dough the same thickness as for pies. Cut in strips from six to ten inches wide and cut the strips into straws or sticks a quarter of an inch in width. Lay upon baking sheets, leaving a space between the straws a third the width of the straws. Grate rich cheese, season to taste with salt and red pepper and scatter thickly over the straws and the spaces between them. Put in the oven where the greatest heat will be at the top and bake ten or fifteen minutes. Cut the cheese in the center of the spaces between the straws, remove from the baking sheet with a limber knife and pile tastily on a plate.

—Emma P. Ewing.

CLAIBORNE AND LEE

The Chinese Cookbook

There are hundreds of ways to make fried rice, some good, some bad or indifferent. The same is true of shrimp toast. This is a remarkably good recipe for shrimp toast with a sesame seed topping.

Shrimp Toast with Sesame Seed Topping

⅛ pound fresh, unsalted fatback
½ pound raw shrimps, shelled and deveined
2 egg whites
Salt to taste
1 teaspoon dry sherry or shao hsing wine*
3 tablespoons cornstarch
1 tablespoon chopped fresh coriander leaves* or parsley
12 thin slices white bread
½ cup sesame seeds,* more or less
1 egg yolk
Peanut, vegetable, or corn oil for deep frying

*Available in Chinese markets and by mail order.

1. Drop the fatback into boiling water and simmer about 5 minutes. Drain and chop enough to make 2 tablespoons.

2. Place the shrimps, 1 egg white, salt, wine, chopped fatback, and 2 teaspoons of the cornstarch into the container of an electric blender. Blend on low speed, stirring down as necessary. Continue blending and stirring down to make a spreadable paste. Spoon and scrape into a mixing bowl and stir in the chopped coriander or parsley.

3. Neatly trim away the crusts from the bread slices. Cut each slice into two 2-inch rounds or into triangles.

4. In a small bowl combine the remaining egg white with 2 tablespoons of the cornstarch and a little salt to taste. Brush one side of each round or triangle of bread with the cornstarch mixture.

5. Spoon equal portions of the shrimp mixture onto each round or triangle of bread on the cornstarch-brushed side, smoothing and rounding the top as the mixture is applied.

6. Pour the sesame seeds onto a piece of waxed paper and dip the top of each shrimp-covered round or triangle in the seeds to coat liberally.

7. Blend the egg yolk with the remaining teaspoon of cornstarch. Brush the bottom of the rounds or triangles with the egg-yolk mixture and set the pieces onto a rack. Cover lightly.

8. In a wok or deep-fryer heat the oil, and when it is just hotter than warm add the pieces with the shrimp side up. The oil must not be too hot when the pieces are added or the sesame seeds will scatter in the fat. Turn the heat to medium and let the pieces simmer quite gently in the oil. You will have to coax and encourage the pieces with a fork or a spoon to keep the shrimp side up, but try to. After about 2 minutes the pieces will become easily manageable in the oil. Turn them shrimp side down and cook about 4 minutes. When nicely golden, increase the heat and cook 6 to 7 minutes longer. They should be cooked a total of about 12 to 14 minutes. Drain on paper toweling and serve hot.

YIELD: 24 PIECES

BURROS AND LEVINE

The Elegant But Easy Cookbook

Sherley's Parmesan Puffs

They disappear like soap bubbles.

Mix to a consistency of softened butter

Mayonnaise
Parmesan cheese, freshly grated

Place in center of

Rounds of white bread, 1 inch in diameter
About ⅛ teaspoon chopped onion

Cover bread round completely with

Mayonnaise-cheese mixture

Refrigerate if desired. To serve broil about 5–8 minutes until puffed and brown. Serve immediately.

THOMAS

The Vegetarian Epicure

Spanakopita

Spinach was never like this when I was little, but would that it had been! This puffy, golden-brown pastry is worth the effort of going to a special store for filo *(a Greek kind of strudel dough) and Feta cheese.*

2 lb. fresh spinach
1 lb. *filo*
7 eggs
½ lb. Feta cheese
1 onion
olive oil
salt and pepper
oregano
butter

To prepare the filling: Wash all the spinach well and put the leaves into a large bowl. Sprinkle them heavily with salt and then rub it into the leaves with your hands as you tear them into small pieces. After a few minutes of this, the spinach will be reduced to a quarter of its former bulk. Rinse the salt off thoroughly and drain.

Beat the eggs, crumble the Feta cheese, and mix together. Add to the spinach. Chop the onion, sauté it in some olive oil until it begins to brown, and add that to the spinach also. Season the mixture with lots of fresh-ground black pepper and a little oregano.

Now choose a large, oblong casserole or baking dish (about 9-inch × 13-inch should do it) and butter it. Melt about 3 to 4 tablespoons of butter in a little pot and stack the pound of filo on a flat surface. Brush the top sheet with melted butter and fit it into the baking pan, with the edges hanging over the sides. The pastry sheets are very large and should extend quite a bit over the edges, even after being fitted against the sides of the pan. Continue in this fashion brushing each sheet with butter and fitting it into the pan on top of the others. Turn each sheet slightly so that the corners fan out around the pan rather than being stacked on top of each other. Do this until you only have two or three pastry sheets left.

Now pour the filling in and then fold over the ends of the pastry sheets to cover it, brushing with a little more butter. You should have sort of a strange-looking, wrinkled crust on top when you finish. Butter the remaining sheets and place them on top of the whole thing, folding them down to the size of the pan. With a sharp knife cut through the top layers to the filling in about three places. Brush the top with butter and bake at 375 degrees for 50 minutes. Cut into squares and serve very hot. Serves 8 generously.

JAFFREY

An Invitation to Indian Cooking

Whole-wheat Samosas

SERVES 8–10

Samosas *are deep-fried patties, filled with potatoes or ground meat. I have a simple version of them. This is how they are made. (For stuffing use recipe for* Sookhe Aloo *or* Kheema.*)*

- 2 cups whole-wheat flour
- 3 tablespoons vegetable oil (plus a little extra for brushing on dough)
- ½ teaspoon salt
- Vegetable oil for deep frying, enough for 3–3½ inches in pot

Combine oil and flour and rub together. Add salt and mix. Add 1 cup water, a little at a time, until you have a firm dough. Knead the dough well for 7 to 10 minutes, until smooth. Form into a ball. Brush with a little oil, and cover with a damp cloth. Set aside until ready for use.

If using *Sookhe Aloo* for stuffing, cook it according to the recipe and then crush potatoes coarsely with the back of a slotted spoon.

If using *Kheema* for stuffing, cook *Kheema* until it is very dry, with no liquid left at all. If any fat has accumulated, it should be discarded.

Divide dough into 28 to 30 equal balls. (Each ball makes 2 *samosas*, so you'll end up with about 60.) Flatten each ball and roll it out on a floured surface until it is 3½ to 4 inches in diameter. Cut each round in half. Taking one semicircle at a time, moisten half the length of the cut edge with a finger dipped in water. Form a wide cone with the semicircle, using the moist section to overlap ¼ inch and hold it closed. Fill *samosa* three-fourths full with the stuffing. Moisten the inside edges of the opening and press it shut. Seal this end by pressing down on the outside with the tip of a fork, as you would a pie crust. Prepare the *samosas* this way and keep them covered with a plastic wrap.

When you are ready to fry them, heat the oil in a wok, *karhai*, or a utensil for deep frying. Keep the heat at medium. When oil is hot, drop a *samosa* in to check the temperature. It should start sizzling immediately. Fry 2 to 3 minutes, or until it looks a warm brown. Remove with slotted spoon and drain on paper towels. Do all *samosas* this way. If they brown too fast, lower your heat.

They can be reheated in a 300° oven.

TO SERVE: Place *samosas* on platter and serve hot or warm with either Fresh Green Chutney with Chinese Parsley and Yogurt or Fresh Mint Chutney with Fruit. The chutney is used as a dip.

MADISON

The Greens Cook Book

Hummous

A smooth and nourishing filling for the Pita Salad Sandwich, hummous can also be included as part of a composed salad plate. The flavors are earthy and bright with lemon and garlic.

1 cup dried chick peas (garbanzo beans), soaked overnight
Salt
6 tablespoons tahini or sesame butter
2 cloves garlic, roughly chopped
5 tablespoons lemon juice
3 tablespoons virgin olive oil
Cayenne pepper
½ cup cooking liquid from the beans or water, as needed

Pour off the soaking water from the chick peas, cover them generously with fresh water, and bring them to a boil. Lower the heat to a slow boil, add ¼ teaspoon salt, and cook until the beans are completely soft, about 1½ hours, or more. Or cook the chick peas in a pressure cooker at 15 pounds for 45 minutes.

Drain the cooked beans, reserving the liquid. Put them in a food processor or a blender with the tahini or sesame butter, garlic, lemon juice, olive oil, salt, and a pinch of cayenne pepper, and process or blend until smooth. When the beans are puréed in a blender, extra liquid may be necessary; use the cooking water from the beans, water, or additional olive oil. Taste and adjust the salt, pepper, lemon, and oil to your liking.

MAKES 3 CUPS

BROWN

Helen Brown's West Coast Cook Book

Guacamole

Here is our favorite dip, another Mexican contribution. I recently saw it spelled, phonetically, "waca molay," but not, I assure you, in a West Coast publication.

You'll want very ripe avocados for this—never mind the blemishes, they are easily cut out. Mash a large one in a bowl that has been rubbed with garlic, and season it with ¼ teaspoon each of salt and chili powder, and a teaspoon of lemon juice. Add 2 teaspoons of very finely minced onion. Now taste it and add more salt if need be, and a little more chili powder, if that's the way you like it. The fleshy part of ripe tomatoes, cut in dice, may be added, or small pieces of canned green chilis, or sliced ripe olives, or crisp and crumbled bacon. Mix well and put in a bowl, covering the top with a thin layer of mayonnaise—this to keep the mixture from blackening. Just before serving, stir it well, and serve with corn chips, corn crisps, or tortillas, fried crisp. Guacamole may be served with spears of raw vegetables, too: green peppers, celery, sweet red onions. . . . And it may be used as a dressing for lettuce or tomato salads.

1 large ripe avocado
¼ teaspoon salt (or more)
¼ teaspoon chili powder (or more)
1 teaspoon lemon juice
2 teaspoons minced onion

JUNIOR LEAGUE OF AUGUSTA

Old and New Recipes from the South

Deviled Eggs

Half cover eggs in cold water, cover with lid and boil for 20 minutes. Remove boiling water from pan and pour cold water over eggs until they are chilled—this makes it easy to remove the egg shells. Remove the shells from the eggs.

Cut the eggs in half, the long way. Remove the yolks. Mash the yolks very fine. Add salt, black pepper, paprika, vinegar and mayonnaise to taste. Then stuff each egg-half gently, so that the half will not lose its shape. If you prefer you may add a little lemon juice to the seasoning—and you may leave out the paprika until the last and then sprinkle it lightly over each egg-half after it is filled.

Deviled eggs are nice for picnics—for salads when used with lettuce or watercress, and in combination with white asparagus (canned) and sliced tomatoes.

For a large salad plate combine cold cuts, stuffed tomatoes, or sliced, asparagus put in green pepper rings and deviled eggs, and place on crisp lettuce leaves.

—Mrs. Owen Cheatham

KELLER
The French Laundry Cookbook

Cornets

Salmon Tartare with Sweet Red Onion Crème Fraîche

CORNETS

¼ cup plus 3 tablespoons all-purpose flour
1 tablespoon plus 1 teaspoon sugar
1 teaspoon kosher salt
8 tablespoons (4 ounces) unsalted butter, softened but still cool to the touch
2 large egg whites, cold
2 tablespoons black sesame seeds

SALMON TARTARE, MAKES ABOUT ¾ CUP

4 ounces salmon fillet (belly preferred), skin and any pin bones removed and very finely minced
¾ teaspoon extra virgin olive oil
¾ teaspoon lemon oil
1½ teaspoons finely minced chives
1½ teaspoons finely minced shallots
½ teaspoon kosher salt, or to taste
Small pinch of freshly ground white pepper, or to taste

SWEET RED ONION CRÈME FRAÎCHE

1 tablespoon finely minced red onions
½ cup crème fraîche
¼ teaspoon kosher salt, or to taste
Freshly ground white pepper to taste

24 chive tips (about 1 inch long)

This is one of my favorite dishes to serve to large groups of people—it's fun to look at, it's distinctive, delicious, and doesn't require a plate or silverware. You can eat it standing up, with a glass of Champagne or wine in one hand. At the French Laundry, I use a specially made Lucite holder to serve these cones, but you might fill a bowl with rock salt, say, or peppercorns, and stand the cones up in this to serve them.

FOR THE CORNETS: In a medium bowl, mix together the flour, sugar, and salt. In a separate bowl, whisk the softened butter until it is completely smooth and mayonnaise-like in texture. Using a stiff spatula or spoon, beat the egg whites into the dry ingredients until completely incorporated and smooth. Whisk in the softened butter by thirds, scraping the sides of the bowl as necessary and whisking until the batter is creamy and without any lumps. Transfer the batter to a smaller container, as it will be easier to work with.

Preheat the oven to 400°F.

Make a 4-inch hollow circular stencil. Place a Silpat on the counter (it is easier to work on the Silpat before it is put on the sheet pan). Place the stencil in one corner of the sheet and, holding the stencil flat against the Silpat, scoop some of the batter onto the back of an offset spatula and spread it in an even layer over the stencil. Then run the spatula over the entire stencil to remove any excess batter. After baking the first batch of cornets, you will be able to judge the correct thickness; you may need a little more or less batter to adjust the thickness of the cornets. There should not be any holes in the batter. Lift the stencil and repeat the process to make as many rounds as you have molds or to fill the Silpat, leaving about 1½ inches between the cornets. Sprinkle each cornet with a pinch of black sesame seeds.

Place the Silpat on a heavy baking sheet and bake for 4 to 6 minutes, or until the batter is set and you see it rippling from the heat. The cornets may have browned in some areas, but they will not be evenly browned at this point.

Open the oven door and place the baking sheet on the door. This will help keep the cornets warm as you roll them and prevent them from becoming too stiff to roll. Flip a cornet over on the sheet pan, sesame seed side down, and place a 4½-inch cornet mold at the bottom of the round. If you are right-handed, you will want the pointed end on your left and the open end on your right. The tip of the mold should touch the lower left edge (at about 7 o'clock on a clock face) of the cornet. Fold the bottom of the cornet up and around the mold and carefully roll upward and toward the left to wrap the cornet tightly around the mold; it should remain on the sheet pan as you roll. Leave the cornet wrapped around the mold and continue to roll the cornets around molds; as you proceed, arrange the rolled cornets, seam side down, on the sheet pan so they lean against each other, to prevent them from rolling.

When all the cornets are rolled, return them to the oven shelf, close the door, and bake for an additional 3 to 4 minutes to set the seams and color the cornets a golden brown. If the color is uneven, stand the cornets on end for a minute or so more, until the color is even. Remove the cornets from the oven and allow to cool just slightly, 30 seconds or so.

Gently remove the cornets from the molds and cool for several minutes on paper towels. Remove the Silpat from the baking sheet, wipe the excess butter from it, and allow it to cool down before spreading the next batch. Store the cornets for up to 2 days (for maximum flavor) in an airtight container.

FOR THE SALMON TARTARE: With a sharp knife, finely mince the salmon fillet (do not use a food processor, as it would damage the texture of the fish) and place it in a small bowl. Stir in the remaining ingredients and taste for seasoning. Cover the bowl and refrigerate the tartare for at least 30 minutes, or up to 12 hours.

FOR THE SWEET RED ONION CRÈME FRAÎCHE: Place the red onions in a small strainer and rinse them under cold water for several seconds. Dry them on paper towels. In a small metal bowl, whisk the crème fraîche for about 30 seconds to 1 minute, or until it holds soft peaks when you lift the whisk. Fold in the chopped onions and season to taste with the salt and white pepper. Transfer the onion cream to a container, cover, and refrigerate until ready to serve for up to 6 hours.

TO COMPLETE: Fill just the top ½ inch of each cornet with onion cream, leaving the bottom of the cone empty. (This is easily done using a pastry bag fitted with a ¼-inch plain tip or with the tip of a small knife.) Spoon about 1½ teaspoons of the tartare over the onion cream and mold it into a dome resembling a scoop of ice cream. Lay a chive tip against one side of the tartare to garnish.

MAKES 24 CORNETS

TO MAKE THE STENCIL: Cut the rim from the top of a plastic container. Trace two concentric circles on the lid, the inner 4 inches in diameter, the outer about 4½ inches. Sketch a thumb tab that will make it easy to lift the stencil off the silicon-coated Silpat. Trim around the tab and outer circle. Remove the inner circle so that you have a hollow ring. The batter gets spread to the stencil's edges, then it's lifted off, leaving perfectly shaped rounds.

BÉGUÉ

Mme. Bégué's Recipes of Old New Orleans Creole Cookery

Shrimp Remoulade

A favorite way of serving cold boiled shrimp in New Orleans. On a bed of crisp, shredded lettuce leaves place the shrimp (after they have been in the ice box for several hours) and over them pour the "sauce remoulade," which is made as follows:

Six tablespoons of olive oil, two tablespoons of vinegar, one tablespoon of paprika, a half teaspoon of pepper, four teaspoons Creole mustard, a little horseradish, celery heart chopped fine, one-half chopped white onion, a little chopped parsley, salt well and give the sauce a good mixing. Chill in the ice box and serve on the chilled shrimp just before placing a wonderful salad before your guests.

ROSSO AND LUKINS

The Silver Palate Cookbook

Salmon Mousse

This has become a Silver Palate classic. It was with us the first day we opened and the only time that it is not in the refrigerator on any given day of the year is when we've sold out. It is light, pretty, refreshing and one of those foods that you enjoy time after time.

1 envelope unflavored gelatin
¼ cup cold water
½ cup boiling water
½ cup Hellmann's mayonnaise
1 tablespoon lemon juice
1 tablespoon finely grated onion
dash of Tabasco
¼ teaspoon sweet paprika
1 teaspoon salt
2 tablespoons finely chopped dill
2 cups finely flaked poached fresh salmon or canned salmon, skin and bones removed
1 cup heavy cream

1. Soften the gelatin in the cold water in a large mixing bowl. Stir in the boiling water and whisk the mixture slowly until gelatin dissolves. Cool to room temperature.

2. Whisk in the mayonnaise, lemon juice, grated onion, Tabasco, paprika, salt and dill. Stir to blend completely and refrigerate for about 20 minutes, or until the mixture begins to thicken slightly.

3. Fold in the finely flaked salmon. In a separate bowl, whip the cream until it is thickened to peaks and fluffy. Fold gently into the salmon mixture.

4. Transfer the mixture to a 6- to 8-cup bowl or decorative mold. Cover and chill for at least 4 hours.

5. Serve on toasts, black bread or crackers. Or serve as a first course, garnished with watercress.

AT LEAST 12 PORTIONS

TROPP

The Modern Art of Chinese Cooking

Strange Flavor Eggplant

In Chinese poetry and art criticism the word kuai *can mean "odd" as in downright weird, or "strange" as in fascinating and unusual. In cooking, there is no such confusion. "Strange flavor" dishes are always extraordinary—spicy, subtle, sweet, tart, and tangy all at the same time, an ineffable blend of tastes. Usually, a strange flavor sauce has sesame paste as a component and is credited with a Szechwanese origin, but mine is clear and thin in a Shanghai mode. Instead of coating the eggplant, it permeates it. • This is an extremely versatile dish, delicious hot or cold, shredded for presentation as a zesty vegetable or puréed for serving as a novel hors d'oeuvre spread with crackers. The complete lack of oiliness and the piquant flavor make it a great favorite. • I prefer the elongated Chinese or Japanese eggplants, which are sweet and not watery, with a pleasantly edible skin. If unavailable, use the large Western variety and pick the smallest good-looking ones on the shelf. Chosen by Chinese standards, the skin should be unblemished and somewhat dull, and the plant should feel firm though not hard to the touch. • The eggplant may be baked a day or two before saucing, and refrigerated another day before serving. The flavors become even fuller if the dish is made in advance.*

TECHNIQUE NOTES:

Cooking eggplant in the oven eliminates the oiliness caused by stir-frying and the wateriness engendered by steaming. It is a Western technique I use gladly in the interest of a better dish.

When adding an assortment of minced condiments that includes red chili pepper to heated oil, add the pepper last. The oil will be somewhat cooled and tempered by the other ingredients, and the chili will be less likely to scorch.

Garnishing a dish with sesame oil just before it leaves the pan imparts aroma and luster. In the case of the eggplant, it also adds a pronounced flavor and a needed touch of oil, without which the eggplant tastes flat.

YIELDS ABOUT 2 CUPS, ENOUGH TO SERVE 4–5 AS A LIGHT VEGETABLE COURSE, 6–8 AS PART OF A MULTICOURSE MEAL, 10–15 AS AN HORS D'OEUVRE SPREAD WITH CRACKERS.

INGREDIENTS

1–1¼ pounds firm eggplant, slender Chinese or Japanese variety recommended

AROMATICS

3–4 large cloves garlic, stem end removed, lightly smashed and peeled (to equal 1 tablespoon minced fresh garlic)
1 large walnut-size nugget fresh ginger (to equal 1 tablespoon minced ginger)
1 hefty whole scallion, cut into 1-inch lengths (to equal 3 tablespoons chopped scallion)
rounded ¼–½ teaspoon dried red chili flakes

LIQUID SEASONINGS

2½–3 tablespoons thin (regular) soy sauce
2½–3 tablespoons packed light brown sugar
1 teaspoon unseasoned Chinese or Japanese rice vinegar
1 tablespoon hot water
2 tablespoons corn or peanut oil
1 teaspoon Chinese or Japanese sesame oil

TO GARNISH

1 tablespoon green scallion rings

BAKING THE EGGPLANT: Preheat the oven to 475° and set the rack in the middle of the oven. Tear off the leaves, rinse the eggplant, and pat dry. Prick in several places with a fork to act as steam vents during baking.

Bake the eggplant in a baking dish or on a baking sheet until it gives easily when you press it with a chopstick or spoon, about 20–40 minutes depending on size. Turn the eggplant over once midway through baking to insure even cooking. Remove to a plate and allow to cool. The eggplant will look like a deflated, wrinkled balloon.

Once cool, the eggplant may be sealed airtight and refrigerated for up to 2 days before saucing.

CUTTING THE EGGPLANT AND READYING THE SAUCE: Discard the stem end and cut the eggplant in half lengthwise.

Peel large Western eggplant fully. The peel should tear off easily with your fingers.

Asian eggplant can be peeled entirely, or you may leave on the bit of peel that inevitably clings to the flesh and is quite good tasting. Drain Western eggplant of any watery liquid, but reserve the thick, brown "liqueur" often exuded by Asian eggplant.

To purée the eggplant, cut it into large chunks, then process in a food processor or blender until completely smooth. For shreds, tear the eggplant into long, pencil-thin strips with your fingers. It is slower than slicing with a cleaver, but the texture is inimitable and the irregular contours drink up the sauce. Once puréed or shredded, the eggplant may be sealed airtight and refrigerated overnight. Bring to room temperature before saucing.

Mince the garlic, ginger, and scallion until fine in the work bowl of a food processor fitted with the steel knife, scraping down as necessary. Alternatively, mince the ingredients by hand. Put in a dish alongside the red pepper. Sealed airtight, the aromatics may be refrigerated for several hours.

Combine the soy, sugar, vinegar, and water, stirring to dissolve the sugar. Use the larger amount of soy sauce and sugar for Western eggplant.

STIR-FRYING THE DISH: Have the eggplant and the remaining ingredients all within easy reach of your stovetop.

Heat a wok or medium-size, heavy skillet over high heat until hot enough to evaporate a bead of water on contact. Add the corn or peanut oil, swirl to glaze the pan, then lower the heat to medium. When the oil is hot enough to sizzle a bit of garlic, add the aromatics, nudging the chili flakes in last. Stir until fully fragrant, about 20–40 seconds, adjusting the heat so they foam without browning. When the fragrance is pronounced, stir the liquids and scrape them into the pan. Stir, wait for the liquid to boil around the edges, then add the eggplant and stir to combine it with the sauce and heat it through. Turn off the heat and taste. Adjust if required with a bit more sugar to bring the spiciness to the fore, then add the sesame oil and stir to combine. Scrape the eggplant into a serving bowl of contrasting color, then smooth the top with the spatula.

Serve the eggplant hot, tepid, at room temperature, or chilled, garnished with scallion. Left to sit for several hours or overnight, the flavors will enlarge and the spiciness will become pronounced. Cover tightly and refrigerate once cool.

Leftovers keep beautifully 3–4 days, sealed airtight and refrigerated.

MENU SUGGESTIONS:

This is an excellent opening to a hot dinner, paired with a Chenin Blanc. As part of a cold table, you might partner it with Tea and Spice Smoked Chicken, Master Sauce Chicken, Scallion and Ginger Explosion Shrimp, *and* Orchid's Tangy Cool Noodles. *In a Western menu, it is a delicious accompaniment to unadorned broiled or grilled poultry or fish.*

KELLER

The French Laundry Cookbook

"Oysters and Pearls"

Sabayon of Pearl Tapioca with Malpeque Oysters and Osetra Caviar

TAPIOCA

⅓ cup small pearl tapioca
1¾ cups milk
16 meaty oysters, such as Malpeque, scrubbed with a brush
1¼ cups heavy cream
Freshly ground black pepper
¼ cup crème fraîche
Kosher salt

SABAYON

4 large egg yolks
¼ cup reserved oyster juice (from above)

SAUCE

3 tablespoons dry vermouth
Remaining reserved oyster juice (from above)
1½ tablespoons minced shallots
1½ tablespoons white wine vinegar
8 tablespoons (4 ounces) unsalted butter, cut into 8 pieces
1 tablespoon minced chives
1 to 2 ounces osetra caviar

Timing is important in the completion of this dish. The cooking should be a continuous process, so have the cream whipped, the water for the sabayon hot, and the remaining ingredients ready.

FOR THE TAPIOCA: Soak the tapioca in 1 cup of the milk for 1 hour. (Setting it in a warm place will speed up the rehydration of the pearls.)

TO SHUCK THE OYSTERS: Trim away the muscle and the outer ruffled edge of each oyster and place the trimmings in a saucepan. Reserve the whole trimmed oysters and strain the oyster juice into a separate bowl. You should have about ½ cup of juice.

TO COOK THE TAPIOCA: In a bowl, whip ½ cup of the cream just until it holds its shape; reserve in the refrigerator.

Drain the softened tapioca in a strainer and discard the milk. Rinse the tapioca under cold running water, then place it in a small heavy pot.

Pour the remaining ¾ cup milk and ¾ cup cream over the oyster trimmings. Bring to a simmer, then strain the infused liquid onto the tapioca. Discard the trimmings.

Cook the tapioca over medium heat, stirring constantly with a wood spoon, until it has thickened and the spoon leaves a trail when it is pulled through, 7 to 8 minutes. Continue to cook for another 5 to 7 minutes, until the tapioca has no resistance in the center and is translucent. The mixture will be sticky and if you lift some on the spoon and let it fall, some should still cling to the spoon. Remove the pot from the heat and set aside in a warm place.

FOR THE SABAYON: Place the egg yolks and the ¼ cup oyster juice in a metal bowl set over a pan of hot water. Whisk vigorously over medium heat for 2 to 3 minutes to incorporate as much air as possible. The finished sabayon will have thickened and lightened, the foam will have subsided, and the sabayon will hold a ribbon when it falls from the whisk. If the mixture begins to break, remove it from the heat and whisk quickly off the heat for a moment to recombine, then return to the heat.

Stir the hot sabayon into the tapioca, along with a generous amount of black pepper. Mix in the crème fraîche and the whipped cream. The tapioca will be a creamy pale yellow with the tapioca pearls suspended in the mixture. Season lightly with salt, remembering that the oysters and the caviar garnish will both be salty. Immediately spoon ¼ cup tapioca into each of eight 4- by 5-inch gratin dishes (with a 3- to 4-ounce capacity). Tap the gratin dishes on the counter so that the tapioca forms an even layer. Cover and refrigerate until ready to use, or for up to a day.

TO COMPLETE: Preheat the oven to 350°F.

FOR THE SAUCE: Combine the vermouth, the remaining reserved oyster juice, the shallots, and vinegar in a small saucepan. Bring to a simmer and simmer until most of the liquid has evaporated but the shallots are glazed, not dry. Whisk in the butter piece by piece, adding a new piece only when the previous one is almost incorporated.

Meanwhile, place the dishes of tapioca on a baking sheet and heat in the oven for 4 to 5 minutes, or until they just begin to puff up.

Add the oysters and the chives to the sauce to warm through.

Spoon 2 oysters and some of the sauce over each gratin and garnish the top with a quenelle, or small oval scoop, of caviar. Serve immediately.

MAKES 8 SERVINGS

NATHAN

Jewish Cooking in America

Mama Batalin's Potato Knishes

Don't be intimidated by this strudel dough. It is easy and fun to make. Try doing it with a friend.

FILLING

4 large onions, sliced
2 tablespoons vegetable oil
2½ pounds russet (baking) potatoes
Salt to taste
1 large egg
½ cup chopped parsley
1 teaspoon salt or to taste
Freshly ground pepper to taste

DOUGH

2 large eggs
½ cup vegetable oil plus additional for rolling the dough
1 cup water
1 tablespoon white vinegar
½ teaspoon salt
4 cups all-purpose flour

1. Slowly cook the onions in the oil in a skillet, covered, over a low heat. Let the onions "sweat" for about 20 minutes, or until they are soft. Then remove the cover and let fry over a medium heat until golden brown. Don't drain.

2. Meanwhile peel the potatoes and cut them in half. Put them in a large pot filled with cold water and salt to taste. Bring to a boil, then turn the heat down, and cook until soft, about 15 minutes. Drain and cool for 5 minutes.

3. Mash the potatoes and add the egg, the parsley, salt, and pepper. Add the onions with the oil and mix well with your hands. Set aside while preparing the dough.

4. Beat the eggs and reserve about 1 tablespoon of egg for the glaze. Mix the rest with the oil, water, vinegar, and salt. Add the flour gradually, beating first with a spoon and eventually your hands as you knead the dough. Continue to add enough flour to make a smooth dough. Shape into 4 balls and let rest, covered with a cloth, about a half hour to relax the gluten.

5. Roll each ball of dough out as thin as possible into a flat rectangle. Flour well and place between 2 sheets of waxed paper. Let sit for about 15 minutes.

6. Using your hands, carefully stretch each rectangle as thin as possible, about 12 to 14 inches long by 4 to 5 inches wide. Spread one quarter of the filling (about 1½ cups) onto approximately one third of the dough, leaving a 1-inch border.

7. Holding onto the waxed paper, roll up the dough like a jelly roll, brushing oil across the top a couple of times as you roll. Using the side of your hand like a knife, divide the roll into 2-inch knishes. Then pinch the open ends shut. Repeat with the remaining balls and dough. Place the knishes, flat side down, on a greased cookie sheet, leaving a 2-inch space between each. You will have to bake in batches.

8. Mix the reserved tablespoon of egg with a little water. Brush the tops with the egg wash and bake in a preheated 375-degree oven for 25 to 30 minutes or until golden brown.

YIELD: APPROXIMATELY 60 KNISHES

SHERATON

From My Mother's Kitchen

Cheese Blintzes

Cheese was the only filling we ever had in blintzes at home, and they were served as desserts, as accompaniments to afternoon or evening coffee, as breakfast, or as a main part of a light dinner. They freeze very well and should be fried without having first been thawed. The optional touch of wheat germ is my own.

CRÈPE BATTER

2 extra-large eggs
⅔ cup milk
⅓ cup water, or as needed
Pinch of salt
6 to 7 heaping tablespoons flour (1 scant cup)

CHEESE FILLING

½ pound dry (uncreamed) pot cheese plus ½ pound farmer cheese, or 1 pound farmer cheese
1 extra-large or jumbo egg
1½ tablespoons sugar, or to taste
½ teaspoon cinnamon, or to taste
1 teaspoon vanilla, or to taste
Pinch of salt
2 heaping tablespoons toasted wheat germ (optional)
Sweet butter, for frying
Sour cream, as accompaniment

Beat the eggs lightly with a fork. Using a rotary beater, beat in the milk and water and a pinch of salt. Gradually beat in the flour, 1 heaping tablespoonful at a time. Be sure each addition is thoroughly absorbed before adding the next. Stop when the batter is the consistency of heavy cream. If there are air bubbles, stir in a little water and hit the bottom of the bowl against the counter top so the bubbles will rise to the surface. Bubbles will become holes in finished crèpes. If the batter has lumps of flour, pour through a fine sieve, rubbing undissolved flour through. Let the batter stand for 30 minutes before frying. Stir before frying.

Prepare the cheese filling by carefully mashing the pot cheese (if you use it) and farmer cheese together. For finest results, both can be rubbed through a sieve. Mix in the egg, sugar, cinnamon, vanilla, salt, and wheat germ, if you use it. Mash together well and adjust the seasoning.

To fry crèpes, it is best to have a traditional crèpe pan or a 6½-inch skillet. Have on hand 4 or 5 tablespoons of melted sweet butter. Batter is most convenient to pour if it is in a pitcher or a bowl with a lip. Add 1 tablespoon melted butter to the batter. Stir the batter between pourings; do not beat.

Spread a thin film of butter on the skillet and heat until a drop of water froths but does not jump or sizzle. Pour in just enough batter to cover the pan. After pouring, tip and rotate the pan so the batter covers the bottom, then quickly pour excess batter back into the bowl. If the batter sets in ripples as it is poured, the pan is too hot; if it slides around without setting, the pan is not hot enough. Work very quickly so excess is poured off before it sets and the crèpe becomes too thick. When the crèpe looks dry around the edges and begins to curl from the pan, invert the pan over a clean towel and drop the crèpe out. Rebutter the pan every 2 or 3 crèpes. Crèpes should not be brown, but a pale golden glaze is acceptable. Ideally, they should be the color of boiled noodles. Be sure you keep the cooked sides up on the towel. Continue until all the crèpes are made; you should have about 14.

The lip or "tab" formed when excess batter is poured back will be convenient for filling the crèpe.

With the tab toward you, on the cooked side of each crèpe place a rounded tablespoonful of cheese filling. Turn tab with filling over once, fold over the side of the crèpes, then continue folding to form a small rectangle. Fill all crèpes before folding, so the amount of filling in each can be adjusted to fill all crèpes evenly.

Place fold side down on a platter and store in the refrigerator until just before serving. Or wrap the blintzes in foil, two to a packet, and freeze.

To fry blintzes, heat enough butter in a frying pan to enable the blintzes to swim slightly. Fry slowly over moderate heat until the first side is golden brown. Turn and fry the second side. If the blintzes are frozen, keep the heat very low and cover the pan for the first 7 or 8 minutes.

By the time the blintzes are golden brown and crisp on both sides, the filling should be thoroughly hot all the way through, so adjust the frying time accordingly.

Serve immediately with beaten sour cream, to be spooned on at the table.

**YIELD: ABOUT 14 BLINTZES;
2 TO 4 BLINTZES PER SERVING**

CASAS
The Foods and Wines of Spain

Empanadillas de Carne

Mini Meat Pies

START PREPARATION AN HOUR AND A HALF IN ADVANCE.

At the busy Bar Coruña in Santiago de Compostela, trays of these spherical meat pies are constantly emerging from the kitchen and are devoured by the two- and three-deep crowds at the bar. The favorite accompaniment is the thick raspberry-colored Ribeiro wine of Galicia.

The pies are made with a light yeast dough and are filled with a spicy meat mixture. They are excellent hot or cold.

MAKES 32 MINI MEAT PIES

DOUGH

1 package dry yeast
¼ cup warm water
3½ cups flour
½ teaspoon salt
1 egg, lightly beaten
1 cup warm milk
2 tablespoons melted butter

FILLING

1 tablespoon olive oil
1 large onion, finely chopped
3 cloves garlic, minced
4 tablespoons minced green pepper
1 pound ground beef
Salt
Freshly ground pepper
3 tablespoons tomato paste
½ cup water
1½ tablespoons dry red wine
¼ teaspoon crushed dried red chili pepper

Oil for frying

To make the dough, dissolve the yeast in the warm water. Mix together in a bowl the flour and salt. Add the egg, then stir in the warm milk, butter, and the yeast mixture. Turn onto a working surface and knead a minute or two, just until the dough is smooth and no longer sticky, adding more flour as necessary. Place the dough in a bowl greased with oil, turning to coat with the oil. Cover with a towel and leave in a warm spot until doubled in bulk, about 1½ hours.

Meanwhile, prepare the filling. Heat the olive oil in a large skillet and sauté the onion, garlic, and green pepper until the green pepper is tender. Add the meat and cook over a high flame until it begins to brown. Season with salt and pepper. Add the tomato paste, water, wine, and red pepper. Cover and cook 10 minutes.

Divide the dough into thirty-two 1½-inch balls. Roll each into a 3-inch circle. Place 1 tablespoon of the filling in the center of each circle, pull up the sides, and pinch to seal.

Heat the frying oil, at least 1 inch deep, in a skillet. Lower the heat to medium and fry the meat pies slowly, turning frequently, until they are golden. Drain.

ROJAS-LOMBARDI

The Art of South American Cooking

Caldudas

Chilean Empanadas

MAKES ABOUT 16 EMPANADAS

While many kinds of empanadas are found in Chile, calduda *is considered* the *Chilean empanada. The meat is slowly cooked in a* caldo, *or stock, and as the stock evaporates to almost nothing, the meat becomes soft as butter and very moist.*

The filling, or pino, *is sweetened with raisins, which also contrast with the tart taste of olives.*

DOUGH

3 cups all-purpose flour
1 teaspoon coarse salt
8 tablespoons (1 stick) unsalted butter, at room temperature, cut in bits
2 egg yolks
2 tablespoons tarragon vinegar or white-wine vinegar
9 tablespoons cold water

FILLING

1 tablespoon Paprika Oil or olive oil mixed with 1 teaspoon Spanish paprika and ⅛ teaspoon cayenne
2 tablespoons unsalted butter
2 medium onions, peeled and finely chopped (2 cups)
½ pound ground lean beef
1 teaspoon finely chopped fresh oregano or ¼ teaspoon dried oregano
2 teaspoons coarse salt
1 bay leaf
½ cup Beef Stock
3 tablespoons seedless raisins
8 Kalamata olives, pitted and chopped
1 hard-boiled egg, chopped

GLAZE

1 egg yolk
1 whole egg
1 tablespoon cold water

1. Sift the flour and salt into a bowl. Add the butter, egg yolks, and vinegar and mix quickly and thoroughly with your fingertips until all ingredients are well incorporated. Add 5 tablespoons of the water and continue mixing, adding just enough of the remaining water, a little at a time, to make a firm dough. Refrigerate until ready to use.

2. For the filling, heat the oil and butter in a sauté pan. Add the onions and sauté over medium heat until light brown around the edges, about 5 minutes. Add the beef, oregano, salt, and bay leaf and cook, until all the liquid has evaporated. Add the stock, and continue cooking until the stock has almost—but not quite—evaporated. Mix in the raisins and olives. Remove from heat and let cool. Stir in the chopped hard-boiled egg. Correct the seasoning with salt to taste; set aside.

3. Preheat the oven to 375 degrees.

4. On a floured board, roll out the dough about ⅛ inch thick, shaping it into a 16-inch square. Cut out circles about 5 inches in diameter. Knead and re-roll the scraps and cut into additional circles. Place a heaping tablespoon of the meat filling about ½ inch from the edge of each circle. Brush the border of the circle with juices from the filling or with water. Fold the dough over to form a half-moon, pressing the edges together with your fingertips or the tines of a fork to seal. Prick the top of each empanada once or twice with the tines of the fork. Repeat this process until all the empanadas are assembled.

5. Make the glaze by beating the egg yolk and egg with the water.

6. Spread parchment paper on a baking sheet. Arrange the empanadas on top and brush with glaze. Bake for 30 minutes, or until golden. Remove the baking tray from the oven, transfer the empanadas to a serving platter or individual plates, and serve hot.

LAGASSE
Emeril's New New Orleans Cooking

Goat Cheese Quesadilla with Guacamole and Pico di Gallo

MAKES 4 FIRST-COURSE SERVINGS

This is an unusual twist on a Tex-Mex favorite; the goat cheese is an unexpected and delightful surprise. Homemade goat cheese would be ideal, and, indeed, we make our own at the restaurant. We were hoping to include a recipe here so you could make your own, too, but found that one ingredient is difficult to come by. That ingredient is rennet, a natural enzyme whose function is to speed the cheese-making process by coagulating the milk. Never mind. Just get yourself some high-quality goat cheese at your local cheese shop.

2 cups Pico di Gallo
1 cup Guacamole
½ pound soft goat cheese, such as Montrachet
2 teaspoons minced shallots
½ teaspoon minced garlic
1 tablespoon chopped fresh cilantro
½ teaspoon ground cumin
½ teaspoon chili powder
½ teaspoon salt
½ teaspoon white pepper
1 tablespoon olive oil
4 teaspoons unsalted butter, softened, in all
8 small (6-inch) corn tortillas (see The Last Word)

1. Prepare the Pico di Gallo, and set aside.

2. Prepare the Guacamole, cover tightly with plastic wrap, and set aside.

3. Combine the goat cheese, shallots, garlic, cilantro, cumin, chili powder, salt, pepper, and oil in a bowl. Mix with a large spoon until thoroughly blended.

4. Spread ½ teaspoon of the butter on 1 side of each of the 8 tortillas and turn them over.

5. Spread one-quarter of the goat cheese mixture on the unbuttered side of each of 4 of the tortillas. Cover the cheese with another tortilla, buttered side up, sandwich-style. Press together lightly, taking care not to squeeze out any of the goat cheese filling.

6. Heat a medium nonstick skillet over medium-high heat. When the skillet is hot, sauté a quesadilla, turning it 3 times, until golden brown and crisp on both sides, for about 4 minutes in all. Repeat the procedure with the remaining quesadillas, keeping those that are finished warm until they're all ready.

7. To serve, cut each quesadilla into 4 wedges, and arrange on a dinner plate. Place ¼ cup of the Guacamole in the center, and drizzle ½ cup of the Pico di Gallo over the Guacamole and between the quesadilla wedges.

THE LAST WORD

Tortillas dry out very quickly; keep them in their bag or keep them covered with a clean, damp towel until you're ready to butter them.

BURROS AND LEVINE
The Elegant But Easy Cookbook

Chafing-Dish Meatballs

50–60 MEATBALLS

Probably the most popular hors d'oeuvres in the book.

Combine

2 lbs. ground meat
1 slightly beaten egg
1 large grated onion
Salt to taste

Mix and shape into small balls. Drop into sauce of:

1 twelve-oz bottle chili sauce
1 ten-oz jar grape jelly
Juice of 1 lemon

Simmer until brown. Refrigerate or freeze. To serve bring to room temperature. Reheat in chafing dish and serve with cocktail picks.

TROPP
The Modern Art of Chinese Cooking

Hunan Pork Dumplings with Hot Sauce

Everything in Hunan is on a grand scale—the dramatic variety and beauty of the terrain, the abundance of the harvest, the sheer spiciness and flavor of the food, and the expansive warmth of the Hunan personality. It is, in many ways, the Texas of China. Even the chopsticks, the bowls, and the dumplings of Hunan are enormous. • For a dumpling-maker, bigger dumplings mean less work. For a dumpling eater, the bonus is a hearty mouthful as opposed to a polite nibble. I cast my vote on both counts and recommend it as a fine place to begin if you are new to making dumplings. • In Hunan, these dumplings are traditionally boiled. You may, however, pan-fry them Peking-style. • The dumplings may be shaped and refrigerated, or even flash-frozen, in advance. To boil them and serve them forth takes only minutes.

TECHNIQUE NOTES

In contrast to steamed dumpling wrappers, the wrappers for water-boiled dumplings are made with cold water. The result is a sturdy, as opposed to a silky, dough that will withstand the hubbub of boiling.

When boiling the dumplings, the repeated addition of a cup of cold water stalls the vigorous boiling without significantly altering the cooking temperature of the water. The skins remain intact, and a minimum of flavor is leached by the water.

YIELDS ABOUT 2 DOZEN LARGE DUMPLINGS, ENOUGH TO SERVE 3–4 AS A SUBSTANTIAL MAIN DISH, 8–12 AS PART OF A MULTICOURSE MEAL.

FOR THE WRAPPERS

2½ cups all-purpose flour
about ¾ cup cold water
additional flour, for rolling out the dough

FOR THE FILLING

½ pound crisp Chinese cabbage leaves, the variety that are evenly broad and a pale white-green
1 teaspoon coarse kosher salt
¾ pound hand-chopped or coarsely ground pork butt
1 tablespoon finely minced fresh ginger
¼ cup coarsely chopped green and white scallion, or 3 tablespoons chopped Chinese chives
1 tablespoon thin (regular) soy sauce
1 tablespoon Chinese rice wine or quality, dry sherry
1 tablespoon Chinese or Japanese sesame oil
1 teaspoon coarse kosher salt
¼ teaspoon freshly ground pepper (optional)

SAUCE INGREDIENTS

¼ cup thin (regular) soy sauce
2 tablespoons white vinegar or unseasoned Chinese or Japanese rice vinegar
2 teaspoons Chinese or Japanese sesame oil
½–¾ teaspoon Chinese chili sauce, or substitute 1–2 teaspoons hot chili oil for the sesame oil above
pinch sugar
2 tablespoons thin-cut green and white scallion rings or coarsely chopped fresh coriander

MAKING THE DOUGH

IF YOU HAVE A FOOD PROCESSOR

Put the flour in the work bowl of a food processor fitted with the steel knife. With the machine running add the water in a thin stream through the feed tube just until the dough clumps in a near-ball around the blade. You may not use all the water or you may need a bit more, depending on the dryness of the flour. After a ball is formed, run the machine 10 seconds more to knead the dough.

Turn the dough out onto a lightly floured board and knead gently by hand about 30 seconds, until it is earlobe-soft and smooth, and will bounce gently back when pressed lightly with a finger. Dust the board only if the dough is sticking. When processed correctly it will need little or no additional flour.

Put the dough in a small bowl, seal airtight with plastic film, then set aside to rest 30 minutes at room temperature or overnight in the refrigerator. Bring to room temperature before rolling out.

IF YOU DO NOT HAVE A FOOD PROCESSOR

Put the flour in a large mixing bowl. Stirring with chopsticks or a large spoon, combine it with enough water dribbled slowly into the bowl to form a stiff dough. Knead gently by hand on a lightly floured board 5–10 minutes, until earlobe-soft, smooth, and elastic enough to spring gently back when pressed lightly with a finger. Seal and let rest as above.

MAKING THE FILLING

Chop the cabbage until pea-size, sprinkle with 1 teaspoon kosher salt, and toss well to combine. Let stand for 10 minutes, drain, then squeeze firmly between your palms or wring out enfolded in cheesecloth to remove excess moisture.

Scatter the cabbage in a large bowl, add the pork, then sprinkle the remaining filling ingredients on top. Stir briskly in one direction until well blended, with chopsticks or a fork, then throw the mixture lightly against the inside of the bowl 5 or 6 times to compact it. (This makes it cohesive enough to go inside the dumpling wrapper, but still loose and coarse enough to have a good texture.) For best flavor, seal the filling airtight with a piece of plastic pressed directly on the surface and let stand 30 minutes at room temperature or up to 24 hours in the refrigerator. Bring to room temperature before using.

ROLLING OUT THE DOUGH AND CUTTING THE WRAPPERS

Remove the dough to a lightly floured board and knead gently with the heel of one hand just until smooth, about 10 seconds. Divide the dough into 3 equal pieces with a sharp knife. Roll out 1 piece at a time, keeping the remainder covered against drying.

Dust the board lightly, then press the first piece of dough into a flat disk and roll out to an even thinness of ⅛ inch, dusting the dough and the board lightly as needed to prevent sticking. Put your eye level to the board and run your fingers over the dough to be sure it is evenly thin.

Use a sharp, floured 3½ inch cutter to cut out as many dough rounds as possible, cutting them right next to one another to minimize scraps. Line up the wrappers on a lightly floured surface and cover them with a dry cloth. Squeeze the scraps into a ball and put aside with the remaining dough.

Fill and shape the first group of wrappers before you roll out the next piece of dough. When all 3 pieces have been rolled out and shaped into dumplings, gently knead the scraps together in a single ball on an unfloured board, then roll out and cut the last wrappers.

FILLING AND SHAPING THE DUMPLINGS

Line a baking sheet with silicone (no-stick) parchment paper to hold the finished dumplings. If you don't have the parchment, flour the baking sheet evenly to prevent the dumplings from sticking. Have the filling, a tablespoon, and the tray alongside the wrappers.

Fill one wrapper at a time, keeping the remaining covered. Put 1 level tablespoon of filling off-center in the wrapper, and nudge it with your finger into a half-moon shape, about 2 inches long. You needn't be precise; shaping the filling simply makes the dumpling easier to seal. Pleat and press the dumpling closed. When you are finished, the dumpling should be sealed tightly and prettily and should curve gracefully into an arc and rest flat on its smooth bottom.

Homemade wrappers are typically soft and moist, and you should have no problem sealing them. If, however, the dough has dried and will not adhere to itself (which is the case with store-bought wrappers), run a moist finger lightly around the edge of the circle before folding and pleating the dough. Do not use too much water, or the dough will turn soggy.

Transfer the finished dumpling to the tray, then cover with a dry cloth to prevent drying. Leave ¾ inch between the dumplings; they will spread a bit as they rest. Check midway to see if the dumplings are sticking to the paper or the sheet, and dust with additional flour if needed.

When all the dumplings are shaped, you may seal the tray airtight with plastic wrap or enfold it in a big bag from the cleaners and refrigerate the dumplings for several hours. Or, you may flash-freeze them on the tray until firm, bag airtight, and freeze for several weeks. Cook frozen dumplings when only partially thawed, while the dough is still firm. Cook refrigerated dumplings directly from the refrigerator.

BOILING THE DUMPLINGS

About 25 minutes before serving, put as many large bowls as you have dumpling eaters in a low oven to warm. Mix the sauce ingredients, and adjust to taste. The sauce should be high-seasoned and spicy.

Fill a 6–7-quart pot with 3 quarts cold unsalted water, cover, and bring to a rolling boil over high heat. Remove the cover, then quickly drop in the dumplings one by one. With chopsticks or a wooden spoon gently stir two or three times to separate the dumplings. Cover the pot and cook *only* until the water returns to a boil. Keep an eye on the lid to see when steam begins to escape, indicating the water is boiling.

Remove the cover, add 1 cup of cold water to the pot, and re-cover. When the water returns to a boil, remove the cover, pour in another cup of cold water, and replace the cover. Repeat this process once more, for a total of 3 cups of cold water. After the third cup, while you are waiting for the water to return to a boil, stir up the sauce and divide it evenly among the individual bowls.

When the water returns to a boil, turn off the heat and uncover the pot. Fish the dumplings from the water with a large Chinese mesh spoon, hold them briefly above the pot to drain, then transfer them swiftly and still dripping a bit of water to the bowls. If you have only a small spoon with which to retrieve the dumplings, transfer them in batches to a large metal colander.

Serve the dumplings at once, accompanied by small Chinese ladles or Western soup spoons, and let each participant toss his or her own dumplings in the sauce.

HOW TO EAT A CHINESE DUMPLING

Traditionally, one scoops a dumpling up on the spoon then steers all or a portion of it into one's mouth with chopsticks, keeping the spoon in readiness at the lips to retrieve what one can't or doesn't wish to bite off. Beware of the first bite! Boiled dumplings are delectably and dangerously juicy, and the hot liquid will squirt out embarrassingly if you are not gentle when you first bite down.

In most Chinese homes the poaching liquid is served up as a hot drink to follow the dumplings, often garnished with a soupçon of soy or chopped scallion, and sometimes profiting from the breakage of poorly sealed dumplings. Try it. It is tummy-soothing.

Cold leftover boiled dumplings are rather wretched, in my opinion, but there is rarely any trouble eating them up while they're hot.

THE COMPLEAT DUMPLING: A STEP-BY-STEP GUIDE

Put filling off-center in wrapper, and nudge it into a half moon with your finger.

Fold wrapper exactly in half over filling. Pinch shut at midpoint.

Beginning to the right of the midpoint, make 3 tiny pleats on the *near* side of the wrapper only, folding the pleats *toward* the midpoint. After each pleat, pinch the dough to join the far, unpleated side of the wrapper. Pinch the extreme right corner of the arc closed. Now half the dumpling is sealed.

Repeat the process to the left of the midpoint, aiming the pleats the other way (that is, still pleating in the direction of the midpoint). Pinch the left corner closed. Then gently pinch all along the arc to insure it is sealed tightly and to thin the ridge of dough. The dumpling is now fully sealed.

The finished dumpling is pleated on one side, smooth on the other, curved prettily into an arc (on account of the pleating), and sitting flat on its bottom.

The genius of this method is that the dough is not overly thick at the top, having been pleated on only one side, and that the dumpling will stand upright on the tray or in the frying pan (if you are making pot stickers). Plus, it is beautiful to look at.

MENU SUGGESTIONS

For a simple dinner, serve the dumplings alongside a bowl of Moslem-Style Hot and Sour Soup, *or* Wine-Explosion Vegetable Chowder. *For a larger spread, add a selection of crisp "Little Dishes," plus* Bong-Bong Chicken or Ma-La Cold Chicken, *and* Dry-Fried Szechwan String Beans *or* Shantung Cold Eggplant with Sesame Sauce.

Soups, Salads, and Sandwiches

SOUPS

COLD

FISHER

The Art of Eating

Cold Buttermilk Soup

- 1½ pounds shrimps, cooked and chopped
- ½ medium cucumber, finely diced
- 1 tablespoon minced fresh dill
- 1 tablespoon prepared mustard
- 1 teaspoon salt
- 1 teaspoon sugar
- 1 quart buttermilk

Mix together shrimps, cucumber and seasonings; stir in buttermilk and chill thoroughly.

YIELD: 6 PORTIONS

SHERATON

From My Mother's Kitchen

Cold Beet Borscht

Beets for this refreshing cold soup were sometimes finely diced, other times coarsely grated. We like best whichever we were being served, and I still alternate, indiscriminately.

- 3 large or 4 medium fresh beets, or the equivalent in russell
- Juice of 1½ lemons, approximately
- Salt
- Pinch of sour salt (optional)
- 5 cups water
- 2 extra-large whole eggs or 4 yolks
- Pinch of sugar, if needed
- White pepper to taste
- *Garnishes:* Sour cream and (optional) boiled potatoes

Wash and peel the beets and cut into fine dice or grate on the coarse side of a grater. Place in a saucepan with the juice of ½ lemon, a pinch each of salt and sour salt, and the 5 cups water. Bring to a boil, reduce the heat, cover, and simmer until the beets are tender, about 40 minutes. Add the juice of another ½ lemon. Remove from the heat.

Using whole eggs results in a creamier, thicker borscht, but it is much trickier to add the hot beet soup to the whole eggs without having them coagulate. If you feel inexperienced with this process, use just the yolks. In either case, beat the eggs with a fork until they are thin and watery. Slowly ladle some of the hot borscht into the eggs, beating constantly. When about half the soup has been added, pour the egg mixture back into the pot with the remaining soup; again pour slowly and beat constantly. When all the egg mixture is beaten into the soup, pour the soup back and forth between the pot and a bowl or pitcher about 10 or 15 times until the mixture is smooth, airy, and creamy. Halfway through, add more lemon juice to produce a winy effect; add a tiny pinch of sugar, if necessary, and salt and white pepper as needed. Continue pouring to blend. Chill thoroughly.

It is best to add sour cream shortly before serving so that the borscht will keep longer. The sour cream can simply be served on the side, to be spooned in at the table. Or you can add sour cream (about 1 heaping tablespoonful per cupful of borscht) to the soup in a jar. Close tightly and shake vigorously to blend. Fluffy, dry, hot boiled potato is wonderful in the middle of this ice-cold soup.

YIELD: 1 TO 1½ QUARTS

VARIATION: Canned beets can also be used for this soup with excellent if slightly less flavorful results. Use whole beets even though you will dice or grate them, as they have more taste and better color. For the above recipe use a 1-pound can of whole beets. Dice or grate. Cook for 10 minutes in a combination of their own canning liquid plus 1½ cans of water, to make a total of 4 cups of liquid. Proceed with the recipe as described above.

DE GROOT

Feasts for All Seasons

Cseresznyelevs— Cold Cherry Soup

FOR 8 TO 10 PEOPLE

This is best with fresh sour cherries, but sweet Bing cherries are also good. If canned fruit has to be used out of season, the first choice is the canned "dietetic" unsweetened sour cherries, the second choice the sweet Bing, without the sugary syrup.

CHECK STAPLES
Aromatics: whole cassia buds, whole stick cinnamon, whole cloves
Granulated instantized flour (about 2 Tbs.)
Granulated white sugar (up to 2 cups, depending on sweetness of cherries)

SHOPPING LIST
Sour cherries (3 lbs., pitted)
Heavy cream (about 1½ cups)
A dry red Hungarian wine, say an Egri Kadarka or, if unavailable, a light young Beaujolais (1 bottle)

THE DAY BEFORE—ABOUT 45 MINUTES TO PREPARE

Put the 3 pounds of cherries, with 5 cups of freshly drawn cold water, into a 3-quart saucepan (preferably enameled or tinned copper to avoid interaction with the acid of the fruit) and bring slowly to simmering heat. Add: 2 teaspoons whole cassia buds, 2 teaspoons whole cloves, a 2-inch stick of cinnamon, and enough sugar to make liquid just sweet, but not too sweet, usually about 1½ cups. Cover and simmer until cherries are soft, usually in 20 to 30 minutes. Then pass through a colander, returning liquid to saucepan and leaving cherries and aromatics to cool slightly. In a small mixing bowl put 2 tablespoons of the flour and gradually liquefy it smoothly with a little of the red wine, added dash by dash, usually 4 or 5 tablespoons. Turn on low heat under saucepan and gradually thicken the cherry liquid by carefully stirring in the liquefied flour, until the liquid assumes the consistency of heavy cream. Then bring up heat until it is just below boiling, stirring continuously. If it is now too thick, add a few dashes of wine. If too thin, more liquefied flour. Turn off heat. Pick cherries in colander out from among the aromatics and drop them back into the saucepan. Aromatics are thrown away. Let saucepan come to room temperature, then pour cherry soup into a covered pot and refrigerate overnight. Also, chill remaining red wine and, of course, the cream.

A FEW MINUTES BEFORE SERVING

Thin the soup with the red wine to about the consistency of light cream; this usually requires 1½ to 2 cups of wine. Then stir in about 1 cup of the cream. Now, by adding more wine and cream, a little at a time, carefully balance the flavor, the thickness, and the color. Put back in refrigerator until ready to serve.

TOKLAS
The Alice B. Toklas Cook Book

Gazpacho of Malaga (Spanish)

4 cups veal broth cooked with 2 cloves of garlic and a large Spanish onion
1 large tomato peeled, with its seeds removed, and cut in minute cubes
1 small cucumber peeled, with its seeds removed, and cut in minute cubes
½ sweet red pepper, skin and seeds removed, cut in minute cubes
4 tablespoons cooked rice
2 tablespoons olive oil

Mix thoroughly and serve ice-cold.

Sufficient for 4 though double the quantity may not be too much!

ROJAS-LOMBARDI
The Art of South American Cooking

Sopa de Tomatitos Verdes

Tomatillo Soup

SERVES 6 TO 8

A tomatillo looks like a small green tomato. It is covered with a papery husk, which is easily peeled off. Though tomatillos can be purplish and may ripen to a yellowish color, they are commonly used green.

Tomatillos are available year-round. Pick firm, medium-size ones, with dry, clean, close-fitting husks; there should be no sign of blackness or mold. They can be stored in the refrigerator, in a paper bag, for about three weeks.

2½ to 3 pounds tomatillos

BOUQUET GARNI
4 sprigs fresh tarragon or thyme
2 to 3 sprigs fresh mint
3 sprigs Italian parsley
3 tablespoons olive oil
1 large onion, peeled and finely chopped (about 2 cups)
4 stalks celery, washed, strings removed, and finely chopped
1 to 2 jalapeño peppers, seeded and chopped
1-inch piece fresh ginger, peeled and chopped
¼ teaspoon sugar

3 cucumbers, peeled, seeded, and chopped (about 2 cups)
3 green bell peppers, seeded and chopped
2½ cups cold water or Chicken Stock
1 tablespoon coarse salt
3 tablespoons chopped fresh cilantro leaves or Italian parsley

1. Peel off the crackly husks and stems of the tomatillos. Wash the tomatillos well and drain.

2. Wrap and tie the sprigs of tarragon, mint, and parsley in a 6-inch-square piece of cheesecloth. Set aside.

3. In an enameled or stainless-steel saucepan, heat the olive oil over medium heat. Add the husked whole tomatillos and sauté them, stirring now and then, until they are golden all around, about 12 minutes. Stir in the onion, celery, hot peppers, ginger, and sugar and cook until the onion is translucent, about 3 to 4 minutes. Add the cucumbers and bell peppers and continue to cook, stirring, for 5 minutes longer. Add the water or stock, salt, and bouquet garni and bring to a boil. Lower the heat and simmer, stirring from time to time, for 15 to 20 minutes, or until the tomatillos have totally collapsed. Remove from the heat and discard the bouquet garni.

4. Force the soup through a food mill, leaving the skins and seeds behind. Place the soup in a double boiler and heat through. Correct the seasoning with salt to taste, sprinkle with chopped cilantro, and serve hot.

NOTE For a smoother texture, blend half or more of the soup in the jar of an electric blender and mix it with the remaining soup, or blend all of it to the desired consistency. Do this only after passing the soup through the food mill to remove the seeds and skins.

VARIATION This soup may be served chilled. Pass the soup through a food mill and puree it in a blender. Cool thoroughly over ice or in the refrigerator for several hours. Correct the seasoning with salt, sprinkle with fresh herbs, and serve.

HOT

LAGASSE

Emeril's New New Orleans Cooking

Dr. E.'s Get-Well Chicken Vegetable Soup

MAKES 16 CUPS, 12 HEALTHY SERVINGS

One of my good friends in New Orleans is Derby Gisclair, one of the last true gentlemen in the world. One day Derby's wife, Claire, called to cancel their dinner reservation because Derby wasn't feeling well. What does a friend do at a time like this? I whipped up a batch of double-strength chicken soup and sent it to the Gisclairs, with instructions from "Dr. E." to bring the soup to a boil and eat it as hot as possible. The next day Derby showed up for lunch at the restaurant, fit as a fiddle. Well, word got around, friends and relatives were putting in orders for "The Cure," and soon I realized these people weren't even sick. Good thing; I didn't want to get busted for practicing medicine without a license.

You'll enjoy this soup even if you're not ailing, but when you prepare it, freeze a couple of individual portions, just in case. One more hint: This is better if it's made a day ahead and reheated.

2 tablespoons olive oil
1 chicken (2½ to 3 pounds), boned, skinned, and visible fat removed (save the bones and the carcass, discard the skin), diced
2½ teaspoons salt
10 turns freshly ground black pepper
1 cup chopped onions
½ cup chopped celery
½ cup diced carrots
½ cup chopped green onions
2 tablespoons minced garlic
¼ cup (loosely packed) fresh parsley leaves
1 tablespoon chopped fresh basil
4 bay leaves
1 tablespoon Emeril's Creole Seasoning
2 cups assorted chopped fresh vegetables, such as beans, zucchini, yellow squash, cabbage, or whatever is in season
1 cup (firmly packed) rinsed and torn spinach leaves
¼ teaspoon crushed red pepper
3 quarts Basic Chicken Stock
2 cups cooked fine or broad noodles

1. Heat the oil in a large heavy pot over high heat. When the oil is hot, add the chicken meat and bones, salt, and pepper and sauté, stirring occasionally, until the meat and bones are brown, for about 5 minutes. Add the onions, celery, carrots, green onions, garlic, parsley, basil, bay leaves, and Creole Seasoning and sauté, stirring once or twice, for about 4 minutes. Add the chopped vegetables, spinach, and crushed red pepper and sauté for 1 minute.

2. Add the stock to the pot and bring it to a boil. Reduce the heat and simmer, uncovered, for about 25 minutes. Add the noodles, bring back to a boil, and simmer for 5 minutes. Remove from the heat. Remove the carcass and loose bones. Unless you're too ill to wait, the soup will taste even better if you refrigerate it overnight. The next day, remove and discard the congealed fat on the top and reheat the soup over medium-low heat.

NATHAN

Jewish Cooking in America

Fluffy Matzah Balls

If you like light, airy matzah balls, you'll like this recipe. It's my son David's favorite, especially when his grandmother makes the matzah balls.

- 4 large eggs
- 2 tablespoons chicken fat or vegetable oil
- ½ cup seltzer or club soda
- 1 cup matzah meal
- Salt and freshly ground pepper to taste

1. Mix the eggs well with a fork. Add the chicken fat or oil, soda water, matzah meal, and salt and pepper and mix well. Cover and refrigerate for several hours.

2. Dip your hands in cold water and make about 12 balls slightly smaller than Ping-Pong balls.

3. Bring water to a boil in a large pot. Add salt and place the matzah balls in the water. Cover and simmer about 30 minutes or until soft.

YIELD: ABOUT 12 LARGE, SOFT MATZAH BALLS

TIP: I often make chicken soup and matzah balls ahead. After cooking the matzah balls I just place them in the warm soup, which I then freeze. The liquid keeps them fluffy. I defrost the soup, reheat, and serve. If you like them more al dente, use large eggs and cook a shorter time.

NOTE: To reduce the cholesterol in this recipe, use 2 egg whites and 2 whole eggs as well as canola oil.

RODEN

A Book of Middle Eastern Food

Beid bi Lamoun (Avgolemono Sauce) for Fried Fish

- 2 cups fish stock (see below)
- Salt and black pepper
- 1 tablespoon cornstarch or flour
- 2–3 egg yolks
- Juice of 1 lemon, or more

Strain the fish stock (made by boiling the discarded heads and tails of the fish with perhaps a celery stalk and a carrot) into the top of a double boiler or a thick-bottomed ordinary pan. Season to taste with salt and pepper. Mix the cornstarch or flour (I much prefer the former) with a little cold water, and introduce the paste gradually into the hot stock, mixing vigorously to avoid lumps. Cook gently, stirring constantly, until the sauce thickens and no longer tastes floury, about 15 to 20 minutes.

Beat the egg yolks in a bowl. Add the lemon juice and stir well. Add a little of the hot sauce, beating well, then return the mixture to the pan with the sauce gradually, stirring with a wooden spoon over low heat until the sauce thickens to a smooth, custard-like consistency. Do not let it come to a boil, or it will curdle. If you use cornstarch, the result will be more jelly-like and translucent.

Serve hot or cold, poured over the fish or in a separate bowl. This sauce is also delicious with poached or baked fish.

BAYLESS
Rick Bayless's Mexican Kitchen

Chilied Tortilla Soup with Shredded Chard

Sopa de Tortilla y Acelgas

Tortilla soup is one of Mexico's most well known soups. I wrote a classic but flexible recipe for it in Authentic Mexican, *but I still have more to say. At Frontera and Topolobampo, we work a little of the traditional toasted pasilla chile garnish into the tomato-flavored broth to deepen it. And I love to simmer in the satisfying complexity of chard—an unexpected addition for a soup this comforting. You can leave out the chard, of course, and serve the soup with diced avocado, even a spoonful of cream . . . but do try it with the greens, since it's a perfect opening to any meal.*

MAKES ABOUT 6 CUPS, SERVING 4 TO 6

- 4 to 6 corn tortillas, preferably stale store-bought ones
- ⅓ cup plus 1 tablespoon vegetable oil
- 4 to 5 medium (about 1½ ounces total) dried pasilla chiles, stemmed and seeded
- 2 garlic cloves, unpeeled
- 1 medium-large round ripe tomato
- 1 medium white onion, sliced ⅛-inch thick
- 6 cups good broth, preferably chicken
- Salt, about ½ teaspoon, depending on saltiness of broth
- 2 cups (8 ounces) shredded Mexican Chihuahua cheese, or other melting cheese such as brick or Monterey Jack
- 1 large lime, cut into 6 wedges
- 4 cups loosely packed, thinly sliced (preferably red) chard leaves (you'll need about ⅔ of a 12-ounce bunch)

1. GETTING STARTED. Slice the tortillas into ⅛-inch-wide strips. Heat ⅓ cup of the vegetable oil in a medium-size (8- to 9-inch) skillet over medium-high. When hot, add about ⅓ of the tortilla strips and fry, turning frequently, until they are crisp on all sides. Remove with a slotted spoon and drain on paper towels. Fry the remaining strips in 2 batches.

Cut chiles into rough 1-inch squares using kitchen shears. Reduce the heat under the oil to medium-low, let cool a minute, then fry the squares very briefly to toast them, 3 or 4 seconds; immediately remove and drain on paper towels. Place ⅓ of the chiles in a small bowl, cover with hot water and let rehydrate for 30 minutes, stirring regularly to ensure even soaking. Drain and discard the water. Set aside the remaining fried chiles.

While the chiles are soaking, roast the unpeeled garlic on an ungreased griddle or heavy skillet over medium heat, turning occasionally, until blackened in spots and soft, about 15 minutes. Cool, then slip off the papery skins.

Roast the tomato on a baking sheet 4 inches below a very hot broiler until blackened and blistered on one side, about 6 minutes; flip and broil the other side. Cool, then peel, collecting any juices.

2. SIMMERING THE BROTH. In a medium-size (4-quart) pot, heat the remaining 1 tablespoon of oil over medium-low. Add the onion and fry until brown, about 10 minutes. Place the rehydrated chiles in a food processor or blender along with the roasted garlic, tomato, and 1 cup of the broth; puree until smooth. Raise the temperature under the pot to medium-high, and, when noticeably hotter, press the tomato-chile puree through a medium-mesh strainer into the fried onion. Stir for several minutes as the mixture thickens and darkens. Mix in the remaining 5 cups of broth, then simmer uncovered over medium-low, stirring occasionally, for 30 minutes. Season with salt.

3. FINISHING THE SOUP. Set out the garnishes: Make mounds of the fried tortilla strips, fried chiles, cheese and lime on a large platter. Just before serving, reheat the soup, add the sliced chard and simmer until the chard is tender, 5 or 6 minutes. Ladle into warm soup bowls and pass the garnishes for each guest to use al gusto.

ADVANCE PREPARATION—The soup itself can be prepared several days ahead. The fried tortillas will keep for a day wrapped in foil on the counter. Reheat the broth and set out the garnishes just before serving.

SHORTCUTS—You can purchase broth (I'd recommend one from the refrigerated or frozen case of a specialty shop rather than canned); if you can buy thickish tortilla chips, they could be broken and used in place of the fried strips.

VARIATIONS AND IMPROVISATIONS

A cup or so of shredded poached or rotisserie chicken makes this a main dish; vegetable stock and a couple cups of roasted or grilled vegetables makes it a vegetarian one.

MEXICAN BEANS-AND-GREENS SOUP—Simmer 8 ounces beans until tender (1½ hours or so) in 5 cups broth; add enough water or additional broth to bring it back to its original level. Prepare the soup as directed, adding the beans-and-broth mixture where the 5 cups of broth are called for.

BRENNAN
The Original Thai Cookbook

Chicken and Coconut Milk Soup

Gaeng Dom Yam Gai

6 TO 8 SERVINGS

A lovely, lemony, creamy soup, Dom Yam Gai *calls for chicken pieces cut through the bone with a heavy cleaver, Chinese style.* If you find gnawing on chicken pieces and delicately trying to remove the bone, vainly searching for a place to deposit it, inhibiting your dinner conversation, you may debone the bird and substitute chicken pieces. In either case, use both dark and light meats for color and nutrition.*

5 cups "Thin" coconut milk
1 small chicken, sectioned and cut into bite-sized pieces (bone in)†
3 stalks lemon grass, bruised and cut into 1" lengths
2 teaspoons Laos powder (Ka)
3 green onions, finely chopped
2 tablespoons coriander leaves, chopped
4 to 6 fresh Serrano chillies, seeded and chopped
Juice of 2 limes
3 tablespoons fish sauce (Nam Pla)

In a saucepan, bring the "Thin" coconut milk to a boil. Add the chicken pieces, lemon grass and Laos powder. Reduce heat and simmer until the chicken is tender, about 15 minutes. Do not cover as this will tend to curdle coconut milk. When the chicken is tender, add the green onions, coriander leaves and chillies. Bring the heat up just below boiling. Remove the pan from heat, stir in the lime juice, fish sauce and serve.

*A whole breast, for instance, should yield 12 pieces when chopped.

†**N.B.** Beef, cut into thin strips or firm white fish pieces may be substituted for chicken.

BRENNAN
The Original Thai Cookbook

Hot and Sour Shrimp Soup

Dom Yam Gung

6 TO 8 SERVINGS

The best known and loved of Thai soups, Dom Yam Gung *is a marvelous combination of tender shrimp floating in a rich broth, liberally spiced with chillies and tangy with lemon grass, lime juice and citrus leaves.*

1 tablespoon vegetable oil
Shells from shrimp (see below)
8 cups chicken stock
1½ teaspoons salt
3 stalks lemon grass, cut into 1" lengths
4 citrus leaves
1 teaspoon lime zest, slivered
2 green Serrano chillies, slivered
2 pounds fresh (green) shrimp (approximately 20 count per pound), shelled and deveined
1 tablespoon fish sauce (Nam Pla)
Juice of 2 limes
1 red Serrano chilli, slivered
2 tablespoons coriander leaves, coarsely chopped
3 green onions (including some green), coarsely chopped

Heat the oil in a saucepan and dry the shells until they turn pink. Add the chicken stock, salt, lemon grass, citrus leaves, lime rind and green chillies. Bring to a boil, cover, reduce heat and simmer for 20 minutes. Strain the mixture through a sieve, return the liquid to a saucepan and bring to a boil. Add the shrimp to this boiling "stock" and cook them for 2 to 3 minutes. Reduce heat to simmer and add the fish sauce and lime juice. Stir and immediately remove from heat to prevent overcooking. Pour the soup in a tureen, sprinkle with red chillies, coriander leaves and green onions. Serve piping-hot.

TSUJI
Japanese Cooking

Miso Soup
Miso-shiru

In many ways, miso *is to Japanese cooking what butter is to French cooking and olive oil is to the Italian way (to paraphrase M. F. K. Fisher), and behind* miso's *omnipresence in the Japanese kitchen lies abundant common sense. Take* miso*-based soups. Not only do they require just a few minutes to prepare (an important criterion for a breakfast food), more important, typical servings provide roughly one-sixth the adult daily requirement of protein.*

It is impossible for miso *soup to be boring. It can be based on any type of* miso*, from salty to sweet, and it is always served with supplementary ingredients and seasonings. In the course of the four seasons, relying on easily available produce and nonseasonal staples, one can make a different miso soup nearly every day without repetition.*

Below is just one of the seemingly limitless variety of miso *soups.*

SERVES 4

3⅓ cups primary *dashi*, or secondary *dashi*, or sardine stock
approximately ½ cup *nameko* mushrooms (or 2 *shiitake* mushrooms, sliced)
⅓ cake *tōfu* (bean curd)
4 Tbsps red *miso*
4 stalks trefoil
ground *sansho* pepper

TO PREPARE: Make the stock of your choice and assemble the supporting ingredients. *Nameko* mushrooms are available fresh and in cans; they are similar to conventional button mushrooms, but have a slippery coating. (Substitute *shiitake* mushrooms.) Drain the *tōfu*.

TO COOK: Soften the *miso* in a medium-sized bowl by adding 2 Tbsps tepid stock and blending with a wire whisk. If you put the *miso* directly into the stock pot, it will not be properly held in solution, and the soup will be full of *miso* pellets.

Gradually ladle the softened *miso* into the stock in a medium-sized pot, simmering over medium heat. (If you want satin-smooth soup, strain the soup from one pot into another.)

When all the *miso* has been added and is dissolved, add the solid ingredients. The *tōfu* can be cut into ½-inch (1½-cm) cubes over the stock pot. Chop the trefoil stalks into small pieces. Keep soup at a simmer a few minutes until the mushrooms and *tōfu* are heated.

Remove from heat just before boiling point. Do not boil—boiling will change the flavor.

TO SERVE: Ladle into individual lacquer bowls, distributing the mushrooms, *tōfu*, and chopped trefoil equally and attractively. Garnish with a shake or two of *sansho* pepper. Cover and serve immediately.

CLAIBORNE AND LEE
The Chinese Cookbook

Hot and Sour Soup

2 large dried black mushrooms*
6 tree ear mushrooms
4 dried tiger lily stems*
1 tablespoon peanut, vegetable, or corn oil
¾ cup finely shredded pork
1 tablespoon light soy sauce*
½ cup finely shredded bamboo shoots*
5 cups Rich Chicken Broth (see recipe)
Salt to taste
2 to 3 tablespoons red wine vinegar, according to taste
1 teaspoon dark soy sauce*
2 tablespoons cornstarch
3 tablespoons water
1½ pads fresh white bean curd,* cut into thin strips
2 eggs, lightly beaten
1 tablespoon sesame oil*
1 teaspoon freshly ground white or black pepper
2 tablespoons chopped scallions, green part included, for garnish
Minced fresh coriander* for garnish (optional)

*Available in Chinese markets and by mail order

1. Place the mushrooms, tree ears, and tiger lily stems in a mixing bowl. Pour very hot or boiling water over them and let stand 15 to 30 minutes, then drain.

2. Cut off and discard the stems of the mushrooms and the harder part of the tree ears. Cut both the mushrooms and tree ears into thin slices. With the fingers, shred the tiger lily stems, and if they are very long cut them in half.

3. Heat a wok or skillet, and when it is hot add the peanut, vegetable, or corn oil and shredded pork. Stir to separate the strands of pork and add the light soy sauce. Add the mushrooms, tree ears, tiger lily stems, and bamboo shoots. Stir quickly about 1 minute and add the chicken broth and salt. Stir in the vinegar and dark soy sauce.

4. Combine the cornstarch and water and stir into the simmering broth. When slightly thickened, add the bean curd, bring to a boil, and turn off the heat for about 30 seconds, to let the broth cool a bit so the eggs won't overcook when they are added.

5. Add the sesame oil and pepper and stir to blend. Pour the soup into a hot soup tureen and gradually add the eggs in a thin stream, stirring in circular motion. Sprinkle with the chopped scallion and the minced fresh coriander, if desired. Serve immediately.

YIELD: ABOUT 6 TO 8 SERVINGS

MACAUSLAND

The Gourmet Cookbook

Soupe à l'Oignon au Fromage

Onion Soup with Cheese

Peel and slice very thinly 4 large onions, separating the rings. Heat ¼ cup butter in a large saucepan, add the onion rings, and cook them very, very gently over a low flame, stirring almost constantly with a wooden spoon, until the rings are an even golden-brown. Sprinkle with 1 tablespoon flour and when this has been well blended, gradually pour into 1½ quarts beef consommé, water, or a mixture of the two, stirring constantly until the soup begins to boil. Lower the heat, cover the pan, and simmer gently for about 20 minutes.

Taste for seasoning and serve in a heated soup tureen or in individual tureens, each one containing a toasted round of French bread heaped with grated Gruyère cheese. Serve toasted rounds of French bread and grated cheese on the side.

French onion soup may also be served *gratinée*. When it is ready to serve, half fill an ovenproof soup casserole with thin rounds of toasted French bread covered with grated Gruyère and pour the onion soup over the toast. Sprinkle the top with more Gruyère and set the casserole under the broiler flame or in a hot oven until the cheese is brown and sizzling.

WATERS

Chez Panisse Vegetables

Kale and Potato Soup

A Portuguese recipe, called caldo verde *(green broth) in Portugal, where cabbage is often substituted for the kale.*

- 1 bunch kale (about 1 pound)
- 2 pounds boiling potatoes
- 2 quarts water
- 1 teaspoon salt
- Optional: 1 garlic sausage
- Extra-virgin olive oil

Remove the stems from the kale, wash the leaves, and cut them into a chiffonade. You should have about 6 to 8 cups.

Peel the potatoes and chop them up very fine (Yellow Finns are good for this—or use some other flavorful boiling potato). Bring the water to a boil with the salt. Add the chopped potatoes, return to a boil, and cook for 2 minutes, covered. Add the kale and cook 2 minutes more. Taste for seasoning. If desired, serve with slices of garlic sausage heated briefly in the soup and a splash of the olive oil.

SERVES 4 TO 6

NOTE: The proportion of kale to potatoes in this soup is not terribly important. Nor do you need to chop the potatoes; but if you slice them, they will need to cook a little longer before you can add the kale. You can also pass the soup through a food mill and serve it as a purée; moisten it with chicken stock instead of water; or enrich it with other vegetables. One very good variation is to stew sliced shallots and garlic apart until they are very soft and caramelized, and then purée them with the kale and potatoes.

HAZAN
The Classic Italian Cook Book

Zuppa di scarola e riso
Escarole and Rice Soup

Scarola *is a broad-leafed salad green from the chicory family. It is marvelous in soup as well as in salads. There are probably as many ways to cook it as there are leaves in a head of escarole, but many make it either too bland and retiring or else too aggressively flavored. This version, where the escarole is first briefly sautéed in butter with lightly browned onions, stays at a happy distance from the two extremes.*

FOR 4 PERSONS

- 1 head of escarole (¾ to 1 pound)
- 2 tablespoons finely chopped yellow onion
- ¼ cup butter
- Salt
- 3½ cups beef broth, or 1 cup canned chicken broth mixed with 2½ cups water, or 2 chicken bouillon cubes dissolved in 3½ cups water
- ½ cup raw rice, preferably Italian Arborio rice
- 3 tablespoons freshly grated Parmesan cheese

1. Detach all the escarole leaves from the head and discard any that are bruised, wilted, or discolored. Wash all the rest in various changes of cold water until thoroughly clean. Cut into ribbons ½ inch wide and set aside.

2. In a stockpot sauté the chopped onion in the butter over medium heat until nicely browned. Add the escarole and a light sprinkling of salt. Briefly sauté the escarole, stirring it once or twice, then add ½ cup of the broth, cover the pot, and cook over very low heat until the escarole is tender—from 25 minutes to more than three-quarters of an hour, depending on the freshness and tenderness of the escarole.

3. When the escarole is tender, add the rest of the broth, raise the heat slightly, and cover. When the broth comes to a boil, add the rice and cover. Cook for 15 to 20 minutes, stirring from time to time, until the rice is *al dente*, firm to the bite. Off the heat, mix in the Parmesan cheese. Taste and correct for salt, spoon into soup plates, and serve.

NOTE: Don't cook the soup ahead of time with the rice in it. The rice will become mushy. If you must do it ahead of time, stop at the end of step 2. About 25 minutes before serving, add the 3 cups of broth to the escarole, bring to a boil, and finish cooking as in step 3.

MENU SUGGESTIONS

Follow the suggestions for Rice and Celery Soup. This can also precede Casserole-Roasted Lamb with Juniper Berries.

WATERS
Chez Panisse Vegetables

French Cream of Cauliflower Soup

- 1 large cauliflower (2 to 3 pounds)
- 1 onion
- 2 tablespoons unsalted butter
- 4 tablespoons crème fraîche
- Salt
- Nutmeg
- Chervil

Cut off the stem of the cauliflower and any green leaves. Break up into flowerets. Wash them in cold water. Reserve a handful of flowerets to garnish the soup.

Peel and slice the onion thin. In a soup pot, stew the onion slices and the flowerets in the butter with a little water for 15 minutes, stirring occasionally, without letting them brown. Add water to cover and cook for 25 minutes, covered, over medium heat. Meanwhile, parboil the reserved flowerets in boiling salted water for 8 minutes or so, keeping them crunchy.

Purée the soup in a blender and reheat gently to just under boiling. Add the crème fraîche and season with salt and nutmeg to taste. Serve the soup very hot, garnished with the whole flowerets and a few sprigs of chervil.

SERVES 4 TO 6

THOMAS

The Vegetarian Epicure

Pea Soup with Butter Dumplings

SOUP

4 cups shelled peas (about 4 lbs. fresh, unshelled)
4½ cups water
1 tsp. brown sugar
salt and fresh-ground black pepper
½ cup light Rhine wine
4½ Tbs. butter
4½ Tbs. flour

DUMPLINGS

6 Tbs. butter
2 eggs
½ cup flour
¼ tsp. nutmeg
salt

SOUP: Cook the peas in the water and sugar until they are quite soft, about ½ hour. Then press the soup through a sieve or put it in the blender for a few moments. Season this thin puree with salt and pepper and stir in the wine.

Melt the butter in a skillet and stir in the flour. Let the roux cook over a very low flame for a few minutes, stirring constantly. Then stir in a cup or two of the soup and whisk until smooth. Return the thickened soup to the rest and blend well.

DUMPLINGS: To make the batter, soften the butter as much as possible, short of melting it. Beat the eggs with the flour and beat in the butter. Season with salt and nutmeg. Drop the batter into gently boiling soup by half-teaspoons. When the dumplings have risen to the top, they will need 5 more minutes before they are done.

SERVES 5 TO 6

KATZEN

The Moosewood Cookbook

Minestrone

4–6 SERVINGS

NOTE: *This recipe calls for cooked pea beans or garbanzo beans (chickpeas). If you use chickpeas, begin soaking them 3½ hours before you make the soup. After 2 soaking hours, cook them in boiling water for about 1½ hours—until comfortably chewable. If you use pea beans, you needn't soak them, but give them 1½–2 hours to cook. In either case, if you cook the beans in plenty of water, save the extra water to use as stock for the soup. You'll have a fuller-flavored, higher-proteined minestrone.*

1½ cups cooked pea or garbanzo beans
(¾ cup raw)
½ cup dry pasta
1 cup fresh chopped tomatoes
parmesan cheese
3 Tbs. olive oil
1 cup chopped onion
4–5 cloves crushed garlic
1 cup minced celery
1 cup cubed carrot
1 cup cubed eggplant or zucchini
1 cup chopped green pepper
2 tsp. salt
¼ tsp. black pepper
1 tsp. oregano
½ cup fresh-chopped parsley
1 tsp. basil
2 cups tomato purée
3½ cups water or stock
3 Tbs. dry red wine

In a soup kettle, sauté garlic and onions in olive oil until they are soft and translucent. Add 1 tsp. salt, carrot, celery and eggplant. (If you use zucchini, add it with the green pepper.) Mix well. Add oregano, black pepper and basil. Cover and cook over low heat 5–8 minutes. Add green pepper, stock, purée, cooked beans and wine. Cover and simmer 15 minutes. Add tomatoes and remaining salt. Keep at lowest heat until 10 minutes before you plan to serve. Then heat the soup to a boil, add pasta, and boil gently until pasta is tender. Serve immediately, topped with parsley and parmesan.

ROBERTSON

Laurel's Kitchen

Greek Lentil Soup

- 2 cups uncooked lentils
- 8 cups water or vegetable stock
- ½ onion, chopped
- 1 small carrot, chopped
- 1 celery stalk, chopped
- 1 small potato, chopped
- 2 tablespoons oil
- 2 bay leaves
- 1½ to 2 teaspoons salt
- 2 teaspoons vinegar

Mix all ingredients except the vinegar in a soup pot and cook until the lentils are very soft, about one hour. Add vinegar at the end and serve.

MAKES ABOUT 8 CUPS

LAPPÉ

Diet for a Small Planet

Lentils, Monastery Style

YIELD: 4 TO 6 SERVINGS

This soup is especially delicious when served with corn muffins.

- ¼ cup of olive oil
- 2 large onions, chopped
- 1 carrot, chopped
- ½ teaspoon thyme
- ½ teaspoon marjoram
- 3 cups seasoned stock
- 1 cup lentils, rinsed
- Salt to taste
- ¼ cup freshly chopped parsley
- One 1-pound can tomatoes
- ¼ cup dry sherry
- ⅔ cup grated Swiss cheese

Heat oil in a large pot and sauté onions and carrot for 3 to 5 minutes. Add herbs and sauté 1 minute. Add stock, lentils, salt, parsley, and tomatoes and cook, covered, until lentils are tender, about 45 minutes. Add sherry.

To serve, put 2 tablespoons cheese in each bowl and fill with soup.

LAPPÉ

Diet for a Small Planet

Turkish Barley-Buttermilk Soup

4 SERVINGS

Don't let the simplicity of this soup fool you. Once I made it for a demonstration of nonmeat cooking, and the moderator could not stop eating it for the entire program.

- 2 tablespoons oil for sautéing
- 2 large onions, chopped
- 1 cup barley
- 5 cups Seasoned Stock
- 2 cups buttermilk or yogurt
- 1 teaspoon dillweed
- 1 pat or more margarine

Heat oil in a heavy pot and sauté onions until translucent. Add barley and sauté, stirring lightly, until translucent and slightly toasty-smelling. When onion is well browned, add stock and cook until barley is well done, 45 minutes to 1 hour (25 minutes in a pressure cooker). Remove from heat, let cool a bit, and slowly add buttermilk, and more stock to thin if necessary. Sprinkle in dill and add margarine.

BASTIANICH

La Cucina di Lidia

Minestra di Funghi Selvatici

Wild Mushroom Soup

SERVES 6

Every cook in our part of Istria had her own version of wild mushroom soup. This one was devised by my Great Aunt Santola, a widow, who cooked the soup for the whole courtyard at Busoler. She would come home and pick over the mushrooms she had gathered, separating those to be sautéed from those earmarked for other uses. Mostly trimmings and stems were reserved for her soup. When I was old enough to begin gathering my own mushrooms, I was allowed to pick only the unmistakably safe varieties, like champignons and porcini, and forbidden to eat any before my aunt approved them. The traditional belief was that the poisonous mushrooms could be detected by cooking them in water with a piece of brass; if the brass turned green, the mushrooms were unsafe. As a further precaution, the oldest woman in a household had the dubious honor of tasting the mushrooms before they were served to other members of the family.

NOTE: The soup is best when made with several varieties of fresh wild mushrooms (porcini, shiitake, chanterelle, hen-of-the-woods, etc.), but even a single variety will produce an excellent soup. Other types of dried mushrooms may be substituted for the dried porcini specified, but porcini are preferable.

FOR THE SOUP

8 pieces (⅔ ounce) dried porcini mushrooms
5 tablespoons olive oil
2 slices bacon, chopped fine
1 medium onion, chopped
2 medium potatoes, peeled
2 medium carrots, whole
1 large shallot, chopped
2½ quarts chicken stock
½ teaspoon salt, or to taste

In 1½ cups of warm water, presoak the dried porcini about 20 minutes, until softened. Drain, reserving all but the last 2 teaspoons of the steeping liquid (to avoid unwanted sediments), remove and rinse the softened porcini.

In the 5-quart pot, heat 5 tablespoons olive oil, add the bacon and onion, and sauté until translucent. Add the potatoes, carrots, and shallot, and cook 2 minutes over medium heat, stirring constantly. Add the stock, drained porcini, reserved soaking liquid, and salt, and bring to a boil. Reduce the heat and keep on low boil about 10 minutes, until the vegetables are tender.

FOR THE FRESH MUSHROOMS

5 tablespoons olive oil
2 pounds wild mushrooms, cleaned and sliced
Freshly ground pepper to taste
¼ cup chopped Italian parsley

To prepare the fresh wild mushrooms, heat the olive oil in the large skillet and sauté them in batches, over medium-high heat, until all water has evaporated, about 7 minutes per batch. Transfer the mushrooms to the soup pot and simmer 30 minutes, skimming occasionally. Add the pepper and parsley, and serve piping hot.

CHILD

From Julia Child's Kitchen

Potages

Potage Parmentier; Potage Bonne Femme

LEEK AND POTATO SOUP

What a delicious soup, you cannot help saying to yourself as you breathe in its appetizing aroma, and then its full homey flavor fills your mouth. There is nothing to mask the taste of those fresh vegetables—no canned chicken stock, no enhancers, preservatives, additives—nothing but the vegetables themselves and a final enriching fillip of cream or butter. This is homemade soup in its primal beauty, to me, and although I love many others, it is leek and potato that I dream of. And it couldn't be simpler to make—sauté the leeks briefly in butter to release their flavor, stir in a little flour to make the light liaison that will hold the vegetables in suspension, add potatoes, water, and salt, and cook until done, as the old books used to say—30 to 40 minutes in a saucepan, or 5 minutes in the pressure cooker. Purée the soup if you wish, or serve it in peasanty chunks; add a dollop of cream for each serving, and that's all there is to it.

Although Potage Parmentier *is in our other books, it is here again with a few changes in technique—the leek sauté and the flour* roux*—plus a piece of absolutely vital information, namely: If, rather than slicing the vegetables, you mince the leeks nicely, and tailor the potatoes into neat ⅜-inch dice, you are then empowered and entitled to call the soup by a new name—*Potage Bonne Femme*. By the way, if you cannot find leeks you can use onions, but leeks are best because of their very special onion-taste-with-a-difference.*

FOR ABOUT 8 CUPS, SERVING 6 TO 8

3 Tb butter in a 3- to 4-quart heavy-bottomed saucepan
3 cups sliced or minced leeks (white part only), or onions, or a combination of both
3 Tb flour
2 quarts hot water (or 4 to 6 cups water plus milk added at the end of cooking)
1 Tb salt; pepper to taste
Optional: A cup or so of tender green part of the leeks, sliced or minced
4 cups (about 1½ pounds) potatoes, peeled, and roughly chopped or neatly diced—in this latter case use "boiling" potatoes that keep their shape
⅓ to ½ cup heavy cream or sour cream, and/or 2 to 3 Tb butter
2 to 3 Tb minced fresh parsley and/or chives

THE SOUP BASE. Melt butter over moderate heat, stir in the leeks and/or onions, cover pan, and cook slowly for 5 minutes without browning. Then blend in the flour, and stir over moderate heat for 2 minutes to cook the flour without browning it either. Remove from heat, let cool a moment, and gradually beat in a cup or so of hot water. Blend thoroughly with the flour and vegetables, then stir in the rest of the water. (If you want to use milk, add it at the end of the cooking—it will curdle if you add it now.) Stir in the salt and pepper, optional green of leek, and the potatoes. Bring to a boil, and simmer partially covered for about 40 minutes, until vegetables are thoroughly tender.

For a peasant-type soup, mash the vegetables in the pan with a mixing fork or a potato masher. For a smoother texture, put through medium blade of a food mill.

Soup base may be completed hours or even a day ahead to this point: when cool, cover and refrigerate; reheat to simmer before proceeding.

FINAL ENRICHMENTS. To serve the soup as is, stir in milk if you are using it, bring to the simmer, and blend in as much of the cream as you wish. Taste carefully, adding more salt and pepper as needed. Off heat, and by tablespoons if you wish, stir in the butter. Decorate each serving with a spoonful more cream, again if you wish to, and a sprinkling of herbs.

ADDITIONS AND VARIATIONS

***SOUPE DU JOUR* (POTATO SOUP WITH LEEKS OR ONIONS AND LEFTOVER VEGETABLES).** Simmer the preceding soup base until the potatoes, onions, and leeks are tender, then add one or all of such cooked vegetables as a cup of squash, a handful of chopped Brussels sprouts, broccoli, cauliflower, or beans, mashed green peas, lettuce leaves from last night's salad, washed and shredded. Simmer 2 to 3 minutes to warm them through. Complete the soup as in the master recipe, mashing the big vegetables into the soup or puréeing all of it through a vegetable mill, and enriching with milk, cream, and/or butter.

***SOUPE AU CRESSON* (WATERCRESS SOUP).** Wash a bunch of watercress 2 to 2½ inches in diameter; pull off most of the leaves and reserve them. Chop the rest, including stems, roughly; stir into the potato and leek soup base after it has simmered about 30 minutes and vegetables are almost tender. Simmer 5 minutes, then purée through a food mill. Stir in the reserved leaves when reheating soup just before serving, and enrich with milk, cream, and/or butter. (This soup is also delicious when served cold; follow general idea of the following recipe for vichyssoise.)

***VICHYSSOISE* (COLD CREAM OF POTATO SOUP WITH LEEKS OR ONIONS).** Simmer the potato and leek or onion soup base (omitting green of leek) in 6 cups of water until vegetables are tender. Puree through fine blade of food mill, or through medium blade and then through a sieve, or through a blender and sieve. Stir in milk and cream to desired consistency, and season carefully with white pepper and salt—oversalt slightly, because chilled soup loses savor. Cover and chill. Taste again for seasoning just before serving, and stir in more chilled cream if you wish; sprinkle each portion with minced fresh chives or parsley.

Since Chef Louis Diat created this soup at the old Hotel Ritz-Carlton in New York, there have been many versions and many additions of chicken stock from the can. I do prefer Diat's simple base of fresh leeks and potatoes, water, milk, cream, and seasonings.

PRESSURE COOKER SOUP. Use the proportions in the main recipe, *Potage Parmentier*. After sautéing the leeks and onions in your pressure cooker, uncovered, blend in the flour, cook it, and blend in the liquid, salt, and potatoes as described. Then cover the pan, bring rapidly to full pressure, and cook exactly 5 minutes. Release pressure at once. If you taste the soup at this point it will have little flavor: for some reason I am ignorant of, it now must simmer 5 minutes or so (or simply sit 15 minutes) for it to develop its taste. Then complete the soup as described in the main recipe or in any of the preceding variations.

TIME-LIFE BOOKS

The Cooking of Provincial France

Potage Crème d'Asperges

Cream of Asparagus Soup

TO SERVE 4 TO 6

2 pounds fresh asparagus
6 cups chicken stock, fresh or canned
1 teaspoon salt
7 tablespoons butter
6 tablespoons flour
2 tablespoons finely chopped shallots or scallions
2 egg yolks
¾ cup heavy cream
2 tablespoons soft butter
Salt
White pepper

With a small sharp knife (*not* a vegetable peeler), peel each asparagus stalk of its skin and tough outer flesh. At the butt end the peeling may be as thick as 1/16 inch, but it should gradually become paper thin as the knife cuts and slides toward the tip. Cut off the tips where the scales end and trim away any oversized scales. Trim and discard about ¼ inch from the butt ends and cut the rest of the stalks into ½-inch lengths; set aside. In a 3- to 4-quart saucepan, bring the chicken stock and the salt to a boil over moderate heat. Drop in the asparagus tips and boil slowly for 5 to 8 minutes, or until they are just tender. Drain the stock into a bowl and set the tips aside in another.

In the same saucepan, melt 5 tablespoons of the butter over moderate heat. Stir in the 6 tablespoons of flour, then cook over low heat, stirring constantly, for 1 or 2 minutes. Do not let this roux brown. Remove the pan from the heat, let it cool for a few seconds, then pour in the stock, beating constantly with a wire whisk to blend the stock and the roux. Return the pan to moderate heat and stir until this cream soup base comes to a boil, thickens and is perfectly smooth. Turn the heat down and let the soup base simmer very gently.

Melt the remaining 2 tablespoons of butter in an 8- to 10-inch enameled or stainless-steel skillet. When the foam subsides, stir in the cut-up asparagus stalks and the shallots, and toss them in the butter over moderate heat for 3 minutes. Stir the stalks and shallots into the simmering soup base and cook over low heat, stirring occasionally, for 15 minutes or until the asparagus is tender.

Purée the soup through a food mill into a mixing bowl and then again through a fine sieve back into the pan. With a wire whisk, blend the egg yolks and cream together in a medium-size mixing bowl. Whisk in the puréed soup, 2 tablespoons at a time, until ½ cup has been added. Then reverse the process and slowly whisk the now-warmed egg-yolk-and-cream mixture into the soup. Bring to a boil, and boil for 30 seconds, stirring constantly. Remove the pan from the heat and stir in the 2 tablespoons of soft butter, 1 tablespoon at a time. Taste the soup and season it with salt and white pepper. Add the reserved asparagus tips and ladle the soup into a tureen or into individual soup bowls.

RORER

Mrs. Rorer's New Cook Book

Cream of Salsify Soup

12 roots of salsify
1 tablespoonful of butter
2 tablespoonfuls of flour
1 teaspoonful of salt
1 quart of milk
1 tablespoonful of grated onion
1 pint of water
1 saltspoonful of pepper

Scrape the salsify, throwing them at once into cold water to prevent discoloration; cut into thin slices, and put into a saucepan with the water and onion; cover and cook slowly for twenty minutes; add the milk. Rub the butter and flour together; add a little of the milk, making a smooth paste; then turn the whole into the kettle; stir constantly until it just reaches the boiling point; add the salt and pepper, and serve at once with oyster crackers. A small bit of salt codfish boiled with the salsify greatly improves the flavor.

BEARD

The Fireside Cook Book

CREAM OF CORN: Heat 1 cup cooked corn kernels in 2 cups chicken broth. Season with salt, pepper, and a little grated onion or finely chopped green pepper. When boiling, pour over 1 cup cream mixed with 2 egg yolks, a little at a time, stirring constantly. Blend well together and rectify the seasoning.

CREAM OF CELERY: Cook 1 cup finely cut celery and tops in 2 cups chicken broth, adding salt. pepper, and parsley for flavoring. You may add 1 tablespoon finely chopped onion as well, if you wish. When tender, puree the celery, return it to broth, and place over hot water. When just at the boiling point, add 1 cup cream mixed with 2 egg yolks. Stir constantly until the soup is lightly thickened. Garnish with chopped parsley and finely chopped celery tops.

The same procedure may be used for other vegetable soups, such as those with broccoli, cauliflower, leeks, onion, peas, spinach, watercress, etc.

RORER

Mrs. Rorer's New Cook Book

Cream of Peanut Soup

- 1 quart of milk
- 1 teaspoonful of grated onion or onion juice
- A tablespoonful of cornstarch
- A dash of paprika
- ½ pint of peanut butter
- A bay leaf
- A saltspoonful of celery seed or a little chopped celery
- ½ teaspoonful of salt
- A dash of white pepper

Put the milk, peanut butter, onion and celery seed into a double boiler; stir and cook until hot. Moisten the cornstarch in a little cold milk, add it to the hot milk, and stir until smooth and thick. Strain through a sieve; add the salt, pepper and paprika, and serve at once with croûtons.

ROSSO AND LUKINS

The Silver Palate Cookbook

Curried Butternut Squash Soup

Squash and apples complement each other naturally; curry adds an exotic note. Feel free to experiment with other types of winter or summer squash.

- 4 tablespoons sweet butter
- 2 cups finely chopped yellow onions
- 4 to 5 teaspoons curry powder
- 2 medium-size butternut squash (about 3 pounds altogether)
- 2 apples, peeled, cored and chopped
- 3 cups Chicken Stock
- 1 cup apple sauce
- salt and freshly ground black pepper, to taste
- 1 shredded unpeeled Granny Smith apple (garnish)

1. Melt the butter in a pot. Add chopped onions and curry powder and cook, covered, over low heat until onions are tender, about 25 minutes.

2. Meanwhile peel the squash (a regular vegetable peeler works best), scrape out the seeds, and chop the flesh.

3. When onions are tender, pour in the stock, add squash and apples, and bring to a boil. Reduce heat and simmer, partially covered, until squash and apples are very tender, about 25 minutes.

4. Pour the soup through a strainer, reserving liquid, and transfer the solids to the bowl of a food processor fitted with a steel blade, or use a food mill fitted with a medium disc. Add 1 cup of the cooking stock and process until smooth.

5. Return puréed soup to the pot and add apple juice and additional cooking liquid, about 2 cups, until the soup is of the desired consistency.

6. Season to taste with salt and pepper, simmer briefly to heat through, and serve immediately, garnished with shredded apple.

4 TO 6 PORTIONS

ROJAS-LOMBARDI

The Art of South American Cooking

Chupe de Quinua

Quinoa Chowder

SERVES 6 TO 8

Quinoa has a good nutritional profile; it is high in protein and other nutrients. It is also exceedingly versatile in the kitchen. It is good by itself and goes well with other foods. A handful of quinoa added to an ordinary vegetable or chicken soup—or any soup for that matter—makes it something special.

8 ounces raw quinoa (1¼ cups)
2 tablespoons olive oil
1 large clove garlic, peeled and minced
1 jalapeño pepper, seeded and minced
¼ teaspoon ground cumin
⅛ teaspoon ground white pepper
1 tablespoon coarse salt
½ pound potatoes, peeled and cut into ¼-inch dice
8 ounces feta, cut into ¼-inch dice
½ pound fresh spinach leaves, shredded about ¼ inch thick
1 or 2 hard-boiled eggs, sliced

1. Rinse the quinoa in a strainer under cold running water. In a saucepan, combine the rinsed quinoa with 6 cups of cold water and bring to a boil over high heat, stirring now and then. Lower the heat and simmer for 10 minutes, or until the quinoa is tender. Remove from the heat, pour through a strainer, and let drain thoroughly. Set aside.

2. In a saucepan, heat the olive oil over low heat. Add the garlic and hot pepper and sauté, stirring, for just a second or two. Do not let the garlic brown. Add the cumin, pepper, salt, and 5 cups of water and bring to a boil. Add the cooked quinoa and the diced potatoes and cook over medium heat for 10 to 15 minutes, or until the potatoes are done.

3. Stir in the cheese and continue to cook for a few seconds, then fold in the shredded spinach leaves. Correct the seasoning with salt to taste and serve hot, garnished with slices of hard-boiled eggs.

VARIATIONS

Add 1½ pounds of lean meat (lamb, beef, pork, or chicken), cut into 1-inch cubes. Thoroughly brown the meat in the olive oil in Step 2; add the garlic and hot pepper and proceed with the recipe.

SOPA DE BETERRAGA Y QUINUA

Beet and Quinoa Soup

Substitute ½ pound of beets for the potatoes. Peel and cut them into ¼-inch cubes and add them in Step 2. They will take a few minutes longer to cook than potatoes. Already-cooked beets may be added too.

SOPA DE QUINUA AL ESTILO HUANCAYO

Fava Bean and Quinoa Soup

Shell and peel 1 to 1½ pounds of fava beans. Substitute them for the potatoes in Step 2.

BÉGUÉ

Mme. Bégué's Recipes of Old New Orleans Creole Cookery

BISQUE OF CRAYFISH. Half bucket of crayfish washed well and boiled three minutes. Separate the tails from the heads. Stuff a number of the heads with a paste of beaten fish to which is added the tails of the crayfish. Pound the remainder of the heads in a mortar and put this latter in a saucepan with a pound of butter, three carrots, two onions, a few pieces of celery, thyme, bay leaves, cloves and grated nutmeg. Boil the whole forty-five minutes. Then add a quart of Marcelas wine and a few tomatoes. Pour into saucepan half gallon good beef stock, add half pound of rice, season with salt, pepper and cayenne and let simmer slowly. Pass through a sifter to remove particles and serve three stuffed heads and six peeled tails to each plate.

BISQUE OF CRAYFISH. Choose about forty nice crayfish and let them have a good boiling. Remove from fire and drain. Clean the heads, keep thirty of the shells and also the remains which you will set to boil in a quart of water. Peel the tails and chop them fine. Make a paste with that meat, to which add a cupful of soaked bread, a large spoonful of fried onions and chopped parsley, and salt and pepper to taste. With this fill the thirty shells and set them aside. Start your soup by frying in butter an onion, some flour for thickening and half a cupful each of green onions and parsley chopped fine, a spray of thyme and two bay leaves. When browned pour in the bouillon made with the remains of the heads, and season with salt and strong pepper; let boil slowly for half an hour. Add more water if needed. When ready to serve take each head, roll it in flour and fry them all in butter until crisp all around, and throw in the soup. Let boil three or four minutes, and serve with very thin slices of toast bread.

JUNIOR LEAGUE OF CHARLESTON
Charleston Receipts

". . . Crab got tuh walk een duh pot demself or dey ain' wut."

SHE-CRAB SOUP

A soup to remember!
The feminine gender
Of crabs is expedient—
The secret ingredient.
The flavor essential
Makes men reverential
Who taste this collation
And cry acclamation.

She-Crab Soup

"She-crab" is much more of a delicacy than "he-crab," as the eggs add a special flavor to the soup. The street vendors make a point of calling "she-crab" loudly and of charging extra for them.

- 1 tablespoon butter
- 1 quart milk
- ¼ pint cream (whipped)
- Few drops onion juice
- ⅛ teaspoon mace
- ⅛ teaspoon pepper
- ½ teaspoon Worcestershire
- 1 teaspoon flour
- 2 cups white crab meat and crab eggs
- ½ teaspoon salt
- 4 tablespoons dry sherry

Melt butter in top of double boiler and blend with flour until smooth. Add the milk gradually, stirring constantly. To this add crab meat and eggs and all seasonings except sherry. Cook slowly over hot water for 20 minutes. To serve, place one tablespoon of warmed sherry in individual soup bowls, then add soup and top with whipped cream. Sprinkle with paprika or finely chopped parsley. Secret: if unable to obtain "she-crabs," crumble yolk of hard boiled eggs in bottom of soup plates. Serves 4–6.

MRS. HENRY F. CHURCH (Rea Bryant)

BÉGUÉ
Mme. Bégué's Recipes of Old New Orleans Creole Cookery

TURTLE SOUP. Select a turtle of the desired size. Clean it well and cut in small pieces. If when bought, some of the inside is added to the meat, scrape well and cut small also. Fry a large onion in hot lard; when done add a spoonful of flour and let the whole brown nicely; put in the meat and let it fry a while. Add tomatoes, the quantity of bouillon needed and a glass each of White and Madeira wine. Season to taste with pepper, a few cloves and bouquet consisting of a couple of bay leaves, thyme and parsley. Lastly add two spoonfuls of Worcestershire sauce. Serve with toast bread.

LUCAS
The Cordon Bleu Cook Book

Clam and Oyster Chowder

- 2 tablespoons butter
- 1 tablespoon oil
- 1 tablespoon mixed scallion, onion, garlic
- 1 dozen raw oysters
- 1 dozen raw hard clams
- 3 cups light cream
- salt
- cayenne pepper
- 4 tablespoons butter
- small handful chopped parsley

Heat butter and oil in a pan and add mixed scallion, onion and garlic. Cook for 2 minutes; then add cut-up oysters and clams. Pour on cream and season with salt and cayenne pepper. Bring very lightly to a boil, then add bit by bit butter and parsley. Simmer a few minutes and serve.

DAVID
French Provincial Cooking

La Bouillabaisse (1)

A whole chapter could be devoted to the bouillabaisse. Every French gastronomic writer and cook for the past hundred years (and some before that) have expounded their theories upon the dish so beloved of the Marseillais, and each one of them gives his own recipe—the only authentic one. And, however many Marseillais, Toulonnais, Antibois or other natives of Provence you ask for the correct recipe, you will never get the same instructions twice.

There is no authentic bouillabaisse without white wine, you are told; it is a heresy of the most deadly kind to add white wine; the best bouillabaisse includes a langouste *and mussels;* langouste *and mussels are only added in Paris because they haven't the other requisite fish; you* must *rub the croûtons with garlic; you must on no account rub the croûtons with garlic, and so on and so on.*

I would not myself think it a great deprivation if I were told that I could never again eat a bouillabaisse. I have had good ones and bad ones but to be quite truthful I have also eaten far superior *dishes of the same sort, call it a soup or a stew or what you like, in Italy, notably on the Adriatic coast (and I hope no Marseillais will ever see these words, for the consequences might be serious).*

However, for those who are interested in both the theory and the practice of the cooking of a bouillabaisse, a few constant factors emerge from all the confusion. They are as follows:

(1) It is useless attempting to make a bouillabaisse away from the shores of the Mediterranean. All sorts of variations can be and are devised in other parts of the world, but it would be foolish to pretend that these have more than a remote relationship to the true bouillabaisse.

(2) The fish must be spanking fresh from the sea, and of diverse kinds. The rascasse is essential, and the fish is always served with its head. If langouste is included, this is cut in half lengthways and served in its shell. Mussels, if part of the bouillabaisse, are likewise left in their shells.

(3) Olive oil and saffron are equally essential.

(4) Furious boiling, so that the olive oil and water (or wine if you are a heretic) amalgamate, is another absolute essential of the success of the dish.

(5) The Toulonnais sometimes add potatoes (a practice which appals a Marseillais). The potatoes are best cut (raw) into thin rounds and added at the same time as the soft fish.

(6) A bouillabaisse is not intended to be a soup. There should merely be enough of the broth, fused with the olive oil by the very rapid boiling, to produce a generous amount of moistening for the slices of bread.

From all the writers who have poured out such eloquent words (very often in verse) on the subject of the bouillabaisse, I have chosen two descriptions to quote and both of these include splendid recipes. But what, I cannot help wondering, would be the consequences if any of these people should chance to see what I with my own eyes have seen—tins, yes tins, ½ pint tins of something called Danish bouillabaisse actually on sale proudly displayed in our most expensive food stores. What unhappy man can have had such a terrible, sad idea? Who are the people who can be induced to buy such concentrated effrontery?

La Bouillabaisse (2)

Austin de Croze, who gives the following recipe in Les Plats Régionaux de France, *says he considers it the best there is. It was contributed by a Marseillais, M. Etienne Fauché, one-time Mayor of Cassis, and subsequently President of the Syndicat d'Initiative of La Sainte Baume, in the Var.*

'The secret of a successful bouillabaisse may be summed up as follows: live fish in large variety; good olive oil and top quality saffron. The only difficulty in executing the dish consists in bringing it to the boil rapidly and fiercely.

'Every locality in Provence has, of course, its claim to the genuine bouillabaisse. But the true one comes from Marseille. For is it not in the waters of the beautiful bay of Marseille that all the requisite varieties of brilliant-hued rock fish, which go to make up the excellence of a bouillabaisse, are to be found?

'Those who have attempted to complicate the simple recipe for a bouillabaisse have succeeded only in spoiling its character; it is a mistake to cook the fish in a previously prepared broth of small fry; it is a culinary heresy to add white wine to a bouillabaisse (although it is indispensable on the table with it). It is superfluous to thicken the sauce, even with a purée of sea-urchins. All such elaborations are simply a fashion of disguising the poverty or lack of freshness of the fish. Bearing these considerations in mind, here is the recipe for bouillabaisse, in its simplicity and integrity.

'For ten people, take about 5 lb. of different fish, comprising rascasse,[i] angler fish [baudroie], weaver [vive], John Dory [St. Pierre], sea-hen [galinette],[ii] whiting and two crawfish [langoustes]. Scale, gut and wash these fish, in sea-water if possible, and cut them in slices.

'In a heavy pan, wider than it is high, put 2 onions, 4 tomatoes and 4 cloves of garlic, all coarsely chopped; moisten with a decilitre (3 oz.) of best quality olive oil, add 2 sprigs of fennel leaves, a bay leaf and a good pinch of powdered saffron; season with ½ oz. of coarse salt and ¼ oz. pepper. Mix all well together, and add the firm fish, keeping the soft ones (galinette, John Dory and whiting) to add 5 minutes later. Pour over boiling water to cover the fish, taking into account those which are to be added. Put the pan over a very fierce flame and give it 12 to 15 minutes at a very rapid boil. It is upon this fast boiling that success depends.

'In the meantime, cut a long loaf into slices; dry them a few seconds in the oven but without letting them take colour.

'When the bouillabaisse is ready, arrange the slices of fish carefully in a dish, and through a sieve pour the bouillon over the bread arranged in a deep vegetable dish. Sprinkle with parsley.

'The bouillabaisse should be served when the guests are at table. Which is to say that it must not wait, but be waited for.

'In a well-cooked bouillabaisse, the particular flavour of each fish should be distinct. The pepper should be slightly dominant; the broth should be naturally thickened by the violent boiling.

'I should advise that the heads of the fish, with the exception of those of the rascasses, should be sacrificed to the broth. Cut them in several pieces and, when the fish has been removed to its serving dish, it will do no harm to the broth to let it boil fiercely another five minutes before straining it over the bread.'

[i] A spiky, spiny rock-fish sometimes called a sea-scorpion.
[ii] A fish of the same family as the gurnard.

KENNEDY
The Cuisines of Mexico

Pozole de Jalisco

Pork and hominy soup

12 TO 14 SERVINGS

This is a superb and unique recipe of the Marín family of Jalisco. The earthy character and flavor of the broth, corn, and meats with the crunchiness of the raw vegetables and the fieriness of the sauce combine to give an incomparable sensation of flavors and textures.

TWO DAYS AHEAD:

1 pound whole hominy or large white dried corn kernels

Put the corn to soak.

ONE DAY AHEAD:

1½ pounds pork, tenderloin or butt without bone
½ pig's head (not more than 3 pounds)
1 pound pork neck bones
Cold water to cover
2 cups *chiles serranos secos* (about 3 ounces)
Cold water to cover

Clean and prepare the hominy for cooking. Cut the pork into large serving pieces and put it, with the head and bones, in cold water to soak overnight. Change the water as often as is practical. Cover the chilies with cold water and let them soak overnight.

ON SERVING DAY:

A very large pot, preferably earthenware, for the pozole
The hominy
14 cups water
A saucepan
The pig's head
Water to cover
The corn
1½ tablespoons salt
The soaked meat and neck bones

Cover the hominy with the cold, unsalted water. Bring to a boil and cook, uncovered, over a brisk flame until it opens up like a flower—about 1 hour. ***Do not stir the corn*** during this time, but, if necessary, skim the surface of the water from time to time.

Cover the head with cold, unsalted water. Bring to a boil, then lower the flame and let it simmer, uncovered, until the flesh can be removed from the bone—but do not overcook—about 1 hour. Set it aside to cool.

When the head is cool enough to handle, remove all the meat, skin, etc., and cut it into serving pieces. Cut the ear up (there should be a piece for everyone) and set the eye aside for the honored guest. Add the pieces of head, and the broth in which it was cooked, to the corn in its pot.

Add the salt. Place the meat on top of the corn and let the *pozole* cook, uncovered, over a gentle flame for about 4 hours. Throughout the cooking time skim the fat from the surface. Keep some water boiling in a kettle at the side to add to the liquid in the pan. On no account should cold water be added. The liquid should be maintained at almost the same level from start to finish.

THE SALSA PICANTE

A blender
A fine sieve
The soaked chilies and the soaking liquid

Blend the chilies with the water in which they were soaking. Strain the sauce through a sieve. Do not add salt.

TO SERVE:
Place the meat onto a serving dish so it can be divided up more easily and everyone can have the part that he likes best. Serve the *pozole* with the corn in large, deep bowls, with the following small side dishes to which everyone can help himself:

The *salsa picante*
Finely chopped onion
Sliced radishes
Finely shredded lettuce
Wedges of lime

NOTE: *Pozole de Jalisco* is not served with oregano, as it is in the neighboring state of Michoacán.

The chili used for the sauce in Jalisco is *chile de árbol*, a long, thin dried red chili; a suitable substitute is *serrano seco*.

The *pozole* should be cooked with plenty of salt; you may need to add more just before the end of the cooking time.

Only those who know the wonderful flavor and consistency of a soup made with the specially prepared corn will appreciate how hard it is for me to say: if you can't get the real corn, used canned. In that case, cook the head first, add the rest of the meat, and an hour later add the drained canned hominy.

MITCHELL
Lüchow's German Cookbook

Barley Soup with Giblets
Graupensuppe Mit Hühnerklein

1 cup pearl barley
Boiling water
1 tablespoon butter
2 quarts beef or chicken bouillon
2 cups broth in which giblets cooked
¼ teaspoon grated nutmeg
Chopped chicken giblets
Salt and pepper
2 tablespoons chopped parsley

Wash barley; drain. Pour boiling water over it twice and drain. Heat butter; cook barley 2 or 3 minutes. Place barley, bouillon, broth from giblets, and nutmeg in soup kettle. Boil slowly 1½ hours. Add giblets for last 20 minutes of cooking. If seasoning is needed, add salt and pepper. Add parsley before serving. Serves 6.

COOKED GIBLETS

Chicken giblets
1 cup white wine
1½ cups chicken stock or bouillon
½ teaspoon salt
¼ teaspoon pepper
¼ teaspoon grated nutmeg

Wash giblets; drain; split and clean gizzard. Add wine, stock, and seasonings. Cover and cook slowly until all are tender, 20 minutes or longer. Drain; chop giblets. Save liquid and use as described above.

KENNEDY
The Cuisines of Mexico

Sopa de Lima

Lime soup

6 SERVINGS

*This is considered to be the soup of Yucatán, and on the hottest day—and that seems to be the year round—you will be served a bowl of sizzling lime soup. Sizzling because of the hot, crisp tortilla pieces that are dropped in at the last moment, and lime because of the unique flavor given it by the rind and juice of the bitter lime—*Citrus limetta. *This lime must be used in other regions, but I have not come across it. It is small, roundish, and pale green when ripe and looks as though it has had its nipple pushed in along the way. Its flavor cannot be compared to that of any other citrus fruit—although there is something of the same astringent quality of the bitter orange, but it is stronger and more fragrant.*

As a substitute for the bitter lime, use a piece of Seville orange and lime—or lime and a little grapefruit peel.

HAVE READY

12 stale tortillas, cut into strips
6 soup bowls
4 small bowls
¾ cup finely chopped onion
⅓ cup fine chopped chile serrano, with seeds
Freshly ground pepper
⅓ cup unpeeled, finely chopped bitter lime

A saucepan
4 chicken gizzards
6 chicken livers (8 ounces)
10 cloves garlic, toasted
¼ teaspoon oregano, toasted
6 peppercorns
1 teaspoon salt
8 cups water

Cover all the ingredients with water and simmer them for about 15 minutes.

2 chicken breasts

Add the chicken breasts and continue cooking for another 15 minutes, or until the meats are tender.

A strainer

Strain the broth and set it aside. Shred the breasts, chop the livers, remove the gristle from the gizzards, and chop them. Set the meats aside.

A small frying pan
1½ tablespoons lard
⅓ cup onion, finely chopped

Heat the lard and gently fry the onion and pepper until they are soft, but not browned.

1 large tomato (about ½ pound), skinned seeded, and mashed
The broth

Add the tomato to the mixture in the pan. Let the mixture cook for about 5 minutes over a medium flame, then add to the broth and let it simmer for about 5 minutes.

Add the salt as necessary, then add the chopped and shredded meats and heat them through.

Squeeze a little of the juice into the broth. Drop the squeezed lime half into the broth for a few seconds only, then remove. Keep the broth warm, and do not put it into the soup bowls until you are draining the fried tortilla strips.

A frying pan
Lard for frying
The tortilla strips
Paper toweling
The soup bowls

Heat the lard until it is smoking and fry the tortilla strips until they are crisp. Drain them on the toweling, and while they are still very hot drop some of them into the broth in each soup bowl.

4 small bowls
The chopped onion
The chopped chile serrano
The freshly ground pepper
The chopped bitter lime

Put each of the last ingredients into a small bowl so that each person can help himself.

ZIEMANN AND GILETTE
The White House Cook Book

Mock Turtle Soup, of Calf's Head

Scald a well-cleansed calf's head, remove the brain, tie it up in a cloth, and boil an hour, or until the meat will easily slip from the bone; take out, save the broth; cut it in small square pieces, and throw them into cold water; when cool, put it in a stewpan, and cover with some of the broth; let it boil until quite tender, and set aside.

In another stewpan melt some butter, and in it put a quarter of a pound of lean ham, cut small, with fine herbs to taste; also parsley and one onion; add about a pint of the broth; let it simmer for two hours, and then dredge in a small quantity of flour; now add the remainder of the broth, and a quarter bottle of Madeira or sherry; let all stew quietly for ten minutes and rub it through a medium sieve; add the calf's head, season with a very little cayenne pepper, a little salt, the juice of one lemon, and, if desired, a quarter teaspoonful pounded mace and a dessert-spoon sugar.

Having previously prepared force meat balls, add them to the soup, and five minutes after serve hot.

ANDREWS
Catalan Cuisine

Escudella i Carn d'olla

Catalan Soup with Boiled Meats and Vegetables, in two courses

There's a Catalan proverb that says, "*No és fa bona olla amb aigua sola*"—"A good soup isn't made with just water." Taking this advice to heart, the people of the *països catalans* tend to like big, serious soups, soups filled almost to excess with assorted meats and vegetables: heroic soups like the *ouillade* or *ollada* of the Roussillon, thick with pork, cabbage, and potatoes, traditionally cooked in two pots simultaneously and then mixed (pots which were never washed out, never allowed to cool), the *olletes* and *gaspatxos* of the *país valencià*, the former rich with white beans and sausages and sometimes huge cornmeal dumplings, the latter (unrelated to the *gazpacho* of Andalusia except in name) crowded with game birds and wild rabbit and performed with aromatic herbs; the legendary "*sopa sens aigua, foch, ni olla*" of the Balearics, made "without water, fire, or pot" (pork and/or chicken and six or eight moist vegetables baked in a hollowed-out pumpkin in the leftover heat of a baker's oven); the many fish soups and *sopes* of Catalonia itself, and the same region's *Escudelles*; and, above all, *Escudella i Carn d'Olla*, the very flesh and blood of Catalan bourgeois cooking—a soup and a stew and practically a way of life, all in the same pot.

Escudella i Carn d'Olla—an *escudella* is a bowl and by extension a bowl of soup; *carn d'olla* is meat from the *olla* or pot—is "the oldest and most traditional dish of Catalan cuisine," author/chef Josep Lladonosa has written. Gironan gastronome Jaume Fàbrega calls it one of the idiom's "culinary chromosomes." Singer/songwriter and food-lover Lluís Llach maintains that it reflects "all the wisdom of the (Catalan) people." Author Manuel Vázquez Montalbán hails it as "the *Summa Theologica* of Catalan cuisine," and says that it was "for the Catalan bourgeoisie its pedigree . . . its credential as a society without pretensions, one that knew how to do things and that had adopted a European, democratic attitude."

And just what is this ancient, definitive, symbolic dish, exactly? It's the Catalan version of *cocido* or *pot au feu* or *bollito misto* or boiled dinner—root vegetables, cabbage, chickpeas, meatballs, chicken, sausages, etc., simmered together for hours to produce a rich, complex broth and then served in two parts: first the broth itself, in which some rice or pasta has been cooked at the last minute, then the vegetables and meats.

Some scholars consider it a direct descendant of the *adafina* of Spain's Sephardic Jews; others point out that the basic notion of such a hodgepodge is common to most of the world's cuisines, developing independently almost everywhere that there were pots, vegetables, and meats. Most Catalans seem content to let anybody think whatever they want about the dish; *they* know it is theirs and theirs alone. During the nineteenth century, which was the period of *Escudella i Carn d'Olla*'s greatest popularity in Catalonia, in fact, many families ate it for dinner six or seven times a week—adding minor variation only by altering the nature of the starch stirred into the soup (rice one day, *fideus* another, semolina another still, and so on, and even this according to the same fixed schedule week after week). Greater love for a dish hath no people.

Escudella i Carn d'Olla

Catalan Soup with Boiled Meats and Vegetables, in two courses

It is said that after the great French Catalan military hero Maréchal Joffre had won the Battle of the Marne in 1914, stopping the German advance on Paris, his chef recited to him a magnificent menu for the victory banquet—to which Joffre responded that what he really had in mind in this moment of glory, thanks, was . . . yes, *Escudella i Carn d'Olla*.

One sees his point. Catalan hyperbole aside, it must be admitted that the dish is indeed an unusually comforting and restorative one—just the thing to soothe travails, salve wounds, revivify beleaguered spirits. It is, indeed, as Garrotxan chef Domènec Moli once wrote, "a sumptuous, splendiferous dish, which marries the virtues of the vegetables with those of the meat, generating an unimprovable broth and a dish both strong and flavorful." True connoisseurs of *Escudella i Carn d'Olla*, in fact, will tell you that that unimprovable broth is the most important aspect of the dish—"an extract of a thousand essences" and "a résumé of the ingredients of the pot," Manuel Vázquez Montalbán has called it.

There's really no secret to the broth's richness—just long, slow cooking and high-quality ingredients—and don't leave out the bones or the pig's foot (the latter of which adds not only flavor but thickness of body). And whether or not *Escudella i Carn d'Olla* sounds like your idea of a good way to celebrate a victory, it certainly can warm a chilly night or feed a hungry multitude.

TO SERVE 8 (AS APPETIZER AND MAIN COURSE)

8 ounces dried chick-peas
6 ounces thick-cut bacon, diced
1 pig's foot, halved
1 small ham bone or 1–1½ pounds ham hocks
1 pound veal or beef bones
1 pound stewing veal, cut into pieces about 2 inches square
1 green cabbage, quartered
2 stalks celery
2 carrots
2 turnips, halved
1 chicken, cut into 8 serving pieces
10 ounces botifarra sausage, casing removed, or 10 ounces ground pork
4 ounces ground veal or beef
2 eggs, lightly beaten
2 cloves garlic, minced
2 sprigs parsley, minced
2 tablespoons breadcrumbs
Pinch of cinnamon
Flour
4 medium potatoes, peeled and halved
2 botifarra negra sausages
Salt and pepper
8 ounces fideus noodles or large shell pasta
Olive oil

Soak the chick-peas overnight in cold water, then drain.

In a large soup pot, add the bacon, pig's foot, ham bone, and veal bones to about 6 quarts of water, bring to a boil, and simmer, partially covered, for ½ hour. Skim as necessary.

Add the veal, cabbage, celery, carrots, and turnips; uncover, and continue simmering for 45 minutes.

After 45 minutes, add the chicken pieces, and cook 45 minutes longer, adding more water if necessary to cover the ingredients.

Meanwhile, crumble the *botifarra* sausage or ground pork into a large bowl, then add the ground veal, eggs, garlic, parsley, breadcrumbs, and cinnamon, and work together thoroughly until all the ingredients are well integrated and slightly sticky. Form the mixture into 2 cylindrical shapes, about 5–7 inches long and 2½–3½ inches thick. Roll the cylinders lightly in flour, and set them aside.

When the chicken has cooked for 45 minutes, add the potatoes and ground meat cylinders to the pot, again, adding more water if necessary, and simmer 20 minutes longer.

After 20 minutes, add the *botifarra negra* sausages, then simmer for 10 minutes longer. Salt and pepper to taste.

Strain out three quarters of the broth, and transfer it to another pot, allowing the meats and vegetables to rest off heat, uncovered, in the original pot.

Bring the transferred broth to a boil; then add pasta, return to a boil, and cook 10–15 minutes or until the pasta is very tender (not *al dente*).

Divide soup and pasta evenly between 8 bowls and serve.

To serve second course, reheat meats and vegetables briefly in remaining broth, then strain out broth, reserving for another use (see below). Divide meats and vegetables evenly between 8 plates, cutting vegetables and *botifarra negra* into 8 pieces each and cutting meat cylinders into 1–1½ inch slices. Drizzle meats and vegetables lightly with olive oil.

NOTE: It is important for this recipe to use dried chick-peas, not canned ones, since they must cook in the broth to lend their flavor to it, and canned ones, already cooked, would disintegrate with long cooking. Leftover broth is delicious by itself, but I also like cooking rice in it as a side dish for pork or veal chops.

SALADS

ALLEN

Mrs. Allen's Cook Book

Waldorf Salad

Large rosy apples
Celery
Walnut meats
Mayonnaise or boiled oil dressing
Lettuce

Form the apples into cups by cutting off the tops and scooping out the pulp with a pointed spoon. Drop the cups into water as soon as made to prevent discoloration, and cut the removed apple pulp into cubes. Add an equal quantity of diced celery, and a fourth the quantity of broken walnut meats. Mix with the salad dressing and pile in the cups. Serve individually, each cup set on a lettuce leaf. Garnish the top of each cup with a sprig of parsley and additional dressing.

JUNIOR LEAGUE OF AUGUSTA

Old and New Recipes from the South

Green Goddess Salad

1 head lettuce
1 head endive
1 lb. tomatoes if desired

Separate lettuce, chop endive, and put in bowl; toss together with following dressing:

1 tablespoon chives, minced
8 tablespoons tarragon vinegar
1 tube anchovy paste
2 tablespoons minced parsley
1 green onion, minced
1 clove garlic
1 pt. mayonnaise

—Mrs. Robert Rood.

WATERS

Chez Panisse Vegetables

Parsley Salad

Pluck the leaves from a large bunch of Italian parsley. Wash them and spin them dry in a salad spinner. Just before serving, drizzle with a small amount of olive oil, enough to coat the leaves; add a squeeze of lemon juice; and grate over a generous amount of Parmesan. Toss and season with salt and pepper. If you wish, garnish with a few thin curls of Parmesan shaved from the block of cheese with a cheese slicer or a swivel bladed vegetable peeler.

CURTIS

Good Housekeeping Everyday Cook Book

Cold Slaw

Chop with one small head of cabbage two hard-boiled eggs. Take one-half cup of sour cream, one tablespoon of sugar, a little salt and pepper, and a teaspoon of celery seed; beat all together, then add one teacup of vinegar, and pour over the cabbage. If this is put in a tight vessel, it will keep several days.

—Mrs Creigh, Omaha.

BAYLESS

Rick Bayless's Mexican Kitchen

Topolo "Caesar" Salad

Ensalada Estilo Topolobampo

Though we're sure this was invented in Mexico (by Italian immigrant Caesar Cardini), I'd never call it traditionally Mexican. In Puebla or Chilpancingo or Oaxaca, its existence is still heresay. I've included it because I love the Mexicanized version I came up with for our restaurant, Topolobampo—green chile and lime, not lemon, in the dressing, cilantro with the greens and queso añejo *or Vella's dry Jack cheese, not Parmesan, over everything.*

It seems there are numerous "original" versions of Caesar salad around, though for me truth always lies with Julia. How can you doubt the one who taught you to master hollandaise and puff pastry? From Julia Child's Kitchen *details a very good original formula that was my starting point here. I've chosen to add a raw egg to the dressing, but to keep it from becoming too thick and mayonnaisy, I whisk in half the oil by hand. If using raw eggs bothers you, make a spicy vinaigrette without the egg for a very good, but different, salad.*

SERVES 4 TO 6; ABOUT 1½ CUPS DRESSING

FOR THE DRESSING (THIS IS THE MINIMUM QUANTITY MANAGEABLE, THOUGH IT MAKES ENOUGH FOR 4 ROUNDS OF THIS SALAD)

1 cup fruity olive oil
1½ tablespoons vinegar, preferably sherry vinegar
4 teaspoons Worcestershire sauce
1 fresh serrano chile, stemmed and halved
The zest (colored part only) of 1½ limes
1 egg
Salt, about ½ teaspoon

FOR THE CROUTONS

¼ cup olive oil
4 garlic cloves, peeled and roughly chopped
2 cups firm bread (preferably sourdough) crusts removed, cut into ½-inch cubes

FOR FINISHING THE SALAD

2 medium-small heads romaine lettuce, tough outer leaves removed, inner leaves rinsed and dried
or 8 ounces (about 8 cups moderately packed) mixed young greens, rinsed and dried
¾ cup finely crumbled Mexican queso añejo, dry Jack or Parmesan cheese
½ cup roughly chopped cilantro

1. THE DRESSING. Combine *½ cup* of the olive oil plus all other dressing ingredients in a food processor or blender and process one full minute. Scrape into a small bowl and slowly whisk in the remaining *½ cup* olive oil. Taste and add more salt if you think necessary.

2. THE CROUTONS. Turn on the oven to 350 degrees. In a small (1- to 1½-quart) saucepan, combine the ¼ cup olive oil and the garlic. Set over the lowest heat and stir every now and again until the garlic is very soft, about 20 minutes. While the garlic is cooking, spread the bread cubes on a baking sheet and bake, stirring occasionally, until completely crisp and dry, about 20 minutes. Gently mash the garlic in the oil to extract as much flavor as possible, then pour the oil through a fine mesh strainer into a small bowl. Toss the oil with the bread cubes to coat evenly, return to the oven and bake until nicely golden, about 5 more minutes.

3. FINISHING THE SALAD. In a large salad bowl, combine the lettuce, ⅓ *cup* of the dressing, *half* of the cheese and all of the cilantro. Toss to coat thoroughly, then divide onto salad plates, top with the remaining cheese and the croutons and serve right away.

ADVANCE PREPARATION—The dressing will keep for several days in a closed jar in the refrigerator. The croutons may be prepared a day or two ahead.

SHORTCUTS—You can buy wonderful garlic oil these days, so feel free to use it. Plain, toasted bread croutons are available in lots of bakeries.

VARIATIONS AND IMPROVISATIONS

TOMATO SALAD—Replace the lettuce with sliced tomatoes. Drizzle them with some of the dressing and sprinkle with cilantro, cheese and croutons. An alternative to croutons is slices of grilled bread smeared with goat cheese.

MEXICAN-FLAVORED BREAD SALAD—Make the croutons using 6 to 8 cups of bread cubes (sourdough bread works well here) and then toss with enough of the dressing to moisten. There should be enough dressing to flavor them but not make them soggy. Stir in 3 or 4 diced tomatoes, ½ cup sliced green onions, a handful of chopped pitted calamata olives and the cheese and cilantro. Serve on crisp romaine leaves.

SCHNEIDER

Uncommon Fruits & Vegetables

Basic Fiddlehead Ferns

One basic preparation will yield pretty, pliant ferns ready to be sauced, sautéed, or dressed for salad. Having experimented with steaming, poaching, braising, and boiling, I find that the last works far better than other methods, retaining texture and color while eliminating the bitterness that is sometimes present in these furled sprouts.

4–6 SERVINGS

1 pound fiddlehead ferns, each about 1–1½ inches in diameter

1. Trim base of each fern, if necessary, to leave only a tiny tail beyond circumference of each circular form. If furry brown covering remains on ferns, rub it off. Rinse briskly under running water.

2. Drop ferns into a large pot of boiling, lightly salted water. Boil until tender throughout—about 5 minutes—testing often; undercooked, the full flavor will not develop. Drain well and serve at once, with melted butter. Or try one of the following alternatives.

FIDDLEHEADS WITH SAUCE

Serve the hot, drained ferns with about 1 cup Hollandaise, Maltaise, cream, or cheese sauce.

FIDDLEHEAD FERNS SAUTÉED IN BUTTER

Drop cooked ferns into ice water to cool. Drain and refrigerate until serving time, covered. At serving time heat 3 tablespoons butter in a large skillet; sauté ferns until heated through.

FIDDLEHEADS FERN VINAIGRETTE

Drop the drained ferns into ice water to cool. Drain and dry well. Combine with ¾ cup light mustard vinaigrette.

NUTMEG CREAM

Prepare ferns as in basic recipe. Serve hot with this intriguing alternative to Hollandaise or cream sauce.

4–6 SERVINGS

1 cup heavy (or whipping) cream (not ultrapasteurized, if possible)
¼ teaspoon salt, approximately
About 1½ teaspoons freshly grated nutmeg
Few drops lemon juice

Whip cream and salt until slightly thickened. Add nutmeg gradually (nutmeg can vary dramatically from one seed to the next, so taste as you add). Add lemon juice and beat until quite firm. Scoop into a cheesecloth-lined sieve, cover with plastic, and refrigerate 1–2 hours before serving.

SCHNEIDER

Uncommon Fruits & Vegetables

Felipe Rojas-Lombardi's Dandelions with Penn Dutch Dressing

Felipe Rojas-Lombardi, the executive chef of the Ballroom Restaurant and Tapas Bar in New York City, draws from a vast culinary vocabulary based on familiarity with the cuisines of many countries. In the simple first-course salad that follows, the influence is from the Pennsylvania Dutch, but I think you'll find the dressing more subtle and less sweet than others of that origin.

6 SERVINGS

- 1¼–1½ pounds dandelion greens, as small and thin as possible, cleaned and trimmed
- ½ pound bacon, diced
- 3 tablespoons flour
- 1 cup milk, approximately
- Approximately ⅓ cup sherry vinegar
- About 1½ teaspoons sugar
- Salt to taste
- About ¼ teaspoon white pepper

1. Dry dandelions thoroughly. Wrap in a towel and chill thoroughly.

2. Fry bacon in skillet until crisp and browned; transfer to paper towels to drain. Discard all but 3 tablespoons bacon fat; strain this to remove all solid bits.

3. Heat fat in small saucepan; add flour, stirring over low heat for several minutes. Add milk and continue stirring over low heat for a few minutes longer. Add ¼ cup vinegar and 1½ teaspoons sugar and stir for a moment; adjust to desired pouring consistency by adding vinegar to taste. Taste for sugar, salt, and pepper. Set aside.

4. Arrange chilled greens on 6 plates. Heat dressing, thinning, if necessary. Pour over greens; sprinkle with bacon, and serve immediately.

RORER

Mrs. Rorer's New Cook Book

Dandelion Salad, German Fashion

- 2 ounces of bacon
- 2 tablespoonfuls of vinegar
- 1 saltspoonful of paprika
- 1 quart of fresh dandelion leaves
- 1 saltspoonful of salt
- 1 tablespoonful of chopped onion or chives

Cut the bacon into strips; put it in a frying pan with two tablespoonfuls of water. Let the water evaporate and the bacon fry carefully until crisp, but not dry. Lift, and stand it aside while you shake the dandelions perfectly dry, and cool the bacon fat. Arrange the dandelions in your salad bowl and put over the slices of bacon. Add to the bacon fat the vinegar, salt, pepper and onion or chives; mix and pour over the dandelions and serve at once.

MADISON

The Greens Cook Book

Wilted Spinach Salad

This salad has been on the menu since the restaurant opened and is still a favorite we make every day. The spinach is tossed with very hot olive oil, which cooks it slightly, sweetening and softening the leaves. As the feta cheese and the olives are both salty, no additional salt is needed.

- 1 small red onion, quartered and thinly sliced
- 3 to 4 slices baguette per person, for croutons
- 6 tablespoons olive oil
- 8 to 12 Kalamata olives
- 1-pound bunch spinach
- 1 clove garlic, finely chopped
- 1 tablespoon mint leaves, finely chopped
- 2 tablespoons sherry vinegar
- 6 ounces feta cheese

Preheat the oven to 400°F. Cover the onion slices with cold water and refrigerate until needed. Brush the bread with some of the olive oil and toast it in the oven until it is crisp and lightly browned, 6 to 8 minutes. Press the olives to split them open, take out the pits, and cut or tear the meats in two.

Remove the spinach stems (or not, as you prefer) and discard any bruised or yellow leaves. Cut the large leaves into halves or thirds; small leaves can be left whole. Wash the spinach, using two changes of water if the spinach is very sandy, and spin dry.

When you are ready to make the salad, drain the onions. Put the spinach in a large metal bowl and toss it with the onions, garlic, mint, olives, and vinegar. Break up the cheese and crumble it over the spinach. Heat the rest of the olive oil until it is very hot but just short of smoking. Immediately pour it over the salad, turning the leaves with a pair of metal tongs so that the hot oil coats and wilts as many leaves as possible. Taste, and season with more vinegar if needed. Serve the salad with the croutons tucked in and around the leaves.

This salad could be accompanied with a moderately dry riesling, or perhaps a zinfandel or Beaujolais.

VARIATIONS: Instead of using only spinach, combine it with curly endive, escarole, or thinly sliced red cabbage—all greens that respond well to being prepared in this way.

MAKES TWO LARGE, OR FOUR TO SIX SMALL SALADS

LEWIS

The Taste of Country Cooking

Wilted Lettuce with Hot Vinegar Dressing

Wilted lettuce was served as a vegetable during the period between spring and summer when there wasn't too much from the garden. The lettuce leaves were washed, crisped, drained dry, and put into a bowl. Then they were seared in a combination of bacon fat, vinegar, and sugar that was boiled up and poured over the lettuce; then sprinkled with finely chopped bacon. For this dish we used Simpson or Grand Rapids lettuce, but iceberg lettuce would be good.

SERVES 4 TO 5

- 1 head iceberg lettuce
- 3 slices bacon
- 1 teaspoon sugar
- ¼ cup vinegar

Remove the outer leaves, using the inside crisp ones. Leave the smaller ones whole. Break away from the stem and reassemble the head loosely in a bowl. Fry 3 slices of good-flavored bacon, then remove the bacon and most of the fat, leaving about 2 tablespoons of fat and residue from the bacon. Now add the sugar and vinegar; bring to a boil, swishing the pan around to stir. Pour this boiling mixture over the lettuce in the bowl. Crumble up the bacon and scatter over the top. Serve while piping hot.

CURTIS

Good Housekeeping Everyday Cook Book

Strawberry Salad

Arrange large ripe strawberries in a glass salad bowl, dust with powdered sugar and a little nutmeg. Pour over a dressing made of two tablespoons of sugar, a gill of sherry, a tablespoon of Maraschino, the juice of one lemon and two oranges; mix the fruit light with a fork and set on ice half an hour before serving.

JUNIOR LEAGUE OF AUGUSTA

Old and New Recipes from the South

Ambrosia

- 6 ripe bananas
- 6 oranges
- 1 grated coconut
- 1 cup sugar

Cut oranges into small thin slices, cut bananas into thin round slices, add sugar, mix, then spread grated coconut on top. Keep cold and serve. This makes a delicious and wholesome dessert. Red cherries may be added.

—MRS. ALFRED BATTEY.

WOLFERT

Couscous and Other Good Food from Morocco

Orange Salads

Moroccan oranges are so good that even Florida and California people begrudgingly admire them. They make marvelous, clean-tasting salads, and superbly refreshing desserts.

ORANGE, LETTUCE, AND WALNUT SALAD (*Shlada Bellecheen*)

INGREDIENTS

1 head romaine lettuce
3 navel or temple oranges
2 tablespoons lemon juice
2 tablespoons granulated sugar
Pinch of salt
Cinnamon
1 tablespoon orange flower water
¾ cup chopped walnuts

EQUIPMENT

Paper towels
Small serrated knife
Small mixing bowls
Slicing knife
Glass serving dish

WORKING TIME: 15 MINUTES
SERVES: 6

1. Wash the romaine lettuce and section into leaves, discarding the tough outer ones. Drain and wrap in paper towels to dry. Store in the refrigerator until needed.

2. Peel the oranges and remove all the outside membranes, using a small serrated knife and employing a seesaw motion. Section the oranges by cutting away all the membranes from the orange flesh. As you work, lift out each section and place in a small mixing bowl. Squeeze the juice from the remainder of the orange over the sections to keep them moist. Cover and keep chilled.

3. Make a dressing by mixing the lemon juice, sugar, salt, ½ teaspoon cinnamon, orange flower water, and 2 tablespoons of the orange juice. Blend well, then taste—the dressing should be sweet.

4. Just before serving, shred the lettuce and arrange in a glass serving dish. Pour the dressing over and toss. Make a design around the edges with overlapping sections of orange, then sprinkle the salad with the chopped walnuts and dust with cinnamon. Serve immediately.

VARIATION

ORANGE AND CHOPPED DATES SALAD: Prepare as in the recipe above, using ¾ cup chopped dates and almonds in place of the chopped walnuts.

SAHNI

Classic Indian Vegetarian and Grain Cooking

Cucumber and Peanut Salad, Maharashtrian-Style

Khamang Kakdi

Khamang kakdi *is one of the most popular salads of Maharashtra. Made with grated cucumber, peanuts, mint, and coriander, it is laced with cumin, mustard, and turmeric. The addition of sugar in the presence of lemon juice is a typical Maharashtrian trademark designed to lend a sweet-sour flavor to food.*

The Brahmins add a pinch of asafetida to perk up their onion- and garlic-free cooking. For best flavor the salad should be served soon after it is made.

FOR 6 PERSONS

3 large cucumbers
⅓ cup roasted peanuts (salted or unsalted), ground to a fine powder
3 tablespoons chopped fresh coriander
1½ tablespoons chopped fresh mint leaves (optional)
2 teaspoons sugar
Juice of 1 small lemon

FOR THE SPICE-PERFUMED BUTTER

2 tablespoons *usli ghee*, or light vegetable oil
¾ teaspoon black mustard seeds
¾ teaspoon cumin seeds
¼ teaspoon ground asafetida
⅛ teaspoon turmeric
8 hot green chilies, shredded
Coarse salt to taste

1. Peel the cucumbers and cut them in half. Using a spoon, scrape out the seeds. Grate the cucumbers, using the coarse blade of a grater or food processor. Put the cucumber in a colander and squeeze hard to extract any excess moisture, and put it in a bowl. Add the next five ingredients and toss well.

2. Heat the *usli ghee* in a small frying pan over high heat. When it is very hot, add the mustard seeds. Keep a pot lid handy, as the seeds may spatter and fly all over. As the seeds are spattering, add the cumin and continue cooking until mixture turns several shades darker (15–20 seconds). Add the asafetida, turmeric, and chilies, shake the pan for a few seconds, and pour the entire contents of the pan over the cucumber. Add salt, and toss well to coat the vegetables with spices.

Serve immediately. If you do not plan to serve immediately, do not add peanuts, sugar, or salt until serving time.

WATERS

Chez Panisse Vegetables

Red and Golden Beets with Blood Orange, Endive, and Walnuts

2 pounds red and golden beets
½ cup shelled walnuts
2 blood oranges
2 tablespoons red wine vinegar
2 tablespoons orange juice
Zest of ½ orange
¼ cup olive oil
Salt and pepper
¼ pound Belgian endive

Preheat the oven to 400°F. Trim and wash the beets and roast them, tightly covered, with a splash of water. While the oven is on, put the walnuts on a baking sheet and toast them in the oven for about 5 minutes. With a sharp paring knife, trim off the top and bottom of each orange. Pare off the rest of the peel, making sure to remove all of the pith. Slice the oranges into ¼-inch rounds.

Make a vinaigrette by mixing together the vinegar, orange juice, and the zest, finely chopped, and stirring in the olive oil. Season with salt and pepper. When the beets are cool enough to handle, peel them and slice into rounds. Toss them gently with the vinaigrette, and arrange the beets on a plate with the orange slices and Belgian endive leaves. Drizzle over any vinaigrette remaining in the bowl, and garnish with the toasted walnuts.

SERVES 4 TO 6

BAILEY

Lee Bailey's Country Weekends

Chopped Beet, Endive, and Red Onion Salad

This can be made with canned beets, but they don't compare with the earthy flavor of fresh ones.

Several bunches of beets
6 medium whole endives
1 medium red onion, peeled and cut into thin rings
Strong Vinaigrette Dressing

Cut off top of beets, leaving roots in place. Cover with water and simmer approximately 30 minutes, or until tender. Allow to cool in juice and slip off skins. Chop into medium-size chunks. Wash and dry endive. Cut into ½-inch rings and separate. Toss beets, endives, and onion together. Dress sparingly with the Strong Vinaigrette.

SERVES 6

SHERATON

From My Mother's Kitchen

Black Radish and Onion Salad

This salad is a lighter, fresher variation on the conserve that my grandmother would prepare when a child or grandchild arrived at her house starving, a frequent occurrence. Pumpernickel seemed always to be on hand to go with it, but it is also very good on matzohs.

2 medium black radishes
½ large Bermuda or Spanish onion
1 to 2 tablespoons schmaltz (rendered chicken fat), or to taste
Salt and black pepper, plenty of both and to taste

Wash and peel the radishes. Grate the radishes and onion on the coarsest side of a four-sided grater, to make long, slim slivers. Toss together gently with a fork, adding schmaltz, salt, and pepper.

YIELD: 2 SERVINGS

MANDEL
Abby Mandel's Cuisinart Classroom

Eleven-Layer Salad

An impressive looking and delicious creation. It must be made well ahead of serving time, but the result is well worth the effort.

LAYERS

½ large head of iceberg lettuce (7 ounces, 200g), cored and cut into wedges to fit the feed tube
1 cup (24 cl) parsley leaves
4 large eggs, hard-boiled, chilled and peeled
Salt
Freshly ground pepper
1 large red pepper (6 ounces, 170g), halved vertically and seeded
4 medium carrots (6 ounces, 170g), peeled and cut into lengths to fit the feed tube horizontally
1 5¾-ounce (163g) can colossal pitted ripe olives, drained and cut flat at ends
¾ pound (340g) green beans, trimmed and cut into uniform lengths to fit feed tube
1 teaspoon dried dillweed
Freshly ground pepper
1 cup large radishes (4 ounces, 155g), washed and trimmed
4 ounces (115g) sharp Cheddar cheese, chilled
½ pound (225g) bacon, crisply cooked, drained and broken into pieces
2 small red onions (3½ ounces total, 110g), peeled

As you process each ingredient, layer it in a 2½ quart (236 cl) glass bowl or soufflé dish, making sure that the edges of each layer are neat and visible. Keep the ingredients and the work bowl dry, patting the ingredients with a paper towel and wiping out the bowl with towels when necessary.

MEDIUM SLICING DISC: Put the lettuce wedges in the feed tube vertically and slice them, using light pressure. Arrange the lettuce in a layer in the glass bowl.

METAL BLADE: Mince the parsley by turning the machine on and off. Reserve 2 tablespoons of it and arrange the rest over the lettuce. Chop the eggs by turning the machine on and off about 8 times and season them with the ½ teaspoon salt and pepper to taste. Arrange them over the parsley.

MEDIUM SLICING DISC: Put the red pepper in the feed tube vertically and slice it, using medium pressure. Arrange it over the eggs.

JULIENNE DISC OR SHREDDING DISC: Put the carrots in the feed tube horizontally and process them, using firm pressure. Arrange them over the red pepper.

MEDIUM SLICING DISC: Stack the olives in the feed tube, flat ends down, and slice them, using light pressure. Arrange them over the carrots.

Fit the green beans tightly into the feed tube and slice them, using medium pressure. Plunge the beans into a saucepan containing 2 quarts (190 cl) boiling water and 2 teaspoons salt. Blanch them for 30 seconds after the water returns to a boil. Drain them in a colander and hold them under cold running water until they are completely cool. Pat them dry with paper towels. Arrange the beans over the olives, and sprinkle with dillweed, 1 teaspoon of salt and pepper to taste.

Put the radishes in the feed tube and slice them, using firm pressure. Arrange them over the beans.

SHREDDING DISC: Put the cheese in the feed tube and shred it, using light pressure. Arrange it over the radishes.

METAL BLADE: Put the bacon in the work bowl, chop it by turning the machine on and off, and arrange it over the cheese.

MEDIUM SLICING DISC: Stack the onions in the feed tube and slice them, using firm pressure. Separate them into rings and arrange them over the bacon so that the red edge is visible through the sides of the bowl.

GREEN SALAD DRESSING

2 cups (47 cl) Basic Mayonnaise
½ cup (12 cl) parsley leaves
1 teaspoon dried basil
1 teaspoon dried dillweed
2 tablespoons sugar
½ cup (12 cl) sour cream

METAL BLADE: Process all the dressing ingredients in the work bowl for 5 seconds. Spoon ½ the dressing over the salad, smoothing it with a spatula. Put the remainder in a serving dish. Sprinkle the salad with the reserved parsley and wipe any dressing from the edges of the bowl. Cover the salad with plastic wrap and refrigerate it for at least 6 hours, or up to 12 hours.

Do not toss the salad. Serve it with 2 long-handled spoons so each person can reach down to the bottom and sample each layer. Pass the remaining dressing separately.

MAKES 8 SERVINGS

LAPPÉ

Diet for a Small Planet

Tabouli

Zesty Lebanese Salad

6 SERVINGS

AVERAGE SERVING = APPROX. 4 G USABLE PROTEIN
9 TO 11% OF DAILY PROTEIN ALLOWANCE

¼ cup dry white or garbanzo beans, cooked and drained
1¼ cups bulgur wheat, raw
4 cups boiling water
1½ cups minced parsley*
¾ cup mint, minced* (if not available, substitute more parsley)
¾ cup minced scallions
3 medium tomatoes, chopped
¾ cup lemon juice
¼ cup olive oil
1–2 tsp salt
freshly ground pepper to taste
raw grape, lettuce, or cabbage leaves

Pour the boiling water over the bulgur and let stand about 2 hours until the wheat is light and fluffy. Drain excess water and shake in a strainer or press with hands to remove as much water as possible. Mix the bulgur, cooked beans, and remaining ingredients. Chill for at least 1 hour. Serve on raw leaves.

This recipe is adapted from a traditional Lebanese dish often served on festive occasions. If you want to be truly authentic, let your guests or family scoop it up with lettuce leaves instead of using spoons. A Lebanese friend once served Tabouli as a party hors d'oeuvre. It was a great hit.

*You can use a blender. A wooden chopstick is good for scraping leaves from sides of blender into blade action.

KATZEN

The Moosewood Cookbook

Gado-Gado

An Indonesian dish with spicy peanut sauce

APPROXIMATELY ONE HOUR TO PREPARE
6–8 SERVINGS

THE SAUCE
1 cup chopped onion
2 medium cloves crushed garlic
1 cup good, pure peanut butter
1 Tbs. honey
¼ tsp. cayenne pepper (more, to taste)
juice of 1 lemon
1–2 tsp. freshly-grated ginger root
1 bay leaf
1 Tbs. cider vinegar
3 cups water
½–1 tsp. salt
dash of tamari
2 Tbs. butter for frying

In a saucepan, cook the onions, garlic, bay leaf and ginger in butter, lightly salted. When onion becomes translucent add remaining ingredients. Mix thoroughly. Simmer on lowest possible heat 30 minutes, stirring occasionally.

UNDERNEATH THE SAUCE:
The sauce goes over an artful arrangement of combined cooked and raw vegetables. Extra protein comes from garnishes of Tofu chunks (bean curd) and hard-cooked egg slices. Base your arrangement on a bed of fresh spinach. Here are some recommended vegetables and garnishes:

GARNISH WITH
a drizzle of sesame oil
apples
lemons
oranges
raisins
toasted seeds & nuts
shredded cabbage (steamed or raw)
carrot slices (steamed or raw)
celery slices (steamed or raw)
broccoli spears (steamed)
fresh, whole green beans (steamed)
fresh, raw mung bean sprouts
tofu chunks, either raw, or sautéed in oil with sesame seeds
pieces of egg

ALFORD AND DUGUID
Seductions of Rice

Spring Pilaf with Fresh Greens

Sabzi Polo

SERVES 6

*A beautiful version of herbed rice using the first greens of spring (*sabzi *means "greens" in Farsi) is traditionally served at Persian New Year, No-Rooz, around the vernal equinox in March. Alongside is presented an herb omelette and, often, fried fish. The rice is prepared as for* chelo, *then it is layered with herbs when it is placed in the pot for steaming. Serve with Golden Chicken Kebabs with Sumac and, if you wish, a chopped salad.*

RICE
2½ cups basmati rice
¼ cup salt
Water

¼ cup finely chopped fresh flat-leaf parsley
¾ cup finely chopped fresh dill
¼ cup finely chopped fresh chives
¼ cup vegetable oil or 4 tablespoons butter
2 tablespoons plain yogurt (whole-milk or 2%)
1 large egg

Following the instructions for Special Everyday Persian Rice, wash and soak the rice, then boil it, drain, rinse, and drain again.

Mix the chopped herbs together and set aside.

If using butter, melt 2 tablespoons in a small saucepan; set aside. In a medium bowl, mix together the yogurt and egg. Add ½ cup of the cooked rice and stir well.

In a large heavy pot, heat 2 tablespoons of the oil or the remaining 2 tablespoons butter with 1 tablespoon water. Place the rice and yogurt mixture into the oil or butter and spread it over the bottom of the pot. Add half the remaining rice, spread on half the herb mixture, and then add another third of the rice, gradually mounding the rice into a cone. Top with the remaining herb mixture and then the remaining rice. Drizzle over the remaining 2 tablespoons oil or the melted butter, cover with a tightly fitting lid wrapped in a cotton cloth, and place over high heat. When steam has built up, after about 2 minutes, reduce the heat to very low and steam for 30 minutes.

Let the rice stand for 10 minutes, then place the pot in 2 inches cold water (in the sink) for a minute or so to help loosen the crust. Remove the cover and turn out onto a platter, mixing the rice and herbs together, and serve the pieces of crust on top.

LA PLACE AND KLEIMAN
Cucina Fresca

Panzanella

Bread Salad

This peasant specialty from Tuscany requires above all good country bread. The bread traditionally used is a large, round, coarse loaf baked in a brick oven. A loaf of French or Italian bread of high quality is an acceptable substitute. In Tuscan dialect Panzanella means "little swamp," an apt description of the juice-soaked bread.

½ loaf day-old country bread, or French or Italian bread
2 tomatoes, peeled, seeded, and cut into ½-inch dice
1–2 tablespoons capers
½ cup fruity olive oil
¼ cup red wine vinegar
Coarse salt and freshly ground pepper to taste
3 cucumbers, peeled, halved, seeded, and cut into ½-inch dice
½ small red onion, peeled and thinly sliced
1 bell pepper, red, yellow, or green, cored, seeded, and cut lengthwise into very thin strips

Cut the bread into ½-inch-thick slices and remove the crusts. Set aside. Mix together in a bowl the tomatoes, capers, oil, vinegar, salt, and pepper. In a wide, shallow bowl or large platter make a layer of bread slices. Scatter the cucumbers, onion, and bell pepper strips over the bread. Pour a ladleful of the tomato mixture over the bread and vegetables. Continue layering until all the ingredients are used up, ending with vegetables and tomato mixture. Set the dish aside at room temperature or in the refrigerator for at least 1 hour. It is important for the bread to absorb the liquid from the vegetables and tomato mixture. If the dish seems too dry, sprinkle on more oil and vinegar. Panzanella can be made a day ahead. Serves 6.

ROJAS-LOMBARDI

The Art of South American Cooking

Ensalada de Papas

Blue-Potato Salad

SERVES 6 TO 8

A spectacular potato salad can be made with blue potatoes, which have a rich flavor and an extraordinary color.

- 3 to 3½ pounds blue potatoes, Yellow Finns, or new potatoes, scrubbed
- ¼ cup red-wine or raspberry vinegar
- 1 large clove garlic, peeled and crushed
- 8 to 10 anchovy fillets, drained and minced
- ¾ cup olive oil
- 2 or 3 jalapeño peppers, seeded and finely chopped
- 8 scallions, trimmed, washed, and thinly sliced
- 1 cup chopped fresh mint leaves
- 1 cup chopped Italian parsley

1. Place the potatoes in a 2½-quart pot. Add 8 cups of water and cook, covered, for 20 minutes, or until the potatoes are done. Remove from the heat, drain off all the water, and place the potatoes on a rack, to let the moisture evaporate as they cool. When the potatoes are cool, peel them. Cut them lengthwise and then crosswise into ½-inch slices. Set aside.

2. Pour the vinegar into a cup and drop in the crushed garlic. With the tines of a fork, mash the garlic and let soak for 10 to 15 minutes, or until ready to use. Remove and discard the garlic. On a plate, mash the anchovy fillets thoroughly with a fork. Mash in 1 tablespoon of the garlic-flavored vinegar and add this to the vinegar in the cup. Mix well.

3. In a bowl large enough to hold the potatoes, combine the garlic-flavored anchovy vinegar and the olive oil. Whisk thoroughly. Stir in the hot peppers and scallions. Add the sliced potatoes and toss gently. Add the mint and parsley and toss again. Correct the seasoning and serve.

STORAGE NOTE This salad will keep well, tightly covered, in the refrigerator for a few days.

MITCHELL

Lüchow's German Cookbook

Hot Potato Salad with Bacon

Speck Salat

- 1 pound (3 medium) potatoes
- 6 slices bacon, diced
- 1 medium-size onion, diced
- ½ cup vinegar
- ½ cup stock or bouillon
- 1 teaspoon salt
- ¼ teaspoon pepper
- 1 teaspoon sugar
- 1 egg yolk, beaten

Scrub potatoes; rinse. Boil in jackets; let cool. Peel and cut in ¼-inch slices.

Cook bacon in hot pan until crisp. Add onion; stir and cook until transparent. Add vinegar, stock or bouillon, and seasonings. Stir; let come to a boil. Stir in egg; remove from heat and pour over potatoes.

SERVES 2 TO 4

HIRTZLER

The Hotel St. Francis Cook Book

CRAB MEAT, À LA LOUISE. Have the crab meat thoroughly chilled, and allow one crab to three or four people, according to the size of the fish. Use small fancy fish plates, or salad plates. Lay on each plate some slices of the white hearts of firm heads of lettuce. Lay on top some canned Spanish pimentos, using the brilliant red variety, which is sweet. On top of this place the crab meat, taking care not to break it too small. Over all pour French dressing made with tarragon vinegar, well-seasoned with freshly-ground black pepper.

CHILD

From Julia Child's Kitchen

Salade Niçoise

Combination Salad with Potatoes, Tomatoes, Green Beans, Anchovies, Tuna Fish, Olives, Capers, and Lettuce

All the elements of this salad may be prepared in advance, but it must not be dressed and arranged until just before serving. I deplore the system employed by many restaurants and even individuals—including some of my best friends—of making a beautiful arrangement in a salad bowl, then pouring on the dressing and mixing it all up. A horrid mess, and it is not right. No! Toss each individual item separately in a separate bowl with the dressing and seasonings, then make your beautiful arrangement, and it stays beautiful for serving.

(*We have* Salade Niçoise *in* Mastering I, *and in* The French Chef Cookbook; *this is a slightly different version.*)

INGREDIENTS FOR 6 TO 8 PEOPLE

FOR THE SAUCE VINAIGRETTE—ABOUT ⅔ CUP

1 clove garlic
Salt
About 1 Tb each lemon juice and wine vinegar
½ tsp dry mustard
½ to ⅔ cup best-quality olive oil
Freshly ground pepper
Fresh or dried herbs, such as basil

FOR THE POTATO SALAD

3 or 4 medium-sized "boiling" or "all-purpose" potatoes
1 Tb finely minced shallot or scallion
Salt and pepper
2 to 3 Tb each white wine or chicken stock, and water

OTHER INGREDIENTS

5 anchovies packed in salt (or a 2-ounce tin of flat fillets in olive oil)
2 to 3 Tb capers
1 large head Boston lettuce, washed, separated into leaves, and chilled
4 ripe red tomatoes, quartered (or cherry tomatoes, halved)
½ lb. fresh string beans, blanched and chilled
2 or 3 hard-boiled eggs, peeled, and halved or quartered
½ to ⅔ cup black olives, preferably the small brine-cured Mediterranean type
A 7-ounce can of tuna fish
2 to 3 Tb chopped fresh parsley

SAUCE VINAIGRETTE. Purée the garlic through a press into a small mortar or bowl, add ¼ teaspoon salt, and mash vigorously with a pestle or wooden spoon to make a very smooth paste. Beat in a tablespoon each of lemon juice and wine vinegar, and the dry mustard. (Strain, if you wish, into another bowl or into a screw-topped jar.) Beat in gradually (or add all at once and shake to blend) ½ cup olive oil—5 to 6 parts of oil to one of vinegar and/or lemon juice is about right, because too tart a dressing will spoil the taste of any wine you are serving. Beat in a grind or two of pepper, a big pinch of herbs, taste carefully, and correct seasoning, beating in more oil, salt, pepper, or herbs as necessary.

POMMES À L'HUILE (Potato salad). Scrub the potatoes under cold water. Place in a vegetable steamer or in a sieve or colander, set over a pan of boiling water, and cover closely. (If steam escapes from sides of steamer, insert a towel around the edges between steamer and pan, to hold in the vapor.) Potatoes should steam until just tender when pierced with a knife—about 20 minutes. Spear each with a fork; peel and cut in half lengthwise, then into slices ⅜-inch thick. Toss the warm potatoes gently in a large bowl with the minced shallot or scallion, sprinkling on ¼ teaspoon of salt and several grinds of pepper. Then toss with the wine or chicken stock and water. Let sit for 5 minutes or so, tossing twice more, and allowing potatoes to absorb as much liquid as they will. Then fold gently with ¼ cup of the dressing, taste, and correct seasoning. Cover and refrigerate until serving time.

ANCHOIS AUX SEL (Salt-packed anchovies). In most Italian markets here, you can buy whole anchovies preserved in salt or in a salt brine. They have an excellent flavor, and keep for several years in a cool place as long as they are surrounded by the coarse (kosher-type) salt that preserves them. To prepare for use, first wash off the salt, then soak the anchovies in several changes of cold water until softened—40 minutes to 2 hours, depending on how long they have been salted. Test by boning one as follows: lay it on a board or on a piece of brown paper, and with 2 forks separate one side (top) from the central bone, then remove the bone from the second side or fillet; run fork along length of each fillet to remove any fins or extraneous matter. Taste a small piece; if still too salty, soak the anchovies (along with the filleted anchovy) in fresh water another 15 minutes or so. Arrange the fillets in a dish and cover with a spoonful of dressing, or with a little olive oil, pepper, oregano, and a spoonful of capers. Refrigerate if not to be used fairly soon, and do not prepare the anchovies more than 2 hours before serving. (To preserve their freshness, open oil-packed canned anchovies only a few minutes before serving, and use as is, or flavor with dressing or herbs as suggested above).

CÂPRES AUX SEL (Salt-packed capers). The very large capers available on the Mediterranean can often be found here in bulk, packed in salt, in Italian markets. To prepare them, wash off the preserving salt, and soak the capers in several changes of cold water for 40 minutes or longer, until the salt has worked itself out. Test by eating one. Drain, squeeze gently to remove excess water, and pack in a screw-top jar; cover with a mixture of wine vinegar and dry white wine or Vermouth. These are now pickled capers, and will keep for months; they need not be refrigerated. (Regular capers, bottled in vinegar, are drained and served as is, although you might improve their flavor when you buy them by pouring out half their vinegar and replacing it with dry white French Vermouth.)

ASSEMBLING THE SALAD. Do this the moment before serving. Choose a deep round platter, or a wide bowl. Toss the lettuce with several spoonfuls of dressing, and arrange the leaves around the edge of the platter or bowl. Turn the potato salad into the middle. Arrange groups of tomatoes around the potatoes; sprinkle with salt and droplets of dressing. Toss the beans with a spoonful of dressing, plus a sprinkling of salt and pepper to taste; arrange in groups between the tomatoes. Distribute eggs, yellow side up, at decorative intervals, and place anchovies and capers over them. Ring the potatoes with a line of black olives; break up the tuna fish and arrange it in the center of the potatoes or at intervals around their edge. Spoon a little of the dressing over the tuna, and dribble the rest over the potatoes. Decorate the tuna with parsley, and the salad is ready to serve.

HIRTZLER
The Hotel St. Francis Cook Book

CHICKEN SALAD, VICTOR. Cut the breast of a boiled soup hen or boiled chicken in half-inch squares, add one-half cup of string beans in cut pieces one inch long, a cup of boiled rice, one peeled tomato cut in small squares and one sliced truffle. Season with salt, fresh-ground black pepper, a little chives, chervil, parsley, one spoonful of tarragon vinegar and two spoonsful of best olive oil. Mix well and serve on lettuce leaves.

ROSSO AND LUKINS
The Silver Palate Cookbook

Tarragon Chicken Salad

After making this salad fresh every day for four years and never tiring of the taste, we think it's safe to say that this one really wears well. It is dressy enough to serve as a main course; delicious enough to have in a sandwich; and so simple to assemble that you will make it often. For a different taste, substitute black walnuts.

boneless whole chicken breasts, about 3 pounds
1 cup *crème fraîche* or heavy cream
½ cup dairy sour cream
½ cup Hellmann's mayonnaise
2 celery ribs, cut into 1-inch-long pencil strips
½ cup shelled walnuts
1 tablespoon crumbled dried tarragon
salt and freshly ground black pepper, to taste

1. Arrange chicken breasts in a single layer in a large jellyroll pan. Spread evenly with *crème fraîche* and bake in a preheated 350°F. oven for 20 to 25 minutes, or until done to your taste. Remove from oven and cool.

2. Shred meat into bite-size pieces and transfer to a bowl.

3. Whisk sour cream and mayonnaise together in a small bowl and pour over chicken mixture.

4. Add celery, walnuts, tarragon, salt and pepper to taste, and toss well.

5. Refrigerate, covered, for at least 4 hours. Taste and correct seasoning before serving.

4 TO 6 PORTIONS

NOTE: Use accumulated juices from jelly-roll pan to enrich soups or sauces.

ALFORD AND DUGUID
Seductions of Rice

Grilled Beef Salad

Yam Neua

SERVES 6 AS PART OF A RICE-BASED MEAL, OR AS AN APPETIZER

When we're at home, beef is not something we prepare all that often. But if we are making food for a party, or for a summer potluck, this grilled beef yam is one of our all-time favorite recipes. We'll even splurge and get a very good cut of meat, such as the tenderloin called for in this recipe.

In Thailand, there are probably as many different versions of yam neua *as there are cooks, each having a different idea about how best to find that perfect balance of hot, sour, and salty. So before serving be sure to taste for yourself.*

- 1 pound beef tenderloin, at room temperature
- About ½ teaspoon freshly ground black pepper
- 2 tablespoons Thai fish sauce, or more to taste
- 5 tablespoons fresh lime juice, or more to taste
- 2 to 3 bird chiles or serrano chiles, minced
- ½ cup thinly sliced shallots
- 4 scallions, cut into ½-inch lengths
- ½ cup packed fresh coriander leaves, plus a few sprigs for garnish
- 2 tablespoons finely chopped fresh mint
- 1 European cucumber, scored lengthwise with a fork and thinly sliced

Preheat a grill or broiler. Halve the tenderloin horizontally to form 2 pieces approximately 1 inch thick. Rub both sides of each piece with the pepper, pressing it into the meat.

TO GRILL, place the meat on the grill and cook until medium-rare, 5 to 8 minutes on each side.

TO BROIL, place the meat on a broiling rack so that the meat is 3 to 5 inches from the broiling element. Broil for 6 to 7 minutes on each side, or until medium-rare.

Let the meat cool for 30 minutes to 1 hour, so that it is easy to slice. (The cooled meat can be put into the refrigerator covered and then sliced several hours later, if more convenient.) Slice the meat as thin as possible with a sharp chef's knife or cleaver, cutting across the grain. In a large bowl, mix the fish sauce, lime juice, and chiles. Add the meat, shallots, and scallions and turn to coat. Mix in the coriander leaves and mint. Taste for a good balance among the salty fish sauce, the tart lime juice, and the hot chiles, and adjust according to your taste.

Arrange the slices of cucumber around the edge of a decorative plate or platter, then mound the salad in the center. Garnish with coriander sprigs and serve.

KASPER
The Splendid Table

Salad of Tart Greens with Prosciutto and Warm Balsamic Dressing

Insalata di Prosciutto e Aceto Balsamico

The good tastes of Emilia-Romagna meet in this unusual salad inspired by the improvisations of several regional cooks. It becomes a light one-dish supper when not served as antipasto.

SERVES 6 TO 8 GENEROUSLY AS AN ANTIPASTO, 6 AS A LIGHT SUPPER

- 1 medium red onion, sliced into thin rings
- ½ cup red wine vinegar
- 1 small head each romaine, radicchio, red-leaf lettuce, and curly endive
- ½ cup (2 ounces) pine nuts, toasted
- 3 to 4 whole scallions, thinly sliced on the diagonal
- 3 ounces Italian Parmigiano-Reggiano cheese, shaved with a vegetable peeler into thin curls
- 3 ounces thinly sliced Prosciutto di Parma, cut into bite-size squares
- 1 cup lightly packed fresh basil leaves
- 1 cup lightly packed fresh Italian parsley leaves
- 8 large cloves garlic, cut into ¼-inch dice
- About ⅔ cup extra-virgin olive oil
- 3 to 6 tablespoons commercial balsamic vinegar
- 3 tablespoons red wine vinegar
- About 1 tablespoon dark brown sugar
- Salt and freshly ground black pepper to taste

METHOD

WORKING AHEAD: The salad can be assembled several hours ahead; cover it with plastic wrap and refrigerate. Serve it lightly chilled. The dressing can be cooked up to several hours ahead. Cover and set aside at room temperature. Reheat just before serving.

ASSEMBLING THE SALAD: Rid the onions of their sharpness by soaking them in the ½ cup vinegar about 30 minutes. Meanwhile, wash and dry the lettuces, throwing away any coarse or bruised leaves. Tear the leaves into bite-size pieces. In a large bowl, toss the greens with all but 3 tablespoons of the pine nuts, most of the scallions, half the cheese, half the prosciutto, and all the basil and parsley. Arrange on a large platter.

MAKING THE DRESSING: In a medium skillet, slowly cook the garlic in the olive oil over very low heat 8 minutes, or until barely colored. Remove with a slotted spoon and reserve. Turn the heat to medium-high, and add the vinegars to the oil. Cook a few moments, or until the acid has diffused slightly. Add brown sugar to taste (this gives some depth to commercial balsamics), and let the mixture bubble slowly 1 minute. Taste for sweet/tart balance (take care to cool the sample, as the hot oil makes this scorching hot). Stir in extra brown sugar or balsamic vinegar to taste. If the dressing is too sharp, simmer for a few moments to boil off some of the vinegar's acid. Stir in the reserved garlic, and season with salt and pepper. Set aside until ready to serve.

TO SERVE: Top with drained red onion, and scatter the rest of the scallions, pine nuts, cheese, and prosciutto over the salad. Reheat the dressing, stir vigorously to blend, and spoon over the salad. Serve immediately.

SUGGESTIONS

WINE: A simple young red, such as a Sangiovese di Romagna from Emilia-Romagna or a Bardolino of the Veneto.

MENU: The salad on its own is a fine one-dish supper. For a full menu, offer small servings before Tagliatelle with Caramelized Onions and Fresh Herbs or the Risotto of Baby Artichokes and Peas, followed by roasted chicken or lamb. For dessert, the Espresso and Mascarpone Semi-Freddo. For a lighter meal, serve before Tagliatelle with Ragù Bolognese, Spaghetti with Shrimps and Black Olives, or Maccheroni with Baked Grilled Vegetables. Dessert could be homey Modena Crumbling Cake or Nonna's Jam Tart.

COOK'S NOTES

The commercial balsamics available in the United States vary greatly in quality.

A SARACEN INVENTION?

Italy comes quite rightly by her antipasto salads, even though many consider them a hallmark of France's nouvelle cuisine. Composed salads of all kinds were very much a part of the elaborate first courses (the forerunner of the antipasto) at Italian Renaissance banquets, when Italy defined much of the dining fashion for all of Europe. Scholars speculate that the first-course salad originated in Italy during the 1400s. I have wondered if the Saracens (Moslems from the Middle East) introduced the concept long before the Renaissance. During their occupation of Sicily in the 9th and 10th centuries, their influence spread far beyond the southernmost portion of Italy. Perhaps then they were serving salads at the opening of meals just as is typical today in North Africa and the Middle East. Perhaps the idea was adopted by Italy's nobles, just as they eagerly took spices, hard wheat, pastry, and confectionery from the Saracens.

JUNIOR LEAGUE OF CHARLESTON
Charleston Receipts

Hopping John

Hopping John, made of cow peas and rice, is eaten in the stateliest of Charleston houses and in the humblest cabins and always on New Year's Day. "Hoppin' John eaten then will bring good luck" is an old tradition.

1 cup raw cow peas (dried field peas)
4 cups water
2 teaspoons salt
1 cup raw rice
4 slices bacon fried with
1 medium onion, chopped

Boil peas in salted water until tender. Add peas and 1 cup of the pea liquid to rice, bacon with grease and onion. Put in rice steamer or double-boiler and cook for 1 hour or until rice is thoroughly done. Serves 8.

MRS. W. H. BARNWELL (Mary Royall)

AIDELLS

Hot Links and Country Flavors

Wild Rice and Pecan Salad with Grilled Venison Sausage

Wild rice and roasted nuts make a splendid combination that complements the flavor of venison beautifully. The salad also works well with Our Wild Boar, Buffalo, or Duck Sausages.

- 1 c. raw wild rice, or 3–4 c. cooked
- ½ tsp. salt
- ½ c. shelled pecans
- 1 tbsp. peanut oil
- 1 lb. Venison Sausage
- 2 green onions or scallions, thinly sliced
- 1 c. chopped fresh Italian flat-leaf parsley
- ¼ c. sherry wine vinegar or red wine vinegar
- ½ c. walnut oil
- Salt and pepper to taste

To prepare wild rice, carefully wash the rice and remove any dirt or foreign material. Bring 3 cups of water to a boil in a heavy 2–3-quart saucepan. Add the rice and salt. When the water returns to a boil, reduce the heat, cover the pot, and simmer for about 40 minutes or longer, until the rice is tender.

While the rice is cooking, roast the pecans in the peanut oil in a medium skillet over medium-low heat for 5 minutes, shaking the pan constantly. When they begin to brown, become crispy, and develop a nutty aroma, immediately remove the nuts, along with any oil remaining, to a large bowl.

Grill or panfry the sausages. Transfer to a platter and let them sit for 5 minutes while you finish the salad.

Add the cooked rice, green onions, parsley, vinegar, and walnut oil to the roasted pecans in the bowl. Toss well to combine the ingredients. The rice should be evenly coated with the oil and vinegar. Season to taste with salt and pepper. Mound the salad on a platter or in a shallow bowl. Slice warm Venison Sausage on an angle, arrange over rice, and serve at once. Makes 4 servings.

SERVE AS A LUNCHEON OR LIGHT DINNER WITH A HEARTY RED WINE LIKE CALIFORNIA SYRAH OR FRENCH RHÔNE.

SANDWICHES

CURTIS

Good Housekeeping Everyday Cook Book

A Club Sandwich

Toast a slice of bread evenly and lightly and butter it. On one half put, first, a thin slice of bacon which has been broiled till dry and tender, next a slice of the white meat of either turkey or chicken. Over one half of this place a circle cut from a ripe tomato and over the other half a tender leaf of lettuce. Cover these with a generous layer of mayonnaise, and complete this delicious "whole meal" sandwich with the remaining piece of toast.—A.W.

WATERS

Chez Panisse Vegetables

Spring Onion Sandwiches

Onion sandwiches were an old favorite of James Beard's. These are best made in May when onions are very sweet. Trim the crusts off thin slices of good white bread. Spread two slices of bread with mayonnaise, on one side. Slice fresh onion very thinly and make a layer of onion slices on one slice of bread. Top that with the other slice of bread. Dip the four side edges of the sandwich into thin mayonnaise and then into chopped parsley.

KELLOGG

Every-day Dishes and Every-day Work

NUT BUTTER SANDWICHES.—Spread slices of thinly cut graham bread with nut butter, and then with chopped dates or figs. Finely minced celery is excellent used in the same manner.

THE TIMES-PICAYUNE
The Original Picayune Creole Cook Book

Oyster Loaf
La Médiatrice

Delicate French Loaves of Bread
2 Dozen Oysters to a Loaf
1 Tablespoonful of Melted Butter

Take delicate French loaves of bread and cut off, lengthwise, the upper portion. Dig the crumb out of the center of each piece, leaving the sides and bottom like a square box. Brush each corner of the box and the bottom with melted butter, and place in a quick oven to brown. Fill each half loaf with broiled or creamed oysters, put the two together and serve.

BROWN
Helen Brown's West Coast Cook Book

MONTE CRISTO AND MONTE CARLO SANDWICHES. These have become very popular of late. They originated, I believe, in San Francisco, but now one finds them everywhere. The Monte Cristo is sliced chicken or turkey and sliced cheese, usually Monterey Jack, though it may be Swiss or a Cheddar. The Monte Carlo has tongue instead of chicken. Both sandwiches are made in 3 layers, buttered ones, with the middle buttered on both sides, and are dipped in egg and milk (2 eggs to 1 cup of milk and ¼ teaspoon of salt), then fried to a golden brown in butter. When this type of sandwich, with either of the above fillings, is cut into little 1-inch squares, they are called Monte Benitos, and are served with cocktails.

BEARD
Cook It Outdoors

San Francisco Style

I seem to be making a complete tour of California in this chapter, and here goes for one of the most fragrant hamburgers I have ever smelled or tasted. It was served to me about midnight when we had driven for miles through one of the magnificent, misty, foggy nights—and I mean magnificent. Nothing in the world was ever so stimulating to the inner regions as this ambrosial hamburger—a good tankard of ale accompanied it—and was nectarious—if I may coin a word.

They were man-sized patties of ground meat—about six by three, and one-half inch thick. Into the pan went about five cloves of garlic, chopped rather fine. This was sautéed very quickly in about two or three tablespoons of butter. The hamburgers were then slipped in and cooked very quickly. Little bits of the garlic adhered to the meat and gave a grand flavor and a strong breath. These bits of pungency were slapped on slabs of French bread split through the middle, toasted well and a-drip with butter. Not exactly the thing to serve for the women's auxiliary, but a dish worthy of the name of San Francisco.

BEARD
Cook It Outdoors

Bagdad Hamburgers

It's a long jump from San Francisco to Bagdad, but we might as well take things as they come. This recipe is a little more trouble, but is a showy enough number for anyone to exhibit.

Slice two medium-size eggplants fairly thin and sprinkle lightly with flour. Sauté them in butter or grill them till they are browned and not cooked to a pulp. These slices may be kept warm somewhere on your grill while you cook the other things.

You will need some barbecue sauce.

Mix two pounds of chopped beef with two tablespoons chopped onion, a clove of garlic, chopped, and two tablespoons heavy cream. Form into patties about three-quarters of an inch thick and about the size of the eggplant slices. Sauté quickly in butter or grill very briskly.

On each plate a slice of eggplant, a hamburger patty and another slice of eggplant. Over this—and salt and pepper as you go—a generous ladle of the barbecue sauce. Hashed brown potatoes are delicious with this dish. Green salad, too. And coffee.

BEARD
Cook It Outdoors

Pig Hamburgers

3 pounds lean pork, ground
½ teaspoon ground ginger
½ teaspoon thyme
½ teaspoon sweet basil
½ teaspoon grated garlic
1 teaspoon salt
freshly ground pepper

Mix the pork and the herbs and spices thoroughly, using fingers to blend it all. Shape into thin cakes about three inches in diameter and grill over the coals. Serve with buns and barbecue sauce.

BEARD
Cook It Outdoors

The Pascal Hamburger

This will fool a lot of people—six, if you serve the recipe.

2 pounds ground lamb or yearling mutton
6 lamb kidneys
6 strips lean bacon, cut rather thick
salt and pepper to taste

Soak the lamb kidneys in milk for two hours and remove the tube. Form cutlets of the chopped lamb around the kidneys and wrap a rasher of bacon. Secure with a metal skewer and broil over coals, being certain that the process is not speeded up too much. Season to your taste and serve with tomatoes you have been grilling at the same time. Grilled slices of onion that are crispy and tangy inside and brown on the outside are also something to be considered. You can manage to watch all of them at the same time and a nice pattern they will make on the grill to be admired by surrounding guests.

Stews, Casseroles, and One-Pot Dishes

BEARD

American Cookery

Oyster Stew

- 5 tablespoons butter
- 1 cup milk
- 2 cups cream
- 1½ pints oysters and liquor
- Salt and freshly ground pepper
- Cayenne
- Chopped parsley or paprika

If there is a traditional Christmas Eve dish in the United States, it is oyster stew.

This may be made with cream only or with milk. Heat soup bowls. Add a good pat of butter to each bowl. Keep piping hot. Drain the oysters, then heat the milk, cream, and oyster liquor to the boiling point. Add the oysters and bring again to the boiling point. Season to taste with salt, pepper, and cayenne. Ladle into the hot bowls and add a sprinkling of chopped parsley or of paprika.

SAUTÉED OYSTER STEW. Combine the oysters and butter in a skillet and cook until the edges curl. Add the hot cream and milk, and bring to the boiling point. Season, ladle into hot bowls, and serve with crisp biscuits or buttered toast.

LAGASSE

Emeril's New New Orleans Cooking

Big Easy Seafood Okra Gumbo

MAKES 12 CUPS, 12 FIRST-COURSE SERVINGS OR 8 MAIN-COURSE SERVINGS

Gumbo—hearty and brimming with fresh seafood and vegetables—seems to be everyone's favorite in Louisiana, and it's gaining popularity throughout the country. But some people hesitate to make gumbo, thinking it requires a great deal of time and energy to prepare. It may have something to do with "rouxphobia," or fear of making roux. This gumbo doesn't have a roux; it's thickened with okra and filé powder, which is ground sassafras leaves. Look for filé powder on your grocer's spice rack. So keep in mind that although the ingredient list for this dish may seem long, once you have everything measured and ready to go, it's a quick and easy gumbo to make.

- 2 tablespoons olive oil
- ½ cup chopped onions
- ¼ cup chopped celery
- ¼ cup chopped green bell peppers
- ¼ cup chopped red bell peppers
- 1 tablespoon salt
- 4 turns freshly ground black pepper
- ½ cup peeled, seeded, and chopped Italian plum tomatoes
- 2 tablespoons minced garlic
- 1 tablespoon minced shallots
- 2 quarts Fish Stock
- ½ pound (about 1 cup) firm-fleshed fish, such as grouper, tilefish, monkfish, or sea bass, diced
- 1 teaspoon Worcestershire sauce
- ½ teaspoon hot pepper sauce
- 6 bay leaves
- 1 tablespoon minced fresh basil
- 1 teaspoon minced fresh oregano
- 1 teaspoon fresh thyme leaves
- 1 cup sliced fresh okra (about 8 large okra)
- 2 teaspoons Emeril's Creole Seasoning
- ½ pound peeled medium fresh shrimp
- 1 cup shucked fresh oysters, with their liquor
- ½ pound (about 1 cup) fresh lump crabmeat, picked over for shells and cartilage
- 1 teaspoon filé powder
- 4 cups cooked long-grain white rice, warm
- ½ to ¾ cup chopped green onions

1. Heat the oil in a large pot over high heat. When the oil is hot, add the onions, celery, and green and red peppers and sauté for 1 minute. Add the salt and pepper and sauté for 1 minute. Add the tomatoes, garlic, and shallots and sauté, stirring occasionally, for about 4 minutes.

2. Stir in the stock, add the fish, Worcestershire, hot pepper sauce, bay leaves, basil, oregano, and thyme, and bring to a boil. Cook over high heat, stirring occasionally, for about 8 minutes. Reduce the heat to medium.

3. Fold in the okra and Creole Seasoning, lower the heat, and simmer for 15 minutes. Skim the impurities from the top of the gumbo, turn the heat to high, and cook for 5 minutes. Fold in the shrimp, oysters, and crabmeat, reduce the heat, and simmer for 5 minutes. Slowly sprinkle in the filé, stirring to incorporate it thoroughly, and simmer, stirring, for 2 minutes. Remove from the heat.

4. To serve as a first course, ladle 1 cup of the

gumbo into each of 12 gumbo bowls or soup plates, and add ⅓ cup of the rice to each; for a main course, allow 1½ cups gumbo and ½ cup of rice. Sprinkle each serving with 1 tablespoon of the green onions.

THE TIMES-PICAYUNE

The Original Picayune Creole Cook Book

Shrimp Gumbo Filé

Gombo aux Crevettes

Lake shrimp are always used in making this gumbo, the river shrimp being too small and delicate. Purchase always about 100 shrimp, or a small basketful, for there are always smaller shrimp in the pile which, when cooked, amount to little or nothing. In making Shrimp Gumbo either "Filé" or okra may be used in the combination, but it must be borne in mind that, while the "Filé" is frequently used, shrimp are far more delicious for gumbo purposes when used with okra. The shrimp should always be scalded or boiled before putting in the gumbo.

- 50 Fine Lake Shrimp
- 2 Quarts of Oyster Liquor
- 1 Quart of Hot Water
- 1 Large White Onion
- 1 Bay Leaf
- 3 Sprigs of Parsley
- 1 Sprig of Thyme
- 1 Tablespoonful of Shortening or Butter
- 1 Tablespoonful of Flour
- Dash of Cayenne
- Salt and Black Pepper to Taste

Shell the shrimp, scald in boiling water and season highly. Put the shortening into a kettle and, when hot, add the flour, making a brown roux. When quite brown, without a semblance of burning, add the chopped onion and the parsley. Fry these, and when brown, add the chopped bay leaf; pour in the hot oyster liquor and the hot water, or use the carefully strained liquor in which the shrimp have been boiled. When it comes to a good boil, and about five minutes before serving, add the shrimp to the gumbo and take off the stove. Then add to the boiling hot liquid about two tablespoonfuls of the Filé, thickening according to taste. Season again with salt and pepper to taste. Serve immediately with boiled rice.

THE TIMES-PICAYUNE

The Original Picayune Creole Cook Book

Okra Gumbo

Gombo Févi

- 1 Chicken
- 1 Onion
- 6 Large Fresh Tomatoes
- 2 Pints of Okra, or Fifty Counted
- ½ Pod of Red Pepper, Without the Seeds
- 2 Large Slices of Ham
- 1 Bay Leaf
- 1 Sprig of Thyme or Parsley
- 1 Tablespoonful of Shortening or 2 Level Spoons of Butter
- Salt and Cayenne to Taste

Clean and cut up the chicken. Cut the ham into small squares or dice and chop the onions, parsley and thyme. Skin the tomatoes, and chop fine, saving the juice. Wash and stem the okra and slice into thin layers of one-half inch each. Put the shortening or butter into the soup kettle, and when hot add the chicken and the ham. Cover closely and let it simmer for about ten minutes. Then add the chopped onions, parsley, thyme and tomatoes, stirring frequently to prevent scorching. Then add the okra, and when well browned, add the juice of the tomatoes, which imparts a superior flavor. The okra is very delicate and is liable to scorch quickly if not stirred frequently. For this reason many Creole cooks fry the okra separately in a frying pan, seasoning with the pepper, Cayenne and salt, and then add to the chicken. But equally good results may be obtained with less trouble by simply adding the okra to the frying chicken, and watching constantly to prevent scorching. The least taste of a "scorch" spoils the flavor of the gumbo. When well fried and browned, add to the boiling water (about three quarts) and set on the back of the stove, letting it simmer gently for about an hour longer. Serve hot, with nicely boiled rice. The remains of turkey may be utilized in the gumbo, instead of using chicken.

In families where it is not possible to procure a fowl, use a round steak of beef or veal, instead of the chicken, and chop fine. But it must always be borne in mind that the Chicken Gumbo has the best flavor. Much, however, depends upon the seasoning, which is always high, and thus cooked, the Meat Gumbo makes a most nutritious and excellent dish.

THE TIMES-PICAYUNE

The Original Picayune Creole Cook Book

Crab Gumbo

Gombo aux Crabes

1 Dozen Hard-Shell or Soft-Shell Crabs
1 Onion
6 Large Fresh Tomatoes
2 Pints of Okra, or Fifty Counted
½ Pod of Red Pepper, Without the Seeds
1 Bay Leaf
1 Sprig of Thyme or Parsley
1 Tablespoonful of Shortening or 2 Level Spoons of Butter
Salt and Cayenne to Taste

This is a great fast day or "maigre" dish with the Creoles. Hard- or soft-shell crabs may be used, though more frequently the former, as they are always procurable, and far cheaper than the latter article, which is considered a luxury. Crabs are always sold alive. Scald the hard-shell crabs and clean according to recipe already given, "taking off the dead man's fingers" and the spongy substances, and being careful to see that the sandbags on the under part are removed. Then cut off the claws, crack and cut the body of the crab in quarters. Season nicely with salt and pepper. Put the shortening into the pot, and when hot throw in the bodies and claws. Cover closely and, after five or ten minutes, add the skinned tomatoes, chopped onions, thyme and parsley, stirring occasionally to prevent scorching. After five minutes add the okra, sliced fine, and when well browned, without the semblance of scorching, add the bay leaf, chopped fine, and the juice of the tomatoes. Pour over about two quarts and a half of boiling water, and set back on the stove and let it simmer well for about an hour, having thrown in the pepper pod. When nearly ready to serve, season according to taste with Cayenne and added salt; pour into a tureen and serve with boiled rice. This quantity will allow two soft-shell crabs or two bodies of hard-shell crabs to each person.

PRUDHOMME

Chef Paul Prudhomme's Louisiana Kitchen

Chicken and Andouille Smoked Sausage Gumbo

MAKES 6 MAIN-DISH OR 10 APPETIZER SERVINGS

1 (2- to 3-pound) chicken, cut up
Salt
Garlic powder
Ground red pepper (preferably cayenne)
1 cup finely chopped onions
1 cup finely chopped green bell peppers
¾ cup finely chopped celery
1¼ cups all-purpose flour
½ teaspoon salt
½ teaspoon garlic powder
½ teaspoon ground red pepper (preferably cayenne)
Vegetable oil for deep frying
About 7 cups Basic Chicken Stock
½ pound andouille smoked sausage (preferred) or any other good pure smoked pork sausage such as Polish sausage (kielbasa), cut into ¼-inch cubes
1 teaspoon minced garlic
Hot Basic Cooked Rice

Remove excess fat from the chicken pieces. Rub a generous amount of salt, garlic powder and red pepper on both sides of each piece, making sure each is evenly covered. Let stand at room temperature for 30 minutes.

Meanwhile, in a medium-sized bowl combine the onions, bell peppers and celery; set aside.

Combine the flour, ½ teaspoon salt, ½ teaspoon garlic powder and ½ teaspoon red pepper in a paper or plastic bag. Add the chicken pieces and shake until chicken is well coated. Reserve ½ cup of the flour.

In a large heavy skillet heat 1½ inches of oil until very hot (375° to 400°). Fry the chicken until crust is brown on both sides and meat is cooked, about 5 to 8 minutes per side; drain on paper towels. Carefully pour the hot oil in a glass measuring cup, leaving as many of the browned particles in the pan as possible. Scrape the pan bottom with a metal whisk to loosen any stuck particles, then return ½ cup of the hot oil to the pan.

Place pan over high heat. Using a long-handled metal whisk, gradually stir in the reserved ½ cup flour. Cook, whisking constantly, until roux is dark red-brown to black, about 3½ to 4 minutes, being careful not to let it scorch or splash on your skin. Remove from heat and immediately add the reserved vegetable mixture, stirring constantly until the roux stops getting darker. Return pan to low heat and cook until vegetables are soft, about 5 minutes, stirring constantly and scraping the pan bottom well.

Meanwhile, place the stock in a 5½-quart saucepan or large Dutch oven. Bring to a boil. Add roux mixture by spoonfuls to the boiling stock, stirring until dissolved between each addition. Return to a boil, stirring and scraping pan bottom often. Reduce heat to a simmer and stir in the andouille and minced garlic. Simmer uncovered for about 45 minutes, stirring often toward the end of cooking time.

While the gumbo is simmering, bone the cooked chicken and cut the meat into ½-inch dice. When the gumbo is cooked, stir in the chicken and adjust seasoning with salt and pepper. Serve immediately.

To serve as a main course, mound ⅓ cup cooked rice in the center of a soup bowl; ladle about 1¼ cups gumbo around the rice. For an appetizer, place 1 heaping teaspoon cooked rice in a cup and ladle about ¾ cup gumbo on top. This is super with Potato Salad on the side.

PRUDHOMME

Chef Paul Prudhomme's Louisiana Kitchen

Chicken and Seafood Jambalaya

MAKES 4 MAIN-DISH OR 8 APPETIZER SERVINGS

This jambalaya may be eaten as is or topped with Creole Sauce.

SEASONING MIX:

2 whole bay leaves
1½ teaspoons salt
1½ teaspoons ground red pepper (preferably cayenne)
1½ teaspoons dried oregano leaves
1¼ teaspoons white pepper
1 teaspoon black pepper
¾ teaspoon dried thyme leaves

2½ tablespoons chicken fat or pork lard or beef fat
⅔ cup chopped tasso (preferred) or other smoked ham (preferably Cure 81), about 3 ounces
½ cup chopped andouille smoked sausage (preferred) or any other good pure smoked pork sausage such as Polish sausage (kielbasa), about 3 ounces
1½ cups chopped onions
1 cup chopped celery
¾ cup chopped green bell peppers
½ cup chicken, cut into bite-size pieces, about 3 ounces
1½ teaspoons minced garlic
4 medium-size tomatoes, peeled and chopped, about 1 pound
¾ cup canned tomato sauce
2 cups Seafood Stock
½ cup chopped green onions
2 cups uncooked rice (preferably converted)
1½ dozen peeled medium shrimp, about ½ pound
1½ dozen oysters in their liquor (we use medium-size ones), about 10 ounces

Combine the seasoning mix ingredients in a small bowl and set aside.

In a 4-quart saucepan, melt the fat over medium heat. Add the tasso and andouille and sauté until crisp, about 5 to 8 minutes, stirring frequently. Add the onions, celery and bell peppers; sauté until tender but still firm, about 5 minutes, stirring occasionally and scraping pan bottom well. Add the chicken. Raise heat to high and cook 1 minute, stirring constantly. Reduce heat to medium. Add the seasoning mix and minced garlic; cook about 3 minutes, stirring constantly and scraping pan bottom as needed. Add the tomatoes and cook until chicken is tender, about 5 to 8 minutes, stirring frequently. Add the tomato sauce; cook 7 minutes, stirring fairly often. Stir in the stock and bring to a boil. Then stir in the green onions and cook about 2 minutes, stirring once or twice. Add the rice, shrimp and oysters; stir well and remove from heat. Transfer to an ungreased 8x8-inch baking pan. Cover pan snuggly with aluminum foil and bake at 350° until rice is tender but still a bit crunchy, about 20 to 30 minutes. Remove bay leaves and serve immediately.

To serve, mold rice in an 8-ounce cup. Place 2 cups on each serving plate for a main course or 1 cup for an appetizer.

BÉGUÉ

Mme. Bégué's Recipes of Old New Orleans Creole Cookery

JAMBALAYA OF CHICKEN. Cut in pieces a young chicken and slices of raw ham. Fry the whole in hot lard and set aside. In the same lard fry an onion and a tomato; when nearly done add a cupful of rice, the chicken and ham, and let all fry together, stirring constantly. Add enough water to cover the whole and let boil slowly until done. Season with strong pepper, bay leaves, chopped parsley and thyme. When cooked let dry a little and serve hot.

THE TIMES-PICAYUNE

The Original Picayune Creole Cook Book

Red Beans and Rice

Haricots Rouges au Riz

1 Quart of Dried Red Beans
1 Carrot
1 Onion
1 Bay Leaf
1 Tablespoonful of Butter
1 Pound of Ham or Salt Meat
Salt and Pepper to Taste

Wash the beans and soak them overnight, or at least five or six hours, in fresh, cold water. When ready to cook, drain off this water and put the beans in a pot of cold water, covering with at least two quarts, for beans must cook thoroughly. Let the water heat slowly. Then add the ham or salt pork, and the herbs and onion and carrot, minced fine. Boil the beans at least two hours, or until tender enough to mash easily under pressure. When tender, remove from the pot, put the salt meat or ham on top of the dish, and serve hot as a vegetable, with boiled rice as an entree, with Veal Saute, Daube à la Mode, Grillades à la Sauce, etc.

DULL

Southern Cooking

Brunswick Stew No. 1

1 pig's head, feet, liver, and heart
4 quarts of peeled, diced Irish potatoes
2 quarts of peeled and diced tomatoes
1 quart of fine cut okra
18 ears of fine cut corn (or two cans)
2 large onions, cut fine
4 garlic buttons, tied in a cheese cloth
1 tablespoon dry mustard
Juice of 1 lemon
½ lemon, put in whole, seed removed
1 bottle Worcestershire sauce
1 medium bottle chili sauce
1 pint bottle tomato catsup
½ lb. butter
Salt, black and red pepper to taste
Sweet pepper, both green and red, may be used if desired

Thoroughly clean pig's head and feet. From the head remove the teeth and gums, upper and lower. Place head, feet, liver and heart into boiling water and cook slowly until meat falls from the bones and will come to pieces. Remove from the liquor, remove all bone and any tough part, pull to pieces and mash or chop until fine. From the liquor remove scum and replace the meat. If not much liquor, add hot water. Add vegetables and seasoning; cook slowly and for several hours. If too thick, add hot water; if thin, add light bread crumbs, one large loaf.

When ready to serve, add half pound of butter. Stir almost constantly during the cooking. If it should stick or scorch, change the vessel, as any scorch will ruin the entire stew. Fresh vegetables are always preferable, canned ones may be used. Cut fine and fry the okra in a little grease. This prevents being slick. Brunswick stew must be served hot. Chili powder and chili peppers are good to use if obtainable.

Tasting when nearly done will help to get the seasoning just right. There should be enough liquor to cover the meat and vegetables to cook. The stew must be thick enough to eat with a fork when served. If bread crumbs are needed add near the end of cooking.

A wash pot of heavy iron should be used for cooking. Chicken, rabbit, squirrel or lamb may be used.

KATZEN
The Moosewood Cookbook

Vegetarian Chili

6–8 SERVINGS

Start beans 4–5 hours early. Several hours to prepare + cook.

2½ cups raw kidney beans
1 cup raw bulghar
1 cup tomato juice
4 cloves crushed garlic
1½ cups chopped onion
1 cup each, chopped:
 celery
 carrots
 green peppers
2 cups chopped, fresh tomatoes
juice of ½ lemon
1 tsp. ground cumin
1 tsp. basil
1 tsp. chili powder (more, to taste)
salt and pepper
3 Tbs. tomato paste
3 Tbs. dry red wine
dash of cayenne (more, to taste)
olive oil for sauté (about 3 Tbs.)

1. Put kidney beans in a saucepan and cover them with 6 cups of water. Soak 3–4 hours. Add extra water and 1 tsp. salt. Cook until tender (about 1 hour). Watch the water level, and add more, if necessary.

2. Heat tomato juice to a boil. Pour over raw bulghar. Cover and let stand at least 15 minutes. (It will be crunchy, so it can absorb more later.)

3. Sauté onions and garlic in olive oil. Add carrots, celery and spices. When vegetables are almost done, add peppers. Cook until tender.

4. Combine all ingredients and heat together gently—either in kettle over double boiler, or covered, in a moderate oven. Serve topped with cheese & parsley.

BAYLESS
Rick Bayless's Mexican Kitchen

VERY, VERY GOOD CHILI—In a large, heavy skillet or Dutch oven filmed with oil or bacon drippings, fry 2 pounds of coarse-ground beef (or half beef, half pork) and one large chopped onion over medium-high heat, stirring to break up clumps, until nicely browned; drain off most of the fat. Add a full recipe of the seasoning, stir for several minutes to temper the raw flavor, then stir in enough water or beef broth so that everything's floating freely. Partially cover and simmer gently for an hour, until it looks like chili; season with salt and a touch of sugar. If you like a less intense flavor, add 1 cup or so of blended canned tomato along with the water, and, if you prefer your chili with thickened juices, mix together a little masa harina and water, and whisk it into the chili during the last few minutes of simmering. I like my chili with whole boiled beans stirred in at the end.

KELLOGG
Every-day Dishes and Every-day Work

SUCCOTASH.—Boil one part Lima beans and two parts sweet corn separately until both are nearly tender. Put them together, and simmer gently till done. Season with salt and sweet cream. Fresh corn and beans may be combined in the same proportion; but as the beans will be likely to require the most time for cooking, they should be put to boil first, and the corn added when the beans are about half done, unless it is exceptionally hard, in which case it must be added sooner.

LAPPÉ

Diet for a Small Planet

Roman Rice and Beans

8–10 SERVINGS
AVERAGE SERVING = APPROX. 11 G USABLE PROTEIN
26 TO 31% OF DAILY PROTEIN ALLOWANCE

1½ cups dried pea beans (cook until tender)
oil as needed
2 large onions, finely chopped
2 garlic cloves, crushed
1–2 carrots, finely chopped
1 stalk celery, chopped (optional)
⅔ cup parsley, chopped
5–6 tsp dried basil
1 tsp dried oregano
2 large tomatoes, coarsely chopped
4–5 tsp salt
pepper to taste
4 cups raw brown rice (cook with 4 tsp salt)
¼–½ cup butter or margarine
1 cup or more grated cheese (parmesan or jack)

Sauté onions, garlic, carrots, celery, parsley, basil, and oregano in oil until onion is golden. Add tomatoes, salt, pepper, and cooked beans. Add butter and cheese to cooked rice. Then add first mixture. Garnish with more parsley and more grated cheese.

BROWNSTONE

The Associated Press Cookbook

Jennie's Rice Torta

This hors d'oeuvre hails from Italy. It's a delicious combination of rice, spinach, cheese and eggs that's baked in a fairly shallow pan. Cut in small pieces, it's great to offer with late-afternoon or before-dinner drinks. All our tasters asked for the recipe.

This torta comes from Piacenza, a town in Northern Italy where rice is a staple and sauces are likely to be made with butter, eggs and cream. In Italy the rice torta goes to the table at the end of the meal along with fruit and cheese. It's so highly regarded that it is usually served on holidays or other festive occasions.

The recipe was contributed by a friend who borrowed it from her Italian-born mother. Our friend says: "I've made a departure from the Italian service of torta because I use it as an hors d'oeuvre nearly every time I entertain a dozen or more friends. It's a perfect do-ahead dish and inexpensive. Recently I served my torta to my mother who pronounced it just right. Although she scorns any spinach that isn't fresh, she didn't even guess that I had used the frozen kind!"

½ cup water
1 package (10 ounces) frozen leaf spinach
3 cups cooked rice
½ pound ricotta cheese
1 cup freshly grated Parmesan cheese
¼ teaspoon salt
1⁄16 teaspoon pepper
4 eggs
Olive oil
Fine dry bread crumbs

In a saucepan bring the water to a boil; add spinach; break up with a fork to thaw and bring to a boil; boil about 1 minute. Drain thoroughly; chop fine; squeeze out any excess water.

In a medium mixing bowl stir together the spinach, rice, ricotta, Parmesan, salt and pepper.

In a small mixing bowl beat together 3 of the eggs until yolks and whites are combined; fold into rice mixture.

With olive oil, grease the bottom and sides of a square cake pan (9 by 9 by 2 inches). Sprinkle bottom and sides with enough bread crumbs to coat. Turn rice mixture into pan.

Beat remaining egg until yolk and white are combined; with a pastry brush, brush over rice mixture.

Bake in a preheated 350-degree oven until firm—about 30 minutes.

Run a small spatula around the sides to loosen edges; cut into 1½-inch squares; remove with spatula. Serve warm as an hors d'oeuvre.

MAKES 36

NOTE: If any of the torta is left over, cut it into large sections; with a wide spatula, loosen carefully and remove; wrap in foil and refrigerate. To reheat, bring to room temperature and then reheat in the foil in a 350-degree oven just until warm—5 or 10 minutes. Recipe may be easily doubled and baked in a 13- by 9- by 2-inch pan at 350 degrees for 30 minutes.

MADISON

The Greens Cook Book

Winter Vegetable Stew

A straightforward stew with robust and well-developed flavors, the vegetables are left whole or cut into good-size pieces so that they maintain their integrity and heartiness throughout the cooking. The sauce, the medium in which the various vegetables are cooked and brought together, uses the Wild Mushroom Stock for its liquid (the Winter Vegetable Stock, reduced by half, could also be used). The stock adds greatly to the overall depth and flavor of the stew, and it can be made in advance.

This stew can be served in different ways. It can be cooked entirely on the stove and served with biscuits or grilled polenta, or it can finish cooking in the oven as a shepherd's pie, or under a buttery crust of puff pastry or cream cheese pastry to make a more special presentation. It is also good reheated the next day.

THE SAUCE

2 tablespoons butter
1 tablespoon olive oil
1 medium yellow onion, cut into ½-inch squares
½ teaspoon dried thyme
½ teaspoon dried tarragon
1 bay leaf
½ teaspoon salt
3 cloves garlic, finely chopped
½ cup red wine
3 tablespoons flour
3 cups Wild Mushroom Stock, heated
2 tablespoons parsley, finely chopped

Heat the butter and the oil in a wide soup pot with a heavy bottom. Add the onion, dried herbs, bay leaf, and salt, and cook over medium heat, stirring frequently, until the onion is nicely browned all over, about 15 minutes. Stir in the garlic and the wine, and reduce by half. Add the flour and cook for 2 minutes; then whisk in the stock. Bring to a boil; then simmer slowly, partially covered, for 25 minutes. Add the parsley and check the seasoning. There will be about 2⅔ cups.

THE STEW

4 to 6 dried shiitake mushrooms
10 ounces boiling onions
4 medium carrots (about 10 ounces)
1 celery root
3 to 4 parsnips (about 10 ounces)
6 ounces mushrooms, wiped clean
1 small cauliflower, broken into large florets
5 ounces brussels sprouts
3 tablespoons butter
2 tablespoons olive oil
Salt
2 cloves garlic, finely chopped
Fresh herbs: parsley, thyme, tarragon, finely chopped
Pepper

Cover the dried mushrooms with a cup of hot water, and set them aside to soak for 20 minutes. Run your fingers over them to loosen any dirt or sand; then remove the caps and cut them into quarters. Strain the soaking water and set aside to use in the stew.

Peel the boiling onions. Leave them whole if they are small, and halve the larger ones, keeping the root end intact. Peel the carrots; then cut them into pieces about 1½ inches long; halve or quarter the thicker ones so that all the pieces are a similar size.

Cut away the gnarly skin of the celery root, cut it into large cubes, and put it in a bowl of water with a little lemon juice until needed. Peel and quarter the parsnips, cut out the cores, and slice them into wide sections. If the mushrooms are small, leave them whole; otherwise cut them into wide, uneven pieces.

Bring a pot of water to a boil, add salt, blanch the cauliflower for 30 seconds, and remove. Parboil the brussels sprouts for 1 minute and remove. Rinse both vegetables with cold water to stop their cooking.

Melt half the butter and a tablespoon of the olive oil in a large skillet or casserole. Add the onions and carrots, and cook over a medium heat about 3 or 4 minutes, until they begin to get a little color. Then add ½ teaspoon salt and ½ cup of the mushroom soaking water, Wild Mushroom Stock, or water. Lower the heat, cover the pan, and cook for 4 to 5 minutes.

In a second pan, heat the remaining butter and oil and add the fresh mushrooms. Cook them briskly over high heat until they begin to brown; then add a little salt, a few tablespoons of soaking water or mushroom stock, and the garlic. Cook another 2 minutes; then add them to the casserole along with the dried mushrooms, celery root, and parsnips. Cook over low heat, covered, for another 3 minutes; then add the sauce, cauliflower, brussels sprouts, and fresh herbs. Season with salt and freshly ground black pepper.

If the stew is to be baked further in the oven, as a shepherd's pie or under a pastry crust, remove it from the heat, transfer it to a suitable casserole, cover it as desired, and bake for 40 minutes at 375°F. Otherwise, continue cooking the stew on top of the stove, slowly, until all the vegetables are tender, 10 to 20 minutes; then serve, garnished with additional fresh herbs. This is a hearty, full-flavored dish that could be served with a zinfandel or a California pinot noir.

SERVES SIX

KATZEN

The Moosewood Cookbook

Gypsy Soup

A spiced and delectable brew of Spanish and Dickensonian origins.

4 SERVINGS

This recipe calls for cooked chickpeas. Begin soaking ¾ cup raw chickpeas at least 3½ hours before soup time. (Allow 1½ hours for them to cook.)

- 3–4 Tbs. olive oil
- 2 cups chopped onion
- 2 cloves crushed garlic
- 2 cups chopped, peeled sweet potatoes or winter squash
- ½ cup chopped celery
- 1 cup chopped, fresh tomatoes
- ¾ cup sweet peppers
- 1½ cups cooked chickpeas
- 3 cups stock or water
- 2 tsp. paprika
- 1 tsp. turmeric
- 1 tsp. basil
- 1 tsp. salt
- dash of cinnamon
- dash of cayenne
- 1 bay leaf
- 1 Tbs. tamari

In a soup kettle or large saucepan sauté onions, garlic, celery and sweet potatoes in olive oil for about five minutes. Add seasonings, except tamari, and the stock or water. Simmer, covered, fifteen minutes. Add remaining vegetables and chickpeas. Simmer another 10 minutes or so—until all the vegetables are as tender as you like them.

NOTE: The vegetables used in this soup are flexible. Any orange vegetable can be combined with green . . . For example, peas or green beans could replace the peppers. Carrots can be used instead of, or in addition to, the squash or sweet potatoes. Etc.

LANG

The Cuisine of Hungary

Layered Cabbage, Basic Recipe, or Kolozsvári Layered Cabbage

Rakottkáposzta vagy Kolozsvári rakott káposzta

6 SERVINGS

- 1½ pounds sauerkraut
- ½ cup uncooked rice
- 1 cup meat broth
- 1 large onion, chopped fine
- 2 tablespoons lard
- 1 pound lean pork, ground
- 1 tablespoon paprika
- 2 garlic cloves, crushed
- ¼ pound smoked bacon, cut into small dice
- ½ pound smoked sausage, sliced
- 1 cup sour cream
- ¼ cup milk

1. Preheat over to 375°F. Squeeze sauerkraut well, and wash it in cold water if it is too sour. Add 1 cup water and cook sauerkraut for 15 minutes.

2. Meantime, cook the rice in the meat broth for 10 minutes.

3. In a separate frying pan fry onion in hot lard for about 5 minutes.

4. Add ground pork, stir it well, and cook for another 15 minutes, breaking up the pork well. Remove from heat and mix in paprika and garlic.

5. Cook bacon dice for a few minutes. Add sliced sausage just to shake it together. Remove both with a slotted spoon.

6. In the bottom of a baking-serving casserole put fat from bacon and spread it all over the inside. Put one third of the sauerkraut in the bottom. On top of sauerkraut place half of the ground pork, then half of the rice and all the sausage and bacon. Sprinkle with half of the sour cream mixed with milk. Cover

with the second third of the sauerkraut, remaining meat and rice, and finally the third part of the sauerkraut. Pour rest of sour cream and milk over, and spread it on top.

7. Bake the casserole, without a cover, in the preheated oven for 1 hour.

VARIATIONS

I. 1. Use sweet cabbage only, and blanch the head to separate leaves. Mix well ½ pound raw veal; 1 pound goose liver, diced (substitute chicken liver if you must); ½ roll soaked in cream, then squeezed and chopped; 1 tablespoon chopped flat parsley; 3 egg yolks; 5 grinds of black pepper; 2 tablespoons sour cream.

2. Butter well an ovenproof pottery mold. Line it carefully with cabbage leaves, spread with some of the filling, and alternate until you come to the top. Finish with cabbage leaves.

3. Stand the dish in a water bath. Bake in a 375°F. oven for 45 minutes. Turn it out onto a serving platter.

II. Top the casserole with thin-sliced pork chops, fried. Some cooks thicken this with 3 tablespoons flour and 2 tablespoons lard cooked to a *roux* and diluted with ½ cup cold water.

III. Line a larded baking mold with sliced boiled ham (freshly made, of course). Fill with sliced hard-cooked eggs, rice and ground pork stuffing, alternating with sauerkraut and sour cream. Bake in a water bath, then turn out on a serving platter.

IV. The oldest recipes use black pepper and white wine with pork and pork sausage. No sour cream or paprika is mentioned.

V. TELEKI LAYERED CABBAGE (*Rakottkáposzta Teleki módra*): Cook sauerkraut with smoked pork chops, smoked goose breast, meaty slab bacon, whole onion, cloves, and sour cream with flour stirred in. Just before serving, fry fresh pork chops separately and put on the serving platter with the finished dish. (Probably first served in Gundel by Chef Rákóczy, and named after the gourmet aristocrat.)

TIME-LIFE BOOKS
A Quintet of Cuisines

Chicorée et Volaille Bruxelloise (Belgium)

Braised Endives Stuffed with Chicken

TO SERVE 6 AS A FIRST COURSE

4 tablespoons unsalted butter, softened, plus 4 tablespoons unsalted butter
6 large firm endives, with tightly closed unblemished leaves
Salt
White pepper
¼ cup strained fresh lemon juice
A 6- to 8-ounce chicken breast, skinned and boned
¼ cup flour
1 cup chicken stock, fresh or canned
1 cup heavy cream
⅛ teaspoon ground nutmeg, preferably freshly grated
1 egg yolk
½ cup freshly grated imported Gruyère cheese
6 slices boiled ham, each ⅛ inch thick and about 6 inches wide and 8 inches long

Preheat the oven to 325°. With a pastry brush, spread 2 tablespoons of the softened butter evenly over the bottom and sides of a baking-serving dish large enough to hold the endives in one layer.

With a small, sharp knife trim off the bases of the endives (making sure not to cut so deep that the leaves separate) and wash the endives under cold running water. Pat them completely dry with paper towels, then arrange them side by side in the buttered dish and with a pastry brush spread them with the remaining 2 tablespoons of softened butter. Sprinkle the endives with ½ teaspoon salt and ¼ teaspoon of white pepper, and pour the lemon juice over them.

Cover the endives with a sheet of wax paper cut to fit flush with the inside rim of the dish. Then bake in the middle of the oven for about 1½ hours, or until the bases of the endives are tender and show no resistance when pierced deeply with the point of a skewer. With tongs or a slotted spatula carefully transfer the endives to a plate. Pour off any liquid remaining in the dish and set the dish aside.

Raise the oven temperature to 375°. In a small flameproof baking pan, melt 1 tablespoon of the butter over moderate heat. When the foam begins to subside, add the chicken breast and turn it about with a spoon until it glistens on all sides. Remove the pan from the heat, sprinkle the chicken with ¼ teaspoon salt and ⅛ teaspoon white pepper, and cover it with wax paper cut to fit inside the pan. Poach the chicken in the middle of the oven for 8 to 10 minutes, or until the flesh feels firm to the touch. Transfer the chicken to a plate and, with a sharp knife, cut it into ¼-inch dice. Place the diced chicken in a small bowl and set aside.

In a heavy 1½- to 2-quart saucepan, melt the remaining 3 tablespoons of butter over moderate heat, stir in the flour, and mix thoroughly. Pour in the chicken stock and, stirring constantly with a wire whisk, cook over high heat until the sauce thickens heavily and comes to a boil. Reduce the heat to low and simmer for about 5 minutes to remove any taste of raw flour, then stir in the cream, nutmeg, ¼ teaspoon of salt and a pinch of white pepper. Taste for seasoning and add more salt or pepper if necessary. Pour about ¼ cup of the sauce over the reserved chicken dice and mix well. Then beat the egg yolk into the remaining sauce and when it is completely absorbed stir in the cheese.

Increase the oven heat to 400°. With a sharp knife, slit each endive in half lengthwise, cutting to within about 1 inch of the base. One at a time, spread the endives open butterfly fashion and flatten one half gently with the side of a cleaver or large knife. Divide the chicken mixture into 6 equal portions. Spread one portion of the chicken on the flattened sides of each endive, then fold the other half of the endive over the filling and wrap each stuffed endive securely in a slice of ham.

Arrange the wrapped endives side by side (seamed side down) in the baking-serving dish and spoon the reserved sauce evenly over the top. Bake in the middle of the oven for about 10 minutes, or until the sauce begins to bubble. Then place the baking dish under a preheated broiler (about 3 inches from the heat) for a minute or so to brown the sauce further. Serve at once, directly from the baking dish.

WELLS

Bistro Cooking

Gratin Dauphinois Madame Laracine

Madame Laracine's Potato Gratin

Wherever I travel in France, I always ask cooks for tips on preparing potato gratins. In the Savoy region, many cooks mentioned the double-cooking method, in which you first cook the potatoes in milk and water, or simply in whole milk, discard the cooking liquid, and then bake the potatoes in a blend of cream and Gruyère cheese. It makes for a rich, satisfying gratin.

It's always dangerous to label anything the best, but in my memory, Madame Laracine—chef-proprietor of a small family ferme-auberge *in the village of Ordonnaz—made a most stunning gratin, prepared with homegrown potatoes, milk and cream from her own cows, and cheese from a nearby dairy.*

- 3 pounds (1.5 kg) baking potatoes, such as russets, peeled and very thinly sliced
- 2 cups (50 cl) whole milk
- 3 garlic cloves, minced
- ¾ teaspoon salt
- 3 imported bay leaves
- Freshly ground nutmeg
- Freshly ground black pepper
- 1 cup (25 cl) crème fraîche or heavy cream
- 2 cups (about 5 ounces; 160 g) freshly grated French or Swiss Gruyère cheese

1. Preheat the oven to 375°F (190°C).

2. Place the potatoes in a large saucepan and cover with the milk and 2 cups (50 cl) of water. Add the garlic, salt, and bay leaves. Bring to a boil over medium-high heat, stirring occasionally so that the potatoes do not stick to the bottom of the pan. Reduce the heat to medium and cook, stirring from time to time, until the potatoes are tender but not falling apart, about 10 minutes.

3. Using a slotted spoon, transfer half of the potatoes to a large, 14 × 9 × 2 inch (35.5 × 23 × 5 cm) gratin dish. Sprinkle with the nutmeg, pepper, half the crème fraîche, and half the cheese. Cover with the remaining potatoes, and sprinkle again with nutmeg, pepper, and the remaining crème fraîche and cheese.

4. Bake the gratin until crisp and golden on top, about 1 hour. Serve immediately.

YIELD: 6 TO 8 SERVINGS

"In 1793 potatoes were considered so indispensable that a decree of the French Republic ordered a census to be taken of luxury gardens, so that they could be devoted to the cultivation of this vegetable. As a result, the principal avenue in the Jardin des Tuileries and the flower beds were turned over to potato cultivation. This is why potatoes were for a long time given the additional name of 'royal oranges.'"

—Alexandre Dumas
Dumas on Food

WELLS
Bistro Cooking

Gratin Dauphinois Madame Cartet

Madame Cartet's Potato Gratin

There are some recipes one can never have too many of in one's repertoire. And potato gratin is one of them. This is one of the easiest potato gratins I know, cooking in just under one hour, a simple but full-flavored blend of potatoes, fresh cream, garlic, and freshly grated Gruyère cheese. Twice each day, Thérèse Nouaille, of Paris's tiny neighborhood bistro Cartet, prepares this gratin for her steady customers: Make it yourself and you'll understand why they keep coming back!

- 1 garlic clove
- 2 pounds (1 kg) baking potatoes, such as russets, peeled and very thinly sliced
- 1 cup (about 3 ounces; 80 g) freshly grated French or Swiss Gruyère cheese
- 1 cup (25 cl) crème fraîche or heavy cream
- Salt

1. Preheat the oven to 350°F (175°C).

2. Thoroughly rub a shallow, 6-cup (1.5 l) porcelain gratin dish with the garlic. Layer half of the potatoes in the dish. Sprinkle with half of the cheese and then half of the crème fraîche. Sprinkle with salt. Add another layer, using the rest of the ingredients.

3. Bake, uncovered, until the gratin is crisp and golden on top, from 50 to 60 minutes. Serve immediately.

YIELD: 4 TO 6 SERVINGS

CHILD, BERTHOLLE, AND BECK
Mastering the Art of French Cooking

Soufflé au Fromage

Cheese Soufflé

This recipe is intended as a detailed guide to those that follow. All main-course soufflés follow this general pattern:

FOR 4 PEOPLE

THE SOUFFLÉ SAUCE BASE

A 6-cup soufflé mold

Preheat oven to 400 degrees.

- 1 tsp butter
- 1 Tb grated Swiss or Parmesan cheese

Measure out all your ingredients. Butter inside of soufflé mold and sprinkle with cheese.

- 3 Tb butter
- A 2½-quart saucepan
- 3 Tb flour
- A wooden spatula or spoon
- 1 cup boiling milk
- A wire whip
- ½ tsp salt
- ⅛ tsp pepper
- A pinch of cayenne pepper
- Pinch of nutmeg

Melt the butter in the saucepan. Stir in the flour with a wooden spatula or spoon and cook over moderate heat until butter and flour foam together for 2 minutes without browning. Remove from heat; when mixture has stopped bubbling, pour in all the boiling milk at once. Beat vigorously with a wire whip until blended. Beat in the seasonings. Return over moderately high heat and boil, stirring with the wire whip, for 1 minute. Sauce will be very thick.

4 egg yolks

Remove from heat. Immediately start to separate the eggs. Drop the white into the egg white bowl, and the yolk into the center of the hot sauce. Beat the yolk into the sauce with the wire whip. Continue in the same manner with the rest of the eggs. Correct seasoning.

*May be prepared ahead to this point. Dot top of sauce with butter. Heat to tepid before continuing.

THE EGG WHITES AND CHEESE

- 5 egg whites
- A pinch of salt
- ¾ cup (3 ounces) coarsely grated Swiss, or Swiss and Parmesan, cheese

Add an extra egg white to the ones in the bowl and beat with the salt until stiff. Stir a big spoonful (about one quarter of the egg whites) into the sauce. Stir in all but a tablespoon of the cheese. Delicately fold in the rest of the egg whites.

BAKING

Turn the soufflé mixture into the prepared mold, which should be almost three quarters full. Tap bottom of mold lightly on the table, and smooth the surface of the soufflé with the flat of a knife. Sprinkle the remaining cheese on top.

Set on a rack in middle level of preheated 400-degree oven and immediately turn heat down to 375. (Do not open oven door for 20 minutes.) In 25 to 30 minutes the soufflé will have puffed about 2 inches over the rim of the mold, and the top will be nicely browned. Bake 4 to 5 minutes more to firm it up, then serve at once.

MADISON

The Greens Cook Book

Black Bean Enchiladas

A delicious enchilada can be prepared using the Black Bean Chili for the filling and the Tomatillo Sauce. Once these are made, it is a simple matter to assemble the enchiladas. The variations list some other ideas for enchilada fillings and sauces. This is hearty fare, so serve it with something light and crisp, such as the Jicama-Orange Salad.

- 3 cups Black Bean Chili
- Tomatillo Sauce
- ½ cup peanut or light corn oil
- 12 corn or wheat tortillas
- 4 ounces Monterey Jack cheese, grated
- Sprigs of cilantro, for garnish

Prepare the black bean chili and the tomatillo sauce, using the variation in which the onions are cooked.

Heat the oil in a large skillet until a tortilla will sizzle when it is put in. Lightly fry the tortillas on each side, about 20 to 30 seconds, not so long that they become crisp, and set them on paper toweling to drain.

Preheat the oven to 400°F. Oil a 9-by-13-inch baking pan, and spread ½ cup of sauce over the bottom. Put another ½ cup or so of sauce aside. Coat each tortilla on both sides with the sauce; then put ¼ cup of chili and a couple tablespoons of cheese in a strip down the middle of the tortilla, and roll the tortilla around the filling. Place them seam side down in the baking pan in a single layer. When they are all assembled, brush the tops with the remaining sauce.

Bake the enchiladas until heated through, 15 to 20 minutes. Garnish with sprigs of cilantro, and serve with the Salsa Picante, if desired.

VARIATIONS: In place of the Tomatillo Sauce, prepare a red sauce such as the Ancho Chili Sauce, or the red sauce in the Mushroom and Fennel Budín.

Replace the Black Bean Chili with a vegetable filling such as that used in Crepas con Queso y Verderas, or the corn-zucchini mixture used to make Corn and Zucchini Timbale.

A more strongly flavored cheese, a smoked cheese or sharp cheddar, for instance, can be used in place of the Monterey Jack.

MAKES 12 ENCHILADAS

LAGASSE

Emeril's New New Orleans Cooking

Southwest Cheese Pie with Pico di Gallo

MAKES 6 TO 8 BRUNCH SERVINGS

There's nothing quite like starting the day with the unique flavors of a Southwestern brunch. This dish could be part of a buffet or served as your main course. The Pico di Gallo, which is a colorful fresh salsa, has a peppery, spicy goodness and is a perfect counterpoint to the creamy cheese pie.

½ recipe Basic Pie Dough
1 tablespoon olive oil
3 strips bacon, diced
½ cup chopped onions
¼ cup diced seeded poblano, green New Mexico, or Anaheim chile peppers
1 teaspoon minced garlic
1 teaspoon Emeril's Southwest Seasoning
½ teaspoon chili powder
½ teaspoon ground cumin
½ teaspoon salt
4 turns freshly ground black pepper
3 tablespoons chopped fresh cilantro
3 large eggs
2 cups heavy cream
2 cups grated jalapeño-flavored Jack cheese
2 cups Pico di Gallo

1. Prepare the Basic Pie Dough for a 9-inch pie shell.

2. Preheat the oven to 375°F.

3. Combine the oil and bacon in a large skillet over high heat and sauté, stirring occasionally, for 3 minutes. Stir in the onions, peppers, garlic, Southwest Seasoning, chili powder, cumin, salt, and pepper and sauté for 2 minutes. Remove from the heat and pour into a bowl.

4. Add the cilantro, whisk in the eggs and cream, fold in the cheese, and pour the mixture into the unbaked pie shell. Bake for 15 minutes at 375°, then turn the oven heat down to 350°, and bake until puffy and golden brown, for about 30 minutes longer. Remove the pie from the oven and let it cool for 10 to 15 minutes before cutting and serving.

5. While the pie is baking, prepare the Pico di Gallo.

6. To serve, cut the pie into 6 or 8 wedges and top each with ⅓ or ¼ cup of the Pico di Gallo.

BAYLESS

Rick Bayless's Mexican Kitchen

Oaxacan Black *Mole* with Braised Chicken

Mole Negro Oaxaqueño

I'd venture to say that anyone who has traveled to Oaxaca, the beautifully preserved colonial city in Southern Mexico, has eaten black mole *at least once. It is the regional specialty—on every restaurant menu, at every fiesta. And, quite expectedly, not all black* moles *are crafted equally. At the touristy* zócalo *("central square") restaurants, it is a lacquered-looking blackness (ever seen drying tar?) that's all sweetness, burn and chocolate. At Abigail Mendoza's now-famous Tlalmanalli restaurant in Teotitlan del Valle, its near-blackness draws you into the layers of complexity, the perfect piquancy, the delicately balanced dulcet char of real* mole negro. *Her version is what dreams are made of.*

Black mole *has to be the star of the meal, so serve it simply with a spoonful of Classic White Rice (you may want to add a little diced cooked carrot and zucchini to the rice as Abigail does) and plenty of hot tortillas. In summer, I'd work hard to locate squash blossoms for Golden Squash Blossom* Crema *or serve Mushroom-Cactus Soup to start. Dessert should stay classic and Oaxacan like Mango-Lime Ice or Tropical "Trifle" of Mango and Almonds.*

Even in Oaxaca, chihuacle chiles are expensive and not always available, so folks have learned to make black mole *with 6 ounces mulato, 2½ ounces pasilla, 1 ounce guajillo and 1 chipotle. For years I collected black* mole *recipes that yielded mediocre results to the point that I just wouldn't offer it at our restaurants. Not until my favorite chile seller, Panchita, in the Oaxaca market really explained the details and her proportions could I get it right. Here's what she taught me.*

SERVES 8 (WITH ABOUT 10 CUPS OF SAUCE, WHICH WILL MEAN LEFTOVERS TO MAKE ENCHILADAS OR MORE CHICKEN WITH)

- 11 medium (about 5½ ounces) dried mulato chiles
- 6 medium (about 2 ounces) dried chihuacle chiles
- 6 medium (about 2 ounces) dried pasilla chiles
- 1 dried chipotle chile (preferably the tan-brown *chipotle meco*)
- 1 corn tortilla, torn into small pieces
- 2 ¼-inch-thick slices of white onion
- 4 garlic cloves, unpeeled
- About 2 cups rich-tasting lard or vegetable oil (for frying the chiles)
- ½ cup sesame seeds, plus a few extra for garnish
- ¼ cup pecan halves
- ¼ cup unskinned or Spanish peanuts
- ¼ cup unskinned almonds
- About 10 cups chicken broth (canned or homemade)
- 1 pound (2 medium-large or 6 to 8 plum) green tomatoes, roughly chopped
- 4 ounces (2 to 3 medium) tomatillos, husked, rinsed and roughly chopped
- 2 slices stale bread, toasted until very dark
- ¼ teaspoon cloves, preferably freshly ground
- ½ teaspoon black pepper, preferably freshly ground
- ½ teaspoon cinnamon, preferably freshly ground Mexican *canela*
- A scant teaspoon oregano, preferably Mexican
- ½ teaspoon dried thyme
- ½ ripe banana
- ½ cup (about 3 ounces) finely chopped Mexican chocolate
- 2 or 3 avocado leaves (if you have them)
- Salt, about 1 tablespoon, depending on the saltiness of the broth
- Sugar, about ¼ cup (or a little more)
- 2 large (3½- to 4-pound) chickens, cut into quarters

1. GETTING STARTED. Pull out the stems (and attached seed pods) from the chiles, tear them open, and shake or scrape out the seeds, collecting them as you go.

Now, do something that will seem very odd: Scoop the seeds into an ungreased medium-size (8- to 9-inch) skillet along with the torn-up tortilla, set over medium heat, turn on an exhaust fan, open a window and toast your seeds and tortilla, shaking the pan regularly, until burned to charcoal black, about 15 minutes. (This is very important to the flavor and color of the *mole*.) Now, scrape them into a fine-mesh strainer and rinse for 30 seconds or so, then transfer to a blender.

Set an ungreased skillet or griddle over medium heat, lay on a piece of aluminum foil, and lay the onion slices and garlic cloves on that. Roast until soft and very dark (about 5 minutes on each side of the onion slices; about 15 minutes for the garlic—turn it frequently as it roasts). Cool the garlic a bit, peel it and combine with the onion in a large bowl.

While the onion and garlic are roasting, turn on the oven to 350 degrees (for toasting nuts), return the skillet to medium heat, measure in a scant 2 cups of the lard or oil (you'll need about ½-inch depth), and, when hot, begin frying the chiles a couple at a time: they'll unfurl quickly, then release their aroma and piquancy (keep that exhaust on and window open) and, after about 30 seconds, have lightened in color and be well toasted (they should be crisp when cool, but not burnt smelling). Drain them well, gather them into a large bowl, cover with hot tap water, and let rehydrate for 30 minutes, stirring regularly to ensure even soaking. Drain, reserving the soaking liquid.

While the chiles are soaking, toast the seeds and nuts. Spread the sesame seeds onto a baking sheet or ovenproof skillet, spread the pecans, peanuts and almonds onto another baking sheet or skillet, then set both into the oven. In about 12 minutes the sesame seeds will have toasted to a dark brown; the nuts will take slightly longer. Add all of them to the blender (reserving a few sesame seeds for garnish), along with 1½ cups of the chicken broth and blend to as smooth a puree as you can. Transfer to a small bowl.

Without rinsing the blender, combine the green tomatoes and tomatillos with another *½ cup* of the broth and puree. Pour into another bowl. Again, without rinsing the blender, combine the onion and garlic with the bread, cloves, black pepper, cinnamon, oregano, thyme, banana and *¾ cup* broth. Blend to a smooth puree and pour into a small bowl.

Finally, without rinsing the blender, scoop in *half* of the chiles, measure in *½ cup* of the soaking liquid, blend to a smooth puree, then pour into another bowl. Repeat with the remaining chiles and another *½ cup* of the soaking liquid.

2. FROM FOUR PUREES TO *MOLE*. In a very large (8- to 9-quart) pot (preferably a Dutch oven or Mexican *cazuela*), heat 3 *tablespoons* of the lard or oil (some of what you used for the chiles is fine) and set over medium-high heat. When very hot, add the tomato puree and stir and scrape for 15 to 20 minutes until reduced, thick as tomato paste, and very dark (it'll be the color of cinnamon stick and may be sticking to the pot in places). Add the nut puree and continue the stirring and scraping until reduced, thick and dark again (this time it'll be the color of black olive paste), about 8 minutes. Then, as you guessed, add the banana-spice puree and stir and scrape for another 7 or 8 minutes as the whole thing simmers back down to a thick mass about the same color it was before you added this one.

Add the chile puree, stir well and let reduce over medium-low heat until very thick and almost black, about 30 minutes, stirring regularly (but, thankfully, not constantly). Stir in the remaining 7 *cups* of broth, the chocolate and avocado leaves (if you have them), partially cover and simmer gently for about an hour. Season with salt and sugar (remembering that sugar helps balance the dark, toasty flavors). Remove the avocado leaves.

In batches in a *loosely* covered blender, puree the sauce until as smooth as possible, then pass through a medium-mesh strainer into a large bowl.

3. FINISHING THE DISH. Return the *mole* to the same pot and heat it to a simmer. Nestle the leg-and-thigh quarters of the chicken into the bubbling black liquid, partially cover and time 15 minutes, then nestle in the breast quarters, partially cover and simmer for 20 to 25 minutes, until all the chicken is done.

With a slotted spoon, fish out the chicken pieces and transfer them to a large warm platter. Spoon a generous amount of the *mole* over and around them, sprinkle with the reserved sesame seeds, and set triumphantly before your lucky guests.

ADVANCE PREPARATION—The *mole* can be completed through step 2 several days ahead (it gets better, in fact); cover and refrigerate. Complete step 3 shortly before serving.

KENNEDY

The Cuisines of Mexico

Mole Poblano de Guajolote

Turkey in mole poblano

10 SERVINGS

The French were somewhat surprised one Christmas Day, during a broadcast from Mexico, to hear the correspondent say: "Today while you eat your turkey and chocolate bûche de Noël *(chocolate log cake), just stop and think that what you are eating came originally from the New World: chocolate and turkeys both came from pre-Columbian Mexico. We, too, are eating them in Mexico today; the only difference is that we are eating them together."*

No special festival is complete without mole poblano de guajolote. *It is prepared with loving care, and even today, more often than not, it is the one dish that brings out the* metate: *chilies, spices, nuts, seeds, and tortillas are all ground on it. In the village fiestas each woman is given her allotted task: some to clean and toast the chilies, others to grind them; there are the turkeys to kill and prepare, the spices to measure, and the maize for the tamales to be soaked and cleaned meticulously.*

It would be impossible to say just how many versions there are; every cook from the smallest hamlet to the grandest city home has her own special touch—a few more mulatos *here, less* anchos, *or a touch of* chipotle *cooked with the turkey; some insist on onion, others won't tolerate it. Many cooks in Puebla itself insist on toasting the chilies, often* mulatos *only, over an open fire and grinding them dry. And so the arguments go on forever.*

The word mole *comes from the Nahuatl word* molli, *meaning "concoction." The majority of people respond, when* mole *is mentioned, with "Oh, yes, I know—that chocolate sauce. I wouldn't like it." Well, it* isn't *a chocolate sauce. One little piece of chocolate (and in Mexico we used to grind toasted cacao beans for the* mole*) goes into a large casserole full of rich dark-brown and russet chilies. And anyone I've ever served this to has been surprised and delighted, for in this, as in other Mexican sauces, the seasonings and spices are not used with such a heavy hand that they vie with each other for recognition, but rather build up to a harmonious whole.*

There are many stories attached to its beginnings but they all agree that the mole *was born in one of the convents in the city of Puebla de los Angeles. The most repeated version, I suppose, is that Sor Andrea, sister superior of the Santa Rosa Convent, wished to honor the Archbishop for having a convent especially constructed for her order; trying to blend the ingredients of the New World with those of the old, she created* mole poblano. *Yet another story goes that the Viceroy, Don Juan de Palafox y Mendoza, was visiting Puebla. This time it was Fray Pascual who was preparing the banquet at the convent where he was going to eat. Turkeys were cooking in* cazuelas *on the fire; as Fray Pascual, scolding his assistants for their untidiness, gathered up all the spices they had been using, and putting them together onto a tray, a sudden gust of wind swept across the kitchen and they spilled over into the* cazuelas. *But, as one present-day Mexican philosopher says, "Whether it was prepared for archbishop or viceroy, by the nuns or the angels, the very thought of it makes your mouth water" (Alfredo Ramos Espinosa,* Semblanza Mexicana, *p. 216).*

THE DAY BEFORE

8 chiles mulatos
5 chiles anchos
6 chiles pasilla
A large frying pan
¼ pound lard (½ cup)

Slit the chilies open with a knife and remove the seeds and veins, reserving at least 1 tablespoon of the seeds.

Heat the lard and quickly fry the chilies on both sides. Take care that they do not burn.

A large bowl
Warm water to cover

Put the chilies into the bowl, cover them with water, and leave them to stand overnight.

ON SERVING DAY

Preheat the oven to 325°.

A 7- to 8-pound turkey

Cut the turkey into serving pieces. Set the giblets aside.

A Dutch oven
6 to 8 tablespoons lard

Melt the lard and brown the turkey pieces well. Drain off the excess fat. Cover the pan and braise the turkey in the oven, without liquid, until it is tender—40 to 60 minutes, depending on toughness.

A saucepan
The turkey giblets
1 small carrot, sliced
1 medium onion, sliced
1 clove garlic, peeled
1 tablespoon salt
6 peppercorns
Water to cover
The pan juices from the turkey

Put the giblets into the pan with the rest of the ingredients. Cover them with water and bring them to a boil. Lower the flame and simmer 1¼ to 1½ hours. Strain the broth and set it aside.

When the turkey is cooked, pour off the juices in the pan and set them aside to cool, then skim off the fat and add them to the giblet broth. Set it aside.

A blender
The soaked chilies
1 cup water
A very large fireproof dish
¼ pound lard (½ cup)
The chili puree

Blend the chilies with the water until smooth—you may have to do them in two or three lots but try not to add more water.

Melt the lard, and when it is hot but not smoking, cook the chili puree over a medium flame for about 10 minutes, stirring it all the time. Keep a lid handy, as it will splatter about. Set it aside.

A blender
½ cup *tomates verdes*, drained

Put the *tomates verdes* into the blender jar.

A spice grinder
4 cloves
10 peppercorns
½-inch stick cinnamon
⅛ teaspoon coriander seeds and
⅛ teaspoon aniseed, toasted together
1 tablespoon reserved chili seeds, toasted separately
7 tablespoons sesame seeds, toasted separately
3 cloves garlic, toasted
A frying pan
6 tablespoons lard
2 tablespoons raisins
20 almonds, unskinned
A *molcajete* or mortar and pestle

Put the spices into the grinder and add the toasted, cooled seeds, reserving 4 tablespoons of the sesame seeds for later use. Grind the spices and seeds finely and transfer them to the blender jar.

Add the toasted garlic to the blender jar.

Melt the lard in the frying pan and fry the raisins briefly, just until they puff up, and transfer them with a slotted spoon to the blender jar. In the same pan fry the almonds, stirring them all the time, until they are well browned. Remove with a slotted spoon and crush them a little before adding them to the blender jar.

2 ounces pumpkin seeds (just over ⅓ cup), hulled and unsalted

In the same pan fry the pumpkin seeds lightly, but have a lid handy, as they pop about explosively. Remove with a slotted spoon and add to the blender.

1 small stale tortilla

In the same pan fry the tortilla until very crisp. Remove with a slotted spoon and crush it a little before adding it to the blender.

3 small rounds stale French bread

In the same pan fry the bread until crisp, then remove with a slotted spoon and crush. Add it to the blender jar.

Turkey broth, if necessary

Blend all the ingredients together until they form a smooth paste. If it is absolutely necessary to add some liquid to blend it effectively, then add a little turkey broth.

The chili sauce

Add the blended mixture to the chile sauce and cook over a brisk flame for about 5 minutes, stirring the mixture constantly.

1 1½-ounce tablet of Mexican chocolate

Break the chocolate into small pieces and add it to the mixture. Continue cooking the *mole* for about 10 minutes more, stirring it all the time so it does not stick.

4 to 5 cups turkey broth
Salt as necessary

Add the broth and continue cooking the *mole* for a minimum of 40 minutes. Add salt as necessary, then add the turkey pieces and heat them through.

The dish should be served with "Blind" Tamales, allowing 2 per serving, and each serving should be sprinkled with some of the reserved toasted sesame seeds.

When it is cooked the sauce should lightly coat the back of a wooden spoon. If it appears to be too thick then add a little more broth. If it is too thin, continue cooking the *mole* until it reduces a little more. You could easily prepare the *mole* several days ahead—in fact it improves in flavor—up to the point of adding the turkey broth. Then braise the turkey and cook the giblets on the day it is needed. Most cooks in Mexico today boil the turkey and then brown it in lard before adding it to the sauce. But it has a far better flavor and texture if cooked in the way I have given—very much as the old cookbooks indicate that it should be cooked. If you have any sauce left over, freeze it and use it to make delicious *enchiladas* at some later date.

The traditional way of grinding the ingredients on a stone *metate* is a long and laborious job, but it is very efficient. All the chilies and particles of seeds and spices get crushed and ground to a paste. The blender cannot do this without the addition of too much liquid. After cooking Mexican food for so many years, I feel strongly that one of the secrets of the unique flavor of a well-prepared sauce is frying the basic ingredients first over a high flame without very much liquid. And since most of these ingredients are briefly cooked alone before being combined, the instructions may seem rather laborious and repetitive. But because this technique best brings out all the flavors, it would be better not to take shortcuts.

CLAIBORNE

The New York Times Cook Book

Chili con Carne

4 SERVINGS

3 tablespoons butter or olive oil
1 large onion, minced
2 cloves garlic, minced
1 pound chopped beef
3 cups water
1⅓ cups canned tomatoes
1 green pepper, minced
½ teaspoon celery seed
¼ teaspoon cayenne
1 teaspoon cumin seed, crushed
1 small bay leaf
2 tablespoons chili powder
⅛ teaspoon basil
1½ teaspoons salt

1. Heat the butter in a skillet, add the onion and garlic and sauté until golden brown. Add the meat and brown.

2. Transfer the meat mixture to a large saucepan and add the remaining ingredients. Bring to a boil, reduce the heat and simmer, uncovered, until the sauce is as thick as desired, or about three hours. If desired, add one can of kidney beans just before serving.

DE GROOT
Feasts for All Seasons

Lemon-Cream Spaghetti with Fish Stuffing

FOR OUR FAMILY OF 4

One of our simplest and most often-repeated pull-back dishes. The fish filling is flexible: canned tuna, as in this version, or canned or frozen crab, lobster, salmon, or lightly cooked fresh fish. It is especially good with salmon or swordfish steaks, fried, then coarsely flaked. It is excellent cold, although not much usually remains.

CHECK STAPLES
Salt butter (¼ lb.)
Lemons (2)
Aromatics: crystal salt, freshly ground black pepper, MSG

SHOPPING LIST
Thin spaghetti (¾–1 lb., according to appetite)
Tuna fish (three 7-oz. cans) or other fish, *see* above (about 3 cups)
Sour cream (1 pt.)

ABOUT 45 MINUTES BEFORE SERVING

Cook the spaghetti in the usual way in about 4 quarts of highly salted, rapidly boiling water. When a single strand twisted around a wooden fork tastes *al dente*, firmly chewy, drain and rinse away excess starch with hot water. Meanwhile coarsely flake or chunk the fish and make the sauce. Mix in a bowl: the pint of sour cream, the juice of the 2 lemons, the ¼ pound of butter, melted, with salt, pepper, and MSG to taste. Turn on oven to 400 degrees. Butter a fairly shallow, open casserole and put about ⅔ of the drained spaghetti into it, lifting with a wooden fork to make sure that it does not pack down. On top put the fish as a single layer. Cover loosely with the rest of the spaghetti. Pour sour cream sauce over the spaghetti and, with a wooden fork, but without disturbing the layer of fish, lift it slightly here and there to encourage sauce to run down. Set the casserole, uncovered, in the center of the oven and bake just long enough to get everything piping hot and bubbly, usually in about 20 minutes. We bring the casserole to the table and plunge the serving spoon straight down, so that each person gets the proper proportion of spaghetti, fish, and sauce.

JUNIOR LEAGUE OF CHARLESTON
Charleston Receipts

Chicken Tetrazzini

6 or 8 large mushrooms
4 tablespoons butter
½ cup good sherry
2 tablespoons flour
2 cups hot milk
Salt and pepper to taste
Sprinkling of nutmeg
1 cup thick cream
2 egg yolks
5 cups diced cooked chicken
1 nine-ounce package thin spaghetti
1 cup grated Parmesan cheese

Sauté mushrooms in 2 tablespoons butter. Add sherry and cook for a few minutes. Make a cream sauce of 2 tablespoons butter and 2 tablespoons flour. Rub these together and add hot milk. Cook in a double-boiler, stirring constantly until smooth and of a good body—about 20 minutes. Season with salt and pepper and nutmeg. Beat the yolks of the eggs into the cream and add to the sauce. Continue to stir. After 5 minutes, add chicken. Season to taste. Add mushrooms. Cook spaghetti. Butter a shallow casserole and put the cooked spaghetti in the bottom. Cover with the creamed chicken mixture. Sprinkle cheese over top and put under broiler until golden brown and bubbling. Serves 6–8.

MRS. HENRY P. STAATS (Juliette Wiles)

BEARD

Cook It Outdoors

If You Should Run Over an Old Hen

Such things happen, this running over a farmer's hen, and there seems to be no reason at the time, but if you follow directions carefully, you will gather what I am driving at.

See that the late, lamented old lady is plucked and drawn and cut up in pieces. Put her in a large stew pot and cover with water, and I mean cover. *Throw in an onion of large proportions, a couple of bay leaves, a pinch of thyme, a stalk of celery, and two or three slices of lemon borrowed from the bar. Cover the pan, set it on the range or hang it on the crane and let it stew for as long as two hours. Test it then with your fork and see what sort of a tenderness it has achieved. If good and tender, and it is close to dinner time, take the chicken out and arrange in a casserole or large dish which may be kept on the back of the stove while you prepare*

THE SAUCE

3 shallots, cut very fine, or 1 medium onion
2 cups sliced mushrooms
4 cups chicken broth
1½ cups heavy cream
3 egg yolks

Dig four cups of the broth out of the pan and pour it over the chopped shallots and mushrooms in a skillet. Allow them to simmer for five minutes. Beat the eggs slightly and stir into the cream. Pour this into the simmering broth mixture very slowly, stirring it constantly. This will take a little time to thicken to a rich, creamy consistency. Salt and pepper to taste, pour the sauce over the chicken and serve up.

Green noodles, or the white ones, as you prefer, with this. Also, try some sweet and sour beets with it and see if they go well.

THOMAS

The Vegetarian Epicure

Lasagne

1½ qt. Tomato and Wine Sauce
about 1½ lbs. spinach (2 cups when chopped and packed)
1 onion
1 to 2 Tbs. olive oil
1 to 2 cloves garlic, minced
2 lbs. Ricotta cheese
¼ lb. grated Romano or Parmesan cheese
3 eggs, beaten
salt and pepper
2 to 3 Tbs. chopped fresh parsley
½ lb. Mozzarella cheese
1 lb. lasagne noodles

Prepare a good 1½ quarts of Tomato and Wine Sauce.

Wash spinach carefully and chop coarsely. You should have about 2 well-packed cups of chopped spinach. Chop the onion and sauté it lightly in the olive oil with the minced garlic. Combine the Ricotta cheese, grated Romano, spinach, sautéed onion, beaten eggs, and mix well. Season the mixture with a little salt, plenty of fresh-ground black pepper, and some chopped parsley.

Grate the Mozzarella coarsely and cook the lasagne noodles until they are just al dente. Now you are ready to assemble the lasagne.

Butter a large, oblong baking dish, or two smaller square ones. Arrange a layer of lasagne noodles in the bottom, then spread on a layer of Ricotta cheese mixture, sprinkle that with Mozzarella, and cover it over smoothly with Tomato and Wine Sauce. Repeat these layers once or twice more, until everything is used up. Be sure to end with sauce on top, regardless of whatever is directly beneath it.

Cover the baking pan with aluminum foil, crimping the edges tightly. Bake the lasagne at 350 degrees for 40 minutes, take off the foil cover, and bake it another 10 to 15 minutes uncovered. Serve very hot, with herb bread or garlic toast, and follow it with a very green, very crisp salad.

SERVES 10 TO 12

MANDEL

Abby Mandel's Cuisinart Classroom

Ratatouille

Ratatouille never had it so easy! The optional topping makes this version unusually delicious as well as more substantial.

- ⅔ cup (16 cl) parsley leaves
- 2 large garlic cloves, peeled
- 2 tomatoes (9 ounces total, 255g), peeled, seeded and quartered
- ½ teaspoon sugar
- 1 eggplant (1¼ pounds, 565g), unpeeled and cut into pieces to fit the feed tube horizontally
- 3 zucchini (1 pound total, 455g), unpeeled and cut into 2-inch (5 cm) lengths
- 1 tablespoon salt
- ⅓ cup (8 cl) olive oil or a mixture of olive oil and vegetable oil
- ½ teaspoon ground coriander
- 1 teaspoon dried thyme
- 2 large onions (8 ounces total, 225g), peeled and quartered
- 2 small green peppers (6 ounces total, 170g), cut flat at the ends, seeded, cored and left whole
- 3 tablespoons tomato sauce
- Salt
- Freshly ground pepper
- ½ teaspoon dried basil

METAL BLADE: Mince the parsley by turning the machine on and off; reserve it. With the machine running, mince the garlic by dropping it through the feed tube. Add the tomatoes and chop them coarsely with the sugar by turning the machine on and off about 6 times; reserve them.

MEDIUM SLICING DISC: Slice the eggplant, using medium pressure. Stack the zucchini in the feed tube horizontally and slice it, using medium pressure. Transfer both eggplant and zucchini to a colander and sprinkle it with the salt. Let it stand for 30 minutes. Pat the vegetables dry with paper towels. In a skillet sauté the vegetables in 3 tablespoons of the oil over high heat for 1 minute. Cover the skillet and let the mixture steam for 3 minutes, shaking the pan several times. Stir in the coriander and thyme and reserve the mixture.

Slice the onions, using firm pressure. Stand the peppers in the feed tube vertically and slice them, using light pressure. In a stainless steel skillet sauté the onions and peppers in the remaining oil over high heat until they are just soft. Stir in the garlic, tomatoes and tomato sauce and cook the mixture, covered, for 5 minutes. Uncover and cook until the juices have evaporated. Season with the salt, pepper and basil and all but 3 tablespoons of the reserved parsley.

Adjust the oven rack to the middle level and preheat the oven to 350°F. (175°C.)

TOPPING

- 4 ounces (115g) imported Parmesan cheese, at room temperature
- 4 ounces (115g) mozzarella cheese, chilled
- 2 large eggs

METAL BLADE: Divide the Parmesan cheese into several pieces of equal size, and put them in the work bowl. Grate them, by turning the machine on and off several times, and leave them in the bowl.

SHREDDING DISC: Shred the mozzarella cheese, using light pressure, and leave it in the bowl.

METAL BLADE: Add the eggs and process for 2 seconds.

ASSEMBLY

Spread ⅓ of the tomato mixture in the bottom of an oiled 1½-quart (142 cl) casserole and cover it with half the eggplant and zucchini mixture. Sprinkle the top with salt and pepper. Add the remaining tomato mixture, spreading it evenly, and the remaining eggplant and zucchini mixture. Sprinkle with salt and pepper and spread the topping over the vegetables. Bake for 40 minutes or until the top is bubbly and brown. Pour off any excess juices and garnish the dish with the reserved parsley.

NOTE: Ratatouille can be baked in advance without the topping. The topping can be mixed in advance, refrigerated and spread on the top before the casserole is reheated.

VARIATION

Baked without the topping, the dish can be served cold or at room temperature.

CHILD, BERTHOLLE, AND BECK
Mastering the Art of French Cooking

Cassoulet de Porc et de Mouton

Beans Baked with Pork Loin, Shoulder of Mutton or Lamb, and Sausage

FOR 10 TO 12 PEOPLE

THE PORK LOIN

2½ lbs. of boned pork loin, excess fat removed (It will taste even better if marinated overnight in salt and spices)

Roast the pork to an internal temperature of 175 to 180 degrees. Set it aside to cool. Reserve cooking juices.

THE BEANS

2 lbs. or 5 cups dry white beans (Great Northern, preferably)
An 8-quart kettle containing 5 quarts of rapidly boiling water

Drop the beans into the boiling water. Bring rapidly back to the boil and boil for 2 minutes. Remove from heat and let the beans soak in the water for 1 hour; they will cook in the soaking water, and the cooking should proceed as soon as possible after the soaking process is completed.

½ lb. fresh pork rind or salt pork rind
A heavy saucepan
Heavy shears

While the beans are soaking, place the rind in the saucepan and cover with 1 quart of cold water. Bring to the boil and boil 1 minute. Drain, rinse in cold water, and repeat the process. Then, with shears, cut the rind into strips ¼ inch wide; cut the strips into small triangles. Cover the rind again with a quart of cold water, bring to the simmer, and simmer very slowly for 30 minutes. Set saucepan aside. This process freshens the rind, and softens it so it will lose itself as it cooks with the beans.

1 1-lb. chunk of fresh, unsalted, unsmoked lean bacon (or very good quality lean salt pork simmered for 10 minutes in 2 quarts of water and drained)
1 cup (4 ounces) sliced onions
The pork rind and its cooking liquid
A large herb bouquet, with garlic and cloves: 6 to 8 parsley sprigs, 4 unpeeled cloves garlic, 2 cloves, ½ tsp thyme, and 2 bay leaves tied in cheesecloth
No salt until later if you have used salt pork; otherwise 1 Tb salt

Place all the ingredients in the kettle with the soaked beans. Bring to the simmer. Skim off any skum which may rise. Simmer slowly, uncovered, for about 1½ hours or until the beans are just tender. Add boiling water if necessary during cooking, to keep beans covered with liquid. Season to taste near end of cooking. Leave beans in their cooking liquid until ready to use, then drain. Reserve cooking liquid. Remove the bacon or salt pork and set aside. Discard the herb packet.

THE LAMB OR MUTTON

2 to 2½ lbs. boned shoulder or breast of mutton or almost mature lamb, fell (skin covering meat) and excess fat removed
4 to 6 Tb rendered fresh pork fat, pork-roast drippings, goose fat, or cooking oil; more if needed
A heavy, 8-quart fireproof casserole
About 1 lb. cracked mutton or lamb bones; some pork bones may be included
2 cups (½ lb.) minced onions

Cut the lamb or mutton into chunks roughly 2 inches square. Dry each piece in paper towels. Pour a ¹⁄₁₆-inch layer of fat into the casserole and heat until the fat is almost smoking. Brown the meat, a few pieces at a time, on all sides. Set the meat on a side dish. Brown the bones and add them to the meat. If fat has burned, discard it and add 3 tablespoons of fresh fat. Lower heat, and brown the onions lightly for about 5 minutes.

4 cloves mashed garlic
6 Tb fresh tomato purée, tomato paste, or 4 large tomatoes peeled, seeded, and juiced
½ tsp thyme
2 bay leaves
3 cups dry white wine or 2 cups dry white vermouth
1 quart brown stock or 3 cups canned beef bouillon and 1 cup water
Salt and pepper

Return the bones and lamb or mutton to the casserole and stir in all ingredients. Bring to the simmer on top of the stove, season lightly with salt. Cover and simmer slowly on top of the stove or in a 325-degree oven for 1½ hours. Then remove the meat to a dish; discard the bones and bay leaves. Remove all but 2 tablespoons fat and carefully correct seasoning of cooking liquid.

FINAL FLAVORING OF BEANS

Pour the cooked and drained beans into the lamb cooking juices. Stir in any juices you may have from the roast pork. Add bean cooking liquid, if necessary, so beans are covered. Bring to the simmer and simmer 5 minutes, then let the beans stand in the liquid for 10 minutes to absorb flavor. Drain the beans when you are ready for the final assembly farther on.

HOMEMADE SAUSAGE CAKES—A SUBSTITUTE FOR SAUCISSE DE TOULOUSE

1 lb. (2 cups) lean fresh pork
⅓ lb. (⅔ cup) fresh pork fat
A meat grinder
A 3-quart mixing bowl
A wooden spoon
2 tsp salt
⅛ tsp pepper
Big pinch allspice
⅛ tsp crumbled bay leaf
¼ cup armagnac or cognac
A small clove mashed garlic
Optional: 1 chopped truffle and the juice from the can

Put the pork and fat through the medium blade of the meat grinder. Place in bowl and beat in the rest of the ingredients on the left. Sauté a small spoonful and taste for seasoning, adding more to the mixture if you feel it necessary. Form into cakes 2 inches in diameter and ½ inch thick. Brown lightly over moderate heat in a skillet. Drain on paper towels.

FINAL ASSEMBLY

An 8-quart fireproof casserole 5 to 6 inches high: brown earthenware glazed inside is typical, but other types of glazed pottery or enameled iron will do nicely
2 cups dry white bread crumbs mixed with ½ cup chopped parsley
3 to 4 Tb pork roasting fat or goose fat

Cut the roast pork into 1½ to 2 inch serving chunks. Slice the bacon or salt pork into serving pieces ¼ inch thick. Arrange a layer of beans in the bottom of the casserole, then continue with layers of lamb or mutton, roast pork, bacon slices, sausage cakes, and beans, ending with a layer of beans and sausage cakes. Pour on the meat cooking juices, and enough bean cooking juice so liquid comes just to the top layer of beans. Spread on the crumbs and parsley, and dribble the fat on top.

(*) Set aside or refrigerate until you are ready to take up the final cooking of about an hour. The *cassoulet* should be served soon after its baking, so it will not dry out or overcook.

BAKING

Preheat oven to 375 degrees. Bring the casserole to the simmer on top of the stove. Then set it in the upper third of the preheated oven. When the top has crusted lightly, in about 20 minutes, turn the oven down to 350 degrees. Break the crust into the beans with the back of a spoon, and baste with the liquid in the casserole. Repeat several times, as the crust forms again, but leave a final crust intact for serving. If the liquid in the casserole becomes too thick during the baking period, add a spoonful or two of bean cooking liquid. The *cassoulet* should bake for about an hour; serve it from its casserole.

VARIATIONS

Here are some additions or substitutions for the meats in the preceding recipe.

PRESERVED GOOSE, CONFIT D'OIE. This is goose, usually from the *foie gras* regions of France, which has been cut into wing, leg, and breast sections, poached in goose fat, and preserved in goose fat. It can usually be bought in cans from one of the food-importing stores. Use it instead of, or even in addition to, the roast pork in the recipe. Scrape the fat off the pieces of goose, and cut the goose into serving portions. Brown them lightly in some of the fat from the can. Arrange the goose in the casserole with the beans and meats for the final baking.

HAM HOCK OR VEAL SHANK. Simmer either of these with the beans. Cut into serving pieces before arranging in the casserole for the final baking.

POLISH SAUSAGE. This sausage can usually be bought in any American market, and is a good substitute for such French sausages as *de campagne, de ménage, à cuire, à l'ail,* or *de Morteau*. First simmer the whole sausage for ½ hour with the beans. Then cut it into ½-inch slices and arrange in the casserole with the beans and the other meats for the final baking. Polish sausage may be used instead of or in addition to the sausage cakes in the recipe.

BITTMAN
How to Cook Everything

Classic Beef Stew

MAKES 4 TO 6 SERVINGS
TIME: 1½ TO 2 HOURS, LARGELY UNATTENDED

Browning the beef before braising adds another dimension of flavor, but isn't absolutely necessary. Try it both ways; skipping the browning step saves time and mess.

Note, too, that stewed beef can be spiced in many different ways; I offer a couple here, but you can also make a chili-like beef stew (add the seasonings from the recipe for Chili con Carne), a beef curry (see Lamb Curry), or a sweet, Thai-flavored stew (see Sweet Simmered Pork Chops). The substitutions are easy and work perfectly.

- 2 tablespoons canola or other neutral oil, or olive oil
- 1 clove garlic, lightly crushed, plus 1 tablespoon minced garlic
- 2 to 2½ pounds beef chuck or round, trimmed of surface fat and cut into 1- to 1½-inch cubes
- Salt and freshly ground black pepper to taste
- 2 large or 3 medium onions, cut into eighths
- 3 tablespoons flour
- 3 cups chicken, beef, or vegetable stock, or water, or wine, or a combination)
- 1 bay leaf
- 1 teaspoon fresh thyme leaves or ½ teaspoon dried thyme
- 4 medium-to-large potatoes, peeled and cut into 1-inch chunks
- 4 large carrots, peeled and cut into 1-inch chunks
- 1 cup fresh or frozen (thawed) peas
- Minced fresh parsley leaves for garnish

1. Heat a large casserole or deep skillet that can later be covered over medium-high heat for 2 or 3 minutes; add the oil and the crushed garlic clove; cook, stirring, for 1 minute, then remove and discard the garlic. Add the meat chunks to the skillet a few at a time, turning to brown well on all sides. Do not crowd or they will not brown properly; cook them in batches if necessary. (You may find it easier to do the initial browning in the oven: Preheat to 500°F and roast the meat with 1 tablespoon of the oil and the garlic clove, shaking the pan to turn them once or twice, until brown all over. Remove the garlic clove before continuing.) Season the meat with salt and pepper as it cooks.

2. When the meat is brown, remove it with a slotted spoon. Pour or spoon off most of the fat and turn the heat to medium. Add the onions. Cook, stirring, until they soften, about 10 minutes. Add the flour and cook, stirring, for about 2 minutes. Add the stock or water or wine, bay leaf, thyme, and meat, and bring to a boil. Turn the heat to low and cover. Cook, undisturbed, for 30 minutes.

3. Uncover the pan; the mixture should be quite soupy (if it is not, add a little more liquid). Add the potatoes and carrots, turn the heat up for a minute or so to resume boiling, then lower the heat and cover again. Cook 30 to 60 minutes until the meat and vegetables are tender. Taste for seasoning and add more salt, pepper, and/or thyme if necessary. (If you are not planning to serve the stew immediately, remove the meat and vegetables with a slotted spoon and refrigerate them and the stock separately. Skim the fat from the stock before combining it with the meat and vegetables, reheating, and proceeding with the recipe from this point.)

4. Add the minced garlic and the peas; if you are pleased with the stew's consistency, continue to cook, covered, over low heat. If it is too soupy, remove the cover and raise the heat to high. In either case, cook an additional 5 minutes or so, until the peas have heated through and the garlic flavor has pervaded the stew. Garnish and serve.

CHILD, BERTHOLLE, AND BECK
Mastering the Art of French Cooking

Boeuf Borguignon

Boeuf à la Bourguignonne
(Beef Stew in Red Wine, with Bacon, Onions, and Mushrooms)

As is the case with most famous dishes, there are more ways than one to arrive at a good boeuf bourguignon. *Carefully done, and perfectly flavored, it is certainly one of the most delicious beef dishes concocted by man, and can well be the main course for a buffet dinner. Fortunately you can prepare it completely ahead, even a day in advance, and it only gains in flavor when reheated.*

VEGETABLE AND WINE SUGGESTIONS

Boiled potatoes are traditionally served with this dish. Buttered noodles or steamed rice may be substituted. If you also wish a green vegetable, buttered peas would be your best choice. Serve with the beef a fairly full-bodied, young red wine, such as Beaujolais, Côtes du Rhone, Bordeaux-St. Emilion, or Burgundy.

FOR 6 PEOPLE

A 6-ounce chunk of bacon

Remove rind, and cut bacon into *lardons* (sticks, ¼ inch thick and 1½ inches long). Simmer rind and bacon for 10 minutes in 1½ quarts of water. Drain and dry.

Preheat oven to 450 degrees.

A 9- to 10-inch fireproof casserole 3 inches deep
1 Tb olive oil or cooking oil
A slotted spoon

Sauté the bacon in the oil over moderate heat for 2 to 3 minutes to brown lightly. Remove to a side dish with a slotted spoon. Set casserole aside. Reheat until fat is almost smoking before you sauté the beef.

3 lbs. lean stewing beef cut into 2-inch cubes

Dry the beef in paper towels; it will not brown if it is damp. Sauté it, a few pieces at a time, in the hot oil and bacon fat until nicely browned on all sides. Add it to the bacon.

1 sliced carrot
1 sliced onion

In the same fat, brown the sliced vegetables. Pour out the sautéing fat.

1 tsp salt
¼ tsp pepper
2 Tb flour

Return the beef and bacon to the casserole and toss with the salt and pepper. Then sprinkle on the flour and toss again to coat the beef lightly with the flour. Set casserole uncovered in middle position of preheated oven for 4 minutes. Toss the meat and return to oven for 4 minutes more. (This browns the flour and covers the meat with a light crust.) Remove casserole, and turn oven down to 325 degrees.

3 cups of a full-bodied, young red wine such as one of those suggested for serving, or a Chianti
2 to 3 cups brown beef stock or canned beef bouillon
1 Tb tomato paste
2 cloves mashed garlic
½ tsp thyme
A crumbled bay leaf
The blanched bacon rind

Stir in the wine, and enough stock or bouillon so that the meat is barely covered. Add the tomato paste, garlic, herbs, and bacon rind. Bring to simmer on top of the stove. Then cover the casserole and set in lower third of preheated oven. Regulate heat so liquid simmers very slowly for 3 to 4 hours. The meat is done when a fork pierces it easily.

18 to 24 small white onions, brown-braised in stock
1 lb. quartered fresh mushrooms sautéed in butter

While the beef is cooking, prepare the onions and mushrooms. Set them aside until needed.

When the meat is tender, pour the contents of the casserole into a sieve set over a saucepan. Wash out the casserole and return the beef and bacon to it. Distribute the cooked onions and mushrooms over the meat.

Skim fat off the sauce. Simmer sauce for a minute or two, skimming off additional fat as it rises. You should have about 2½ cups of sauce thick enough to coat a spoon lightly. If too thin, boil it down rapidly. If too thick, mix in a few tablespoons of stock or canned bouillon. Taste carefully for seasoning. Pour the sauce over the meat and vegetables.

(*) Recipe may be completed in advance to this point.

- Parsley sprigs

FOR IMMEDIATE SERVING: Cover the casserole and simmer for 2 to 3 minutes, basting the meat and vegetables with the sauce several times. Serve in its casserole, or arrange the stew on a platter surrounded with potatoes, noodles, or rice, and decorated with parsley.

FOR LATER SERVING: When cold, cover and refrigerate. About 15 to 20 minutes before serving, bring to the simmer, cover, and simmer very slowly for 10 minutes, occasionally basting the meat and vegetables with the sauce.

WELLS

Bistro Cooking

Daube de Boeuf Auberge de la Madone aux Cèpes et à l'Orange

Auberge de la Madone's Beef Stew with Wild Mushrooms and Orange

I am convinced that in Provence there are as many recipes for daube, *or beef stew, as there are households. This version, flavored with mushrooms and orange, comes from a favorite family restaurant—Auberge de la Madone—situated just north of Nice, in the village of Peillon. Although chef Christian Millo uses wild cèpe mushrooms, I find that when they are not available, fresh domestic mushrooms are a worthy substitute. Serve with the same wine used in cooking, a sturdy red such as Nice's Bellet, Château de Crémat.*

- 4½ pounds (2.25 kg) stewing beef, preferably a combination of beef round and beef chuck, cut into large pieces (each weighing about 4 ounces; 125 g)
- 4 carrots, peeled and cut into rounds
- 3 medium onions, coarsely chopped
- 2 garlic cloves
- 1 sprig of fresh parsley
- 1 celery rib, thickly sliced
- 3 imported bay leaves
- 1 tablespoon fresh thyme or 1 teaspoon dried
- ¼ cup (6 cl) marc de Provence or Cognac
- 1 bottle (75 cl) sturdy red wine, such as Côtes-du-Provence
- ¼ cup (6 cl) plus 1 tablespoon extra-virgin olive oil
- 1 teaspoon whole black peppercorns
- 3 whole cloves
- 3 tablespoons (1½ ounces; 45 g) unsalted butter
- 1 pound (500 g) fresh wild cèpe mushrooms or cultivated mushrooms
- 1 tablespoon tomato paste
- Salt and freshly ground pepper
- Grated zest and juice of 1 orange

1. One day before serving the stew: In a large nonreactive bowl, combine the meat with the carrots, onions, garlic, parsley, celery, bay leaves, thyme, marc, red wine, and the 1 tablespoon olive oil. Tie the peppercorns and cloves in a piece of cheesecloth; add to the bowl and toss well. Cover and refrigerate for 24 hours, stirring once or twice.

2. Let the meat and vegetables return to room temperature. With a slotted spoon, remove the meat from the marinade. Drain well; pat dry on paper towels. Set the vegetables aside. Transfer the liquid and the cheesecloth bag to a nonreactive large heatproof casserole. Bring to a boil over medium-high heat. Boil for 5 minutes to reduce slightly. Remove from the heat.

3. In a large skillet, melt the butter in the remaining ¼ cup (6 cl) olive oil over high heat. When the foam subsides, add half of the meat. Sauté, tossing, until browned all over, about 5 minutes. With a slotted spoon, transfer the meat to the liquid in the casserole. Repeat with the remaining meat.

4. In the same skillet, sauté the reserved vegetables until browned, about 7 minutes. Transfer the vegetables to the casserole. Add the mushrooms to the skillet. Sauté until lightly browned, about 5 minutes; set aside.

5. Stir the tomato paste into the casserole. Bring to a simmer over medium-low heat. Reduce the heat to very low and simmer, skimming occasionally, until the meat is very tender, 3½ to 4 hours. Stir in salt and pepper to taste, the mushrooms, and the orange zest and juice. Discard the cheesecloth bag of cloves and peppercorns. (The recipe can be prepared 2 to 3 days ahead and refrigerated. Reheat before serving.) Serve with potatoes, rice, or pasta.

YIELD: 8 SERVINGS

Vegetables and Legumes

FISHER

The Art of Eating

HOW TO BE CONTENT WITH A VEGETABLE LOVE

If he's content with a vegetable love which would certainly not suit me,

Why, what a most particularly pure young man this pure, young man must be!

—*Patience*, W. S. GILBERT

Purity may have something to do with a vegetable love, but is almost certain to have nothing to do with a love of vegetables, since petits pois à la Française *have been known to appeal to the lowest as well as the loftiest emotions of at least one hardened sinner.*

[There is, of course, an excellent recipe for this naive and delicate dish in Escoffier and many another cookbook. And like many another cook I seldom pay any attention to it. Instead I fit the ways to the means: I use uniformly mediocre frozen peas in preference to unpredictably uneven market peas, if I cannot pick my own from a now vanished garden. If I have good garden shallots or onions I use them. If I have my own lettuces I am happiest, but I have often settled, with silent resignation, for a small tight head of tasteless "Alaska" (which is insultingly called Los Angeles Lettuce in salad-happy San Francisco!). I use salted butter, for want of the sweet. And so on and so on. My petits pois *more-or-less* à la Française *always please me . . . as long as I manage not to have the telephone ring at the moment they should be done, and let them turn pale or puckered.*

Petits Pois à la Française

½ cup water
1 head lettuce
6 green onions
handful of parsley
2 pounds peas
¼ pound good butter
salt, fresh pepper

Put water in heavy casserole or pot; shred lettuce coarsely into it; add onions split and cut in 2-inch pieces, using tops; chop parsley and add. Put peas on this bed, and put chunk of butter on top. Cover tightly and bring slowly to boil, shaking now and then. Lower heat, let cook for about five minutes, and serve at once, mixing all well together and seasoning to taste. There should be almost no liquid. More butter can be added at the last if it seems desirable.]

TOKLAS

The Alice B. Toklas Cook Book

Green Peas à la Good Wife

Put 12 young onions in a saucepan over medium heat with 3 tablespoons butter and ½ cup fat back of pork previously boiled for 5 minutes, drained and cut in cubes of ½ inch. When the onions are lightly browned, remove with the cubes of back fat. In the saucepan stir 1 tablespoon flour. Mix well and gradually add 1¾ cups veal *bouillon*. Allow to boil for 15 minutes and salt. Then add 4 cups shelled green peas, the diced pork fat and the onions. Cover and cook from 15 to 25 minutes according to the size and age of the peas.

TRUAX

Ladies' Home Journal Cookbook

Artichoke Hearts in Lemon Butter

2 (15 oz.) cans artichoke hearts
½ cup minced onion
½ clove garlic crushed
2 tablespoons butter
¾ cup canned chicken broth
3 tablespoons lemon juice
1½ teaspoons salt
1 teaspoon orégano
¼ teaspoon grated lemon rind

Sauté the onion and garlic in butter until tender. Add the chicken broth and the artichoke hearts. Season with lemon juice, salt, orégano, and lemon rind. Simmer gently until the artichokes are heated through, about 10 minutes. Six servings.

LA PLACE AND KLEIMAN
Cucina Fresca

Artichokes Roman-Style

People always rave about these rich-tasting and meaty artichokes flavored with mint and garlic. Look for heavy artichokes with stems. Cleaned according to the directions, the whole artichoke is completely edible including the stem. Provide bread to soak up the savory juices. When served whole, this dish is good as a first course. To present the artichoke in a buffet style, however, prepare them as indicated, but first quarter the vegetable, remove the choke, and then braise with the herbs.

1 lemon, halved
4 large artichokes with stems
Coarse salt to taste
¼ cup fresh mint leaves, chopped, or
1 tablespoon dried mint leaves, crumbled
1 tablespoon minced garlic
½ cup olive oil

Use half of the lemon to rub surfaces as you work. Snap back and pull down the leaves and discard, working around the artichoke until the pale yellow leaves are exposed. Trim away about 2 inches from the top of the artichokes. With a paring knife, cut away the dark green around the base. Cut away the dark green exterior of the stalk until the pale green, tender part is exposed. With a small spoon, dig into the center of the artichoke and remove the fuzzy choke, scraping against the heart until it is completely clean. Remove any interior leaves that have prickly tips. Fill a large bowl with water and add the juice of the remaining half lemon. Immerse each finished artichoke in the acidulated water to prevent discoloration.

Drain the artichokes. Salt the interiors. Combine the mint, garlic, and a little of the olive oil in small bowl. Add salt to taste. Put the mixture in the center of each artichoke, dividing it equally. Arrange the artichokes stem-side up in a pot just large enough to contain them. Lightly salt them and drizzle with the remaining olive oil. Add enough water to come one-third up to the heart. Bring to a boil. Lower the heat to medium and cover with a tight-fitting lid. Cook until tender but firm; the tip of a knife should slide into the artichoke heart with just the slightest resistance. The time will vary greatly depending on size. Remove the artichokes from the pot with a slotted spoon to a platter. Bring the remaining liquid to a boil and reduce slightly, if necessary. The liquid should be syrupy. Pour the liquid over the artichokes. These can be made up to 2 days in advance but are best when served the same day they are cooked. Serves 4.

WATERS
Chez Panisse Vegetables

Grilled Asparagus with Blood Oranges and Tapenade Toast

1 shallot
3 blood oranges
1½ teaspoons balsamic vinegar
½ teaspoon red wine vinegar
Extra-virgin olive oil
Salt and pepper
1½ pounds fat asparagus (25 to 30 spears)
4 slices country-style bread
Tapenade

Peel and chop the shallot fine and macerate for 30 minutes in the juice of ½ orange and the balsamic and red wine vinegars. Whisk in the olive oil to taste to make a vinaigrette, and season with salt and pepper. Peel just the zest from one of the oranges, chop it very fine, and add it to the vinaigrette.

Cut away all the rind and pith from all the oranges and slice them, crosswise, into thin rounds. Parboil and grill the asparagus. At the same time, grill the bread. When the bread is toasted, cut the slices into thirds and spread with tapenade. Arrange the asparagus on a platter with the orange slices on top. Drizzle the vinaigrette over and garnish with the tapenade toast.

SERVES 4

HIRTZLER
The Hotel St. Francis Cook Book

CELERY VICTOR. (SALAD.) Wash six stalks of large celery. Make a stock with one soup hen or chicken bones, and five pounds of veal bones, in the usual manner, with carrots, onions, bay leaves, parsley, salt and whole pepper. Place celery in vessel and strain broth over same, and boil until soft. Allow to cool in the broth. When cold press the broth out of the celery gently with the hands, and place on plate. Season with salt, fresh-ground black pepper, chervil, and one-quarter white wine tarragon vinegar to three-quarters of olive oil.

GREENE
Greene on Greens

Drunken Leeks in Red Wine

This heavenly first course is a Francophile offering: green leek stalks soused with butter, garlic, and good red wine, baked, and eaten either hot or cold as you wish. My choice? Room temperature.

3 tablespoons unsalted butter
6 to 8 small leeks, trimmed of green tops, washed
1 large clove garlic
¼ teaspoon salt
½ cup red wine
1 teaspoon red wine vinegar
Freshly ground black pepper
2 tablespoons chopped fresh parsley

1. Melt the butter in a large heavy skillet over medium heat. Add the leeks and garlic. Cook 3 minutes. Turn the leeks over and sprinkle with the salt and red wine. Cook, covered, 10 minutes. Remove the cover and cook until the leeks are tender, about 5 minutes longer. Discard the garlic. Transfer the leeks to a serving dish and keep warm.

2. Add the vinegar to the sauce in the skillet. Mix well, and pour over the leeks. Sprinkle with pepper to taste and the chopped parsley.

SERVES 4

DELFS
The Good Food of Szechwan

Gan-bian Si-ji-dou
Dry-Fried String Beans

Occasionally you may see "four-season beans" (si-ji dou) in a Chinese grocery store. They are longer than Western string, or French, beans but their taste is similar. If available, use them in this recipe. In making this dish, the green beans are first deep fried, then cooked with pork, Szechwan vegetable, dried shrimp and green onion. The result is very unusual for there is no sauce to speak of. Substitute bacon for pork in this recipe—the smoky flavor of bacon doesn't seem at all out of place.

1–1½ lbs. fresh "four season beans" or green beans
3–4 dried shrimp
2 Tbsps. finely chopped Szechwan vegetable
¼ lb. pork
2 Tbsps. finely chopped green onion

SEASONINGS
2–3 Tbsps. soy sauce
2–3 Tbsps. rice wine or dry sherry
1½ tsps. sugar
1 tsp. salt
3 Tbsps. water
2–3 Tbsps. sesame oil
½–1 cup oil

TO PREPARE

1. Wash the green beans, drain, pat dry, cut off the ends and remove strings. Cut into 2- or 3-inch lengths.

2. Chop shrimp finely. Wash the red pickling material off the Szechwan vegetable and chop the vegetable finely. Chop the pork meat and green onion finely.

3. Mix the SEASONINGS in a small bowl.

TO COOK

1. Heat about ½–1 cup cooking oil in a *wok* or large frying pan until very hot. Add the green beans, only one handful at a time. Deep fry until the skin of the green beans becomes crackled and wrinkled and the beans darken and become soft. When each batch has deep fried, remove it from the *wok* with a slotted spoon and drain. Allow the oil to reheat between batches if necessary.

2. When all the green beans have been deep fried, remove all but 2–3 Tbsps. of the cooking oil from the *wok*. Heat these few tablespoons cooking oil over high heat and add the finely chopped pork. Stir-fry until the pork is well cooked, or past the white-colored stage, and is beginning to brown.

3. Then add the chopped Szechwan vegetable and chopped dried shrimp. Toss together over high heat until these ingredients are thoroughly heated.

4. Add the prefried green beans. Continue to toss until the green beans are reheated. Then add the SEASONINGS. Stir.

5. Add the finely chopped green onion. Continue to cook over high heat until the liquid has almost disappeared. At this stage of preparation, all the chopped ingredients should be well distributed through the dish, adhering slightly to the beans. (If this is not the case, add a very small amount of cornstarch mixed with a little water at this time and stir it well.) Transfer to a serving dish and serve hot.

CALLAHAN

The California Cook Book

Mexican Chiles Rellenos

These cheese-stuffed green chile peppers, so popular at the best Mexican restaurants, look difficult to make, but are really easy as can be. What is more, they can be stuffed, dipped, and fried several hours or even a day ahead of time, then heated in the tomato sauce just before serving.

To make them, cut Monterey cream cheese, or mild American cheese, into domino-shaped pieces, about ½ × 1 × 2 inches. Wrap each piece in a strip of peeled green chile pepper, fresh or canned. Make a fluffy batter, allowing 1 egg and 1 tablespoon flour for each 2 whole green chiles: beat the egg whites stiff, beat the yolks, fold in the flour, then fold yolks into whites. Drop a cheese-stuffed pepper into the batter, lift out with a spoon, and place in moderately hot oil (375° F.) about 1½ inches deep in a frying pan. Turn immediately. (If you don't, you'll find it hard to make them stay turned over!) Fry until golden brown all over. Drain on paper towels and let stand. The puffy coating will deflate, but don't let that worry you.

Shortly before serving time make a thin sauce this way: Mince 1 small onion and 1 clove garlic fine, and fry in a little oil until transparent. Add 2 cups tomato puree (solid-pack canned tomatoes forced through a wire strainer), and 2 cups chicken broth or meat stock. When boiling, season with 1½ teaspoons salt, ½ teaspoon pepper and 1 teaspoon oregano (rub this between the palms of your hands into the sauce). Drop the stuffed chiles into the boiling sauce and heat about 5 minutes, until they are heated through and puffed up again. Serve with some of the sauce. Allow 2 (or more!) chiles rellenos per person.

COST

Bruce Cost's Asian Ingredients

Yow Choy with Black Vinegar

A little black vinegar is the perfect foil for the slightly bitter, fibrous yow choy, my favorite of the bok choy–type vegetables.

YIELD: 6 SERVINGS

- 2 pounds yow choy
- 1½ tablespoons black vinegar
- 1½ teaspoons sugar
- 1 teaspoon salt
- 1 tablespoon Shaoxing wine
- 1 tablespoon water
- 3 tablespoons fresh lard or peanut oil
- ½ tablespoon finely slivered fresh ginger
- 1 tablespoon finely slivered Smithfield ham

Cut off and discard the bottom 1 or 2 inches of the tough stems of the yow choy, and cut the remainder into 2-inch lengths, leaves and all. Set aside.

Mix the vinegar, sugar, salt, wine, and water, and set aside.

Over high heat, heat a wok and add the lard or oil. When it is hot, add the ginger and yow choy. Cook, stirring, until wilted. Add the seasoned vinegar and stir briefly. Cover, reduce the heat, and steam briefly. Take off the cover, turn the heat to high, and cook, stirring, until most of the liquid has been absorbed, another 2 minutes or so. Stir in the ham and serve.

TROPP

The Modern Art of Chinese Cooking

Dry-Fried Szechwan String Beans

This is a stir-fry of deep-fried *string beans, tossed with zesty condiments and bits of pork, then glazed with a sauce that one lets nearly evaporate in order to concentrate its flavor (this being what is known as dry-frying). It is one of the dishes for which Szechwan is famed—yet it hasn't a speck of chili in it. What makes it typically Szechwanese is the liberal use of dried and pickled condiments to create a pungency that moves one to eat more. • Tender, young, and full-flavored beans are a prerequisite for this dish. Leathery Kentucky Wonders or overgrown and gnarled Chinese longbeans are simply not worth trying, and the otherwise lovely French* haricots verts *(which are now grown in Mexico) are here too delicate. The perfect bean should be tasty and tender enough to enjoy raw, yet possessed of enough body to withstand the deep-frying. Jersey beans are ideal, to praise my native state. • This is a good dish hot, but is even better made in advance and served at room temperature when its flavors have had a chance to marry.*

TECHNIQUE NOTES

When deep-frying anything that cools the oil significantly (on account of its bulk or water content), it is crucial to allow the oil to regain its original high temperature before deep-frying the next batch. Oil used to fry even a scant half-pound of beans may require a full 5 minutes to climb back to 400°, depending on your stove. Be patient. If you rush the next batch, it will turn out greasy because the oil was too cool.

Serves 4 as a substantial vegetable course, 6–8 as part of a multicourse meal. For large parties, I go to the market and count out a loose fistful of beans per guest, then weigh and tally them with the recipe.

1½ pounds fresh young string beans, or tender Chinese longbeans

CONDIMENTS

2 rounded tablespoons dried shrimp
1 small walnut-size nugget fresh ginger
2 ounces (6 tablespoons) Tientsin preserved vegetable
2 ounces ground pork butt

4–6 cups corn or peanut oil, for deep-frying

LIQUID SEASONINGS

1 tablespoon sugar
¾ teaspoon coarse kosher salt
¼ cup light, unsalted chicken stock or water

1 tablespoon well-aged Chinese black vinegar or balsamic vinegar
1 teaspoon Chinese or Japanese sesame oil
1 tablespoon chopped green and white scallion

TO GARNISH

1 tablespoon freshly chopped scallion

PREPARATIONS:

Cut off the tips of the beans and cut longbeans into even lengths about 5 inches long. Rinse with cool water, then dry thoroughly to avoid spattering when fried.

Soak the shrimp in very hot tap water to cover until you can chew on one and enjoy its saltiness, about 15 minutes. Drain and pick through to discard any bits of shell.

Mince the ginger in the work bowl of a food processor fitted with the steel knife. Add shrimp and process with on-off turns until coarsely chopped. Add the preserved vegetable, process with 2 on-off turns to expose new surface, then scrape the mixture into a dish alongside the pork.

Alternatively, mince the ginger and coarsely chop the shrimp and preserved vegetable by hand.

The above may be done up to a day in advance of cooking. Seal the beans and condiments airtight and refrigerate. Bring to room temperature before cooking.

DEEP-FRYING THE BEANS:

Divide the beans into 2 equal batches and put each on a flat plate. Have the beans, cooking chopsticks or a long wooden spoon, a large Chinese mesh spoon, a bowl to hold the fried beans, and a large lid all within easy reach of your stovetop.

Heat a wok or a large, very deep, heavy skillet over high heat until hot. Add the oil, leaving 3–4 inches free at the top of the pot to accommodate bubbling. Heat the oil to the dense-haze stage, 400° on a deep-fry thermometer, when a thick haze is visible above the surface but the oil has not yet begun to smoke. Adjust the heat so the temperature does not climb, then test the oil with a single bean. It should come immediately to the surface surrounded by white bubbles.

Return the heat to high and slide the first plate of beans into the oil. Shield yourself from spatters by holding the pot lid several inches above the oil and angled away from you. Do not cover the pot. Give the beans a gentle stir to even them. After about 30 seconds, the bubbling will die down and you can put the lid aside.

Fry the beans over high heat for about 4 minutes or until thoroughly wrinkled, stirring occasionally. Remove them from the oil with the mesh spoon, hold briefly above the pot to drain, then transfer to the empty bowl or pot. If fried properly, the beans will look limp and pitiful.

Wait a full 3–4 minutes or longer for the oil to regain a temperature of 400°. Test again with a single bean, then repeat the process with the next batch. When both batches are fried, tip the bowl to drain off excess oil. The beans may be left uncovered at room temperature for several hours before continuing.

Once the oil cools, strain and bottle it for future use.

STIR-FRYING THE BEANS:

Combine the sugar and salt with the stock, and leave the spoon in the bowl. Have the beans, the minced condiments, the combined liquids, and the remaining ingredients all within easy reach of your stovetop.

Heat a wok or large, heavy skillet over high heat until hot enough to evaporate a bead of water on contact. Add 2½ tablespoons of the deep-frying oil and swirl to coat the pan. When the oil is hot enough to sizzle a bit of ginger, add the minced mixture and pork. Stir-fry briskly, chopping and poking the pork to break it into tiny bits, adjusting the heat so it sizzles without scorching.

When the pork is 90 percent gray, give the liquids a stir and add them to the pan. Stir to blend, then raise the heat to bring the mixture to a simmer. Add the beans and toss to combine until most all the liquid has evaporated. Rapidly sprinkle in the vinegar, fold in the sesame oil and scallion, then turn off the heat.

Taste and adjust if needed with a bit more salt, sugar, or vinegar. The taste should be very zesty. When you have the taste you want, scrape the mixture into a large serving bowl or plate.

For best flavor, let the beans stand several hours at room temperature or refrigerate overnight once cool, stirring occasionally. Serve at room temperature, not cold, to enjoy the full flavor and aroma. Just before serving, garnish with a fresh sprinkling of scallion.

Leftovers keep beautifully, sealed airtight and refrigerated, for 3–4 days. Bring to room temperature before eating, stirring up the oils and seasonings from the bottom of the dish.

MENU SUGGESTIONS:

I love this dish in tandem with cold dishes such as Orchid's Tangy Cool Noodles, Scallion and Ginger Explosion Shrimp, Master Sauce Chicken, or Tea and Spice Smoked Chicken. It will also add zest to a simple dinner of Hunan Pork Dumplings with Hot Sauce, Moslem-Style Beef or Lamb Pot Stickers, or Pan-Fried Meat Pies. Saucy Potted Pork and Tea and Spice Smoked Fish are also dishes that mate well with the beans.

GREENE

Greene on Greens

Farm-Style Braised Kale

My prototypical kale recipe is borrowed from a farm kitchen. Not just one, however, for I have uncovered the very same recipe performance with ever so slight variations at homespun stoves everywhere from Caen to Kansas City. And inevitably dined well on each offering.

Serve this dish hot off the stove with any main dish you have up your sleeve and gather the hurrahs with confidence!

- 2 strips bacon
- 1 tablespoon unsalted butter
- 1 small onion, finely chopped
- 1 pound kale, stems removed, roughly chopped
- Salt and freshly ground black pepper
- Pinch of ground allspice
- 1 tablespoon red wine vinegar
- 2 lemons, sliced thin

1. Sauté the bacon strips in a large skillet until crisp. Drain on paper towels. Crumble and reserve.

2. Add the butter to the bacon drippings in the skillet. Cook the onion over medium-low heat until golden, about 5 minutes.

3. Meanwhile, rinse the kale in cold water.

4. Add the kale to the skillet, with just the water that clings to the leaves. Cook, covered, stirring occasionally, until tender, 15 to 20 minutes. Add salt and pepper to taste, the allspice, and the vinegar. Sprinkle with the reserved bacon and garnish with lemon slices.

SERVES 4

ROBERTSON
Laurel's Kitchen

Chinese Vegetables & Tofu

This recipe is endlessly adaptable. There are a few fixed ingredients and some that may vary with seasonal changes and differing tastes. Where amounts are given, they are for 6 servings.

THE MUSTS

1 onion, preferably red
celery
green pepper
¼ cup oil
1 teaspoon chopped fresh ginger root
½ cup vegetable stock or water
tofu
soy sauce
or
salt to taste

THE VARIABLES

green beans
carrots
broccoli
cauliflower
zucchini
snow peas
mushrooms
bok choy or chard
Chinese or Western cabbage
peas
bean sprouts
coarsely ground sesame seeds

Allow at least 1 cup of vegetables per person. Cut them all in diagonal shapes. Cut the onion in thin wedges. If a vegetable doesn't lend itself to the diagonal cut (cabbage, for example), dice or cut in square pieces.

Heat the oil in heavy saucepan or wok. Sauté the onion, green pepper, ginger, and celery over medium heat for 5 minutes.

Add each of the longer-cooking vegetables in turn. Sauté for a few minutes between additions and stir occasionally.

Add some stock, put faster-cooking vegetables and leafy greens over other vegetables, and place cubes of tofu over this. Cover all and steam about 10 minutes until vegetables are just tender.

Gently stir in bean sprouts if desired. (Allow sprouted soybeans to cook a full 5 minutes.) Add soy sauce or salt to taste.

Sprinkle with coarsely ground sesame seeds and serve right away, with a steaming hot bowl of brown rice.

SAHNI
Classic Indian Vegetarian and Grain Cooking

Indian Cheese and Red Peppers in Fragrant Spinach Sauce

Saag Paneer

Indian cheese (paneer) *is a delicacy all Indians—particularly vegetarians—love. Popular all through the north from Bengal in the east to Gujarat and Punjab in the west,* paneer *is cooked in an onion-and-cumin-laced spinach sauce. I add sweet red peppers, as the brilliant red peppers and ivory-white cheese pieces look stunning against the glazed moss-green sauce.*

FOR 4–6 PERSONS

Indian cheese (*paneer*) made with 8 cups milk or 8 ounces farmer's cheese or 2 cakes *tofu*, sliced as *paneer*
2 cups cooked spinach
1 sweet green pepper, cored and seeded
6–8 tablespoons light vegetable oil
⅓ cup all-purpose flour for dusting
1½ cups finely chopped onion
2 tablespoons grated or crushed fresh ginger
½ teaspoon turmeric
4 hot green chilies, minced
½ cup water
1 teaspoon coarse salt, or to taste
2 medium-size sweet red peppers, cored, seeded, and cut into 1-inch-wide strips
2 teaspoons *garam masala*

1. Lay the *paneer*, farmer's cheese, or *tofu* pieces in a single layer on a cookie sheet lined with paper towels and let dry for 10 minutes (this will enable them to hold their shape better during cooking).

2. Puree the spinach and green pepper together in a food processor or blender. The puree should be as fine and velvety as you can make it.

3. Heat 4 tablespoons of the oil in a large, heavy, nonstick pan over medium heat. Dust the *paneer* pieces lightly with flour and add them to the pan. Fry them in batches, turning and tossing them until they turn light golden (about 2 or 3 minutes per batch). Watch carefully to ensure that they do not burn. Take them out and put on a dish and set aside.

4. Add 2 more tablespoons of oil to the same pan, along with the onion. Fry the onion, stirring constantly, until brown (about 20 minutes). Add the ginger and fry for an additional 2 minutes. Add the turmeric and green chilies, stir for a few seconds, then add the spinach puree along with ½ cup water, salt, and sweet red peppers. Mix well and bring to a boil. Lower heat and cook, covered, for 2 minutes. Add the fried *paneer* pieces, mix again thoroughly, and continue cooking for 2 more minutes. Stir in the *garam masala*.

When ready to serve, heat thoroughly and, if desired, fold in the remaining 2 tablespoons of oil to glaze and mellow the sauce.

Saag paneer, *rich in many nutrients including protein, makes an excellent luncheon entrée accompanied by* Fresh Corn Bread *or* Corn Bread with Radish. *You may also serve a refreshing beverage such as* Low-Calorie Papaya Drink *or* Iced Yogurt Drink with Mint. *For an elaborate meal add* Eggplant and Potatoes Laced with Fenugreek.

SAHNI

Classic Indian Vegetarian and Grain Cooking

Bengali Green Beans and Potatoes Smothered in Mustard Oil

Bangla Aloo Sem

This delicately sautéed bean dish in mustard oil with turmeric, chili peppers, garlic, and mustard seeds represents the essence of Bengali cooking. For best results use only young, tender bean pods.

FOR 4 PERSONS

- 2 tablespoons mustard oil (or light vegetable oil and ½ teaspoon dry mustard powder)
- 1 teaspoon black mustard seeds
- ⅓ teaspoon turmeric
- 2 large cloves garlic, peeled and sliced
- 4 dry red chili pods, broken into bits
- 1 pound fresh green beans, trimmed and left whole
- 1 large baking potato (about ½ pound), peeled and cut into ⅜-inch-thick matchsticks
- Approximately ¼ cup water
- ¾ teaspoon coarse salt, or to taste
- Lemon juice

1. Put the mustard oil in a heavy skillet and heat to smoking. Turn off the heat and let the oil cool briefly. (Omit this step if you are using light vegetable oil. Do not add mustard powder yet.)

2. Measure out the spices and place them right next to the stove in separate piles. Heat the oil again over medium-high heat. When it is hot, add the mustard seeds. Keep a pot lid handy, as the seeds may spatter and fly all over. When the spattering subsides, add the turmeric, garlic, and chili pieces and fry, shaking the pan, until the garlic turns light golden (about 20 to 30 seconds).

3. Add the beans and potatoes. Let the vegetables sizzle undisturbed for 1 minute (if necessary reduce the heat to medium). Fry the vegetables, turning them, for 5 minutes. Add about ¼ cup water along with the salt. If you are using light vegetable oil, add the mustard powder now and mix well. Reduce the heat to low or medium-low and cook, covered, until the vegetables are thoroughly cooked (about 25 minutes). There will be a little liquid left in the pan. Uncover and continue cooking, turning and tossing the vegetables until they look dry and glazed (3–4 minutes). If necessary increase the heat a little. Turn off the heat. Sprinkle on a little lemon juice (about 1–2 teaspoons) to taste.

NOTE: For a milder dish, discard the seeds of the chili pods.

These beans are delicious, even cold as a salad. Although cooked in the authentic Bengali style, the beans go well with any northern or western Indian menu. To maintain the Bengali flavor serve Bengali Pointed Squash in Spicy Gravy, Bengal Red Lentils with Spices *accompanied by plain cooked rice, or* Deep-Fried Puffy Bread with Poppy Seeds. Indian Mango Ice Cream *would be ideal to conclude this lovely eastern-flavored meal.*

CURTIS

Good Housekeeping Everyday Cook Book

Tomatoes Stuffed

Cut a thin slice off the tops of eight large, firm tomatoes and with a spoon carefully lift out the pulp. Rub it through a sieve, discarding the seeds. To the juice add half a cup of stale bread crumbs, two tablespoons of melted butter, a dust of salt, pepper and paprika and half a teaspoon of minced parsley. Stuff the tomato shells with this, put a bit of butter on top of each and set in a hot oven for ten minutes.

BROWN

Helen Brown's West Coast Cook Book

Figs and Bacon

Soak dried figs overnight, egg and crumb, and fry in bacon fat. Serve with bacon—try it.

BAILEY

Lee Bailey's Country Weekends

Peppered Peaches

This dish is East Indian in origin and has a nice tang that goes well with poultry and meat dishes.

6 large peaches, peeled, pitted, and halved
3 tablespoons fresh lemon juice
2 tablespoons sugar
1 teaspoon salt
Black pepper and cayenne pepper

To peel peaches, dip in boiling water for 6 seconds. Skins should then slip off easily. Put peach halves in a single layer on a plate and coat with lemon juice. Sprinkle sugar and salt over all. Add black pepper and cayenne pepper sparingly. After you have made this once, you can increase the amounts of peppers to suit your taste.

This dish can be prepared up to 3 hours in advance. Don't refrigerate. The lemon juice keeps the peaches from discoloring.

SERVES 6

JAFFREY

An Invitation to Indian Cooking

Stuffed Whole Okra

SERVES 4–6

This recipe, which comes from my maternal grandmother, is perhaps the most delicious way to cook okra. Fresh young okra pods are slit and stuffed with a mixture of fried onions, fennel, cumin, and fenugreek. Then they are lightly fried and allowed to simmer until cooked. Stuffing the slim okra requires a little patience, but don't let that stop you. The most confirmed okra hater will be converted and the ooooh's and aaaah's of your guests will be ample reward for your trouble.

10 medium-sized onions, peeled and finely chopped
8 cloves garlic, peeled and minced
A piece of fresh ginger, about 2 inches by 1½ inches by 1 inch, peeled and grated
2 teaspoons whole cumin seeds
4 teaspoons whole fennel seeds
20 whole fenugreek seeds
10 tablespoons vegetable oil
1 teaspoon ground turmeric
Salt
4 teaspoons garam masala
2 tablespoons lemon juice
1 pound fresh young okra

THE STUFFING

Since this dish is to be cooked in two 10-inch skillets to accommodate all the okra, divide the onions, garlic, and ginger into two equal piles. Make two separate equal piles of the cumin, fennel, and fenugreek seeds.

Heat 5 tablespoons of oil in each skillet over medium heat, and when hot, put in the cumin, fennel, and fenugreek seeds. As they begin to pop and change color (5 to 10 seconds), put half the onion, garlic, and ginger and ½ teaspoon turmeric into each skillet. Stir and fry over medium heat for about 12 minutes until the onions look a rich brown. Stir frequently.

Add ½ teaspoon salt and 1 teaspoon *garam masala* to each skillet and stir. Turn off heat under both skillets. Using a slotted spoon, remove onion mixture from skillets, leaving as much of the cooking fat behind as possible. You will need it later. Collect the onion mixture from both skillets in a bowl, add 2 more teaspoons *garam masala* and the lemon juice, mix, and set aside to cool.

THE OKRA

Wash the okra and pat it dry with paper towels. Trim off the head and the lower tip.

Since the stuffing of the okra takes a little time, place the okra, the bowl of stuffing, a clean platter, and a small sharp knife on a table, and settle yourself on a chair. Pick up one okra pod at a time. Make a slit along its length, being sure that you do not go through the opposite side and that you leave about ⅛ inch at the top and bottom unslit.

Assuming you are right-handed, slip your left thumb into the pod to keep the slit open. With your right thumb and fingers, pick up a little stuffing at a time and push it into the slit. You will need from ¼ to 1 teaspoon of stuffing for each pod, depending on its size. As each pod is stuffed, set it aside on the platter.

Turn on the flame under both skillets and keep on medium-low heat. Divide the okra between the two skillets and lay them slit side up in the pans in a single layer if possible (a few overlapping won't matter). Cook for 5 minutes, shake salt (about ¼ teaspoon to each skillet) over okra, add 2 tablespoons warm water to each pan, cover, lower flames to very, very low, and cook gently for 30 minutes or until the okra is tender.

TO SERVE: Lift out gently and arrange on warm platter. Serve with *Lamb Pullao* or Rice with Peas, Pork Chops à la Jaffrey, and Potatoes with Asafetida and Cumin. It also goes very well with all Indian breads.

TSUJI

Japanese Cooking

Grilled Mushrooms with *Ponzu* Sauce

Yaki-Shiitake Ponzu-Ae

When using shiitake *mushrooms, be careful not to overcook them or their subtle aroma will disappear and they will dry out. Good as a cocktail snack or as a garnish with grilled or deep-fried dishes.*

4 SERVINGS

12 large fresh *shiitake* mushrooms, wiped and trimmed

FOR "INSTANT" PONZU

4 Tbsps lemon juice
4 Tbsps dark soy sauce
splash *mirin*

1 Tbsp finely chopped, green onion, rinsed

TO PREPARE: Salt mushrooms lightly. Grill stem side first, then cap side, over a hot charcoal fire for no longer than 5 minutes total. To pan-broil, cook both sides of mushrooms in a frying pan over medium-high heat in a scant amount of oil for about 3 minutes total. (Oven broiling does not give good results.)

Mix the ponzu sauce and stir in the finely chopped green onion.

TO ASSEMBLE AND SERVE: The mushrooms must be served really *hot*. As they come off the grill or out of the pan, cut mushrooms in half. One serving is six halves, serve in small individual dishes and top each with 1 Tbsp of ponzu sauce.

Combines well with *tempura on rice.*

COST

Bruce Cost's Asian Ingredients

A simple dish, good hot or at room temperature, this makes good use of the smoky Chinese black vinegar.

Sautéed Eggplant with Black Vinegar

YIELD: 4 TO 6 SERVINGS

1 ¼ pounds Asian eggplants
3 tablespoons Gold Plum "Chinkiang" vinegar or other Chinese black vinegar
2 teaspoons sugar
¾ teaspoon salt
⅓ cup peanut oil
1 teaspoon crushed dried red chili pepper
2 tablespoons finely chopped scallions, green part included

Cut the eggplants in half and then into wedges no more than ½ inch wide. Cut the wedges into strips measuring 2 inches by ½ inch. Blend the vinegar, sugar, and salt, and set aside.

Heat a skillet over medium-high heat and add the oil. When it is hot, add the eggplant and cook, stirring constantly, about 5 minutes or until lightly browned and thoroughly wilted. Add the dried chili pepper and stir briefly. Add the vinegar mixture and cook another minute or two, until the liquid is thoroughly absorbed. Stir in the scallions and turn off the heat. Serve warm or at room temperature.

CALLAHAN

The California Cook Book for Indoor and Outdoor Eating

Syrian Stuffed Eggplant

I got this recipe in a decidedly unusual way—from a friendly Western Union operator who liked the sound of a recipe I was describing in a wire to Good Housekeeping, *and who offered this one in exchange for a copy of mine! Try it, and I think you'll mark it as one of your special favorites, as it is mine. To serve 6 to 8, you will need:*

1 pound lamb shoulder, cut in small cubes (or 1 to 2 cups diced cold cooked lamb)
4 tablespoons olive oil
½ cup uncooked rice
1 large eggplant (or 2 small ones)
1 clove garlic, minced
1 small onion, minced
2 tablespoons diced green pepper
¼ cup piñons (pine nuts)
1 tomato, peeled and diced
Salt, celery salt, and pepper
A tiny sprinkle of cinnamon
¼ to ½ cup red table wine
1 cup crumbled goat cheese or ½ cup grated Parmesan

Brown lamb slowly in olive oil in a heavy skillet. (If uncooked meat is used, cover after browning and let it braise until tender.) Meanwhile boil the rice tender, drain, and set aside; also parboil the whole eggplant for 15 minutes in boiling salted water. After parboiling, cut eggplant in half lengthwise, and hollow out, leaving a shell about ¼ inch thick. (Save the part you have removed; it is to be added to the meat a little later.)

When the meat is well browned and tender, add garlic, onion, and green pepper, and let braise until almost brown. Then add piñons, diced tomato, chopped eggplant, season to taste with salt, celery salt, pepper, and that tiny touch of cinnamon, and stir in just enough red wine to make a rather loose mixture. Fill eggplant shells with this, spread cheese over the top, and bake in an uncovered pan in moderate oven (350° F.) 30 to 40 minutes. Finally, slide the whole thing under the broiler to brown the top lightly.

ROBERTSON
Laurel's Kitchen

Cauliflower Eggplant Curry

1 cauliflower
1 eggplant
1 cup peas
2 potatoes
2 to 4 tablespoons oil
1 teaspoon black mustard seed
½ teaspoon turmeric powder
1 teaspoon curry powder
1 teaspoon salt
¼ cup water
1 tomato, chopped
or
1 tablespoon tomato paste
juice of 1 lemon

This combination of vegetables is popular all over India.

Remove thick stems of cauliflower and cut into small pieces. Separate carefully into flowerets and slice.

Cut eggplant into ½ inch cubes.

Heat oil in a large, heavy pot with a lid. When hot add mustard seed and brown, covered. Be careful not to burn it. Stir in turmeric, curry powder, and salt.

Add cauliflower and stir to coat with spices and oil. Add ¼ cup water and eggplant. Cube potatoes and boil them separately until partially cooked before adding them.

Continue cooking over medium heat, adding 1 or 2 tablespoons of water from time to time, stirring gently. Peas should be added about 5 minutes before serving. At the last minute add a finely chopped tomato or tomato paste. Turn off heat and add lemon juice. The cooking time will depend on how crisp you like your vegetables.

SERVES 6 TO 8

RODEN
A Book of Middle Eastern Food

Imam Bayildi / "The Imam Fainted"

This is a Turkish specialty. Widely conflicting stories are told about the origins of its name. Some say that the dish acquired it when an imam, or Turkish priest, fainted with pleasure on being served these stuffed eggplants by his wife. Others believe that the imam fainted when he heard how expensive the ingredients were, and how much olive oil had gone into the making of the dish.

The dish is delightful and, in fact, not very expensive. It makes a splendid first course.

6 long medium-sized eggplants
Filling VI
½ cup olive oil
1 teaspoon sugar, or more
Salt
Juice of 1 lemon

Prepare the eggplants for filling. Stuff them with Filling VI.

Arrange the eggplants side by side in a large pan. Pour over them the oil and enough water to cover (about ½ cup) mixed with a little sugar, salt to taste, and the lemon juice.

Cover the pan and simmer gently until the eggplants are very soft, about 1 hour. Remove from the heat and allow to cool. Turn out onto a serving dish. Serve cold.

FILLING VI

For vegetables prepared à la Imam Bayildi, *to be eaten cold, and sometimes called* yalangi dolma, *or "false dolma," because of the lack of meat. A very popular filling in Turkey.*

¾ lb. onions
4 tablespoons olive oil
2–3 large cloves garlic, crushed
A bunch of parsley, finely chopped
¾ lb. tomatoes, skinned, seeded, and chopped
Salt

Slice the onions thinly. Soften them gently in olive oil, but do not let them color. Add garlic and stir for a minute or two until aromatic. Remove from the heat and stir in parsley and tomatoes. Season to taste with salt, and mix well.

SHERATON

From My Mother's Kitchen

Eggplant Caviar, Two Ways

My mother and grandmother prepared this two ways, the first as a puree bound with tomato that was kept for a day or two and was as rich as a conserve. The second is a fresher, lighter puree that should be served within two or three hours of the time it is made. In both, the smoky flavor of the broiled eggplant adds the distinctive and characteristic touch.

EGGPLANT CAVIAR I

1 medium-sized ripe eggplant
¼ cup vegetable oil, preferably olive, or as needed
1 small onion, peeled and finely minced
1 large clove garlic, minced
3 small canned tomatoes, drained and pureed, or 3 tablespoons tomato puree (not paste)
Salt, pepper, and lemon juice to taste
Garnishes: 1 tablespoon finely minced parsley, salty black olives, and (optional) chopped raw onion

There are two methods for broiling eggplant. The slightly better, if more tedious way, is to hold it over an open flame with a long-handled carving or barbecue fork, turning slowly until the outside skin is evenly charred and the inside is almost completely tender. This will take about 20 to 30 minutes.

The simpler method is broiling. Cut the whole, unpeeled eggplant in half vertically and remove only the leaves of the stem end. Place a piece of aluminum foil on the pan of your broiler. Brush the cut side of each eggplant half with oil, and place cut side down on the foil. Broil about 4 inches below the flame or coil until the skin is charred and the flesh is tender.

When the eggplant has been cooked by either method, peel, scrape out the seeds, and chop the flesh fine. Heat 2 tablespoons of the oil in a heavy-bottomed saucepan and in it slowly sauté the minced garlic and onion until soft but not brown. Stir in the eggplant and tomato puree and trickle in enough oil to enable the mixture to simmer.

Simmer over very low heat for about 30 minutes, adding trickles of oil as needed to prevent scorching, and stirring frequently and vigorously with a wooden spoon until the mixture is smooth and thick.

Add salt, pepper, and a few drops of lemon juice to taste. Chill at least several hours. Serve garnished with the minced parsley, salty black olives, and chopped raw onion, if you like.

YIELD: ABOUT ¾ CUP

EGGPLANT CAVIAR II

This is almost exactly like the Middle Eastern baba gannouj.

1 medium eggplant
1 clove garlic, lightly crushed and peeled
Pinch of kosher (coarse) salt
About ¼ cup olive, sesame, or sunflower oil
1 to 2 tablespoons lemon juice
Salt and white pepper to taste
Garnishes: 1 small onion, peeled and finely chopped, and/or 1 small ripe tomato, cut in coarse chunks, and/or minced parsley

Cook the eggplant either over an open flame or under a flame, as described in the preceding recipe. Peel, remove the seeds, and chop. Rub a small mixing bowl with the crushed garlic clove and coarse salt. Leave the garlic in the bowl. Add the chopped eggplant and, with a wooden spoon, beat the eggplant as you slowly add trickles of oil, much as you would for mayonnaise. The final result should be thick and smoothly silky, but not liquidy. Stir in lemon juice, salt, and pepper to taste. Let stand from 1 to 3 hours in the refrigerator so the flavor will develop.

Serve with any or all of the garnishes sprinkled on top or stirred into the puree. This is especially good with dark bread or with Middle Eastern pita bread.

YIELD: ABOUT ¾ CUP

DAVID

French Provincial Cooking

Tarte à l'Oignon, or Zewelwaï

Onion and Cream Tart

This is the famous Alsatian speciality. It makes a truly lovely first course.

For the pastry: 4 oz. plain flour, 2 oz. butter or 1 oz. each of butter and meat dripping, 1 egg, salt, water.

For the filling; 1½ lb. onions, the yolks of 3 eggs, a good ¼ pint of thick cream, seasonings including nutmeg and plenty of freshly-milled pepper, butter and oil for cooking the onions.

Make a well in the sieved flour, put the butter cut in small pieces, the egg and a good pinch of salt in the middle. Blend quickly and lightly but thoroughly, with the fingertips. Add a very little water, just enough to make the dough moist, but it should come cleanly away from the bowl or board. Place the ball of dough on a floured board and with the heel of your palm gradually stretch the paste out, bit by bit, until it is a flat but rather ragged-looking sheet. Gather it up again, and repeat the process. It should all be done lightly and expeditiously, and is extremely simple although it sounds complicated written down. Roll it into a ball, wrap it in greaseproof paper and leave it to rest in a cold larder or refrigerator for a minimum of 2 hours, so that it loses all elasticity and will not shrink or lose its shape during the baking. This is one version of the pâte brisée or pâte à foncer used for most open tarts in French cookery. Without being as rich or as complicated as puff pastry, it is light and crisp. But those who already have a satisfactory method for tart and flan pastries may prefer to stick to their own. In spite of all the cookery rules, the making of pastry remains a very personal matter. I find myself that the easiest and most generally successful tart pastry is the one described for the cheese dish in the next recipe.

For the filling, peel and slice the onions as finely as possible, taking care to discard the fibrous parts at the root of the onions. Melt 2 oz. of butter and a little oil in a heavy frying-pan. In this cook the onions, covered, until they are quite soft and pale golden. They must not fry, and they should be stirred from time to time to make sure they are not sticking. They will take about ½ hour. Season with salt, nutmeg and pepper. Stir in the very well-beaten yolks and the cream, and leave until the time comes to cook the tart.

Oil an 8-inch tart or flan tin. Roll out your pastry as thinly as possible (the great thing about this dish, as also the quiches of Lorraine, is that there should be a lot of creamy filling on very little pastry). Line the tin with the pastry, pressing it gently into position with your knuckle. Pour in the filling, cook in the centre of a fairly hot oven, with the tin standing on a baking sheet at Gas No. 6, 400 deg. F., for 30 minutes. Serve very hot.

TIME-LIFE BOOKS

Cooking of Scandinavia

Rårakor med Gråslök

Lacy Potato Pancakes with Chives

TO SERVE 4

- 4 medium-sized baking potatoes
- 2 tablespoons chopped fresh chives
- 2 teaspoons salt
- Freshly ground black pepper
- 2 tablespoons butter
- 2 tablespoons vegetable oil

Peel the potatoes and grate them coarsely, preferably into tiny slivers, into a large mixing bowl. Do not drain off the potato water that will accumulate in the bowl. Working quickly to prevent the potatoes from turning brown, mix into them the chopped chives, salt and a few grindings of pepper.

Heat the butter and oil in a 10- to 12-inch skillet over high heat until the foam subsides. The pan must be very hot, but not smoking. Using 2 tablespoons of potato mixture for each pancake, fry 3 or 4 at a time, flattening them out with a spatula to about 3 inches in diameter. Fry each batch of pancakes over medium-high heat for 2 or 3 minutes on each side, or until they are crisp and golden. Serve at once.

GREENE

Greene on Greens

Fritterra

My favorite scallion chomp (after raw) is the following tender-hearted patty, Israeli in heritage. It was a gift from a taxi driver, who related it in pieces—each time we stopped for a light.

- 12 whole scallions, bulbs and green tops
- 2 eggs, lightly beaten
- ¼ teaspoon freshly grated nutmeg
- ½ teaspoon salt
- Freshly ground black pepper
- ¼ cup fresh bread crumbs
- 1½ cups cold mashed potatoes
- 1 tablespoon olive oil
- 2 tablespoons vegetable oil

1. Wash and trim the scallions, leaving about 2 inches of green stems. Cook in boiling water until tender, about 5 minutes. Drain and chop.

2. Place the scallions in a medium-size bowl. Add the eggs, nutmeg, salt, pepper to taste, bread crumbs, and mashed potatoes. Mix well.

3. Heat the oils in a large skillet until hot but not smoking. Shape the onion-potato mixture into patties, using 2 rounded tablespoons of the mixture for each patty. Sauté, about six at a time, until golden brown on both sides, 2 or 3 minutes per side. Keep warm while sautéing the remaining patties.

SERVES 4

LANG

The Cuisine of Hungary

Lecsó

In Hungary vegetables are not just "cooked"; they are "prepared." The difference between an American vegetable dish and a Hungarian one is similar to the difference between plain boiled meat and a meat stew.

Hungary is famed for its vegetable gardens. The Hungarian name for green peas is cukorborsó, *which means "sugar peas," and without additional flourishes they do taste like a sugared vegetable. Yet you will rarely find a Hungarian housewife simply steaming, boiling or sautéing peas; she would consider that as only the first step. Plain boiled vegetables are incomprehensible to a Hungarian.*

I am not recommending the exclusive use of this complex treatment of vegetables, but since the simple preparations are already only too familiar, I will describe the preparations I grew up with. What makes these dishes unusual is that many of them can be eaten by themselves for luncheons, and a few will serve as appetizers.

4 TO 8 SERVINGS

2 tablespoons lard
1 medium-sized onion, sliced
1 pound green Italian or frying peppers, sliced
3 large, very ripe tomatoes, peeled and diced
½ tablespoon sugar
½ tablespoon salt
1 tablespoon paprika

1. Heat the lard, add sliced onion, and cook over very low heat for 5 minutes.

2. Add green pepper slices and cook for an additional 10 minutes.

3. Add tomatoes, sugar, salt and paprika. Cook for 8 to 10 minutes longer. Adjust sugar and salt to taste.

VARIATION: Put ½ pound beef tenderloin on a board. Hold it with one hand, and start scraping it with the dull edge of a strong knife (the same way you make a proper steak tartare). It will take 10 minutes to scrape the whole piece. Heat 1 teaspoon lard till very hot, coat the bottom of the frying pan completely, and throw in the meat pulp. Work very fast and squeeze-stir to make sure that within seconds, or certainly in less than 1 minute, the meat browns. Do not let it stick together; in other words don't make a hamburger out of it, but rather something more like meat crumbs. Then mix it with the *lecsó*. Adjust salt.

This variation comes from the great chef Emil Turós.

NOTE: This is one of the most ingeniously used vegetable dishes in the Hungarian kitchen. First of all it is used in an appetizer; for this amount ¼ cup cooked rice or ¼ pound thin-sliced smoked sausage are added; or at the last minute 4 eggs are beaten into it.

With the same additions *lecsó* can also be used as a luncheon main course, particularly if you cook it with larger sections of smoked or fresh sausage, or frankfurter (*virsli*).

Lecsó is also used as an ingredient for stews and other dishes, especially when no fresh tomatoes or green peppers are available in Hungary.

Do not use bell peppers, for they have no taste to speak of. Italian frying peppers or banana peppers are better. And do not make this dish unless you have ripe tomatoes.

The sugar must be adjusted according to the ripeness of the tomatoes; if you have vine-ripened fruit you can usually eliminate sugar altogether.

Reduce salt if you use smoked sausage, for sausage is salty.

Curiously enough, this most Hungarian of dishes originated in Serbia and is very closely related to their *djuvets*.

NATHAN
Jewish Cooking in America

Crispy Traditional Potato Pancakes

Ever since I visited a tiny French village in the Ardèche where I tasted a "craque," an extraordinary crisp thin potato pancake as large as a plate, I have changed my view of the taste of potato pancakes. For me they should be thin and crisp. This is only possible if you squeeze out as much water as possible from the grated potato, omit flour or matzah meal as fillers, and gently flatten the pancakes on a very hot skillet. Although the taste of hand-grated potato latkes is superior to that of those grated in the food processor, the difference is definitely marginal. So don't feel guilty if you don't want to use elbow grease and cut your fingers.

2 pounds russet (baking) or Yukon Gold potatoes
1 medium onion
½ cup chopped scallions, including the green part
1 large egg, beaten
Salt and freshly ground pepper to taste
Vegetable oil for frying

1. Peel the potatoes and put in cold water. Using a grater or a food processor coarsely grate the potatoes and onions. Place together in a fine-mesh strainer or tea towel and squeeze out all the water over a bowl. The potato starch will settle to the bottom; reserve that after you have carefully poured off the water.

2. Mix the potato and onion with the potato starch. Add the scallions, egg, and salt and pepper.

3. Heat a griddle or nonstick pan and coat with a thin film of vegetable oil. Take about 2 tablespoons of the potato mixture in the palm of your hand and flatten as best you can. Place the potato mixture on the griddle, flatten with a large spatula, and fry for a few minutes until golden. Flip the pancake over and brown the other side. Remove to paper towels to drain. Serve immediately. You can also freeze the potato pancakes and crisp them up in a 350-degree oven at a later time.

YIELD: ABOUT 2 DOZEN PANCAKES

VARIATION: If you want a more traditional and thicker pancake, you can add an extra egg plus ⅓ cup of matzah meal to the batter.

KANDER
"The Settlement" Cook Book

Potato Cakes

Take cold mashed potatoes and make into round cakes, one-half inch thick. Put them in a hot greased frying pan, fry well on one side until golden brown, then turn over and brown the other side.

TIME-LIFE BOOKS
A Quintet of Cuisines

Rösti

Fried Shredded Potato Cake

TO SERVE 4 TO 6

9 medium-sized baking potatoes (about 3 pounds)
½ teaspoon salt
¼ cup vegetable oil
2 tablespoons butter

Drop the potatoes into enough boiling water to cover them completely and cook briskly for about 10 minutes, or until the point of a knife can be inserted about 1 inch into a potato before meeting any resistance. Drain the potatoes. When cool enough to handle, peel them with a small, sharp knife, cover with plastic wrap, and refrigerate for at least an hour. Just before frying the potatoes grate them into long strips on the tear-shaped side of a four-sided stand-up grater. Toss lightly with the salt.

In a heavy 10-inch slope-sided skillet (preferably one with a nonstick cooking surface), heat the oil and butter over moderate heat until a drop of water flicked over them splutters and evaporates instantly. Drop in the potatoes and, with a spatula, spread them evenly in the pan. Fry uncovered for 8 to 10 minutes, using a spatula to gently lift up a side of the potatoes to check their color as they brown. When the underside of the potato cake is as brown as you can get it without letting it burn, place a plate upside down over the skillet. Grasping the skillet and plate firmly together, invert them quickly. Then carefully slide the potato cake, browned side up, back into the skillet. (If you are not using a pan with a nonstick surface, add more butter and oil before returning the potatoes to the pan.) Fry for 6 to 8 more minutes, or until the bottom side of the potatoes is as evenly browned as the top and the edges are crisp.

Slide the potato cake onto a heated platter and serve at once.

NOTE: *Rösti* potatoes are often made with onions or bacon. Sauté ½ cup of finely chopped onions in 3 tablespoons of butter until they are soft and transparent. Drop half the shredded potatoes into the skillet, pat them flat and smooth and spread the onions evenly over them before adding the remaining potatoes, patting them down as before. Or fry ½ cup of finely diced bacon until the bits are crisp, drain on paper towels and spread the bacon over half of the potatoes as described for the onions.

SAHNI

Classic Indian Vegetarian and Grain Cooking

Eggplant and Potatoes Laced with Fenugreek

Aloo Baigan

Eggplant and potatoes are a popular combination throughout northern India. They can be spiced Moghul-style (as is done in Indian restaurants) or with regional flavorings. My favorite is a version from the eastern extremities of the Northern Province near Nepal, in which the vegetables are first fried to develop a roasted flavor and then steamed in their own moisture. Cayenne pepper, fenugreek, and tart mango powder bring out the essence of that region's cooking.

FOR 4 PERSONS

- 1 pound eggplant (five 7-inch long, 1½-inch-thick eggplants, or 1 pear-shaped eggplant)
- 1 pound potatoes (about 4 medium-size)
- ¾ teaspoon turmeric
- 1½ tablespoons ground coriander
- ½–1 teaspoon cayenne pepper
- 1½ teaspoons coarse salt
- 4 tablespoons light vegetable oil
- ¾ teaspoon fenugreek seeds
- 1 teaspoon mango powder

1. Cut the eggplant, unpeeled, into 1-inch pieces or cubes. Peel the potatoes and cut them into 1-inch cubes. Put the vegetables in a bowl. Sprinkle on the turmeric, coriander, cayenne, and salt, and mix well to coat evenly with spices.

2. Heat the oil in a large skillet over high heat for 3 minutes. Add the fenugreek seeds and fry until they turn dark brown (10–15 seconds). Add the vegetables, shake the pan a few times, and let the vegetables sizzle undisturbed for 1 or 2 minutes. Fry the vegetables, turning them for 5 minutes or until the spices start clinging to the vegetables and the eggplant looks limp and begins to steam. Lower the heat and cook, covered, for 20 minutes, turning the vegetables often to ensure that they are cooking evenly. Be careful not to break the fragile pieces of vegetables. Sprinkle on the mango powder and fry uncovered, turning them regularly, for 5 minutes or until they look glazed. Serve warm or at room temperature.

Aloo baigan can be served with any meal as long as it doesn't contain potatoes or eggplant. I love it by itself with Deep-Fried Puffy Bread with Poppy Seeds, Creamy Mint Dressing, *and* Punjab Five-Jewel Creamed Lentils.

LANG

The Cuisine of Hungary

Inces' Stuffed Cabbage

Incék töltött káposztája

6 TO 8 SERVINGS

(Stolen from the secret files of Peggy and the late Alexander Ince)

- 1 head of fresh cabbage
- ¼ cup uncooked rice
- ½ cup beef broth
- 2 medium-sized onions, chopped
- 3 tablespoons bacon drippings
- ½ pound lean pork, ground
- ½ pound beefsteak, ground
- Dash of freshly ground pepper
- ½ teaspoon salt
- 1 raw egg
- 3 tablespoons flour
- 1 tablespoon paprika
- 2 pounds sauerkraut
- 1 tomato, sliced
- 2 smoked pig knuckles
- 1 pound fresh sausage
- ½ pound oxtails
- 1 pound *dagadó*, or smoked spareribs
- 1 cup sour cream

¼ cup heavy sweet cream
Paprika Essence

1. Separate the cabbage leaves and place in hot water to make them limp enough not to crack when rolled.

2. Cook rice in beef broth for 10 minutes.

3. Fry 1 onion in 1 tablespoon bacon drippings for 5 minutes. Mix ground meats with fried onion, pepper and salt, ½ cup water, 1 egg and the semi-cooked rice.

4. Place mixture in separated cabbage leaves, and roll or squeeze together in clean napkins so the rolls won't come apart when cooking.

5. Fry the other chopped onion in remaining drippings for 5 minutes. Add flour, stir, and cook for 5 or 6 minutes. Add paprika and 1 cup cold water, whip, and pour over sauerkraut.

6. Line the bottom of a large casserole with the stuffed cabbage leaves; put sauerkraut layer over. Add tomato and 2 cups water, or enough to cover the sauerkraut layer. Top with meats, neatly arranged. Cook it over very, very low heat for 2 to 2½ hours. Lift cover as few times as you can.

7. Take a huge, low-sided casserole or platter. Put sauerkraut on bottom. Place stuffed cabbage leaves around and the meats cut into individual portions in the center. Sprinkle with sour cream mixed with sweet cream and the paprika essence.

NOTE: I've eaten this superb dish cooked by Sándor Incze, whose spirit, I hope, lingers over this book!

GREENE
Greene on Greens

Mucver

Turkish Squash Cakes

From the Pilgrims on, summer squash has had its detractors. When this vegetable crossed the Atlantic to England in the late seventeenth century it was known as "harrow marrow," for only cattle would eat it. The French were no better; when the famed geese of Strasbourg choked on summer squash seeds, they gave the entire vegetable a bad name, calling it malmain *("bad hand").*

Only the Turks consumed summer squash with any relish. They reputedly acquired a taste for it when a ship bound for Russia with a cargo of fodder in the hold sank in the harbor at Constantinople. All hands were lost but the squash floated across the isthmus and took root. Fact or fiction is utterly beside the point: squash certainly became part of the Middle Eastern diet shortly afterward. For further evidence, try these delicate squash and cheese fritters.

½ pound crookneck squash (about 2 small), trimmed, grated
2 tablespoons crumbed feta cheese
2 tablespoons ricotta cheese
2 tablespoons finely chopped fresh dill
2 tablespoons finely chopped fresh mint
1 tablespoon finely chopped fresh parsley
¼ teaspoon salt, plus extra to taste
⅛ teaspoon fresh ground black pepper
1 egg, lightly beaten
½ cup all-purpose flour
Oil for frying

1. Combine the squash, cheeses, dill, mint, parsley, salt, and pepper in a bowl. Add the egg and flour; mix thoroughly.

2. Heat ¾ inch of oil in a heavy skillet until hot but not smoking. Drop rounded tablespoons of the mixture, a few at a time, into the oil. Fry until golden, about 2 minutes per side. Drain on paper towels. Sprinkle with salt to taste before serving.

MAKES 8 TO 10; SERVES 4

GREENE
Greene on Greens

Winter Squash Crème Brûlée

An aureate crème brûlée *compounded of winter squash and more deviltry than a deep-dyed Puritan could shake a stick at and crusted to the nines with burnt sugar.*

- 3 cups heavy or whipping cream
- ½ cup granulated sugar
- 6 egg yolks
- ⅓ cup puréed cooked winter squash
- ¼ teaspoon ground cinnamon
- ⅛ teaspoon ground ginger
- Pinch of ground cloves
- 1 tablespoon dark rum
- ⅓ cup packed light brown sugar

1. Preheat the oven to 325°F. Heat the cream and granulated sugar in the top of a double boiler over hot water until the sugar has dissolved. Remove from the heat.

2. Beat the egg yolks in a medium bowl until light. Add the squash, cinnamon, ginger, and cloves. Whisk in the hot cream mixture. Stir in the rum.

3. Pour the squash mixture into a 1½-quart soufflé dish. Place the dish in a roasting pan and add boiling water to the pan to come halfway up the sides of the dish. Bake until the center is fairly firm, about 1½ hours. Remove from the water and allow to cool. Refrigerate overnight.

4. About 15 minutes before serving, preheat the broiling unit. Sprinkle the brown sugar over the custard. Place the dish in a pan and surround it with ice cubes. Heat it under the broiler, gently shaking the pan, until the sugar melts. Serve immediately.

SERVES 6 TO 8

GREENE
Greene on Greens

Bashed Neeps

Mashed Rutabagas and Potatoes

The French call rutabaga navet de Suède, *while the English dub them* Stockholms, *Italians know them as* rapa svedese, *and the Spanish tag them* nabo sueco*—which are all variations of the same moniker when you come down to it. But not the Scottish handle, for a rutabaga is referred to as a "neep" from Edinburgh to the Orkneys. Scots have a way with this vegetable: they* bash *them with a mix of white potatoes, lots of butter and nutmeg—and they are the best thing I have ever tasted in Scotland or anywhere else a rutabaga is rooted.*

- 1 pound rutabagas, peeled, cut into cubes
- ½ pound potatoes, peeled, cut into cubes
- 2 tablespoons unsalted butter
- ¼ teaspoon freshly grated nutmeg
- Salt and freshly ground black pepper

1. Cook the rutabagas in boiling salted water for 10 minutes. Add the potatoes; cook until both vegetables are tender, about 15 minutes longer. Drain.

2. Mash the rutabagas and potatoes with the butter until smooth. Add the nutmeg, and salt and pepper to taste. Place over low heat to warm through.

SERVES 4

SCHNEIDER
Uncommon Fruits & Vegetables

Richards' Mashed Celeriac and Potatoes

Richard Sax, co-author of From the Farmers' Market, *learned this simple method of preparing aromatic celery root from Richard Olney, the chief consultant for the Time-Life Good Cook Series, when they worked together on those books. No milk, no cream, just full-strength good vegetable flavor. The butter, when added after the vegetables have cooked, binds, mellows, and softens the purée.*

4–6 SERVINGS

- 2 medium-large celery roots (2 pounds, weighed without leaves)
- 3 medium all-purpose potatoes (1 pound)
- 2 medium garlic cloves, smashed and peeled
- Salt and white pepper
- Nutmeg
- 2 tablespoons cold unsalted butter

1. Trim, peel, and chunk celery roots (should equal about 4–5 cups). Peel and chunk potatoes (should equal 2½ generous cups).

2. Combine vegetables and garlic in saucepan with cold water to cover; salt lightly and bring to a boil, covered. Boil gently, covered, until very tender, 25–30 minutes.

3. Drain vegetables thoroughly, reserving cooking liquid. Press through food mill or sieve, using pestle or large wooden spoon. Season with salt, pepper, and nutmeg. Add cooking liquid gradually until purée has a fairly soft consistency—as much as 1–2 cups.

4. Reheat, stirring, over low heat. Remove from heat; stir in butter. Serve at once.

BAILEY
Lee Bailey's Country Weekends

Turnip Custard

Turnips prepared this way are mild and have a subtle flavor that is perfect with fish.

- 12 ounces white turnips (weigh after peeling)
- 1 3-ounce white potato (weigh after peeling)
- 3 tablespoons butter
- 2 large eggs
- ½ cup milk
- 3 tablespoons evaporated skimmed milk
- ½ teaspoon nutmeg
- ½ teaspoon salt, or to taste
- Chopped parsley

Put kettle of water on to boil. Butter a 9-inch cake pan and set the oven rack in the middle position. Preheat to 375 degrees.

Boil the turnips until very tender, about 30 minutes. If they are large, cut into several pieces. Cut the potato into pieces and boil it until tender. Do this separately. In a food processor with a metal blade, process the turnips and butter until puréed, about 10 seconds. You may have to stop and scrape down the sides of the bowl. Add the remaining ingredients, except the potato, and process for 30 seconds. Push the potato through a fine sieve, add to the mixture. Adjust seasoning if necessary.

Pour the mixture into the cake pan and set it into a larger ovenproof pan. Surround with boiling water to come up ½ inch. Put in the oven and cook for 30 minutes, until the custard sets. Remove from water bath and let rest. If you have trouble getting the pan out of the bath, you can remove the hot water with a bulb baster. When ready to serve, run a knife around the edge and invert onto a platter. Decorate with chopped parsley.

NOTE: This custard can be prepared ahead and set aside, unmolded. Reheat by putting in water bath and simmering for 30 minutes on top of stove. When unmolding it, if parts should stick, carefully remove them with a spatula and mold the parts together with your hands. You will hardly be able to see the seams, and the parsley garnish will always help hide any imperfections.

SERVES 6

THOMAS

The Vegetarian Epicure

Russian Vegetable Pie

PASTRY

1¼ cups flour
1 tsp. sugar
1 tsp. salt
4 oz. softened cream cheese
3 Tbs. butter

FILLING

1 small head cabbage (about 3 cups shredded)
½ lb. mushrooms
1 yellow onion
to taste:
basil
marjoram
tarragon
salt and fresh-ground pepper
3 Tbs. butter
4 oz. softened cream cheese
4 to 5 hard-cooked eggs
dill

Make a pastry by sifting together the dry ingredients, cutting in the butter, and working it together with the cream cheese. Roll out ⅔ of the pastry and line a 9-inch pie dish. Roll out the remaining pastry and make a circle large enough to cover the dish. Put it away to chill.

Shred a small head of cabbage coarsely. Wash the mushrooms and slice them. Peel and chop the onion.

In a large skillet, melt about 2 tablespoons butter. Add the onion and cabbage, and sauté for several minutes, stirring constantly. Add at least ⅛ teaspoon each of marjoram, tarragon, and basil (all crushed), and some salt and fresh-ground pepper. Stirring often, allow the mixture to cook until the cabbage is wilted and the onions soft. Remove from the pan and set aside.

Add another tablespoon of butter to the pan and sauté the mushrooms lightly for about 5 or 6 minutes, stirring constantly.

Spread the softened cream cheese in the bottom of the pie shell. Slice the eggs and arrange the slices in a layer over the cheese. Sprinkle them with a little chopped dill, then cover them with the cabbage. Make a final layer of the sautéed mushrooms and cover with the circle of pastry.

Press the pastry together tightly at the edges, and flute them. With a sharp knife, cut a few short slashes through the top crust.

Bake in a 400-degree oven for 15 minutes, then turn the temperature down to 350 degrees and continue baking for another 20 to 25 minutes, or until the crust is light brown.

SERVES 4 TO 6

SCHNEIDER

Uncommon Fruits & Vegetables

Plantain Baked in Its Skin

For the simplest, most basic dish, plantain needs nothing more than to be baked in its skin, like a potato. Choose brown to black-ripe plantain for full flavor and softness. Baked without adornment, the plantain will be tender, not mushy, with a fruity sweetness. It is just firm enough to remove whole from the peel to be served as a vegetable accompaniment to roasted or fried meats or stews, with which it is particularly compatible. Or sprinkle over sugar, butter, and spices once the peel has baked enough to split open, then continue baking until caramelized: a truly no-fuss dessert.

Rinse and dry as many plantain as needed, usually figuring one medium-sized per person. Trim off tips. Cut lengthwise slit in each fruit. Set slit-side up in a foil-lined pan and bake in 375-degree oven until creamy-tender, about 40 minutes. When it is baked, you can peel and serve whole, or separate in lengthwise strips along the natural seed divisions, or slice crosswise in rounds or diagonals.

VARIATIONS FOR BAKED PLANTAIN:

- Cut in thin, diagonal slices and drizzle with melted butter.

- Slice in thick diagonals, sprinkle with lime juice, butter, and pure mild chili powder; heat through in the oven.
- Bake in the oven while you roast meat, then serve with pan juices or gravy.
- Prepare chili or meat sauce (figuring on ⅓–½ cup per ½ pound plantain). Pour over sliced fruit and bake at 375 degrees for about 20 minutes, until puffed and soft.
- Reheat in wide skillet with sweet dessert sauce, such as rum, caramel, or citrus.
- Slice and arrange in buttered baking dish; top with chopped pineapple, butter, brown sugar, and nuts or coconut. Bake in hot oven until bubbling.

DE GROOT

Feasts for All Seasons

Fruit and Chestnut Stuffing

FOR A 16-POUND BIRD

CHECK STAPLES

Salt butter (about ¾ lb.)
Aromatics: crystal salt, freshly ground black pepper, MSG, marjoram, rosemary, thyme
Yellow onions (3 medium)
Parsley (small bunch)
Stale white bread (small loaf) or packaged "Herb Stuffing"
Olive oil, for cooking chestnuts (2 to 3 Tbs.)

SHOPPING LIST

The choice of fruit is flexible—it should be tart and juicy—we like a combination of the following, when in season:

Tangerines (6)
Cranberries (up to ½ lb.)
Fresh Swedish lingonberries (up to ½ lb.)

White celery (1 heart)
Fresh chestnuts (2 lbs.)
Fresh mushrooms (½ lb.)
Corn bread (small loaf); we bake our own
Pork sausage meat (1 lb.); we use our homemade

THE DAY BEFORE—ADVANCE PREPARATION OF CHESTNUTS, CORN BREAD AND FRUIT IN ABOUT 1 HOUR

We bake, shell, and skin the 2 pounds of chestnuts according to our basic rule. We quickly mix and bake a batch of Johanna's crackling corn bread or we use a commercially baked corn loaf or crumbled corn muffins. We grind the stale white loaf to crumbs or use a bag of pre-crumbed "herb stuffing." While chestnuts and corn bread are baking, assemble the vegetables: the 3 onions, peeled and finely chopped; the white celery heart, washed and finely chopped; the ½ pound of mushrooms, wiped clean (never washed) and sliced lengthwise into hammer shapes, plus a handful of parsley, finely chopped. Separately assemble the fruit: the 6 tangerines, peeled, sectioned, and pitted; the ½ pound each of fresh cranberries and lingonberries, washed; or any other fruits, prepared and cut to a uniform size. We put the pound of our own homemade sausage meat or commercial sausage meat into a sauté pan and fry it, crumbling it with a fork, until lightly brown. Our own sausage meat has very little fat, but with commercial meat, the excess fat must be drained off. Now add to sauté pan ½ pound of the butter plus the chopped vegetables and sauté lightly for 4 or 5 minutes, then turn off heat. Now mix all ingredients, except fruits. Coarsely mash chestnuts with a steel fork or pass them through the grinder with the coarse cutter in position, then put into largest mixing bowl. Blend in about 2 cups of crumbled corn bread and about 1 cup of white bread crumbs, using judgment as to exact amount, remembering that corn bread gives body, the chestnuts, weight, and the bread crumbs, lightness. Now blend aromatics into warm contents of sauté pan: 1 teaspoon each of marjoram, rosemary, and thyme, plus about 3 tablespoons salt, a dozen or so grinds of black pepper, and MSG to taste. Now lightly work entire contents of sauté pan into chestnut-bread mixture. Finally, taste and adjust both seasonings and texture. For more body, add more corn bread. For more lightness, use more white bread crumbs. For more moisture, add more melted butter. Above all, use a light touch in mixing, preferably with a wooden fork. When mixture seems right, cover and refrigerate overnight. Separately cover and refrigerate prepared fruits.

ABOUT 3 HOURS BEFORE TURKEY IS READY TO BE STUFFED

Take both parts of stuffing out of refrigerator and let come to room temperature.

WHEN TURKEY IS READY—THE FINAL ASSEMBLY

Sometimes the most efficient tool in the kitchen is a set of clean fingers. The mixing must be thorough, yet so light that none of the fruit is crushed. Then loosely fill the turkey and proceed.

WEAVER
Pennsylvania Dutch Country Cooking

Hickory Nut Dumplings

Hickerniss-Gnepp

YIELD: 24 DUMPLINGS, OR 6 SERVINGS

1¼ cups (100 g) ground hickory nuts (see note)
¼ cup (30 g) white breadcrumbs (*Mutschelmehl*)
¼ teaspoon sugar
¼ teaspoon ground mace
¼ teaspoon baking soda
1 large egg
⅓ cup (80 ml) milk
spelt flour
oil or fat for deep frying

Combine the ground hickory nuts, breadcrumbs, sugar, mace, and baking soda. Beat the egg and milk together. Combine with the crumb mixture. Form into 24 small dumplings. Roll in spelt flour and let stand, uncovered, for 15 minutes before cooking. Heat the oil or fat in a deep fryer to 375°F (190°C) and fry the dumplings until golden brown (about 2 minutes). Drain and set aside to cool. Store overnight for use the next day.

NOTE: The hickory nuts must be ground to a cornmeal texture. The best tool for this is a Swedish *mandelkvarn*, a small hand grinder that can be mounted to the top of a table. A coffee grinder will work, but not a food processor, which will not reduce the nuts to a fine enough texture.

Fresh hickory nut dumplings have a hard crust, which softens as they stand overnight. Fresh, crispy hickory nut dumplings can be rolled in confectioners' sugar and served like doughnuts or served with stewed peaches and sugar.

WEAVER
Pennsylvania Dutch Country Cooking

Chickweed Pie

Hinkeldarremkuche

This very old recipe was never written down until I convinced an elderly cousin of mine to work through it so that I could weigh and measure step-by-step. I am certain that the pie was originally baked in a yeast-raised crust, but sometime in the nineteenth century there was a shift to short pastry. I now have the redware dish that my cousin used all her life to bake the pie in. After I had baked it myself several times, I was startled to learn from a ceramics specialist that it dated from the 1790s. Had the Bucklich Mennli *known, surely it would have cracked in half right before my eyes.*

Although it is best served hot, Chickweed Pie will keep for 1 to 2 days in the refrigerator and can be reheated in a microwave oven.

Some advice about harvesting chickweed. Stellaria media *grows like a mat against the ground. It is at its peak for culinary purposes right before it blooms. When the plant blossoms, it is covered with tiny white starlike flowers. These go to seed, and in the early fall another crop appears.*

YIELD: 6 TO 8 SERVINGS

3 cups (250 g) finely chopped chickweed
1 cup (185 g) diced slab bacon
½ cup (75 g) finely chopped onion
3 large eggs
1½ cups (375 ml) sour cream
1 tablespoon all-purpose flour
½ teaspoon grated nutmeg

Preheat the oven to 325°F (165°C). Line a 10-inch (26-cm) pie dish with short crust. Make a raised border around the rim to prevent the filling from overflowing during baking. Pick the chickweed clean of dead leaves and twigs that may have become tangled in it as it grew. Trim off the root ends of the stems, reserving only the greenest and leafiest parts. Rinse thoroughly in a colander, then pat dry with paper towels.

Bunch the chickweed together into a ball and chop it with a sharp knife, or put it into a food processor and process with the chopping blade until reduced to a confetti texture. Measure out 3 cups (250 g) and place into a large bowl.

Fry the diced bacon in a skillet until it begins to brown, then add the onion. Cook until the onion wilts (about 3 minutes). Remove the bacon and onion mixture with a slotted spoon and add to the chickweed. Discard the drippings from the pan. Beat the eggs until lemon colored, then add the sour cream, flour, and nutmeg. Combine the egg mixture with the chickweed and bacon.

Spread the filling evenly in the prepared pie shell, and pat down firmly with a spoon. Bake for 1 hour. The pie is done when it has set in the center and has developed a golden tinge across the top.

NOTE: Less adventuresome cooks may substitute 4 cups (260 g) finely chopped spinach for the chickweed. This, of course, changes the recipe to *Schpinatkuche* (Spinach Pie).

Common chickweed (Stellaria media) *makes a delicious lunch pie in early spring or fall.*

ROBERTSON

Laurel's Kitchen

Falafel

1 medium potato
1 large bunch parsley or coriander
2 small onions
3 tablespoons oil
3 cups cooked, ground garbanzo beans
¼ cup sesame seed meal
1 tablespoon yogurt
⅛ teaspoon garlic powder
1 tablespoon salt
dash cayenne
⅛ teaspoon pepper
1 teaspoon paprika
juice of 1 lemon

Traditionally, falafel (garbanzo balls) are served as a filling for Arab Bread with fresh shredded vegetables and yogurt. The result is somewhat like a taco, but with its own quite distinctive savour.

Cook and mash potato and set aside. Mince leaves of parsley.

Preheat oven to 350°.

Chop onions fine and sauté in oil until soft. Stir in parsley and cook briefly. Add to ground beans. Mix well with remaining ingredients. Form into balls or shape into patties, using about 2 tablespoons of the mixture for each one. Place on greased cookie sheets and bake for 10 minutes on each side.

MAKES ABOUT 24

KAFKA

Microwave Gourmet

Soft Polenta

The Italians are the most convincing thieves in the culinary business. They took our tomatoes and made us think they were as Italian as pasta. Then they took our cornmeal mush and convinced us they knew more about it. They do grind corn differently than we do, coarser; but whether using Italian-grind polenta or American cornmeal, yellow or white, this is a wonderful accompaniment to all sorts of foods. You can serve it (with or without Gorgonzola cheese) drizzled with the pan juices of roasted meats or birds, with grilled fish or with rich stews.

I think polenta has been less popular than potatoes because, cooked on top of the stove, it demands long and constant stirring, and even then there are likely to be lumps. Also, it has always worked best in quantity: no polenta for one or two. With the microwave oven, the polenta is stirred only once during the entire cooking time; it is guaranteed lumpless, and it can be made for one or for a crowd. If you can cook this in a serving dish, choose one with a cover; it will prevent the polenta from forming a skin and will, at the same time, keep it hot. **SERVES 8 AS A SIDE DISH.**

4 cups water
¾ cup yellow or white cornmeal
2 teaspoons kosher salt
3 tablespoons unsalted butter
⅛ teaspoon freshly ground black pepper
¼ cup softened Gorgonzola cheese or ¼ cup additional butter

1. Combine water, cornmeal, and salt in a 2-quart soufflé dish. Cook, uncovered, at 100% for 6 minutes. Stir well, cover loosely with paper toweling, and cook for 6 minutes more. (If using a small oven, cook uncovered for 9 minutes; cover loosely and cook for 9 minutes.)

2. Remove from oven. Uncover and stir in butter, pepper, and cheese (or additional butter). Let stand for 3 minutes. Serve hot.

TO SERVE 1 OR 2. Quarter all ingredients (use 3 tablespoons cornmeal). Proceed as for Soft Polenta, cooking in a soup bowl for 1 minute 30 seconds, uncovered, and then for another 1 minute 30 seconds, covered.

TO SERVE 3 OR 4. Combine 2½ cups water, ½ cup cornmeal, and 1 teaspoon salt in an 8-cup glass measure. Cook as for Soft Polenta for 5 minutes. Stir and continue cooking for 5 minutes longer. Finish as for Soft Polenta, stirring in 2 tablespoons butter and a pinch of pepper.

VARIATION

SPICY POLENTA Use Monterey Jack or fresh goat cheese instead of Gorgonzola and add 1 jalapeño pepper, stemmed, seeded, and chopped.

BASTIANICH
La Cucina di Lidia

Polenta con Fonduta e Funghi Porcini

Polenta with Fontina and Porcini Mushrooms

SERVES 6

This dish derives from a Piedmontese specialty. Polenta and cheese are quite complementary, and porcini work well with both.

- ½ pound Italian Fontina cheese
- 1 cup milk
- 2 tablespoons soft unsalted butter
- 2 egg yolks
- Salt to taste
- 1 walnut-size white truffle from Alba, brushed clean (optional)
- Polenta
- ½ pound porcini
- Olive oil to sauté

Preheat the broiler. Cut the Fontina in ½" cubes and soak in the milk for 1 hour. Transfer to a double boiler and cook gently until cheese is melted. Add the soft butter and the egg yolks, one at a time, and mix well. Add salt to taste. If used, shave the rough corners of the truffle into the *fonduta,* and mix.

Grill or pan-brown the polenta slices for a few minutes on each side. Place in a large gratin dish in a single layer and top with very hot *fonduta.* Set under the broiler until golden, about 1 minute. In the meantime, sauté the porcini and serve with the polenta, shaving truffle over the dish if desired.

RECOMMENDED WINE—On a chilly fall evening, my choice would be either a Gattinara or a Spanna. Reliable producers include Antoniolo, Nervi, Trovaglini, and Vallana.

FARMER
The Boston Cooking-School Cook Book

Fried Corn Meal Mush, or Fried Hominy

Pack corn meal or hominy mush in greased, one pound baking-powder boxes, or small bread pan, cool, and cover. Cut in thin slices, and sauté; cook slowly, if preferred crisp and dry. Where mushes are cooked to fry, use less water in steaming.

FARMER
The Boston Cooking-School Cook Book

Boston Baked Beans

Pick over one quart pea beans, cover with cold water, and soak over night. In morning, drain, cover with fresh water, heat slowly (keeping water below boiling point), and cook until skins will burst,—which is best determined by taking a few beans on the tip of a spoon and blowing on them, when skins will burst if sufficiently cooked. Beans thus tested must, of course, be thrown away. Drain beans, throwing bean-water out of doors, not in sink. Scald rind of one-half pound fat salt pork, scraped, remove one-fourth inch slice and put in bottom of bean-pot. Cut through rind of remaining pork every one-half inch, making cuts one inch deep. Put beans in pot and bury pork in beans, leaving rind exposed. Mix one tablespoon salt, one tablespoon molasses, and three tablespoons sugar; add one cup boiling water, and pour over beans; then add enough more boiling water to cover beans. Cover bean-pot, put in oven, and bake slowly six or eight hours, uncovering the last hour of cooking, that rind may become brown and crisp. Add water as needed. Many feel sure that by adding with seasonings one-half tablespoon mustard, the beans are more easily digested. If pork mixed with lean is preferred, use less salt.

The fine reputation which Boston Baked Beans have gained, has been attributed to the earthen bean-pot with small top and bulging sides in which they are supposed to be cooked. Equally good beans have often been eaten where a five-pound lard pail was substituted for the broken bean-pot.

Yellow-eyed beans are very good when baked.

LA PLACE AND KLEIMAN
Cucina Fresca

White Beans with Sage

This dish is served at the most elegant Florentine restaurants. Americans tend to scorn the bean, considering it a lowly budget-stretcher. That it is economical cannot be denied, but served as a side dish with a tablespoon of fine extra-virgin olive oil, White Beans with Sage often outclasses the accompanying entrée. The elegance of the dish, however, rests in its whole-bean presentation. Overcooked, or cooked too rapidly, the beans can split and become mushy and unappealing. They should be cooked slowly over very low heat so that they do not move with the movement of the water. Cooked this way just until tender, each bean remains separate and whole.

- 1 pound dry small white, or Great Northern beans
- 2½ quarts water
- 1 large garlic clove, peeled
- 1 handful fresh sage leaves, or 1 teaspoon dried sage leaves, crumbled
- Coarse salt and freshly ground pepper to taste
- Fruity olive oil

Place the beans, water, garlic, sage, and salt in a heavy cooking pot, preferably earthenware. Cover and place on heat so low that it will take almost an hour for the water to boil. Once the liquid comes to a boil, regulate the heat so that the liquid barely simmers. The beans must not move around during the cooking as it will cause them to break up. If the water level drops greatly, carefully add boiling water. The length of time it takes for the beans to cook depends on their age, but count on at least 3 hours. The beans should retain their shape but be tender to the bite. Cool to room temperature and serve as a side dish. Season to taste. Have fruity olive oil on the table to drizzle on top. **SERVES 6 TO 8.**

SAHNI
Classic Indian Vegetarian and Grain Cooking

Bengal Red Lentils with Spices

Bengali Masar Dal

Of all the legumes available in India, the Bengalis favor red lentils the most, and they inevitably prepare them in one classic way. In this technique the lentils are first cooked with turmeric and green chilies until they become a puree. This smooth puree is infused with two flavorings. The first, consisting of fixed seasonings, is added near the end, while the lentils are cooking. The second, the perfumed butter with chili pods, garlic, and whole spices, is gently folded into the dal *just before it is served. The resulting dal is spicy, utterly delicious, and my very favorite. I love it with plain rice and a simple vegetable preparation on the side.*

FOR 6–8 PERSONS

FOR COOKING THE *DAL*
- 1½ cups red lentils (*masar dal*)
- 6 hot green chilies
- ½ teaspoon turmeric
- 4½ cups water
- 1½ teaspoons coarse salt, or to taste

FOR FLAVORING THE *DAL*
- 4 tablespoons *usli ghee* or light vegetable oil
- 1 cup minced onion
- 1 tablespoon grated or crushed fresh ginger
- 1 cup finely chopped tomatoes

FOR THE SPICE-PERFUMED BUTTER
- 2 tablespoons *usli ghee*, or light vegetable oil
- 1 tablespoon *panch phoron* mix
- 4 bay leaves
- 4 dry red chili pods
- 2 teaspoons minced garlic (optional)

1. Pick clean, wash, and cook the *dal* using red lentils, green chilies, turmeric, salt, and 4½ cups of water.

2. While the lentils are cooking, heat the *usli ghee* in a large frying pan over medium-high heat. When it is hot, add the onion and fry, stirring constantly, until golden brown (about 10 minutes). Add the ginger and tomatoes and continue frying until the tomatoes are cooked and the contents reduce to a thick pulp (about 8 minutes). Stir constantly to prevent sticking and burning.

3. Blend the fried onion-tomato paste and salt to taste into the dal; continue cooking for an additional 10 to 15 minutes or until the flavors have blended in. Keep the dal on a low simmer while you make the spice-perfumed butter.

4. Measure out the spices and place them right next to the stove in separate piles. Heat the *usli ghee* in a small frying pan over medium-high heat. When it is hot, add the *panch phoron* spice blend. When the mustard seeds are spattering and the cumin turns a little darker (about 15 seconds), add the bay leaves and chili pods. Continue frying until the chili turns dark (15–20 seconds), turning and tossing them. Turn off the heat, add the garlic, and let mixture fry, sizzling for 25 seconds or until it looks light golden. Pour the entire contents of the pan over the *dal*, mix well, and serve.

RODEN

A Book of Middle Eastern Food

Megadarra

Here is a modern version of a medieval dish called mujadarra, *described by al-Baghdadi as a dish of the poor, and still known today as Esau's favorite. In fact, it is such a great favorite that although said to be for misers, it is a compliment to serve it.*

An aunt of mine used to present it regularly to guests with the comment: "Excuse the food of the poor!"—to which the unanimous reply always was: "Keep your food of kings and give us megadarra *every day!"*

The proportions for this lentil and rice dish vary with every family. Here is my family recipe for rather a large quantity. Whereas I have used twice the weight of rice to lentils, many other people use equal amounts. Today, meat is not included as it was in the medieval recipe.

- 2 cups large brown lentils, soaked if required
- 1 onion, finely chopped
- Oil
- Salt and black pepper
- 1 cup long-grain rice, washed
- 2 onions, sliced into half-moon shapes

Boil lentils in a fresh portion of water to cover for ¾ to 1½ hours, or until tender. Fry the chopped onion in 2 tablespoons oil until soft and golden. Add it to the lentils and season to taste with salt and pepper. Mix well and add rice, together with enough water to make the liquid in the pan up to 2 cups. Season again and simmer gently, covered, for about 20 minutes until the rice is soft and well cooked, adding a little more water if it becomes absorbed too quickly.

Fry the sliced onions in 2 tablespoons very hot oil until they are dark brown and sweet, almost caramelized.

Serve the rice and lentils on a large shallow dish, garnished with fried onion slices.

This dish is delicious served either hot or cold, and accompanied by yogurt.

Condiments, Pickles, and Jams

ZIEMANN AND GILETTE
The White House Cook Book

Tomato Catsup. No. 1

Put into two quarts of tomato pulp (or two cans of canned tomatoes) one onion, cut fine, two tablespoonfuls of salt and three tablespoonfuls of brown sugar. Boil until quite thick; then take from the fire and strain it through a sieve, working it until it is all through but the seeds. Put it back on the stove, and add two tablespoonfuls of mustard, one of allspice, one of black pepper and one of cinnamon, one teaspoonful of ground cloves, half a teaspoonful of cayenne pepper, one grated nutmeg, one pint of good vinegar; boil it until it will just run from the mouth of a bottle. It should be watched, stirred often, that it does not burn. If sealed tight while *hot*, in large-mouthed bottles, it will keep good for years.

RORER
Mrs. Rorer's New Cook Book

Mushroom Catsup

Wash and slice two quarts of mushrooms. Put a layer in the bottom of a stone jar. Sprinkle over a teaspoonful of salt, then another layer of mushrooms, another teaspoonful of salt, and so continue until the jar is full. Cover and stand aside over night. Next day drain the liquor from the mushrooms and chop them fine. Measure the liquor; put it into a porcelain lined kettle and to each pint allow a saltspoonful of pepper, a blade of mace, two whole cloves, a teaspoonful of mustard seed, a saltspoonful of ground ginger, and two bay leaves. Boil five minutes; strain; add the mushrooms; boil again five minutes, take from the fire, add a half cup of port wine, bottle, cork and seal.

HIRTZLER
The Hotel St. Francis Cook Book

Thousand Island dressing, for salads

Two soupspoonfuls of mayonnaise, one soupspoonful of Chili sauce, one soupspoonful of French dressing, one teaspoonful of chopped pimentos, one-half teaspoonful of chopped olives, salt and pepper, all well mixed. Use a very cold salad bowl.

HAZAN
The Classic Italian Cook Book

Blender Pesto

ENOUGH FOR ABOUT 6 SERVINGS OF PASTA

- 2 cups fresh basil leaves (see note below)
- ½ cup olive oil
- 2 tablespoons pine nuts
- 2 cloves garlic, lightly crushed with a heavy knife handle and peeled
- 1 teaspoon salt
- ½ cup freshly grated Parmesan cheese
- 2 tablespoons freshly grated Romano pecorino cheese
- 3 tablespoons butter, softened to room temperature

1. Put the basil, olive oil, pine nuts, garlic cloves, and salt in the blender and mix at high speed. Stop from time to time and scrape the ingredients down toward the bottom of the blender cup with a rubber spatula.

2. When the ingredients are evenly blended, pour into a bowl and beat in the two grated cheeses by hand. (This is not much work, and it results in more interesting texture and better flavor than you get when you mix in the cheese in the blender.) When the cheese has been evenly incorporated into the other ingredients, beat in the softened butter.

3. Before spooning the pesto over pasta, add to it a tablespoon or so of the hot water in which the pasta has boiled.

NOTE: The quantity of basil in most recipes is given in terms of whole leaves. American basil, however, varies greatly in leaf sizes. There are small, medium, and very large leaves, and they all pack differently in the measuring cup. For the sake of accurate measurement, I suggest that you tear all but the tiniest leaves into two or more small pieces. Be gentle, so as not to crush the basil. This would discolor it and waste the first, fresh droplets of juice.

COST

Bruce Cost's Asian Ingredients

This delicious green sauce, to be tossed with warm or cold fresh egg noodles, captures the essential flavors of Southeast Asia. Many who have tasted it prefer it to its Italian counterpart. It will keep for a week or so in a jar in the refrigerator if topped with a little oil.

Asian "Pesto"

(A Southeast Asian Herb Sauce for Noodles)

YIELD: 2½ CUPS

- 1½ cups Asian basil leaves (tightly packed)
- ¼ cup Asian mint leaves (tightly packed)
- ¼ cup coriander leaves (tightly packed)
- 1 cup peanut oil
- ½ cup raw peanuts
- 2 small fresh green chili peppers
- 1 tablespoon coarsely chopped ginger
- 4 large garlic cloves
- 1½ teaspoons salt
- 1 teaspoon sugar
- 3 tablespoons fresh lemon juice

Combine the herbs in a small bowl and set aside.

Heat the oil in a small skillet until nearly smoking, then remove from the heat and add the peanuts. Allow to sit until lightly browned. Remove the nuts with a slotted spoon and drain, reserving the oil.

Put the peanuts in a food processor or blender and blend to a rough paste. Add the chilis, ginger, and garlic, and continue to blend. Add the herbs and a little of the reserved oil, and continue to blend. Add the salt, sugar and lemon juice, and blend until the herbs are very finely minced.

Transfer the mixture to a serving bowl and stir in the remaining oil. Serve alongside warm or cold noodles, and allow each eater to spoon sauce to taste over a helping of noodles.

NOTE: This quantity of pesto, about 2½ cups, will be more than adequate for a pound of fresh noodles.

LAUREL

Living on the Earth

Yogurt

Heat milk to wrist temperature (don't boil) and stir in one tablespoon yogurt per pint of milk. Pour into small glass jars. Leave them in the sun all day if it is warm and sunny. Or leave in a warm place (near stove). Or if it's sunny, but not warm, leave jars in a black box in the sun all day. Or put yogurt in a thermos bottle. Instant milk can also be used—or even evaporated milk—restored to normal consistency.

Store in a cool place after it reaches desired tanginess. Yogurt culture destroys toxic bacteria in the colon.

LA PLACE AND KLEIMAN

Cucina Fresca

Homemade Ricotta

This ricotta must be served just as it cools to really enjoy the farm-fresh dairy flavor, aroma, and light, moist texture. Refrigeration destroys the delicacy of the homemade cheese. Serve with green olives, lemon wedges, and good bread.

- 2 quarts whole milk
- 1 cup heavy cream
- 2–4 tablespoons lemon juice
- Coarse salt and freshly ground pepper to taste
- Fruity olive oil

Bring the milk and cream to a simmer very slowly in a saucepan. Turn off heat. Add the lemon juice a little at a time and stir. Use only enough lemon juice needed to curdle the milk and cream. The mixture should separate into curds and whey in a matter of seconds. When the mixture curdles, pour into a colander lined with a double thickness of dampened cheesecloth. Allow to drain at least 1 hour or until very thick. Place the drained ricotta on a serving platter. As soon as it has cooled, sprinkle with a generous amount of salt and a grind of black pepper. Drizzle with olive oil. Makes 2 cups. Serves 4 to 6 as a first course.

JAFFREY

An Invitation to Indian Cooking

Cucumber Raita

SERVES 4–6

This is a refreshing, cool yogurt and cucumber relish. In the hot summer months, it really takes the place of a salad.

1 cucumber
16 ounces (2 containers) plain yogurt
1 teaspoon salt
⅛ teaspoon freshly ground black pepper
½ teaspoon roasted, ground cumin seeds
⅛ teaspoon cayenne peppers (optional)
⅛ teaspoon paprika (for garnishing)

Peel and grate the cucumber.

Empty the yogurt into serving bowl and beat it well with a fork until it is smooth and pastelike.

Add the cucumber, salt, black pepper, roasted cumin (reserve a pinch for garnish), and cayenne to the bowl with the yogurt.

Sprinkle with paprika and the pinch of roasted cumin. Cover and refrigerate until ready to serve.

TO SERVE: Bring bowl of cold yogurt to the table. This relish goes well with nearly all Indian meals.

WOLFERT

Couscous and Other Good Food from Morocco

Preserved Lemons

Preserved lemons, sold loose in the souks, *are one of the indispensable ingredients of Moroccan cooking, used in fragrant lamb and vegetable* tagines, *recipes for chicken with lemons and olives, and salads. Their unique pickled taste and special silken texture cannot be duplicated with fresh lemon or lime juice, despite what some food writers have said. In Morocco they are made with a mixture of fragrant-skinned* doqq *and tart* boussera *lemons, but I have had excellent luck with American lemons from Florida and California.*

Moroccan Jews have a slightly different procedure for pickling, which involves the use of olive oil, but this recipe, which includes optional herbs (in the manner of Safi), will produce a true Moroccan preserved-lemon taste.

The important thing in preserving lemons is to be certain they are completely covered with salted lemon juice. With my recipe you can use the lemon juice over and over again. (As a matter of fact, I keep a jar of used pickling juice in the kitchen, and when I make Bloody Marys or salad dressings and have a half lemon left over, I toss it into the jar and let it marinate with the rest.)

Sometimes you will see a sort of lacy, white substance clinging to preserved lemons in their jar; it is perfectly harmless, but should be rinsed off for aesthetic reasons just before the lemons are used. Preserved lemons are rinsed, in any case, to rid them of their salty taste. Cook with both pulps and rinds, if desired.

INGREDIENTS
5 lemons
¼ cup salt, more if desired

OPTIONAL SOFT MIXTURE
1 cinnamon stick
3 cloves
5 to 6 coriander seeds
3 to 4 black peppercorns
1 bay leaf
Freshly squeezed lemon juice, if necessary

EQUIPMENT
Shallow bowl
Sterile 1-pint mason jar
Sharp knife

WORKING TIME: 10 MINUTES
RIPENING TIME: 30 DAYS

1. If you wish to soften the peel, soak the lemons in lukewarm water for 3 days, changing the water daily.

2. Quarter the lemons from the top to within ½ inch of the bottom, sprinkle salt on the exposed flesh, then reshape the fruit.

3. Place 1 tablespoon salt on the bottom of the mason jar. Pack in the lemons and push them down, adding more salt, and the optional spices, between layers. Press the lemons down to release their juices and to make room for the remaining lemons. (If the juice released from the squashed fruit does not cover them, add freshly squeezed lemon juice—not chemically produced lemon juice and not water.*)
Leave some air space before sealing the jar.

4. Let the lemons ripen in a warm place, turning the jar upside down each day to distribute the salt and juice. Let ripen for 30 days.

To use, rinse the lemons, as needed, under running water, removing and discarding the pulp, if desired—and there is no need to refrigerate after opening. Preserved lemons will keep up to a year, and the pickling juice can be used two or three times over the course of a year.

VARIATION

AZIZA BENCHEKROUN'S FIVE-DAY PRESERVED LEMON SPECIAL

If you run out of preserved lemons, or decide on just a few days' notice to cook a chicken, lamb, or fish dish with lemons and olives and need preserved lemons in a hurry, you can use this quick five-day method taught to me by a Moroccan diplomat's wife. Lemons preserved this way will not keep, but are perfectly acceptable in an emergency.

With a razor blade, make 8 fine 2-inch vertical incisions around the peel of each lemon to be used. (Do not cut deeper than the membrane that protects the pulp.) Place the incised lemons in a stainless-steel saucepan with plenty of salt and water to cover and boil until the peels become very soft. Place in a clean jar, cover with cooled cooking liquor, and leave to pickle for approximately 5 days.

*According to the late Michael Field, the way to extract the maximum amount of juice from a lemon is to boil it in water for 2 or 3 minutes and allow it to cool before squeezing.

LESEM

The Pleasures of Preserving and Pickling

Spiced Cherries

Although spiced cherries set like jelly, they're more of a relish than a spread. Sometimes I add blanched halved or slivered almonds during the last 5 minutes of cooking to make a conserve. Either way, they're good with pork or turkey.

- 2 pounds ripe dark sweet cherries
- 3 cups sugar
- ¾ cup red wine vinegar
- ½ teaspoon ground mace
- ½ teaspoon ground cinnamon
- ⅛ teaspoon ground cloves
- ¼ to ½ cup blanched almond halves or slivers (optional)

Stem and pit the fruit, preferably with a plunger-type pitter that leaves the cherries whole.

Combine remaining ingredients in a wide 4-quart saucepan; bring quickly to boil, stirring to dissolve sugar. When the syrup boils, add the cherries all at once. Boil steadily, stirring occasionally, about 40 minutes, or until a teaspoon of syrup thickens in 2 to 3 minutes on a prechilled saucer in the coolest part of the refrigerator.

Pour while hot into hot, sterilized half-pint jars, and seal. Store at least 1 month. Makes about 4½ cups without almonds, about 5 cups with them.

WEAVER

Pennsylvania Dutch Country Cooking

Green Apple Pap

Griene Ebbelbrei

Pap *is an old-fashioned word for any food that is soft and purée-like. In this case the pap is served as a relish with poultry, such as cold fried chicken, or as a sauce.*

YIELD: 4 TO 6 SERVINGS

- 14 ounces (440 g) unripe green apples, peeled and cored (see note)
- ⅔ cup (160 ml) dry white wine
- 3 tablespoons (45 ml) extra-virgin olive oil
- ½ teaspoon ground mace
- ½ cup (100 g) sugar
- grated zest of 1 lime
- ¼ teaspoon cayenne pepper

Put the apples, wine, olive oil, mace, sugar, lime zest, and cayenne in a food processor and puree to a smooth, creamy consistency. Serve immediately

NOTE: Unripe Summer Rambos, Yellow Transparents, and Gravensteins are excellent choices for this recipe.

LESEM

The Pleasures of Preserving and Pickling

Bermuda Marmalade

This pale amber-colored marmalade is both an unusual spread for bread and a versatile cooking ingredient. Melted with orange or grapefruit juice, it makes a good glaze for baked ham or sautéed ham steak. It is also delicious in baked apples and as a glaze for baked or sautéed bananas. I've named it for Bermuda because it was inspired by a recipe in a collection called What's Cooking in Bermuda *by Betsy Ross (Elizabeth Ross Hunter).*

1 small (about ¾ pound) grapefruit
1 medium (about ¼ pound) lime
6 cups water
Sugar

Cut the grapefruit, lengthwise, into sixths, and the lime into quarters. Discard the white cores and remove seeds to a small pan of at least 1½ cups' capacity. Cover seeds with 1 cup of the water, and set aside at least 2 to 3 hours.

Strip peel from pulp. Slice pulp a scant ¼ inch thick. Slice peel ⅛ inch thick and 1½ to 2 inches long. Measure. You should have about 2¼ cups, packed, of pulp, juice, and peel. Place the mixture in a 2½- or 3-quart bowl. Cover with remaining 5 cups of water and let stand at least 2 or 3 hours.

Boil seeds 10 minutes to extract pectin while you bring the pulp, juice, peel, and water mixture quickly to boil in a wide 2½-quart saucepan. Strain the seed water into the larger pan, and continue boiling it for a total of about 1 hour, until peel is very tender.

Remove from heat and measure. You should have about 4⅓ cups. Stir in the same amount of sugar until no crystals remain. Measure about 4 cups of the stock back into the saucepan, bring quickly to a boil, stirring occasionally, and boil rapidly 10 to 15 minutes, or until peel is transparent and jell tests done. Stir and skim, if necessary, about 5 minutes to prevent floating peel. Pour into hot, scalded half-pint or 4-ounce glasses or jars, and seal. Repeat process, using remainder of stock. You'll probably need to cook the second batch the shorter time, because there's less stock for it than for the first batch. Store at least one week before using. Makes about 5 cups.

Amber Marmalade

This is a good example of making lots out of little. I first improvised the recipe to use up two oranges, a lemon, and a lone stalk of rhubarb left over from other recipes. The result was a lovely, amber-colored spread that tastes like mild, sweet orange marmalade. Try it some time on the bottom of the crust you use for apple pie.

2 medium oranges and 1 medium lemon
(total weight about 1 pound)
1 2- to 3-ounce stalk of rhubarb
Sugar

Thinly slice oranges and lemon, reserving seeds. Tie seeds loosely in two thicknesses of dampened cheesecloth or place in a metal tea ball. Measure fruit; you should have about 2 cups, tightly packed. Place the fruit in a 4-quart mixing bowl. Add three times as much water as you have fruit. Let stand, uncovered, about 24 hours.

The next day, slice rhubarb ¼ inch thick, discarding leaves. Place rhubarb-citrus mixture and bag of seeds in a wide 4-quart saucepan, bring quickly to boil, and boil rapidly 20 to 30 minutes, or until peel is tender and rhubarb has broken up. Stir occasionally.

Remove from heat and let stand uncovered about 24 hours more.

The next day, discard seed bag. Measure fruit mixture. You should have 5½ to 6 cups.

Place 3 cups of mixture in a wide 2½-quart saucepan. Add 3 cups of sugar, stir to dissolve, and bring to boil over medium heat, stirring occasionally. Boil rapidly 15 to 20 minutes, or until jell tests done.

Remove from heat, and skim and stir for about 5 minutes to prevent floating peel. Pour into hot, scalded half-pint jars or glasses and seal at once.

Repeat with remaining fruit mixture and an equal amount of sugar.

Store at least 1 week. Makes about 6 cups.

LESEM

The Pleasures of Preserving and Pickling

Mystery Marmalade

I call this mystery marmalade because few who see and taste it for the first time guess that the primary ingredient is carrots. The natural sweetness of carrots lends itself well to marmalade. And the color is splendid. The recipe is based on one published by the Royal Horticultural Society in London in 1928.

- 1½ pounds carrots, peeled and coarsely grated (about 4 cups)
- Juice and finely diced or ground peel of 2 small lemons
- 3¼ cups sugar

Cook grated carrots in water to cover in a wide 2½-quart saucepan about 15 minutes, or until tender, or steam until tender. Drain well.

Return cooked carrots to the pan. Add lemon juice and peel and sugar. Stir to dissolve sugar. Place over medium heat and continue to stir constantly until sugar has dissolved completely and mixture reaches boil.

Boil steadily about 45 minutes, or until thick, stirring occasionally to prevent sticking.

Ladle into hot, scalded half-pint jars and seal. This is best put up in screw-top jars instead of glasses. The marmalade texture makes a perfect paraffin seal hard to obtain.

Let stand at least 1 week to mellow. Makes about 3½ cups.

SAHNI

Classic Indian Vegetarian and Grain Cooking

Sweet and Spicy Tamarind Chutney

Imli Chatni

This is a very popular north Indian sauce for dipping fried food. For variation add a cup of peeled chopped unripe mango.

MAKES ABOUT 3 CUPS

- 4 ounces tamarind (about 1 tangerine-size ball)
- 2½ cups boiling water
- 1½ tablespoons paprika
- 1 tablespoon cayenne pepper
- 1 teaspoon dry ginger powder
- 2 teaspoons dry mango powder (or 2 tablespoons lemon juice)
- ½ teaspoon garam masala
- 2 teaspoons ground roasted cumin
- 1 teaspoon coarse salt, or to taste
- ¼ cup sugar

1. Put tamarind in a nonmetallic bowl and add 2 cups boiling water. Let soak for 30 minutes. Strain liquid, squeezing and mashing pulp to extract as much juice as possible, into another bowl. Add another ½ cup boiling water to the residue. When cool enough to handle, squeeze pulp again and strain the liquid. Measure the tamarind liquid. There should be 2¾ cups; if not, repeat until you have the required amount. Discard the fibrous residue.

2. Add all the other ingredients, mix well to blend, and serve.

Keeps well for three days, covered, in the refrigerator, and for six months in the freezer.

CUNNINGHAM
The Breakfast Book

Rhubarb Ginger Jam

This jam has an arresting, different taste. It is splendid on rye or coarse wheat toast. The rhubarb flavor is not hindered by the piquant ginger.

FOUR CUPS

About 2 pounds rhubarb, washed and cut into small pieces (to make 4 cups)
4 cups sugar (if tartness is desired, use only 3 cups)
¼ cup chopped unpeeled gingerroot

Put a layer of rhubarb in a shallow bowl, sprinkle with a layer of sugar, and continue layering until the last layer of rhubarb is covered with sugar. Cover the dish with plastic wrap and leave covered for 36 hours. Lots of juice will accumulate. Pour the juice into a saucepan. Tie the chopped ginger in a piece of muslin or cheesecloth. Put the ginger into the saucepan with the juice and boil for about 5 minutes. Add the rhubarb and simmer for about 15 minutes, or until the rhubarb begins to look translucent. Cool and transfer to sealed jars if storing for an indefinite time; or cover and refrigerate until needed. This will keep for a couple of weeks in the refrigerator, or a few months in the freezer.

JUNIOR LEAGUE OF CHARLESTON
Charleston Receipts

Shrimp Paste

1 plate or 1½ pounds shrimp
¼ pound butter
Dash of mace
¼ to ½ teaspoon dry mustard
Salt and black pepper
10 drops onion juice
1 tablespoon sherry wine

Boil shrimp in salted water, peel and pound in mortar or run through fine meat grinder. Mix thoroughly with butter and add rest of ingredients. Let chill in refrigerator until ready to serve.

Mrs. Lawrence Lucas (Nell Hall)

JUNIOR LEAGUE OF AUGUSTA
Old and New Recipes from the South

Green Tomato Pickle

1 peck green tomatoes
2 bell peppers
8 large onions

Sprinkle over this 4 tablespoons salt and let stand overnight. Make a sauce of:

1 lb. brown sugar
1 lb. white sugar
1 dime box mustard
1 tablespoon each of celery seed and mustard seed
½ box turmeric
Teaspoon black pepper
Teaspoon cloves

Put all together and cook until tender.

—Mrs. Will Evans, Waynesboro, Ga.

DULL
Southern Cooking

Watermelon Rind Pickles

½ gallon of cut watermelon rind
1 quart apple vinegar
½ ounce whole cloves
½ ounce whole mace
1 ounce white mustard seed
2 lbs. sugar

Cut the rind in small pieces, about two-inch cubes; pack in brine until ready to use. Put a layer of rind and a light layer of salt; let stand until ready to make up. Soak in water over-night or until they are fresh. Then boil in weak alum water until they are firm and brittle. Boil again in plain water to remove the alum, and the rinds clear.

Put sugar and spices into vinegar; boil together for five minutes. Add rind and boil gently for 10 minutes. Put rinds into a jar; pour the hot vinegar over, having the jar full; seal. They will be ready to use in a few days.

LESEM

The Pleasures of Preserving and Pickling

Mustard Pickles

Crispness, tartness, and a pronounced mustard flavor are what I look for in this type of pickle. The vegetables remain crunchy because they're not cooked, but only heated, first in the soaking water and then in the sauce. On a hot summer's day, I like mustard pickles with cold roast beef, pumpernickel bread, and a glass of cold beer. They're also good with any cold meat or sausages.

- 1 pound small, unwaxed cucumbers (preferably no more than 1-inch diameter), cut in ½-inch crosswise slices (about 1 quart)
- ¾ pound small white onions (1-inch diameter), scalded and peeled
- 1 pound hard green cherry tomatoes, halved, or larger tomatoes, cut in 1-inch chunks
- ½ pound cauliflowerets (about 2½ cups)
- ½ pound bell peppers, stemmed, seeded, and cut in ¼-inch chunks (about 1⅓ cups)
- ½ cup uniodized table salt or pickling salt or ½ cup plus 3 tablespoons coarse (kosher) salt
- 5 cups water
- ½ cup flour
- 1 teaspoon ground turmeric
- 3 tablespoons dry mustard
- 1 teaspoon celery seed
- 1 teaspoon mustard seed
- ½ teaspoon each whole cloves and whole allspice, tied loosely in a double thickness of damp cheesecloth or placed in a metal tea ball
- 1 cup packed, light brown sugar
- 4 cups cider vinegar

Place cucumbers, onions, tomatoes, cauliflowerets, peppers, salt, and water in a 3-quart bowl (not aluminum), Stir well to dissolve salt. Weight the vegetables with a plate and a jar filled with water. Let stand 18 to 24 hours.

The next day, heat the vegetables in the brine in a wide 4-quart saucepan, stirring often, until they are hot to the touch. Drain well in colander.

While the vegetables heat, mix the flour, spices, and sugar in a wide 4-quart saucepan, Gradually stir in the vinegar. Place over medium heat, and stir constantly until mixture is as thick as heavy cream sauce.

Add the hot, well-drained vegetables and continue stirring until they are very hot and sauce is boiling. Adjust heat to keep mixture hot while you quickly pack the pickles in hot, sterilized pint jars. Vegetables should come within ¾ inch of top, and sauce should cover them within ¼ inch of top. Seal. Store at least a month before using. Makes about 5 pints.

Pasta, Noodles, and Rice

PASTA AND NOODLES

BUGIALLI

The Fine Art of Italian Cooking

Fresh Pasta

This is the basic "yellow" egg pasta. It is cut into taglierini, tagliatelle *(fettucine)*, pappardelle, farfalle, *homemade spaghetti, and* penne *to be eaten with sauce. It is cut into* taglierini *(again) and* quadrucci *to be eaten with broth. And finally, it is used to make the stuffed pasta:* tortelli *(ravioli)*, tortellini, *and* cappelletti *(smaller tortellini for broth) and* cannelloni. *The squares made for* cannelloni *are also used to make the layered lasagne.*

- 1 cup all-purpose flour, preferably unbleached
- 1 "extra-large" egg
- 1 teaspoon olive oil or other vegetable oil
- Pinch of salt

The proportion of ingredients to each other is given, rather than a fixed amount per serving, because the amounts vary depending on which dish the pasta is being made for. Definite amounts are given in ingredients for each recipe.

FLOUR: Unbleached all-purpose flour in America is not significantly different from Italian flour used for making pasta. (Semolina is almost never used in Italy to make fresh pasta.) Indeed, since much of the wheat used in Italy is imported, some of it is probably American. The difference in method of grinding becomes significant only for dark flour used in making bread. Unbleached flour is preferable, but bleached is also usable. All-purpose flour is generally partially sifted and states this on the package. Use it as it comes, without additional sifting.

EGGS: If you use "large" instead of "extra-large" eggs, you will need an extra egg for every 5 or 6. If the eggs are still smaller, add an extra one for every 3 or 4. Flour absorbs less egg in damp weather, so you may have to add a little more egg under such conditions.

OIL: If you do not use olive oil, be sure that the vegetable oil you do use is one such as safflower or peanut oil, which does not have a strong taste.

Tuscan fresh pasta varies from that of the Bologna region. Oil and salt are used in Tuscany, and the pasta is generally rolled finer. A little oil makes the pasta more flexible so it can be rolled a little finer, and is lighter when cooked. This pasta when stuffed can be sealed without being dampened, or if left to dry a little, may be sealed by being dampened very slightly with a finger dipped in water.

I repeat that the amount of pasta necessary for each serving varies, especially according to whether it is used with sauce or with broth, or again whether it is to be filled. The proportion of the ingredients remains the same. See each individual recipe for specific amounts.

Making fresh pasta is an area in which I take a slightly heretical position. I believe that pasta made with a pasta machine is at least as good as that rolled out with a wooden rolling pin. Perhaps this is because I have the Tuscan preference for pasta that is fine and soft. (The Bolognese *sfoglia* of 1 millimeter is too thick for my taste.) Taking the pasta machine's roller to the last notch, it can be made even finer. The little oil in the Tuscan pasta makes that fineness possible, without holes.

Hand-rolled pasta is necessary, however, for dishes that require a large single sheet, wider than is possible with the machine, such as the *rotolo di pasta ripieno*, where the hand rolling process is described. Even by hand, however, I still prefer it finer than the thickness that is usual in Bologna or in the south of Italy.

PASTA BOARD: A pasta board 18 × 26 inches provides a good wooden surface to work on.

ROLLING PIN: The long, thin Italian rolling pin is difficult to find here, but I see no reason why the American rolling pin, which is shorter and rotates, cannot be used equally well. The rotary action actually makes it easier to use.

PASTA MACHINE: When you invest in a pasta machine, be careful of the trademark. They are not equally good, and some of the brands that are most often imported are inferior. Among the brands I find satisfactory is the Imperia. Use of the different parts of the machine is explained below.

MAKING FRESH PASTA

Place the flour in a mound on a pasta board. Make a well in the center and put in the egg, olive oil, and salt. With a fork, first mix together the yolk, white, oil, and salt, then begin to incorporate the flour from the inner rim of the well, always incorporating fresh flour from the lower part, pushing it under the dough to keep the dough detached.

When half of the flour has been absorbed, start kneading, always using the palms of your hands, not the fingers. Continue absorbing the flour until almost all of it has been incorporated. The small fraction of flour that remains unabsorbed should be passed through a sifter to remove bits of dough and kept to coat dough during the succeeding steps. Now you are ready to use the pasta machine.

The machine has two main parts, one for rolling, the other for cutting. The first part of the machine consists of two rollers, the distance between which can be adjusted by a little wheel on the side. On the opposite side fits a detachable handle, to turn the rollers. The second part, for cutting, is sometimes detachable. It consists of two rows of teeth, one to cut into narrow strips (*taglierini*), the other wide (the width of *tagliatelle*).

Attach the machine to your table by tightening the clamp at the bottom. Set the wheel for the rollers at the widest setting.

If the dough has been made with more than one egg, cut it into the same number of pieces as eggs. Repeat the following steps with each piece of dough.

Turning the handle, pass the dough through the rollers. Fold the dough into thirds and press down. Sprinkle with flour and repeat the rolling and folding eight to ten times, until the dough is very smooth. (These steps take the place of hand kneading.)

Move the wheel to the next notch, which places the rollers a little closer together. Pass dough through rollers once; do not fold. Move the wheel to each successive notch, each time passing the dough through the rollers once. After passing each time, sprinkle the dough with a little flour. Each successive notch produces a thinner layer of pasta. Stop when the layer reaches the thickness desired; I always go to the last notch.

CAUTION: Beginning with the step in which you first pass the pasta through the rollers without folding, do not hold it with your fingers, but let it hang over your whole left hand.

When the long sheet of pasta has finished passing through the rollers, take the end gently in your fingers and carefully pull the layer out to its full length, free of folds. Sprinkle a cotton dishtowel with flour and lay the sheet of pasta upon it to dry for 10 minutes before cutting. If the kitchen is hot or drafty, cover the pasta with another dishtowel.

BUGIALLI
The Fine Art of Italian Cooking

Spaghetti alla Fiaccheraia

Spaghetti, Coachmen's Style

SERVES 4

A very spicy red-peppery dish that is Tuscan, but also close to similar dishes in other parts of Italy—a dish that should give lie to the idea that red-peppery dishes exist only in the south of Italy. The name means "in the style of coachmen," who are supposed to be the prototypical tough, rough-hewn city types in Italy.

- 2 ounces *pancetta* or 1 pounce of boiled ham plus 1 ounce of salt pork
- 5 tablespoons olive oil
- 1 small red onion
- 1 cup canned tomatoes
- 1 tablespoon tomato paste
- Salt and freshly ground black pepper to taste
- ½ teaspoon hot pepper flakes
- 1 pound spaghetti
- ¼ cup freshly grated Parmigiano or Romano cheese

Chop the *pancetta* (or boiled ham and salt pork) coarsely.

Heat the olive oil in a saucepan. When it is hot, add the *pancetta* and sauté until golden brown (about 15 minutes). Meanwhile, chop the onion coarsely.

Remove the *pancetta* from the saucepan with a slotted spoon and set it aside. Add the onion to the oil in the saucepan and sauté gently until soft and golden brown (about 15 minutes). Add the tomatoes and tomato paste, then taste for salt and pepper and add the hot pepper flakes. Reduce the sauce very slowly for about 20 minutes.

While the sauce is reducing, place a stockpot containing a large quantity of salted water on the heat. When the water boils, add the spaghetti and cook until al dente (about 12 minutes, depending on the brand).

When the sauce is reduced and the spaghetti almost cooked, place the *pancetta* back in the sauce and simmer it for 1 minute more. Remove the pan from the flame.

Drain the spaghetti in a colander and place it in a serving bowl. Pour the sauce on top and sprinkle with the Parmigiano. Toss very well and serve hot.

NOTE: No extra cheese should be added at the table.

ROSSO AND LUKINS
The Silver Palate Cookbook

Pasta Puttanesca

It is not known whether the Italian ladies of the night (the puttane*) who gave their name to this racy pasta sauce did so because they were short of time or cash or both. In any case,* puttanesca *is quick and cheap and we hope it offends no one's memory to say so.*

This dish, with its zesty nuggets of garlic, capers, olives and anchovies, is not for the faint-hearted. Serve it to food-loving friends and pour an earthy red wine. With practice you can have this sauce ready to eat in 20 minutes.

- 1 pound spaghetti, linquine or other thin dried pasta
- 2 cans (2 pounds, 3 ounces each) peeled Italian plum tomatoes
- ¼ cup best-quality olive oil
- 1 teaspoon oregano
- ⅛ teaspoon dried red pepper flakes, or to taste
- ½ cup tiny black Niçoise olives
- ¼ cup drained capers
- 4 garlic cloves, peeled and chopped
- 8 anchovy fillets, coarsely chopped
- ½ cup chopped Italian parsley, plus additional for garnish
- 2 tablespoons salt

1. Bring 4 quarts water to a boil in a large pot. Add salt and stir in the spaghetti. Cook until tender but still firm. Drain immediately when done and transfer to 4 heated plates.

2. While spaghetti is cooking, drain the tomatoes, cut them crosswise into halves, and squeeze out as much liquid as possible.

3. Combine tomatoes and olive oil in a skillet and bring to a boil. Keep the sauce at a full boil and add remaining ingredients except pasta, one at a time, stirring frequently.

4. Reduce heat slightly and continue to cook for a few minutes, or until sauce has thickened to your liking. Serve immediately over hot pasta and garnish with additional chopped parsley.

4 MAIN-COURSE PORTIONS

BUGIALLI
The Fine Art of Italian Cooking

DRIED PASTA

There are scores of varieties of dried pasta. Italians feel that a particular shape and thickness lends itself best to certain sauces or treatments. And, conversely, each sauce has a particular dried pasta, or perhaps two, especially suited to it.

Dried pasta made in the south of Italy is still in a class by itself. For this reason I would recommend not merely imported pasta, but pasta made in Naples or Abruzzo. It is lighter and more finely made than versions made outside Italy, and fortunately it is widely available, especially in Italian markets in America.

Of the multitude of dried pasta dishes, I am going to suggest a limited number that I feel have culinary distinction, though they are often simple enough. Spaghetti (from spaghi, *meaning "little strings") remains the prototype and the most popular kind of dried pasta. I include five treatments that are best for this type of pasta and two more recipes, one for* chiocciole *(snails or shells) and another for* penne *(short tubular pasta). Most of these are Tuscan treatments, but several come from other parts of Italy. My principal criterion has been that they retain a relative lightness consistent with the approach in the rest of the book.*

Al dente cooking time for dried pasta is given as 12 minutes. With some brands, it may be as little as 8 minutes. Check package instructions.

Spaghetti alla Carbonara

Spaghetti with Egg-Pancetta Sauce

SERVES 4

This Roman dish is sometimes called "spaghetti with bacon and eggs" on tourist menus. Pancetta, *of course, is not bacon, because it is not smoked; do not substitute bacon. To make it well and with as much lightness as possible, cook the* pancetta *slowly to remove the fat. This recipe contains just enough* pancetta *fat and eggs to have all the sauce well incorporated. There is nothing worse in* carbonara *than to have excess fat and unincorporated egg sitting on the bottom. This version should give a spicy, but not greasy,* carbonara, *one that is as light as the dish can be.*

- 4 ounces *pancetta* or salt pork
- 2 large cloves garlic
- 3 tablespoon olive oil

- ½ teaspoon hot pepper flakes
- Salt
- 2 eggs
- ⅓ cup freshly grated Parmigiano cheese
- 1 pound spaghetti
- Freshly ground black pepper

Put a large quantity of salted water in a stockpot. Set on the heat.

While the water is heating, cut *pancetta* into small pieces and chop the garlic very fine. Put the *pancetta* and garlic in a saucepan with the olive oil, salt, and hot pepper flakes. (Salt should be added depending on the saltiness of the *pancetta; alla carbonara* should be rather salty.) Place the saucepan on very low heat for 12 to 15 minutes. The pancetta should brown very, very slowly, so that all the fat is rendered out.

In the meantime, beat the eggs and combine with the grated Parmigiano.

When the water reaches the boiling point, add the pasta and cook until it is al dente (about 12 minutes). Drain the spaghetti well, then place it in a serving bowl. Quickly spoon the hot contents of saucepan over it. Toss; then, just as quickly, add the eggs and Parmigiano. Grind black pepper plentifully over the dish, as it should be very peppery, then toss very well and serve hot.

DULL

Southern Cooking

Macaroni and Cheese

- ½ pound macaroni
- 1 cup cheese chips
- 3 tablespoons butter
- 1 teaspoon salt
- ⅛ teaspoon cayenne pepper
- ½ cup milk
- 1 egg
- ½ cup buttered bread crumbs

Break and boil macaroni in salt water until tender (about 20 minutes). Blanch in cold water to prevent sticking. Cover bottom of baking dish with layer of macaroni, a sprinkle of cheese, bits of butter, salt and pepper.

Continue until all is used, having cheese on top.

Mix milk and egg together, pour over the dish, cover top with crumbs, bake in moderate oven long enough to brown top and cook egg and milk. Serve in the same dish.

A thin white sauce is sometimes used instead of the milk and egg.

This dish, when left over, makes nice croquettes. Serve with tomato sauce.

KASPER

The Splendid Table

An Unusual Tortellini Pie

Pasticcio di Tortellini con Crema di Cannella

A lavish piece of the past, this tall pie with its sweet crust and layering of tortellini, ragù, and tiny meatballs is well-known feasting food in Emilia-Romagna, especially in Bologna and Romagna. What sets this recipe apart is the sweet, cinnamon-scented custard that is added just before the top crust is put in place. It accents the meaty flavors of the pie's filling.

Save tortellini pie for the most important of occasions. Although time-consuming to make, it is fully worth the effort. Prepare in easy stages. Each component can be done days ahead, and the pie is assembled and in the oven before guests arrive. The meatballs, ragù, and custard also stand on their own, as a fine antipasto, a dressing for pasta, and a sauce for desserts.

SERVES 12 AS A FIRST COURSE, 8 TO 10 AS A MAIN DISH

PASTRY

- 3½ cups (14 ounces) all-purpose unbleached flour (organic stone-ground preferred)
- 1 cup (4 ounces) cake flour
- ¼ teaspoon salt
- ¾ cup (5 ounces) sugar
- ½ teaspoon baking powder
- 1 teaspoon grated lemon zest
- 11 tablespoons (5½ ounces) unsalted butter, chilled, cut into chunks
- 3 large egg yolks
- 5 to 8 tablespoons dry white wine

WORKING AHEAD: *The pastry can be made 2 days ahead; wrap and refrigerate. Or freeze it up to 3 months. The custard keeps, covered, in the refrigerator 3 days, but it cannot be frozen. The meatballs can be made a day ahead and refrigerated overnight. Do not freeze them. The Baroque Ragù can be refrigerated, covered, up to 3 days, and frozen up to 1 month. Skin the fat from it before using.*

FOOD PROCESSOR METHOD: Combine the dry ingredients and the lemon zests in a food processor fitted with the steel blade. Blend 10 seconds. Add the butter, and process with the on/off pulse until the mixture looks like coarse meal. Turn off the machine. In a small bowl, beat together the yolks and 5 tablespoons of the wine. Add the mixture to the processor. Process with the on/off pulse until the dry ingredients are moistened and the dough begins to collect in clumps. If the dough seems dry, sprinkle with 2 or more tablespoons of wine, and process a second or two. Turn the pastry out onto a counter, gather it into a ball, wrap in plastic wrap, and chill at least 1 hour. Remove from the refrigerator about 30 minutes before rolling it out.

HAND METHOD: Using a fork, mix together the dry ingredients and the lemon zest in a large bowl. Add the butter. Use your fingertips to rub together the flour and butter until the mixture resembles coarse meal. Do not worry if there are a few larger pieces of butter. Make a well in the center; add the yolks and 5 tablespoons of wine. Beat the liquids with the fork to thoroughly blend. Toss with the dry ingredients. Avoid stirring or beating, which toughens the dough. If the dough is dry, sprinkle with another 2 or more tablespoons of wine, and toss to moisten. Once the dough is moist enough to be gathered into a ball, wrap in plastic wrap and refrigerate at least 1 hour. Remove from the refrigerator 30 minutes before rolling it out.

CINNAMON CUSTARD

4 egg yolks
5 tablespoons sugar
2 tablespoons plus 2½ teaspoons all-purpose unbleached flour (organic stone-ground preferred)
Dash of salt
2 cups milk, scalded
2 tablespoons unsalted butter
2 generous pinches of ground cinnamon

COOKING THE CUSTARD: In a heavy nonaluminum 3- to 4-quart saucepan, whisk together the yolks and sugar until light in color. Beat in the flour and salt. Slowly whisk in the hot milk until the custard is smooth. Set the saucepan over medium heat, and stir constantly with a wooden spatula to make sure nothing sticks to the bottom of the pan. Cook 3 minutes, or until the custard comes to a bubble. Then stir continuously at a slow bubble another 5 minutes, or until the custard is thick enough to coat the spatula with a sheet of custard that does not slip off easily. Check for doneness by tasting and making sure there is no flavor of raw flour. Pour the custard through a strainer into a bowl, stir in the butter and cinnamon, and cool. Lay a film of plastic wrap over the surface of the custard, and refrigerate it.

MEATBALLS

2 to 3 ounces Italian Parmigiano-Reggiano cheese, cut in chunks
7 tablespoons minced Italian parsley
1 large clove garlic
1 medium onion, coarsely chopped
10 ounces chicken thighs, boned, skinned, and cut into chunks
6 ounces pancetta, chopped
10 ounces ground lean beef round
1 tablespoon imported Italian tomato paste
¼ cup dried bread crumbs
1 egg, beaten
¼ teaspoon salt
⅛ teaspoon freshly ground black pepper
4 tablespoons vegetable oil
About ½ cup water

PREPARING THE MEATBALLS: Grate the cheese in a food processor fitted with the steel blade. Add the parsley, garlic, and onion. Run the processor about 3 seconds to mince but not purée the ingredients. Drop in the chicken pieces and pancetta. Use the on/off pulse to grind quite fine. Add the beef and process only a second or two. Turn everything into a bowl, and blend in the tomato paste, bread crumbs, egg, salt, and pepper. Shape into 1-inch balls.

COOKING THE MEATBALLS: Line a baking sheet with a triple thickness of paper towels. Heat the oil in a large sauté pan over medium-high heat. Cook half the meatballs 7 to 8 minutes, or until dark brown and crusty on all sides. Lift out the browned meatballs with a slotted spoon, and drain on the paper towels. Repeat with the second batch. Once they are cooked and drained, place in a bowl. Pour all the fat out of the pan, and add the water. Bring to a boil, scraping up the brown bits in the pan, and boil down to about 4 tablespoons. Pour this over the meatballs, and cool. Cover and refrigerate.

ASSEMBLING AND BAKING THE PIE

Unsalted butter
Sweet Pastry
1 recipe Tortellini, or 2½ pounds store-bought meat-filled tortellini

8 quarts Quick Stock or water
Salt
Double recipe Baroque Ragù
1½ cups (6 ounces) freshly grated Italian Parmigiano-Reggiano cheese
2 eggs, beaten
Meatballs
Cinnamon Custard
Lemon leaves, spruce sprigs, grapes, or sprigs of bay leaves for garnish

WORKING AHEAD: *The pastry dough must be rolled out 1 hour before assembling the pie. Although the pie cannot be assembled far in advance, it requires about 1½ hours of unattended baking and resting before serving. This allows plenty of time for conversation, drinks, and a first course.*

PREPARING THE PASTRY: Butter the bottom, sides, and rim of a 10½- to 11-inch springform pan. On a floured surface, roll out two thirds of the pastry to form a ⅛-inch-thick round. Fit it into the springform pan, covering the bottom and sides. Trim the edges at the rim so there is a 1-inch overhang. Save the scraps for decorations. Roll out the remaining dough to about ⅛ inch thick, and trim it to form a 13-inch round. Cover a cookie sheet with foil, and lift the pastry onto it. Arrange the scraps around the pastry. Chill both pastries about 30 minutes.

COOKING THE TORTELLINI: Stock is the traditional cooking medium here. It can be saved for future use once the tortellini are drained. If you are using water instead of stock, add 2 tablespoons salt. Bring the stock or water to a fierce boil. Drop in the tortellini and cook 3 to 8 minutes, or until tender but firm enough to have resilience or "bite." Drain well and turn into a large bowl.

ASSEMBLING: Gently warm the ragù. Wrap the meatballs in foil and warm them 10 minutes in a 350°F oven. Remove the meatballs and turn the heat to 400°F. Add two thirds of the ragù (save the rest for another use) to the tortellini, along with half the Parmigiano-Reggiano cheese and about two thirds of the beaten egg. Gently fold together until well blended.

Take the springform pan and cookie sheet out of the refrigerator. Spoon half the meatballs over the bottom of the crust, and sprinkle with 1 tablespoon of cheese. Spread half the tortellini over the meatballs, pressing them down gently with the back of a large spoon. Top with the remaining meatballs and another spoonful of cheese. Add the remaining tortellini, gently pressing into them the filling with the back of the large spoon. Dust with the rest of the Parmigiano-Reggiano. Spread the cinnamon custard over all. Brush the overhanging crust with beaten egg. Seal the reserved pastry round to the rim of the pie by pinching the two pieces together. Form a thick upstanding rim by rolling the edge in toward the center of the pie. Crimp or flute all around the crust. Brush the entire surface with more beaten egg.

DECORATING THE CRUST: Roll out the leftover dough. Cut 4-inch-long ovals of dough to resemble long California bay leaves. Cut a 1-inch-diameter steam hole in the center of the crust, and arrange the leaves in a sunburst pattern around it, overlapping them slightly toward the center. Small leaves could be arranged in clusters around the pie's rim. Brush all the decorations with beaten egg, and set the pie on a baking sheet.

BAKING: Place the baking sheet in the lower third of the oven, and bake 40 minutes. Lower the heat to 350°F and bake another 40 minutes. Let the pie stand in the turned-off oven with the door open halfway 10 to 20 minutes before serving.

THE PRESENTATION: Unmold by setting the springform pan on three large cans. Release the springform and let it drop down to the counter. Place the pie on a large silver tray or china platter garnished with clusters of lemon leaves, spruce sprigs, grapes, or bouquets of fresh bay leaves. Cut the pie at the table.

SUGGESTIONS

WINE: The sweet undertones of this dish present challenges in selecting a wine. An aged red Recioto della Valpolicella Amarone from the Veneto is ideal with the pie.

MENU: Although traditionally a first course at festive meals, the pie is a spectacular main dish for buffets and special dinners. In keeping with the pie's lineage, start with Almond Spice Broth. Afterward pass platters of fresh fennel and chunks of Parmigiano-Reggiano to eat with the last of the red wine. Dessert could be Strawberries in Red Wine or Meringues of the Dark Lake.

COOK'S NOTES

STORE-BOUGHT TORTELLINI: Look for fresh or frozen tortellini made with pasta sheer enough to detect the filling through it. Dried tortellini sold in boxes and needing no refrigeration are unacceptable.

BASTIANICH
La Cucina di Lidia

Gnocchi di Susine

Plum Gnocchi

YIELDS 16 PIECES

This is an Istrian specialty of Austro-Hungarian derivation, and a particular favorite of my brother Franco's. When our plums were fully ripened, we had these gnocchi as a main dish—not as dessert. If any were left over, we'd eat them at room temperature the next day.

Preferably, these dumplings should be made with Italian-type prune plums, which make a tidier, more symmetrical little package, but half their number of round red or purple plums (easier to find in this country) may be substituted. In either case, the fruits should be fully ripened but still firm.

- 16 Italian-type prune plums or 8 round red or purple plums
- ⅓ cup sugar
- ½ recipe potato gnocchi dough, made without pepper
- 6 tablespoons unsalted butter
- 1¾ cups unseasoned bread crumbs
- 2 teaspoons cinnamon

If using Italian-type plums, halve them lengthwise, remove the pits, fill each cavity with ½ teaspoon of the sugar, and re-form the plums by pressing the halves together.

If using larger round plums, halve them crosswise, separate the halves, neatly remove the pits with a small melon baller, and fill the cavities with sugar as above. Do not press halves together.

Hand-roll the dough to form a cylinder 2" in diameter, and slice it evenly into 16 rounds. Flatten each round in the palm of one hand, place a plum (or half plum) in the center of each, and carefully gather the dough up around the fruit, enclosing it completely with no breaks or tears in the dough. Pat the covered plums between your hands to seal and even the dough.

To a wide pot of boiling water, add the gnocchi 8 at a time, stirring gently to prevent sticking, and cook 5 minutes after they surface. Remove the gnocchi with a slotted spoon, set them aside, and keep them warm while proceeding with the second batch.

Meanwhile, melt the butter in a heavy skillet. Add the bread crumbs and toast over medium heat, stirring almost constantly, until golden brown, about 7 minutes. Add the remaining sugar and the cinnamon, and blend thoroughly.

Roll the cooked and drained gnocchi in the bread crumb mixture until all are well coated. Arrange on a serving plate and sprinkle with any bread crumbs remaining in the skillet.

SCHNEIDER
Uncommon Fruits & Vegetables

Spaghetti with Radicchio, Anchovies, and Garlic

When I first saw cooked radicchio, I was taken aback: where was the gorgeous garnet leaf with its sturdy crispness? But after a few tastes I began to understand the subtle changes the escarole-like leaf underwent when subjected to heat: an intensification of flavor and a broadening of range reveal its bitter-to-mellow-to-sweet spectrum. Although its brilliant red is lost once sautéed, radicchio gains an altogether new taste coloring.

4 SERVINGS

- 1 pound spaghetti
- ⅓ cup full-flavored olive oil
- 2–3 teaspoons finely minced garlic, to taste
- 1 pound radicchio (preferably 2 heads), cored, rinsed, and slivered
- 2-ounce can anchovies in olive oil, sliced (do not discard oil)
- 2 tablespoons minced chives
- ¼ cup minced flat-leaf parsley
- Black pepper to taste
- 1 cup finely grated provolone (about 2 ounces)

1. Drop spaghetti into a large kettle of well-salted boiling water; stir until water returns to a boil. Cook until just barely tender.

2. Meanwhile, heat oil in a large skillet; stir in garlic; cook over moderately low heat until just golden. Add radicchio and toss for a few minutes over high heat, until just wilted.

3. Drain pasta and toss in a heated bowl with the anchovies and oil. Add radicchio, chives, parsley, and plenty of pepper and toss well. Add half the cheese and toss. Serve at once with the remaining cheese on the side.

KASPER
The Splendid Table

Linguine with Braised Garlic and Balsamic Vinegar

Linguine con Aglio e Balsamico

This dish is a garlic lover's paradise, taking Italy's popular pasta with garlic and oil into a new realm. Balsamic vinegar spooned over the finished pasta is the all-important refinement. The dish comes together in almost no time.

SERVES 6 TO 8 AS A FIRST COURSE, 4 TO 6 AS A MAIN DISH

- 3 tablespoons extra-virgin olive oil or unsalted butter
- 8 large cloves garlic, cut into ¼-inch dice
- 6 quarts salted water
- 1 pound imported dried linguine, or 1 recipe Egg Pasta cut into tagliarini
- 3 tablespoons extra-virgin olive oil or unsalted butter
- Salt and freshly ground black pepper to taste
- 1 to 1½ cups (4 to 6 ounces) freshly grated Italian Parmigiano-Reggiano cheese
- 8 to 10 teaspoons artisan-made or high-quality commercial balsamic vinegar (if using commercial, blend in 1 teaspoon brown sugar)

WORKING AHEAD: *The garlic can be braised up to 8 hours ahead. Set it aside, covered, at room temperature. The dish is best finished and eaten right away.*

BRAISING THE GARLIC: In a large heavy skillet, heat the 3 tablespoons oil or butter over medium-low heat. Add the garlic, and lower the heat to the lowest possible setting. Cook, covered, 5 minutes, Uncover and continue cooking over the lowest possible heat 8 minutes, or until the garlic is barely colored to pale blond and very tender. Stir it frequently with a wooden spatula. Do not let the garlic turn medium to dark brown, as it will be bitter.

COOKING THE PASTA: Warm a serving bowl and shallow soup dishes in a low oven. As the garlic braises, bring the salted water to a fierce boil, and drop in the pasta. Stir occasionally. Cook only a few moments for fresh pasta, and up to 10 minutes for dried pasta. Taste for doneness, making sure the pasta is tender but still firm to the bite. Spoon about 3 tablespoons of the cooking water into the cooked garlic just before draining the pasta. Drain in a colander.

FINISHING AND SERVING: Remove the garlic from the heat and add the hot drained pasta. Add the additional 3 tablespoons of oil or butter (the fresh taste of uncooked oil or butter brightens the dish), and toss with two wooden spatulas. Season with salt and pepper. Now toss with all of the cheese.

Turn into the heated serving bowl. As you serve the pasta, sprinkle each plateful with a teaspoon or so of the vinegar.

SUGGESTIONS

WINE: A simple but fruity white, like Trebbiano del Lazio or Frascati.

MENU: Serve before simple or complex dishes: Herbed Seafood Grill, Braised Eel with Peas, Christmas Capon, Beef-Wrapped Sausage, Lamb with Black Olives, or Rabbit Roasted with Sweet Fennel. Offer as a main dish after Prosciutto di Parma, Mousse of Mortadella, Garlic Crostini with Pancetta, Chicken and Duck Liver Mousse with White Truffles, or Valentino's Pizza. Have Riccardo Rimondi's Spanish Sponge Cake for dessert.

COOK'S NOTES

VARIATION WITH FRESH BASIL: In summer add 1 cup coarsely chopped fresh basil leaves to the braised garlic a few seconds before tossing with the pasta. Let the basil warm and its aromas blossom, then add the pasta to the pan.

KASPER
The Splendid Table

Lasagne of Emilia-Romagna

Lasagne Verdi al Forno

This is one of the most sumptuous yet restrained dishes found in Emilia-Romagna's repertoire. Yes, the lasagne is rich. But for all its richness, the dish maintains an elegance rarely surpassed by any other lasagne in Italy.

Although strongly identified with Bologna, this lasagne is found throughout the region. Its ragù sauce may change slightly from one area to another, but the dish is always a vivid expression of the "less is more" philosophy of cooking. Mere films of béchamel sauce and meat ragù coat the sheerest spinach pasta.

Parmigiano-Reggiano cheese dusts each layer. There is nothing more; no ricotta, no piling on of meats, vegetables, or cheeses; little tomato, and no hot spice. Baking performs the final marriage of flavors. The results are splendid.

SERVES 8 TO 10 AS A FIRST COURSE, 6 TO 8 AS A MAIN DISH

- 4 tablespoons (2 ounces) unsalted butter
- 4 tablespoons all-purpose unbleached flour (organic stone-ground preferred)
- 2⅔ cups milk
- Salt and freshly ground black pepper to taste
- Freshly grated nutmeg to taste
- 10 quarts salted water
- 1 recipe Spinach Pasta cut for lasagne, or 1 pound imported dried lasagne
- 1 recipe Country-Style Ragù
- 1 cup (4 ounces) freshly grated Italian Parmigiano-Reggiano cheese

WORKING AHEAD: *The ragù and béchamel sauces can be made 3 days ahead; cover and refrigerate. The ragù also freezes well up to 1 month. The pasta can be rolled out, cut, and dried up to 24 hours before cooking. The assembled lasagne can wait at room temperature about 1 hour before baking. Do not refrigerate it before baking, as the topping of béchamel and cheese will overcook by the time the center is hot.*

MAKING THE BÉCHAMEL: Melt the butter in a 3- to 4-quart saucepan over medium-low heat. Sprinkle with the flour and whisk until smooth. Stir without stopping about 3 minutes. Then whisk in the milk a little at a time, keeping the mixture smooth. Bring to a slow bubble, and stir 3 to 4 minutes, or until the sauce thickens. Cook, stirring, 5 minutes, or until all raw flour taste has disappeared. Season with salt, pepper, and a hint of nutmeg.

ASSEMBLING THE INGREDIENTS: Have the pasta, ragù sauce, béchamel, and cheese at hand. Have a large perforated skimmer and a large bowl of cold water next to the stove. Spread a double thickness of paper towels over a large counter space. Rewarm the sauces gently over medium heat. Preheat the oven to 350°F. Oil or butter a 3-quart shallow baking dish.

COOKING THE PASTA: Bring the salted water to boil. Drop about four pieces of pasta in the water at a time. Cook about 2 minutes. If you are using dried pasta, cook about 4 minutes, taste, and cook longer if necessary. The pasta will continue cooking during baking, so make sure it is only barely tender. Lift the lasagne from the water with a skimmer, drain, and then slip into the bowl of cold water to stop cooking. When cool, lift out and dry on the paper towels. Repeat until all the pasta is cooked.

ASSEMBLING THE LASAGNE: Spread a thin film of béchamel over the bottom of the baking dish. Arrange a layer of about four overlapping sheets of pasta over the béchamel. Spread a thin film of béchamel (about 3 or 4 spoonfuls) over the pasta, and then an equally thin film of the ragù. Sprinkle with about 1½ tablespoons of the cheese. Top with another layer and repeat the process. Reserve about ⅓ cup of the béchamel and about ⅓ cup of the cheese for the top of the lasagne. Spread the sauce to completely cover the last layer of pasta. Then top with a generous dusting of cheese.

BAKING AND SERVING THE LASAGNE: Cover the baking dish lightly with foil, taking care not to let it touch the top of the lasagne. Bake 40 minutes, or until almost heated through. Remove the foil and bake another 10 minutes, or until hot in the center. Test by inserting a knife in the center. If it comes out very warm, the dish is ready. Take care not to brown the cheese topping. It should be melted, creamy-looking, and barely tinged with a little gold. Let the lasagne rest in the turned-off oven with the door ajar about 10 minutes. Then serve. This is not a solid lasagne, but a moist one that slips a bit when it is cut and placed on a dinner plate.

SUGGESTIONS

WINE: From Emilia-Romagna, a full and generous red Cabernet Sauvignon Colli Bolognesi, a Sangiovese di Romagna Riserva, or a Barbarossa. From other parts of Italy, drink a round and rich Piemontese Barbera d'Alba, or a Tuscan Chianti Classico.

MENU: In Emilia-Romagna it is offered in small portions as a first course. I find it complex and interesting enough to also hold its own as a main dish. Keep the other dishes simple and direct. Everything should be a prelude or aftermath to the lasagne. Start with a few slices of salami or coppa and Balsamic Vegetables, or Spring Salad with Hazelnuts. Finish the meal with Baked Pears with Fresh Grape Syrup and Sweet Cornmeal Biscuits.

VARIATIONS: Other ragùs are also excellent in the lasagne. Try The Cardinal's Ragù, A Lighter Contemporary Ragù Bolognese, or Baroque Ragù.

For a meatless lasagne, Winter Tomato Sauce or Piacenza's Porcini Tomato Sauce can stand in for the meat ragùs. Egg Pasta can be substituted for Spinach Pasta.

COOK'S NOTES

DRIED PASTA: Boxed lasagne pasta should be as sheer as possible.

IT'S A GIRL! According to Emilia-Romagna folklorist Piero Camporesi, for many families in Emilia-Romagna a lasagne celebrated the birth of a girl.

NATHAN

Jewish Cooking in America

Eggplant and Green Pepper Kugel (Casserole)

Here is an eggplant kugel *for Passover I first tasted in Jerusalem, the world's capital of international eggplant dishes. The recipe was brought there by American immigrants.*

1 large eggplant (about 2 pounds)
1 onion, diced
1 green pepper, diced
2 tablespoons pine nuts
¼ cup olive oil
2 tablespoons chopped fresh basil
Salt and freshly ground pepper to taste
2 large eggs, lightly beaten
1 matzah, crumbled
2 tablespoons butter or margarine

1. Peel the eggplant and dice in 2-inch cubes. Cook in simmering salted water to cover until the eggplant is tender—about 20 minutes. Drain and mash.

2. Meanwhile, sauté the onion, pepper, and pine nuts in olive oil over medium heat until the vegetables are tender but not crisp. Combine with the basil and salt and pepper.

3. Mix the eggplant with the lightly beaten eggs as well as the vegetable mixture. Add the matzah and mix well. Place in a greased casserole and dot with butter or margarine. Bake in a preheated 350-degree oven for 35 minutes or until golden brown on top and crusty on the sides.

YIELD: 6 TO 8 SERVINGS

MITCHELL

Lüchow's German Cookbook

Goulash Spätzle

1 pound (3¼ cups) sifted flour
1 teaspoon salt
½ teaspoon grated nutmeg
4 eggs, beaten
Milk
2 quarts boiling salted water
4 or 5 tablespoons butter
½ cup toasted bread crumbs

Sift dry ingredients together. Beat eggs in. Add milk gradually to make heavy dough. Force through large-hole colander into kettle of rapidly boiling salted water. (Use 1 teaspoon salt to 1 quarter water.) Boil 6 to 8 minutes.

Remove Spätzle with large strainer-spoon and put in colander. Dash with cold water; drain. Sauté in butter until golden. Sprinkle with crumbs and serve. Serves 6 or more.

CLAIBORNE AND LEE

The Chinese Cookbook

Cold Noodles with Spicy Sauce

1 whole chicken breast
4 ounces fine egg noodles
1 teaspoon plus 1 tablespoon sesame oil*
¼ cup sesame paste*
3 tablespoons brewed tea or water
2 tablespoons hot oil* (optional)
3 tablespoons light soy sauce*
3 tablespoons red wine vinegar
2 teaspoons sugar
Salt to taste
¼ teaspoon monosodium glutamate (optional)
¼ cup peanut, vegetable, or corn oil
2 tablespoons chopped garlic

*Available in Chinese markets and by mail order.

1. In a kettle or large saucepan, bring about 6 cups of water to a boil and add the chicken breast. Do not add salt. Return to a boil and simmer about 10 to 15 minutes. Do not overcook, or the meat will be dry. Remove the chicken breast, but leave the water in the kettle.

2. Bring the water to a boil again. Do not add salt. Add the noodles and cook, stirring occasionally, until they are tender, 7 minutes or less. Drain in a colander and run under cold water until they are thoroughly chilled and the strands are separated. Drain. Sprinkle with the teaspoon of sesame oil and toss to coat. Set aside.

3. To make the sauce, spoon the sesame paste into a mixing bowl and add the tea or water gradually, stirring with chopsticks or a fork. Stir in the remaining ingredients and the 1 tablespoon sesame oil.

4. Arrange the noodles on a serving dish. Cut the chicken into uniform shreds and arrange neatly over the noodles. Spoon the sauce over all and serve cold.

YIELD: 2 TO 4 SERVINGS

TSUJI
Japanese Cooking

Homemade Japanese Noodles

Teuchi Udon or *Soba*

Using only all-purpose white flour, the result is udon-*type noodles;* soba *noodles are made with buckwheat flour and wheat flour at a ratio of about 4 buckwheat to 1 wheat. These noodles can be frozen. Cook after defrosting.*

4 POUNDS (1¾ KG)—6 SERVINGS

- 1¾ cups water (about)
- 3⅓ Tbsps salt
- 2 egg yolks (optional)
- 8⅓ cups (2¼ pounds or 1 kg) all-purpose flour

TO PREPARE: Dissolve salt in cold water. (If using eggs, beat yolks, mix with water, then dissolve salt in this mixture.) Make a well in the center of the flour and gradually work in the liquid with your hands to a stiff dough. This recipe is based on standard Japanese flours. Adjust the amount of liquid to the flour you use. Knead vigorously until dough is smooth and soft but firm—"like your earlobe," is the traditional Japanese guide. Cover with a damp kitchen cloth and let rest 8 hours in winter or 3 hours in summer for the best results, but 2 hours are adequate.

On a flour-dusted board or pastry cloth, roll out dough in an even width (a rectangular shape, *not* a round) till ⅛ inch (½ cm) thick or slightly thinner. Sprinkle sheet of rolled-out dough with flour and fold. Cut with a sharp knife or cleaver across the folded sheet into ⅛-inch (½-cm) strips. After cutting, insert a long chopstick or long skewer into the center fold and shake out the strands.

Udon noodles can be frozen or will keep refrigerated for 3–4 days in a closed container. *Soba* are more delicate—the flavor does not keep well. See below for cooking directions.

Besides *udon*, *soba*, and *somen*, which are the three most commonly used Japanese noodles, there are others, which are not noodles. *Harusame* ("spring rain") is made from various starches and comes in the form of fine, translucent filaments. *Shirataki* ("white waterfall"), a transparent, ropy, gelatinous filament often used in SUKIYAKI or other one-pot dishes, is made from the starchy root of the devil's tongue plant, *konnyaku*. Both *harusame* and *shirataki* are made by an extrusion process, not cut with a knife. They are often called vermicelli, an unfortunate misnomer. They do not fit any Western category, so they are called filaments in this book—not the best word, but adequate.

As mentioned above, the instant noodle preparations gaining worldwide attention are the result of Japanese ingenuity, but the type of noodle is Chinese and is not a part of Japanese cuisine. Like fried rice, fried noodles (*yakisoba*), too, are Chinese, not Japanese, though part of the ambience of every Japanese festival (as is cotton candy).

There are two places to look for noodles in a Japanese store: dried noodles are on the grocery shelf; both fresh uncooked and cooked ones are in the refrigerator case. You may at first feel overwhelmed by the wide selection of packaged noodles to chose from (this is certainly true in Japan), but merely pick out the basic kind of noodle you want—*udon*, *somen*, *soba*, or whatever. There are many regional variations, and manufacturers often specialize in one noodle for which they have become famous. There are thus any number of different *sobas* or *udons*, etc. Outside Japan, the variety is less, and the choice is easier.

Cooked noodles do *not* freeze well and must be used within 1 or 2 days of purchase; uncooked fresh *udon* noodles keep 2 weeks refrigerated and also freeze well; dried noodles keep indefinitely. Manufacturers of fresh cooked noodles in Japan often include concentrated noodle broth (to be mixed with hot water) and other seasonings in plastic packets, in cans, or in some form.

Before going on to some noodle recipes, a description of how to cook both freshly made and dried noodles will be helpful. If the package includes its own directions, follow them, or use this basic method:

TO COOK FRESH AND DRIED NOODLES
Bring about 2 quarts (2 L) unsalted water to a rolling boil in a large pot. There should be enough water and the pot should be big enough so that the noodles are not crowded and boiling water circulates around them—just as with any pasta. Add noodles to boiling water gradually so as not to stop the boiling entirely. Stir slowly to keep noodles from sticking to the bottom of the pot. Let water come to a full rolling boil again, then add 1 cup cold water. Repeat this 3–4 times, and cook until noodles are a bit tenderer than *al dente*. To test, remove a strand from the boiling water, run it under cold water, and bite into it. The noodle should be cooked through to the center (no hard core), but still quite firm. Test frequently to avoid overcooking. Drain noodles in a colander and rinse under cold running water, rubbing vigorously with the hands to remove surface starch.

To reheat cooked noodles, place in a colander or deep, handled sieve and plunge into a pot of boiling water just until heated. Separate strands by shaking the colander or sieve. Noodles, if not served floating in a mild broth, are almost always eaten with a slightly stronger-flavored dipping sauce. Since both the broth (*kake-jiru*), literally "soup for pouring on," and dipping sauce (*tsuke-jiru*), freely rendered, "soup on the side" are standard recipes, they are included here. Take time to master the noodle broth (*kake-jiru*), for its flavor naturally affects the flavor of the whole dish, and an overseasoned broth as well as an insipid one can dim the experience of good noodles, homemade or otherwise.

RICE

BROWN
The South American Cook Book

Rice with Palm Hearts
Arroz com Palmito

- 1 tablespoon olive oil
- 1 medium onion, chopped
- 1 tomato, peeled and chopped
- 1 herb bouquet (bay leaf, parsley, celery)
- ½ pound smoked sausage
- 3 slices salt pork, cut thin
- 1 cup boiling water
- ½ cup rice, well washed
- 3 cups palmetto, sliced thick

Heat oil. Add onion and slowly fry until lightly browned and tender. Add tomato, herbs, sausage and pork. Cover and let simmer, stirring occasionally. Add water and rice. Cover and continue slow simmering. When rice is swollen add more boiling water and increase heat. Boil rapidly until rice is tender and fairly dry, frequently shaking pan to make sure it does not scorch.

Meanwhile cook palmetto in salted boiling water, or if canned palmetto is used heat it in its own liquor.

Arrange rice on hot platter, using cut-up sausage and pork as a garnish, and heap drained palmetto in center.

Palmettos and hearts of palm are the creamy inside meat of young palm shoots and the buds of cabbage palm and other palms, including the royal. During ten years in Brazil we ate different kinds of palmettos every day in every way, and they always made a hit with guests from home. Frederick Stief, author of Eat, Drink and Be Merry in Maryland, *met his first palmettos there and liked them so well he used to cable us several times a year to ship him a few tins with which to thrill Baltimore guests. But domestic palm hearts can be had in plenty from Florida today, where they're looked upon as almost as necessary a vegetable as potatoes.*

John Crashley, an Englishman who ran the only Anglo-Saxon bookshop in Rio de Janeiro, used to tell us of his first encounter with palmettos when he was a youngster fresh from London. Employed on a Brazilian farm in Nicteroy, just across Rio's beautiful bay, it was his job to row the farmer's green stuff across to the city market every morning. There he saw for the time piles of palm shoots selling at very good prices and recalled that he'd seen similar sprouts on an apparently abandoned island en route.

So one morning he cut down a boatload of them and took them to market on his own, expecting to earn a month's wages in one. But the marketmen laughed at his ignorance—for he'd cut down a farmer's whole field of newly planted banana palms, which are inedible.

ALFORD AND DUGUID

Seductions of Rice

Thai Sticky Rice

Khao Neeo

MAKES APPROXIMATELY 6½ CUPS RICE

Sticky rice is eaten as a staple in northern and northeastern Thailand. It is long-grain and opaque white in color before cooking. A different variety from jasmine rice, it becomes "sticky" when cooked because its starch component is different (it has very low amylose and a high proportion of amylopectin compared to nonsticky rices. Asian sticky rice is sometimes sold labeled "sweet rice" or "glutinous rice." The rice from Thailand will often be marked pin kao, *or with the Vietnamese term for sticky rice,* gao nêp.

Sticky rice is soaked overnight in cold water, then steam-cooked in a basket or steamer over boiling water. The long soaking time gives it a very good flavor, but you can use the short-cut method instead and soak in very warm water for two hours. Many Thais in the north and northeast save a little cooked rice each day to soak with their next batch of raw rice. They say it gives extra depth of flavor.

Sticky rice tends to be a big hit with children and adults alike. It has a slightly sweet grain taste and sticks to itself but not to your hands. You just pick up a small clump from the serving basket and lightly squeeze it into a ball, before dipping it in some sauce or using it to pick up a little grilled meat or piece of salad, rather as you might use a tortilla chip.

Knowing how much sticky rice to prepare for a meal can be a tricky proposition. We used to buy Thai sticky rice in five-pound packages, the size most commonly available in Asian groceries here in North America. For a dinner for four hungry adults, we would cook one third of a package (or about three cups of uncooked rice). But people tend to eat a lot of sticky rice, or at least we do and so do our friends, so now I prepare four to five cups for four hungry adults and several children. And now we buy our sticky rice in twenty-pound bags.

There are several different options for steaming sticky rice. If you can shop in a Thai, Lao, or Vietnamese grocery, chances are that they will have for sale a conical basket used for cooking sticky rice as well as the lightweight pot the basket rests in as it steams. Otherwise, use a steamer or a large sieve, lined with cheesecloth or muslin and placed over a large pot of water.

3 cups long-grain Thai sticky rice

Put the rice in a container that holds at least twice the volume of the rice, cover with 2 to 3 inches of cold water, and soak for 8 to 24 hours. Or, if you need to accelerate the soaking time, soak in warm (about 100°F) water for 2 hours.

Drain the rice and place in a steamer basket or in a steamer or large sieve lined with cheesecloth or muslin. Set over several inches of boiling water in a large pot or a wok. *The rice must not be touching the boiling water.* Cover and steam for 25 minutes, or until the rice is shiny and tender. Be careful that your pot doesn't run dry; add more water if necessary, making sure to keep it from immersing the rice.

Turn the rice out into a basket or a bowl, break up into smaller lumps, and then cover with a cloth or lid. (In Thailand and Laos, cooked sticky rice is kept warm and moist in covered baskets.) The rice dries out if exposed to the air for long as it cools, so keep covered until serving, then serve directly from the basket or bowl.

ALFORD AND DUGUID
Seductions of Rice

Classic Thai Fried Rice

Khao Pad

SERVES 1

*Fried rice is a Thai classic. No matter where you are, no matter what time of day, you can always order fried rice—*khao pad*—and it will almost always be very good. You can order it with chicken, pork, squid, green vegetables, mushrooms, extra garlic, any way you like—something like ordering a pizza here. Our favorite is* khao pad pak sai khai dao, *vegetable fried rice with a fried egg on top (eggs in Thailand are full of flavor).*

But khao pad *is much more than a neighborhood restaurant dish. It is also cooked at home, almost daily, probably the best way of turning leftover Thai jasmine rice into a quick delicious meal. It is versatile and always satisfying, light and nourishing. If your larder is almost bare, make it only with garlic, lots of garlic. If you have a few mushrooms or a little chicken or pork, slice thinly and add to the wok once the garlic is golden. Whatever you might add, be sure to brown the garlic first, to use* nam pla *(fish sauce), and, if possible, to start with fragrant Thai rice—these are the elements that make* khao pad *so uniquely good.*

Thai fried rice is ideally accompanied by a squeeze of fresh lime, a sprinkling of fresh coriander leaves, a few slices of cucumber, and nam pla prik *(fish sauce with hot chiles). We've seen many a chile hater turn into a chile lover all on account of Thai fried rice and* nam pla prik.

This recipe is for one serving. If you have a large wok, the recipe is easily doubled to serve two; increase your cooking time by about thirty seconds. If you are serving more than two, prepare the additional servings separately. The cooking time is very short, so once all your ingredients are prepared it is easy to go through the same cooking process twice, or more—simply clean out the wok and wipe it dry each time. It is much easier to prepare khao pad *when your wok isn't overly full.*

Total preparation time is about six minutes; cooking time is about four minutes. Street vendors normally prepare khao pad *one plate at a time, while you wait.*

2 tablespoons peanut oil or vegetable oil
4 to 8 cloves garlic, minced (even more if not using optional ingredients)
1 cup sliced oyster mushrooms or other mushrooms (optional)
2 cups cooked rice, cooled (preferably Thai jasmine or American jasmine rice)
2 scallions, cut into ½-inch slivers (optional)
1 medium tomato, finely chopped (optional)
2 teaspoons Thai fish sauce or to taste
1 teaspoon soy sauce

GARNISH AND ACCOMPANIMENTS

About ¼ cup packed fresh coriander leaves
About 6 thin cucumber slices
1 scallion, trimmed
½ tomato, sliced (optional)
2 to 3 lime wedges
¼ cup Fish Sauce with Hot Chiles
Leaf lettuce (optional)

Heat a medium to large wok over high heat. When it is hot, add the oil and heat until very hot. Add the garlic and fry until just golden, about 20 seconds. Add the mushrooms, if using, and cook, stirring constantly, until softened, about 1 minute. Add the rice, breaking it up with your fingers as you toss it into the wok. With your spatula, keep moving the rice around the wok. At first it may stick, but scoop and toss the rice and soon it will be more manageable. Try to visualize "frying" each little bit of rice, sometimes pressing the rice against the wok with the back of your spatula. Good fried rice should have a faint seared-in-the-wok taste. Cook for approximately 1½ minutes. Add the optional scallions and tomato, the fish sauce, and soy sauce. Stir-fry for 30 seconds to 1 minute.

Turn out onto a dinner plate. Garnish with fresh coriander. Around the rice, lay a row of overlapping cucumber slices, a scallion, the optional tomato slices and one or two lettuce leaves, and wedges of lime. The lime should be squeezed onto the rice as you eat it. Serve with the *nam pla prik*—the salty hot taste of the sauce brings out the full flavor of the rice.

NOTE: Once you've tossed the garlic in the hot oil, you can add about ½ teaspoon (or more) of Red Curry Paste. It adds another layer of flavor and a little heat too.

ALTERNATIVE: Many people (we're among them) like to eat a fried egg (with a soft yolk) on top of their fried rice. Wipe out your wok, heat about 2 teaspoons oil, and quickly fry the egg in the wok, then turn it out onto the rice. It's delicious. Try it!

KAFKA

Microwave Gourmet

Shrimp and Spring Vegetable Risotto

This dish is so beautiful that when The New York Times *asked me to provide a microwave recipe that would be photographed for their entertaining issue, this is the one I chose. Italians use ambra rice rather than arborio in this recipe, both for its pale golden color and for its lighter, less glutinous consistency, but arborio can be substituted.*

SERVES 6 AS A MAIN COURSE, 10 AS A FIRST COURSE

- 3 tablespoons unsalted butter
- 3 tablespoons fruity olive oil
- ½ cup chopped scallion (white part only)
- 2 celery stalks, peeled and chopped
- ½ cup (packed) chopped flat-leaf parsley
- 2 cups ambra rice
- 4 cups Fish Broth, Clam Broth, Chicken Broth or canned chicken broth
- ¾ pound asparagus, trimmed, peeled and cut into 2-inch lengths
- 1 pound medium shrimp, peeled, deveined and cut in half crosswise
- ¾ cup shelled fresh peas or frozen tiny peas, defrosted in a sieve under warm running water
- 1 to 2 teaspoons kosher salt
- ½ teaspoon freshly ground black pepper
- ¼ cup chopped scallion (green part only)
- ½ cup freshly grated Parmesan cheese

1. Heat butter and oil in a 14" × 11" × 2" dish, uncovered, at 100% for 3 minutes. Add scallion whites, celery, parsley, and rice and stir to coat. Cook, uncovered, at 100% for 4 minutes.

2. Stir in broth and cook, uncovered, at 100% for 12 minutes. Add asparagus, shrimp, and peas and stir well. Cook, uncovered, for 12 minutes more.

3. Remove from oven. Stir in salt and pepper. Cover loosely with paper toweling and let stand for 8 to 10 minutes. Uncover, sprinkle with scallion greens and cheese, and serve.

ANDREWS

Catalan Cuisine

Paella Valenciana amb Mariscos

Valencian Paella with Shellfish

This is a paella in more familiar form—with mussels and shrimp and/or crayfish added. Again, the recipe is based on the formula offered by Llorenç Millo in La Taula i la cuina.

TO SERVE 8–10 (AS APPETIZER) OR 6–8 (AS MAIN COURSE)

- 2 pounds chicken, cut into small serving pieces
- Olive oil
- 5½ cups chicken stock
- 12 mussels, cleaned
- ½ pound shrimp and/or small prawns (scampi), heads and shells on
- ½–¾ pound assorted white beans, butter beans, and Italian-style broad beans or string beans, cooked and drained
- 1 tomato, seeded and grated or peeled, seeded, and chopped
- 1 tablespoon sweet paprika
- 6–8 threads saffron, lightly toasted
- 1⅓ pounds short-grain rice
- Salt

In a paella, cassola, or other wide, flat-bottomed pan, sauté the chicken pieces in a small amount of oil until golden-brown; then remove them, drain, and set aside.

Meanwhile, bring stock to a boil; then reduce the heat and simmer.

Pour off excess fat from the paella; then add the mussels and shrimp and/or the crayfish, beans, tomato, and paprika, and stir well.

Add the stock, and simmer for 10 minutes; then crumble saffron into pan, and salt to taste.

Stir in the rice; then cook over a medium-high flame without stirring for 20–25 minutes or until the rice is done and the liquid has evaporated. (Do not allow the rice to burn; a dark brown crust on the bottom and sides of the pan, however, is desirable.)

When paella is finished, carefully arrange the mussels and shrimp and/or crayfish on top of the rice, using tongs and being careful not to leave the rice uneven (top should be flat); then let stand 5–10 minutes off heat before serving.

CASAS
The Foods and Wines of Spain

Arroz con Pollo

Rice and Chicken

Arroz con Pollo *is more or less a simplified version of* paella, *appropriate for those who don't or cannot eat seafood and good to prepare on a last-minute basis because its ingredients can all be found in the supermarket.*

SERVES 4–6

- A 3-pound chicken, cut in small serving pieces
- Salt
- 6 tablespoons olive oil
- 2 green peppers, chopped
- 1 onion, chopped
- 2 cloves garlic, minced
- 2 fresh tomatoes, skinned and chopped
- 2 pimientos, homemade or imported, chopped
- 3 teaspoons paprika
- ¼ teaspoon saffron
- 2 cups short-grain rice
- 3½ cups strong chicken broth, preferably homemade
- ½ cup dry white wine
- Freshly ground pepper
- 1 tablespoon minced parsley for garnish

Sprinkle the chicken pieces with salt. Heat the oil in a metal *paella* pan with about a 15-inch base and fry the chicken until golden on all sides. Remove to a warm platter. Add the green pepper, onion, and garlic and sauté until the green pepper is tender. Stir in the tomato and pimiento and cook, uncovered, 10 minutes more. Add the paprika and saffron, then add the rice and stir to coat well with the oil. Pour in the broth, boiling hot, the wine, salt, and pepper. Boil over medium heat, uncovered and stirring occasionally, for about 7 minutes, or until the rice is no longer soupy, but not yet dry. Arrange the chicken pieces over the rice and place in a 325° F oven, uncovered, for 15 minutes. The liquid should be absorbed, but the rice still "al dente." Remove and let sit, lightly covered with foil, for 10 minutes more. Sprinkle with the parsley. An Ensalada a la Almoraina and a light red wine like Diamante are the only accompaniments necessary.

ALFORD AND DUGUID
Seductions of Rice

Baked Persian Rice with Chicken

Tahchin

SERVES 6 TO 8

Though around the world most rice is cooked in some form of pot or pan over a flame or other heat, there is a whole category of baked savory rice dishes. These include not only Italian bomba de riso *and South Carolina baked perloo, but also their probable ancestor,* tahchin, *baked Persian rice. The same principles apply to baked rice as to* katteh *and* chelo: *The goal is fluffy separate grains of rice and a tasty crust, though in this case the bottom layer of rice is thicker and studded with small pieces of chicken.*

The chicken is simmered, then placed in a yogurt marinade enlivened with a little dried orange peel (available from Middle Eastern groceries or by mail order). The rice is soaked and boiled, as for chelo *or* katten *or* polo, *then placed with the chicken in an ovenproof dish to bake slowly until done. Though this dish was traditionally cooked in a tandoor oven (probably in the waning heat after baking the day's breads), it does very well in a modern electric or gas oven. All you need is a wide heavy ovenproof pot sealed with a tight-fitting lid (or aluminum foil), and several hours cooking time (during which you can forget about it).*

The baked rice is a golden round about two inches high. It is inverted onto a large plate, the well-browned crust forming the top surface, then sliced into wedges. Pieces of succulent chicken are buried in the rice and crust. The texture is firm and the slices of the rice hold together well, so they can be eaten as finger food (a pleasure for children especially). Accompany with moist side dishes such as Oasis Salad, a yogurt sauce, and a plate of greens and fresh herbs such as tarragon, mint, scallions, and salad greens.

FILLING

2 tablespoons butter or vegetable oil
1½ to 1¾ pounds boneless skinless chicken breasts, cut into 1- to 2-inch pieces and trimmed of fat
1 onion, minced
2 tablespoons lemon juice
1 teaspoon salt
Generous teaspoon of dried orange peel (see Glossary)
½ cup plain yogurt (whole-milk or 2%)
2 large eggs

RICE

3 cups basmati rice
Water
2 tablespoons salt

About 2 tablespoons melted butter

At least 5 hours before you wish to serve the dish, prepare the filling: Heat the butter or oil in a large heavy nonreactive skillet over medium heat. Add the chicken and onion and cook for 10 minutes. Add the lemon juice and salt, cover, and simmer for 40 minutes.

Meanwhile, prepare the orange peel: Bring a small pot of water to a vigorous boil, toss in the peel, and boil for 5 minutes, then drain. In the same pot, bring another 2 cups water to a boil and add the peel, then remove from the heat and let stand for at least 10 minutes. Drain and coarsely chop.

When the chicken is cooked, remove from the heat and stir in the yogurt and orange peel. Cool to room temperature, then cover and place in the refrigerator to marinate for 2 to 24 hours.

Wash the rice thoroughly and put it in a large bowl with 8 cups water mixed with 1 tablespoon of the salt. Let soak for 30 minutes to 3 hours.

When ready to proceed, preheat the oven to 375°F.

Drain the soaked rice, then boil the rice following the directions for Special Everyday Persian Rice; drain, rinse, and drain again.

Butter or oil a wide (12-inch diameter) casserole or heavy ovenproof pot.

Remove the chicken pieces from the marinade and set aside. Break the eggs into a small bowl and beat well. Stir into the marinade mixture. Mix in 3 cups of the cooked rice. Spread the rice mixture over the bottom and up the sides of the casserole or pot. Distribute the chicken pieces over the rice, then add the remaining rice to cover, smoothing it level. Drizzle on the melted butter.

Bake, tightly covered with a lid or aluminum foil, for 45 minutes. Lower the heat to 350°F and bake for 1¼ hours longer, or until the top of the rice is golden brown.

Just before removing the casserole from the oven, fill your kitchen sink with about 2 inches of cold water.

Remove the casserole from the oven and place in the cold water for several minutes; this will help keep the rice from sticking to the pot. Slide a thin-bladed knife along the sides of the pot to loosen the rice. Place a large plate over the pot and invert; the rice should drop onto the plate (this is easiest with two people). Serve cut into wedges.

Eggs, Breakfast, and Brunch

EGGS

OLNEY
Simple French Food

Scrambled Eggs

Correctly prepared, the softest of barely perceptible curds held in a thickly liquid, smooth, creamy suspension, scrambled eggs number among the very great delicacies of the table. They, like omelets, should be beaten but lightly with an addition of butter and, whether they be prepared over low, direct heat or in a bain-marie (their cooking utensil immersed in another containing nearly boiling water), they should be contained in a generously buttered heavy pan, preferably copper, which absorbs heat slowly and retains it for a long time. It is not only easier to precisely control the heat in a bain-marie, but also the cooking time is shortened, thanks to the heat's being absorbed through the sides of the utensil as well as from the bottom. The eggs should be stirred constantly with a wooden spoon during their preparation, the sides and the bottom of the pan being repeatedly scraped, and they should be removed from the heat some moments before the desired consistency is achieved and stirred continuously for another minute or so, for they continue to cook from an absorption of heat contained in the pan. It is wise to remove them two or three times from the heat toward the end of the cooking to control more exactly the degree of creaminess and, once removed definitively, from contact with heat, a small amount of heavy cream may be stirred in, arresting at once the cooking and underlining at the same time their caressing consistency. They may be served in butter-crisp containers carved out of crustless bread. Otherwise, if one is among friends, it is preferable to serve them directly from the cooking vessel onto warm, but not hot, plates and a wonderful additional garnish is the crisp, brown-butter note of croutons, either scattered over the surface or stirred into the eggs at the moment of serving.

The complication of such rich garnishes as foie gras, game, crayfish, or lobster with their corresponding Périgueux, Salmis, Nantua, or Américaine sauces seems only to detract from the purity of the thing. But for truffles (the black ones incorporated, slivered, sliced, or chopped before the cooking; the fresh white ones sliced paper thin over the surface the moment the eggs are done) and morels (fresh or dried, stewed in butter before being incorporated into the eggs), scrambled eggs ally themselves the most beautifully with a single vegetable—be it tender asparagus tips, parboiled and sweated in butter (or, Oriental-wise, slivered, raw, on the bias, parboiled for but a few seconds, and tossed for no more than a minute in hot butter), artichoke hearts stewed in butter, finely sliced zucchini sautéed in butter or in olive oil, shredded sorrel stewed in butter, tender peas, rapidly parboiled . . . The same herbs that find a place in omelets are good, alone or in combination with vegetables, in scrambled eggs.

It is said that eggs and wine do not marry. I, personally, take great pleasure in drinking a young, light-bodied, relatively dry white wine with scrambled eggs.

Both the following recipes, though traditional, stray from the classical formula.

EGGS SCRAMBLED WITH TOMATO AND BASIL
Brouillade de Tomates au Basilic

FOR 4

3 or 4 medium tomatoes, peeled, seeded, chopped coarsely
Salt
3 or 4 cloves garlic, crushed
Bouquet garni (bay leaf, thyme, celery branch—or a pinch of crumbled mixed dried herbs)
½ teaspoon sugar
¼ cup olive oil
¼ cup butter
8 to 10 eggs
Pepper
Handful fresh basil leaves and flowers

Cook the tomatoes, salted, with the garlic, bouquet garni, and sugar in the olive oil over a low flame, tossing from time to time, until the free liquid is evaporated and the tomatoes seem only to be coated with oil. Discard the garlic and the bouquet garni.

Add the butter, cut into small pieces, to the eggs, season to taste, beat them lightly with a fork and, with a wooden spoon, stir them into the tomato mixture, keeping it over a low flame and continuing to stir constantly, adding when the eggs begin to thicken the basil, chopped at the last minute to avoid its blackening. Remove from the flame just before the desired consistency is achieved and continue stirring.

EGGS SCRAMBLED WITH CHEESE AND WHITE WINE

Fondue à la Comtoise

FOR 4

- 3 cloves garlic, crushed, peeled, chopped finely
- 1 cup dry white wine
- ¼ cup butter
- 10 eggs
- 5 ounces freshly grated Swiss Gruyère (it must be a dry and nutty-tasting cheese with only a few very tiny holes; Emmental-type cheese is too bland and too sweet)
- Salt, pepper

Simmer the chopped garlic in the white wine, covered, in a small saucepan for about ½ hour. The wine should, at this point, be reduced to about ⅓ cup—if it is not sufficiently reduced, turn the heat up with the lid off for a minute or so. Strain, discarding the fragments of garlic, and leave to cool.

Butter liberally the interior of an earthenware casserole and cut the rest of the butter into small pieces. Add all the ingredients, grinding in a generous amount of pepper. Beat with a small whisk. Install the casserole over a fairly high heat, using an asbestos pad to protect it from the direct flame, and stir the mixture with the whisk, first slowly, then, as the pieces of butter begin to melt, more rapidly, scraping constantly the sides and the bottom. As soon as the mixture begins to thicken noticeably, remove the casserole from the heat and continue stirring for a minute or so. The consistency should be that of a thick, but "pourable" cream. Serve directly from the cooking utensil onto well-warmed plates.

ALLEN

Mrs. Allen's Cook Book

Shirred Eggs

Butter individual baking dishes, and carefully slip in one or two eggs, as desired. Dust lightly with salt and pepper, and add a bit of butter. Set the dishes in a pan of boiling water, and cook the eggs gently in the oven until they are set. It will take about ten minutes for medium-soft eggs. They can be cooked directly in the oven without the hot water medium in a shorter time, but they will not be so digestible.

CHILD, BERTHOLLE, AND BECK

Mastering the Art of French Cooking

Omelettes

A good French omelette is a smooth, gently swelling, golden oval that is tender and creamy inside. And as it takes less than half a minute to make, it is ideal for a quick meal. There is a trick to omelettes, and certainly the easiest way to learn is to ask an expert to give you a lesson. Nevertheless, we hope the technique we describe will enable you, if you have never made an omelette before, to produce a good one. The difficulty with all written recipes for omelettes is that before you even start to make one you must read, remember, and visualize the directions from beginning to end, and practice the movements. For everything must go so quickly once the eggs are in the pan that there is no time at all to stop in the middle and pore over your book in order to see what comes next. Learning to make a good omelette is entirely a matter of practice. Do one after another for groups of people every chance you get for several days, and even be willing to throw some away. You should soon develop the art, as well as your own personal omelette style.

OMELETTE PANS

An omelette cannot be made in a stick pan. The eggs must be able to slide around freely. This is why it is a good idea to have one pan that is reserved for omelettes only. Various omelette makers like different kinds of pans: stainless steel, plain or treated aluminum, or plain or enameled iron. We prefer the French type of plain iron pan ⅛ inch thick. Eggs never stick to it when the pan is properly cared for; and its 2-inch sloping sides and long handle make it a perfect shape for omelettes done in the professional manner. Such pans are inexpensive and can be ordered from one of the shops importing French kitchenware, or can be bought in many restaurant supply houses. Ask for a Number 24 chef's iron pan with a bottom diameter of 7 inches. This is the perfect size for the 2- to 3-egg omelette. The pan must be treated before you use it. First scrub it with steel wool and scouring powder. Rinse and dry it. Then heat it for a minute or two, just until its bottom is too hot for your hand. Rub it with cooking oil and let it stand overnight. Just before making your first omelette, sprinkle a teaspoon of table salt in the pan, heat it, and rub vigorously for a minute with paper towels. Then rub the pan clean and it is ready for an omelette. If the pan is used only for omelettes, it needs no washing afterwards; merely rub it clean with paper towels. If the pan is washed, you should dry, warm, and oil it before putting it away. If the pan sticks a bit after a period of non-use, heat it gently, and rub it with salt. Never allow any type of pan to sit empty over heat; this does something to its internal structure so that foods stick to it ever after.

EGGS AND HOW TO BEAT THEM

An omelette can contain up to 8 eggs, but the individual 2- to 3-egg omelette is usually the tenderest, and by far the best size to practice making. At under 30 seconds an omelette, a number of people can be served in a very short time. In fact, unless you are extremely expert and have a restaurant-size heat source, we do not recommend larger omelettes at all. But if you do want to attempt them, be sure to have the correct size of pan. The depth of the egg mass in the pan should not be over ¼ inch, as the eggs must cook quickly. A pan with a 7-inch bottom is right for the 2- to 3-egg omelette; a 10- to 11-inch pan is required for 8 eggs.

Just before heating the butter in the pan, break the eggs into a mixing bowl and add salt and pepper. With a large table fork, beat the eggs only enough to blend the whites and yolks thoroughly. From 30 to 40 vigorous strokes should be sufficient.

If you are making several 2- to 3-egg omelettes, beat the necessary number of eggs and seasonings together in a large mixing bowl, and provide yourself with a ladle or measure. Two U.S. large eggs measure about 6 tablespoons; 3 eggs, about 9 tablespoons. Measure out the required quantity for each omelette as you are ready to make it, giving the eggs 4 or 5 vigorous beats before dipping them out with your measure.

TRANSFERRING THE OMELETTE FROM PAN TO PLATE

In the method described, the finished omelette ends up in the far lip of the pan. This is the way to transfer it from the pan to the plate.

Hold the plate in your left hand. Turn the omelette pan so its handle is to your right. Grasp the handle with your right hand, thumb on top. Rest the lip of the pan slightly off the center of the plate so the omelette will land in the middle of the plate. Then tilt plate and pan against each other at a 45-degree handle.

Quickly turn the pan upside down over the plate and the omelette will drop into position.

If it has not formed neatly, push it into shape with the back of a fork. Rub the top of the omelette with softened butter and serve as soon as possible, for omelettes toughen if they are kept warm.

L'OMELETTE BROUILLÉE
Scrambled Omelette

This is best in a French omelette pan, but a skillet can be used.

FOR 1 OMELETTE, 1 TO 2 SERVINGS
TIME: LESS THAN 30 SECONDS OF COOKING

2 or 3 eggs
Big pinch of salt
Pinch of pepper
A mixing bowl
A table fork

Beat the eggs and seasonings in the mixing bowl for 20 to 30 seconds until the whites and yolks are just blended.

CHILD
From Julia Child's Kitchen

L'omelette nature
Plain French Omelette

The best omelettes are single servings made from 2 or 3 eggs, since tenderness depends on the speed with which you make them. You will find the scrambled omelette-making technique (shaking the pan in one hand and stirring the eggs with the back of a fork in the other hand) both in Volume 1 of Mastering *and* The French Chef Cookbook. *The following no-hands technique forces the omelette to form itself by the manner in which you toss and shake the omelette pan. The whole process takes but a few seconds.*

FOR EACH OMELETTE
2 eggs (or 3 eggs, but start first with 2 "large" eggs until you are expert)
Salt and pepper
Optional: 1 Tb water
2 Tb butter

EQUIPMENT
A beating bowl and a table fork; a nonsticking frying pan 7 to 7½ inches bottom diameter; a warm dinner plate beside you.

Break the eggs into the bowl, add a pinch of salt and pepper, the optional water (to make a more perfect blending) and beat vigorously about 30 strokes of the fork to mix yolks and whites. Set the omelette pan over highest heat, add 1½ tablespoons of the butter; tilt pan in all directions to film bottom and sides. When melted, the butter will foam; when foam begins to subside and butter is on the point of browning, pour in the beaten eggs. They should sizzle as they hit the pan, indicating pan is hot enough.

Wait 4 or 5 seconds for a film of coagulated egg to form in the bottom of the pan.

Grasp pan by its handle and swish it about right and left to distribute the eggs for several seconds.

Then jerk pan roughly toward you several times, throwing egg mass against far edge of pan, and forcing it to roll over upon itself; continue the movement, lifting handle slightly up as you do so.

When omelette is nicely formed—in a matter of several seconds and 4 or 5 tossing movements—let it rest over heat in the edge of the pan 5 seconds or so, and unmold as follows.

Immediately grasp pan handle with your right hand, palm underneath, fingers on top, and hold warm plate in left hand. Tilt plate and far edge of pan together.

Quickly turn pan over upside down onto plate, to unmold the omelette.

Push omelette into shape with fork, if necessary, brush a bit of the remaining butter over the top to glaze it, and serve immediately. The omelette should be soft inside, the eggs barely set. The outside has hardly a hint of brown; it is golden yellow. (The late great Dione Lucas, by the way, was firm about not browning the omelette at all; however, the equally famous doyenne of omelettes, Madame Romaine de Lyon, lets her butter brown very lightly and produces a more golden omelette, while the omelette king, Rudy Stanish, follows the Lucas school.)

FILLED OMELETTES

Omelettes with cheese, potatoes, chicken livers, or other fillings make a whole quick main course, or are amusing for informal omelette parties. As an example, suppose you have a big bowl of seasoned and beaten eggs beside you, and a myriad of different fillings all ready in separate bowls on an electric warming tray. If one omelette takes less than 20 seconds to make, you can produce 3 omelettes a minute. Then suppose there are five of you tossing and serving omelettes together. The five of you could make 15 omelettes a minute, meaning you could easily serve a party of 300 people in 20 minutes! It works out on paper, anyway, and here are a few filling suggestions.

OMELETTES AUX FINES HERBES. Beat a tablespoon of fresh minced herbs into the eggs before making the omelette—parsley, chives, tarragon, chervil for instance.

OMELETTE AU CRESSON. Chop a small handful of watercress leaves and tender stems, and beat into the eggs before making the omelette.

OMELETTE AU FROMAGE. Have a bowl of coarsely grated Swiss cheese at your side. When eggs have settled in pan, and you have swished them once or twice, rapidly sprinkle on 2 to 3 tablespoons of the cheese; finish the omelette.

OMELETTE AU LARD ET AUX POMMES DE TERRE. Cut chunk bacon into half-inch dice, sauté to brown lightly, then add diced boiled potatoes and sauté together to brown; season to taste and keep warm. Proceed as for the cheese omelette.

CREAMED MUSHROOMS, CREAMED LOBSTER OR CRAB, CHICKEN LIVERS, ETC. Have these warm at your side—3 to 4 tablespoons per omelette. Either proceed as above, or slit top of finished omelette, and spoon in the filling, letting it also act as a decorative top to the omelette.

DE GOUY
The Gold Cook Book

Asparagus Tip Omelet

If you wish a perfect omelet, blanch the asparagus tips first. Add a tender diced artichoke heart and sauté both gently in butter but to not brown. Nothing else, no parsley, chervil or chives.

The asparagus and artichoke, singing in the butter, make a harmonious duet, to which no other voice should be added unless it be that of a truffle cut in thin blades, but then this would be a dream rather than an omelet.

The Flemish serve asparagus with quartered hard-cooked eggs and plain melted butter with a profusion of chopped parsley; the Italians sprinkle it first with grated Parmesan cheese, then with melted butter, and just before serving, glaze this delectable dish under the flame of the broiling oven; the Polish sprinkle it with sieved yolk of hard-cooked eggs mixed with finely chopped parsley and when ready to serve, cover the whole with freshly made fine breadcrumbs toasted to a light golden color in butter; the Germans serve it with brown sauce; the French like it "au gratin" and à la vinaigrette; the Spanish with a highly seasoned sauce into which both garlic and onion enter; while the British and Americans—more prosaic and practical—prefer the Hollandaise, or the Mousseline sauces, or sometimes the delicious Maltaise sauce; everyone to his liking—there is no accounting for taste.

I have often served asparagus with Bearnaise sauce, slightly flavored with tomato.

When served cold, asparagus, in addition to vinaigrette or French dressing, loves mayonnaise, especially when it is blended with an equal part of whipped cream. A fine dish for a summer luncheon. However, according to gourmets and connoisseurs, asparagus patty, when combined with button mushrooms and diced, cooked sweetbreads, is the apogee of its gastronomic preparation and a bottle of Chablis, or Montrachet will never be amiss with such a regal dish.

Green asparagus contains more bitter and resinous principles than the white.

THE CHEMICAL COMPOSITION OF AN EDIBLE PORTION OF FRESH ASPARAGUS IS AS FOLLOWS: WATER, 94.0%; PROTEIN, 1.8%; FAT, 0.2%; CARBOHYDRATES, 3.3%; ASH OR MINERAL SALTS, 0.7%; FUEL VALUE, (CALORIES) 1.05%, AND VITAMINS B AND C.

OLNEY

Simple French Food

Hot Onion Omelet with Vinegar

Omelette à la Lyonnaise

Lyons, to everyone in France, is known as the gastronomic capital of the world. What that means depends on who mouths the words. For the guidebooks and the foreigners it usually means elegant pike quenelles *in crayfish sauce, truffled chickens, artichokes stuffed with foie gras, salmon in Champagne, bass in pastry—the fare of the starred and sometimes very good restaurants, for instance, that of the famous mères* Lyonnaises *and their successors and that of Point and his successors. To others—*les vicieux*—it means the* mâchon, *a morning meal of hearty and attractively vulgar preparations washed down with a cool abundance of Beaujolais, vibrant in its tender youth. Typical of this food are boiled pigs' tails and rinds, quaint salads of lambs' trotters and testicles, agrestic terrines, sausages poached in white wine with boiled potatoes, tripes in every conceivable form—and the following omelet. Sautéed onions and a pan washed up with vinegar melt into a single recurrent theme in Lyonnaise cooking.*

3 large sweet onions (about 12 ounces), halved and finely sliced
¼ cup butter
3 eggs
Salt, pepper
1 tablespoon wine vinegar

Choose a relatively small, heavy pan in which to cook the onions so as to have a thick layer of onions—scattered loosely over a large surface, even with the tiniest of flames, they color too rapidly, their moisture being immediately evaporated. Cook them for at least ½ hour in 2 tablespoons of butter over a very low flame, tossing or stirring from time to time. They should be yellowed and very soft, but not browned.

Beat the eggs lightly with the seasonings, stir in the onions and prepare the omelet (hot pan, pour in the mixture when the butter stops foaming, stir a couple of times, lift the edges to let liquid run beneath, toss and, a couple of seconds later, slip it onto a warm plate—just done), add a tablespoon of butter to the pan, return to the heat, and, when the butter has stopped foaming and starts to turn brown, pour it over the omelet. Add the vinegar to the pan, swirl it around, and dribble it over the omelet.

HIRTZLER

The Hotel St. Francis Cook Book

EGGS BENEDICT. Cut an English muffin in two, toast, and put on platter. Put a slice of broiled ham on top of each half, a poached egg on top of the ham, cover all with Hollandaise, and lay a slice of truffle on top of the sauce.

BROWN
The South American Cook Book

Paraguayan Eggs with Tomato Sauce

Huevos con Salsa de Tomate

Devil eggs by removing yolks from hard-cooked eggs. Mix with a little salt, onion and melted butter, then replace in the whites. Put on platter in slow oven for 8 minutes and then pour over them a rich tomato sauce made by boiling tomatoes, salt, pepper, onion and a taste of vinegar until thick.

LUCAS
The Cordon Bleu Cook Book

Quiches Lorraine

- 2 cups flour
- 2 hard-boiled egg yolks
- 4 raw egg yolks
- 5 heaping tablespoons fat
- ⅛ teaspoon dry mustard
- salt
- 1 teaspoon paprika
- 4 tablespoons grated cheese
- 5 slices bacon
- 2 whole eggs
- ¼ cup cream
- cayenne pepper

PASTRY: Put the flour on a slab, make a well in the center and put in the strained, hard-boiled egg yolks. Add 3 raw egg yolks, fat, mustard, 1 teaspoon salt, paprika and 2 tablespoons grated cheese. Work center ingredients to a smooth paste. Work in the flour and roll out not too thick. Line a flan ring with wax paper. Sprinkle with rice and bake for 20 minutes in a 350° F. oven. Remove and fill with the following:

Cook finely shredded bacon until crisp in a hot pan; in the meantime beat 2 eggs and 1 egg yolk in a bowl. Add cream, 2 tablespoons grated cheese, salt, cayenne pepper, crisp bacon and bacon fat. Fill into the tart and put to set for 15 minutes in a slow oven. Remove and eat hot.

GREENE
Greene on Greens

Broccoli Frittata, Parma Style

This is the very best Italian frittata I have ever sampled.

- 5 tablespoons unsalted butter
- 1 tablespoon olive oil
- 1 medium onion, chopped
- 1 clove garlic, minced
- ½ cup cooked chopped ham or Canadian bacon
- 2 cups small broccoli flowerets (from about 1¼ pounds broccoli)
- 20 strands cooked spaghetti, roughly chopped (leftover is fine)
- 6 eggs
- ½ cup freshly grated Parmesan cheese
- ½ teaspoon crushed dried hot red pepper

1. Heat 3 tablespoons of the butter with the oil in a heavy 10-inch skillet over medium heat. Sauté the onion until golden. Add the garlic and ham; cook 3 minutes. Stir in the broccoli flowerets and spaghetti; toss until well coated with the mixture. Remove from the heat.

2. Beat the eggs in a large bowl until light. Add the broccoli mixture and all but 2 tablespoons of the Parmesan cheese.

3. Melt 1 tablespoon of the butter in the same skillet over medium heat. Pour in the broccoli-egg mixture. Immediately reduce the heat to low; cook, without stirring, 20 minutes.

4. Using a long spatula, carefully loosen the edges of the frittata and run the spatula underneath to loosen the bottom. Place a shallow plate over the skillet and quickly invert the frittata onto it.

5. Melt the remaining 1 tablespoon butter in the same skillet over medium-low heat. Carefully slide the frittata back into the pan. Sprinkle it with the crushed pepper and the remaining Parmesan cheese. Cook 5 minutes longer. Serve from the pan, in wedges—hot, cold, or at room temperature.

SERVES 4 TO 6

CASAS
The Foods and Wines of Spain

Tortilla Española

Potato Omelet

The tortilla *is a way of life in Spain and is loved by all, natives and tourists alike. A Spanish tortilla has nothing in common with its Mexican counterpart except its Latin root—*torte, *meaning a round cake. Although a Spanish* tortilla *is simply a potato omelet, it is not as simple to prepare as you might expect, unless you know the technique involved. And it is much more delicious than you might think a dish of such limited ingredients could be.*

Tortilla *is a great favorite with my family and friends. We often have it, cut in wedges, for dinner, accompanied by fried peppers and sausages. For large parties, I cut the* tortilla *into 1-inch squares to be picked up with toothpicks. It is good hot, but usually preferred at room temperature.*

SERVES 4–6

- 1 cup olive oil, or a mixture of olive and salad oils
- 4 large potatoes, peeled and cut in ⅛-inch slices
- Coarse salt
- 1 large onion, thinly sliced
- 4 large eggs

Heat the oil in an 8- or 9-inch skillet and add the potato slices one at a time to prevent sticking. Alternate potato layers with the onion slices and salt the layers lightly. Cook slowly, over a medium flame, lifting and turning the potatoes occasionally, until they are tender but not brown. (The potatoes will remain separated, not in a "cake.")

Meanwhile, in a large bowl beat the eggs with a fork until they are slightly foamy. Salt to taste. Remove the potatoes from the skillet and drain them in a colander, reserving about 3 tablespoons of the oil. (The potatoes give the oil a delicious flavor, so reserve the rest for future use.) Add the potatoes to the beaten eggs, pressing the potatoes down so that they are completely covered by the egg. Let the mixture sit 15 minutes.

Heat 2 tablespoons of the reserved oil in a large skillet until very hot (you may use the same skillet as long as absolutely nothing is stuck on the bottom). Add the potato-and-egg mixture, rapidly spreading it out in the skillet with the aid of a pancake turner. Lower the heat to medium-high and shake the pan often to prevent sticking. When the potatoes begin to brown underneath, invert a plate of the same size over the skillet. Flip the omelet onto the plate. Add about 1 tablespoon more of oil to the pan, then slide the omelet back into the skillet to brown on the other side. (If your skillet was not hot enough, some of the omelet may stick to the pan. If this happens, don't despair—scrape off the pieces and fit them into their places on the omelet. With subsequent flips, the pieces will mesh with the omelet.)

Lower the heat to medium. Flip the omelet 2 or 3 more times (this helps to give it a good shape) cooking briefly on each side. It should be slightly juicy within. Transfer to a platter and serve hot or at room temperature. I prefer it after it has been sitting for several hours. Serve with a Valdepeñas or Valencia wine.

MACAUSLAND
The Gourmet Cookbook

Jellied Egg Salad Gourmet

Puncture the narrow end of a dozen eggs and chip away a hole about ½ inch in diameter. Hold the open end over a dish and twist and turn the shells until the egg white slowly pours out. Blow out whatever egg white remains in the shell. Then break away just enough of the shell to remove the egg yolks. Reserve the yolks and whites for some other use. Rinse the empty shells in hot water, then in cold, and invert them in an egg carton to dry.

Soften 3 envelopes gelatin in ¼ cup sherry for 5 minutes. Dissolve the gelatin in 4 cups hot chicken broth, clarified with egg whites and shells, and highly seasoned with salt, cayenne, and 1 teaspoon each grated onion, finely chopped parsley, and chives. Add 2 teaspoons curry powder and blend thoroughly. Let the gelatin mixture cool to the congealing point, then combine it with 1 scant cup finely chopped smoked tongue, mixing well. Pour this mixture into the egg shells, filling the shells as full as possible, since gelatin tends to shrink in solidifying. Chop coarsely the remaining gelatin and use as a garnish for the platter. Let the shells chill in the refrigerator until serving time.

Crack the shells, remove them carefully, and arrange the jelly eggs in a row on a bed of water cress in the center of an oblong platter. On each side of the eggs lay rows of overlapping thin slices of cold tongue, cold liver sausage, roast beef, and slices of smoked turkey rolled cornucopia shape and filled with the chopped gelatin. Between the rows of meat there should be lines of white cabbage coleslaw, red cabbage coleslaw, and mayonnaise mixed with chopped celery and apples. Garnish the platter with half slices of ripe tomato. Top the slices with mayonnaise, and sprinkle them with a little paprika.

DE SILVA

In Memory's Kitchen

Gefüllte Eier [kalt] Pächter

Koche 10 Eier hart, schneide selbe durch. Nehme die Dotter heraus, passiere selbe gib dann 5 dkg Butter, 2 passierte Sardellen, etwas Senf, 3–4 Tropfen Maggi, 1/8 l geschlagenes Schlagobers, Petersilie, Zitronensaft. Nun gebe die Eier auf die Schüssel, übergiesse selbe mit Aspik vorher lasse der Fantasie freien Lauf, indem die Eier mit Schinken, Lachs, Kaviar, Kaperln verziert werden. Dann kann man die Eier in Papier Manschetten geben und serviert dazu heiße Semmelschnitten.

Cold Stuffed Eggs Pächter

Hard boil 10 eggs, cut them in half. Remove yolks and press them through a sieve. Add 5 decagrams butter, 2 anchovies pressed through a sieve, a little mustard, 3–4 drops Maggi [liquid seasoning], 1/8 liter whipped heavy cream, parsley, lemon juice. Now put eggs on a platter. Pour [liquid] aspic over. Before [pouring on the aspic] let fantasy run free and the eggs are garnished with ham, [smoked] salmon, caviar, capers. One can put the eggs into paper cuffs and serve them with hot sliced rolls.

BEARD

American Cookery

Scotch Eggs

6 hard-boiled eggs
1 pound well-seasoned sausage meat
Flour
2 eggs, lightly beaten
Bread crumbs

Peel the eggs and flour them lightly. Divide the sausage meat into six portions and flatten each section a bit. Flour your hands and wrap the sausage meat around the eggs to form a firm egg-shaped covering. Flour the eggs, dip in beaten eggs and roll in crumbs. Fry in deep fat at 375 degrees until nicely browned and cooked through. Drain on absorbent towels. Serve either whole or carefully cut in halves. Best served cold.

TOKLAS

The Alice B. Toklas Cook Book

Oeufs Francis Picabia

Break 8 eggs into a bowl and mix them well with a fork, add salt but no pepper. Pour them into a saucepan—yes, a saucepan, no, not a frying pan. Put the sauce over a very, very low flame, keep turning them with a fork while very slowly adding in very small quantities ½ lb. butter—not a speck less, rather more if you can bring yourself to it. It should take ½ hour to prepare this dish. The eggs of course are not scrambled but with the butter, no substitute admitted, produce a suave consistency that perhaps only gourmets will appreciate.

TSUJI
Japanese Cooking

Savory Cup Custard
Chawan-mushi

Though the word "custard" evokes images of sweet eggy desserts, this is a delicate, stock-enriched, nonsweet egg custard containing chicken, shrimp, and assorted vegetables. Inventive cooks will be able to come up with any number of variations: you can add anything that complements the taste of the savory custard base, including sliced mushroom, small strips of lemon rind, parboiled carrot slices, or, as Japanese do, parboiled bamboo shoot slices, slices of fish paste (kamaboko), *or even* udon *noodles.*

Attesting to the general popularity of this dish, special lidded chawan-mushi *cups are available in Japan wherever china is sold. You may safely use heatproof cups or conventional custard cups.*

Chawan-mushi *is one of the few Japanese dishes eaten with both chopsticks and a spoon. Even though the egg completely sets in steaming, the stock and juices released from various ingredients make the dish a little soupy. In fact, this dish is regarded by many as a soup and is often served as a soup course. In cold months it is brought to table piping hot, and in summer it is very good chilled.*

4 SERVINGS

2½–3 ounces (70–80 g) chicken breast
about 1 tsp *saké*
about 1 tsp light soy sauce
4 small raw shrimp, shelled and deveined
1 lily root (*yuri-ne*) (optional)
12 stalks trefoil (or equivalent amount of young spinach or watercress)
12–16 raw ginkgo nuts, shelled and peeled (if available)
4 raw chestnuts, peeled and slices

CUSTARD

4 medium eggs
2½ cups *dashi* or light chicken stock
½ tsp salt
1 Tbsp *mirin*
1 Tbsp light soy sauce

TO PREPARE: Prepare all the solid ingredients first. Cut chicken breast into ½-inch (1½-cm) morsels. Marinate in a scant amount of *saké* and light soy sauce for about 15 minutes. Drain; discard marinade.

Blanch shrimp in hot water for 30 seconds, remove, and pat dry. Leave whole, but if very large, slit half-open down the belly, press out flat, and cut in half crosswise.

Lily root is worth trying if you can find it. Its shape is somewhat like a flattened garlic bulb, but its flavor is mild and it has a pleasant, delicate texture. Separate bulb into segments and parboil gently in lightly salted water for 4–5 minutes. Drain. Wash trefoil or other greens, pat dry, and chop coarsely.

Shell and peel gingko nuts and use whole, if you are able to find fresh ones. Peel and slice chestnuts.

TO ASSEMBLE, STEAM, AND SERVE: Beat eggs in a medium-sized bowl. In another bowl mix the room-temperature *dashi*, salt, *mirin*, and light soy sauce. This recipe is one in which chicken stock is as good as *dashi*, not just a substitute. Pour stock mixture in a thin stream into beaten egg. Mix well, but do not beat. The surface of the mixture should be free of bubbles or foam. Strain. The seasoned stock mixture should be 3 times the volume of beaten egg, so apply this ratio of 3:1 in adjusting this recipe to the number of diners.

Divide the prepared solid ingredients between 4 cups, except for chopped trefoil or greens. Ladle the egg stock mixture into the cups, filling them to about ½ inch (1½ cm) from the top. Add chopped greens.

Cover each cup with plastic wrap or foil and set in a hot steamer. Cover steamer and steam over medium heat for 20 minutes, or place foil-covered cups in a bain-marie and cook in a preheated 425°F/220°C oven for 30 minutes.

The *chawan-mushi* is done when a toothpick inserted in the center comes out clean. The custard should be set but still jiggle freely. The volume of the custard will not increase much. It is overdone if the top is pocked or cracked and tough looking.

Serve hot or chilled and eat with a spoon and chopsticks. If you intend to serve chilled *chawan-mushi*, omit the chicken, which might develop an odor in refrigeration.

BREAKFAST AND BRUNCH

KELLOGG

Every-day Dishes and Every-day Work

Granola

Granola is a preparation of oats and wheat ready cooked. It is excellent eaten with milk or cream, either hot or cold. It may also be served with fruit juices, or it may be used in place of bread crumbs for scalloped vegetables, and for sprinkling the tops of prepared dishes.

KELLOGG

Every-day Dishes and Every-day Work

Oatmeal Mush

GRANOLA MUSH.—Granola makes a most appetizing and quickly prepared breakfast dish. Into a quart of boiling water sprinkle a pint of granola. Milk may be used instead of water, if preferred; then a little less granola will be needed. Cook for two or three minutes, and serve hot with cream.

GRANOLA FRUIT MUSH.—Prepare the mush as directed, and stir into it, when done, a large cupful of nicely steamed, seedless raisins. Serve hot with cream. Milk may be used instead of water, if preferred.

GRANOLA PEACH MUSH.—Instead of the raisins directed in the preceding recipe, add to the mush, when done, a pint of sliced yellow peaches. Finely cut, mellow sweet apples, sliced bananas, or blueberries may be used in a similar way.

RASPBERRY GRANOLA MUSH.—For this, use the freshly extracted juice of red raspberries, diluted with one part of water, or the juice from canned red raspberries. Heat a quart of the juice to boiling, sprinkle in sufficient granola to thicken (about one pint will be needed), cook for two or three minutes, and serve hot, with or without cream.

CUNNINGHAM

The Breakfast Book

The Coach House Bread and Butter Pudding

TEN SERVINGS

This is the best bread pudding ever. The recipe comes generously from Leon Lianides, owner of the legendary New York restaurant The Coach House. Don't overbake the pudding—remove it from the oven when the center still trembles slightly.

- 12 or 13 slices French bread, crusts removed (not sourdough)
- 8 tablespoons (1 stick) butter, room temperature
- 5 eggs
- 4 egg yolks
- 1 cup granulated sugar
- ⅛ teaspoon salt
- 4 cups milk
- 1 cup heavy cream
- 1 tablespoon vanilla extract
- Confectioners' sugar for sprinkling

Preheat the oven to 375°F.

Butter one side of each slice of bread and set aside.

Put the eggs, yolks, granulated sugar, and salt in a large bowl and beat until thoroughly mixed.

Pour the milk and cream into a heavy-bottomed saucepan and heat until scalded (tiny bubbles will form around the edge of the pan). Remove from the heat and, whisking briskly, slowly add the egg mixture. Stir in the vanilla.

Have ready enough boiling water to come 2½ inches up the sides of a pot large enough to hold a 2-quart baking dish. Layer the bread, buttered side up, in the baking dish. Strain the custard into the dish (the bread will float to the top). Put the pot of boiling water into the oven and then put the custard-filled dish into it.

Bake about 45 minutes, or until the custard is set except for a slight tremble in the center. Remove from the oven and sprinkle confectioners' sugar on top. It is delicious hot or cold, and just perfect with a little unsweetened heavy cream poured over.

JUNIOR LEAGUE OF CHARLESTON
Charleston Receipts

Breakfast Shrimp

1½ cups small, peeled raw shrimp
2 tablespoons chopped onion
2 teaspoons chopped green pepper
3 tablespoons bacon grease
Salt and pepper to taste
1 teaspoon Worcestershire sauce
1 tablespoon tomato catsup
1½ tablespoons flour
1 cup water or more

Fry onion and green pepper in bacon grease. When onion is golden, add shrimp; turn these several times with onion and pepper. Add enough water to make a sauce—about 1 cup. Do not cover shrimp with water or your sauce will be tasteless. Simmer 2 or 3 minutes and thicken with flour and a little water made into a paste. Add seasoning, Worcestershire sauce and catsup. Cook slowly until sauce thickens. Serve with hominy. Serves 4.

Mrs. Ben Scott Whaley (Emily Fishburne)

VARIATIONS: A variation to the above receipt says that cooked shrimp may be floured and fried with onions browned in butter. Hot water is slowly added and shrimp allowed to simmer under cover for several minutes or until a thick gravy forms. Stir constantly.

Fish and Seafood

FISH

LAUREL
Living on the Earth

How to Smoke Fish

A smoke house should be cool enough so that it doesn't cook the meat. This can be accomplished by funneling stove smoke into a wooden box or by building a little smoke house of cardboard. Reinforce a cardboard carton with strips of wood along the corners and 2 sets of strips on opposing sides, one set near the top and one set near the middle.

Cut off the bottom of the box and cut out a door 10 inches by 12 inches folding at the hinge. Pierce the box to insert rods (2 at the top to keep the flaps up, 3 just above the upper set of strips and 2 just above the lower set of strips. Place a screen over the lower rods to catch fish that fall.

Scale, decapitate and disembowel the fish (leave collar bones). Soak in brine (4 cups salt to 1 gallon water) 1 hour (or less for little fish). Rinse in clear water, hang on wire and let dry ½ hour or until surface shines. Use heavy wire: under the collar bone, around backbone and up on other side of collar bone. Place big fish on the screen. Prepare a fire on flat ground of green hardwood sticks 1 inch in diameter (oak, hickory, beech, sweet bay, alder, apple, citrus and corn cobs or coconut husks).

Hang fish from the 3 rods above the upper strips. Close the top flaps. Place the box over the fire with door facing wind. Cover all openings and pile dirt around sides (make it airtight). Stoke fire every ½ hour. Check at 3 hours and every hour after that. Fish is done when flesh separates from backbone. Remove house. Cool.

PÉPIN
La Technique

Gravlax à la Française

Salt-Cured Salmon with Green Peppercorns

Gravlax, or Gravlaks, is a Scandinavian salmon dish. It is customarily made by boning out a fresh salmon and pickling it with lots of sugar and a dash of salt. It is heavily seasoned with dill. After a day or so, the fillets are sliced and served raw with a sweet mustard and dill sauce. Our version, à la française, is pickled with salt instead of sugar and is seasoned with a number of fresh herbs and a lot of green peppercorns. It is served sprinkled with capers, virgin oil and a dash of vinegar. One 7- to 8-pound salmon will serve about 30 persons.

1. Choose the freshest possible salmon with bright and glossy eyes and red, plump gills. Cut off the head, sliding your knife under the bone near the gills.

2. Using a sharp knife, start cutting along, and just above, the backbone.

3. Follow the central bone. Try to leave as little meat as possible on the bone.

4. Do not cut through, but follow the shape of the rib cage, sliding your knife, almost flat, along the ribs. Finish by "lifting up" the whole fillet.

5. Cut under the backbone and follow the same method as described in steps 3 and 4. The central bone is now on top of the knife.

6. Go slowly and be careful not to cut into the meat with your knife. Keep the blade almost flat. Separate the flesh and the rib cage, without going through the ribs.

7. Central bone completely separated. Note the rib cage.

8. Using small pliers, pull out the bones which go straight down in a line, almost in the center of each fillet. Start at the head. (This is the same technique used to clean smoked salmon.)

9. You can feel the bones by rubbing the tip of one finger from the head down to the tail of the fillet. The bones go about three-quarters down the fillet and there are about 30.

10. Using a large, stiff knife, begin to remove the skin.

11. Keep the blade on a 30-degree angle so you do not cut through the skin. Pull on the skin with one hand, and cut forward in jigsaw fashion, scraping the skin clear of all meat.

12. Remove the skin and discard.

13. Remove, as thin as you possibly can, the white skin on the inside and thinner side of each fillet.

14. Turn the fillets over. All along the central line you will notice a dark brownish strip of flesh. Cut it off, going all the way down the center line.

15. The meat should be completely pink and cleaned of brown meat, bones and gristle. Seven to 8 pounds of salmon will yield two fillets between 2¼ and 2½ pounds each.

16. For each fillet, mix together ⅓ cup coarse (kosher) salt and 2 teaspoons granulated sugar. Place the fillets on a large piece of aluminum foil. Rub the salt and sugar mixture on both sides of the fillet. Reduce the salt and sugar mixture if the fillets are smaller.

17. Cover with another sheet of foil and fold the edges carefully.

18. The fillets should be well wrapped and tight in the foil. Place on a tray in the refrigerator for a day and a half. Turn the fillet upside down and let pickle for another day and a half. (If the fillets are smaller or thinner, cut the curing time to 2 days instead of 3.)

19. After 3 days, unwrap the fillets. Mash 4 tablespoons green peppercorns (you need the soft green canned peppercorns from Madagascar) into a purée. Chop ½ cup of fresh herbs (chervil, tarragon and thyme mixed together). Spread on both sides of the fillets (¼ cup for one fillet). (If green peppercorns are not available, you can use a tablespoon of coarsely ground black peppercorn instead.)

20. Wrap again in foil and place between 2 cookie sheets. Place about 8 to 10 pounds of weight on top of the cookie sheets to flatten the fillets. Keep refrigerated and pressed for 12 to 24 hours. Slice and serve. (The peppercorns and herbs may discolor the salmon in spots. This does not impair its flavor.)

NATHAN
Jewish Cooking in America

Like Mr. Leibner's father, first-generation immigrants tried to catch live fish. The late Jack Bloom, one of the founders of the Jewish community in Albuquerque, New Mexico, fished carp until his death at eighty-one. He traveled regularly to the irrigation ditches of the Rio Grande, near the Isleta Pueblo, requested a fishing permit from the Indians, and fished for fresh carp for the "bubbies and zaydes," who, he said, needed it for the Jewish holidays.

My mother-in-law does not insist on live fish, but she is a very demanding customer; she would never accept the first fish offered by a fishmonger. She has even been very reluctant to use my food processor for grinding the fish and is aghast when I suggest poaching the patties for less than 2 hours. (Gefilte fish cooks in less than 20 minutes.) Until I married into this "start-from-scratch" gefilte fish family, we graced our Passover table with the jarred variety. What a difference homemade makes! Now gefilte fish-making has become a welcome twice-yearly ritual in our house—at Rosh Hashanah and Passover. At our Passover seder, we all wait with baited breath for my husband's opinion. "Peshke, *your gefilte fish is better than ever!" gets a broad grin from his Jewish mother.*

The gefilte fish recipe we use today came with my husband's family from the DP camps.

Classic Gefilte Fish

Gefilte fish is one of those recipes where touch and taste are essential ingredients. A basic recipe goes this way: "You put in this and add that." If you don't want to taste the raw fish, add a bit more seasoning than you normally would. What makes this recipe Galicianer (southern Polish) is the addition of sugar. For some reason the farther south in Poland, the more sugar would be added. A Lithuanian Jew would never sweeten with sugar but might add beets to the stock. I have added ground carrot and parsnip to the fish, something that is done in the Ukraine, because I like the slightly sweet taste and rougher texture. If you want a darker broth, do not peel the onions and leave them whole.

7 to 7½ pounds whole carp, whitefish, and pike, filleted and ground*
4 quarts cold water or to just cover
3 teaspoons salt or to taste
3 onions, peeled
4 medium carrots, peeled
2 tablespoons sugar or to taste
1 small parsnip, chopped (optional)
3 to 4 large eggs
Freshly ground pepper to taste
½ cup cold water (approximately)
⅓ cup matzah meal (approximately)

*Ask your fishmonger to grind the fish. Ask him to reserve the tails, fins, heads, and bones. Be sure he gives you the bones and trimmings. The more whitefish you add, the softer your gefilte fish will be.

1. Place the reserved bones, skin, and fish heads in a wide, very large saucepan with a cover. Add the water and 2 teaspoons of the salt and bring to a boil. Remove the foam that accumulates.

2. Slice 1 onion in rounds and add along with 3 of the carrots. Add the sugar and bring to a boil. Cover and simmer for about 20 minutes while the fish mixture is being prepared.

3. Place the ground fish in a bowl. In a food processor finely chop the remaining onions, the remaining carrot, and the parsnip; or mince them by hand. Add the chopped vegetables to the ground fish.

4. Add the eggs, one at a time, the remaining teaspoon of salt, pepper, and the cold water, and mix thoroughly. Stir in enough matzah meal to make a light, soft mixture that will hold its shape. Wet your hands with cold water, and scooping up about ¼ cup of fish form the mixture into oval shapes, about 3 inches long. Take the last fish head and stuff the cavity with the ground fish mixture.

5. Remove from the saucepan the onions, skins, head, and hones and return the stock to a simmer. Gently place the fish patties in the simmering fish stock. Cover loosely and simmer for 20 to 30 minutes. Taste the liquid while the fish is cooking and add seasoning to taste. Shake the pot periodically so the fish patties won't stick. When gefilte fish is cooked, remove from the water and allow to cool for at least 15 minutes.

6. Using a slotted spoon carefully remove the gefilte fish and arrange on a platter. Strain some of the stock over the fish, saving the rest in a bowl.

7. Slice the cooked carrots into rounds cut on a diagonal about ¼ inch thick. Place a carrot round on top of each gefilte fish patty. Put the fish head in the center and decorate the eyes with carrots. Chill until ready to serve. Serve with a sprig of parsley and horseradish.

YIELD: ABOUT 26 PATTIES

ROJAS-LOMBARDI

The Art of South American Cooking

Cebiche de Atún

Tuna Ceviche

SERVES 6 TO 8

Anyone who has lived on the Pacific coast of South America knows and appreciates the flavorful fish known as bonito, *which resembles a small tuna. Both tuna and bonito work well in a ceviche. Be sure to use a very sharp knife with a smooth blade to cut the fish; otherwise the edges of the fish cubes will shred when they are marinated.*

2½ pounds fresh tuna
1 cup lemon juice (about 6 lemons)
1 cup lime juice (about 6 limes)
1½-inch piece fresh ginger, grated (2 tablespoons)
2 jalapeño or serrano peppers, seeded and chopped
6 scallions, thinly sliced (½ cup)
2 tablespoons coarse salt
1 red bell pepper, very finely diced
3 tablespoons olive oil
¼ cup finely chopped fresh cilantro leaves

1. Wipe the fish with a damp cloth. Remove any skin and bones and cut into ¼-inch cubes. Set aside.

2. In a large stainless-steel, porcelain, or glass bowl, combine the lemon and lime juices, ginger, peppers, scallions, salt, and the tuna cubes. Marinate, covered, in the refrigerator for 2 hours.

3. Toss the diced red pepper with the olive oil and add to the marinated tuna cubes. Just before serving, correct the seasoning with salt to taste and gently toss in the cilantro.

PÉPIN
La Technique

Sole Meunière

Sole Sautéed in Butter

Whereas the sole bercy *is cooked with the little side bones intact (they are removed after cooking),* sole meunière *is cooked without them. The reason is that where the trimmings enhance the stock the* sole bercy *is cooked in, they just absorb the butter used to sauté the* sole meunière. *They do not add any extra flavor to the meat of the sole. Therefore, even though the sole will look smaller, it is preferable to remove the side bones before cooking.*

1. Clean the sole, leaving the white skin on. With a pair of scissors, remove the bones on the side of the fillets.

2. Sprinkle the sole with salt and a small dash of pepper. Dredge in flour.

3. Melt ⅓ stick of butter in a skillet. Place sole in the hot butter, skin side down, and cook on medium to low heat for 6 to 7 minutes on each side.

4. Bring the skillet directly to the table. Using a spoon and fork, lift up the top fillets and place on each side of the sole.

5. Remove the central bone and discard.

6. Place the bottom fillets on a hot plate and cover with the top fillets. The sole is reconstructed and completely boned.

7. Add 1 tablespoon of hot brown gravy all around (optional) and the drippings of the skillet.

8. Cover with slices of lemon dipped in chopped parsley and serve immediately.

THIS RECIPE SERVES 2 AS A FIRST COURSE

BITTMAN
How to Cook Everything

Skate with Brown Butter

MAKES 2 SERVINGS
TIME: 20 MINUTES

Skate—which, along with ray, appears in every fictional depiction of the deep sea—actually lives fairly close to the shore. It's an unusually structured fish, but easy to eat: Just lift the meat off the central cartilage and you have a perfect fillet. Usually this is done after cooking, as it is here. One warning: Never buy skate that has not been skinned; the skin is virtually impossible to remove at home.

- 1 skate wing, 1½ to 2 pounds, skinned
- About 4 cups Fast Fish Stock or a mixture of 4 cups water and ½ cup white or white wine vinegar
- Salt to taste (optional)
- 1 onion, cut in half (optional)
- 1 bay leaf
- 1 tablespoon drained capers, lightly crushed
- 2 tablespoons minced fresh parsley leaves
- 4 tablespoons (½ stick) butter
- 1 tablespoon wine vinegar, red or white

1. Place the skate in a deep, wide saucepan or skillet and add enough liquid to cover. Salt the liquid if necessary and add the onion if desired and the bay leaf. Bring to a boil, skim off any foam, turn the heat to medium-low, and poach the skate until you can easily lift the meat off the cartilage at the wing's thickest point, about 10 minutes.

2. Remove the skate, drain it, and place it on a hot platter. If you like, you can lift the top half of the meat with a broad spatula, remove the cartilage, and replace the meat (it's not as difficult as it sounds). Top the fish with the capers and parsley.

3. During the last 5 minutes of the poaching, prepare the brown butter: Heat the butter over medium heat. After it foams it will turn golden and then darken; just when it becomes dark brown, take it off the heat and drizzle it over the skate. Rinse the saucepan with the vinegar and pour that over everything. Serve instantly.

PÉPIN
La Technique

Saumon Poché en Gelée

Poached Salmon Glazed with Aspic

There is nothing more glorious than a large, decorated, glazed salmon for a buffet. It is not difficult to make but it requires some time and effort. You will need a fish poacher, preferably one that is made of tin or stainless steel because aluminum tends to discolor the broth. For a 6½- to 7-pound salmon, the poacher should be 28 to 30 inches long. Make the vegetable stock and poach the salmon in it one day ahead. (If there's any salmon left over, the meat can be molded in aspic and served very attractively with vegetable garnishes.

- 2 cups coarsely chopped green of leek
- 2 cups diced carrots
- 2 cups coarsely chopped leafy celery
- 2 tablespoons salt
- 1 teaspoon black peppercorns
- 4 bay leaves
- 2 thyme leaves

1. Place all the ingredients in a large kettle, cover with water and boil on a high heat for 30 minutes. Pour the stock and vegetables into the fish poacher.

2. Place the removable perforated rack on top of the vegetables. Lay the fish on top and fill with cold water, enough to cover the fish. The stock should be barely lukewarm. Bring to a simmer on medium to high heat. As soon as the stock starts simmering, reduce the heat to very low and let the fish poach (just under a simmer) for 30 minutes. (This is equal to 10 minutes per inch of thickness at the thickest point.) Remove from heat and let the fish cool off gently in the broth overnight.

3. Lift from the broth. (The salmon should be intact. It if is split, it boiled too fast.) Let it drain and set for a good hour. Then slide the salmon onto the working table. Cut through the thick skin in a decorative pattern near the head.

4. Pull the skin off. It should come easily.

5. Using a small pair of pliers or tweezers, pull off the bones that stick out along the back of the fish.

6. Scrape off the top of the flesh, especially along the middle line to remove darkish brown fatty flesh. The salmon should be nice and pink all over. When the salmon is all cleaned, slide it onto a large serving platter. If you do not own a platter large enough to accommodate the salmon, cut an oval piece of plywood, pad with a towel, cover with a piece of white cloth and staple underneath.

7. Using vegetable flowers, decorate the salmon. First, place long strips of blanched green of leeks near the head and tail to outline the edge of the skin. Next, place strips down both sides of the salmon to frame the area to be decorated.

8. Make a flowerpot with thin slices of cooked carrots and green of leek.

9. Make flowers using your imagination. Simulate the eye of the fish with the white of a hard-boiled egg and the black of an olive.

10. Make an aspic with the poaching broth by thoroughly mixing together 5 egg whites, 3 cups greens (a mixture of leeks, scallions, parsley and celery) and 5 to 6 envelopes of plain gelatin. Add 10 cups of strong, flavorful poaching liquid. Bring the mixture to a boil, stirring to avoid scorching. Let it come to a strong boil; then shut the heat off. Let the mixture settle for 10 minutes, then pour through a sieve lined with wet paper towels. Chill the mixture on ice until syrupy, and glaze the salmon. Repeat until the whole surface is coated with aspic.

11. Prepare the garnishes. Fill artichoke bottoms with vegetable salad.

12. Slit, without going through, a large wedge of tomato. Pull open and

13. Set a quarter of a hard-boiled egg in the opening.

14. Cut two tomatoes in half. Squeeze the seeds and some juice out. Compress the flesh inside to make a receptacle and fill it with the vegetable salad.

15. Decorate the top of the garnishes with strips or cut-outs of tomatoes, leeks, eggs and the like. Decorate around the salmon with lettuce leaves and the garnishes. Carve in the dining room.

THE SALMON WILL SERVE 15 TO 18

TIME-LIFE BOOKS
Russian Cooking

Kulebiaka

Flaky Salmon or Cabbage Loaf

TO SERVE 8 TO 10

PASTRY
4 cups all-purpose flour
½ pound chilled unsalted butter, cut into bits
6 tablespoons chilled vegetable shortening
1 teaspoon salt
10 to 12 tablespoons ice water

SALMON FILLING
2 cups dry white wine
1 cup coarsely chopped onions
½ cup coarsely chopped celery
1 cup scraped, coarsely chopped carrots
10 whole black peppercorns
4½ teaspoons salt
2½ pounds fresh salmon, in one piece
8 tablespoons unsalted butter (¼-pound stick)
½ pound fresh mushrooms, thinly sliced
3 tablespoons fresh, strained lemon juice
Freshly ground black pepper
3 cups finely chopped onions
½ cup unconverted, long-grain white rice
1 cup chicken stock, fresh or canned
⅓ cup finely cut fresh dill leaves
3 hard-cooked eggs, finely chopped

CABBAGE FILLING
3-pound head of white cabbage, quartered, cored, then coarsely shredded
4 tablespoons butter
2 large onions, coarsely chopped
4 hard-cooked eggs, finely chopped
¼ cup finely cut fresh dill leaves
2 tablespoons finely chopped parsley
1 tablespoon salt
½ teaspoon sugar
Freshly ground black pepper

2 tablespoons butter, softened
1 egg yolk, mixed with 1 tablespoon cream
1 tablespoon butter, melted
1 cup melted butter, hot but not brown, or sour cream

PASTRY: In a large, chilled bowl, combine the flour, butter, shortening and salt. Working quickly, use your fingertips to rub the flour and fat together until they blend and resemble flakes of coarse meal. Pour 10 tablespoons of the water over the mixture all at once, toss together lightly and gather into a ball. If the dough seems crumbly, add up to 2 tablespoons more ice water by drops. Divide the dough in half, dust each half with flour, and wrap them separately in wax paper. Refrigerate 3 hours, or until firm.

SALMON FILLING: Combine 3 quarts of water, the wine, the coarsely chopped onion, celery, carrots, peppercorns, and 3 teaspoons of the salt in a 4- to 6-quart enameled or stainless-steel casserole. Bring to a boil over high heat, then lower the salmon into the liquid and reduce the heat to low. Simmer 8 to 10 minutes, or until the fish is firm to the touch. With a slotted spatula, transfer the fish to a large bowl, remove the skin and bones, if any, and separate into small flakes with your fingers or a fork.

Melt 2 tablespoons of the butter in a heavy 10- to 12-inch skillet set over high heat. Add the mushrooms, reduce the heat to moderate, and, stirring occasionally, cook for 3 to 5 minutes, or until the mushrooms are soft. With a slotted spoon, transfer the mushrooms to a small bowl and toss them with lemon juice, ½ teaspoon of salt and a few grindings of pepper.

Melt 4 more tablespoons of butter in the skillet over high heat and drop in all but 1 tablespoon of the finely chopped onions. Reduce the heat to moderate and, stirring occasionally, cook 3 to 5 minutes, or until the onions are soft but not brown. Stir in the remaining 1 teaspoon of salt and ¼ teaspoon of pepper and with a rubber spatula, scrape into the mushrooms.

Now melt the remaining 2 tablespoons of butter in the skillet over high heat. Drop in the remaining tablespoon of chopped onion, reduce the heat to moderate and stirring frequently, cook for 2 to 3 minutes, or until soft but not brown. Stir in the rice and cook 2 or 3 minutes, stirring almost constantly, until each grain is coated with butter. Pour in the chicken stock, bring to a boil, and cover the pan tightly. Reduce the heat to low and simmer for 17 minutes, or until the water is completely absorbed and the rice is tender and fluffy. Off the heat, stir in the dill with a fork. Add the cooked mushrooms and onions, rice and chopped, hard-cooked eggs to the bowl of salmon and toss together lightly but thoroughly. Taste for seasoning.

CABBAGE FILLING: Over high heat, bring 4 quarts of lightly salted water to a boil in an 8- to 10-quart pot and drop in the cabbage. Reduce the heat to moderate and cook uncovered for 5 minutes. Then drain the cabbage in a colander and set it aside.

Melt the butter over high heat in a deep skillet or 3- to 4-quart casserole. Add the chopped onions, reduce the heat to moderate, and cook 5 to 8 minutes, or until the onions are soft and lightly colored. Drop in the cabbage and cover the pan. (The pan may be filled to the brim, but the cabbage will shrink as it cooks.) Simmer over low heat for 30 to 40 minutes, or until the cabbage is tender, then uncover the pan, raise the heat to high and boil briskly until almost all of the liquid in the pan has evaporated. Drain the cabbage in a colander and combine it with the chopped eggs, dill and parsley. Stir in the salt, sugar and a few grindings of pepper and taste for seasoning.

TO ASSEMBLE: Preheat the oven to 400°. Place one ball of dough on a floured surface and roll it into a rough rectangle about 1 inch thick. Dust with flour and roll until the dough is about ⅛ inch thick, then trim it to a rectangle 7 inches wide by 16 inches long.

Coat a large cookie sheet with 2 tablespoons of butter, drape the pastry over the rolling pin and unroll it over the cookie sheet. Place the filling along the length of the pastry, leaving a 1-inch border of dough exposed around it. With a pastry brush, brush the exposed rim of dough with the egg-yolk- and-cream mixture. Roll the other half of the dough into a rectangle about 9 inches wide and 15 inches long, drape over the pin and unroll over the filling. Seal the edges by pressing down hard with the back of a fork. Or use your fingertips or a pastry crimper to pinch the edges into narrow pleats. Cut out a 1-inch circle from the center of the dough. If you like you may gather any remaining pastry scraps into a ball, roll them out again, and with a cookie cutter or small, sharp knife, cut out decorative shapes such as leaves or triangles and decorate the top of the loaf. Coat the entire surface of the pastry with the remaining egg-yolk-and-cream mixture, place any pastry shapes on top, and refrigerate for 20 minutes. Pour 1 tablespoon of melted butter into the opening of the loaf and bake the kulebiaka in the center of the oven for 1 hour, or until golden brown. Serve at once, accompanied by a pitcher of melted butter or sour cream.

CONSTRUCTING THE CLASSIC "KULEBIAKA"

A delicate filling of salmon, mushrooms, onions, rice, eggs and herbs is mounded high on a 7-by-16-inch rectangle of dough that has been set on a buttered cookie sheet. With a pastry brush, coat the exposed rim of dough with an egg-yolk-and-cream mixture, then drape a 9-by-18-inch rectangle of dough over a rolling pin (below) and unroll it over the filling.

One way of sealing the loaf begins with a gentle brushing of the edges with the yolk-and-cream mixture.

Turn up the border of dough to make a shallow rim around filling. Be careful not to stretch the dough.

With a pastry crimper, pinch the rim in narrow pleats (or simply make shallow cuts with a small knife).

If you like, you may gather any remaining pastry scraps into a ball, roll them out again and, with a cookie cutter, cut out such decorative shapes as leaves. Use a small knife to make leaf veinings on the dough. Cut out a small circle from the center of the loaf and brush the entire surface of the loaf with the egg-yolk-and-cream mixture. Then arrange the pastry leaves around the opening and refrigerate before baking.

FARMER
The Boston Cooking-School Cook Book

Baked Cod with Oyster Stuffing

Clean a four-pound cod, sprinkle with salt and pepper, brush over with lemon juice, stuff, and sew. Gash, skewer, and bake as Baked Halibut with Stuffing. Serve with Oyster Sauce.

OYSTER STUFFING

1 cup cracker crumbs
¼ cup melted butter
½ teaspoon salt
⅛ teaspoon pepper
1½ teaspoons lemon juice
½ tablespoon finely chopped parsley
1 cup oysters

Add seasonings and butter to cracker crumbs. Clean oysters, and remove tough muscles; add soft parts to mixture with enough oyster liquor to moisten.

ANDREWS
Catalan Cuisine

Bacallà amb Mel

Salt Cod with Honey

I remember a game I used to play with friends, in younger years, of trying to invent the most unlikely or revolting-sounding food combinations possible—things, I recall, like raw oysters with chocolate sauce and pineapple-clam cake. This dish, I imagine, must sound a bit like one of those to many readers or at least like some mindless nouvelle (or nova) excess. In fact, though, salt cod with honey is neither nouvelle nor revolting. It's an old Catalan mountain dish, first mentioned in print in the seventeenth century and said to have been an invention of necessity—the union of two easily stored, well preserved ingredients, eaten together simply to provide a kind of calorie-loading, essential for survival in cold climates during the cropless winter months.

As for the way it tastes—well, think of something Moroccan (a honey-flavored chicken tajine*, for instance) or Chinese (sweet-and-sour fish, say); if sweet and salt are balanced skillfully the result can be extraordinary. Even in Catalonia I must admit,* Bacallà amb Mel *can be a sort of rough-and-ready dish, lacking in subtlety. Not so this version, which comes from one of the more imaginative restaurants in Barcelona, Petit París (which is not at all French, incidentally: It's on a street called París, and is indeed* petit*—which is a Catalan word as well as a French one). As ex-architect Climent Maynés, who runs the place with his wife Gloria Blanco, notes, his version of the dish contrasts not only sweet and salt but also the sharpness of vinegar and the fresh green crunch of escarole.*

TO SERVE 4 (AS MAIN COURSE) OR 6 (AS APPETIZER)

⅓ cup flour
1 teaspoon dry yeast
Salt
1 egg, lightly beaten
2 tablespoons honey, preferably Provençal or Spanish
Olive oil
1½ pounds thick-cut salt cod, desalted, skinned, boned, and cut into 1½-inch cubes
1 head young escarole or 2–3 bunches watercress, finely chopped
Honey vinegar or white wine vinegar

Combine the flour and yeast in a mixing bowl with a pinch of salt.

In another bowl, mix the egg, 1 tablespoon of the honey, and about ¼ cup of water together to form a batter; then stir in the flour mixture and mix together well. (Add more water if the batter seems too thick.)

In another bowl, mix the remaining honey with ¼–½ cup of warm water (depending on the sweetness desired), and set aside.

Fill a cassola or other deep pan with at least 1 inch of oil (or use a deep-fryer), and heat the oil to 375°.

Dip the salt cod cubes into the batter, and fry them in batches until golden-brown; then drain on paper towels.

Divide the chopped escarole or watercress into equal portions on individual plates, and dress with a few drops of vinegar (or more to taste).

Divide the salt cod pieces equally among the plates, and drizzle with honey water.

CRAB

GAIGE

New York World's Fair Cook Book

Baltimore Crab Cakes

This is more of a home dish.

1 pound crab meat
1½ teaspoons salt
1 teaspoon white pepper
1 teaspoon English dry mustard
2 teaspoons Worcestershire sauce
1 egg yolk
2 teaspoons cream sauce or mayonnaise
flour
beaten eggs
bread crumbs
1 teaspoons chopped parsley

Put crab meat into mixing bowl; add mustard, Worcestershire sauce, egg yolk, cream sauce or mayonnaise, and chopped parsley. Mix well, making four crab cakes; press together, dip into flour, then into beaten eggs, then into bread crumbs. Fry the cakes in a hot greased pan.

HIBBEN

The National Cook Book

Crab-Flake Cakes (Baltimore)

2 cups crab meat
1 cup milk
yolk 1 egg
2 tablespoons flour
½ teaspoon onion juice
2 tablespoons butter
1 teaspoon Worcestershire sauce
salt and pepper
bread crumbs
rice cream sauce

Melt the butter in a saucepan and add to it the flour; when well mixed, add the milk gradually, stirring constantly until smooth. Add the egg yolk beaten up with Worcestershire sauce and onion juice, and the crab flakes, seasoning with salt and pepper. As soon as this mixture is cool enough, put it in the icebox to get very cold. Form into flat cakes; dredge in finely sifted bread crumbs and fry on both sides in either lard or butter. Serve on a hot platter with rich cream sauce poured over the cakes.

The crab meat used must be from the body part of the crab, and must be very carefully picked over.

COST

Bruce Cost's Asian Ingredients

This is a wonderful Chinese solution to the American soft-shell crab. A friend who has traveled around the world, after tasting this dish made with crabs barely out of the water, remarked that it was the best dish he ever had, period.

Soft-Shell Crabs with Ginger, Lemon, and Black Beans

YIELD: 6 SERVINGS

6 soft-shell crabs, cleaned of their gills and ready to cook
½ cup + 1½ tablespoons cornstarch
¼ cup finely shredded fresh ginger
1 tablespoon shredded lemon zest (yellow part only)
2 small fresh red chili peppers, shredded
3 scallions, cut into 1-inch lengths
1½ tablespoons minced garlic
1 tablespoon salted and fermented black beans
1 tablespoon Shaoxing wine or dry sherry
1½ cups fresh chicken or fish stock
1 tablespoon grated lemon zest
2 tablespoons oyster sauce
1 tablespoon light soy sauce
1 teaspoon sugar
Pinch of salt
¼ cup water
Peanut oil for deep-frying
¼ cup peanut oil
Coriander sprigs for garnish

Cut the crabs in half through the top of the shell. Put about ½ cup cornstarch in a bowl, and dip the cut part of each crab into it. Set them aside.

Combine the ginger, shredded lemon zest, chili peppers, and scallions and set aside. Combine the garlic, black beans, and wine and set aside. Blend the stock with the grated lemon zest, oyster sauce, soy sauce, sugar, and salt, and set aside. Combine 1½ tablespoons cornstarch with ¼ cup water, and set aside.

Heat the frying oil in a wok or deep skillet until very hot but not smoking, and add half the crab pieces. Cook for 2 to 4 minutes, turning them in the oil until red and crisp. Remove and drain. Repeat with the other pieces.

Over high heat, heat a clean wok or skillet and add ¼ cup oil. When it is hot, add the ginger combination and cook, stirring, until just fragrant, about 10 seconds. Add the black bean mixture and cook, stirring, another 20 seconds. Add the seasoned stock and bring to a boil. Give the cornstarch and water a quick stir and add it to the sauce. When the sauce is thickened and glossy, turn off the heat. Arrange the crabs on a serving platter, pour the sauce over, and serve garnished with the coriander sprigs.

SHELLFISH AND SQUID

DE GOUY

The Gold Cook Book

Mussels Mariniere

Prepare 2 generous cups of white wine court-bouillon; strain through a fine-meshed wire sieve into a kettle and add 3 quarts of mussels, scrubbed clean. Cook over a bright flame until the mussels open, thus adding their salty juice to the broth. Taste for seasoning, being careful about salt and generous with black pepper. Serve in heated soup plates as indicated for Mussels Bonne Femme.

ANDREWS

Catalan Cuisine

Calamars Farcits amb Salsa de Xocolata

Stuffed Squid with Chocolate Sauce

At first glance, this unusual combination of squid, ground pork, and chocolate will probably sound about as unlikely and unappetizing as the aforementioned salt cod with honey (page 479)—but, like that dish, it is quite wonderful and quite traditionally Catalan.

TO SERVE 4 (AS MAIN COURSE)

1 pound squid, cleaned and thoroughly dried
½ pound ground pork
1 onion, finely diced
1 small carrot, finely diced
2 cloves garlic, minced
2 sprigs parsley, minced
Olive oil
¼ cup breadcrumbs
½ cup pine nuts, lightly toasted
Salt and pepper
1 cup fish, shellfish, or chicken stock
½ cup dry white wine
10–12 almonds, blanched and roasted
1 ounce chocolate
2 slices fried bread

Remove the heads and tentacles from the squid, and set the bodies aside. Mince the head and tentacles, then mix them well with the ground pork. (The mixture may be processed in a food processor if desired.)

In a cassola or large skillet, make a *sofregit* of the onion, carrot, garlic, and parsley in oil, then add the pork mixture, breadcrumbs, and half the pine nuts, mixing together well and cooking until the meat is well done. Salt and pepper to taste, then remove the mixture from the cassola, and drain on paper towels or in a colander.

Preheat the oven to 350°.

When the pork mixture is cool, lightly stuff the reserved squid bodies with it. (Do not overstuff, or the squid will shrink and tear while cooking.)

Bake the squid in a single layer, uncovered, in a lightly oiled baking dish, for about 20 minutes.

Meanwhile, deglaze the cassola with the stock and wine, simmering until it is reduced by about half.

While the liquid reduces, make a *picada* of the almonds, remaining pine nuts, chocolate, and fried bread, moistened with a bit of the liquid to make a thick paste.

Add the *picada* to the reduced liquid, stir in well, return to the boil, and salt and pepper to taste.

Pour over the stuffed squid, or spoon onto serving plates, and set the squid on top of the sauce.

LOBSTER

DE GOUY

The Gold Cook Book

It was for Bonaparte that chef Bailly created the world-wide known recipe for Lobster Thermidor. *When the dish was first presented to Napoleon, he inquired the name of the chef, who forthwith was called to see His Majesty the Emperor. When Napoleon asked for the name of the dish, the chef simply answered: "Lobster à la Napoléon." "Not at all," replied the emperor. "We should call this indescribable creation of goodness Lobster Thermidor."*

AUTHOR'S NOTE: *Thermidor used to be the eleventh month of the first French Republic, from July 19th to August 17th. And so the name "Thermidor" remained tagged to this lobster dish.*

Lobster Thermidor

Split from the middle, lengthwise, 3 live lobsters of 2 pounds each; clean, season to taste with mixed salt and pepper and broil very slowly under the flame of the broiling oven, basting frequently with melted sweet butter. Remove the meat from the shell and cut in small piece, slantwise; pour in each of the six shells 1 tablespoon or two of rich cream sauce (No. 258), to which has been added a scant teaspoon of dry English mustard (more or less according to taste); refill the shells with sliced lobster and cover with the same sauce and dust tops of the shells with a little paprika. Glaze quickly under the flame of the boiling oven. Arrange on a hot platter; garnish with fresh parsley or young crisp watercress and quartered lemons and serve with a side dish of thinly sliced cucumber salad in French dressing. If desired, stir into the sauce a little sherry wine—but this is optional, the original recipe not calling for such luxury.

MACAUSLAND
The Gourmet Cookbook

Lobster Newberg

Cook 3 lobsters, weighing 1½ pounds each, in boiling salted water for 20 minutes. Remove the meat from the shells, cut it into ½-inch slices, and refrigerate until wanted.

Melt 4 tablespoons butter in the top pan, or blazer, of a chafing dish. Add the lobster meat and sauté it over a direct flame until the outside membrane becomes bright red. Sprinkle with ½ teaspoon paprika, add ½ cup sherry or Madeira, and cook until the wine is almost completely cooked away. Place the pan over the hot-water pan, add 1½ cups cream blended with 4 well-beaten egg yolks, and stir gently until the sauce is thickened. Add 1 tablespoon cognac. Turn the lamp low and keep hot over the hot-water pan. Serve on freshly made toast with a touch of lobster coral or paprika.

KELLER
The French Laundry Cookbook

"Macaroni and Cheese"

Butter-Poached Maine Lobster with Creamy Lobster Broth and Mascarpone-Enriched Orzo

2 cups Creamy Lobster Broth
½ cup orzo (rice-shaped pasta)
2 tablespoons mascarpone
Kosher salt
Three 1½- to 2-pound lobsters, "steeped" and meat removed (reserve knuckle meat for another use)
1½ cups Beurre Monté
1 tablespoon minced chives
Coral Oil, in a squeeze bottle
6 Parmesan Crisps

We serve so much lobster at the restaurant that creating new lobster dishes is always an exciting challenge. I used to do an actual gratin with lobster and macaroni, but now I use orzo with mascarpone, the lobster on top, and Parmesan crisps—an echo of the crisp texture of a traditional gratin dish. The coral oil rings the orzo for bright color, and I finish the plate with chopped coral. This is an enormously satisfying dish to eat.

Place the lobster broth in a saucepan and bring it to a simmer. Reduce the broth to a sauce consistency; you should have 1 to 1¼ cups. Set aside in the pan.

Cook the orzo in boiling lightly salted water until just tender. Drain the cooked pasta in a strainer and rinse under cold water. Shake the strainer to remove excess water and add the orzo to the lobster broth.

TO COMPLETE: If the lobster pieces have been refrigerated, bring them to room temperature.

Heat the orzo and lobster broth to a simmer. Add the mascarpone and season with salt to taste. Let simmer for a minute, then remove the pan from the heat and keep warm.

Meanwhile, place the lobster pieces in one layer in a large saucepan. Pour in the beurre monté; the lobster should almost be covered. Heat gently to warm the lobster.

Stir the chives into the orzo. Pipe a 2-inch circle of coral oil in the center of each serving dish. Place about ⅓ cup of orzo in the center of the oil, allowing it to spread the oil out into a larger circle. Arrange a piece of lobster tail and a claw in the center of the orzo and top each serving with a Parmesan crisp.

MAKES 6 SERVINGS

ANDREWS
Catalan Cooking

Civet de Llagosta
Spiny Lobster Stew

Llagosta *is a favorite shellfish all over the* països catalans, *even in the inland reaches of the Roussillon. In fact, the wine region of Maury, just northwest of Perpignan, considers* llagosta *to be one of its most important local specialties—and the day after major holidays, such as the annual Maury town fete, the garbage is said to be literally strewn with lobster shells. "People even used to make a point of keeping the carapaces whole," according to winery proprietor Bernard Dauré, "and arranging them on the top of their garbage sacks so that the garbage collector would notice them and spread the word that so-and-so had* eight *or* ten *or* twelve *for his holiday dinner. It became such a status symbol that there were even people who would collect carapaces and sell them to others who wished to exaggerate their consumption."*

This recipe, a classic of French Catalonia, is more typical of the seaside than of Maury, but it is a rich, serious, quite extraordinary preparation of this honored crustacean. It comes from French Catalan food writer Eliane Thibaut-Comelade's comprehensive two-volume work, La Cuisine catalane *(L. T. Jacques Lanore, 131 rue P. V Couturier, 92242 Malakoff, France).*

TO SERVE 4–6 (AS MAIN COURSE)

4 spiny lobsters, each cut into 4–6 serving pieces, with the coral and the creamy interior of the head removed and set aside
Olive oil
6 ounces cognac
1 tablespoon lard
2 onions, chopped
3 shallots, minced
2 carrots, diced
1 tomato, seeded and grated or peeled, seeded, and chopped
½ pound European-style ham (prosciutto or Black Forest type), diced
½ bottle medium-dry Banyuls, medium-dry sherry, or tawny port
1½ cups fish or shellfish stock
1½ cups veal or beef stock
Bouquet garni of 1 sprig each of fresh thyme, rosemary, and parsley, or ¼ teaspoon each of dried thyme, rosemary, and parsley, mixed together well and wrapped securely in cheesecloth
6 cloves garlic, minced
1 sprig parsley, minced
Cayenne
Salt and pepper

In a cassola, Dutch oven, or large pot, sauté the lobster quickly in a small amount of oil until it turns red, then flame it with cognac, and when the flames burn out, remove the lobster, and set it aside.

Add the lard to the cassola, with more oil if necessary, and make a *sofregit* of the onions, shallots, carrots, and tomato. When the *sofregit* is cooked, add the ham, mix well, and cook an additional 3 minutes.

Add the Banyuls, both stocks, the bouquet garni, garlic, parsley, a pinch of cayenne, and salt and pepper to taste and bring to a boil.

Simmer the contents of the cassola, partially covered, for about 20 minutes, or until the mixture has thickened slightly. Add the reserved lobster, and cook for about 10 minutes more, or until the lobster is heated through.

Remove the lobster pieces from the cassola, and arrange them on a warm serving platter.

Add the coral and creamy interior of the lobster head, stir well, and reduce over medium heat for about 1 minutes.

Pour the sauce over the lobster, and serve.

KELLER
The French Laundry Cookbook

"Peas and Carrots"
Maine Lobster Pancakes with Pea Shoot Salad and Ginger-Carrot Emulsion

LOBSTER GLACE

2 tablespoons canola oil
3 lobster bodies (reserved from lobsters), cut into 2-inch pieces
1 tomato quartered
1 small carrot, cut into 1-inch pieces
2 sprigs thyme
3 to 4 cups water

LOBSTER FILLING

Three 1¼-pound lobsters, "steeped" and meat removed (about 2 cups [¾ pound] meat)
¼ cup chopped chives
1 tablespoon finely minced shallots
½ cup mascarpone

Kosher salt and freshly ground black pepper

3 to 4 tablespoons (2 ounces) unsalted butter, melted

8 crêpes

GINGER-CARROT EMULSION

3 pounds carrots, trimmed

One 1-inch (1-ounce) slice ginger

2 tablespoons heavy cream

12 tablespoons (6 ounces) cold unsalted butter, cut into pieces

PEA SHOOT SALAD

½ cup pea shoot leaves, in ice water

Few drops of lemon oil

Pinch of minced shallots

Kosher salt and freshly ground black pepper

Carrot Powder

When I hear "peas and carrots," my mind goes directly to the frozen food section of the grocery store, with its boxes of Jolly Green Giant peas and carrots. I'm not sure why anyone put the two vegetables together, but I think in most Americans' minds, it's a common pairing. So when J.B., one of my early poissonniers, and I were thinking of things to do with lobster, which we were serving with a carrot-emulsion sauce, we thought "Why not serve it with peas?" I use pea shoots to make the peas-and-carrots connection, dressed lightly with a little lemon-infused oil.

FOR THE LOBSTER GLACE: Heat the canola over medium-high heat in a sauté pan that will hold the shells in one layer. Add the lobster bodies and sauté for about 4 minutes, turning the shells occasionally, until the shells have turned red (be careful not to burn them). Add the tomato, carrot, thyme, and water just to cover. Simmer gently for 1¼ hours.

Strain the stock through a large strainer or China cap, pressing firmly on the solids to extract as much liquid as possible. Discard the bodies and strain the liquid through a chinois. There will be 1½ to 2 cups of stock. Place the stock in a saucepan and reduce over medium heat until it has thickened to a glaze (1 to 2 tablespoons). The glaze can be refrigerated in a covered container for several days or frozen. Bring to room temperature before using for the filling.

FOR THE LOBSTER FILLING: Cut the lobster meat into small dice (do not use the claw tips, as they will detract from the texture of the filling). Mix the lobster meat with the chives, shallots, 1 tablespoon of the lobster glace, and the mascarpone. Season to taste with salt and pepper. The filling can be covered and refrigerated until you are ready to fill the crêpes.

TO FILL THE CRÊPES: Brush a baking sheet with some of the melted butter. Place the crêpes (nicest side down) on a work surface. Scoop about ¼ cup of the filling into the center of each crêpe. (A 2-ounce ice-cream scoop works well for this, but be careful not to rip the pancakes with the scoop.) One by one, fold one edge of each crêpe over the filling and then, working clockwise, continue folding the crêpe over the filling, pleating it as you go to form a round packet. Place the packets seam side down on the buttered pan. Lightly brush the tops with more butter. The filled crêpes can be refrigerated for several hours.

FOR THE GINGER-CARROT EMULSION: Run the carrots and ginger through a juicer (you can save the carrot pulp to make carrot powder). You should have 2 to 2¼ cups of juice. Place the juice in a saucepan, bring to a simmer, and remove the first layer of foam that rises to the top. Simmer for 12 to 15 minutes, or until the juice is reduced to ½ to ¾ cup and is the consistency of baby food. Do not skim again; the body is needed to yield a purée rather than a sauce. Remove from the heat and set aside. The purée can be made up to a day ahead and stored in the refrigerator.

TO COMPLETE: Preheat the oven to 350°F.

Heat the carrot purée in a saucepan. Whisk in the cream and reduce slightly, to regain the consistency it had before the cream was added. With the purée at a gentle simmer, whisk in the butter a piece at a time, adding a new piece only when the last piece is almost incorporated. Remove the sauce to a blender and blend until it is emulsified. Keep the sauce in a warm spot, but do not place it over direct heat, or it will break.

Heat the lobster pancakes in the oven for 8 to 10 minutes, or until hot throughout.

MEANWHILE, FOR THE PEA SHOOT SALAD: Drain the pea shoot leaves, then dry in a salad spinner. Toss the leaves in a bowl with the lemon oil, shallots, and salt and pepper to taste.

Place a spoonful of carrot emulsion on each serving plate. Use the back of a spoon to spread the sauce into a circle that will extend slightly beyond the edges of the pancake. Center the pancakes on the sauce and garnish the tops with the pea shoot salad. Dust each plate with a little carrot powder.

MAKES 8 SERVINGS

CRÊPES

Scant 1 cup (4 ounces) all-purpose flour
Pinch of kosher salt
3 large eggs, lightly beaten
1¼ cups milk
4 tablespoons (2 ounces) unsalted butter, melted
1 tablespoon minced chives

You can make crêpes savory or sweet, depending on the dish you're serving.

Place the flour and salt in a bowl and create a well in the center of the flour. Whisk the eggs and milk together and pour into the well. Whisk the flour and egg mixture together, then whisk in the butter. Strain the batter through a fine-mesh strainer and stir in the chives.

Heat an 8½-inch nonstick crêpe pan over medium heat until hot. Spray with a non-stick spray, then use a 1-ounce ladle to pour the batter into the center of the skillet (or add 2 tablespoons of batter to the skillet). Rotate the skillet in a circular motion to cover the bottom of the pan evenly with the batter (if you hear it sizzle in the pan, your heat is too high). Cook for 30 to 45 seconds to set the batter. Then use a small narrow spatula to gently flip the crêpe. Cook for only 10 to 15 seconds more, to set the second side.

Remove the crêpe and place it with the nicer side down on a paper towel. Repeat for the remaining crêpes, spraying the pan as needed, and layer the paper towels and crêpes.

When you are ready to fill the crêpes, just lift up the towels and fill the crêpes—the best side of the crêpes will be on the outside.

MAKES 14 TO 18 CRÊPES

DESSERT CRÊPES: Omit the chives. Add 1 tablespoon of sugar to the dry ingredients. Add 1 teaspoon pure vanilla extract with the eggs.

SHRIMP

LAGASSE

Emeril's New New Orleans Cooking

André's Barbecued Shrimp and Homemade Biscuits

MAKES 4 MAIN-COURSE SERVINGS OR 6 FIRST-COURSE SERVINGS

This is a new twist on an old New Orleans sacred cow, which I had the audacity to tamper with. I decided my version was good enough to be a signature dish for the restaurant; but I was so busy putting the restaurant together, I didn't have time to refine it for customer consumption. So I turned it over to my friend and sous chef André Begnaud, who edited and retested it until it was just right for Emeril's. Today it's one of the most popular dishes on the menu, served as an appetizer or a main course with perfect bite-size Southern biscuits.

2 pounds medium-large shrimp in their shells, about 42 shrimp
2 tablespoons Emeril's Creole Seasoning, in all
16 turns freshly ground black pepper, in all
2 tablespoons olive oil, in all
¼ cup chopped onions
2 tablespoons minced garlic
3 bay leaves
3 lemons, peeled and sectioned
2 cups water
½ cup Worcestershire sauce
¼ cup dry white wine
¼ teaspoon salt
12 mini Buttermilk Biscuits
2 cups heavy cream
2 tablespoons unsalted butter

1. Peel the shrimp, leaving only their tails attached. Reserve the shells, sprinkle the shrimp with 1 tablespoon Creole Seasoning and 8 turns of the black pepper. Use your hands to coat the shrimp with the seasonings. Refrigerate the shrimp while you make the sauce base and biscuits.

2. Heat 1 tablespoon of the oil in a large pot over high heat. When the oil is hot, add the onions and garlic and sauté for 1 minute. Add the reserved shrimp shells, the remaining 1 tablespoon Creole Seasoning, the bay leaves, lemons, water, Worcestershire, wine, salt, and the remaining 8 turns black pepper. Stir well and bring to a boil. Reduce the heat and simmer for 30 minutes. Remove from the heat, allow to cool for about 15 minutes, and strain into a small saucepan. There should be about 1½ cups. Place over high heat, bring to a boil, and cook until thick, syrupy, and dark brown, for about 15 minutes. Makes about 4 to 5 tablespoons of barbecue sauce base.

3. Prepare the Buttermilk Biscuits, and keep warm.

4. Heat the remaining 1 tablespoon of oil in a large skillet over high heat. When the oil is hot, add the seasoned shrimp and sauté them, occasionally shaking the skillet, for 2 minutes.

5. Add the cream and all of the barbecue base. Stir and simmer for 3 to 5 minutes. Remove the shrimp to a warm platter with tongs and whisk the butter into the sauce. Remove from the heat. Makes about 2 cups.

6. To serve 4, allow ½ cup of sauce, about 10 shrimp, and 3 biscuits each; for 6 servings; ⅓ cup sauce, about 7 shrimp, and 2 biscuits.

PRUDHOMME

Chef Paul Prudhomme's Louisiana Kitchen

Shrimp Diane

MAKES 2 SERVINGS

This dish is best if made only two servings at a time. If you want to make more than two servings, do so in separate batches but serve while piping hot.

- 1¾ pounds medium shrimp with heads and shells (see Note)
- 6 tablespoons, *in all*, Basic Shrimp Stock
- ⅜ pound (1½ sticks) unsalted butter, *in all*
- ¼ cup very finely chopped green onions
- ¾ teaspoon salt
- ½ teaspoon minced garlic
- ½ teaspoon ground red pepper (preferably cayenne)
- ¼ teaspoon white pepper
- ¼ teaspoon black pepper
- ¼ teaspoon dried sweet basil leaves
- ¼ teaspoon dried thyme leaves
- ⅛ teaspoon dried oregano leaves
- ½ pound mushrooms, cut into ¼-inch-thick slices
- 3 tablespoons very finely chopped fresh parsley
- French bread, pasta or hot Basic Cooked Rice

NOTE: If shrimp with heads are not available, buy 1 pound of shrimp without heads but with shells for making the stock.

Rinse and peel the shrimp; refrigerate until needed. Use shells and heads to make the shrimp stock.

In a large skillet melt *1 stick* of the butter over high heat. When almost melted, add the green onions, salt, garlic, the ground peppers, basil, thyme and oregano; stir well. Add the shrimp and sauté just until they turn pink, about 1 minute, shaking the pan (versus stirring) in a back-and-forth motion. Add the mushrooms and *¼ cup* of the stock; then add the remaining 4 tablespoons butter in chunks and continue cooking, continuing to shake the pan. Before the butter chunks are completely melted, add the parsley, then the remaining 2 tablespoons stock: continue cooking and shaking the pan until all ingredients are mixed thoroughly and butter sauce is the consistency of cream.

Serve immediately in a bowl with lots of French bread on the side, or serve over pasta or rice.

ROJAS-LOMBARDI
The Art of South American Cooking

Cebiche de Calamares

Squid Ceviche

SERVES 6 TO 8

When I get my hands on baby squid—maybe three or four inches long—I cannot help but see it as a candidate for ceviche. The squid must be cut in circles at an angle, no more than a quarter of an inch thick. Larger squid should be cut even thinner, about an eighth of an inch, for best taste and texture.

Blanching is key: it should be done in a flash. Overcooked squid becomes yellowish and tough. Properly cooked squid is white and tender, a real treat.

2 to 2½ pounds squid
8 scallions, white parts only, julienned
1 red bell pepper, seeded and julienned
2 or 3 jalapeño or serrano peppers, seeded and julienned
1 large clove garlic, peeled and crushed
1 tablespoon coarse salt
1 cup lime juice (about 6 limes)
¼ cup olive oil

1. Clean the squid. Slice the squid on the diagonal about ¼ inch thick. If the tentacles are small, leave them whole; if they are large, cut them in half or quarters. Blanch all the pieces for less than 1 minute in 8 cups of boiling water. Drain and drop the pieces in a bowl containing ice water, and let them cool. Drain thoroughly and set aside.

2. Place the julienned scallions, bell pepper, and hot peppers in ice water for 10 minutes. Drain well and set aside.

3. In a small bowl, combine the garlic, salt and lime juice and let sit, undisturbed, at room temperature for 10 minutes. Discard the garlic and save the flavored lime juice.

4. In a ceramic, porcelain, or glass bowl, combine the squid, scallions, bell pepper, and hot peppers. Add the flavored lime juice and oil, toss, correct the seasoning with salt to taste, and serve.

BAYLESS
Rick Bayless's Mexican Kitchen

Chipotle Shrimp

Camarones Enchipotlados

These shrimp were a revelation the first time I bit into one at Carmen Ramírez Degollado's table! Spicy, garlicky, smoky and (like the best barbecued shrimp) not too saucy. You can pick them up with your fingers and pop them right into your mouth, one after another after another. They are wonderful party food for the not-too-timid, though truthfully I can't imagine that all won't eventually be won over to these glowing flavors.

Like all of Carmen's specialties, this shrimp dish is a great rendition of classic Veracruz cooking. If you take the time to make Carmen's Sweet-and-Smoky Chipotle Seasoning Salsa, the dish will take on incredible depth of flavor. Still, I'd never turn them down made the quick way with chopped canned chipotles. With Classic White Rice to serve alongside the shrimp, you'll have the perfect summer meal. And since they're good at room temperature, carry them on a picnic or pass around a platter sprinkled with chopped cilantro, as the starter for a great feast. This is beer food, in my opinion—icy Bohemia or Negra Modelo taste great here.

SERVES 6 GENEROUSLY

6 garlic cloves, unpeeled
1 small white onion, sliced ¼ inch thick
6 ounces (1 medium-small or 2 to 3 plum) ripe tomatoes
¾ teaspoon black pepper, preferably freshly ground
⅛ teaspoon cloves, preferably freshly ground
2 tablespoons olive oil
2 to 4 tablespoons Essential Sweet-and-Smokey Chipotle Seasoning Salsa or 2 to 4 tablespoons very finely chopped canned chipotle chiles, drained before chopping
Salt, about ½ teaspoon
2 pounds (about 50) medium-large shrimp

1. **ROASTING THE FLAVORINGS.** On an ungreased griddle or heavy skillet set over medium, roast the garlic cloves, turning occasionally, until soft (they will blacken in spots), about 15 minutes. Cool and peel.

While the garlic is roasting, lay the onion out on a small square of foil, set on the griddle and let sear, brown and soften, about 5 minutes per side.

Roast the tomatoes on a baking sheet set 4 inches below a very hot broiler until blackened in spots and soft, about 6 minutes; flip and roast the other side. Cool and peel, collecting all the juices with the tomatoes.

2. THE SAUCE. Combine all the roasted ingredients in a food processor or blender, along with the pepper, cloves and ¼ cup water. Process to a medium-smooth puree.

In a very large (12-inch) skillet, heat the oil over medium-high. When hot enough to make a drop of the puree sizzle noisily, add it all at once. Stir for several minutes as the mixture sears and darkens, then reduce the heat to medium-low and continue to cook, stirring regularly, until very thick, about 5 minutes. A tablespoon at a time, stir in the Chipotle Seasoning Salsa (or chopped chipotles), tasting until the thick salsa suits your own penchant for spiciness. (I think these are best when they've reached the upper levels of heat.) Taste, season with salt and remove from the heat.

3. THE SHRIMP. Peel the shrimp, leaving the final joint and the tail intact. One at a time, devein the shrimp by laying them flat on your work surface and making a shallow incision down the back, exposing the (usually) dark intestinal tract and scraping it out.

Return the skillet with the sauce to medium-high heat. Add the shrimp, then slowly stir and turn for about 3 to 4 minutes, until the shrimp are just cooked through. (The sauce should nicely coat the shrimp, though it won't really pool around them.) Taste a shrimp, sprinkle on a little more salt if necessary, then pile up the crustaceans on a rustic platter and carry them to the table.

ADVANCE PREPARATION—The sauce (steps 1 and 2) may be made several days ahead; cover and refrigerate. Finish step 3 just before serving if you want them hot or several hours ahead for room-temperature shrimp.

VARIATIONS AND IMPROVISATIONS—You can take this same approach with scallops (preferably medium-size for even cooking with this method), or with beef (grill about 2 pounds of anything tender enough to be a grillable steak, cut into ¾-inch cubes, toss with the warm sauce and serve). For a casserole to serve on a buffet, toss the sauce with roasted potatoes or spread it on grilled eggplant, sprinkle with melting cheese, and run under the broiler until bubbly and brown.

PRUDHOMME

Chef Paul Prudhomme's Louisiana Kitchen

Crawfish (or Shrimp) Etouffée

MAKES 8 SERVINGS

SEASONING MIX:
- 2 teaspoons salt
- 2 teaspoons ground red pepper (preferably cayenne)
- 1 teaspoon white pepper
- 1 teaspoon black pepper
- 1 teaspoon dried sweet basil leaves
- ½ teaspoon dried thyme leaves

- ¼ cup chopped onions
- ¼ cup chopped celery
- ¼ cup chopped green bell peppers
- 7 tablespoons vegetable oil
- ¾ cup all-purpose flour
- 3 cups, *in all*, Basic Seafood Stock
- ½ pound (2 sticks) unsalted butter, *in all*
- 2 pounds peeled crawfish tails or medium shrimp
- 1 cup very finely chopped green onions
- 4 cups hot Basic Cooked Rice

Thoroughly combine the seasoning mix ingredients in a small bowl and set aside. In a separate bowl combine the onions, celery and bell peppers.

In a large heavy skillet (preferably cast iron), heat the oil over high heat until it begins to smoke, about 4 minutes. With a long-handled metal whisk, gradually mix in the flour, stirring until smooth. Continue cooking, whisking constantly, until roux is dark red-brown, about 3 to 5 minutes (be careful not to let it scorch in the pan or splash on your skin). Remove from heat and immediately stir in the vegetables and 1 tablespoon of the seasoning mix with a wooden spoon; continue stirring until cooled, about 5 minutes.

In a 2-quart saucepan bring 2 cups of the stock to a boil over high heat. Gradually add the roux and whisk until thoroughly dissolved. Reduce heat to low and cook until flour taste is gone, about 2 minutes, whisking almost constantly (if any of the mixture scorches, don't continue to scrape that part of the pan bottom). Remove from heat and set aside.

Heat the serving plates in a 250° oven.

In a 4-quart saucepan melt 1 stick of the butter over medium heat. Stir in the crawfish (or shrimp) and the green onions; sauté about 1 minute, stirring almost constantly. Add the remaining stick of butter, the stock mixture and the remaining 1 cup stock; cook until butter melts and is mixed into the sauce, about 4 to 6 minutes, constantly shaking the pan in a back-and-forth motion (versus stirring). Add the remaining seasoning mix; stir well and remove from heat (if sauce starts separating, add about 2 tablespoons more of stock or water and shake pan until it combines). Serve immediately.

To serve, mound ½ cup rice on each heated serving plate. Surround the rice with ¾ cup of the etouffée.

LAGNIAPPE

A certain percentage of oil is released when butter is melted; shaking the pan in a back-and-forth motion and the addition of stock keep the sauce from separating and having an oily texture—stirring doesn't produce the same effect.

CASAS

The Foods and Wines of Spain

Gambas al Ajillo "Rincón de España"

Garlic Shrimp

SERVES 6

- 4 tablespoons olive oil
- 2 tablespoons butter
- ¾ pound small or medium shrimp, in their shells
- 4 cloves garlic, peeled and sliced
- 2 tablespoons lemon juice
- 2 tablespoons dry sherry
- ½ teaspoon paprika
- 1 dried red chili pepper, cut in 3 pieces, seeds removed
- Salt
- Freshly ground pepper
- 1 tablespoon minced parsley

Heat the oil and butter in a shallow casserole. Add the shrimp and garlic and sauté over high heat about 3 minutes. Add the lemon juice, sherry, paprika, chili pepper, salt, and pepper. Sprinkle with parsley and serve immediately, preferably in the cooking dish.

Fowl

DUCK

ESTES
Good Things to Eat, as Suggested by Rufus

ROASTED CANVAS-BACK DUCK—Procure a fine canvas-back duck, pick, singe, draw thoroughly and wipe; throw inside a light pinch of salt, run in the head from the end of the head to the back, press and place in a roasting pan. Sprinkle with salt, put in a brisk oven, and cook for eighteen minutes. Arrange on a very hot dish, untruss, throw in two tablespoons of white broth. Garnish with slices of fried hominy and currant jelly. Redhead and mallard ducks are prepared the same way.

MACAUSLAND
The Gourmet Cookbook

Caneton à l'Orange, or à la Bigarade

Duckling with Orange

Wipe with a damp cloth a 5- to 6- pound duckling and truss it. Rub it with salt and pepper and roast the bird in a hot oven for 15 minutes. Reduce the heat to moderate and continue to roast, allowing 20 minutes to the pound in all. Baste several times during the cooking period with 1 cup dry white wine.

In a small pan melt 1 tablespoon sugar and blend in 1 tablespoon vinegar until it caramelizes. Remove the roasted duck from the oven and set it aside to keep warm. Remove the excess fat from the pan and add slowly to what remains of 1 cup white wine, scraping the bottom of the pan well. Add the juice of 4 oranges and 1 small lemon and 2 tablespoons brandy, blend well, and add the vinegar caramel. Cook the sauce slowly for 10 minutes.

Carve the duckling and arrange it on a large heated platter, pour the sauce over it, and sprinkle the grated rind or julienne of 2 bitter oranges over the duck. Surround the platter by orange wedges, blanched, and water cress.

GOOSE

CHILD, BERTHOLLE, AND BECK
Mastering the Art of French Cooking

Goose

Oie

Goose, like duck, can only be considered gastronomically interesting when it is under 6 months old, and that is probably the only kind you will find in American markets. It usually comes frozen, and should be defrosted either in the refrigerator or in a pan with cold, running water. It is prepared for cooking like duck.

GOOSE FAT

Goose fat is extremely good as a sauté or basting medium, or as a flavoring for braised cabbage or sauerkraut. Once rendered, it will keep for weeks in the refrigerator. To render the fat, pull out all the loose fat from inside the goose. Chop it up into ½-inch pieces. Simmer it in a covered saucepan with 1 cup of water for 20 minutes to draw the fat out of the tissues. Then uncover the pan and boil the liquid slowly to evaporate the water. As the moisture evaporates, the fat will make spluttering noises. As soon as these have stopped, the fat is rendered, the liquid will be a pale yellow, and the fat particles will have browned very lightly. Strain the liquid into a jar.

Frittons
Grattons
(Goose Cracklings)

The browned fat particles may be turned into a spread for *croûtons*, toast, or crackers. Pound them in a mortar or put them through the meat grinder. Warm them briefly in a skillet and stir in salt, pepper, and allspice to taste. Pack them into a jar. When cold, pour a ⅛-inch layer of hot goose fat over them to seal them. They will keep for several weeks in the refrigerator.

GOOSE STOCK

A good goose stock is easy to make with the gizzard, neck, heart, and wing tips of the goose. The liver may be included, unless you wish to treat it like chicken liver, or add it to your stuffing. Follow the general procedure for chicken stock. It should simmer for 2 hours or so.

STUFFINGS FOR GOOSE

Goose may be cooked with or without a stuffing. Besides the prune and *foie gras*, and the chestnut stuffing, another good one for goose is an apple and sausage mixture. Count on ¾ to 1 cup of stuffing for each ready-to-cook pound of goose. An 8-lb. bird, for instance, will take 6 to 8 cups of stuffing. Although you may prepare a stuffing ahead of time, never stuff the goose until just before cooking, or both goose and stuffing may spoil.

TIMETABLE FOR ROAST OR BRAISED GOOSE

The following table is based on unstuffed, unchilled goose cooked to the well-done stage—when its juices run pale yellow. Be sure not to overcook your goose, or the breast meat especially will be dry and disappointing. You will see in the table that the larger the goose, the less time per pound it takes to cook. A 9-lb. goose requires about 2 hours, and a 12½-lb. bird, only about 30 minutes longer. The best sizes to buy are from 9 to 11 lbs.; larger geese may be a bit older and tougher. Oven temperature for roasting is 350 degrees; for braising, 325 degrees. A meat thermometer should register 180 degrees.

READY-TO-COOK WEIGHT	NUMBER OF PEOPLE SERVED	APPROXIMATE TOTAL COOKING TIME (UNSTUFFED GOOSE)*
8 lbs.	6	1 hour and 50 to 55 minutes
9 lbs.	6 to 8	About 2 hours
9½ lbs.	8 to 9	2 hours and 10 to 15 minutes
10½ lbs.	9 to 10	2 hours and 15 to 20 minutes
11½ lbs.	10 to 12	2 hours and 20 to 30 minutes
12½ lbs.	12 to 14	2 hours and 30 to 40 minutes

*For a stuffed goose, add from 20 to 40 minutes to the times given.

OIE RÔTIE AUX PRUNEAUX

Roast Goose with Prune and Foie Gras *Stuffing*

Goose is roasted exactly like duck, the only exception being that the goose is basted every 15 to 20 minutes with boiling water to help in the dissolution of its subcutaneous fat, which is more copious for goose than for duck. Prunes and goose are an exceptionally fine combination. With the goose you can serve braised onions and chestnuts, and a full red wine such as a Burgundy or Châteauneuf-du-Pape.

FOR 6 TO 8 PEOPLE
ESTIMATED ROASTING TIME: ABOUT 2½ HOURS

NOTE: A good brown goose stock will give you an excellent sauce, but it must be prepared in advance; see preceding remarks.

PRUNE AND FOIE GRAS STUFFING

32 "tenderized" prunes

Soak the prunes in hot water for 5 minutes. Pit them as neatly as possible.

1 cup white wine or ⅔ cup dry white vermouth
2 cups brown goose stock, brown stock, or canned beef bouillon

Simmer them slowly in a covered saucepan with the wine and stock or bouillon for about 10 minutes, or until they are just tender. Drain them and reserve the cooking liquid.

The goose liver, minced
2 Tb finely minced shallots or green onions
1 Tb butter

Sauté the goose liver and shallots or onions in butter, using a small skillet, for 2 minutes. Scrape into a mixing bowl.

⅓ cup port

Boil the wine in the same skillet until it is reduced to 2 tablespoons. Scrape it into the mixing bowl with the liver.

½ cup or 4 ounces of *foie gras* (goose liver), or very good liver paste
Pinch of allspice
Pinch of thyme
Salt and pepper to taste

Blend the *foie gras* or liver paste and flavorings into the mixing bowl with the sautéed liver. Taste carefully for seasoning. Fill each prune with a teaspoon of the stuffing.

A 9-lb. ready-to-cook young roasting goose
1 tsp salt
A shallow roasting pan

Preheat oven to 425 degrees.

Salt the cavity of the goose. Stuff it loosely with the prunes. Sew or skewer the vent. Secure the legs, wings, and neck skin to the body. Prick the skin over the thighs, back, and lower breast. Dry thoroughly, and set it breast up in the roasting pan.

Boiling water
A bulb baster

Following directions for roast duck, brown the goose for 15 minutes in the hot oven. Turn goose on its side, lower heat to 350 degrees, and continue roasting. Baste every 15 to 20 minutes with 2 or 3 tablespoons of boiling water, and remove excess accumulated fat. A bulb baster is useful for this; tilt the pan and suck the fat out. Turn goose on its other side at the halfway mark, and on its back 15 minutes before the end. The goose should be done in 2 hours and 20 to 30 minutes, when the drumsticks move slightly in their sockets, and, when the fleshiest part of one is pricked, the juices run a pale yellow. Do not allow the goose to overcook or the meat will dry out.

When done, discard trussing strings and set the goose on a platter.

The prune cooking juices
Optional: ⅓ to ½ cup port
Salt and pepper
2 Tb softened butter

Tilt the pan and spoon out the fat, but leave the brown roasting juices. Pour in the prune cooking juices and optional port. Boil down rapidly, scraping up coagulated roasting juices, until liquid has reduced and is full of flavor. Correct seasoning. Off heat and just before serving, swirl in the enrichment butter by bits. Pour into a warmed sauceboat, spoon a bit of sauce over the goose, and serve.

(*) **AHEAD-OF-TIME NOTE:** Roast goose may wait for 30 to 40 minutes in the turned-off hot oven with its door ajar.

OIE BRAISÉE AUX MARRONS

Braised Goose with Chestnut and Sausage Stuffing

There are many who prefer braised goose to roast goose because the meat is more tender and more flavorful, and the closed, moist cooking of a braise renders out more fat than open-pan roasting. A good combination to go with this would be more chestnuts, either braised or puréed, and braised lettuce, onions or leeks. Brussels sprouts, or braised green or red cabbage are other choices. Serve a red Burgundy, Côtes du Rhône, Châteauneuf-du-Pape, or chilled Alsatian Traminer.

FOR A 9-LB. BIRD, SERVING 8 TO 10 PEOPLE—BECAUSE OF THE MEAT STUFFING THE GOOSE WILL GO FURTHER
ESTIMATED ROASTING TIME: 2½ HOURS

SAUSAGE AND CHESTNUT STUFFING (8 CUPS)

1½ pounds of fresh chestnuts, or 4 cups of drained, canned, and unsweetened chestnuts

If using fresh chestnuts, peel them, and simmer them in stock and seasonings.

4 cups of the fresh ground veal and pork stuffing
The goose liver, chopped, and sautéed in butter

Prepare the stuffing and beat the sautéed liver into it. Sauté a spoonful to check seasoning.

A 9-lb. ready-to-cook young roasting goose
½ tsp salt
A shallow roasting pan

Preheat oven to 450 degrees.

Season the cavity of the goose with salt. Starting with the meat stuffing, loosely pack alternate layers of stuffing and of chestnuts into the goose, leaving a good inch of unfilled space at the vent. Sew or skewer the vent, truss the goose, and prick its skin. Dry it thoroughly, and set it breast up in the roasting pan.

Brown the goose lightly in the hot oven for 15 to 20 minutes, turning it several times so it will color evenly.

1 tsp salt
A covered roaster just large enough to hold the goose easily

Salt the goose and place it breast up in the roaster. Turn oven down to 325 degrees.

The goose neck, wing tips, gizzard, and heart
1½ cups sliced onions
½ cup sliced carrots
4 Tb rendered goose fat, rendered fresh pork fat, or cooking oil
A skillet

Brown the goose bits and vegetables in hot fat in the skillet.

6 Tb flour

Stir the flour into the skillet and brown slowly for several minutes.

4 cups boiling brown stock or canned beef bouillon
3 cups dry white wine or 2 cups dry white vermouth

Off heat, blend in the boiling stock or bouillon, and then the wine. Simmer for a moment. Then pour the contents of the skillet into the roaster around the goose. Add additional stock if necessary, so liquid reaches about one third the way up the goose.

Bring to the simmer on top of the stove. Cover, and set in the middle level of the preheated 325-degree oven.

A bulb baster

Braise for about 2 hours and 20 to 30 minutes, regulating oven heat so liquid simmers very quietly. Basting is not necessary. Accumulated fat may be removed occasionally with the bulb baster. The goose is done when its drumsticks move slightly in their sockets, and, when their fleshiest part is pricked, the juices run pale yellow.

Remove the goose to a serving platter and discard trussing strings.

Salt and pepper to taste
⅓ to ½ cup port

Skim the fat out of the roaster, boil the cooking liquid down rapidly until it has thickened enough to coat a spoon lightly. Correct seasoning. Stir in the port and simmer a minute or two to evaporate its alcohol. Strain the sauce into a bowl or a saucepan, pressing juice out of the ingredients. You should have about 5 to 6 cups of sauce. Pour a spoonful over the goose, and serve.

(*) **AHEAD-OF-TIME NOTE:** For a 30- to 40-minute wait, return the goose to the roaster, and set the cover askew. Place in turned-off hot oven with its door ajar, or over barely simmering water.

DE SILVA

In Memory's Kitchen

Ganshals mit Griess gefüllt

Der Ganshals wird auf der schmalen Seite zugenäht mit folg. farce gefüllt. 10–15 dkg Griess, ½ fein geschnittene Semmel, Salz, Pfeffer, Ing. das Ganze mit 2–3 Löffel kochendem Fett gebrüht mit heisser G. Suppe zu einem Brei vermengt, und gefüllt. Der Hals zugenäht, in der Suppe 25 Min. gekocht dann auf Fett gebraten.

Goose Neck Stuffed with Farina

Sew the small side of the gooseneck [skin] together and fill it with the following farce: 10–15 decagrams farina, ½ fine-cut roll, salt, pepper, ginger. Scald [mixture] with 2–3 spoons boiling fat and enough hot goose broth to form farce. Stuff [the gooseneck]. Sew the neck together. Boil it in the [goose] broth 25 minutes, then roast on fat.

TURKEY

ROMBAUER

The Joy of Cooking

Roast Turkey

Clean a turkey and fill it with bread or chestnut dressing. Spread the entire surface of the fowl with salt and follow this with a coat of ⅓ cup of butter creamed with ¼ cup of flour. If the fowl is clean, a piece of salt pork may be put across the breast. Place the turkey on a dripping rack in a roasting pan in a hot oven 500°. If the turkey browns too fast, cover it with a piece of buttered paper. When it is well browned (15 minutes) reduce the heat to a slow oven 275°, pour 1 cup of stock over it, cover it and roast it until it is done, basting it every 15 minutes. Remove the pork and cook it uncovered for the last half hour (optional). Turn the turkey so that it may brown evenly. Add additional stock, if necessary. The time for cooking a 12 lb. turkey by this method is approximately 3 hours.

ESTES

Good Things to Eat, as Suggested by Rufus

TURKEY TRUFFLES—Take a fat turkey, clean and singe it. Take three or four pounds of truffles, chopping up a handful with some fat bacon and put into a saucepan, together with the whole truffles, salt, pepper, spices and a bay-leaf. Let these ingredients cook over a slow fire for three-quarters of a hour, take off, stir and let cool. When quite cold place in body of turkey, sew up the opening and let the turkey imbibe the flavor of the truffles by remaining in a day or two, if the season permits. Cover the bird with slices of bacon and roast.

PIGEON, PHEASANT, AND SQUAB

ZIEMANN AND GILETTE

The White House Cook Book

Pigeon Pie

Take half a dozen pigeons; stuff each one with a dressing the same as for turkey; loosen the joints with a knife, but do not separate them. Put them in a stewpan with water enough to cover them, let them cook until nearly tender, then season them with salt and pepper and butter. Thicken gravy with flour, remove and cool. Butter a pudding dish, line the sides with a rich crust. Have ready some hard-boiled eggs cut in slices. Put in a layer of egg and birds and gravy until the dish is full. Cover with a crust and bake.

COST

Bruce Cost's Asian Ingredients

Tea-Smoked Squabs

These little birds, best eaten at room temperature, should sit for 8 hours or overnight in a cool place (not the refrigerator) before they are served.

YIELD: 8 TO 10 SERVINGS

4 squabs, with heads and feet
2 tablespoons coarse salt
2 teaspoons Sichuan peppercorns
6 star anise
2 2-inch cinnamon sticks

FOR SMOKING

½ cup uncooked rice
½ cup light brown sugar
¼ cup black tea leaves
2 teaspoons dark soy sauce
Oil for deep-frying

Cut the feet off the squabs, and rinse and dry the birds thoroughly. Toast the salt and spices in a dry skillet, shaking over medium heat until they begin to smoke and the salt begins to brown. Allow to cool. Discard the star anise and cinnamon, and rub the salt and peppercorns over the squabs, inside and out. Hang the squabs by strings in a cool airy place for 8 hours or overnight.

Place the squabs, breast side down, on a heatproof plate, and steam them for 30 minutes in a steamer or a covered wok fitted with a rack. Allow to cool, then rub each squab with ½ teaspoon dark soy sauce.

Cover the bottom of a wok with aluminum foil and add the rice, brown sugar, and tea. Put a rack in the wok, and arrange the squabs breast side up on the rack. Cover the wok, and ring the edge of the cover with dampened paper towels to keep the smoke from escaping. Turn the heat to medium-high and when you smell smoke, leave the heat on for 15 minutes. Turn the heat off and allow the birds to stay in the covered wok for another 45 minutes.

In a large wok or deep-fryer, heat a large amount of oil to nearly smoking. Add the squabs one at a time and fry them, continuously spooning the oil over them, for about 5 minutes. Remove and drain. Pat dry with paper towels. (The frying gives the skin an interesting texture.)

You can of course eat these warm, but the smoke and spice flavors seem to mellow and permeate the birds after they sit for 8 hours, or preferably overnight. Serve Chinese-style, chopped into bite-size pieces.

FISHER

The Art of Eating

Sausage Pie (or Sardine Pie)

Shrimps are good in this pie too; indeed, it came from Portugal, where they used to grow on bushes, practically.

Left-over meats are always fun to cope with, and one of the nicest ways, which for some reason always surprises people, is in Canelloni. Canelloni are simply small unsweetened pancakes like delicate enchiladas, which are filled with what the recipe discreetly calls "any plausible mixture": meat, fish, herbs, egg yolks, on and on.

They are rolled and laid in a shallow dish, on spinach purée if you like. Then they are sprinkled with grated cheese and browned quickly. [A nice thing about them is that the pancakes can be made several hours in advance (they should be thin, like French crêpes). So can the "mixture." They should be combined at the last. If something in a sauce is used for the filling, like creamed chicken, some of the sauce should be put over the whole.]

There are always curries, of course, which are really not curries at all, but simply left-over meat served in a gravy flavored with curry powder. [This is a horrible definition, and only the next sentence saves me from gastronomical guilt.] They can be very good or ghastly, according to the cook.

½ pound sausage [or bacon] (or ½ can sardines)
tomato sauce
biscuit-mix
1 teaspoon grated onion or chopped green onion

Spread sausage [or bacon or fish] thin in pie-pan or shallow casserole. Let heat in quick oven and pour off almost all fat. (Leave oil on sardines.)

Make one-half usual baking powder biscuit, mixing with tomato sauce [. . . or meat stock. It is a question of flavors. One good combination with bacon strips is milk in the biscuit-mix, plus a generous half-cup of grated cheese.] instead of milk or water. Add the onion and any chopped herbs you like. Pour over the sausage, and bake in hot oven until firm and brown [. . . about 20 minutes].

CHICKEN

DULL

Southern Cooking

Fried Chicken

Select a young chicken weighing from 1½ to 2 lbs. Dress and disjoint, chill. When ready, have a deep fry pan with grease at least two inches deep.

Sift enough flour in which to roll the chicken pieces (a cup and a half or two cups). Add salt and pepper to the flour, roll each piece in flour and place in the hot grease. Put the largest pieces in first and on the hottest part of the pan. When all is in, cover for 5 minutes. Remove top and turn when the underside is well browned. Replace top for another 5 minutes, remove and cook in open pan until the bottom side is browned. About 30 minutes in all will be required for cooking chicken if it is not too large. Do not turn chicken but once; too much turning and too long cooking will destroy the fine flavor which is there when well cooked.

The fat should be deep enough to cover the pieces when it boils up.

TO MAKE CREAM GRAVY: Pour off the grease, leaving 2 to 3 tablespoons in the pan with the browned crumbs. Add 2 tablespoons butter, 4 tablespoons flour, blend and cook until a golden brown; add 1 cup milk and 1 cup hot water. Stir until smooth and the right thickness and add salt and black pepper. Pour into a gravy boat and serve with hot biscuit or dry rice. Never pour gravy over chicken if you wish Georgia fried chicken.

BITTMAN

How to Cook Everything

Simple Roast Chicken

MAKES 4 SERVINGS
TIME: ABOUT 1 HOUR

We associate roast chicken with elegance, but it's also great weeknight food, since it takes just about an hour from start to finish. This method gives you a nicely browned exterior without drying out the breast meat, and it's easily varied (the variations I offer are a fraction of the possibilities). Use kosher or free-range chicken if at all possible.

- 1 whole (3- to 4-pound) chicken, trimmed of excess fat, then rinsed and patted dry with paper towels
- 3 tablespoons olive oil
- 2 teaspoons chopped fresh thyme, rosemary, marjoram, oregano, or sage leaves, or 1 teaspoon dried
- Salt and freshly ground black pepper to taste
- Chopped fresh herbs for garnish

1. Preheat the oven to 500°F.

2. Place the chicken, breast side down, on a rack in a roasting pan. Begin roasting. Mix together the olive oil, herbs, salt, and pepper.

3. After the chicken has roasted for about 20 minutes, spoon some of the olive oil mixture over it, then turn the bird breast side up. Baste again, then again after 7 or 8 minutes; at this point the breast should be beginning to brown (if it hasn't, roast a few more minutes). Turn the heat down to 325°F, baste again, and roast until an instant-read thermometer inserted into the thickest pan of the thigh reads 160° to 165°F. Total roasting time will be under an hour.

4. Before removing the chicken from the pan, tip the pan to let the juices from the bird's cavity flow into the pan (if they are red, cook another 5 minutes). Remove the bird to a platter and let it rest for about 5 minutes. While it is resting, pour the pan juices into a clear measuring cup, and pour or spoon off as much of the fat as you can. Reheat the juice, carve the bird, garnish, and serve with the pan juices.

ROAST CHICKEN WITH SOY SAUCE: Step 1 remains the same. In Step 2, replace the olive oil mixture with a combination of ¼ cup soy sauce; 2 tablespoons peanut (or vegetable) oil; 2 tablespoons honey; 1 teaspoon minced garlic; 1 teaspoon peeled and grated or minced fresh ginger or ½ teaspoon ground ginger; and ¼ cup minced scallions. Steps 3 and 4 remain the same.

ROAST CHICKEN WITH CUMIN, HONEY, AND ORANGE JUICE: Step 1 remains the same. In Step 2, replace the olive oil mixture with a combination of 1 tablespoon olive oil; 2 tablespoons freshly squeezed orange juice; 2 tablespoons honey; 1 teaspoon minced garlic; 2 teaspoons ground cumin; and salt and pepper to taste. Steps 3 and 4 remain the same.

BURROS AND LEVINE
The Elegant But Easy Cookbook

Chicken Florentine

6 SERVINGS

Cook according to package directions

2 ten-oz packages frozen chopped spinach

Drain well. Then melt

1 tablespoon butter

Cook in it and stir constantly

1 clove garlic, mashed
Dash basil
Dash marjoram

Add and mix well

1 tablespoon flour

Add

⅓ cup medium or heavy cream
Spinach

Place mixture on bottom of casserole. Cover with

Meat from 1 five-lb stewed chicken

Melt

3 tablespoons butter

Add and blend well

3 tablespoons flour

Stir in and cook until thickened

¾ cup cream
Salt and pepper to taste
¾ cup chicken stock

Pour sauce over chicken. Cover with

1 cup grated Parmesan cheese

Refrigerate or freeze. When ready to serve, return to room temperature; bake at 400° F for 20 minutes or until cheese is bubbling.

PADDLEFORD
How America Eats

Flannel Cakes with Chicken Hash

2 cups sifted flour
¾ teaspoon baking soda
1 teaspoon salt
2½ cups buttermilk
2 tablespoons melted butter or margarine
2 eggs, separated
Chicken hash

Sift together flour, soda and salt into bowl. Beat in buttermilk and melted shortening. Beat in egg yolks. Fold in stiffly beaten whites. Bake on hot griddle. When brown, place a generous tablespoon of hash on cake, roll cake and fasten with toothpick. Place in rows on baking pan. Heat in a 350°F. oven or under low broiler.

YIELD: 12 CAKES

CHICKEN HASH

3 tablespoons butter or margarine
2 tablespoons minced onion
3 tablespoons flour
1 cup chicken or turkey broth
⅓ cup minced celery
2 teaspoons minced parsley
½ cup light cream
2 cups cold chicken or turkey, cut in small pieces
Salt and pepper

Melt butter. Add onion and sauté until tender. Add flour and cook 4 minutes, stirring constantly. Add broth, celery and parsley and simmer for 5 minutes. Add cream and stir well. Add chicken. Heat to boiling point and season. Set aside to thicken while Flannel Cakes are baking.

BROWNSTONE

The Associated Press Cookbook

Country Captain

How did Country Captain, a chicken dish with a delectable reputation, get its name? No one could ever tell us.

So we searched American cookbooks of an earlier day until we found the explanation in "Miss Leslie's New Cookery Book" published in 1857. Miss Leslie wrote:

"This is an East India dish, and a very easy preparation of curry. The term 'country captain' signifies a captain of the native troops (or Sepoys), in the pay of England; their own country being India, they are there called generally the country troops. Probably this dish was first introduced at English tables by a Sepoy officer."

The recipe for Country Captain that has been treasured for more than 50 years is the one given by Alexander Filippini, famed chef of New York's old Delmonico restaurant, in his 1906 The International Cook Book.

Here is our version of the Filippini recipe. Of all the chicken dishes we have adapted, this is the prime favorite.

1 frying chicken, about 2½ pounds
¼ cup flour
1 teaspoon salt
¼ teaspoon pepper
4 to 5 tablespoons butter
⅓ cup finely diced onion
⅓ cup finely diced green pepper
1 clove garlic, crushed
1½ teaspoons curry powder
½ teaspoon dried crushed thyme
1 can (1 pound) stewed tomatoes
3 tablespoons dried currants, washed and drained
Blanched toasted almonds

Have chicken cut so there are 2 pieces of breast, 2 wings, 2 legs, 2 second joints, 2 pieces of bony back. (Wing tips, neck and giblets may be used for stock for another dish.) Wash and clean chicken pieces in cold water; drain.

Mix flour, salt and pepper; coat chicken pieces with mixture, rubbing it in where necessary.

Heat butter in 10- or 12-inch skillet until very hot; add chicken and brown well on all sides. If 10-inch skillet is used, squeeze in bony back pieces at sides. Start with 4 tablespoons butter and add remaining tablespoon if necessary to brown chicken well or if there are not enough drippings in pan for next step.

Remove chicken pieces; add onion, green pepper, garlic, curry powder and thyme to drippings in skillet. Stir over low heat to get up browned particles and cook slightly; add stewed tomatoes, including liquid in can.

Return chicken to skillet, skin side up. Cover skillet and cook slowly until tender—20 to 30 minutes. Stir currants into sauce. Serve accompanied by almonds.

MAKES 4 SERVINGS

ALLEN

Mrs. Allen's Cook Book

Old-Fashioned Chicken Pot-Pie

1 (3-pound) fowl
½ cupful fat salt pork, diced
3 cupfuls boiling water
4 tablespoons flour
½ cupful cream
Salt and pepper to taste
Short biscuit crust

Clean and disjoint the fowl. Heat a small iron pot and put the salt pork in it. Try out the fat, then toss in the chicken, and cook until well-browned. Add the water, cover and let simmer over the heat or in the oven till tender. Season, add the flour and cream, blended, let boil up once and set the paste in position in a casserole as follows: Cut a strip two inches wide and line the inside of the casserole. Pour in the chicken mixture, set a round cover in place over the top of the boiling liquid, and pinch the two edges together; set in the oven and bake till light brown. Invert on a platter, and serve surrounded with buttered peas or asparagus tips.

ROSSO AND LUKINS
The Silver Palate Cookbook

Chicken Marbella

This was the first main-course dish to be offered at The Silver Palate, and the distinctive colors and flavors of the prunes, olives and capers have kept it a favorite for years. It's good hot or at room temperature. When prepared with small drumsticks and wings, it makes a delicious hors d'oeuvre.

The overnight marination is essential to the moistness of the finished product: the chicken keeps and even improves over several days of refrigeration; it travels well and makes excellent picnic fare.

Since Chicken Marbella is such a spectacular party dish, we give quantities to serve 10 to 12, but the recipe can successfully be divided to make a smaller amount if you wish.

4 chickens, 2½ pounds each, quartered
1 head of garlic, peeled and finely puréed
¼ cup dried oregano
coarse salt and freshly ground black pepper to taste
½ cup red wine vinegar
½ cup olive oil
1 cup pitted prunes
½ cup pitted Spanish green olives
½ cup capers with a bit of juice
6 bay leaves
1 cup brown sugar
1 cup white wine
¼ cup Italian parsley or fresh coriander (cilantro), finely chopped

1. In a large bowl combine chicken quarters, garlic, oregano, pepper and coarse salt to taste, vinegar, olive oil, prunes, olives, capers and juice, and bay leaves. Cover and let marinate, refrigerated, overnight.

2. Preheat oven to 350°F.

3. Arrange chicken in a single layer in one or two large, shallow baking pans and spoon marinade over it evenly. Sprinkle chicken pieces with brown sugar and pour white wine around them.

4. Bake for 50 minutes to 1 hour, basting frequently with pan juices. Chicken is done when thigh pieces, pricked with a fork at their thickest, yield clear yellow (rather than pink) juice.

5. With a slotted spoon transfer chicken, prunes, olives and capers to a serving platter. Moisten with a few spoonfuls of pan juices and sprinkle generously with parsley or cilantro. Pass remaining pan juices in a sauceboat.

6. To serve Chicken Marbella cold, cool to room temperature in cooking juices before transferring to a serving platter. If chicken has been covered and refrigerated, allow it to return to room temperature before serving. Spoon some of the reserved juice over chicken.

16 PIECES, 10 OR MORE PORTIONS

CHILD
From Julia Child's Kitchen

COQ AU VIN VERSUS CHICKEN FRICASSEE

Chicken, onions, and mushrooms—simmer them in red wine for Coq au Vin, *served brown and hearty; in white wine for old-fashioned chicken fricassee, all suave and creamy. Except for small details, the two recipes are parallel in technique yet so different in taste you would never dream they were sisters under the sauce, and to illustrate their twinship, I've combined them together into a single recipe. (You may notice the procedure is slightly different here than for either recipe in our other books.) Both dishes are useful cook-in-advance ones for parties since they lose none of their special qualities when cooked, refrigerated, and then reheated a day later. Serve the* Coq au Vin *with rice, noodles, or boiled potatoes; the fricassee with rice. You need no other vegetable accompaniment, although fresh buttered peas or broccoli flowerets make a nice touch of green. The red wine to serve with* Coq au Vin *can be either the same used in the cooking, or one of the regional Burgundies or Côtes du Rhône, or domestic Pinot Noir. Serve either a red Bordeaux or a white Burgundy or Pinot Blanc with the fricassée.*

Coq au vin

Chicken in Red Wine

Chicken fricassee

Chicken in White Wine

FOR 4 TO 6 PEOPLE

FOR BOTH COQ AU VIN AND CHICKEN FRICASSEE

2½ lbs. ready-cut frying chicken (a selection of parts, or all one kind), thoroughly dried
Salt and pepper
16 to 20 small white onions, peeled (or double the amount if you want to use tiny frozen peeled raw onions)
3 Tb flour
1 quart (¾ lb.) fresh mushrooms, trimmed, washed, and quartered
Optional enrichment: 2 to 3 Tb butter

FOR COQ AU VIN ONLY

Optional: ½ cup lardons (fresh fat-and-lean pork strips, ¼ by 1½ inches)
2 or more Tb olive oil or cooking oil
Optional: ¼ cup Cognac or Armagnac
1 imported bay leaf and ¼ tsp thyme
2 cups red wine (Burgundy, Côtes du Rhône, or Pinot Nair)
About 2 cups brown chicken stock or beef bouillon
1 or 2 cloves of garlic, mashed or minced
About 1 Tb tomato paste

FOR FRICASSEE ONLY

3 to 4 Tb butter
½ tsp tarragon
2 cups dry white wine or 1½ cups dry white French Vermouth
About 2 cups chicken bouillon
About ½ cup heavy cream
Drops of fresh lemon juice

EQUIPMENT FOR BOTH

A large heavy frying pan, casserole, or electric skillet; tongs; wooden spoon and fork

COQ AU VIN. If you are using *lardons*, sauté several minutes in 2 tablespoons oil until lightly browned; remove *lardons* to a side dish and leave fat in pan. (Otherwise, film pan with ⅛ inch of oil.) Heat fat or oil in pan to moderately hot, add chicken, not crowding pan; turn frequently to brown nicely on all sides. Pour in the optional Cognac, shake pan a few seconds until bubbling hot, then ignite Cognac with a match. Let flame a minute, swirling pan by its handle to burn off alcohol; extinguish with pan cover.

CHICKEN FRICASSEE. Over moderate heat, cook butter in pan until foaming. Add chicken pieces and turn frequently in the butter for several minutes, regulating heat so chicken does not brown. Meat should stiffen slightly in contrast to its squashy raw state, and become a golden yellow.

FOR BOTH. Then season chicken pieces with salt and pepper; add bay leaf and thyme to *Coq au Vin*, tarragon to Chicken Fricassee. Place the onions around the chicken. Cover and cook slowly 10 minutes, turning once. Uncover pan, sprinkle on the flour, turning chicken and onions so flour is absorbed; cook 3 to 4 minutes more, turning once or twice. Remove from heat, gradually stir and swirl in the wine and enough stock or bouillon almost to cover the chicken. (Add the browned *lardons*, garlic, and tomato paste to the *Coq au Vin*.) Cover pan and simmer slowly 25 to 30 minutes, then test chicken; remove those pieces that are tender, and continue cooking the rest a few minutes longer. If onions are not quite tender, continue cooking them; then return all chicken to pan, add mushrooms, and simmer 4 to 5 minutes. Taste carefully, and correct seasoning.

COQ AU VIN. Sauce should be just thick enough to coat chicken and vegetables lightly. If too thin, boil down rapidly to concentrate; if too thick, thin out with spoonfuls of bouillon.

CHICKEN FRICASSEE. Add ½ cup of cream, and bring to the simmer, thinning out if necessary with spoonfuls of more cream until sauce coats chicken and vegetables lightly. Correct seasoning again, adding drops of lemon juice to taste.

SERVING AND HOLDING NOTES FOR BOTH. For immediate serving, arrange the chicken and vegetables on a platter, surrounded by the rice or whatever else you are including; swirl the optional butter enrichment by tablespoons into the sauce, and spoon sauce over chicken. For later serving, baste chicken with its sauce, and let cool, uncovered, to room temperature; then cover and refrigerate. To reheat, simmer slowly, covered; baste and turn chicken every 2 minutes until thoroughly warmed through (6 to 8 minutes), but do not overcook.

OLNEY

Simple French Food

Garlic Chicken

Poulet "aux 40 Gousses d'Ail"

FOR 4

The garlic, squeezed from its hull and spread onto grilled crisp slices of rough country bread as one eats the chicken, will be appreciated by all who do not share the mental antigarlic quirk: if the bread can be grilled over hot coals, the light smoky flavor will be found to marry particularly well with the garlic puree.

For variety's sake, turn, quarter, and choke 3 or 4 tender young artichokes, coating them immediately in the recipe's olive oil before mixing all the ingredients together.

- 1 chicken, cut up as for a sauté (or 4 legs, thighs and drumsticks, separated)
- 4 heads (6 ounces) firm garlic, broken into cloves, cleared of loose hulls, but unpeeled
- ⅔ cup olive oil
- Salt, pepper
- 1 teaspoon finely crumbled mixed dried herbs (thyme, oregano, savory)
- 1 large bouquet garni: large branch celery, parsley and root (if available), bay leaf, leek greens, small branch lovage (if available)
- Flour for dough

Put everything except the bouquet into an earthenware casserole, turning around and over repeatedly with your hands to be certain of regularly dispersed seasoning and liberal and even coating of oil. Force the bouquet into the center, packing the chicken around and filling all interstices with garlic cloves. Prepare a dough of flour, water, and a dribble of oil, roll it into a long cylindrical band on a floured board, moisten the ridge of the casserole, press the roll of paste into place, and press the lid on top. Cook in a 350° oven for 1 hour and 45 minutes and break the seal of paste at the table.

WELLS

Bistro Cooking

Poulet au Vinaigre Le Petit Truc

Le Petit Truc's Chicken with Tarragon Vinegar

While the regional bistro shares many common traits with its Parisian counterpart—the decor borders on the haphazard, the ambiance is frankly familial, the rarely varying menu could well be engraved in stone—each manages to take on a character all its own, reflecting the gastronomic style and rhythm of every section of France. Often, as in the now defunct Burgundian bistro Le Petit Truc, it's also the personality of the owner. Here, the youthful, blonde Edith Remoissenet-Cordier ran her tiny restaurant with a will of iron. If you didn't reserve a table, you just didn't get in! But if you played by the rules, all usually went well.

At Le Petit Truc Madame Remoissenet-Cordier offered a medley of homey fare, including this special version of chicken with tarragon vinegar.

- 3 tablespoons extra-virgin olive oil
- 3 tablespoons (1½ ounces; 45 g) unsalted butter
- 1 chicken (3 to 4 pounds; 1.5 to 2 kg), well rinsed, patted dry, cut into 8 serving pieces, at room temperature
- Salt and freshly ground black pepper
- ½ cup (12.5 cl) dry white wine, such as Mâcon-Villages
- 4 shallots, minced
- 2 medium tomatoes, peeled, cored, seeded, and chopped
- ½ cup (12.5 cl) white wine tarragon vinegar
- 1 bunch of tarragon leaves, minced

"Poultry is for the cook what canvas is for the painter." —BRILLAT-SAVARIN

1. In a deep-sided nonreactive, 12-inch (30 cm) skillet, heat the oil with 1 tablespoon (½ ounce; 15 g) of the butter over high heat. Season the chicken liberally with salt and pepper. When the fats are hot but not smoking, add the chicken and cook on both sides until the skin turns an even, golden brown and the chicken is cooked to the desired doneness, about 12 minutes on each side. Carefully regulate the heat to avoid scorching the skin. (If you do not have a pan large enough to hold all of the chicken pieces in a single layer, do this in several batches.)

2. Transfer the chicken to a serving platter; cover loosely with aluminum foil. Keep warm.

3. Pour off the fat in the skillet. Return the skillet to medium-high heat and add the wine. Deglaze the pan, scraping up any bits that cling to the bottom. Add the shallots and tomatoes and cook for several minutes. Raise the heat to high and slowly add the vinegar. Cook for an additional 2 to 3 minutes. Whisk in the remaining 2 tablespoons (1 ounce; 30 g) butter; cook for 1 more minute. Return the chicken to the skillet; coat well with the sauce. Cover and continue cooking over medium heat until the chicken absorbs some of the sauce, just 2 or 3 minutes. Sprinkle with the tarragon and turn the chicken pieces to coat. Serve immediately, accompanied by sautéed potatoes.

YIELD: 4 TO 6 SERVINGS

A Burgundian Dinner

This is typical of the meals served in Burgundian family homes, starting with cheese puffs and a chilled white Chablis, finishing off with a young red Burgundy.

GOUGÈRE FRANÇOISE POTEL
Françoise Potel's Cheese Puffs

POULET AU VINAIGRE LE PETIT TRUC
Le Petit Truc's Chicken with Tarragon Vinegar

QUARTIERS DE POMMES DE TERRE SAUTÉS DANS LEUR PEAU
Potato Quarters Sautéed in Their Skins

TARTE AUX POMMES FRANÇOISE POTEL
Françoise Potel's Apple Tart

DAVID
French Provincial Cooking

Poulet à l'Estragon
Chicken with Tarragon

Tarragon is a herb which has a quite remarkable affinity with chicken and a poulet à l'estragon, *made with fresh tarragon, is one of the great treats of the summer. There are any amount of different ways of cooking a tarragon-flavoured chicken dish: here is a particularly successful one.*

For a plump roasting chicken weighing about 2 lb. when plucked and drawn, knead a good ounce of butter with a tablespoon of tarragon leaves, half a clove of garlic, salt and pepper. Put this inside the bird, which should be well coated with olive oil. Roast the bird lying on its side on a grid in a baking dish. Turn it over at half-time (45 minutes altogether in a pretty hot oven or an hour in a modern oven should be sufficient; those who have a roomy grill might try grilling it, which take about 20 minutes, and gives much more the impression of a spit-roasted bird, but it must be constantly watched and turned over very carefully, so that the legs are as well done as the breast).

When the bird is cooked, heat a small glass of brandy in a soup ladle, set light to it, pour it flaming over the chicken and rotate the dish so that the flames spread and continue to burn as long as possible. Return the bird to a low oven for 5 minutes, during which time the brandy sauce will mature and lose its raw flavour. At this moment you can, if you like, enrich the sauce with a few spoonfuls of thick cream and, at la Mère Michel's Paris restaurant, from where the recipe originally came, they add Madeira to the sauce. Good though this is, it seems to me a needless complication.

MACAUSLAND
The Gourmet Cookbook

Chicken Cacciatore

Chop coarsely 1 large onion and brown it slightly in 2 tablespoons olive oil. Remove the onion pieces from the pan and reserve for later use. Cut a 3- to 3½-pound roasting chicken into serving pieces and dredge them with flour seasoned with salt and pepper. Sauté the chicken until well browned on all sides in the oil in which the onion was browned, adding 2 more tablespoons olive oil. Add 2 cups fresh or canned tomatoes and 1 cup coarsely chopped sweet green peppers, with white ribs and seeds removed. Return the browned onion to the pan and simmer chicken and vegetables together, covered, for 15 minutes over a very low flame. Add a little chicken stock or consommé to the liquid in the pan. Again cover the pan and continue to simmer for about 45 minutes, or until the chicken is tender.

KASPER
The Splendid Table

Balsamic Roast Chicken

Pollo al Forno con Aceto Balsamico

In Modena and Reggio cooks rub garlic and fresh rosemary into a chicken before roasting. At the table, the dish is finished with a few spoonfuls of the family's own balsamic vinegar. I do not exaggerate in saying that few sauces, no matter how intricate, can equal the distinction of a great balsamic. And few dishes equal the simple elegance of this one.

SERVES 4 TO 6

- 4- to 4½-pound frying or roasting chicken (organic free-range preferred)
- 1 tablespoon fresh rosemary leaves, or 1 teaspoon dried rosemary
- 1 large clove garlic
- ¼ teaspoon salt
- 2 tablespoons extra-virgin olive oil
- Freshly ground black pepper
- 8 sprigs fresh rosemary
- 3 to 4 tablespoons artisan-made tradizionale balsamic vinegar, or a high-quality commercial balsamic blended with ½ teaspoon brown sugar

WORKING AHEAD: *Season the chicken and refrigerate 24 hours before cooking. Although leftovers are excellent, the chicken is best eaten hot from the oven.*

SEASONING THE CHICKEN: Rinse the chicken under cold running water. Dry it thoroughly inside and out. Set it on a dinner plate. Mince together the rosemary leaves and garlic in the salt. Rub the olive oil over the chicken, then rub in the herb mixture. Sprinkle with pepper. Put two rosemary sprigs in the bird's cavity, and refrigerate 24 hours, lightly covered with plastic wrap. Keep the remaining rosemary sprigs for garnishing.

ROASTING THE CHICKEN: Preheat the oven to 350°F. Truss the chicken if desired. Rub into the chicken any of the seasoning that might have fallen onto the dinner plate. Use a small heavy roasting pan, and place the chicken in it breast side down. Roast 20 to 25 minutes per pound (about 1¼ to 1¾ hours), or until a thermometer tucked into the thickest part of the thigh or leg reads 170°F. Baste every 15 minutes or so with the pan juices. During the last 30 minutes of roasting, turn the chicken over to brown the breast. If the chicken is not deep golden brown when the cooking time is up, turn the heat to 475°F and brown it about 10 minutes, turning once.

FINISHING WITH BALSAMIC AND SERVING: Transfer the chicken to a heated serving platter. Present it whole, drizzled with the balsamic vinegar, and carve at the table. Or use poultry shears to cut it into eight pieces in the kitchen. Spoon the balsamic vinegar over them, and scatter with the remaining rosemary sprigs. Serve immediately.

SUGGESTIONS

WINE: Drink Bologna's Cabernet Sauvignon Colli Bolognesi, a Sangiovese di Romagna Riserva, or a fine Amarone Reciota della Valpolicella from the Veneto.

MENU: Traditionally Tortellini in Broth Villa Gaidello is served at special dinners. Priest's Soup or Modena's Spiced Soup of Spinach and Cheese is lighter and excellent before the chicken. In Modena style, have Torta Barozzi for dessert, or the old-style Frozen Zuppa Inglese.

COOK'S NOTES

VARIATION WITH CAPON: Even more festive than chicken is a 6- to 7-pound capon. Double the seasoning and the amount of vinegar. Season the capon as described for chicken. Roast it breast down at 325°F 20 to 25 minutes per pound, or until a thermometer inserted into the thigh reads 170°F. Turn the breast up during the last 30 minutes of roasting. Baste frequently with pan juices. Carve the capon as you would a turkey, then spoon the balsamic vinegar over it and serve.

VARIATION IN ROMAGNA: Rigging a new fishing boat is often celebrated with roast chicken made just like this one, but served without the balsamic vinegar.

JUST A FEW DROPS OF *BALSAMICO*

The little town of Spilamberto, near Modena, is home to the oldest of Modena and Reggio's three balsamic vinegar consortiums. The Consorteria dell'Aceto Balsamico is the spiritual mother to Modena and Reggio's organizations. Every year the Consorteria evaluates over a thousand of members' vinegars until one is singled out. On June 24, the festival of Saint John the Baptist, the highest honor a balsamic vinegar artisan can receive is awarded in Spilamberto. Before visiting a Spilamberto tasting, I dined with three men whose families had been making the vinegar for generations. As plates of vegetable fritters arrived, one of my hosts took a small silver flask bearing his family crest from his pocket. Removing the medicine-dropper top, he offered some of his private balsamico for my pleasure. With only a few drops of the brown liquid, that simple fritter became unforgettable. With each new course I waited in silent but eager anticipation, hoping he would again offer the special condiment. I was not disappointed. The final pleasure was droplets of the vinegar over small crocks of caramelized baked custard.

WOLFERT

Couscous and Other Good Food from Morocco

Four Different Ways to Make Chicken with Lemon and Olives

Chicken with lemon and olives is one of the great combinations in Moroccan cookery, the dish that most often seduces foreigners and turns them into devotees of Moroccan tagines. *There are numerous variations on this exquisite theme; I have included four, each one delicious, each one unique:* Djej masquid bil beid*—a glorious variation enriched by the addition of whipped and baked eggs;* Djej emshmel*—a multispiced classic served in a plentiful onion-based sauce;* Djej bil zeetoon meslalla*—a tangy variation literally smothered with whole or cracked green olives; and* Djej makalli*—a more subtle though no less delicious variation, flavored with ginger and saffron and served with a thick sauce enriched by additional mashed chicken livers. I recommend that you try them all.*

Before the recipes, however, a few words about lemons and olives. I could barely contain my rage and my scorn when I read the following paragraph in an American women's magazine: "You needn't brine your lemons in order to taste a close reproduction of the Moroccan lemon chicken; fresh lemons do very well as a substitute. What you miss by making it with fresh lemons is the 'preserved' flavor (much like bottled lime juice)." This same writer then described the olives in her recipe as, simply, "green."

There is, and I cannot emphasize this enough, no substitute for preserved lemons *in Moroccan food. (There is also not much similarity between the taste of preserved lemons and the taste of bottled lime juice, and, of course, no similarity as far as texture is concerned.) To not use preserved lemons is to completely miss the point, and also to miss a whole dimension of culinary experience. Preserved lemons are easy to make* *(page 434)**, and if carefully put up they will keep almost a year.*

As for olives, I have written about them at length. One does use "green olives" to smother Djej bil zeetoon meslalla*—not California or Spanish ones, but unripened ones cracked and soaked in brine. (If you cannot get Moroccan olives, buy Greek ones.)*

For the other three recipes the classic olive to use is the ripe reddish-brown Moroccan mchqouq *perfumed with citrus juice. When they are not available I have had excellent luck with Gaetas from Italy, Kalamatas from Greece, and also Greek Royal-Victorias that have been rinsed to rid them of bitterness.*

Chicken with Eggs, Lemons, and Olives

Djej Masquid Bil Beid

This is one of my favorite Moroccan dishes.

INGREDIENTS

2 chickens, cut up and prepared
1 cup chopped parsley
3 cloves garlic, peeled and chopped
¾ cup grated Spanish onion
Salt to taste
½ rounded teaspoon ground ginger
Pinch of pulverized saffron
¾ teaspoon freshly ground black pepper
¼ cup sweet butter, melted
3 large or 6 small cinnamon sticks
10 eggs
2 preserved lemons (see page 434)
8 "red-brown" olives, such as Kalamatas, pitted and chopped
½ cup lemon juice

EQUIPMENT

5½-quart casserole with cover
Shallow, 2½-quart ovenproof serving dish
Mixing bowl
Whisk
Chopping knife
Aluminum foil

WORKING TIME: 30 MINUTES
COOKING TIME: 1 HOUR 30 MINUTES
SERVES: 6

1. Place the cleaned chicken in the casserole. Add ⅔ cup of the chopped parsley, the chopped garlic, grated onion, salt, spices, half the butter, and the cinnamon sticks. Add 2 cups water and bring to a boil. Simmer, covered, about 1 hour or until the chickens are very tender and the flesh is almost falling off the bone. (During the cooking you may need to add more water.)

2. Preheat oven to 350°.

3. Transfer the chickens (but not the sauce) to the serving dish. Remove any loose bones and cinnamon sticks from the sauce in the casserole and, by boiling rapidly, uncovered, reduce to 2 cups of thick, rich sauce. Pour over the chickens.

4. Beat the eggs to a froth with the remaining parsley. Rinse and dice the preserved lemons, using the pulp if desired. Stir the lemons and chopped olives into the eggs and pour the egg mixture over the chickens. Cover the dish with aluminum foil and bake on the middle shelf of the oven for 20 minutes. Raise the oven heat to highest setting, remove the aluminum cover, and dot the eggs with the remaining melted butter. Transfer the dish to the upper shelf of the oven and bake 10 minutes more, or until the eggs are completely set and the chickens have browned slightly. Sprinkle with lemon juice and serve at once.

NOTE: Six Moroccan pigeons or 3 squabs may be substituted for the chickens, in which case the dish is called *Frach masquid bil beid.*

Chicken with Lemons and Olives Emshmel

Djej Emshmel

I first ate this dish in a home in the city of Meknes, sometimes called the City of Olives. Djej emshmel *(pronounced* meshmel or emsharmel*) is a classic Moroccan dish—chicken served in an intricately spiced, creamy, lemony, and sublime sauce with a scattering of pale-hued olives.*

INGREDIENTS

2 to 3 chickens, whole or quartered, with their livers
6 cloves garlic, peeled
Salt
1 teaspoon ground ginger
1 teaspoon sweet paprika
¼ teaspoon ground cumin
¼ teaspoon ground black pepper
¼ cup salad oil
2½ cups grated onion, drained
¼ teaspoon pulverized saffron (mixed with turmeric, if desired)
½ cup mixed, chopped fresh herbs (green coriander and parsley)
1½ cups ripe "green-brown" olives, such as Royal-Victorias
2 preserved lemons (see page 434)
2 to 3 fresh lemons

EQUIPMENT

Large bowl
Paring knife
6-quart casserole with cover
Strainer, if necessary
Small mixing bowl

WORKING TIME: 30 MINUTES
COOKING TIME: 1 HOUR (APPROXIMATELY)
SERVES: 8

1. The day before, using 4 cloves of the garlic and 2 tablespoons salt, prepare the chickens, then marinate both chickens and livers in 1 teaspoon salt, the remaining 2 cloves of garlic, sliced thin, the spices, and the oil. Refrigerate, covered.

2. The next day, place the chickens, livers, and marinade in the casserole. Add ½ cup of the grated onion, the saffron, herbs, and 2 cups water. Bring to a boil, cover, and simmer 30 minutes, turning the chickens often in the sauce.

3. While the chickens are cooking, rinse and pit the olives. (If they seem a little bitter, cover with cold water, bring to a boil, and drain.) Set aside.

4. Remove the chicken livers from the casserole and mash them fine. Return to the casserole with the remaining grated, drained onions. (This will give a good deal of heftiness to the sauce.) Add water, if necessary. Continue cooking 20 minutes, partially covered.

5. Rinse the preserved lemons (discarding the pulp, if desired) and quarter. Add the olives and preserved lemon quarters to the sauce when the chickens are very tender and the flesh falls easily from the bone. Continue cooking 5 to 10 minutes, uncovered.

6. Transfer the chickens to a serving dish and spoon the olives and lemons around them. Cover and keep warm. By boiling rapidly, uncovered, reduce the sauce to 1½ cups. Add the juice of 2 fresh lemons to the sauce in the pan. Add more salt (and more lemon juice, if desired) to taste. Pour the sauce over chickens and serve at once.

Chicken Smothered with Green, Cracked Olives

Djej Bil Zeetoon Meslalla

For this recipe you can use the bitter green olives often sold "cracked" and packed in brine in Greek specialty stores; to get rid of the bitterness boil them three times. When I first learned this dish in Morocco I wondered how the olives were going to be pitted, since they were already cracked on one side. The Moroccans had a solution—they put them on the stone floor of the kitchen, tapped each of them smartly with a smooth stone, and the pits popped right out. I have often served this dish with uncracked Moroccan green olives, with great success.

INGREDIENTS

2 chickens, whole or cut up, with giblets
1 teaspoon ground ginger
1 teaspoon freshly ground black pepper
¼ teaspoon pulverized saffron (mixed with turmeric, if desired)
1 tablespoon finely chopped garlic
¾ cup grated onion, drained
1 cup finely chopped mixed herbs (parsley and green coriander)
⅓ cup salad oil
½ teaspoon ground cumin
½ teaspoon sweet paprika
Salt to taste
4 cups green olives (2 pounds), preferably Agrinon or Nafpiou
½ cup lemon juice, or more to taste

EQUIPMENT

5½-quart casserole with cover
Paring knife or smooth stone
1½-quart saucepan
Sieve
Large serving platter

WORKING TIME: 45 MINUTES
COOKING TIME: 1 HOUR (APPROXIMATELY)
SERVES: 6 TO 8

1. Place the prepared chickens in the casserole with all the ingredients except the olives and lemon juice. Cover with 4 cups water and bring to a boil, then reduce the heat, cover, and simmer 30 minutes, turning the chickens often in the sauce.

2. Meanwhile, pit the olives, using a paring knife or just smashing each one with a smooth stone. Cover the olives with water, bring to boil, and boil 5 minutes. Drain, cover with fresh water, bring to a boil, and boil 5 more minutes. Repeat the procedure one more time. Taste olives—they should no longer be bitter: if they are, boil them again. Drain and add to the casserole after the chicken has cooked 30 minutes.

3. Pour in the lemon juice and continue cooking until the chickens are very tender and the sauce is thick. Transfer the chickens to an ovenproof serving platter and place in a hot oven to brown. Reduce the liquid in the casserole to a thick gravy and adjust salt and lemon juice to taste.

4. To serve, cover the chickens completely with olives. Pour the sauce over and serve at once.

Chicken with Lemon and Olives, Makalli

Djej Makalli

INGREDIENTS

1 chicken, cut in 6 pieces, with 2 chicken livers
6 to 7 cloves garlic, peeled
Salt
1 teaspoon ground ginger
¼ teaspoon freshly ground black pepper
1 preserved lemon, rinsed (see page 434)
¼ cup salad oil
¼ teaspoon pulverized saffron (mixed with turmeric)
½ cup grated onion, drained
6 sprigs green coriander, tied together with a thread
½ cup "red-brown" olives, such as Kalamatas or Gaetas

EQUIPMENT

Electric blender
Large bowl
Plastic wrap
4½-quart casserole with cover
Small mixing bowl
Olive pitter or paring knife (optional)

WORKING TIME: 30 MINUTES
COOKING TIME: 45 TO 50 MINUTES
SERVES: 4

1. The day before, using 4 cloves of the garlic and 2 tablespoons salt, prepare the chicken. (Be sure to rinse well after rubbing with the garlic and salt.) Using the blender, combine the ginger, a little salt, the pepper, 2 to 3 cloves garlic, the pulp only of the preserved lemon (reserving the peel), and the oil into a sauce. Rub the sauce over the pieces of chicken and the livers. Cover with plastic wrap and refrigerate overnight.

2. The next day, place the chickens, livers, and sauce in the casserole. Add the saffron, onion, bundle of green coriander sprigs, and 2½ cups water. Stir and bring to a boil. Partially cover and simmer gently 30 minutes. Turn and baste the chickens often.

3. Remove the livers and mash, then return to the sauce. Rinse the olives and pit them, if desired. Add the quartered preserved lemon peel and olives for the final 15 minutes' cooking. Transfer the chicken to a hot oven to brown. By boiling rapidly, uncovered, reduce the sauce to a wry thick gravy, about ¾ cup. Remove the coriander sprigs. Spoon the sauce over the chicken, decorate with the lemon peel and olives, and serve at once.

CLAIBORNE
The New York Times Cook Book

Chicken à la Kiev

6 SERVINGS

Chicken à la Kiev is a dish created during the Czarist days in Russia. It is, in effect, rolled boneless breast of chicken stuffed with butter and chives. When a knife slices into it, the butter should spurt forth. This is a dish still found on menus in Moscow.

3 whole breasts of chicken with or without main wing bones attached, boned and halved
½ cup chilled, firm butter
Salt and freshly ground black pepper
2 tablespoons chopped chives
Flour for dredging
2 eggs, lightly beaten
1 cup fresh bread crumbs
Fat for deep frying

1. Place the chicken breasts between pieces of waxed paper and pound until thin with a mallet or the flat side of a butcher knife. Do not split the flesh. Remove the waxed paper.

2. Cut the butter into six finger-shaped pieces. Place a piece in the middle of each breast, sprinkle with salt, pepper and chives and roll up, envelope fashion, letting the wing bone protrude and making the sides overlap. The flesh will adhere without skewers.

3. Dredge each roll lightly with flour, dip into the beaten eggs and roll in bread crumbs. Refrigerate one hour or more so the crumbs will adhere.

4. Fill a fryer or kettle with enough fat to completely cover the breasts. Heat until hot (360° F.). Add chicken gradually and brown on all sides. Drain on absorbent paper and place a paper frill on the main wing bones before serving.

LANG
The Cuisine of Hungary

Paprika Chicken

Paprikás csirke

4 SERVINGS

2 medium-sized onions, peeled and minced
2 tablespoons lard
1 plump chicken, about 3 pounds, disjointed, washed, and dried
1 large ripe tomato, peeled and cut into pieces
1 heaping tablespoon "Noble Rose" paprika
1 teaspoon salt
1 green pepper sliced
2 tablespoons sour cream
1 tablespoon flour
2 tablespoons heavy cream
Egg Dumplings

1. Use a 4- or 5-quart heavy casserole with a tight-fitting lid. Cook the onions in the lard, covered, over low heat for about 5 minutes. They should become almost pasty, but definitely not browned.

2. Add chicken and tomato and cook, covered, for 10 minutes.

3. Stir in paprika. Add ½ cup water and the salt. Cook, covered, over very low heat for 30 minutes. In the beginning, the small amount of water will create a steam-cooking action. Toward the end of the 30-minute period, take off lid and let the liquid evaporate. Finally let the chicken cook in its own juices and fat, taking care that it does not burn. (If the chicken is tough, you may have to add a few more tablespoons of water.)

4. Remove chicken pieces. Mix the sour cream, flour and 1 teaspoon cold water, and stir in with the sauce till it is very smooth and of an even color. Add green pepper, replace chicken parts, adjust salt. Put lid back on casserole and over very low heat cook until done.

5. Just before serving whip in the heavy cream. Serve with egg dumplings.

NOTE: The combination of sour cream and heavy cream is the almost forgotten, but ideal way to prepare this dish. Today, more often than not, the heavy cream is omitted. In Hungary, the lily is gilded by spreading several tablespoons of additional sour cream on top of the chicken in the serving platter.

BRENNAN
The Original Thai Cookbook

Green Chicken Curry

Gaeng Keo Wan Gai

6 TO 8 SERVINGS

This curry should properly contain pea eggplants, Makeua Pong, *a tiny, bitter vegetable of the eggplant/tomato family slightly larger than a pea. It is not commercially obtainable in the United States at this time, but it is being experimentally grown and should be available in Thai markets shortly. Some Thai restaurants substitute green peas for appearance.*

2½ to 3 pounds frying chicken, boned, skinned and cut into small chunks
2 cups "Thick" coconut milk
2 tablespoons fish sauce (*Nam Pla*)
3 pieces dried Laos (*Ka*)
3 tablespoons green curry paste (*Krung Gaeng Keo Wan*)
2 cups "Thin" coconut milk
½ cup fresh sweet basil leaves (1 tablespoon dried may be substituted)
6 to 8 young citrus leaves
2 to 3 pea eggplants (*Makeua Pong*) (optional)
6 green Serrano chillies

In a wok, boil together the chicken, "Thick" coconut milk, fish sauce and Laos until the meat is tender. Remove the chicken to a plate with a slotted spoon and continue boiling until the milk thickens and becomes oily. Add the curry paste and continue cooking, stirring to help mix the paste, for a few more minutes. Return the chicken to the wok when the mixture is smooth and the paste has released its aroma. Pour in the "Thin" coconut milk and return to the boil. Reduce heat and simmer for 5 to 10 minutes. Add the basil and citrus leaves, pea eggplant, and chillies. Increase heat and boil again for 5 minutes. Serve over rice.

BRENNAN
The Original Thai Cookbook

Sate

Satay

6 SERVINGS

The generic term Sate *refers more to a fashion of cooking, barbecued on skewers, rather than a specific dish or food.*

Southeast Asians, as other Orientals, have great difficulty pronouncing any two consonants together, particularly s *in conjunction with* t *or* p. *(The popular soda pop in Thailand, Green Spot, generally is heard as "Galeen Supot.") The common reference is that the name* Satay *is merely a corruption stemming from Asian attempts at the word "steak." Satay is indigenous to Indonesia but this way of cooking has spread up through Malaysia and is commonplace in Thailand. Thai restaurants, here in the United States, almost universally feature Satay on their menus, causing many Americans to believe that it is an original Thai specialty.*

1 pound beef, pork or chicken, very thinly sliced and cut into strips ½" wide x 2" long

MARINADE

2 cloves garlic, smashed and chopped
½ onion, chopped
1 tablespoon palm or brown sugar
Juice of 1 lime
1 tablespoon fish sauce (Nam Pla)
½ teaspoon tamarind pulp, dissolved in 2 tablespoons hot water
1 tablespoon vegetable oil

SAUCE

8 tablespoons crunchy peanut butter
1 onion, finely chopped
1 cup "Thick" coconut milk
1 tablespoon palm or brown sugar
1 teaspoon red chilli powder (Cayenne)
1 stalk lemon grass, finely chopped
1 tablespoon fish sauce (Nam Pla)
1 tablespoon dark, sweet soy sauce

Place all the Marinade ingredients in a food processor or blender and process or blend until smooth. Thread the meat strips like a ribbon on 12" wooden skewers, 3 or 4 to each stick, and place in a large, shallow dish. Pour the Marinade over the Satay and let stand for 30 to 60 minutes, rotating each stick occasionally.

If cooking over charcoal, light the coals and let them come to a temperature that creates a white, chalky film. If using a broiler, turn it on and let it come to a full heat for at least 10 minutes before you start to grill or broil. The *Satay* should be grilled, barbecued or broiled near high heat.

In a saucepan, combine all the Sauce ingredients and bring to a boil, stirring. Remove from heat and pour into small bowls for accompaniment.

Remove the *Satay* from the Marinade and cook fiercely and quickly. (The cooking time will vary with the type and density of meat used, the amount of heat and proximity thereto, but should never exceed a total of 5 minutes for all sides.)

Serve with the Sauce, and side bowls of *Taeng Kwa Brio Wan*.

CLAIBORNE AND LEE
The Chinese Cookbook

Kung Pao Chicken

The following dish was named for a high-ranking Chinese official, Ting Kung Pao, who fled to Szechwan as a political refugee a few hundred years ago during the Ching Dynasty. It became popular in many provinces where the inhabitants dote on hot foods, such as Hunan and Kweichow. An interesting spiced dish, it is redolent with garlic and chili paste, hot peppers, and bean sauce.

1 large whole chicken breast, boned but not skinned
½ egg white (beat the egg white lightly, then divide in half)
2 teaspoons cornstarch
Salt to taste
2 tablespoons bean sauce*
1 tablespoon hoi sin sauce*
1 tablespoon chili paste with garlic (Szechwan paste)*
1½ teaspoons sugar
1 tablespoon dry sherry or shao hsing wine*
¼ teaspoon monosodium glutamate (optional)
1 tablespoon red wine vinegar
4 cloves garlic, peeled and flattened but not chopped
2 cups peanut, vegetable, or corn oil
12 to 16 hot dried red peppers,* cut in half
1 cup raw shelled and hulled fresh unsalted peanuts*

*Available in Chinese markets and by mail order.

1. Cut the chicken into ¾-inch cubes. Combine with the egg white, cornstarch, and salt. Refrigerate for 30 minutes.

2. Combine the bean sauce, hoi sin sauce, chili paste with garlic, sugar, wine, monosodium glutamate, vinegar, and garlic and set aside.

3. Heat the 2 cups of oil in a wok or skillet, and when it is almost boiling hot but not smoking turn the heat off and add the peanuts. The peanuts should turn light golden brown from retained heat, but if they don't, turn the heat on and cook briefly, watching carefully—they cook very fast and will continue to cook after being removed from the heat. Drain and reserve the oil.

4. Heat 1 cup of the reserved oil in the pan (save the rest for another use). When the oil is hot, add the chicken mixture. Cook quickly, only about 45 seconds, stirring, until the chicken becomes translucent. Do not brown. Remove the chicken and drain well. Pour off all but about 2 tablespoons of the oil from the wok.

5. Add the peppers and cook until dark—about 15 seconds longer. Add the sauce and the chicken and cook about 1 minute. Serve sprinkled with the peanuts.

YIELD: 4 TO 8 SERVINGS

DELFS

The Good Food of Szechwan

Gong-bao Ji-ding

Chicken with Charred Red Peppers and Cashews

The story is that when a certain Ting Kung-pao of Kweichow received all appointment as an imperial official to Szechwan, he prepared a dinner for his friends that included this dish, which then took his name. Gong-bao Ji-ding, *in one form or another, is one of the best known and most often prepared Szechwanese foods, especially outside China. Whole dried red peppers are purposely cooked until they are burnt, flavoring the oil in which the chicken is to be cooked. The final dish should be somewhat sweet and slightly spicy and also hot from the charred red peppers of which there should be an adequate supply. Many restaurants skimp on the red peppers and add red oil and the result is a dull* Gong-bao Ji-ding. *Be careful when you cook this dish because the volatile oil of red peppers tends to be released into the air while the peppers are cooking. If you don't have a hood and fan over your stove, open all the windows and keep doors to other rooms closed while charring the peppers.*

½ chicken breast, about ½ lb. when boned

MARINADE

2 tsps. cornstarch
2 tsps. soy sauce
1 Tbsp. rice wine or dry sherry
½–1 egg white
½ tsp. salt

10 dried red peppers, or a few more
2 tsps. finely chopped fresh ginger
1 green onion
¼ cup cashews, or peanuts or almonds

SEASONINGS

2 tsps. cornstarch
2 tsps. rice wine or dry sherry
1–2 Tbsps. soy sauce
1 tsp. vinegar
½ tsp. salt (omit if using salted nuts)
1–2 tsps. sugar
2 tsps. sesame oil (optional—in this dish I prefer omitting the sesame oil)

4 Tbsps. oil

TO PREPARE: 1. Bone the chicken breast and cut the meat into pieces, 1-inch or slightly smaller.

2. Make the MARINADE by mixing the cornstarch with 2 tsps. soy sauce and 1 Tbsp. wine, then adding the salt and egg white. Mix the MARINADE with the chicken and marinate at least 15 minutes.

3. Cut off the ends of the dried red peppers and shake out the seeds. Chop the ginger very finely and cut the green onion into ¾-inch lengths.

4. In a small bowl, mix the SEASONINGS, first mixing the cornstarch with the soy sauce and wine and then mixing in the other ingredients.

TO COOK: 1. Heat about 4 Tbsps. cooking oil in a *wok* or large frying pan. Add the red peppers, cooking over a medium flame until they start to char. Turn the fire up as high as possible and as soon as the peppers are black, add the chicken pieces. Reduce flame to medium.

2. Stir-fry until the chicken is white, then add the ginger and green onion. Cook, stirring for a few more seconds, then add the cashews or other nuts

and the SEASONINGS (give it a quick stir first). When the sauce has thickened slightly and is glaze-like, remove to a serving dish and serve hot.

TROPP

The Modern Art of Chinese Cooking

Bong-Bong Chicken

Bong-bong *means "club-club," a description of the pounding process that gives this cold chicken its special softness. Satisfying and filling, this is Szechwanese fare at its earthy best—simple to prepare, complexly flavored, and gutsily good. • The classic formula calls for sesame sauce and shredded mung bean sheets to accompany the chicken. I find peanut sauce equally tasty and bean threads (glass noodles) easier to handle. Cucumber is a traditional variation for color and crunch. • This is great party or picnic food. Cheap and easy, it can be made in quantity, well in advance.*

TECHNIQUE NOTES:

To achieve its special character, the chicken must be bashed lightly—not to flatten it, but to spread the fibers. A lightweight rolling pin does the job perfectly. The blunt end of a cleaver handle is a good second choice.

SERVES 2–3 AS A MAIN COURSE, 4–6 AS PART OF A MULTICOURSE MEAL

1½ pounds fresh whole chicken breasts, with skin and bone in, cooked the "no-poach" way

TOPPINGS (CHOOSE ONE)

½–⅔ cup Chinese sesame sauce of your choice
½–⅔ cup Spicy Szechwan Peanut Sauce

SALAD BASES (USE ONE OR BOTH)

½–2 ounces bean threads (glass noodles)
¾ pound very firm seedless cucumbers, or 1½ pounds very firm cucumbers with seeds

OPTIONAL GARNISH

3–4 tablespoons fresh coriander leaves, coarsely chopped

CUTTING AND CLUBBING THE CHICKEN:
Skin and bone the cooked chicken, keeping the meat in as much of one piece as possible. Separate fillet and main pieces. Discard any membranes, tendons, or hard spots. Cut the meat against the grain into strips ¼ inch wide. With a rolling pin, lightly club each strip in 2 or 3 places to separate the fibers and loosen the meat. Be gentle with the delicate fillets. Pull the strips into 2 or 3 pieces; they should come apart easily. Tightly sealed, the chicken may be refrigerated overnight.

PREPARING THE SALAD BASE:
Soak the noodles until soft and silky, then cut into 3- or 4-inch lengths.

Cut off the tips of the cucumbers. Peel and seed, if necessary. To remove seeds, cut the cucumbers in half lengthwise, then scoop out the seeds with a small spoon. Cut the cucumbers into thin strips, which is traditional, or into small arcs, which is a pretty treatment for seeded cucumbers.

If you are working in advance, the noodles may be drained and left at room temperature. The cucumbers may be sealed airtight and refrigerated up to several hours.

ASSEMBLING THE DISH:
Drain the noodles thoroughly so they will not dilute the sauce. Spread the noodles on a large platter, then layer the cucumbers and chicken on top. For a nice presentation, choose a platter of contrasting color, and arrange the layers so that each is rimmed by a border of the one underneath. Just before serving, pour thin streams of sauce over the chicken; do not smother it. Garnish with the coriander, if desired, and serve a bowl of sauce alongside. Invite each guest to dress and toss his or her own portion.

Unsauced and ungarnished, the dish may be sealed and refrigerated for an hour before serving. The salad may be served slightly chilled, but the sauce should be at room temperature for peak flavor.

Unsauced leftovers will keep 1–2 days, refrigerated and sealed airtight. For a change, try dressing them with *Dijon Mustard Sauce*.

MENU SUGGESTIONS:

This is a gutsy dish, most at home in the company of simple foods with striking flavors, such as *Strange Flavor Eggplant* and *Orchid's Tangy Cool Noodles*. For a luncheon, I often star it on its own surrounded by a colorful assortment of "Little Dishes." To accompany the chicken, try a light red wine with bite—a California Gamay Beaujolais or a Beaujolais.

DELFS

The Good Food of Szechwan

Guai-wei Ji

"Strange-Taste" Chicken

Guai-wei, *or "strange taste," in the name of this dish refers to the flavors of sweetness, sourness, hotness, saltiness and spiciness that are all blended with no single flavor predominating. Since the strength of the various ingredients varies, the measures below may have to be adjusted slightly. If the taste of any ingredient is noticeably stronger than that of any other, reduce the amount of that ingredient a little the next time. Serve at room temperature.*

1 whole small chicken

SEASONINGS (PER LB. OF MEAT)

4 tsps. finely chopped fresh ginger
2 Tbsps. finely chopped green onion
4 tsps. finely chopped garlic
4 tsps. sesame paste
2 Tbsps. soy sauce
4 tsps. red oil
4 tsps. vinegar
4 tsps. sesame oil
2 tsps. sugar
1 tsp. Szechwan pepper

TO COOK AND SERVE: 1. Place the whole chicken in a *wok* or pot in enough boiling water to cover. Boil until tender but not overdone. Remove and drain. When cool cut the meat into bite-sized pieces. Arrange attractively on a platter.

2. Chop the ginger, green onion and garlic finely and then mix all the SEASONINGS ingredients in a small bowl. Mix well.

3. Pour the SEASONINGS over the pieces of cooled chicken. Garnish with parsley. Serve at room temperature.

NOTE: If you add 2 or 3 thin slices of fresh ginger, 2 green onions cut into 3-inch lengths and 10–12 Szechwan peppercorns to the water in which the chicken is to boil, you may omit the ginger and ground Szechwan pepper (but not the chopped green onion) from the SEASONINGS.

WOLFERT

Couscous and Other Good Food from Morocco

Bisteeya

Note that bisteeya *is made either with pigeons (squabs) or chicken; I do not recommend Cornish hens—they are too dry. In Morocco the poultry inside a* bisteeya *is often left unboned, and the bones usually end up strewn all over the table. However, I can think of no earthly reason why the bones should not be removed before the poultry is placed inside the pie.*

Bisteeya *is customarily served as a first course, and should be hot to the fingertips. To eat it Moroccan style, plunge into the burning pastry with the thumb and first two fingers of your right hand and tear out a piece as large or as delicate as you want. You will burn your fingers, of course, but you will have a lot of fun and the pain will be justified by the taste.*

Note that the sugar and cinnamon design on the top is always abstract; it is definitely not traditional to stencil on pictures of animals or other recognizable motifs—Muslim practice forbids it. Lattice designs of crisscrossed ground cinnamon always look good.

INGREDIENTS

4 squabs or 1½ frying chickens (4 pounds), quartered, with giblets
5 cloves garlic (approximately), peeled
Salt
1 cup chopped parsley, mixed with a little chopped fresh green coriander
1 Spanish onion, grated
Pinch of pulverized saffron
¼ teaspoon turmeric
1 scant teaspoon freshly ground black pepper
¾ teaspoon ground ginger
3 cinnamon sticks
1 cup butter
¼ cup salad oil
¾ pound whole, blanched almonds
Confectioners' sugar
Ground cinnamon
¼ cup lemon juice
10 eggs
½ to ¾ pound phyllo pastry or strudel leaves, or 40 *warka* leaves (approximately)

EQUIPMENT

5½-quart cast-iron enameled casserole with cover
12-inch skillet

Paper towels
Rolling pin or nut grinder
Mixing bowls
Whisk
Colander
Small saucepan
13-inch cake pan, or pizza pan, or paella pan
Large baking sheet (at least 12 inches wide)
Spatula
Serving plate

WORKING TIME: 1½ HOURS
COOKING TIME: 1 HOUR 20 MINUTES
BAKING TIME: 30 TO 40 MINUTES
SERVES: 12 (AS PART OF A MOROCCAN DINNER)

1. Wash the poultry well and pull out as much fat as possible from the cavities. Crush the garlic and make a paste of it with 2 tablespoons salt. Rub the poultry with the paste, then rinse well and drain. Put the squabs or chickens in the casserole with the giblets, herbs, onion, spices, half the butter, a little salt, and 3 cups water. Bring to a boil, then lower the heat, cover, and simmer for 1 hour.

2. Meanwhile, heat the vegetable oil in the skillet and brown the almonds lightly. Drain on paper towels. When cool, crush them with a rolling pin until coarsely ground, or run them through a nut grinder. Combine the almonds with ⅓ cup confectioners' sugar and 1½ teaspoons ground cinnamon. Set aside.

3. Remove the poultry, giblets, cinnamon sticks, and any loose bones from the casserole and set aside. By boiling rapidly, uncovered, reduce the sauce in the casserole to approximately 1¾ cups, then add the lemon juice. Beat the eggs until frothy, then pour into the simmering sauce and stir continuously until the eggs cook and congeal. (They should become curdy, stiff, and dry.) Transfer the egg mixture to a colander and let drain (this will insure against a soggy *bisteeya*). Taste for salt and set aside.

4. Remove all the bones from the squabs or chickens. Shred the poultry into 1½-inch pieces and chop the giblets coarsely.

5. Heat the remaining butter. When the foam subsides, clarify it by pouring off the clear liquid butter into a small bowl and discarding the milky solids. *Up to this point the dish can be prepared in advance, even the day before.*

6. Preheat the oven to 425°.

7. Unroll the pastry leaves, keeping them under a damp towel to prevent them from drying out. Brush some of the clarified butter over the bottom and sides of the cake pan, then cover the bottom of the pan with a pastry leaf. Arrange 6 more leaves so that they half cover the bottom of the pan and half extend over the sides. (The entire bottom of the pan should be covered.) Brush the extended leaves with butter so they do not dry out. (If you are using *warka*, arrange about 15 to 18 leaves around the bottom and sides; there is no need to butter extended leaves.)

8. Fold 4 leaves in half and bake in the oven for 30 seconds, or until crisp but not too browned, or fry the leaves on an oiled skillet. (This is unnecessary if using *warka*.)

9. Place chunks of poultry and giblets around the inner edges of the pan, then work toward the center so that the pastry is covered with a layer of shredded poultry. Cover this layer with the well-drained egg mixture from step 3, and the four baked or fried pastry leaves (or *warka* leaves).

10. Sprinkle the almond-sugar mixture over the pastry. Cover with all but 2 of the remaining pastry leaves, brushing each very lightly with butter.

11. Fold the overlapping leaves in over the top to cover the pie. Brush lightly with butter. Put the remaining 2 leaves over the top, lightly buttering each, and fold these neatly under the pie (like tucking in sheets). Brush the entire pie again with butter and pour any remaining butter around the edge. (Use the same procedure for *warka*.)

12. Bake the pie in 425° oven until the top pastry leaves are golden brown, about 70 minutes. Shake the pan to loosen the pie and run a spatula around the edges. If necessary, tilt the pan to pour off excess butter (which should be reserved). Invert the pie onto a large, buttered baking sheet. Brush the pie with the reserved butter and return to the oven to continue baking another 10 to 15 minutes, or until golden brown. (You can bake the pie made with *warka* leaves, but it is more traditional to gently fry the pie over low heat until golden brown on both sides.)

13. Remove the *bisteeya* from the oven. Tilt to pour off any excess butter. Put a serving plate over the pie and, holding it firmly, invert. (The traditional upper filling is always the almond layer.) Dust the top of the pie with a little confectioners' sugar and run crisscrossing lines of cinnamon over the top. *Serve very hot.*

VARIATION

*This makes a superior—but more expensive—*bisteeya.

Proceed as directed above, but double the quantity of almonds. Partially drain the browned almonds and run through a meat grinder, then knead with sugar and cinnamon (to taste) to form an oily paste. Roll the paste into 1-inch nuggets. Arrange the nuggets over the baked pastry leaves and proceed as directed in step 10.

JAFFREY

An Invitation to Indian Cooking

Tandoori Chicken—my version

SERVES 6–8

The chickens used for the tandoor *in India are usually spring chickens, weighing 2–2½ pounds each. They are cooked whole, with only wings and neck removed, on all sides at once. I find it more convenient to marinate and cook the chicken cut in pieces (it is also easier to serve and to eat this way). I buy the legs and breasts of broiling or frying chickens. (You may have an odd member of the family who just loves wings, and who will need to be placated some other way at some other time.) Also, I should point out again that Indians seem to dislike the chicken skin and always remove it before cooking.*

The chicken in this recipe should be marinated for about 24 hours. Assuming that most people like both dark and light meat, I am allocating one whole leg and half a breast for each of 6 people.

1 medium-sized onion, peeled and coarsely chopped
6 whole cloves garlic, peeled and coarsely chopped
A piece of fresh ginger, about 2 inches long and 1 inch wide, peeled and coarsely chopped
3 tablespoons lemon juice
8 ounces (1 container) plain yogurt
1 tablespoon ground coriander
1 teaspoon ground cumin
1 teaspoon ground turmeric
1 teaspoon *garam masala*
¼ teaspoon ground mace
¼ teaspoon ground nutmeg
¼ teaspoon ground cloves
¼ teaspoon ground cinnamon
4 tablespoons olive oil (or vegetable oil)
2 teaspoons salt
¼ teaspoon freshly ground black pepper
¼–½ teaspoon cayenne pepper (optional, or use as desired)
½–1 teaspoon orange food coloring (use the Spanish *bijol*, or Indian powdered food coloring, or American liquid kind; its use is optional)
6 broiler *or* fryer chicken legs
3 broiler *or* fryer chicken breasts, halved

GARNISH

1 medium-sized onion
2 lemons
Extra lemon juice (optional)

Make the marinade first. Put the chopped onions, garlic, ginger, and lemon juice in an electric blender, and blend to a smooth paste, about 1 minute at high speed. Place this in a bowl large enough to accommodate the chicken. Add the yogurt, coriander, cumin, turmeric, *garam masala*, mace, nutmeg, cloves, cinnamon, olive oil, salt, black pepper, cayenne, and food coloring. Mix thoroughly.

Skin the chicken legs and breasts. With a sharp knife make 3 diagonal slashes on each breast section, going halfway down to the bone. Make 2 diagonal slashes on each thigh, also going halfway down to the bone. With the point of a sharp knife, make 4 or 5 jabs on each drumstick.

Put the chicken in the marinade and rub the marinade into the slashes with your finger. Cover and leave refrigerated for 24 hours. Turn 4 or 5 times while the chicken is marinating.

About 1½ hours before serving, light your charcoal. It should take 20 to 30 minutes to get red hot. Place the grill on its lowest notch.

Peel the onion for garnishing and slice it paper-thin. Separate the rings and set in a small bowl of ice water, cover, and refrigerate.

When the fire is hot, lift out the chicken pieces and place on the grill. Cook about 7 or 8 minutes on each side, then raise the grill a few notches to cook more slowly for another 15 to 20 minutes on each side. Baste with marinade as you cook.

TO SERVE: Warm a large platter. Place the chicken pieces on it. Drain the water from the onion rings and lay them on top of the chicken. Quarter the lemons lengthwise and place them around the chicken. The chicken tastes very good with extra lemon juice squeezed on it.

This chicken is considered a delicacy and can be served at a banquet with *Pullao, naans*, a few vegetable dishes, and onions pickled in vinegar.

Try it also with Rice with Spinach and Yogurt with Potatoes.

BUGIALLI

The Fine Art of Italian Cooking

Pollo in Porchetta

Chicken Made in the Manner of Suckling Pig

SERVES 4

The famous porchetta, *or suckling pig, is cooked filled with a large quantity of herbs, spices, and* pancetta. *This treatment is also very good with both chicken and duck. After the bird is stuffed, it is closed up tightly by sewing, and put in the oven. Suckling pig is indeed evoked, and one can make this dish more often than the* porchetta, *which after all requires a very special occasion.*

FOR THE STUFFING

4 ounces *pancetta* or 2 ounces boiled ham plus 2 ounces salt pork
14 large leaves sage, fresh or under salt
10 juniper berries
1 large bay leaf
1 tablespoon rosemary leaves
6 or 7 whole black peppercorns
Salt and freshly ground black pepper

FOR THE CHICKEN

1 broiler chicken (about 3½ pounds), left whole
¼ cup olive oil

Prepare the stuffing by coarsely chopping the *pancetta*, 10 of the sage leaves, the juniper berries, bay leaf, and rosemary leaves, then mix in the peppercorns, 2 level teaspoons of salt, and ½ teaspoon pepper.

Preheat the oven to 400°.

Wash the chicken inside and out; leave in all the chicken fat. Fill the cavity of the chicken with the stuffing mixture and sew up both ends, placing the 4 remaining sage leaves in the neck end before sewing it up, then tie the chicken up as you would a roast.

Abundantly salt and pepper the outside of the chicken and place in a roasting pan along with the olive oil. Cook in the preheated oven for about 65 minutes.

Transfer the chicken to a serving dish and serve hot.

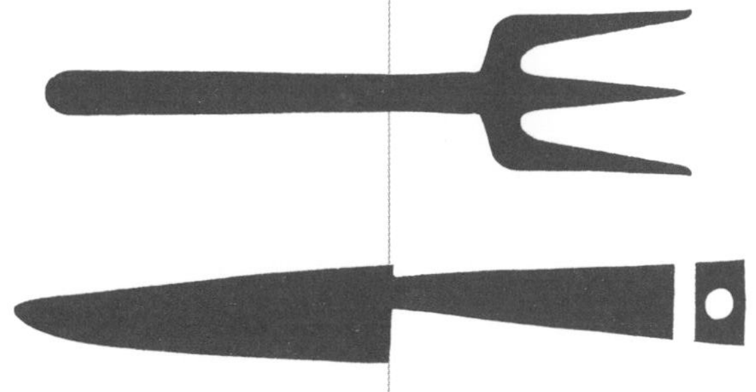

Stocks and Sauces

MADISON
The Greens Cook Book

Summer Vegetable Stock

1 tablespoon butter
1 tablespoon olive oil
1 onion, chopped into ½-inch squares
8 branches parsley
2 bay leaves
Several large basil leaves or 1 teaspoon dried basil
Several branches marjoram or 1 teaspoon dried marjoram
Other fresh summer herbs, such as savory, lovage, borage leaves
1 teaspoon nutritional yeast (optional)
1 potato, diced
2 medium carrots, peeled and diced
2 celery stalks, diced
4 tomatoes, coarsely chopped
4 summer squash, sliced
1 handful green beans, roughly chopped
4 chard leaves and their stems, chopped
1 cup eggplant, diced
4 ounces mushrooms, chopped
1 teaspoon salt
8 cups cold water

Heat the butter and oil in a soup pot; add the onion, herbs, and nutritional yeast, if using. Cook briskly over a medium-high flame for several minutes to lightly color the onion, stirring as needed; then add the other vegetables. Cook them for 12 to 15 minutes; then add the water, bring to a boil, and simmer for 45 minutes. Strain the stock. If the stock is to be used in a pasta or ragout, reduce it further to strengthen the flavor.

MAKES 6 CUPS

TSUJI
Japanese Cooking

Basic Stock
Dashi

Dashi, *Japan's all-purpose soup stock and seasoning, stands figuratively if not literally at the right hand of every Japanese chef. Different varieties of* dashi *lend subtle depth to a wide variety of soups and entrées.* Dashi *provides Japanese cuisine with its characteristic flavor, and it can be said without exaggeration that the success or failure (or mediocrity) of a dish is ultimately determined by the flavor and quality of the* dashi *that seasons it. Making good* dashi *is the first secret of the simple art of Japanese cooking.*

Before the age of instant mixes, obviously dashi *had to be made fresh. This (usually) involved* katsuo-bushi *and* konbu. *The former is dried fillet of bonito, and the latter dried giant kelp. Today, most Japanese home cooks often rely on instant* dashi, *packaged granules that dissolve in hot water, generically called* dashi-no-moto, *or "stock essence." You will probably turn to this instant preparation too, but it is important to understand the traditional method of preparation, for the sake of knowing how to make the highest quality, most delicious* dashi *as well as for the satisfaction of understanding the theory behind this basic stock. While some instant mixes are excellent, and none is bad, nothing compares in subtle flavor and delicate fragrance with* dashi *made from freshly shaved dried bonito.*

A stick of katsuo-bushi *looks like a 6- to 8-inch (15- to 20-cm) long brownish hunk of wood. A bonito yields four fillets, two dorsal and two ventral. These are dried in shade in the open air in a complex process involving many steps and taking six months. One guide in buying a dried fillet is weight in relation to size: the denser the better. Two* katsuo-bushi *struck together should emit a metallic sound. It should have an ash-white coating of mold; green mold means it is too watery, and yellow too acid. For the best flavor,* katsuo-bushi *should be used as quickly as possible. However, it keeps well in a moisture-free container. Store it in a can in a cool, dark, dry place or wrap well in plastic wrap and refrigerate.*

The best-tasting dashi *is made with flakes shaved immediately prior to use. The dried bonito fillet is transformed into pinkish-tan curls or flakes by a shaver that looks like a carpenter's plane fixed above a single-drawer box (in fact, you can use a sharp carpenter's plane). Shaving* katsuo-bushi *takes time and it is an activity requiring a certain amount of skill and practice. Perhaps for these reasons, commercially prepared and packed flakes (called* hana-katsuo *or* kezuri-katsuo*) are available. These are convenient, and stock made with commercially shaved flakes is good, but does not compare with the flavor and aroma obtained from just-shaved bonito flakes.*

Konbu, *giant kelp, is the second main ingredient. (Some restaurants ignore the* konbu *and make* dashi *with bonito alone.) The most prized variety of* konbu *is harvested in the subarctic waters off tiny Rebun Island in Hokkaido. Good quality is signified by thick, wide leaves, a dark amber color in the dried product, and a whitish powder encrusting the surface. The whitish powder holds much of the flavor of this seaweed, so the standard practice no matter what the recipe is to wipe it before using with only a few sweeps of a clean damp cloth. Washing this seaweed would dissolve away its flavor.*

Lacking any or all of these ingredients, use instant dashi *for basic stock. There are a number of such instant* dashi *preparations; check directions on jar or packet. Instant* dashi *or* dashi-no-moto *is often sold with dried Chinese foods in American supermarkets.*

Of course many substitutes for dashi *are possible, but without* dashi, *dishes are merely* à la japonaise *and lack the authentic flavor. Chicken stock is only used in Japanese cooking when chicken is the main ingredient of a dish. But the flavor of chicken may be added to* dashi *by making the stock with water in which chicken has been boiled for 10 minutes. Keep all flavors* light.

Because it has a lovely fragrance, fresh primary dashi *is best for clear soups. A Japanese clear soup should be thin enough to allow one to clearly perceive the flavors of the other ingredients present. Its bouquet disappears quickly and is lost if the* dashi *is not used immediately. For use as a basic seasoning, however, primary (and secondary)* dashi *made well ahead of time is perfectly fine. Leftover* dashi *may be stored in a sealed bottle in the refrigerator for up to 3 days or may be frozen, but flavor and aroma are lost.*

PRIMARY DASHI
Ichiban Dashi

MAKES 1 QUART (1 L); SERVES 6 AS BASE FOR CLEAR SOUP

1 quart (1 L) cold water
1 ounce (30 g) giant kelp (*konbu*)
1 ounce (30 g) dried bonito flakes (*hana-katsuo*)

TO PREPARE: Fill a medium-sized soup pot with 1 quart (1 L) cold water and put in the kelp. Heat, uncovered, so as to reach the boiling point in about 10 minutes. IMPORTANT: Kelp emits a strong odor if it is boiled, so remove *konbu* just *before* water boils.

Insert your thumbnail into the fleshiest part of the kelp. If it is soft, sufficient flavor has been obtained. It tough, return it to the pot for 1 or 2 minutes. Keep from boiling by adding approximately ¼ cup cold water.

After removing the *konbu* bring the stock to a full boil. Add ¼ cup cold water to bring the temperature down quickly and immediately to add the bonito flakes. No need to stir. Bring to a full boil and remove from the heat at once. If bonito flakes boil more than a few seconds, the stock becomes too strong, a bit bitter, and is not suitable for use in clear soups. If you make this mistake, all is not lost, use the stock as a base for thick soups, in simmered foods, and so on.

Allow the flakes to start to settle to the bottom of the pot (30 seconds to 1 minute). Remove foam, then filter through a cheesecloth-lined sieve. Reserve the bonito flakes and kelp for secondary *dashi*.

SECONDARY DASHI
Niban Dashi

While primary dashi *is best suited for clear soups by virtue of its fragrance, subtle taste, and clarity, secondary* dashi *does noble service as a basic seasoning—for thick soups, for noodle broths, as a cooking stock for vegetables, and in many other ways.*

MAKES 3–4 CUPS

bonito flakes and giant kelp reserved from primary *dashi*
1½ quarts (1½ L) cold water
⅓–½ ounce (10–15 g) dried bonito flakes (*hana-katsuo*)

TO PREPARE: Place the bonito flakes and giant kelp reserved from the primary *dashi* in 1½ quarts (1½ L) cold water in a medium-sized soup pot. Place over high heat just until the boiling point, then reduce heat and keep at a gentle simmer until the stock is reduced by ⅓ or ½, depending on the flavor desired. This reduction takes about 15–20 minutes.

Add the fresh *hana-katsuo* and immediately remove from heat. Allow the flakes to start to settle to the bottom of the pot (30 seconds to 1 minute), and remove foam from the surface. Filter liquid through a cheesecloth-lined sieve.

Discard the *hana-katsuo* flakes and *konbu*.

KELP STOCK
Konbu Dashi

Since the flavor and nutrients of giant kelp pass quickly into clear water, it is not actually necessary to subject it to heat to produce a delicate stock. A lengthy soaking, 8 hours or overnight, yields what is considered to be a delicious and subtle liquid. In many homes, this liquid is used in primary dashi *in lieu of heating the kelp in water—just heat this seaweed liquor and begin the primary* dashi *recipe midway with the addition of the dried bonito flakes.* Konbu dashi *is also the base in preparing sardine stock (below).*

MAKES 1 QUART (1 L)

1½ ounces (40 g) giant kelp (*konbu*)
1 quart (1 L) cold water

TO PREPARE: Wipe kelp lightly with a damp cloth. Fill a medium-sized bowl with the cold water and add kelp. Let stand at room temperature at least 8 hours, or overnight.

Remove kelp and reserve for use in other recipes.

SARDINE STOCK
Niboshi Dashi

A type of fish stock is made from small sun-dried sardines called niboshi. *Wooden or basketwork drying pallets on quays, spread full of these tiny silvery fish, are a part of fishing village scenes in Japan. Savory sardine stock is much stronger than bonito* dashi *and makes a very good base for thick and rich* miso *soups. It is also often used in broth for* udon *noodles.* Niboshi *vary considerably in size; about 2 inches (5 cm) is average. Good-quality* niboshi *should have whole bodies that are relatively straight and well formed.*

MAKES 1 QUART (1 L)

1⅓ ounces (40 g) dried small sardines (*niboshi*)
1 quart (1 L) cold water or cooled KELP STOCK

TO PREPARE: To prevent the stock from being bitter or sour, pluck off heads and pinch away entrails of dried sardines.

Place the sardines in 1 quart (1 L) cold water or cooled KELP STOCK (above) in a medium-sized soup pot and place over high heat to bring quickly to the boiling point. Reduce heat and simmer for 7–8 minutes.

Remove from heat and strain through cheesecloth.

Use as required.

TSUJI
Japanese Cooking

Ponzu Sauce
Ponzu

Also widely used as a dressing for vinegared foods (sunomono) *and with one-pot dishes, such as* SHABU-SHABU.

ABOUT 2½ CUPS

1 cup lemon juice or combination lemon-lime (in Japan, *sudachi* citron or other very acid citrus fruits are used)
⅓ cup plus 2 Tbsps rice vinegar
1 cup dark soy sauce
2 Tbsps *tamari* sauce
3 Tbsps *mirin*, alcohol burned off
⅓ ounce (10 g; 1 small handful) dried bonito flakes (*hana-katsuo*)
2-inch (5-cm) square giant kelp (*konbu*)

Mix all ingredients and let stand 24 hours. Strain through cheesecloth and mature 3 months in a cool dark place, or refrigerate. Keeps indefinitely, but should be used within 1 year for best flavor.

ANDREWS
Catalan Cuisine

Catalan cuisine is built around four basic sauces: allioli, sofregit, picada, *and* samfaina. *It must be pointed out, however, that these aren't really sauces in the conventional French or Italian sense:* Allioli*—an emulsion of garlic, olive oil, and (inauthentically but very commonly) eggs—is sometimes stirred into a dish for added emphasis, but it is primarily a condiment, to be dabbed or slathered onto this or that at table;* sofregit, *which is made by cooking onions and usually tomatoes (and occasionally herbs and/or other vegetables) down almost to melting, is a* base *for sauces rather than a sauce itself;* picada, *a dense paste usually composed of garlic, almonds, fried bread, and olive oil, with such other possible additions as parsley, hazelnuts, pine nuts, chocolate, and saffron (among other things), is a thickening and flavoring agent—a sort of glorified roux; and* samfaina *is a ratatouillelike vegetable mixture, which can be made* into *a sauce by puréeing (with or without cream or some other dilution), but which is also eaten as a side dish or used as a coarsely textured cloak (hardly a sauce) for meat, fish, and fowl.*

If these four basic sauces aren't really sauces, however, they certainly are *basic—especially* sofregit *and* picada, *which are almost always used in tandem (one to start the preparation of a dish and the other to finish it), and which seem to appear in almost every traditional Catalan soup, sauce, or stew recipe. And if you learn how to make all four of them in their simplest forms, you will have understood the very foundations of Catalan cuisine.*

Allioli

Allioli *might be called the Catalan catsup—though of course it is better and far more reputable gastronomically than catsup. It's the all-purpose tabletop relish, the diner's friend, the enhancer of good food and disguiser of bad. In one form or another, it can go on or into almost anything—seafood, noodle and rice dishes, soups, stews, vegetables, snails. It is all but obligatory with grilled meats, especially pork, rabbit, and chicken. It even gets spread plain on bread. For all I know, folks take baths in it.*

Strictly speaking, the name is the recipe: all *(garlic),* i *(and),* oli *(oil). The oil, of course, is olive oil; that's a given in the* països catalans. *Salt, of course, is added, another given. Anything else, claim purists, is just (shall we say) gilding the lily. Well,* maybe *a few drops of lemon juice or vinegar or a combination of the two, if you insist upon a tingle of acidity. ("Heaven and hell are both full of people who eat* allioli *with lemon juice and without, with vinegar and without," suggests author Manuel Vázquez Montalbán.) But a little crustless white bread to thicken it, as some sources recommend? No. And eggs? Never. "*Allioli *made with eggs," an old-school Catalan bartender announced to me one evening as we were discussing the subject, "isn't* allioli *at all. It's just fancy mayonnaise." The fact that* allioli's *closest relatives, the aïoli of Provence and the lesser-known* aïllade *of the Languedoc, always do include eggs—and thus really* are *"fancy mayonnaise"—is taken by some Catalans simply as further proof of what they have long suspected: that the French don't know very much about food after all. Big talk aside, however, the plain truth is that the vast majority of the* allioli *served in Catalonia and vicinity today is made with eggs, especially in restaurants—and purism be damned. The eggless variety is just too difficult to whip up, and too fragile—capable of instantaneous and capricious breakdown.*

Where allioli *came from in the first place is hard to say. "As in the case of Homer," notes Valencian gastronome Llorenç Millo, "dozens of cities dispute the honor of having been its birthplace." Millo does reveal, however, that Pliny the Elder (*A.D. *23–79), who served as* procurator *in Roman Tarragona for a year, gives what is apparently the first written recipe for the sauce in one of his manuscripts. "When garlic is beaten with oil and vinegar," he observes (approximately), "it is wondrous how the foam increases." Wherever it might come from, though,* allioli *has been popular in the* països catalans *for hundreds of years (it's even mentioned in the* Libre del coch*), and is indeed a thing, as Joseph Cunill de Bosch has said, "*purament catalana*"—purely Catalan.*

Here are some recipes for allioli *both with and without eggs, a recipe for mayonnaise, and several variations on the theme.*

ALLIOLI AUTÈNTIC
Authentic Allioli

Allioli *in its purest form is white and shiny, rather like lemon sorbet in appearance. It is very strong in garlic flavor, and a little goes a long way—except among the garlic-mad, of course. It is, as noted, practically de rigueur in Catalan cooking to accompany grilled meat and fowl (especially chicken, rabbit, and pork), and is traditional as well with snails and with many kinds of fish and shellfish. Fishermen are famous for their mastery of its manufacture, in fact, as are rural mothers and grandmothers—while some of the region's most famous chefs openly admit that they can't always get the damned thing to work. The tricky part is coaxing an emulsion to form without eggs or other thickeners, and this takes a lot of practice. In answer to the obvious question, no, you cannot make* Allioli Autèntic *in a food processor, at least in my experience; the very thought is sacrilege to a good Catalan (that's part of his heritage you're threatening to throw into that machine, for heaven's sake). More to the point, though, the oil and garlic get too homogenized in a processor, and the emulsion doesn't hold. If all this doesn't discourage you, and you'd still like to, er, try your hand at making the real thing, this is how it's done:*

TO MAKE 1–1¼ CUPS

- 6 cloves garlic (or more to taste), peeled
- ½ teaspoon salt
- 1 cup mild extra-virgin olive oil (see note)

Cut each clove of garlic in half lengthwise and discard any green pieces, then mince the garlic finely.

Scatter salt in the bowl of a large mortar and add the garlic. Mash the garlic gently with a pestle, mixing it with the salt until it takes on the consistency of a thick paste.

Add the olive oil very slowly, a few drops at a time, while stirring the mixture with the pestle, using slow, even motions and always stirring in the same direction. Continue adding oil until an emulsion forms. Less than a full cup might be sufficient to obtain this result, in which case do not use the rest, as it will "break" the emulsion.

Serve immediately.

NOTE: It is very important for the success of the emulsion that all the ingredients be at room temperature—even the garlic.

ALLIOLI AMB OUS
Allioli with Eggs

This, as noted, is by far the most common kind of allioli *in the* països catalans *today—and, tradition aside, the fact is that there's nothing wrong with it at all. Some Catalans even prefer it to the original version, because it's subtler and adds garlic character to dishes without overpowering them.* Allioli *with eggs* can *be made in a food processor quite easily, though it's not particularly difficult by hand either. The following recipe, a plain and simple formula based on the preceding one, will work equally well (with minor variation) for either method. I haven't included lemon juice or vinegar in the recipe, incidentally, because I like my* allioli *without their added bite; but a few drops of either (or both) stirred in at the last minute won't affect the emulsion and will cut the sauce's richness a bit.*

TO MAKE 1–1¼ CUPS

- 6 cloves garlic (or more to taste), peeled
- ½ teaspoon salt
- 2 egg yolks (or 1 egg yolk and 1 whole egg; see below)
- 1 cup mild extra-virgin olive oil

BY HAND:
Prepare a garlic paste as in the previous recipe.

Add the egg yolks to the mortar, mix with the garlic paste, and then proceed as in previous recipe, adding the oil slowly until an emulsion forms.

BY FOOD PROCESSOR:
Again, prepare a garlic paste as in the previous recipe.

Put the paste into the work bowl of a food processor, and then add 1 egg yolk and 1 whole egg (instead of 2 egg yolks).

Process for several seconds, then, with the machine still running, pour a slow, steady stream of oil through the feed tube, until an emulsion forms.

Serve immediately (although, unlike the eggless version, this *allioli* will hold its emulsion for several days at least if refrigerated).

ALLIOLI NEGAT
"Drowned" Allioli

"Allioli negat, dòna'l al gat," *says the proverb—"Give 'drowned'* allioli *to the cat." Disregard this advice. Drowned* allioli, *a specialty of the Costa Brava, is broken* allioli, allioli *with its molecules unclasped,* allioli *that has turned from a creamy emulsion into a bath of liquid oil swamping (drowning) the minced, crushed garlic it contains. It is an intentional mistake, in other words—regular* allioli, *with or without eggs, deliberately pushed too far, made to shatter. The result is delicious, and somehow even more unctuous than its emulsified forebear.* Allioli Negat *is always stirred* into *something—most often* fideus *noodles and fish soups or stews—and it adds much character to them. The cat has character enough already.*

TO MAKE 1¼–1½ CUPS

- 6 cloves garlic (or more to taste), peeled
- ½ teaspoon salt
- 2 egg yolks or 1 egg yolk and 1 whole egg (optional)
- 1–1¼ cups mild extra-virgin olive oil (see note)

Follow the instructions in one of the two preceding recipes, for *allioli* with or without eggs, but continue adding oil after an emulsion forms, until it breaks again, and the sauce thins. The amount of oil necessary to achieve this effect will vary. Watch the *allioli* carefully, and don't add more than you need to get it to break. The finished *Allioli Negat* should look curdled.

NOTE: Again, make sure that all the ingredients are at room temperature before beginning.

ALLIOLI AMB FRUITA
Allioli with Fruit

Allioli *admits of more possibilities than might be apparent at first. It can be simultaneously thickened and flavored, for instance, with honey; in Majorca and some parts of Catalonia, boiled potatoes or tomatoes are stirred into it; in France, under the guide of* aïllade à la toulousaine, *it includes blanched, pulverized walnuts. And in the Catalonian Pyrénées and Pyrenean foothills, it is sometimes elaborated with puréed fruit—most notably quince (a specialty of the* comarques *of the Pallars Sobirà and Pallars Jussà), apples, and pears. These fruit* alliolis *make superb and unusual accompaniments to grilled and roasted meats—again, above all, to rabbit, chicken, and pork. They can be made with eggs if you wish, but there's really no reason to do so, since the fruit and oil alone will form a very nice emulsion. This recipe is eggless, then.*

TO MAKE 1½–1¾ CUPS

- 1 large ripe quince or 2 small ripe apples or pears
- 3–4 cloves garlic, peeled
- ½ teaspoon salt
- 3–4 ounces mild extra-virgin olive oil

Peel and core the fruit and cut it into large cubes, then cook in water to cover in a covered pot for about 5 minutes, or until the fruit is soft but not mushy. Drain and cool.

Prepare a garlic paste as for *Allioli Autèntic*, then stir the fruit into the mortar and work with the pestle until smooth.

Add the oil slowly, as for *Allioli Autèntic* until an emulsion forms.

Correct the salt if necessary, and serve immediately, or refrigerate until ready.

BUGIALLI

The Fine Art of Italian Cooking

Balsamella

Béchamel

MAKES 2 TO 2½ CUPS

Though this sauce was given the name béchamel *by the French in the eighteenth century, it probably existed long before that in Italy. The fifteenth-century recipe for* crema di miglio fritta *starts with a technique very close to this.*

Balsamella *is a basic sauce used in making many dishes. It is placed on top in some, used as a base inside of others, and ties together the ingredients of still others. It also serves as the base for several other sauces.*

- 4 tablespoons butter
- ¼ cup flour
- 1½ to 2 cups milk, depending on thickness desired
- Salt to taste

Melt the butter in a heavy saucepan over a low, steady flame. (It is important to use a heavy pan and a low flame so the sauce will thicken without burning.) When the butter has reached the frothing point, add the flour. Mix very well with a wooden spoon, then let cook until the color is golden brown. Remove the pan from the flame and let rest for 10 to 15 minutes.

While the butter-flour mixture is resting, heat the milk in another pan until it is very close to the boiling point. Put the first saucepan back on the flame and very quickly add all of the hot milk. Be careful not to pour the milk in slowly; that can create lumps in the sauce. Begin mixing with a wooden spoon while you pour and keep mixing, always stirring in the same direction, to prevent lumps from forming.

When the sauce reaches the boiling point, add the salt and continue to stir gently while the sauce cooks slowly for 12 to 14 minutes more. Remove from the flame; the sauce is ready to use.

DE GOUY

The Gold Cook Book

Mornay Sauce

Appropriate for almost any kind of fish, shellfish, crustaceans, eggs, asparagus, artichoke bottoms, broccoli, cauliflower, and so forth.

To each cup of Cream Sauce or Hot Béchamel Sauce add ¾ scant cup of dry white wine and let this reduce to ⅓ its volume over a bright flame, stirring frequently. Then stir in 2 tablespoons of your favorite grated cheese or equal parts of two different kinds. When ready to use, blend in 1 tablespoon of sweet butter and taste for seasoning.

HOME STYLE. Simply add ⅓ cup of grated cheese to each cup of cream sauce and stir until the cheese is melted. It is merely a cheese sauce.

When using Mornay Sauce to top a dish to be made au gratin, it is usually, in the French cuisine, considered improved if a tablespoon or two of whipped cream is folded into each half cup of Mornay Sauce before spreading over top of fish or other main ingredient. The top then takes on an even golden brown glaze.

CAUTION: This sauce cannot be boiled when it is made, lest it curdle, so, if for any reason it has to stand, keep it over hot, never boiling, water. This applies to any sauce containing eggs.

MANDEL
Abby Mandel's Cuisinart Classroom

Béarnaise Sauce

3 large shallots (3 ounces, 85g)
¼ cup (6 cl) white tarragon vinegar
¼ cup (6 cl) dry white wine
1 tablespoon plus 1 teaspoon dried tarragon
3 large egg yolks
1 tablespoon warm water
½ teaspoon dry mustard
1 teaspoon salt
½ to 1 pound (255 to 455g) unsalted butter, bubbling hot
2 teaspoons lemon juice
1 tablespoon parsley leaves

METAL BLADE: Mince the shallots by dropping them through the feed tube with the machine running. Simmer them in a saucepan with the vinegar, wine and 1 tablespoon of tarragon until the liquid is reduced to 2 tablespoons. Strain it into the work bowl and add the egg yolks, water, mustard and salt. Process the mixture for 1 minute, or until it is well combined and slightly thickened. With the machine running, pour ½ the hot melted butter through the feed tube in a thin steady stream. Add butter only when the previous amount has been incorporated into the egg yolks. Repeat the process with the remaining hot butter. Add the lemon juice and parsley and the remaining tarragon and process for 3 seconds. Add salt and pepper to taste, and transfer the sauce to a serving dish.

MAKES 1¼ TO 2¼ CUPS (30 TO 53 CL)

VARIATIONS

1. Make Choron Sauce by cutting a peeled tomato shell into ¼-inch (.60 cm) dice and using the diced tomato as a garnish for Béarnaise Sauce.

2. Dice a 2-ounce (55g) jar of pimientos and use the pimiento as a garnish for Béarnaise Sauce.

NOTE: Béarnaise Sauce can be made in advance and kept warm over hot, but not boiling, water. It can be made with ½ to 1 pound (225 to 455g) of butter, depending on the amount of sauce desired.

SCHNEIDER
Uncommon Fruits & Vegetables

Sorrel Cream Sauce for Vegetables

This astonishingly simple sauce provides tart and complex dressing for asparagus, yellow or green beans, cauliflower, summer squash, or other quite crisp, not-too-strong vegetables. The amount provided below will enrich about 1 pound of vegetables.

MAKES ABOUT ¾ CUP SAUCE

About 3 ounces fresh sorrel, rinsed and stripped
About ⅓ cup heavy (or whipping) cream
Big pinch salt

1. With stainless-steel knife, cut the leaves into thin strips, slivering enough to make about 1¾ cups light packed leaves. (Save one or two for garnish.)

2. Combine ⅓ cup cream and salt in a small, nonaluminum saucepan and bring to a boil. Add sorrel; simmer, stirring and mashing the leaves until the sauce is thickened slightly and sorrel incorporated evenly, which takes about 4–5 minutes. Adjust seasoning and cream, as desired.

3. Serve hot over steaming blanched vegetables; garnish with a few strips of slivered sorrel leaves.

CLAIBORNE
The New York Times Cook Book

Basic Tomato Sauce

ABOUT 3 PINTS

2 cups chopped onion
3 cloves garlic, chopped
3 tablespoons olive oil
3½ cups canned Italian-style plum tomatoes, undrained
2 small cans tomato paste
2 cups water or meat broth, approximately
1 bay leaf
½ teaspoon salt
¼ teaspoon freshly ground black pepper
½ teaspoon orégano, or ¼ teaspoon each orégano and basil

1. Sauté the onion and garlic in the olive oil until brown, stirring often. Add the tomatoes, tomato paste, water, bay leaf, salt and pepper. Simmer uncovered, stirring occasionally, about two hours. Add more water as necessary.

2. Add the orégano and continue cooking about fifteen minutes. Remove the bay leaf. The sauce should be thick. Serve over cooked spaghetti or use as an ingredient in such dishes as eggplant parmigiana, meat loaf, soups and stews.

VARIATIONS

MEAT TOMATO SAUCE: Brown one-half pound chopped beef in the fat before adding the onions and garlic.

TOMATO AND WINE SAUCE: Substitute one cup dry red wine for one of the cans of tomato paste.

ROBERTSON

Laurel's Kitchen

Tomato Ginger Sauce

Vegetables and grain dishes alike take on a distinctly Oriental air when served with this flavorful sauce.

¼ cup oil
½ onion, cut in thin slices
¼ cup whole wheat flour
2 cups vegetable or soybean stock
2 tablespoons tomato paste
½ teaspoon finely minced fresh ginger root
soy sauce to taste

Sauté onions in oil until soft. Stir in flour and cook several minutes. Slowly add the stock and tomato paste, stirring all the time. Add ginger. Bring to a boil, then simmer gently for about 15 minutes. Add soy sauce and serve.

MAKES ABOUT 2½ CUPS

KENNEDY

The Cuisines of Mexico

Salsa de Jitomate Cocida

Cooked tomato sauce

ABOUT 2 CUPS

A blender
3 medium tomatoes (1 pound), broiled
¼ onion, roughly chopped
1 small clove garlic, peeled and roughly chopped

Blend the ingredients to a fairly smooth sauce—it should have some texture.

A small frying pan
2 tablespoons peanut or safflower oil
The sauce
¼ teaspoon salt, or to taste

Heat the oil, add the sauce and salt, and cook over a medium flame for about 8 minutes until it has thickened and is well seasoned.

This is a simple sauce to use with Tortitas de Papa and Calabacitas Rellenas de Elote.

HAZAN

The Classic Italian Cook Book

Ragù

Meat Sauce, Bolognese Style

Ragù *is not to be confused with* ragoût. *A* ragoût *is a French meat stew, while* ragù *is Bologna's meat sauce for seasoning its homemade pasta. The only thing they share is a common and justified origin in the verb* ragoûter, *which means "to excite the appetite."*

A properly made ragù *clinging to the folds of homemade noodles is one of the most satisfying experiences accessible to the sense of taste. It is no doubt one of the great attractions of the enchanting city of Bologna, and the Bolognese claim one cannot make a true* ragù *anywhere else. This may be so, but with a little care, we can come very close to it. There are three essential points you must remember to make a successful* ragù:

- *The meat must be sautéed just barely long enough to lose its raw color. It must not brown or it will lose delicacy.*

• *It must be cooked in milk* before *the tomatoes are added. This keeps the meat creamier and sweeter tasting.*

• *It must cook at the merest simmer for a long, long time. The minimum is 3½ hours; 5 is better.*

The union of tagliatelle *and ragù is a marriage made in heaven, but* ragù *is also very good with* tortellini, *it is indispensable in* lasagne, *and it is excellent with such macaroni as* rigatoni, ziti, conchiglie, *and* rotelle. *Whenever a menu lists* pasta alla bolognese, *that means it is served with* ragù.

FOR 6 SERVINGS, OR 2¼ TO 2½ CUPS

2 tablespoons chopped yellow onion
3 tablespoons olive oil
3 tablespoons butter
2 tablespoons chopped celery
2 tablespoons chopped carrot
¾ pound ground lean beef, preferably chuck or the meat from the neck
Salt
1 cup dry white wine
½ cup milk
⅛ teaspoon nutmeg
2 cups canned Italian tomatoes, roughly chopped, with their juice

1. An earthenware pot should be your first choice for making *ragù*. If you don't have one available, use a heavy, enameled cast-iron casserole, the deepest one you have (to keep the *ragù* from reducing too quickly). Put in the chopped onion, with all the oil and butter, and sauté briefly over medium heat until just translucent. Add the celery and carrot and cook gently for 2 minutes.

2. Add the ground beef, crumbling it in the pot with a fork. Add 2 teaspoons salt, stir, and cook only until the meat has lost its raw, red color. Add the wine, turn the heat up to medium high, and cook, stirring occasionally, until all the wine has evaporated.

3. Turn the heat down to medium, add the milk and the nutmeg, and cook until the milk has evaporated. Stir frequently.

4. When the milk has evaporated, add the tomatoes and stir thoroughly. When the tomatoes have started to bubble, turn the heat down until the sauce cooks at the laziest simmer, just an occasional bubble. Cook, uncovered, for a minimum of 3½ to 4 hours, stirring occasionally. Taste and correct for salt. (If you cannot watch the sauce for such a long stretch, you can turn off the heat and resume cooking it later on. But do finish cooking it in one day.)

NOTE: *Ragù* can be kept in the refrigerator for up to 5 days, or frozen. Reheat until it simmers for about 15 minutes before using.

Meats

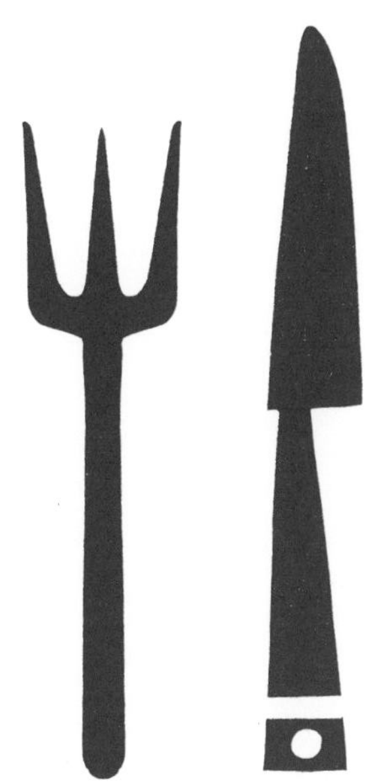

PORK

CLAIBORNE
The New York Times Cook Book

Herbed Pork Chops

4 SERVINGS

1 teaspoon rosemary
½ teaspoon sage
½ clove garlic, chopped
Salt and freshly ground black pepper
4 large pork chops, about 1 inch thick
1 cup water
½ cup dry white wine

1. Mix the rosemary, sage, garlic, salt and pepper. Rub the chops with the mixture.

2. Place the chops in a large greased skillet, add the water and cover. Simmer until all the water has evaporated, about forty-five minutes. Remove the cover and brown the chops in their own fat.

3. Add the wine and cook about one minute, turning the chops occasionally. The wine should be almost evaporated before service.

CLAIBORNE
The New York Times Cook Book

Pork Chops with Paprika

6 SERVINGS

6 loin pork chops, ⅓ inch thick
1 clove garlic, finely chopped
1 teaspoon caraway seeds
2 teaspoons paprika
Salt and freshly ground black pepper to taste
1 cup dry white wine

1. Arrange the chops in a shallow heatproof casserole so that they do not touch. Mix the garlic, caraway seeds, paprika, salt and pepper and sprinkle over the chops. Add the wine. Cover and let the chops marinate in the refrigerator two to three hours.

2. Preheat oven to slow (300° F.).

3. Bake the chops in the marinade, uncovered, until tender, about one hour. Add more wine if necessary. Serve with buttered noodles and the pan sauce.

CLAIBORNE
The New York Times Cook Book

Pork Chops with Basil

8 SERVINGS

Flour for dredging
Garlic salt to taste
8 loin pork chops, trimmed
Olive oil
2 teaspoons chopped fresh basil, or ½ teaspoon dried basil
½ cup Marsala wine, apricot or plum juice

1. Preheat oven to slow (250° F.).

2. Combine flour and garlic salt in a paper bag, add the chops and toss lightly until they are thoroughly coated with the mixture. Brown chops in a heavy skillet, using just enough olive oil to cover bottom of skillet.

3. Arrange the chops neatly in a shallow ungreased baking dish without letting them overlap. Sprinkle with basil. Cover the dish closely with aluminum foil.

4. Bake until the chops are tender, about one and one-half hours. Skim off the fat. Add the wine or fruit juice to the baking dish, remove the cover and continue to cook, basting occasionally, until the liquid bubbles.

CLAIBORNE
The New York Times Cook Book

Key West Pork Chops

6 SERVINGS

3 tablespoons salad oil
6 lean pork chops
1½ cups raw rice
Salt to taste
6 large onion slices
6 lime or lemon slices
6 tablespoons chili sauce
3 cups tomato juice or water
½ teaspoon Tabasco sauce

1. Preheat oven to moderate (325° F.).

2. In a Dutch oven, heat the oil, add the chops and brown on both sides. Remove the chops and drain off all but four tablespoons of the fat. Stir in the raw, dry rice, coating all the grains with fat. Arrange the chops on top and sprinkle with the salt.

3. Place a slice of onion, a slice of lime and a spoonful of chili sauce on each chop. Add the tomato juice and Tabasco, cover closely and bake until the chops are tender, about one hour.

THE TIMES-PICAYUNE

The Original Picayune Creole Cook Book

Pork Chops Zingara

4 SERVINGS

4 loin pork chops
1 small white onion, chopped
¼ pound mushrooms, cut in thin strips julienne style
1 cup tomato sauce
2 tablespoons julienne-cut cooked ham
2 tablespoons julienne-cut cooked tongue
3 tablespoons dry sherry
Salt and freshly ground black pepper to taste

1. In a lightly greased skillet brown the chops on both sides over brisk heat. Cover, reduce the heat and cook slowly until the chops are almost tender, about twenty minutes.

2. Add the onion and mushrooms and cook slowly, covered, until the chops are tender and the onion is soft, about five minutes.

3. Add the tomato sauce, heat to simmering and add the remaining ingredients.

NOTE: If desired, finish off by adding bits of butter to the sauce just before serving and swirling it in to give the sauce a gloss.

CLAIBORNE AND LEE

The Chinese Cookbook

Cantonese Roast Pork

2½ pounds lean loin of pork or other boneless cut in one piece
1 tablespoon bourbon whiskey, cognac, or rum
½ cup light soy sauce*
9 tablespoons sugar
1 teaspoon five spices powder,* commercially prepared or homemade
Salt to taste
2 tablespoons red bean curd sauce*
2 tablespoons bean sauce*
1 tablespoon sesame paste*
2 tablespoons or more dark soy sauce*
1 cup white or dark corn syrup or honey

*Available in Chinese markets and by mail order.

1. Cut the meat into strips approximately 8 to 10 inches long and 1½ to 2 inches thick. The length will depend, of course, on the size of the meat. There should be about 6 strips. Place the strips in one layer in a dish just large enough to hold them.

2. Combine the liquor, ¼ cup of light soy sauce, half the sugar, the five spices powder, and salt. Blend well. Pour the sauce over the meat, turning the pieces until the meat is coated. Let stand about 30 minutes.

3. Meanwhile, blend together the red bean curd sauce, bean sauce, 1 tablespoon of the light soy sauce, 1½ tablespoons of the sugar, and the sesame paste.

4. Preheat the oven to 450 degrees.

5. Take the meat from the original marinade but do not dry. Smear each piece of meat with the red bean curd sauce mixture.

6. Place a rack on top of a roasting pan. The rack should be about 2 inches above the bottom of the pan. Arrange the pieces of meat parallel to each other but without the sides touching. Bake 30 minutes, then turn each piece of meat and bake 15 minutes longer.

7. Brush each piece of meat with approximately ½ teaspoon dark soy sauce. Bake 5 minutes.

8. Turn each piece of meat and brush that side with dark soy sauce. Continue baking 10 minutes.

9. Meanwhile, in a saucepan blend the remaining 3 tablespoons of light soy sauce, 3 tablespoons of the sugar, 1 tablespoon of dark soy sauce, and the corn syrup. Heat briefly and stir to blend. Let cool slightly, then pour the mixture into a mixing bowl.

10. When the pieces of pork are done, add them to the last sauce. Coat well and remove. Let stand 10 minutes, then dip again to coat well. Dip 3 or 4 times in all.

11. Serve thinly sliced, at room temperature.

YIELD: 8 TO 12 SERVINGS

NOTE: Unused portions of both the red bean curd sauce and the bean sauce may be kept in properly sealed containers in the refrigerator for several weeks.

DELFS

The Good Food of Szechwan

Hui-guo Rou

Twice-cooked Pork

Another dish which has become very well known outside China, Hui-guo Rou *literally means "returned-to-the-pot pork," for the pork is first boiled in one large piece, then cooled, sliced, and finally fried with other ingredients. The recipe below calls for ½ pound pork loin or rump. However, the most practical way to prepare this dish is to buy a small roast (enough to prepare this dish several times) and to boil the entire piece. Cut off what you need and then refrigerate or freeze the rest. The remaining pork can be used to make Twice-cooked Pork again or in other recipes such as Cold White Pork with Garlic.*

½ lb. pork, loin or rump

STOCK

1 green onion, cut into 3-inch lengths
1 slice fresh ginger

1-3 green peppers, depending on size
½ tsp. salt
3 pieces yellow, dry *dou-fu* (optional)*
1 tsp. finely chopped fresh ginger (optional)
1-2 tsps. coarsely chopped garlic
1-2 green onions
½-1 Tbsp. hot bean sauce
4½ tsps. sweet bean sauce

SEASONINGS

1 tsp. wine or sherry
1 Tbsp. soy sauce
1 tsp. sugar
½-1 tsp. salt

approximately ¾ cup oil

*This ingredient is pretty difficult to find even at Chinese grocery stores. Keep trying.

TO PREPARE: 1. Bring enough water to cover the pork to boil in a *wok* or pot. Add the STOCK ingredients and let boil for a few minutes. Add the pork and gently boil until the pork is tender. Test with a fork. Depending on the size of the pork roast, it will take from 20–30 minutes. Remove and allow to cool. Strain and use the broth for pork stock in other recipes, if desired.

2. Cut the pork into very thin slices, about the size of potato chips. The fatty parts are considered a delicacy and should not be removed.

3. Top and seed the green pepper and cut into bite-sized sections, about 1-inch pieces. Slice the yellow, dry *dou-fu* thinly. Chop the ginger finely and the garlic coarsely. Cut the green onion into 1½-inch lengths.

4. Mix the SEASONINGS in a cup or small bowl.

TO COOK: 1. Heat the ¾ cup cooking oil until very hot in a *wok* or large frying pan. Add green pepper and sprinkle with ½ tsp. salt. Toss quickly for 5–15 seconds until the peppers are covered with oil and heated. Remove and drain. Reheat any remaining oil (it may be necessary to add 3–4 Tbsps. more oil) until very hot. Add yellow, dry *dou-fu* and toss until pieces are heated. Remove and drain.

2. Heat only 4–6 Tbsps. cooking oil left from the previous step in the wok. Add the slices of boiled pork roast. Toss for 10–15 seconds. If there seems to be too much oil, pour some off. Then add the hot bean sauce, sweet bean sauce, garlic and ginger. Toss until the pork is coated with the sauces and everything is heated. Then add the green onion lengths, green pepper, yellow, dry *dou-fu* and SEASONINGS. Stir over heat until everything is well mixed and smells good. Check for salt, remove to a serving dish and serve hot.

CLAIBORNE AND LEE
The Chinese Cookbook

Sweet and Sour Pork

Sweet and sour pork is, of course, one of the best-known dishes in all the world. Like anything else, a good sweet and sour pork is one thing and an ordinary sweet and sour pork is quite another. This is an excellent one. It is best if all the recommended ingredients are used, but license may be taken. For example, substitute fresh or canned mushrooms for the dried ones, and so on.

1 pound lean pork, cut into ¾-inch cubes
1 tablespoon dark soy sauce*
1 tablespoon dry sherry or shao hsing wine*
1 cup plus 2 tablespoons cornstarch
4 dried black mushrooms*
½ cup green and red sweet peppers, cut into 1-inch cubes (or use all green if red is not available)
2 tablespoons sliced carrot
½ cup onion, cut into 1-inch cubes
¼ cup thinly sliced bamboo shoots*
⅓ cup drained pineapple chunks or sliced pineapple cut into bite-size pieces
⅓ cup pickled scallions,* each cut in half (optional)
4 cloves garlic, peeled, crushed, and left whole
4 thin slices fresh ginger,* peeled
1¼ cups water
½ cup sugar
⅓ cup red wine vinegar
1 tablespoon light soy sauce*
Salt to taste
Peanut, vegetable, or corn oil
12 drops red food coloring

*Available in Chinese markets and by mail order.

1. Using the back of a kitchen knife or cleaver, pound each piece of pork lightly, then place in a mixing bowl and add the dark soy sauce and the wine. Mix with the fingers.

2. Place 1 cup of the cornstarch on a large sheet of waxed paper and dredge the pork, one piece at a time, in the cornstarch. Dredge each piece liberally and massage gently to coat well. Discard the leftover cornstarch.

3. Place the mushrooms in a mixing bowl and add hot water to cover. Let stand 15 minutes or so until softened.

4. In a mixing bowl combine the pepper cubes, carrot, onion, bamboo shoots, pineapple, scallions, garlic, and ginger.

5. Drain the mushrooms and squeeze to extract the moisture. Cut off the stems and slice the mushrooms into thin pieces. Add them to the vegetables and set aside.

6. Heat oil for deep frying to the boiling point in a wok or deep-fryer and drop in the pork pieces, a few at a time. Cook 5 to 8 minutes, or until the pork is cooked through and golden brown and crisp. Remove and drain on paper toweling.

7. Pour off all but ¾ cup of the oil and add the vegetable mixture. Cook, stirring, 4 to 5 minutes.

8. Meanwhile, in a saucepan combine 1 cup of the water, the sugar, vinegar, light soy sauce, and salt. Bring to a boil and stir until the sugar is dissolved.

9. Blend the remaining 2 tablespoons of cornstarch with the remaining ¼ cup of water and stir into the simmering sweet and sour sauce. Stir in the food coloring, then stir in 2 tablespoons of fresh oil to "glaze" the sauce. Pour the sauce over the vegetables and bring to a boil.

10. Transfer the pork to a serving dish. Customarily in America the sauce and vegetables are poured over the pork before serving. We prefer to serve the pork on one platter, the sauce with vegetables separately, so that each guest may help himself.

YIELD: 4 TO 8 SERVINGS

NOTE: The pork may be cooked twice to make the pieces crisper. Cook 5 minutes the first time, and remove the pieces. Let the oil reheat until it is almost smoking and put back the pork, cooking for 1 or 2 minutes, or until it is brown and crisp.

CALLAHAN
The California Cook Book for Indoor and Outdoor Eating

Chinatown Spareribs

These sweet-sour spareribs are simple to make, when you know how! Have your meat man chop the ribs into 2-inch lengths. To serve 4, you'll need:

- 2 pounds spareribs
- 1 tablespoon peanut oil or pork fat
- 2 tablespoons brown sugar
- 2 tablespoons cornstarch
- ½ teaspoon salt
- ¼ cup vinegar
- ¼ cup cold water
- 1 cup pineapple juice
- 1 tablespoon soy sauce
- 1 bouillon cube
- ¼ cup boiling water
- ¼ cup diced onions
- ⅓ cup diced pineapple
- ⅓ cup diced carrot
- ⅓ cup diced green pepper

Separate ribs, cover with boiling salted water, cover kettle, and simmer 1 hour, or until tender. Drain. Brown ribs slowly in oil. Mix sugar, cornstarch, salt; stir in vinegar, cold water, pineapple juice, soy sauce; add bouillon cube dissolved in boiling water. Add this mixture to ribs and cook, stirring constantly, until the sauce is transparent. Add onion, pineapple, carrot, and green pepper, and cook until vegetables are tender but still crisp. Serve with rice or fried noodles.

BEARD
The Fireside Cook Book

Spareribs

Spareribs may be broiled, boiled, baked, or braised, and are most savory. Buy the meatiest ones, getting at least a pound per person, for the bone content is large.

BROILED SPARERIBS

Cut spareribs into serving pieces. Season with salt and pepper, and place on the rack of a preheated broiler. Place the rack 4 inches from the flame and broil for 20 minutes. Turn and continue broiling until spareribs are nicely browned and crisp and cooked through. Serve with a spicy sauce.

BAKED SPARERIBS

Arrange seasoned spareribs in a lightly oiled baking dish or pan. Place in a preheated modern oven (350°) and allow them to roast for approximately 1 hour.

WEAVER
Pennsylvania Dutch Country Cooking

Scrapple
Panhaas

Much commercial Panhaas *is fatty because of what is thrown into it. Homemade Panhaas does not need to have any fat in it at all, even though a small amount does help give it its distinctive texture and flavor.*

The recipe here is based on my great-great-grandfather's, but most of the fat has been eliminated. Best of all, the recipe can easily be made at home, without starting with a whole pig.

YIELD: 9 6-INCH (15-CM) LOAVES (APPROXIMATELY 72 SERVINGS)

- 1 pork heart (approximately 8 ounces/250 g)
- 1 pound (500 g) meaty pork ribs (mix of fatty and lean)
- 2 pounds (1 kg) pork liver
- 2 cups (250 g) organic yellow cornmeal
- 1½ cups (210 g) organic buckwheat flour
- 2½ tablespoons (30 g) sea salt
- 1½ tablespoons freshly grated pepper
- 2½ tablespoons (25 g) ground sage
- ½ teaspoon ground clove

Trim the fat from around the top of the heart and remove the so-called deef ears, or sinews. Cut the heart into 4 pieces and put it in a heavy stewing kettle with the pork ribs and liver. Add 3 quarts (3 liters) of water, cover, and simmer gently for 3 hours or until the meat is falling from the bones.

Strain the broth into a clean pan. Pick the meat and fat from the ribs. Discard the bones and run the meat through a meat grinder or food processor. The texture should be somewhat coarse. Then grind the heart and liver as fine as possible. Mix the 2 textures of ground meat together and stir into the strained broth. Bring to a simmer over medium heat.

Sift together the cornmeal, buckwheat flour, salt, pepper, sage, and clove. Gradually add to the simmering meat mixture, stirring to eliminate lumps. Cook for 30 minutes, stirring almost constantly to prevent scorching on the bottom. Add extra hot water if the batter becomes too dry. After 30 minutes, the scrapple should acquire a thick, mashed-potato-like consistency. It is now ready to pour into pans.

Lightly grease 9 bread pans 6 by 3½ inches (15 by 8.5 cm) and fill with the batter. Set the pans on racks to cool. When cool, cover with plastic wrap and set in the refrigerator overnight. The next day, turn the scrapple loaves out onto a clean surface and cut each loaf into 8 slices. Use immediately or wrap individually with plastic wrap. Put the wrapped slices in freezer bags and store in the freezer for later use.

To fry fresh scrapple, dust each slice with flour. Lightly grease a skillet and get it very hot over high heat. Lower the heat to medium and add the slices. When they develop a thick crust on the bottom, turn them over and brown the other side. Serve very hot with a choice of typical Pennsylvania Dutch condiments: Pepper Hash, Pepper Vinegar, or molasses. I do not like molasses on *Panhaas*, but the Dutch of Lehigh County won't eat it any other way.

NOTE: Freezing causes scrapple to become loose and crumbly; therefore frozen scrapple should never be fried. So much the better for those who want to eliminate fried foods from their diet. Preheat the oven to 375°F (190°C). Lay the thawed scrapple slices on an ungreased cookie sheet and bake for 45 minutes. Turn each piece at least once so that it browns evenly on both sides. Serve immediately.

HAZAN

The Classic Italian Cook Book

Arrosto di maiale al latte

Pork Loin Braised in Milk

Whenever I teach this dish I am greeted by more or less polite skepticism, which usually turns to enthusiasm at the first taste. Pork cooked by this method turns out to be exceptionally tender and juicy. It is quite delicate in flavor because it loses all its fat and the milk, as such, disappears, to be replaced by clusters of delicious, nut-brown sauce.

FOR 6 PERSONS

2 tablespoons butter
2 tablespoons vegetable oil
2 pounds pork loin in one piece, with some fat on it, securely tied
1 teaspoon salt
Freshly ground pepper, 3 or 4 twists of the mill
2½ cups milk

1. Heat the butter and oil over medium-high heat in a casserole large enough to just contain the pork. When the butter foam subsides add the meat, fat side facing down. Brown thoroughly on all sides, lowering the heat if the butter starts to turn dark brown.

2. Add the salt, pepper, and milk. (Add the milk slowly, otherwise it may boil over.) Shortly after the milk comes to a boil, turn the heat down to medium, cover, but not tightly, with the lid partly askew, and cook slowly for about 1½ to 2 hours, until the meat is easily pierced by a fork. Turn and baste the meat from time to time, and, if necessary, add a little milk. By the time the meat is cooked the milk should have coagulated into small nut-brown clusters. If it is still pale in color, uncover the pot, raise the heat to high, and cook briskly until it darkens.

3. Remove the meat to a cutting board and allow to cool off slightly for a few minutes. Remove the trussing string, carve into slices ⅜ inch thick, and arrange them on a warm platter. Draw off most of the fat from the pot with a spoon and discard, being careful not to discard any of the coagulated milk clusters. Taste and correct for salt. (There may be as much as 1 to 1½ cups of fat to be removed.) Add 2 or 3 tablespoons of warm water, turn the heat to high, and boil away the water while scraping and loosening all the cooking residue in the pot.

Spoon the sauce over the sliced pork and serve immediately.

MENU SUGGESTIONS
This is a Bolognese dish, and is often preceded by Tagliatelle with Bolognese Meat Sauce or Baked Green Lasagne with Meat Sauce. If this appears to be too substantial, try the Baked Semolina Gnocchi, or an assortment of Italian cold cuts. As a vegetable Fried Artichoke Wedges or Crisp-Fried Whole Artichokes are excellent accompaniments.

BEARD

American Cookery

Baked Ham

TO PREPARE HAMS FOR BAKING

DRIED HAMS. The dried hams from Italy, France, England, and other countries—and the adaptations of those hams made in the United States—require no cooking before eating. They are sliced paper-thin and served for a first course seasoned with freshly ground pepper or accompanied by melon quarters, fresh figs, pineapple fingers, or pears. The Italian Parma ham (prosciutto) is also used in some cookery.

AGED HAMS. Nowadays one seldom finds a ham aged more than two or three years. Formerly it was not uncommon to find them aged six and seven years, especially from Virginia or Kentucky. They were black, covered with mold, and looked uninviting to the average person, but they gave promise of fine feasting to the ham fancier. Aged hams must be scrubbed with a brush and soapy water, not perfumed detergent but soap such as Ivory, for there is sometimes a patina of spice, dust, and mold that needs to be removed. The ham is then soaked 24 to 48 hours, depending upon its age and dryness, then cooked in water. Finally, the skin is removed and it is baked (see below).

To cook, cover the ham with fresh water, bring it to a boil, and boil 5 minutes or so, removing any scum that forms on the top. From this point on, there are two methods of cooking:

(1) Cover the ham and let it simmer at the barest ripple for 20 minutes per pound. The small bone at the shank end of the ham will be very loose when the ham is thoroughly cooked. Remove the ham from the water at once and allow it to cool.

(2) The other method is to let the ham simmer 2½ hours exactly, then let it cool in the liquid.

To remove the skin from the ham, use a sharp boning knife. When the ham is cool enough to handle, loosen the skin at the butt end, and run your fingers under the skin to loosen it further. Then pull the skin over the shank end, leaving ham covered with a blanket of creamy fat. If the fat is too heavy, carefully trim some of it off with the boning knife. Do not, of course, cut away all the fat, or the ham will dry out during baking.

COUNTRY HAMS. For the most part, producers of the various country hams, such as MacArthur's Smokehouse in Millerton, New York, the Talmadge Farms in Georgia, and the Great Valley Mills in Pennsylvania, are very good about providing printed directions with their hams. However, in the South one occasionally finds hams cured at small farms, and these require your own judgment in preparing them. The smell and feel of the ham should guide you. If it is dry, very hard to the touch, and has a fairly heavy smoky smell, I would treat it as an aged ham.

READY-TO-EAT AND TENDERIZED HAMS. The type of ham one ordinarily buys in the store or supermarkets is usually marked "ready to eat" or "tenderized." These hams usually need no boiling before you bake them.

CANNED HAMS. These are becoming increasingly standard for many people. They are convenience food at its most unattractive—boned, cooked, defatted, deflavored, and ready to eat! There is absolutely no relationship between an artificially flavored canned pork and a real ham. If you must use them, bake them in a crust or coat with a chaudfroid sauce, a cold sauce made with aspic, or a glaze.

BAKED AGED COOKED HAM

Traditionally the ham fat is covered with brown sugar and crumbs, studded with cloves, and baked in a 350-degree oven to glaze. In my opinion too many cloves overwhelm the flavor, and they are a nuisance to insert, besides. I like to break with tradition and either spread the ham with crumbs, brown sugar, and some dry mustard, or use a glaze.

Aged hams should be served tepid or cold, cut in paper-thin slices with a very sharp ham slicing knife. Spoon bread, hominy in cream, or creamed potatoes are traditional accompaniments. All are excellent. This is also usually the place for watermelon pickles, pickled peaches, or crabapples, perhaps hot biscuit or beaten biscuit, and certainly some preserves.

BAKED COUNTRY HAM

If there are no directions with the ham, cook as above (baked aged cooked ham)—most country hams fare well if they are boiled and baked like aged hams, with or without presoaking. Or they should be prepared as follows. After the skin is removed, place the ham fat side down in a large pan and pour water, wine, cider, or ginger ale into the pan to cover about two-thirds of the ham. Cover tightly with foil. Bake at 325 degrees, allowing approximately 18 minutes per pound. Two-thirds of the way through the cooking, remove the foil and turn the ham. Cover with the foil again and continue cooking. Remove the ham and cool. Cover with crumbs, brown sugar, and mustard or a glaze. Bake at 350 degrees for 1 hour. Serve with spoon bread or corn pudding and a purée of fresh spinach prepared with butter and a touch of nutmeg.

BAKED READY-TO-EAT OR TENDERIZED HAM

These hames are quite wet, and if you like a dry texture, be certain to pierce the ham with a fork in several places before baking. The skin can usually be loosened with a knife and pulled off before baking. Glaze the ham, or rub crumbs, brown sugar, and mustard into the surface. Stud with cloves if you like, first scoring the fat in parallel lines with a sharp knife so as to form perfect squares. A clove can be inserted in the center of each square. Bake the ham at 325 degrees approximately 10 to 12 minutes per pound.

NOTE: You may bake tenderized or ready-to-eat hams fat side down in a pan with a pint of sherry, Madeira, apple cider, or ginger ale. Baste the ham with the liquid from time to time during baking.

LAMB

OLNEY

Simple French Food

Shanks with Garlic

Souris aux Aulx

FOR 4

2 or 3 pounds lamb shanks, outside fat removed
Salt
3 tablespoons olive oil
15 to 20 cloves garlic, unpeeled
A few tablespoons water
½ teaspoon finely crumbled mixed dried herbs
½ cup dry white wine
Pepper

Use, if possible, a heavy copper pan of just a size to hold the shanks at their ease. It should have a tight-fitting lid. Brown the shanks, salted, lightly in the oil, toss in the garlic, and cook over very low heat, covered, turning them occasionally, for about 1½ hours, or longer to be very tender. An asbestos pad may be necessary to disperse the heat—the shanks should only very gently stew in their own juices. In heavy copper their natural juices will hold for about 1 hour—in other metals, for a much shorter time. When all liquid has disappeared and they begin to sizzle in fat, add a spoonful of water from time to time so that a film of liquid remains always in the bottom of the pan. Sprinkle with the herbs after about an hour's time.

As the meat approaches the desired tenderness, stop moistening with water so that all the liquid evaporates. When the meat begins again to sizzle in pure fat, remove it to a plate, pour off the fat, deglaze the pan with the white wine, scraping and stirring with a wooden spoon to dissolve all caramelized adherences, put the juice and garlic through a sieve to rid them of the garlic hulls, return to the pan, reduce the liquid to the staccato bubbling stage, and return the meat to the pan—there should be only enough sauce to just coat the pieces. Grind over pepper to taste.

BASTIANICH
La Cucina di Lidia

Agnello di Latte Arrosto
Roast Baby Lamb
SERVES 6

I always had mixed emotions about this dish as a little girl. Traditionally, it was served at the first meal after Lent, a joyous occasion to which everyone looked forward, including me. Still, there was an element of personal sadness: My pet was being eaten. At Busoler I spent long hours playing in the fields with lambs and young goats, and always found sentiment struggling with appetite at Easter. When the appearance of the first peas of the season coincided with Easter, they'd be shelled and added to the dish at the last moment.

5-pound baby lamb shoulder with bone, cut in 2" cubes
2 ribs celery, coarsely chopped
2 medium carrots, coarsely chopped
1 large onion, sliced
1 cup dry white wine
½ cup olive oil
¼ cup balsamic vinegar
3 small sprigs fresh rosemary
¼ teaspoon freshly ground pepper
½ teaspoon salt
2 cups beef stock

In a large bowl, toss all ingredients except the beef stock until well blended. Cover and refrigerate 24 hours, tossing occasionally.

Preheat the oven to 425° F. Transfer the contents of the refrigerated bowl to a roasting pan large enough to accommodate a single layer of vegetables covered by a single layer of meat. Add the stock and roast, basting and turning the lamb frequently, until the meat is very tender, about 1 hour 45 minutes.

Reduce the oven temperature to 350° F. Remove the lamb from the pan and set it aside. Skim and discard as much fat as possible from the pan liquids. Place the pan over high heat and boil until the liquids reduce to about 1¼ cups. Transfer the meat to a smaller roasting pan and strain the reduced sauce over it. Place the meat in the oven and roast, turning the meat every 10 minutes, until extremely tender, brown, and caramelized, about 30–40 minutes.

Strain the juices from the pan and, if necessary, reduce further over moderately high heat; there should be ½ cup of finished sauce. Transfer the lamb to a serving platter and spoon the sauce over it.

RECOMMENDED WINE—I like Abbazia di Rosazzo's Ronco dei Roseti with roast baby lamb.

BROWN
The South American Cook Book

Argentine Lamb Stew
Cazuela de Cordero

3 pounds lamb
3 quarts boiling water
1 tablespoon salt
2 tablespoons butter
1 onion, chopped
1 carrot, sliced
1 celery heart, minced
1 garlic clove, minced
½ teaspoon marjoram (dry)
A tiny pinch cumin seeds
1 cup green peas
2 cups green beans, cut fine
1 ear green corn
6 cubes of squash
Salt and pepper to taste
6 small potatoes
1½ tablespoons rice
1 egg yolk
4 tablespoons milk
1 teaspoon parsley, minced

Cut lamb into 6 portions. Cover with water. Add salt and let cook gently. Melt butter in frying pan and fry in it onion, carrot, celery, garlic and herbs slowly. When onion is soft turn mixture into the lamb stew. Add peas, beans, squash cubes and ear of corn cut into 6 pieces. When meat is nearly done, about 25 minutes before serving, add potatoes. Season to taste and add rice. When all are done beat egg yolk with milk. Remove stew from heat. Stir in egg mixture. Add parsley and serve at once in deep bowls, portioning each with meat and vegetables.

The original recipe calls for goat's milk, but since so little is used in it, cow's milk will do as well.

WOLFERT

Couscous and Other Good Food from Morocco

Lamb Tagine with Artichokes, Lemon, and Olives

The small artichokes found in Italian markets in the spring are especially good in this tagine. *Note that canned artichoke bottoms and frozen artichoke hearts will* not *produce a good dish.*

INGREDIENTS

2½ to 3 pounds lamb shoulder, cut into 1½ inch chunks
2 cloves garlic, peeled and crushed
Salt to taste
¼ teaspoon freshly ground pepper
1½ teaspoons ground ginger
Pinch of pulverized saffron
½ teaspoon turmeric
¼ cup vegetable oil, or less
¼ cup grated onion
8 to 10 small artichokes (about 2½ pounds)
¾ to 1 preserved lemon (see page 434), rinsed
½ cup "red" olives, such as Kalamatas or Gaetas
2 tablespoons lemon juice

EQUIPMENT

Paring knife
5½ quart enameled cast-iron or stainless steel casserole with cover
Vegetable peeler
Olive pitter (optional)
Shallow serving dish

WORKING TIME: 30 MINUTES
COOKING TIME: 2 HOURS
SERVES: 4 TO 6

1. Trim excess fat from the lamb. In the casserole toss the lamb chunks with the garlic, salt, spices, oil, and onion. Cover with 1 cup water and bring to a boil. Reduce the heat, cover, and simmer over moderate heat for 1½ hours, turning the pieces of meat often in the sauce and adding water whenever necessary.

2. Prepare the artichokes by removing the outside leaves and trimming the bases. Halve each one and remove the hairy choke. Place in acidulated water (water with 2 tablespoonfuls of vinegar added) to keep from blackening while trimming the rest. Rinse and drain before using.

3. Place the artichokes over the pieces of meat after the meat has cooked 1½ hours. Place the rinsed preserved lemon, cut in quarters, on top. Cover tightly and cook 30 minutes. Sprinkle with the lemon juice and olives and cook a few minutes all together.

4. Place the lamb in center of the serving dish. Arrange the artichokes, flat side up, facing in one direction around the rim. By boiling rapidly, uncovered, reduce the sauce to a thick gravy. Readjust the seasoning of the sauce. Swirl the pan once to combine and pour over the meat. Decorate with preserved lemons and olives and serve at once.

NOTE: An alternative sauce includes a peeled and seeded tomato cooked with the sauce.

TOKLAS

The Alice B. Toklas Cook Book

Gigot de la Clinique

A surgeon living in the provinces, as fond of good cheer as he was learned, invented this recipe which we acquired by bribing his cook. No leg of venison can compare with a simple leg of mutton prepared in the following manner. Eight days in advance you will cover the leg of mutton with the marinade called Baume Samaritain, composed of wine—old Burgundy, Beaune or Chambertin—and virgin olive oil. Into this balm to which you have already added the usual condiments of salt, pepper, bay leaf, thyme, beside an atom of ginger root, put a pinch of cayenne, a nutmeg cut into small pieces, a handful of crushed juniper berries and lastly a dessertspoon of powdered sugar (effective as musk in perfumery) which serves to fix the different aromas. Twice a day you will turn the *gigot*. Now we come to the main point of the preparation. After you have placed the *gigot* in the marinade you will arm yourself with a surgical syringe of a size to hold ½ pint which you will fill with ½ cup of cognac and ½ cup of fresh orange juice. Inject the contents of the syringe into the fleshy part of the *gigot* in three different spots. Refill the syringe with the same contents and inject into the *gigot* twice more. Each day you will fill the syringe with the marinade and inject the contents into the *gigot*. At the end of the week the leg of mutton is ready to be roasted; perfumed with the condiments and the spices, completely permeated by the various flavours, it has been transfused into a strange and exquisite venison. Roast and serve with the usual venison sauce to which has been added just before serving 2 tablespoons of the blood of a hare.*

Everyone thought that the syringe was a whimsy, that Madame Pierlot was making mock of them. Not at all. Years later I found it in that great collection of French recipes, Bertrand Guegan's *Le Grand Cuisinier Français*. The Baronne Pierlot's recipe is classified, it has entered into the *Grande Cuisine Française*.

*__NOTE.__ A marinade is a bath of wine, herbs, oil, vegetables, vinegars and so on, in which fish or meat destined for particular dishes repose for specified periods and acquire virtue.

WELLS

Bistro Cooking

Gigot Rôti au Gratin de Monsieur Henny

Roast Lamb with Monsieur Henny's Potato, Onion, and Tomato Gratin

This is a simple, satisfying dish to make—the sort of one-dish meal that French village women used to bring to the local baker for cooking in the community's bread oven. In Provence, it's become our "house special." In this recipe offered to me by my village butcher Monsieur Roland Henny, the lamb's wonderful juices drip into the gratin, a mixture of tomatoes, potatoes, and onions, as it cooks. While more traditional recipes call for baking the lamb right in the gratin, I like to let it sit an inch or so above the gratin on a sturdy cake stand or oven rack that rests atop the gratin dish. This allows the lamb to roast and not steam. Serve with a solid red wine, such as a Côtes-du-Rhône-Villages or a Châteauneuf-du-Pape.

6 garlic cloves, 1 clove split, the rest chopped
2 pounds (1 kg) baking potatoes, such as russets, peeled and very thinly sliced
Salt and freshly ground black pepper
1 tablespoon fresh thyme
2 large onions, very thinly sliced
5 medium tomatoes (about 1 pound; 500 g), cored and thinly sliced
⅔ cup (16 cl) dry white wine
⅓ cup (8 cl) extra-virgin olive oil
1 leg of lamb, bone-in (6 to 7 pounds; 3 to 3.5 kg)

1. Preheat the oven to 400°F (205°C).

2. Rub the bottom of a large oval porcelain gratin dish about 16 × 10 × 2 inches (40.5 × 25.5 × 5 cm) with the split garlic clove. Arrange the potatoes in a single layer. Season generously with the salt, pepper, and some of the thyme and chopped garlic. Layer the sliced onions on top; season as with the potatoes. Layer the tomatoes on top of the onions. Season with salt, pepper, and the remaining thyme and garlic. Pour on the white wine, and then the oil.

3. Trim the thicker portions of fat from the leg of lamb. Season the meat with salt and pepper. Place a sturdy cake rack or oven rack directly on top of the gratin dish. Set the lamb on the rack, so that the juices will drip into the gratin.

4. Roast, uncovered, for about 1 hour and 15 minutes for rare lamb. (For well-done lamb, roast an additional 30 to 40 minutes.) Turn the lamb every 15 minutes, basting it with liquid from the dish underneath. Remove from the oven and let the lamb sit for 20 minutes before carving.

5. To serve, carve the lamb into thin slices and arrange on warmed dinner plates or on a serving platter, with the vegetable gratin alongside.

YIELD: 8 TO 10 SERVINGS

"Gourmandise is a capital sin. So, therefore, my brothers, let us guard against being gourmands. Let's be gourmets."

—Saint Ignatius of Loyola,
founder of the Jesuit order

BEEF

BITTMAN
How to Cook Everything

Grilled Steak, American-Style

MAKES 2 TO 4 SERVINGS
TIME: ABOUT 10 MINUTES, PLUS TIME TO BUILD THE FIRE

Straightforward and simple. Start with the right steak (prime, if you can find it, is worth it in this instance) and don't overcook. This is one of those times where a gas grill simply will not do the trick; you need a blazing hot fire and no cover if you want your steak crisp and slightly charred on the outside and rare inside; use real hardwood charcoal if at all possible. In this single case, pan-grilling is closer to grilling than broiling, since most home broilers just don't get hot enough.

2 sirloin strip, rib-eye, or other steaks, 8 ounces each and about 1 inch thick
Salt and freshly ground black pepper to taste

1. Remove the steaks from the refrigerator and their packaging if you have not already done so. Build a medium-hot charcoal fire; you should not be able to hold your hand 3 inches above it for more than 2 or 3 seconds. The rack should be 3 or 4 inches from the top of the coals.

2. Dry the steaks with paper towels. Grill them without turning for 3 minutes (a little more if they're over an inch thick, a little less if they're thinner or you like steaks extremely rare). Turn, then grill for 3 minutes on the other side. Steaks will be rare to medium-rare.

3. Check for doneness. If you would like the steaks better done, move them away from the most intense heat and grill another minute or two longer per side; check again. When done, sprinkle with salt and pepper and serve.

GRILLED PORTERHOUSE (T-BONE) STEAK: These are best when very thick, 1½ inches or more, and weigh about 2 pounds, in which case they will easily serve 4 to 6 people. In Step 2, grill for 4 to 5 minutes per side, taking care not to burn the meat; the leaner tenderloin (the smaller of the two pieces on either side of the bone) is best very rare, so keep it toward the coolest part of the fire. Check for doneness, preferably with an instant-read thermometer and in both the sirloin and the tenderloin sections. If not done to your liking, move the steak to a cooler part of the grill and cook for another 2 to 3 minutes per side before checking again.

BROILED STEAK: Remember that a broiler is little more than an upside-down grill. The major difference is that melting fat can build up in your broiling pan and catch fire, so it's best to broil on a rack. Turn the broiler to maximum, preheat it, and broil 3 to 4 inches from the heat source (any more, and you won't brown the steak; any less, and you'll burn it). Proceed as for grilling, with this exception: If your broiler heat is not intense enough to brown the steak well, don't turn it, but cook it the entire time on one side only. It will cook reasonably evenly, and should develop a nice crust on the top.

PAN-GRILLED STEAK: A terrific option for 1-inch-thick steaks (not much thicker, though), as long as you have a decent exhaust fan; otherwise, see the next option. Preheat a cast-iron or other sturdy skillet just large enough to hold the steaks over medium-high heat for 4 to 5 minutes; the pan should be really hot—in fact, it should be smoking. Sprinkle its surface with coarse salt and put in the steaks. Clouds of smoke will instantly appear; do not turn down the heat. The timing remains the same as for grilled steaks.

PAN-GRILLED/OVEN-ROASTED STEAK: An excellent alternative to grilling for homes without good exhaust systems. Turn the oven to its maximum temperature, at least 500°F, and set a rack in the lowest possible position (if you can place a skillet directly on the oven floor, so much the better). Preheat a cast-iron or other sturdy, ovenproof skillet large enough to hold the steaks over medium-high heat for 4 to 5 minutes; the pan should be really hot, just about smoking. Sprinkle its surface with coarse salt and put in the steaks. Immediately transfer the skillet to the oven (wearing a thick oven mitt to protect your hand); timing remains the same as for grilled steaks.

BISTRO STEAK: After cooking, top each steak with 1 teaspoon to 1 tablespoon of any compound butter. For example, try parsley butter mixed with a little garlic (with some minced anchovy, if you like).

TUSCAN STEAK: Drizzle some flavorful extra-virgin olive oil over the steak when it is done; top with freshly squeezed lemon juice to taste.

CLAIBORNE
The New York Times Cook Book

Flank Steak with Herb Stuffing

6 SERVINGS

1 two-pound flank steak
2 tablespoons butter
½ large onion, minced (optional)
½ cup chopped mushrooms
¼ cup pistachio nuts, coarsely chopped (optional)
¼ cup chopped parsley
1½ cups soft bread cubes
⅓ teaspoon poultry seasoning, or a mixture of orégano and basil
½ teaspoon salt
Freshly ground black pepper to taste
1 egg, slightly beaten
½ cup water, dry table wine or bouillon

1. Preheat oven to moderate (350° F.). Pound the steak or score it lightly on both sides.

2. In a skillet heat the butter, add the onion and garlic and cook until lightly browned. Add the mushrooms and cook three minutes. Add the nuts, parsley, bread cubes, poultry seasoning, salt, pepper and egg and mix.

3. Spread the mixture on the steak. Roll lengthwise, as for jelly roll, and tie with string at two-inch intervals.

4. Brown the meat on both sides in a little fat in a skillet or heavy Dutch oven. Add the liquid, cover and bake two hours. To serve, cut into one-inch slices and serve with the pan drippings.

DE GOUY
The Gold Cook Book

Swiss Steak

The original name of this recipe was "Schmor Braten." It is three centuries old.

Select a 3-pound piece of round steak, top round preferred about 2½ inches thick. Rub about ½ a cup of salted and peppered flour into the meat on both sides. Heat to the smoking point 2 tablespoons of drippings or lard; put the meat in it, and brown nicely on both sides. Transfer to a stewpot; add 2 cups of boiling water, with 1 large onion, thinly sliced, and season to taste with salt and black pepper. Now add 1 bouquet garni composed of 1 extra large or 2 small bay leaves, 8 sprigs of fresh parsley, 1 sprig of thyme and 2 sprigs of green celery leaves all tied together with white kitchen thread, 2 whole cloves, and a blade of garlic. Let simmer very gently, covered, over a low flame for an hour. Then stir in 1 cup of tomato purée, 1 teaspoonful of good prepared mustard and 1½ tablespoons of tomato catsup, cover again and continue simmering for another hour, or until done, and the meat may be cut with the fork. If there is not enough liquid, add more beef stock; thicken, if needed, with a little flour; taste for seasoning and serve steak and half of the gravy in a heated deep platter, the remainder of the gravy separately with a side dish of plain boiled potatoes.

BEARD

The Fireside Cook Book

Leftover Roast Beef

COLD ROAST BEEF

Cold beef is far more palatable and flavorful when it has not been too thoroughly chilled in the refrigerator. Either allow the cold roast to stand in a cooler or remove it from the refrigerator an hour or two before serving. Serve slices of rare beef, all excess fat removed, with salad (potato or vegetable salad is an excellent accompaniment). Or combine slices of beef with other cold cuts for luncheon or for a buffet supper.

DEVILED BEEF BONES

Men are usually very fond of the rib bones—with some meat left on them, of course! The bones are dipped in beaten egg and rolled in dry bread crumbs, and cooked very quickly in butter in a large skillet until nicely browned on all sides. Serve with devil sauce.

DEVILED BEEF SLICES

Slices of rare roast beef, prepared as deviled beef bones are, will be most delicious for dinner on a roast's second or third day.

Roast Beef Tenderloin

The tenderloin of beef, which usually weighs 4 to 6 pounds, is considered by many to be the choicest of all cuts. It has a tendency to be stringy and rather dry, although exceedingly tender. It slices perfectly because there is no tendon or bone, and is, although expensive per pound, a truly economical cut. Count on about ½ pound per person.

Tenderloin should be larded before cooking. Run strips of very fat salt pork through the flesh with a larding needle or have the roast thoroughly wrapped and tied with flattened pieces of beef suet. Place the tenderloin on a rack in a roasting pan and roast in either a very hot oven (450°), allowing 13 minutes per pound, or a moderately slow oven (325°), allowing 18 minutes per pound.

TENDERLOIN ON A SPIT

This is a dish for cooking outdoors. Lard the tenderloin. Secure to a roasting spit and toast over the coals, allowing about 15 minutes per pound.

It is a good idea to slice the meat thin and serve on large French rolls or pieces of toasted French bread with a pungent barbecue sauce.

This is an ideal way to serve a large number of people outdoors. A 6-pound tenderloin will serve 12 people easily.

Pot Roasts of Beef

A pot roast is one of the less tender cuts of beef. Pot roasts are covered and then cooked very slowly in liquid (water, wine, or stock) on top of the stove or in the oven. It may be marinated before cooking. The meat is always served well done and has tenderness and flavor. It is hearty fare and one that is relished by all who are blessed with good appetites.

The best cuts for pot roast are top round, rump, chuck, or bottom round. There should be an ample amount of fat on the meat.

Allow 1 pound per person, for a pot roast will shrink.

Wipe the roast well with a damp cloth. Brown quickly on all sides in hot fat. Season. Place in a heavy, covered kettle or pot, add liquid, and simmer on top of stove or in a slow oven until tender. Allow about 25 minutes per pound for a pot roast.

PLAIN POT ROAST

Choose a piece of beef weighing 4 to 6 pounds. Have it larded or not, as you wish.

Dredge the meat with flour, pepper, and salt. Melt 4 tablespoons butter in a deep kettle and sear meat on all sides very quickly until nicely browned. Add ½ to 1 cup liquid. (This may be water, stock, wine, or tomato juice.)

Reduce the heat, cover tightly, and simmer slowly for 25 minutes per pound or until meat is tender. The meat should be tender enough to cut easily, but not stringy and mushy. If the liquid evaporates, add more. (Serves 4 to 6.)

LEWIS
The Taste of Country Cooking

Oven Brisket or Rolled Chuck

Beef was more available in the spring and summer and it was inexpensive as well, being locally butchered. We would take a big piece so that we could have some left for slicing cold during the busy season. Usually it was the rib roast. It was dusted with flour, salt, pepper, cooked to perfection, and served cold after the first or second meal. Locally grown beef had such a great flavor. None was ever left to spoil.

Because of the lack of flavor in beef today, I have searched and found that the more unpopular cuts have a bit more taste. Brisket, rolled chuck, which is also sold sliced as chicken steak, and flanken all have more flavor than some of the other more expensive, better-known cuts.

For preparing this dish of brisket or chuck, purchase half as many onions as beef.

SERVES 6

3 pounds beef brisket or chuck
Vegetable oil or lard
1 tablespoon butter
1½ pounds onions, peeled and sliced
Fresh-ground black pepper
3 or 4 whole allspice
1 bay leaf
Salt

Wipe the meat with a damp cloth. Heat a skillet hot, grease lightly with oil or lard, and add the beef, searing well on all sides until well browned. Place the seared meat in a heavy pot or pan. Wipe the skillet out and then add a tablespoon of butter and put in the onions. Stir the onions until they are pretty well browned. Sprinkle the meat over with fresh-ground black pepper and now add the browned onions, allspice, and bay leaf. Cover closely and see that the pan is good and hot before placing it in the oven. Set into a preheated 400° oven until the meat begins to cook. Turn the oven to 225° and leave to cook undisturbed for 2½ hours. When finished, remove the meat and press the onions through a sieve. Add to pan drippings and season this sauce with salt and pepper to taste. Serve hot with the beef.

PRUDHOMME
Chef Paul Prudhomme's Louisiana Kitchen

Cajun Meat Loaf

MAKES 6 SERVINGS

This is best using both ground pork and ground beef, as the pork gives more flavor diversity. However, you can make it with ground beef only.

SEASONING MIX
2 whole bay leaves
1 tablespoon salt
1 teaspoon ground red pepper (preferably cayenne)
1 teaspoon black pepper
½ teaspoon white pepper
½ teaspoon ground cumin
½ teaspoon ground nutmeg

4 tablespoons unsalted butter
⅓ cup finely chopped onions
½ cup finely chopped celery
½ cup finely chopped green bell peppers
¼ cup finely chopped green onions
2 teaspoons minced garlic
1 tablespoon Tabasco sauce
1 tablespoon Worcestershire sauce
½ cup evaporated milk
½ cup catsup
1½ pounds ground beef
½ pound ground pork
2 eggs, lightly beaten
1 cup very fine dry bread crumbs

Combine the seasoning mix ingredients in a small bowl and set aside.

Melt the butter in a 1-quart saucepan over medium heat. Add the onions, celery, bell peppers, green onions, garlic, Tabasco, Worcestershire and seasoning mix. Sauté until mixture starts sticking excessively, about 6 minutes, stirring occasionally and scraping the pan bottom well. Stir in the milk and catsup. Continue cooking for about 2 minutes, stirring occasionally. Remove from heat and allow mixture to cool to room temperature.

Place the ground beef and pork in an ungreased 13 × 9-inch baking pan. Add the eggs, the cooked vegetable mixture, removing the bay leaves, and the bread crumbs. Mix by hand until thoroughly combined. In the center of the pan, shape the mixture into a loaf that is about 1½ inches high, 6 inches wide and 12 inches long. Bake uncovered at 350° for 25 minutes, then raise heat to 400° and continue cooking until done, about 35 minutes longer. Serve immediately as is or with *Very Hot Cajun Sauce for Beef.*

MITCHELL

Lüchow's German Cookbook

Cold Sauerbraten à la Mode in Aspic

Leftover Sauerbraten makes a delicious dish in madeira-flavored aspic. Place a piece of Sauerbraten in a serving dish or mold. Cover and surround with aspic; decorate with fancy-cut raw and cooked vegetables; chill and serve.

TIME-LIFE BOOKS

Scandinavia

Små Köttbullar

Small Swedish Meatballs

TO SERVE 6 TO 8 (ABOUT 50 MEATBALLS)

1 tablespoon butter
4 tablespoons finely chopped onion
1 large boiled potato, mashed (1 cup)
3 tablespoons fine dry bread crumbs
1 pound lean ground beef
⅓ cup heavy cream
1 teaspoon salt
1 egg
1 tablespoon finely chopped fresh parsley (optional)
2 tablespoons butter
2 tablespoons vegetable oil
1 tablespoon flour
⅓ cup light or heavy cream

In a small frying pan, melt the tablespoon of butter over moderate heat. When the foam subsides, add the onions and cook for about 5 minutes, until they are soft and translucent but not brown.

In a large bowl, combine the onions, mashed potato, bread crumbs, meat, cream, salt, egg and optional parsley. Knead vigorously with both hands or beat with a wooden spoon until all of the ingredients are well blended and the mixture is smooth and fluffy. Shape into small balls about 1 inch in diameter. Arrange the meatballs in one layer on a baking sheet or a flat tray, cover them with plastic wrap and chill for at least 1 hour before cooking.

Over high heat, melt the 2 tablespoons of butter and 2 tablespoons of oil in a heavy 10- to 12-inch skillet. When the foam subsides, add the meatballs, 8 to 10 at a time. Reduce the heat to moderate and fry the balls on all sides, shaking the pan almost constantly to roll the balls around in the hot fat to help keep their shape. In 8 to 10 minutes the meatballs should be brown outside and show no trace of pink inside when one is broken open with a knife. Add more butter and oil to the skillet as needed, and transfer each finished batch to a casserole or baking dish and keep warm in a 200° oven.

If the meatballs are to be served as a main course with noodles or potatoes, you may want to make a sauce with the pan juice. Remove from the heat, pour off all of the fat from pan, and stir in 1 tablespoon of flour. Quickly stir in ¾ cup of light or heavy cream and boil the sauce over moderate heat for 2 or 3 minutes, stirring constantly, until it is thick and smooth. Pour over the meatballs and serve.

If the meatballs are to be served as an hors d'oeuvre or as part of a smörgåsbord, they should be cooked as above, but formed into smaller balls and served without the sauce.

BRENNAN
The Original Thai Cookbook

Beef Balls in Peanut Sauce

Panaeng Neua

4 TO 6 SERVINGS

Panaeng Neua *is sold by the Thai street vendors as an occasional snack. It is also commonly served as one of the dishes to complement a Thai dinner. This rich curry/peanut sauce transforms the plain meatballs into a savory delight. It is delicious and* farangs, *Westerners living in Thailand, find it a popular cocktail* hors d'oeuvre.

- 1 pound medium lean ground beef
- ½ cup all-purpose flour
- 2 tablespoons vegetable oil
- 4 cloves garlic, coarsely chopped
- 2 tablespoons red curry paste (*Krung Gaeng Ped*)
- 1 cup "Thick" coconut milk
- 2 tablespoons chunky peanut butter or ground peanuts
- 1½ tablespoons granulated sugar
- 2 tablespoons fish sauce (*Nam Pla*)
- 1 teaspoon fresh mint or sweet basil leaves, chopped

Shape the beef into small, firm balls about 1" in diameter. Press and roll the balls in the flour, dusting off the excess. Heat the oil in a wok until a haze forms and fry the garlic for 1 minute. Add the floured meatballs and continue frying until brown, stirring and tilting the wok to cook the balls uniformly. Remove with a slotted spoon and drain on paper towels. In the remainder of the oil in the wok, fry the Red Curry Paste for about 2 minutes, stirring well to prevent sticking. Add the "Thick" coconut milk and stir in the peanut butter. Continue cooking and stirring until you have a smooth, uniform consistency. Season with sugar and fish sauce. Return the meatballs to the sauce and simmer over low heat for 5 minutes or until they return to temperature. Remove to a serving dish and garnish with mint or sweet basil sprinkled over the top.

DELFS
The Good Food of Szechwan

Gan-bian Niu-rou-si

Dry-Fried Beef with Carrots and Celery

- 1 lb. beef, any cut, sirloin steak is the best
- ⅓–½ lb. celery
- 1–2 carrots, depending on size*
- 3 fresh or dried red peppers
- 1 green onion
- 1 tsp. finely chopped ginger
- 2 tsps. finely chopped garlic
- 1–1½ Tbsps. hot bean sauce (optional)
- 2 tsps. sweet bean sauce
- 1 Tbsp. rice wine or dry sherry
- 1½ tsp. salt
- 1 tsp. sugar
- ½ tsp. ground Szechwan pepper
- 2 tsps. sesame oil
- 1 tsp.–2 Tbsps. red oil (optional)
- 9 Tbsps. oil or lard

*If this ingredient is omitted, increase the amount of celery used and add ½ tsp. sugar

TO PREPARE: 1. Cut the meat into very thin slices about ⅛-inch thick, and then into very narrow shreds, about ⅛-inch wide. Cutting is easier if the meat is frozen.

2. Remove the leaves and base of the celery, wash the celery thoroughly and cut it into 1-inch pieces. Peel the carrots and cut them into fine shreds, about 2½–3-inches long. Top and seed the red peppers and cut them lengthwise into fine shreds. If using dried red peppers, soak them in warm water until softened and then seed and cut them into fine shreds. Cut the green onion into ½-inch lengths or smaller.

3. Chop the ginger and the garlic as finely as possible. Have the other ingredients at hand.

TO COOK: 1. Heat 3 Tbsps. of the cooking oil or lard in a wok or large frying pan until very hot. Add the celery and carrots and ½ tsp. of the salt. Toss over high heat briefly until the vegetables are partially cooked. Remove and drain.

2. Heat 6 Tbsps. of the cooking oil or lard in the wok until very hot, then allow to cool slightly. Add the beef shreds and cook over a medium fire, stirring constantly. (If the juices stick to the sides of the wok, they will soon char and ruin the flavor of the beef. If this begins to happen, immediately remove the beef, discard the oil, clean the wok and start over with another 6 Tbsps. cooking oil or lard.) Cook the beef evenly and thoroughly and, using chopsticks or another utensil, keep the beef shreds from sticking together while cooking. Cook, tossing frequently, until the beef has turned a dark color and has become dry looking and stiff—about 10 minutes.

3. When the beef is thoroughly cooked, add the hot bean sauce and the sweet bean sauce, red peppers, garlic, about half the green onion, the remaining salt and the rice wine. Stir well. When the smell of the garlic and bean sauces is noticeable, add the prefried celery and carrots. Continue to stir until the celery and carrots are reheated, then at the last minute add the sugar, ginger, remaining green onion, Szechwan pepper and sesame oil. Stir for 20–30 seconds. Taste and check for saltiness and hotness and add more salt or the red oil if you desire. Remove to a serving dish and serve hot.

TSUJI
Japanese Cooking

Steak Teriyaki
Gy niku Teriyaki

Teri *means "glossy luster," and the secret is to achieve this effect by reducing the sauce without overcooking the meat.*

4 SERVINGS

4 sirloin steaks, about 1 inch (2½ cm) thick and 6–8 ounces (180–225 g) each
salt
2 Tbsps vegetable oil
4 Tbsps *saké*
3 Tbsps *mirin*
2 Tbsps dark soy sauce
mustard paste

TO PAN-BROIL: Salt the meat lightly on both sides to extract juices.

Heat a scant amount of oil in a large frying pan and brown on one side, covered, over high heat, about 3 minutes. Turn once only. While the meat is frying on the second side, splash on the *saké*. Cover the pan and fry for another 2 or 3 minutes. This browning will produce quite a lot of smoke; the meat will be seared on the outside and will be quite rare on the inside.

Remove steaks to a side plate. Over heat add the *mirin* and dark soy sauce to the meat juices in the pan (this forms the *teriyaki* sauce). As soon as meat glaze is dissolved, return the steaks to the pan to coat with the sauce, about 30 seconds on each side.

TO SERVE: Cut the steaks across the grain into ½-inch (1½–cm) slices. This slicing is necessary only for eating with chopsticks. Arrange on individual plates. Spoon over some of the *teriyaki* sauce. Garnish with a dollop of prepared mustard.

Combines well with ASPARAGUS WITH MUSTARD DRESSING and BEATEN EGG SOUP.

CLAIBORNE
The New York Times Cook Book

Beef Stroganoff

ABOUT 6 SERVINGS

1½ pounds beef fillet, sirloin or porterhouse steak
Salt and freshly ground black pepper to taste
3 tablespoons butter
1 tablespoon flour
1 cup beef broth or canned consommé
1 teaspoon prepared mustard
1 onion, sliced
3 tablespoons sour cream, at room temperature

1. Remove all the fat and gristle from the meat. Cut into narrow strips about two inches long and one-half inch thick. Season the strips with salt and pepper and refrigerate two hours.

2. In a saucepan melt one and one-half tablespoons of butter, add the flour and stir with a wire whisk until blended. Meanwhile, bring the consommé to a boil and add all at once to the butter-flour mixture, stirring vigorously with the whisk until the sauce is thickened and smooth. Stir in the mustard.

3. In a separate pan heat the remaining butter, add the meat and sliced onion and brown quickly on both sides. Remove the meat to a hot platter, discarding the onion.

4. Add the sour cream to the mustard sauce and heat over a brisk flame for three minutes. Pour sauce over meat and serve.

ROMBAUER
The Joy of Cooking

Beef Wellington or Filet de Boeuf en Croûte

ABOUT 12 SERVINGS

If time is no object and your aim is to out-Jones the Joneses, you can serve this twice-roasted but rare beef encased in puff paste—but don't quote us as devotees.

Double the recipe for:

Puff Paste

which can be prepared the day before and reserved in the refrigerator.

Preheat oven to 425°.

Rub with butter:

a 5-lb. fillet of beef

Roast on a rack 25 minutes or until thermometer reads 120°—very rare. On taking meat from oven, you may flambé with:

(⅓ cup brandy)

Let meat cool to room temperature. You may then thinly coat with:

(Paté de foie gras or de volaille)

Now roll out part of the puff paste into a rectangle bout 1½ inches larger in width and length than the fillet. Spread the rectangle with:

Duxelles

that have been well cooled. Preheat oven again to 425°. Center the fillet on the rolled-out dough. Roll out remaining dough and shape it over the entire fillet. Secure top and bottom pieces together, finger-pinching all around after brushing edges with:

White of egg

Use any excess dough for decorations, which you can stick to the surface with more of the egg white. Brush exposed surfaces with:

French Egg Wash

Place the covered fillet on a greased baking sheet. Bake 10 minutes. Reduce heat to 375° and bake until crust is golden, about 20 minutes more. Allow to stand 15 minutes before serving on a garnished platter. Carve with a very sharp knife into slices about ¾ inch thick. Serve with:

Sauce Périgueux or
Bordelaise Sauce

EDITOR'S NOTE: This recipe first appeared in the 1975 edition of *The Joy of Cooking*.

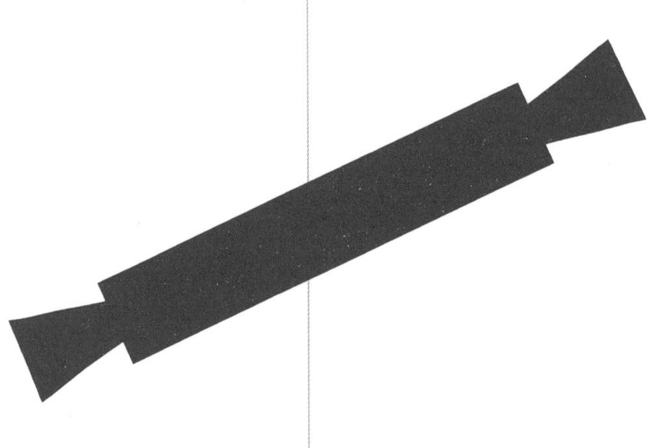

VEAL

HAZAN
The Classic Italian Cook Book

Scaloppine

The perfect scaloppina *is cut across the grain from the top round. It is cut a shade more than ¼ inch thick and flattened to a shade less than ¼ inch. It is a solid slice of meat without any muscle separations. The problem lies in finding a butcher to cut it. I have discussed this with many American butchers, and I know exactly the answer yours will give you. With varying degrees of politeness it will be, "That is not the way we do it." One solution is to allow the butcher to cut a thin slice across the entire leg, which you can then divide into its separate muscles. This, however, will give you scaloppine of uneven texture and, while acceptable, will not be wholly satisfactory. A better alternative is to look for the kind of butcher who is willing to cooperate with you, and give you what you want—at a price. It may be expensive, but it will save you much heartache.*

Once you have found this paragon, make sure not only that he cuts the scaloppine *from a single muscle but also that he cuts them across the grain. If* scaloppine *are cut any other way, the muscle fibers will contract in the cooking, producing a wavy, shrunken, tough slice of meat.*

SCALOPPINE DI VITELLO AL MARSALA
Sautéed Veal Scaloppine with Marsala

FOR 4 PERSONS

- 3 tablespoons vegetable oil
- 1 pound veal *scaloppine*, very thinly sliced and pounded flat
- ⅓ cup all-purpose flour, spread on a dinner plate or waxed paper
- ½ teaspoon salt
- Freshly ground pepper, 5 to 6 twists of the mill
- ½ cup dry Marsala
- 3 tablespoons butter

1. Heat the oil over medium-high heat in a heavy skillet.

2. Dip the veal *scaloppine* in flour, coating them on both sides and shaking off any excess. When the oil is quite hot slip the *scaloppine* into the pan and quickly brown them on both sides, which should take less than a minute for each side if the oil is hot enough. (If you can't get all of them into your skillet at one time, do them a few at a time but dip them in flour only as you are ready to brown them, otherwise the flour will get soggy and the *scaloppine* won't brown properly.) Transfer the browned meat to a warm platter and season with salt and pepper.

3. Tip the skillet and draw off most of the fat with a spoon. Turn the heat on to high, add the Marsala, and boil briskly for less than a minute, scraping up and loosening any cooking residue stuck to the pan. Add the butter and any juices that may have been thrown off by the *scaloppine* in the platter. When the sauce thickens, turn the heat down to low and add the *scaloppine*, turning them and basting them with sauce once or twice. Transfer meat and sauce to a warm platter and serve immediately.

MENU SUGGESTIONS
An elegant first course would be Italian Pancakes Filled with Spinach, Meat-Stuffed Pasta Rolls, or Yellow and Green Noodles with Cream, Ham, and Mushroom Sauce. Risotto with Parmesan Cheese or either vegetable risotto would also be a good choice. The vegetable: Sautéed Green Beans with Butter and Cheese or Sautéed Finocchio with Butter and Cheese.

SCALOPPINE DI VITELLO AL LIMONE
Sautéed Veal Scaloppine with Lemon Sauce

FOR 4 PERSONS

- 2 tablespoons vegetable oil
- ¼ cup butter
- 1 pound veal *scaloppine*, thinly sliced and pounded flat
- ⅓ cup all-purpose flour, spread on a dish or on waxed paper
- Salt and freshly ground pepper to taste
- 2 tablespoons lemon juice
- 2 tablespoons finely chopped parsley
- ½ lemon, thinly sliced

1. Heat the oil and 2 tablespoons of the butter in a skillet, over medium-high heat. (It should be quite hot. Thinly sliced veal must cook quickly or it will become leathery.)

2. Dip both sides of the *scaloppine* in flour and shake off the excess. Slip the *scaloppine*, no more than will fit comfortably in the skillet at one time, into the pan. If the oil is hot enough the meat should sizzle.

3. Cook the *scaloppine* until they are lightly browned on one side, then turn and brown the other side. (If they are very thin they should be completely cooked in about 1 minute.) When done, transfer to a warm platter and season with salt and pepper.

4. Off the heat, add the lemon juice to the skillet, scraping loose the cooking residue. Swirl in the remaining 2 tablespoons of butter. Add the parsley, stirring it into the sauce.

5. Add the *scaloppine*, turning them in the sauce. Turn on the heat to medium very briefly, just long enough to warm up the sauce and *scaloppine* together—but do not overdo it, because the *scaloppine* are already cooked.

6. Transfer the *scaloppine* to a warm platter, pour the sauce over them, garnish with the lemon slices, and serve immediately.

MENU SUGGESTIONS

These exquisite *scaloppine* should be preceded by a first course that has both delicacy and character. It could be spaghetti with Tomato Sauce III, Fettuccine Tossed in Cream and Butter, Tortelloni Filled with Swiss Chard, with either Butter and Cheese or Tomato and Cream Sauce, Risotto with Asparagus, Rice and Peas, or Spinach and Ricotta Gnocchi, with either of the two sauces recommended. Some of the vegetables that can accompany the *scaloppine* are Fried Artichoke Wedges, Gratinéed Jerusalem Artichokes, Sautéed Green Beans with Butter and Cheese, Cauliflower Gratinéed with Butter and Cheese, and Zucchini Fried in Flour and Water Batter.

SCALOPPINE DI VITELLO ALLA PIZZAIOLA

Veal Scaloppine with Tomatoes

FOR 4 PERSONS

- 2½ tablespoons vegetable oil
- 3 cloves garlic, peeled
- 1 pound veal *scaloppine*, very thinly sliced and pounded flat
- ⅓ cup all-purpose flour, spread on a dinner plate or waxed paper
- Salt
- Freshly ground pepper, 4 to 5 twists of the mill
- ⅓ cup white wine
- 3 teaspoons tomato paste diluted in ½ cup warm water
- 1 tablespoon butter
- ½ teaspoon oregano
- 2 tablespoons capers

1. In a heavy-bottomed skillet heat the oil over high heat and sauté the garlic cloves. When they are browned, remove them.

2. Dip both sides of the veal *scaloppine* in the flour, shake off the excess, and sauté very rapidly on both sides in the hot oil. (Do not overcook. It is sufficient to brown them lightly, which should take a minute or less each side. And never dip the *scaloppine* in flour until you are just ready to cook them. If you do it ahead of time the flour becomes damp and they won't brown properly.) Transfer the *scaloppine* to a warm platter and season with salt and pepper.

3. Tip the skillet and draw off most of the fat with a spoon. Turn on the heat to moderately high, add the wine, and scrape up and loosen the cooking residue in the pan. Then add the diluted tomato paste, stir, add the butter, stir, and continue cooking for a few minutes, until the liquids thicken into sauce. Add the oregano and the capers, stirring them into the sauce. Cook for another minute, then add the sautéed *scaloppine*, turning them quickly once or twice in the sauce. Transfer to a warm platter, pouring the sauce over the veal, and serve immediately.

HAZAN

The Classic Italian Cook Book

Ossobuco alla milanese (oss bus)

Braised Veal Shanks, Milan Style

Ossobuco, oss bus *in Milanese dialect, literally means "bone with a hole," or hollow bone. It is made with the shanks of milk-fed veal, very slowly braised in broth with vegetables and herbs, and it turns, when done, into one of the most tender morsels of meat one can eat. A properly cooked* ossobuco *needs no knife; it can be broken up with a fork. The hind shanks are better than the front ones for* ossobuco *because they are meatier and more tender. When the butcher prepares your shanks, have him saw off the two ends, which contain mostly bone and little meat (you can use them in a broth). Have him cut the shanks into pieces no more than 2 inches long, the size at which* ossobuco *cooks best, making sure he doesn't remove the skin enveloping the shanks. It helps to hold the* ossobuco *together and it has a delectable, creamy consistency when cooked.*

FOR 6 PERSONS

- 1 cup finely chopped yellow onion
- ⅔ cup finely chopped carrot
- ⅔ cup finely chopped celery
- ¼ cup butter
- 1 teaspoon finely chopped garlic
- 2 strips lemon peel
- ½ cup vegetable oil
- 2 shanks of veal, sawed into 8 pieces about 2 inches long, each securely tied around the middle
- ⅓ cup all-purpose flour, spread on a plate or on waxed paper
- 1 cup dry white wine
- 1½ cups Homemade Meat Broth or canned beef broth, approximately
- 1½ cups canned Italian tomatoes coarsely chopped, with their juice
- ¼ teaspoon dried thyme
- 4 leaves fresh basil (optional)
- 2 bay leaves
- 2 or 3 sprigs parsley
- Freshly ground pepper, about 6 twists of the mill
- Salt, if necessary

1. Preheat the oven to 350°.

2. Choose a heavy casserole with a tight-fitting lid that is just large enough to contain the veal pieces later in a single layer. (If you do not have a casserole large enough for all the veal, use two small ones, dividing the chopped vegetables and butter in two equal parts, but adding 1 extra tablespoon of butter per casserole.) Put in the onion, carrot, celery, and butter and cook over medium heat for 8 to 10 minutes, until the vegetables soften and wilt. Add the chopped garlic and lemon peel at the end. Remove from the heat.

3. Heat the oil in a skillet over medium-high heat. Turn the trussed pieces of veal in the flour, shaking off any excess. When the oil is quite hot (test it with the corner of one of the pieces of veal: a moderate sizzle means the heat is just right), brown the veal on all sides. (Brown the veal as soon as it has been dipped in flour, otherwise the flour may dampen and the meat won't brown properly.) Stand the pieces of veal side by side on top of the vegetables in the casserole.

4. Tip the skillet and draw off nearly all the fat with a spoon. Add the wine and boil briskly for about 3 minutes, scraping up and loosening any browning residue stuck to the pan. Pour over the pieces of veal in the casserole.

5. In the same skillet, bring the broth to a simmer and pour into the casserole. Add the chopped tomatoes with their juice, the thyme, basil, bay leaves, parsley, pepper, and salt. (Hold off on salt until after cooking if you are using canned beef broth. It is sometimes very salty.) The broth should come up to the top of the veal pieces. If it does not, add more.

6. Bring the contents of the casserole to a simmer on top of the stove. Cover tightly and place in the lower third of the preheated oven. Cook for about 2 hours, carefully turning and basting the veal pieces every 20 minutes. When done, they should be very tender when pricked with a fork, and their sauce should be dense and creamy. (If, while the veal is still cooking, there is not enough liquid in the casserole, you may add up to ⅓ cup of warm water. If the reverse is true, and the sauce is too thin when the veal is done, remove the meat to a warm platter, place the uncovered casserole on top of the stove, and over high heat briskly boil the sauce until it thickens.) Pour the sauce over the veal and serve piping hot.

NOTE: When transferring the veal pieces to the serving platter, carefully remove the trussing strings without breaking up the shanks.

GREMOLADA

The traditional recipe for ossobuco *calls for a garnish of herbs, grated lemon peel, and garlic called* gremolada, *which is added to the veal shanks as they finish cooking. Tradition deserves respect, but art demands sincerity, and cooking is, above all else, an art. In the light of modern taste, I find that the gremolada overloads with unnecessary pungency a beautifully balanced and richly flavored dish. I never serve* ossobuco *with* gremolada. *If you feel, however, that you absolutely must try it for yourself, here are the recommended ingredients:*

- 1 teaspoon grated lemon peel
- ¼ teaspoon very finely chopped garlic
- 1 tablespoon finely chopped parsley

Some old recipes also include sage and rosemary, but that, I think, is going too far. *Gremolada* is sprinkled over the veal shanks just as they finish cooking.

MENU SUGGESTIONS

The natural accompaniment for *ossobuco* is Risotto, Milan Style. It is not served separately, but together with ossobuco. If you would just as soon not have *risotto*, you can precede *ossobuco* with Potato Gnocchi with Gorgonzola Sauce, or with Artichokes, Roman Style. *Ossobuco* can be served without any vegetables on the side, but if you are willing to make the effort, Sautéed Peas with Prosciutto make a very happy accompaniment. Follow *ossobuco* with a fine salad. An excellent one would be Jerusalem Artichoke and Spinach Salad.

MITCHELL
Lüchow's German Cookbook

Breaded Veal Cutlet

Wiener Schnitzel

- 4 6-ounce veal cutlets
- Flour
- 3 tablespoons grated Parmesan cheese
- 1 egg, beaten
- 1 teaspoon minced parsley
- ½ teaspoon salt
- ¼ teaspoon pepper
- ¼ teaspoon grated nutmeg
- ½ cup milk
- 6 tablespoons butter
- Juice ⅓ lemon
- Parsley for garnish

Wipe meat with damp cloth; pound very thin; dip lightly in flour. Mix cheese, 2 tablespoons flour, egg, parsley, salt, pepper, nutmeg, and milk. Beat smooth. Dip floured cutlets in this batter. Cook over low heat in 4 tablespoons butter until golden and tender.

Remove cutlets to warmed serving platter and keep them hot. Heat remaining butter until darkened; add lemon juice. Stir and pour over cutlets. Garnish with parsley. Serves 4.

HAZAN
The Classic Italian Cook Book

Vitello tonnato

Cold Sliced Veal with Tuna Sauce

This is one of the loveliest and most versatile of all cold dishes. It is an ideal second course for a summer menu, a beautiful antipasto for an elegant dinner, a very successful party dish for small or large buffets. It requires quite some time and patience in the preparation, but, since it must be prepared at least 24 hours in advance, you can set your own pace and make it at your convenience.

Vitello tonnato *is common to both Lombardy and Piedmont, and there are many ways of making it. Most recipes call for braising the veal either partly or wholly in white wine. You may try it if you like. I find it gives the dish a tarter flavor than it really needs.*

In this recipe, do not under any circumstances use prepared, commercial mayonnaise.

Veal tends to be dry. To keep it tender and juicy, cook it in just enough water to cover (the method indicated below—put the meat in, add water to just cover, and then remove the meat—is the simplest way to gauge the exact amount); add veal to its cooking liquid only when the liquid is boiling; never *add salt to the liquid; allow the meat to cool in its own broth.*

FOR 6 TO 8 PERSONS

- 2 to 2½ pounds lean, boneless veal roast, preferably top round, firmly tied
- 1 medium carrot
- 1 stalk celery, without leaves
- 1 medium yellow onion
- 4 sprigs parsley
- 1 bay leaf

THE TUNA SAUCE

- Mayonnaise, made with 2 egg yolks, 1¼ cups olive oil, 2 to 3 tablespoons lemon juice, ¼ teaspoon salt
- 1 seven-ounce can Italian tuna in olive oil
- 5 flat anchovy fillets
- 1¼ cups olive oil
- 3 tablespoons lemon juice
- 3 tablespoons tiny capers
- Salt, if necessary

1. In a pot just large enough to contain the veal, put in the veal, the carrot, celery, onion, parsley, bay leaf, and just enough water to cover. *Now remove the veal and set aside.* Bring the water to a boil, add the meat, and when the water comes to a boil again, cover the pot, reduce the heat, and keep at a gentle simmer for 2 hours. (If you are using a larger piece of veal, cook proportionately longer.) Remove the pot from the heat and allow the meat to cool in its broth.

2. Prepare the mayonnaise, remembering that all ingredients for the mayonnaise must be at room temperature.

3. In a blender mix the tuna, anchovies, olive oil, lemon juice, and the capers at high speed for a few seconds until they attain a creamy consistency. Remove the mixture from the blender jar and fold it carefully but thoroughly into the mayonnaise. Taste to see if any salt is required. (None may be necessary, depending upon how salty the anchovies and capers are.)

4. When the meat is quite cold, transfer it to a cutting board, remove the strings, and cut into thin and uniform slices.

5. Smear the bottom of a serving platter with some of the tuna sauce. Arrange the veal slices over this in a single layer, edge to edge. Cover the layer well with sauce. Lay more veal over this and cover again with sauce; set aside enough sauce to cover well the topmost layer. (The more layers you make the better. It prevents the veal from drying.)

6. Refrigerate for 24 hours, covered with plastic wrap. (It keeps beautifully for up to 2 weeks.) Before serving you may garnish it with lemon slices, olive slices, whole capers, and parsley leaves.

MENU SUGGESTIONS

If you are using this as a second course, precede it with Cold Vegetable Soup and Rice, Milan Style, Rice and Peas, or Trenette with Potatoes and Pesto. No vegetable, but follow it with a simple salad, such as Green Bean Salad.

As an introduction to a memorable meal, follow it with Molded Risotto with Parmesan Cheese and Chicken-Liver Sauce, and follow the *risotto* with Pan-Roasted Squab.

BAILEY
Lee Bailey's Country Weekends

Eating at the beach can be comparable to finding yourself at a big buffet supper with a too-small plate overloaded with food in one hand and a napkin, knife and fork, and glass of wine in the other . . . and no place to sit. Only at the beach you have sand, too. Plan carefully and prepare simple, easy-to-eat foods that are neither too perishable nor too fragile. Also, because people are always hungry in sea air, the meal should be generous. Big napkins and premoistened towelettes are a great help. And make it red wine, which needn't be chilled.

This menu is based on the assumption that you have the marinated vegetables already prepared in your refrigerator. I usually do have a combination of some sort on hand for quick lunches and to eat with sandwiches. I would also plan to cook the peppers the day before, so that all I had to deal with on the day of the outing would be the corn bread, which takes only 45 minutes to cook. Although it keeps well for a day or so, it is best on the day it is cooked.

Veal-Stuffed Sweet Red Peppers

This recipe produces a rather dense stuffing. Any leftover cooked stuffing is good sliced thinly (this takes a very sharp knife) for open-face sandwiches. Use a thin, softish rye or whole-wheat bread spread with a bit of butter and mustard. Top with strips of the red pepper and sprinkle with capers.

8 medium sweet red peppers
2 pounds ground veal
3 teaspoons salt
1 teaspoon ground black pepper
2 tablespoons Worcestershire sauce
1½ cups finely chopped onion
2 cups cooked rice
4 tablespoons chopped parsley
1 egg
Freshly grated nutmeg (optional)

Preheat oven to 350 degrees.

Slice tops off stem end of peppers and clean out cavity. Even off bottoms so they will stand on end, being careful not to cut away so much that a hole is made. Add boiling water to just cover, parboil for 4 minutes, then hold in cold water.

Mix all the remaining ingredients except egg and nutmeg. This is best done with the hands. Beat egg lightly and incorporate.

Drain peppers and put a kettle of water on to boil. Dry interiors of the peppers and pack with stuffing, finishing off with a mounded top. Put them in a greased ovenproof dish into which they fit snugly. Sprinkle tops of each generously with salt and pepper (and a touch of nutmeg if you like). Pour boiling water into pan to come halfway up the sides of the peppers. Cover loosely with foil and bake for approximately 45 minutes. Remove foil to finish. Total cooking time is from 1 to 1¼ hours. Remove from pan to a rack to cool. Do not refrigerate.

SERVES 8

LANG
The Cuisine of Hungary

Veal Pörkölt

Borjúpörkölt

4 TO 6 SERVINGS

- 2 pounds young veal, cut from the leg or leaner part of the breast and shoulder
- 2 tablespoons lard (amount depends on fattiness of meat)
- 1 large onion, minced
- 1 heaping tablespoon paprika
- 1 garlic clove, chopped and mashed (optional)
- 1 scant teaspoon salt
- 1 medium-sized very ripe tomato, or 2 drained canned Italian tomatoes
- 1 green pepper, cored and diced

1. Cut the veal into 1-inch dice.

2. Melt the lard in a heavy stewing casserole or Dutch oven and fry onion till it is light brown.

3. Remove from heat and mix in paprika, garlic (if used), salt and veal. Cover, and start cooking over very low heat.

4. The simple but tricky secret of this dish is to let the meat cook in the steam from its own juices and the juices of the onion. Just before the stew starts burning, add a few tablespoons of water; repeat this during the first 10 minutes of cooking whenever liquid evaporates.

5. Meantime, blanch tomato, peel, and dice.

6. When meat is beginning to get soft, in 10 to 15 minutes, add tomato and green pepper. Cook for another 10 to 20 minutes, depending on the age of the veal. Continue to add water bit by bit whenever the moisture evaporates.

7. When meat is done, let the liquid reduce as much as possible without burning it. At that point you should have a rich dark red and gold sauce-gravy, neither too thin nor too heavy, somewhat like a good American beef stew, but the texture must be achieved without any thickening.

8. Serve with Little Dumplings, Baked Egg Barley, or rice.

VARIATIONS

I. Try this dish once without adding any tomato.

II. To make veal *paprikás*, reduce paprika to ½ tablespoon and use a small onion and no garlic. When meat is almost done, let the liquid evaporate so the meat is seared in remaining fat. Mix 1 cup sour cream with 1 tablespoon flour and stir into stew. Cook covered over very, very low heat until the meat is cooked. This dish should have a much milder, gentler taste than *pörkölt*, almost like a feminine version of it.

III. Use any red meat, including game, for *pörkölt* or *paprikás* made according to this recipe.

NOTE: The character of this dish derives from the careful addition of liquid—no more than ½ cup at a time for this amount of meat. Also the meat must be cooked just as the last of the liquid is evaporated so that the meat is "singed" in the last few minutes.

GAME

HAZAN
The Classic Italian Cook Book

Coniglio in padella
Stewed Rabbit with White Wine

Now that factory chicken has completely replaced free-roaming yard-raised chicken, one of the best tasting "fowls" you can eat is rabbit. Rabbit meat is lean and not as flabby as most chicken, and its taste is somewhere in between very good breast of chicken and veal. Frozen young rabbit of excellent quality is now widely available cut up in ready-to-cook pieces. It is so good that there is really little need to bother dismembering whole fresh rabbit. I recommend it without reservation.

In France and Germany rabbit is sometimes subjected to a lengthy preliminary marinade which gives it somewhat the taste of game and partly breaks down its texture. The method given here is very straightforward. Without sautéing, rabbit is stewed in practically nothing but its own juices. It is then simmered in white wine with a little rosemary and a touch of tomato. It is a familiar northern Italian approach, and it succeeds marvelously well in drawing out the delicate flavor of rabbit and in maintaining its fine texture intact.

FOR 6 PERSONS

3 to 3½ pounds frozen cut-up rabbit, thawed overnight in the refrigerator (see note)
½ cup olive oil
¼ cup finely diced celery
1 clove garlic, peeled
⅔ cup dry white wine
1½ teaspoons rosemary
2 teaspoons salt
Freshly ground pepper, 6 to 8 twists of the mill
1 bouillon cube
2 tablespoons tomato paste
¼ teaspoon sugar

1. Rinse the rabbit pieces in cold running water and pat thoroughly dry with paper towels.

2. Choose a deep covered skillet large enough to contain all the rabbit pieces in a single layer. Put in the oil, celery, garlic, and the rabbit, cover, and cook over low heat for 2 hours. Turn the meat once or twice, but do not leave uncovered.

3. After 2 hours, you will find that the rabbit has thrown off a great deal of liquid. Uncover the pan, turn up the heat to medium, and cook until all the liquid has evaporated. Turn the meat from time to time. When the liquid has evaporated, add the wine, rosemary, salt, and pepper. Simmer, uncovered, until the wine has evaporated. Dissolve the bouillon cube, tomato paste, and sugar in ⅔ cup warm water, pour it over the rabbit, and cook gently for another 12 to 15 minutes, turning and basting the rabbit two or three times. Serve immediately or reheat gently before serving.

NOTE: Do not use wild rabbit in this recipe, only rabbit raised for food.

If using fresh rabbit, soak in abundant cold water for 12 hours or more, then rinse in several changes of cold water and thoroughly pat dry. It may be refrigerated while soaking.

The rabbit may be prepared entirely ahead of time. When reheating, add 2 to 3 tablespoons of water and warm up slowly in a covered pan over low heat, turning the meat from time to time.

JUNIOR LEAGUE OF CHARLESTON
Charleston Receipts

Roast 'possum

1 opossum
1 onion, chopped
1 tablespoon fat
¼ teaspoon Worcestershire sauce
1 cup bread crumbs
1 hard-boiled egg
1 teaspoon salt
Water

Rub opossum with salt and pepper. Brown onion in fat. Add opossum liver and cook until tender. Add bread crumbs, Worcestershire sauce, egg, salt and water. Mix thoroughly and stuff opossum. Truss like a fowl. Put in roasting pan with bacon across back and pour 1 quart of water into pan. Roast uncovered in moderate oven (350°) until tender. (About 2½ hours.) Serve with sweet potatoes.

R. O. Dion

SAUSAGES AND OFFAL

MITCHELL

Lüchow's German Cookbook

Pork and Veal Sausage

Bratwurst
½ pound fresh veal
1 pound pork loin
1½ teaspoons salt
1 teaspoon pepper
½ teaspoon grated nutmeg
½ teaspoon mace
Pork casings

Combine all ingredients; put through grinder 3 times. Mix with about ½ cup water; fill pork casings. To serve, prepare:

BROILED BRATWURST: Cover bratwurst with hot water. Bring to a boil and remove from heat immediately. Let stand in the hot water a few minutes until firm. Drain; dip bratwurst in milk. Place in broiler and cook until golden brown under low-to-moderate heat. Serves 4.

AIDELLS

Hot Links and Country Flavors

Smoked Country Sausage

In the South smoked sausage is usually seasoned with the same spices used to make fresh sausage. As always, there are regional variations, but most smoked country sausage contains the basic mix of pork and sage, with red and black pepper for emphasis. Often, smoked sausage is not tied into individual links. Instead, a continuous rope of sausage is coiled around a stick in large, one-foot loops. Customers simply say to the butcher, "I'll take a foot or two of that smoked sausage there," and it is sliced off and wrapped.

2¼ lbs. pork butt
¾ lb. pork back fat
1 tbsp. brown sugar
2 tsp. red pepper flakes
1 tsp. ground sage
1 tsp. dried thyme
1 tbsp. paprika
Pinch ground allspice
1 tbsp. kosher salt
¾ tsp. curing salts (optional)
½ c. water
Medium hog casings

Grind the pork butt through a ⅜-inch plate, the fat through a ¼-inch. Mix together with the sugar and spices. If you are going to cold smoke the sausage for later use, you must add curing salts. Dissolve the optional curing salts in the water and add to the mixture. If you are going to smoke-cook (hot smoke) and eat the sausage directly after making it, you won't need any curing salts. Just add the water to the meat and spices, and knead everything together thoroughly. Stuff into medium hog casings, coiling the sausage as you go. To cold smoke, loop 1-foot lengths of sausage over a smoke stick of ½-inch doweling 3–4 feet long, and air-dry in a cool place in front of a fan overnight until the surface is dry to the touch. Cold smoke for 8–10 hours. You can keep cold-smoked sausage for 10–12 days in the refrigerator or up to 2 months in the freezer. If you are going to smoke-cook the sausage, it will keep fresh for a week in the refrigerator or 2 months in the freezer. Makes 3 pounds.

Hickory is the most common wood for smoking sausage, bacon, and ham in the South, but depending on the area, maple, apple, cherry, oak, or pecan can also be used.

OLNEY

Simple French Food

Rabbit Sausages

Boudins de Lapin

18 TO 20 BOUDINS

In old cookbooks, andouillette, boudin, *and* saucisse *are more or less interchangeable terms, the first two identifying practically any bound and precooked mixture that takes the form of a sausage, is usually but not necessarily stuffed into a sausage casing, and is reheated by grilling (an* andouille *is a large* andouillette *and shares with cornichon the additional and derogatory meaning of "dolt");* Le Cuisinier Méridional *(1855), for instance, gives one recipe for* andouillettes *whose stuffing is a truffled mixture of lambs' sweetbreads, chopped roast chicken, chicken livers, and the roof of beef mouth, bound with a stiff velouté and eggs and another of pounded, cooked white meats, cow's udder, and* panade *with beaten egg whites added.*

Today andouillette *means chitterling sausage and* boudin *most often* boudin noir, *or blood sausage (*boudin blanc *is casing stuffed with a pounded raw white meat—chicken or pork—and* panade quenelle *forcemeat and poached).*

Prepare these sausages in advance (they may be kept refrigerated for several days—or they may be deep frozen) and, before being served, bring them to room temperature, rub them with olive oil, and grill over hot wood coals (or broil) until golden and slightly crisp—about 10 minutes, turning every 2 or 3 minutes. A generously buttered, fine-textured lentil purée accompanies them perfectly—as does a potato purée.

Chopping the different meats separately by hand, to varying degrees of finesse, is a valuable refinement, but, pressed for time, you may put everything together through a meat grinder with satisfactory results.

If you cannot get blood, eliminate it rather than discarding the recipe; if you cannot find sausage casing, fashion the boudins *by hand, rolling them in flour, place them in a large, buttered* plat à sauter *or skillet, pour in boiling water (against the side of the pan so as not to disturb the* quenelles*) to cover generously and poach at the suggestion of a simmer, covered, for 10 minutes; remove to a pastry grill to drain and cool and wrap individually in plastic or aluminum foil for storing. Dip in egg and roll in breadcrumbs, cooking until crisp and golden in half butter and half olive oil (or baste with butter and grill).*

PANADE

1 cup milk
3 ounces stale bread, crusts removed, crumbled

8 ounces finely chopped lean pork tenderloin
1 rabbit, all flesh removed (about 1 pound) from bones and chopped, less finely than the pork, lungs, heart, and liver are chopped
6 ounces fresh pork fatback, chopped or cut into tiny cubes
6 ounces sweet onions, finely chopped, gently stewed in 2 tablespoons butter until soft and yellowed but not browned
The rabbit's blood (beaten with a tablespoon of vinegar and strained) or ⅓ cup pork blood (from pork specialty butcher)
2 ounces shelled, unroasted pistachios, put for a minute or so in boiling water, drained, rubbed vigorously in a towel to remove skins, coarsely chopped
5 eggs
1 teaspoon powdered mixed dried herbs
1 teaspoon (if available) finely chopped flowers and leaves of fresh marjoram
Salt, pepper, cayenne, allspice
About 4 yards of sausage casing (pork specialty butcher)

Boil the milk and the bread together, stirring and, finally, beating with a wooden spoon until the *panade* is stiff and homogeneous. Add to the chopped meats, mixing loosely.

Add the blood to the stewed onions and cook over very gentle heat for about 5 minutes, stirring. Stir into the bread and meat mixture—enough to attenuate the heat, then add all the other ingredients, mixing and squishing with hands. Taste for seasoning (not very pleasant in this condition—spit out).

Soak the intestinal membrane in tepid water acidulated with vinegar until soft and supple. Lacking professional material, it is easier to cut the casing into 2-foot lengths. Use a large plastic funnel to stuff them, gently stretching one end up and around the funnel tube to receive the stuffing and leaving the other end untied until the entire length of casing is stuffed (to avoid trapping air inside). Force the stuffing through the funnel with your fingers and into place in the casing, squeezing or forcing with your hands, and molding each 2-foot length into 4 very loosely packed sausages, no air bubbles remaining inside. Tie the ends with string and twist, tying at intervals to form the sausages.

Slip them into a large pot of hot but not boiling water, bring barely to the boiling point, and poach at the suggestion of a simmer for 10 minutes. Drain, drop them into a basin of cold water until cooled, and then drain on absorbent paper, gently sponging them dry before wrapping to store.

AIDELLS
Hot Links and Country Flavors

Venison Sausage

Venison sausage often suffers from lack of fat, which makes it too dry, and from too many overpowering ingredients, which can mask the rich flavor of the meat. In this recipe we use herbs that complement the flavor of venison, and we allow the meat to marinate and mellow with these herbs overnight. The sausages are delicious grilled and served with a Cumberland Sauce for Game Sausages along with Oven-Roasted Garlic-Rosemary Potatoes. A good hearty red wine from the Côtes du Rhône is the best match.

1½ lbs. venison shoulder
1 lb. pork butt
¾ lb. pork back fat
½ lb. slab bacon, rind removed
1 tsp. minced garlic
1 tsp. minced shallots
2 tsp. minced juniper berries
4 tsp. kosher salt
2 tsp. coarsely ground black pepper
1 tsp. fresh rosemary or ½ tsp. dried
2 tbsp. brandy
3 tbsp. dry red wine
Medium hog casings

Cut the meat, fat, and bacon into 2-inch strips. In a large bowl, mix the meat, fat, and bacon with all the ingredients except casings. Cover and place in the refrigerator to marinate overnight.

The next day, grind the mixture through a ¼-inch plate. Add any juices remaining in the bowl. Knead to blend all the ingredients thoroughly. Stuff into hog casings and tie into 6-inch links. Dry the sausage, uncovered, in the refrigerator overnight before grilling or pan-frying. Will keep for 3 days refrigerated, 2 months frozen.

MAKES 4 POUNDS

To bring out the earthy flavors of these tangy sausages, serve them with other wild ingredients such as wild rice, morels or other wild mushrooms, and steamed wild greens (young dandelions, mâche, fiddleheads).

CASAS
The Foods and Wines of Spain

Chorizo

Spanish Sausage

Prepare several days in advance.

Spanish cuisine would be unthinkable without chorizo, *a sausage heavily spiced with paprika and garlic. It is used as an appetizer—cold, fried, or baked—or as an ingredient in omelet, tripe, soup, meat, and vegetable dishes, to which it imparts a special flavor. There are recipes scattered throughout this book that need* chorizo *in their preparation.*

Chorizo *is cured but eaten uncooked, like salami, or used in cooking like sausage. However, it is not advisable to consume homemade* chorizo *uncooked. If you wish to eat it as a cold cut, the commercially made product must be used.*

MAKES 6–8 SAUSAGE LINKS

¾ pound lean pork loin, cut in ½-inch cubes
¼ pound pork fat or unsalted fatback, cut in ¼-inch cubes
¼ pound pork fat or unsalted fatback, ground
2 teaspoons coarse salt
¼ teaspoon freshly ground pepper
2 tablespoons paprika
¼ teaspoon ground cumin
½ teaspoon ground or crushed coriander seeds
½ teaspoon sugar
3 tablespoons dry red wine
2 cloves garlic, crushed
1 teaspoon crushed dried red chili pepper
½ teaspoon saltpeter
Sausage casings

Mix together the cubed pork and the cubed and ground fat. Add the remaining ingredients except the sausage casings. Cover and refrigerate overnight.

Stuff the sausage casings, twisting and tying every 4 inches. Hang to dry at room temperature for 3 days, then refrigerate, loosely covered with wax paper, and continue to dry several more days before using. They will keep for a few weeks in the refrigerator.

NOTE: Miniature *chorizos*, called *choricitos*, are popular as appetizers, fried. To make them, twist and tie the sausage every 1½ inches (makes about 16–20).

WEAVER
Pennsylvania Dutch Country Cooking

Stuffed Pig's Stomach, Or "Dutch Goose"

Seimawe genannt "Deitscher Gans"

When Pennsylvania Dutch cooks choose to show their mettle, this is the test of accomplishment. The best indication of failure is that, when pierced with a knife, Seimawe *deflates and burps its filling all over the plate. Keep in mind that* Seimawe *is a species of sausage meant to be cut in slices. The secret is in the way it is sewn up so that no leakage occurs during boiling; otherwise, the filling will be runny. A large needle and strong thread are mandatory. The right texture is not difficult to accomplish.*

My recipe is easier and better than most of those I have tasted in Alsace and not nearly as fatty too.

YIELD: 10 TO 12 SERVINGS

- 1 cleaned pig's stomach
- 1½ cups (8 ounces/240 g) diced lean slab bacon
- 3 cups (350 g) chopped onion
- 1½ cups (12 ounces/375 g) ground beef, pork, or venison
- 1½ teaspoons coarsely grated pepper
- ¼ teaspoon ground cayenne
- 1 tablespoon ground marjoram
- ½ teaspoon ground cardamom
- 1 teaspoon dried savory
- 2 teaspoons sea salt
- ½ cup (50 g) rye breadcrumbs or spelt breadcrumbs
- 3 large eggs
- 6 cups (2½ pounds/1.5 kg) diced cooked red potatoes, peeled or unpeeled
- clarified butter

Soak the pig's stomach 2 to 5 hours in salted water, then rinse and drain. Put the slab bacon in a large skillet and fry over medium heat until it begins to brown. Remove the bacon with a slotted spoon and pour out the fat. Do not clean the skillet. Put the skillet back on the stove and add the onion. Fry over medium heat until soft, then add the ground meat. Cook until the meat changes color, then transfer the meat and onion mixture to a deep mixing bowl. Add the reserved bacon, pepper, cayenne, marjoram, cardamom, savory, salt, and breadcrumbs. Beat the eggs until lemon colored, then add to the meat mixture. Fold in the cooked potatoes.

Turn the stomach inside out. Using a needle and thread, sew up the 2 smallest holes in the stomach so that they are absolutely tight and will not leak. Turn the stomach right side out and fill it with the stuffing until it is tightly packed and there is no room for air pockets. Sew up the large opening as tightly as possible, leaving only a small space inside for the expansion of the filling.

Bring 2 gallons (8 liters) of salted water to a hard boil. Reduce the heat and add the stomach. Simmer, uncovered, for 3 hours. At the end of 3 hours, preheat the oven to 375°F (190°C). Remove the stomach from the water and set it in a baking dish, seam side down. Bake for 20 to 25 minutes, basting often with clarified butter only until the surface of the *Seimawe* achieves a deep golden brown color. Serve immediately on a hot platter.

ALLEN
Mrs. Allen's Cook Book

Fried Liver and Bacon

Cover with boiling water slices of liver cut one-half inch thick; let stand five minutes to draw out the blood, drain, wipe and remove the thin outside skin and veins. Sprinkle with salt and pepper, dip in flour and fry in the fat remaining from baked bacon.

Fried Liver with Onions

Prepare the liver for frying as in the preceding recipe. For a pound of liver, peel and slice six onions. Fry them gently until done in bacon fat, remove from the fat and cook the liver in it. Put the liver on a platter, spread the onions over it and dust lightly with salt and pepper.

BÉGUÉ

Mme. Bégué's Recipes of Old New Orleans Creole Cookery

LIVER À LA BÉGUÉ. Secure a fine bit of calf liver, fresh and of good color. Skin well. Have quantity of lard in frying pan, well heated. Slice liver in thick pieces. Place in lard and let cook slowly after seasoning with pepper and salt. Let lard cover liver. Simmer on slow fire and when cooked drain off grease and serve on hot plate.

DE SILVA

In Memory's Kitchen

Leberknödel

Weiche 4–5 Semmel ein. Jetzt zerschneide ½ kg Kalbsleber oder noch besser Gansleber & dünste auf Zwiebel und Fett ab. Jetzt zerwiege die Leber mit dem Hackmesser ganz fein. Gebe sie in die abgetriebenen geweichten Semmeln gebe dazu einen grossen Löffel Gansfett, 5 Dotter, Salz & Pfeffer & Ingwer von den Eiweiss Schnee; man kann auch die Eier ganz geben, gebe dazu etwas Petersilie, 20 Deca Semmelbrösel & 20 Deca Mehl, forme daraus Knödel. Obenauf Zwiebel in Fett, Semmelbrösel bestreuen. Dazu Rotkraut oder Kohlrabi Kraut. Nicht zerschneiden, im Ganzen servieren.

Liver Dumplings

Soak 4–5 rolls. Now cut ½ kilogram calves liver, or, even better, goose liver and stew on onion and fat. Now mince the liver with a chopping knife. Add to the softened mashed rolls. Add 1 large spoon goose fat, 5 egg yolks, salt & pepper & ginger and from [stiffly beaten] egg whites snow. One can also add whole eggs. Add a little parsley, 20 decagrams breadcrumbs & 20 decagrams flour. Form into dumplings. [The boiling of the dumplings is omitted.] Top with onion [sautéed] in fat [and] sprinkle breadcrumbs. Accompany with red cabbage or kohlrabi cabbage. Do not cut [dumplings], serve them whole.

DAVID

French Provincial Cooking

Terrine de Campagne

Pork and Liver Pâté

This is the sort of pâté you get in French restaurants under the alternative names of pâté maison *or* terrine du chef.

The ingredients are 1 lb. each of fat pork (belly) and lean veal, ½ lb. of pig's liver, an after-dinner coffee-cup of dry white wine, 2 tablespoons of brandy, a clove of garlic, half a dozen each of black peppercorns and juniper berries, a teaspoon of ground mace, 4 oz. of fat bacon or, better still, if your butcher will provide it, of either flare fat, or back fat, which is the pork fat often used for wrapping round birds for roasting.

An obliging butcher will usually mince for you the pork, veal and liver, provided he is given due notice. It saves a great deal of time, and I always believe in making my dealers work for me if they will.

To the minced meats, all thoroughly blended, add 2 oz. of the fat bacon or pork fat cut in thin, irregular little dice, the seasonings chopped and blended (half a dessertspoon of salt will be sufficient), and the wine and brandy. Mix very thoroughly and, if there is time, leave to stand for an hour or two before cooking, so that the flavours penetrate the meat. Turn into one large 2-pint capacity terrine, or into 2 or 3 smaller ones, about 2 to 2½ inches deep. Cut the remaining fat or bacon into thin strips and arrange it across the top of the pâté. Place the terrines in a baking tin filled with water and cook, uncovered, in a slow oven, Gas No. 2, 310 deg. F. for 1¼ to 1½ hours. The pâtés are cooked when they begin to come away from the sides of the dish.

Take them from the oven, being careful not to spill any of the fat, and leave them to cool. They will cut better if, when the fat has all but set, they are weighted. To do this, cover with greaseproof paper and a board or plate which fits inside the terrine and put a weight on top. However, if this proves impractical, it is not of very great importance. If the terrines are to be kept longer than a week, cover them completely, once they are cold, with just melted pure pork lard.

When cooking the pâtés remember that it is the *depth* of the terrine rather than its surface area which determines the cooking time. The seasonings of garlic and juniper berries are optional.

Serve these pâtés as a first course, with toast or French bread. Some people like butter as well, although they are quite rich enough without.

Lastly, the proportions of meat, liver and seasonings making up the pâtés can be altered to suit individual tastes, but always with due regard to the finished texture of the product. A good pâté is moist and fat without being greasy, and it should be faintly pink inside, not grey or brown. A dry pâté is either the result of overcooking, or of too small a proportion of fat meat having been used. And ideally all the meat for pâtés should be cut up by hand rather than put through the mincing machine, which squeezes and dries the meat. But this is a counsel of perfection which few people nowadays would care to follow.

ALTERNATIVE PROPORTIONS FOR THOSE WHO LIKE MORE LIVER AND LESS MEAT: 1 lb. 2 oz. pig's liver, 1¼ lb. belly of pork, ½ lb. lean veal, a coffee-cup of dry white wine, 2 tablespoons brandy, 2 cloves garlic, 6 to 8 juniper berries (optional), 1 dessertspoon salt, 4 black peppercorns, mace, 4 oz. of back pork fat or 4 rashers of fat bacon.

The procedure is exactly as in the first recipe.

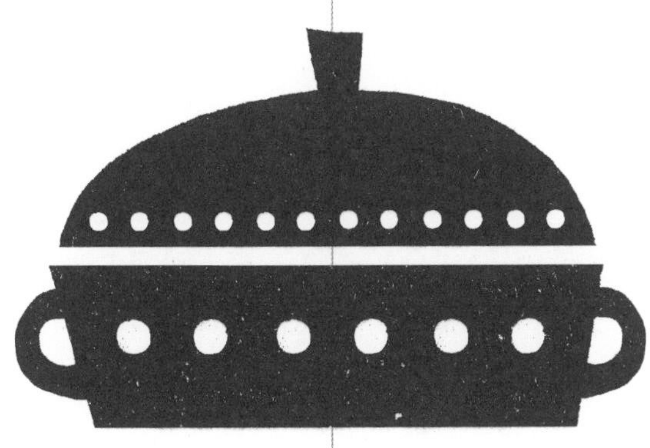

BEARD
The Fireside Cook Book

Tongue Rolls

1 teaspoon chopped onion
2 teaspoons horseradish
½ teaspoon dry mustard
1 package cream cheese
Salt
Parsley, chopped
12 thin cold tongue slices

Blend onion, horseradish, and mustard with cheese and salt to taste (about ½ teaspoon). Trim edges of tongue slices and spread slices with cream cheese mixture. Roll very tightly, being careful not to break the meat slices. Secure with toothpick and dip ends into finely chopped parsley.

Baked Goods and Desserts

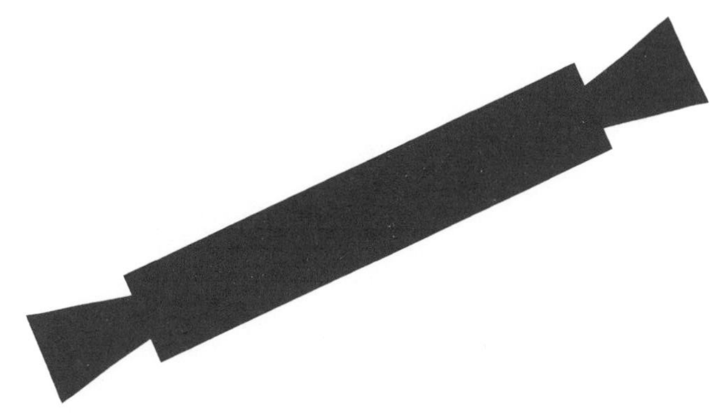

BREADS

LEWIS

The Taste of Country Cooking

Parker House Rolls

The cooks of Freetown loved making yeast bread. Rolls were particularly good for sopping up sauces or gravies from the braised rabbits, quail, and guinea fowl we ate in the fall. We made rolls in a variety of shapes, and the Parker House rolls always reminded me of a folded envelope as we flipped the dough over.

MAKES 1½ TO 2 DOZEN

- 1 cake (½ ounce) yeast or 1 package dry active yeast
- ¼ cup lukewarm water
- 1 tablespoon plus 1 teaspoon sugar
- 2 tablespoons butter plus extra for dough
- 2 tablespoons lard
- 1 teaspoon salt
- 2 cups milk
- 4 cups sifted flour

Dissolve the yeast in ¼ cup lukewarm water with 1 teaspoon sugar. Place the remaining sugar, 2 tablespoons butter, lard, and salt in a bowl. Heat the milk to a scald and pour into the bowl containing the butter mixture. Stir until all is dissolved. When lukewarm, add flour and stir well. When halfway mixed add in the dissolved yeast. Mix well, knead the dough for about 5 minutes, place in a draft-free place of approximately 80°, cover with a towel, and set to rise until it is double in bulk. Push the dough down gently and spoon onto a flour-dusted surface and roll out a little less than ½ an inch thick. Cut with a round biscuit cutter. Butter the surface of each circle of dough. Fold in half and as they are finished and place side by side almost touching in a baking pan. This should be done very quickly; the yeast dough will be rising all the while. Preheat the oven to 425°. When rolls have risen to almost double their size and are light to the touch, set them into the oven, turn oven down to 375°, and bake for 20 minutes.

CROCKER

Betty Crocker's Picture Cook Book

Sweet Dough Yeast Breads for Delectable Rolls and Coffee Cakes

SWEET DOUGHS (🔑 RECIPES)
MAKE EITHER TYPE AS DESIRED.

Mix together

SWEET DOUGH	RICHER SWEET DOUGH
2 cups lukewarm milk	1 cup
½ cup sugar	½ cup
2 tsp. salt	1 tsp.

For excellent eating and keeping quality, keep doughs as soft as possible, almost sticky . . . just so you're able to handle.

Crumble into mixture

*2 cakes compressed yeast	*2 cakes

Stir until yeast is dissolved.

Stir in

2 eggs	2 eggs
½ cup soft shortening	½ cup
7 to 7½ cups sifted GOLD MEDAL Flour	4½ to 5 cups

Add flour in 2 additions, using the amount necessary to make it easy to handle. Handle and knead the dough.

AMOUNT:

4 DOZ. PLAIN ROLLS	3 DOZ. ROLLS
or	*or*
1 LARGE PAN ROLLS	1 LARGE PAN
or	*or*
1 COFFEE CAKE 2 DOZ. PLAIN ROLLS	1 COFFEE CAKE 1 DOZ. ROLLS

*For dry yeast, see recipe below.

AFTER SECOND RISING, divide dough for desired rolls and coffee cake. Round up, cover, and let rest 15 min. so dough is easy to handle.

Shape doughs, let rise until light (15 to 30 min.) and bake according to directions for each type of roll or coffee cake.

PLAINER SWEET DOUGH

For plain biscuits or rolls.

Follow 🔑 recipe for Sweet Dough—*except* use only ¼ cup shortening, only 1 egg.

DOUGHS WITH DRY YEAST

Follow either 🔑 recipe above—*except* omit ½ cup of milk. In place of compressed yeast, soak 2 pkg. dry granular yeast in ½ cup lukewarm water for 5 min. without stirring. Stir well before adding.

ROLLS OF ALL SHAPES

Follow either of 🔑 recipes above. Shape dough as desired. Let rise until light (15 to 20 min.). Bake on lightly greased pan. Serve piping hot.

TEMPERATURE: 425° (hot oven).
TIME: Bake 12 to 20 min. (depending on size).

DINNER ROLLS

Roll dough into cylindrical shapes with tapered ends and place on pan.

PARKERHOUSE ROLLS

Roll dough ¼" thick. Cut with biscuit cutter. Brush with melted butter. Make crease across each. Fold so top half slightly overlaps. Press edges together at crease. Place close together on pan.

OLD-FASHIONED BISCUITS

Form dough into ⅓ size desired. Place close together in a greased round pan.

CLOVERLEAF ROLLS

Form bits of dough into balls about 1" in diameter. Place 3 balls in each greased muffin cup. Brush with butter for flavor.

TO USE EGG YOLKS IN THESE DOUGHS: use 2 yolks plus 1 tbsp. water in place of 1 whole egg.

For all twisted shapes, roll dough a little less than ½" thick into a long oblong 12" wide. Spread with soft butter. Fold ½ of dough over the other half. Trim edges to square the corners. Cut into strips ½" wide and 6" long.

FIGURE 8'S

Hold one end of strip in one hand and twist the other end . . . stretching it slightly until the two ends when brought together on greased baking sheet will form a figure 8.

TWISTS

Same as Figure 8's, but give strip additional twist before placing it on baking sheet.

SNAILS

Twist and hold one end of the strip down on baking sheet. Wind strip around and around. Tuck end underneath.

CLOTHESPIN CRULLERS

Wrap strip around greased clothespin so edges barely touch. When baked, twist clothespin and pull out. May be filled with one of Fruit Fillings.

KNOTS

Twist and tie each strip into a knot. Press ends down on greased baking sheet.

TOAD-IN-HOLE (TURK'S CAP)

Twist and tie each strip with a knot in one end of strip. Then pull the longer end through center of knot.

BUTTERFLY ROLLS

Roll dough only ⅛" thick into an oblong 6" wide. Spread with soft butter, and roll up like jelly roll. Cut into 2" pieces. Make a deep impression with narrow wooden handle in middle of each roll (to resemble butterfly).

CRESCENTS (BUTTERHORNS)

Roll dough scarcely ¼" thick into a 12" circle. Spread with soft butter. Cut into 16 pie-shaped pieces. Beginning at rounded edge, roll up. Place on pan, point underneath.

BUTTER FLUFFS (FAN TANS)

Roll dough ⅛" thick into a long oblong 9" wide. Spread with soft butter. Cut into 6 long strips 1 ½" wide. Stack 6 strips evenly, one on top of other. Cut into 1" pieces. Place cut-side-down in greased muffin cups.

SALT STICKS

Roll dough very thin into oblong 8" wide. Cut into 4" squares. Starting at a corner, roll each square diagonally to opposite corner. Round the ends. Brush with egg yolk and sprinkle with coarse salt.

PICNIC BUNS

Use ½ of Plainer Sweet Dough. Divide into 2 parts. Roll each into 7½" sq. (½" thick). Cut into 2½" squares. Place on greased baking sheet. Cover with damp cloth, let rise until double (30 to 45 min.). Bake.

TEMPERATURE: 400° (mod. hot oven).
TIME: Bake 12 to 15 min.

AMOUNT: 1½ DOZ. BUNS

CLAYTON
The Complete Book of Breads

Cottage Bread

TWO CASSEROLE LOAVES

Cottage Bread is moist and flaky. It has, however, a somewhat coarser texture than other white loaves. Baked in a casserole, it is easy to prepare and can go in the oven in about an hour. When it comes out of the oven an hour later, brush with melted butter, sprinkle with salt and serve. It is a surprisingly tasty loaf for such little work.

INGREDIENTS

2¾ cups warm water (105–115°)
2 packages dry yeast
3 tablespoons sugar
1 tablespoon salt
2 tablespoons vegetable shortening
6½ cups all-purpose flour
Vegetable oil
Melted butter, salt

BAKING PANS

Two 1½ quart casseroles, greased or Teflon. If glass, reduce oven heat 25°.

PREPARATION
10 mins.
Place the warm water in a mixing bowl and sprinkle with yeast. Stir briskly to dissolve. Blend in sugar, salt, shortening, and 3 cups of flour. Beat with an electric mixer for 2 minutes at medium speed, or for an equal time with a wooden spoon.

Gradually add remaining flour, a half-cup at a time, and beat until smooth and somewhat stiff.

FIRST RISING
40 mins.
Cover the bowl with plastic wrap and put in a warm place (80°–85°) until the batter has doubled in volume, about 40 minutes.

FORMING
5 mins.
Stir down the batter and beat for 30 seconds with a wooden spoon. Turn half the batter into one casserole and the balance into the other. With moist fingers, pat the tops smooth.

SECOND RISING
30 mins.
Cover casseroles with wax paper and return them to the warm place until the dough is level with the edge of the casserole, about 30 minutes. In the meantime, heat the oven to 375°.

BAKING
375°
40–50 mins.
Brush the loaves with oil and place them in the moderately hot oven until they are light brown and test done when a metal testing pin or skewer inserted in the center of the loaf comes out clean and dry, about 40 to 50 minutes. (If moist particles cling to the probe, return loaves to the oven for an additional 10 minutes.)

FINAL STEP
Remove the loaves from the casseroles and place on wire rack to cool. Brush tops with melted butter and sprinkle with a little salt.

CLAYTON
The Complete Book of Breads

Sprouted Wheat Bread

TWO BIG LOAVES

A little gardening effort is called for to first produce a cup of whole wheat sprouts in a period of 3 or 4 days. When a sprout has grown the length of the seed, proceed with the bread baking. The liquid called for in the recipe is the water drained from the sprouting wheat.

It is a delicious deep-crusted loaf that has the rich wheaty flavor to be found only in an all-wheat loaf.

INGREDIENTS

¼ cup wheat seeds or berries
2 cups warm water (80°–90°)
2 packages dry yeast
2 cups liquid from wheat soaking, warm (100°)
¼ cup *each* brewer's yeast and honey
3 tablespoons oil
5 cups whole wheat flour, approximately
1 tablespoon salt

BAKING PANS

Two large loaf pans (9 × 5), greased or Teflon, glass or metal. If glass, reduce oven heat 25°.

SPROUTING

3–4 days

Three or four days beforehand, place ¼ cup of whole wheat seeds or berries in a quart jar. Cover mouth with cheesecloth and fasten securely with a rubber band or string. Don't remove during the growing period—about 3 or 4 days. Soak in water. Turn the jar on its side. Keep the berries moist, warm and dark in a kitchen closet. Twice a day, rinse the berries in tepid water (80°–85°) poured through the cheesecloth; drain and reserve the water for a total of 2 cups needed in the recipe.

When the sprouts are as long as the seed, continue with the bread making.

(The first time I made this bread I inadvertently used beef stock as the liquid ingredient rather than the water saved from soaking the wheat berries. The result was an exceptional loaf of bread. I heartily recommend it.)

15 mins.

On bake day, sprinkle the yeast over ½ cup of the reserved stock poured into a large mixing bowl. Stir briskly with a fork or whisk. Put aside for 3 or 4 minutes until the yeast begins to work and bubble. Stir in the balance of the stock, brewer's yeast, honey and oil. Blend well. Measure in 3 cups of whole wheat flour and the salt. Beat vigorously for 3 minutes until the batter is smooth.

FIRST RISING

1 hour

Cover with plastic wrap and put in a warm place (80°–85°) to rise.

KNEADING

8 mins.

Stir down. Add the sprouts and about 1 cup of whole wheat flour. Turn onto the work surface and surround the dough with about 1 cup of whole wheat flour. As you work the dough, brush a bit of the flour onto the ball of dough and over the hands to help control the stickiness. Use the side of a spatula or a wide putty knife to scrape the film off the work surface as it accumulates. Use the spatula or putty knife to turn over the dough as you knead, thus lessening the opportunity it has to stick to the hands. Soon, however, it will become elastic and smooth, and not stick.

SECOND RISING

50 mins.

Return the dough to the bowl, pat with greased fingers and cover the bowl tightly with plastic wrap. Put in the warm place until the dough has doubled in size.

SHAPING

12 mins.

Punch down the dough and knead for 30 seconds to press out the bubbles. Divide the dough evenly into two pieces. Shape into balls and let rest on the counter top for 3 or 4 minutes. Form the loaf by pressing each ball of dough into a flat oval, roughly the length of the baking pan. Fold the oval in half, pinch the seam tightly to seal, tuck under the ends, and place in the pan, seam down. Repeat with the second loaf.

THIRD RISING

45 mins.

Place the pans in the warm place, cover with wax paper and leave until the center of the dough has risen slightly above the level of the edge of the pan.

BAKING

375°
25 mins.
300°
35 mins.

Preheat oven to 375°. Bake in the moderately hot oven for 25 minutes, reduce heat to 300° and continue baking for an additional 35 minutes. When the loaves are golden brown and tapping the bottom crust yields a hard and hollow sound, the bread is done. If not, return to the oven for an additional 10 minutes. Midway in the bake period and again near the end of it, shift the pans so the loaves are exposed equally to temperature variations in the oven.

FINAL STEP

Remove bread from the oven, turn loaves from pans and place on a metal rack to cool before serving. This bread makes delicious toast. The loaf freezes well, and will keep thus for several months.

FARMER
The Boston Cooking-School Cook Book

Boston Brown Bread

1 cup rye-meal
1 cup granulated corn-meal
1 cup Graham flour
¾ tablespoon soda
1 teaspoon salt
¾ cup molasses
2 cups sour milk, or 1¾ cups sweet milk or water

Mix and sift dry ingredients, add molasses and milk, stir until well mixed, turn into a well-buttered mould, and steam three and one-half hours. The cover should be buttered before being placed on mould, and then tied down with string; otherwise the bread in rising might force off cover. Mould should never be filled more than two-thirds full. A melon-mould or one-pound baking powder boxes make the most attractive-shaped loaves, but a five-pound lard pail answers the purpose. For steaming place mould on a trivet in kettle containing boiling water, allowing water to come half-way up around mould, cover closely, and steam, adding, as needed, more boiling water.

CLAYTON
The Complete Book of Breads

Old Milwaukee Rye Bread

TWO TO FOUR LOAVES

This is a two or three day affair that produces a fine rye loaf. It can be made into 2 large round loaves—good for husky family sandwiches—or 3 or 4 long, slender loaves, best for the buffet.

Under the taut plastic wrap covering the bowl, the sponge will rise and fall as it bubbles to its maximum goodness in approximately 3 days, give or take a few hours. After a day or so, a whiff of the fermented sponge will make manifest the historic connection between the baker and the brewer.

I have made several hundred loaves of this wonderful bread, probably more than any other, and each time I have a warm thought for Bernadine Landsberg of Milwaukee, who sent me the recipe a long time ago.

INGREDIENTS

The sponge: 1 package dry yeast
1½ cups warm water (105°–115°)
2 cups medium rye flour
1 tablespoon caraway seed

All of the sponge
1 package dry yeast
1 cup warm water (105°–115°)
¼ cup molasses
1 tablespoon caraway seed
1 egg, room temperature
1 tablespoon salt
1 cup rye flour
5 to 5½ cups all-purpose flour, approximately
3 tablespoons vegetable shortening

Glaze: 1 egg
1 tablespoon milk
1 tablespoon caraway seed

Baking sheet, greased or Teflon.

PREPARATION

1–3 days

Set the sponge in a large bowl by dissolving yeast in the water. Stir in rye flour. Add caraway seeds. Cover the bowl snugly with plastic wrap so that the sour loses none of its moisture which condenses on the plastic and drops back into the mixture. The dark brown paste will rise and fall as it develops flavor and a delicious aroma. The sponge, which will resemble a wet mash that's too thick to pour and too thin to knead, may be used anytime after 6 hours although the longer the better—up to three days when it will have ceased fermenting.

20 mins.

On bake day, uncover the sponge bowl, sprinkle on the new yeast and add water. Blend well with 25 strokes of a wooden spoon. Add molasses, caraway, egg, salt, rye flour, and about 2 cups of the white flour. Beat till smooth—about 100 strokes. Add shortening. Stir in the balance of the flour, a half cup at a time, first with the spoon and then by hand. The dough should clean the sides of the bowl but it will be sticky due to the rye flour.

KNEADING

5 mins.

Turn the dough out on a floured surface—counter top or bread board. Knead until the dough is smooth. It may help to grease fingers to keep the dough from sticking.

FIRST RISING
1 hour 10 mins.
Return the dough to the large bowl, pat the surface well with butter or shortening and place plastic wrap tightly over the top of the bowl. Put in a warm place (80°–85°) for about 1 hour, or until the dough has doubled in bulk. Punch down and let rise 10 additional minutes.

SHAPING
20 mins.
Divide the dough with a sharp knife. For two round loaves, mold each into a smooth ball and place on the baking sheet. For the long slender loaves, roll out a long rectangle of dough with a rolling pin. Starting at one long edge, roll tightly and pinch together firmly at the seam. Place these side by side on a baking sheet.

SECOND RISING
40 mins.
Cover the loaves with wax paper supported on glass tumblers so that paper will not touch the dough. Return to the warm place until loaves have doubled in bulk.

BAKING
375°
40 mins.
Preheat oven to 375°. With a sharp razor carefully slash 3 or 4 diagonal cuts on the top of each loaf. Brush the tops with water (for an unglazed crust) or a whole egg mixed with 1 tablespoon of milk for a shiny crust. Sprinkle the moist glaze with caraway seeds.

Bake the loaves in the oven. When tapping the bottom crust yields a hard and hollow sound, they are done. If the loaves appear to be browning too quickly, cover with a piece of foil or brown sack paper.

FINAL STEP
Remove from the oven and allow to cool on metal racks. This bread keeps for at least a week or more and freezes well.

ESPE BROWN
The Tassajara Bread Book

Tassajara Yeasted Bread

The fundamental Tassajara Yeasted Bread recipe

FOUR LOAVES

I. 6 c lukewarm water (85–105°)
2 T yeast (2 packages)
½–¾ c sweetening (honey, molasses, brown sugar)
2 c dry milk (optional)
7–9 c whole wheat flour (substitute 2 or more cups unbleached white flour if desired)

II. 2½ T salt
½–1 c oil (or butter, margarine, etc.)
6–8 c additional whole wheat flour
2–3 c whole wheat flour (for kneading)

Dissolve yeast in water.

Stir in sweetening and dry milk.

Stir in whole wheat flour until thick batter is formed.

Beat well with spoon (100 strokes).

Let rise 60 minutes.

Fold in salt and oil.

Fold in additional flour until dough comes away from sides of bowl.

Knead on floured board, using more flour as needed to keep dough from sticking to board, about 10–15 minutes until dough is smooth.

Let rise 50 minutes.

Punch down.

Let rise 40 minutes.

Shape into loaves.

Let rise 20 minutes.

Bake in 350° oven for one hour.

Remove from pans and let cool, or eat right away.

TIME-LIFE BOOKS
The Cooking of the British Isles

Irish Soda Bread

TO MAKE ONE 8-INCH ROUND LOAF

1 tablespoon butter, softened
4 cups all-purpose flour
1 teaspoon baking soda
1 teaspoon salt
1 to 1½ cups buttermilk

Preheat the oven to 425°. With a pastry brush coat a baking sheet evenly with the tablespoon of softened butter.

Sift the flour, soda and salt together into a deep mixing bowl, Gradually add 1 cup of the buttermilk, beating constantly with a large spoon until the dough is firm enough to be gathered into a ball. If the dough crumbles, beat up to ½ cup more buttermilk into it by the tablespoon until the particles adhere.

Place the dough on a lightly floured board, and pat and shape it into a flat circular loaf about 8 inches in diameter and 1½ inches thick. Set the loaf on the baking sheet. Then with the tip of a small knife, cut a ½-inch-deep × into the dough, dividing the top of the loaf into quarters.

Bake the bread in the middle of the oven for about 45 minutes, or until the top is golden brown. Serve at once.

TRUAX
Ladies' Home Journal Cookbook

Apricot Nut Bread

1½ cups dried apricots
¾ cup sugar
5 teaspoons baking powder
½ teaspoon salt
½ teaspoon baking soda
2¾ cups flour
1 egg
1 cup buttermilk
1 tablespoon melted shortening or salad oil
1 cup chopped walnuts

Wash and drain the apricots and cut into thin strips. Sift the sugar, baking powder, salt and baking soda with the flour. (Save out 1 tablespoon of flour to dredge apricots.) Mix the well-beaten egg with buttermilk and add to dry ingredients with melted shortening or oil, stirring only until mixed. Fold in the nuts and apricots which have been dredged with the 1 tablespoon of flour. Pour into greased 9 × 5 × 2¾ inch loaf pan. Bake in moderate oven, 350°, for about an hour. Turn out and cool on rack. Wrap in aluminum foil. This bread slices better the second day. Yield: 1 loaf.

BITTMAN
How to Cook Everything

Banana Bread

MAKES 1 LOAF
TIME: ABOUT 1 HOUR

I love all banana bread (especially toasted, the next day, with peanut butter), but I have been making them for thirty years and I do think this one is the ultimate—the coconut is what does it, although the butter helps too.

8 tablespoons (1 stick) butter, plus some for greasing the pan
1½ cups (about 7 ounces) all-purpose flour
½ cup whole wheat flour
1 teaspoon salt
1½ teaspoons baking powder
¾ cup sugar
2 eggs
3 very ripe bananas, mashed with a fork until smooth
1 teaspoon vanilla extract
½ cup chopped walnuts or pecans
½ cup grated dried unsweetened coconut

1. Preheat the oven to 350°F. Grease a 9 × 5-inch loaf pan.

2. Mix together the dry ingredients. Cream the butter and beat in the eggs and bananas. Stir this mixture into the dry ingredients; do not mix more than necessary. Gently stir in the vanilla, nuts, and coconut.

3. Pour the batter into the loaf pan and bake for 45 to 60 minutes, until nicely browned. A toothpick inserted into the center of the bread will come out fairly clean when it is done, but because of the

bananas this bread will remain moister than most. Do not overcook. Cool on a rack for 15 minutes before removing from the pan. To store, wrap in waxed paper.

MANDEL
Abby Mandel's Cuisinart Classroom

Banana Bread

Make several loaves in sequence by processing all the dry ingredients and nuts for each recipe first. You won't have to wash the work bowl between batches of batter for each loaf.

- 2 cups unbleached all-purpose flour (10 ounces, 285g)
- 1 teaspoon baking soda
- 1 teaspoon double-acting baking powder
- ½ teaspoon salt
- ½ cup walnut pieces (2 ounces, 55g)
- 2 large ripe bananas (13 ounces total, 370g), peeled and cut into 1-inch (2.5 cm) pieces
- 1 cup sugar (7 ounces, 200g)
- 3 large eggs
- 1 stick unsalted butter (4 ounces, 115g), at room temperature and quartered
- ½ cup (12 cl) buttermilk
- 2 teaspoons vanilla extract

Preheat the oven to 350° F. (175° C.) and adjust the rack to the middle level.

METAL BLADE: Put the flour, baking soda, salt and nuts in the work bowl and process for 10 seconds, or until the nuts are coarsely chopped. Remove the mixture and reserve it. Process the bananas for 1 minute, or until they are puréed. Add the sugar and eggs and process the mixture for 1 minute. Add the butter and process for 1 minute. With the machine running, pour the buttermilk and vanilla through the feed tube. Blend in the reserved nut mixture by turning the machine on and off 3 to 5 times, or until the flour just disappears. Do not overprocess the batter.

Pour the batter into a buttered and floured 7-inch (18 cm) loaf pan and bake for 1 hour, or until the bread is brown and a cake tester inserted in the center comes out clean. Turn the bread out on a wire rack and let it cool.

MAKES 1 LOAF

TIME-LIFE BOOKS
The Cooking of Italy

Pizza

All of these ingredients can be used in various combinations to garnish a pizza: chopped beef, peperoni (sausage), prosciutto (dry cured ham), mushrooms and salami, capers, green peppers, garlic, shrimp and anchovies.

TO MAKE 4 TEN-INCH PIZZAS

- 2 packages or cakes of dry or compressed yeast
- Pinch of sugar
- 1¼ cups lukewarm water
- 3½ cups all-purpose or granulated flour
- 1 teaspoon salt
- ¾ cup olive oil
- Corn meal
- 2 cups pizza sauce
- 1 pound mozzarella cheese, coarsely grated or cut in ¼-inch dice
- ½ cup freshly grated imported Parmesan cheese

Sprinkle the yeast and a pinch of sugar into ¼ cup of lukewarm water. Be sure that the water is lukewarm (110° to 115°—neither hot nor cool to the touch). Let it stand for 2 or 3 minutes, then stir the yeast and sugar into the water until completely dissolved. Set the cup in a warm place (a turned-off oven would be best) for 3 to 5 minutes, or until the yeast bubbles up and the mixture almost doubles in volume. If the yeast does not bubble, start over again with fresh yeast,

Into a large mixing bowl, sift the all-purpose flour and salt, or pour in the granulated flour and salt. Make a well in the center of the flour and pour into it the yeast mixture, 1 cup of lukewarm water and ¼ cup of the olive oil. Mix the dough with a fork or your fingers. When you can gather it into a rough ball, place the dough on a floured board and knead it for about 15 minutes, or until it is smooth, shiny and elastic. (If you have an electric mixer with a paddle and dough hook, all the ingredients can be placed in a bowl and, at medium speed, mixed with the paddle until they are combined. Then at high speed knead them with the dough hook for 6 to 8 minutes.) Dust the dough lightly with flour, place it in a large clean bowl and cover with a plate or pot lid. Set the bowl in a warm draft-free spot (again, an oven with the heat turned off is ideal) for about 1½ hours, or until the dough has doubled in bulk.

Now preheat the oven to 500°. Punch the dough down with your fists and break off about one fourth of it to make the first of the 4 pizzas. Knead the small piece on a floured board or pastry cloth for a minute or so, working in a little flour if the dough seems sticky. With the palm of your hand, flatten the ball into a circle about 1 inch thick. Hold the circle in your hands and stretch the dough by turning the circle and pulling your hands apart gently at the same time. When the circle is about 7 or 8 inches across, spread it out on the floured board again and pat it smooth, pressing together any tears in the dough. Then roll the dough with a rolling pin, from the center to the far edge, turning it clockwise after each roll, until you have a circle of pastry about 10 inches across and about ⅛ inch thick. With your thumbs, crimp or flute the edge of the circle until it forms a little rim. Dust a large baking sheet lightly with corn meal and gently place the pizza dough on top of it. Knead, stretch and roll the rest of the dough into 3 more pizzas. Pour 1½ cup of the tomato sauce on each pie and swirl it around with a pastry brush or the back of a spoon. To make a cheese pizza, sprinkle the sauce with ½ cup of grated *mozzarella* and 2 tablespoons of grated Parmesan cheese. Dribble 2 tablespoons of the olive oil over the pizza and bake it on the lowest shelf or the floor of the oven for about 10 minutes, or until the crust is lightly browned and the filling bubbling hot.

ALTERNATIVE GARNISHES: You may top the pizza with almost any sort of seafood, meat or vegetable you like, using or omitting the *mozzarella* or Parmesan. Swirl the pie with ½ cup of tomato sauce first, as for a cheese pizza. Then top with such garnishes as shrimp, anchovies, sausage or *peperoni* slices, prosciutto slivers, tiny meatballs, garlic slices, strips of green pepper, capers, whole or sliced mushrooms. They may be used alone or on suitable combinations. Dribble 2 tablespoons of olive oil over the pizza after garnishing and before baking it.

SALSA PIZZAIOLA

Pizza Sauce

TO MAKE ABOUT 3 CUPS

3 tablespoons olive oil
1 cup finely chopped onions
1 tablespoon finely chopped garlic
4 cups Italian plum or whole-pack tomatoes, coarsely chopped but not drained
1 six-ounce can tomato paste
1 tablespoon dried oregano, crumbled
1 tablespoon finely cut fresh basil or 1 teaspoon dried basil, crumbled
1 bay leaf
2 teaspoons sugar
1 tablespoon salt
Freshly ground black pepper

In a 3- to 4-quart enameled or stainless-steel saucepan, heat the 3 tablespoons of olive oil and cook the finely chopped onions in it over moderate heat, stirring frequently, for 7 or 8 minutes. When the onions are soft and transparent but are not brown, add the tablespoon of finely chopped garlic and cook for another 1 or 2 minutes, stirring constantly. Then stir in the coarsely chopped tomatoes and their liquid, the tomato paste, oregano, basil, bay leaf, sugar, salt and a few grindings of black pepper. Bring the sauce to a boil, turn the heat very low and simmer uncovered, stirring occasionally, for about 1 hour.

When finished, the sauce should be thick and fairly smooth. Remove the bay leaf. Taste and season the sauce with salt and freshly ground black pepper. If you wish a smoother texture, puree the sauce through a food mill, or rub it through a sieve with the back of a large wooden spoon.

JAFFREY

An Invitation to Indian Cooking

Naan

SERVES 6

Naan *is a leavened flat bread shaped like a teardrop. It is best when cooked in the clay oven called the* tandoor. *While meats, chicken, and fish broil on large skewers inside the* tandoor, *moistened* naans *are stuck to its walls to bake.*

- 3 cups all-purpose white flour
- ½ cup plus 3 tablespoons milk
- 1 egg, beaten
- ¾ teaspoon salt
- 2 teaspoons sugar
- 1 teaspoon baking powder
- ½ packet dry yeast
- 2 tablespoons vegetable oil, plus a little more for brushing on dough later
- 4 tablespoons plain yogurt
- ¼ teaspoon black onion seeds (kalonji), or poppy seeds as substitute

Sift the flour into a bowl. Place the milk in a small pot and warm slightly. Remove from heat. In another bowl combine the egg, salt, sugar, baking powder, yeast, 2 tablespoons oil, yogurt, and 5 tablespoons of the warm milk.

Mix well. Pour mixture over flour and rub it in with the hands.

Add 1 tablespoon of warm milk at a time to the flour, and begin kneading. Add up to 6 tablespoons or enough so that all the flour adheres and kneading is easy. Knead well for about 10 minutes or until dough is elastic. Form into a ball, brush with oil, cover with damp cloth, and leave in a warm place to rise. If the temperature is above 80° it should take only 2 hours. Otherwise it may take about 3 hours.

Preheat broiler to about 550°.

Line 3 cookie sheets with aluminum foil. Brush them lightly with oil.

Knead the dough again for a minute or two and divide into 6 balls. Flatten the balls one at a time, keeping the rest covered, and stretch them and pat them with your hands until you have a teardrop shape about 11 inches long and 4 inches wide. Do all balls this way, placing 2 *naans* on each baking sheet as you do so. Cover with moistened cloths and leave for 15 minutes in a warm place.

Remove moistened cloths. Brush the center portion of each *naan* with water, leaving a ½-inch margin. Sprinkle the center portion with the onion or poppy seeds.

Place sheets under the broiler, about 2½–3 inches away from the heat and broil quickly for about 2½ minutes on each side or until lightly browned.

TO SERVE: Serve *naans* hot with *Tandoori* Chicken, *Seekh Kabab*, Lamb Cooked in Dark Almond Sauce, or Chicken *Moghlai*.

PÉPIN
La Technique

Pâte à Brioche

Brioche Dough

Brioches are the small, moist and butter cakes eaten for breakfast throughout France. In parts of the country, like Lyon, this yeast-risen dough is used to encase sausage, goose liver, game and other pâtés. The brioche dough is not as difficult to make as pâte feuilletée. *It is easiest to use a large mixer rather than beating by hand, but both methods give excellent results. The dough should be very satiny and elastic.* A brioche mousseline, *which is especially good, is a brioche dough loaded with butter. This recipe will make from 18 to 20 small brioches.*

- ½ teaspoon sugar
- ¼ cup lukewarm water
- 1 (¼-ounce) package dry yeast, or ½ cake fresh yeast
- 2¼ cups all-purpose flour
- 4 large eggs
- 2 sticks (½ pound) sweet butter, at room temperature and cut into ½-inch pieces
- ½ teaspoon salt

In a bowl, mix the sugar, water and yeast until smooth. Set the mixture aside and let it "work" for 5 minutes (the yeast will make it foam or bubble). Place the remaining ingredients in the bowl of an electric mixer. Using the flat beater, start mixing on low, adding the yeast mixture slowly. When all the ingredients hold together, scrape the sides and bottom, picking up any loose pieces. Place on medium speed and beat for 8 minutes. Scrape the sides and bottom twice more during the process so the ingredients are well blended. The dough should be elastic, velvety and hold into a lump around the beater. It should separate easily from the beater if pulled.

1. If you are making the dough by hand instead of machine, work it for at least 10 minutes. Grab the dough on both sides,

2. Lift it from the table and

3. Flip it over, slapping it on the table.

4. It should come up in one lump from an unfloured table. Place the dough in a bowl, set in a draftless, lukewarm place, cover with a towel and let rise until it has doubled in bulk (about 1½ to 2 hours).

5. Break the dough down by pushing and lifting with your fingers. If you are not going to use the dough immediately, wrap it in a towel and plastic wrap and place it in the refrigerator (the cool meat drawer) to prevent the dough from developing too much. It can be made a day ahead.

6. To make small brioches, generously butter individual brioche molds. Divide the dough into balls the size of a golf ball (about 2½ to 3 ounces) and roll on the table in a circular motion to give body to the brioche.

7. With the side of your hand, "saw" a small piece of the brioche in a back and forward motion.

8. This forms a small lump which should remain attached to the body of the brioche.

9. Lift the brioche by the "head" and place in the buttered mold.

10. Push the head down into the brioche.

11. Brush with an egg wash (1 whole egg, beaten).

12. A large brioche (*brioche parisienne*) is done similarly, but slits are cut all around to give texture to the finished brioche.

13. Let the brioches rise in a warm place for 1½ to 2 hours.

14. Bake the small brioches in a 400-degree preheated oven for approximately 25 minutes, and the large ones for approximately 45 minutes. They should be golden. Keep in a plastic bag to avoid drying out.

FIELD

The Italian Baker

Ciabatta

Slipper-Shaped Bread from Lake Como

I can't think of a way to describe the fabulous and unusual taste of ciabatta *except to say that once you've eaten it, you'll never think of white bread in the same way again. Everyone who tries this bread loves it.* Ciabatta *means slipper in Italian; one glance at the short stubby bread will make it clear how it was named.* Ciabatta *is a remarkable combination of rustic country texture and elegant and tantalizing taste. It is much lighter than its homely shape would indicate, and the porous chewy interior is enclosed in a slightly crunchy crust that is veiled with flour. Eat for breakfast or slice an entire* ciabatta *horizontally and stuff it with salami and cheese.*

This dough should be made in the mixer, although it also works in the processor. I have made it by hand but wouldn't recommend it unless you are willing to knead the wet, sticky mass between your hands—in mid-air—turning, folding, and twisting it rather like taffy, your hands covered with dough. You can't put it on the table because the natural inclination is to add lots of flour to this very sticky dough and pretty soon you wouldn't have a ciabatta. *Resist the temptation to add flour and follow the instructions. The dough will feel utterly unfamiliar and probably a bit scary. And that's not the only unusual feature—the shaped loaves are flat and look definitely unpromising; even when they are puffed after the second rise, you may feel certain you've done it all wrong. Don't give up. The loaves rise nicely in the oven.*

MAKES 4 LOAVES, EACH ABOUT THE WIDTH OF A HAND AND THE LENGTH OF THE ARM FROM WRIST TO ELBOW

1 teaspoon active dry yeast or ⅓ small cake (6 grams) fresh yeast
5 tablespoons warm milk
1 cup plus 3 tablespoons water, room temperature
1 tablespoon olive oil
2 cups (500 grams) Biga
3¾ cups (500 grams) unbleached all-purpose flour
1 tablespoon (15 grams) salt
Cornmeal

BY MIXER
Stir the yeast into the milk in a mixer bowl; let stand until creamy, about 10 minutes. Add the water, oil, and starter and mix with the paddle until blended. Mix the flour and salt, add to the bowl, and mix for 2 to 3 minutes. Change to the dough hook and knead for 2 minutes at low speed, then 2 minutes at medium speed. Knead briefly on a well-floured surface, adding as little flour as possible, until the dough is velvety, supple, very springy, and moist.

BY PROCESSOR
Refrigerate the starter until cold. Stir the yeast into the milk in a large bowl; let stand until creamy, about 10 minutes. Add 1 cup plus 3 tablespoons cold water, the oil, and starter and mix, squeezing the starter between your fingers to break it up. Place the flour and salt in the food processor fitted with the dough blade and process with several pulses to sift. With the machine running, pour the starter mixture through the feed tube and process until the dough comes together. Process about 45 seconds longer to knead. Finish kneading on a well-floured surface until the dough is velvety, supple, moist, and very springy.

FIRST RISE. Place the dough in an oiled bowl, cover with plastic wrap, and let rise until doubled, about 1¼ hours. The dough should be full of air bubbles, very supple, elastic, and sticky.

SHAPING AND SECOND RISE. Cut the dough into 4 equal pieces on a well-floured surface. Roll up each piece into a cylinder, then stretch each into a rectangle, about 10 × 4 inches, pulling with your fingers to get it long and wide enough. Generously flour 4 pieces of parchment paper on peels or baking sheets. Place each loaf, seam side up, on a paper. Dimple the loaves vigorously with your fingertips or knuckles so that they won't rise too much. The dough will look heavily pockmarked, but it is very resilient so don't be concerned. Cover loosely with dampened towels and let rise until almost doubled, 1½ to 2 hours. The loaves will look flat and definitely unpromising but don't give up for they will rise more in the oven.

BAKING. Thirty minutes before baking, heat the oven with baking stones in it to 425° F. Just before baking, sprinkle the stones with cornmeal. Carefully invert each loaf onto a stone. If the dough sticks a bit, just work it free from the paper gently. Bake for 20 to 25 minutes, spraying 3 times with water in the first 10 minutes. Cool on racks.

FIELD
The Italian Baker

Panmarino

Rosemary Bread

The lovely pungent flavor of rosemary is often kneaded into the breads of Tuscany and Liguria, but this panmarino *comes from Ferrara, the invention of an ebullient, mustachioed baker named Luciano Pancalde, whose surname aptly translates as "hot bread." Years ago, while reading a biography of the d'Este family who once ruled Ferrara, he discovered that one of the numerous spectacular court banquets featured a rosemary bread with a crust described as sparkling with diamonds. Luciano baked and baked again before he came up with this wonderful dome-shaped bread that is aromatic with fresh rosemary. But there's no need to go to Tiffany's for any of the ingredients. Just before baking, he slashes the top in the pattern of a star and sprinkles chunky crystals of sea salt into the crevices. The salt really does sparkle like diamonds.*

I make this bread all the time, not only because it is so easy and takes relatively little time from beginning to end, but also because it goes well with so many foods. It is wonderful with roast pork, chicken, or lamb and has an affinity with white fish, especially swordfish. Because the recipe makes two loaves, the second usually ends up sliced for sandwiches or a platter of cold meat.

If you use the electric mixer, you will have to stop the motor several times to push down the dough because the recipe proportions are just at the edge of the machine's capacity. Be sure not to let the dough fully double in its second rise or it won't spring to its full height in the oven. And there's no sense in not having a spectacular-looking bread to bring to the table.

MAKES 2 ROUND LOAVES

3¾ teaspoons active dry yeast or 1½ small cakes (27 grams) fresh yeast
1 cup warm water
1 cup milk, room temperature
⅓ cup less 1 tablespoon olive oil
3½ to 4 tablespoons finely chopped fresh rosemary or 1½ tablespoons dried
1 tablespoon plus 1 teaspoon (20 grams) salt
About 6¾ cups (900 grams) unbleached all-purpose flour
1 to 1½ teaspoons coarse sea salt

BY HAND

Stir the yeast into the water in a large mixing bowl; let stand until creamy, about 10 minutes. Stir in the milk and oil. Combine the rosemary, salt, and flour and stir into the yeast mixture in 3 or 4 additions. Stir until the dough comes together. Knead on a floured surface until velvety, elastic, and smooth, 8 to 10 minutes. It should be somewhat moist and blistered.

BY MIXER

This recipe is slightly large for the mixer, so that you'll have to stop and push the dough down frequently while the mixer is kneading it. Stir the yeast into the water in a mixer bowl; let stand until creamy, about 10 minutes. Stir in the milk and oil with the paddle. Combine the rosemary, salt, and flour and add to the yeast mixture. Mix until the flour is absorbed, 1 to 2 minutes. Change to the dough hook and knead on medium speed until velvety, elastic, smooth, and somewhat moist, about 3 minutes. Finish kneading briefly by hand on a lightly floured surface.

BY PROCESSOR

Make sure your food processor can handle the volume of this dough. Even when done in 2 batches there will be about 3½ cups flour plus liquid to be processed. If you have a large-capacity machine, use the dough blade. Stir the yeast into ¼ cup warm water in a small bowl; let stand until creamy, about 10 minutes. Place the rosemary, salt, and flour in a food processor fitted with the dough or steel blade and process briefly to mix and chop the rosemary. Stir the oil into the dissolved yeast. With the machine running, pour the yeast mixture, cold milk, and ¾ cup cold water in a steady stream through the feed tube and process until the dough gathers into a ball. Process 45 seconds longer to knead. Finish kneading by hand on a lightly floured surface until smooth, velvety, elastic, and slightly moist, 2 to 3 minutes.

FIRST RISE. Place the dough in an oiled bowl, cover tightly with plastic wrap, and let rise until doubled, about 1½ hours.

SHAPING AND SECOND RISE. Gently punch the dough down on a lightly floured surface, but don't knead it. Cut the dough in half and shape each half into a round ball. Place the loaves on a lightly floured peel or a lightly oiled baking sheet, cover with a towel, and let rise 45 to 55 minutes (but not until truly doubled).

BAKING. Heat the oven to 450° F. If you are using a baking stone, turn the oven on 30 minutes before baking and sprinkle the stone with cornmeal just before sliding the loaves onto it. Just before you put the loaves in the oven, slash the top of each loaf in an asterisk with a razor blade and sprinkle half the sea salt into the cuts of each loaf. Bake 10 minutes, spraying 3 times with water. Reduce the heat to 400° F and bake 30 to 35 minutes longer. Cool completely on racks.

CLAYTON

The Complete Book of Breads

Challah

TWO BRAIDED LOAVES

Challah (pronounced hal-la) is a lovely yellow egg-rich and light textured white bread steeped in history. While the word "challah" has come to mean this loaf of braided bread, the preparation of the dough for baking in the Jewish kitchen is "the act of Challah" in which the woman takes a small part of the dough to burn in the oven as an offering. She thereby reenacts her origin at the Creation when she sprang from man's rib. The remaining dough may then be baked as she chooses, usually in the braided form.

The Hebrew law of Challah requires that the quantity of flour to be kneaded into dough be no less than the weight of 43 and one-fifth eggs, or 2½ quarts or 3½ pounds. The portion to be separated as the Challah offering is to be no less than the size of an olive.

1 package dry yeast
5 cups all-purpose flour, approximately
2 tablespoons sugar
1½ teaspoons salt
⅓ cup butter or margarine, room temperature
1 cup hot tap water (120°–130°)
1 pinch saffron
3 eggs and 1 egg white, room temperature
Glaze: 1 yolk (from egg above)
2 tablespoons sugar
1 teaspoon cold water
½ teaspoon poppy seeds, to sprinkle

Large baking sheet, greased or Teflon

PREPARATION

15 mins.

In a large bowl mix yeast, 2 cups flour, sugar, salt and butter or margarine. Gradually add water to dry ingredients and beat at medium speed of electric mixer for 2 minutes. Scrape bowl occasionally. Add saffron, 3 eggs and 1 egg white (reserving the yolk). The batter will be thick. Beat for 2 minutes at high speed. Put aside the electric beater and continue mixing in flour with a wooden spoon. Add about 3 additional cups of flour, one at a time, until the rough mass is no longer sticky. If it is moist, add small amounts of flour until the dough cleans the side of the bowl.

KNEADING

8 mins.

Turn the dough out onto a floured surface and knead until the dough is smooth and elastic. (Six minutes with a dough hook.)

FIRST RISING

1 hour

Return dough to the mixing bowl which has been washed or wiped clean and greased. Turn the dough so that it is oiled on all sides.

Cover the bowl tightly with a length of plastic wrap and place it in a warm draft-free place until dough has doubled in bulk.

SHAPING

25 mins.

Punch the dough down and knead out the bubbles. Divide the dough in half.

To braid, divide each half into three equal pieces. With the hands roll each piece into a 12-inch length. Lay rolls parallel to each other. Start the braid in the middle and work to one end. Pinch the ends securely together. Turn around and complete the other end. Repeat with second piece.

Place the two braids on baking sheet.

Beat together remaining egg yolk, sugar and cold water. Carefully brush braids with the mixture. Sprinkle with poppy seeds.

SECOND RISING

1 hour

Don't cover the braids for the second rise. They will double in bulk.

BAKING

400°

30 mins.

Preheat oven to 400°. Bake in the oven until the braids test done when a wooden toothpick inserted in the center comes out clean and dry. The loaves will be a shiny golden brown.

FINAL STEP

Remove bread from the oven. Carefully remove from baking sheet and cool on wire racks. A long braided piece fresh from the oven is fragile and should be handled with care (and a spatula) until it cools and has stiffened a bit.

LA PLACE AND KLEIMAN

Cucina Fresca

Torta Rustica

Rustic Country Tart

Country cooking that pleases the most sophisticated palate. Cutting into the tart reveals a brilliant mosaic of colors. To make even more substantial, add cubes of Arista. Or, if Black Forest ham proves difficult to find, substitute any high-quality smoked meat.

- 6 packages (10 ounces each) frozen chopped spinach
- 1 tablespoon butter
- 1 tablespoon olive oil
- 1 small onion, peeled and minced
- 4 eggs
- 1 cup grated Parmesan cheese
- ½ cup bread crumbs
- Coarse salt and freshly ground pepper to taste
- 4 large red bell peppers, or a 1-pound can good quality peeled red peppers
- 1 recipe Soft Tart Dough
- ½ pound Italian fontina, rind removed, sliced
- ½ pound Black Forest ham, sliced ⅛ inch thick
- 1 egg beaten with 2 tablespoons milk

Cook the spinach according to the package directions. Drain in a colander and rinse under cold water to cool. Drain the spinach and with your hands squeeze out the excess moisture. The spinach should be almost completely dry. Set aside. Heat the butter and oil together in a small skillet. Sauté the minced onion until it becomes translucent and begins to color. Mix together the spinach, sautéed onion, eggs, Parmesan, bread crumbs, salt, and pepper in a bowl. Set aside.

To peel the peppers, place them over a gas burner or under a broiler and turn with tongs until they are blackened all over. Place them in plastic bags, close the top, and let them sweat for 10 minutes. Remove the peppers from the plastic bag and rinse the skins off under cold running water. Lay on paper towels to dry. Carefully remove the stems, open the peppers, and discard the seeds and white ribs. Cut the peppers to lie flat in one piece. Set aside.

To assemble the tart, roll out two-thirds of the Soft Tart Dough on parchment, wax paper, aluminum foil, or plastic wrap into a circle approximately 14 inches in diameter. Line a medium mixing bowl with plastic wrap. Invert the 14-inch circle of dough into the bowl. Peel off the paper or plastic wrap and pat the dough against the sides of the bowl. Now begin to layer the ingredients. First, place a thin layer of spinach mixture, then a layer of red pepper, fontina, and ham. Continue layering in a pattern you like, but finish with a layer of spinach at least ½ inch thick.

Roll out the remaining dough on parchment, wax paper, aluminum foil, or plastic wrap into a circle large enough to cover the filling. Invert the dough onto the tart filling and peel off the paper or plastic wrap. Trim the edges of the circle (which will become the bottom crust). Brush the edge of the circle with the egg wash and fold over the extra dough from the larger circle (which will be the top of the tart). Make sure the edges are well sealed. Carefully invert the tart onto a baking sheet and remove the bowl. Peel off the plastic wrap that lined the bowl.

Bake the tart in a preheated 375° oven for approximately 40 minutes or until the crust is a deep golden brown. If you desire a sheen to the crust, brush it with the egg wash before placing it in the oven and once or twice during baking. Serve the tart at room temperature, cut into pie-shaped wedges. Serves 10 to 12.

FIELD

The Italian Baker

Grissini Torinesi

Breadsticks from Turin

Most Americans know grissini *from the pale breadsticks in the elongated waxen envelopes that appear on the tables of Italian restaurants, but they bear about as much resemblance to authentic* grissini *as packaged industrial white bread does to true country loaves. Real* grissini *are made of yeast, flour, water, and either olive oil, lard, or butter. They are shaped between the hands by gently vibrating and stretching the dough to about the span of the baker's arms, and are then baked directly on the floor of a wood-burning oven. They are as thick and irregular as knobby fingers and look like cordwood when stacked. They have crunch and an earthy taste. Even when made at home with the methods and recipes that follow, they are still redolent of the countryside and the old ways.*

Although there is some dispute about who came up with the first grissini, *there is no question that they first appeared in Turin sometime in the seventeenth century. Some say that a baker in Turin invented them in 1668 in response to inquiries from the doctor of the young duke Vittorio Amadeo II, who had stomach disturbances, for a bread that would be good for the duke's digestion. The baker stretched out the traditional local bread dough so long that it became a long, thin, crunchy stick that was essentially all crust. Although there is no word of their effect on the patient's health, it is safe to assume that they met with great success, because* grissini *were well known all over Italy by the next century when Napoleon discovered "les petits batons de Turin." Napoleon was so enthusiastic about the breadsticks that he instituted a fast postal service expressly for transporting them to court every day. The most popular rival story to that of the young duke credits a Florentine abbot on a diplomatic mission near Turin in 1643 with the discovery of "a thin bread as long as an arm and very, very fine."*

Serve grissini *with eggs, green salad, prosciutto and smoked beef, and with all imaginable kinds of antipasti. Some Italians eat them for breakfast with milk or coffee, an old, once widespread custom.*

MAKES 20 TO 22 BREADSTICKS

- 1¾ teaspoons active dry yeast or ⅔ small cake (12 grams) fresh yeast
- 1 tablespoon malt syrup
- 1¼ cups warm water
- 2 tablespoons olive oil, plus additional for brushing the dough
- 3¾ cups (500 grams) unbleached all-purpose flour
- 1½ teaspoons (8 grams) salt
- ½ cup semolina flour for sprinkling

BY HAND
Stir the yeast and malt into the warm water in a large mixing bowl; let stand until foamy, about 10 minutes. Stir in 2 tablespoons oil. Add the flour and salt and stir until the dough comes together. Knead on a lightly floured surface until smooth, soft, velvety, and elastic, 8 to 10 minutes.

BY MIXER
Stir the yeast and malt into the water in a mixer bowl; let stand until foamy, about 10 minutes. Mix in the 2 tablespoons oil with the paddle. Add the flour and salt and mix until the dough comes together. Change to the dough hook and knead at low speed about 3 minutes. Finish kneading briefly by hand on a lightly floured surface.

BY PROCESSOR
Stir the yeast and malt into ¼ cup warm water in a small bowl; let stand until foamy, about 10 minutes. Place the flour and salt in a standard food processor fitted with the dough blade or a large (over 7 cups capacity) processor fitted with the steel blade and process with several pulses to sift. Mix 1 cup cold water and 2 tablespoons oil. With the machine running, pour the water mixed with oil and the dissolved yeast through the feed tube and process until the dough comes together. Process 45 seconds longer to knead. Finish kneading by hand on a lightly floured surface.

FIRST RISE. Pat the dough with your hands into a 14 × 4-inch rectangle on a well-floured surface. Lightly brush the top with oil. Cover with plastic wrap and let rise until doubled, about 1 hour.

SHAPING. Sprinkle the dough with semolina flour before cutting and stretching. The baker's method of shaping breadsticks is ingenious, simple, and quick, for he certainly doesn't have time to roll out individual *grissini*. Cut the dough crosswise into 4 equal sections and then cut each section crosswise again into 5 strips, each about the width of a fat finger. The dough is so elastic that you can simply pick up each piece and stretch it between your hands to fit the width of a baking sheet. Place the breadsticks several inches apart on lightly oiled baking sheets (unless they are rimless, I find it easier to use the backs of the baking sheets).

BAKING. Heat the oven to 400° F. If you are using a baking stone, turn the oven on 30 minutes before baking. Bake the breadsticks for 20 minutes. If you like crunchy breadsticks, bake directly on the baking stone, which has been sprinkled with cornmeal or semolina flour, for the last 5 minutes. Cool on racks.

VARIATIONS. For *Grissini Siciliani*, sprinkle the dough with ½ cup sesame seeds instead of semolina flour before cutting and shaping.

For *Grissini al Papavero,* sprinkle the dough with ½ cup poppy seeds instead of semolina flour before cutting and shaping.

GRISSINI INTEGRALI
Whole-Wheat Breadsticks

MAKES 20 TO 22 BREADSTICKS

- 1¾ teaspoons active dry yeast or ⅔ small cake (12 grams) fresh yeast
- 1¼ cups warm water
- 1 tablespoon malt syrup
- ¼ cup olive oil, plus additional for brushing the dough
- 2¼ teaspoons (10 grams) lard
- 1 cup less 2 tablespoons (125 grams) unbleached all-purpose flour
- 2⅔ cups (375 grams) whole-wheat flour
- 1½ teaspoons (8 grams) salt

Follow the directions for *Grissini Torinesi* (recipe precedes), adding the lard with the oil. Omit sprinkling the dough with semolina flour.

GRISSINI ALLE CIPOLLE

Onion Breadsticks

MAKES 20 TO 22 BREADSTICKS

- 1 large yellow onion
- 4 tablespoons olive oil, plus additional for brushing the dough
- 1¾ teaspoons active dry yeast or ⅔ small cake (12 grams) fresh yeast
- 1¼ cups warm water
- 1 tablespoon malt syrup
- 2 tablespoons (25 grams) lard
- 3¾ cups (500 grams) unbleached all-purpose flour
- 2 teaspoons (10 grams) salt

Cut the onion into small dice and sauté in 2 tablespoons of the oil over low to medium heat until golden and almost dry roasted, 10 to 15 minutes. Watch that it doesn't burn.

Follow the directions for *Grissini Torinesi* (recipe precedes), adding the lard with the remaining 2 tablespoons oil. Work the onion into the dough at the very end of the kneading. Omit sprinkling the dough with semolina flour.

GRISSINI AL FORMAGGIO

Cheese Breadsticks

MAKES 20 TO 22 BREADSTICKS

- 1¾ teaspoons active dry yeast or ⅔ small cake (12 grams) fresh yeast
- 1⅓ cups warm water
- 2 tablespoons olive oil, plus additional for brushing the dough
- 3¾ cups (500 grams) unbleached all-purpose flour
- 1½ teaspoons (8 grams) salt
- 2 ounces (60 grams) grated Parmesan cheese

Follow the directions for *Grissini Torinesi* (recipe precedes). Work the cheese into the dough at the very end of the kneading. Omit sprinkling the dough with semolina flour. Bake at 450° F for 12 to 15 minutes.

GRISSINI CRIC-CRAC ALLA SALVIA

Sage Breadsticks from Como

I suppose you could call this recipe and the variations that follow grissini nuovi, *for they are imaginative departures from the classical breadstick of Turin.* Cric-crac *is really a musical bit of onomatopoeia.*

MAKES 20 TO 22 BREADSTICKS

- 1¾ teaspoons active dry yeast or ⅔ small cake (12 grams) fresh yeast
- 1¼ cups warm water
- 1 tablespoon malt syrup
- ¼ cup olive oil, plus additional for brushing the dough
- 3¾ cups (500 grams) unbleached all-purpose flour
- 1½ teaspoons (8 grams) salt
- ¼ cup chopped fresh sage

Follow the directions for *Grissini Torinese* (recipe precedes), adding the malt with the yeast to the water. Work in the sage at the very end of the kneading. Omit sprinkling the dough with semolina flour.

VARIATIONS.

CRIC-CRAC ALLA PANCETTA: Substitute 2 ounces (60 grams) diced *pancetta* for the sage.

CRIC-CRAC AL SALAME. Substitute 2 ounces (60 grams) diced salami for the sage.

CRIC-CRAC ALLA GORGONZOLA. Substitute 2 ounces (60 grams) softened Gorgonzola for the sage.

CRIC-CRAC AGLI SPINACI. Substitute 2 ounces (60 grams) frozen chopped spinach, thawed and well drained, for the sage.

SWEET BREADS

FIELD
The Italian Baker

Panettone

Panettone is a delicate and porous rich egg bread studded with raisins and bits of candied citron and orange that is traditionally eaten by the Milanese on Christmas. These days it can be found all over Italy and America as well and not only during the holidays. Many panettones from Italy are made with a special natural yeast, and they seem to last almost forever. I received one once that had been two months in transit and still tasted fresh and delicious. Panettones made at home probably will not keep for such a long time, but I have never had panettone around long enough to see.

No bread has more stories of its origins. The most reasonable explanation of the name is that the Milanese passion for terms of affection led them to call regular bread panett*, so that when a larger or richer bread was made, it was inevitable that it be called* panettone. *Some point instead to the Middle Ages when bakers were divided into two groups: those who baked for the poor with millet and other inexpensive grains and those who baked for the rich with wheat flour. Only at Christmas could bakers for the poor make an enriched bread with butter, eggs, sugar, raisins, and candied fruit, which became known as a* pan di tono*, or rich and fancy bread.*

The most famous story of the origins of panettone involves a wealthy young Milanese noble in the fifteenth century who fell in love with the daughter of a poor baker named Tony. He wanted to marry the girl and so put at her father's disposal the means to buy the best flour, eggs, and butter, as well as candied orange and citron and fat sultana raisins. The bread he created, known as pan di Tonia*, was a great success. It made Tony's reputation as well as his fortune and, as a dividend, Tony's backer got the baker's daughter.*

If the beginnings of panettone are clouded with mystery, it is well known that panettone was politicized after the uprisings of 1821 when red candied cherries were substituted for raisins and green citron was added so that the bread symbolized the tricolored Italian flag and liberty itself.

In fact, panettone was a much shorter and less dramatic bread until Angelo Motta founded his industrial company in 1921 and used natural yeast and his own tall cylindrical form to make the dazzlingly tall, domed panettone. The soft and delicate bread was such an immediate success that the following year Motta's friend Giacchino Allemagna set up a rival company making equally light and airy panettones. Today those two firms together turn out more than fifty-five million pounds of panettone a year and have made porous, delicately sweetened breads synonymous with Italy and Christmas. There is nothing better with coffee or cappuccino for breakfast or with tea at midday, but the Milanese insist that it is best at Christmas with cream or, even better, fresh Mascarpone. And they traditionally put aside a piece to eat on February 3rd, the feast day of Saint Biagio, the protector of the throat.

MAKES 2 PANETTONE

SPONGE

2½ teaspoons (1 package) active dry yeast or 1 small cake (18 grams) fresh yeast
⅓ cup warm water
½ cup (70 grams) unbleached all-purpose flour

Stir the yeast into the water in a small bowl; let stand until creamy, about 10 minutes. Stir in the flour. Cover tightly with plastic wrap and let rise until doubled, 20 to 30 minutes.

FIRST DOUGH

2½ teaspoons (1 package) active dry yeast or 1 small cake (18 grams) fresh yeast
3 tablespoons warm water
2 eggs, room temperature
1¼ cups (180 grams) unbleached all-purpose flour
¼ cup (50 grams) sugar
½ stick (115 grams) unsalted butter, room temperature

BY HAND
Stir the yeast into the water in a mixing bowl; let stand until creamy, about 10 minutes. Add the sponge and beat thoroughly together. Add the eggs, flour, and sugar and mix well. Stir in the butter thoroughly. The entire process will take 5 to 6 minutes. Cover with plastic wrap and let rise until doubled, 1 to 1¼ hours.

BY MIXER
Stir the yeast into the water in a mixer bowl; let stand until creamy, about 10 minutes. Add the sponge, eggs, flour, and sugar and mix with the paddle. Add the butter and mix until the dough is smooth and consistent, about 3 minutes.
Cover with plastic wrap and let rise until doubled, 1 to 1¼ hours.

SECOND DOUGH

- 2 eggs
- 3 egg yolks
- ¾ cup (150 grams) sugar
- 2 tablespoons honey
- 1½ teaspoons vanilla extract
- 1 teaspoon (5 grams) salt
- 2 sticks (225 grams) unsalted butter, room temperature
- About 3 cups (420 grams) unbleached all-purpose flour, plus ¾ cup for kneading

BY HAND

Place the first dough in a large mixing bowl, if it isn't already. Add the eggs, egg yolks, sugar, honey, vanilla, and salt and mix well. Add the butter and stir until blended. Stir in the flour and keep stirring until smooth. The dough will be soft, a bit like cookie dough. Knead gently on a well-floured surface with well-floured hands until it is smooth and holds its shape. You may need as much as ¾ cup additional flour during the kneading.

BY MIXER

Add the eggs, egg yolks, sugar, honey, vanilla, and salt to the first dough and mix thoroughly with the paddle. Add the butter and mix until smooth. Add the flour and mix again until smooth. The dough will be soft, a bit like cookie dough. Change to the dough hook and knead until smooth and soft, about 2 minutes. Finish by kneading on a lightly floured work surface, using a little additional flour as necessary.

FIRST RISE. Place the dough in a lightly oiled bowl, cover with plastic wrap, and let rise until tripled, 2½ to 4 hours. The dough can also rise overnight at a cool room temperature (65° to 68° F).

FILLING

- 1½ cups (250 grams) golden raisins
- ½ cup (75 grams) chopped candied citron
- ½ cup (75 grams) chopped candied orange peel
- Grated zest of 1 orange
- Grated zest of 1 lemon
- 2 to 3 tablespoons unbleached all-purpose flour

At least 30 minutes before the end of the first rise, soak the raisins in cool water to cover. Drain and pat dry. Cut the dough in half on a floured surface. Combine the raisins, candied citron and orange, and orange and lemon zests and dust with 2 to 3 tablespoons flour. Pat each piece of dough into an oval and sprinkle each with a quarter of the fruit mixture. Roll up into a log. Gently flatten the dough again to create as much surface as possible, sprinkle with the remaining fruit mixture, and roll up again.

SHAPING AND SECOND RISE. Shape each piece into a ball and slip into 2 well-buttered panettone molds or 2-pound coffee cans lined with a parchment-paper circle on the bottom. For this panettone, which is as light and airy as the traditional bakery panettone, the pan is very important—if you use a charlotte mold, springform pan, or soufflé dish, you will not get the same spectacular height or delicate porous texture.

Cut an × in the top of each loaf with a razor. Cover with a towel and let rise until doubled, about 2 hours. If your kitchen is cold, warm the oven at the lowest possible setting for 3 minutes, place a large pan of hot water on the lowest rack, and let the dough rise in the warm, slightly moist atmosphere. With a gas oven, the heat of the pilot light may be enough.

BAKING. Heat the oven to 400° F. Just before baking, cut the × in each loaf again. Some bakers insert a nut of butter into the cut. Bake 10 minutes. Reduce the heat to 375° F and bake 10 minutes. Reduce the heat to 350° F and bake until a tester inserted in the center comes out clean, 30 minutes. Cool on racks for 30 minutes; then carefully remove from the molds and place the loaves on their sides on pillows to cool. If you place the warm panettone on a rack to cool, it will collapse.

FIELD
The Italian Baker

Panforte

Traditional Fruitcake of Siena

Panforte *means "strong bread" in Italian, and this phenomenal dessert is the best fruitcake you could ever imagine, denser than sweet bread and only slightly less rich than candy. The monks of Siena may have been among the first to find pleasure in its rich nutty flavors, and Crusaders may have taken it as a long-lasting food to give them quick bursts of energy on their rigorous pilgrimages. No one is quite sure when* panforte *was first prepared, although there are stories that it dates back to the year 1000 when Siena was one of the first cities in Italy to use sugar and rare spices, including the white pepper that gives* panforte *its authentic medieval taste.*

These days panforte *remains the true Christmas treat of Siena. I remember reading an article once by Sean O'Faolain in which he expressed amazement that some people went to Siena only for this remarkable chewy sweet. It's true that Siena has numerous other enchantments—its extraordinary* Campo, *which may be the most beautiful piazza in all the world, its sinuous curving streets of pink and gray stone buildings, its almond-eyed madonnas, and its moment of collective madness in a horse race called the* Palio—*but surely there is also fascination in finding your way to Siena in a quest for* panforte, *one of the best dolci Italy has to offer.*

MAKES ONE 9-INCH CAKE

- 1 cup (115 grams) whole hazelnuts, coarsely chopped
- 1 cup (115 grams) blanched almonds
- 1 cup (130 grams) coarsely chopped candied orange peel
- 1 cup (130 grams) finely chopped citron
- 1 teaspoon grated lemon zest
- ½ cup (70 grams) unbleached all-purpose flour
- 1 teaspoon ground cinnamon
- ¼ teaspoon ground coriander
- ¼ teaspoon ground cloves
- ¼ teaspoon freshly ground nutmeg
- Pinch ground white pepper
- ¾ cup (150 grams) granulated sugar
- ¾ cup honey
- 2 tablespoons (30 grams) unsalted butter
- Confectioners' sugar

Heat the oven to 350° F. Toast the hazelnuts on a baking sheet until the skins pop and blister, 10 to 15 minutes. Rub the skins from the hazelnuts in a kitchen towel. Toast the almonds on a baking sheet until very pale golden, about 10 to 15 minutes. Chop the almonds and hazelnuts very coarsely. Mix the nuts, orange peel, citron, lemon zest, flour, cinnamon, coriander, cloves, nutmeg, and pepper together thoroughly in a large mixing bowl.

Butter a 9-inch springform pan; line the bottom and sides with parchment paper and then butter the paper. Heat the granulated sugar, honey, and butter in a large heavy saucepan over low heat, stirring constantly, until the syrup registers 242° to 248° F on a candy thermometer (a little of the mixture will form a ball when dropped into cold water). Immediately pour the syrup into the nut mixture and stir quickly until thoroughly blended. Pour immediately into the prepared pan and smooth the top with a spatula. The batter will become stiff and sticky very quickly, so you must work fast.

BAKING. Heat the oven to 300° F. Bake about 30 to 40 minutes. The *panforte* won't color or seem very firm even when ready, but it will harden as it cools. Cool on a rack until the cake is firm to the touch. Remove the side of the pan and invert the cake onto a sheet of waxed paper. Peel off the parchment paper. Dust heavily with the confectioners' sugar.

VARIATION. To make *Panforte Scuro* (dark), add 2 ounces (60 grams) coarsely chopped dried figs and 1 to 2 tablespoons unsweetened cocoa powder.

CLAYTON
The Complete Book of Breads

Dresden Christmas Fruit Bread

TWO LONG LOAVES

A stollen-type Yule bread, shaped in a long rectangle rather than as a crescent, it begins with rum poured over dried and candied fruit and left to soak for at least an hour—or, better still, overnight. Exchanged throughout Germany as a holiday gift, the loaf will keep through the festive season wrapped in foil.

- 1 cup mixed candied citrus peel
- ¼ cup candied angelica, if available
- ½ cup dried currants
- ½ cup seedless raisins
- ½ cup candied cherries, halved
- ½ cup rum, light or dark
- ¼ cup warm water (105°–115°)
- 2 packages dry yeast
- 1 pinch of sugar
- 2 tablespoons flour (to dredge fruit)
- 1 cup milk
- ¾ cup sugar
- 1 tablespoon salt
- ½ teaspoon almond extract
- ½ teaspoon grated lemon peel
- 6 cups of all-purpose flour, approximately
- 2 eggs, room temperature
- ¾ cup (1½ sticks) butter, room temperature and cut into bits
- 1 cup blanched and slivered almonds
- 4 tablespoons melted butter
- ¼ cup confectioners' sugar to brush dough

One 11 x 17 baking sheet, greased or Teflon.

PREPARATION
45 mins.

An hour or more before baking (or even the night before) combine in a small bowl the citrus peel, angelica, currants, raisins and cherries—and pour the rum over them. Stir the mixture to moisten all the pieces, and set aside.

Pour the water into a small bowl and sprinkle yeast on top. Add a pinch of sugar to help start the yeast action. Stir with a fork or small metal whip to completely dissolve the yeast.

Drain the fruit, reserving the rum, and pat the fruit dry with paper towels. Place the fruit in a paper sack with 2 tablespoons of flour and shake vigorously to coat the pieces. Set aside.

In a medium saucepan, combine milk, ½ cup of the sugar and salt; heat to lukewarm, stirring constantly, until sugar is dissolved. Off the heat, stir in reserved rum, almond extract, lemon peel and yeast mixture. In a large bowl pour 3 cups of flour and with a wooden spoon slowly stir in the yeast mixture. Beat the eggs until frothy. Stir them into the bowl, followed by small pieces of the softened butter which can either be room temperature or melted. Beat 100 times. Add more flour, about 2 cups. When the dough can be gathered into a soft ball, turn it out on the counter top or a bread board sprinkled generously with flour.

KNEADING
12 mins.

Knead the dough, adding flour if it is sticky. When the kneading is finished, gently work the fruit and almonds into the dough. Don't work it unnecessarily long, for some of the fruit, especially the raisins, may discolor the dough.

FIRST RISING
2 hours

Place the dough in a bowl and cover tightly with plastic wrap. Put the bowl in a warm spot (80°–85°) in the kitchen until the dough doubles.

SHAPING
25 mins.

Turn out the dough, punch it down and knead it for a few seconds to press out the bubbles.

Divide into two pieces, and put one back in the bowl until you are ready to shape the second loaf. With a rolling pin work the dough into a rectangle about 12 inches long, 8 inches wide, and about ½ inch thick. Brush the dough with warmed butter and sprinkle with 2 tablespoons of sugar. Fold one long side just over the center of the strip. Fold the other long edge over the seam—overlapping by about 1 inch. Press both of the outside edges firmly but lightly to prevent the top from lifting up during proofing and baking. The ends of the loaf should be tapered slightly by patting them. Also push the sides together to mound the loaf in the center. The finished loaf will be about 13 inches long and about 3½ to 4 inches wide. Repeat with second piece.

SECOND RISING
1 hour
Place the loaves on an 11 × 17 baking sheet. Brush them with melted butter. Cover with wax paper (resting on glass tumblers to keep the paper off the dough) and set in a warm place until doubled in bulk.

BAKING
375°
50 mins.
Preheat oven to 375°. Bake in the oven until golden brown and crusty. Midway through the baking period, turn the loaves halfway around so that they are equally exposed to any temperature variations in the oven.

FINAL STEP
Remove bread from the oven. Transfer to wire racks. Either serve warm from the oven, or let it mature 3 days before reheating and serving. Just before serving, coat heavily with confectioners' sugar sprinkled from a sifter or small sieve.

CHILD
From Julia Child's Kitchen

Mrs. Child's Famous Sticky Fruitcake

A Christmas Cake

This cake isn't sticky at all, but it started out that way during my first experiments, and the name has remained, as a family joke. I decided to work up a very fruity and nutty mixture that was easy to do all alone, with no friendly helping hands, and this is it. It's not a budget cake, unfortunately, since a large amount of fruits and nuts can never be an economy affair. But it is so rich and filled with good things that only a small slice should suffice, meaning that one luxury cake can go a long way. It is my habit to make a large amount of anything like this, particularly since it keeps for months and small fruitcakes make wonderful gifts, but you may cut the recipe in half or in thirds if you wish.

FOR 16 CUPS OR MORE OF FRUITCAKE BATTER, TO FILL A 16-INCH ANGEL LOAF PAN 4¼ INCHES DEEP, OR TWO 9-INCH 8-CUP PANS, OR WHATEVER COMBINATION AND SIZE OF PANS YOU WISH, INCLUDING MINIATURE 1-CUP LOAF PANS

THE FRUIT AND NUT MIXTURE: TO BE MACERATED 12 HOURS
4 pounds (2 quarts) diced mixed glacéed fruits: part of this may be diced dried dates, pitted tenderized dried prunes or apricots, or raisins, or currants
1 pound (2 cups) prepared store-bought mincemeat
1 pound (1 quart) mixed unsalted whole or chopped nut meats (such as walnuts, pecans, almonds, cashews, filberts)
⅔ cup dark Jamaican rum
⅓ cup Cognac or Bourbon
1 Tb instant coffee (espresso coffee suggested)
¼ cup dark molasses
1 tsp cardamom
½ tsp each: cinnamon, cloves, allspice, mace
1½ tsp salt

THE DRY INGREDIENTS
30 cups all-purpose flour (measure by dipping dry-measure cups into flour and sweeping off excess)
1 Tb double-action baking powder

THE REMAINING INGREDIENTS
½ pound (2 sticks) butter
2 cups white sugar
⅓ cup light-brown sugar
2 Tb vanilla
6 "large" eggs

OPTIONAL DECORATION AFTER BAKING
1 to 1½ cups apricot glaze (apricot jam pushed through a sieve, boiled to the thread stage [228 degrees] with 2 Tb sugar per cup of strained jam)
A dozen or so glacéed cherries
A dozen or so whole pecan or walnut halves

MACERATING THE FRUITS AND NUTS. Turn the candied fruits into a very large mixing bowl, pour on boiling water to cover, stir about for 20 to 30 seconds, then drain thoroughly; this is to wash off any preservatives. Return fruit to bowl, add the mincemeat, nuts, liquors, instant coffee, molasses, spices, and salt; stir about. Cover airtight, and let macerate for 12 hours (or longer).

COMPLETING THE CAKE MIXTURE. Stir half the flour into the fruits and nuts, sprinkle over the baking powder and the rest of the flour, and stir to blend. Using an electric mixer, beat the butter and sugars together in a separate bowl until light and fluffy, then beat in the vanilla, and the eggs, one at a time, beating 30 seconds after the addition of each egg. Blend the egg-sugar mixture into the fruits.

BAKING. Preheat the oven to 275 degrees. Butter your cake pan (or pans), line bottom with wax paper, butter that, roll flour around in the pan to coat interior, and knock out excess flour. Turn the batter into the pan, filling it to within ¼ inch of rim (and mold any extra cake mixture in a muffin tin). Bake in middle level of oven for 2 to 2¾ hours or longer, depending on size and shape of pan. Cake will rise about ¼ inch, top will crack in several places, and it is done when it shows the faintest line of shrinkage around edge of pan in several places; a skewer, plunged down into cake through a crack, should come out clean (or, at most, showing a residue of sticky fruit). Remove cake from oven and place pan on a rack to cool for 20 to 25 minutes; cake should shrink a little more from sides, showing it is ready to unmold. Turn cake upside down on rack and give a little shake to unmold it. Peel paper off bottom, and turn cake carefully right side up—you will need some fancy maneuvering if this is a big cake, like boards for bracing and turning.

ADDITIONAL FLAVORING. If you wish more Cognac or rum or Bourbon flavoring, pour a spoonful or two over the cake 2 or 3 times as it cools.

**Storing the cake.* When cold, wrap in plastic, then in foil, and store in a cool place. Will keep for months, and flavor matures with age, although the cake makes delicious eating when still warm from the oven.

OPTIONAL DECORATION. If you wish to make a luxurious spectacle of this cake, first paint the top and sides with warm apricot glaze (be sure glaze has really boiled to the thread stage, so it will not remain sticky when cool).

Press halved glacéed cherries and nut meats into the glaze and, for a loaf cake, make a line of cherries down the center flanked on either side by nut meats.

Paint a second coating of glaze over the fruits and the top of the cake. Let set for half an hour at least. allowing the glaze to dry and lose its stickiness. (Although you can still store the cake after glazing, I usually glaze it the day I serve it.)

HEATTER

Maida Heatter's Book of Great Desserts

Texas Fruit Cake

12 SLICES

This cake is so thick with fruit and nuts it is almost a confection. Recipe may be multiplied by any number provided you have a very large container for mixing it in. In place of a large bowl use a roasting pan or a dish pan.

- 8 ounces (1 cup) pitted dates, left whole
- 1 cup candied cherries, tightly packed and left whole
- 1 cup (4–5 slices) candied pineapple, each slice cut in 8–10 wedges
- ½ cup sifted all-purpose flour
- 8 ounces (2½ cups) mixed walnut and pecan halves, left whole
- ½ teaspoon double-acting baking powder
- ¼ teaspoon salt
- 2 eggs, separated
- ½ cup sugar
- ½ teaspoon vanilla extract
- 2 tablespoons bourbon

Adjust oven rack one-third of the way up from the bottom. Preheat oven to 325 degrees. Butter a 9 × 5 × 3-inch loaf pan. Then cut two strips of aluminum foil to line the pan, one for the length and one for the width. Put them into place carefully; the foil should remain smooth. Brush with melted butter and dust lightly with fine, dry bread crumbs. Set aside.

Pick over the dates carefully to see that there are no pits or stems left in them. Rinse the cherries quickly in cold water and dry them thoroughly between paper towels.

Place the dates, cherries, and pineapple in a large mixing bowl. Add 2 tablespoons of the flour and toss with your fingers to separate and coat each piece of fruit thoroughly. Add the nuts and toss again. Set aside.

Sift the remaining flour with the baking powder and salt and set aside.

In small bowl of electric mixer at high speed beat the egg yolks and sugar for about 3 minutes until light. Reduce the speed to low and add the vanilla, bourbon, and then the sifted dry ingredients, scraping the bowl with a rubber spatula, and beating only until smooth.

Beat the egg whites until they hold a firm shape, or are stiff but not dry. Fold the egg whites into the egg yolk mixture.

Pour the batter over the prepared fruit and nuts. With your hand, fold together, and then, with your hand, transfer to prepared pan. With your fingers and the palm of your hand, press down very firmly, especially in the corners of the pan. Make the top as level as possible.

Bake 1½ hours until the cake is semi-firm to the touch, covering the top loosely with foil for the last half hour of baking. Remove from oven and cool in pan for 20 minutes. Cover with a rack and invert. Remove pan and aluminum foil. Cover with another rack and invert again to cool, right side up.

When cool, wrap airtight and refrigerate for at least several hours, or a day or two if you wish. Freeze for longer storage.

It is best to slice the cake in the kitchen, and arrange the slices on a tray, or wrap them individually in clear cellophane. Turn the cake upside down to slice it. Use a very sharp, thin knife. If you have any trouble, hold the knife under running, hot water before cutting each slice. Cut with a sawing motion. It is difficult to cut this cake into very thin slices; for smaller portions cut each slice in half.

NOTE: Fruit cakes slice best if very cold; I think they also taste best when cold.

MUFFINS & WHATNOT

HIBBEN

The National Cook Book

Muffin Cakes (Colorado)

yolks 8 eggs
⅔ cup butter
1 cup sugar
½ cup milk
1½ cups flour (sifted twice)
1 teaspoon vanilla
3½ teaspoons baking-powder

Beat the yolks until they are thick and lemon colored; add the sugar gradually, beating all the time. Add the butter, creamed until soft and fluffy, then add flour and vanilla, and last of all the baking-powder. Grease muffin-pans and dredge them with flour; then invert the pans and tap the bottoms lightly so that no loose flour remains. Put a very little of the batter in each muffin-pan, as it rises considerably. Bake in fairly hot oven until brown. Serve the same day as baked. These cakes will fall a little when taken from the oven, which is as it should be.

TRUAX

Ladies' Home Journal Cookbook

Bran Muffins

1 cup whole bran
¾ cup milk
¼ cup sugar or molasses
2 tablespoons shortening
1 egg
1 cup flour
2½ teaspoons baking powder
½ teaspoon salt

Soak the bran in milk in a mixing bowl for 5 minutes. Mix the sugar or molasses and shortening, and add the well-beaten egg. Mix—do not beat. Combine with the soaked bran. Sift the flour, baking powder and salt together, and add to the mixture all at once. Stir just enough to blend the ingredients. The mixture need not be smooth. Fill greased muffin pans ⅔ full. Bake in hot oven, 400°, for about half an hour. Yield: 10–12 medium muffins.

BITTMAN

How to Cook Everything

Yorkshire Pudding

To accompany Prime Rib Roast for a Small Crowd, 1 (3-rib) roast, about 5 pounds: Essentially a large popover, this will serve at least 6; make 2 separate ones if you're going to serve 12 or more. The batter can be made ahead: Beat 3 eggs until foamy and light; add 1 cup milk and beat some more. Add salt to taste and 1 cup all-purpose flour; stir gently, only enough to combine ingredients. Refrigerate until 10 minutes before the roast is done. At that time, place a large cast-iron skillet or a 9-inch square baking pan in the oven to preheat. When you take the roast from the oven, put 3 tablespoons of its drippings into the pan, working carefully to avoid getting burned. Turn the heat to 450°F and put the pan back in the oven until your oven reaches that temperature. Carefully pour the batter into the pan. Bake 10 minutes, then lower the heat to 350°F and reverse the pan back to front once during cooking so the pudding browns evenly. Bake another 10 minutes, or slightly more, until the pudding is high and brown. Cut up and serve immediately, with the carved roast and its juices.

PECK

The Art of Fine Baking

Croissants

After years of experimentation with croissant recipes, I have finally discovered the knack of making perfect, flaky croissants at home. Actually, the proportions given in almost any standard recipe for croissants could be followed, if only the method for making and shaping them were made clear.

- 2 packages dry yeast or 1 ounce fresh yeast
- 1 tablespoon sugar
- 2 teaspoons salt
- 4 cups flour
- 1½ cups sweet butter
- 1 cup cold milk (approximately)
- 2 egg yolks mixed with 2 teaspoons cream

It is most important to use only a small amount of yeast in croissants so that the dough never rises before it is placed in the oven.

If dry yeast is used, follow directions on package. If fresh yeast is used, cream it with sugar and salt to make a syrup.

Place 3½ cups flour in a large bowl. Make a well in the center. Add yeast, 2 tablespoons butter cut into pieces, and enough cold milk to make a medium-firm dough—not as firm as a bread dough, but not sticky. Knead dough a few minutes, only until it is smooth, not elastic. If the dough is kneaded too long, the croissants will not be tender and flaky. Place dough in refrigerator to rest for 10 minutes.

While dough is resting, shape butter into a flattened brick, rolling it in some of remaining flour to prevent sticking. Place butter on a sheet of wax paper. Sprinkle it with flour and cover with another sheet of wax paper. Then roll out butter into a square ¼ inch thick. Cut square in half. Wrap pieces in wax paper and place in refrigerator.

Remove dough from refrigerator and roll it out on a cloth well dusted with flour, making a rectangle about 3 times longer than it is wide.

Brush off excess flour from surface of dough. Place a piece of butter in center. Fold one end of dough over butter. Place remaining butter on top. Fold second end of dough over butter. Press edges together.

Place dough on cloth so that the short ends are parallel to the edge of the table nearest you. Roll out on floured cloth into a long rectangle as before. Brush off excess flour. Fold both ends to meet in the center. Then fold once more, in half, as if you were closing the pages of a book, making 4 layers.

Press all edges together. Wrap and chill for one hour. Place dough on floured cloth, again being sure that the short ends are parallel to the edge of table nearest you. Roll out dough. Fold ends to meet in the center, then fold once again as before.

Chill dough at least two or three hours, or until it is very cold.

Cut dough in half. Roll out each half separately into a sheet ⅛ inch thick. Cut into long strips 5 inches wide. Divide strips into triangles. Roll up widest side of triangles toward opposite point fairly tightly, stretching slightly as you roll to make them longer. Do not try to shape further now. First chill rolls, preferably in freezer, for ½ hour.

Then, removing only 4 or 5 at a time, make each into a thinner, longer, and more compact shape by rolling it firmly against the pastry cloth with open palm of hand. Place on greased baking sheet, curving each into a croissant. Chill again until very cold.

Set oven at 475 degrees.

Brush with egg yolks mixed with cream. Place in preheated oven for 5 minutes. Reduce heat to 400 degrees. Continue baking about 8 minutes longer, or until croissants are golden brown.

YIELD: APPROXIMATELY 3 DOZEN

NOTE: These freeze well after baking.

ESPE BROWN

The Tassajara Bread Book

Mustard Gingerbread

A requested recipe.

(9" x 9" x 2" pan or loaf pan of suitable size)

2¼ c sifted whole wheat flour
1½ t baking powder
½ t salt
½ t soda
½ t cloves
1 t powdered mustard
1 t cinnamon
1 t ginger
½ c liquid oil or shortening
1 c unsulphured molasses
1 large egg
1 c hot water
(Whipped cream)

Sift together flour, baking powder, and salt. Add soda and spices to oil and blend carefully. Beat in molasses and egg. Add flour mixture alternately with hot water. Beat mixture ½ minute and turn into a well-greased and lightly-floured pan. Bake 350° for 45–50 minutes. Cool in pan 10 minutes. Turn onto wire rack, bread board or plate to finish cooling. May be served with whipped cream or fruit sauce.

KANDER

"The Settlement" Cook Book

Gingerbread No. 1.

½ cup sugar
3 tablespoons butter
1 egg
1½ cups flour
⅛ teaspoon salt
1 tablespoon ginger
1 teaspoon cinnamon
1 teaspoon soda
½ cup milk or hot water
½ cup molasses

Mix butter and sugar to a soft, creamy paste; add beaten egg. Mix spices, salt and soda with flour, and add a small portion. Add molasses and milk mixed together, and flour alternately. Bake 30 to 45 minutes.

ALLEN

Mrs. Allen's Cook Book

Old-Fashioned Strawberry Shortcake

1 quart strawberries
1 cupful sugar—more or less
Thick cream

Make a biscuit shortcake. Split and butter it liberally and fill with halved strawberries which have been allowed to stand with the sugar on them for at least an hour. Pile strawberries on the top, and serve warm with the cream.

BISCUIT SHORTCAKE

2½ cupfuls flour
4 teaspoonfuls baking powder
½ teaspoonful salt
1 tablespoonful sugar
1 cupful milk
3 tablespoonfuls butter or oleo margarine

Mix the dry ingredients, thoroughly. Work in in the shortening with the fingertips, and add the milk slowly. Toss on a floured board, divide into 2 parts, pat out and fit into 2 layer-cake pans. Bake 15 minutes in a hot oven.

CURTIS
Good Housekeeping Everyday Cook Book

Buttermilk Biscuits

Sift a quart of flour, add a tablespoon of lard, half a teaspoon of salt, one teaspoon of soda, sour buttermilk to make soft dough, roll thin, cut into biscuits, and bake in a very quick oven.

BEARD
American Cookery

Baking Powder Biscuits

- 2 cups sifted all-purpose flour
- 1 tablespoon baking powder
- ½ teaspoon salt
- ¼ cup shortening
- ¾ cup milk
- 1 tablespoon sugar (optional)

In former times, biscuits were the bread of many people. Breakfast, lunch, and dinner brought them to the table hot, light, and fresh. Made with butter, lard, bacon fat, chicken fat, or vegetable shortening, they were also commonly used as topping for savory pies—fried, of course—and for shortcakes. They are still standard countrywide, but homemade varieties have been supplanted by the advent of refrigerated biscuits, which may be bought and with very little preparation (brushing or dipping in melted butter does make a great difference), placed on a cookie sheet and baked. They are so good that I sometimes feel it is foolish to put these biscuits together from scratch. (Cream biscuits and shortcake are another matter.)

Sift the flour, baking powder, and salt (and sugar if used) into a bowl. Cut in the shortening (butter, lard, vegetable shortening, chicken fat—what you will). The pieces of fat should be quite fine. Add the milk and stir quickly until the dough clings together. Turn out on a floured board, knead a few times, and pat or roll out to ¼ to ½ inch thickness. Cut into rounds with a floured cutter 1 to 2 inches in diameter. Place on a buttered cookie sheet, or, if you like biscuits crisp on top and bottom and soft in the center, place in a buttered 9 × 9 inch pan. Bake at 450 degrees 12 to 15 minutes, or until light and brown.

NOTE: For richer biscuits, turn each one in a bowl or pan of melted butter before placing on the baking sheet.

CREAM BISCUITS. These were a specialty of mother's. I find them very light and thoroughly different from other biscuits. Use no shortening, but add ¾ to 1 cup heavy cream to make a light dough. Pat or roll ½ inch thick. Melt 4 tablespoons butter in a 9 × 9-inch baking pan or a small skillet. Dip each biscuit in the melted butter and place either in the pan or on a cookie sheet. Bake as above.

ESPE BROWN
The Tassajara Bread Book

Flakey Biscuits

Very rich and tender, also suitable for making cinnamon rolls and shortcake.

12–16 BISCUITS

- 1 c unbleached white flour
- 1 c whole wheat flour
- ½ c butter or margarine
- 3 t baking powder
- ½ t salt
- 2 eggs
- ½ c milk

Cut butter or margarine into flour, powder, and salt with pastry cutter or two knives, or rub gently between hands until butter or margarine is in mostly pea-sized pieces. Make well in center and add eggs and ½ c milk. Beat eggs and milk with a fork until smoothish. Then continue stirring with fork, gradually incorporating flour, until moistened. Knead dough just enough to bring it together.

Roll dough out on floured board ½" thick. Fold in thirds. Repeat rolling and folding. (The rolling and folding makes a flakier biscuit.) Roll out to ½" thick cut in rounds with cutter or glass. Place on ungreased sheet. Bake at 450–500° for about 8–10 minutes.

For variation add ½ c roasted sesame seeds or roasted sunflower seeds.

LEWIS

The Taste of Country Cooking

Ham Biscuits

The women of Freetown were amazing because they participated in the work of the fields and barnyard and yet would step right out of the field work when an unexpected friend or traveler turned up. They would make a quick fire in the wood cookstove, and in a few minutes emerge from the kitchen with a pot of hot coffee, a plate of biscuits—flannel-soft, a thin slice of ham inserted in each—a bowl of home-canned peaches, and perhaps some sugar cookies. Often the biscuits were made with chipped pieces of ham—the remains after the ham was sliced—and that is what this recipe calls for. Ham biscuits were usually served at ball games and suppers, and always at Sunday Revival.

Follow the recipe below and add 1 cup finely minced ham just after you have added the milk.

MAKES ABOUT 1 ½ DOZEN

3 cups sifted flour
1 scant teaspoon salt
½ teaspoon baking soda
4 teaspoons Royal Baking Powder
⅔ cup lard
1 cup plus 2 tablespoons buttermilk
(If sweet milk is being used, omit the baking soda and the 2 tablespoons of milk; sweet milk is more liquid than sour and therefore these are not needed.)

Take a large bowl, sift into it the measured flour, salt, soda, and baking powder. Add the lard and blend together with a pastry blender or your fingertips until the mixture has the texture of cornmeal. Add the milk all at once by scattering it over the dough. Stir vigorously with a stout wooden spoon. The dough will be very soft in the beginning but will stiffen in 2 or 3 minutes. Continue to stir a few minutes longer. After the dough has stiffened, scrape from sides of bowl into a ball and spoon onto a lightly floured surface for rolling. Dust over lightly with about a tablespoon of flour as the dough will be a bit sticky. Flatten the dough out gently with your hands into a thick, round cake, and knead for a minute by folding the outer edge of the dough into the center of the circle, giving a light knead as you fold the sides in overlapping each other. Turn the folded side face down and dust lightly if needed, being careful not to use too much flour and causing the dough to become too stiff. Dust the rolling pin and the rolling surface well. Roll the dough out evenly to a ½-inch thickness or a bit less. Pierce the surface of the dough with a table fork. (It was said piercing the dough released the air while baking.) Dust the biscuit cutter in flour first; this will prevent the dough sticking to the cutter and ruining the shape of the biscuit. Dust the cutter as often as needed. An added feature to your light, tender biscuits will be their straight sides. This can be achieved by not wiggling the cutter. Press the cutter into the dough and lift up with a sharp quickness without a wiggle. Cut the biscuits very close together to avoid having big pieces of dough left in between each biscuit. Trying to piece together and rerolling leftover dough will change the texture of the biscuits.

Place the biscuits ½ inch or more apart on a heavy cookie sheet or baking pan, preferably one with a bright surface. The biscuits brown more beautifully on a bright, shining pan than on a dull one, and a thick bottom helps to keep them from browning too much on the bottom. Set to bake in a preheated 450° oven for 13 minutes. Remove from the oven and let them rest for 3 to 4 minutes. Serve hot.

BROWN

Helen Brown's West Coast Cook Book

Sourdough Biscuits

An all-time favorite with pioneers and miners, and still beloved by prospectors, sheep herders, or anyone who has ever tasted them. There's something about the flavor of sourdough that never can be equaled or imitated. It's a bit difficult to get started on a sour dough unless the right yeasts are in the air. That's why the old-timers guarded their "starter" as they did their gold hoard. The dough was used for flapjacks, for biscuits, or for bread—in other words, they all but lived in it. There are several approved methods of starting a sour dough. Some used stale bread, some flour and milk, and some flour and water. The last is the surest, as some breads don't "work," and pasteurized milk cannot be used.

Mix 2 cups of flour, 2 cups of warm water, and 1 teaspoon of salt, and let it stand in a warm place for 2 to 4 days until sour and bubbly. This is your "souring." For biscuits a little of this was mixed with some "sody" and poured right into the top of a bag of flour, then worked around until it had taken up sufficient flour. Or, to be less primitive, the desired amount of "starter" was put in a dish, flour, shortening (often drippings), and salt and soda added by ear, and all mixed with water or milk to the proper consistency for whatever was to be made. Always some of the sourings were kept, usually smelling to heaven, for wild yeasts are hard to tame. But the worse the smell, the better the dough. Many sourdough experts have never started from scratch—they were originally given some starter by an old-timer, and have never allowed it to give out. One story goes that the original came over with Columbus. At any rate, every sheep herder and prospector in the Northwest knows how to make sourdough, and knows it's the best bread there is.

CUNNINGHAM

The Breakfast Book

Dried Fruit Cream Scones

ONE DOZEN SCONES

2 cups all-purpose flour
1 tablespoon baking powder
½ teaspoon salt
¼ cup sugar
½ cup chopped dried fruit (apricots, prunes, or figs)
¼ cup golden raisins
1¼ cups heavy cream

GLAZE

3 tablespoons butter, melted
2 tablespoons sugar

Preheat the oven to 425°F. Use an ungreased baking sheet.

Combine the flour, baking powder, salt, and sugar in a bowl, stirring with a fork to mix well. Add the dried fruit and raisins. Still using a fork, stir in the cream and mix until the dough holds together in a rough mass (the dough will be *quite* sticky).

Lightly flour a board and transfer the dough to it. Knead the dough 8 or 9 times. Pat into a circle about 10 inches round. For the glaze, spread the butter over the top and side of the circle of dough and sprinkle the sugar on top. Cut the circle into 12 wedges and place each piece on the baking sheet, allowing about an inch between pieces.

Bake for about 15 minutes, or until golden brown.

GAIGE

New York World's Fair Cook Book

Leavenworth Corn-bread Sticks

2 cups corn meal
1 teaspoon soda
2 cups thick sour milk
1 teaspoon salt
¼ cup sugar
2 well-beaten eggs
2 tablespoons melted fat

Sift dry ingredients together. Add milk to beaten eggs and melted fat. Combine mixtures. Put batter in oiled pans. Bake in hot oven (400°F.) about twenty-five minutes.

HIBBEN

The National Cook Book

Rhode Island Johnny Cake

2 cups Rhode Island corn meal
1 scant teaspoon salt
boiling water

Put the meal in the oven to heat; take it out and add salt and enough boiling water to "chop" off the spoon easily. Beat hard for about 4 minutes. Have an iron frying-pan very hot, with ½ inch of bacon or sausage drippings. Drop the cakes far enough apart to keep each quite separate, and fry brown on each side. They should be about 3½ inches in diameter, and about ½ inch thick. Serve immediately, and split open and butter at table.

If the greyish Rhode Island meal is not available, white corn meal can be used, but never yellow.

LEWIS
The Taste of Country Cooking

Spoon Bread

SERVES 5

- 1 cup water-ground white cornmeal
- ½ teaspoon salt
- 2 teaspoons sugar
- ⅓ teaspoon baking soda
- 2 teaspoons Royal Baking Powder
- 3 medium-sized eggs, beaten
- 3 tablespoons butter
- 2 cups buttermilk

- 1 8 × 8 × 2-inch baking pan, or a 1½-quart soufflé dish

Preheat oven to 400°. Sift the cornmeal, salt, sugar, soda, and baking powder together into a mixing bowl. Make a well in the center and add the beaten eggs. At this time put the butter in the baking pan and set it in the oven to heat. Stir the eggs into the meal vigorously, then pour in the buttermilk, stirring well again. Remove the hot pan from the oven and tilt it around to butter the entire surface. Pour the excess butter into the meal batter, stir quickly, and pour the batter into the hot baking dish. Bake for 35 minutes in a 400° oven. Serve in the pan right from the oven with loads of fresh butter.

ROBERTSON
Laurel's Kitchen

Tennessee Corn Pone

A homesick friend from Knoxville described a dish his grandma used to make. After several false starts, we came up with this—a dead ringer, he says, and certainly one of our favorites.

- 4 cups very juicy cooked and seasoned beans (especially pinto or kidney)
- 2 cups cornmeal
- 2 teaspoons baking soda
- 1 teaspoon salt
- 1 quart buttermilk
- 2 eggs, slightly beaten
- ⅓ cup margarine

Heat beans until quite hot and pour into a lightly greased 9" × 13" baking dish.

Preheat oven to 450°.

Mix the cornmeal, baking soda, and salt in a large bowl. Melt the margarine and combine with buttermilk and eggs.

Stir the wet and dry ingredients together until smooth and pour them over the hot beans. Bake on the top rack of your oven until bread is a rich golden color and the sides of the corn bread pull away from the sides of the pan. This takes about 30 minutes.

SERVES 10 TO 12

WAFFLES & PANCAKES

BÉGUÉ
Mme. Bégué's Recipes of Old New Orleans Creole Cookery

LOST BREAD OR PAIN PERDU. Take six thick slices of stale bread and soak in sugared milk, to which has been added a large spoonful of brandy. Drain and when ready to use turn each slice in beaten eggs. Fry in hot lard, brown well on both sides, sprinkle with powdered sugar and serve hot.

CUNNINGHAM
The Breakfast Book

Buttermilk Pancakes

FOURTEEN 3-INCH PANCAKES

Among buttermilk pancakes, I don't think you can beat these. They are slightly sourish and light, easy to make, and the batter holds well for several days in the refrigerator.

- 1 cup buttermilk
- 1 egg, room temperature
- 3 tablespoons butter, melted
- ¾ cup all-purpose flour
- ½ teaspoon salt
- 1 teaspoon baking soda

Put the buttermilk, egg, and melted butter in a mixing bowl. Stir briskly until the mixture is smooth and blended.

Stir the flour, salt, and baking soda together in a small bowl so they are well blended. Stir into the buttermilk mixture only until the dry ingredients are moistened—leave the lumps.

Heat a skillet or griddle to medium hot. Grease lightly and spoon out about 3 tablespoons of batter per pancake. Spread the batter with the back of the spoon so it is thinned out a little. Cook until a few bubbles break on top. Turn the pancake over and cook briefly. Keep pancakes warm until enough are cooked to serve.

RYE BUTTERMILK PANCAKES: Use ½ cup all-purpose flour and ¼ cup rye flour.

WHOLE WHEAT BUTTERMILK PANCAKES: Replace up to ½ cup all-purpose flour with an equivalent amount of whole wheat flour.

YELLOW CORNMEAL BUTTERMILK PANCAKES: Substitute ¼ cup yellow cornmeal for ¼ cup of the flour in the recipe.

CUNNINGHAM
The Breakfast Book

Bridge Creek Heavenly Hots

FIFTY TO SIXTY DOLLAR-SIZE PANCAKES

These are the lightest sour cream silver-dollar-size hotcakes I've ever had—they seem to hover over the plate. They are heavenly and certainly should be served hot.

- 4 eggs
- ½ teaspoon salt
- ½ teaspoon baking soda
- ¼ cup cake flour
- 2 cups sour cream
- 3 tablespoons sugar

Put the eggs in a mixing bowl and stir until well blended. Add the salt, baking soda, flour, sour cream, and sugar, and mix well. All of this can be done in a blender, if you prefer.

Heat a griddle or frying pan until it is good and hot, film with grease, and drop small spoonfuls of batter onto the griddle—just enough to spread to an approximately 2½-inch round. When a few bubbles appear on top of the pancakes, turn them over and cook briefly.

KANDER
"The Settlement" Cook Book

German Pancakes

- 1 pint flour
- 1 pint milk
- 3 eggs, whites separate

Heat butter in deep sauce pan so as to boil, drop a large spoonful of the batter into hot butter and fry quickly. Rub up the edges of the pancake as it fries, and turn over; drain on butchers' paper and serve with lemon and sugar.

SAX
Classic Home Desserts

Reuben's Legendary Apple Pancake

Reuben's was the legendary Times Square after-theatre hangout for generations of New Yorkers, the place where they tucked into Reuben's 12-inch apple pancake, along with the famed cheesecake, as a late-night snack. Researching the origins of this archetypal pancake, food journalist Marian Burros was directed to three very different recipes (all of which claimed to be the authentic original). Finally, she tracked down Arnold Reuben, Jr., the owner's son.

"We had a specialist make the pancakes," Mr. Reuben explained. "We had special, well-seasoned big iron skillets and we never washed them." After buying a 12-inch cast-iron skillet, learning how to caramelize the sugar properly and encountering the biggest hurdle of all, "trying to flip a 12-inch pancake," Ms. Burros concluded that the recipe would work better if halved and made in a smaller skillet.

She's right. I've streamlined it further by cooking the pancake in a nonstick skillet and by cutting back on butter and sugar. But it still tastes like Reuben's, glazed and gilded with caramel syrup—a great way to get your apple a day.

Try it for a late-night snack or a leisurely breakfast.

SERVES 2

1 large green apple, such as Granny Smith
2 tablespoons raisins
9 tablespoons (½ cup plus 1 tablespoon) sugar
½ teaspoon ground cinnamon
3 large eggs
½ cup milk
1 teaspoon pure vanilla extract
½ cup all-purpose flour
4–6 tablespoons unsalted butter

1. Peel and core the apple; slice ¼ inch thick. Place in a bowl with the raisins, 1½ tablespoons of the sugar and the cinnamon. Mix well; cover and set aside, stirring occasionally, until needed.

2. In a bowl, beat the eggs with the milk and vanilla; whisk in the flour to make a smooth batter. Do not overmix.

3. Preheat the oven to 400 degrees F, with a rack in the center. In an 8-inch ovenproof nonstick skillet, heat 1 tablespoon of the butter over medium heat until it sizzles. Pour off any liquid that has accumulated, and add the apple and raisin mixture to the pan. Cook, stirring, until the apples soften, about 5 minutes.

4. Add 1 tablespoon butter and let it melt. Pour in the batter to cover completely. Cook over medium-high heat, pulling the set sides of the pancake away from the edges and allowing the runny batter to flow under and cook, shaking the pan occasionally to prevent sticking, until the pancake begins to firm, about 3 minutes. Sprinkle about 1½ tablespoons of the sugar evenly over the top.

5. You can either flip the pancake or invert it onto a plate and slide it back into the skillet. If you are brave enough to flip it, first add another 1½ tablespoons of butter, cut into pats, slipping it underneath the edges and center of the pancake. Flip the pancake. If you are inverting it onto a plate, do it decisively. Melt 1 tablespoon of butter in the empty pan, sprinkle with about 1 tablespoon sugar and slide the pancake back in.

6. Cook the second side, allowing the sugar to caramelize on the bottom. When it begins to brown (after 3 or 4 minutes), sprinkle the top with about 2 tablespoons of the sugar. If the pancake seems to stick, add a little more butter. Flip or invert the pancake again and allow the sugar to caramelize on the bottom, about 4 minutes.

7. Sprinkle about 2 tablespoons of sugar on top. Add more butter to the pan if needed. Flip or invert the pancake once again and continue to caramelize, shaking the pan occasionally, about 3 or 4 minutes longer.

8. Sprinkle the top of the pancake lightly with another tablespoon of sugar. Place the skillet in the oven and bake until the surface is golden brown, 8 to 15 minutes. Serve hot, dividing the pancake in the pan and transferring it to plates with a spatula.

MACAUSLAND
The Gourmet Cookbook

Crêpes Suzette

Make *crêpes gourmet* 5 to 5½ inches across. Place them on a hot dish to keep warm while preparing the sauce.

Rub 4 lumps of loaf sugar on the rind of an orange. Put the sugar on a plate with 3 tablespoons sweet butter and crush together with a fork, mixing until creamy. Put another 2 tablespoons butter in a chafing dish or in a flat pan and add the juice of 1 orange, a few drops of lemon juice, and ½ cup curaçao, Cointreau, benedictine, or Grand Marnier. When this comes to the boil, stir in the other mixture. Place the *crêpes* in this sauce, spooning it over them liberally. A teaspoon of ground filberts or grated almonds may be put in the center of each *crêpe*. Fold each *crêpe* in quarters, like a handkerchief. Sprinkle with ½ cup hot brandy and ignite. Serve with the sauce over them.

TARTS AND PIES

CHILD, BERTHOLLE, AND BECK
Mastering the Art of French Cooking

La Tarte des Demoiselles Tatin

Upside-down Apple Tart—hot or cold

This is an especially good tart if your apples are full of flavor. It is cooked in a baking dish with the pastry on top of the apples. When done, it is reversed onto a serving dish and presents a lovely mass of caramelized apples.

FOR 8 PEOPLE

4 lbs. crisp cooking or eating apples
⅓ cup granulated sugar
Optional: 1 tsp cinnamon
2 Tb softened butter
A baking dish 9 to 10 inches in diameter and 2 to 2½ inches deep (Pyrex is practical, as you can see when the tart is done)
½ cup granulated sugar
6 Tb melted butter
Aluminum foil, if needed
A fireproof serving dish
Powdered sugar, if needed
Chilled sweet short paste (proportions for 1 cup of flour)
2 cups heavy cream, or *crème fraîche*

Quarter, core, and peel the apples. Cut into lengthwise slices ⅛ inch thick. Toss in a bowl with the sugar and optional cinnamon. You should have about 10 cups of apples.

Butter the baking dish heavily especially on the bottom. Sprinkle half the sugar in the bottom of the dish and arrange a third of the apples over it. Sprinkle with a third of the melted butter. Repeat with a layer of half the remaining apples and butter, then a final layer of apples and butter. Sprinkle the rest of the sugar over the apples.

Preheat oven to 375 degrees.

Roll out the pastry to a thickness of ⅛ inch. Cut it into a circle the size of the top of the baking dish. Place it over the apples, allowing its edges to fall against the inside edge of the dish. Cut 4 or 5 holes about ⅛ inch long in the top of the pastry to allow cooking steam to escape.

Bake in lower third of preheated oven for 45 to 60 minutes. If pastry begins to brown too much, cover lightly with aluminum foil. Tart is done when you tilt the dish and see that a thick brown syrup rather than a light liquid exudes from the apples between the crust and the edge of the dish.

Immediately unmold the tart onto serving dish. If the apples are not a light caramel brown, which is often the case, sprinkle rather heavily with powdered sugar and run under a moderately hot broiler for several minutes to caramelize the surface lightly.

Keep warm until serving time, and accompany with a bowl of cream. (May also be served cold, but we prefer it warm.)

BROWN

Helen Brown's West Coast Cook Book

A CALIFORNIA PIONEER APPLE PIE, 1852, said Mrs. B. C. Whiting in *How We Cook in Los Angeles* (1894), was made with a filling of soda crackers made tart with citric acid, moist with water, and flavored with brown sugar and cinnamon. "The deception was most complete and readily accepted. Apples at this early date were a dollar a pound, and we young people all craved a piece of Mother's apple pie to appease our homesick feelings."

SAX

Classic Home Desserts

The World's Best Lemon Tart

Tarte au Citron Nézard

After tasting my way through just about every tarte au citron *in Paris, I came back again and again to the simple version baked at Nézard, a tiny unknown pâtisserie on the Left Bank near Montparnasse. Nowhere else did the lemon burst with such sharp citrus zing in each mouthful. No other tart cut so cleanly, each slice standing neat and trim on the plate, its unadorned surface of baked lemon curd glazed with gold.*

There's still no dessert more refreshing after dinner, whether in winter, when there's little other fruit around, or in summer, served with a few fresh berries on the side.

MAKES ONE 9- OR 10-INCH TART; SERVES ABOUT 8

Rich Tart Dough for 1 shell

LEMON CURD FILLING

Juice of 2 lemons
6 large eggs
1 scant cup sugar
10 tablespoons (1 stick plus 2 tablespoons) cold unsalted butter, cut into pieces
Finely grated zest of 3 lemons
3 tablespoons apricot preserves or orange marmalade
1 paper-thin lemon slice

1. Roll out the dough on a lightly floured surface into a large circle; the crust for this tart should be very thin. Gently fold the dough in half, and fit it, without stretching, into a lightly buttered 9- or 10-inch fluted tart or quiche pan with a removable bottom. Trim off the excess dough, leaving a ¾-inch overhang. Tuck in the overhang, pressing the edges of the dough against the sides of the tart pan to form a high, smooth border. Chill the tart shell while you preheat the oven to 400 degrees F, with a rack in the center.

2. Line the tart shell with a sheet of lightly buttered foil, buttered side down. Weigh down with dried beans, rice or pie weights; place the shell on a heavy baking sheet. Bake until the edges are set, 8 to 10 minutes. Very carefully lift out the weights and foil; prick the dough lightly with a fork. Continue to bake until the pastry is very pale gold, about 8 minutes longer. Cool slightly on a wire rack; leave the oven on.

3. LEMON CURD FILLING: In the top of a double boiler or a heatproof bowl, whisk together the lemon juice, eggs and sugar until blended. Add the butter, and set over simmering water. Whisk the mixture constantly until thick and smooth, about 8 minutes. Do not let the mixture boil; be sure to scrape the bottom as you whisk. Remove from the heat. Strain the mixture into a clean bowl; whisk in the lemon zest. (If you are not going to use the custard immediately, lay a sheet of wax paper or plastic wrap directly on the surface and refrigerate.)

4. Pour the custard into the tart shell. Bake until the filling is set and lightly golden, about 30 minutes. Cool the tart to room temperature on a wire rack, 1 to 2 hours.

5. Strain a thin layer of the preserves directly over the surface of the tart (if you are using a stiff marmalade, it may need to be warmed before straining). Gently brush it over the surface of the tart, glazing evenly (brush gently so you don't tear the custard). Lay the thin slice of lemon in the center of the tart; glaze the lemon slice with the preserves. Remove the tart from the rim of the pan and serve at room temperature.

VARIATION

FRESH ORANGE TART: For the lemon zest and juice, substitute the zest of 1 orange and 1 lemon, ¼ cup fresh orange juice and the juice of ½ lemon.

BROWNSTONE

The Associated Press Cookbook

Strawberry Deep Dish Pie

1¼ cups sugar
⅓ cup cornstarch
¼ teaspoon salt
4 pints fresh strawberries, halved
2 tablespoons butter, melted
1⅓ cups flour, stir before measuring
½ teaspoon salt
½ cup solid all-vegetable shortening
2 tablespoons butter
3 tablespoons water
½ egg white, beaten slightly
1 teaspoon sugar

In a large bowl stir together 1¼ cups sugar, cornstarch and salt. Add strawberries and melted butter; mix well; let stand while you prepare pastry.

In a medium sized bowl stir together the flour and salt. Cut in shortening until the size of small peas; cut in butter until the size of large peas. Sprinkle with water, toss with a fork and press into a square. On a lightly floured surface roll out pastry to a 10-inch square. Cut 10 1-inch strips with pastry wheel.

Turn strawberry mixture into a 9-inch square (2 quart) oven-glass baking dish. Weave pastry strips over strawberries to form lattice top. Brush with egg white; sprinkle with 1 teaspoon sugar. Bake in a preheated 425-degree oven 30 minutes or until crust is golden brown. Serve warm in bowls with vanilla ice cream.

MAKES 8 SERVINGS

NOTE: Toward the end of the baking time, if the strawberry juice bubbles up and looks as if it's going to run over, place a piece of foil on a lower rack under the baking dish to collect the syrup and save you oven washing.

TIME-LIFE BOOKS

American Cooking

Prune and Apricot Pie

TO MAKE ONE 9-INCH PIE

2½ cups all-purpose flour
8 tablespoons chilled vegetable shortening or lard
4 tablespoons chilled butter, cut into ¼-inch pieces
¼ teaspoon salt
6 tablespoons ice water

FILLING

1½ cups dried pitted prunes
1½ cups dried apricots
1 cup shelled walnuts, coarsely chopped
½ cup sugar
1 teaspoon grated lemon rind
1 teaspoon vanilla
8 tablespoons (½ cup) melted butter, plus 1 tablespoon
1 cup heavy cream, whipped (optional)

In a large mixing bowl, combine the flour, vegetable shortening or lard, butter and salt. Working quickly, use your fingertips to rub the flour and fat together until they look like flakes of coarse meal. Pour 6 tablespoons of ice water over the mixture, toss together, and press and knead gently with your hands until the dough can be gathered into a compact ball. Dust very lightly with flour, wrap in wax paper and chill for at least ½ hour.

Lightly butter a 9-inch pie plate and divide the ball of dough into 2 parts, one a third larger than the other. On a floured surface, roll out the larger half of dough into a circle about ⅛ inch thick and 13 to 14 inches in diameter. Lift it up on the rolling pin and unroll it over the pie plate. Be sure to leave enough slack in the middle of the pastry to enable you to line the plate without pulling or stretching the dough. Trim the excess pastry with a sharp knife, so that the pastry is even with the outer rim of the pie plate. Roll the smaller half of the dough into a rectangle 12 inches long and about ⅛ inch thick. With a sharp knife or pastry wheel, cut it into 6 strips about 1 inch wide. Refrigerate both the pie shell and the pastry strips while you make the filling.

Place the prunes and apricots in a small enameled or stainless-steel saucepan, and pour in enough water to cover them by about an inch. Bring the water to a boil. Boil rapidly for 4 to 5 minutes, then drain in a sieve. Dry the fruit with paper towels, and cut each prune and apricot into

4 pieces. Combine them in a mixing bowl with the walnuts, sugar, grated lemon rind and vanilla. Add the melted butter and, with a large spoon, mix together thoroughly. Spoon the filling into the pie shell. Arrange the reserved 3 strips of dough ¾ of an inch apart across the top of the pie and crisscross the other 3 strips of dough over them. With your fingers, tuck the ends firmly under the rim of the pie plate to secure them.

Preheat the oven to 350°. Brush the crisscross strips of pastry with the 1 tablespoon of melted butter and bake the pie in the middle of the oven for about 1 hour, or until the pastry is golden brown and the fruit is tender.

Serve warm or at room temperature, accompanied by unsweetened whipped cream if you like.

BEARD

American Cookery

Fresh Fruit Pie (Two-Crust)

4 to 5 cups prepared fruit
¾ to 1½ cups sugar
Flour
¼ teaspoon salt
Spice (optional)
1 to 2 tablespoons butter
Pastry for two-crust 9-inch pie

Prepare the pastry and roll out the bottom crust. Fit without stretching into the pan and trim the edge. Roll out the top crust. Prepare the fruit, and mix with the sugar, flour, salt, and spice. Turn the filling into the pie, and dot with butter. Moisten the edge of the bottom crust, place the top crust on it, and cut slits in it to allow the steam to escape. Trim the crust and crimp the edges to seal it. Bake in a 450-degree oven 15 minutes. Reduce the heat to 350 degrees, and bake about 25 to 30 minutes. Do not overbake. The pie will continue to cook after it is out of the oven. Cool the pie on a rack, unless it is to be served warm.

PEACH PIE: Peel, pit, and slice peaches about ½ inch thick. Very sweet peaches will be improved in flavor by the addition of 1 or 2 tablespoons lemon juice. Use 4 tablespoons flour combined with the sugar and salt. For very firm varieties of peaches, bake the pie slightly longer. For early peaches, generally of a very loose texture, bake the pie a total of about 40 minutes.

BURROS AND LEVINE

The Elegant But Easy Cookbook

Fruit Torte

8 SERVINGS

This gets a 10-star rating on our list.

Cream

1 cup sugar
½ cup butter

Add

1 cup flour, sifted
1 teaspoon baking powder
Salt
2 eggs

Place in 9-inch spring form. Add to top and cover entire surface with one of the following or a combination of:

1 pint blueberries
24 halves pitted Italian plums (skin side up)
Sliced apples
Sliced peaches

(In winter, frozen or canned blueberries or peaches may be substituted. If using canned, drain and wash off syrup well.)

Sprinkle top with

Sugar
Lemon juice
Flour (if fruit is very juicy)
Cinnamon (use a heavy hand)

Bake at 350° F for one hour. Delicious when served with vanilla ice cream or whipped cream. Best served slightly warm. Refresh in oven, if desired.

SAX

Classic Home Desserts

Mixed Fruit Cobbler

The cobbler prototype: light buttermilk biscuit topping, "cobbled" (cut in individual biscuit rounds) and placed over fruit. The juices are left runny. Serve this warm in bowls, not plates, with a pitcher of cream or a scoop of ice cream (or frozen or chilled vanilla or plain yogurt).

Make this cobbler with any soft fruit, using similar quantities and adjusting for sweetness. Add a touch of grated fresh or minced crystallized ginger, ground spices or a few berries to a pear cobbler; add a sliced quince to an apple cobbler; add a handful of dried cherries, blueberries or cranberries to a peach cobbler.

SERVES 4 TO 6

FRUIT

4 firm-ripe nectarines
3 firm-ripe peaches
Juice of 1 lemon
2 plums, halved, stoned and sliced
1½–2 cups blueberries or a combination of blueberries and blackberries, picked over
½ teaspoon minced or grated peeled fresh ginger
¼ cup packed light brown sugar
3 tablespoons sugar
1 tablespoon cornstarch
½ teaspoon ground cinnamon

LIGHT BISCUIT DOUGH

1½ cups all-purpose flour
⅓ cup sugar
1 teaspoon baking powder
½ teaspoon baking soda
½ teaspoon salt
¼ cup (½ stick) cold unsalted butter, cut into pieces
½ teaspoon pure vanilla extract
⅔ cup buttermilk (or ⅓ cup plain yogurt thinned either with ¼ cup skim milk or with cold water)
Milk and sugar, for glaze

Ice cream, frozen yogurt or heavy cream, for topping

1. **FRUIT:** Peel the nectarines and the peaches by immersing them in a large pot of boiling water for about 30 seconds; rinse under cold water in a colander. The skins should slip off easily. Halve the fruit, remove the stones and cut into thick wedges, letting them fall into a mixing bowl and tossing them with the lemon juice to prevent discoloration. Pour off any excess liquid, leaving the fruit somewhat moist. Add the plums, berries and ginger; toss.

2. In a small bowl, stir together the brown and white sugars, the cornstarch and the cinnamon with a fork or small whisk until free of lumps. Sprinkle this mixture over the fruit and toss gently with your fingers or 2 large spoons until thoroughly mixed. Transfer the mixture to an 8-inch square baking pan, oval gratin dish or other shallow baking dish with a capacity of about 2 quarts.

3. **LIGHT BISCUIT DOUGH:** In a food processor, combine the flour, sugar, baking powder, baking soda and salt, pulsing once or twice. Add the butter and process, pulsing, until the mixture is crumbly. Add the vanilla and dribble most, but not all, of the buttermilk or yogurt mixture over the dry mixture; pulse to combine. If necessary, add the remaining buttermilk; the dough should hold together and should be moist, but not sticky. Gather the dough onto a floured sheet of plastic wrap or wax paper, patting it together to form a cohesive disk. (The dough can be made several hours in advance; wrap and refrigerate until needed.)

4. Preheat the oven to 400 degrees F. Pat out the dough on a lightly floured sheet of wax paper to about ¾ inch thick. Cut with a biscuit cutter or glass dipped in flour; reroll and cut the scraps. Brush the biscuit rounds with milk; then arrange them over the fruit. Lightly sprinkle the biscuits with sugar.

5. Place the cobbler in the oven with a sheet of foil underneath to catch any drips. Bake the cobbler until the biscuits are golden and the fruit is bubbly, 30 to 35 minutes. Cool briefly on a wire rack. Serve warm, with ice cream, frozen yogurt or cream.

VARIATIONS

SUMMER

Blueberries/Blackberries
Blackberries/Nectarines/Plums
Raspberries/Peaches/Red Currants
Sweet and Sour Cherries/Nectarines

WINTER

Cranberries/Apples/Pears
Pears/Dried Cherries/Ginger
Pears/Bananas/Mangoes

PECK
The Art of Fine Baking

Linzer Torte

This traditional Viennese cake looks more like a tart than a torte.

1 cup unblanched almonds
1¼ cups sifted flour
1 cup soft butter
2 hard-cooked egg yolks, mashed
2 raw egg yolks
½ cup sugar
2 tablespoons dark, unsweetened cocoa
⅛ teaspoon ground cloves
¼ teaspoon cinnamon
1 teaspoon vanilla
1 teaspoon grated lemon rind
1 egg, beaten with
2 teaspoons light cream
1½ cups thick raspberry jam

Set oven at 350 degrees. Lightly grease a cooky sheet.

Grate almonds fine. Mix flour and grated almonds together in a bowl. Make a well in the center. In well, place butter, mashed hard-cooked egg yolks, raw yolks, sugar, cocoa, spices, vanilla, and lemon rind. Combine these ingredients into a paste, gradually incorporating the flour and almonds to make a dough. If dough is very soft, chill it slightly.

Roll ½ the chilled dough between sheets of wax paper to a thickness of ½ inch. Using a plate or pan as a pattern, cut out a round of dough 6 inches in diameter. Place on prepared cooky sheet. Brush lightly with egg mixed with cream.

Roll out remaining half of dough into a rectangle ¼ inch thick between sheets of wax paper. Cut into strips ¼ inch wide. Make a border on circle with some of the strips, pressing to make certain they are set on firmly. Brush with egg.

Fill shell with 1 cup raspberry jam. Using most of remaining strips, make a lattice across top of the torte. The ends of each strip should rest on the border. Brush ends of strips with egg. Make a second border on top of first, using last of strips. Press down firmly with the tines of a fork. Chill torte (or you can freeze it for baking later).

Set oven at 350 degrees. Brush lattice and border with egg. Bake 40 to 50 minutes or until torte is lightly browned. Jam will have darkened in baking. While torte is still hot, use remaining jam for color to fill in between lattice strips.

DE GOUY
The Gold Cook Book

Pecan Pie

Cream ⅓ cup of butter until light; gradually adding ½ cup of brown sugar and creaming until light and fluffy. Add 3 eggs, one at a time, beating well after each addition, also ¼ teaspoon of salt, 1 cup of dark corn syrup and ½ teaspoon of vanilla. Blend thoroughly, and finally stir in 1 cup of chopped slightly floured pecans. Line a 9-inch pie plate with pastry, crimping the edge, pour filling into it as evenly as possible, and bake in a hot oven (450° F.) for 10 minutes to set the pastry. Then reduce the heat to moderately slow (300–325° F.) and continue baking for about 30 minutes, or until a silver knife inserted in the center comes out clean.

NOTE: The filling browns very quickly. To avoid over-browning before filling is cooked, allow the oven door to remain open a minute when temperature is reduced, to make sure that heat is reduced at once. Watch closely for remainder of baking period.

TROPP
The Modern Art of Chinese Cooking

Mendocino Lemon Tart

Mendocino is a picturesque spot on the north California coast, where the cliffs drop steeply to the sea, and the mist rushing over the weather-worn trees reminds me of Japan. In a corner of the town is a charming rose-ringed Victorian house, my friend Margaret's Café Beaujolais. It is there one can find extraordinary desserts, including this smooth and tangy lemon tart. This is a simple, foolproof dessert, perfect for beginners. The rich, cookie-type crust is made in minutes in a food processor, then pressed into place by hand. The filling, a smooth lemon curd, requires nothing more than an arm to beat it. You may garnish the tart with plain or fancy nuts or whipped cream rosettes, all depending on your mood and the style of the occasion. The recipe will make two 9-inch tarts. The crust for one or both may be frozen. The lemon curd may be refrigerated for 2 weeks, or frozen for a longer period if you like, with no loss of flavor or texture. Frozen lemon curd should be defrosted in the refrigerator, then beaten 2–3 seconds in a food processor, or thoroughly with a wire whisk before using.

TECHNIQUE NOTES:

If your lemons are the least bit old or hard, put them in a preheated 150° oven for 10–20 minutes. Even the hardest ones will soften and become easy to juice.

Cooking in the top of a double boiler provides a gentle, indirect heat. Do not let the water touch the bottom of the pan or rise above a steaming near-simmer. Otherwise, you risk curdling the eggs.

Freezing the crust partially or fully before baking minimizes shrinkage. It also, by firming the butter, contributes to a flakier crust with a more pronounced layering.

YIELDS TWO 9-INCH TARTS
EACH TART SERVES 8–10

FOR THE CRUST

2 cups all-purpose flour
2 tablespoons sugar
medium-grated zest of 2 lemons (use box grater; do not grate any of the white pith)
½ pound room temperature sweet butter, cut into large cubes
pinch salt

FOR THE LEMON CURD

3 whole large eggs
3 large yolks
medium-grated zest of 2 lemons (use box grater; do not grate any of the white pith)
½ cup freshly squeezed, strained lemon juice
⅔ cup plus 2 teaspoons sugar
¼ teaspoon salt
¼ pound room temperature sweet butter, cubed

TO GARNISH

freshly toasted sliced almonds
or
Crystalline Walnut Halves
or
about ½ cup chilled heavy (whipping) cream, whipped to stiff peaks with powdered confectioners' sugar and pure vanilla extract to taste

MAKING THE DOUGH:

Add the flour, sugar, and lemon zest to the dry work bowl of a food processor fitted with the steel knife. Process 5 seconds to mix. Distribute ½ of the butter cubes evenly on top of the flour mixture, turn on the machine, and drop the remaining cubes one by one through the feed tube. Process about 20–30 seconds, until well blended. The dough will look crumbly. It will not form a ball around the blade.

If you do not have a food processor, blend the ingredients in a mixer or by hand until crumbly and well combined.

Press the dough into 2 compact balls. At this point the dough for one or both crusts may be refrigerated or frozen, wrapped separately in wax paper, then sealed airtight. The dough should be soft and at room temperature when you shape the crust.

PRESSING THE DOUGH INTO THE PAN:

Use ball of dough for each 9-inch removable-bottom tart pan.

Begin with a big wad of dough to form the wall and the outer rim of the base. Use your thumb to press the dough into the side of the pan, turning the pan as you go, removing most of the excess from the top, and pressing on a slight diagonal, so after one full turn you have the wall and the outer rim pressed into place. Go around again, if necessary, to even the dough. The wall should be evenly 3⁄16 of an inch thick, becoming slightly thicker where it slopes to meet the base, and should bulge ⅛ inch above the pan to allow for shrinkage during baking. Then use the flat of your fingers to press the remaining dough into the bottom of the pan, to form an even base 3⁄16 inch thick. The whole process will take 10 minutes or less once you get the hang of it.

Chill the crust in the freezer, loosely covered, for a full 30 minutes before baking. For longer freezing, seal airtight once firm, then bake directly from the freezer without defrosting.

BAKING THE CRUST:

Bake the crust on the middle level of a preheated 375° oven for about 20 minutes, until pale golden, rotating the pan after 10 minutes to insure even browning.

Remove to a rack, then let the crust cool completely in the pan. Once cooled, it may be kept at room temperature several hours before filling.

COOKING AND CHILLING THE LEMON CURD:

Beat the whole eggs and the egg yolks until combined.

In the top of a double boiler over very low heat, combine the grated zest, lemon juice, sugar, and salt. Add the beaten eggs, then whisk gently for 15 minutes, until the mixture is thick enough to coat a spoon. Add the butter, stir to melt, then remove the pot from the heat.

Strain the mixture through a sieve to remove the bits of zest and coagulated egg. Chill uncovered in the refrigerator for 4 hours, until thoroughly cold and thick. To hasten the process, you may chill the lemon curd in the freezer for 1–2 hours, but be diligent about stirring it up from the bottom every 15 minutes, so it does not begin to freeze.

ASSEMBLING THE TART:
Just before serving, remove the metal collar from the tart pan by centering it on your palm or the top of a large can. Leave the fragile crust on the metal base and put it on a doily-lined serving plate. Fill the shell evenly with lemon curd to come ⅛–3⁄16 inch below the top of the crust, then smooth the top lightly with a spatula. Garnish with a border of sliced toasted almonds, Crystalline Walnut Halves, or whipped cream rosettes pressed from a pastry bag fitted with a star tip.

Slice the tart at the table, or—Cafe Beaujolais-style—serve each slice on an individual doily-lined plate, with a fresh tea rose alongside.

Eat the tart promptly. It quickly wilts.

MENU SUGGESTIONS

This tart is zesty and simple enough to follow a "dressy" meal of mildly seasoned foods or an informal meal of lightly spiced dishes with equal ease. It is especially good when served on the heels of deep-fried foods and smoked foods, when the lemony taste of the tart is wonderfully refreshing. For the same reason, it is a very good ending to a meal featuring fish. To serve alongside the tart, try a California Angelica, which is reappearing again long after its popularity in the nineteenth century.

HIBBEN

The National Cook Book

Jelly Pie (Arkansas)

4 eggs
½ cup currant jelly
½ cup butter
1½ cups sugar
1 teaspoon lemon juice

Cream the butter and add the sugar and beat well. Add well-beaten yolks and jelly, and fold in the whites of eggs. Add lemon juice and bake without upper crust.

ROMBAUER

The Joy of Cooking

FOR A NINE INCH PIE SHELL

Rule for Meringue

2 egg whites
⅛ teaspoon salt
4 tablespoons sugar, granulated or powdered
½ teaspoon vanilla

Add the salt to the egg whites and beat them on a platter, using a flat wire whisk, until they stand up in peaks and are stiff, but not dry. Add the sugar very slowly, ½ teaspoon at a time, beating constantly. Beat in the vanilla and bake the meringue in a slow oven—300°—for about 12 minutes.

NOTE: The success of the meringue will depend upon the proper beating of the egg whites, the slow addition of the sugar and the slow oven.

ZIEMANN AND GILETTE

The White House Cook Book

Boston Cream Pie

CREAM PART.—Put on a pint of milk to boil. Break two eggs into a dish and add one cup of sugar and half a cup of flour previously mixed; after beating well, stir it into the milk just as the milk commences to boil; add an ounce of butter and keep on stirring one way until it thickens; flavor with vanilla or lemon.

CRUST PART.—Three eggs beaten separately, one cup of granulated sugar, one and a half cups of sifted flour, one large teaspoonful of baking powder and two tablespoonfuls of milk or water. Divide the batter in half and bake on two medium-sized pie-tins. Bake in a rather quick oven to a straw color. When done and cool, split each one in half with a sharp broad-bladed knife, and spread half the cream between each. Serve cold.

The cake part should be flavored the same as the custard.

WASHINGTON PIE

This recipe is the same as "Boston Cream Pie" (adding half an ounce of butter). In summer time, it is a good plan to bake the pie the day before wanted; then when cool, wrap around it a paper and place it in the ice box so as to have it get *very cold*; then serve it with a dish of fresh strawberries or raspberries. A delicious dessert.

PADDLEFORD

How America Eats

Boston Marlborough Pie

Tell me where your grandmother came from and I can tell you how many kinds of pie you serve for Thanksgiving. In the Midwest two is the usual, mince and pumpkin. In the South no pie but wine jelly, tender and trembling, topped with whipped cream. Down East it's a threesome, cranberry, mince and pumpkin, a sliver of each, and sometimes, harking back to the old days around Boston, four kinds of pie were traditional for this feast occasion—mince, cranberry, pumpkin and a kind called Marlborough, a glorification of everyday apple.

I had heard about Marlborough pie but never met one face to face. Then came a letter from Miss Susan L. Ball, of Lexington. She had lost one of my recipes and offered to trade two versions of her Marlborough pie if I'd replace the loss. I sent the recipe along and said, "Thank you very much, and may I come to see you when I travel into New England again?"

I found Miss Ball at home on Bloomfield Street, Lexington, in the tall white house under ancient elms where she has lived for the past 30 years. I had telephoned from Boston that I was heading her way after the promised recipes. She had them ready. One is taken from an old Deerfield Cook Book, the second version a hand-down belonging to Mrs. Helen Judd, who lived with Miss Ball, this recipe from the Judd family of Boston.

We sat in the library of the 100-year-old house to talk about pies. Miss Ball said, "This house is no age at all compared to the historic old houses of Lexington."

I said, "Apple pies for Thanksgiving?" Pumpkin, yes, and mince and cranberry. But wasn't apple too every-day?

"But not just any apple pie went to the holiday table," she explained. "It's the Marlborough for celebration, sharp of lemon rind and juice and thickened with eggs."

She told me that where apple pie to a modern cook means the ordinary two-crust kind made of raw apples sliced and sweetened, to our down-east grandmothers the baking of apple pie meant making a choice among a dozen different recipes.

1 cup tart applesauce, sieved
3 tablespoons lemon juice
1 cup sugar (to taste)
4 eggs, slightly beaten
2 tablespoons butter or margarine, melted
½ teaspoon nutmeg (if desired)
½ teaspoon salt

1 9-inch unbaked pastry shell (deep)

Combine applesauce with lemon juice, sugar, eggs, butter, nutmeg and salt. Blend thoroughly. Pour into pastry shell. Bake at 450°F. for 15 minutes; reduce heat to 275°F. and bake 1 hour or longer. The pie should be a rich yellow and cut like firm jelly. Yield: 1 9-inch pie.

SAX

Classic Home Desserts

Best-Ever Pumpkin Pie

One autumn while cooking at a restaurant on Martha's Vineyard, I became obsessed with pumpkin pie, testing one recipe after another, making yet a few more adjustments each time, in search of the perfect pie. I could "taste" this one in my head—simple and custardy, light but with some body to cut through, the flavor subtly rounded with vanilla and complex spicing, but with the pumpkin, not the spice, predominant.

MAKES ONE DEEP 9½-INCH PIE; SERVES ABOUT 8

Basic Pie Dough for a 1-crust pie
2 cups pumpkin puree, preferably homemade; if you use canned pumpkin, be sure it's unsweetened puree, not pie filling)
⅔ cup packed dark or light brown sugar
⅓ cup sugar
1 tablespoon all-purpose flour
½ teaspoon salt
1½ teaspoons ground cinnamon
½ teaspoon fresh-grated nutmeg
½ teaspoon ground ginger
¼ teaspoon ground allspice
Pinch freshly ground pepper
1 cup heavy cream
⅓ cup milk

2 large eggs, lightly beaten
3 tablespoons bourbon or rum
1½ teaspoons pure vanilla extract
Whipped cream flavored with pure maple syrup or pure vanilla extract, for serving

1. Roll out the dough on a lightly floured surface to a large circle about ⅛ inch thick. Fit it, without stretching, into a buttered deep 9½-inch pie pan. Trim off the excess dough, leaving a ¾-inch overhang. Fold under the edge of the dough, pressing along the rim of the pan and forming a fairly high fluted border. Chill the dough while you preheat the oven to 400 degrees F, with a rack in the lower third.

2. Line the dough with a lightly buttered sheet of foil, buttered side down. Bake the pie shell for about 8 minutes. Very gently remove the foil; prick the dough all over with a fork. Bake the crust until the surface of the dough is dry, but has not yet baked all the way through, about 5 minutes longer. Set the pie shell aside until needed; leave the oven on.

3. Meanwhile, whisk together the pumpkin puree, brown and white sugars, flour, salt, spices, pepper, cream, milk, eggs, spirits and vanilla in a large bowl. Taste and correct the seasonings. Pour the mixture into the pie shell.

4. Bake until the filling is set but still slightly wobbly in the center, usually about 45 minutes.

5. Cool the pie on a wire rack. Serve with the flavored whipped cream.

VARIATIONS
If you like, substitute about 3 tablespoons pure maple syrup for an equal amount of the white sugar. A tablespoonful of minced crystallized ginger (in addition to the other spices) gives the flavor a nice edge, too, but don't let it take over.

PERFECT PIE

Once I got it right, I've baked this pie every year at Thanksgiving. When I first met my friend Mick, as autumn was livening up New York City, he told me that when he was a kid, he always ate pie for breakfast. Ever the cook-provider, I baked him a pumpkin pie and carried it downtown to Bleecker Street in a shopping bag.

Every year after that, I would bake this pie for our Thanksgiving dinner, even if—especially if—it was just two for the holiday feast. Now that it's just me, this pie will always remind me of feeding him.

SAX
Classic Home Desserts

Buttermilk Silk Pie

Like chess pie and pecan pie, buttermilk pie can be baked in any season, when there's little fresh fruit in the larder. If you've never tried it, buttermilk pie is like custard pie, but with a gently mellow flavor that's almost like cheesecake. It's plain and wonderfully smooth. I like it best without the meringue that often tops it.

MAKES ONE 9-INCH PIE; SERVES ABOUT 8

Basic Pie Dough for a 1-crust pie
1 cup sugar
3 tablespoons cornstarch
1 large whole egg
3 large egg yolks
6 tablespoons (¾ stick) unsalted butter, melted
1½ cups buttermilk
1½ teaspoons pure vanilla extract
¼ teaspoon salt

1. Roll out the dough on a lightly floured surface into a large circle about ⅛ inch thick. Fit it, without stretching, into a buttered 9-inch pie pan. Trim the edge, leaving a ¾-inch overhang. Fold under the edge of the dough, pressing along the rim of the pan and forming a high, fluted border. Chill the pie shell while you preheat the oven to 350 degrees F, with a rack in the lower third.

2. Bake the pie shell, gently pricking any air bubbles with a fork until it is partially baked (it will not take on much color at this point), 8 to 10 minutes. Cool the pie shell on a wire rack; leave the oven on.

3. Meanwhile, in a bowl, whisk together the sugar and cornstarch until there are no lumps. Add the egg, egg yolks, melted butter, buttermilk, vanilla and salt and mix well. Pour the filling into the partially baked pie crust.

4. Bake until the surface is a very pale golden color and the custard is set but still slightly wobbly in the center (the mixture will set up more as it cools; do not overbake), about 40 minutes.

5. Cool the pie to room temperature on a wire rack. Serve at room temperature or slightly chilled.

BASTIANICH

La Cucina di Lidia

Torta di Ricotta

Ricotta Cheesecake

SERVES 6

This is my region's version of the universal Italian cheesecake. We made it in Busoler with our own goat's milk ricotta, and whenever we did, the goats would be fed stale market bread soaked in the whey produced during the cheese-making process. The egg whites folded into the cake mixture give it a texture I like very much.

1 pound ricotta cheese
⅓ cup raisins
2 tablespoons dark rum
3 eggs, separated
½ cup sugar
1 pinch salt
Grated zest of 1 lemon
Grated zest of 1 orange
⅓ cup pignoli (pine nuts)
Softened butter and bread crumbs, for the pan

Drain the ricotta overnight in a cheesecloth-lined sieve.

Soak the raisins in the rum. Preheat the oven to 375° F. Beat the egg yolks with the sugar until pale yellow. Add the drained ricotta, salt, and citrus zests, and blend thoroughly. Add the pignoli and the raisins and rum, blending well. Beat the egg whites until they form stiff peaks and fold them into the cake mixture. Brush a 6" springform pan with softened butter, coat the inner surfaces with bread crumbs, and shake out the excess.

Pour the cake mixture into the prepared pan, bake 30 minutes, and cool before serving.

FARMER

The Boston Cooking-School Cook Book

Custard Pie

2 eggs
3 tablespoons sugar
⅛ teaspoon salt
1½ cups milk
Few gratings nutmeg

Beat eggs slightly, add sugar, salt, and milk. Line plate with paste, and build up a fluted rim. Strain in the mixture and sprinkle with few gratings nutmeg. Bake in quick oven at first to set rim, decrease the heat afterwards, as egg and milk in combination need to be cooked at low temperature.

HEATTER

Maida Heatter's Book of Great Desserts

Walnut Fudge Pie à la Mode with Hot Fudge Sauce

6 TO 8 PORTIONS

Although this is called a pie, it does not have a crust. It is a dense chocolate cake, almost like Brownies baked in a pie plate.

2 ounces (2 squares) unsweetened chocolate
¼ pound (½ cup) butter
1 teaspoon vanilla extract
1 cup sugar
2 eggs, separated
2 tablespoons hot water
⅓ cup sifted all-purpose flour
½ cup walnuts, cut in medium-size pieces
Pinch of salt

Adjust rack to center of oven. Preheat oven to 350 degrees. Line a 9-inch ovenproof glass pie plate with a large piece of aluminum foil. Brush the foil well with soft or melted butter.

In the top of a small double boiler over hot water melt the chocolate. Remove from heat and set aside.

In small bowl of electric mixer cream the butter. Add the vanilla and sugar and beat for a minute or two. Beat in the egg yolks and then the chocolate. When smooth add the hot water and then the flour, scraping bowl with a rubber spatula as necessary and beating only until smooth. Remove from mixer and stir in the walnuts.

Beat the whites with the salt until they hold a peak, stiff but not dry, and fold them into the chocolate mixture. Turn into pie plate and spread the top level.

Bake 35 minutes. During baking the cake will rise and then sink—correctly. The top will have formed a crust but it will be soft inside. Cool in the plate on a rack. When completely cool, let stand for about ½ to 1 hour to become firm and then cover with a cookie sheet or a rack and invert. Remove pie plate and aluminum foil. Replace pie plate over pie and invert again.

Just before serving place scoops of ice cream on the top of the pie; or place a ring of whipped cream (1 cup heavy cream beaten with ¼ cup confectioners sugar and 1 scant teaspoon vanilla) around the edge and fill the center with ice cream.

With this, pass Hot Fudge Sauce, or any other chocolate sauce.

CAKES

BEARD

American Cookery

Pound Cake

2 cups butter
2 cups sugar
8 to 10 large eggs, separated
2 tablespoons rum, brandy, or orange juice
1 teaspoon vanilla
4½ cups sifted cake flour
¾ teaspoon salt

Every homemaker in the late nineteenth and early twentieth century kept a loaf or two of this cake in the pantry to serve to unexpected callers. As in 1-2-3-4 cakes, the name is derived from the quantity of the ingredients—a pound each of butter, sugar, eggs, and flour.

Cream the butter until very fluffy, easiest done with an electric mixer. Cream in the sugar, or reserve ½ cup for the egg whites. The butter and sugar mixture should be like sweetened whipped cream in texture. If using a mixer, drop the egg yolks in one at a time with mixer on medium to high speed. If mixing by hand, beat the yolks with a rotary beater or whisk until very light and lemon-colored. Add to the butter and sugar mixture and beat vigorously. The mixture should be even lighter after the egg yolks are added. Stir or beat in the flavorings. It is customary to use several flavorings—that is, a combination of orange juice and vanilla or rum, or brandy with a little vanilla, or 1 tablespoon each of rum and brandy. (Some cooks insist that pound cake should also have 1 teaspoon of nutmeg or mace added, which was invariably true of New England pound cakes.) Sift the flour with salt, then sift several times more, holding the sifter high to incorporate as much air as possible. Stir into the creamed mixture until well blended. If using an electric mixer, do this at lowest speed. In any event, be sure to keep the batter wiped down from the sides and bottom of the bowl with a rubber or plastic spatula. Beat the egg whites until foamy, and if you like add 1 teaspoon lemon juice or cream of tartar at this point to stabilize the egg whites. If you have reserved ½ cup of sugar, add it gradually during beating of whites. Beat until stiff but not dry—the mixture should hold soft peaks. Fold into the cake batter with a rubber spatula. Turn immediately into two buttered and lightly floured loaf pans 9 × 5 × 3 inches. Or use smaller loaf pans, filling a little more than half full. (This cake works better in loaf than in sheet cake pans.) Bake in a moderately slow 325-degree oven for about an hour, depending upon size of the pans used—it may take 1¼ hours. Test by pressing the center of the cake lightly with the finger. When the cake springs back, and it has pulled away from the sides of the pan, it is done. Transfer to a rack and cool about 15 minutes before loosening from the pan and turning out on the rack to cool. Pound cake is generally considered best after a day or two of "resting." Store in a tightly covered container or place in plastic bags and seal. If kept for several weeks, it is better if stored in the refrigerator. It freezes well. Pound cake is not frosted.

SEED CAKE: A variation of pound cake, which itself is made in a variety of ways in different sections of the country, true seed cake supposedly uses only 1 teaspoon to 1 tablespoon of caraway seed, stirred in with the flour. Other variations include adding, with the seeds, ½ cup finely shaved citron and 1 teaspoon grated lemon rind, and adding 4 teaspoons baking powder with the flour.

BERANBAUM

The Cake Bible

All-Occasion Downy Yellow Butter Cake

SERVES 12

If I had to choose among all my cakes, this one would win first place because it is delicious by itself yet versatile enough to accommodate a wide range of buttercreams. The cake combines the soft texture of white cake with the buttery flavor of yellow cake. Using all yolks instead of whole eggs produces a rich yellow color, fine texture, and delicious flavor.

Two 9-inch by 1½-inch cake pans greased, bottoms lined with parchment or wax paper, and then greased again and floured.

FINISHED HEIGHT

Each layer is 1¼ inches.

STORE

Airtight: 2 days room temperature, 5 days refrigerated, 2 months frozen. Texture is most perfectly moist the same day as baking.

COMPLEMENTARY ADORNMENTS

- A simple dusting of powdered sugar.
- One recipe: Any buttercream, glaze, or fondant.

SERVE

Room temperature.

INGREDIENTS	MEASURE	WEIGHT	
room temp	volume	ounces	grams
6 large egg yolks	3.5 fluid oz	4 oz	112 g
milk	1 liquid cup	8.5 oz	242 g
vanilla	2¼ tsps	-	9 g
sifted cake flour	3 cups	10.5 oz	300 g
sugar	1½ cups	10.5 oz	300 g
baking powder	1 tbs + 1 tsp	-	19.5 g
salt	¾ tsp	-	5 g
unsalted butter (must be softened)	12 tsp	6 oz	170 g

Preheat the oven to 350°F.

In a medium bowl lightly combine the yolks, ¼ cup milk, and vanilla.

In a large mixing bowl combine the dry ingredients and mix on low speed for 30 seconds to blend. Add the butter and remaining ¾ cup milk. Mix on low speed until the dry ingredients are moistened. Increase to medium speed (high speed if using a hand mixer) and beat for 1½ minutes to aerate and develop the cake's structure. Scrape down the sides. Gradually add the egg mixture in 3 batches, beating for 20 seconds after each addition to incorporate the ingredients and strengthen the structure. Scrape down the sides.

Scrape the batter into the prepared pans and smooth the surface with a spatula. The pans will be about ½ full. Bake 25 to 30 minutes or until a tester inserted near the center comes out clean and the cake springs back when pressed lightly in the center. *The cakes should start to shrink from the sides of the pans only after removal from the oven.*

Let the cakes cool in the pans on racks for 10 minutes. Loosen the sides with a small metal spatula and invert onto greased wire racks. To prevent splitting, reinvert so that the tops are up and cool completely before wrapping airtight.

VARIATION

MAPLE BUTTER CAKE: This cake has a deep golden color and a real New England flavor. It is superb frosted with Neoclassic Maple Buttercream and encrusted with toasted walnuts, coarsely chopped.

To make this cake, simply replace the sugar with an equal weight of maple sugar (or 2 cups). Decrease the vanilla to ¾ teaspoon and add 1 teaspoon of maple flavoring.

NOTE: Maple sugar is available in specialty stores such as Dean & DeLuca. It is expensive, but the resulting cake, frosted with Maple Buttercream, is uniquely delicious.

UNDERSTANDING

Compared to Perfect Pound Cake, this cake has more than double the baking powder, less than half the butter, and no egg whites. The decrease in butter is responsible for the lighter and softer texture. The increased baking powder further lightens the cake and also makes it more tender.

FARMER

The Boston Cooking-School Cook Book

Angel Cake

- 1 cup white of eggs
- ¾ cup sugar
- ¼ cup corn-starch
- ⅓ cup flour
- ½ teaspoon salt
- 1 teaspoon cream of tartar
- 1 teaspoon vanilla

Beat whites of eggs until stiff and dry, add sugar gradually and continue beating, then add flavoring. Cut and fold in corn-starch, flour, salt, and cream of tartar, mixed and sifted. Bake forty-five to fifty minutes in an unbuttered angel cake pan in a moderate oven.

STEWART

Weddings

Whipped Cream Cake

MAKES 1 ROUND LAYER—2 X 9 INCHES
APPROXIMATELY 5 CUPS BATTER

Caroline Damerell wanted everything "barely" pink for her wedding to Carmine Santandrea. As a wedding gift, I created my "Rose Cake" and floral arrangements, using blooms from my rose gardens. The cake was quite small, four 2-inch-thick layers of whipped cream cake, a white cake of unusual richness and excellent texture. The icing was tinted slightly with red food coloring, and it was applied in vertical stripes with ruffled edges and swags.

- 2 cups sifted cake flour
- ½ teaspoon salt
- 3 teaspoons baking powder
- 3 egg whites
- 1 cup (½ pint) heavy cream
- 1½ cups sugar
- ½ cup cold water
- 1 teaspoon vanilla extract
- ½ teaspoon almond extract

Preheat oven to 350°. Butter and flour the pan, then line with parchment paper.

Sift the flour, salt, and baking powder together three times, and set aside.

Beat the egg whites until stiff but not dry.

Whip cream until stiff and fold into eggs. Add sugar gradually and mix well, folding in with a rubber spatula.

Add dry ingredients alternately with water in small amounts, mixing well. Add extracts and blend well.

Pour batter into pan and bake for about 40 to 50 minutes. If the center is still soft, reduce the oven temperature to 325° and bake until the center is set.

Let cool in the pan for about 10 minutes, then remove to a wire rack and cool thoroughly.

Tiny rosebuds and roses were used to decorate each layer of the cake, and more roses completely lined my silver tray.

LEWIS
The Taste of Country Cooking

Coconut Layer Cake

Coconut layer cake was one of the most famous desserts we baked. Coconuts were only available at Christmas, so that was the only time we could enjoy a feathery light coconut cake; other times it was topped with dried coconut. The batter was mixed with great care. When the cake was baked and frosted it was sprinkled generously with the sweet, grated coconut.

¼ teaspoon salt
3 teaspoons Royal Baking Powder
2 cups sifted all-purpose unbleached flour
½ cup (1 stick) butter
1¼ cups finely granulated sugar
2 egg yolks, beaten
2 teaspoons vanilla extract
2 teaspoons freshly squeezed lemon juice
1 cup milk, at room temperature
3 egg whites

2 9-inch cake pans

Add salt and baking powder to sifted flour. Sift again and reserve until ready to be used. Place the butter in a mixing bowl and mix it with a wooden spoon until it becomes a bit shiny in appearance. Add the sugar in quarters, stirring well after each addition. When the mixture has become light and most of the granulated quality of the sugar has disappeared, add the beaten egg yolks, which will further dissolve the grainy texture. Continue to stir well and add the vanilla and lemon juice. Stir in ½ cup of the mixed flour and add in ¼ cup of milk, stirring until the batter is smooth. Continue to alternate the flour and milk until the ingredients are used up. (Be sure to end with the flour.) Then beat the whites of eggs to soft peaks and fold them carefully into the batter. Spoon the batter into the two cake pans that have been greased and dusted with flour on the bottom. Be sure that each pan has an equal amount of batter. Set the pans on the middle rack in the center of the oven preheated to 375° and bake for 30 minutes.

Check the cake to see if it has shrunk away from the sides of the pan, or pick the cake pan up and listen for any quiet noises in the cake. If you hear faint sounds, remove from oven and turn the cakes out of the pans onto a wire cake rack. After 10 minutes of cooling, cover the layers with a light, clean cloth until the cakes are ready to be frosted. It is important to cover the cakes in time before they become hard and crusty on the surface.

BOILED WHITE FROSTING

A successful boiled white frosting was the desire of every cook. The greatest achievement was to have a crusty outside and a creamy inside. However, when using coconut on top the outside will remain soft.

The most important step in making a good frosting is to see that the syrup spins a definite thread. When a spoon is placed in the boiling syrup and then held up above the pan, the drippings should become a thin thread waving in the air. The eggs should be beaten to firm peaks before the syrup is slowly poured in, then beaten again until the icing stands in peaks and holds the shape it falls in. Then you can add the flavoring and cool a bit before frosting the cake.

1 cup plus 2 tablespoons sugar
¼ cup cold water
3 egg whites (medium to large eggs)
1 teaspoon fresh lemon juice
Coconut

Place the sugar and water in a quart saucepan and leave it for 15 minutes until the water is absorbed. Place the saucepan and contents over a medium-high heat. Watch carefully to keep the syrup from burning around the edges of the pan. Begin beating the egg whites. When the syrup has reached the point where it spins a thread when it falls from the spoon, turn off the heat. Quickly finish beating the egg whites until they hold their shape, then pour the hot syrup slowly into the beaten egg whites. Continue to beat the mixture until the frosting falls in peaks or holds its shape. Add lemon juice or extract. Cool the frosting a few minutes.

Prepare the cake by dusting off any crumbs to prevent them from falling off into the frosting. Place the first layer on a serving plate and spread over with a generous amount of frosting, leaving enough for the top and sides of the cake. Frost the second layer, making sure it is flush with the bottom. Pour the rest of the frosting onto the center of the cake and quickly spread it over the top and around the sides, then sprinkle the grated coconut over the top and sides. A frosted coconut cake is even better when served the next day.

THE COCONUT

1 medium-sized coconut

It is a good idea to purchase two coconuts just in case one isn't sweet enough. Pick heavy coconuts that sound like they contain a lot of liquid.

Grating the coconut was great fun. After cracking the nut in half with a stout hatchet, catching the water and passing it around for everyone to taste, the meat was pried out with a blunt knife, the brown skin peeled off, and any brown specks were carefully wiped away. The cleaned pieces were grated on the large holes of a four-sided grater and sprinkled over the top and sides of the cake. Press the coconut on lightly with your hand. Be sure and save enough to be sprinkled over in the end to give the cake a fluffy appearance.

LEWIS

The Taste of Country Cooking

Caramel Layer Cake

MAKES 1 9-INCH LAYER CAKE

5 tablespoons butter
1 cup sugar
¼ teaspoon salt
2 medium-sized eggs, at room temperature
2 cups sifted flour
⅔ cup milk, at room temperature
2 teaspoons vanilla extract
1 teaspoon freshly squeezed lemon juice
4 teaspoons Royal Baking Powder

2 9-inch cake pans

Put the butter in a large mixing bowl and with a wooden spoon work the butter until it becomes shiny, about 4 minutes. Add sugar and salt. Blend together until the mixture becomes quite light. Add in an egg and stir one way, clockwise. Add second egg and stir until all the grains of sugar disappear. Sift in ½ cup of flour, stir in, but not too thoroughly. Add ¼ cup of milk and stir vigorously. Alternate the rest of the flour and milk, ending with flour. Mix the flour and milk in a way that keeps the batter from separating. Pour the milk into the flour before it is completely mixed in. This will keep the batter completely smooth. Before sifting in the last bit of flour, add flavoring. Then add the baking powder to the last batch of flour, sift in together, and stir well. Spoon the batter into the buttered and floured cake pans. Set in the center of the middle shelf of a preheated 375° oven. Bake 25 minutes without opening the oven. Test to see if done by noticing if cake has shrunk from the sides of the pan. Also, listen for any quiet noises from the cake. If there are none, that's a sign it is done. Remove from oven, run a spatula around sides of pan, and turn out right away on a wire rack. Cool for 5 minutes, then cover with a clean towel until ready to ice it.

CARAMEL ICING

1 cup heavy cream
2¼ packed cups light-brown sugar (not brownulated)
2 tablespoons butter
2 teaspoons vanilla extract

Heat the cream until hot in a saucepan but do not allow it to boil. Add in the sugar and mix well. Boil gently on a medium-high burner and cook to soft stage—that is, when it forms a soft mass when a little is dropped into a cup of cold water. You should be able to pick it up even though it is soft. Remove from burner when this stage is reached. Set the saucepan in a bowl of cold water, add butter and vanilla, stirring continuously until the mixture becomes thick enough to spread. Remove pan from the bowl of cold water. Place one layer of cake on serving platter. Spread about one third of the icing over the top. Place second layer on iced layer and pour remaining icing in the center of the top layer and spread it over top and down the sides. (If the icing becomes too thick to spread, add a tablespoon or two of cream to soften.)

Set the cake in a dry tin. It is better not to store cake in the refrigerator. It becomes heavy and loses its light, fluffy quality.

ZIEMANN AND GILETTE
The White House Cook Book

Election Cake

Three cups milk, two cups sugar, one cup yeast; stir to a batter and let stand over night; in the morning add two cups sugar, two cups butter, three eggs, half a nutmeg, one tablespoonful cinnamon, one pound raisins, a gill of brandy.

Brown sugar is much better than white for this kind of cake, and it is improved by dissolving a half-teaspoonful of soda in a teaspoonful of milk in the morning. It should stand in the greased pans and rise some time until quite light before baking.

CUNNINGHAM
The Breakfast Book

Great Coffee Cake

ONE 10-INCH TUBE CAKE

This makes a moist, rich cake adaptable to many changes. Some very good variations to this splendid basic cake follow the recipe.

- ½ pound (2 sticks) butter, room temperature
- 1 cup sugar
- 3 eggs
- 2½ cups all-purpose flour
- 2 teaspoons baking powder
- 1 teaspoon baking soda
- 1 teaspoon salt
- 1 cup sour cream

Preheat the oven to 350°F. Grease and flour a 10-inch tube pan or Bundt pan.

Put the butter in a large mixing bowl and beat for several seconds. Add the sugar and beat until smooth. Add the eggs and beat for 2 minutes, or until light and creamy. Put the flour, baking powder, baking soda, and salt in a bowl and stir with a fork to blend well. Add the flour mixture to the butter mixture and beat until smooth. Add the sour cream and mix well. Spoon the batter into the pan. Bake for about 50 minutes, or until a straw comes out clean when inserted into the center. Remove from the oven and let rest for 5 minutes in the pan. Invert onto a rack and cool a little bit before slicing. Serve warm.

RAISIN AND SPICE COFFEE CAKE: Add 1 teaspoon mace and 1 teaspoon nutmeg when combining the dry ingredients. Stir ¾ cup raisins and ½ cup currants into the batter after adding the sour cream, and proceed with the basic recipe.

CROCKER
Betty Crocker's Picture Cook Book

Maraschino Cherry Cake (Recipe)

A lovely pink, high cake. Olga Stage of our Staff especially likes it for February parties.

FOR LARGE CAKE	SMALL CAKE
Grease and flour	
2 9" layer pans or 13 × 9" oblong pan or 9" square pan	2 8" layer pans
Cream together until fluffy	
⅔ cup soft shortening (half butter for flavor)	½ cup
1½ cups sugar	1⅛ cups
Sift together	
3 cups sifted SOFTASILK or 2¾ cups sifted GOLD MEDAL Flour	2¼ cups or 2 cups
2½ tsp. baking powder	2 tsp.
1 tsp. salt	¾ tsp.
Add alternately with	
¼ cup cherry juice	¼ cup
¾ cup milk	½ cup
Stir in	
½ cup chopped nuts	⅜ cup
16 maraschino cherries cut in eighths	12 cherries
Fold in	
5 egg whites (⅔ cup) stiffly beaten	4 whites (½ c.)

Pour into prepared pans. Bake. Cool. Finish with cooked white frosting made with cherry juice in place of water. Decorate with red stemmed cherries.

TEMPERATURE: 350° (mod. oven).
TIME: Bake layers 30 to 35 min., square or oblong 30 to 35 min.

POPPY SEED CAKE

Luscious! An old German recipe sent in years ago by Mrs. P. R. Aust of Minneapolis.

Soak ⅓ cup poppy seeds in ½ cup water for 2 hr. Drain off water. Add seeds to creamed mixture. Prepare 2 8" layer pans. Follow 🔑 recipe above for method. Use:

¾ cup soft shortening (half butter)
1½ cups sugar

the drained poppy seeds

2¼ cups *sifted* SOFTASILK *or* 2 cups *sifted* GOLD MEDAL Flour
2 tsp. baking powder
½ tsp. salt

1 cup water
4 egg whites (½ cup), stiffly beaten

Pour into prepared pans. Bake. Cool. Use Cream Filling between layers and finish with a cooked white frosting.

ALL YOU HAVE TO DO—TO USE THE EGG YOLKS:
- bake a Gold Cake or Sponge Cake
- make a Cream Filling for a cake
- make Hollandaise Sauce for vegetables
- make eggnogs for the children

BERANBAUM
The Cake Bible

Perfect Pound Cake

SERVES 8

One 8-inch by 4-inch by 2½-inch loaf pan (4 cups)—most attractive size—or any 6-cup loaf or fluted tube pan, greased and floured. If using a loaf pan, grease it, line the bottom with parchment or wax paper, and then grease again and flour.

FINISHED HEIGHT

IN A 4-CUP LOAF: 2¼ inches at the sides and 3½ inches in the middle. In a 6-cup loaf: 1¾ inches at the sides and 2½ inches in the middle. In a 6-cup fluted tube: 2¼ inches in the middle.

STORE

AIRTIGHT: 3 days room temperature, 1 week refrigerated, 2 months frozen. Texture is most evenly moist when prepared at least 8 hours ahead of serving.

COMPLEMENTARY ADORNMENT

A simple dusting of powdered sugar.

SERVE

Room temperature

INGREDIENTS	MEASURE	WEIGHT	
room temp	volume	ounces	grams
milk	3 tbs	1.5 oz	45 g
3 large eggs	scant 5 fl oz	5.25 oz	150 g
vanilla	1½ tsp	-	6 g
sifted cake flour	1½ cups	5.25 oz	150 g
sugar	¾ cup	5.25 oz	150 g
baking powder	¾ tsp	-	3.7 g
salt	¼ tsp	-	-
unsalted butter (must be softened)	13 tbs	6.5 oz	184 g

Preheat the oven to 350°F.

In a medium bowl lightly combine the milk, eggs, and vanilla.

In a large mixing bowl combine the dry ingredients and mix on low speed for 30 seconds to blend. Add the butter and half the egg mixture. Mix on low speed until the dry ingredients are moistened. Increase to medium speed (high speed if using a hand mixer) and beat for 1 minute to aerate and develop the cake's structure.

Scrape down the sides. Gradually add the remaining egg mixture in 2 batches, beating for 20 seconds after each addition to incorporate the ingredients and strengthen the structure. Scrape down the sides.

Scrape the batter into the prepared pan and smooth the surface with a spatula. The batter will be almost ½ inch from the top of the 4-cup loaf pan. (If your pan is slightly smaller, use any excess batter for cupcakes.) Bake 55 to 65 minutes (35 to 45 minutes in a fluted tube pan) or until a wooden toothpick inserted in the center comes out clean. Cover loosely with buttered foil after 30 minutes to prevent overbrowning. The cake should start to shrink from the sides of the pan only after removal from the oven.

To get an attractive split down the middle of the crust, wait until the natural split is about to develop (about 20 minutes) and then with a lightly greased sharp knife or single-edged razor blade make a shallow mark about 6 inches long down the middle of the cake. This must be done quickly so that the oven door does not remain open very long or the cake will fall. When the cake splits, it will open along the mark.

Let the cake cool in the pan on a rack for 10 minutes and invert it onto a greased wire rack. If baked in a loaf pan, to keep the bottom from splitting, reinvert so that the top is up and cool completely before wrapping airtight.

UNDERSTANDING

In creating this recipe I started out with the classic pound cake proportions: equal weights of flour, sugar, eggs, and butter and no leavening. But I soon discovered that the traditional balance of ingredients benefits from a few minor alterations: A small amount of milk adds marvelous moisture and also strengthens the cake's structure by gelatinizing the flour and joining the gluten-forming proteins enough to be able to hold some extra butter. More butter adds flavor and tenderizes the crumb, producing that "melt-in-the-mouth" quality. A very small amount of baking powder opens the crumb slightly, contributing more tenderness and less of that heavy chewiness characteristic of the original pound cake.

Over forty trials have led me to believe that there is no way to get this melting texture in a pound cake that is larger so it is best to keep the cake small. If you happen to prefer a denser, chewier cake, however, replace the regular sugar with equal weight powdered sugar (1¼ cups unsifted) and reduce the butter to 10½ tablespoons (5.25 ounces/150 grams) and the baking powder to ½ teaspoon. (The smooth grains of the powdered sugar do not trap air the way the sharp-edged grains of granulated sugar do. The cornstarch added to powdered sugar to prevent lumping also increases the chewy quality of the cake.)

POINTERS FOR SUCCESS

Be sure to use a wooden toothpick to test for doneness. The cake will spring back when pressed lightly in the center even before it is done. If the cake is underbaked, it will have tough, gummy spots instead of a fine, tender crumb.

LEMON POPPY SEED POUND CAKE

This is perhaps my favorite way to eat pound cake! The fresh light flavor of lemon blends beautifully with the buttery flavor of pound cake. The lemon syrup tenderizes, adds tartness, and helps to keep the cake fresh for a few days longer than usual. Poppy seeds add a delightful crunch. Lemon blossoms and lemon leaves make a lovely and appropriate garnish.

- 1 tablespoon (6 grams) loosely packed grated lemon zest
- 3 tablespoons (1 ounce/28 grams) poppy seeds
- ¼ cup + 2 tablespoons sugar (2.75 ounces/75 grams)
- ¼ cup freshly squeezed lemon juice (2 ounces/63 grams)

Add the lemon zest and poppy seeds to the dry ingredients and proceed as above. Shortly before the cake is done, prepare the Lemon Syrup: In a small pan over medium heat, stir the sugar and lemon juice until dissolved. As soon as the cake comes out of the oven, place the pan on a rack, poke the cake all over with a wire tester, and brush it with ½ the syrup. Cool in the pan for 10 minutes. Loosen the sides with a spatula and invert onto a greased wire rack. Poke the bottom of the cake with the wire tester, brush it with some syrup, and reinvert onto a greased wire rack. Brush the sides with the remaining syrup and allow to cool before wrapping airtight. Store 24 hours before eating to give the syrup a chance to distribute evenly. The syrup will keep the cake fresh a few days longer than a cake without syrup.

FISHER

The Art of Eating

Tomato Soup Cake

This is a pleasant cake, which keeps well and puzzles people who ask what kind it is. It can be made in a moderate oven while you are cooking other things, which is always sensible and makes you feel rather noble, in itself a small but valuable pleasure.

Another excellent way to use any space left from cooking meat or a casserole or anything that wants a moderate heat, is, as I have already argued, to make baked apples. They are good hot or cold, stuffed with raisins or with brown sugar. [Or mincemeat or leftover jam. Canelloni are also a fine dessert made with jam.] They can make a whole supper, with plenty of hot buttered toast, or they can be the rather heavy but savory and wholesome dessert of a dinner, served with sour cream or my grandmother's recipe for Cinnamon Milk.

3 tablespoons butter or shortening
1 cup sugar
1 teaspoon soda
1 can tomato soup
2 cups flour
1 teaspoon cinnamon
1 teaspoon nutmeg, ginger, cloves mixed
1½ cups raisins, nuts, chopped figs, what you will

Cream butter, add the sugar, and blend thoroughly. Add the soda to the soup, stirring well, and add this alternately to the first mixture with the flour and spices sifted together. Stir well, and bake in a pan or loaf-tin at 325°.

SAX
Classic Home Desserts

Applesauce-Carrot Cake with Lemon Cream Cheese Frosting

The applesauce keeps this carrot cake moist, dense and richly flavored, and the lemon brightens the frosting nicely.

MAKES ONE 10-INCH TUBE CAKE OR TWO 8-×-4-INCH LOAVES; SERVES 10 TO 12

CAKE
2 cups all-purpose flour
2 teaspoons baking powder
2 teaspoons baking soda
¾ teaspoon salt
1 tablespoon ground cinnamon
1 teaspoon each ground allspice and fresh-grated nutmeg
½ cup drained canned crushed pineapple in unsweetened juice
¼ cup raisins
½ cup pecan or walnut pieces
1 cup sugar
3 large eggs
1 cup packed dark brown sugar
1¼ cups bland vegetable oil
½ cup applesauce
2 teaspoons pure vanilla extract
2 cups finely shredded peeled carrots (about 4)
⅔ cup shredded sweetened coconut

FROSTING
8 ounces cream cheese (regular or "light" but not nonfat), softened
¼ cup (½ stick) unsalted butter, softened
1 cup confectioners' sugar
Grated zest and juice of 1 small lemon
½ teaspoon pure vanilla extract
¼ teaspoon lemon extract

1. **CAKE:** Preheat the oven to 350 degrees F. Lightly oil a 10-inch Bundt or tube pan, or two 8-×-4-inch loaf pans; set aside. Sift the flour, baking powder, baking soda, salt and spices onto a sheet of wax paper; set aside.

2. In a food processor, pulse the pineapple, raisins, nuts and ¼ cup of the sugar until minced; do not overprocess or puree; set aside.

3. In a large bowl with an electric mixer on medium-high speed, combine the remaining ¾ cup sugar, eggs, brown sugar, oil, applesauce, vanilla and the minced pineapple-nut mixture; beat until well combined. Lower the speed to slow and gradually add the sifted dry ingredients. Stir in the carrots and coconut just until combined. Pour into the prepared pan(s).

4. Bake until the cake is golden brown, the edges shrink slightly away from the pan(s), and a toothpick inserted in the center(s) emerges clean, usually 50 to 60 minutes in a tube pan, about 45 minutes for loaves.

5. Cool the cake(s) to room temperature in the pan(s) on a wire rack.

6. **FROSTING:** Beat all of the ingredients together with an electric mixer until very smooth and light.

7. Run the tip of a knife around the cake to loosen it from the sides and tube of the pan; unmold and turn right side up if necessary. Split the cake(s) horizontally into 2 layers. Spread some of the frosting over the bottom layer; spread the remainder over the top. Chill if not serving immediately. Serve cool or chilled.

CROCKER
Betty Crocker's Picture Cook Book

Upside Down Cake (🔑 Recipe)

Handsome dessert to serve at table.

FIRST, PREPARE THE PAN
Melt ⅓ cup butter in heavy 10" skillet or baking dish. Sprinkle ½ cup brown sugar evenly over butter. Arrange drained cooked fruit in attractive pattern on the butter-sugar coating.

Make the Cake Batter and pour it over fruit. Bake until wooden pick thrust into center of cake comes out clean. Immediately turn upside-down on serving plate. Do not remove pan for a few minutes. Brown sugar mixture will run down over cake instead of clinging to pan. Serve warm with plain or whipped cream.

CAKE BATTER

Beat until thick and lemon-colored (5 min.)

2 eggs

Gradually beat in . . .

⅔ cup sugar

Beat in all at once . . .

6 tbsp. juice from fruit
1 tsp. flavoring

Sift together and beat in all at once . . .

1 cup sifted GOLD MEDAL Flour or SOFTASILK Cake Flour
⅓ tsp. baking powder
¼ tsp. salt

TEMPERATURE: 350° (mod. oven).
TIME: Bake 45 min.

PINEAPPLE UPSIDE-DOWN CAKE

Follow 🔑 recipe above—using vanilla for flavoring. Arrange slices of pineapple over butter-sugar coating, and garnish with maraschino cherries and pecan halves.

BERANBAUM
The Cake Bible

Orange Glow Chiffon Cake

SERVES 14

Moist, billowy, light as a feather, and perfumed with fresh orange juice and zest, this is an incomparably refreshing cake. If you live in a part of the world where oranges grow, you could not ask for a more appropriate and aromatic adornment than orange blossoms, but fresh daisies also convey the lighthearted spirit of this lovely cake. A serving contains only 129 mg. of cholesterol.

One ungreased 10-inch two-piece tube pan.

FINISHED HEIGHT
4½ inches high in the middle.

STORE
3 days room temperature, 10 days refrigerated, 2 months frozen.

COMPLEMENTARY ADORNMENTS
A light sprinkling of powdered sugar and/or decorate the base and center with orange blossoms or fresh daisies. Candied Orange Zest scattered on top also makes an attractive and flavorful addition.

SERVE
Room temperature or lightly chilled. Cut with a serrated knife.

INGREDIENTS	MEASURE	WEIGHT	
room temp	volume	ounces	grams
sifted cake flour	2¼ cups	8 oz	225 g
sugar	1½ cups	10.5 oz	300 grams
baking powder	2 teaspoons	-	10 g
salt	½ teaspoon	-	3.5 g
safflower oil	½ liquid cup	3.75 oz	108 g
7 large eggs, separated, + 3 additional whites			
yolks	½ liquid cup	4.5 oz	130 g
whites	1¼ liquid cups	10.5 oz	300 g
orange juice, freshly squeezed	¾ liquid cup	6.25 oz	182 g
grated orange zest	2 tablespoons	-	12 grams
vanilla	1 teaspoon	-	4 grams
cream of tartar	1¼ teaspoons	-	4 grams

Preheat the oven to 325°F.

In a large mixing bowl combine the flour, all but 2 tablespoons of the sugar, baking powder, and salt and beat 1 minute to mix. Make a well in the center.

Add the oil, egg yolks, orange juice, orange zest, and vanilla and beat 1 minute or until smooth.

In another large mixing bowl beat the egg whites until frothy, add the cream of tartar, and beat until soft peaks form when the beater is raised. Beat in the remaining 2 tablespoons sugar and beat until stiff peaks form when the beater is raised slowly. Gently fold the egg whites into the batter with a large balloon wire whisk, slotted skimmer, or angel food cake folder until just blended.

Pour into the tube pan (the batter will come to 1 inch from the top) and bake for 55 minutes or until a cake tester inserted in the center comes out clean and the cake springs back when lightly pressed in the center. Invert the pan, placing the tube opening over the neck of a soda or wine bottle to suspend it well above the counter, and cool the cake completely in the pan (this takes about 1½ hours).

Loosen the sides with a long metal spatula and remove the center core of the pan. Dislodge the bottom and center core with a metal spatula or thin, sharp knife. (A wire cake tester works well around the core. To keep the sides attractive, press the spatula against the sides of the pan and avoid any up-and-down motion.) Invert onto a greased wire rack and reinvert onto a serving plate. Wrap airtight.

POINTERS FOR SUCCESS

An angel food cake folder, large balloon whisk, or slotted skimmer is ideal for folding in the flour with the least amount of air loss. If using the whisk, periodically shake out the batter which collects inside.

RODEN

A Book of Middle Eastern Food

Sephardic Cakes

Among the minority dishes of the Middle East, there are some which are particularly Sephardic Jewish in origin. Besides peculiarities due to their religious dietary laws, such as the use of oil and vegetable cooking fats instead of butter or samna (clarified butter), the Jews brought with them their favorite dishes from previous homelands. The main feature of Sephardic cooking as distinct from Middle Eastern cooking, which the Jews also practice, is the evidence of Spanish and Portuguese influence.

During the fourteenth and fifteenth centuries, the time of the Inquisition, thousands of Jews left Spain and Portugal after a thousand years of life in the Peninsula. Many headed toward the countries of the Middle East. The local Arab Jews, overwhelmed by their superior intellect, high rank, and refined social manners, copied and adopted their language, manners, and customs, as well as their dishes. These dishes, similar to those prepared in Spain today—some still bearing Spanish names—are still faithfully prepared by Middle Eastern Jews. Among them are cakes baked specially for the Jewish Passover, made with ground almonds instead of flour. During Passover dried bread crumbs are not used either, nor is the baking pan floured. Instead, fine matzo meal is substituted for both.

These cakes, which are half pudding, half cakes, can never fail. If they are undercooked they make a fine dessert with cream. They are too moist ever to be overcooked or to dry up.

ORANGE AND ALMOND CAKE

2 large oranges
6 eggs
1½ cups ground almonds
1 cup sugar
1 teaspoon baking powder

Butter and flour, for cake pan

Wash and boil the oranges (unpeeled) in a little water for nearly 2 hours (or ½ hour in a pressure cooker). Let them cool, then cut them open and remove the pips. Turn the oranges into a pulp by rubbing them through a strainer or by putting them in an electric blender.

Beat the eggs in a large bowl. Add the other ingredients, mix thoroughly, and pour into a buttered and floured cake pan with a removable base if possible. Bake in a preheated moderately hot oven (400°) for about 60 minutes. Have a look at it after 1 hour—this type of cake will not go any flatter if the oven door is opened. If it is still very wet, leave it in the oven for a little longer. Cool in the pan before turning out. This is a very moist cake.

ANOTHER ORANGE AND ALMOND CAKE

5 eggs
½ cup sugar
⅓ cup ground almonds
3 tablespoons matzo meal or fine dry white bread crumbs
1 tablespoon grated orange rind
1 tablespoon orange blossom water

Butter and flour, for cake pan

Beat the eggs well in a large bowl. Add the remaining ingredients and mix thoroughly. Pour the mixture into a buttered and floured cake tin and bake in a preheated moderate oven (375°) for about ¾ to 1 hour. Cool in the pan, then turn out.

LEWIS
The Taste of Country Cooking

Blueberry Cake with Blueberry Sauce

Blueberry cake was a surprisingly good, quick dessert made at the last minute. When canning, there was always some leftover fruit that was not enough to fill a jar and it was usually used for the next meal to make a pudding, pie, plain compote, or blueberry cake.

SERVES 4 TO 5 (WITH LEFTOVERS)

2 cups sifted unbleached flour
¼ teaspoon salt
4 tablespoons butter
1 egg
1 cup milk
2 teaspoons vanilla
3 teaspoons Royal Baking Powder
1½ cups stewed blueberries
⅓ cup sugar
¼ teaspoon cinnamon

1 8 × 8 × 2-inch buttered baking pan

Sift the flour and salt into a mixing bowl. Add the butter and blend with fingertips or, even better, with a pastry blender until the mixture becomes grainy, fine, and a bit more coarse than cornmeal. Beat the egg and mix in the milk, then add to the dough, stirring all the while. Add the vanilla and continue stirring, then last, add the baking powder. Mix well and spoon into a well-buttered baking pan. Drain the blueberries and quickly scatter them over the dough. Combine the sugar and cinnamon and sprinkle over the top. Set the cake into a preheated 425° oven. Close the door and turn the oven down to 375°. Cook for 25 to 28 minutes.

NOTE: Draining the juice from the berries is to keep the cake from becoming too soggy while cooking. If using fresh berries, stew them for 3 to 4 minutes before putting on the dough. Drain away the juice and make into a sauce by boiling the juice, adding sugar to taste, and a teaspoon of cornstarch dissolved in a little cold water.

MEDRICH
Cocolat

Chocolate Banana Charlotte

SERVES 10–12

⅓ cup plus 2–3 tablespoons sugar
2½ tablespoons dark rum
1½–2 ripe bananas
8-inch springform or cheesecake pan with removable bottom, lined, bottom and sides, with Ladyfingers
Chocolate Velvet Mousse, made with rum
2 cups heavy cream
2 teaspoons vanilla extract
Chocolate shavings (optional)
Bright colored ribbon (optional)

SPECIAL EQUIPMENT
Pastry bag fitted with closed star tip

Don't pass up this recipe because you dread the usually fussy and time-consuming task of lining a mold with ladyfingers. The professional trick of making them in one continuous strip reduces the task to child's play.

1. Combine ⅓ cup sugar and 3 tablespoons cold water in a very small saucepan. Simmer, covered, for 1–2 minutes, to dissolve sugar. Allow to cool. Stir in rum; set aside.

2. Slice bananas about ½ inch thick. Pour the rum syrup over them; set aside for at least 15 minutes, or until needed.

3. Drain the bananas, reserving the syrup. Using a pastry brush, moisten all of the inside surfaces of the ladyfingers in the mold with the reserved rum syrup. Place drained pieces of banana all over the bottom of the lined mold, overlapping if necessary.

4. Make Chocolate Velvet Mousse. Turn immediately into lined pan. Chill for at least 3–4 hours, until set. Dessert may be completed to this point, wrapped, and refrigerated in the mold, up to 2 days in advance.

5. Whip cream with vanilla and remaining 2–3 tablespoons sugar until fairly stiff. Scrape whipped cream into pastry bag. Pipe decorative swirls all over mousse so that it peaks up and above the ladyfingers. Decorate with chocolate shavings, if desired. Dessert may be completed up to 12 hours in advance of serving. Refrigerate in a covered container until needed. Do not freeze.

Remove the sides of the mold and transfer the charlotte to a serving platter. If desired, tie a pretty ribbon around the dessert to present.

ROMBAUER
The Joy of Cooking

Chocolate Custard Cake—Devils' Food

This is a smooth, fine grained chocolate cake. When the larger amount of chocolate is used, it is a black, rich Devils' Food.

- 2 to 4 ounces bitter chocolate
- ½ cup sweet milk
- 1 cup granulated sugar
- 1 egg yolk

Cook these ingredients in a saucepan over a very low flame. When they are thick and smooth, set them aside to cool.

CUSTARD
- ½ cup butter
- 1 cup light brown sugar
- 2 egg yolks
- 2 cups flour
- ½ cup sweet milk
- 1 teaspoon vanilla

Cream the butter and the sugar and add the other ingredients, alternating the flour with the milk. Add the custard and 1 teaspoon soda, dissolved in ¼ cup boiling water. Fold in the 2 egg whites, stiffly beaten. Bake the cake in two greased layer pans in a moderate oven 375°. Ice it with White Icing, or Boiled Chocolate Icing.

PADDLEFORD
How America Eats

Aunt Sabella's Black Chocolate Cake

It was down in the mushroom country I heard tell of a pair of chocolate cakes, so famous people drive one hundred miles and more to eat a slice fresh cut from one or the other. The cakes stand shoulder to shoulder in popular favor. The kinds—chocolate icebox and Aunt Sabella's black chocolate.

Chocolate cake, now that's my meat. I headed the car east out of Coatesville, took a left turn, second crossroad on Lincoln Highway, Route 30. Then to the Dutch Cupboard's door, home of the chocolate-cake twins. I ate a light luncheon, then settled for double dessert, one slice of each cake.

Want my honest opinion? I liked the chocolate icebox cake a wee bit better. But as everyone says, Aunt Sabella's black chocolate "is out of this world."

I talked to Eleanor Taylor of the Eleanor-and-Jackson-Taylor (Mr. and Mrs.) team who own the Dutch Cupboard. Aunt Sabella, Eleanor told me, was her father's sister, Sabella Nye Chapman, of Cayutaville, New York. She gave the recipe to Eleanor's mother, who gave it to Eleanor when the restaurant was opened.

- 1¼ cups sifted flour
- 1 teaspoon salt
- ⅓ cup butter or margarine
- 1 cup sugar
- 2 egg yolks
- 2 squares unsweetened chocolate, melted and cooled
- 1 cup sour milk
- 1 teaspoon baking soda

Sift together flour and salt. Cream butter and sugar thoroughly. Beat in egg yolks. Blend in melted chocolate. Add flour mixture alternately with sour milk, to which the soda is added. Beat well after each addition. Pour into greased 8 × 8-inch cake pan. Bake at 350°F. for about 35 minutes. Ice with caramel icing or 7-minute frosting. Yield: 1 8-inch square cake.

HEATTER
Maida Heatter's Book of Great Desserts

Queen Mother's Cake

12 PORTIONS

Jan Smeterlin, the eminent pianist, picked up this recipe on a concert tour in Austria. He loves to cook, and when he baked this to serve to the Queen Mother of England, she asked for the recipe and then served it frequently at her royal parties. If there could be only one cake in the whole world, this would be my choice.

- 6 ounces sweet or semisweet chocolate, coarsely cut or broken (I prefer Maillard Eagle Sweet)
- 6 ounces (¾ cup) butter
- ¾ cup sugar
- 6 eggs, separated
- 6 ounces (1¼ cups) almonds, finely ground
- ⅛ teaspoon salt

Adjust rack to one-third up from the bottom of the oven. Preheat oven to 375 degrees. Butter a 9 × 2½- or 3-inch spring-form pan and line the bottom with wax paper or baking pan liner paper. Butter the paper and dust allover it lightly with fine, dry bread crumbs.

Melt chocolate in the top of a small double boiler over hot water on low heat. Remove from heat and set aside to cool slightly.

In the small bowl of an electric mixer cream the butter. Add sugar and beat at moderately high speed for 2 to 3 minutes. Add yolks one at a time, beating until each addition is thoroughly incorporated.

Beat in the chocolate and then, on lowest speed, gradually beat in the almonds, scraping the bowl with a rubber spatula as necessary to keep mixture smooth. Transfer to a large mixing bowl.

In the large bowl of an electric mixer beat the salt with the whites until they hold a definite shape, or are stiff but not dry. Stir a large spoonful of the whites into the chocolate and then, in three additions, fold in the balance. Turn into pan. If necessary, level top by rotating pan briskly from side to side.

Bake for 20 minutes at 375 degrees. Reduce oven temperature to 350 degrees and bake for an additional 50 minutes. (Total baking time is 1 hour and 10 minutes.) Do not overbake. Cake should remain soft and moist in the center.

Wet and slightly wring out a folded towel and place it on a smooth surface. Remove spring form from oven and place it directly on the wet towel. Let stand 20 minutes. Remove sides of spring form. Place a rack over the cake and carefully invert. Remove bottom of form and paper lining. Cover with another rack and invert again to cool right side up. The cake will be about 1¾ inches high.

When the cake is completely cool, place four strips of wax paper around the edges of a cake plate. Gently transfer the cake to the plate, bottom up. Prepare the following:

ICING FOR QUEEN MOTHER'S CAKE

- ½ cup heavy cream
- 2 teaspoons instant coffee
- 8 ounces sweet or semisweet chocolate, coarsely cut or broken (I prefer Maillard Eagle Sweet)

Scald the cream in a medium-size heavy saucepan over moderate heat until it begins to form small bubbles around the edge or a skin on top. Still over heat, add instant coffee and stir briskly with a small wire whisk until dissolved. Add chocolate. After 1 minute remove from heat and stir with wire whisk until chocolate is melted and mixture is smooth. Transfer to a small bowl or place the bottom of the saucepan in cold water to stop the cooking.

Let mixture stand at room temperature for 15 minutes or more, stirring occasionally until it reaches room temperature. Stir (do not beat) and pour all over the top of the cake. Use a long narrow metal spatula to smooth the top, letting a bit of the icing run down the sides. Use a small metal spatula to smooth the sides. After about 5 minutes remove the wax paper strips, pulling each one out by a narrow end (see page 18) before the icing hardens.

NOTES: 1. The cake may rise and crack unevenly during baking—O.K. It will level almost completely while cooling.

2. If you have a turntable or a Lazy Susan, use it when icing the cake.

PECK
The Art of Fine Baking

Gênoise

Gênoise, the French butter spongecake, is the most versatile cake you can make. It is rich, yet light and delicate. Any dessert cake made with layers of gênoise *is unforgettably delicious. It is a 1-bowl cake and not at all difficult to make when directions are followed.*

Note that an alternate method is given for mixing gênoise *batter. For those who do not own an electric beater, the second method is much easier, cutting down the beating time by at least half. Cakes made by the alternate method have a slightly less fluffy texture, which is actually preferred by some people.*

6 large eggs
1 cup sugar
1 cup sifted flour
½ cup sweet butter, melted and clarified
1 teaspoon vanilla

Set oven at 350 degrees. Grease and lightly flour 1 of the following:

two 9-inch layer-cake tins
three 7-inch layer-cake tins
one 11 × 16 jelly-roll pan
two shallow 10-inch layer-cake tins

In a large bowl combine eggs and sugar. Stir for a minute, or until they are just combined. Set bowl over a saucepan containing 1 or 2 inches of hot water. Water in pan should not touch bowl; nor should it ever be allowed to boil. Place saucepan containing bowl over low heat for 5 to 10 minutes, or until eggs are lukewarm. Heating the eggs helps them whip to greater volume.

It is not necessary to beat them continuously as they are warming. *They should, however, be lightly stirred 3 or 4 times to prevent them from cooking at bottom of bowl.*

When eggs feel lukewarm to your finger and look like a bright yellow syrup, remove bowl from heat. Begin to beat, preferably with an electric mixer. Beat at high speed for 10 to 15 minutes, scraping sides of bowl with a rubber spatula when necessary, until syrup becomes light, fluffy, and cool. It will almost triple in bulk and look much like whipped cream. It is the air beaten into the eggs that gives *gênoise* its lightness.

Beating by hand with a good rotary beater will take about 25 minutes.

Sprinkle flour, a little at a time, on top of the whipped eggs. Fold in gently, adding slightly cooled, clarified butter and vanilla. Folding can be done with electric mixer turned to lowest speed, or by hand. Be especially careful not to overmix.

Pour batter into prepared pans. Bake in preheated oven 25 to 30 minutes, or until cakes pull away from sides of pans and are golden brown and springy when touched lightly on top.

Remove from pans immediately and cool on cake rack.

ALTERNATE METHOD FOR MIXING *GÊNOISE*
Separate eggs. Add vanilla to egg yolks.

Beat egg whites until they hold soft peaks. Beat in sugar, a tablespoon at a time, beating well after each addition. Continue to beat until egg whites are very stiff, about 5 minutes in all.

Fold about ¼ of egg whites into yolks. Pour over remaining stiffly beaten whites. Sprinkle flour lightly on top. Fold eggs and flour gently but thoroughly together, adding cooled clarified butter at the same time. Fold only until flour and butter disappear into batter.

CHOCOLATE *GÊNOISE*

Follow the recipe for *gênoise*. Substitute ½ cup dark unsweetened Dutch cocoa for ½ cup of flour. Sift cocoa and flour together once before folding into batter.

MEDRICH
Cocolat

Chocolate Hazelnut Torte

SERVES 10–12

Torte tastes best if baked at least one day ahead.

6 ounces semisweet or bittersweet chocolate, cut into small pieces
6 ounces sweet butter, cut into pieces
4 large eggs, separated
¾ cup sugar
½ cup (2 ounces) ground toasted hazelnuts
¼ cup (1 ounce) flour
⅛ teaspoon cream of tartar
Bittersweet Chocolate Glaze or Chocolate Honey Glaze
12 plain or caramelized hazelnuts (optional), for decoration, or 1 ounce each, milk and white chocolate, for piped decoration (optional)

SPECIAL EQUIPMENT
8-inch corrugated cake circle
Parchment paper cone(s) for piping decoration (optional)

1. Preheat oven to 375°. Line bottom of an 8 × 3-inch round cake pan or springform pan with a circle of parchment or waxed paper.

2. Melt chocolate and butter in a small bowl placed in a barely simmering water bath on low heat, stirring occasionally until completely melted. Remove from heat. Or, microwave on medium (50%) for about 2 minutes. Stir until smooth and completely melted.

3. Beat egg yolks with ½ cup of sugar until pale and thick. Stir in warm chocolate mixture, nuts, and flour. Set aside.

4. Beat the egg whites and cream of tartar at medium speed until soft peaks form. Gradually sprinkle in remaining ¼ cup sugar, beating at high speed until stiff but not dry. Fold one-fourth of whites into chocolate batter to lighten it. Quickly fold in remaining whites. Turn mixture into prepared pan and smooth top if necessary. Bake for 40–45 minutes, or until a toothpick or wooden skewer plunged into center of torte shows moist crumbs.

5. Cool torte completely in pan on a rack. It will have risen and then fallen in the center, leaving a higher rim of cake around sides and possibly some cracking. Level and unmold torte onto an 8-inch corrugated cake circle. Torte may be completed to this point, wrapped and kept at room temperature up to 3 days in advance. Or freeze for up to 3 months. Let come to room temperature before glazing.

6. Glaze with Bittersweet Chocolate or Chocolate Honey Glaze. To decorate place plain or caramelized hazelnuts around the top edge of the cake or pipe overlapping zigzags of melted white and milk chocolate. Do not refrigerate.

TIME-LIFE BOOKS
The Cooking of Vienna's Empire

Sachertorte

Sacher Cake

TO MAKE 1 NINE-INCH ROUND CAKE
6½ ounces semisweet chocolate, broken or chopped in small chunks
8 egg yolks
8 tablespoons (¼-pound stick) unsalted butter, melted
1 teaspoon vanilla extract
10 egg whites
Pinch of salt
¾ cup sugar
1 cup sifted all-purpose flour
½ cup apricot jam, rubbed through a sieve

THE GLAZE
3 ounces unsweetened chocolate, broken or chopped into small chunks
1 cup heavy cream
1 cup sugar
1 teaspoon corn syrup
1 egg
1 teaspoon vanilla extract

Preheat the oven to 350°. Line two 9-by-1½-inch round cake pans with circles of wax paper.

In the top of a double boiler, heat the chocolate until it melts, stirring occasionally with a wooden spoon. In a small mixing bowl, break up the egg yolks with a fork, then beat in the chocolate, melted butter and vanilla extract.

With a wire whisk or a rotary or electric beater, beat the egg whites and pinch of salt until they foam, then add the sugar, 1 tablespoon at a time, continuing to beat until the whites form stiff, unwavering peaks on the beater when it is lifted from the bowl.

Mix about ⅓ of the egg whites into the yolk-chocolate mixture, then reverse the process and pour the chocolate over the remaining egg whites. Sprinkle the flour over the top. With a rubber spatula, using an over-and-under cutting motion instead of a mixing motion, fold the whites and the chocolate mixture together until no trace of the white remains. Do not overfold.

Pour the batter into the 2 lined pans, dividing it evenly between them. Bake in the middle of the oven until the layers are puffed and dry and a toothpick stuck in the center of a layer comes out clean.

Remove the pans from the oven and loosen the sides of the layers by running a sharp knife around them. Turn them out on a cake rack and remove the wax paper. Let the layers cool while you prepare the glaze.

THE GLAZE: In a small heavy saucepan, combine the chocolate, cream, sugar and corn syrup. Stirring constantly with a wooden spoon, cook on low heat until the chocolate and sugar are melted, then raise the heat to medium and cook without stirring for about 5 minutes, or until a little of the mixture dropped into a glass of cold water forms a soft ball. In a small mixing bowl beat the egg lightly, then stir 3 tablespoons of the chocolate mixture into it. Pour this into the remaining chocolate in the saucepan and stir it briskly. Cook over low heat, stirring constantly, for 3 or 4 minutes, or until the glaze coats the spoon heavily. Remove the pan from the heat and add the vanilla. Cool the glaze to room temperature.

When the cake layers have completely cooled, spread one of them with apricot jam and put the other layer on top. Set the rack in a jelly-roll pan and, holding the saucepan about 2 inches away from the cake, pour the glaze over it evenly. Smooth the glaze with a metal spatula. Let the cake stand until the glaze stops dripping, then, using two metal spatulas, transfer it to a plate and refrigerate it for 3 hours to harden the glaze. Remove it from the refrigerator ½ hour before serving.

KASPER

The Splendid Table

Torta Barozzi

A sensational specialty, made only in the castle town of Vignola outside Modena, Torta Barozzi *is to chocolate cake what a diamond is to zircon. It looks like yet another flourless chocolate cake, but one mouthful banishes any sense of the mundane. This is a chocolate essence, moist and fudgy, with secret ingredients known only to the baker. Serve the rich cake cut in small wedges, and do tell the story of Modena's obsession with a seemingly conventional chocolate cake.*

MAKES 1 CAKE, SERVING 6 TO 8

½ cup (2 ounces) blanched almonds, toasted
2 tablespoons confectioner's sugar
3 tablespoons cocoa (not Dutch process)
1½ tablespoons unsalted butter
3 to 4 tablespoons all-purpose unbleached flour (organic stone-ground preferred)
8 tablespoons (4 ounces) unsalted butter, at room temperature
½ cup plus 2 tablespoons (4 ounces) sugar
3½ tablespoons smooth peanut butter
4 large eggs, separated
5½ ounces bittersweet chocolate, melted and cooled
½ ounce unsweetened chocolate, melted and cooled
1½ tablespoons instant espresso coffee granules, dissolved in 1 tablespoon boiling water
1½ teaspoons dark rum
1 teaspoon vanilla extract

DECORATION

1 tablespoon cocoa
½ tablespoon confectioner's sugar

METHOD

WORKING AHEAD: *The* Barozzi *can be baked ahead and has admirable keeping qualities, It may be slightly better tasting in the first 24 hours after baking, but the cake keeps all its flavor when tightly wrapped and stored in the refrigerator up to 3 days. It freezes well 2 months. Serve at room temperature.*

MAKING ALMOND POWDER: Combine the almonds, 2 tablespoons confectioner's sugar, and 3 tablespoons cocoa in a food processor fitted with the steel blade. Process until the almonds are a fine powder.

BLENDING THE BATTER: Butter the bottom and sides of an 8-inch springform pan with the 1 tablespoon of butter, Cut a circle of parchment paper to cover the bottom of the pan. Butter the paper with ½ tablespoon butter and line the pan with it, butter side up. Use the 3 to 4 tablespoons flour to coat the entire interior of the springform, shaking out any excess. Preheat the oven to 375°F, and set a rack in the center of the oven. Using an electric mixer fitted with the paddle attachment or a hand-held electric mixer, beat the butter and sugar at medium speed 8 to 10 minutes, or until almost white and very fluffy. Scrape down the sides of the bowl several times during beating. Beating the butter and sugar to absolute airiness ensures the *torta*'s fine grain and melting lightness. Still at medium speed, beat in the peanut butter. Then beat in the egg yolks, two at a time, until smooth. Reduce the speed to medium-low, and beat in the melted chocolates, the dissolved coffee, and the rum and vanilla. Then use a big spatula to fold in the almond powder by hand, keeping the batter light.

Whip the egg whites to stiff peaks. Lighten the chocolate batter by folding a quarter of the whites into it. Then fold in the rest, keeping the mixture light but without leaving any streaks of white.

BAKING: Turn the batter into the baking pan, gently smoothing the top. Bake 30 minutes. Then reduce the oven heat to 325°F and bake another 15 to 20 minutes, or until a tester inserted in the center of the cake comes out with only a few small flecks. The cake will have puffed about two thirds of the way up the sides of the pan. Cool the cake 10 minutes in the pan set on a rack. The cake will settle slightly but will remain level. Spread a kitchen towel on a large plate, and turn the cake out onto it. Peel off the parchment paper and cool the cake completely. Then place a round cake plate on top of the cake and hold the two plates together as you flip them over so the *torta* is right side up on the cake plate.

SERVING: *Torta Barozzi* is moist and fudgy. Just before serving, sift the tablespoon of cocoa over the cake. Then top it with a sifting of the confectioner's sugar. (Or for a whimsical decoration, cut a large stencil of the letter "B" out of stiff paper or cardboard. Set it in the center of the cake before dusting the entire top with the confectioner's sugar. Carefully lift off the stencil once the sugar has settled.) Serve the *Barozzi* at room temperature, slicing it in small wedges.

SUGGESTIONS

WINE: In Vignola, homemade walnut liqueur (*Nocino*) is sipped with the *Barozzi*. Here, the black muscat-based Elysium dessert wine from California does well with the cake's intense chocolate.

MENU: Serve after Modena dishes such as Giovanna's Wine-Basted Rabbit, Beef-Wrapped Sausage, Balsamic Roast Chicken, and Rabbit Dukes of Modena, or after light main dishes and first courses.

COOK'S NOTES

CHOCOLATE: Use a chocolate rich in deep fruity flavors, such as Tobler Tradition or Lindt Excellence.

PEANUT BUTTER: Peanut butter is the surprise ingredient in the cake, and an important one. I use creamy Skippy, but no doubt other brands work well too.

WHIPPED CREAM: Although not served this way in Vignola, the *Barozzi* is superb topped with dollops of unsweetened whipped cream. Count on whipping 1 cup of heavy cream to serve 6 to 8.

"IT'S ALL THERE ON THE BOX"

Cracking the code of Torta Barozzi *is Modena's favorite food game. For decades local cooks have tried to unravel its mystery, without success. When a Modenese dinner party gets dull, ask about* Torta Barozzi *and settle back. The heat of the debate will warm you for the rest of the evening. Eugenio Gollini invented the cake in 1897 at his Pasticceria Gollini in Vignola. The cake commemorated the birthday of Renaissance architect Jacopo Barozzi, a native son of Vignola who invented the spiral staircase. Today Gollini's grandsons, Carlo and Eugenio, still make* Barozzi *at the same pasticceria. Its recipe is secret, although its ingredients are stated on the cake's box. Family members have sworn never to reveal nor change the formula. But Eugenio Gollini smiles serenely when he tells you it is all there in plain sight.*

Gollini offered no clue of how peanuts—a startling and definitely non-Italian ingredient—became part of the cake. I speculate that late 19th-century cooks considered these nuts, brought from Africa, to be exotic and intriguing. Perhaps in experimenting with them, the elder Gollini discovered how good they are with chocolate. Then he might have found that peanuts pureed into peanut butter ensured a smoother and even more melting Torta Barozzi. *Historian Renato Bergonzini explained why the people of Vignola believe the cake's secret eludes discovery: "Barozzi left the last step of his spiral staircase unfinished. No one knows why, and no one would presume to finish it. To imitate the torta is like trying to finish Barozzi's staircase: impudent and foolish. Only the master himself can complete his work." I confess to both impudence and foolishness, but also to success. This recipe comes tantalizingly close to the original.*

LANG

The Cuisine of Hungary

Ilona Torte

12 OR MORE SERVINGS

5 ounces semisweet chocolate
1 cup sugar
6 tablespoons sweet butter
8 eggs, separated
½ pound walnuts, ground
2 tablespoons white bread crumbs
Pinch of salt
1 teaspoon ice water
Butter
Flour
Mocha Filling I (below)
2 tablespoons chopped walnuts

1. Preheat oven to 375°F. Heat chocolate with sugar and ¼ cup water. This will take 5 to 6 minutes, with constant stirring. Heat and stir till a smooth syrup is formed.

2. In a mixing bowl whip butter with egg yolks till light and foamy. Add the chocolate syrup, ground walnuts and bread crumbs.

3. Adding salt and ice water, whip egg whites till so stiff a spoon will stand in them; then very, very gently fold them into the chocolate mixture.

4. Butter a 10-inch torte pan 3 inches deep and sprinkle with flour. Shake out excess. Pour the batter into the pan, and bake in the preheated oven for 20 to 25 minutes. Cool the cake completely.

5. Make filling.

6. Cut the cooled torte into 2 layers. Fill the layers with two thirds of the filling. Use the rest as frosting. Finally, sprinkle with chopped walnuts. Serve chilled.

MOCHA FILLING I

¼ pound semisweet chocolate
¼ cup prepared very strong espresso coffee
½ teaspoon instant coffee
2 egg yolks
⅓ pounds sweet butter
⅓ cup vanilla confectioners' sugar

1. Heat chocolate and coffee together for a few minutes, until chocolate is melted and the mixture is smooth. Let it cool completely.

2. In a mixing bowl whip the egg yolks with butter and sugar till light and foamy.

3. Whip in the cooled chocolate-coffee mixture.

NOTE: This cake is perhaps closer to me than any other for the sentimental reason that it is named after my mother and my daughter, Andrea Ilona. The origin of this torte was lost in the second half of the nineteenth century, when most of these recipes were formalized and written down. It is perhaps the richest of all chocolate tortes.

DE SILVA

In Memory's Kitchen

Ausgiebige Schokolade Torte

10 dkg Butter, 10 dkg Zucker, 4 Dotter, 14 dkg erweichte Schokol. abtreiben; 4 Schnee, 3 dkg Mehl. Eine dünne Platte in einer Tortenform backen, den Rest am Blech und zerbröseln. In der Form immer eine Lage Creme, 1 Lage Brösel obenauf Glasur, oder Sahne. Creme: 14 dkg Schok. m. 5 dkg Zucker, 2 Löffel Wasser am Feuer verrühren, ½ l Schlagsahne hinein.

Rich Chocolate Cake

Beat 10 decagrams butter, 10 decagrams sugar, 4 egg yolks, 14 decagrams softened chocolate. Fold in 4 [egg whites stiffly beaten to] snow, 3 decagrams flour. Bake a thin layer in a cake pan. [Pour] the test [of the batter] on a baking sheet, [bake] and make crumbs [from it]. In cake pan always put a layer [of] cream, a layer [of] crumbs. Top with glaze or cream. Cream: 14 decagrams choc. with 5 decagrams sugar, 2 spoons water. Mix over fire. Fold in ½ liter whipped heavy cream.

MEDRICH
Cocolat

Queen of Sheba

SERVES 10–12

Torte tastes best if baked at least one day ahead.

- 6 ounces semisweet or bittersweet chocolate, cut into pieces
- 6 ounces sweet butter, cut into pieces
- 3 tablespoons brandy
- ⅛ teaspoon almond extract
- 4 large eggs, separated
- ¾ cup sugar
- ½ cup (2 ounces) ground blanched almonds
- ¼ cup (1 ounce) flour
- ⅛ teaspoon cream of tartar
- Bittersweet Chocolate Glaze
- 1 ounce each white and/or dark chocolate (optional) if you plan to marble the glaze
- ½ cup (about 2 ounces) sliced toasted almonds

SPECIAL EQUIPMENT

8-inch round corrugated cake circle

1. Preheat oven to 375°. Line bottom of 8 × 3-inch springform pan with parchment or waxed paper.

2. Combine chocolate and butter in a small bowl placed in a barely simmering water bath over low heat, stirring occasionally until melted and smooth. Remove from heat. Or, microwave on medium (50%) for about 2 minutes. Stir until completely melted and smooth. Stir in brandy and almond extract. Set aside.

3. In bowl, whisk egg yolks with ½ cup sugar until pale and thick. Stir in the warm chocolate mixture, almonds, and flour. Set aside.

4. Beat the egg whites and cream of tartar at medium speed until soft peaks form. Gradually sprinkle in remaining ¼ cup sugar, beating at high speed until stiff but not dry. Fold about one-quarter of the egg whites completely into the chocolate batter to lighten it. Quickly fold in remaining whites. Turn mixture into the prepared pan and smooth top if necessary. Bake for 40–45 minutes, until a toothpick or wooden skewer plunged into the center of the cake shows moist crumbs (the center of the cake should be neither completely dry nor runny).

5. Cool torte completely in pan on a rack. It will have risen and then fallen in the center, leaving a higher rim of cake around sides and possibly some cracking. Level and unmold torte onto an 8-inch corrugated cake circle. Torte may be prepared to this point up to 3 days in advance. Wrap well and store at room temperature until needed, or freeze for up to 3 months. Bring to room temperature before serving, glazing, or decorating.

6. Glaze torte with Bittersweet Chocolate Glaze, plain or marbled, and press sliced toasted almonds around the sides.

BERANBAUM
The Cake Bible

Swiss Black Forest Cake

Schwarzwalder Kirschtorte

SERVES 10 TO 12

My version of this classic was inspired by Confiserie Tschirren in Berne, Switzerland. They brought the recipe from Germany after World War II; and it has since become the national cake of Switzerland.

The Swiss rendition is far lighter and more delicate than the original German one, which also includes buttercream. A lofty layer of whipped cream studded with liqueur-soaked cherries is sandwiched between two thin, light layers of liqueur-moistened chocolate génoise. The chocolate flakes on top dissolve like snowflakes on the tongue.

In Switzerland, the Black Forest Cake is served in all *confiseries and konditorei for afternoon tea, but the cake is elegant enough for fancy dinner parties as well.*

TIMING

The cake should be assembled 4 to 12 hours ahead.

SERVE

Chilled.

SPECIAL EQUIPMENT

- 8⅝-inch by 2⅜-inch (22-centimeter by 6-centimeter) French flan ring. Or a 9-inch springform or loose-bottom pan fitted with cardboard rounds until a depth of 2½ inches is achieved. Molding the cake this way makes it perfectly symmetrical. The French flan ring is the ideal size because the 9-inch cake layer shrinks to just that size after baking. The springform pan also works but the sides of the finished cake will not be quite as even.
- Pastry bag and a large number 6 star tube

CAKE COMPONENTS

- 1 recipe Brandied Burgundy Cherries, well drained and the syrup reserved
- ¼ cup kirsch or brandy
- ½ recipe (1 layer) Moist Chocolate Génoise, top and bottom crusts removed and split in half horizontally to make (2) ½" layers
- 3 times the quantity of recipe for Super-Stabilized Whipped Cream or Real Old-Fashioned Whipped Cream. The Real Old-Fashioned Whipped Cream is lighter in texture, but the cake cannot be held at room temperature for more than 15 to 30 minutes.
- ½ cup Chocolate Snowflakes

METHOD FOR ASSEMBLING CAKE

1. Place the flan ring on a serving plate or cut out a cardboard round to fit the diameter of the ring. Or use a loose-bottom or springform pan fitted with cardboard rounds to a depth of 2½ inches.

2. Add the kirsch or brandy to the reserved cherry syrup to make ½ cup. Sprinkle each side of the cake layers with 2 tablespoons syrup.

3. Reserve 12 whole cherries for decor and cut the remaining cherries in half if they are large.

4. Reserve 2¼ cups whipped cream for the top of the cake and the rosettes. (This may be refrigerated for up to 6 hours).

5. Place 1 cake layer in the bottom of the flan ring and top with the remaining whipped cream.

6. Poke the cherries into the whipped cream, pressing some of the cut sides against the pan.

7. Use a small angled spatula to level the cream and top with the second cake layer.

8. Spread with 1 cup of the reserved whipped cream. Use a long metal spatula to create a smooth top, allowing the blade to rest on the sides of the ring to create a very even surface.

9. Cover with foil and refrigerate for at least 4 hours.

10. Wipe the sides of the ring with a warm damp towel and lift away the ring or remove the sides of the pan.

11. Use the remaining whipped cream to decorate the top with rosettes using a large number 6 star tube. Top the rosettes with the reserved whole cherries. Spoon the chocolate snowflakes in the center.

VARIATION

Three times the quantity of recipe for White Ganache or 1½ times the quantity of recipe for Light Whipped Ganache may be used in place of whipped cream for a more chocolaty effect.

BERANBAUM

The Cake Bible

Blueberry Swan Lake

SERVES 12

The fanciful image of this cake reflects the flavor within: soft-as-swan's-down white butter cake, silky lemon buttercream, and a shimmering lake of dark blueberry topping.

The Victorian dessert spoons in the picture were found at an antiques fair held in a Moravian church in Hope, New Jersey. I spent a small fortune on them because they reminded me of swans' wings.

This cake is lovely to serve any time of year and satisfying yet light enough as the finale for a grand dinner.

TIMING

The cake can be assembled 1 day ahead and refrigerated except for the blueberry topping and swans, which should be placed on the cake no more than 2 hours before serving. The frosted cake (without the swans or blueberry topping) can be frozen 2 months.

SERVE

If the cake has been refrigerated, allow it to come to room temperature before serving (at least 2 hours). Cut into wedges radiating from the center.

SPECIAL EQUIPMENT NEEDED

- Plastic swans can be used in place of piped meringue swans. They are available at party supply stores and can be painted with a thin coating of Royal Icing.
- Two 9¼-inch x 6⅝-inch oval pans
- Oval platter or board, flat portion at least 10 inches by 7 inches
- Pastry bag and number 22 star tube

CAKE COMPONENTS

- 2 meringue swans and ¼ cup Stabilized Whipped Cream
- 1 recipe White Chocolate Whisper Cake, baked in two 9¼-inch by 6⅝-inch oval cake pans
- 1 recipe Neoclassic or Classic Lemon Buttercream
- 1 recipe Winter Blueberry Topping

METHOD FOR ASSEMBLING CAKE

1. Frost directly on a serving plate, using strips of wax paper slid under the sides. Or make a cardboard base, using one of the cake pans as a template.

2. Spread a little buttercream on the base so that the cake will stick to it.

3. Fill and frost the layers with a ¼-inch thick layer of buttercream. Use a small metal spatula to create vertical lines to represent waves on the sides.

4. With the remaining buttercream pipe a board of sideways shells (reverse shell technique without altering direction), using a number 22 star tube. Chill for 30 minutes.

5. Up to 2 hours before serving, carefully, so as not to damage the border, spoon room temperature Winter Blueberry Topping smoothly over the cake.

6. Complete the swans by piping the whipped cream and securing the heads and necks and set on the cake.

STEWART

Weddings

Orange Almond Cake

MAKES 1 ROUND LAYER—2 × 11 INCHES
APPROXIMATELY 6½ CUPS BATTER

This cake, which I made for Allison Zucker's wedding, I call my "Rose Swag Cake." The frosting decoration is quite simple to execute, yet flamboyant looking. A smooth undercoating was applied to each of the five layers and then a swag was applied with a wide rose tip. The same tip was used to create the ruffled edging.

The interior of this cake was the orange-almond cake, a French cake made with fresh orange juice, grated orange rind, and egg whites for leavening. It is a dense, rich, melt-in-the-mouth cake, and a favorite of brides.

1 cup plus 3 tablespoons sugar
6 eggs, separated
Grated rind of 2 oranges
⅔ cup freshly squeezed, strained orange juice
½ teaspoon almond extract
1½ cups finely ground blanched almonds
1½ cups sifted cake flour
Pinch of salt
½ pound (2 sticks) unsalted butter, melted and cooled

Preheat the oven to 350°. Butter and flour the cake pan, line it with parchment paper, and butter and flour the paper.

With an electric mixer, beat 1 cup sugar with the egg yolks until the mixture is thick and pale yellow. Beat in the orange rind and juice and almond extract. Quickly stir in the ground almonds; then beat in the flour.

In a separate bowl, beat the egg whites to soft peaks. Add the salt and remaining tablespoons sugar and beat until stiff but not dry.

Quickly fold the melted butter into the batter, a bit at a time, until incorporated. Gently fold the beaten egg whites into the batter, taking care not to deflate them. Immediately spoon the batter into the prepared pan and bake for 35 minutes, or until the center tests done. Cool on a wire rack for 10 minutes; remove the cake from the pan and cool completely.

I used old roses from my garden, in shades of apricot, to decorate Allison's cake.

BERANBAUM

The Cake Bible

Cordon Rose Chocolate Christmas Log

Bûche de Noël

SERVES 12

I made this traditional holiday cake for Christmas dinner in France some years ago in the home of my dear friends the Brossolets. (Something like bringing coals to Newcastle!) It quickly became a family project, with Martin, the youngest, running out to the corner store to purchase parchment for piping the meringue mushrooms and Nadège sneaking her husband's oldest rum for the ganache, saying he would have a fit if he knew it was being used for a cake. The best part, however, was when Max (Papa) contributed his antique toy buglers for the decoration.

My version uses a moist chocolate roll and whipped cream instead of the usual yellow cake roll and chocolate buttercream, which I always found too rich and heavy under the chocolate "bark."

TIMING:

The cake can be assembled and refrigerated 2 days ahead. The meringue mushrooms should not be set on the log until serving day.

SERVE:
Lightly chilled or room temperature. Cut diagonal slices with a thin, sharp knife.

CAKE COMPONENTS
- 1 recipe Chocolate Cloud Roll
- 1 recipe Perfect Whipped Cream
- 1 recipe Dark Ganache Frosting

OPTIONAL DECOR
- Meringue Mushrooms
- Pistachio Marzipan Ivy Leaves
- Green Tea Pine Needles

METHOD FOR ASSEMBLING CAKE

1. Fill the Chocolate Cloud Roll with the Perfect Whipped Cream.

2. Chill for at least 1 hour.

3. Cut a diagonal slice from one end of the roll and place on top to form a knot.

4. Spread the ganache frosting over the log and use the tines of a fork to make lines resembling bark. Make a few round swirls with the fork on top of the knot.

5. Decorate with the meringue mushrooms, marzipan leaves, green tea pine needles, and any small appropriate figures such as porcelain elves or trumpeters.

6. Refrigerate 1 hour before serving.

STEWART
Weddings

Croquembouche

Pastry chef Maurice Bonté does not like to make the croquembouche commercially because it is very delicate. But if the weather permits, or if you are entertaining in an air-conditioned space, this fantasy dessert is both romantic and extremely delicious. I often make these free-form, tall, cone-shaped mounds of pastry-cream filled cream puffs as a supplementary wedding dessert. Only rarely does a bride request a croquembouche as her sole wedding cake, I like to decorate this confection with full-blown pink roses and golden puffs of spun sugar.

PÂTE À CHOUX
MAKES APPROXIMATELY 60 PUFFS

1½ cups water
12 tablespoons (1½ sticks) unsalted butter, cut into small pieces
¼ teaspoon salt
1 teaspoon sugar
1½ cups all-purpose flour
6 large eggs

GARNISH
1 egg beaten with 1 teaspoon water

CRÈME PATISSIÈRE (PASTRY CREAM)
6 egg yolks
½ cup sugar
½ cup sifted all-purpose flour
2 cups scalded milk
3 tablespoons unsalted butter
1 teaspoon vanilla extract
2 tablespoons Cognac
Pinch of salt

CARAMEL
2 cups sugar
⅔ cup water
2 tablespoons light corn syrup

GARNISH
spun sugar

To make the puffs, put the water in a small heavy saucepan, add the butter, and bring the water to a boil. When the butter is melted add the salt and sugar. Remove the saucepan from the heat and add the flour, stirring until smooth.

Return the pan to high heat and continue stirring until the mixture forms a smooth mass and the bottom of the pan is coated with a thin film. (This indicates that the flour is cooked.) Remove the pan from the heat and put the mixture into a mixing bowl. Let it cool slightly.

Add the eggs, one at a time, beating the batter until very smooth. Once the eggs have been added, the mixture can remain covered at room temperature for an hour or two.

Preheat the oven to 425°. Lightly butter or line several baking sheets with parchment paper.

Place the dough in a pastry bag fitted with a ½-inch round tip. Pipe the mixture onto the prepared baking sheets, forming mounds 1 inch in diameter and ¾ inch high. Lightly brush each with the egg glaze, gently smoothing the top of each puff. Bake for 10 minutes.

Reduce the oven temperature to 375° and continue baking until the puffs are golden brown, about 20 minutes more. Reduce the oven temperature to 325° and bake until the puffs are firm and the insides are not sticky or doughy. Let the puffs cool on a wire rack while you prepare the crème patissière.

Bear the egg yolks, gradually adding the sugar until the mixture is thick and pale yellow. Beat in the flour.

Add all but ½ cup of the scalded milk to the egg mixture in dribbles. Set aside remaining ½ cup of scalded milk. Return the mixture to the pot in which the milk was scalded, and stir over high heat until it comes to a boil. Stir vigorously; the mixture may become lumpy at first but will smooth out. Be careful, however, not to scorch the bottom of the pan. The cream should be thick, but if it is too thick to pipe, add a bit more scalded milk.

Remove the crème patissière from the heat and add the butter, a tablespoon at a time. Stir in the vanilla, Cognac, and salt, and let the pastry cream cool completely.

When the pastry cream has cooled, place it in a pastry bag fitted with a ¼-inch tip. Make a small hole in the side of each pâte à choux puff with the tip, and pipe the pastry cream into each one. Set aside. (Try to find a pastry-cream tip for filling the puffs for it makes the job easier.)

To make the caramel, bring the sugar, water, and corn syrup to a boil over high heat. Swirl the pan to dissolve the sugar, but do not stir or the mixture may become cloudy. Cover the pan to allow the steam to dissolve any crystals that might form, still boiling the syrup, for approximately 5 minutes. Uncover the pan and boil the mixture several more minutes, or until it turns amber colored. Reduce the heat to keep the syrup from hardening.

Dip the cream-filled puffs into the caramel syrup, one by one, and arrange in a cone shape to resemble a pyramid. Decorate the entire croquembouche with Spun Sugar. Garnish with flowers.

NOTE: The croquembouche cannot be refrigerated because the caramel and spun sugar will soften, so it must be assembled as close to serving time as possible (2 to 3 hours). However, the pâte à choux puffs and the crème patissière can be prepared in advance. The puffs freeze very well and can be thawed the morning of the wedding and filled. Refrigerate filled puffs until ready to assemble.

The completed croquembouche—a fantasy of pâte à choux puffs, spun sugar, golden caramel, and delicate pink roses.

BAILEY

Lee Bailey's Country Weekends

Lord Baltimore Cake

This cake can be made in either 2 or 3 layers. If you do it in 3, use pans with removable bottoms as the layers will be thin and sometimes rather reluctant to come out.

2½ cups cake flour
4 teaspoons baking powder
12 tablespoons (1½ sticks) unsalted butter
1½ cups sugar
8 egg yolks
¾ cup milk
½ teaspoon vanilla

FROSTING

2½ cups sugar
¾ cup water
3 egg whites
½ teaspoon cream of tartar
¾ teaspoon orange juice
3 teaspoons lemon juice
18 candied cherries, cut into quarters
¾ cup macaroons, crumbled
¾ cup pecans, coarsely chopped
¾ cup blanched almonds, coarsely chopped

Preheat oven to 350 degrees. Grease 2 or 3 9-inch cake pans and dust lightly with flour, shaking out the excess.

Sift the flour and baking powder together twice and set aside. Cream butter and sugar together thoroughly. Add egg yolks all at one time and beat well. Add flour alternately with milk and beat well after each addition. Stir in vanilla.

Pour into the prepared pans and bake 25 minutes for a double-layer cake, slightly less for a triple-layer one. Remove from oven and allow to cool in the pans a few minutes. Run a knife around the edges and invert onto a cooling rack. Rap the pan gently so that cake will come out. If it doesn't, allow to cool 10 minutes or so longer. Try again.

To make frosting, dissolve sugar in the water and bring to a boil. Continue until syrup spins a thread (238 degrees on a candy thermometer). Beat egg whites stiffly and add the cream of tartar (have these ready to go when the syrup is ready to be added). Continue beating while you add the syrup in a steady stream. Add lemon and orange juice and mix. Set aside ½ the icing, and pour the other ½ in with the remaining ingredients. Use the first ½ of the icing to frost between the 3 layers of the cake, securing them with toothpicks. Frost the top and sides of the cake with the other batch.

SERVES 12

TRUAX
Ladies' Home Journal Cookbook

Burnt-Sugar Cake

BURNT-SUGAR SIRUP
¾ cup sugar
¾ cup very hot strong coffee

CAKE
3 cups cake flour
¾ teaspoon salt
1 tablespoon baking powder
¾ cup butter
1¼ cups sugar
3 eggs
½ cup milk
1 teaspoon vanilla

BURNT-SUGAR BUTTER FROSTING
6 tablespoons butter
3¼ cups sifted confectioners' sugar
Pinch salt
½ teaspoon vanilla
Light cream

BURNT-SUGAR SIRUP: Heat sugar slowly in a skillet. Stir gently and when completely melted and dark amber in color, remove from heat and stir in coffee. This will boil up a great deal. Return to low heat. Stir gently until all the caramelized sugar is dissolved. Cool to room temperature before using.

CAKE: Sift cake flour, salt and baking powder together. Cream the butter. Gradually add sugar and beat until light and fluffy. Add egg yolks, one at a time, beating well after each addition. Mix ½ cup burnt-sugar sirup and the milk. Add ¼ of the dry ingredients to batter. Beat at medium speed on mixer (or by hand) until all flour is moistened. Add ⅓ of the liquid and continue beating until the liquid is absorbed. Repeat, using all ingredients and ending with an addition of flour. Stir in vanilla. Beat egg whites until they are stiff but still shiny. Fold thoroughly into the batter. Divide evenly between two 9-inch layer-cake pans which have been lined with waxed paper. Bake in a moderate oven, 350°, half an hour. Cool slightly, remove from pans, pull off paper, and cool thoroughly.

BURNT-SUGAR BUTTER FROSTING: Cream butter. Gradually add sifted confectioners' sugar alternately with ⅓ cup burnt-sugar sirup. Finally add salt and vanilla. If frosting seems a bit dry, add a little light cream to soften to spreading consistency. Eight to ten servings.

STEWART
Weddings

Chocolate Ganache Groom's Cake

This is one of my favorite cakes to assemble. I like working with the two textures of ganache—the creamy whipped undercoat, which covers and smooths the baked layers of chocolate almond cake, and the thin, shiny ganache, which can virtually be poured over the entire stacked cake and smoothed to perfection with a small metal spatula. When doubled, this recipe is enough to ice a 4-layer cake.

Layers of Chocolate-Almond Wedding Cake

CHOCOLATE GANACHE

(MAKES 3 CUPS)

1 pound semisweet chocolate, cut into bits
2 cups heavy cream

GARNISH
Chocolate Curls

Bake as many layers of the Chocolate-Almond Wedding Cake as desired.

To make the ganache, melt the chocolate with the cream in a heavy saucepan and cook over very low heat until the mixture is smooth and glossy.

Place half of the mixture in a mixing bowl and beat until it becomes thick. Use this mixture as the undercoat for the cake layers.

Stack the layers as desired, using chopsticks for support, and pour the shiny, thin other half of the ganache over the entire stacked cake, smoothing with a metal spatula. The mixture must be relatively liquid to do this, but if it is too thin, gently stir over ice to thicken it slightly.

Top the iced cake layers with chocolate curls and chill the cake before serving.

COOKIES

CROCKER

Betty Crocker's Picture Cook Book

Sugar Jumbles (🔑 Recipe)

Little sugar cakes of old-time goodness.

Mix together thoroughly . . .

½ cup soft shortening (part butter)
½ cup sugar
1 egg
1 tsp. vanilla

Sift together and stir in . . .

1⅛ cups *sifted* GOLD MEDAL Flour
¼ tsp. soda
½ tsp. salt

Drop rounded teaspoonfuls about 2" apart on lightly greased baking sheet. Bake until delicately browned . . . cookies should still be soft. Cool slightly . . . then remove from baking sheet.

TEMPERATURE: 375° (quick mod. oven).
TIME: Bake 8 to 10 min.
AMOUNT: About 3 doz. 2" cookies.

CHOCOLATE CHIP COOKIES

The glamorous Toll House cookies . . . first introduced to American homemakers in 1939 through my series of radio talks on "Famous Foods from Famous Eating Places."

Follow 🔑 recipe above—*except* in place of ½ cup sugar use ¾ cup (half brown, half white). Then mix into the dough ½ cup cut-up nuts and one 7-oz. package chocolate pieces (about 1¼ cups).

FARMER

The Boston Cooking-School Cook Book

Peanut Butter Cookies

ABOUT 50 COOKIES

¼ pound (115 g) butter
½ cup (1 dL) chunk-style peanut butter
½ cup (100 g) granulated sugar
½ cup (1 dL) dark-brown sugar
1 egg
½ teaspoon vanilla
½ teaspoon salt
½ teaspoon baking soda
1 cup (140 g) flour

Preheat the oven to 350°F (180°C) and grease some cookie sheets. Cream the butter and peanut butter together. Beat in the two sugars, then add the egg and the vanilla and mix well. Mix together the salt, baking soda, and flour and add to the first mixture, combining thoroughly. Arrange by teaspoonfuls on the cookie sheets, about 1½ inches apart. Press each one flat with the back of a floured spoon. Bake about 7 minutes or until firm.

CUNNINGHAM

The Breakfast Book

Oatmeal Bran Breakfast Cookies

THREE DOZEN COOKIES

These chewy, crunchy cookies need no introduction.

¾ cup vegetable shortening
1 cup brown sugar
⅓ cup granulated sugar
¼ cup strong coffee
1 egg
2½ cups rolled oats
1 cup all-purpose flour
1 teaspoon salt
½ teaspoon baking soda
1½ cups All-Bran cereal

Preheat the oven to 350°F. Don't grease the baking sheet(s).

Put the shortening, sugars, coffee, and egg in a mixing bowl and beat until smooth and blended. Add the oats, flour, salt, and baking soda. Stir very well so the dough is well mixed.

Spread the All-Bran cereal out on a piece of waxed paper. This is a sticky dough, so wet your fingers with cold water before pinching off about 2 tablespoons of dough at a time and rolling it in the All-Bran. Don't worry if you can't get a heavy coating of cereal on each piece of dough; if just a little of the All-Bran sticks, it will give a nice texture to the cookies.

Place the dough pieces about 1½ inches apart on the baking sheet(s). Bake 12 to 15 minutes. Remove from the oven and cool on racks.

DULL

Southern Cooking

Mother Dull's Tea Cakes

- 2 cups sugar
- 1 cup of lard and butter mixed
- ½ cup buttermilk
- 3 eggs
- ½ teaspoon soda
- 2 teaspoons baking powder
- 1 teaspoon vanilla
- Flour sufficient to make a soft dough

Cream butter and lard, add sugar then the beaten eggs. Into one cup flour sift soda and baking powder. Add this to the sugar mixture. Add milk and vanilla, now sufficiently more flour to make a soft dough.

Turn onto a floured board, knead until smooth, roll out one-fourth inch thick, cut into any shape, bake in moderate oven until brown and done, about ten minutes. Do not put close enough to touch, as this would spoil the shape. This recipe makes 120 cakes.

If a hard brittle cake is liked, by kneading into the dough dry sugar this will give a brittle cake. Divide dough into two parts, using half cup of sugar, half cup of flour for one part roll, cut and bake and you will have some of both.

If these cakes are iced over top or two put together with icing, they are unusually good.

This is without any exception the best tea cake or cookie recipe I have ever used.

RORER

Mrs. Rorer's New Cook Book

Peanut Wafers

Mix a half cup of peanut meal with a half cup of peanut butter; beat thoroughly, then add gradually one and a half cups of sugar. Dissolve a half teaspoonful of soda in a half cup of warm water; add to the nut mixture and then work in about three cups of Graham meal. The dough must be rather hard. Roll out into a very thin sheet, and cut into squares of two inches. Bake in a very slow oven until a golden brown.

JUNIOR LEAGUE OF CHARLESTON

Charleston Receipts

Benne Seed Wafers

"According to legend among descendants of negro slaves along the coast of Charleston, benne is a good luck plant for those who eat thereof or plant in their gardens. It was originally brought in by the slaves from West Africa to this Coastal region."

- 2 cups brown sugar
- 1 cup plain flour
- ½ teaspoon baking powder
- ¼ teaspoon salt
- ¾ cup toasted benne seed
- 1 egg, beaten
- 1 block butter, or ¾ cp cooking oil or oleo
- 1 teaspoon vanilla

Cream the butter and sugar, add beaten egg, then flour sifted with salt and baking powder. Add vanilla and benne seed. Drop by teaspoon or less on greased cookie sheet. Bake in moderate oven 325°. Cook quickly. Allow to cool one minute before removing from pan. This makes a transparent wafer. Yield: about 100.

Mrs. Gustave P. Richards (Lizetta Wagener)

WEAVER
Pennsylvania Dutch Country Cooking

Christmas Gingerbread Men, or "Mummeli"

Grischdaags Mennli, odder Mummeli

This is one of the earliest types of gingerbread that I have come across in Pennsylvania Dutch cookery. The basic recipe was brought to America in the eighteenth century by immigrants from Hessia. Mummeli *are still baked in the New Berlin area of Union County and other parts of central Pennsylvania.*

Traditionally, Mummeli *are made with spelt and barley flours, which create a distinct texture and flavor; the mix was once believed to impart certain magical properties to the little men. If spelt and barley flours are unavailable, substitute whole-wheat flour.*

YIELD: 4 MUMMELI, 9 TO 10 INCHES (22.5 TO 25 CM) TALL

- ½ ounce (14 g) active dry yeast
- 2 cups (500 ml) lukewarm milk
- 5½ cups (770 g) organic spelt flour
- 5 cups (700 g) organic barley flour
- ½ cup (125 g) unsalted butter
- ¾ cup (180 ml) honey
- 4 large eggs
- 1 tablespoon grated nutmeg
- 1 teaspoon sea salt
- 2 tablespoons (30 ml) unsulfured molasses
- 2 tablespoons (30 ml) saffron water (see note)

Proof the yeast in the lukewarm milk mixed with 1 cup (250 ml) warm water. Sift together the spelt and barley flours and put 3 cups (420 g) in a deep bowl. Make a well in the center of the flour and stir in the yeast to form a thick slurry. Cover and set in a warm place until the slurry has risen and is completely covered with bubbles, then stir it down.

Cream the butter and honey. Beat the eggs until lemon colored and blend with the butter mixture. Add this mixture to the slurry. Sift together the remaining flour mixture, the nutmeg, and the salt, and gradually stir into the slurry. Add only enough flour so that the dough is not sticky when handled. (In humid weather, an additional ½ cup/70 g of spelt flour may be necessary.)

Knead the dough for 15 minutes on a clean work surface. Then mold into 4 equal-sized balls. Break off a small piece from each dough ball, and roll out to form 20-inch (50-cm) ropes of equal length. Form the large balls into Mummeli figures. Lay them on greased baking sheets. Decorate the figures with the ropes of dough by tying them around the necks and across the chests. Set the Mummeli aside to recover in a warm place for 20 minutes. While they are rising, preheat the oven to 375°F (190°C). Once the Mummeli are fully risen, bake them for 30 minutes. Remove them from the oven and glaze with a mixture of molasses and saffron water. Return to the oven and bake an additional 15 minutes. Cool on racks.

NOTE: To make saffron water, dissolve ½ teaspoon of powdered saffron (the contents of a 10-grain vial) in 2 tablespoons (30 ml) of water. To make the saffron-molasses glaze, mix the saffron water with the molasses in the recipe above.

TIMES-PICAYUNE
The Original Picayune Creole Cook Book

Bonbons et Sucreries Créoles

Creole Candies occupy a unique position among confections in the United States, and it has often been said that the old French Quarter could apply for a patent for its delicious "Pacanes à la Creme," "Praline Blanc," "Pistaches Pralinées," "La Colle," "Mais Tactac," "Dragées," "Guimauves," "Pastilles," "Nougats" and other exclusive products of the Creole cuisine. The term "Praline" is not of Creole origin, being a common enough word in the vocabulary of the French nation. With the mother country of Louisiana it simply means "sugared," and has no reference whatever to the delightful confections that had their origin in the old Creole homes of New Orleans. There is, indeed, a traditional recipe of the great Viart, "Homme de Bouche," as he called himself, who tickled the palate of Charles X, in the jocund days of the Bourbon restoration, and another old tradition that the Praline was a species of Dragée, which derived its name from the Maréchal de Plessin-Pralin, who was very fond of almonds, and whose butler one day advised him to have them coated with sugar to avoid indigestion. Again, there is an old French rhyme of Gresset's which has become incorporated in the banquette games of the little Creole children of New Orleans, and which runs thus:

> *"Soeur Rosalie au retour de matines,*
> *Plus d'une fois lui porta des pralines."*

But all these songs and stories simply refer to any sugar-coated nut. It was reserved for the gentle descendants of these old French ancestral homes to evolve from the suggestiveness of the word "Praline" dainty and delightful confections that have, for upwards of 150 years, delighted the younger generations of New Orleans, and the older ones, too.

WHITE PRALINES

Pralines Blanches de Coco

2 Cups of Fine White Sugar (Granulated)
1 Freshly-Grated Coconut (Small Size)
4 Tablespoons of Water

Use a farina boiler or a porcelain-lined saucepan. Put the sugar in the saucepan with the water and let it boil well. When it begins to form a syrup, take from the fire and stir in the freshly grated coconut. Mix thoroughly and return to the fire, and let it boil until you can draw it like a thread between your finger and thumb. Be careful to stir constantly from the time you add the coconut. When it begins to bubble, take from the stove, for it will have reached the above-mentioned state in two or three minutes. This will be sufficient if you wish the praline to be light and flaky. Have ready a cleanly washed and somewhat wet marble slab or buttered dish. Take a kitchen spoon and drop the mixture into cakes on the slab, spreading them out with the spoon and rounding with a fork till they form a neat round cake of about a quarter of an inch in thickness and four or five inches in diameter. Let them dry; and then take a knife and gently raise them from the slab. You will have the dainty white pralines that are such peculiar Creole confections and which are also much sought after by strangers visiting New Orleans.

Increase the quantity of sugar in proportion to the size of the coconut, using 6 cups of finest white sugar for a very large coconut, and never boil the coconut more than a few minutes in the sugar.

PINK PRALINES

Pralines Rose de Coco

2 Cups of Fine White Sugar (Granulated)
1 Freshly Grated Coconut (Small Size)
4 Tablespoonfuls of Water
1 Tablespoonful of Cochineal

Proceed in exactly the same manner as above, only add about a tablespoonful of Cochineal to the pralines, just before taking off the fire. Proceed to drop on a marble slab, as above.

PECAN PRALINES

Pralines aux Pacanes

2 Cups of Brown Sugar
½ Pound of Freshly-Peeled and Cut Louisiana Pecans
1 Spoon of Butter
4 Tablespoons of Water

Set the sugar to boil, and as it begins to boil add the pecans, which you will have divested of their shells, and cut some into fine pieces, others into halves and others again into demihalves. Let all boil till the mixture begins to bubble, and then take off the stove and proceed to lay on a marble slab, as above, to dry. These pecan pralines are delicious.

Be careful to stir the mixture in the above recipe constantly till the syrup begins to thicken and turn to sugar. Then take from the stove and proceed to turn on the marble slab. One pound of unshelled pecans will make a half pound shelled. In using water, add just sufficient to melt the sugar.

CREAM PECANS

Pacanes à la Crème

1 Pound of Pecans
The White of an Egg
⅝ Cup of Finest White Confectionary Sugar

Under this suggestive term is known a species of confection that is much used by the Creole as an addition to the most fashionable and recherche feast. Peel the pecans in halves, being careful not to break the meat. Then take the white of an egg and beat well with its weight in water till it forms a cream. Then work in with your fingers the finest white confectionary sugar till it forms a smooth paste. Take a small piece of this paste, roll it, and put it between two halves of the pecans, and then lightly roll in the paste, flattening the pecan somewhat. This coating outside must be very, very light, so that the delicate brown of the pecan meat shows through. Set the pecans to dry, and serve on dainty china saucers, setting a saucer to each guest.

ALMOND PRALINES
Amandes Pralinées

1 Pound of Beautiful New Almonds
2 Cups of Sugar
½ Glass of Water
A Pinch of Carmine

Peel the almonds whole, and then rub them well with a linen cloth, to take off any dust. Put them into a skillet with 2 cups of the finest white sugar, and a dash of Carmine, if you wish to tinge them to a beautiful rose. But they are very beautiful when a snowy white. Place the skillet on the fire, stirring all the time until the almonds crackle hard. Then take off the fire and work until the sugar becomes sandy and well-detached from the almonds. Then separate one part of the sugar, and again put the almonds on the fire, stirring them lightly with a spoon as they again pick up the sugar, paying strict attention to the fire, that it be not too quick. When the almonds have taken up this part of the sugar, put in that which you have reserved, and continue to parch until they have taken up all the sugar. Then take a piece of paper and put it in a sieve, and throw the almonds upon it, shaking around so as to separate those which still cling together. Each almond must be separate and incrusted with sugar.

PEANUT PRALINES
Pistaches Pralinées

1 Pound of Peanuts
2 Cups of Sugar
½ Glass of Water
A Pinch of Carmine

Peanuts, which have been dubbed "Pistaches" by the Creoles, may be made into delightful confections by procedure as outlined above for "Amandes Pralinées."

PEANUT PRALINES
Pralines aux Pistaches

1 Pound of Peanuts
2 Cups of Brown Sugar
4 Tablespoonfuls of Water
1 Tablespoonful of Butter

Shell the peanuts and break into bits. Then set the sugar and water to boil, and as it begins to simmer add the peanuts and the butter. Stir constantly and as it bubbles up once take from the fire, pour from the spoon on the marble slab or a buttered plate, and set away to harden.

OTHER DESSERTS AND SWEETS

GAIGE
New York World's Fair Cook Book

Elephants' Ears

Beat three eggs, add pinch of salt and a tablespoon of milk. Mix very stiff with flour. Pinch off a piece about the size of a walnut, roll out very thin, fry in deep hot fat. Serve with hot maple syrup.

ZIEMANN AND GILLETTE
The White House Cook Book

Dessert Puffs

Puffs for dessert are delicate and nice; take one pint of milk and cream each, the whites of four eggs beaten to a stiff froth, one heaping cupful of sifted flour, one scant cupful of powdered sugar, add a little grated lemon peel and a little salt; beat these all together till very light, bake in gem-pans, sift pulverized sugar over them and eat with sauce flavored with lemon.

THE TIMES-PICAYUNE
The Original Picayune Creole Cook Book

Sweet Entremets
Des Entremêts Sucrés

Sweet entrees and entremets are not the least part of the real Creole cuisine. The ancient French colonists brought the custom of serving sweet entremets and entrees, such as Beignets, Compotes, Soufflés, Gelées, etc., from the old mother country to Louisiana. The Creoles applied these to the various delightful and refreshing fruits which abound in Louisiana. When the little Creole children, taking a peep into the kitchen as children will do in every clime, saw that the fat and cheery old negro cook was going to make Apple Fritters, Orange Fritters or cook fried bananas for dinner, there was always some very endearing term applied to the old Creole cuisiniere, and she never failed to respond in the wholesome and practical way that the Creole cooks of those days did, by handing a beautiful golden beignet, piled with snowy sugar, to the expectant little ones.

Fritters

Des Beignets

The most important rule to be observed in making fritters, whether of fruit or plain, is to have the batter of the proper consistency. This is particularly important in making fruit fritters. "La Pâte à Beignets," as the Creoles call the batter, must be of sufficient consistency to envelop in one single immersion the fruit or other substance with which it is intended to make the fritters.

FRITTER BATTER À LA CRÉOLE

Pâte de Beignets à la Créole

1 Cup Flour
2 Eggs
2 Tablespoonfuls Brandy
¼ Teaspoonful of Salt
Cold Water
1 Tablespoonful Butter, Melted

Beat the yolks of the eggs well and add the flour, beating very light. Now add the melted butter and the Brandy, and thin with water to the consistency of a very thick starch. Add the whites of eggs, beaten to a stiff froth, and then dip the fruit into this, immersing well at one dipping. Lift out with a large cooking spoon, drop into the boiling shortening and fry to a golden brown. The batter must be thick enough to coat the fruit all around in one immersion, yet it must not be so thick as to be overheavily coated or tough.

Many of the Creoles substitute, according to the fruit which they intend to make into fritters, White wine or Sherry or lemon juice for the Brandy. A fruit fritter must always be sprinkled nicely and lightly with powdered sugar, and if served as an entremet, it must be hot. Fruit fritters often take the place of desserts among the poorer Creole families.

FRENCH FRITTER BATTER

Pâte de Beignets à la Française

1 Cup of Sifted Flour
½ Cup of Cold Water
2 Eggs
½ Cup of Sugar
1 Tablespoonful of Best Olive Oil
2 Tablespoonfuls of Brandy or Orange Flower Water
¼ Teaspoonful of Salt

Beat the whites well into a stiff froth. Beat the yolks of the eggs into the flour until very light, and add the sugar, blending well. Add Brandy or orange flower water, and beat light, and then add the water and oil, making the batter of the consistency of a very thick starch. Now add the whites of the egg, beat well, and proceed to drop in the fruit, as in above recipe.

PLAIN FRITTERS

Beignets de Pâte

2 Cups Sifted Flour
1 Pint of Milk
1 Teaspoonful of Baking Powder
4 Eggs
The Outer Skin of Half a Lemon
¼ Cup of Sugar
Flavoring to Taste
½ Teaspoonful of Salt

Beat the yolks of the eggs and the whites separate. Sift the baking powder into the flour, and add the yolks of the eggs, well beaten. Beat well, and add the milk, and flavoring of orange, vanilla or Brandy to taste. (The flavoring may be omitted altogether.) Add the outer skin of a lemon, grated very fine, and salt in quantity given above. Lastly, add the whites, beaten to a stiff froth, and have the batter of such consistency that it will pour from the spoon. Drop it in the boiling shortening by large kitchen spoonfuls and let it fry to a golden yellow. Lift out with a skimmer, and drain and place on a heated dish, and sprinkle freely with powdered white sugar, and serve hot. In arranging them in the dish make the fritters rise into a pretty pyramid and sprinkle with the sugar. Never pierce fritters with a fork, as it will cause the steam to evaporate and make the fritters heavy. A fritter that is well made should be light and puffy.

PLAIN FRITTER BATTER FOR MEATS, POULTRY, ETC.

Pâte de Beignets pour les Viandes, la Volaille, etc.

1 Cup Flour
1 Cup of Water
2 Eggs
½ Teaspoonful of Salt
1 Tablespoonful of Melted Butter

Beat the yolks of the eggs and the flour together, and add the melted butter and the salt. Then add the water and beat well, and finally add the whites of the eggs, beaten to a stiff froth. Some add a half teaspoonful of baking powder. This is according to taste. If the eggs are well beaten, there will be no need for the baking powder.

This batter is used in making pork, kidney or chicken fritters, or fritters of left-over meats, and also for all meats or fish which must be rolled in batter.

APPLE FRITTERS

Beignets de Pommes

3 Fresh Apples
½ Cup of Brandy or Rum (if desired)
Grated Peel of ½ Lemon
Powdered Sugar

Peel and core the apples, which will be all the nicer if they are a little tart. Take out the seeds and core. Cut them into slices, more or less thick or thin, according to taste. The thin slices are recommended. Soak them in Brandy or good Whiskey, or Rum, for the space of two hours, sprinkling with the grated outer skin of a lemon and sugar, according to judgment. Two tablespoonfuls of sugar should be sufficient for the rind of half a lemon. Make a batter à la Creole and have ready a deep saucepan of boiling shortening. Drain the apples. Dip the slices, one at a time, into the batter, lift out with a large kitchen spoon, drop into the boiling shortening, and fry to a golden brown. Then lift out with a skimmer, and set on brown paper in the mouth of the oven, and drain. Sift powdered white sugar over them, and serve hot, piling high in pyramidal shape, and sprinkling again with powdered white sugar. Serve as an entremet or as a dessert. The liquor may be omitted, and the apples simply cut into very thin slices; then proceed with the dropping in batter and frying.

APRICOT FRITTERS

Beignets d'Abricots

6 Fresh or a Half Can of Apricots
1 Glass of Madeira Wine
3 Tablespoonfuls of Sugar
Grated Lemon Peel

If the apricots are fresh, peel and stone them, and cut into halves. Then sprinkle them with the grated outer skin of a lemon and sugar, and pour over them sufficient Madeira wine to thoroughly saturate. Cover and set aside for two hours. Then drain off the liquor. Make a Fruit Fritter Batter à la Creole, and have ready a saucepan filled deep with boiling shortening. Dip the apricots, one by one, into the batter, and drop from the spoon into shortening, and let them fry to a golden brown. In serving, proceed in exactly the same manner as in the directions given for Apple Fritters. (See recipe.)

BANANA FRITTERS

Beignets de Bananes

3 Bananas
Fritter Batter à la Creole

Make a Fritter Batter à la Creole. Peel the bananas and then cut them in halves. Slice them nicely, according to length. Dip in the fritter batter, and proceed to cook and serve as in the recipe for Apple Fritters. The bananas may also be cut into round slices. In this case two or three slices at a time must be put in each fritter. The method of cutting by lengths is recommended.

BANANA FRITTERS WITH COGNAC OR RUM

Beignets de Bananes au Cognac ou au Rhum

3 Bananas
Fritter Batter à la Creole

If "Beignets de Bananes au Cognac," or "au Rhum," are desired, slice the banana and sprinkle with sugar and cover with sufficient Cognac or Rum to saturate well. Set them aside for half an hour, then drain, and proceed as in Apple Fritters.

BRIOCHE FRITTERS
Beignets de Brioches

3 Small Brioches
1 Tablespoonful of Essence of Vanilla, Lemons or Orange Flower Water
Creole Fritter Batter
Powdered White Sugar

Cut the Brioche into slices, more or less thin, and soak them in sweetened milk, to which you have added the essence of orange flower water, vanilla or lemon. Drop them into a light fritter batter, or simply drop them into boiling shortening, fry to a golden yellow, sprinkle with white sugar and serve.

CHERRY FRITTERS
Beignets de Cerises

1 Pint of Fine Cherries
1 Egg
1 Pint of Milk
1 Tablespoonful of Madeira or Malaga Wine
1 Tablespoonful of Sugar
The Grated Outer Skin of a Lemon

Prepare the cherries by taking out the stones. Make them into a thick marmalade, adding a tablespoonful of Madeira or Malaga wine. Soak nice slices of bread in milk and egg, seasoned well with a tablespoonful of sugar and the grated outer skin of a lemon. Take the slices, when well-soaked, and spread the marmalade well over them, making it adhere very thickly and closely into the meshes of the bread. Then fry in boiling shortening, sprinkle nicely with powdered sugar, and serve hot. Or mix the cherries in Creole Fritter Batter, drop by spoonfuls into the boiling shortening, fry to a golden brown, drain in the oven and sprinkle with powdered white sugar and serve hot.

KANDER
"The Settlement" Cook Book

Good Kuchen

4 cups flour
1 cup lukewarm milk
1 cent's worth yeast

Of these ingredients make a sponge.
Add:

3 whole eggs
½ cup sugar
½ cup melted butter
Lemon rind
Pinch of salt

Slightly heat all materials before mixing them together. Beat one-half hour. Let rise in a warm place, make into desired forms, let rise and bake.

Roll kuchen dough one-half inch thick on floured board, spread with melted butter, add chopped walnuts and brown sugar. Roll as jelly roll. Place in greased pan, spread melted butter over top, let rise again and bake well until brown.

BERLINER PFANN KUCHEN

Make a good kuchen dough, roll one-inch thick, cut into rounds with biscuit cutter. Place a piece of jelly or preserves in the center of one-half of them. Brush edges with white of egg and cover with the other half. Press edges neatly. Place on well floured board, let raise very light and fry in deep fat.

DE GOUY
The Gold Cook Book

Almond Fritters (Hot)

Beat 2 egg yolks and 2 tablespoons of sugar together until creamy, then stir in ¼ cup of blanched, peeled and ground almonds, ½ teaspoon of vanilla extract, a few grains of salt, 2 tablespoons of pastry flour (more or less) and beat well. Lastly stir in very gently 2 stiffly beaten egg whites. When ready to serve, drop by teaspoons into clear, clean, hot, deep fat and fry until of a pale brown color. Drain and serve on a folded napkin on a hot platter.

TRUAX

Ladies' Home Journal Cookbook

Cream Puffs

½ cup butter
1 cup water
1 cup flour
Pinch salt
4 eggs
Confectioners' sugar (optional)

Put the butter in a saucepan, add water and bring to a boil. Add the flour, all at once, and the salt. Beat until the mixture makes a ball that comes away from the sides of the pan. Remove from heat and add 1 unbeaten egg at a time, beating until smooth after each addition. Drop mixture from a spoon onto greased baking sheet. Bake in hot oven, 400°, for 20 minutes, until the puffs have really puffed; then reduce heat to moderate, 350°, and bake another 25 minutes. This prevents their falling. Let cool; then slit 1 side and fill with whipped cream or Custard Filling. Dust with sugar if you wish. Yield: 8 large puffs.

ESTES

Good Things to Eat, as Suggested by Rufus

MAPLE PARFAIT—Beat four eggs slightly in a double boiler, pour in one cup of hot maple sirup, stirring all the time. Cook until thick, cool, and add one pint of thick cream beaten stiff. Pour into a mold and pack in equal parts of ice and salt. Let stand three hours.

HEATTER

Maida Heatter's Book of Great Desserts

Raspberry-Strawberry Bavarian

9 PORTIONS

This obviously is not an authentic Bavarian. It is, however, the most popular dessert I make. Most of my students have said that this is so easy that they feel like they're cheating when they make it.

6 ounces strawberry-flavored gelatin
2 cups boiling water
1 cup sour cream
1 pint strawberry ice cream
1 tablespoon lemon juice
2 10-ounce packages frozen raspberries (whole berries packed in syrup)
1 10-ounce package frozen, sliced strawberries (halves, packed in syrup)

Place gelatin in large bowl. Add boiling water and stir to dissolve. Add sour cream and beat with wire whisk or egg beater until smooth. Cut the frozen ice cream into the gelatin mixture, cutting it into about ten pieces. Stir until melted and smooth. Add lemon juice and frozen fruit. Use a fork to break up the frozen fruit a bit, then use your bare hands until there are no pieces larger than a single piece of fruit. It feels cold, but it does the best job. (Adding the fruit while it is frozen helps to set the gelatin mixture, so that by the time the fruit is broken up and separated, the Bavarian is firm enough to keep the fruit from sinking.)

Quickly pour mixture into a pitcher and pour into nine large glasses, each with about a 9-ounce capacity. (See Note 1.) Leave a generous amount of headroom on each. Refrigerate. Do not freeze. This will be ready to serve in an hour or two, or it may stand overnight.

Top with the following:

WHIPPED CREAM

- 2 cups heavy cream
- 1½ teaspoons vanilla extract
- ½ cup confectioners sugar

In a chilled bowl with chilled beaters, whip above ingredients until cream holds a shape. Place a large spoonful on each dessert. Decorate, if and as you wish. I use chopped green pistachio nuts, glacéed cherries, and chocolate leaves or slabs.

NOTES: 1. I prepare this in heavy, stemmed beer glasses. This must be prepared for individual servings—it is too delicate to serve from one large bowl.

2. About ½ teaspoon each of strawberry and raspberry flavorings, added with the lemon juice, emphasizes the flavor and is a welcome addition. I use Flavor Mill brand flavorings, available at specialty stores. They may be ordered by mail.

3. If both frozen raspberries or frozen strawberries are not available, use 3 packages of whichever one you can get.

HIRTZLER
The Hotel St. Francis Cook Book

PEACH MELBA. Peel some large fresh peaches, and cook them whole in a light syrup; or use whole preserved peaches. From vanilla ice cream, that is frozen very hard, cut some round pieces about three inches in diameter and an inch thick. Place the ice cream on plates, place a peach on the center of each, and pour Melba sauce over them.

HIRTZLER
The Hotel St. Francis Cook Book

STRAWBERRIES ROMANOFF. Put some nice ripe strawberries into a bowl, pour some Curaçao over them, and serve with well-sweetened whipped cream, flavored with vanilla, on top. Serve very cold.

TOKLAS
The Alice B. Toklas Cook Book

Scheherezade's Melon

This dessert and a complicated Bavarian cream which had a similar flavour from its including the same fruits and precisely the same liqueurs and cordials were early favourites. The recipe for Scheherezade's Melon is preserved in my mother's handwritten cook-book.

Cut a piece from the stem end of the melon. Scoop out in as large pieces as convenient as much of the pulp as is possible without piercing the melon. Empty all the juice, dice the pulp in equal quantities (this will depend upon the size of the melon) as well as pineapple and peaches. Add bananas in thin slices, and whole strawberries and raspberries. Sugar to taste. When the sugar mixed with the fruit has dissolved put the fruit and their juice in the melon. Cover with four parts very dry champagne and one part each of Kirsch, Maraschino, Crème de Menthe and Roselio.* Put in refrigerator overnight.

***NOTE:** Roselio is a Catalan liqueur or cordial which is also made round about Perpignan. It has not been imported into England since the war: Grenadine might replace it.

ESTES
Good Things to Eat, as Suggested by Rufus

CRANBERRY SHERBET–This is often used at a Thanksgiving course dinner to serve after the roast. To make it boil a quart of cranberries with two cupfuls of water until soft, add two cupfuls of sugar, stir until dissolved, let cool, add the juice of one or two lemons and freeze. This may be sweeter if desired. Serve in sherbet glasses.

FISHER
The Art of Eating

Borderland

Almost every person has something secret he likes to eat. He is downright furtive about it usually, or mentions it only in a kind of conscious self-amusement, as one who admits too quickly, "It is rather strange, yes—and I'll laugh with you."

Do you remember how Claudine used to crouch by the fire, turning a hatpin just fast enough to keep the toasting nubbin of chocolate from dripping off? Sometimes she did it on a hairpin over a candle. But candles have a fat taste that would taint the burnt chocolate, so clean and blunt and hot. It would be like drinking a Martini from silver.

Hard bitter chocolate is best, in a lump not bigger than a big raisin. It matters very little about the shape, for if you're nimble enough you'll keep it rolling hot on the pin, as shapely as an opium bead.

When it is round and bubbling and giving out a dark blue smell, it is done. Then, without some blowing all about, you'll burn your tongue. But it is delicious.

However, it is not my secret delight. Mine seems to me less decadent than Claudine's, somehow. Perhaps I am mistaken. I remember that Al looked at me very strangely when he first saw the little sections lying on the radiator.

That February in Strasbourg was too cold for us. Out on the Boulevard de l'Orangerie, in a cramped dirty apartment across from the sad zoo half full of animals and birds frozen too stiff even to make smells, we grew quite morbid.

Finally we counted all our money, decided we could not possibly afford to move, and next day went bag and baggage to the most expensive pension *in the city.*

It was wonderful—big room, windows, clean white billows of curtain, central heating. We basked like lizards. Finally Al went back to work, but I could not bear to walk into the bitter blowing streets from our warm room.

It was then that I discovered how to eat little dried sections of tangerine. My pleasure in them is subtle and voluptuous and quite inexplicable. I can only write how they are prepared.

In the morning, in the soft sultry chamber, sit in the window peeling tangerines, three or four. Peel them gently; do not bruise them, as you watch soldiers pour past and past the corner and over the canal towards the watched Rhine. Separate each plump little pregnant crescent. If you find the Kiss, the secret section, save it for Al.

Listen to the chambermaid thumping up the pillows, and murmur encouragement to her thick Alsatian tales of l'intérieure. *That is Paris, the interior, Paris or anywhere west of Strasbourg or maybe the Vosges. While she mutters of seduction and French bicyclists who ride more than wheels, tear delicately from the soft pile of sections each velvet string. You know those white pulpy strings that hold tangerines into their skins? Tear them off. Be careful.*

Take yesterday's paper (when we were in Strasbourg L'Ami du Peuple *was best, because when it got hot the ink stayed on it) and spread it on top of the radiator. The maid has gone, of course—it might be hard to ignore her belligerent Alsatian glare of astonishment.*

After you have put the pieces of tangerine on the paper on the hot radiator, it is best to forget about them. Al comes home, you go to a long noon dinner in the brown dining-room, afterwards maybe you have a little nip of quetsch *from the bottle on the* armoire. *Finally he goes. Of course you are sorry, but—*

On the radiator the sections of tangerine have grown even plumper, hot and full. You carry them to the window, pull it open, and leave them for a few minutes on the packed snow of the sill. They are ready.

All afternoon you can sit, then, looking down on the corner. Afternoon papers are delivered to the kiosk. Children come home from school just as three lovely whores mince smartly into the pension's *chic tearoom. A basketful of Dutch tulips stations itself by the tram-stop, ready to tempt tired clerks at six o'clock. Finally the soldiers stump back from the Rhine. It is dark.*

The sections of tangerine are gone, and I cannot tell you why they are so magical. Perhaps it is that little shell, thin as one layer of enamel on a Chinese bowl, that crackles so tinily, so ultimately under your teeth. Or the rush of cold pulp just after it. Or the perfume. I cannot tell.

There must be some one, though, who knows what I mean. Probably everyone does, because of his own secret eatings.

SAX

Classic Home Desserts

Sour Cherry Clafouti

A clafouti (the older spelling is clafoutis) is a French country dessert, with fruit baked in a batter that ends up being something between a custard and a pancake, puffed, golden and crisp. This is a version of the rustic original, an amalgam of several French recipes, including one from my friend, cookbook author Martha Rose Shulman.

SERVES 6 TO 8

- 2½ cups (about 1 pound) sour red cherries
- 1¼ cups milk
- ¼ cup sugar, plus more for sprinkling
- 3 large eggs
- 1 tablespoon pure vanilla extract or 2 teaspoons vanilla and 1 tablespoon cognac or kirsch
- Pinch salt
- ½ cup sifted all-purpose flour
- Sugar, for sprinkling

1. Preheat the oven to 350 degrees F, with a rack in the center. Butter the bottom and sides of an 8- or 9-inch round or oval gratin dish or pie pan.

2. Rinse, stem and pit the cherries, placing them in a colander set over a bowl to catch the juices.

3. In a blender or food processor, combine the milk, sugar, eggs, vanilla (or vanilla and cognac or kirsch), salt, flour and the reserved cherry juices. Process just until blended and smooth, no longer. (If you aren't using a machine, whisk together al the batter ingredients except the flour and cherry juices in a bowl. Whisk in the cherry juices, and then the flour; do not overmix.)

4. Place the cherries in the buttered dish. Pour the batter over the cherries (or strain it over, if it's slightly lumpy). Sprinkle the top with sugar.

5. Bake until the edges are dark golden and a toothpick inserted in the center emerges clean, usually 45 to 50 minutes. The clafouti will fall when it comes out of the oven; cool on a wire rack. Serve warm.

BROWN

Helen Brown's West Coast Cook Book

Fried Cream

Gourmets who visit San Francisco enthuse about this dessert, which is to be found at a few of the best hotels and restaurants. It's not often served at home, apparently because most cooks don't dare risk it, but it's really very simple to make. It turns up in a San Diego cook book, under the name of "Bonfire Entré." It was called that because the fried cream was cut in sticklike pieces and stacked up on individual plates like miniature and roofless log cabins. A couple of lumps of sugar, brandy-soaked, went into the center of each pile of "logs," and matches graced the side of each plate. The lights were lowered, and everyone lit up. Whoopee!

- 1 pint heavy cream
- 2 teaspoons Jamaica rum
- ⅓ teaspoon salt
- ¼ cup sugar
- ½-inch stick of cinnamon
- 5 tablespoons cornstarch
- 3 tablespoons milk
- 3 egg yolks
- Grated almonds
- Beaten egg
- Cracker crumbs

Scald a pint of heavy cream and add to it 2 teaspoons of Jamaica rum, ⅛ teaspoon of salt, ¼ cup of sugar, a ½-inch stick of cinnamon, and 5 tablespoons of cornstarch moistened in 3 tablespoons of milk. Cook long enough to remove the starch taste, then beat in 3 egg yolks and cook over hot water, whisking continuously, until thick. Remove cinnamon and pour mixture, about ¾ of an inch deep, into a flat dish (an oblong Pyrex dish is perfect) to become cold. Turn out on a board, cut into squares or oblongs, and roll in very finely grated almonds. Now dip in beaten egg, and then in finely crushed salted crackers, Chill again, then fry in deep fat at 390° just long enough to brown the nuts. Pour on heated rum, set afire, and serve flaming.

SERVES 8

ROJAS-LOMBARDI
The Art of South American Cooking

Manjar Blanco
Quick Milk Pudding

MAKES 4 CUPS

5 14-ounce cans sweetened condensed milk (8½ cups)
1 4-inch cinnamon stick

1. Combine the milk and cinnamon stick in an enameled saucepan. Bring to a boil, lower the heat to very low, and let simmer, stirring and scraping the bottom of the pan every 10 to 15 minutes to prevent the pudding from sticking to the pan, for 2½ hours, or until the mixture has a puddinglike consistency and the spoon leaves a track on the bottom of the pan. If the milk sticks or starts to burn while simmering, stop stirring and strain it into a clean enameled saucepan. Add the cinnamon stick and continue simmering.

2. Remove from the heat and beat the pudding for a few minutes with a spoon until light in color. Let cool.

KENNEDY
The Cuisines of Mexico

Flan a la Antigua
Old-fashioned flan

6 SERVINGS

A very solid version of a caramel custard, this cuts better if made the day before.

HAVE READY
A flan mold coated with caramel
A saucepan
1 quart milk
½ cup granulated sugar
A vanilla bean or a stick of cinnamon (about 2 inches)
A pinch of salt
4 whole eggs
6 egg yolks
A fine cheesecloth or strainer
A water bath

Preheat oven to 350°.

Heat the milk, add the sugar, vanilla bean or cinnamon, and salt and let it simmer briskly for about 15 minutes. The milk should be reduced by about ½ cup. Set it aside to cool.

Beat the eggs and egg yolks together well. Add them to the cooled milk and stir well.

Pour the mixture through the strainer into the coated mold. (Rinse the vanilla bean, let it dry, and store it for use again.)

Cover the mold and set it in a water bath on the lowest shelf in the oven. Cook the flan for 2 hours and test to see if it is done. When it is done, set it aside to cool.

MACAUSLAND
The Gourmet Cookbook

Petits Pots de Crème à la Vanille
Pot Creams

Scald 2 cups cream with a 1-inch piece of vanilla bean and ½ cup sugar and cool it slightly. Beat 6 egg yolks until they are light and lemon-colored and add the milk, stirring constantly. Strain the mixture through a fine sieve and pour into small earthenware pots or custard cups. Set the pots in a pan of water, cover the pan, and bake them in a moderately slow oven for about 15 minutes, or until a knife inserted in the center comes out clean. Serve chilled.

CHOCOLATE POT CREAMS

Follow the directions for *petits pots de crème à la vanille*, substituting 4 ounces sweet chocolate, melted, for half the sugar.

COFFEE POT CREAMS

Follow the directions for *petits pots de crème à la vanille*, substituting 1 tablespoon coffee essence for the vanilla.

SAX

Classic Home Desserts

Panna Cotta and Poached Pears in Merlot Syrup

Panna cotta—the name literally means "cooked cream"—is a smooth, alabaster white, rich molded custard. After years of being unknown outside of its native Piedmont in northern Italy, panna cotta is turning up on restaurant menus all over this country. In its simplest form, it is sweetened heavy cream, flavored with lemon and vanilla and sometimes rum, set with gelatin (not baked) and unmolded in individual servings.

I first enjoyed this beautifully composed panna cotta as the conclusion to an unforgettable tall feast at the guest house of Livio Felluga, whose wines are among the best in Friuli, the region east of Venice. The custard's gleaming surface was counterpointed by a warm poached pear half, sliced but still joined at the stem, both fruit and panna cotta perfumed by a heady syrup made with Merlot wine. This recipe is from Leda and Claudio Della Rovere, the brother and sister who own Ristorante Romea in nearby Manzano.

I've cut back on the fat of this custard a little; the proportions below are a happy compromise, clean but just rich enough. You can also serve panna cotta without the pears and syrup; just scatter a few berries alongside.

SERVES 6

PANNA COTTA

2⅓ cups milk
⅔ cup heavy cream
1 vanilla bean, split lengthwise, or 1 teaspoon pure vanilla extract
Strips of zest of 1 lemon
1½ envelopes (3¾ teaspoons) unflavored gelatin
⅓ cup sugar

PEARS AND MERLOT SYRUP

2¼ cups Italian or American Merlot wine
⅓ cup plus 1 tablespoon sugar
3 firm-ripe pears, such as Bosc, Bartlett or Anjou, peeled with stems left on, halved and cored

1. **PANNA COTTA:** In a saucepan, combine 2 cups of the milk, the cream, vanilla bean and lemon zest. (If using vanilla extract, do not add it now.) Set the pan over medium-high heat, cover and bring just to a boil. Remove from the heat and let steep, covered, for about 1 hour.

2. Sprinkle the gelatin over the remaining ⅓ cup milk. Return the milk and cream mixture to a simmer. Remove from the heat and whisk in the dissolved gelatin and sugar until smooth. Strain the mixture into a pitcher; if using vanilla extract, add it now. Scrape the vanilla seeds out of the bean and stir them into the cream. Pour into six ½-cup ramekins or other small molds. Chill until set, at least 2 hours.

3. **PEARS AND MERLOT SYRUP:** Bring the wine and sugar to a simmer in a wide nonreactive sauté pan; stir to dissolve the sugar. Gently slip the pear halves into the syrup. Cover and poach them gently over low heat until tender, 10 to 20 minutes, depending on the pears. Remove the pears with a slotted spoon; arrange in a layer on a plate. Cover and set aside.

4. Boil the poaching liquid over high heat until lightly syrupy, about 10 minutes or slightly longer. Remove from the heat and set aside.

5. To serve, rewarm the pears in the Merlot syrup. Run the tip of a knife around each ramekin of cream; unmold onto a serving plate. Gently place a warm pear next to each cold cream. Make 4 or 5 lengthwise cuts in each pear half, leaving the pear joined at the stem end. Spoon some of the warm syrup over and around the pear and serve immediately.

TOKLAS

The Alice B. Toklas Cook Book

Haschich Fudge

(which anyone could whip up on a rainy day)

This is the food of Paradise—of Baudelaire's Artificial Paradises: it might provide an entertaining refreshment for a Ladies' Bridge Club or a chapter meeting of the DAR. In Morocco it is thought to be good for warding off the common cold in damp winter weather and is, indeed, more effective if taken with large quantities of hot mint tea. Euphoria and brilliant storms of laughter; ecstatic reveries and extensions of one's personality on several simultaneous planes are to be complacently expected. Almost anything Saint Theresa did, you can do better if you can bear to be ravished by 'un évanouissement réveillé.'

Take 1 teaspoon black peppercorns, 1 whole nutmeg, 4 average sticks of cinnamon, 1 teaspoon coriander. These should all be pulverised in a mortar. About a handful each of stoned dates, dried figs, shelled almonds and peanuts: chop these and mix them together. A bunch of *canibus sativa* can be pulverised. This along with the spices should be dusted over the mixed fruit and nuts, kneaded together. About a cup of sugar dissolved in a big pat of butter. Rolled into a cake and cut into pieces or made into balls about the size of a walnut, it should be eaten with care. Two pieces are quite sufficient.

Obtaining the *canibus* may present certain difficulties, but the variety known as *canibus sativa* grows as a common weed, often unrecognised, everywhere in Europe, Asia and parts of Africa; besides being cultivated as a crop for the manufacture of rope. In the Americas, while often discouraged, its cousin, called *canibus indica*, has been observed even in city window boxes. It should be picked and dried as soon as it has gone to seed and while the plant is still green.

EDITOR'S NOTE: This recipe appeared in the 1984 edition.

MEDRICH
Cocolat

Classic Chocolate Truffles

MAKES ABOUT 30 BITE-SIZE TRUFFLES

I began Cocolat *with these simple, classic, cocoa-dusted dark chocolate truffles. Although we've developed over a hundred variations since then, these are still my favorite! They make a rare and exquisite gift.*

- 8 ounces semisweet or bittersweet chocolate, cut into bits
- 3 ounces sweet butter, cut into pieces
- 1 egg yolk
- ½ cup unsweetened cocoa powder

SPECIAL EQUIPMENT

- 5 × 9-inch loaf pan, or any shallow pan with a similar dimension, bottom and sides lined with parchment or waxed paper or foil
- Fluted paper candy cups* (optional)

*Available from kitchenware and specialty stores, or by mail order.

1. Melt chocolate with butter and ¼ cup water in a bowl set in a barely simmering water bath. Stir from time to time until mixture is melted and smooth. Or, microwave on medium (50%), stirring once or twice, for about 2 minutes. Off heat, whisk in the egg yolk just until incorporated. Do not mix or beat more than necessary. Strain truffle mixture into the lined pan and chill, without stirring, until firm, about 1 hour.

2. Remove pan from refrigerator. Unmold and cut into ¾-inch squares. (If chocolate is too firm to cut without breaking, wait 15–20 minutes to soften slightly.)

3. Put cocoa in a shallow dish. Roll truffle squares in cocoa, rounding them between the palms of your hands. Dust your hands with cocoa as necessary to keep truffles from sticking. (If the truffles are too hard to shape, wait until they soften slightly. If they are too soft, refrigerate until firmer.) Truffles look more authentic if they are a little irregular, so don't try for perfectly smooth round balls. Shake truffles gently in a dry strainer, if necessary, to remove excess cocoa.

4. Truffles may be made and stored in an airtight container in the refrigerator for 10 days, or frozen for 3 months. Remove from refrigerator about 30 minutes before serving to soften slightly. Serve heaped in a candy dish, or place each truffle in an individual fluted paper candy cup.

HEATTER
Maida Heatter's Book of Great Desserts

Chocolate Mousse Heatter

6 PORTIONS

It has been said that chocolate is the sexiest of all flavors. If so, this is the sexiest of all desserts.

- ½ pound bittersweet chocolate (I use Tobler Tradition or Lindt Excellence)
- 1 tablespoon instant coffee
- ⅓ cup boiling water
- 5 eggs, separated
- Pinch of salt

Break up the chocolate into a small, heavy saucepan. Dissolve the coffee in the boiling water and pour it over the chocolate. Place over low heat and stir occasionally with a small wire whisk until mixture is smooth. Remove from heat and set aside to cool for about 5 minutes.

In the small bowl of an electric mixer at high speed, beat the egg yolks for 3 to 4 minutes until pale lemon-colored. Reduce the speed and gradually add the slightly warm chocolate mixture, scraping the bowl with a rubber spatula and beating only until smooth. Remove from mixer.

Add the salt to the whites and beat until they hold a definite shape but are not dry. (See Note 1.) Without being too thorough, gently fold about one-quarter of the beaten whites into the chocolate mixture, then fold in a second quarter, and finally fold the chocolate into the remaining whites, folding only until no whites show.

Gently transfer the mousse to a wide pitcher and pour it into six large dessert or wine glasses, each with about a 9-ounce capacity. Do not fill the glasses too full; leave generous headroom on each. (This mousse must be prepared in individual portions. It just won't work if it is all done in one large container.)

Cover with plastic wrap or aluminum foil and refrigerate 3 to 6 hours. (The mousse may stand longer—12 to 24 hours, if you wish. The texture will become more spongy and less creamy. Delicious both ways.)

Prepare the following:

MOCHA CREAM

- 1 cup heavy cream
- ¼ cup confectioners sugar
- 1 tablespoon instant coffee

In a chilled bowl with chilled beaters, beat the heavy cream only until it begins to thicken. Add sugar and coffee and beat until thickened to the consistency of a heavy custard sauce, not stiff. Pour or spoon onto desserts to completely cover the tops.

OPTIONAL: Top with a light sprinkling of coarsely grated chocolate.

NOTES: 1. I beat the whites with the salt in the large bowl of the mixer, beating at high speed only until the whites thicken or hold a very soft shape. Then I finish the beating with a large wire whisk so that there is less chance of overbeating.

2. This recipe may easily be doubled, if you wish.

3. Purely as a matter of interest, the chocolate mousse served at most of the fine hotels and restaurants is generally made with the addition of whipped cream folded into the chocolate mixture.

MEDRICH
Cocolat

Chocolate Velvet Mousse

MAKES ABOUT 4½ CUPS

Yet another favorite mousse, with a texture all its own. This one, without butter, is lightened with egg whites and made rich with cream. It is stiff enough to slice and stars in Chocolate Ruffle Torte, Chocolate Banana Charlotte, etc.

- 12 ounces semisweet or bittersweet chocolate, cut into bits
- 2 teaspoons powdered instant coffee (not freeze-dried), dissolved in ¼ cup water
- ¼ cup Curaçao or rum
- 2 egg yolks
- 4 egg whites, at room temperature
- ¼ teaspoon cream of tartar
- 2 tablespoons sugar
- ½ cup heavy cream

1. Melt chocolate, dissolved coffee, and Curaçao in a medium bowl set in a barely simmering pan of water. Stir frequently to hasten melting. Or, melt in a microwave on medium (50%) for about 2 minutes and 15 seconds. Stir until smooth. When mixture is warm and smooth, whisk in egg yolks and combine well. Remove from heat and set aside.

2. In a clean, dry mixing bowl, beat egg whites and cream of tartar on medium speed until soft peaks form. Gradually sprinkle in 2 tablespoons sugar, beating on high speed until stiff but not dry. Fold one-fourth of the egg whites into chocolate mixture to lighten it. Scrape all of the remaining whites on top of mousse and set aside while you beat the cream. Beat cream until it holds its shape softly (do not beat until stiff).

3. Scrape whipped cream over egg whites and chocolate. Fold together just until incorporated. Turn the mousse immediately into lined mold.

BASTIANICH
La Cucina di Lidia

Crema di Caffè

Espresso Mousse

SERVES 8

Italians in general are passionate about coffee in almost any form and make particularly good use of it in all sorts of desserts. I wish I could remember where I picked up this recipe, but I can't. I think you'll like the flavor of the dish as much as I do.

- 1 tablespoon unflavored gelatin
- ½ cup cold water
- 1 cup sugar
- 3 drops fresh lemon juice
- 1 cup milk
- 1¾ cups heavy cream
- 3 eggs, separated
- ½ cup strong espresso coffee (see Note)
- ¼ teaspoon vanilla extract
- Coffee beans or shaved chocolate for garnish

Sprinkle the gelatin over ¼ cup of the cold water and allow it to soften.

In a medium-size heavy saucepan, combine the sugar with ¼ cup of water and the lemon juice. Bring to a boil and cook until the sugar caramelizes to a rich dark brown, about 7 minutes. (Do not stir as it cooks.)

Meanwhile, in a second pan, scald the milk. When the caramel is ready, remove it from the heat and immediately add ¾ cup of the heavy cream. (Stand back because it may splatter.) Whisk the cream and caramel together, blending thoroughly, then whisk in the scalded milk.

In a bowl, beat the egg yolks. Add some of the caramel mixture and whisk well, then pour the contents of the bowl into the saucepan and whisk to blend. Return to moderately low heat and cook, stirring with a wooden spoon, until the custard coats the back of a spoon, about 9 minutes.

Off the heat, blend in the softened gelatin and stir well until thoroughly dissolved. Add the coffee and vanilla extract and combine well. Transfer the mixture to a bowl and refrigerate 30 minutes, stirring occasionally, until it begins to thicken.

Meanwhile, whip the remaining 1 cup heavy cream until stiff and keep chilled. When the mousse mixture has thickened, beat the egg whites until stiff. Fold them into the espresso custard, then fold in the whipped cream, lightly but thoroughly.

Pour into individual serving dishes or a large serving bowl and chill 3–4 hours. To serve, allow the mousse to rest about 10 minutes at room temperature to develop flavor, and decorate with coffee beans or shaved chocolate.

NOTE: 2 tablespoons instant espresso dissolved in ½ cup water can be substituted.

KAFKA
Microwave Gourmet

Steamed Chocolate Pudding

Even if you have never tried a steamed pudding, you must try this rich and moist one, a dessert to dream about. Serves 8

- ¼ pound plus 2 tablespoons unsalted butter
- 8 ounces semisweet chocolate
- ½ cup (packed) light brown sugar
- 1 teaspoon vanilla extract
- ½ cup heavy cream
- ⅓ cup cake flour, sifted
- ½ teaspoon baking powder
- 3 eggs
- Heavy cream, for serving (optional)

1. Butter a 9" × 4" ceramic bowl or a 4-cup pudding basin with 2 tablespoons of the butter.

2. Grate chocolate in a food processor. Add remaining ¼ pound butter, cut into 1-tablespoon pieces, and sugar. Process until thoroughly combined.

3. Add remaining ingredients except cream and process to a smooth mixture.

4. Pour into prepared bowl. Cover tightly with microwave plastic wrap. Cook at 100% for 5 minutes, until set.

5. Remove from oven. Pierce plastic with the tip of a sharp knife and cover top of bowl with a heavy plate; this will keep the pudding hot. Let stand for 10 minutes.

6. Unmold pudding onto a serving plate. Serve warm or cold, with whipped cream if desired.

TO MAKE INDIVIDUAL PUDDINGS: Cook in 2 batches of four ½-cup ramekins each for 1 minute 30 seconds.

TO MAKE A SINGLE, SMALLER PUDDING: Halve all ingredients and halve cooking time; cook in a smaller bowl (7" × 4") or 3-cup pudding basin. From this quantity you can, of course, prepare 1 batch of individual puddings.

MADISON

The Greens Cook Book

Semolina Pudding with Blood Orange Syrup

A soft sweet pudding of Greek origin, this can be served warm or cooled with the syrup. The blood oranges give it a rose-pink hue, but if they are not available, use regular oranges.

THE PUDDING

1 vanilla bean or 2 teaspoons vanilla extract
4 cups milk
1 cup sugar
¾ cup semolina, or Cream of Wheat
½ cup butter
2 teaspoons grated orange peel
5 eggs

Preheat the oven to 350°F and generously butter a 9-by-12-inch baking dish.

Split the vanilla bean in half lengthwise and scrape the seeds into the milk. Add the pods and the sugar and heat slowly, stirring to dissolve the sugar. When the milk is hot but not boiling, gradually pour in the semolina, stirring continuously. Cook the cereal, continuing to stir, until it has thickened, about 10 minutes. Remove it from the heat, take out the vanilla pods, and stir in the butter and the orange peel.

Separate the eggs. Beat the yolks with a little of the cereal to gradually warm them; then stir them into the pot of cooked semolina. Beat the egg whites in a large bowl until they form firm peaks; then add them to the semolina and gently fold everything together with a wide rubber spatula. Pour the batter into the baking dish and place it in the center of the oven. Bake for 1 hour and 10 minutes, until the center is firm and the top is browned. (If it seems that the top is browning too much, cover it loosely with foil.) Remove the pudding from the oven and let it cool.

BLOOD ORANGE SYRUP

Several pieces orange peel
1 cup blood orange juice, about 2 to 3 oranges
1 cup sugar
1 tablespoon Grand Marnier (optional)
3 cloves
1-inch piece of cinnamon stick

Remove the orange peel with a vegetable peeler and cut it into fine strips. Combine with the remaining ingredients and bring to a boil. Simmer slowly for 10 minutes.

Cut the pudding into diamond-shaped pieces, and serve it with some syrup and a few of the candied peels spooned over the top.

SERVES TEN

FARMER

The Boston Cooking-School Cook Book

Snow Pudding I

¼ box gelatine or
1¼ tablespoons granulated gelatine
¼ cup cold water
1 cup boiling water
1 cup sugar
¼ cup lemon juice
Whites 3 eggs

Soak gelatine in cold water, dissolve in boiling water, add sugar and lemon juice, strain, and set aside in cool place; occasionally stir mixture, and when quite thick, beat with wire spoon or whisk until frothy; add whites of eggs beaten stiff, and continue beating until stiff enough to hold its shape. Mould, or pile by spoonfuls on glass dish; serve cold with Boiled Custard. A very attractive dish may be prepared by coloring half the mixture with fruit red.

Snow Pudding II

Beat whites of four eggs until stiff, add one-half tablespoon granulated gelatine dissolved in three tablespoons boiling water, heat until thoroughly mixed, add one-fourth cup powdered sugar, and flavor with one-half teaspoon lemon extract. Pile lightly on dish, serve with Boiled Custard.

RORER
Mrs. Rorer's New Cook Book

Banana Pudding

Slice six bananas and stew them with very little water. When done, beat them to a pulp; add four tablespoonfuls of sugar, and turn them into a baking dish. Put a tablespoonful of butter and one of flour in a saucepan, mix and add a half pint of cocoanut milk; stir until boiling. Take from the fire, and when cold add the yolks of three eggs. Beat the whites to a froth, adding the custard gradually to them, beating all the while; add four tablespoonfuls of powdered sugar, a quarter of a grated nutmeg; pour this over the bananas and bake in a moderate oven a half hour.

PADDLEFORD
How America Eats

Ellin North's Plum Pudding

1 pound seeded raisins
1 pound currants
½ pound citron, finely chopped
1 pound white suet
4 to 5 apples
2 cups soft breadcrumbs (from day-old bread)
1 tablespoon salt
1½ tablespoons nutmeg
1½ tablespoons ginger
1 tablespoon flour
8 eggs, well beaten
2 cups milk
2 cups sugar
1 wine glass brandy

Combine raisins, currants and citron; dredge with flour. Chop suet and apples into small pieces. Mix bread crumbs, salt, spices and the tablespoon of flour. Combine eggs, milk and sugar. Add breadcrumb mixture, suet and apples. Add brandy. Pour into a well-greased 3-quart mold. Cover tightly. Steam for 4 hours. Yield: 1 3-quart pudding.

SAUCE:
Cream ¾ cup sugar and ¼ pound butter or margarine thoroughly. Add 2 eggs, well beaten. Heat only until smooth. Add 1 cup sherry wine. Yield: about 2 cups sauce.

PECK
The Art of Fine Baking

Swiss Meringue

For making such delightful pastries as vacherin, meringue layers and shells.

5 egg whites, at room temperature
¼ teaspoon cream of tartar
¼ teaspoon salt
1 teaspoon vanilla
1¼ cups sugar

Grease and flour 2 baking sheets, Combine egg whites, cream of tartar, salt and vanilla in a large bowl. Beat (at medium speed if a mixer is used) until egg whites hold soft peaks. Gradually add ¾ cup sugar, a tablespoon at a time, beating continuously. Continue beating until meringue is very stiff and dull. It has been beaten enough when a bit, rubbed between thumb and finger, is no longer grainy. The meringue should be stiff enough to hold its shape when formed with a pastry tube. Gently fold in remaining sugar.

Meringues should actually be dried rather than baked. Herein lies the secret of making meringues which are tender, delicate, and light-colored, rather than overly crisp, tough, and too dark to be either attractive or delicious. The best meringues are baked by the following method:

Set oven temperature at 200 degrees before beginning to beat the egg whites. After shaping the meringue mixture on baking sheets, place in the preheated oven for 15 minutes. Then turn off the oven heat. Allow the meringues to remain in the oven with the heat turned off for at least 4 to 5 hours—the longer the better. If your oven has a pilot light, the meringues will be ready a little sooner. The meringues should be totally dry before removing them from the oven. If you can, leave them in the oven overnight.

For many of us, however, time is a factor. If you can't take the time to bake meringues this slow, slow way, accept second best and simply bake them slowly, setting the oven temperature for 200 degrees or less if possible. At 200 degrees, meringue layers will need to bake for about 40 minutes; small meringues may take a little less time.

Whatever method you use, it is important to prevent the meringues from coloring, since even a light tan color changes their texture and taste as well as their appearance. When thoroughly dry, meringues can be kept covered in a dry airy place (not in a tightly covered box) for several weeks.

ALTERNATE MIXING METHOD BY ELECTRIC BEATER FOR SWISS MERINGUE

Combine egg whites, cream of tartar, salt, ½ cup sugar and vanilla in large bowl. Beat at high speed until egg whites hold peaks. Add ½ cup sugar, all at once. Beat at high speed until mixture is very stiff and there are no grains of undissolved sugar. Fold in remaining sugar.

TO SHAPE SWISS MERINGUE

Grease and flour a large baking sheet. Press the rim of a 9-inch layer cake pan or a 2-inch cooky cutter lightly into the flour on baking sheet to make guides. If Baking Pan Liner Paper is used, the guiding circles will have to be traced with a pencil. Spread mixture within circles.

PÉPIN
La Technique

Oeufs à la Neige
Floating Islands

1. To make tender floating islands, the egg whites should be poached in water that doesn't exceed a temperature of 170 degrees. Beat 6 egg whites with a dash of salt in the electric mixer or by hand. When the egg whites are firm, add ¾ cup sugar and continue beating for 30 seconds. Stop the beating and fold in another ¼ cup sugar.

2. Using an ice-cream scoop, dish the whites out. Round the top of the scoop with your finger to get an "egg" as round as possible.

3. Drop the eggs into the hot (170 degrees) water.

4. Poach for 1½ to 2 minutes on one side, then turn the eggs on the other side.

5. Poach for another 1½ to 2 minutes; then lift the eggs onto a paper-lined tray.

6. Prepare a crème anglaise, let it cool and place in the bottom of an oval or round dish. Arrange the cold eggs on top of the cream.

7. Mix ¼ cup sugar with ¼ cup corn syrup. Cook until it turns into caramel. Let cool for a few minutes so the mixture thickens. Using a fork, drip the hot caramel over the eggs. The threads should be scattered all over the eggs. Do not refrigerate but keep in a cool place until serving time. Serve cool.

This recipe serves 8 to 10.

ESTES
Good Things to Eat, as Suggested by Rufus

SIMPLE WAY OF SUGARING FLOWERS—A simple way of sugaring flowers where they are to be used at once consists of making the customary sirup and cooking to the crack degree. Rub the inside of cups with salad oil, put into each cup four tablespoons of the flowers and sugar, let stand until cold, turn out, and serve piled one on top of the other.

PADDLEFORD
How America Eats

Iowa Ice Cream

1¼ cups sugar
1 pint heavy cream
6 eggs, separated
2 quarts milk
1½ tablespoons vanilla extract
⅛ teaspoon salt
Milk

Mix sugar with cream, stirring to dissolve thoroughly and turn into 1-gallon can of freezer. Beat egg yolks until thick and mix with milk; add vanilla and salt. Combine the two mixtures. Whip egg whites until stiff but not dry. Blend into mixture, then add enough milk to fill within 1 inch of the top. Freeze, using 8 parts ice to 1 part salt. Yield: 1 gallon.

BIBLIOGRAPHY

Books Considered by the Advisory Committee

Adam, H. Pearl. *Kitchen Ranging: A Book of Dish-cover-y.* New York: Jonathan Cape & Harrison Smith, 1929.

Aidells, Bruce. *Hot Links and Country Flavors: Sausages in American Regional Cooking.* New York: Alfred A. Knopf, 1990.

Aidells, Bruce. *Real Beer and Good Eats: The Rebirth of America's Beer and Food Traditions.* New York: Alfred A. Knopf, 1992.

Alford, Jeffrey, and Naomi Duguid. *Flatbreads & Flavors: A Baker's Atlas.* New York: William Morrow, 1995.

Alford, Jeffrey, and Naomi Duguid. *Hot Sour Salty Sweet: A Culinary Journey through Southeast Asia.* New York: Artisan, 2000.

Alford, Jeffrey, and Naomi Duguid. *Seductions of Rice.* New York: Artisan, 1998.

Allen, Ida Cogswell Bailey. *Mrs. Allen's Cook Book.* Boston: Small, Maynard & Company, 1917.

Allen, Ida Cogswell Bailey. *Food for Two.* Garden City, NY: Garden City Publishing Co., 1947.

Anderson, Jean. *The Doubleday Cookbook: Complete Contemporary Cooking.* Garden City, NY: Doubleday, 1975.

Anderson, Jean. *The Family Circle Cookbook.* New York: The Family Circle, Inc., 1974.

Andoh, Elizabeth. *An American Taste of Japan.* New York: Morrow, 1985.

Andrews, Colman. *Catalan Cuisine: Europe's Last Great Culinary Secret.* New York: Atheneum, 1988.

Arnold, Augusta Foote. *The Century Cook Book.* New York: The Century Company, 1906.

Ash, John, and Sid Goldstein. *From the Earth to the Table: John Ash's Wine Country Cuisine.* New York: Dutton, 1995.

Bailey, Lee. *Lee Bailey's Country Weekends: Recipes for Good Food and Easy Living.* New York: C.N. Potter, 1983.

Baird, Edith Harbison. *365 Chafing-Dish Recipes: A Chafing-Dish Recipe for Every Day in the Year.* Philadelphia: G.W. Jacobs and Company, 1912.

Bar-David, Molly Lyons. *The Israeli Cookbook: What's Cooking in Israel's Melting Pot.* New York: Crown Publishers, 1964.

Bastianich, Lidia. *La Cucina di Lidia: Recipes and Memories from Italy's Adriatic Coast.* New York: Broadway, 1990.

Batali, Mario. *Simple Italian Food: Recipes from My Two Villages.* New York: Clarkson Potter, 1998.

Batchelder, Ann. *Ann Batchelder's Cook Book.* New York: M. Barrows and Company, 1949.

Batmanglij, Najmieh. *Food of Life: A Book of Ancient Persian and Modern Iranian Cooking and Ceremonies.* Washington, DC: Mage Pub., 1986.

Bayless, Rick. *Rick Bayless's Mexican Kitchen: Capturing the Vibrant Flavors of a World-Class Cuisine.* New York: Scribner, 1996.

Beard, James. *American Cookery.* Boston: Little, Brown and Company, 1972.

Beard, James. *Cook It Outdoors.* New York: M. Barrows and Company, 1941.

Beard, James. *The Fireside Cook Book.* New York: Simon & Schuster, 1949.

Beard, James. *Hors d'Oeuvre and Canapés: With a Key to the Cocktail Party.* New York: M. Barrows and Company, 1940.

Beard, James. *James Beard's Treasury of Outdoor Cooking.* New York: Golden Press, 1960.

Beard, James. *Theory & Practice of Good Cooking.* New York: Alfred A. Knopf, 1977.

Beard, James, and Sam Aaron. *How to Eat Better for Less Money.* New York: Simon & Schuster, 1970.

Beck, Phineas (Samuel Chamberlain). *Clementine in the Kitchen.* New York: Hastings House, 1949.

Beck, Simone, Louisette Bertholle, and Julia Child. *Mastering the Art of French Cooking, Volumes I and II.* New York: Alfred A. Knopf, 1961–1970.

Bégué, Elizabeth Kettenring. *Mme. Bégué's Recipes of Old New Orleans Creole Cookery.* New Orleans: Harmanson, 1937.

Beranbaum, Rose Levy. *The Cake Bible.* New York: William Morrow, 1988.

Berkowitz, George and Jane Doerfer. *The Legal Sea Foods Cookbook.* Boston: Main Street Books, 1988.

Berolzheimer, Ruth, ed. *The American Woman's Cook Book.* Chicago: Published for Culinary Arts Institute by Consolidated Book Publishers, 1938.

Betty Crocker's Picture Cook Book. Minneapolis: General Mills, 1950.

Bittman, Mark. *How to Cook Everything: Simple Recipes for Great Food.* New York: Macmillan, 1998.

Bollock, Helen. *The Williamsburg Art of Cookery.* Williamsburg: Printed for Colonial Williamsburg, Inc., on the Press of A. Dietz and his Son, near the great prison at Richmond, Virginia, 1938.

Boni, Ada. *Italian Regional Cooking.* New York: Dutton, 1969.

Bracken, Peg. *The I Hate to Cook Book.* New York: Harcourt Brace, 1960.

Braker, Flo. *Sweet Miniatures: The Art of Making Bite-Size Desserts.* New York: William Morrow, 1991.

Brennan, Jennifer. *The Original Thai Cookbook.* New York: Richard Marek Publishers, 1981.

Brizova, Joza. *The Czechoslovak Cookbook.* New York: Clarkson Potter, 1965.

Brown, Cora, Rose, and Robert. *The South American Cook Book: Including Central America, Mexico and the West Indies.* New York: Doubleday, Doran and Co., 1939.

Brown, Edward Espe. *The Tassajara Bread Book.* Berkeley: Shambala, 1970.

Brown, Helen Evans. *Helen Brown's West Coast Cook Book.* Boston: Little, Brown and Company, 1952.

Brownstone, Cecily. *Cecily Brownstone's Associated Press Cookbook.* New York: David McKay Company, 1972.

Bugialli, Giuliano. *The Fine Art of Italian Cooking.* New York: New York Times Book Co., 1977.

Bugialli, Giuliano. *The Foods of Sicily & Sardinia and the Smaller Islands.* New York: Rizzoli International, 1996.

Bugialli, Giuliano. *Giuliano Bugialli's Foods of Tuscany.* New York: Stewart, Tabori & Chang, 1992.

Burros, Marian. *The Elegant But Easy Cookbook.* New York: Macmillan, 1967.

Burros, Marian Fox. *20-Minute Menus: Time-Wise Recipes & Strategic Plans for Freshly Cooked Meals Every Day.* New York: Simon & Schuster, 1989.

Callahan, Genevieve. *The California Cook Book for Indoor and Outdoor Eating.* New York: M. Barrows and Company, 1946.

Cameron, Angus, and Judith Jones. *The L.L. Bean Game & Fish Cookbook.* New York: Random House, 1983.

Carpenter, Hugh, and Teri Sandison. *Pacific Flavors: Oriental Recipes from a Contemporary Kitchen.* New York: Workman Publishing, 1988.

Carroll, John P. *California: The Beautiful Cookbook.* San Francisco: Collins Publishers, 1991.

Casas, Penelope. *The Foods and Wines of Spain.* New York: Alfred A. Knopf, 1982.

Chamberlain, Narcissa G. *The Omelette Book.* New York: Alfred A. Knopf, 1956.

Chan, Shiu Wong. *The Chinese Cook Book.* New York: Frederick A. Stokes, 1917.

Chao, Buwei Yang. *How to Cook and Eat in Chinese.* New York: John Day Co., 1949.

Chen, Joyce. *Joyce Chen Cook Book.* Philadelphia: Lippincott, 1962.

Child, Julia. *From Julia Child's Kitchen.* New York: Alfred A. Knopf, 1972.

Claiborne, Craig. *The New York Times Cookbook.* New York: Harper & Row, 1961.

Claiborne, Craig, and Virginia Lee. *The Chinese Cookbook.* Philadelphia: Lippincott, 1972.

Clancy, John. *John Clancy's Christmas Cookbook.* New York: Hearst Books, 1982.

Clayton Jr., Bernard. *The Complete Book of Breads.* New York: Simon & Schuster, 1973.

Cobb, Robert H. *The Brown Derby Cookbook.* Garden City, NY: Doubleday, 1952.

Colquitt, Harriet Ross. *The Savannah Cook Book: A Collection of Old Fashioned Receipts from Colonial Kitchens.* New York: Farrar and Rinehart, Inc., 1933.

Colwin, Laurie. *Home Cooking: A Writer in the Kitchen.* New York: Alfred A. Knopf, 1988.

Connolly, Vera Leona; United States Dept. of Agriculture; United States Food Administration. *Uncle Sam's Advice to Housewives.* New York: The Christian Herald, 1917.

Cook's Illustrated: The Best Recipe. Brookline, MA: Boston Common Press, 1999.

Corbitt, Helen. *Helen Corbitt's Cookbook.* Boston: Houghton Mifflin, 1957.

Corriher, Shirley. *CookWise: The Hows and Whys of Successful Cooking.* New York: William Morrow, 1997.

Cost, Bruce. *Bruce Cost's Asian Ingredients: Buying and Cooking the Staple Foods of China, Japan and Southeast Asia.* New York: William Morrow, 1989.

Craddock, Harry. *The Savoy Cocktail Book.* New York: Richard R. Smith, 1930.

Cunningham, Marion. *The Breakfast Book.* New York: Alfred A. Knopf, 1987.

Cunningham, Marion. *The Fannie Farmer Baking Book.* New York: Alfred A. Knopf, 1984.

Cunningham, Marion. *The Fannie Farmer Cookbook.* New York: Alfred A. Knopf, 1979.

Cunningham, Marion. *The Fannie Farmer Cookbook.* New York: Alfred A. Knopf, 1990.

Curtis, Isabel Gordon. *Good Housekeeping Everyday Cook Book.* New York: The Phelps Publishing Company, 1903.

Cushing, Frank Hamilton. *Zuñi Breadstuff.* New York: Museum of the American Indian, 1920.

Daley, Rosie. *In the Kitchen with Rosie: Oprah's Favorite Recipes.* New York: Alfred A. Knopf, 1994.

David, Elizabeth. *French Provincial Cooking.* New York: Harper and Row, 1962.

David, Elizabeth. *Italian Food.* New York: Penguin, 1963.

Davidson, Alan. *Seafood: A Connoisseur's Guide and Cookbook.* New York: Simon & Schuster, 1989.

de Gouy, Louis Pullig. *The Gold Cook Book.* New York: Greenberg, 1947.

de Groot, Roy Andries. *Feasts for All Seasons.* New York: Alfred A. Knopf, 1966.

DeKnight, Freda. *A Date with a Dish, A Cook Book of American Negro Recipes.* New York: Hermitage Press, 1948.

De Silva, Cara, ed. *In Memory's Kitchen: A Legacy from the Women of Terezín.* Northvale, NJ: Jason Aronson, 1996.

Del Conte, Anna. *Gastronomy of Italy.* New York: Prentice Hall Press, 1987.

Delfs, Robert A. *The Good Food of Szechwan: Down-to-Earth Chinese Cooking.* New York: Kodansha, 1974.

de Monteiro, Longtiene and Katherine Neustadt. *The Elephant Walk Cookbook.* Boston: Houghton Mifflin Harcourt, 1998.

de Vries, Peter. *Comfort Me with Apples.* Boston: Little, Brown and Company, 1956.

Dodge, Jim. *The American Baker: Exquisite Desserts from the Pastry Chef of the Stanford Court.* New York: Simon & Schuster, 1987.

Donon, Joseph. *The Classic French Cuisine.* New York: Alfred A. Knopf, 1959.

Dull, Mrs. S. R. *Southern Cooking.* New York: Grosset & Dunlap, 1941. First edition, 1928.

East, Anna Merritt. *Kitchenette Cookery.* Boston: Little, Brown and Company, 1917.

Embury, David A. *The Fine Art of Mixing Drinks.* Garden City, NY: Doubleday, 1948.

Ephron, Nora. *Heartburn.* New York: Alfred A. Knopf, 1983.

Esen Algar, Ayla. *The Complete Book of Turkish Cooking.* New York: Paul Kegan International, 1988.

Estes, Rufus. *Good Things to Eat, as Suggested by Rufus: A Collection of Practical Recipes for Preparing Meats, Game, Fowl, Fish, Puddings, Pastries, Etc.* Chicago: The Author, 1911.

Evans, Meryle. *The American Heritage Cookbook and Illustrated History of Eating and Drinking*. Rockville, MD: American Heritage Publishing Co., 1964.

Fabricant, Florence. *New Home Cooking: Feeding Family, Feasting Friends*. New York: Clarkson Potter, 1991.

Farmer, Fannie Merritt. *A Book of Good Dinners for My Friend; or "What to Have for Dinner."* New York: Dodge Publishing Company, 1914.

Farmer, Fannie Merritt. *The Boston Cooking-School Cook Book*. Boston: Little, Brown and Company, 1896.

Farmer, Fannie Merritt. *A New Book of Cookery*. Boston: Little, Brown and Company, 1915.

Farmer, Fannie Merritt. *What to Have for Dinner*. New York: Dodge Publishing Company, 1905.

Field, Carol. *The Italian Baker: The Classic Tastes of the Italian Countryside—Its Breads, Pizza, Focaccia, Cakes, Pastries, and Cookies*. New York: Harper & Row, 1985.

Field, Michael. *Michael Field's Cooking School*. New York: Holt, Rinehart, and Winston, 1965.

Filippini, Alexander. *The International Cook Book: Over 3,300 Recipes Gathered from All Over the World, Including Many Never Before Published in English*. New York: Doubleday, 1906.

Fisher, M.F.K. *The Art of Eating*. New York: Macmillan, 1954.

Fisher, M.F.K. *Consider the Oyster*. New York: Duell, Sloan, Pearce, 1941.

Fisher, M.F.K. *How to Cook a Wolf*. New York: Duell, Sloan, and Pearce, 1942.

Foster, Pearl Byrd. *Classic American Cooking*. New York: Simon & Schuster, 1983.

Fox, Minerva Carr. *The Blue Grass Cook Book*. New York: Fox, Duffield, 1904.

Franey, Pierre. *The New York Times 60-Minute Gourmet*. New York: Times Books, 1979.

Frolov, Wanda L. *Katish: Our Russian Cook*. New York: Farrar Strauss, 1947.

Gaige, Crosby. *Dining with My Friends: Adventures with Epicures*. New York: Crown Publishers, 1949.

Gaige, Crosby. *New York World's Fair Cook Book: The American Kitchen*. New York: Doubleday, Doran & Co., 1939.

Garmey, Jane. *Great British Cooking: A Well-Kept Secret*. New York: Random House, 1981.

Gold, Rozanne. *Recipes 1-2-3: Fabulous Food Using Only Three Ingredients*. New York: Viking, 1996.

Grausman, Richard. *At Home with the French Classics*. New York: Workman Publishing, 1988.

Gray, Patience. *Honey from a Weed: Fasting and Feasting in Tuscany, Catalonia, the Cyclades and Apulia*. New York: Harper and Row, 1986.

Greene, Bert, *Greene on Greens*. New York: Workman Publishing, 1984.

Greenspan, Dorie. *Sweet Times: Simple Desserts for Every Occasion*. New York: Willliam Morrow, 1991.

Greenstein, George. *Secrets of a Jewish Baker: Authentic Jewish Rye & Other Breads*. Freedom, CA: Crossing Press, 1993.

Hagen, Uta. *Uta Hagen's Love for Cooking*. New York: Macmillan, 1976.

Hazan, Marcella. *The Classic Italian Cook Book: The Art of Italian Cooking*. New York: Harper's Magazine Press, 1973.

Hazelton, Nika. *American Home Cooking*. New York: Viking Press, 1980.

Heatter, Maida. *Maida Heatter's Book of Great Desserts*. New York: Alfred A. Knopf, 1974.

Hertzberg, Ruth, Beatrice Vaughan, and Janet Greene. *Putting Food By*. Brattleboro, VT: Stephen Greene Press, 1973.

Hibben, Sheila. *American Regional Cookery*. Boston: Little, Brown and Company, 1946.

Hibben, Sheila. *The National Cookbook: A Kitchen Americana*. New York: Harper & Brothers, 1932.

Hill, Janet McKenzie. *The American Cook Book: Recipes for Everyday Use*. Revised and Updated Edition. Boston: Boston Cooking-School Magazine, 1929. First edition, 1914.

Hill, Janet McKenzie. *Dainty Desserts for Dainty People: Knox Gelatine*. Johnstown, NY: Charles B. Knox Co., ca. 1909.

Hines, Duncan. *Adventures in Good Eating: Good Eating Places Along the Highways and in the Cities of America*. Bowling Green, KY: Adventures in Good Eating, Inc., 1936.

Hirtzler, Victor. *The Hotel St. Francis Cook Book,* Chicago: The Hotel Monthly Press, 1919.

Hom, Ken. *Easy Family Recipes from a Chinese-American Childhood*. New York: Alfred A. Knopf, 1997.

Hom, Ken. *Ken Hom's Chinese Cookery*. New York: Perennial Library, 1986.

Huguenin, Mary Vereen; Anne Montague Stoney; Junior League of Charleston (S.C.). *Charleston Receipts*. Charleston, SC: The League, 1950.

Idone, Christopher. *Christopher Idone's Glorious American Food*. New York: Random House, 1985.

Jaffrey, Madhur. *An Invitation to Indian Cooking*. New York: Alfred A. Knopf, 1973.

Johnston, Mireille. *The Cuisine of the Sun: Classical French Cooking from Nice and Provence*. New York: Random House, 1976.

Jones, Evan. *American Food: The Gastronomic Story*. New York: Dutton, 1975.

Jones, Evan and Judith. *The L.L. Bean Book of New New England Cookery*. New York: Random House, 1987.

Junior League of Augusta. *Old and New Recipes from the South*. Augusta, GA: Junior League of Augusta, 1940.

Kafka, Barbara. *Microwave Gourmet*. New York: William Morrow, 1987.

Kafka, Barbara. *Roasting: A Simple Art*. New York: William Morrow, 1995.

Kamman, Madeleine. *The Making of a Cook*. New York: Atheneum, 1971.

Kamman, Madeleine. *When French Women Cook: A Gastronomic Memoir with over 250 Recipes*. New York: Atheneum, 1976.

Kander, Mrs. Simon, and Others. *"The Settlement" Cookbook: The Way to a Man's Heart*. Milwaukee, WI: The Settlement, 1901 (Second edition, 1903).

Kasper, Lynne Rossetto. *The Splendid Table: Recipes from Emilia-Romagna, the Heartland of Northern Italian Food*. New York: William Morrow, 1992.

Katzen, Mollie. *The Moosewood Cookbook: Recipes from Moosewood Restaurant, Ithaca, New York*. Berkeley: Ten Speed Press, 1977.

Keller, Thomas. *The French Laundry Cookbook*. New York: Artisan, 1999.

Kellogg, Ella. *Every-day Dishes and Every-day Work*. Battle Creek, MI: Modern Medicine Publishing Company, 1897.

Kennedy, Diana. *The Cuisines of Mexico*. New York: Harper & Row, 1972.

Kent, Louise Andrews. *Mrs Appleyard's Kitchen*. Boston: Houghton Mifflin Co., 1942.

Kleiman, Evan, and Viana La Place. *Cucina Fresca: Italian Food, Simply Prepared*. New York: Harper and Row, 1985.

Kovi, Paul. *Paul Kovi's Transylvanian Cuisine: History, Gastronomy, Legend, and Lore from Middle Europe's Most Remarkable Region*. New York: Crown, 1985.

Kragen, Jinx, and Judy Perry. *Saucepans and the Single Girl*. Garden City, NY: Doubleday, 1965.

Kremezi, Aglaia. *The Foods of the Greek Islands: Cooking and Culture at the Crossroads of the Mediterranean*. Boston: Houghton Mifflin Harcourt, 2000.

Kuo, Irene. *The Key to Chinese Cooking*. New York: Alfred A. Knopf, 1977.

Kwak, Jenny. *Dok Suni: Recipes from My Mother's Korean Kitchen*. New York: St. Martin's Press, 1998.

Lach, Alma. *Hows and Whys of French Cooking*. Chicago: University of Chicago Press, 1974.

Lagasse, Emeril. *Emeril's New New Orleans Cooking*. New York: William Morrow, 1993.

Lang, George. *The Cuisine of Hungary*. New York: Antheneum, 1971.

Lappé, Frances Moore. *Diet for a Small Planet*. New York: Ballantine Books, 1971.

Laurel, Alicia Bay. *Living on the Earth: Celebrations, Storm Warnings, Formulas, Recipes, Rumors, Country Dances Harvested*. Berkeley: The Bookworks, 1970.

Leader, Daniel, and Judith Blahnik. *Bread Alone: Bold Fresh Loaves from Your Own Hands*. New York: William Morrow, 1993.

Lesem, Jeanne. *The Pleasures of Preserving and Pickling*. New York: Alfred A. Knopf, 1975.

Lewis, Edna. *The Taste of Country Cooking*. New York: Alfred A. Knopf, 1976.

Los Angeles Times. *The Times Cook Book No. 2*. Los Angeles: Times-Mirror Co., 1905.

Lucas, Dione. *The Cordon Bleu Cookbook*. Boston: Little, Brown and Company, 1947.

Lucas, Dione. *The Dione Lucas Meat and Poultry Cook Book*. Boston: Little, Brown and Company, 1955.

Lukins, Sheila, and Julee Rosso. *The Silver Palate Cookbook*. New York: Workman Publishing, 1982.

Lustig, Lillie, S. Claire Sondheim, and Sarah Rensel, eds. *The Southern Cook Book of Fine Old Recipes*. Reading, PA: Culinary Arts Press, 1935.

Lynch, Reah Jeannette. *"Win the War" Cook Book*. St. Louis, MO: St. Louis County Unit, Woman's Committee, Council of National Defense, Missouri Division, 1918.

MacAusland, Earle R. *The Gourmet Cookbook*. New York: Gourmet, 1950.

Madison, Deborah. *The Greens Cook Book: Extraordinary Vegetarian Cuisine from the Celebrated Restaurant*. New York: Bantam Books, 1987.

Malgieri, Nick. *Nick Malgieri's Perfect Pastry*. New York: Macmillan, 1989.

Mandel, Abby. *Abby Mandel's Cuisinart Classroom*. Greenwich, CT: Cuisinart Cooking Club, 1980.

McCall's Cook Book. New York: Random House, 1963.

McCulloch-Williams, Martha. *Dishes & Beverages of the Old South*. New York: McBride, Nast and Co., 1913.

McCully, Helen. *Nobody Ever Tells You These Things about Food and Drink*. New York: Holt, Rinehart and Winston, 1967.

McLaughlin, Michael. *The Manhattan Chili Co. Southwest-American Cookbook: A Spicy Pot of Chilies, Fixins', and Other Regional Favorites*. New York: Crown, 1986.

Medrich, Alice. *Cocolat: Extraordinary Chocolate Desserts*. New York: Warner Books, 1990.

Miller, Gloria Bley. *The Thousand Recipe Chinese Cookbook*. New York: Atheneum, 1966.

Mitchell, Jan. *Lüchow's German Cookbook: The Story and the Favorite Dishes of America's Most Famous German Restaurant*. Garden City, NY: Doubleday, 1952.

Modesto, Maria de Lourdes. *Traditional Portuguese Cooking*. Lisbon: Verbo, 1989.

Morash, Marian. *The Victory Garden Cookbook*. New York: Alfred A. Knopf, 1982.

My New Better Homes & Gardens Cook Book. Des Moines: Meredith Publishing Co., 1937.

Nathan, Joan. *Jewish Cooking in America*. New York: Alfred A. Knopf, 1994.

Neal, Bill. *Biscuits, Spoonbread, & Sweet Potato Pie*. New York: Alfred A. Knopf, 1990.

Nidetch, Jean. *The Weight Watchers Program Cookbook*. Great Neck, NY: Hearthside Press, 1973.

O'Neill, Molly. *New York Cookbook*. New York: Workman Publishing, 1992.

Olney, Richard. *The French Menu Cookbook*. Simon & Schuster, 1970.

Olney, Richard. *Simple French Food*. New York: John Wiley & Sons, 1974.

Ortiz, Elisabeth Lambert. *The Book of Latin American Cooking*. New York: Knopf, 1979.

Ortiz, Elisabeth Lambert. *The Complete Book of Caribbean Cooking*. New York: M. Evans & Co., 1973.

Owen, Jeanne, and Richardson Wright. *A Wine Lover's Cook Book*. New York: M. Barrows and Company, 1940.

Owen, Sri. *Indonesian Regional Cooking*. New York: St. Martin's Press, 1995.

Owen, Sri. *The Rice Book: The Definitive Book on Rice, with Hundreds of Exotic Recipes from Around the World*. New York: St. Martin's Press, 1993.

Paddleford, Clementine. *How America Eats*. New York: Charles Scribner & Sons, 1960.

Peck, Paula. *The Art of Fine Baking: Cakes and Pastries, Coffeecakes, Breads with a Continental Flavor*. New York: Simon & Schuster, 1961.

Pépin, Jacques. *La Technique: An Illustrated Guide to the Fundamental Techniques of Cooking*. New York: Times Book Co., 1976.

Peters, Lulu Hunt. *Diet and Health with Key to the Calories*. Chicago: The Reilly and Lee Company, 1918.

Pillsbury Company. *Best of the Bake-Off Collection: Pillsbury's Best 1,000 Recipes*. Chicago: Consolidated Book Publishers, 1959.

Platt, June. *June Platt's Party Cookbook*. Boston: Houghton Mifflin Company, 1936.

Platt, June. *June Platt's Plain and Fancy Cookbook*, Boston: Houghton Mifflin Company, 1941.

Plotkin, Fred. *Recipes from Paradise: Life and Food on the Italian Riviera*. Boston: Little, Brown, 1997.

Prudhomme, Paul. *Chef Paul Prudhomme's Louisiana Kitchen*. New York: William Morrow, 1984.

Puckett, Susan, and Angela Meyers, eds. *A Cook's Tour of Mississippi*. Jackson: Jackson Daily News, 1980.

Raichlen, Steven. *The Barbecue! Bible*. New York: Workman Publishers, 1998.

Randelman, Mary Urrutia. *Memories of a Cuban Kitchen: More than 200 Classic Recipes*. New York: John Wiley & Sons, 1996.

Rawlings, Marjorie Kinnan. *Cross Creek Cookery*. New York: C. Scribner's Sons, 1942.

Rhett, Blanche S., ed. Lettie Gay. *Two Hundred Years of Charleston Cooking*. New York: J. Cape and H. Smith, 1930.

Robertson, Laurel, Carol Flinders, and Bronwen Godfrey. *Laurel's Kitchen: A Handbook for Vegetarian Cookery & Nutrition*. Berkeley: Nilgiri Press, 1976.

Roden, Claudia. *A Book of Middle Eastern Food*. New York: Alfred A. Knopf, 1972.

Roden, Claudia. *The Book of Jewish Food: An Odyssey from Samarkand to New York*. New York: Alfred A. Knopf, 1996.

Rojas-Lombardi, Felipe. *The Art of South American Cooking*. New York: HarperCollins Publishers, 1991.

Rombauer, Irma. *The Joy of Cooking*. St. Louis: A.C. Clayton Printing Company, 1931.

Rorer, Sarah Tyson. *How to Use a Chafing Dish*. Philadelphia: Arnold & Co., 1912.

Rorer, Sarah Tyson. *Mrs. Rorer's New Cook Book*. Philadelphia: Arnold & Co., 1902.

Saberi, Helen. *Afghan Food & Cookery*. New York: Hippocrene, 2000.

Sahni, Julie. *Classic Indian Vegetarian and Grain Cooking*. New York: William Morrow, 1985.

Sax, Richard. *Classic Home Desserts: A Treasury of Heirloom and Contemporary Recipes from Around the World*. Shelburne, VT: Chapters Publishing, 1994.

Schneider, Elizabeth. *Uncommon Fruits & Vegetables: A Commonsense Guide*. New York: Harper & Row, 1986.

Schwartz, Arthur. *Cooking in a Small Kitchen*. Boston: Little, Brown and Company, 1979.

Seely, Lida. *Mrs. Seely's Cook Book: A Manual of French and American Cookery, with Chapters on Domestic Servants, Their Rights and Duties and Many Other Details of Household Management*. New York: Macmillan, 1902.

Seranne, Ann. *The Art of Egg Cookery: 448 Unusual, Appetizing, Economical Dishes Prepared with Eggs, including Omelets, Souffles, Mousses, Meringues, Baked Alaskas, Custards, Creams, Sauces, Cakes, and Drinks*. Garden City, NY: Doubleday, 1949.

Sheraton, Mimi. *From My Mother's Kitchen: Recipes and Reminiscences*. New York: Harper & Row, 1979.

Sheraton, Mimi. *The German Cookbook: A Complete Guide to Mastering Authentic German Cooking*. New York: Random House, 1965.

Shircliffe, Arnold. *Edgewater Beach Hotel Salad Book*. Chicago: The Hotel Monthly Press, 1926.

Shurtleff, William, and Akiko Aoyagi. *The Book of Tofu*. Brookline, MA: Autumn Press, 1975.

Silverton, Nancy. *Desserts*. New York: Harper & Row, 1986.

Silverton, Nancy. *Nancy Silverton's Breads from the La Brea Bakery: Recipes for the Connoisseur*. New York: Villard, 1996.

Smart-Grosvenor, Vertamae. *Vibration Cooking: or, The Travel Notes of a Geechee Girl*. Garden City, NY: Doubleday, 1970.

Somerville, Annie. *Fields of Greens: New Vegetarian Recipes from the Celebrated Greens Restaurant*. New York: Bantam, 1993.

Southworth, May E. *One Hundred & One Mexican Dishes*. San Francisco: Paul Elder and Co., 1906.

Stern, Jane and Michael. *Roadfood: The Coast to Coast Guide to over 400 of America's Great Inexpensive Regional Restaurants All Within 10 Miles of a Major Highway*. New York: Random House, 1978.

Stewart, Martha. *Entertaining*. New York: Clarkson Potter, 1982.

Stewart, Martha. *Weddings*. New York: Clarkson Potter, 1987.

Strybel, Robert and Maria. *Polish Heritage Cookery*. New York: Hippocrene, 1993.

Thomas, Anna. *The Vegetarian Epicure*. New York: Vintage Books, 1972.

Time-Life American Regional Cookbook. Boston: Little, Brown and Company, 1978.

Time-Life Books. *Foods of the World*. 27 Volumes. New York: Time-Life Publishers, 1968–70.

Times-Picayune Publishing. *The Original Picayune Creole Cook Book: Containing Recipes Using Wines and Liquors Customary in Early Creole Cookery*. New Orleans: Times-Picayune Publishing Company, 1901.

Toklas, Alice B. *The Alice B. Toklas Cook Book*. First American Edition. New York: Harper, 1954.

Torres, Marimar. *The Spanish Table: The Cuisines and Wines of Spain*. Garden City, NY: Doubleday, 1986.

Tower, Jeremiah. *Jeremiah Tower's New American Classics*. New York: Harper & Row, 1986.

Townsend, Doris. *The Cook's Companion*. New York: Crown Publishers, 1978.

Tropp, Barbara. *The Modern Art of Chinese Cooking*. New York: William Morrow, 1982.

Trotter, Charlie. *Charlie Trotter's*. Berkeley: Ten Speed Press, 1994.

Truax, Carol. *Ladies' Home Journal Cookbook*. New York: Doubleday, 1960.

Tsuji, Shizuo. *Japanese Cooking: A Simple Art*. New York: Kodansha International Ltd., 1980.

Uvezian, Sonia. *The Cuisine of Armenia*. New York: Harper & Row, 1974.

Van Aken, Norman. *Norman Van Aken's Feast of Sunlight*. New York: Ballantine, 1988.

Villas, James. *American Taste: A Celebration of Gastronomy Coast to Coast*. New York: Arbor House, 1982.

Villas, James. *Villas at Table: A Passion for Food and Drink*. New York: Harper & Row, 1988.

Voltz, Jeanne. *The California Cookbook*. Indianapolis: Bobbs-Merrill, 1970.
Waters, Alice. *Chez Panisse Café Cookbook*. New York: HarperCollins, 1999.
Waters, Alice. *Chez Panisse Vegetables*. New York: HarperCollins Publishers, 1996.
Weaver, William Woys. *Pennsylvania Dutch Country Cooking*. New York: Abbeville Press, 1993.
Weiss-Armush, Anne Marie. *The Arabian Delights Cookbook: Mediterranean Cuisines from Mecca to Marrakesh*. Los Angeles: Lowell House, 1994.
Wells, Patricia. *Bistro Cooking*. New York: Workman Publishing, 1989.
Wells, Patricia. *Food Lover's Guide to Paris*. New York: Workman Publishing, 1999.
White, Jasper. *Jasper White's Cooking from New England: More Than 300 Traditional and Contemporary Recipes*. New York: Harper & Row, 1989.
Willan, Anne. *La Varenne Pratique: The Complete Illustrated Cooking Course; Techniques, Ingredients, and Tools of Classic Modern Cuisine*. New York: Crown, 1989.
Williams, Chuck. *The Williams-Sonoma Cookbook and Guide to Kitchenware*. New York: Random House, 1986.
Witty, Helen, and Elizabeth Schneider Colchie. *Better Than Store-Bought: A Cookbook*. New York: Harper & Row, 1979.
Wolcott, Imogene. *The Yankee Cook Book; An Anthology of Incomparable Recipes from the Six New England States and a Little Something about the People Whose Tradition for Good Eating Is Herein Permanently Recorded by Imogene Wolcott, from the Files of Yankee Magazine and from Time Worn Recipe Books and Many Gracious Contributors*. New York: Coward-McCann, 1939.
Wolfert, Paula. *The Cooking of the Eastern Mediterranean: 215 Healthy, Vibrant, and Inspired Recipes*. New York: HarperCollins, 1994.
Wolfert, Paula. *The Cooking of Southwest France: Recipes from France's Magnificent Rustic Cuisine*. New York: The Dial Press, 1983.
Wolfert, Paula. *Couscous and Other Good Food from Morocco*. New York: Harper & Row, 1973.
Wolfert, Paula. *Mediterranean Cooking*. New York: Quadrangle/New York Times Book Co., 1977.
Worthington, Diane Rossen. *The California Cook: Casually Elegant Recipes with Exhilarating Taste*. New York: Bantam Books, 1994.
Wright, Clifford A. *A Mediterranean Feast: The Story of the Birth of the Celebrated Cuisines of the Mediterranean, from the Merchants of Venice to the Barbary Corsairs, with More than 500 Recipes*. New York: William Morrow, 1999.
Zelayeta, Elena Emilia. *Elena's Famous Mexican and Spanish Recipes*. San Francisco: Dettners Printing House, 1944.
Ziemann, Hugo, and Mrs. F. L. Gilette. *The White House Cook Book: A Comprehensive Cyclopedia of Information for the Home, Containing Cooking, Toilet and Household Recipes, Menus, Dinner-giving, Table Etiquette, Care of the Sick, Health Suggestions, Facts Worth Knowing, etc.* Chicago: The Werner Company, 1900.

ABOUT THE ADVISORY COMMITTEE

MICHAEL BAUER is the executive food and wine editor and restaurant critic for the *San Francisco Chronicle* and is in charge of the largest food and wine staff on any newspaper in the United States. In 2002 he launched the Wine section, the first freestanding weekly newspaper section of its kind in the country. Much of the content has been syndicated by King Features and is now published in some of the largest newspapers in the country. In May 2003 the Food and Wine staff moved into a separate building behind the *Chronicle* outfitted with a 20,000-bottle wine cellar, test kitchen, and rooftop herb garden. Bauer grew up in the food business, working at his father's meat market while he was an undergraduate in journalism at Kansas State University and while working on a master's degree in mass communications at Kansas State University. He began his journalism career as a feature writer specializing in behavioral sciences at the *Kansas City Star,* where he eventually switched to food reporting. He then went to the *Dallas Times Herald* as the restaurant critic and wine editor before coming to the *San Francisco Chronicle* in 1986. He is a past president of the Association of Food Journalists, a current member of the James Beard Foundation Restaurant Awards Committee, and a 2004 inductee in the foundation's Who's Who of Food & Beverage in America.

PAT BROWN is an editor and writer who began in publishing at *The New Yorker* and went on, after other magazine posts, to edit the food magazines *Bon Appétit* and *Cuisine* as well as books on food, wine, and entertaining for HarperCollins. For five years she devised and oversaw regular special sections on Italian food and wine for *The New York Times* with Lidia Bastianich. She has written for many other publications and was editor and project manager for *The Loews Hotels Family Cookbook*. Brown acted as consultant to the March of Dimes on its successful fundraising Gourmet Galas in forty-five United States cities, and for twenty years was a member (and chair) of the James Beard Foundation Book Awards Committee. She also served on the Advisory Board of the School of Food and Nutrition at New York University. Currently she serves on the Board of Directors of the Bowdoin International Music Festival in Maine, where she chairs its annual scholarship fundraiser Dine On. She is a member of Les Dames d'Escoffier and the Wine Media Guild.

MARIAN BURROS is an author and journalist. For more than half a century she has reported on the seismic changes that have taken place in American kitchens and restaurants and on America's farms, authoring thirteen cooking and food books along the way that reflect these changes. The first book, *Elegant But Easy Cookbook* (coauthor Lois Levine, 1959), from which the Plum Torte recipe emerged to become one of the most requested recipes that ever appeared in *The New*

York Times, also included recipes that used convenience foods (deleted from the 1998 revision). But the bulk of her work reflects a rebellion against industrialized foods and, instead, concentrates on efforts to help people cook from scratch without relying on products filled with ingredients that never grew on a farm. *20 Minute Menus, You've Got It Made, Pure and Simple*, and *Eating Well Is the Best Revenge* are books that also reflect her work as a reporter covering the politics of food for *The New York Times,* from which she retired in 2008, the *Washington Post*, and the NBC station in Washington, D.C., WRC-TV. Her latest book, *Cooking for Comfort*, published in 2003, reflects America's desire for a return to less complicated times, to artisanal, local, and organic ingredients and grass-fed meats. Burros covers First Lady Michelle Obama's child obesity initiative, Let's Move, and writes for *Politico, Rodale,* and *Flavor* magazines, and for *The New York Times*.

DALIA CARMEL GOLDSTEIN is an independent scholar, book collector, and specialist on the cuisines of the world with a strong knowledge of Middle Eastern cooking. Carmel was born in Israel and grew up in Jerusalem. She was enlisted in the Israeli army and served a little more than three years, part in compulsory service and part in regular service. For two of the years, she served as secretary to the chief of intelligence and spent some time in London. In 1960 she was sent to the United States and worked for a short time for the State of Israel Bonds. From there she took a position with El Al Israeli Airlines, where she worked for thirty-seven years in the claims department. Her love of food, music, and photography salved her from the headaches and issues of her job. Carmel didn't know how to boil water when she left home. A cookbook club introduced her to the world of food writing. She could get three books the first month for just $1.00. So she "chose the fattest books, not knowing which book was appropriate for a novice." The first three books: *The Joy of Cooking, The New York Times Cook Book,* and *Mastering the Art of French Cooking* were the foundation of her collection. Over the following years, Carmel would amass more than 11,000 cookbooks, with a specialization in world foods written about in their original languages. To date, Carmel has given 11,000 books to the Food Studies Collection at the Fales Library, enriching its holdings of world cuisines immeasurably.

MITCHELL DAVIS is the vice president of the James Beard Foundation, a cookbook author, food journalist, and scholar with a PhD in Food Studies from New York University's Department of Nutrition, Food Studies, and Public Health. His academic work focuses on restaurants, media, and taste, particularly how restaurant reviews influence food preferences. At the Beard Foundation, Davis has spearheaded "Sustainability on the Table," national dialogue on sustainability and public health in the food-service industry. In addition to his work at the foundation, Davis frequently writes about and reviews restaurants. He holds a chair on the academy of the London-based World's 50 Best Restaurants program. He has written four cookbooks, most recently *Kitchen Sense* (Clarkson Potter), and he is a regular contributor to the *Art of Eating* and *Gastronomica*. His television appearances include the Food Network's *Food(ography), Throwdown with Bobby Flay*, and *Best in Smoke,* on which he is a regular judge.

MERYLE EVANS is a food journalist and culinary historian who has written extensively about the world's cuisines for more than thirty years. She was an editor of *The American Heritage Cookbook, The Horizon Cookbook,* the eighteen-volume Southern Heritage Cookbook Library, and the Antique American Cookbook series of reprints. As a contributing editor to *Food Arts*, Evans has covered cooking and culture from Australia to Tunisia, for the past twenty-two years. She was an associate editor for the *Oxford Encyclopedia of Food and Drink in America* (2004) and has written for *Diversion* and *Gastronomica*. Evans has also lectured on various aspects of culinary history to organizations such as the American Institute of Wine and Food, the Oxford Symposium, Colonial Williamsburg, and the U.S. Pastry Alliance. She donated her large collection of early American cooking utensils to the Johnson & Wales Culinary Archives in Providence, Rhode Island. Her enthusiasm for American cultural history was fostered during a seven-year tenure as supervisor of public relations at The New-York Historical Society, and a five-year stint as co-creator and associate producer of *Bicentennial Minutes* on the CBS Television Network.

FLORENCE FABRICANT is a food and wine writer for *The New York Times*. She contributes the weekly "Food Stuff" and "Off the Menu" columns, and frequently writes features that appear in the Dining and Travel sections. Her blog called Dear FloFab, which responds to questions about entertaining and dining out, is a feature on the Diner's Journal section of the *New York Times* online edition. She has written eleven cookbooks: *Park Avenue Potluck* and *Park Avenue Potluck Celebrations* (Rizzoli) are two recent ones. Fabricant is a Phi Beta Kappa graduate of Smith College, with an MA in French from New York University Graduate School of Arts and Sciences. She holds L'Ordre National du Mérite from the French government, and is a member of Who's Who of Food and Beverage in America. She lives in Manhattan and in East Hampton, New York, with her husband, Richard, a lawyer with a great metabolism who loves to eat. They have two children: Robert Fabricant, a graduate of the Interactive Telecommunications Program at New York University's Tisch School of the Arts, is a creative director of Frog Design. Patricia Fabricant, an artist and a graphic designer, has collaborated with her mother on five cookbooks. Florence and Richard also have two granddaughters.

BARBARA FAIRCHILD is presently a freelance food and travel writer, columnist, editor, speaker, and consultant. For ten years Fairchild was the editor-in-chief of *Bon Appétit* magazine, based in Los Angeles. She stepped down in November 2011 when the magazine was relocated to New York. Her career with *Bon Appétit* spanned more than three decades, beginning as an editorial assistant in 1978. A prominent leader in the epicurean world, Fairchild was inducted into the James Beard Foundation's Who's Who of Food & Beverage in May 2000. She is also the author of three successful cookbooks. Fairchild makes frequent appearances on television and radio. She is a member of more than a dozen professional organizations and devotes time to many charities, focusing on children and hunger, culinary careers for high school students (C-CAP), literacy, and cancer prevention. Fairchild and her life partner, Paul Nagle, a consultant for the global think tank KPMG, divide their time between residences in Los Angeles, New York, and Washington, D.C.

BETTY FUSSELL is a scholar, author, and journalist who for the past fifty years has been writing articles and books on the subject of what it is to be an American, first looking at movies and theater, and then at food. Her most recent, and eleventh, book is *Raising Steaks: The Life and Times of American Beef* (2008). In this she takes up the historical epic she began in *The Story of Corn* (1992), which won the International Association of Culinary Professional's Jane Grigson Award for Scholarship. In between she wrote a food memoir, *My Kitchen Wars* (1999), which was performed in Hollywood and New York as a one-woman show by actress Dorothy Lyman. In 2007 she won a James Beard Foundation Award for Journalism for "American Prime" in *Saveur*'s Steak Issue of July of that year. She was recently celebrated, along with other winners of the Silver Spoon Award, by *Food Arts Magazine*, for which she has long been a contributing authority. Over the decades, her writing has appeared in literary publications such as *Sewanee Review, Hudson Review, Ontario Review, New York Literary Forum,* and *Culture Front.* Food and travel articles have appeared in *The New York Times, The Los Angeles Times, Holiday, Travel and Leisure, Connoisseur, Journal of Gastronomy, Gastronomica, Country Journal, Wine and Food, Bon Appétit, Gourmet, Saveur, Cooking Light, Redbook, Ladies' Home Journal, More, Kitchen Gardener, Metropolitan Home,* and *Edible Manhattan.*

JONATHAN GOLD is *LA Weekly*'s restaurant critic and the author of *Counter Intelligence: Where to Eat in the Real Los Angeles.* He has been restaurant critic for *California*, the *Los Angeles Times, Los Angeles,* and *Gourmet*, and he has won seven James Beard Awards for his magazine and newspaper restaurant reviews. In 2007 Gold became the first food writer to win the Pulitzer Prize for criticism; in 2011 he was again a finalist for the award.

BARBARA KIRSHENBLATT-GIMBLETT is university professor and professor of Performance Studies at New York University, where she teaches a course on food and performance. She has served on the editorial boards of the *Encyclopedia of Food and Culture*, *Gastronomia*, and *Cuizine,* and contributed entries on Jewish food and Jewish cookbooks to *Encyclopedia Judaica, YIVO Encyclopedia of Jews in Eastern Europe,* and *Encyclopedia of Food and Culture.* She is currently leading the Core Exhibition Planning Team for the Museum of the History of Polish Jews on the site of the former Warsaw Ghetto.

JENIFER LANG is a chef, author, and restaurateur. From 1990 to 2009 Lang was the managing director of the Café des Artistes, one of the most popular restaurants in New York City. Lang began her culinary career as the first woman cook in the kitchens of New York's famous '21' Club Restaurant. She enrolled at the Culinary Institute of America in order to apply professional chef's training to her journalism skills, which she had practiced at CBS Network News and at *Family Circle*. She had further culinary training as assistant to Marcella Hazan in Bologna, Italy. After graduating, Lang began a column in the *Washington Post* titled "The Resolute Shopper." As an outgrowth of that column, she spent four years working on a major book for Crown titled *Tastings: The Best From Ketchup to Caviar*. For a period of fifteen years, Lang pursued a successful career as a food journalist. Her articles on food, restaurants, and consumer subjects, many including recipes she developed, appeared frequently in national food and general interest magazines. She was a television guest on many national shows, including NBC's *Today* show, *Good Morning America, The CBS Morning News*, and *Live with Regis and Kelly,* as well as on CNN and the Food Network. She was the American editor for the penultimate edition of *Larousse Gastronomique,* the definitive encyclopedia of French cuisine. Lang was named to the Alumni Advisory Board of the Culinary Institute of America. She also served on the founding board of Women Chefs and Restaurateurs, and is a member of Les Dames d'Escoffier. Lang's latest book, *Jenifer Lang Cooks for Kids*, was published by Harmony Books.

MARION NESTLE is Paulette Goddard Professor in the Department of Nutrition, Food Studies, and Public Health, which she chaired from 1988 to 2003, and professor of Sociology at New York University. She holds a PhD in molecular biology and an MPH in public health nutrition from University of California, Berkeley. Her research examines scientific and socioeconomic influences on food choice, obesity, and food safety, with an emphasis on the role of food marketing. She is the author of several prize-winning books, among them *Food Politics, Safe Food*, and *What to Eat*. Her latest book, coauthored with Malden Nesheim, is *Why Calories Count.* She writes the "Food Matters" column for the San Francisco Chronicle, blogs at www.foodpolitics.com, and twitters @marionnnestle.

SCOTT PEACOCK is one of the nation's most respected and influential chefs. He has been at the forefront of the local food movement since the early 1990s, when he and his longtime friend and collaborator, the culinary legend Edna Lewis, cofounded the Society for the Revival and Preservation of Southern Food. They organized symposiums that drew the participation of highly respected writers and food professionals, laying the groundwork for what is now the nationally revered Southern Foodways Alliance. Born and raised in rural Alabama, Peacock was chosen in 1987, at the age of twenty-four, to man the kitchen of the Georgia Governor's Mansion. In 1995 he became the opening chef of Atlanta's Horseradish Grill. In 1998 he joined Watershed restaurant in Decatur as executive chef, where both he and the restaurant received numerous honors. The James Beard Foundation named him Best Chef in the Southeast in 2007, and a semifinalist for Outstanding Chef in America in 2009. In 2003 Peacock and Lewis published the best-selling cookbook *The Gift of Southern Cooking*, which was a nominee for best regional cookbook in both the James Beard and International Association of Culinary Professionals cookbook competitions. An accomplished writer, speaker, and media personality, Peacock has since 2010 produced the monthly "American Classics" column for *Better Homes and Gardens* magazine, and he appears regularly on the *Today* show. Peacock left the restaurant business in 2010 to focus on writing and on producing a documentary about the traditional foodways of Alabama, as told through oral histories of its longest-living citizens.

MICHAEL POLLAN is an author, journalist, and food writer. For the past twenty-five years, he has been writing books and articles about the places where nature and culture intersect: on our plates, in our farms and gardens, and in the built environment. He is the author of four *New York Times* bestsellers: *Food Rules* (2010), *In Defense of Food* (2008), *The Omnivore's Dilemma* (2006), and *The Botany of Desire* (2001). *The Omnivore's Dilemma* was named one of the ten best books of 2006 by both *The New York Times* and the *Washington Post*. It also won the California Book Award, the Northern California Book Award, and the James Beard Award, and was a finalist for the National Book Critics Circle Award. *The Botany of Desire* was recognized as a best book of the year by the American Booksellers Association and Amazon.com. PBS premiered a documentary based on *The Botany of Desire* in fall 2009. Pollan is also the author of *A Place of My Own* (1997) and *Second Nature* (1991). He was named to the 2010 *TIME* 100, the magazine's annual list of the world's hundred most influential people. In 2009 he was named by *Newsweek* as one of the top ten "New Thought Leaders." In 2003 Pollan was appointed the John S. and James L. Knight Professor of Journalism at UC Berkeley's Graduate School of Journalism, and the director of the Knight Program in Science and Environmental Journalism.

RUTH REICHL is editorial advisor to *Gilt Taste* and editor at large at Random House. From 1999 to 2009 she was editor in chief of *Gourmet* magazine. She began her career as restaurant critic for *New West* and *California* magazines, and went on to be the restaurant critic and food editor of the *Los Angeles Times*. From 1993 to 1999 she served as restaurant critic for *The New York Times*. Reichl began writing about food in 1972, when she published *Mmmmm: A Feastiary*. Since then, she has authored four memoirs, *Tender at the Bone*, *Comfort Me with Apples*, *Garlic and Sapphires*, and *For You, Mom, Finally*. She is the editor of The Modern Library Food Series, which currently includes ten books. She is executive producer and host of the public television series *Adventures with Ruth*. She is also a producer on the Fox 2000 movie *Garlic and Sapphires*. At the moment she is at work on a novel and a cookbook.

CELIA SACK was born and raised in San Francisco. During her seven-year tenure at Pacific Book Auction, she channeled her passion for rare books into a private antiquarian cookbook collection. In 2008 she opened Omnivore Books on Food, San Francisco's only culinary bookshop. Featuring new and antiquarian titles, her store has become the destination for internationally known food writers touring their new books and for collectors expanding their shelves.

LAURA SHAPIRO was a columnist at *The Real Paper* (Boston) before beginning a sixteen-year run at *Newsweek*, where she covered food, women's issues, and the arts, and won several journalism awards. Her essays, reviews, and features have also appeared in *The New Yorker, The New York Times, Condé Nast Traveler, Gourmet, Gastronomica, Slate*, and many other publications. Her first book was *Perfection Salad* (1986), which the University of California Press recently reissued with a new afterword. She is also the author of *Something from the Oven* (2004) and *Julia Child* (2007), which won the award for Literary Food Writing from the International Association of Culinary Professionals. Her work is represented in the Library of America's *American Food Writing, The Virago Book of Food*, and *Best Food Writing 2002*. She is a frequent speaker and panelist on culinary history, and contributed a regular column on a wide range of food topics to the *Gourmet* magazine website. From 2009 to 2010 she was a fellow at the Cullman Center for Scholars and Writers at the New York Public Library.

ANDREW F. SMITH is a freelance writer who teaches food history, food controversies, and professional food writing at the New School University in New York City. He is the author or editor of twenty-one books, including his most recent books, *Starving the South*, from St. Martin's Press, and *Eating History*, from Columbia University Press. He serves as the editor of the *Oxford Encyclopedia on Food and Drink in America*, a second edition of which is currently underway. He has written more than three hundred articles in academic journals, popular magazines, and newspapers, including *Gastronomica, Martha Stewart Living, Saveur*, and the *Los Angeles Times*. Smith is the editor for the Edible Series at Reaktionbooks in the United Kingdom, and he serves on the editorial board for the American Society for Food Studies journal, *Food, Culture, and Society*. He has been regularly interviewed on radio and television, including National Public Radio, the History Channel, and the Food Network. He has served as historical consultant to several television series, including PBS's *What We Eat and Why* and *The History Detectives*, the Food Network's *Heavyweights*, the History Channel's *American Eats*, and Discovery's *How Stuff Is Made*. His website is www.andrewfsmith.com.

MARVIN J. TAYLOR is a curator, academic, and director of the Fales Library and Special Collections at New York University. He began his studies as a musician at Indiana University's prestigious School of Music, before moving on to receive a degree in Comparative Literature and a master's in Library Science. While at Indiana, he worked at the Lilly Library, the rare book and manuscript repository for the university, which is known for, among other things, the Gernon Cookbook Collection. He moved to New York City in 1987 to take a position at Columbia University's Rare Book and Manuscript Library. In 1993 he became director of the Fales Library and set about revitalizing the collections through new modes of acquisitions. He founded the Downtown New York Collection, which documents the art scene that flourished in SoHo and the Lower East Side from the 1970s to the 1990s. He edited *The Downtown Book*, the first book to look at this explosive period of artistic creativity in New York. At the instigation of Dr. Marion Nestle, he founded the Food Studies Collection at the Fales Library in 2003. The collection is now the largest in the United States, holding more than 55,000 volumes related to food. Taylor also writes about gender and sexuality in the Victorian and modern periods, postmodern fiction, and the epistemology of libraries and archives.

ALICE WATERS is a chef, author, and the proprietor of Chez Panisse Restaurant in Berkeley, California. Waters is a pioneer of a culinary philosophy based on using only the freshest organic products, served only in season. Over the course of thirty-nine years, Chez Panisse has developed a network of local farmers and purveyors whose dedication to sustainable agriculture assures the restaurant a steady supply of pure, fresh ingredients. Waters's commitment to education led to the creation of the Edible Schoolyard, a one-acre garden and kitchen classroom at Berkeley's Martin Luther King, Jr., Middle School. The Edible Schoolyard, started in 1996, is a model public education program that gives students the knowledge and values they need to build a humane and sustainable future by actively involving them in all aspects of the food cycle: planting, harvesting, and cooking. The success of the Edible Schoolyard has led to the School Lunch Initiative, which has as its national agenda the integration of a nutritious daily lunch and gardening experience into the academic curriculum of all the public schools in the United States. Waters is Vice President of Slow Food International, a nonprofit organization that promotes and celebrates local artisanal food traditions and has more than 100,000 members in more than 130 countries. She is the author of eight books, including *The Art of Simple Food* and her most recent book, *In the Green Kitchen*.

CLARK WOLF, chair of the Advisory Committee, is a special advisor to the Food Studies Collection at New York University's Fales Library and Special Collections, where he hosts the well-regarded Critical Topics in Food Series. He was the Academic Advisory Committee Chair in the development of the Steinhardt School's Food Studies program, aiding Dr. Marion Nestle in the formulation and launch of the first of its kind BS, MA, and PhD program in America. Wolf is a James Beard Awards Who's Who winner, a Food Arts Silver Spoon recipient, author of *American Cheeses* (2008, Simon & Schuster), host of *The Food Show* on Northern California's station KFTY, regular columnist for the Voices section of the *San Francisco Chronicle*'s food-focused website Inside Scoop, and president of his restaurant and food business consulting firm, Clark Wolf Company, since 1986. Wolf's degree is in English Literature from San Francisco State University. He was the director of the famed San Francisco Oakville Grocery when it opened in 1980, where he brought arugula to the West Coast, sold wild mushrooms by the pound, cream-top milk in bottles, and America's first world-class goat cheese, Laura Chenel Chèvre. He was brought to New York in 1982 by then *Vogue* food editor and restaurant consultant Barbara Kafka. In New York he was fed weekly by the legendary James Beard, whom he'd befriended in San Francisco. He helped form and launch the American Institute of Wine and Food with Julia Child and Robert Mondavi. Wolf is active in educational and business activities on two coasts, splitting his time between Manhattan and a hundred-year-old loggers' cabin in the redwoods by the Russian River in northwestern Sonoma, California. His websites include www.clarkwolfcompany.com and www.clarkwolf.com.

CONVERSION CHARTS

All conversions are approximate.

LIQUID CONVERSIONS

U.S.	METRIC
1 tsp	5 ml
1 tbs	15 ml
2 tbs	30 ml
3 tbs	45 ml
¼ cup	60 ml
⅓ cup	75 ml
⅓ cup + 1 tbs	90 ml
⅓ cup + 2 tbs	100 ml
½ cup	120 ml
⅔ cup	150 ml
¾ cup	180 ml
¾ cup + 2 tbs	200 ml
1 cup	240 ml
1 cup + 2 tbs	275 ml
1¼ cups	300 ml
1⅓ cups	325 ml
1½ cups	350 ml
1⅔ cups	375 ml
1¾ cups	400 ml
1¾ cups + 2 tbs	450 ml
2 cups (1 pint)	475 ml
2½ cups	600 ml
3 cups	720 ml
4 cups (1 quart)	945 ml (1,000 ml is 1 liter)

WEIGHT CONVERSIONS

U.S. / U.K.	METRIC
½ oz	14 g
1 oz	28 g
1½ oz	43 g
2 oz	57 g
2½ oz	71 g
3 oz	85 g
3½ oz	100 g
4 oz	113 g
5 oz	142 g
6 oz	170 g
7 oz	200 g
8 oz	227 g
9 oz	255 g
10 oz	284 g
11 oz	312 g
12 oz	340 g
13 oz	368 g
14 oz	400 g
15 oz	425 g
1 lb	454 g

OVEN TEMPERATURES

°F	GAS MARK	°C
250	½	120
275	1	140
300	2	150
325	3	165
350	4	180
375	5	190
400	6	200
425	7	220
450	8	230
475	9	240
500	10	260
550	Broil	290

ACKNOWLEDGMENTS

I would like to thank Clark Wolf and Marion Nestle for having faith that I could write this book. Clark's vision and assistance was invaluable, especially for putting together the selection Advisory Committee, planning the essays, and compiling the recipes. Marion's unwavering belief that we need to build library collections in food studies helped me in more ways than I can express. This book was really a joint effort.

I'd like to thank the Fales staff: Lisa Darms, Brent Phillips, and Charlotte Priddle for keeping the library open while I was writing, and Fales graduate students Esti Brennan, Rachel Greer, and Caitlin Klein for all the help pulling books, checking page numbers, and copying recipes. Researchers Tosca Giamatti, Janet Lo, and Waverley Aufmuth helped compile lists and research recipes. Thanks to Gioia Stevens and Frederick Courtright for help with permissions, to Andrea Thompson for her beautiful photography, and to Patricia Fabricant for her outstanding design.

We could not have done this without the generous assistance of the Advisory Committee, who volunteered their time and, in many cases, also wrote essays about some of the books and authors. I'd also like to send special thanks to Christopher Steighner from Rizzoli for thinking of this book as a project for the Fales Food Studies Collection. We are grateful as well to everyone at Rizzoli who worked to make this book a success, particularly Maria Pia Gramaglia for her production expertise and Nicki Clendening for her publicity acumen. Thanks to Carol A. Mandel, dean of the NYU Libraries, for allowing me a sabbatical during which I wrote most of the manuscript. And, as always, greatest thanks go to my partner Michael Gillespie. There is no better editor that I know and no greater supporter.

Finally, none of this would have happened without the donors who helped us create the Food Studies Collection. I'd especially like to thank Dalia Carmel, Betty Fussell, Sara Moulton, Rozanne Gold, Jenifer and George Lang, Andrew F. Smith, Les Dames d'Escoffier of New York, the James Beard Foundation, The Ladies' Home Journal, and all the others who have made our collection the largest of its kind in the United States.

—Marvin J. Taylor

First and foremost I want to thank Marvin J. Taylor for his wonderful work and words in this book and for making such a good and valuable, vibrant and dynamic home for the Food Studies Collection—and for all of the very special everything that lives at Fales. Without his tireless and generous efforts, significant tenacity, broad (!) worldview, unique humor, and the respect he garners from colleagues, students, friends, and visitors—this collection of books, papers, and assorted materials would not be what it is today. Working with him is a pleasure and a privilege. Working on this book has been a serious joy.

And then there's Marion Nestle, without whom this Collection would never have happened. She keeps us focused and lively, our standards high, and our thinking clear. We three have an awfully good time working away at things we love. Her ongoing nurturing and support for all of the many activities connected to the Collection is unceasing. She is, as everyone knows, the real deal. I also want to thank Florence Fabricant who made the introduction that led to the making of this book, gave us a wonderful essay, and joined us as a member of an extraordinary Advisory Committee.

In fact, that list of advisors, which appears at the front of this book, with biographies in the back, is a fairly stellar artifact itself. The collected experience and knowledge of the group is vast and deep, and I thank them all sincerely for giving of their time and expertise. They represent some of the finest talents and accomplishments, certainly of the twentieth century and now of this new manic era, in many areas of food. We're grateful and honored to have had their help.

I want to thank my talented team, all grads of the master's program in Food Studies at the Steinhardt School: Tosca Giamatti, Janet Lo, Waverley Aufmuth, and, more recently, just at the important end, Rachel Hannon. They are well aware of the value and import of this work and their contribution to it all.

I also want to express appreciation for special guidance and specific support, to Judith Jones, who provides a rigorous benchmark and the occasional well-directed good words in ways others only hope to. Her essay on Julia is a delight.

In fact, all those who gave us the wonderful essays—neatly slipped between the tomes—deserve our very special thanks. These are unique and personal works that add enormously to what we've gathered here.

To this I'd add special thanks to dear friends who have listened to me prattle and fuss over this book for the last year: Marian Burros, Scott Peacock, Jon Tisch, Tammie Fraser, and Scott Mitchell.

Finally, to Christopher Steighner from Rizzoli, for guiding us along the way and bringing these opinionated and disparate voices together with a pleasing cohesion and a resonant result. You rock.

—Clark Wolf

PERMISSIONS

Bruce Aidells, recipes from *Hot Links and Country Flavors: Sausages in American Regional Cooking*. Copyright © 1990 by Bruce Aidells. Used by permission of Alfred A. Knopf, a division of Random House, Inc.

Jeffrey Alford and Naomi Duguid, recipes from *Seductions of Rice*. Copyright © 1998 by Jeffrey Alford and Naomi Duguid. Reprinted with the permission of Artisan Publishers, a division of Workman Publishing Co., Inc.

Colman Andrews, recipes from *Catalan Cuisine*. Copyright © 1988 by Coleman Andrews. Reprinted with the permission of John Wiley & Sons, Inc.

Lee Bailey, recipes from *Lee Bailey's Country Weekends*. Copyright © 1983 by Lee Bailey. Used by permission of Clarkson N. Potter, a division of Random House, Inc.

Lidia Bastianich, recipes from *La Cucina di Lidia*. Copyright © 1990 by Lidia Bastianich. Used by permission of Broadway Books, a division of Random House, Inc.

Rick Bayless, recipes from *Rick Bayless's Mexican Kitchen*. Copyright © 1996 by Rick Bayless. Reprinted with the permission of The Doe Coover Agency. Cover photo: Chris Casaburi; interior photos: Maria Robledo.

James Beard, recipes from *Cook It Outdoors*. Copyright 1941 by James Beard. Reprinted with the permission of Reed College and John Ferrone. Recipes from *The Fireside Cook Book*. Copyright 1949 by James Beard. Reprinted with the permission of Simon & Schuster. Recipes from *American Cookery*. © 1972 by James A. Beard. Reprinted with the permission of Little, Brown and Company. All rights reserved.

Simone Beck, Louisette Bertholle, and Julia Child, recipes from *Mastering the Art of French Cooking, Volumes I & II*. Copyright © 1961–1970 by Simone Beck, Louisette Bertholle, and Julia Child. Used by permission of Alfred A. Knopf, a division of Random House, Inc.

Rose Levy Berenbaum, recipes from *The Cake Bible*. Copyright © 1988 by Rose Levy Berenbaum. Reprinted by permission of HarperCollins Publishers.

Mark Bittman, recipes from *How to Cook Everything*. Copyright © 1998 by Mark Bittman. Reprinted by permission of John Wiley & Sons, Inc.

Jennifer Brennan, recipes from *The Original Thai Cookbook*. Copyright © 1981 by Jennifer Brennan. Used by permission of G. P. Putnam's Sons, a division of Penguin Group (USA) Inc. and the Robert Cornfield Literary Agency.

Cora Brown, recipes from *The South American Cook Book: Including Central America, Mexico, and the West Indies*. Copyright 1939 by Cora Brown. Used by permission of Doubleday, a division of Random House, Inc.

Edward Espe Brown, recipes from *Tassajara Bread Book*. Copyright © 1970 by Edward Espe Brown. Reprinted with the permission of Shambhala Publications, Inc.

Cecily Brownstone, recipes from *The Associated Press Cookbook*. Copyright © 1972 by Cecily Brownstone. Used by permission of Random House, Inc.

Giuliano Bugialli, recipes from *The Art of Fine Italian Cooking*. Copyright © 1989 by Giuliano Bugialli. Used by permission of Times Books, a division of Random House, Inc.

Marian Burros, recipes from *The Elegant But Easy Cookbook*. Copyright © 1967 by Marian Burros and Lois Levine. Reprinted with the permission of Scribner, a division of Simon & Schuster, Inc.

Penelope Casas, recipes from *The Foods and Wines of Spain*. Copyright © 1982 by Penelope Casas. Used by permission of Alfred A. Knopf, a division of Random House, Inc.

Julia Child, recipes from *From Julia Child's Kitchen*. Copyright © 1972 by Julia Child. Used by permission of Alfred A. Knopf, a division of Random House, Inc.

Craig Claiborne, recipes from *The New York Times Cookbook*. Copyright © 1961 and renewed 1989 by Craig Claiborne. Reprinted by permission of HarperCollins Publishers.

Craig Claiborne and Virginia Lee, recipes from *The Chinese Cookbook*. Copyright © 1972 by Craig Claiborne and Virginia Lee. Reprinted by permission of HarperCollins Publishers.

Bernard Clayton, Jr., recipes from *The Complete Book of Breads*. Copyright © 1973 by Bernard Clayton. Reprinted with the permission of Simon & Schuster, Inc. All rights reserved.

Bruce Cost, recipes from *Bruce Cost's Asian Ingredients*. Copyright © 1988 by Bruce Cost. Reprinted with the permission of the author.

Marion Cunningham, recipes from *The Breakfast Book*. Copyright © 1987 by Marion Cunningham. Used by permission of Alfred A. Knopf, a division of Random House, Inc.

Elizabeth David, recipes from *French Provincial Cooking*. Copyright © 1962 by Elizabeth David. Used by permission of Viking Penguin, a division of Penguin Group (USA) Inc.

Roy Andries de Groot, recipes from *Feasts for All Seasons*. © 1966 by Roy Andries de Groot. Used by permission of Alfred A. Knopf, a division of Random House, Inc.

Louis P. de Guoy, recipes from *The Gold Cook Book*. Copyright 1947 by Louis P. de Guoy, renewed © 1975 by Jacqueline S. Dooner. Reprinted with the permission of James D. Dooner, Sr., and Michael F. Dooner.

Robert A. Delfs, recipes from *The Good Food of Szechwan*. Copyright © 1974 by Robert A. Delfs. Reprinted by permission.

Cara de Silva (ed.), recipes from *In Memory's Kitchen: A Legacy from the Women of Terezin*. Reprinted with the permission of Rowman & Littlefield Publishing Group.

Mrs. S. R. Dull, recipes from *Southern Cooking*. Copyright 1928, 1941 by Mrs. S. R. Dull. Copyright © 1968 by Grosset & Dunlap. Used by permission of Grosset & Dunlap, Inc., a division of Penguin Group (USA) Inc.

Carol Field, recipes from *The Italian Baker*. Copyright © 1985 by Carol Field. Used by permission of Ten Speed Press, a division of Random House, Inc.

M.F.K. Fisher, recipes from *The Art of Eating*. Copyright 1954 by M.F.K. Fisher. Reprinted with the permission of John Wiley & Sons, Inc., and Lescher & Lescher, Ltd.

Crosby Gaige, recipes from *New York World's Fair Cook Book: The American Kitchen*. Copyright 1939 by Crosby Gaige. Used by permission of Doubleday, a division of Random House, Inc.

General Mills Company, recipes from *Betty Crocker's Picture Cook Book*. Copyright 1950 by General Mills, Inc. Reprinted with the permission of John Wiley & Sons, Inc.

Bert Greene, recipes from *Greene on Greens*. Copyright © 1984 by Bert Greene. Reprinted with the permission of Artisan Publishers, a division of Workman Publishing Co., Inc.

Marcella Hazan, recipes from *The Classic Italian Cookbook: The Art of Italian Cooking*. Copyright © 1973 by Marcella Hazan. Used by permission of Alfred A. Knopf, a division of Random House, Inc.

Maida Heatter, recipes from *Maida Heatter's Book of Great Desserts*. © 1974 by Maida Heatter. Used by permission of Alfred A. Knopf, a division of Random House, Inc.

Madhur Jaffrey, recipes from *An Invitation to Indian Cooking*. Copyright © 1973 by Madhur Jaffrey. Used by permission of Alfred A. Knopf, a division of Random House, Inc.

Junior League of Augusta, recipes from *Old and New Recipes from the South*. Copyright 1940 by The Association of Junior Leagues International, Inc. Reprinted with permission.

Junior League Cookbooks, recipes from *Charleston Receipts*. Copyright 1950 by The Association of Junior Leagues International, Inc. Reprinted with permission.

Barbara Kafka, recipes from *Microwave Gourmet*. Copyright © 1987 by Barbara Kafka. Reprinted by permission of the author.

Lynne Rossetto Kasper, recipes from *The Splendid Table: Recipes from Emilia-Romagna, the Heartland of Northern Italian Food*. Copyright © 1992 by Lynne Rossetto Kasper. Reprinted by permission of HarperCollins Publishers.

Mollie Katzen, recipes from *The Moosewood Cookbook*. Copyright © 1977 by Mollie Katzen. Used by permission of Ten Speed Press, a division of Random House, Inc.

Thomas Keller, recipes from *The French Laundry Cookbook*. Copyright © 1999 by Thomas Keller. Reprinted with the permission of Artisan Publishers, a division of Workman Publishing Co., Inc.

Diana Kennedy, recipes from *The Cuisines of Mexico*. Copyright © 1972 by Diane Kennedy. Used by permission of Clarkson Potter, a division of Random House, Inc.

Evan Kleiman and Viana La Place, recipes from *Cucina Fresca*. Copyright © 1985 by Evan Kleiman and Viana La Place. Reprinted by permission of HarperCollins Publishers.

George Lang, recipes from *The Cuisine of Hungary*. Copyright © 1971, 1982 by George Lang. Reprinted with the permission of Scribner, a division of Simon & Schuster, Inc.

Frances Moore Lappé, recipes from *Diet for a Small Planet*. Copyright © 1971 by Frances Moore Lappe. Reprinted with the permission of the author.

Alicia Bay Laurel, recipes from *Living on the Earth: Storm Warnings, Formulas, Recipes, Rumors, Country Dances Harvested by Alicia Bay Laurel*. Copyright © 1971 by Alicia Bay Laurel. Used by permission of Random House, Inc.

Emeril Lagasse, recipes from *Emeril's New New Orleans Cooking*. Copyright © 1993 by Emeril Legasse. Photographs copyright © 1993 by Brian Smale. Reprinted by permission of HarperCollins Publishers.

Jeanne Lesem, recipes from *Pleasures of Preserving and Pickling*. Copyright © 1975 by Jeanne Lesem. Used by permission of Alfred A. Knopf, a division of Random House, Inc.

Edna Lewis, recipes from *The Taste of Country Cooking*. Copyright © 1976 by Edna Lewis. Used by permission of Alfred A. Knopf, a division of Random House, Inc.

Felipe Rojas-Lombardi, recipes from *The Art of South American Cooking*. Copyright © 1991 by Felipe Rojas-Lombardi. Reprinted with the permission of HarperCollins Publishers and the Robert Cornfield Literary Agency.

Dione Lucas, recipes from *The Cordon Bleu Cookbook*. Copyright 1947 by Dione Lucas, © 1975 by Mark Lucas. Reprinted by permission.

Sheila Lukins and Julee Rosso, recipes from *The Silver Palate Cookbook*. Copyright © 1982 by Sheila Lukins and Julee Rosso. Reprinted with the permission of Workman Publishing Co., Inc.

Earle MacAusland, recipes from *The Gourmet Cookbook*. Copyright 1950 by Earl MacAusland. Reprinted with the permission of Condé Nast Publications, Inc.

Deborah Madison, recipes from *The Greens Cookbook: New Vegetarian Recipes from the Celebrated Greens Restaurant*. Copyright © 1987 by Deborah Madison. Used by permission of Bantam Books, a division of Random House, Inc.

Abby Mandel, recipes from *Abby Mandel's Cuisinart Classroom: The World's Most Successful Food Processor*

Recipes. Copyright © 1980 by Abby Mandel. Reprinted by permission of HarperCollins Publishers.

Alice Medrich, recipes from *Cocolat: Extraordinary Chocolate Desserts* (New York: Warner Books, 1990). Copyright © 1990 by Alice Medrich. Reprinted with the permission of Dystel & Goderick Literary Management.

Jan Mitchell, recipes from *Lüchow's German Cookbook*. Copyright 1952 by Jan Mitchell. Used by permission of Doubleday, a division of Random House, Inc.

Joan Nathan, recipes from *Jewish Cooking in America*. Copyright © 1994 by Alfred A. Knopf, a division of Random House, Inc. Used by permission.

Marion Nestle, parts of the Foreword were previously published in the essay "Writing the Food Studies Movement," in *Food, Culture, and Society* 2010 (vol. 13, no. 2, pages 159–168). Used by permission.

Richard Olney, recipes from *Simple French Food*. Copyright © 1974 by Richard Olney. Reprinted with the permission of John Wiley & Sons, Inc.

Richard Olney, "Essay by Alice Waters" from *Reflexions* (New York: Brick Tower Press, 1999). Copyright © 1999 by Alice Waters. Reprinted with the permission of Brick Tower Press.

Clementine Paddleford, recipes from *How America Eats*. Copyright © 1960 by Clementine Paddleford. Reprinted with the permission of Rizzoli.

Paula Peck, recipes from *The Art of Fine Baking*. Copyright © 1961, 1966 by Paula Peck, renewed 1989 by Peter Klousner and 1994 by Theodore W. Adler and John Freeman. Reprinted with the permission of Samuel Peck, Charles Peck, and Simon & Schuster, Inc.

Jacques Pépin, recipes from *La Technique*. Copyright © 1976 by Jacques Pépin. Used by permission of Times Books, a division of Random House, Inc.

Paul Prudhomme, recipes from *Chef Paul Prudhomme's Louisiana Kitchen*. Copyright © 1984 by Paul Prudhomme. Reprinted by permission of HarperCollins Publishers.

Laurel Robertson, Carol Flinders, and Bronwen Godfrey, recipes from *Laurel's Kitchen*. Copyright © 1976 by Laurel Robertson, Carol Flinders, and Bronwen Godfrey. Reprinted with the permission of Nilgiri Press.

Claudia Roden, recipes from *A Book of Middle Eastern Food*. Copyright © 1968 by Claudia Roden. Used by permission.

Irma Rombauer and Marion Rombauer Becker, recipes from *The Joy of Cooking*. Copyright 1931, 1936, 1941, 1943, 1946, 1951, 1952, 1953, © 1962, 1963, 1964, 1975 by Simon & Schuster, Inc. Copyright © 1997 by Simon & Schuster, Inc., The Joy of Cooking Trust, and The MRB Revocable Trust. Reprinted with the permission of Scribner, a division of Simon & Schuster, Inc.

Julie Sahni, recipes from *Classic Indian Vegetarian and Grain Cooking*. Copyright © 1985 by Julie Sahni. Reprinted by permission of HarperCollins Publishers.

The Savoy Hotel, recipes from *The Savoy Cocktail Book*. Reprinted with the permission of Constable & Robinson.

Richard Sax, recipes from *Classic Home Desserts: A Treasury of Heirloom and Contemporary Recipes from Around the World*. Copyright © 1994 by Richard Sax. Used by permission of Houghton Mifflin Harcourt Publishing Company and Lescher & Lescher, Ltd. All rights reserved.

Elizabeth Schneider, recipes from *Uncommon Fruits & Vegetables*. Copyright © 1986 by Elizabeth Schneider. Reprinted by permission of the author and HarperCollins Publishers.

Mimi Sheraton, recipes from *From My Mother's Kitchen: Recipes and Reminiscences*. Copyright © 1979 by Mimi Sheraton. Reprinted with the permission of the author.

Martha Stewart, recipes from *Weddings*. Copyright © 1987 by Martha Stewart. Used by permission of Clarkson N. Potter, a division of Random House, Inc.

Anna Thomas, recipes from *The Vegetarian Epicure*. Copyright © 1972 by Anna Thomas. Used by permission of Random House, Inc.

Time-Life Publishers, recipes from *Time-Life Foods of the World Series*, 27 volumes. Copyright © 1972 by Time-Life Publishers. Reprinted by permission.

Alice B. Toklas, recipes from *The Alice B. Toklas Cook Book*. Copyright 1954 by Alice B. Toklas, renewed © 1982 by Edward M. Burns. Reprinted by permission of HarperCollins Publishers and Penguin Group (UK) Ltd.

Barbara Tropp, recipes form *The Modern Art of Chinese Cooking*. Copyright © 1982 by Barbara Tropp. Reprinted by permission of HarperCollins Publishers.

Carol Truax (ed.), recipes from *The Ladies' Home Journal Cookbook*. Copyright © 1960 by Carol Truax. Used by permission of Doubleday, a division of Random House, Inc.

Shizuo Tsuji, recipes from *Japanese Cooking: A Simple Act*. Copyright © 1980 by Tsuji Shizuo. Reprinted by permission.

Alice Waters, recipes from *Chez Panisse Vegetables*. Copyright © 1996 by Alice Waters. Reprinted by permission of HarperCollins Publishers and Lescher & Lescher, Ltd.

William Woys Weaver, recipes from *Pennsylvania Dutch Country Cooking*. Copyright © 1993 by William Woys Weaver. Reprinted with the permission of Abbeville Press and the author.

Patricia Wells, recipes from *Bistro Cooking*. Copyright © 1989 by Patricia Wells. Reprinted with the permission of Workman Publishing Co., Inc.

Paula Wolfert, recipes from *Couscous and Other Good Food from Morocco*. Copyright © 1973 by Paula Wolfert. Reprinted by permission of HarperCollins Publishers.

INDEX

C

P